A Publication of the Law School Admission Council

The Official Guide to

U.S. Law Schools

FROM THE PRODUCERS OF THE LSAT

LAW
Services

TIMES **T** BOOKS

RANDOM HOUSE

ISBN: 0-8129-9046-3
ISSN: 0886-3342

Library of Congress Catalog Number: 99-70214

The Law School Admission Council is a nonprofit corporation that provides
services to the legal education community. Its members are 196 law schools in
the United States and Canada. For information, write: Communications, Law
School Admission Council, Box 40, 661 Penn Street, Newtown, PA 18940-0040.

LSAT®; *The Official LSAT PrepTest*®; *LSAT: The Official TriplePrep*®; and the
Law Services logo are registered marks of the Law School Admission
Council, Inc. Law School Forum is a service mark of the Law School
Admission Council, Inc. *LSAT: The Official TriplePrep Plus; The Whole Law
School Package; The Official Guide to U.S. Law Schools;* and *LSACD* are
trademarks of Law School Admission Council, Inc.

Law School Admission Council fees, policies, and procedures relating to, but
not limited to, test registration, test administration, test score reporting,
misconduct and irregularities, and other matters may change without notice at
any time. To remain up to date on Law School Admission Council policies and
procedures, you may obtain a new *Registration and Information Book*, or you
may contact our candidate service representatives.

Special Sales
Times Books are available at special discounts for bulk purchases for sales
promotions or premiums. Special editions, including personalized covers,
excerpts of existing books, and corporate imprints, can be created in large
quantities for special needs. For more information, write to Special Markets,
Times Books, 201 East 50th Street, New York, NY 10022, or call (800) 800-3246.

Published simultaneously in Canada

Table of Contents

How to Use This Book

The Official Guide to U.S. Law Schools is both a resource book for individuals seeking broad information about law school in general, and an up-to-date, detailed guide to the 181 LSAC-member law schools.

In the school profiles section, which comprises the bulk of this book, you will find several pages of information on each of the LSAC-member law schools in the United States. This information is provided by the individual schools each fall and includes current data on the school's admission process, programs of study, enrollment and student body, faculty, library and physical facilities, career services, financial aid, and more. We also offer a visual geographic guide to law schools across the country. We provide information on school and city populations on these pages as well. Most schools include an admission profile grid displaying information on the number of applicants and admitted students grouped by their LSAT scores and GPA numbers.

The first 13 chapters of the *Official Guide* are geared toward answering your questions if you are

- considering a law school education after graduation from college;

- preparing to enter law school in the near future;

- thinking about law as a possible career choice; or

- contemplating a change from your current career.

The *Guide* gives answers to the most commonly asked questions regarding law as a career, preparation for and application to law school, the choice of a school to attend, and the financing of a law school education. Additionally, the *Guide* addresses the important issue of opportunities in law for minority men and women. Information can be found both within the individual school descriptions and, more specifically, in Chapter 7. This book also contains recent information regarding admission to the bar and job prospects, including useful statistics based on the experiences of 1997 law school graduates.

No guidebook on legal education can rightly claim to be a final authority on the many questions that the law school applicant will encounter. Whether you are choosing a school, selecting courses or other activities, or investigating career opportunities, you will be faced with decisions that, in the final analysis, will be yours alone to make. As you seek counsel from those who have been to law school, those who teach law school, those who admit students to law school, and those who successfully practice law, you are likely to meet strongly divergent viewpoints on the numerous points that concern you. Regarding various aspects of legal education, there is no single school of thought, but rather ongoing, vigorous discussion of numerous important issues. Your research will help you to make **informed** choices, which will increase your chances of success in meeting your own goals. We urge you to review carefully the information in this book and understand its limitations. Additionally, you should seek information from as many sources as possible, particularly from the law schools themselves. The information provided in this volume is one way to start.

Chapter 1: Being a Lawyer

Lawyers and Their Skills

Law practice is so diverse that it is not possible to describe the so-called typical lawyer. Each lawyer works with different clients and different legal problems. Ordinarily, certain basic legal skills are required of all lawyers. They must know

- how to **analyze** legal issues in light of the existing state of the law, the direction in which the law is headed, and relevant policy considerations;

- how to **synthesize** material in light of the fact that many issues are multifaceted and require the combination of diverse elements into a coherent whole;

- how to **advocate** the views of groups and individuals within the context of the legal system;

- how to give intelligent **counsel** on the law's requirements;

- how to **write** and **speak** clearly; and

- how to **negotiate** effectively.

■ Analyzing

Lawyers must be able to determine the fundamental elements of problems. They spend much time discerning the nature and significance of the many issues in a particular problem. In every issue, the lawyer must study the relationship between each element in order to arrive at an answer, result, or solution.

■ Synthesizing

Lawyers must learn that because of the complexities of many issues and the number of laws either directly or tangentially relevant, they must be able to pull together in a meaningful, focused, cogent manner often large amounts of material.

■ Advocating

As an advocate, the lawyer's role is to represent his or her client's particular point of view and interests as vigorously as possible. The American judicial system assumes that equitable solutions will emerge from the clash of opposing interests. The success of this adversarial system of American law depends upon the talents and training of the lawyers who work as advocates within it. Lawyers must be able to use their advocacy skills to marshal evidence and present arguments as to why a particular outcome is desirable.

■ Counseling

Lawyers also spend a good deal of their time giving clients legal advice. Few ventures in the modern world can be undertaken without some understanding of the law. Through their knowledge of what the law involves, lawyers advise clients about partnerships, decisions, actions, and many other subjects. In many cases, the lawyer's role as a counselor serves as much to prevent litigation as to support it.

■ Writing and Speaking

Whether in the courtroom or the law office, lawyers must be effective communicators. If lawyers could not translate thoughts and opinions into clear and precise English, it would be difficult for the law to serve society. After all, the law is embodied in words, and many of the disputes that give birth to laws begin with language—its meaning, use, and interpretation. Litigation leads to written judicial opinions; congressional enactments are recorded as printed statutes; and even economic transactions must be expressed as formal, written contracts.

■ Negotiating

One of the lawyer's primary roles is reconciling divergent interests and opinions. When the parties to a proposed transaction disagree, the lawyer, acting as a facilitator, may be able to help them negotiate to a common ground. Although the client's interests are a lawyer's first priority, often those interests are served best after compromise and conciliation have paved the way to an equitable settlement. Because lawyers are trained to see the implications of alternative courses of action, they are often able to break an impasse.

Fields of Law

Lawyers are central figures in the life of a democratic country. They may deal with major courtroom cases or minor traffic disputes, complex corporate mergers or straightforward real estate transactions. Lawyers may work for giant industries, small businesses, government agencies, international organizations, public interest groups, legal aid offices, and universities—or they may work for themselves. They represent both the impoverished and the wealthy, the helpless and the powerful. Lawyers may work solo, in a small group, or in a large law firm.

About 72.9 percent of American lawyers are in private practice, most in small, one-person offices and some in large firms. Roughly 8.2 percent of the profession works for government agencies, 9.5 percent works for private industries and associations as salaried lawyers or as managers, 1.1 percent works for legal aid or as public defenders, and one percent is in legal education. (About 4.6 percent are retired or inactive.) Many lawyers develop expertise in a particular field of law. Large law firms that provide a full range of legal services tend to employ more specialists. The sole practitioner, who must handle a variety of problems alone, may have greater opportunity to work in several areas. Of course, there are lawyers in large firms who maintain general practices, and lawyers in one-person offices who concentrate on a particular legal issue. Both specialized and general practice can be rewarding. One offers the satisfaction of mastering a particular legal discipline, and the other the challenge of exploring new fields. Following are brief descriptions of selected areas of specialization, though there are many areas of the law that can rightly fall into more than one category:

■ Corporate and Securities Law

The corporate lawyer helps clients conduct their business affairs in a manner that is efficient and consistent with the law. The responsibilities of a corporate lawyer can range from preparing the initial articles of incorporation and bylaws for a new enterprise to handling a corporate reorganization under the provisions of federal bankruptcy law. Examples of other areas of corporate law practice include (but are not limited to) contract, intellectual property, legislative compliance, and liability matters.

Securities law is an extremely complex area that almost always requires the services of a specialist. In the past, lawyers who acquired this specialty were involved with the formation, organization, and financing of corporations through securities such as stock. However, in recent years, such lawyers also have become involved in mergers, acquisitions, and corporate takeovers.

■ Criminal Law

Criminal defense lawyers represent clients accused of crimes. Their public counterparts are the prosecutors and district attorneys who represent the interests of the state in the prosecution of those accused of crimes. Both types of criminal lawyers deal with fundamental issues of the law and personal liberty. They defend many of the basic rights considered crucial to the preservation of a free and just society.

■ Environmental Law

Environmental law was born out of widespread public and professional concern about the fate of our natural resources. Lawyers in this field may tackle legal and regulatory issues relating to air and water quality, hazardous waste practice, natural gas transportation, oil and gas exploration and development, electric power licensing, water rights, toxic torts, public land use, marine resources, and energy trade regulation. They may work directly for governmental agencies that address environmental problems or represent corporations, public interest groups, and entities concerned about protecting the environment.

■ Family Law

Family, or domestic relations, law is concerned with relationships between individuals in the context of the family. Many lawyers who practice this kind of law are members of small law firms or are sole practitioners. They specialize in solving problems that arise among family members and in creating or dissolving personal relationships through such means as adoption or divorce.

■ Intellectual Property Law

Intellectual property law is concerned with the protection of inventors' rights in their discoveries, authors' rights in their creations, and businesses' rights in their identifying marks. Often, an intellectual property lawyer will specialize in a particular area of the law. For example, for those attorneys with a technical background, patent law is a way to combine one's scientific and legal background into one practice. A copyright attorney counsels authors, composers, and artists on the scope of their rights in their creations, and even personal identities, negotiates contracts, and litigates to enforce these rights. In recent years, copyright law has also focused on technological advances, particularly developments in electronic publishing. Additionally, in today's global economy, intellectual property issues are at the forefront of international trade negotiations.

■ International Law

International law has grown significantly as a field of practice, reflecting the increasing interdependence of nations and economies. Public international law provides a limited range of job opportunities, particularly with national governments or international institutions or with public interest bodies. Immigration and refugee law also assumes increasing importance as more people move more frequently across national boundaries for business, tourism, or permanent resettlement. Private international law may offer more extensive employment opportunities, either through law firms or for corporations, banks, or telecommunications firms. Fluency in another language or familiarity with another culture can be a decided advantage for law school graduates who seek to practice in the international arena.

■ Tax Law

In the past 50 years, the importance and complexity of federal, state, and local taxes have necessitated a specialty in this field of law. It is one area of the law where change is constant. The federal Internal Revenue Code and its associated regulations are now several thousand pages in length. New statutes, court decisions, and administrative rulings are issued frequently, and the tax lawyer must be alert to these changes. Economic planning usually includes attention to taxes, and the tax lawyer often assists clients in understanding and minimizing their tax liabilities.

Chapter 2: Becoming a Lawyer

A legal education is both challenging and rewarding. You will develop your analytical, synthesizing, creative, and logical thinking skills, and you will strengthen your reading and debating abilities. A legal education is necessary to become a lawyer in the United States, but it is also excellent preparation for many other careers, both because of the framework for organizing knowledge it provides and the analytical approach it brings to problems. Many teachers, business people, and writers first obtained a legal education before pursuing careers other than law.

Juris Doctor Degree

ABA-approved law schools generally require three years of full-time study to earn the Juris Doctor (J.D.) degree. Most schools with part-time programs require four years of part-time study to earn the J.D. degree. Most law schools share a common approach to training lawyers. However, they differ in the emphasis they give to certain subjects and teaching methods, such as opportunities for independent study, legal internships, participation in clinical programs, and involvement with governmental affairs.

Law school can be an intense, competitive environment. Students have little time for other interests, especially during the first year of law school. The ABA requires that no full-time student hold an outside job for more than 20 hours a week. Most schools encourage their students to become totally immersed in reading, discussing, and thinking about the law.

■ The First Year

The newness of the first year of law school is exciting for many and anxiety-provoking for almost all. Professors expect you to be prepared in class, but in most courses, grades will be determined primarily from examinations administered at the end of the semester or, at some schools, the end of the year. The professor may give little feedback until the final examination.

■ The Case Method Approach

The "case method" is what first-year law students are likely to find least familiar. By focusing on the underlying principles that shape the law's approach to different situations, you will learn to distinguish among subtly different legal results and to identify the critical factors that determine a particular outcome. Once these distinctions are mastered, you should be able to apply this knowledge to new situations.

The case method involves the detailed examination of a number of related judicial opinions that describe an area of law. You will also learn to apply the same critical analysis to legislative materials and scholarly articles. The role of the law professor is to provoke and stimulate. For a particular case, he or she may ask questions designed to explore the facts presented, to determine the legal principles applied in reaching a decision, and to analyze the method of reasoning used. In this way, the professor encourages you to relate the case to others and to distinguish it from those with similar but inapplicable precedents. In order to encourage you to learn to defend your reasoning, the professor may adopt a position contrary to the holding of the case.

Because this process places much of the burden of learning on the student, classroom discussions can be exciting. They are also demanding. However uninformed, unprepared, or puzzled you may be, you will be required to participate in these discussions.

■ The Ability to Think

The case method reflects the general belief that the primary purpose of law school is not to teach substantive law but to teach you to think like a lawyer. Teachers of law are less concerned about rules and technicalities than are their counterparts in many other disciplines. Although the memorization of specifics may be useful to you, the ability to be analytical and literate is considerably more important than the power of total recall. One reason for this approach to legal education is that in our common-law tradition, the law is constantly evolving and changing; thus, specific rules may quickly lose their relevance.

Law is more an art than a science. The reality lawyers seek in analyzing a case is not always well-defined. Legal study, therefore, requires an attentive mind and a tolerance for ambiguity. Because many people believe incorrectly that the study of law involves the memorization of rules in books and principles dictated by learned professors, law schools often attract those people who especially value structure, authority, and order. The study of law does **not** involve this kind of certainty, however; complex legal questions do not have simple legal solutions. Law professors rarely have the answers and they prefer to encourage students to develop their own responses to legal issues.

■ The Curriculum

As a first-year law student, you will follow a designated course of study that may cover many of the following subjects:

- **Civil procedure**—the process of adjudication in the United States; i.e., jurisdiction and standing to sue, motions and pleadings, pretrial procedure, the structure of a lawsuit, and appellate review of trial results.

- **Constitutional law**—the legislative powers of the federal and state governments, and questions of civil liberties and constitutional history, including detailed study of the Bill of Rights and constitutional freedoms.

- **Contracts**—the nature of enforceable promises and rules for determining appropriate remedies in case of nonperformance.

- **Criminal law and criminal procedure**—bases of criminal responsibility, the rules and policies for enforcing sanctions against individuals accused of committing offenses against the public order and well-being, and the rights guaranteed to those charged with criminal violations.

- **Legal method**—students' introduction to the organization of the American legal system and its processes.

- **Legal writing**—research and writing component of most first-year programs; requires students to research and write memoranda dealing with various legal problems.

- **Property law**—concepts, uses, and historical developments in the treatment of land, buildings, natural resources, and personal objects.

- **Torts**—private wrongs, such as acts of negligence, assault, and defamation, that violate obligations of the law.

In addition to attending classes, you may be required to participate in a moot court exercise in which you take responsibility for arguing a hypothetical court case.

After the first year, you will probably have the opportunity to select from a broad range of courses. Generally, you will take courses in administrative law, civil litigation, commercial law, corporations, evidence, family law, professional responsibility, taxation, and wills and trusts before completing your degree. These universal courses are basic to legal education. Every law school supplements this basic curriculum with additional courses, such as international law, environmental law, conflict of laws, labor law, criminal procedure, and jurisprudence.

■ Opportunities to Practice What Is Learned

Legal education is primarily academic, in that students devote most of their time to mastering general concepts and principles that shape the law. Most schools offer a variety of professional skills courses as well. Law schools place less emphasis on matters such as legal drafting and law office management than on legal principles. However, a number of schools have programs designed to offer students direct experience in legal practice. These programs allow second- and third-year students to participate in court trials and appeals, render counseling, undertake legislative drafting, and do other legal work for academic credit. Schools differ in the range and variety of practical education they offer, but the trend toward integrating this experience with theoretical study continues to grow.

■ Extracurricular Activities

Student organizations greatly supplement classroom learning. Typically, these organizations are dedicated to advancing the interests of particular groups of law students, such as black, women, or Hispanic students; or to promoting greater understanding of specific legal fields, such as environmental or international law; or to providing opportunities for involvement in professional, social, and sports activities.

A unique feature of American law schools is that law students manage and edit most of the legal profession's principal scholarly journals. Membership on the editorial staffs of these journals, also called law reviews, is considered a mark of academic distinction. Selection is ordinarily based on outstanding academic performance, writing ability, or both, as discussed on page 19 of this book.

Bar Associations

Bar associations are membership organizations designed to raise the standards of the legal profession and to encourage professional unity. Each state has its own bar association. There are also a variety of national, state, local, and special-interest bar associations.

The largest national organization of attorneys in the United States is the American Bar Association (ABA), which sponsors a number of programs dealing with legal education, law reform, judicial selection, and professional responsibility. The ABA publishes the *Model Rules of Professional Conduct*, a set of regulations governing ethical standards in the practice of law. Attorneys who violate such standards are subject to censure, suspension, or disbarment by the state bar admitting authorities.

Many bar associations sponsor programs intended to broaden the availability of legal services and to familiarize the public with the legal profession. They also conduct extensive continuing legal education programs to help members update their skills and their knowledge of the law.

■ Admission to the Bar

To practice law in the United States, every lawyer must be admitted to a state bar. Standards for admission to state bars are regulated by each state and differ from state to state. In order to be admitted to the bar, most states require that candidates:

- Possess a law degree from an ABA-approved law school;

- Pass state examinations that test their knowledge of the law, skill in reasoning, and understanding of legal ethics and professional responsibility; and

- Show evidence of fitness to practice law, understanding of legal ethics, and sound character.

Lawyers may practice only in the state or states where they are members of the bar in good standing. However, many states will admit a lawyer to its bar if the lawyer has been admitted to the bar of another state and has practiced law actively for a certain number of years. This is known as reciprocity. Courts often grant temporary bar admission to out-of-state lawyers for the duration of a specific case.

Many states have student practice rules that, in conjunction with students' academic programs, admit advanced law students who are under the close supervision of an admitted lawyer. A few states require law students to register with the board of bar examiners before graduation or, in some cases, soon after they're enrolled in law school, if they intend to practice in those states. So, if you're planning to attend law school, you should check the bar admission requirements for those states in which you may wish to practice after graduation.

Federal courts set their own standards for admission. The most basic requirement for federal district court admission is that the lawyer be admitted to the bar in the state in which the federal district is located.

A good source of information regarding bar admission requirements is the latest edition of the ABA's *Comprehensive Guide to Bar Admission Requirements*, which should be available in any law school library.

■ Bar Approval and School Selection

A number of law schools have not been approved by the American Bar Association. Some states permit graduates of these schools to take the bar examination or will admit to their bars one who has been admitted to the bar of another state (even though he or she graduated from a school not approved by the ABA), but most do not. Before you enroll in a law school not approved by the ABA, contact the bar admission authorities in your state for more information about the limitations that may result from obtaining a degree from these programs.

A few institutions offer correspondence courses purporting to provide a legal education. The ABA expressly disapproves of correspondence law courses. Correspondence law school graduates are not eligible to take the bar examination in any state except California, and even there only under special conditions.

Legal Education and Bar Admission Statistics

Year	Total J.D. Enrollment*	Total J.D. Women Enrollment*	First Year Enrollment*	Total LSAT Administrations	Est. ABA Applicants†	J.D. or LL.B. Awarded*	New Admissions to the Bar*
1981-82	120,879	43,245	42,521	119,291	72,912	35,598	45,382
1982-83	121,791	45,539	42,034	112,125	71,755	34,846	42,905
1983-84	121,201	46,361	41,159	105,076	63,801	36,389	41,684
1984-85	119,847	46,897	40,747	95,563	60,338	36,687	42,630
1985-86	118,700	47,486	40,796	91,848	61,304	36,829	42,450
1986-87	117,813	47,920	40,195	101,235	65,145	36,121	40,247***
1987-88	117,997	48,920	41,055	115,988	74,938	35,478	39,918***
1988-89	120,694	50,932	42,860	137,088	82,741	35,701	46,528
1989-90	124,471	53,113	43,826	138,865	88,303	35,520	47,174
1990-91	127,261	54,097	44,104	152,685	94,026	36,385	43,286***
1991-92	129,580	55,110	44,050	145,567	91,954	38,800	54,577
1992-93	128,212	54,644	42,793	140,054	86,184**	39,425	57,117
1993-94	127,802	55,134	43,644	132,028	84,574	40,213	51,152
1994-95	128,989	55,808	44,298	128,553	78,391**	39,710	57,875
1995-96	129,318	56,923	43,676	114,756	70,724	39,191	56,613
1996-97	128,623	57,123	43,245	105,313	66,137	39,920	56,629
1997-98	125,886	56,915	42,186	103,990	67,063	40,114	N/A

*   Sources for these figures include the *Official American Bar Association Guide to Approved Law Schools*, 1999 Edition.
**   Revised figure.
*** Data was not complete for these years; this figure is lower than prior years.
†   Numbers noted in this column include only current-year applicants.

Chapter 3: Preparing for Law School

Acquire a Well-Balanced Education

Students interested in legal study should get the most from their undergraduate education. A college education should stand on its own merits as preparation for a lifetime of active involvement in a diverse and changing society.

Admission committees are usually impressed by applicants who can convincingly demonstrate that they've challenged their thinking and reasoning skills in a diverse course of undergraduate study. Law schools prefer students who can think, read, and write well, and who have some understanding of what shapes human experience. Because a lawyer's work involves most aspects of our complex society, a broad liberal arts curriculum is the preferred preparation for law school.

Maintain a Rigorous Courseload

High academic standards are important when selecting your undergraduate courses. The range of acceptable majors is broad; the quality of the education you receive is most important. Undergraduate programs should reveal your capacity to perform well at an academically rigorous level. An undergraduate career that is narrow, unchallenging, or vocationally oriented is not the best preparation for law school.

Law school admission committees want to see how the courses you chose relate to one another, and they want a sense of how you rise to intellectual challenge, whether in the sciences, the liberal arts, the business curriculum, or elsewhere. In assessing how favorably a law school will view your application, you should examine your courses. Try to fit them into this sort of overview. To what extent can they be seen as part of a whole, and to what extent do the parts seem to coalesce intellectually?

The Pros and Cons of a "Prelaw" Major

Unlike the premedical curriculum that contains specific courses, some obligatory, there is no recommended set of prelaw courses. Law schools prefer that you reserve your legal study for law school and fill your undergraduate curriculum with broad, diverse, and challenging courses. Prelaw courses that introduce you to broad legal principles may present you with enough information to decide whether you want to continue with a legal educa- tion, but they are rarely taught with the same depth and rigor as actual law school courses. A prelaw curriculum that is designed to encompass a broad array of liberal arts courses, however, can be excellent preparation for law school. Be sure you know precisely what is meant by "prelaw" when choosing your undergraduate course of study.

Prelaw Advisors

Prelaw advisors at undergraduate institutions are a good source of information before and during the law school admission process. If you are considering law school, you should introduce yourself to a prelaw advisor as soon as possible. The advisor knows his or her school's course offerings quite well and will be able to direct you to courses that will better prepare you for law school. The prelaw advisor should also be quite helpful during the law school application process. Advisors have the latest information on the Law School Admission Test (LSAT), the Law School Data Assembly Service (LSDAS), and even on many law school requirements. In addition, they may be able to point you toward law schools that would be particularly well suited to your needs and interests.

If you are considering law school but are not currently enrolled in a university, you may be able to obtain counsel from the undergraduate prelaw advisor at the college from which you graduated. Most prelaw advisors will be happy to answer any questions you may have.

(See also Appendix D, Preparation for Legal Education, page 434.)

Chapter 4: LSAT and Other Criteria for Admission

How Law Schools Select Applicants

No concrete principles exist for predicting who will perform well in law school, so admission committees seek the most qualified from the pool of applicants. In order to be fair, schools rely heavily upon selection criteria that bear on expected performance in law school and can be applied objectively to all candidates. Law schools consider a variety of factors in admitting their students, and no single qualification will independently guarantee acceptance or rejection. However, the two factors that usually outweigh the rest are prior academic performance and the Law School Admission Test score.

The most difficult admission decisions are those regarding candidates who are neither so well qualified nor so deficient as to present a clear-cut case for acceptance or rejection. These applicants constitute the majority of the applicant pool at many law schools and are the candidates that most law schools spend the bulk of their time reviewing.

■ Criteria That May Be Considered by Law School Admission Committees

- LSAT score
- Undergraduate grade-point average
- Undergraduate course of study
- Graduate work, if any
- College attended
- Improvement in grades and grade distribution
- College curricular and extracurricular activities
- Ethnic/racial background
- Individual character and personality
- Letters of recommendation
- Writing skills
- Personal statement or essay
- Work experience or other postundergraduate experiences
- Community activities
- Motivation to study and reasons for deciding to study law
- State of residency
- Difficulties that you have overcome
- Precollege preparation
- Past accomplishments and leadership
- Anything else that stands out in an application

The Law School Admission Test (LSAT)

All American Bar Association (ABA)-approved law schools and many non-ABA-approved law schools require that you take the LSAT. (On rare occasions, exceptions may be made for people with certain disabilities.)

The test consists of five 35-minute sections of multiple-choice questions, in three different item types. A 30-minute writing sample is administered at the end of the test. Four of the five sections contribute to the test taker's score. The fifth section typically is used to pretest new test items and to preequate new test forms. Law Services does not score the writing sample. Copies of the writing sample are sent to all law schools to which you apply.

Some schools place greater weight than others on the LSAT; still, low LSAT scores will hamper your chances for admission, particularly at the most competitive schools. Most law schools do make a genuine effort to evaluate your full credentials.

■ What the Test Measures

The LSAT is designed to measure skills that are considered essential for success in law school: the reading and comprehension of complex texts with accuracy and insight; the organization and management of information and the ability to draw reasonable inferences from it; the ability to think critically; and the analysis and evaluation of the reasoning and argument of others.

The three item types in the LSAT are:

Reading Comprehension Questions
These questions measure your ability to read, with understanding and insight, examples of lengthy and complex materials similar to those commonly encountered in law school work. The reading comprehension items consist of passages of approximately 450 words, each followed by five to eight questions that test reading and reasoning abilities.

Analytical Reasoning Questions
These questions are designed to measure your ability to understand a structure of relationships and to draw logical conclusions about that structure. You are asked to make deductions from a set of statements, rules, or conditions that describe relationships among entities such as persons,

places, things, or events. They simulate the kinds of detailed analyses of relationships that a law student must perform in solving legal problems.

Logical Reasoning Questions

These questions are designed to evaluate your aptitude for understanding, analyzing, criticizing, and completing a variety of arguments. Each logical reasoning question requires you to read and comprehend a short passage, then answer one or two questions about it. The questions test a variety of abilities involved in reasoning logically and thinking critically.

■ Your Score as a Predictor of Law School Performance

The LSAT, like any admission test, is not a perfect predictor of law school performance. The predictive power of an admission test is limited by many factors, such as the complexity of the skills the test is designed to measure and the unmeasurable factors that can affect students' performances, such as motivation, physical and mental health, or work and family responsibilities. In spite of these factors, the LSAT compares very favorably with admission tests used in other graduate and professional fields of study. (For additional information about the predictive value of LSAT scores, refer to the 1999-2000 edition of the *LSAT/LSDAS Registration and Information Book*.)

■ Test Preparation

Most law school applicants familiarize themselves with test mechanics and question types, practice on sample tests, and study the information available on test-taking techniques and strategies. Though it is difficult to say when examinees are sufficiently prepared, very few people achieve their full potential without some preparation.

Law Services publishes a variety of materials to help you prepare for the LSAT.

10 Actual, Official LSAT PrepTests®

This book contains *PrepTests 7, 9, 10, 11, 12, 13, 14, 15, 16,* and *18*—10 previously administered LSATs with answer keys, writing samples, and score conversion tables. (Please note: this book contains *PrepTests* that are also featured in the *Official TriplePrep* books.)

The Official LSAT PrepTest®

Each *Official LSAT PrepTest* contains a previously administered LSAT, an answer key, and a conversion table that helps you compute your score. The PrepTest allows you to prepare for the LSAT by simulating actual test condi-

tions and checking your answers to see which question types you might need to practice. The disclosed tests are made available approximately six weeks after they are administered. *The Official LSAT Sample PrepTest* (the June 1991 test) is included as part of the *LSAT/LSDAS Registration and Information Book* which is available through the mail from Law Services, or at law school admission offices, undergraduate schools, and testing and counseling centers.

LSAT: The Official TriplePrep®

Three PrepTests provide more practice than one, and buying three together in one book costs less than buying them separately. *TriplePrep—Volume 1* contains PrepTests 2 (October 1991 LSAT), 4 (February 1992 LSAT), and 5 (June 1992 LSAT). *TriplePrep—Volume 2* contains PrepTests 3 (December 1991 LSAT), 6 (October 1992 LSAT), and 7 (February 1993 LSAT). *TriplePrep—Volume 3* contains PrepTests 8 (June 1993 LSAT), 9 (October 1993 LSAT), and 10 (February 1994 LSAT). *TriplePrep* contains answer keys, writing samples, and score-conversion tables for all three PrepTests.

*LSAT: The Official TriplePrep **Plus** with Explanations*™

This is the only official LSAC product that contains explanations for all three LSAT-item types. *TriplePrep **Plus*** also contains 50 previously administered writing sample prompts in addition to three complete PrepTests—11 (June 1994 LSAT), 12 (October 1994 LSAT), and 13 (December 1994 LSAT). These PrepTests are also sold separately.

Candidates may order publications directly from Law Services by mail, by telephone, or online (*http://www.LSAC.org*), using a VISA, MasterCard, American Express, or DISCOVER credit card. For further information, or to order publications, contact:

> **Law Services**
> **Box 2400**
> **661 Penn Street**
> **Newtown, PA 18940-0977**
> **215.968.1001**
> **URL: http://www.LSAC.org**

For further information about your LSAT score and on the question of taking the test more than one time, please refer to your *LSAT/LSDAS Registration and Information Book*.

Academic Record

Undergraduate performance is generally an important indicator of how someone is likely to perform in law school. Hence, many law schools look closely at college grades when considering individual applications.

Course selection also can make a difference in admission evaluations. Applicants who have taken difficult or advanced courses in their undergraduate study often are evaluated in a more favorable light than students who have concentrated on easier or less advanced subjects.

Many law schools consider undergraduate-performance trends along with a student's numerical average. Thus, they may discount a slow start in a student's undergraduate career if he or she performs exceptionally well in the later school years. Similarly, admission committees may see an undergraduate's strong start followed by a mediocre finish as an indication of less potential to do well in law school. Candidates are advised to comment on irregular grade trends in their personal statement.

Grade Conversion Table

LSDAS Conversion	Grades as Reported on Transcripts				
4.0 Scale	A to F	1 to 5	100-0*	Four Passing Grades	Three Passing Grades
4.33	A+	1+	98-100	Highest Passing Grade (4.0)	Highest Passing Grade (4.0)
4.00	A	1	93-97		
3.67	A-	1-	90-92		
3.50	AB				
3.33	B+	2+	87-89	Second Highest Passing Grade (3.0)	Middle Passing Grade (3.0)
3.00	B	2	83-86		
2.67	B-	2-	80-82		
2.50	BC				
2.33	C+	3+	77-79	Third Highest Passing Grade (2.0)	Lowest Passing Grade (2.0)
2.00	C	3	73-76		
1.67	C-	3-	70-72		
1.50	CD				
1.33	D+	4+	67-69	Lowest Passing Grade (1.0)	
1.00	D	4	63-66		
0.67	D-	4-	60-62		
0.50	DE or DF				
0.00	E and F	5	Below 60	Failure (0.0)	Failure (0.0)

*In some instances, a school's numeric grading scale might be converted differently than shown here.

Additional Admission Decision Factors

Most law schools consider more than academic records and LSAT scores when evaluating applicants. These factors are particularly significant after the preliminary review of an application.

Letters of Recommendation

The most effective letters of recommendation are those from professors who have known you well enough to write with candor, detail, and objectivity about your academic and personal achievements and potential. Work supervisors also can write in support of your applica-

tion. Letters that compare you to your academic peers are often considered the most useful. Most schools do not consider general, unreservedly praiseworthy letters helpful. Some schools do not require letters at all, and some of those schools will not read letters of recommendation if they receive them.

Work Experience

Law schools want diverse, interesting classes, representative of a variety of backgrounds. A candidate who applies to law school several years after completing his or her undergraduate education, and who has demonstrated an ability to succeed in a nonacademic environment, is sometimes more motivated than one who continues his or her education without a break. In fact, only about 40 percent of law students enter directly from college.

Interviews

In general, interviews are not a part of the law school admission process. You are encouraged to visit law schools to gather information, and often an appointment with admission personnel will be a part of the visit. The purpose of your conversation with the admission staff usually will be informational rather than evaluative and will not become a part of your admission file. An occasional school will grant an interview, and some may even request it, but, in general, you should not count on an interview as a means to state your case for admission; this is best done in the personal statement.

Graduate or Professional Study

Prior success or failure in other graduate or professional school work, including other law schools, may also be a factor in the admission committee's decision. In any case, you are required to report such work to any law school to which you apply.

Minority Applicants

Almost all law schools actively seek students who are members of minority groups to help ensure greater minority representation in the legal profession and to maintain a diversity of views in the classroom. Law schools strongly encourage minority applicants. (See Chapter 7 for further details on minority recruitment and enrollment.)

International Applicants

Students from other countries are enrolled at U.S. law schools, most frequently in graduate programs (usually called LL.M. programs) that are designed to meet the needs of people who already hold a recognized law degree from another country, but want to learn about the legal system of the United States. Being a foreign student, however, is **not** the same as being from a United States minority group that is underrepresented in the American legal profession. Therefore, foreign applicants should be aware that most information in law school catalogs that is directed to minority students may not apply to them.

Procedures and requirements for foreign applicants for the J.D. or LL.M. programs vary from school to school.

You should contact the individual schools that interest you to learn about that school's particular requirements. Most schools will ask applicants for whom English is not their native language to take a standardized test such as the Test of English as a Foreign Language (TOEFL) or the Test of Written English (TWE). Each school sets its own standard for required minimal scores on the tests, but a score of 650 is typical.

Some schools may use a credential-evaluation service to translate documents, inspect them for authenticity, and evaluate a student's grades and degrees for U.S. admission committees. The student is responsible for the cost of this service, and some law schools will require you to use a specific service.

Foreign students must also demonstrate the ability to pay for schooling in this country in order to apply for a student visa (F-1 form). You may be asked to complete a certification of finances form from the law school; if the school is satisfied that the student can pay, it will issue a form (I-20) to submit to the Immigration and Naturalization Service (INS) as part of your application for a student visa.

Your Personal Essay

Each candidate to law school has something of interest to present. Maybe you've had some experience, some training, or some dream that sets you apart from others. Law schools want to recruit men and women who are qualified for reasons beyond grades and scores. The essay or personal statement in your application is the place to tell the committee about yourself.

In general, your evaluation of actual experiences and past accomplishments has more value to the committee than speculation about future accomplishments. Also, if you have overcome a serious obstacle in your life to get where you are today, by all means let the admission committee know about it. Any noteworthy personal experience or accomplishment may be an appropriate subject for your essay; however, be sure to do more than just state it. Describe your experience briefly but concretely, and why it had value to you, whether it is a job, your family, a significant accomplishment, or your upbringing. You are simultaneously trying to add information and create structure. **Be brief, be factual, be comprehensive, and be organized.**

You are a storyteller here. You want a living person—**you**—to emerge. The statement is your opportunity to become vivid and alive to the reader, and it is an opportunity to demonstrate your ability to write and present a prose sample in a professional manner.

Assessing Yourself Realistically

When selecting law schools to which you will apply, the general philosophy is that you should have a threefold plan: dream a little, be realistic, and be safe. Most applicants have no trouble selecting dream schools—those that are almost, but not quite, beyond their grasp—or safe schools—those for which admission is virtually certain. A common strategic error made by applicants is failure to evaluate realistically their chances for admission to a particular law school. The best source of this information, because it comes directly from the law schools, is a law school's admission profile in this book.

■ Use Admission Profile Grids in This Book

Check your qualifications against the admission profile of the law schools that interest you. Most schools publish a grid that indicates the number of applicants with LSAT scores and GPAs like yours who were admitted in the most recent admission year. This gives you a general sense of your competitiveness at that school. These charts will help you determine which schools are your dream schools, your realistic schools, and your safe schools. If your profile meets or exceeds that of a school, it is likely that that school will be as interested in admitting you as you are in being admitted. Other statistics are often contained in the school's text entry, so that material should be read with care as well. A few words of caution: First, law schools consider many other factors beyond the LSAT score and GPA, as described in the previous section ("Additional Admission Decision Factors"), and the grids and data about these credentials only give you part of the story. Second, you should make your final decision about where you will apply only after reading the materials sent directly from law schools so that you are aware of features of the school beyond your admissibility on the numbers.

■ Research Specific Law Schools That Interest You

Other sources of information include:

- **The school's admission office.** This is a good source for general information about the school and your chances for admission. Do not hesitate to request admission counseling. Be sure to obtain current catalogs from each law school you are considering.

- **Your college or university prelaw advisor.** Your prelaw advisor can often provide you with reliable information about which law schools fit your personal profile. He or she may also be able to tell you which law schools have accepted students from your school in the past and provide you with an overview of the admitted students' credentials. This will help you to

determine how law schools have treated applicants from your school in the recent past.

- **Law School Forums.** The Law School Forums, organized by the Law School Admission Council, are excellent opportunities to talk with law school representatives from around the country in one central, urban location—usually a hotel exhibit hall. Recent forums have been held in Atlanta, Boston, Chicago, Dallas, Los Angeles, New York City, and Washington, DC. In 1998, 168 of the 181 U.S. LSAC-member law schools participated in the forums, and 16,437 people registered as attendees. Because the costs of traveling to a number of law schools can be expensive, many prospective law students find the forums to be the most productive means of gathering information and making school contacts. Approximately 19.6 percent of the forum attendees traveled over 100 miles to get to a forum. Forum admission is free; for dates and locations of 1999 Law School Forums, see the list toward the end of this book.

- **School representatives and alumni.** Take advantage of opportunities to talk with law school representatives and alumni. When you talk with alumni, remember that law schools sometimes change fairly quickly. Try to talk to a recent graduate or to one who is active in alumni affairs and therefore knowledgeable about the school as it is today.

- **School visits.** Law schools encourage you to visit. You can learn a surprising amount about a school from talks with students and faculty members. Many law schools have formal programs in which a currently enrolled student will take you on a tour of the campus and answer your questions. Such a first-hand experience can be quite valuable in assessing how you would fit into the school.

- **The Internet.** Our Web site, *http://www.LSAC.org*, provides links to the Web sites of most LSAC-member law schools.

■ Keep Your Options Open

Flexibility is a key word in the law school admission process. Keep your options open. Even during the early stages of the admission process, you should continually reevaluate your prospects and prepare alternative plans. For example, don't set your sights on only one law school and one plan of action. You could severely limit your potential and your chance to practice law.

Chapter 5: Applying to Law School

Working With Law Services: Registering for the LSAT, Subscribing to the LSDAS

Law Services administers the LSAT and serves as a liaison for much of the communication between you and the law schools. You are expected to send your individual law school application **directly to each law school** to which you apply; however, your test scores, transcripts, and other academic information and biographical data are sent to the law schools through the Law School Data Assembly Service (LSDAS).

Comprehensive information about LSAT registration and LSDAS subscription is set forth in complete detail in the *LSAT/LSDAS Registration and Information Book,* published annually. This publication is available at no charge through Law Services or at any of 3,500 national distribution sites located on undergraduate campuses (principally prelaw advising offices and career centers) and at law schools. (Law Services operators will provide a list of distribution locations nearest your zip code; call 215.968.1001.)

You need not subscribe to the LSDAS at the same time you register for the LSAT, but doing so will simplify the process. Application deadlines for the law schools to which you apply dictate when you should subscribe to the LSDAS.

■ Planning Ahead for Law School Deadlines

Most law schools have a variety of application requirements and deadlines that you **must** meet to be considered for admission. If you are applying to a number of schools, the various deadlines and requirements can be confusing. It probably will be helpful if you set up a detailed calendar that will remind you of when and what you must do to complete an application.

You will also want to be sure you can make an LSAT score available to a law school before its application deadline. In registering for the LSAT, be sure to give yourself enough time to select a convenient testing location and prepare for the actual test.

Below is a chart listing all scheduled test administrations, including alternate dates for Saturday Sabbath observers, along with corresponding deadlines and fees.

Basic LSAT Date and Deadline Information (1999-2000)

All scheduled administrations of the LSAT, both for regular test takers and test takers who are Saturday Sabbath observers, are listed below along with corresponding regular registration deadlines. Dates shown represent **postmark** deadlines for mail registrations and receipt deadlines for telephone and online registration. The basic fee for the LSAT is $88 (published test centers only). For information on deadlines and fees for late registrations and nonpublished test centers (domestic and foreign), partial refunds, and early score reporting by telephone (TelScore), please refer to the current *LSAT/LSDAS Registration and Information Book,* or call Law Services directly at 215.968.1001. You can also find complete registration information on our World Wide Web site at *http://www.LSAC.org.*

Test Dates

■ Regular	Monday, June 14, 1999	Saturday, Oct. 2, 1999	Saturday, Dec. 4, 1999	Saturday, Feb. 12, 2000 Nondisclosed*
■ Saturday Sabbath Observers		Monday, Oct. 4, 1999 Nondisclosed*	Monday, Dec. 6, 1999 Nondisclosed*	Monday, Feb. 14, 2000 Nondisclosed*
■ Score Report mailed (approx.)	July 13, 1999	Nov. 1, 1999	Jan. 6, 2000	March 10, 2000

Regular Registration Deadline (mail, telephone, and online)

■ Domestic	May 14, 1999	Sept. 3, 1999	Nov. 5, 1999	Jan. 14, 2000
■ Foreign	May 7, 1999	Aug. 27, 1999	Oct. 29, 1999	Jan. 7, 2000

* Persons who take a nondisclosed test receive only their scores. They do not receive their test questions, answer key, or individual responses.

The Law School Data Assembly Service (LSDAS)

Nearly all LSAC-member law schools in the United States require applicants to subscribe to the LSDAS. Many nonmember law schools require this as well.

The LSDAS provides a means of centralizing and standardizing undergraduate academic records to simplify the law school admission process. The service organizes, analyzes, and summarizes biographical and academic information for law school applicants and subsequently prepares an LSDAS Law School Report to be sent within two weeks to all law schools from which a report request has been received.

If you subscribe to the LSDAS, every undergraduate, graduate, and professional school you have attended—including law school—must send an official transcript to Law Services. An official transcript is one that is signed, sealed, and sent by the registrar to Law Services. Do not send your own transcripts directly to Law Services; these will be returned to you unprocessed. Letters of recommendation may also be sent to Law Services. Up to three letters received by LSAC will be sent with the LSDAS report to the LSDAS-participating law schools to which you apply. Letter of Recommendation forms and instructions are included in the *Registration and Information Book*.

You may subscribe to the LSDAS through our online registration service (*http://www.LSAC.org*). Or you can call our Automated Telephone System at 215.968.1001; be sure to complete the worksheet in the front of the *LSAT/LSDAS Registration and Information Book*. You can also subscribe to the LSDAS by using the same registration form you use to register for the LSAT in the *Registration and Information Book*. Complete information on transcripts, LSDAS Law School Reports, and other LSDAS subscription information can be found in this book as well. Be sure to follow all directions carefully.

Information on LSDAS fees is as follows:

- **LSDAS subscription fee**   **$93**
  12 months of service (includes reporting to one law school requiring the LSDAS)

- **LSDAS Law School Reports**   **$9 each**
  (ordered when you subscribe to the LSDAS and pay the $93 LSDAS subscription fee)

- **Additional LSDAS Law School**   **$11 each**
  Reports (ordered after you subscribe to the LSDAS initially)

- **LSDAS subscription renewal**   **$55**

■ Fee Waivers for Law Services

Fee waivers are available for the LSAT, LSDAS, and *TriplePrep **Plus*** (see the *Registration and Information Book*). For U.S. citizens, U.S. nationals, or permanent resident aliens of the United States with an Alien Registration Receipt Card (I-151 or I-551), fee waivers can be authorized by Law Services or LSAC-member law schools, which are listed in the *Registration and Information Book*. Canadian citizens must submit their fee waiver request to a Canadian LSAC-member law school even if they plan to apply for admission to a U.S. law school. Fee waivers cannot be granted by financial aid offices of undergraduate institutions, non-LSAC-member law schools, prelaw advisors, or any other individual organization. See the *Registration and Information Book* or contact a law school admission office for details.

The Admission Process

Law school applicants can expect that the admission process will be competitive. Nationally, there are more applicants than spaces available in first-year classes and this means that, at some law schools, there will be considerable competition for seats. However, it is probably true that, if you assess your credentials accurately, your likelihood of admission to an ABA-accredited law school is strong.

■ The Importance of Complete Files

Remember that law schools require complete files before making their decisions. A law school will consider your file complete when it has received your application form; LSDAS Law School Report (or LSAT Law School Report if the law school does not require the LSDAS); letters of recommendation (if required); any requirements unique to the particular school; and application fee.

■ Rolling Admission

Many law schools operate what is known as a rolling admission process: the school evaluates applications and informs candidates of admission decisions on a continuous basis over several months, usually beginning in late fall and extending to midsummer for waiting-list admissions.

At such schools, it is especially important for you to apply at the earliest possible date. The earlier you apply, the more places the school will have available. Most schools try to make comparable decisions throughout the admission season, even those that practice rolling admission. Still, it is disadvantageous to be one of the last applicants to complete a file. Furthermore, the more decisions you receive from law schools early in the process, the better able you will be to make your own decisions, such as whether to apply to more law schools or whether to accept a particular school's offer.

Applying to More Than One School

The average applicant applies to 4.3 law schools. You should be sure to place your applications at schools representing a range of admission standards. Even if you have top qualifications, you should apply to at least one safety school where you are almost certain of being admitted. This is your insurance policy. If you apply to a safety school in November, and are accepted in January or February, you may be disappointed but not panicked if you are later rejected by your top choices.

The Preliminary Review of an Application

Applicants whose qualifications more than fulfill the school's admission standards are usually accepted during the first round of decisions. Candidates whose credentials fall below the school's standards are usually rejected. Full admission committees may never even examine these files.

Most applications are not decided upon immediately. They are usually reviewed in depth by a committee that bases its admission decision on many facets of each application (see "How Law Schools Select Applicants," page 7).

The length of time it takes the committee to review an application varies; consult the individual law schools to which you apply.

Waiting Lists

If you have strong qualifications, but you do not quite meet the competition of those currently being admitted at a particular law school, you may be placed on a waiting list for possible admission at a later date. The law school will send you a letter notifying you of its decision as early as April or as late as July.

It is up to you whether you wish to wait for a decision from a school that has put you on a waiting list or accept an offer from a school that accepted you at an earlier date.

Most schools rank students who are on the waiting list. Some law schools will tell you your rank. If a law school doesn't tell you, you might ask the admission office how many students have been placed on the waiting list.

Seat Deposits

Many law schools use seat deposits to help keep track of their new classes. For example, a typical fee is $200, which is credited to your first-term tuition if you actually register at the school; if you don't register, the deposit may be forfeited or returned partially. A school may require a larger deposit around July 1, which is also credited to tuition. If you decline the offer of admission after you've paid your deposit, a portion of the money may be refunded, depending on the date you actually decline the offer. At some schools, you may not be refunded any of the deposit.

The official position of the Law School Admission Council is:

> Except under early decision plans, law schools should permit applicants to choose among offers of admission as well as offers of scholarships, grants, and loans without penalty **until April 1**. Admitted applicants who have submitted a timely financial aid application should not be required to commit to enroll until notified of financial aid awards that are within the control of the law school.

Misconduct and Irregularities in the Admission Process

The Law School Admission Council has established procedures for dealing with instances of possible candidate misconduct or irregularities on the LSAT or in the law school admission process. Misconduct or irregularity in the admission process is a serious offense with serious consequences. Intent is not an element of a finding of misconduct or irregularity. Misconduct or irregularity is defined as the submission, as part of the law school admission process, of any information that is false, inconsistent, or misleading, or the omission of information that may result in a false or misleading conclusion, or the violation of any regulation governing the law school admission process, including any violation of LSAT test center regulations.

Examples of misconduct and irregularities include, but are not limited to: submission of an altered or a nonauthentic transcript; submission of an application containing false, inconsistent, or misleading information; submission of a fraudulent letter of recommendation; falsification of records; impersonation of another in taking the LSAT; switching of LSAT answer sheets with another; taking the LSAT for purposes other than applying to law school; copying on, or other forms of cheating on, the LSAT; obtaining advance access to test materials; theft of test materials; working, marking, erasing, reading, or turning pages on sections of the LSAT during unauthorized times; submission of false, inconsistent, or misleading information to the Law School Data Assembly Service (LSDAS); false, inconsistent, or misleading statements or omissions of information requested on the LSAT/LSDAS Registration Form or on individual law school application forms; or falsification of transcript information, school attendance, honors, awards, or employment. A charge of misconduct or irregularity may be made prior to a candidate's admission to law school, after matriculation at a law school, or after admission to practice.

When alleged misconduct or irregularity brings into question the validity of LSAC data about a candidate, the school may be notified of possible data error, and transmission of LSAT scores and LSDAS reports will be withheld until the matter has been resolved by the Law School Admission Council's Misconduct and Irregularities in the Admission Process Subcommittee.

The Council will investigate all instances of alleged misconduct or irregularities in the admission process in accordance with the *LSAC Rules Governing Misconduct and Irregularities in the Admission Process*.

A subcommittee representative will determine whether misconduct or an irregularity has occurred. If the subcommittee representative determines that a preponderance of the evidence shows misconduct or irregularity, then a report of the determination is sent to all law schools to which the individual has applied, subsequently applies, or has matriculated. Notation that a misconduct or irregularity report is on file is also included on LSAT/LSDAS Law School Reports. Such reports are retained indefinitely. In appropriate cases, state and national bar authorities and other affected persons and institutions may also receive notification. Individual law schools and bar authorities determine what action, if any, they will take in response to a finding of misconduct or irregularity. Such action may include the closing of an admission file, revocation of an offer of admission, dismissal from law school through a school's internal disciplinary channels, or disbarment. Thus, a finding of misconduct or irregularity is a very serious matter. More information regarding misconduct and irregularity procedures may be obtained by writing to: **Law School Admission Council Misconduct and Irregularities in the Admission Process Subcommittee, Box 40, 661 Penn Street, Newtown, PA 18940-0040**

Chapter 6: Choosing a Law School

For some people, the choice of which law school to attend is an easy one. The most outstanding students will probably be able to go anywhere, and they will select the schools they perceive to be the most prestigious or which offer a program of particular interest. Others who need to stay in a particular area, perhaps because they have a family or a job they don't want to leave, will choose nearby schools and schools with part-time programs.

However, the majority of applicants will have to weigh a variety of personal and academic factors to come up with a list of potential schools. Then, once they have a list, and more than one acceptance letter, they will have to choose a school. Applicants should consider carefully the offerings of each law school before making a decision. The quality of a law school is certainly a major consideration; however, estimations of quality are very subjective. Factors such as the campus atmosphere, the school's devotion to teaching and learning, and the applicant's enthusiasm for the school also are very important. Remember that the law school is going to be your home for three years. Adjusting to law school and the general attitudes of a professional school is difficult enough without the additional hardship of culture shock. Don't choose a law school in New York City if you can't bear subway commutes, noise, and the fast pace. And, if you've lived your entire life in New York, can you face the change you will experience in Kentucky? You also may want to ask yourself if you are already set in an unshakable lifestyle or if you are eager for a new environment.

■ Applicants With Disabilities

If you are a student with a disability, you need not permit your disability to govern choices of where to further your education. You should decide which schools you are interested in attending, based on your interests and qualifications, regardless of disability.

Often law schools give weight to the fact that an applicant has successfully overcome obstacles to build a solid record of academic and professional performance. By law, schools are not permitted to ask about an applicant's disability status, except in very limited circumstances; thus whether or not you disclose on your application that you have a disability is entirely up to you.

The HEATH Resource Center can help you throughout the admission process. For more information on how to contact this organization, see page 39.

Ranking Law Schools

■ Law Schools and Reputation

Many people will tell you to apply to the schools that take students in your GPA and LSAT ranges, and then enroll in the best one that accepts you. Law school quality can be assessed in a number of ways.

There is a hierarchy of law schools based on reputation, job placement success, strength of faculty, and the prestige of the parent institution (if there is one). In fact, a study done at one university suggests that undergraduate students perceive schools not only in terms of a hierarchy but also in terms of hierarchical clusters. In other words, certain schools are grouped together in terms of equivalent quality and prestige. Also, there are books or magazine articles that assign law schools purported numerical quality rankings. According to the ABA:

> No rating of law schools beyond the simple statement of their accreditation status is attempted or advocated by the official organizations in legal education. Qualities that make one kind of school good for one student may not be as important to another. The American Bar Association and its Section of Legal Education and Admissions to the Bar have issued disclaimers of any law school rating system. Prospective law students should consider a variety of factors in making their choice among schools.[1]

Since there is no official ranking authority, you should be cautious in using such rankings. The factors that make up a law school's reputation—strength of curriculum, faculty, career services, ability of students, quality of library facilities, and the like—don't lend themselves to quantification. Even if the rankings were more or less accurate, the school's reputation is only one factor among many for you to consider.

■ What's in a Name?

While going to a "name" school may mean that you will have an easier time finding your first job, it doesn't necessarily mean that you will get a better legal education than if you go to a lesser-known law school. Some schools that were at their peaks years ago are still riding on the wave of that earlier reputation. Others have greatly improved their programs and have recruited talented faculty, but have not yet made a name for themselves. Of course, schools already considered excellent have a stake in maintaining their status.

Once admitted, many applicants elect to attend "name" schools. However, in making this decision you should consider a variety of factors, such as the contacts you may acquire at a school in the area where you hope to practice, the size of the school, and cost. The substantive differences between schools should be your focus when making this important choice rather than the school's reputed ranking.

■ The Parent University

About 90 percent of ABA-approved law schools are part of a larger university. The reputation of an undergraduate school may influence the reputation of the law school so you might want to investigate the college before committing to the law school.

In addition, there may be some advantages to attending a law school that is part of a university. Such law schools may have more options for joint-degree programs or for taking a nonlaw school course or two. They also may have more academic and social activities, campus theater groups, sports teams, and everything else that comes with university life. Perhaps most important, the university can act as a support system for the law school by providing a wealth of facilities, including student housing and support for career services.

■ National, Regional, and Local Schools

A **national** school will generally have an applicant population and a student body that draws almost indistinguishably from the nation as a whole and will have many international students as well. A **regional** school is likely to have a population that is primarily from the geographic region of its location, though many regional schools have students from all over the country as well; a number of regional schools draw heavily from a particular geographical area, yet graduates may find jobs all over the country. Generally speaking, a **local** school is drawing primarily on applicants who either come from or want to practice in the proximate area in which the school is located. Many local law schools have excellent reputations and compete with the national schools in faculty competence, in research-supporting activities, and in resources generally. Check the school's catalog or talk with the admission and placement staff to get a clear breakdown on where their students come from and where they are finding jobs.

[1] The American Bar Association Standards for Approval of Law Schools, General Information of the Council for the Section of Legal Education and Admissions to the Bar, Number 8, "Rating of Law Schools," p. 161, American Bar Association, Indianapolis, IN, 1998.

Evaluating Law Schools

The best advice on how to select a law school is to choose the school that is **best for you**. The law schools invest substantial time and effort in evaluating prospective students, and applicants should evaluate law schools with equivalent care. The following are some features to keep in mind as you systematically evaluate law schools. (Costs and other financial criteria are not included below; they are discussed in Chapter 8.)

Each listing in this *Guide* provides school-specific information in the following categories as well.

■ Enrollment/Student Body

The academic qualifications of the student body are important to consider. It's a good idea to select a law school where you will be challenged by your classmates. Use the admission profile grids in this book to check the LSAT scores and GPAs for the previous year's entering class. Try to select a school where your averages will not be significantly different from those of your fellow law students. This is especially true for those with high scores and high GPAs, who would do well at any law school. Because of the important role of student participation in law school classes, your legal education might not be as rewarding as it could be if you are not challenged by your classmates.

You might also inquire about the diversity of the student body. Are a majority of the students the same age, race, sex, and so on? Remember, differences among students will expose you to various points of view; this will be an important aspect of your law school education.

Find out how many students are in a typical class. Much of the learning in law school depends on the quality of class discussion. Small classes provide essential interaction; large classes and the Socratic method provide diversity, challenge, and a good mix of reactions, opinions, and criticism.

It is also important to find out the total number of students enrolled at the school. Not surprisingly, the larger law schools tend to offer a larger selection of courses. Of course, more doesn't always mean better, and no one student has time to take all the courses offered at a large school. However, if you think you want to sample a wide range of courses, you are apt to have more opportunity to do so at a law school with a large faculty.

Part of the law school learning experience takes place after class with fellow students and with members of the faculty. Check to see whether faculty and students are on campus for a substantial part of the day.

Larger schools may also offer more extracurricular programs, greater student services, and a larger library. However, faculties and administrators at smaller schools may be able to give students more attention, and students at smaller schools may experience greater camaraderie. The size of a school is a personal consideration. Some students thrive in large schools; others prefer a smaller student community. Ask yourself which kind of student you are.

■ Faculty

You will undoubtedly wish to assess the faculties of the law schools you are considering. School catalogs will give you some idea of the backgrounds of the full-time faculty—where they went to school, what specialties they have, and what they have published. If the catalog tells you only where degrees were earned, ask for more information. You may also want to check the latest edition of the AALS's *Directory of Law Teachers* available at law school libraries. It may help you to know that some of the faculty have interests similar to your own.

- **Is the faculty relatively diverse with respect to race, ethnic background, gender, degrees in other fields, and breadth of experience?** A faculty with diverse backgrounds will have various points of view and experiences. This diversity will enrich your legal education, broaden your own point of view, and help prepare you for the variety of clients you will work with after law school.

- **How many full-time professors teach how many students—that is, what is the faculty/student ratio?** Although some of the most prestigious law schools are famous for their large sections in the introductory courses, they also provide smaller classes, clinics, simulations, and seminars in advanced subjects. According to the ABA's *Standards for Approval of Law Schools*, it is not favorable to have a full-time faculty to full-time student ratio of 30 to one or more. (The ABA, for purposes of its calculations only, counts as "full-time" those teachers who are employed as full-time teachers on the tenure track or an equivalent, and who do not hold an administrative office. In addition, the ABA considers three part-time students equivalent to two full-time students.)

- **Are some of the teachers recognized as authorities in their respective fields through their writings and professional activities?** Law school catalogs vary widely regarding information about faculty. Some merely list each faculty member's name along with schools attended and degrees earned. Others may provide details about publications, professional activities, and noteworthy achievements, particularly when an individual is an authority in his or her field.

- **Are there visiting professors, distinguished lecturers and visitors, symposiums and the like at the schools you are considering?** Law school lectureship programs are a good means of presenting the knowledge and views of academics outside of the particular law school you attend.

■ The Library and Other Physical Facilities

Chances are you will spend more time in the library than anywhere else, so take stock of the place before you get there. There are five factors to consider when assessing a law school library: the quality of its holdings, cataloging methods, staff, and facilities; and the hours the library remains open.

Whether a library has 250,000 volumes or 2.5 million volumes tells you little about the actual usefulness of the library. It may have an unfathomable number of volumes, but many of them may be outdated, irrelevant, or not readily available to students. All ABA-approved law schools must maintain a library that has the research materials considered essential for the study of law.

Beyond that, find out if the school has any special collections and whether it subscribes to a computerized legal research service such as LEXIS or WESTLAW. Also, find out how many copies of essential materials are available, particularly for large classes.

Even if the library has all the materials you need, you won't be able to get your hands on those materials if the cataloging is years behind. Find out about the quality of the library's professional staff. Is there an adequate number of reference librarians for the number of students and faculty being served? Is the staff helpful?

Be sure the library has an adequate number of comfortable seats with at least enough carrels to accommodate a reasonable number of students at any given time. There should also be conference rooms that students may use for group discussions.

Because you will need to spend much of your time in the library, make sure its hours will accommodate just about any schedule you might have. It should open its doors by the start of classes and remain open well into the night, with a professional library staff available to assist students.

■ Curriculum

The range and quality of academic programs is one of the most important factors to consider when choosing a law school.

Almost all law schools follow the traditional first-year core curricula of civil procedure, criminal law, contracts, torts, and property (see Chapter 2). Do not assume that all law schools have programs that suit your personal needs and special interests. If you don't have any specific interests in mind—and many beginning students don't—try to make sure the school offers a wide range of electives so that you will have many options. A thorough grounding in basic legal theory will enable you to apply the principles learned to any area of law to which they pertain.

In fact, you shouldn't overemphasize your search for specialties; most law students are not specialists when they graduate, nor do they need to be. Generally speaking, new lawyers begin to find their specialties only in the second to fifth years of their careers. A well-rounded legal education from a respected law school is the best preparation for almost any career path you take. The schools' catalogs and the descriptions in this book will tell you a good deal about academic programs. You may also wish to ask school representatives questions such as: Does the school offer a variety of courses, or is it especially strong in certain areas; what sizes are the classes; are seminars and small-group classroom experiences available; and are there ample opportunities for developing writing, researching, and drafting skills?

Beyond the content of law school courses, other academic program considerations may be of interest to you as a prospective law student.

■ Special Programs and Academic Activities

Joint-degree Programs

Joint-degree programs allow you to pursue law school and graduate degrees simultaneously. Almost every combination is available at some institutions. Among the more popular degrees are the J.D./ M.B.A. and the J.D./M.A. in such areas as economics or political science. For details, check individual school catalogs and Chapter 12 in this book (Key Facts About LSAC-Member Law Schools).

Master of Laws (LL.M.) Programs and Special-Degree Programs

Many law schools offer advanced degrees that allow students to take graduate-level law courses. The LL.M. degree is quite common and usually is tailored to individual interests. Some schools offer master of laws degrees with particular concentrations, such as a master of laws in taxation and master of comparative law. Students may enroll in LL.M. programs only after having received the J.D. degree.

A few schools also offer very specific, special-degree programs. Some of these specialties include a Doctorate in Civil Law, Doctor of Juridical Science, and Doctor of Jurisprudence and Social Policy. Finding out what types of advanced degrees a law school offers may help you determine the emphases of the school.

Part-Time and Evening Programs

Part-time programs may be offered either in the evening or the day. For the past 10 years, approximately 17 percent of law students have been enrolled in part-time programs. The conventional wisdom is that if you are financially able to attend law school full-time, you ought to do so.

Part-time programs generally take four years to complete instead of three years. If you wish to enroll in such a program, you may be limiting your options somewhat since less than half of the law schools offer part-time programs.

Clinical Programs and Moot Court Competition

Many law schools offer students authentic experiences as lawyers by involving them with clients and providing opportunities to rehearse trial and appellate advocacy in trial team and moot court competitions. It is important that students become adept at using interviewing, counseling, negotiating, and investigating skills.

The best clinical programs involve students in actual legal situations, simulations of such situations, or a combination of both, either at the school itself or in the community. Clinical programs at some schools offer a team-teaching approach; practical, professional skills are taught along with traditional classroom theory. In this manner, faculty can advise and work closely with students.

Law Reviews

Most law schools have a law review—a journal of scholarly articles and commentaries on the law. Writing for the law review of a school can be important to both your legal education and your career in law. Thus, evaluating the law review at a particular law school may be worthwhile when trying to choose the right school to attend.

Traditionally, student law review editors are chosen on the basis of academic standing—usually from the top 10 percent of the class—but writing ability may also be a criterion. Today, a growing number of schools select law review editors by holding a competition in which students submit a previously assigned writing sample to the current editorial board of the review. If you are on the law review, employers may assume you are either one of the brightest in your class, or an outstanding writer—or both.

If possible, check the law reviews of the schools you are considering. The character of the review may be a reflection of the character of the institution that supports it.

Order of the Coif

Many law schools have a chapter of the Order of the Coif, a national honor society for outstanding students. Students are elected to Coif on the basis of scholarship and character. Check to see if the schools you are considering include such a chapter.

Academic Support Programs

Programs for students who need or who are expected to need assistance with legal analysis and writing are offered by most law schools. Students are invited to participate in these programs on the basis of either their entering credentials or their demonstrated academic performance. This assistance may be offered in the summer prior to beginning law school, during the academic year, or both. The aim of academic support programs is to ensure that students have an equal opportunity to compete in law school. For further information about academic assistance programs, consult the admission office at the law school.

■ Student Organizations

You can also tell something about a law school's intellectual resources and its students by the number and range of student associations and organizations sponsored on campus. Many schools have chapters of the American Bar Association—Law Student Division; a student bar association; associations for minority groups, such as the Asian, Black, Hispanic, and Native American Law Student Associations; and associations based on religious affiliations. Some, but not all, schools sponsor an environmental law society, a gay and lesbian law student society, a legal assistance society, a postconviction assistance project, an

ACLU group, a federalist society, a volunteer income-tax assistance program, a law student spouses' club, an international law society, a law and technology society, or a client-counseling society. Determine which associations are important to you and check individual law school catalogs to see which law schools offer what you need.

■ Career Services and Employment

One of the tests of a good law school is the effort the institution makes to help its students and graduates understand their career options and find satisfying employment. Planning a career in law requires students to integrate their legal education and personal goals in the context of the employment marketplace. Some students begin law school with a clear idea of how they expect to use their legal education (although they may change their minds along the way). Others are uncertain, or see a number of tempting possibilities. The career services office, faculty, and alumni/ae of the school are valuable resources in the process of understanding and selecting among the many opportunities available to lawyers.

The first role of the career services office is to educate students about career opportunities in all sectors, including government and public service, law firms of all sizes and specialties, corporations, and so forth. To accomplish such a task, a law school may arrange panel presentations, meetings with practicing lawyers in different fields, and a library of career information materials. Career services professionals also teach students job-search strategies, such as effective interviewing skills and employment research, and discuss students' individual interests, options, and presentation.

One of the most visible career services provided by many law schools is the opportunity to interview with employers on campus for summer and full-time jobs. Ideally, the recruiters should represent a broad range of legal options (small and large firms, government agencies, public interest groups, corporate law departments) and sufficient geographic diversity to meet your needs. Be aware that the number of recruiters at the law school does not necessarily reflect the range of options open to students.

In most schools, only a small percentage of the class gets jobs through on-campus interviewing. Therefore, it is important to investigate the additional support provided by the career services staff and the experiences of the school's students and graduates in finding jobs.

Career services offices are concerned about all students, not just those at the top of the class rankings. Most spend a great deal of time and effort working with students individually and marketing the school to potential employers in order to increase students' options.

Here are some questions you may want to ask about a school's career services:

- What programs does the school offer to introduce students to career options? Do they seem interesting, relevant, and timely?

- Are the career-counseling professionals accessible, respected, well-qualified, and supportive?

- Are the school's faculty and graduates involved in educating students about their career options?

- What types of employers, and how many, recruit on-campus each year? What are the average number of interviews and offers per student? What percentage of students obtain jobs through the on-campus interviewing process?

- What positions have graduates taken in recent years? What work do students do during the summers? In what locales do students and graduates work? Are these employment profiles changing?

- What are the average or median salaries for the school's graduates?

- What percentage of students have accepted positions by graduation; within six months of graduation?

- Does the school offer career counseling and information for its graduates?

Chapter 7: Opportunities in Law for Minority Men and Women

A Career in Law for Minority Group Members

The legal profession is cognizant of the minority exclusion and underrepresentation that has historically pervaded American society. The legal system, which greatly values and benefits from multicultural perspectives, acknowledges the importance of diverse legal representation.

Many minority men and women seek a career in law as a way to address social and political issues. A law career provides a singular opportunity to effect change both on an individual level—by representing the interests of a client—

and on a global level—by setting policy or establishing a precedent in the governmental or business arenas.

Although minority participation in law school and the legal profession is increasing every year, more can and is being done to attract minority men and women to the profession. Outreach efforts by the legal system can and do counteract the shortage of minority lawyers. So does the realization on the part of minority men and women that law can be a rewarding and fulfilling career.

Acquiring a Legal Education

Individual law schools and legal organizations have worked hard to assure continued progress toward alleviating the historic shortage of minority lawyers. For example, the Law School Admission Council established a Minority Affairs Committee and appropriated $1.2 million to be used for projects designed to increase the number of minority men and women who attend law schools. The American Bar Association adopted a law school standard calling for specific commitments to provide full opportunities for members of minority groups.

The Association of American Law Schools also requires that member schools provide full opportunities in legal education for minorities and has programs to increase the number of minority faculty.

A legal education can provide you with considerable opportunity. You will have spent approximately three years thinking critically, reading broadly, and debating forcefully, and these skills are worthwhile in most everything you do.

Admission to Law School

Admission to law school is competitive—sometimes very competitive. However, getting into law school may be less difficult than you expect. Because there are many law schools and varied admission standards, it is advisable for you to do sufficient research and be selective.

- Read and reread the information in this book and study law school catalogs.

- *Thinking About Law School: A Minority Guide* offers realistic tips on how to assess your chances for admission, select the right law school, and finance your legal education. It also includes personal accounts by law school graduates who represent the kind of ethnic diversity law schools seek to achieve. (The book is published by and available free of charge from Law Services.)

- Get advice from a prelaw advisor, an academic counselor, a minority affairs advisor, or a practicing lawyer. Let the law schools you have selected know that you are

interested. Often a school will have a specific program, a minority organization, designated personnel, or a law student to provide assistance for minority applicants.

Don't be intimidated by the law school admission process. Many minority men and women have been surprised by how well their credentials served them in getting into law school. The schools take all aspects of candidates' applications into account when they evaluate them. Personal and social background are considered, as are undergraduate records, LSAT scores, and letters of recommendation. It is to your advantage to include information on your racial or ethnic identity (even if not requested on the application); such information helps to present a complete picture of you. Similarly, interesting life experiences and past employment experiences also count.

For information on the number and percentages of specific minority students and specific minority faculty at ABA-approved law schools, consult the Key Facts for Minority Law School Applicants on the following pages.

Once You Are in Law School

Once you are in law school, you will encounter a difficult but manageable academic program. Very often minority student groups will advise, assist, and support newcomers. Most minority students perform successfully in law school; they are also able to make effective use of their law degrees, whether practicing law or following other career avenues.

Key Facts for Minority Law School Applicants

The chart that follows is based on figures supplied by the majority of Law School Admission Council-member law schools in the fall of 1998. Not all schools use the same classifications for minority groups; as a compromise we are using the classifications defined at the end of this chart.

This information was reported by the schools in Fall 1998, thus the figures may have changed.	Total No. of Students (Full-time + Part-time)	Number and Percentage of Minority Students						Total No. of Full-time Faculty	Number and Percentage of Full-time Minority Faculty						No. of Part-time Minority Faculty	Total No. of Full-time Visiting Minority Faculty	% of Minority Students Receiving Scholarships or Grants	Average Amount Per Scholarship or Grant
		AI/AN	A/PI	B/A-A	H/L	Other	Total No. of Minority Students		AI/AN	A/PI	B/A-A	H/L	Other	Total No. and % of Full-time Minority Faculty				
University of Akron School of Law	579	3 0.5%	8 1.4%	32 5.5%	8 1.4%	2 0.3%	53 9.2%	27	-	1 3.7%	3 11.1%	-	-	4 14.8%	4	-	-	-
The University of Alabama School of Law	550	5 0.9%	3 0.5%	37 6.7%	5 0.9%	-	50 9.1%	38	-	-	3 7.9%	-	-	3 7.9%	1	-	100	$3,000
Albany Law School of Union University	691	3 0.4%	35 5.1%	56 8.1%	28 4.1%	2 0.3%	124 17.9%	36	-	2 5.6%	3 8.3%	-	-	5 13.9%	5	-	74	$8,300
American University—Washington College of Law	1194	11 0.9%	117 9.8%	110 9.2%	85 7.1%	-	323 27.1%	53	-	2 3.8%	5 9.4%	1 1.9%	-	8 15.1%	6	-	37	$8,600
University of Arizona College of Law	460	20 4.3%	27 5.9%	14 3%	54 11.7%	-	115 25%	32	1 3.1%	-	2 6.3%	1 3.1%	-	4 12.5%	3	-	65	$3,480
Arizona State University College of Law	482	32 6.6%	17 3.5%	16 3.3%	51 10.6%	-	116 24.1%	30	1 3.3%	-	-	2 6.7%	-	3 10%	-	-	-	n/a
University of Arkansas School of Law—Fayetteville	364	6 1.6%	4 1.1%	15 4.1%	2 0.5%	-	27 7.4%	33	1 3%	-	3 9.1%	1 3%	-	5 15.2%	-	-	63	varies
University of Arkansas at Little Rock School of Law	420	2 0.5%	4 1%	36 8.6%	7 1.7%	-	49 11.7%	29	-	1 3.4%	2 6.9%	-	-	3 10.3%	2	-	20	$5,989
University of Baltimore School of Law	972	7 0.7%	31 3.2%	122 12.6%	31 3.2%	60 6.2%	251 25.8%	45	-	-	5 11.1%	-	-	5 11.1%	-	-	8	$5,300
Baylor University School of Law	423	3 0.7%	8 1.9%	3 0.7%	21 5%	6 1.4%	41 9.7%	20	-	-	1 5%	-	-	1 5%	-	-	-	n/a
Benjamin N. Cardozo School of Law Yeshiva University	888	4 0.5%	82 9.2%	48 5.4%	46 5.2%	-	180 20.3%	46	-	-	3 6.5%	-	-	3 6.5%	-	-	-	-
Boston College Law School	827	3 0.4%	58 7%	62 7.5%	35 4.2%	-	158 19.1%	53	-	4 7.5%	5 9.4%	1 1.9%	-	10 18.9%	1	3	63	n/a
Boston University School of Law	947	3 0.3%	104 11%	32 3.4%	59 6.2%	-	198 20.9%	58	-	1 1.7%	3 5.2%	1 1.7%	-	5 8.6%	7	-	55	$10,000
Brigham Young University—J. Reuben Clark Law School	456	9 2%	26 5.7%	4 0.9%	22 4.8%	6 1.3%	67 14.7%	28	1 3.6%	-	1 3.6%	1 3.6%	-	3 10.7%	-	-	95	$2,500
Brooklyn Law School	1430	4 0.3%	127 8.9%	80 5.6%	71 5%	-	282 19.7%	62	-	1 1.6%	2 3.2%	1 1.6%	-	4 6.5%	5	1	46	$5,130
University at Buffalo, State University of New York School of Law	657	4 0.6%	17 2.6%	29 4.4%	15 2.3%	-	65 9.9%	50	-	1 2%	5 10%	-	-	6 12%	3	-	30	$10,000
University of California at Berkeley School of Law (Boalt Hall)	846	7 0.8%	178 21%	28 3.3%	69 8.2%	-	282 33.3%	65	-	4 6.2%	1 1.5%	3 4.6%	-	8 12.3%	5	-	70	$5,138

School of Law, University of California—Davis	505	6 1.2%	60 11.9%	13 2.6%	34 6.7%	5 1%	118 23.4%	29	-	3 10.3%	1 3.4%	2 6.9%	-	6 20.7%	2	3	79	$5,243
University of California—Hastings College of the Law	1130	7 0.6%	219 19.4%	54 4.8%	83 7.3%	4 0.4%	367 32.5%	46	-	4 8.7%	4 8.7%	2 4.3%	-	10 21.7%	8	1	-	$1,000–$4,000
University of California at Los Angeles School of Law	976	11 1.1%	184 18.9%	38 3.9%	97 9.9%	-	330 33.8%	80	-	4 5%	4 5%	3 3.8%	-	11 13.8%	-	-	-	-
California Western School of Law	699	12 1.7%	80 11.4%	30 4.3%	73 10.4%	-	195 27.9%	43	-	-	4 9.3%	2 4.7%	-	6 14%	5	-	32	-
Capital University Law School	765	2 0.3%	14 1.8%	58 7.6%	12 1.6%	-	86 11.2%	31	-	4 12.9%	4 12.9%	-	-	4 12.9%	-	-	86	$3,000–$4,000
Case Western Reserve University School of Law	657	2 0.3%	31 4.7%	37 5.6%	2 0.3%	-	72 11%	41	-	2 4.9%	2 4.9%	1 2.1%	-	2 4.9%	-	-	91	$12,800
The Catholic University of America—Columbus School of Law	902	-	30 3.3%	113 12.5%	34 3.8%	-	177 19.6%	47	-	-	6 12.8%	1 2.1%	-	7 14.9%	7	-	-	-
Chapman University School of Law	187	2 1.1%	26 13.9%	3 1.6%	18 9.6%	-	49 26.2%	17	-	2 11.8%	1 5.9%	1 5.9%	-	4 23.5%	1	-	-	$8,082
University of Chicago Law School	560	-	55 9.8%	25 4.5%	29 5.2%	-	109 19.5%	49	-	-	4 8.2%	-	-	4 8.2%	1	-	70	$11,000
Chicago-Kent College of Law—Illinois Institute of Technology	1176	4 0.3%	84 7.1%	64 5.4%	52 4.4%	-	204 17.3%	69	-	-	3 4.3%	2 2.9%	-	5 7.2%	3	-	59	$7,777
University of Cincinnati College of Law	368	1 0.3%	5 1.4%	39 10.6%	8 2.2%	1 0.3%	54 14.7%	26	2 7.7%	2 7.7%	-	-	4 15.4%	8 30.8%	-	-	83	$7,846
City University of New York School of Law at Queens College	372	3 0.8%	44 11.8%	66 17.7%	44 11.8%	7 1.9%	164 44.1%	36	-	4 11.1%	7 19.4%	3 8.3%	-	14 38.9%	3	1	49	varies
Cleveland State University—Cleveland-Marshall College of Law	866	3 0.3%	26 3%	83 9.6%	12 1.4%	7 0.8%	131 15.1%	45	-	2 4.4%	2 4.4%	2 4.4%	-	4 8.9%	2	1	27	$1,330
University of Colorado School of Law	487	14 2.9%	20 4.1%	15 3.1%	28 5.7%	-	77 15.8%	35	-	1 2.9%	2 5.7%	2 5.7%	-	5 14.3%	5	1	55	$2,861
Columbia University School of Law	1132	7 0.6%	155 13.7%	135 11.9%	84 7.4%	1 0.3%	381 33.7%	75	-	7 9.3%	7 9.3%	1 1.3%	-	9 12%	4	1	37	$11,482
University of Connecticut School of Law	581	2 0.3%	36 6.2%	28 4.8%	24 4.1%	-	90 15.5%	43	-	-	3 7%	1 2.3%	-	4 9.3%	2	-	45	$7,562
Cornell University Law School	543	12 2.2%	77 14.2%	39 7.2%	22 4.1%	-	150 27.6%	39	-	1 2.6%	3 7.7%	-	-	4 10.3%	1	-	57	$11,110
Creighton University School of Law	424	3 0.7%	7 1.7%	9 2.1%	20 4.7%	-	39 9.2%	24	-	-	1 4.2%	-	-	1 4.2%	-	-	59	$10,500
University of Dayton School of Law	500	2 0.4%	20 4%	50 10%	23 4.6%	12 1.1%	95 19%	27	-	-	1 3.7%	1 3.7%	-	2 7.4%	-	-	53	$9,500
University of Denver College of Law	1041	9 0.9%	33 3.2%	14 1.3%	37 3.6%	-	93 8.9%	42	2 4.8%	2 4.8%	2 4.8%	2 2.4%	-	5 11.9%	6	4	62	$6,900
DePaul University College of Law	1093	2 0.2%	48 4.4%	55 5%	60 5.5%	-	177 16.2%	48	1 2.1%	1 2.1%	2 4.2%	1 2.1%	-	4 8.3%	4	-	72	$8,000
Detroit College of Law at Michigan State University	741	8 1.1%	22 3.0%	48 6.5%	14 1.9%	-	92 12.4%	29	-	-	2 6.9%	1 3.4%	-	3 10.3%	6	1	39	n/a

This information was reported by the schools in Fall 1998, thus the figures may have changed.	Total No. of Students (Full-time + Part-time)	Number and Percentage of Minority Students						Total No. of Full-time Faculty	Number and Percentage of Full-time Minority Faculty						No. of Part-time Minority Faculty	Total No. of Full-time Visiting Minority Faculty	% of Minority Students Receiving Scholarships or Grants	Average Amount Per Scholarship or Grant
		AI AN	A PI	B A-A	H L	Other	Total No. of Minority Students		AI AN	A PI	B A-A	H L	Other	Total No. and % of Full-time Minority Faculty				
University of Detroit Mercy School of Law	429	2 0.5%	9 2%	51 11.2%	4 0.9%	-	65 14.3%	24	-	-	2 10.0%		-	2 10.0%	3	-		-
University of The District of Columbia—The David A. Clarke School of Law	172	1 0.6%	8 1.9%	37 8.6%	7 1.6%	-	54 12.6%	20	-	-	2 10.0%	-	-	2 10.0%	3	0	-	-
Drake University Law School	397	3 0.8%	5 1.3%	19 4.8%	15 3.8%	5 1.3%	47 11.8%	27	-	-	1 3.7%	-	-	1 3.7%	2	-	66	$12,809
Duke University School of Law	608	-	37 6.1%	67 11%	14 2.3%	12 2%	130 21.4%	33	-	1 3.0%	3 9.1%	-	-	4 12.1%		-	72	$23,181
Duquesne University School of Law	691	-	4 0.6%	26 3.8%	3 0.4%	-	33 4.8%	23	-	1 4.3%	1 4.3%	1 4.3%	-	3 13.0%	5	-	60	$7,000
Emory University School of Law	635	1 0.2%	37 5.8%	54 8.5%	36 5.7%	7 1.1%	135 21.3%	38	-	-	2 5.3%	-	-	2 5.3%		-	36	$13,066
University of Florida College of Law	1191	5 0.4%	40 3.4%	109 9.2%	122 10.2%	-	276 23.2%	74	-	-	5 6.8%	2 2.7%	-	7 9.5%		-	43	$14,194
The Florida State University College of Law	654	7 1.1%	10 1.5%	80 12.2%	62 9.5%	2 0.3%	161 24.6%	43	1 2.3%	-	3 7%	2 4.7%	-	6 14%	2	-	54	$11,447
Fordham University School of Law	1476	-	118 8%	130 8.8%	112 7.6%	-	360 24.4%	62	-	1 1.6%	3 4.8%	1 1.6%	-	5 8.1%	13	-	66	$6,800
Franklin Pierce Law Center	384	3 0.8%	26 6.8%	9 2.3%	16 4.2%	16 4.2%	70 18.2%	20	-	-	-	-	-	-	1	-	72.3	$5,906
George Mason University School of Law	741	4 0.5%	41 5.5%	19 2.6%	20 2.7%	-	84 11.3%	33	-	1 3%	1 3%	-	-	2 6.1%	8	-	11	up to full tuition
George Washington University Law School	1403	5 0.4%	134 9.6%	186 13.3%	91 6.5%	-	416 29.7%	65	-	2 3.1%	5 7.7%	2 3.1%	-	9 13.8%	14	-	47	$8,000
Georgetown University Law Center	2030	11 0.5%	195 9.6%	211 10.4%	114 5.6%	-	531 26.2%	99	-	3 3.0%	8 8.1%	1 1.0%	-	12 12.1%	9	1	-	$8,400
University of Georgia School of Law	633	2 0.3%	17 2.7%	50 7.9%	6 0.9%	-	75 11.8%	44	1 2.3%	1 2.3%	1 2.3%	-	-	3 6.8%	3	-	21	$3,500
Georgia State University College of Law	662	3 0.5%	25 3.8%	84 12.7%	9 1.4%	43 6.5%	164 24.8%	40	1 2.5%	2 5.0%	3 7.5%	-	-	6 15.0%	6	-	6	$2,500
Golden Gate University School of Law	585	3 0.5%	72 12.3%	23 3.9%	55 9.4%	-	153 26.2%	37	-	4 10.8%	2 5.4%	1 2.7%	-	7 18.9%	10	-	8	$8,500
Gonzaga University School of Law	487	11 2.3%	32 6.6%	16 3.3%	16 3.3%	-	75 15.4%	34	-	-	-	3 8.8%	-	3 8.8%	1	1	36	up to full tuition
Hamline University School of Law	488	6 1.2%	21 4.3%	22 4.5%	6 1.2%	5 1%	60 12.3%	28	1 3.6%	-	1 3.6%	-	-	2 7.1%	-	7	29	up to full tuition
Harvard University Law School	1656	11 0.7%	208 12.6%	152 9.2%	89 5.4%	10 0.6	470 28.4%	112	1 0.9%	-	12 10.7%	6 5.4%	-	19 17%	9	4	54	$8,672

University of Hawai'i at Manoa—William S. Richardson School of Law	240	4 1.7%	144 60%	2 0.8%	3 1.3%	3 1.3%	156 65%	17	-	5 29.4%	-	-	-	5 29.4%	16	-	48	$5,280
Hofstra University School of Law	799	-	50 6.3%	50 6.3%	42 5.3%	2 0.3%	144 18%	40	-	-	3 7.5%	1 2.5%	-	4 10%	-	-	58	$4,810
University of Houston Law Center	1002	8 0.8%	76 7.6%	33 3.3%	104 10.4%	-	221 22.1%	46	-	-	3 6.5%	3 6.5%	-	6 13%	6	-	30	$2,000
Howard University School of Law	405	1 0.3%	13 3.2%	362 89.4%	12 3.0%	15 3.7%	403 99.5%	31	-	1 3.2%	24 77.4%	-	1 3.2%	26 83.9%	19	2	37	$8,700
University of Idaho College of Law	300	1 0.3%	2 0.7%	-	14 4.7%	-	17 5.7%	21	-	-	-	-	-	-	-	-	6	$600 - $2,500
University of Illinois College of Law	592	2 0.3%	49 8.3%	74 12.5%	50 8.4%	10 1.7%	175 29.6%	44	-	2 4.5%	4 9.1%	2 4.5%	-	8 18.1%	-	-	64	$6,300
Indiana University School of Law—Bloomington	622	1 0.2%	35 5.6%	46 7.4%	19 3.1%	-	101 16.2%	43	-	-	3 7%	-	-	3 7%	-	-	64	$2,000-full tuition
Indiana University School of Law—Indianapolis	883	5 0.6%	31 3.5%	49 5.5%	19 2.2%	10 1.1%	114 12.9%	33	-	-	2 6.1%	-	-	2 6.1%	-	-	10	$6,000
University of Iowa College of Law	654	14 2.1%	31 4.7%	43 6.6%	31 4.7%	-	119 18.2%	47	1 2.1%	1 2.1%	3 6.4%	1 2.1%	-	6 12.8%	-	-	70	$6,240
The John Marshall Law School	1167	9 0.8%	72 6.2%	96 8.2%	55 4.7%	-	232 19.9%	56	-	-	3 5.4%	1 1.8%	-	4 7.1%	13	-	11	$6,000
University of Kansas School of Law	536	9 1.7%	9 1.7%	20 3.7%	20 3.7%	-	58 10.8%	29	1 3.4%	-	1 3.4%	2 6.9%	-	4 13.8%	-	-	60	up to $8,500
University of Kentucky College of Law	418	-	4 1%	17 4.1%	-	3 0.7%	24 5.7%	27	-	-	2 7.4%	-	-	2 7.4%	1	-	83	tuition
Lewis and Clark, Northwestern School of Law	647	6 0.9%	41 6.3%	8 1.2%	17 2.6%	19 2.9%	91 14.1%	37	-	1 2.7%	1 2.7%	1 2.7%	1 2.7%	4 10.8%	-	-	24	$4,449
Louis D. Brandeis School of Law at the University of Louisville	418	1 0.2%	9 2.2%	24 5.7%	6 1.4%	-	40 9.6%	30	-	-	3 10%	1 3.3%	-	4 13.3%	-	-	80	$5,500
Loyola University Chicago School of Law	725	5 0.7%	59 8.1%	46 6.3%	29 4%	15 2.1%	154 21.2%	36	1 2.8%	-	3 8.3%	-	-	4 11.1%	2	-	66	$3,287
Loyola Law School, Los Angeles, Loyola Marymount University	1343	21 1.6%	284 21.1%	64 4.8%	191 14.2%	-	560 41.7%	64	-	4 6.3%	4 6.3%	5 7.8%	-	13 20.3%	8	-	27	$15,281
Loyola University—New Orleans, School of Law	660	6 0.9%	15 2.3%	88 13.3%	47 7.1%	3 0.5%	159 24.1%	36	-	-	5 13.9%	1 2.8%	-	6 16.7%	-	-	58	$500 to full tuition
University of Maine School of Law	289	1 0.3%	3 1%	7 2.4%	3 1%	-	14 4.8%	18	-	-	-	-	-	-	-	-	80	$2,500 to full tuition
Marquette University Law School	542	-	10 1.8%	13 2.4%	17 3.1%	-	40 7.4%	31	-	-	2 6.5%	1 3.2%	-	3 9.7%	4	-	-	$500 to full tuition
University of Maryland School of Law	847	2 0.2%	82 9.7%	123 14.5%	27 3.2%	9 1.1%	243 28.7%	53	-	1 1.9%	8 15.1%	-	-	9 17%	6	-	75	20% of need-based award
McGeorge School of Law, University of the Pacific	1095	20 1.8%	132 12.1%	34 3.1%	83 7.6%	-	269 24.6%	49	-	1 2%	2 4.1%	1 2%	-	4 8.2%	2	-	44	$1,000 to full tuition
The University of Memphis—Cecil C. Humphreys School of Law	478	1 0.2%	5 1%	51 10.7%	5 1%	-	62 13%	26	-	-	2 7.7%	-	-	2 7.7%	2	-	89	varies

This information was reported by the schools in Fall 1998, thus the figures may have changed.	Total No. of Students (Full-time + Part-time)	Number and Percentage of Minority Students						Total No. of Full-time Faculty	Number and Percentage of Full-time Minority Faculty						No. of Part-time Minority Faculty	Total No. of Full-time Visiting Minority Faculty	% of Minority Students Receiving Scholarships or Grants	Average Amount Per Scholarship or Grant
		AI AN	A PI	B A-A	H L	Other	Total No. of Minority Students		AI AN	A PI	B A-A	H L	Other	Total No. and % of Full-time Minority Faculty				
Mercer University—Walter F. George School of Law	407	4 1%	11 2.7%	26 6.4%	6 1.5%	4 1%	51 12.5%	27	-		2 7.4%	-		2 7.4%	-	-	29	$15,275
University of Miami School of Law	1254	4 0.3%	48 3.8%	114 9.1%	263 21%	-	429 34.2%	52	-		4 7.7%	3 5.8%		7 13.5%	-	2	18	$12,331
University of Michigan Law School	1030	17 1.7%	89 8.6%	76 7.4%	50 4.9%	-	232 22.5%	68			7 10.3%	1 1.5%		8 11.8%	2	-	-	need-based: $8,760 resident; $11,364 nonresident
University of Minnesota Law School	789	8 1%	80 10.1%	22 2.8%	37 4.7%	-	147 18.6%	44	1 2.3%	1 2.3%	3 6.8%			5 11.4%	1	5	64	$1,000 to full tuition
The University of Mississippi School of Law	485	8 1.6%	4 0.8%	47 9.7%	4 0.8%	-	63 13%	27	1 3.7%		4 14.8%			5 18.5%	1	-	92	varies
Mississippi College School of Law	401	3 0.7%	3 0.7%	31 7.7%	3 0.7%	1 0.2%	41 10.2%	20			2 10%			2 10%	2	-	21	$9,564
University of Missouri—Columbia School of Law	550	3 0.5%	10 1.8%	30 5.5%	5 0.9%	-	48 8.7%	35	1 2.9%		2 5.7%			3 8.6%	1	-	90	$2,097
University of Missouri—Kansas City School of Law	485	7 1.4%	10 2.1%	23 4.7%	16 3.3%	-	56 11.5%	31			2 6.5%			2 6.5%	1	1	62	varies
University of Montana School of Law	253	12 4.7%	3 1.2%	1 0.4%	6 2.4%	-	22 8.7%	16	1 6.3%					1 6.3%	1	-	72	$500-$5,908
University of Nebraska College of Law	393	1 0.3%	14 3.6%	11 2.8%	7 1.8%	-	33 8.4%	28			2 7.1%			2 7.1%	1	-	88	varies
New England School of Law	937	9 1%	48 5.1%	56 6%	50 5.3%	21 2.2%	184 19.6%	36		1 2.8%	2 5.6%			3 8.3%	2	-	47	varies
University of New Mexico School of Law	335	20 6%	9 2.7%	8 2.4%	89 26.6%	-	126 37.6%	32	2 6.3%		1 3.1%	6 18.8%		9 28.1%	6	1	25	varies
New York Law School	1405	5 0.4%	97 6.9%	127 9%	109 7.8%	-	338 24.1%	51		2 3.9%	3 5.9%	2 3.9%		7 13.7%	5	-	39	$500-$20,000
New York University School of Law	1368	1 0.1%	141 10.3%	93 6.8%	79 5.8%	-	314 23%	95	0	1 1.1%	8 8.4%	1 1.1%		10 10.5%	-	5	-	-
University of North Carolina School of Law	690	4 0.6%	30 4.3%	91 13.2%	11 1.6%	-	136 19.7%	44			3 6.8%			3 6.8%	2	-	-	$2,800
North Carolina Central University School of Law	373	4 1.1%	8 2.1%	200 53.6%	2 0.5%	5 1.3%	219 58.7%	19			12 63.2%			12 63.2%	6	1	44	varies
University of North Dakota School of Law	204	7 3.4%	3 1.5%	1 0.5%	2 1%	-	13 6.4%	13							-	-	54	varies
Northeastern University School of Law	614	3 0.5%	57 9.3%	60 9.8%	40 6.5%	-	160 26.1%	29		1 3.4%	3 10.3%	2 6.9%		6 20.7%	5	-	58	$10,350
Northern Illinois University College of Law	290	1 0.3%	25 8.6%	21 7.2%	16 5.5%	2 0.7%	65 22.4%	29		1 3.4%	4 13.8%	1 3.4%		6 20.7%	2	-	33	varies
Northern Kentucky University—Salmon P. Chase College of Law	392	2 0.5%	-	16 4.1%	4 1%	-	22 5.6%	24			1 4.2%			1 4.2%	2	-	33	varies

Northwestern University School of Law	642	6 0.9%	59 9.2%	46 7.2%	49 7.6%	–	160 24.9%	54	–	1 1.9%	4 7.4%	–	–	5 9.3%	9	1	76	varies
Nova Southeastern University—Shepard Broad Law Center	953	3 0.3%	21 2.2%	74 7.8%	168 17.6%	–	266 27.9%	48	–	1 2.1%	4 8.3%	4 8.3%	–	9 18.8%	5	2	43	varies
Ohio Northern University—Claude W. Pettit College of Law	305	–	10 3.3%	25 8.2%	11 3.6%	11 3.6%	57 18.7%	20	–	–	–	–	–	–	–	–	50	$10,000
The Ohio State University College of Law	638	2 0.3%	27 4.2%	32 5%	8 1.3%	–	69 10.8%	40	–	1 2.5%	6 15%	–	–	7 17.5%	–	–	77	varies
University of Oklahoma College of Law	575	39 6.8%	24 4.2%	15 2.6%	18 3.1%	–	96 16.7%	34	–	–	1 2.9%	2 5.9%	–	3 8.8%	–	1	20	varies
Oklahoma City University School of Law	509	34 6.7%	18 3.5%	19 3.7%	23 4.5%	–	94 18.5%	30	1 3.3%	–	1 3.3%	–	–	2 6.7%	2	–	–	n/a
University of Oregon School of Law	499	5 1%	28 5.6%	14 2.8%	13 2.6%	–	60 12%	38	1 2.6%	1 2.6%	3 7.9%	1 2.6%	–	6 15.8%	–	–	–	varies
Pace University School of Law	757	2 0.3%	35 4.6%	50 6.6%	44 5.8%	–	131 17.3%	34	–	1	3 8.8%	–	–	3 8.8%	–	–	36	$3,509
University of Pennsylvania Law School	767	4 0.5%	62 8.1%	69 9%	54 7%	–	189 24.6%	51	–	1 2%	2 3.9%	–	–	3 5.9%	8	–	–	–
The Pennsylvania State University, The Dickinson School of Law	508	2 0.4%	9 1.8%	15 3%	8 1.6%	–	34 6.7%	31	–	1 3.2%	1 3.2%	–	–	2 6.5%	–	1	63	$6,372
Pepperdine University School of Law	652	6 0.9%	41 6.3%	35 5.4%	24 3.7%	–	106 16.3%	39	–	1 2.6%	2 5.1%	1 2.6%	–	4 10.3%	–	–	57	$10,295
University of Pittsburgh School of Law	727	2 0.3%	15 2.1%	45 6.2%	14 1.9%	7 1%	83 11.4%	42	–	2 4.8%	2 4.8%	–	–	4 9.5%	2	–	60	$7,100
Quinnipiac College School of Law	758	5 0.7%	24 3.2%	42 5.5%	35 4.6%	–	106 14%	42	–	1 2.4%	2 4.8%	–	–	3 7.1%	1	–	–	varies
Regent University School of Law	398	2 0.5%	13 3.3%	28 7%	12 3%	1 0.3%	56 14.1%	28	–	2 7.1%	3 10.7%	2 7.1%	–	7 25%	3	–	82	$4,000
University of Richmond School of Law	476	1 0.2%	32 6.7%	43 9%	8 1.7%	15 3.2%	99 20.8%	27	–	2 7.4%	2 7.4%	–	1 3.7%	3 11.1%	–	2	71	$7,410
Roger Williams University School of Law	383	–	5 1.3%	14 3.7%	6 1.6%	8 1%	25 6.5%	26	–	–	1 3.8%	–	–	1 3.8%	–	–	50	$3,000
Rutgers—The State University—School of Law—Camden	751	2 0.3%	45 6%	60 8%	25 3.3%	–	132 17.6%	41	–	–	2 4.9%	–	–	2 4.9%	4	–	30	varies
Rutgers University School of Law—Newark	688	–	55 8%	97 14.1%	68 9.9%	–	220 32%	46	–	2 4.3%	7 15.2%	2 2.2%	–	10 21.7%	4	–	34	$1,934
St. John's University School of Law	1034	3 0.3%	79 7.6%	78 7.5%	75 7.3%	4 0.4%	239 23.1%	53	–	1 1.9%	2 3.8%	2 3.8%	–	5 9.4%	–	–	–	–
Saint Louis University School of Law	824	4 0.5%	29 3.5%	66 8.0%	17 2.1%	8 1%	124 15.0%	39	–	1 2.6%	3 7.7%	–	–	4 10.3%	–	–	90	$5,600
St. Mary's University	733	3 0.4%	23 3.1%	42 5.7%	259 35.3%	–	327 44.6%	36	–	1 2.8%	1 2.8%	6 16.7%	–	7 19.4%	3	1	–	varies
St. Thomas University School of Law	487	6 1.2%	13 2.7%	52 10.7%	130 26.7%	3 0.6%	204 41.9%	22	–	9 9.1%	3 13.6%	2 9.1%	–	7 31.8%	6	–	28	$8,767
Samford University, Cumberland School of Law	605	–	4 0.7%	36 6%	8 1.3%	–	48 7.9%	32	–	1 3.1%	3 9.4%	–	–	4 12.5%	5	–	80	$10,000

This information was reported by the schools in Fall 1998, thus the figures may have changed.	Total No. of Students (Full-time + Part-time)	Number and Percentage of Minority Students						Total No. of Full-time Faculty	Number and Percentage of Full-time Minority Faculty						No. of Part-time Minority Faculty	Total No. of Full-time Visiting Minority Faculty	% of Minority Students Receiving Scholarships or Grants	Average Amount Per Scholarship or Grant
		AI AN	A PI	B A-A	H L	Other	Total No. of Minority Students		AI AN	A PI	B A-A	H L	Other	Total No. and % of Full-time Minority Faculty				
University of San Diego School of Law	1133	21 / 1.9%	136 / 12%	20 / 1.8%	80 / 7.1%	-	257 / 22.7%	60	-	2 / 3.3%	2 / 3.3%	4 / 6.7%	-	8 / 13.3%	3	-	-	up to full tuition
University of San Francisco School of Law	645	4 / 0.6%	80 / 12.4%	27 / 4.2%	44 / 6.8%	-	155 / 24%	24	-	1 / 4.2%	3 / 12.5%	1 / 4.2%	-	5 / 20.8%	7	1	-	$5,000
Santa Clara University School of Law	917	5 / 0.5%	174 / 19%	33 / 3.6%	67 / 7.3%	35 / 3.8%	314 / 34.2%	32	-	2 / 6.3%	4 / 12.5%	1 / 3.1%	-	7 / 21.9%	5	-	70	up to full tuition
Seattle University School of Law	841	15 / 1.8%	85 / 10.1%	51 / 6.1%	33 / 3.9%	-	184 / 21.9%	36	-	2 / 5.6%	2 / 5.6%	-	-	4 / 11.1%	6	-	35	up to full tuition
Seton Hall University School of Law	1255	4 / 0.3%	67 / 5.3%	83 / 6.6%	89 / 7.1%	69 / 5.5%	312 / 24.9%	51	-	2 / 3.9%	5 / 9.8%	-	-	7 / 13.7%	4	-	44	$5,074
University of South Carolina School of Law	746	1 / 0.1	8 / 1.1	64 / 8.6	2 / 0.3	-	75 / 10.1	44	-	-	2 / 4.5%	-	-	2 / 4.5%	-	-	30	$1,500
University of South Dakota School of Law	214	6 / 2.8%	3 / 1.4%	3 / 1.4%	-	-	12 / 5.6%	15	1 / 6.7%	-	-	-	-	1 / 6.7%	1	-	33	$900
South Texas College of Law affiliated with Texas A&M University	1206	11 / 0.9%	62 / 5.1%	53 / 4.4%	126 / 10.4%	-	252 / 20.9%	57	1 / 1.8%	1 / 1.8%	2 / 3.5%	2 / 3.5%	-	6 / 10.5%	2	-	-	varies
University of Southern California Law School	620	2 / 0.3%	90 / 14.5%	73 / 11.8%	83 / 13.4%	-	248 / 40%	46	-	1 / 2.2%	2 / 4.3%	1 / 2.2%	-	4 / 8.7%	2	2	65	up to full tuition
Southern Illinois University School of Law	381	3 / 0.8%	16 / 4.2%	22 / 5.8%	5 / 1.3%	-	46 / 12.1%	23	-	-	1 / 4.3%	-	-	1 / 4.3%	-	-	65	varies
Southern Methodist University School of Law	751	6 / 0.8%	31 / 4.1%	34 / 4.5%	45 / 6%	-	116 / 15.4%	36	-	1 / 2.8%	2 / 5.6%	3 / 8.3%	1 / 2.8%	7 / 19.4%	-	1	80	up to full tuition
Southern University Law Center	311	-	-	206 / 66.2%	-	-	206 / 66.2%	30	-	1 / 3.3%	19 / 63.3%	-	-	20 / 66.7%	9	-	20	$4,000
Southwestern University School of Law	902	8 / 0.9%	167 / 18.5%	64 / 7.1%	96 / 10.6%	-	335 / 37.1%	47	-	1 / 2.1%	3 / 6.4%	2 / 4.3%	-	6 / 12.8%	8	-	30	$5,100
Stanford University Law School	541	14 / 2.6%	46 / 8.5%	45 / 8.3%	64 / 11.8%	-	169 / 31.2%	51	-	-	5 / 9.8%	1 / 2%	-	6 / 11.8%	-	3	52	up to full tuition
Suffolk University Law School	1700	3 / 0.2%	68 / 4%	56 / 3.3%	47 / 2.8%	32 / 1.9%	206 / 12.1%	60	-	1 / 1.7%	3 / 5%	1 / 1.7%	-	5 / 8.3%	6	-	80	$5,000
Syracuse University College of Law	751	2 / 0.3%	62 / 8.3%	57 / 7.6%	34 / 4.5%	26 / 3.5%	181 / 24.1%	38	-	-	4 / 10.5%	-	-	4 / 10.5%	-	2	61	$4,278
Temple University School of Law	1104	6 / 0.5%	80 / 7.2%	130 / 11.8%	43 / 3.9%	18 / 1.6%	277 / 25.1%	55	-	2 / 3.6%	8 / 14.5%	2 / 3.6%	-	12 / 21.8%	17	-	26	$2,984
University of Tennessee College of Law	489	4 / 0.8%	6 / 1.2%	47 / 9.6%	4 / 0.8%	-	61 / 12.5%	31	-	-	2 / 6.5%	-	-	2 / 6.5%	-	3	48	$8,474
The University of Texas School of Law	1394	12 / 0.9%	92 / 6.6%	41 / 2.9%	123 / 8.8%	21 / 1.5%	289 / 20.7%	74	-	1 / 1.4%	3 / 4.1%	3 / 4.1%	1 / 1.4%	8 / 10.8%	8	-	78	$2,378
Texas Southern University—Thurgood Marshall School of Law	600	-	-	-	-	-	-	32	-	-	22 / 68.8%	3 / 9.4%	-	25 / 78.1%	17	3	7	$1,000

Texas Tech University School of Law	619	4 0.6%	4 0.6%	11 1.8%	63 10.2%	19 3.1%	101 16.3%	22	-	-	1 4.5%	-	1 4.5%	2 9.1%	1	-	87	$1,000 to full tuition
Texas Wesleyan University School of Law	558	9 1.6%	15 2.7%	25 4.5%	45 8.1%	6 1.1%	100 17.9%	26	-	-	2 7.7%	2 7.7%	-	4 15.4%	2	1	-	-
Thomas M. Cooley Law School	1694	19 1.1%	67 4%	276 16.3%	80 4.7%	39 2.3%	481 28.4%	58	-	-	5 8.6%	-	-	5 8.6%	-	-	-	n/a
Thomas Jefferson School of Law	563	6 1.1%	42 7.5%	22 3.9%	50 8.9%	-	120 21.3%	26	-	-	1 3.8%	1 3.8%	-	2 7.7%	2	-	-	-
The University of Toledo College of Law	550	6 1.1%	8 1.5%	24 4.4%	8 1.5%	-	46 8.4%	33	-	-	3 9.1%	-	-	3 9.1%	-	1	31	$5,537
Touro College—Jacob D. Fuchsberg Law Center	704	-	36 5.1%	89 12.6%	42 6%	2 0.3%	169 24%	37	-	-	2 5.4%	-	-	2 5.4%	4	-	75	$1,000 to full tuition
Tulane University Law School	942	4 0.4%	54 5.7%	79 8.4%	62 6.6%	15 1.6%	214 22.7%	58	-	1 1.7%	4 6.9%	1 1.7%	-	6 10.3%	3	-	28	$10,403
University of Tulsa College of Law	583	51 8.7%	17 2.9%	19 3.3%	21 3.6%	-	108 18.5%	37	1 2.7%	1 2.7%	1 2.7%	3 8.1%	-	6 16.2%	1	-	16	$7,924
University of Utah College of Law	360	3 0.8%	15 4.2%	4 1.1%	21 5.8%	5 1.4%	48 13.3%	27	1 3.7%	1 3.7%	-	3 11.1%	-	5 18.5%	1	1	71	$3,250
Valparaiso University School of Law	420	3 0.7%	8 1.9%	33 7.9%	14 3.3%	6 1.4%	64 15.2%	29	-	-	2 6.9%	-	-	2 6.9%	-	-	50	1/4 to full tuition
Vanderbilt University Law School	550	-	52 9.5%	63 11.5%	11 2%	2 0.4%	128 23.3%	34	-	-	1 2.9%	-	-	1 2.9%	3	-	75	$9,500
Vermont Law School	500	5 1%	15 3%	4 0.8%	16 3.2%	-	40 8%	38	2 5.3%	1 2.6%	-	-	-	3 7.9%	-	-	48	$6,710
Villanova University School of Law	713	3 0.4%	42 5.9%	28 3.9%	26 3.6%	9 1.3%	108 15.1%	42	1 2.4%	1 2.4%	2 4.8%	1 2.4%	-	5 11.9%	-	2	21	-
University of Virginia School of Law	1105	6 0.5%	51 4.6%	74 6.7%	10 0.9%	-	141 12.8%	64	-	1 1.6%	3 4.7%	-	-	4 6.3%	1	-	51	$12,334
Wake Forest University School of Law	475	3 0.6%	10 2.1%	22 4.6%	2 0.4%	-	37 7.8%	34	-	-	2 5.9%	-	-	2 5.9%	3	1	-	-
Washburn University School of Law	435	3 0.7%	15 3.4%	19 4.4%	18 4.1%	-	55 12.6%	27	-	2 7.4%	3 11.1%	2 7.4%	-	7 25.9%	-	-	60	$3,460
University of Washington School of Law	500	8 1.6%	86 17.2%	17 3.4%	32 6.4%	-	143 28.6%	47	-	2 4.3%	3 6.4%	-	-	5 10.6%	-	-	50	$1,200
Washington and Lee University School of Law	367	3 0.8%	12 3.3%	14 3.8%	2 0.5%	2 0.5%	33 9%	33	-	1 3%	3 9.1%	-	-	4 12.1%	-	1	76	7,950
Washington University School of Law	627	11 1.8%	54 8.6%	53 8.5%	14 2.2%	3 0.5%	135 21.5%	48	-	1 2.1%	3 6.3%	-	-	4 8.3%	8	-	35	$15,000
Wayne State University Law School	736	2 0.3%	20 2.7%	78 10.6%	16 2.2%	-	116 15.8%	35	-	-	3 8.6%	-	-	3 8.6%	5	1	95	$2,500
West Virginia University College of Law	439	2 0.5%	9 2.1%	12 2.7%	4 0.9%	-	27 6.2%	25	-	-	2 8%	-	-	2 8%	-	-	95	$11,168
Western New England College School of Law	599	5 0.8%	12 2%	29 4.8%	22 3.7%	4 0.7%	72 12%	26	-	-	-	-	-	-	1	-	19	$4,193
Western State University—College of Law	732	6 0.8%	102 13.9%	50 6.8%	86 11.7%	-	244 33.3%	20	1 5%	1 5%	1 5%	3 15%	-	6 30%	4	-	26	$3,337

This information was reported by the schools in Fall 1998, thus the figures may have changed.	Total No. of Students (Full-time + Part-time)	Number and Percentage of Minority Students						Total No. of Full-time Faculty	Number and Percentage of Full-time Minority Faculty						No. of Part-time Minority Faculty	Total No. of Full-time Visiting Minority Faculty	% of Minority Students Receiving Scholarships or Grants	Average Amount Per Scholarship or Grant
		AI/AN	A/PI	B/A-A	H/L	Other	Total No. of Minority Students		AI/AN	A/PI	B/A-A	H/L	Other	Total No. and % of Full-time Minority Faculty				
Whittier Law School	651	9 1.4%	93 14.3%	41 6.3%	95 14.6%	-	238 36.6%	27	-	-	2 7.4%	1 3.7%	-	3 11.1%	3	-	26	$8,342
Widener University School of Law	1510	5 0.3%	28 1.9%	51 3.4%	19 1.3%	15 1%	118 7.8%	78	-	-	4 5.1%	-	-	4 5.1%	4	-	29	$6,940
Willamette University College of Law	407	5 1.2%	30 7.4%	5 1.2%	8 2%	-	48 11.8%	31	-	-	-	1 3.2%	-	1 3.2%	1	-	56	$7,172
College of William and Mary School of Law	533	4 0.8%	25 4.7%	79 14.8%	6 1.1%	-	114 21.4%	27	-	-	3 11.1%	-	-	3 11.1%	2	1	44	$2,388
William Mitchell College of Law	1021	14 1.4%	38 3.7%	35 3.4%	23 2.3%	-	110 10.8%	33	-	2 6.1%	1 3%	-	-	3 9.1%	6	-	76.4	$2,948
University of Wisconsin Law School	805	23 2.9%	39 4.8%	73 9.1%	50 6.2%	-	185 23%	47	1 2.1%	-	3 6.4%	2 4.3%	-	6 12.8%	-	-	55	$5,000
University of Wyoming College of Law	226	-	2 0.9%	1 0.4%	7 3.1%	-	10 4.4%	14	-	-	-	-	-	-	-	-	-	-
Yale Law School	594	2 0.3%	82 13.8%	58 9.8%	41 6.9%	-	183 30.8%	53	-	4 7.5%	3 5.7%	-	-	7 13.2%	-	-	-	n/a

Minority Key Facts

AI/AN American Indian/Alaskan Native
A/PI Asian/Pacific Islander (i.e., Chinese, Japanese, Korean, Vietnamese, etc.)
B/A-A Black/African American
H/L Hispanic/Latino (i.e., Mexican American, Chicano, Puerto Rican, etc.)
Other

Note: Enrollment figures listed in this Minority Key Facts chart may not directly correspond to figures listed on the Key Facts chart. The discrepancies are due to differences in enrollment definitions used by schools. For example, some schools include part-time students as well as full-time students in their totals; others do not. Several schools included LL.M. candidates, dual-degree students, or other graduate students in their total on one chart but not the other. For the most up-to-date and accurate figures, contact individual schools directly.

Chapter 8: Financing Your Legal Education

The Cost of a Legal Education

The cost of attending law school is a figure that includes tuition, fees, books, housing, and other living expenses for the academic year. It can vary significantly from one school to another. Tuition alone can range from a few thousand dollars a year to more than $25,000 per year. After adding in housing, food, books, and personal expenses, the figure *could* exceed $125,000 for a three-year law school education.

The cost of attending a particular law school is only one of the many factors you should consider in making your choice.

Financial Aid: A Student's Responsibility

The first step in applying for financial aid for law school is to complete the Free Application for Federal Student Aid (FAFSA), available from your college or university financial aid office or from the law school to which you are applying. The FAFSA is a need analysis tool developed by the U.S. Government, Department of Education. It asks for information about your income, assets, and other financial resources. The information you provide on the financial aid form will be used to compute how much you and your family should contribute toward your legal education. Most schools also require copies of annual federal tax returns to verify financial information; some schools also require students to fill out a supplemental form to be considered for institutional aid. Once the analysis is completed, the financial aid officer at the school can determine what types of aid you will need—such as scholarships, grants, loans, or work-study—to pay your law school expenses.

A brochure published by the Law School Admission Council, *Financial Aid for Law School: A Preliminary Guide,* is available at most law school financial aid offices. For complete and individualized information on financing your law school education, contact the financial aid office at the individual law school(s) to which you apply.

Determining How You Will Pay

There are three basic types of financial aid:

- **Scholarships, Grants, and Fellowships**—These types of awards, which do not have to be repaid, are given according to need and/or merit. *Their availability is quite limited,* and they are usually awarded by the law schools themselves. The law school's financial aid office can give you more information.

- **Federal Work-Study**—Federal Work-Study is a program that provides funding for students to work part time during the school year and full time during the summer months. Students sometimes may work on campus in a variety of settings or in off-campus nonprofit agencies. Additional information is available from any law school financial aid office.

- **Loans**—Education loans may be awarded directly by the school or through other private agencies. The largest student loan programs are funded or guaranteed by the federal government. Some are awarded on a need basis, while others are not need-based. Some types of loans will require a credit check. Student loans are usually offered at interest rates lower than consumer loans, and the repayment of principal and interest usually begins after the end of your educational program.

Debt Management

Approximately 80 percent of law school students rely on education loans as their primary source of financial aid for law school. An education loan is a serious financial obligation that must be repaid. Dealing with this long-term financial obligation can be made easier through the implementation of sound debt management practices—both while you are in law school and following your graduation.

■ Credit History

It is very important that you have a good credit history. In today's society, most students have already established a credit history through their repayment records as reported by financial institutions and major retail stores to national credit bureaus. Lenders refer to these credit bureau records to determine your credit worthiness. The credit bureaus report the amounts you borrowed or charged, your outstanding balances, and the promptness by which payments have been made. Failure to pay your financial obligations in a prompt and timely manner will jeopardize your eligibility for some education loans.

If you have been denied credit in the past—or if you even suspect a problem with your credit history—it is wise to get a copy of your credit report. Usually, you can obtain it from a credit bureau in your area. Contact the bureau in writing, giving your name, address, and social security number. You can expect to pay a nominal fee unless you have been denied credit recently, in which case the report may be free. Review your report carefully and clear up any problems you can. Keep in mind that it takes time—possibly months—to clear up errors or other problems, so do not wait until the last minute.

■ Loan Default or Delinquency

These two terms are often confused: **delinquency** occurs when you have begun repayment on a loan or other obligation and have missed one or more payment dates; **default** generally occurs when a delinquency goes beyond 150-180 days.

Delinquencies appear on credit records and may hinder you from qualifying for an education loan that requires a credit check. Defaults are even more serious and are likely to prevent you from receiving federal financial aid as well as disqualifying you for most other education loans. If you are in a default status, you must take steps to change your status if you wish to apply for a federally guaranteed loan for law school. Contact the servicer of your loan(s) for more information on this subject.

■ Planning Ahead: Repayment of Your Loan

Your income after law school is an important factor in determining what constitutes manageable payments on your education loans. Although it may be difficult to predict what kind of job you will get (or want) after law school, or exactly what kind of salary you will receive, it is important that you make **some** assessment of your goals for the purpose of sound debt management. In addition to assessing expected income, you must also create a realistic picture of how much you can afford to pay back on a monthly basis and maintain the lifestyle that you desire. You may have to adjust your thinking about how quickly you can pay your loans back, or how much money you can afford to borrow, or just how extravagantly you expect to live in the years following your graduation from law school.

Your education loan debts represent a serious financial commitment which must be repaid. A default on any loan engenders serious consequences, including possible legal action against you by the lender and/or the government.

There are alternatives available to you to lessen the burden of repayment following law school, including the Federal Consolidation Loan program. The financial aid office at your law school can advise you about repayment issues.

Chapter 9: Finding a Job

Employment Prospects

Because the number of practicing lawyers in the United States continues to increase, it may become more difficult for recent graduates to find jobs in some fields and in certain parts of the country. Opportunities will vary from locality to locality and among legal disciplines. Future lawyers may have to devote considerable time and energy to secure a first job that they consider acceptable. Competition for certain positions will continue to be intense, while opportunities in other fields may expand.

Future demand for people with legal training is almost impossible to predict. Demand for legal services is substantially influenced by the state of the economy. Rising caseloads in the nation's courts and continuing federal and state regulation suggest that the need for lawyers is growing. Whether this expanding need will match or fall short of the parallel growth in the number of practicing lawyers is a question no one can answer with certainty. Lawyers with outstanding academic credentials will continue to obtain desirable positions.

The legal profession itself may adapt to changing job markets by encouraging the entry of lawyers into relatively new fields of law, such as environmental law, intellectual property law, immigration law, and other fields. In addition, certain parts of the country are underrepresented by lawyers.

■ Career Satisfaction

A job search strategy requires careful self-assessment in much the same way as a school search strategy does. A legal career should meet the interests, abilities, capacities, and priorities of the individual lawyer. Career satisfaction is a result of doing what you like to do, and being continually challenged by it. It is up to you to determine what skills you are comfortable using, and to discern which skills are required in the specialties or types of practice you are considering.

■ Gathering Information

Take advantage of any programs and workshops offered by the career services office at your law school. (See page 20 for more on the role of the career services office.) Place your name on file in the office, and be sure to maintain contact with the staff even after you leave school.

The National Association for Law Placement (NALP) is an important source of information (see page 39 for details). This chapter includes a number of charts and graphs compiled by NALP that provide current information relating to employment of law school graduates.

■ Nonlegal Careers for Lawyers

Law-trained individuals pursue a wide variety of careers, and the skills discussed in the first section of this chapter provide excellent training for law school graduates who pursue directions outside the practice of law itself. Lawyers work in the media; as teachers of college, graduate school, and law school; and in law enforcement, public relations, foreign service, politics, and administration.

National Association for Law Placement (NALP) Employment Report and Salary Survey

■ Types of Employment

Data collected on employer types help us understand how new graduates are absorbed into various sectors of the economy. As in all prior years that NALP has collected data, the most common employment setting was that of private practice within a law firm. Of graduates known to be employed, 55.6 percent obtained their first job in a law firm. This remains virtually unchanged from the Class of 1996 and is well below the peak of 64.3 percent for the Class of 1988.

The second most frequent employment setting, accounting for 27.4 percent of employed graduates, was in public service. This total consisted of government (including the military) at 13.5 percent, judicial clerkships at 11.1 percent, and public interest at 2.8 percent. This total compares with 26.5 percent for last year. A small decrease in the percentage of these jobs that were judicial clerkships and an increase in the percentage that were in public interest organizations is noted. Business and industry, accounting for 14.0 percent of jobs, decreased very slightly, after posting steady increases every year from 1989 to 1996.

**Types of Employment
Class of 1997*
(as of February 1998)**

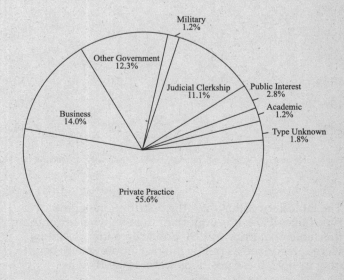

*Represents 82.6% of survey respondents

Twenty-Four-year Perspective of Six Employer Types

Year	Academic	Public Interest	Business	Government	Clerkship	Private Practice
1974	3.5	5.3	9.7	18.5	8.4	51.9
1975	3.3	5.4	9.2	19.3	9.3	49.2
1976	3.3	4.9	9.6	18.5	8.7	50.4
1977	3.3	5.2	9.9	18.2	8.8	52.1
1978	3.4	5.8	10.4	17.0	8.7	51.8
1979	3.0	5.3	10.4	16.2	9.7	53.0
1980	3.0	4.2	10.8	15.5	9.9	54.0
1981	3.1	3.4	11.0	13.4	10.2	56.6
1982	3.0	2.9	10.4	12.1	10.6	57.5
1983	1.2	2.8	10.1	12.8	11.9	58.9
1984	1.8	3.3	11.1	12.2	10.5	58.9
1985	1.5	3.3	10.4	12.0	12.0	60.6
1986	1.6	3.0	9.0	11.8	12.1	62.3
1987	1.0	3.0	7.9	12.2	12.4	63.5
1988	1.0	3.1	6.9	12.0	12.7	64.3
1989	1.0	3.4	5.8	11.4	12.2	62.4
1990	0.8	2.1	6.9	13.7	12.7	62.9
1991	1.0	2.3	7.5	13.4	12.4	60.8
1992	1.1	2.4	8.9	13.4	12.4	59.0
1993	1.1	2.3	10.6	12.6	12.3	57.1
1994	1.3	2.8	12.0	13.1	12.0	55.0
1995	1.2	2.0	13.4	12.8	11.8	56.1
1996	1.3	2.5	14.2	12.6	11.4	55.7
1997	1.2	2.8	14.0	13.5	11.1	55.6

Charts, tables, and copy adapted with permission from the National Association for Law Placement's Class of 1997 Employment Report and Salary Survey (ERSS).

The table above illustrates the distribution of employer types since 1974. It is important to note, when examining this table, that prior to 1990 public defender positions were categorized as public interest employment; beginning in 1990, these positions were reclassified as government employment. In addition, prior to 1983, the academic category included those pursuing an advanced degree full time.

■ Salary as an Employment Factor

The average starting salary for the class of 1997 was $48,986, and the median starting salary for the class of 1997 was $41,000. The median figure compares with $40,000 for last year and is at the highest level since 1985, when these numbers were first compiled.

Nearly 40 percent of all salaries were in the $30,000-40,000 range, and salaries of $30,000 and $35,000 were the most frequently reported. The data also show that the highest paying jobs were the exception rather than the rule: salaries of more than $70,000 accounted for roughly one in five salaries reported. It is worth noting that, over the last two years, the share of salaries of more than $70,000 increased from 11.2 percent to 18.5 percent, while the proportion of salaries in the $55,001-$70,000 range decreased from 15.2 percent to 13.1 percent.

Median Starting Salaries* In:

	Private Practice	Business & Industry	Government
Atlanta	$63,000	$45,000	$38,000
Boston	$75,000	$55,000	$32,669
Chicago	$73,000	$47,000	$35,000
Dallas/ Ft. Worth	$60,000	$46,000	$35,500
Houston	$62,000	$50,000	$36,000
Los Angeles	$78,000	$56,000	$40,000
New York City	$86,000	$60,000	$39,000
Philadelphia	$66,000	$50,000	$34,000
San Francisco	$75,000	$50,000	$46,500
Washington, DC	$75,000	$45,000	$38,380

*Full-time jobs only

Note: The median is the mid-point in a ranking of *all* full-time salaries reported for a given employer type. However, because so many reported salaries are identical and especially cluster at round dollar amounts, such as $40,000, the median should generally be interpreted as the point at which half the salaries are at or above that figure and half are at or below it.

Full-Time Salary Median by Employer Type*

General Category	Legal Jobs Only	Other Jobs
Academic	$36,000	$36,500
Business/Industry	$45,000	$47,000
Government	$34,758	$40,000
Private Practice	$55,000	$31,600
Public Interest	$30,000	$33,000
All Types	$40,000	$44,750

*Based on 1997 Salary Data, full-time jobs only

■ Geography as an Employment Factor

Geographic considerations provide yet another perspective on the placement of new law graduates.

Jobs by City

The 20 cities with the largest number of jobs reported accounted for 39.5 percent of all jobs with a known location. Of these 20 cities, listed in the table, 13 correspond to the 20 largest cities in terms of population. The three largest cities in the country—New York, Los Angeles, and Chicago—continue to be major employment centers for new law graduates. Not surprisingly, New York City accounts for the largest number of jobs, 9 percent of the total. Chicago is among those cities which have lost population from 1990 to 1996.

Seven of the 20 cities providing the most jobs, however, are not among the largest cities in the country. Some of these seven cities are older industrial cities that have been eclipsed in population by the rapidly growing cities of the south and west. Even though Washington, DC no longer ranks as one of the 20 largest cities in terms of population, its importance in the legal market is unlikely to correspondingly diminish.

Jobs by State

States vary widely in the number of jobs each provides, again reflecting the distribution of the total population. However, the top 10 states in terms of total reported jobs taken by law graduates have remained the same over the past six years, with New York and California consistently ranked first and second. Other states have fluctuated to varying degrees in their ranking.

Cities With the Largest Number of Jobs Reported

	City	Number of Jobs
1.	New York City	2,695
2.	Washington, DC	1,570
3.	Chicago	1,238
4.	Los Angeles	1,012
5.	Boston	706
6.	San Francisco	565
7.	Houston	559
8.	Philadelphia	525
9.	Atlanta	521
10.	Dallas/Fort Worth	516
11.	San Diego	405
12.	Minneapolis/St. Paul	378
13.	Miami	349
14.	Cleveland	301
15.	Seattle	283
16.	St. Louis	275
17.	Columbus	250
18.	Baltimore	245
19.	Phoenix	237
20.	Indianapolis	230

Jobs by Region

The distribution by region of jobs taken by law graduates reflects the overall distribution of population. Two regions, Mid-Atlantic and South Atlantic, dominated the job market, accounting for about 40 percent of the jobs for which a location was reported. The East North Central and Pacific states each accounted for an additional 14-15 percent of jobs. The East South Central and Mountain states continued to provide the fewest jobs.

Place of Work Versus Place of School

Comparing the locations of graduates' law school training with the location of their first job offers some insight into the way each geographic market attracts and absorbs graduates from within that market. Some of the underlying factors at work are the supply and demand for new law graduates in each market, the perceived attractiveness of each market, and individual preferences.

Nationally, about 77 percent of graduates accepted jobs within the region where they attended law school. The Mountain region was markedly below this average: 56.4 percent of jobs in the Mountain region were taken by graduates from that region. In contrast, about 85 percent of jobs in the East North Central, West North Central, and West South Central regions were obtained by regional graduates.

These percentages may reflect, in part, variations in each region's ability to attract new lawyers. There appears to be some correlation also between a region's supply of graduates and the extent to which employers hired from that supply.

States With Largest Number of Jobs Per State
1992-1997

Rank	1992	1993	1994	1995	1996	1997
1.	New York	New York	New York	New York	New York	New York
2.	California	California	California	California	California	California
3.	Pennsylvania	Texas	Texas	Texas	Illinois	Texas
4.	Illinois	Illinois	Illinois	Illinois	Texas	Illinois
5.	Wash DC	Pennsylvania	Wash DC	Wash DC	Wash DC	Wash DC
6.	Texas	Wash DC	Florida	Florida	Florida	Florida
7.	Massachusetts	Florida	Pennsylvania	Pennsylvania	Pennsylvania	Pennsylvania
8.	Florida	New Jersey	New Jersey	New Jersey	Ohio	Ohio
9.	New Jersey	Massachusetts	Massachusetts	Massachusetts	Massachusetts	Massachusetts
10.	Ohio	Ohio	Ohio	Ohio	New Jersey	New Jersey

Jobs and Graduates by Region*

Region

	New England	Mid-Atlantic	East North Central	West North Central	South Atlantic	East South Central	West South Central	Mountain	Pacific	Total
Graduates With Known Employment Status	3,181	6,092	5,640	2,418	6,909	1,430	3,357	1,242	4,936	35,205
Graduates With Known Job Location*	2,723	5,136	4,890	2,161	5,813	1,318	2,775	1,054	4,126	29,996
Jobs Reported in Region	1,847	6,101	4,288	1,815	5,819	1,221	2,622	1,471	4,577	29,761
Graduates Staying in Region	1,482	4,336	3,655	1,554	4,260	957	2,237	830	3,564	22,875
Percentage of Jobs to Region Graduates	80.2%	71.1%	85.2%	85.6%	73.2%	78.4%	85.3%	56.4%	77.9%	76.9%
Percentage of Graduates Staying in Region	54.4%	84.4%	74.7%	71.9%	73.3%	72.6%	80.6%	78.7%	86.4%	76.3%

*Includes foreign locations

*U.S. Census Bureau Regions

	Region	States Included
1.	New England	CT, ME, MA, NH, RI, VT
2.	Mid-Atlantic	NJ, NY, PA
3.	East North Central	IL, IN, MI, OH, WI
4.	West North Central	IA, KS, MN, MO, NE, ND, SD
5.	South Atlantic	DE, DC, FL, GA, MD, NC, SC, VA, WV
6.	East South Central	AL, KY, MS, TN
7.	West South Central	AR, LA, OK, TX
8.	Mountain	AZ, CO, ID, MT, NV, NM, UT, WY
9.	Pacific	AK, CA, HI, OR, WA

Chapter 10: Organizations You Should Know About

You may have questions concerning a variety of issues while you are applying to law school, once you are in law school, and even after you have your degree. The following organizations may provide you with the answers you need.

American Association of Law Libraries (AALL)

The American Association of Law Libraries exists to provide leadership in the field of legal information, to foster the professional growth of law librarians, to develop the profession of law librarianship, and to enhance the value of law libraries to the legal community and to the public. AALL members come from all sizes and types of libraries: the Library of Congress, legislative libraries, academic law libraries, law firm libraries, bar association libraries, county law libraries, court libraries, and law libraries in business and industry. The association publishes a scholarly journal, a monthly magazine (*AALL Spectrum*), and an annual directory and handbook (which includes a minority law librarians directory).

For more information, contact:

American Association of Law Libraries
53 W. Jackson Blvd., Suite 940
Chicago, IL 60604
Phone: 312.939.4764
URL: http://www.aallnet.org

American Bar Association (ABA)

The American Bar Association is the national organization of the legal profession. It is composed principally of practicing lawyers; judges; court administrators; law teachers; public service attorneys; many nonpracticing lawyers who are business executives, government officials and so forth; and law students. Although the ABA does not have the power to discipline attorneys or enforce rules, the association leads by serving as the national voice of the profession.

The ABA, with about 350,000 members and 35,000 law student members, is the world's largest voluntary professional association. It serves a dual role as advocate for the profession and for the public. During the past decade, the association has initiated hundreds of programs addressing a wide range of public concerns. Response to these concerns is made possible by thousands of volunteers who contribute both time and money.

The Council of the Section of Legal Education and Admissions to the Bar of the ABA is identified by the U.S. Department of Education as the "nationally recognized accrediting agency for professional schools of law." The role that the American Bar Association plays as a central accrediting body has allowed accreditation to become national in scope rather than fragmented among the 50 states, District of Columbia, the Commonwealth of Puerto Rico, and other territories. Most admitting jurisdictions require applicants for admission to be graduates of law schools approved by the American Bar Association.

The ABA may be contacted for information on the accreditation of law schools and the role of lawyers in the legal profession:

Office of the Consultant on Legal Education
American Bar Association
Indiana University
550 West North Street, Third Floor
Indianapolis, IN 46202
Phone: 317.264.8340
URL: http://www.abanet.org/legaled

Association of American Law Schools (AALS)

The Association of American Law Schools was founded for "the improvement of the legal profession through legal education." It is an association of law schools that serves as the law teachers' learned society. The association requires quality teaching and scholarship of its 162 member schools.

The organization provides a range of services to law schools. Among them are professional development workshops and conferences for law faculty, facilitation of law faculty recruitment, publication of the *AALS Directory of Law Teachers*, and interpretation of the mission and needs of legal education as the principal representative to other national higher education organizations, the federal government, and learned societies.

The AALS may be contacted for specific information about the role of legal education in the profession:

Association of American Law Schools
1201 Connecticut Ave., NW
Suite 800
Washington, DC 20036-2605
Phone: 202.296.8851
URL: http://www.aals.org

HEATH Resource Center

The American Council on Education operates the HEATH Resource Center, the national clearinghouse on postsecondary education for individuals with disabilities. HEATH can provide information about requesting disability-related accommodations, ascertaining the level of physical and programmatic access available at law schools, and thinking through disability issues surrounding the application process. A reprint of "Students with Disabilities and Law School" from the HEATH newsletter is available at no charge.

For more information, contact:

HEATH Resource Center
One Dupont Circle, NW
Suite 800
Washington, DC 20036-1193
Phone: 202.939.9320 (Voice/TDD)
URL: http://www.acenet.edu

Law School Admission Council

The Law School Admission Council (LSAC) is a non-profit corporation whose members are 196 law schools in the United States and Canada. It was founded in 1947 to coordinate, facilitate, and enhance the law school admission process. The organization also provides programs and services related to legal education. All law schools approved by the American Bar Association (ABA) are LSAC members. Canadian law schools recognized by a provincial or territorial law society or government agency are also included in the voting membership of the Council.

The services provided by Law Services include: The Law School Admission Test (LSAT); the Law School Data Assembly Service (LSDAS); the Candidate Referral Service (CRS); and various publications and LSAT preparation tools. The LSAT, the LSDAS, and CRS are provided to assist law schools in serving and evaluating applicants. LSAC does not engage in assessing an applicant's chances for admission to any law school; all admission decisions are made by individual law schools.

LSAC exists to serve both the law schools and their candidates for admission. Last year, LSAC administered about 104,000 tests, and processed 135,000 transcripts, 303,000 law school report requests, and 398,000 law school reports.

For more information on the LSAT, the LSDAS, and law school admission, contact:

Law School Admission Council
Box 2000
661 Penn Street
Newtown, PA 18940-0998
Phone: 215.968.1001
URL: http://www.LSAC.org

For information on minority opportunities in law, contact:

Law School Admission Council
Minority Opportunities in Law
Box 40
661 Penn Street
Newtown, PA 18940-0040
Phone: 215.968.1338
URL: http://www.LSAC.org

National Association for Law Placement (NALP)

The National Association for Law Placement is a professional organization of law schools and legal employers. NALP's mission is to provide information, coordination, and standards for fair recruiting for all of the participants in the legal recruiting process. NALP provides a forum for discussion of recruiting trends and problems among school and employer representatives; provides professional education and resources for law school career services professionals and legal employers, recruiting directors, and hiring attorneys; and conducts research on legal employment.

NALP publishes resource materials that assist students in making informed career choices. NALP publications are available through law school career services offices and may be ordered directly through NALP. However, NALP is not an employment agency, and does not offer specific job listings or maintain comprehensive employment statistics on attorneys other than recent graduates.

NALP believes that each law school offers unique programs and opportunities and, like the American Bar Association and the Law School Admission Council, does not rate law schools or career services offices.

For further information, write or call:

National Association for Law Placement
Suite 325
1666 Connecticut Avenue, NW
Washington, DC 20009-1039
Phone: 202.667.1666
URL: http://www.nalp.org

Chapter 11: Prelaw Readings: Books of Interest

The following list of prelaw readings offers prospective law students an overview of selected classics and current titles in certain subjects: law school and legal education, the legal profession, biography, jurisprudence and legal issues, and financing a law school education. Some of these publications list sources for financial aid, but students will need to call or write the individual organizations for the most up-to-date information.

This list should not be construed as the official bibliography of Law School Admission Council; it is beyond the scope of this publication to provide any sort of definitive catalog of prelaw readings.

Some of these books have already withstood the test of time, and are as relevant today as when they were first written and published, generations ago. Examples are: Richard Kluger's *Simple Justice*—a rare glimpse into the private workings and deliberations of the Supreme Court; and Karl Llewellyn's *The Bramble Bush*—a classic study of how legal education shapes our legal institutions.

Some titles simply reflect the most current writing on the subjects listed above and are not necessarily recommended simply because they appear on this list. It will be up to you to search out the titles that pique your interest and make your own determination of their worth. The aim of our list is merely to give you a head start. We hope that those interested in pursuing legal studies will find the issues raised and the ideas discussed in these works helpful in making the decision to choose law as a career.

■ Law School and Legal Education

Balancing the Scales: Minorities and Law School. [video, 20 min.] Newtown, PA: Law School Admission Council, 1995.

Barber, David H. *Winning in Law School: Stress Reduction.* 2d ed. Dillon, CO: Spectra, 1986.

Bay, Monica. *Careers in Civil Litigation.* Chicago: American Bar Association/Law Student Division, 1990.

Bell, Susan J. *Full Disclosure: Do You Really Want to Be a Lawyer?* Princeton, NJ: Peterson's Guides, 1989.

Bell, Susan J. *Interviewing for Success and Satisfaction.* Chicago: American Bar Association/Young Lawyers Division, 1989.

Briggs, Amy Thompson. *Degrees of Difference: A How-to Guide to Choosing a Law School.* Washington, DC: National Association of Law Placement, 1998.

Calamari, John D. and Joseph M. Perillo, eds. *How to Thrive in Law School.* Pelham Manor, NY: Hook Mountain Press, 1984.

Carter, Lief H. *Reason in Law.* Boston: Little, Brown & Company, 1988.

Chase, William C. *The American Law School and the Rise of Administrative Government.* Madison, WI: University of Wisconsin Press, 1982.

Curry, Boykin, ed. *Essays That Worked for Law Schools: 35 Essays from Successful Applications to the Nation's Top Law Schools.* New York: Fawcett Book Group, 1991.

Deaver, Jeff. *The Complete Law School Companion: How to Excel at America's Most Demanding Post-Graduate Curriculum.* New York: John Wiley & Sons, 1992.

Dworkin, Elizabeth, Jack Himmelstein, and Howard Lesnick. *Becoming a Lawyer: A Humanistic Perspective on Legal Education and Professionalism.* St. Paul, MN: West Publishing, 1989.

Farnsworth, Edward A. *An Introduction to the Legal System of the United States.* 2d ed. Dobbs Ferry, NY: Oceana Publications, 1983.

Gillers, Stephen, ed. *Looking at Law School: A Student Guide From the Society of American Law Teachers.* 3d ed. New York: NAL/Dutton, 1990.

Goldfarb, Sally F. *Inside the Law Schools: A Guide by Students for Students.* 6th ed. New York: Plume, 1993.

Goodrich, Chris. *Anarchy and Elegance: Confessions of a Journalist at Yale Law School.* Boston: Little, Brown & Company, 1991.

Kaplin, William A. *The Concepts and Methods of Constitutional Law.* Durham, NC: Carolina Academic Press, 1992.

Law School: Achieving the Dream. [video, 20 min.] Newtown, PA: Law School Admission Council, 1995.

Legal Education and Professional Development—An Educational Continuum. Report of the Task Force on Law Schools and the Profession: Narrowing the Gap. Chicago: American Bar Association, Section of Legal Education and Admissions to the Bar, July 1992.

Lichtenstein, Elissa, ed. *Law School Public Interest Law Support Programs: A Directory.* Chicago: American Bar Association/Division for Public Services, 1995.

Llewellyn, Karl N. *The Bramble Bush: On Our Law and Its Study.* rev. ed. Dobbs Ferry, NY: Oceana Publications, 1981.

Margulies, Sheldon and Kenneth Lasson. *Learning Law: The Mastery of Legal Logic.* Durham, NC: Carolina Academic Press, 1993.

Martinson, Thomas H., J.D., and David P. Waldherr, J.D. *Getting Into Law School: Strategies for the 90s.* New York: Prentice Hall, 1992.

Mayfield, Craig K. *Reading Skills for Law Students.* Charlottesville, VA: Michie Co., 1980.

Moliterno, James E. and Fredric Lederer. *An Introduction to Law, Law Study, and the Lawyer's Role.* Durham, NC: Carolina Academic Press, 1991.

Morgan, Rick L. and Kurt Snyder. *Official American Bar Association Guide to Approved Law Schools.* New York: Macmillan, 1999.

Roth, George. *Slaying the Law School Dragon: How to Survive—and Thrive—in First-Year Law School.* 2d ed. New York: John Wiley & Sons, 1991.

Schlag, Pierre and David Skolver. *Tactics of Legal Reasoning.* Durham, NC: Carolina Academic Press, 1986.

Shapo, Helene and Marshall Shapo. *Law School Without Fear: Strategies for Success.* New York: Foundation Press, 1996.

Simonhoff, Mark. ed. *My First Year as a Lawyer.* New York: Walker & Company, 1994.

So You Want to Be a Lawyer: A Practical Guide to Law as a Career. Newtown, PA: Law School Admission Council, 1996.

Stevens, Robert. Law School: *Legal Education in America from the 1850s to the 1980s*. Chapel Hill, NC: University of North Carolina Press, 1983.

Stover, Robert V. *Making It and Breaking It: The Fate of Public Interest Commitment During Law School*. Urbana, IL: University of Illinois Press, 1989.

Swygert, Michael I. and **Robert Batey**, eds. *Maximizing the Law School Experience: A Collection of Essays*. St. Petersburg, FL: Stetson University College of Law, 1983.

Turow, Scott. *One L.: An Inside Account of Life in the First Year at Harvard Law School*. New York: Penguin Books, 1978.

Vanderbilt, Arthur T. *Law School: Briefing for a Legal Education*. New York: Penguin Books, 1981.

VerSteeg, Russ. *Essential Latin for Lawyers*. Durham, NC: Carolina Academic Press, 1990.

Williams, Glanville. *Learning the Law: A Book for the Guidance of the Law Student*. 11th ed. London: Stevens, 1982.

Wydick, Richard C. *Plain English for Lawyers*. 2d ed. Durham, NC: Carolina Academic Press, 1985.

■ Legal Profession

Abel, Richard L. *American Lawyers*. New York: Oxford University Press, 1989.

Arron, Deborah. *Running From the Law: Why Good Lawyers Are Getting Out of the Legal Profession*. Berkeley, CA: Ten Speed Press, 1991.

Arron, Deborah. *What Can You Do With a Law Degree? A Lawyer's Guide to Career Alternatives Inside, Outside, and Around the Law*. Seattle: Niche Press, 1992.

Bailey, F. Lee. *To Be a Trial Lawyer*. New York: John Wiley & Sons, 1985.

Caplan, Lincoln. *Skadden: Inside the Business of Law in America*. New York: Farrar, Strauss & Giroux, 1993.

Carey, William T. *Law Students: How to Get a Job When There Aren't Any*. Durham, NC: Carolina Academic Press, 1986.

Couric, Emily. *The Trial Lawyers: The Nation's Top Litigators Tell How They Win*. New York: St. Martin's Press, 1988.

Delaney, John. *Learning Legal Reasoning: Briefings, Analysis and Theory*, rev. ed. Bogota, NJ: John Delaney Publications, 1987.

Epstein, Cynthia Fuchs. *Women in Law*. 2d ed. Urbana, IL: University of Illinois Press, 1993.

Foonberg, Jay G. *How to Start and Build a Law Practice*. 3d ed. Chicago: American Bar Association/Law Student Division, 1991.

Fox, Ronald W. *Lawful Pursuit: Careers in Public Interest Law*. Chicago: American Bar Association, Career Series, 1995.

Galanter, Marc and **Thomas Palay.** *Tournament of Lawyers: The Transformation of the Big Law Firm*. Chicago: University of Chicago Press, 1991.

Glendon, Mary Ann. *A Nation Under Lawyers: How the Crisis in the Legal Profession is Transforming American Society*. New York: Farrar, Straus & Giroux, 1994.

Greene, Robert Michael. *Making Partner: A Guide for Law Firm Associates*. Chicago: American Bar Association, Section of Law Practice Management, 1992.

Harrington, Mona. *Women Lawyers: Rewriting the Rules*. New York: Alfred A. Knopf, 1994.

Henslee, William D. *Careers in Entertainment Law*. Chicago: American Bar Association/Law Student Division, 1990.

Kelly, Michael J. *Lives of Lawyers: Journeys in the Organizations of Practice*. Ann Arbor: University of Michigan Press, 1994.

Killoughey, Donna M. ed. *Breaking Traditions: Work Alternatives for Lawyers*. Chicago: American Bar Association, Section of Law Practice Management, 1993.

Kronman, Anthony T. *The Lost Lawyer: Failing Ideals of the Legal Profession*. Cambridge, MA: Harvard University Press (Belknap Press), 1993.

Linowitz, Sol M., with **Martin Mayer.** *The Betrayed Profession: Lawyering at the End of the Twentieth Century*. New York: Charles Scribner's Sons, 1994.

López, Gerald P. *Rebellious Lawyering: One Chicano's Vision of Progressive Law Practice*. Boulder, CO: Westview Press, 1992.

Luney, Percy R., Jr. *Careers in Natural Resources and Environmental Law*. Chicago: American Bar Association/Law Student Division, 1987.

Mayer, Martin. *The Lawyers*. Westport, CT: Greenwood Press, 1980.

Moll, Richard W. *The Lure of the Law: Why People Become Lawyers, and What the Profession Does to Them*. New York: Penguin Books, 1990.

Munneke, Gary A. *The Legal Career Guide: From Law Student to Lawyer*. Chicago: American Bar Association Career Series, 1992.

Munneke, Gary A. and **William D. Henslee** *Nonlegal Careers for Lawyers*. Chicago: American Bar Association, 1994.

O'Neill, Suzanne B. and **Catherine Gerhauser Sparkman.** *From Law School to Law Practice: The New Associate's Guide*. Philadelphia: American Law Institute/American Bar Association Committee on Continuing Professional Education, 1989.

Shaffer, Thomas L., with **Mary M. Shaffer.** *American Lawyers and Their Communities: Ethics in the Legal Profession*. Notre Dame, IN: University of Notre Dame Press, 1991.

Short Stories from the Real World of Law. [video, 20 min.] Newtown, PA: Law School Admission Council, 1997.

Shropshire, Kenneth. *Careers in Sports Law*. Chicago: American Bar Association/Law Student Division, 1990.

Smith, Janet. *Beyond L.A. Law: Break the Traditional "Lawyer" Mold*. Chicago: Harcourt, Brace, 1998.

Smith, J. Clay, Jr. *Rebels in Law: Voices in History of Black Women Lawyers*. Ann Arbor: The University of Michigan Press, 1998.

Speiser, Stuart M. *Lawyers and the American Dream*. New York: M. Evan and Co., 1993.

Stewart, James B. *The Partners*. New York: Simon & Schuster, 1983.

Thorner, Abbie Willard, ed. *Now Hiring: Government Jobs for Lawyers (1990-1991 edition)*. Chicago: American Bar Association/Law Student Division, 1990.

Wayne, Ellen. *Careers in Labor Law*. Chicago: American Bar Association/Law Student Division, 1985.

■ Biography

Auchincloss, Louis. *Life, Law and Letters: Essays and Sketches*. Boston: Houghton Mifflin Co., 1979.

Baker, Leonard. *John Marshall: A Life in Law*. New York: Macmillan, 1974.

Barth, Alan. *Prophets With Honor: Great Dissents and Great Dissenters in the Supreme Court*. New York: Vintage Books, 1975.

Cray, Ed. *Chief Justice: A Biography of Earl Warren*. New York: Simon & Schuster, 1997.

Darrow, Clarence. *The Story of My Life*. New York: Charles Scribner's Sons, 1932.

Davis, Deane C. *Justice in the Mountains: Stories & Tales by a Vermont Country Lawyer*. Shelburne, VT: New England Press, 1980.

Davis, Lenwood G. *I Have a Dream: The Life and Times of Martin Luther King*. Westport, CT: Negro Universities Press, 1973.

Davis, Michael D. and Hunter R. Clark. *Thurgood Marshall: Warrior at the Bar, Rebel on the Bench*. New York: Birch Lane Press/Carol Publishing Group, 1993.

Douglas, William O. *Go East Young Man: The Early Years*. New York: Random House, 1974.

Douglas, William O. *Court Years, 1939-1975: The Autobiography of William O. Douglas*. New York: Random House, 1980.

Dunne, Gerald T. *Hugo Black and the Judicial Revolution*. New York: Simon & Schuster, 1977.

Frankfurter, Felix. *Felix Frankfurter Reminisces*. New York: Reynal & Co., 1960.

Goldman, Roger, with David Gallen. *Justice William J. Brennan, Jr.: Freedom First*. New York: Carroll & Graf Publishers, Inc., 1994

Griffith, Kathryn. *Judge Learned Hand and the Role of the Federal Judiciary*. Norman, OK: University of Oklahoma Press, 1973.

Griswold, Erwin N. *Ould Fields, New Corne: The Personal Memoirs of a Twentieth Century Lawyer*. St. Paul, MN: West Publishing, 1992.

Gunther, Gerald. *Learned Hand: The Man and the Judge*. New York: Alfred A. Knopf, 1994.

Howe, Mark deWolfe. *Justice Oliver Wendell Holmes*. Cambridge, MA: Harvard University Press, 1957 (vol. 1), 1963 (vol. 2).

Jeffries, John, Jr. *Justice Lewis F. Powell*. New York: Scribner, 1994.

Kahlenberg, Richard D. *Broken Contract: A Memoir of Harvard Law School*. New York: Farrar, Straus & Giroux, 1992.

Lynn, Conrad J. *There Is a Foundation: The Autobiography of a Civil Rights Lawyer*. Westport, CT: Hill & Company, 1978.

Marke, Julius J. *The Holmes Reader*. Dobbs Ferry, NY: Oceana Publications, 1964.

Mason, Alpheus. *Harlan Fiske Stone: Pillar of the Law*. New York: Viking Press, 1956.

Nizer, Louis. *Reflections Without Mirrors: An Autobiography of the Mind*. New York: Doubleday, 1978.

Noonan, John T., Jr. *Persons and Masks of the Law: Cardozo, Holmes, Jefferson, and Wythe as Makers of the Masks*. New York: Farrar, Straus & Giroux, 1976.

Pusey, Merlo J. *Charles Evans Hughes*. New York: Macmillan, 1951.

Rosenkranz, E. Joshua and Bernard Schwartz. *Reason and Passion: Justice Brennan's Enduring Influence*. New York: Norton, 1997.

Rowan, Carl T. *Dream Makers, Dream Breakers. The World of Justice Thurgood Marshall*. Boston: Little Brown & Company, 1993.

Schwartz, Bernard. *Super Chief, Earl Warren and His Supreme Court—A Judicial Biography*. New York: New York University Press, 1983.

Simon, James F. *Independent Journey: The Life of William O. Douglas*. New York: Harper & Row, 1980.

Strum, Phillippa. *Brandeis: Beyond Progressivism*. Lawrence, KS: University Press of Kansas, 1993.

Thomas, Evan. *The Man to See: Edward Bennett Williams, Ultimate Insider; Legendary Trial Lawyer*. New York: Simon & Schuster, 1991.

Urofsky, Melvin I. *Louis D. Brandeis and the Progressive Tradition*. Boston: Little, Brown and Company, 1981.

Westin, Alan F. *Autobiography of the Supreme Court: Off-the-Bench Commentary by the Justices*. Westport, CT: Greenwood Press, 1978.

White, G. Edward. *Earl Warren: A Public Life*. New York: Oxford University Press, 1982.

White, G. Edward. *Justice Oliver Wendell Holmes: Law and the Inner Self*. New York: Oxford University Press, 1993.

Wigdor, David. *Roscoe Pound: Philosopher of Law*. Westport, CT: Greenwood Press, 1974.

■ Jurisprudence and Legal Issues

Berry, Mary Frances. *Black Resistance, White Law: A History of Constitutional Racism in America*. New York: Allen Lane/Peguin Press, 1994.

Bickel, Alexander M. *The Least Dangerous Branch: The Supreme Court at the Bar of Politics*. 2d ed. New Haven: Yale University Press, 1986.

Bodenhamer, David J. and James E. Ely, Jr., eds. *The Bill of Rights in Modern America*. Bloomington, IN: Indiana University Press, 1993.

Cahn, Edmond. *The Moral Decision: Right and Wrong in the Light of American Law*. Bloomington, IN: Indiana University Press, 1955.

Cardozo, Benjamin N. *The Nature of the Judicial Process*. New Haven: Yale University Press, 1921.

Fine, Toni M. *American Legal Systems: A Resource and Reference Guide.* Cincinnati, OH: Anderson Publishing, 1997.

Finkel, Norman J. *Insanity on Trial.* New York: Plenum, 1988.

Friedman, Lawrence M. and **Harry N. Scheiber**, eds. *Legal Culture and the Legal Profession.* Boulder, CO: Westview Press, 1996.

Greenberg, Jack. *Crusaders in the Courts: How a Dedicated Band of Lawyers Fought for the Civil Rights Revolution.* New York: Basic Books, 1994.

Guinier, Lani. *The Tyranny of the Majority: Fundamental Fairness in Representative Democracy.* New York: Martin Kessler Books (The Free Press), 1994.

Hoban, Thomas More and **Richard Oliver Brooks**. *Green Justice: The Environment and the Courts.* Boulder, CO: Westview Press, 1996.

Irons, Peter and **Stephanie Guitton**, eds. *May It Please the Court: The Most Significant Oral Arguments Made Before the Supreme Court Since 1955* [audiocassette]. New York: New Press, 1993.

Kennedy, Caroline and **Ellen Aldeman**. *The Right to Privacy.* New York: Knopf, 1995.

Kluger, Richard. *Simple Justice: The History of Brown vs. Board of Education and Black America's Struggle for Equality.* New York: Alfred A. Knopf, 1976.

Lewis, Anthony. *Gideon's Trumpet.* New York: Random House, 1964.

Lewis, Anthony. *Make No Law: The Sullivan Case and the First Amendment.* New York: Random House, 1991.

Pound, Roscoe. *Law and Morals.* South Hackensack, NJ: Rothman Reprints, 1969.

Rehnquist, William H. *The Supreme Court: How It Was, How It Is.* New York: Quill Press, 1987.

Savage, David. *Turning Right: The Making of the Rehnquist Supreme Court.* New York: John Wiley & Sons, 1992.

Schwartz, Bernard. *A History of the Supreme Court.* New York: Oxford University Press, 1992.

Shapiro, Fred R. *The Oxford Dictionary of American Legal Quotations.* New York: Oxford University Press, 1993.

Shapiro, Joseph P. *No Pity: People With Disabilities Forging a New Civil Rights Movement.* New York: Random House, 1993.

Simon, James F. *The Antagonists: Hugo Black, Felix Frankfurter and Civil Liberties in Modern America.* New York: Simon & Schuster, 1989.

Spence, Gerry. *With Justice for None.* New York: Penguin, 1990.

Stone, Geoffrey R., Richard Epstein, and **Cass R. Sunstein**, eds. *The Bill of Rights in the Modern State.* Chicago: University of Chicago Press, 1992.

Sunstein, Cass R. *Democracy and the Problem of Free Speech.* New York: The Free Press, 1993.

Treanor, Richard Bryant. *We Overcame: The Story of Civil Rights for Disabled People.* Falls Church, VA: Regal Direct Publishing, 1993.

Tribe, Laurence H. *God Save This Honorable Court: How the Choice of Supreme Court Justices Shapes Our History.* New York: Penguin/Mentor, 1986.

Tushnet, Mark V. *Making Civil Rights Law: Thurgood Marshall and the Supreme Court, 1936-1961.* New York: Oxford University Press, 1994.

Tushnet, Mark, ed. *The Warren Court in Historical and Political Perspective.* Charlottesville, VA: University Press of Virginia, 1993.

Vandevelde, Kenneth J. *Thinking Like a Lawyer: An Introduction to Legal Reasoning.* Boulder, CO: Westview Press, 1996.

Walker, Samuel. *Hate Speech: The History of an American Controversy.* Lincoln, NB: University of Nebraska Press, 1994.

Walker, Samuel. *In Defense of American Liberties: A History of the ACLU.* New York: Oxford University Press, 1990.

Williams, Patricia J. *The Alchemy of Race and Rights.* Cambridge, MA: Harvard University Press, 1991.

Wishman, Seymour. *Anatomy of a Jury.* New York: Penguin, 1987.

■ Financing Law School

Johnson, Willis L. *The Big Book of Minority Opportunities: Directory of Special Programs for Minority Group Members.* Garrett Park, MD: Garrett Park Press, 1997.

Financial Aid for Minorities in Business and Law. Garrett Park, MD: Garrett Park Press, 1995.

Schlachter, Gail Ann. *Directory of Financial Aid for Women, 1997-99.* El Dorado Hills, CA: Reference Service Press.

Schlachter, Gail Ann and **R. David Weber.** *Financial Aid for African Americans, 1997-99.* El Dorado Hills, CA: Reference Service Press.

Schlachter, Gail Ann and **R. David Weber.** *Financial Aid for Asian Americans, 1997-99.* El Dorado Hills, CA: Reference Service Press.

Schlachter, Gail Ann and **R. David Weber.** *Financial Aid for Hispanic Americans, 1997-99.* El Dorado Hills, CA: Reference Service Press.

Schlachter, Gail Ann and **R. David Weber.** *Financial Aid for Native Americans, 1997-99.* El Dorado Hills, CA: Reference Service Press.

Schlachter, Gail Ann and **R. David Weber.** *Financial Aid for the Disabled and Their Families, 1998-2000.* El Dorado Hills, CA: Reference Service Press.

Schlachter, Gail Ann and **R. David Weber.** *Financial Aid for Veterans, Military Personnel, and Their Dependents, 1998-2000.* El Dorado Hills, CA: Reference Service Press.

Chapter 12: Key Facts About LSAC-Member Law Schools

This information was reported by the schools in Fall 1998, thus the figures may have changed. The reader is cautioned against making direct comparisons of complex information limited to chart form. Be sure to go beyond the table, indeed beyond the two-page descriptions that follow, if you wish to inform yourself adequately about a particular school. Symbols and footnotes are explained on the last page of this chart.

School	Full-time	Part-time	% Women	% Minority	Faculty Total full-time	Faculty Total part-time	Part-time	Evening division	Total credits from required classes	Total credits required to obtain J.D.	Joint degrees offered	Graduate law study available	Transferable summer courses offered	Summer matriculation for first-year students	Midyear matriculation for first-year students	Academic Support Programs offered	Library Number of full-time staff	Number of volumes and equivalents	In-state, full-time	Out-of-state, full-time	In-state, part-time	Out-of-state, part-time	Application fee	Application deadline for fall admission	Financial aid application deadline	Official Guide page number	Grid included with narrative school description
ALABAMA																											
The University of Alabama School of Law	550	-	38	9	38	42			36	90	•					•	7	364,537	$4,490	$9,484			$25	03/01	03/01	68	
Samford University, Cumberland School of Law	605	-	36.9	7.9	32	32			53	90		•	•	•		•	7	247,324	$18,350	$18,350			$40	05/01	03/01	322	•
ARIZONA																											
University of Arizona College of Law	460	-	50	25	32	48			39	85	•	•	•			•	22	374,000	$4,538	$11,490			$45	03/01	03/01	74	•
Arizona State University College of Law	482	-	44	24	30	21			40	87	•	•	•			•	13	368,919	$4,536	$11,488			$45	03/01	03/01	76	•
ARKANSAS																											
University of Arkansas School of Law—Fayetteville	364	-	40	7.4	33	12			44	90	•	•	•			•	5	252,000	$4,168	$9,136			-	04/01	05/01	78	•
University of Arkansas at Little Rock School of Law	276	144	47	12	29	23	•	•	50	87	•		•			•	14	262,000	$4,500	$10,200	$150h	$340h	$40	05/01	3/01	80	•
CALIFORNIA																											
University of California at Berkeley School of Law (Boalt Hall)	846	-	52	33	65	87			31	85	•	•	•			•	34	760,000	$10,814	$20,198			$40	02/01	03/02F	98	•
University of California—Davis School of Law	505	-	51	23	29	20			35	88	•	•				•	15	401,343	$10,859	$20,243			$40	02/01	03/01	100	•
University of California—Hastings College of the Law	1130	-	48	33	46	44			34	86	•					•	19	612,117	$11,167	$19,937			$40	02/16	02/16	102	•
University of California at Los Angeles School of Law	976	-	48.6	34	80	24			33	87	•	•	•			•	11	554,000	$10,972	$20,356			$40	02/01	03/01	104	•
California Western School of Law	667	32	53.5	27.9	43	46	•		45	89	•	•	•		•	•	7	265,077	$20,500	$20,500	$7,350	$7,350	$45	04/01	03/20	106	•

School										Vols.	Tuition A	Tuition B	Room/Bd A	Room/Bd B	Fee	Deadline 1	Deadline 2	Page
Chapman University School of Law	74	113	48	26	17	15	•	48	88	12	219,386	$20,000	$20,000	$13,750	$13,750	$40	rolling	rolling	116
Golden Gate University School of Law	415	170	58	26	37	94	•	55	88	12	226,140	$19,981	$19,981	$13,091	$13,091	$40	03/01	04/15	176
Loyola Law School, Los Angeles, Loyola Marymount University	968	375	47	41.7	64	84	•	43	87	30	475,000	-	$21,674	$14,526	-	$50	03/02	02/01	218
McGeorge School of Law, University of the Pacific	745	350	48	24.6	49	62	•	54	88	22	436,384	$20,724	$20,724	$13,286	$13,286	$40	-	05/15d; none—e	228
Pepperdine University School of Law	652	-	45	16	39	42	•	57	88	12	265,000	$22,830	$22,830	-	-	$50	05/01	03/01	294
University of San Diego School of Law	788	345	43	22.7	60	56	•	48	85	25	445,000	-	$20,980	$14,890	-	$40	03/02	02/01p	324
University of San Francisco School of Law	518	127	55.7	24.2	24	68	•	48	86	12	288,678	$20,938	$20,938	$748u	$748u	$40	02/15	04/01	326
Santa Clara University School of Law	629	288	49	34.2	32	44	•	45	86	18	275,160	-	$20,782	$15,078	-	$40	03/01	03/01	328
University of Southern California Law School	620	-	46	40	46	40	•	33	88	21	340,000	$25,052	$25,052	-	-	$60	02/15	02/01	340
Southwestern University School of Law	616	286	51.3	37.1	47	37	•	51	87	21	394,090	$21,040	$21,040	$13,362	$13,362	$50	06/01	06/30	348
Stanford University Law School	541	-	43	31	51	76	•	26	86	34	470,000	$25,080	$25,080	$11,580	$11,580	$65	03/15	02/01	350
Thomas Jefferson School of Law	333	230	37.8	21.3	26	26	•	55	88	16	121,180	$18,780	$18,780	-	-	$35	-	raf	372
Western State University—College of Law	231	501	42	33	20	44	•	51	88	8	149,000	$18,900y	$18,900y	$12,600y	$12,600y	$50	04/16	08/01	410
Whittier Law School	392	259	48	37	27	35	•	40	87	8	310,000	$21,030	$21,030	$12,618	$12,618	$50	06/1F	03/15	412
COLORADO																		
University of Colorado School of Law	487	-	47	16	35	42	•	43	89	17	370,000	$17,086	$5,411	-	-	$45	asap	02/15	128
University of Denver College of Law	751	290	52	10	42	49	•	47	90	12	321,596	$19,282	$19,282	$12,440	$12,440	$45	02/15	05/01	140
CONNECTICUT																		
University of Connecticut School of Law	420	161	46	15.5	43	52	•	36	86	18	461,903	$22,420	$10,630	$782c	$371c	$30/45	04/01	04/01	132
Quinnipiac College School of Law	491	267	43	14	42	40	•	53	86	6	339,979	$19,992	$19,992	$833ch	$833ch	$40	04/01	rolling	302
Yale Law School	594	-	43	31	53	64	•	24	82	50	800,000	-	$25,550	-	-	$65	03/15	02/15	426
DELAWARE																		
Widener University School of Law	885	625	45	7.8	78	84	•	51	87	31	572,000	$18,550	$18,550	$13,930	$13,930	$60	-	05/15	414
DISTRICT OF COLUMBIA																		
American University—Washington College of Law	883	311	60	27	53	152	•	34	86	10	425,049	$22,590	$22,590	$881ch	$881ch	$55	03/01	03/01	72
The Catholic University of America—Columbus School of Law	643	259	49	19.6	47	88	•	32	84	17	300,000	$23,014	$23,014	$836ch	$836ch	$55	03/15	03/01	114
University of The District of Columbia—The David A. Clarke School of Law	172	-	53	74	21	9	•	62	90	6	180,000	$14,000	$7,000	-	-	$35	04/30	04/01	148
George Washington University Law School	1165	238	43	30	65	177	•	34	84	32	509,753	$23,955	$23,955	$808c	$808c	$55	03/01	03/01	168
Georgetown University Law Center	1553	477	48	26.2	99	177	•	29	83	70	933,290	$24,530	$24,530	$855c	$855c	$65	03/01	02/01F 03/01e	170
Howard University School of Law	405	-	53	99.5	31	25	•	30	88	17	250,000	$12,425	$12,425	-	-	$60	04/01	04/30	190

This information was reported by the schools in Fall 1998, thus the figures may have changed. The reader is cautioned against making direct comparisons of complex information limited to chart form. Be sure to go beyond the table, indeed beyond the two-page descriptions that follow, if you wish to inform yourself adequately about a particular school. Symbols and footnotes are explained on the last page of this chart.

School	Fall 1998 Enrollment/Student Body				Faculty				Programs								Library		Tuition				Miscellaneous				
	Full-time	Part-time	Percentage of Women	Percentage of Minority	Total full-time	Total part-time	Part-time	Evening division	Total credits from required classes	Total credits required to obtain J.D.	Joint degrees offered	Graduate law study available	Transferable summer courses offered	Summer matriculation for first-year students	Midyear matriculation for first-year students	Academic Support Programs offered	Number of full-time staff	Number of volumes and equivalents	In-state, full-time	Out-of-state, full-time	In-state, part-time	Out-of-state, part-time	Application fee	Application deadline for fall admission	Financial aid application deadline	Official Guide page number	Grid included with narrative school description
FLORIDA																											
University of Florida College of Law	1191	-	42.9	23	74	12			34	88	•		•		•	•	25	591,800	$4,466	$15,022			$20	02/01F 05/15S	04/01F 07/01S	158	•
The Florida State University College of Law	654	-	45	25	43	15			35	88	•		•			•	18	401,020	$4,495	$14,874			$20	02/15	04/01	160	•
University of Miami School of Law	1043	211	43	34.2	52	99	•	•	76	88	•	•	•			•	26	490,000	$21,956	$21,956	$16,168	$16,168	$50	03/08p	03/01	234	•
Nova Southeastern University—Shepard Broad Law Center	784	169	46.1	28	48	65	•		44	90	•		•			•	12	300,689	$19,770	$19,770	$14,832	$14,832	$50	03/01p	03/01	276	•
St. Thomas University School of Law	487	-	39.6	41.8	22	37			41	90				•	•	•	19	287,385	$19,975	$19,975			$40	04/30	04/15	320	•
Stetson University College of Law	644	-	57	21	44	34		•	55	88	•					•	27	350,000	$19,750	$19,750			$50	02/15	02/15	352	•
GEORGIA																											
Emory University School of Law	635	-	50	21.3	38	48			43	88	•		•			•	22	300,000	$23,175	$23,175			$50	03/01	02/15	156	•
University of Georgia School of Law	633	-	46	12	44	29			33	88	•		•			•	20	462,731	$4,200	$14,940			$30	03/01	03/01	172	•
Georgia State University College of Law	414	248	50.5	24.8	40	27	•	•	43	90	•		•			•	6	262,000	$3,132	$12,528	$2,552	$10,208	$30	03/15	04/01	174	•
Mercer University—Walter F. George School of Law	407	-	49	12.5	27	18			53	90	•		•			•	14	273,000	$18,590	$18,590			$45	03/15	04/01	232	•
HAWAII																											
University of Hawai'i at Manoa—William S. Richardson School of Law	240		53	65	17	33			42	89							-	257,679	$8,520	$14,832			$30	03/01	03/01	184	
IDAHO																											
University of Idaho College of Law	300	-	30	6	21	6			31	88						•	9	174,395	$4,076	$10,076			$40	02/01	02/15	192	•
ILLINOIS																											
University of Chicago Law School	560	-	42	19.5	49	39			40	105	•	•				•	20	628,000	$25,149	$25,149			$60	02/01	04/15	118	•
Chicago-Kent College of Law—Illinois Institute of Technology	832	344	49	17.3	69	109	•	•	42	87	•	•	•			•	26	530,000	$20,680	$20,680	$14,915	$14,915	$45	04/01	04/15	120	•
DePaul University College of Law	766	327	51	16	48	86	•	•	40	86	•	•	•			•	26	343,000	$19,800	$19,800	$13,400	$13,400	$40	04/01	03/01	142	•
University of Illinois College of Law	592	-	40	30	44	34			34	90	•	•	•			•	3.5	687,963	$8,412	$18,786			$40	03/15	03/15	194	•

The John Marshall Law School	739	428	44	20	56	125	•	52	90	•	•	•	•	22	362,000	19,500	19,500	11,780	11,780	$50	03/01	rolling	204	•
Loyola University Chicago School of Law	518	207	53	21.2	36	103	•	46	86	•	•	•	•	18	346,663	22,000	22,000	16,500	16,500	$45	04/01	03/01	216	•
Northern Illinois University College of Law	267	23	38	22	29	13	•	38	90	•	•	•	•	12	204,000	5,450	10,900	182ch	364ch	$40	05/15p	03/01p	268	•
Northwestern University School of Law	642	–	51	30	54	162	•	32	86	•	•	•	•	31	634,272	23,974	–	–	–	$70	02/15	03/15	272	•
Southern Illinois University School of Law	376	5	36	12	23	10	•	48	90	•	•	•	•	18	350,000	5,654	14,884	–	–	$25	03/01p	–	342	•
INDIANA																								
Indiana University School of Law—Bloomington	614	8	41	16.2	43	10	•	38	86	•	•	•	•	10	610,000	6,717	17,229	216c	555c	$35	raf	03/01	196	•
Indiana University School of Law—Indianapolis	563	320	45	13	33	34	•	37	90	•	•	•	•	23	492,000	6,499	15,786	4,193	10,185	$35	03/01	–	198	•
Notre Dame Law School	550	–	40	20	40	26	•	52	90	•	•	•	•	23	485,000	21,500	21,500	–	–	$50	03/01	03/01	274	•
Valparaiso University School of Law	367	53	46	15	29	29	•	46	90	•	•	•	•	11	262,000	17,580	17,580	660h	660h	$30	04/15	03/01	384	•
IOWA																								
Drake University Law School	384	13	44	12	27	36	•	41	90	•	•	•	•	12	275,000	16,950	16,950	565ch	565ch	$35	03/01	03/01	150	•
University of Iowa College of Law	654	–	39	18	47	9	•	34	90	•	•	•	•	30	909,842	6,510	16,426	–	–	$30d $50f	03/01	03/01	202	•
KANSAS																								
University of Kansas School of Law	536	–	41	10.8	29	9	•	45	90	•	•	•	•	11	325,000	5,729	12,820	239ch	–	$40	03/15	03/15	206	•
Washburn University School of Law	435	–	43.2	12.6	27	35	•	36	90	•	•	•	•	17	311,932	7,210	10,780	239ch	358ch	$30	03/15	04/01	396	•
KENTUCKY																								
University of Kentucky College of Law	418	–	43	6	27	30	•	37	90	•	•	•	•	17	350,000	5,426	14,036	–	–	$25	03/01	04/01	208	•
Louis D. Brandeis School of Law at the University of Louisville	313	105	40	10	30	10	•	44	90	•	•	•	•	14	303,000	5,330	13,940	4,789	12,559	$30	03/01	06/30	212	•
Northern Kentucky University—Salmon P. Chase College of Law	201	191	41	6	24	105	•	61	90	•	•	•	•	6	248,646	5,390	14,000	227sh	585sh	$30	03/01	02/01	270	•
LOUISIANA																								
Louisiana State University, Paul M. Hebert Law Center	658	–	46	9	33	14	•	39	97	•	•	•	•	9	578,034	1,976	4,654	–	–	$25	02/01	03/01	214	•
Loyola University—New Orleans, School of Law	493	167	46	24	36	41	•	50-56	90	•	•	•	•	23	265,089	18,941	18,941	12,831	12,831	$20	05/01p	–	220	•
Southern University Law Center	311	–	50	66	30	11	•	75	96	•	•	•	•	17	400,270	3,128y	7,728y	–	–	$25	03/31	04/15	346	•
Tulane University Law School	942	–	46.7	22.6	58	48	•	31	88	•	•	•	•	19	501,000	23,588	23,588	–	–	$50	05/01	02/15	378	•
MAINE																								
University of Maine School of Law	289	–	42	5	18	8	•	44	89	•	•	•	•	12	300,000	9,360	17,012	–	–	$25	02/15	02/01	222	•
MARYLAND																								
University of Baltimore School of Law	648	324	52	25.8	45	78	•	38	90	•	•	•	•	17	295,200	9,006	15,624	426c	666c	$35	05/01	04/01	82	•
University of Maryland School of Law	581	266	53	28.7	53	60	•	38-39	85	•	•	•	•	22	375,304	9,517	17,410	7,083	13,001	$50	03/01	03/15	226	•

This information was reported by the schools in Fall 1998, thus the figures may have changed. The reader is cautioned against making direct comparisons of complex information limited to chart form. Be sure to go beyond the table, indeed beyond the two-page descriptions that follow, if you wish to inform yourself adequately about a particular school. Symbols and footnotes are explained on the last page of this chart.

School	Full-time	Part-time	% Women	% Minority	Total full-time faculty	Total part-time faculty	Part-time	Evening division	Total credits from required classes	Total credits required to obtain J.D.	Joint degrees offered	Graduate law study available	Transferable summer courses offered	Summer matriculation for first-year students	Midyear matriculation for first-year students	Academic Support Programs offered	Number of full-time staff	Number of volumes and equivalents	In-state, full-time	Out-of-state, full-time	In-state, part-time	Out-of-state, part-time	Application fee	Application deadline for fall admission	Financial aid application deadline	Official Guide page number	Grid included with narrative school description
MASSACHUSETTS																											
Boston College Law School	827	-	51.6	19.1	53	59			38	85	•					•	22	382,629	$23,420	$23,420	-	-	$65	03/01	03/15	88	•
Boston University School of Law	947	-	49	21	58	71		•	29	84	•					•	26	550,000	$23,138	$23,138	-	-	$50	03/01	04/01	90	•
Harvard University Law School	1656	-	42	28	112	64			30	82						•	91	1,962,871	$23,900	$23,900	-	-	$70	02/01	03/01	182	•
New England School of Law	573	364	50	19.6	36	76	•	•	43	84		•				•	17	290,000	$14,950	$14,950	$11,210	$11,210	$50	03/15p	04/15	252	
Northeastern University School of Law	614	-	65.8	26.1	29	38			48	99	•		•			•	14	285,000	$22,500	$22,500	-	-	$55	03/01	-	266	•
Suffolk University Law School	1050	650	50	12	60	95	•	•	44	84	•		•			•	28	300,080	$20,250	$20,250	$15,188	$15,188	$50	03/01	03/01	354	•
Western New England College School of Law	357	242	50	12	26	34	•	•	42	88	•		•			•	13	351,000	$17,750	$17,750	$13,312	$13,312	$45	raf	04/01	408	•
MICHIGAN																											
Detroit College of Law at Michigan State University	555	186	39	12	29	33	•		60	85	•		•			•	11	200,000	$535c	$535c	$535c	$535c	$50	04/15F	03/15	144	•
University of Detroit Mercy School of Law	243	186	50	13	20	24	•	•	45	90			•			•	12	298,557	$18,000	$18,000	$13,800	$13,800	$50	04/15	03/01	146	•
University of Michigan Law School	1030	-	39.3	22.5	68	52			31	83	•	•	•			•	44	823,967	$17,910	$23,880	-	-	$70	02/15	03/01	236	
Thomas M. Cooley Law School	406	1288	44	28	58	100	•	•	63	90	•		•	•	•	•	34	395,151	$550ch	$550ch	$550ch	$550ch		-	-	370	•
Wayne State University Law School	516	220	46	15.7	35	48	•	•	35	86	•	•		•		•	14	500,000	$7,698	$15,828	$4,170	$8,506	$20	03/15	04/30	404	•
MINNESOTA																											
Hamline University School of Law	463	25	50	12.3	28	45	•		34	88						•	34	220,000	$16,460	$16,460	$11,852	$11,852	$40	03/01p	-	180	
University of Minnesota Law School	789	-	50	19	44	100			32	88	•	•	•			•	29	850,000	$9,000	$15,300	-	-	$40	03/01	03/01	238	•
William Mitchell College of Law	471	550	48	10.8	33	100	•	•	46	86	•	•	•			•	18	286,000	$17,230	$17,230	$12,510	$12,510	$45	07/01	03/15	420	•
MISSISSIPPI																											
The University of Mississippi School of Law	481	4	37	13	27	10			55-58	90			•	•		•	12	287,000	$3,581y	$7,503y	-	-	$25	3/01	03/01	240	
Mississippi College School of Law	401	-	38	10	20	-			34	88	•		•			•	10	293,000	$14,291	$14,291	-	-	$25	05/01	05/01	242	•

MISSOURI

University of Missouri—Columbia School of Law	550	-	40	9	35	12				57	89	•	•	•				•	14	315,000	$8,842	$17,116	-	-	$40	rolling	03/01	244	•
University of Missouri—Kansas City School of Law	454	31	53	11.5	31	47	•			52	91	•	•	•				•	8	277,843	$8,824	$17,098	$315ch	$611ch	$25	rolling	-	246	•
Saint Louis University School of Law	563	261	46	15	39	15	•		•	36	88	•	•	•				•	9	530,000	$19,170	$19,170	$14,360	$14,360	$40	03/01	04/01	316	•
Washington University School of Law	627	-	47	21.5	48	77				35	85	•	•	•					17	563,292	$23,080	$23,080	-	-	$50	03/01	03/01	402	•

MONTANA

University of Montana School of Law	253	-	41	8.7	16	23				59	90	•						•	6	101,990	$6,742	$12,113	-	-	$60	03/01	03/01	248	•

NEBRASKA

Creighton University School of Law	409	15	42	9.2	24	36	•			39	94	•		•				•	14	240,000	$15,684	$15,684	$525ch	$525ch	$40	05/01	03/01	136	
University of Nebraska College of Law	392	1	41	8	28	31				45	96	•						•	12	349,419	$5,050	$11,116			$25	03/01	03/01	250	

NEW HAMPSHIRE

Franklin Pierce Law Center	373	11	39	18.2	20	55				39	84	•	•	•				•	6	213,019	$16,475	$16,475	-	-	$45	05/01	-	164	

NEW JERSEY

Rutgers—The State University—School of Law—Camden	592	159	46	18	41	57	•	•		34	84	•						•	20	404,075	$9,682	$14,206	$401	$591	$50	03/01	03/01	310	•
Rutgers University School of Law—Newark	493	195	45	25	46	27	•	•		31	84	•		•				•	10	386,000	$9,682	$14,206	$401ch	$592ch	$50	03/15	03/01	312	•
Seton Hall University School of Law	920	335	44	25	51	96	•	•		46-47	85	•	•	•				•	23	386,000	$21,980	$21,980	$16,096	$16,096	$50	04/01	04/15	332	

NEW MEXICO

University of New Mexico School of Law	335	-	53	38	32	35				42	86	•						•	35	346,000	$3,984	$13,338	-	-	$40	02/16	03/01	254	•

NEW YORK

Albany Law School of Union University	656	35	53	18	36	45	•			31	87	•		•				•	17	536,218	$19,425	$19,425	$14,600	$14,600	$50	03/15	-	70	•
Benjamin N. Cardozo School of Law Yeshiva University	888	-	48	20.3	46	98				38-39	84	•	•		•	•	•	•	19	427,385	$21,760	$21,760			$60	04/01 Ma,Se	04/15 Ma,Se	86	
Brooklyn Law School	946	484	47.7	19.7	62	94	•	•		35	86	•		•	•			•	21	475,457	$22,000	$22,000	$16,500	$16,500	$60		03/01	94	
University at Buffalo, State University of New York School of Law	657	-	48	10	50	31				39	87	•		•				•	19	517,226	$7,850	$12,500	-	-	$50	02/15	03/15	96	
City University of New York School of Law at Queens College	372	-	62	44	36	12				66	91							•	12	242,632	$3,225s	$4,840s			$40	12/01S; 03/15	07/01	124	
Columbia University School of Law	1132	-	45	34	75	75				32	83	•	•					•	55	980,461	$26,570	$26,570	-	-	$65	02/15	03/01	130	
Cornell University Law School	543	-	44	28	39	15				36	84	•	•	•				•	22	600,442	$24,100	$24,100	$24,100	$24,100	$65	02/01	03/15	134	
Fordham University School of Law	1108	368	45	24.4	62	152	•	•		45	83	•	•					•	11	450,000	$23,600	$23,600	$17,700	$17,700	$60	03/01	03/01	162	•
Hofstra University School of Law	799	-	45	18	40	35				39	87	•		•				•	21	488,617	$22,210	$22,210			$60	04/15	05/15	186	
New York Law School	921	484	47	24	51	70	•	•		37	86	•						•	23	451,199	$22,114	$22,114	$16,588	$16,588	$50	04/01	04/15	256	•
New York University School of Law	1368	-	50	23	95	97				37	82	•	•	•				•	60	944,969	$26,100	-	-		$65	02/01	05/01	258	

This information was reported by the schools in Fall 1998, thus the figures may have changed. The reader is cautioned against making direct comparisons of complex information limited to chart form. Be sure to go beyond the table, indeed beyond the two-page descriptions that follow, if you wish to inform yourself adequately about a particular school. Symbols and footnotes are explained on the last page of this chart.

School	Enroll. Full-time	Enroll. Part-time	% Women	% Minority	Faculty Total full-time	Faculty Total part-time	Part-time	Evening division	Total credits from required classes	Total credits required to obtain J.D.	Joint degrees offered	Graduate law study available	Transferable summer courses offered	Summer matriculation for first-year students	Midyear matriculation for first-year students	Academic Support Programs offered	Library full-time staff	Volumes and equivalents	Tuition In-state, full-time	Tuition Out-of-state, full-time	Tuition In-state, part-time	Tuition Out-of-state, part-time	Application fee	Application deadline for fall admission	Financial aid application deadline	Official Guide page number	Grid included
Pace University School of Law	449	308	51	17	34	64	•	•	40	90	•	•	•			•	8	318,430	$21,600	$21,600	$16,300	$16,300	$55	02/15	02/01	288	•
St. John's University School of Law	752	282	39	23	53	27	•	•	50	85	•	•	•			•	8	440,000	$22,000	-	$16,500	-	$50	03/01	04/01	314	•
Syracuse University College of Law	736	15	46	24	38	44	•	•	40	87	•	•	•			•	16	368,407	$22,224	$22,224	$956ch	$956ch	$50	04/01	03/01	356	•
Touro College—Jacob D. Fuchsberg Law Center	419	285	46.6	24	37	30	•	•	55-56	87	•	•	•		•	•	22	380,000	$19,920	$19,920	$15,450	$15,450	$50	rolling	05/01	376	•
NORTH CAROLINA																											
Campbell University—Norman Adrian Wiggins School of Law	323	-	45	8	20	15			70	90							7	156,342	$16,500	$16,500	-	-	$40	03/31	-	108	
Duke University School of Law	608	-	44	21	33	31			30	84	•	•	•			•	25	510,000	$24,400	$24,400	-	-	$65	02/01	02/01	152	•
University of North Carolina School of Law	690	-	50.5	19.7	44	40			39	86	•	•	•	•		•	19	456,558	$3,169	$15,269	-	-	$60	02/01	03/01	260	•
North Carolina Central University School of Law	265	108	55.8	58.7	19	20	•	•	65	88	•		•			•	15	292,173	$2,700	$10,997	$2,700	$10,997	$30	04/15	02/01	262	
Wake Forest University School of Law	475	-	39	7.7	34	35			41	89	•	•	•			•	13	330,585	$20,450	$20,450	-	-	$60	03/15	05/01	394	•
NORTH DAKOTA																											
University of North Dakota School of Law	204	-	40	6	13	8		•	34	90	•	•	•			•	9	255,991	$4,250	$8,896	-	-	$35	04/01	05/01	264	•
OHIO																											
University of Akron School of Law	351	228	46	9.2	27	43	•	•	44	88	•	•	•			•	12	250,978	$7,718	$13,166	$6,034	$10,290	$35	-	05/01	66	•
Capital University Law School	430	335	45	11.2	31	53	•	•	42	86	•	•	•			•	12	237,500	$15,370	$15,370	$10,070	$10,070	$35	05/01	04/01	110	•
Case Western Reserve University School of Law	640	17	45	11	41	7	•		33	88	•	•	•			•	26	358,621	$20,500	$20,500	$854ch	$854ch	$40	04/01	05/01	112	•
University of Cincinnati College of Law	368	-	51	15	26	68			37	90	•	•	•	•		•	24	379,242	$7,704	$14,808	-	-	$35	04/01	03/01	122	•
Cleveland State University—Cleveland-Marshall College of Law	555	311	48	15	45	30	•	•	46-56	87	•	•	•			•	-	400,000	$7,391	$14,782	$285sh	$569sh	$35	04/01	04/01	126	•
University of Dayton School of Law	500	-	44	19	27	30			36	87	•	•	•			•	12.5	262,739	$18,750	$18,750	-	-	$40	05/01	03/01	138	•

Ohio Northern University— Claude W. Pettit College of Law	305	-	36	18.7	20	23			55	87	•		•			•	11	265,000	$18,980	$18,980	-	-	$40	-	-	278	•
The Ohio State University College of Law	638	1	52.3	10.8	40	36			37	88	•					•	19	665,317	$7,692	$17,086	-	-	$30	03/15	03/01	280	•
The University of Toledo College of Law	387	163	45	8	33	23	•	•	40	89	•		•			•	6.5	306,450	$7,351	$14,174	$307sh	$591sh	$30	03/15	04/01	374	•
OKLAHOMA																											
University of Oklahoma College of Law	575	-	41	17	34	16			40	90	•		•			•	17	300,896	$4,140	$12,924	-	-	$50	04/15	03/01	282	•
Oklahoma City University School of Law	364	145	41	19	30	33	•	•	45	90	•		•				7	262,000	$15,624	$15,624	$10,080	$10,080	$40	07/15	-	284	•
University of Tulsa College of Law	459	124	44	19	37	34	•		28-31	88	•		•		•	•	30	270,325	$16,000	$16,000	$10,600	$10,600	$30	-	-	380	•
OREGON																											
Lewis and Clark, Northwestern School of Law	491	156	47	14	37	61	•	•	35-40	86		•	•			•	-	443,000	$18,265	$18,265	$13,697	$13,697	$50	03/15	02/01	210	•
University of Oregon School of Law	499	-	51	12	38	16			40	85	•		•			•	6	360,000	$10,238	$13,986	-	-	$50	03/01	02/01	286	•
Willamette University College of Law	401	6	45	12	31	21			39	88	•		•			•	11	280,076	$17,700	$17,700	-	-	$50	04/01	03/01	416	
PENNSYLVANIA																											
Duquesne University School of Law	359	332	45	4.7	28	44	•	•	33	86	•		•				16	215,000	$14,942	$14,942	$11,378	$11,378	$50	04/01d	05/01e	154	
University of Pennsylvania Law School	767	-	43	25	51	59			34	89	•	•					14	672,000	$25,780	$25,780	-	-	$65	03/01	03/01	290	•
The Pennsylvania State University, The Dickinson School of Law	508	-	43	7	31	60			41	88	•	•	•			•	14	393,000	$15,040	$15,040	$650ch	$650ch	$50	03/01	02/15	292	•
University of Pittsburgh School of Law	717	10	42	11.4	42	38	•		37	88	•					•	18	375,000	$11,912	$18,618	$11,912	$18,618	$50	03/01	03/01	296	•
Temple University School of Law	758	346	49	25	55	165	•	•	38	86	•	•					16	497,575	$8,926	$15,632	$7,140	$12,506	$50	03/01	03/01	358	•
Villanova University School of Law	713	-	47	15	42	35			45	87	•	•				•	23	430,000	$19,410	$19,410	-	-	$75	03/01	-	390	
Widener University School of Law	885	625	45	7.8	78	84	•	•	51	87	•	•	•			•	31	572,000	$18,550	$18,550	$13,930	$13,930	$60	05/15	-	414	
PUERTO RICO																											
Inter American University School of Law	376	352	56	-	30	27	•	•	62	92		•	•				9	174,934	$8,480	-	$6,360	-	$63	03/31	-	200	
Pontifical Catholic University of Puerto Rico, Faculty of Law**	328	190	51	-	19	15	•	•	82	94	•		•				23	176,914	$4,250s	-	$3,000s	-	$60	04/15	10/02 02/05	298	
University of Puerto Rico School of Law	352	221	55	-	33	33	•	•	70	92			•				10	328,113	$2,320	$3,570	$1,570	$3,500	$15	02/16	04/15	300	•
RHODE ISLAND																											
Roger Williams University School of Law	207	176	44	6.5	26	28	•	•	54	90	•		•			•	13	220,000	$19,100	$19,100	$14,655	$14,655	$60	05/15	04/01	308	•
SOUTH CAROLINA																											
University of South Carolina School of Law	746	-	43	10	44	25			45-47	90	•		•			•	5	326,000	$7,228	$14,986	$304	$626	$25	02/15	04/15	334	•
SOUTH DAKOTA																											
University of South Dakota School of Law	214	-	40.6	5.6	15	2			43-44	90	•		•			•	5	182,522	$103ch	$298.50ch	-	-	$15	03/01	-	336	•

This information was reported by the schools in Fall 1998, thus the figures may have changed. The reader is cautioned against making direct comparisons of complex information limited to chart form. Be sure to go beyond the table, indeed beyond the two-page descriptions that follow, if you wish to inform yourself adequately about a particular school. Symbols and footnotes are explained on the last page of this chart.

School	Full-time	Part-time	% Women	% Minority	Faculty Total full-time	Faculty Total part-time	Part-time	Evening division	Total credits from required classes	Total credits required to obtain J.D.	Joint degrees offered	Graduate law study available	Transferable summer courses offered	Summer matriculation for first-year students	Midyear matriculation for first-year students	Academic Support Programs offered	Library full-time staff	Number of volumes and equivalents	In-state, full-time	Out-of-state, full-time	In-state, part-time	Out-of-state, part-time	Application fee	Application deadline for fall admission	Financial aid application deadline	Official Guide page number	Grid included with narrative school description
TENNESSEE																											
The University of Memphis—Cecil C. Humphreys School of Law	446	32	45	13	26	38	•		56	90	•	•				•	12	272,454	$4,580	$11,376	$206h	$501h	$15	02/15	04/01	230	•
University of Tennessee College of Law	489	-	45	12.5	31	23			45	89	•		•			•	21	452,892	$4,502	$11,424	-	-	$15	02/01	02/14	360	•
Vanderbilt University Law School	550	-	42	23	34	30			33	88	•						22	521,151	$22,780	$22,780	-	-	$50	03/01	2/28	386	
TEXAS																											
Baylor University School of Law	423	-	39	9.7	20	36			62	126	•	•	•	•	•	•	3	198,500	$12,259	$12,259	-	-	$40	03/01	05/31	84	•
University of Houston Law Center	773	229	45	22	46	77	•	•	35	90	•	•	•	•		•	24	480,000	$4,960	$9,920	$160ch	$320ch	$50	02/15	04/01	188	•
St. Mary's University School of Law	733	-	50	45	36	43			47	90	•					•	8	320,000	$545ch	-	-	-	$45	03/01	3/31	318	•
South Texas College of Law affiliated with Texas A&M University	812	394	44	21	57	32	•	•	42	90						•	22	357,491	$15,400	$15,400	$10,500	$10,500	$40	03/01	05/01	338	•
Southern Methodist University School of Law	733	18	45.4	15	36	58	•		33	90	•	•	•		•	•	20	500,000	$21,900	$21,900	-	-	$50	modified rolling	05/01	344	•
The University of Texas School of Law	1394	-	45	20.7	74	73	•		38	90	•	•	•		•	•	43	927,000	$7,234	$15,034	-	-	$65	02/01	03/31	362	•
Texas Southern University—Thurgood Marshall School of Law	600	-	49	87	32	21			71	86						•	8	300,000	$3,960	$7,860	-	-	$40	rolling	05/01	364	•
Texas Tech University School of Law	619	-	43	16	22	13			55	90	•		•			•	14	250,000	$160ch	$329ch	-	-	$50	02/01	-	366	•
Texas Wesleyan University School of Law	303	255	40	17.9	26	31	•	•	50	88			•			•	11	147,750	$13,450	$13,450	$450c	$450c	$50	rolling	-	368	•
UTAH																											
Brigham Young University—J. Reuben Clark Law School	456	-	34	15	28	37			32	90	•	•				•	14	421,912	$5,120	$7,680	-	-	$30	02/01	05/01	92	•
University of Utah College of Law	360	-	38	13.3	27	33			36	88	•	•	•			•	23	300,000	$4,856	$10,822	-	-	$40	02/01	02/15	382	•

School																					Page	
VERMONT																						
Vermont Law School	500	-	48	8	38	27		42	84	•	•	•				•	13	220,000	$19,415	$19,415	-	-	$50	02/01	02/15	388	•
VIRGINIA																						
George Mason University School of Law	379	362	39	11	33	90	•	v	84	•	•	•				•	13	374,000	$7,644	$18,214	$273sh	$650sh	$35	03/01	-	166	•
Regent University School of Law	367	33	43	14.1	28	30	•	67	90	•	•	•				•	10	300,000	$15,840	$15,840	$495ch	$495ch	$40	06/01	03/01	304	•
University of Richmond School of Law	475	1	54	21	27	68		35	86	•						•	14	267,224	$19,195	$19,195	$960ch	$960ch	$35	01/15	02/25	306	•
University of Virginia School of Law	1105	-	37	13	64	65		25	86	•						•	27	788,674	$14,533	$20,633	-	-	$65	01/15	02/28	392	•
Washington and Lee University School of Law	367	-	40	9	33	12	•	37	85	•	•					•	26	350,065	$17,470	$17,470	-	-	$40	02/01	02/15	400	•
College of William and Mary School of Law	533	-	45	21	27	39		36	90	•		•				•	20	350,000	$8,494	$17,940	-	-	$40	03/01	02/15	418	•
WASHINGTON																						
Gonzaga University School of Law	469	18	43	15	34	27		58	90	•	•	•				•	11	225,400	$610c 18,300y	$610c 18,300y	$610c 12,200y	$610c 12,200y	$40	03/15	05/01	178	•
Seattle University School of Law	652	189	60	22	36	51	•	45	90	•	•	•				•	18	322,520	$17,880	$17,880	$14,900	$14,900	$50	04/01	03/01	330	•
University of Washington School of Law	500	-	53	28.6	47	45		54q	135	•	•	•				•	32	508,000	$5,800	$14,200	-	-	$50	01/15	02/28	398	•
WEST VIRGINIA																						
West Virginia University College of Law	423	16	47	6.2	25	25	•	52	93	•						•	13	255,000	$5,296	$12,568	$297ch	$625ch	$45	03/01	03/01	406	•
WISCONSIN																						
Marquette University Law School	449	93	44	7.4	31	41	•	43	90	•	•	•				•	17	262,540	$18,370	$18,370	$760ch	$760ch	$40	04/01	03/01	224	•
University of Wisconsin Law School	757	48	47	23	47	-		60	90	•	•					•	13	400,000	$6,206	$16,382	$260c	$680c	$45	02/01	03/01	422	•
WYOMING																						
University of Wyoming College of Law	226	-	40	4	14	3		52	88	•	•					•	6	174,000	$4,234	$9,322	-	-	$35	03/15	02/15	424	•

Key Facts Abbreviations and Footnotes

•	yes	ch	per credit hour	h	per hour
-	not available	d	day(s)	hr	hour(s)
asap	as soon as possible	e	evening(s)	Ja	January
c	per credit	F	Fall semester	Ma	May

nr	nonresident	raf	rolling application deadline for fall admission	Se	September	y	per year
p	priority deadline			sh	per semester hour
q	per quarter credits	S	Spring semester	u	per unit
r	resident	s	per semester	v	varies

** 1997/1998 information

Chapter 13: Geographic Guide to Law Schools in the United States (by region)*

New England

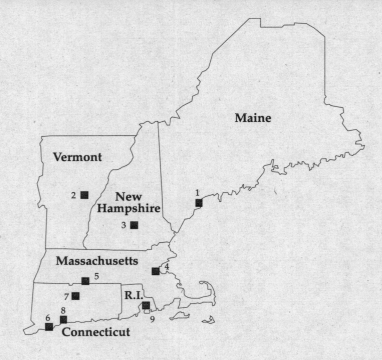

Maine
1. **Portland—Population: 64,358**
   University of Maine—Enrollment: 289/NA

Vermont
2. **South Royalton—Population: 2,500**
   Vermont Law School—Enrollment: 500/NA

New Hampshire
3. **Concord—Population: 36,006**
   Franklin Pierce—Enrollment: 373/11

Massachusetts
4. **Boston—Population: 574,283**
   Boston College—Enrollment: 827/NA
   Boston University—Enrollment: 947/NA
   Harvard (Cambridge, MA)—Enrollment: 1656/NA
   New England—Enrollment: 573/364
   Northeastern—Enrollment: 614/NA
   Suffolk—Enrollment: 1050/650
5. **Springfield—Population: 156,983**
   Western New England College—
   Enrollment: 357/242

Connecticut
6. **Bridgeport—Population: 141,686**
   Quinnipiac—Enrollment: 491/267
7. **Hartford—Population: 139,739**
   University of Connecticut—Enrollment: 420/161
8. **New Haven—Population: 130,474**
   Yale—Enrollment: 594/NA

Rhode Island
9. **Bristol—Population: 21,625**
   Roger Williams—Enrollment: 207/176

"Enrollment" represents the numbers of total full-time/total part-time students unless otherwise indicated. NA stands for "Not Applicable."

*Population information is derived from the U.S. Bureau of the Census, Population Division, Washington, DC. Data is accurate as of the 1990 Census. City populations reflect the number of people residing in the city proper, not the metropolitan area which would include outlying suburbs as well. Donald P. Racheter, director of the prelaw program at Central University of Iowa, also contributed data for these regional maps.

Northeast

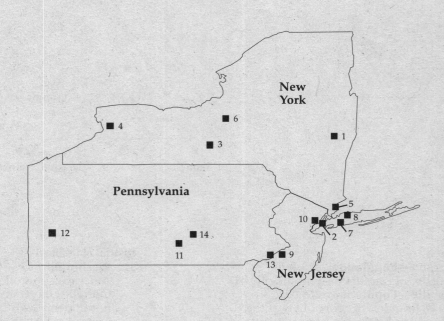

New York
1. **Albany—Population: 101,082**
    Albany—Enrollment: 656/35
2. **New York City—Population: 7,322,564**
    Benjamin N. Cardozo—Enrollment: 888/NA
    Brooklyn—Enrollment: 946/484
    City University of New York—Enrollment: 372/NA
    Columbia—Enrollment: 1132/NA
    Fordham—Enrollment: 1108/368
    The New York Law School—Enrollment: 921/484
    New York University—Enrollment: 1368/NA
    St. John's University (Jamaica, NY)—
    Enrollment: 752/282
3. **Ithaca—Population: 29,541**
    Cornell—Enrollment: 543/NA
4. **Buffalo—Population: 328,123**
    University at Buffalo—Enrollment: 657/NA
5. **White Plains—Population: 48,718**
    Pace—Enrollment: 449/308
6. **Syracuse—Population: 163,860**
    Syracuse—Enrollment: 736/15
7. **Hempstead—Population: 725,639**
    Hofstra—Enrollment: 799/NA
8. **Huntington—Population: 18,243**
    Touro—Enrollment: 419/285

New Jersey
9. **Camden—Population: 87,492**
    Rutgers–Camden—Enrollment: 592/159
10. **Newark—Population: 275,221**
    Rutgers–Newark—Enrollment: 493/195
    Seton Hall—Enrollment: 920/335

Pennsylvania
11. **Carlisle—Population: 18,419**
    The Pennsylvania State University,
    Dickinson—Enrollment: 508/NA
12. **Pittsburgh—Population: 369,879**
    Duquesne—Enrollment: 359/332
    University of Pittsburgh—Enrollment: 717/10
13. **Philadelphia—Population: 1,585,577**
    University of Pennsylvania—Enrollment: 767/NA
    Temple—Enrollment: 758/346
    Villanova (Villanova, PA)—Enrollment: 713/NA
14. **Harrisburg—Population: 52,376**
    Widener—(see Delaware—Midsouth region)

Midsouth

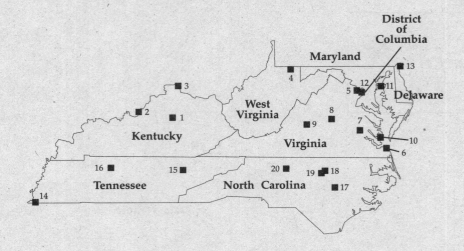

Kentucky
1. **Lexington—Population: 225,366**
    University of Kentucky—Enrollment: 418/NA
2. **Louisville—Population: 269,063**
    Louis D. Brandeis School of Law at the
    University of Louisville—Enrollment: 313/105
3. **Highland Heights—Population: 4,223**
    Northern Kentucky University—
    Enrollment: 201/191

West Virginia
4. **Morgantown—Population: 25,879**
    West Virginia—Enrollment: 423/16

Virginia
5. **Arlington—Population: 170,936**
    George Mason—Enrollment: 379/362
6. **Virginia Beach—Population: 393,069**
    Regent—Enrollment: 367/33
7. **Richmond—Population: 203,056**
    University of Richmond—Enrollment: 475/1
8. **Charlottesville—Population: 40,341**
    University of Virginia—Enrollment: 1105/NA
9. **Lexington—Population: 6,959**
    Washington and Lee—Enrollment: 367/NA
10. **Williamsburg—Population: 11,530**
    College of William and Mary—Enrollment: 533/NA

Maryland
11. **Baltimore—Population: 736,014**
    University of Baltimore—Enrollment: 648/324
    University of Maryland—Enrollment: 581/266

District of Columbia
12. **Washington, DC—Population: 606,900**
    American—Enrollment: 883/311
    Catholic University of America—
    Enrollment: 643/259
    District of Columbia—Enrollment: 172/NA
    George Washington—Enrollment: 1165/238
    Georgetown—Enrollment: 1553/477
    Howard—Enrollment: 405/NA

Delaware
13. **Wilmington—Population: 71,529**
    Widener—Enrollment: 885/625

Tennessee
14. **Memphis—Population: 610,337**
    University of Memphis—Enrollment: 446/32
15. **Knoxville—Population: 165,121**
    University of Tennessee—Enrollment: 489/NA
16. **Nashville—Population: 488,374**
    Vanderbilt—Enrollment: 550/NA

North Carolina
17. **Buies Creek—Population: 2,085**
    Campbell—Enrollment: 323/NA
18. **Durham—Population: 136,611**
    Duke—Enrollment: 608/NA
    North Carolina Central—Enrollment: 265/108
19. **Chapel Hill—Population: 38,719**
    University of North Carolina—Enrollment: 690/NA
20. **Winston-Salem—Population: 143,485**
    Wake Forest—Enrollment: 475/NA

Southeast

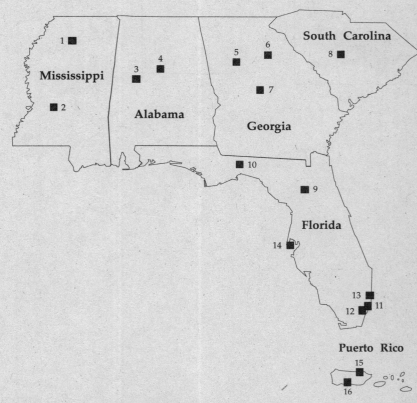

Mississippi
1. **Oxford—Population: 9,984**
   University of Mississippi—Enrollment: 481/4
2. **Jackson—Population: 196,637**
   Mississippi College—Enrollment: 401/NA

Alabama
3. **Tuscaloosa—Population: 77,759**
   University of Alabama—Enrollment: 550/NA
4. **Birmingham—Population: 265,968**
   Samford University, Cumberland School of Law
   Enrollment: 605/NA

Georgia
5. **Atlanta—Population: 394,017**
   Emory—Enrollment: 635/NA
   Georgia State—Enrollment: 414/248
6. **Athens—Population: 45,734**
   University of Georgia—Enrollment: 633/NA
7. **Macon—Population: 106,612**
   Mercer—Enrollment: 407/NA

South Carolina
8. **Columbia—Population: 98,052**
   University of South Carolina—Enrollment: 746/NA

Florida
9. **Gainesville—Population: 84,770**
   University of Florida—Enrollment: 1191/NA
10. **Tallahassee—Population: 124,773**
    Florida State—Enrollment: 654/NA
11. **Miami—Population: 358,548**
    St. Thomas—Enrollment: 487/NA
12. **Coral Gables—Population: 40,091**
    University of Miami—Enrollment: 1043/211
13. **Ft. Lauderdale—Population: 149,377**
    Nova—Enrollment: 784/169
14. **St. Petersburg—Population: 238,629**
    Stetson—Enrollment: 644/NA

Puerto Rico
15. **San Juan—Population: 437,745**
    Inter American—Enrollment: 376/352
    University of Puerto Rico—Enrollment: 352/221
16. **Ponce—Population: 187,749**
    Pontifical Catholic University—
    Enrollment: 328/190

South Central

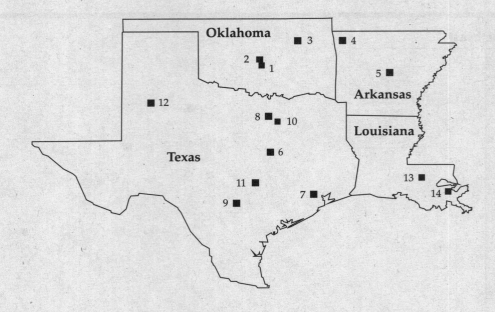

Oklahoma

Arkansas

Louisiana

Texas

Oklahoma
1. **Norman—Population: 80,171**
   University of Oklahoma—Enrollment: 575/NA
2. **Oklahoma City—Population: 444,719**
   Oklahoma City—Enrollment: 364/145
3. **Tulsa—Population: 367,302**
   University of Tulsa—Enrollment: 459/124

Arkansas
4. **Fayetteville—Population: 42,099**
   University of Arkansas–Fayetteville—
   Enrollment: 364/NA
5. **Little Rock—Population: 175,795**
   University of Arkansas–Little Rock—
   Enrollment: 276/144

Texas
6. **Waco—Population: 103,590**
   Baylor—Enrollment: 423/NA
7. **Houston—Population: 1,630,553**
   University of Houston—Enrollment: 773/229
   Texas A&M—Enrollment: 812/394
   Texas Southern—Enrollment: 600/NA
8. **Irving—Population: 155,037**
   Texas Wesleyan—Enrollment: 303/255

9. **San Antonio—Population: 935,933**
   St. Mary's—Enrollment: 733/NA
10. **Dallas—Population: 1,006,877**
    Southern Methodist—Enrollment: 733/18
11. **Austin—Population: 465,622**
    University of Texas–Austin—Enrollment: 1394/NA
12. **Lubbock—Population: 186,206**
    Texas Tech—Enrollment: 619/NA

Louisiana
13. **Baton Rouge—Population: 219,531**
    Louisiana State—Enrollment: 658/NA
    Southern—Enrollment: 311/NA
14. **New Orleans—Population: 496,938**
    Loyola–New Orleans—Enrollment: 493/167
    Tulane—Enrollment: 942/NA

Mountain West

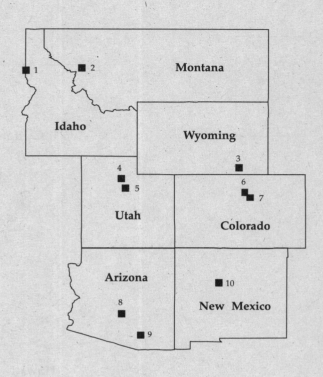

Idaho
1. **Moscow—Population: 18,519**
   University of Idaho—Enrollment: 300/NA

Montana
2. **Missoula—Population: 42,918**
   University of Montana—Enrollment: 253/NA

Wyoming
3. **Laramie—Population: 26,687**
   University of Wyoming—Enrollment: 226/NA

Utah
4. **Salt Lake City—Population: 159,936**
   University of Utah—Enrollment: 360/NA
5. **Provo—Population: 86,835**
   Brigham Young—Enrollment: 456/NA

Colorado
6. **Boulder—Population: 83,312**
   University of Colorado—Enrollment: 487/NA
7. **Denver—Population: 467,610**
   University of Denver—Enrollment: 751/290

Arizona
8. **Tempe—Population: 141,865**
   Arizona State—Enrollment: 482/NA
9. **Tucson—Population: 405,390**
   University of Arizona—Enrollment: 460/NA

New Mexico
10. **Albuquerque—Population: 384,736**
   University of New Mexico—Enrollment: 335/NA

Far West

California

1. **Anaheim—Population: 266,406**
   Chapman—Enrollment: 74/113
2. **Fullerton—Population: 114,144**
   Western State—Enrollment: 231/501
3. **Los Angeles—Population: 3,485,398**
   University of California–Los Angeles—
   Enrollment: 976/NA
   Loyola–Los Angeles—Enrollment: 968/375
   Pepperdine—Enrollment: 652/NA
   University of Southern California—
   Enrollment: 620/NA
   Southwestern—Enrollment: 616/286
   Whittier—Enrollment: 392/259
4. **Sacramento—Population: 369,365**
   University of California–Davis (Davis, CA)—
   Enrollment: 505/NA
   McGeorge—Enrollment: 745/350

5. **San Diego—Population: 1,110,549**
   California Western—Enrollment: 667/32
   University of San Diego—Enrollment: 788/345
   Thomas Jefferson—Enrollment: 333/230
6. **San Francisco—Population: 723,959**
   University of California–Berkeley (Berkeley, CA)—
   Enrollment: 846/NA
   University of California–Hastings—
   Enrollment: 1130/NA
   Golden Gate—Enrollment: 415/170
   University of San Francisco—Enrollment: 518/127
   Stanford (Stanford, CA)—Enrollment: 541/NA
7. **Santa Clara—Population: 93,613**
   Santa Clara—Enrollment: 629/288

Hawaii
8. **Honolulu—Population: 365,272**
   University of Hawai'i—Enrollment: 240/NA

Northwest

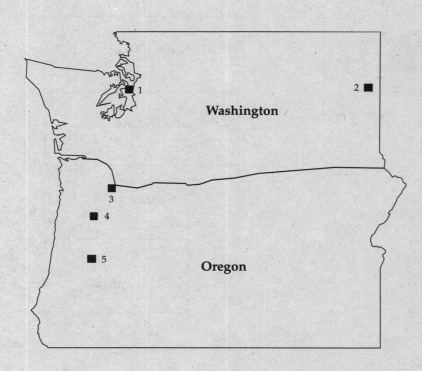

Washington

Oregon

Washington
1. **Seattle—Population: 516,259**
   University of Washington—Enrollment: 500/NA
   Seattle University—Enrollment: 652/189
2. **Spokane—Population: 177,196**
   Gonzaga—Enrollment: 469/18

Oregon
3. **Portland—Population: 437,319**
   Lewis & Clark—Enrollment: 491/156
4. **Salem—Population: 107,786**
   Willamette—Enrollment: 401/6
5. **Eugene—Population: 112,669**
   University of Oregon—Enrollment: 499/NA

Midwest

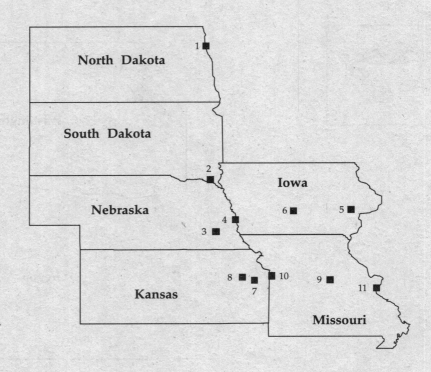

North Dakota
1. **Grand Forks—Population: 49,425**
    University of North Dakota—Enrollment: 204/NA

South Dakota
2. **Vermillion—Population: 10,034**
    University of South Dakota—Enrollment: 214/NA

Nebraska
3. **Lincoln—Population: 191,972**
    University of Nebraska—Enrollment: 392/1
4. **Omaha—Population: 335,795**
    Creighton—Enrollment: 409/15

Iowa
5. **Iowa City—Population: 59,738**
    University of Iowa—Enrollment: 654/NA
6. **Des Moines—Population: 193,187**
    Drake—Enrollment: 384/13

Kansas
7. **Lawrence —Population: 65,808**
    University of Kansas—Enrollment: 536/NA
8. **Topeka—Population: 119,883**
    Washburn—Enrollment: 435/NA

Missouri
9. **Columbia—Population: 69,101**
    University of Missouri–Columbia—
    Enrollment: 550/NA
10. **Kansas City—Population: 435,146**
    University of Missouri–Kansas City—
    Enrollment: 454/31
11. **St. Louis—Population: 396,685**
    St. Louis—Enrollment: 563/261
    Washington University—Enrollment: 627/NA

Great Lakes

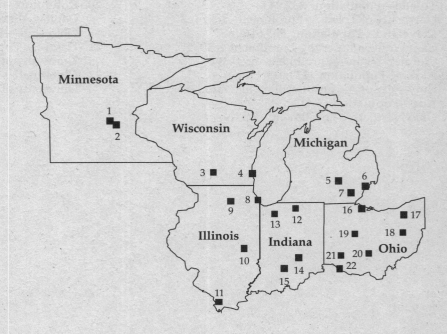

Minnesota

1. **Minneapolis—Population: 368,383**
   University of Minnesota—Enrollment: 789/NA
2. **St. Paul—Population: 272,235**
   Hamline—Enrollment: 463/25
   William Mitchell—Enrollment: 471/550

Wisconsin

3. **Madison—Population: 191,262**
   University of Wisconsin—Enrollment: 757/48
4. **Milwaukee—Population: 628,088**
   Marquette—Enrollment: 449/93

Michigan

5. **Lansing—Population: 127,321**
   Thomas M. Cooley —Enrollment: 406/1288
   Detroit College of Law—Enrollment: 555/186
6. **Detroit—Population: 1,027,974**
   University of Detroit, Mercy—Enrollment: 243/186
   Wayne State—Enrollment: 516/220
7. **Ann Arbor—Population: 109,592**
   University of Michigan—Enrollment: 1030/NA

Illinois

8. **Chicago—Population: 2,783,726**
   University of Chicago—Enrollment: 560/NA
   Chicago-Kent—Enrollment: 832/344
   DePaul—Enrollment: 766/327
   John Marshall—Enrollment: 739/428
   Loyola–Chicago—Enrollment: 518/207
   Northwestern—Enrollment: 642/NA
9. **DeKalb—Population: 34,925**
   Northern Illinois—Enrollment: 267/23
10. **Champaign—Population: 63,502**
    University of Illinois—Enrollment: 592/NA
11. **Carbondale—Population: 27,033**
    Southern Illinois—Enrollment: 376/5

Indiana

12. **South Bend—Population: 105,511**
    Notre Dame—Enrollment: 550/NA
13. **Valparaiso—Population: 24,414**
    Valparaiso—Enrollment: 367/53
14. **Indianapolis—Population: 731,327**
    Indiana–Indianapolis—Enrollment: 563/320
15. **Bloomington—Population: 60,633**
    Indiana–Bloomington—Enrollment: 614/8

Ohio

16. **Toledo—Population: 332,943**
    University of Toledo—Enrollment: 387/163
17. **Cleveland—Population: 505,616**
    Case Western Reserve—Enrollment: 640/17
    Cleveland State—Enrollment: 555/311
18. **Akron—Population: 223,019**
    University of Akron—Enrollment: 351/228
19. **Ada—Population: 5,413**
    Ohio Northern—Enrollment: 305/NA

20. **Columbus—Population: 632,910**
    Capital—Enrollment: 430/335
    Ohio State—Enrollment: 638/1
21. **Dayton—Population: 182,044**
    University of Dayton—Enrollment: 500/NA
22. **Cincinnati—Population: 364,040**
    University of Cincinnati—Enrollment: 368/NA

Chapter 14: LSAC-Member Law School Descriptions

The descriptions that follow were prepared by each law school under editorial and formatting guidelines provided by Law Services. The schools were encouraged to use the bulleted lead-ins to each section for quantitative data that did not require a narrative explanation, and to use the descriptive text to provide details on the unique features of the school. Most schools also include admission profiles that illustrate admission prospects based on a combination of LSAT score and GPA.

The purpose of this book is to provide a brief introduction to the programs, facilities, and admission requirements of each ABA-approved law school. For a balanced view of each law school, it is important not only to look at all of the elements included in each school's description on these pages, but also to obtain the catalog and admission materials of each school that interests you. The data in the school descriptions and admission profiles are for the 1998-99 academic year unless otherwise noted, and represent full-time, day programs unless otherwise noted.

There are factors that may not predict law school performance but may otherwise affect an admission decision. Many law schools give special admission consideration to members of minority and disadvantaged groups because traditionally they have been underrepresented in the legal profession. Footnotes to the admission grids generally will note any special information about the composition of the applicant pool.

Please Note:

- Unless otherwise indicated, bulleted details in the school descriptions under the heading "Enrollment/Student Body" refer to the total student body of the law school.

- In the bulleted section called "Enrollment/Student Body," law schools provide percentile information on GPA and LSAT scores for the 1998 entering class. One-quarter (25 percent) of the first-year class has credentials that are *below* the number given for the 25th percentile. Three-quarters (75 percent) of the first-year class has credentials that are *below* the number given for the 75th percentile. For example, if a school reports a 25th/75th percentile GPA—3.01/3.47, then 25 percent of this first-year class had a GPA of *less than* 3.01, while 75 percent of this class had a GPA of *less than* 3.47. The same principle holds for 25th/75th percentile LSAT score.

- **Full-time** students are those registered for the number of units that would constitute a full-time load to complete the J.D. in the normal three-year period.

- **Part-time** is anything less than the above.

- **Range of first-year class size** is the range from the smallest first-year class section to the largest. This differs from the size of the entire first-year class.

- **Total full-time faculty** represents permanent faculty appointments teaching full time.

- **Total part-time faculty** represents part-time and adjunct appointments.

- **Total credits from required classes** are nonelective courses needed to obtain the J.D.

University of Akron School of Law

Office of Admissions
Corner of Wolf Ledges and University Avenue
Akron, OH 44325-2901

E-Mail: lawadmissions@uakron.edu
URL: http://www.uakron.edu/law
Phone: 800.4.AKRON.U or 330.972.7331; Fax: 330.258.2343

■ Introduction

Located just 45 minutes south of Cleveland, Ohio, the University of Akron (UA) is one of the 50 largest universities in the country. UA is a comprehensive research and teaching university with degree programs ranging from the associate to the doctoral level. Founded in 1870, UA has celebrated over 125 years of academic excellence, while forging ahead to meet complex needs of today's students.

The Akron law school was founded in 1921 and merged with UA in 1959. More than 5,000 students have graduated from the law school since 1921. The University of Akron School of Law has alumni practicing throughout the U.S. and abroad. The School of Law is accredited by the American Bar Association and is a member of the Association of American Law Schools.

■ Enrollment/Student Body

fall 1998 entering class: ➼ *1,032 completed applications* ➼ *503 admit offers* ➼ *full-time 25th/75th percentile GPA—3.00/3.59* ➼ *part-time 25th/75th percentile GPA—2.83/3.45* ➼ *full-time 25th/75th percentile LSAT—148/154* ➼ *part-time 25th/75th percentile LSAT—150/157* ➼ *199 enrolled—day, 123; evening, 76* ➼ *13% students of color* ➼ *52.7% women* ➼ *entering class represented by 19 states, 78 undergraduate schools, 7 graduate schools, 64 undergraduate majors, 9 majors* ➼ *average age—day, 25; evening, 31* ➼ *age range—day, 21-50; evening, 21-51* *1998-99 law student body:* ➼ *579 students—day, 351; evening, 228* ➼ *9.2% students of color* ➼ *46% women*

■ Faculty

➼ *70 total* ➼ *27 full-time* ➼ *43 part-time* ➼ *28 women—full-time, 12; part-time, 16* ➼ *8 minority—full-time, 4; part-time, 4*

■ Tuition and Financial Aid (annual)

➼ *resident—full-time, $7,718; part-time, $6,034* ➼ *nonresident—full-time, $13,166; part-time, $10,290* ➼ *books—full-time, $600 to $700; part-time, $500 to $600*

All first-year students are considered for full or partial scholarships. Nearly half of the fall 1998 entering class received scholarships. Merit- and need-based loans available. File FAFSA early.

■ Admission

In order to be considered for law school admission, the prospective applicant must submit the application form, personal statement, and $35 fee. The applicant must also take the LSAT and register for the LSDAS before the file may be sent to the Admission Committee. An applicant may apply during his/her final year of undergraduate studies. The bachelor's degree must be conferred prior to law school matriculation. Decisions are made on a "rolling basis" as soon as the files are complete. Recommended

deadline: March 1. For more details on admission and/or to access the application on the World Wide Web, please see our Web site at www.uakron.edu/law.

Students enrolled in an ABA-accredited law school may apply for transfer or transient status. A law student who has completed not more nor less than one year (approx. 30 semester credit hours) and is in good academic standing may apply for transfer. A law student who has permission from his/her dean to visit UA for one or two semesters may apply for transient status. Consult www.uakron.edu/law and/or our catalog for details.

■ Physical Facilities

Three connected buildings house the law school facilities. It is one stop shopping for law students as everything is under one roof—legal clinic, law library, moot courtrooms, classrooms, faculty offices, deans' offices, lounge, student organization offices, etc. The law school is within one block of the Akron Municipal Court, the Court of Common Pleas, and the Ninth District Court of Appeals. The Federal Court is a couple of blocks from those buildings. While the law school is in the downtown Akron area, the campus is a green one bordered by grassy areas, decorative plantings, and fountains.

■ Curriculum/Special Programs

➼ *88 semester hours required to graduate* ➼ *3 year or 2 1/2 year full-time, day* ➼ *4 year or 3 1/2 year part-time, evening* ➼ *students matriculate in fall (Aug.)* ➼ *4 juris doctor tracks offered (see details below)* ➼ *3 joint degrees available (see details below)*

The first-year curriculum is traditional. Courses include a wide range of substantive areas suited to developing the analytical skills essential to lawyering. Private and public law, judicial and legislative process, and research and writing are all subsumed in this curriculum. A comprehensive writing program designed to enhance students' skills in exposition, drafting, and argumentation is an integral part of the curriculum. **Four Juris Doctor(J.D.)Tracks**: Litigation, corporate, taxation, and general. Other specialty areas include criminal, intellectual property, international, labor and employment, public, and diverse course offerings. **Three Joint Degrees**: J.D./Master in Business Administration, J.D./Master in Taxation, J.D./Master in Public Administration. **Center for Intellectual Property**: Some of the many intellectual property courses offered include patent law, patent prosecution, trademark law, copyright law, cyber law, trade secrets, law and genetics, and media law. **Competition Teams**: The National Institute for Trial Advocacy ranked UA trial teams among the top 16 law schools nationally, and categorized them among the "best of the best" champions of trial advocacy. As a result, UA teams compete, by invitation only, in the most elite student mock trial competition in the nation. **Legal Clinic**: A variety of opportunities for clinical training are offered. Students can experience the actual practice of law in a variety of supervised settings. Programs offered include Trial Litigation Clinic, Appellate Review, Clinical Seminar, and Inmate Assistance.

■ Library

➤ *over 250,000 volumes & equivalents* ➤ *library hours: Mon.-Fri., 8:00 A.M.-11:00 P.M.; Sat., 9:00 A.M.-6:00 P.M.; Sun., NOON-11:00 P.M.* ➤ *LEXIS* ➤ *NEXIS*
➤ *WESTLAW* ➤ *Internet* ➤ *OhioLINK*
➤ *World Wide Web* ➤ *12 CD-ROM databases*
➤ *6 full-time librarians* ➤ *library seats 295*
➤ *Federal Government Depository* ➤ *interactive video disk*
➤ *computer based education terminals*
➤ *network & television cables in all classrooms*

OhioLINK, an online public access catalog system, connects the library by daily courier service to eight other Ohio law schools and virtually all colleges and universities in Ohio. Any item available for checkout at any member library can be requested online. These systems are also accessible via home computer. Over 60 databases are available through this system, some of which are full text.

Materials for conducting research on federal law and the law of every state are available. Group study rooms are available, some equipped with VCRs/TVs, others with interactive video. The student microcomputer network in the law library has 40 workstations with full Internet access. Students are eligible to register for free e-mail, free Web access, and can create free Web pages through the university.

■ Career Planning and Placement

The class of 1997 consisted of 166 graduates. Of those, 165 or 99.4 percent replied to our six-month post-graduation employment survey. The respondents were 66.1 percent male, 33.9 percent female, and minorities represented 7.9 percent. This class had an employment rate of 96.6 percent, which is above the national average of 89.2 percent. These graduates are located in 18 states and 3 foreign countries. The average starting salary was $35,463, which ranged from $16,000 to $85,000.

Applicant Group for the 1998-1999 Academic Year

University of Akron School of Law
This grid includes only applicants who earned 120-180 LSAT scores under standard administrations.

LSAT Score	GPA																		
	3.75 +		3.50 - 3.74		3.25 - 3.49		3.00 - 3.24		2.75 - 2.99		2.50 - 2.74		2.25 - 2.49		2.00 - 2.24		Below 2.00		No GPA		Total	
	Apps	Adm	Apps	Adm	Apps	Adm	Apps	Adm	Apps	Adm	Apps	Adm	Apps	Adm	Apps	Adm	Apps	Adm	Apps	Adm	Apps	Adm
160-180	3	3	7	6	7	6	8	7	9	8	5	5	2	2	0	0	1	0	0	0	42	37
154-159	13	12	18	17	23	22	26	26	29	28	17	16	11	11	6	5	0	0	1	1	144	138
150-153	10	9	29	27	43	42	42	41	29	23	27	23	17	12	8	4	2	0	0	0	207	181
145-149	12	12	21	14	53	35	45	20	53	15	54	8	22	6	11	1	6	0	0	0	277	111
120-144	4	2	15	7	28	1	64	5	80	8	70	4	44	0	35	0	10	0	0	0	350	27
Total	42	38	90	71	154	106	185	99	200	82	173	56	96	31	60	10	19	0	1	1	1020	494

Apps = Number of Applicants
Adm = Number Admitted

The University of Alabama School of Law

Box 870382
Tuscaloosa, AL 35487-0382

E-Mail: admissions@law.ua.edu
URL: http://www.law.ua.edu
Phone: 205.348.5440

■ Introduction

The University of Alabama School of Law was established on the university's main campus in Tuscaloosa in 1872. The law school has served the state and the nation as the training ground for leaders of the legal profession, business, and government. The curriculum is traditional but broad, with Alabama law emphasized only in a few elective courses. The school has a national reputation for excellence in teaching, although the faculty is also committed to scholarly research and writing. The school is accredited by the ABA and AALS.

■ Enrollment/Student Body

➡ *759 applicants*   ➡ *340 admitted first-year class 1998*
➡ *179 enrolled first-year class 1998*   ➡ *full-time 25th/75th percentile GPA—2.98/3.50*   ➡ *full-time 25th/75th percentile LSAT—154/159*   ➡ *550 total full-time*   ➡ *9% minority*
➡ *38% women*   ➡ *13 states represented (entering class)*
➡ *53 degree-granting schools (entering class)*

■ Faculty

➡ *80 total*   ➡ *38 full-time*   ➡ *42 part-time or adjunct*
➡ *14 women*   ➡ *4 minority*

■ Library and Physical Facilities

➡ *257,121 volumes & 107,416 equivalents*   ➡ *library hours: weekdays, 7:30 A.M.-MIDNIGHT; Sat., 9:00 A.M.-10:00 P.M.; Sun., 10:00 A.M.-MIDNIGHT; varies during holidays*
➡ *LEXIS*   ➡ *NEXIS*   ➡ *WESTLAW*   ➡ *DIALOG,*
➡ *OCLC*   ➡ *Alabama on disc*   ➡ *7 full-time librarians*
➡ *library seats 562*

The physical facility is among the nation's finest law school buildings. The Law Center building is graphic evidence of the school's dynamic growth and progressive spirit. Each level of the three-story facility provides an efficient and aesthetically stimulating environment. The Law Center's library provides students, faculty, attorneys, and other users with a substantial research collection of Anglo-American and international legal materials.

■ Curriculum

➡ *Academic Support Program*   ➡ *90 credits required to graduate*   ➡ *degrees available: J.D.; J.D./M.B.A.; M.C.L.; LL.M. (in Taxation)*   ➡ *semesters, start in Aug.*
➡ *range of first-year class size—96-Section I, 95-Section II*

■ Special Programs

The clinical program enables law students to gain valuable practical experience in interviewing clients, preparing cases, and participating in courtroom presentations. The joint-degree program enables students to earn the J.D./M.B.A. (Master of Business Administration). The LL.M. in taxation is awarded to qualified graduates of law schools upon completion of 24 graduate hours. The

M.C.L. (Master of Comparative Law) degree is offered to a limited number of international lawyers. The law school also offers a five-week summer program at the University of Fribourg in Fribourg, Switzerland. During the program students may earn four hours of credit; included are a course surveying Swiss law and a comparative doctrinal course.

■ Admission

➡ *Bachelor's degree required*   ➡ *application postmark deadline—March 1; Feb. 1 for M.C.L. applicants*
➡ *LSAT, LSDAS required*   ➡ *application fee—$25*

A student must obtain a bachelor's degree at an accredited institution before enrolling but may apply during the senior year. Applicants must register for and take the LSAT, preferably no later than the December before enrollment, and subscribe to LSDAS for transcript analysis. Transcripts must show all schools attended and include at least three-fourths of the hours needed for graduation. Students are admitted only for the next immediate fall semester and only for full-time study. Application materials are available in September each year. Students are encouraged to submit applications early. The committee considers all information available about an applicant; however, the LSAT score and undergraduate GPA are by far the most important. Other factors considered include honors, activities, work experience, difficulty of undergraduate course of study, trends in academic performance, leadership ability, writing ability, and the applicant's personal statement. Admission decisions will also be influenced by the law school's commitment to racial, ethnic, cultural, economic, and geographic diversity. Special programs and support are available to members of minority and other diversity groups. Written letters of recommendation are not required. Personal interviews are usually not recommended.

Summer school is open to students who have completed the first year of law school (including students in good standing at other law schools), and graduation can be accelerated one semester by summer coursework. The full-time faculty of 32 is comprised of graduates of leading American law schools.

■ Student Organizations

Student organizations represent diverse interests. They include: Student Bar Association, Black Law Students Association, Environmental Law Society, Trial Advocacy Association, Dorbin Association (women's support group), International Law Society, American Civil Liberties Union Tuscaloosa/University Chapter, and Christian Legal Society.

■ Activities

A broad range of student activities adds to the students' law school experience. The *Alabama Law Review*, edited by students, devotes substantial space to national issues as well as issues relevant to Alabama. Three additional publications involve student participation: *The Journal of* the *Legal Profession*; the *Law and Psychology Review*; and the *American Journal of Tax Policy* (American College of Tax Fellows). Trial advocacy teams have enjoyed exceptional success over the years, advancing 10 teams from regional to national competition in the last eight years. The appellate advocacy program also is very strong. Seven appellate advocacy teams have advanced from regional to national competition in the last five years. All 193 Alabama teams have won regional, national, and international brief awards; captured a national championship; and won individual, regional, and national oral advocacy awards. The Student Bar Association (SBA) provides several student services and sponsors academic and social activities.

■ Expenses and Financial Aid

➡ *tuition & fees—resident per semester, $2,245; nonresident per semester, $4,742; estimated 1999-2000*
➡ *estimated additional expenses—$500 books, first-year*
➡ *scholarships available*   ➡ *minority scholarships available*
➡ *financial aid available; Family Financial Statement required; March 1 deadline*

The great majority of the students enrolled in the School of Law finance their legal education through loans, savings, earnings, and/or contributions from their families. Scholarships are awarded to approximately 30 percent of the first-year students. Scholarship recipients are identified on the basis of their applications for admission, and scholarship applications are necessary. Scholarships are sometimes renewable during the second and third years, often depending upon funding availability, the student's need, and whether the recipients maintain stated levels of academic achievement. Limited law school scholarship funds are available to assist extremely needy students. Applicants who have been admitted to the first-year class and who believe they qualify for these need-based scholarships should apply, using the form supplied by the School of Law and available upon request, not later than May 1 preceding the anticipated enrollment. Scholarship applications are required for renewal of law school scholarships. Aid is also available for law students from the university's Financial Aid Office. Further information can be obtained by writing to Director of Student Financial Services, The University of Alabama, Box 870162, Tuscaloosa, AL 35487-0162. Phone: 205.348.6756.

The School of Law provides significant support. Outstanding nonresident students may receive a nonresident fee waiver.

■ Career Services Program

The Career Services Program is designed to assist all students in their efforts to find employment. Extensive on-campus interviewing occurs.

The office has an excellent Career Resource Library. Seminars are presented on résumé writing, interviewing techniques, and job-search techniques to help students refine their job-search skills. Panel discussions are scheduled, and job fairs are supported as part of the Career Services Program. More than 95 percent of each year's graduating class is employed within six months of graduation. Well over 90 percent of the graduates pass a bar exam the first time. More than 96 percent of the 1998 graduating class passed the bar exam the first time.

■ Housing

The university maintains residence halls and apartment units for students; however, most law students live off campus. For information, students may write to the Office of Housing and Residential Life, The University of Alabama, Box 870399, Tuscaloosa, AL 35487-0399. Phone: 205.348.6676.

Applicant Profile Not Available

Albany Law School of Union University

80 New Scotland Avenue
Albany, NY 12208

E-Mail: admissions@mail.als.edu
URL: http://www.als.edu
Phone: 518.445.2326

■ Introduction

Albany Law School, founded in 1851, is one of the nation's oldest law schools. A midsize, private law school, it is joined by Union College, Albany Medical College, and Albany College of Pharmacy to form Union University, a historic linkage dating back to 1873. The Law School offers both full-time and part-time day programs.

Albany Law School, a member of the AALS, is accredited by the ABA.

The City of Albany is located 150 miles from New York City and 160 miles from Boston. Albany is an exceptional laboratory for the study of law. Long established here are the agencies of state government, the legislature, executive offices, and the state's highest court, the Court of Appeals. Through programs at the Law School and positions available in state government, the Albany Law School student has the opportunity to participate in those processes.

■ Enrollment/Student Body

➡ *1,220 applicants*   ➡ *804 admitted first-year class 1998*
➡ *238 enrolled first-year class 1998*   ➡ *full-time 25th/75th percentile GPA—2.90/3.41*   ➡ *full-time 25th/75th percentile LSAT—145/154 (if multiple LSAT scores—higher score used)*
➡ *656 total full-time*   ➡ *35 total part-time*
➡ *18% minority*   ➡ *53% women*
➡ *22 states & foreign countries represented*
➡ *143 undergraduate schools represented*

Nearly 16 percent of our students completed their undergraduate studies five or more years before starting their legal education, and more than half of our students graduated from college at least one year prior to entering law school.

Additionally, 52 percent of the class entering in the fall of '98 were women and 22 percent were people of color.

■ Faculty

➡ *81 total*   ➡ *36 full-time*   ➡ *45 part-time or adjunct*

The Albany Law School faculty is noted for its accessibility to the students. The full-time professors, clinical and legal research and writing instructors possess law degrees from 35 different law schools, including Harvard, Yale, Columbia, Stanford, New York University, Northwestern, St. John's, Howard, Georgetown, and Oxford University. In addition, adjunct professors enrich the curriculum with their expertise in specific practical areas of the law.

■ Library and Physical Facilities

➡ *536,218 volumes & equivalents*   ➡ *library hours: Mon.-Thurs., 8:00 A.M.-MIDNIGHT; Fri., 8:00 A.M.-10:00 P.M.; Sat., 9:00 A.M.-9:00 P.M.; Sun., 10:00 A.M.-MIDNIGHT*
➡ *LEXIS*   ➡ *NEXIS*   ➡ *WESTLAW*
➡ *DIALOG*   ➡ *NETSCAPE*
➡ *7 full-time librarians*   ➡ *library seats 488*
➡ *58 personal computers available for student use*

In 1986 the Schaffer Law Library, one of the finest law libraries in the country, was added to Albany Law School. In addition, a new computerized classroom, moot courtroom, gymnasium, student lounge, and open-air courtyard complement the law school complex.

■ Curriculum

➡ *Academic Support Program*   ➡ *87 credits required to graduate*   ➡ *104 courses available*   ➡ *4 in-house clinical options and 110 externships available*   ➡ *degrees available: J.D./M.B.A.; J.D./M.P.A.; J.D.*   ➡ *terms start in Aug. only*
➡ *range of first-year class size—24-91*

An "Introduction to Lawyering" course offers a unique, year-long case simulation that combines legal writing, clinical methodology, and professional skills development designed to introduce first-year students to what lawyers do and how the legal system works.

Students have the option of electing a concentration after the first year in any one of these eleven areas: Business Law, Civil and Constitutional Rights, Civil Litigation, Criminal Law, Environmental Law, Estate Planning, Family and Elder Law, Governmental Administration and Regulation, Health Law, International Law, and Labor and Employment Law.

■ Special Programs

Clinical Legal Studies provide opportunities for upperclassmen to work and study for credit. They offer students a chance to view the legal system first-hand and to begin participating in that system as professionals. Students may choose to participate in the AIDS Law Clinic, Disabilities Law Clinic, Domestic Violence Law Clinic, Civil Litigation Clinic, or the Placement Clinics which include Albany County District Attorney's Office, Environmental Protection Bureau, U.S. District Court, U.S. Court of Appeals, NYS Supreme Court, Legal Aid Society, NYS Assembly, and the U.S. Attorney's Office. Additionally, students may choose an externship. There are over 30 public law offices in which to work and study as externs.

The Government Law Center (GLC) was established in 1978 to facilitate multidisciplinary study and research in government and the problems facing the government; to introduce students to policy analysis and to public service; and to provide a resource to government in the resolution of specific problems. The GLC sponsors conferences, symposia, and seminars on a variety of topics.

■ Admission

➡ *Bachelor's degree required*   ➡ *application deadline— March 15*   ➡ *applicants encouraged to apply early*
➡ *LSAT, LSDAS required*   ➡ *application fee—$50*
➡ *students with exceptional academic credentials may apply if 90 semester-hours towards a bachelor's degree are completed in a regionally accredited institution*

An Admissions Committee, consisting of four full-time faculty members, reviews all parts of all applications. Albany Law School does not participate in any type of screening process whereby applicants are automatically accepted or denied. The Committee attempts to select a highly qualified, diverse student body and, therefore, takes many factors into consideration, including LSAT scores, previous scholastic achievement, employment experience, socio-economic status, minority status, recommendations, and any exceptional circumstances pertaining to the applicant. Evaluative interviews are not part of the process. Rather, applicants are encouraged to submit a written statement detailing all information that might be relevant for an admission decision.

A small number of transfer students are usually admitted to the second-year class based on above average academic performance at another ABA accredited law school.

■ Student Activities

Students at Albany Law School are provided with opportunities to participate in educational, as well as social, activities. *Albany Law Review* is published four times a year. The *Albany Law Journal of Science & Technology* is a student publication dedicated to the development of the law as it relates to the sciences and the effect technology has upon society. Nationwide moot court competitions help students develop their legal research and advocacy skills. In addition, the recently renovated gymnasium also provides students with an opportunity to participate in a variety of organized intramural athletic programs.

■ Expenses and Financial Aid

➺ *tuition & fees—$19,425, full-time; $14,600, part-time*
➺ *merit scholarships awarded on the basis of UGPA & LSAT score* ➺ *diversity scholarships awarded to students with unusual backgrounds including minorities*
➺ *scholarships range from $5,000 to $19,295*
➺ *need-based grants from $1,000 to $5,700/yr.*

More than 43 percent of students receive some type of institutional scholarship or grant award, and more than 85 percent also qualify for loan and/or employment assistance. Financial aid applicants must file the FAFSA form, Albany Law School Request for Financial Assistance, and their 1998 Federal Income Tax form. Applicants should file the FAFSA as soon after January 1 as possible regardless of whether or not an admission decision has been received. Accepted applicants who list Albany Law School's code (G02886) on their FAFSA will receive an estimate of their eligibility for aid.

Most students live off-campus in moderately priced, privately owned housing. The Admissions Office maintains a listing of available accommodations. Additionally, a dormitory houses 84 law students in single rooms. Room and food for the academic year is approximately $5,900.

■ Career Services

The Career Planning Office provides career information and assistance to all students and alumni. Panels, workshops, and individual consultations are offered. Students can participate in on-campus and off-campus recruitment programs. Statistics from the past few years show an employment rate of over 96 percent for graduates.

Applicant Group for the 1998-1999 Academic Year

Albany Law School of Union University
If multiple LSAT scores are earned, placement on the grid is determined by the highest score.

LSAT Score	3.75 +		3.50 - 3.74		3.25 - 3.49		3.00 - 3.24		2.75 - 2.99		2.50 - 2.74		2.25 - 2.49		2.00 - 2.24		Below 2.00		No GPA		Total	
	Apps	Adm	Apps	Adm	Apps	Adm	Apps	Adm	Apps	Adm	Apps	Adm	Apps	Adm	Apps	Adm	Apps	Adm	Apps	Adm	Apps	Adm
175-180	0	0	0	0	0	0	1	1	0	0	0	0	0	0	0	0	0	0	0	0	1	1
170-174	0	0	1	1	1	1	0	0	0	0	0	0	3	3	1	1	0	0	0	0	6	6
165-169	3	3	3	3	1	1	5	4	1	1	3	3	0	0	1	1	0	0	1	1	18	17
160-164	9	9	7	7	11	11	14	13	15	13	6	6	2	2	2	2	0	0	2	2	68	65
155-159	17	17	27	26	34	34	36	35	22	20	24	23	16	9	3	2	0	0	9	9	188	175
150-154	14	13	32	31	50	49	72	70	70	68	44	29	13	1	6	1	1	0	6	5	308	267
145-149	13	12	24	24	55	52	71	60	78	38	47	19	22	3	11	0	3	0	7	2	331	210
140-144	2	1	20	12	19	14	43	14	50	11	35	10	16	0	7	0	2	0	4	0	198	62
135-139	1	0	3	0	4	0	9	0	16	1	13	0	9	0	4	0	0	0	3	0	62	1
130-134	0	0	0	0	0	0	4	0	1	0	1	0	2	0	1	0	1	0	3	0	13	0
125-129	0	0	1	0	0	0	0	0	2	0	0	0	0	0	0	0	0	0	0	0	3	0
120-124	0	0	0	0	1	0	0	0	0	0	0	0	0	0	0	0	0	0	0	0	1	0
Total	59	55	118	104	176	162	255	197	255	152	173	90	83	18	36	7	7	0	35	19	1197	804

Apps = Number of Applicants
Adm = Number Admitted

American University—Washington College of Law

4801 Massachusetts Avenue, N.W.
Washington, DC 20016

E-Mail: wcladmit@wcl.american.edu
URL: http://www.wcl.american.edu
Phone: 202.274.4101

■ Introduction

American University's Washington College of Law offers opportunity for the study of law in the center of the nation's legal institutions. The law school is minutes from downtown Washington, but at the same time offers the facilities and ambiance of a true campus environment in one of the city's most beautiful residential neighborhoods.

Founded in 1896 by two women, the law school is national in character. It is committed to the development of the intellectual abilities and practical skills required to prepare lawyers to practice in an increasingly complex and transnational world. The school is noted for the accessibility of faculty and administration to its students.

■ Enrollment/Student Body (First-Year Class)

➡ *4,500 applicants*   ➡ *1,935 admitted*   ➡ *393 enrolled*
➡ *full-time 25th/75th percentile GPA—3.09/3.51*
➡ *part-time 25th/75th percentile GPA—2.85/3.31*
➡ *full-time 25th/75th percentile LSAT—153/158*
➡ *part-time 25th/75th percentile LSAT—148/155*
➡ *296 total full-time*   ➡ *97 total part-time*
➡ *30% minority*   ➡ *63% women*   ➡ *36 states & 3 foreign countries represented*   ➡ *190 undergraduate schools represented*

■ Faculty

➡ *205 total*   ➡ *53 full-time*   ➡ *152 part-time*
➡ *61 women*   ➡ *14 minority*

■ Library and Physical Facilities

➡ *425,049 volumes & equivalents*   ➡ *library hours: Mon.-Thurs., 8:00 A.M.-2:00 A.M.; Fri., 8:00 A.M.-MIDNIGHT; Sat., 9:00 A.M.-MIDNIGHT; Sun., 10:00 A.M.-2:00 A.M.*
➡ *LEXIS*   ➡ *WESTLAW*   ➡ *10 full-time librarians*
➡ *library seats 649*

Opened in 1996, our state-of-the-art facility allows an unparalleled opportunity not only to house all of the law school's programs under one roof, but also to develop a structure that will prepare lawyers for practice in the twenty-first century.

The two-story library is the heart of the complex. It is approximately two and one-half times the size of the old facility and seats over 600 students. Approximately half of the total seats are equipped with data ports so a student can plug in a portable computer and have access to all Internet and campus-wide research databases. The library collection includes European Community and U.S. Government depositories and the Baxter Collection in International Law. The library was recently designated as the repository for the National Equal Justice Library, which is an archive of primary and public-defender programs. Students also have access to the university's library, the Library of Congress, specialized agency libraries, and other area law libraries to which the school is electronically linked.

■ Curriculum

The law school offers full-time and part-time programs leading to the J.D. degree, which is awarded after satisfactory completion of 86 credit hours, 34 of which are prescribed. All degree candidates must also fulfill an upper-level writing requirement. The Socratic method is the basic form of instruction in the first year. Its purpose is to develop the skills of critical analysis, provide perspectives on the law and lawyering, and deepen understanding of fundamental legal principals. In the Legal Method program, basic legal research and writing skills are taught to groups of 14 students by practicing attorneys and upper-level assistants. In the second and third years, students elect a course of study drawing from advanced courses, seminars, independent research, externships, and clinical programs. Students are exposed to a variety of teaching processes by the law school's distinguished full-time faculty of 53 and our many adjunct professors.

■ Special Programs

While many of the advanced courses take place in a traditional classroom setting, a variety of other innovative teaching modes is available to enhance research skills and provide professional training. The Washington College of Law Clinical Programs enjoy a national reputation for clinical education. Second-year and third-year students may participate in the Civil Practice Clinic, the Community and Economic Development Law Clinic, and the International Human Rights Clinic; third-year students may also develop their lawyering abilities in the Criminal Justice Clinic, the DC Civil Litigation Clinic, the Domestic Violence Clinic, and the Tax Clinic. The Women and the Law Program also includes a clinical component in which students represent indigent women in family law cases in the District of Columbia courts. This program also offers several public-education projects each year, and is designed to integrate women's legal studies into the overall curriculum and to heighten awareness about legal issues affecting women.

Complementing its outstanding curriculum in International Law, the university offers a combined J.D./M.A. in International Affairs with the School of International Service. Combined-degree programs also include a J.D./M.S. in Justice, Law, and Society with the School for Public Affairs and a J.D./M.B.A. with the Kogod College of Business Administration. Graduate study is available leading to either an LL.M. degree in International Legal Studies or Law and Government.

The externship program places upper-level students in many governmental, nonprofit, and public interest entities throughout the DC metropolitan area. Field components, taken simultaneously with a seminar, include such areas as security and commodities markets regulation. The Program for Advanced Studies in the Federal Regulatory Process, offered each summer, provides an intensive analysis of the federal regulatory process through lectures and optional field placements in a myriad of federal agencies and nonprofit organizations.

■ Admission

➡ *Bachelor's degree from accredited college or university required* ➡ *application deadline—March 1* ➡ *rolling admission, early application preferred* ➡ *LSAT, LSDAS required* ➡ *application fee—$55*

Applicants to the law school are admitted on the strength of their entire academic and related records. The faculty admission committee gives primary emphasis to the undergraduate record, LSAT scores, and other major accomplishments and achievements, whether academic, work-related, or extracurricular. The benefits the school derives from racial, ethnic, cultural, and geographical diversity among its students are considered in admission decisions. Members of disadvantaged and minority groups are encouraged to apply. Admission to the law school is highly competitive and operates on a rolling admission basis, so early application is strongly encouraged.

■ Student Activities

The *Law Review*, the *International Law Review*, the *Administrative Law Review*, and the *Journal of Gender and the Law* are edited and published by students selected on the basis of scholarship and creative research. The Moot Court Board sponsors intraschool competitions for first-year and upper-level students, and selects representatives for a number of interschool competitions, including the National Moot Court Competition. Other student activities include active chapters of the Black Law Students Association, the Women's Law Association, the Environmental Law Society, the Hispanic Law Student Association, the Asian Pacific American Law Student Association, the National Lawyers Guild, the Equal Justice Foundation, the Federalist Society, the Lambda Law Students Association, and many other student groups.

■ Expenses and Financial Aid

➡ *tuition—$22,590; part-time, $881/credit* ➡ *fees—full-time, $382; part-time, $242* ➡ *estimated additional expenses—$11,934 (room, board, books)* ➡ *need-based scholarships available* ➡ *FAFSA form due by March 1; Need Access diskette due by Feb. 15 for scholarships*

■ Career Services

The Office of Career Services provides individual assistance to students on career counseling and the techniques of job searching. The office arranges for both on- and off-campus recruitment for summer and permanent legal positions and participates in a variety of hiring consortia. Graduates from 1997 report employment in the following areas of practice: private practice, 39 percent; business and industry, 15 percent; government, 19 percent; judicial clerkships, 13 percent; public interest, 6 percent. A majority of the law school's alumni practice in the Washington, DC metropolitan area; however, its graduates can be found in every state and many foreign countries.

Applicant Group for the 1998-1999 Academic Year

American University—Washington College of Law
This grid includes only applicants who earned 120-180 LSAT scores under standard administrations.

LSAT Score	3.75 +		3.50 - 3.74		3.25 - 3.49		3.00 - 3.24		2.75 - 2.99		2.50 - 2.74		2.25 - 2.49		2.00 - 2.24		Below 2.00		No GPA		Total	
	Apps	Adm	Apps	Adm	Apps	Adm	Apps	Adm	Apps	Adm	Apps	Adm	Apps	Adm	Apps	Adm	Apps	Adm	Apps	Adm	Apps	Adm
175-180	0	0	0	0	2	2	3	3	1	1	0	0	0	0	0	0	0	0	0	0	6	6
170-174	6	6	5	4	6	6	3	3	9	8	5	3	0	0	0	0	0	0	1	1	35	31
165-169	18	18	17	17	33	32	31	28	24	21	15	7	4	2	3	0	1	1	1	1	147	127
160-164	52	50	106	99	157	150	131	110	82	49	35	13	11	4	9	0	0	0	5	3	588	478
155-159	97	86	221	182	323	214	268	136	172	58	80	20	39	8	14	0	0	0	11	5	1225	709
150-154	58	33	176	79	306	102	262	62	179	47	97	16	39	6	12	0	4	0	14	4	1147	349
145-149	27	14	64	19	128	29	161	30	138	18	100	8	47	3	19	1	6	0	10	1	700	123
140-144	10	1	33	4	74	9	71	9	75	7	82	1	30	0	12	3	4	0	16	0	407	34
135-139	3	0	11	0	13	0	30	3	30	1	29	0	22	0	13	0	2	0	10	0	163	4
130-134	0	0	2	0	2	0	8	0	12	0	11	0	17	0	7	0	1	0	4	0	64	0
125-129	1	0	0	0	0	0	0	0	3	0	4	0	1	0	2	0	0	0	3	0	14	0
120-124	0	0	0	0	0	0	0	0	0	0	0	0	0	0	0	0	0	0	1	0	1	0
Total	272	208	635	404	1044	544	968	384	725	210	458	68	210	23	91	4	18	1	76	15	4497	1861

Apps = Number of Applicants
Adm = Number Admitted
Reflects 99% of the total applicant pool.

University of Arizona College of Law

James E. Rogers Law Center
P.O. Box 210176
Tucson, AZ 85721-0176

E-Mail: admissions@nt.law.arizona.edu
URL: http://www.law.arizona.edu
Phone: 520.621.3477; 520.621.9949

■ Introduction

The University of Arizona College of Law was founded in 1915, is the oldest law school in Arizona, and has a rich and distinguished history. The college is an integral part of the University of Arizona, one of the nation's leading research institutions. The College of Law has a national reputation for providing its students a high quality education in a collegial, friendly, and intellectually challenging atmosphere. The College of Law is located in Tucson, an environmentally beautiful and culturally rich city of 750,000, which is home to an active legal and judicial community. The college is approved by the ABA, has been a member of the AALS since 1931, and has a chapter of Order of the Coif.

■ Enrollment/Student Body

➡ 1,499 applicants ➡ 408 admitted first-year class 1998 ➡ 152 enrolled first-year class 1998 ➡ full-time 25th/75th percentile GPA—3.11/3.66 ➡ full-time 25th/75th percentile LSAT—157/164 ➡ 460 total full-time ➡ 25% minority ➡ 50% women ➡ 40 states & foreign countries represented ➡ 165 undergraduate schools represented ➡ 3% persons with disabilities

The students of the College of Law bring varied work and life experiences to the College. The average age of students entering in the fall of 1998 was 26, with 19 percent of the class age 30 or above and 12 percent of the class holding graduate degrees.

■ Faculty

➡ 80 total ➡ 32 full-time ➡ 48 part-time or adjunct ➡ 23 women ➡ 4 minority

With a ratio of 14 to 1, the college has one of the most favorable student-faculty ratios of any American law school. Many members of the faculty are nationally recognized legal scholars.

■ Library and Physical Facilities

➡ 374,000 volumes & equivalents ➡ library hours: Mon.-Thurs., 7:00 A.M.-11:45 P.M.; Fri., 7:00 A.M.-10:00 P.M.; Sat., 8:00 A.M.-8:00 P.M.; Sun., 9:00 A.M.-11:45 P.M. ➡ LEXIS ➡ NEXIS ➡ WESTLAW ➡ OCLC ➡ DIALOG ➡ Internet ➡ 8 full-time librarians ➡ library seats 368

The College of Law occupies the James E. Rogers Law Center, a modern building, which was expanded and refurbished in 1997 and is fully wheelchair accessible, with outstanding classroom, library, and conference facilities. The Arizona State Supreme Court convenes annually at the college and hears arguments on a variety of cases. The library, housing a major research facility, is one of the foremost legal research facilities in the Southwest. There is an expanding foreign law collection emphasizing Latin America and an International Commercial Law Center within the library. The library is networked and contains a student computer laboratory equipped with state-of-the-art technology.

■ Curriculum

➡ Academic Support Program ➡ BRIDGE (a two-week long prelaw program for traditionally underrepresented enrollees) ➡ 85 credits required to graduate ➡ 116 courses available ➡ degrees available: J.D.; J.D./Ph.D. (Economics, Philosophy, Psychology); J.D./M.A. (Economics, American Indian Studies); J.D./M.B.A.; J.D./M.P.A. ➡ LL.M. in International Trade Law ➡ semesters, start in Aug.

The college has committed substantial faculty resources to the first-year curriculum and the development of research and writing skills. Each first-year student meets in a section of approximately 25 students in one of the first-semester courses. In addition to the substantive course material, the student receives instruction in legal research and writing. Students must also complete a special writing seminar during the second or third year.

After completing the first-year requirements, students have considerable flexibility in considering second- and third-year coursework. The college offers a rich variety of courses taught by nationally recognized faculty, including courses in Business and Corporate Law, Securities, Employment Law, Criminal Law, Constitutional Law, Remedies, International Law, Tax, Estates and Trusts, Indian Law, Family Law, Immigration Law, Environmental Law, Legal History, Water Law, and a wealth of Trial Advocacy offerings.

The college has varied clinical opportunities which combine classroom instruction and field placements in the Domestic Violence Clinic, Immigration Clinic, Criminal Defense and Prosecution Clinics, Child Advocacy Clinic, Tribal Law Clinic, and the Judicial Clerking program.

In addition, the college sponsors several congressional internships, a state legislative internship, and internship programs with the Navajo, Pascua Yaqui, White Mountain Apache, and Tohono O'Odham tribal governments.

The course of study leading to the J.D. degree is normally completed in six semesters of resident study; a cumulative average of 2.0 (C) is required to graduate.

■ Admission

➡ Bachelor's degree required ➡ application deadline—March 1, rolling admission Nov. through May, early applications welcome ➡ LSAT, LSDAS required ➡ application fee—$45

Admission to the College of Law is selective. There are two ways to be admitted to the College: through the Presumptive Admission process and through the Admission Committee. In the Presumptive process, all applicants are initially ranked according to an index score combining undergraduate grade-point average and LSAT score in a formula. Some applicants are then admitted primarily based upon their index rankings. In the Admission Committee process, a portion of those applicants who are not admitted on the basis of their index score in the presumptive process are selected for further consideration by the Admission Committee. In making decisions, the Admission Committee considers all relevant personal information, including graduate education; nature of undergraduate experience; distinctive ethnic or cultural backgrounds; work and travel experience; unique talents, interests, accomplishments; special personal goals; extracurricular activities; substantial public or community service; or other circumstances which have influenced the candidate's life or given it direction. The college is very committed to enrolling students who bring diverse perspectives to the college and the legal profession, and encourages applications from minority, disadvantaged, and disabled candidates and candidates who bring varied life experiences to the educational process. Students begin their studies in the fall only and must have completed an undergraduate degree from an accredited four-year college. The deadline for completed applications, including transcripts, LSAT scores, and two letters of recommendation, is March 1. To complete a timely application, applicants must take the LSAT no later than the February of the year of expected enrollment. A waiver of the fee is available when requested and explained in writing and substantiated by a financial aid award letter or a tax return.

Student Activities

The *Arizona Law Review* and *The Arizona Journal of International and Comparative Law* are well-known, student-operated and student-edited scholarly journals on current legal problems. The law school newspaper, *The Arizona Advocate*, serves as a voice for student and faculty opinions on a variety of issues. *The Journal of Psychology, Public Policy and Law* is of special interest to concurrent degree students in law and psychology. The students in the moot court program participate in national and state appellate advocacy competitions.

The student body is self-governing through the Student Bar Association. Students also participate in making law school policy by serving as voting members of student-faculty committees. There are over 20 law student organizations which are an important part of institutional and student life.

Special Programs

The College of Law cooperates with other colleges at the University of Arizona and offers joint J.D./Ph.D. programs in philosophy, psychology, or economics; J.D./M.A. programs in economics and American Indian Studies; a J.D./M.B.A. program; and a J.D./M.P.A. The college also offers a 24-unit LL.M. program in International Trade Law.

Expenses and Financial Aid

➺ *tuition & fees—full-time residents, $4,538 (annually); nonresidents, $11,490 (annually)* ➺ *estimated additional expenses—$12,000 (room, board, travel, books, misc.)* ➺ *scholarships available: need-based & merit-based; tuition waivers* ➺ *minority scholarships available: Native American Scholarships, Cordova Scholarships, cash awards* ➺ *financial aid available* ➺ *FAFSA required—due March 1*

The cost of living in Tucson is relatively modest.

Applicant Group for the 1998-1999 Academic Year

University of Arizona College of Law
This grid includes only applicants who earned 120-180 LSAT scores under standard administrations.

LSAT Score	3.75 +		3.50 - 3.74		3.25 - 3.49		3.00 - 3.24		2.75 - 2.99		2.50 - 2.74		2.25 - 2.49		2.00 - 2.24		Below 2.00		No GPA		Total	
	Apps	Adm	Apps	Adm	Apps	Adm	Apps	Adm	Apps	Adm	Apps	Adm	Apps	Adm	Apps	Adm	Apps	Adm	Apps	Adm	Apps	Adm
175-180	0	0	1	1	1	0	2	2	0	0	0	0	0	0	0	0	0	0	0	0	4	3
170-174	2	2	3	3	7	7	1	1	6	5	4	3	0	0	0	0	0	0	0	0	23	21
165-169	16	16	25	25	21	21	13	9	11	6	7	4	4	0	0	0	0	0	1	0	98	81
160-164	44	33	59	44	58	38	64	29	36	12	15	1	4	1	3	0	0	0	3	3	286	161
155-159	45	11	77	18	100	22	76	16	50	6	22	4	9	2	3	0	0	0	5	0	387	79
150-154	28	5	69	7	72	7	63	7	56	6	16	2	13	1	9	0	1	0	2	0	329	35
145-149	14	2	31	6	36	1	44	3	28	0	13	0	11	0	1	0	1	0	2	0	181	12
140-144	5	0	13	0	24	0	22	0	25	0	16	0	6	0	3	0	1	0	2	0	117	0
135-139	1	0	5	0	5	0	2	0	2	0	3	0	4	0	3	0	4	0	4	0	33	0
130-134	0	0	0	0	1	0	2	0	5	0	2	0	3	0	0	0	1	0	2	0	16	0
125-129	0	0	0	0	0	0	0	0	0	0	1	0	0	0	1	0	1	0	0	0	3	0
120-124	0	0	0	0	0	0	0	0	0	0	0	0	0	0	0	0	0	0	0	0	0	0
Total	155	69	283	104	325	96	289	67	219	35	99	14	54	4	23	0	9	0	21	3	1477	392

Apps = Number of Applicants
Adm = Number Admitted
Reflects 99% of the total applicant pool.
This grid is to be used as a general guide only. Qualitative factors, including each candidate's personal statement, letters of recommendation, and life experiences, play an important role in the evaluation process.

Arizona State University College of Law

Box 877906
Tempe, AZ 85287-7906

URL: http://www.law.asu.edu
Phone: 602.965.1474

■ Introduction

The College of Law is located on the campus of the Arizona State University in Tempe, a suburb of Phoenix. Established in 1966, the law school was accredited by the AALS and ABA in 1969. In the fall of 1992, the college celebrated its 25th anniversary and the accomplishments it has achieved in a relatively short time.

■ Enrollment/Student Body

➽ *1,691 applicants* ➽ *380 admitted first-year class 1998*
➽ *161 enrolled first-year class 1998* ➽ *full-time 25th/75th percentile GPA—2.96/3.59* ➽ *full-time 25th/75th percentile LSAT—154/161* ➽ *482 total full-time* ➽ *24% minority*
➽ *44% women* ➽ *37 states & foreign countries represented*
➽ *140 undergraduate schools represented*
➽ *1998 entering class: 75% resident, 25% nonresident*

■ Faculty

➽ *51 total* ➽ *30 full-time* ➽ *21 part-time or adjunct*
➽ *13 women* ➽ *3 minority*

■ Library and Physical Facilities

➽ *368,919 volumes & equivalents* ➽ *library hours: Mon.-Thurs., 7:00 A.M.-MIDNIGHT; Fri., 7:00 A.M.-10:00 P.M.; Sat., 8:00 A.M.-10:00 P.M.; Sun., 10:00 A.M.-MIDNIGHT*
➽ *LEXIS* ➽ *WESTLAW* ➽ *7 full-time librarians*
➽ *library seats 590*

Armstrong Hall, a modern, air-conditioned structure, is architecturally designed for the special functions of legal education. Among its features are classrooms with seating on elevated tiers to facilitate dialogue between professors and students; the Willard H. Pedrick Great Hall, seating 400, which serves not only as a courtroom, but also as a location for campus events; and a trial courtroom which is equipped to permit videotaping of trials and other advocacy exercises to facilitate instruction in litigation techniques. Armstrong Hall houses a legal clinic, providing easy access for law student interns.

The John J. Ross—William C. Blakley Law Library is housed in a dramatic and functional building that opened in August 1993. The collection includes growing special collections in the areas of international law, Indian law, Mexican law, and law and technology. The library has a 30-station computer lab, as well as LEXIS and WESTLAW rooms each containing 10 stations, 27 meeting and study rooms, and a microforms facility.

■ Curriculum

➽ *Academic Support Program*
➽ *Law School Clinic, Prosecutor Clinic, Externship Programs*
➽ *87 units/credits required to graduate* ➽ *85 courses available*
➽ *degrees available: J.D.; J.D./M.B.A.; J.D./M.H.S.A.; J.D./Ph.D. Justice Studies* ➽ *fall semester starts in Aug.,*

spring semester starts in Jan. ➽ *range of first-year class size—30-135*

The College of Law awards the J.D. degree following a three-year course of study. The first year consists of a required curriculum. In the following years, the student selects from a wide number of legal courses, including small-group seminars, clinic internships, independent and interdisciplinary study, and a trial practice program. Many students also choose to enhance their theoretical classroom knowledge with the practical experience of an externship. The college offers a variety of externship opportunities with agencies and governmental offices.

■ Center for the Study of Law, Science, and Technology

The Center for the Study of Law, Science, and Technology was established in 1984 in response to the increasing number of social and legal questions arising out of new scientific and technological development in areas such as computers, communications, medicine, genetics, space technology, and nuclear power.

The center conducts research, engages in curricular development, sponsors papers and conferences, and brings visiting scholars to the law school. The College of Law coedits the *Jurimetrics Journal*, a quarterly journal of the ABA Section of Science and Technology.

■ Clinical Programs

The College of Law offers a variety of clinical courses. In the Law School Clinic students gain experience in interviewing, legal research and writing, fact investigation, discovery, pretrial procedure, and oral advocacy in the courtroom. Students may be assigned to a variety of civil matters. Prosecutor Clinic interns prosecute misdemeanor charges in city courts in Tempe and neighboring communities. Students also have an opportunity to participate in a Public Defender clinic and a Mediation Clinic.

■ Indian Legal Program

The Indian Legal Program (ILP) at the Arizona State University College of Law actively recruits American Indian students and promotes Indian legal education in the course curriculum. The ILP also seeks to provide public service to American Indian tribes and tribal governments.

The ASU College of Law student body typically includes students from 15-25 different American Indian tribes.

■ Student Activities

The Student Bar Association sponsors numerous activities including lectures and social events. Second- and third-year students publish a professional law review, *Arizona State Law Journal*. Students also direct the moot court program and participate in national and international moot court competitions. In addition, law students publish a newspaper, *Devil's Advocate,* and have formed such independent organizations as Women's Law Student Association, Chicano/Latino Law Students Association, American Indian Law Students, Asian Law Students Association, legal fraternities, and a chapter of the Black Law Students Association. Many students participate in pro bono activities including the Volunteer Income Tax Assistance program and the Homeless Legal Assistance Project. Students also serve as voting members of several College of Law committees.

■ Admission

➡ *Bachelor's degree required from an accredited institution* ➡ *application deadline—March 1* ➡ *LSAT, LSDAS required* ➡ *application fee—$45*

With approximately 12 applicants for each place in the first-year class, admission to the College of Law is highly selective. Such varied factors as the undergraduate education, LSAT score, trend of college grades, course-selection patterns, quality and grading patterns of undergraduate institutions, work or other nonacademic experience, and cultural or socioeconomic background are considered in the admission decision.

Transfer applications will be considered on a space-available basis for students with excellent records.

Students who are members of minority groups are encouraged to apply. The College of Law has a vital diversity admission policy, a policy to which the college is enthusiastically committed. Students from diverse cultural, ethnic, and racial backgrounds enrich the educational experience of all students and faculty and ultimately increase the number of minority lawyers in the country.

■ Expenses and Financial Aid

➡ *tuition & fees—full-time resident, $4,536/yr.; nonresident, $11,488* ➡ *estimated additional expenses— $10,500 (living expenses, books/9-month academic year)* ➡ *scholarships available: merit- & need-based* ➡ *minority scholarships available* ➡ *financial aid available*

■ Placement

The law school Placement Office provides assistance to students and alumni seeking employment. Placement services include a computerized job line and bulletin board of job openings, a resource library, an alumni mentor program, and workshops on résumé writing, interviewing, and research techniques. Special-interest workshops are offered on various topics such as clerkship positions and public interest law opportunities. The Placement Office also arranges for on-campus interviews with law firms and governmental agencies.

Applicant Group for the 1998-1999 Academic Year

Arizona State University College of Law
This grid includes only applicants with 120-180 LSAT scores earned under standard administrations.

LSAT Score	3.75 +		3.50 - 3.74		3.25 - 3.49		3.00 - 3.24		2.75 - 2.99		2.50 - 2.74		2.25 - 2.49		2.00 - 2.24		Below 2.00		No GPA		Total	
	Apps	Adm	Apps	Adm	Apps	Adm	Apps	Adm	Apps	Adm	Apps	Adm	Apps	Adm	Apps	Adm	Apps	Adm	Apps	Adm	Apps	Adm
175-180	1	1	1	1	0	0	0	0	0	0	0	0	0	0	0	0	0	0	0	0	2	2
170-174	2	2	2	1	2	1	2	2	2	2	3	2	0	0	0	0	0	0	0	0	13	10
165-169	8	7	4	3	10	9	10	9	8	6	5	4	3	1	0	0	0	0	1	0	243	160
160-164	31	26	37	27	52	38	57	34	39	25	14	7	8	2	4	1	0	0	1	0	243	160
155-159	37	13	70	24	105	21	89	21	66	9	29	5	14	3	4	0	1	0	8	1	423	97
150-154	38	7	79	12	86	6	85	4	65	5	33	2	19	2	8	0	0	0	3	1	416	39
145-149	18	1	33	10	36	1	65	4	52	5	28	1	21	1	9	0	1	0	5	0	268	23
140-144	7	0	21	0	25	2	24	4	38	1	27	0	11	0	6	0	0	0	5	0	164	7
135-139	2	0	9	1	8	0	8	0	11	0	9	1	11	0	2	0	3	0	5	0	68	2
130-134	0	0	1	0	0	0	3	0	2	0	4	0	7	0	1	0	1	0	2	0	21	0
125-129	0	0	0	0	0	0	0	0	0	0	0	0	0	0	2	0	1	0	0	0	3	0
120-124	0	0	0	0	0	0	0	0	0	0	0	0	0	0	0	0	0	0	0	0	0	0
Total	144	57	257	79	324	78	343	78	283	53	152	22	94	9	36	1	7	0	29	2	1669	379

Apps = Number of Applicants
Adm = Number Admitted
Reflects 99% of the total applicant pool.

University of Arkansas School of Law—Fayetteville

Robert A. Leflar Law Center
Fayetteville, AR 72701

URL: http://law.uark.edu/
Phone: 501.575.3102

■ Introduction

The University of Arkansas School of Law is located on the main university campus at Fayetteville, a city of 49,000 in Northwest Arkansas. The School of Law was established in 1924 and has continuously sought to provide high quality legal education in a university community. In 1926 the School of Law was approved by the ABA, and in 1927 the school became a member of the AALS.

■ Enrollment/Student Body

➼ *624 applicants* ➼ *320 admitted first-year class 1998* ➼ *125 enrolled first-year class 1998* ➼ *full-time 25th/75th percentile GPA—2.97/3.63* ➼ *full-time 25th/75th percentile LSAT—148/157* ➼ *364 total full-time* ➼ *7.4% minority* ➼ *40% women* ➼ *30 states & foreign countries represented* ➼ *114 undergraduate schools represented*

Although 80 percent of the students are Arkansas residents, others are from every part of the United States. Since the school has no undergraduate course prerequisites, the academic backgrounds and nonacademic experiences of students are varied.

■ Faculty

➼ *45 total* ➼ *33 full-time* ➼ *12 part-time or adjunct* ➼ *12 women* ➼ *5 minority*

■ Library and Physical Facilities

➼ *252,000 volumes & equivalents* ➼ *library hours: Mon.-Thurs., 7:00 A.M.-MIDNIGHT; Fri., 7:00 A.M.-10:00 P.M.; Sat., 9:00 A.M.-10:00 P.M.; Sun., 1:00 P.M.-MIDNIGHT; 107 total hours* ➼ *LEXIS* ➼ *WESTLAW* ➼ *Legislate* ➼ *5 full-time librarians* ➼ *library seats 346*

The library is expanding at a rate of over 10,000 volumes a year. Students are trained in the techniques of computer-assisted legal research as well as in the traditional research methods. The law library is a federal and state depository for government documents.

■ Curriculum

➼ *90 credits required to graduate* ➼ *102 courses available* ➼ *degrees available: J.D.; J.D./M.B.A.; J.D./M.P.A.* ➼ *semesters, start in Aug.* ➼ *range of first-year class size—25-63*

The primary function of the University of Arkansas School of Law is to prepare lawyers who will render the highest quality of professional service to their clients, who are interested in and capable of furthering legal process and reform, and who are prepared to fill the vital role of the lawyer as a community leader. The school offers a full-time, three-year program leading to the J.D. degree. The degree is conferred upon satisfactory completion of 90 semester hours, including 44 hours of required courses. The first-year curriculum is required. A broad selection of elective second- and third-year courses is available. Students who have completed the first year of law school may earn up to 12 semester hours of credit in summer school, and graduation can be accelerated one semester by summer coursework. The School of Law offers a joint J.D./M.B.A. program with the College of Business Administration. If a student is accepted into both programs, a maximum of six hours of approved upper-level elective law courses may be used on duplicative credit toward the M.B.A. degree and a maximum of six hours of approved graduate courses in business administration may be used as duplicative credit toward the J.D. degree. The Department of Political Science, the graduate school, and the School of Law cooperate in offering a dual-degree program that allows a student to pursue the M.P.A. and the J.D. degrees concurrently. Students must be admitted to the M.P.A. program, the School of Law, and the dual-degree program. The Graduate Program in Agricultural Law provides opportunities for advanced study, creative research, and specialized professional training in this rapidly developing area of law. The program is designed to prepare a small number of carefully selected attorneys as specialists in the legal problems of agricultural production, distribution, and marketing. Applicants for admission as candidates for the Master of Laws (LL.M.) in Agricultural Law must have earned a J.D. or LL.B. degree from a fully accredited law school.

■ Admission

➼ *B.A. required* ➼ *application deadline—April 1, rolling admission, early application preferred* ➼ *LSAT, LSDAS required*

First-year students are admitted in the fall and only for full-time study. Prior to enrolling in the School of Law, applicants must have completed all requirements for an undergraduate degree from an accredited four-year college. Admission is based on the applicant's LSAT score and undergraduate GPA. In a small percentage of cases, additional criteria such as vocational or professional experience, graduate work, ethnicity, and progressive improvement in college work are considered by a faculty admissions committee. A preference is given to Arkansas residents; for the current status of this preference, contact the school. A nonrefundable tuition deposit is required of all admitted candidates. The law school's application deadline is April 1 of the year in which admission is sought; however, applicants are requested to apply by January 1 to expedite the selection and notification process. Applicants must take the LSAT no later than February. Applications completed after April 1 will be considered only on a space-available basis.

■ Housing

Housing for single students is available in campus dormitories; apartments are also available for married students.

Applicants should write to the Housing Office, University of Arkansas, Fayetteville, AR 72701. A variety of private off-campus housing is available in Fayetteville and surrounding communities, within easy commuting distance of the law school.

■ Student Activities

The *Arkansas Law Review* is a legal periodical published quarterly by the students of the School of Law in cooperation with the Arkansas Bar Association. Candidates for the *Review* are selected on the basis of scholarship and writing ability. Students in their second and third years are encouraged to compete in an intramural moot court competition, and Arkansas students participate in national moot court competitions. The University of Arkansas School of Law also participates in the ABA Law Student Division Client Counseling Competition. The law school operates a legal aid clinic providing counseling and representation for university students and indigent persons seeking legal assistance. An Arkansas Supreme Court Rule permits senior law students, upon certification and under supervision, to appear in court on a no-fee basis. The Student Bar Association sponsors a variety of academic and social activities. All students are also eligible for membership in the Law Student Division of the Arkansas Bar Association. Three of the largest national legal fraternities, Delta Theta Phi, Phi Alpha Delta, and Phi Delta Phi, maintain active chapters at the school. The Women's Law Student Association was organized to provide an opportunity for women to discuss and work with common professional interests and problems. Members of the Arkansas Chapter of Black Law Students Association work as a collective body to inform black students of the available and advantages of a legal education, to promote the academic success of black law students at Arkansas, and to increase the awareness and commitment of the legal profession to the black community.

■ Expenses and Financial Aid

➤ *tuition & fees—full-time resident, $4,168; nonresident, $9,136*
➤ *scholarships available*   ➤ *minority scholarships available*

Students are expected to make sufficient financial arrangements for the first year of study without the necessity of seeking employment. All law students are required to be full-time students. All financial aid in the form of Perkins Loans (formerly NDSL), higher education loans, and work-study grants is processed by the University of Arkansas Office of Student Financial Aid, University of Arkansas, Fayetteville, AR 72701. A limited number of law school-administered scholarships are available to entering students. Applications are distributed following fall registration in August.

■ Career Services

The law school maintains a Career Services Office with a full-time, highly qualified director and staff to assist and advise students and graduates. Services offered by the office include: on-campus interviews for permanent and summer employment; individual career counseling sessions; workshops and handbooks regarding résumé preparation, interviewing skills and techniques, and job searches; panels of lawyers who present programs on a variety of topics; a bi-monthly jobs bulletin; and a comprehensive placement library. The office also maintains employment and salary statistics.

Applicant Group for the 1998-1999 Academic Year

University of Arkansas School of Law—Fayetteville
This grid includes only applicants who earned 120-180 LSAT scores under standard administrations.

LSAT Score	GPA																					
	3.75 +		3.50 - 3.74		3.25 - 3.49		3.00 - 3.24		2.75 - 2.99		2.50 - 2.74		2.25 - 2.49		2.00 - 2.24		Below 2.00		No GPA		Total	
	Apps	Adm	Apps	Adm	Apps	Adm	Apps	Adm	Apps	Adm	Apps	Adm	Apps	Adm	Apps	Adm	Apps	Adm	Apps	Adm	Apps	Adm
175-180	0	0	0	0	0	0	0	0	0	0	0	0	0	0	0	0	0	0	0	0	0	0
170-174	1	1	0	0	0	0	1	1	0	0	0	0	0	0	0	0	0	0	0	0	2	2
165-169	1	1	0	0	1	1	4	4	2	2	1	1	0	0	0	0	0	0	1	1	10	10
160-164	10	10	11	11	7	7	9	9	4	4	3	2	1	0	0	0	0	0	1	0	46	43
155-159	20	20	19	19	13	12	19	19	21	14	10	4	7	2	5	1	0	0	3	2	117	93
150-154	15	13	24	23	20	19	28	19	22	11	9	0	10	2	0	0	1	0	4	1	133	88
145-149	12	11	28	22	23	14	20	8	26	5	18	1	9	0	2	1	1	0	6	0	145	62
140-144	3	2	12	4	13	2	17	4	22	2	14	1	11	0	4	1	0	0	1	0	97	16
135-139	0	0	1	0	3	0	5	0	5	0	7	0	4	0	6	0	0	0	3	0	34	0
130-134	0	0	0	0	0	0	3	0	3	0	3	0	3	0	1	0	0	0	3	0	16	0
125-129	0	0	0	0	0	0	1	0	0	0	1	0	0	0	0	0	0	0	0	0	2	0
120-124	0	0	0	0	0	0	0	0	0	0	0	0	0	0	0	0	0	0	0	0	0	0
Total	62	58	95	79	80	55	107	64	105	38	66	9	45	4	18	3	2	0	22	4	602	314

Apps = Number of Applicants
Adm = Number Admitted
Reflects 97% of the total applicant pool.

University of Arkansas at Little Rock School of Law

1201 McAlmont St.
Little Rock, AR 72202-5142

E-Mail: lawadm@ualr.edu
URL: http://www.ualr.edu/~lawschool/
Phone: 501.324.9439

■ Introduction

The School of Law is located in the heart of metropolitan Little Rock, close to the Capitol, the state's largest law firms, and state government offices. The law school enrolls 420 students out of a total UALR enrollment of 10,541.

The UALR School of Law is fully accredited by the American Bar Association and is a member of the Association of American Law Schools. The university is fully accredited by the North Central Association of Colleges and Schools.

UALR is known for cost-effective legal education that blends theory with practice, at a school that is an integral part of the Arkansas and national legal community.

■ Enrollment/Student Body

➡ *390 applicants* ➡ *224 admitted first-year class 1998*
➡ *146 enrolled first-year class 1998* ➡ *full-time 25th/75th percentile GPA—3.11/3.70* ➡ *part-time 25th/75th percentile GPA—2.79/3.42* ➡ *full-time 25th/75th percentile LSAT—145/160* ➡ *part-time 25th/75th percentile LSAT—148/154* ➡ *276 total full-time* ➡ *144 total part-time*
➡ *12% minority* ➡ *47% women* ➡ *21 states & foreign countries represented* ➡ *102 undergraduate schools represented*

■ Faculty

➡ *52 total* ➡ *29 full-time* ➡ *23 part-time or adjunct*
➡ *18 women* ➡ *3 minority*

■ Library and Physical Facilities

➡ *262,000 volumes & equivalents* ➡ *99 library hours/wk.*
➡ *LEXIS* ➡ *NEXIS* ➡ *WESTLAW* ➡ *DIALOG*
➡ *Lois & Case-Base* ➡ *Netscape Internet access*
➡ *6 full-time librarians* ➡ *library seats 385*

Since 1992, the law school has been housed in a completely renovated, 140,000-square-foot building, adjacent to MacArthur Park, a 40-acre expanse containing greenery, ponds, and an art museum. The new building contains multiple courtrooms, ample room for student activities, and a breathtaking library built around a four-story atrium blending print and computer resources. The library serves the county bar as well, offering a unique working environment for law students. Library resources range from handwritten 19th century Arkansas Supreme Court briefs to Internet Netscape access.

■ Curriculum

➡ *Academic Support Program* ➡ *87 credits required to graduate* ➡ *94 courses available* ➡ *degrees available: J.D.; J.D./M.B.A.* ➡ *semesters, start in Aug.*
➡ *range of first-year class size—20-100*

The School of Law offers a program of legal education in both day and evening divisions. The day division operates a full-time program, with an average courseload of 15 hours per semester. A full-time student will normally complete the course of study in three years. The average courseload per semester in the part-time evening program is 10 hours; the maximum load is 11 hours. The part-time course of study is normally completed in four years. The first-year curriculum is prescribed.

■ Special Programs

The School of Law is noted for its required Trial Advocacy course, in which students serve as counsel in both a bench trial and a jury trial. Other upper-level skills and simulation courses are available to students, as well as a strong internal clinic, where students represent real clients in court under the supervision of attorneys and may engage in mediation as a part of a broader dispute resolution program. The School of Law also offers a joint J.D./M.B.A. degree with the UALR College of Business Administration.

■ Admission

➡ *Bachelor's degree required* ➡ *application deadline—May 1*
➡ *LSAT, LSDAS required* ➡ *application fee—$40*
➡ *rolling admission, early application preferred*

The School of Law enrolls 125 to 135 students each year. At least 80 percent of the entering students are Arkansas residents. The majority are selected on the basis of LSAT scores and undergraduate GPAs ("Index Admission"), while approximately 40 percent are selected by using additional criteria ("Non-Index Admission"), such as letters of recommendation, work experience, graduate education, extracurricular activities, evidence of strong motivation and maturity, ethnicity disadvantages, underrepresentation of minorities in the legal profession, and diversity of backgrounds. Nonresident students are selected on the basis of LSAT scores and undergraduate GPAs.

A specific prelaw curriculum is not required. The School of Law subscribes to the comments found in the introduction to this handbook. Each applicant must hold a degree from an accredited college or university. Prospective applicants should contact the Admissions Office for details about admission requirements. Students are enrolled only in the fall. Application should be made as early as possible and may not be considered unless completed by May 1 of the calendar year of desired admission.

■ Housing

UALR does not maintain student residence halls for law students; however, affordable private housing is available within easy commuting distance of the law school.

■ Activities

Many activities are open to UALR law students. The most prestigious are service on the *UALR Law Review*, a student-run scholarly publication which publishes articles written by both students and attorneys, and service on the Moot Court Board, which coordinates participation in local, regional, and national moot court competitions of various kinds. All students are automatic members of the Student Bar Association, which is the student governance body as well as a social group. Students can also join a multitude of other organizations, such as the American Bar Association, Arkansas Bar Association, Black Law Students Association, Community Outreach Opportunity League (an umbrella organization which sponsors various public service projects), the Federalist Society, Christian Legal Society, Environmental Law Society, and a number of others, including several legal fraternities. The Arkansas Bar Association and Arkansas Association of Women Lawyers also sponsor mentoring programs to bring students and practitioners together. Upper-class students may be invited to join the Overton Inn of Court, modeled on the British inns of court, which are social and educational bodies where attorneys, judges, professors, and students convene to discuss aspects of trial practice.

■ Expenses and Financial Aid

➡ *full-time tuition—resident, $4,500/yr.; nonresident, $9,072/yr.* ➡ *part-time tuition—resident, $150/credit hour; nonresident, $340/credit hour* ➡ *average part-time tuition—resident, $3,300 (22 hours)/yr.; nonresident, $7,480/yr.* ➡ *estimated additional expenses—$400/semester (books)* ➡ *scholarships available* ➡ *financial aid available* ➡ *application for Federal Student Aid due March 1*

The UALR School of Law has dramatically increased the number of scholarships available to entering students with strong credentials. An applicant who meets the minimum criteria is automatically awarded a scholarship. Maximum awards provide full tuition, fees, and books for three to four years of study for both residents and nonresidents admitted into the full- or part-time division. Tuition waivers for nonresidents and partial tuition awards are also available.

A growing number of scholarships are also available to second- and third-year students who demonstrate financial need and possess strong academic records. The School of Law participates in the Federal Family Education Loan programs (subsidized and unsubsidized Stafford Loans) and Federal College Work-Study programs. A minimum number of emergency short-term student loans are also available. Applicants for federal financial aid must complete the Free Application for Federal Student Aid. Requests for financial assistance should be addressed to the Director of Student Financial Services, UALR, 2801 South University, Little Rock, AR 72204. Phone: 501.569.3035.

■ Career Services

The law school maintains an active Career Services Program within the Office of Student Services. Its objectives are: (1) to assist students in defining and exploring career goals, (2) to increase students' awareness of effective job search strategies, and (3) to serve as the liaison between students and alumni and potential employers, allowing the opportunity for mutual consideration for employment opportunities. Career Services provides workshops on job search strategies, including networking, résumé writing, and interviewing preparation. The office also makes available current position openings, locally and statewide, as well as nationally and internationally; hosts employers for on-campus interviews; and provides a résumé referral service to employers. Career Services also provides a number of resources, including WESTLAW access, allowing individuals to explore career possibilities and employment opportunities.

Applicant Group for the 1998-1999 Academic Year

University of Arkansas at Little Rock School of Law
This grid includes only applicants who earned 120-180 LSAT scores under standard administrations.

LSAT Score	3.75 + Apps	Adm	3.50 - 3.74 Apps	Adm	3.25 - 3.49 Apps	Adm	3.00 - 3.24 Apps	Adm	2.75 - 2.99 Apps	Adm	2.50 - 2.74 Apps	Adm	2.25 - 2.49 Apps	Adm	2.00 - 2.24 Apps	Adm	Below 2.00 Apps	Adm	No GPA Apps	Adm	Total Apps	Adm
175-180	0	0	0	0	0	0	0	0	0	0	0	0	0	0	0	0	0	0	0	0	0	0
170-174	0	0	0	0	0	0	0	0	0	0	0	0	0	0	0	0	0	0	0	0	0	0
165-169	0	0	2	2	0	0	0	0	0	0	1	1	0	0	0	0	0	0	1	0	4	3
160-164	4	4	6	6	6	6	3	3	2	2	1	1	1	1	0	0	0	0	0	0	23	23
155-159	2	2	9	9	9	8	9	9	6	6	4	3	1	0	3	1	0	0	2	1	45	39
150-154	7	6	11	11	15	15	18	16	13	12	4	2	5	3	1	0	1	0	0	0	75	65
145-149	13	13	21	21	13	10	12	9	17	11	14	5	7	0	3	2	0	0	4	1	104	72
140-144	4	4	10	5	11	5	8	1	13	2	10	1	16	1	0	0	3	0	2	0	77	18
135-139	0	0	1	1	0	0	5	0	7	0	6	0	4	0	7	0	1	0	4	0	35	1
130-134	0	0	1	0	0	0	4	0	2	0	2	0	3	0	0	0	0	0	2	0	14	0
125-129	0	0	0	0	0	0	1	0	1	0	1	0	1	0	0	0	0	0	1	0	5	0
120-124	0	0	0	0	0	0	0	0	0	0	0	0	0	0	0	0	1	0	0	0	1	0
Total	30	29	61	55	54	44	60	38	61	33	43	13	38	4	17	3	3	0	16	2	383	221

Apps = Number of Applicants
Adm = Number Admitted
Reflects 96% of the total applicant pool.

University of Baltimore School of Law

1420 North Charles Street
Baltimore, MD 21201

E-Mail: lwadmiss@ubmail.ubalt.edu
URL: http://www.ubalt.edu/www/law
Phone: 410.837.4459, Fax: 410.837.4450

■ Introduction

Founded in 1925, the University of Baltimore is one of thirteen institutions in the University System of Maryland. The School of Law has a distinguished history of offering high quality legal education in a vibrant urban environment that provides a wide range of opportunities for students to put their legal knowledge into practice. In both day and evening divisions, the school offers a comprehensive curriculum that gives students core substantive and procedural classes, as well as excellent training in legal skills. A broad selection of elective courses completes the curriculum. The school's midtown location puts it only eighteen blocks from Baltimore's Inner Harbor, Oriole Park at Camden Yards, and the new Baltimore Ravens Stadium. Also nearby are state and federal courts, large law firms, government offices, symphony concerts, theater productions, and excellent museums. The law school is on the light-rail line that leads to downtown attractions, as well as northern and southern suburbs, and one block from the Amtrak station. The School of Law is accredited by the American Bar Association and is a member of the Association of American Law Schools.

■ Enrollment/Student Body

➡ *1,565 applicants: 877 admitted, 277 enrolled in 1998 entering class* ➡ *full-time 25th/75th percentile GPA—2.64/3.31* ➡ *part-time 25th/75th percentile GPA—2.56/3.18* ➡ *full-time 25th/75th percentile LSAT—147/152* ➡ *part-time 25th/75th percentile LSAT—146/153* ➡ *1998 first-year class: 196 day, 81 evening* ➡ *23.5% minority first-year class 1998* ➡ *52% women first-year class 1998* ➡ *25% nonresidents from 16 states and Washington, DC* ➡ *114 undergraduate schools represented*

■ Faculty

➡ *123 total* ➡ *45 full-time (17 women, 5 minority)* ➡ *78 adjunct* ➡ *faculty/student ratio—1:13*

■ Library and Physical Facilities

➡ *295,200 volumes & equivalents* ➡ *library hours: Mon.-Sun., 8:00 A.M.-MIDNIGHT* ➡ *8 full-time librarians*

The library's two computer labs are open to law students during library hours and provide access to word processing, Lexis, Westlaw, computer-assisted learning programs, and other resources.

■ Curriculum

➡ *Academic Support Program* ➡ *Juris Doctor (J.D.) requires 90 credits* ➡ *full-time day & part-time evening and day programs available* ➡ *135 courses offered* ➡ *fall semester entry only* ➡ *summer abroad comparative law program in Scotland* ➡ *Joint degrees offered: J.D. with M.B.A., M.P.A., M.S. in Criminal Justice, LL.M. in Taxation, or Ph.D. in Policy Science*

■ Special Programs

Areas of Concentration—The School of Law has introduced an innovative curriculum that allows students to develop an area of study focused on one or more areas of the law, while still providing them with the basic first-year curriculum and many electives. Students may take courses in one of 12 areas of concentration: Business Law, Criminal Practice, Environmental Law, Estate Planning, Family Law, General Practice, Intellectual Property, International and Comparative Law, Litigation and Advocacy, Public Interest Law, Real Estate Practice, and Theories of the Law.

The Center for International and Comparative Law—promotes the study and understanding of international and comparative law and the political and economic institutions that support the international legal order. The center places special emphasis on environmental law, human rights, intellectual property, and international business transactions.

Clinical, Advocacy, and Internship Programs—Professional development is fostered through clinics in which students represent individuals and organizations in litigation and transactional matters. Clinics include: the **Appellate Practice Clinic**, which enables students to brief and argue a case in the Maryland Court of Special Appeals; the **Civil Clinic**, which focuses on such issues as consumer protection, public benefits cases, and landlord-tenant disputes; the **Community Development Clinic**, which represents non-profit community organizations in a variety of housing, economic, social and cultural development areas; the **Criminal Practice Clinic**, in which students handle misdemeanor and felony matters in the district and circuit courts; the **Disability Law Clinic**, which provides representation to patients in involuntary commitment hearings; and the **Family Law Clinic**, where students represent low income clients seeking child custody, support, divorce, and protection from domestic violence. The **Internship Programs** give students experience clerking for academic credit in the public and private sector, including positions in the executive, legislative, and judicial branches of state, and local government.

Law reviews, journals, and other periodicals give students an opportunity to hone their skills in research, analysis, and writing. The *University of Baltimore Law Review, Journal of Environmental Law,* and *Intellectual Property Law Journal* offer in-depth analyses of issues of current concern to practioners and judges alike. The *Law Forum* specializes in articles that trace developing trends in the law.

■ Admission

➡ *Baccalaureate degree, LSAT & LSDAS registration required* ➡ *rolling admission—May 1* ➡ *strongly recommend all material be submitted before April 1* ➡ *application fee—$35*

The School of Law has established an admission policy designed to obtain a diverse and well-qualified student body. In evaluating applicant files, the Admission Committee considers not only the cumulative undergraduate grade-point average and the LSAT score, but also nontraditional factors that may be relevant in determining an applicant's ability to succeed in law school. Applicants are encouraged to discuss fully in a personal statement or an attached explanation any such factors they wish the committee to consider in evaluating their application. Although interviews are not a part of the application process, frequent group information programs and several open houses are conducted by the admission staff.

■ Expenses and Financial Aid

➡ *annual full-time tuition & fees—in-state, $9,006; out-of-state, $15,624* ➡ *part-time, per credit hour— in-state, $426; out-of-state, $666* ➡ *all fees included*
➡ *FAFSA & financial aid transcripts required*
➡ *Financial Aid application deadline—April 1*

The university's Financial Aid Office administers federal, state, and institutional loan programs. First-year and transfer applicants are advised to apply for financial aid well in advance of the April 1 deadline. Law Scholarships are awarded by the School of Law on the basis of the same traditional and nontraditional factors considered for admission. Financial need is not required for scholarships, although it is a factor. Applicants should submit scholarship forms and a copy of the FAFSA they filed with the Financial Aid Office to the Office of Law Admission.

■ Career Services

Ninety percent of the class of 1997 as employed six months after graduation. The Career Services Center is dedicated to assisting law students in articulating, developing, and attaining their professional goals. The CSC provides career counseling, offers a broad array of programs and workshops, maintains an extensive resource library, and is online with both LEXIS and WESTLAW.

Applicant Group for the 1998-1999 Academic Year

University of Baltimore School of Law
This grid includes only applicants who earned 120-180 LSAT scores under standard administrations.

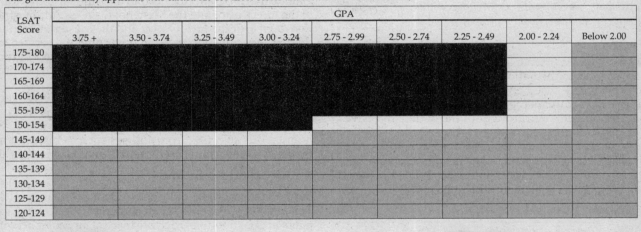

LSAT Score	GPA								
	3.75 +	3.50 - 3.74	3.25 - 3.49	3.00 - 3.24	2.75 - 2.99	2.50 - 2.74	2.25 - 2.49	2.00 - 2.24	Below 2.00
175-180									
170-174									
165-169									
160-164									
155-159									
150-154									
145-149									
140-144									
135-139									
130-134									
125-129									
120-124									

■ Very Competitive   □ Competitive   ▨ Less Competitive

Baylor University School of Law

P.O. Box 97288
Waco, TX 76798

E-Mail: law_support@baylor.edu
URL: http://law.baylor.edu
Phone: 800.BAYLOR.U. or 254.710.1911

■ Introduction

Baylor University School of Law is a private, ABA-approved law school and is a member of the American Association of Law Schools. Formally organized in 1857, Baylor law school is the oldest law school in Texas. The School of Law is located on the campus of Baylor University in Waco, Texas. Waco is located in the heart of Texas, has a population of over 200,000, and offers a diverse and rich array of cultural and recreational opportunities.

Baylor law school stands today at the forefront of practice-oriented law schools nationally. Baylor is singularly clear about its mission—to equip students to practice law effectively. That's the key difference. Students are trained and mentored in all facets of law including: theoretical analysis, practical application, legal writing, advocacy, and negotiation and counseling skills. Baylor surrounds students with faculty mentoring and a culture of caring and support to ensure their success.

■ Enrollment/Student Body

➡ 729 applicants ➡ 279 admitted first-year class 1998 ➡ 57 enrolled first-year class 1998 ➡ full-time 25th/75th percentile GPA—3.31/3.73 ➡ full-time 25th/75th percentile LSAT—156/161 ➡ 423 total full-time ➡ 35 minority ➡ 166 women ➡ 38 states & foreign countries represented ➡ 154 undergraduate schools represented

■ Faculty

Baylor law school is first a teaching school, and one of the only law schools in the nation in which the granting of tenure is primarily based on a professor's teaching effectiveness. Faculty members hold degrees from law schools and universities throughout the nation and have a strong dedication to teaching and scholarship.

Faculty members are experts in their areas and have significant practical experience. They have produced a significant amount of legal scholarship which has led to their demand as speakers at legal institutes and civic functions.

■ Library and Physical Facilities

➡ 198,500 volumes & equivalents ➡ LEXIS ➡ NEXIS ➡ WESTLAW ➡ DIALOG ➡ OCLC ➡ automated online card catalog ➡ 4 full-time librarians

Classrooms, practice courtrooms, computer labs, study lounges, faculty offices, and the law library are all located in a self-contained building. The law library houses two computer labs and legal research centers. Both labs feature IBM-compatible personal computers and provide access to the World Wide Web, the LEXIS and WESTLAW databases, and student e-mail accounts.

■ Curriculum

➡ Academic Support Program ➡ 126 quarter hour credits required to graduate ➡ 84 courses available

➡ degrees available: J.D.; J.D./M.B.A.; J.D./M.Tax; & J.D./M.P.P.A. ➡ quarters, start in Aug., Nov., Feb., & May ➡ range of first-year class size—30-70 ➡ 6 areas of concentration

All students receive a well-rounded education by completing a broad course of study in the fundamentals of legal theory and doctrine and by participating in skills training exercises. The required curriculum is structured to provide a logical progression for legal study from fundamental legal doctrine in first-year courses to increasingly more sophisticated and complex second- and third-year courses. The challenging curriculum, along with the opportunity to perform specialized lawyering tasks under the direct supervision of accomplished lawyers, prepares students for the rigors of any type of modern legal practice. Additionally, students have the opportunity to complete a more concentrated course study and training in six areas of interest: General Civil Litigation, Business Litigation, Criminal Practice, Business Transactions, Estate Planning, and Administrative Practice.

■ Special Programs

Baylor law school offers three joint-degree programs. The law school and the Hankamer School of Business offer joint-degree programs that lead to the simultaneous award of the Juris Doctor and the Master of Business Administration degree, or the Juris Doctor and the Master of Taxation degree. Students interested in governmental service can complete their law degree along with a Master of Public Policy and Administration degree offered by the political science department of Baylor University.

Each August, Baylor law school offers a two-week study abroad program at the Universidad Autonoma de Guadalajara in Mexico. Students may earn up to five quarter-hour credits selecting from courses such as International Business Transactions and International Human Rights.

■ Individual Attention

Baylor law school has a target student population of 400. This smaller size allows for all students to be active participants in class and to participate in extracurricular activities.

One of the distinctive features of the school is that professors maintain unrestricted hours for student consultation. They are actively involved in all intraschool and interscholastic competitions. Every professor is available for lending advice and guidance in all academic and other matters of concern to students.

■ The Quarter System

The school year at the law school is divided into four quarters. A full curriculum is offered during each quarter, enabling a student to graduate in as little as 27 months. After completing the first three quarters, a student generally may elect at any time during the year, to take time off from their legal studies to pursue a clerkship, internship, or other program to allow the student to apply the principles and skills developed in school. Full-time study is required. Evening classes are not offered.

■ Admission

➡ *three entering classes*   ➡ *fall application deadline—March 1*   ➡ *spring application deadline—Nov. 1*
➡ *summer application deadline—Feb. 1*
➡ *LSAT, LSDAS required*   ➡ *application fee—$40*
➡ *reapplication fee—$20*

The law school has three entering classes—the fall, spring, and summer quarter. Admission for each class is competitive; however, admission to the spring or summer is slightly less competitive than admission to the fall.

The law school considers such factors as the Law School Admission Test score, the undergraduate grade-point average, work experience, demonstrated leadership potential, cocurricular and extracurricular activities, academic performance trends, undergraduate major, caliber of undergraduate school, circumstances of particular disadvantage, and any other relevant information submitted by the applicant.

■ Student Activities

Each year, Baylor student teams enter several interscholastic mock trial, moot court, negotiation, and client counseling competitions. A number of regional and national championships have been won in recent years by the law school.

The *Baylor Law Review* gives outstanding students an opportunity to develop legal-writing ability. *Baylor Law Review* candidates are selected on the basis of academic performance or through a writing competition. The Student Bar Association, affiliated with the Law Student Division

of the ABA, is the student government in the law school. Three national legal fraternities have active chapters at the law school and sponsor an array of activities. Other student organizations include the Christian Legal Society, the Minority Law Student Association, the Texas A&M Club, and the Association of Women Law Students.

■ Expenses and Financial Aid

➡ *tuition & fees—$12,896*   ➡ *academic merit scholarships available (ranging from amounts equal to 1/3 to full tuition)*
➡ *financial aid available: Texas Tuition Equalization Grant, Perkins Loans, Baylor Revolving Loans, Stafford Loans, Law Access Loans, supplemental loans, & College Access Loans*

Baylor has one of the lowest tuitions of all of the private law schools in the nation. Generally, first-year scholarships are based upon undergraduate GPA and LSAT, and second- and third-year scholarships are based upon law school academic performance. Special scholarships are available to graduates of certain Texas undergraduate institutions and outstanding university debaters and advocates. Also, special consideration for scholarships will be given to persons with evidence of academic achievement despite significant disadvantage.

■ Career Services

Employers value Baylor lawyers. The Director of Career Services is an attorney and she helps prospective graduates plan career strategies, identify job opportunities, market themselves, and improve their interviewing skills. Equally important, the Career Services Office does an exceptional job participating in job fairs in Dallas, Houston, Austin, Chicago, and Washington, DC. Each year over 200 local, regional, and national recruiters interview our students.

Applicant Group for the 1998-1999 Academic Year

Baylor University School of Law
This grid includes only applicants who earned 120-180 LSAT scores under standard administrations.

LSAT Score	GPA 3.75 +		3.50 - 3.74		3.25 - 3.49		3.00 - 3.24		2.75 - 2.99		2.50 - 2.74		2.25 - 2.49		2.00 - 2.24		Below 2.00		No GPA		Total	
	Apps	Adm	Apps	Adm	Apps	Adm	Apps	Adm	Apps	Adm	Apps	Adm	Apps	Adm	Apps	Adm	Apps	Adm	Apps	Adm	Apps	Adm
175-180	0	0	1	1	0	0	0	0	0	0	0	0	0	0	0	0	0	0	0	0	1	1
170-174	3	2	0	0	1	1	2	2	1	1	1	1	1	0	1	0	0	0	0	0	10	7
165-169	6	6	4	4	9	9	5	4	2	2	5	5	0	0	1	0	0	0	1	1	33	31
160-164	25	24	27	27	30	28	23	21	17	17	5	5	2	0	1	0	0	0	1	1	131	123
155-159	34	32	58	50	67	51	65	31	38	11	15	5	4	2	3	0	1	0	1	0	286	182
150-154	28	23	56	28	63	20	51	12	32	1	20	1	9	0	2	0	0	0	2	1	263	86
145-149	8	0	20	1	31	1	28	1	34	1	20	0	9	0	3	0	2	0	2	0	157	4
140-144	1	0	8	0	14	0	25	2	18	0	12	0	4	0	5	0	0	0	2	0	89	2
135-139	0	0	2	0	3	0	7	0	5	0	9	0	3	0	1	0	0	0	1	0	31	0
130-134	0	0	1	0	1	0	2	0	4	1	3	0	1	0	1	0	1	0	0	0	14	1
125-129	0	0	0	0	0	0	0	0	1	0	0	0	0	0	0	0	0	0	1	0	2	0
120-124	0	0	0	0	0	0	0	0	0	0	0	0	0	0	0	0	0	0	0	0	0	0
Total	105	87	177	111	219	110	208	73	152	34	90	17	33	2	18	0	4	0	11	3	1017	437

Apps = Number of Applicants   Adm = Number Admitted   Reflects 99% of the total applicant pool.

Benjamin N. Cardozo School of Law Yeshiva University

55 Fifth Avenue
New York, NY 10003

E-Mail: lawinfo@ymail.yu.edu
URL: http://www.yu.edu/cardozo
Phone: 212.790.0274; Fax: 212.790.0482

■ Introduction

Benjamin N. Cardozo School of Law offers students a stimulating and supportive educational experience. Its curriculum combines practical training in basic skills and legal doctrine, sophisticated study of recent developments in legal theory, and interdisciplinary approaches to the study of law. A wide variety of courses provide depth and breadth in all the standard subjects of legal study, as well as many more specialized ones including intellectual property law and legal theory. Extensive clinical and externship opportunities provide practical lawyering experiences in civil and criminal litigation as well as in alternative methods of settling disputes. A Cardozo education challenges students to think critically, teaches them to express themselves concisely and persuasively, and emphasizes ethics and the pursuit of intellectual excellence.

■ Enrollment/Student Body

➡ *2,380 applicants* ➡ *enrolled—Jan., 45; May, 32; Sept., 253* ➡ *full-time 25th/75th percentile GPA— 3.03/3.57* ➡ *full-time 25th/75th percentile LSAT—154/159* ➡ *student population, 888* ➡ *minorities: 20.3%* ➡ *women: 48% (54.3% of first-year class)* ➡ *32 states and 12 foreign countries represented* ➡ *234 undergraduate schools represented*

■ Faculty

➡ *46 full-time* ➡ *98 part-time or adjunct* ➡ *30 % women*

Cardozo's faculty ranked 15th nationwide and 2nd in New York City, in a recent survey of faculty productivity, and 25th nationwide in a study of academic reputation and scholarly impact. Over half of Cardozo's faculty hold advanced degrees in other disciplines such as philosophy, political science, and comparative literature.

■ Library

➡ *427,385 volumes & equivalents* ➡ *LEXIS* ➡ *NEXIS* ➡ *WESTLAW* ➡ *OCLC* ➡ *Integrated Automated Library System* ➡ *19 full-time staff* ➡ *library seats 500* ➡ *full internet access and e-mail*

■ Location

Located in an elegant residential neighborhood in the heart of Greenwich Village, Cardozo is easily reached from any point of New York City. The Manhattan courts, Wall Street, Midtown, and the art and music centers on the Upper East and West Sides are easily accessible from the law school.

■ Curriculum

➡ *84 credits required to graduate* ➡ *160 courses available* ➡ *degrees available: J.D.; LL.M. in Intellectual Property & General Studies* ➡ *range of first-year class size—9-102*

First-year courses consist of Civil Procedure, Constitutional Law, Contracts, Criminal Law, Elements of Law, Property, Torts and Legal Writing, and Appellate Advocacy. Upper-level courses are elective except for a course in Professional Responsibility, completion of Advanced Legal Research, an upper-level writing requirement, and fulfillment of minimal distribution requirements.

■ Special Programs/Clinical Opportunities

Intellectual life extends beyond the classroom. The school offers many panels and symposia which enrich the educational climate. Special programs include **The Jacob Burns Institute for Advanced Legal Studies** (supports legal scholarship, lectures, conferences, and faculty research); **The Samuel and Ronnie Heyman Center on Corporate Governance** (sponsors conferences on issues related to corporate and business law); and **The Howard M. Squadron Program in Law, Media, and Society** (sponsors conferences on issues related to telecommunications, publishing, and entertainment law).

Externships: Cardozo has numerous programs arranging for-credit outside placements. Among others, the **Intellectual Property Law Program**, combines a specialized curriculum with related externships in this burgeoning area of practice; the **Summer Institute for Placement and Career Development** offers seminars linked to field placements in specialty areas such as international trade law, bankruptcy, entertainment law, environmental law, and civil and criminal litigation; the **Alexander Judicial Fellows Program** places outstanding third-year students in clerkships with prominent federal judges; and the **U.S. Attorney's Office Externship** allows students to work with Assistant U.S. Attorneys handling white collar prosecutions.

Clinics: Students in the **Criminal Law Clinic** represent defendants in the Manhattan Criminal Court; the **Criminal Appeals Clinic** trains students in appellate advocacy and allows them to argue the appeal; the **Innocence Project** assists prisoners whose innocence may be proved through DNA testing; in the **Prosecutor Practicum**, students work in the Manhattan District Attorney's office; the **Bet Tzedek Legal Services Clinic** provides legal assistance to the elderly and disabled; the **Mediation Clinic** provides training in alternate dispute resolution; **Tax Clinic** participants represent taxpayers in cases before the United States Tax Court; and the **Immigration Law Clinic** allows students an opportunity to obtain practical experience in the field of immigration law; Cardozo's clinical faculty also oversees the simulation based **Intensive Trial Advocacy Program**.

Public Interest Opportunities: The **Cardozo Public Interest Summer Stipend Program** funds students working with such underrepresented groups as the elderly, the homeless, recent immigrants, and juveniles; **Telford Taylor Fellowships** are available for summer internships in public international law and international human rights.

■ Admission

➡ *Bachelor's degree required*   ➡ *application deadlines: Dec. 1 for Jan.; April 1 for May & Sept.*
➡ *LSAT, LSDAS required*   ➡ *application fee—$60*

Students may begin legal studies at Cardozo in September, January, or May. September's entering class is a traditional three-year program; January and May classes are Accelerated Entry Plans (AEP), designed so students may complete six semesters of law school in two-and-one-half years. AEP programs are particularly appealing to mid-year graduates and some returning students.

Each applicant's LSAT score, undergraduate and graduate records, letters of recommendation, and materials reflecting character, academic achievements, and aptitude for law study are carefully considered.

■ Housing

The Cardozo residence hall is located on an attractive, tree-lined street just one block south of the main building. A limited number of studio and one-bedroom apartments —all of which are air conditioned, attractively furnished, and have a full kitchen— are available for incoming students.

■ Publications/Student Activities

Cardozo sponsors four student-run journals: *Cardozo Law Review, Cardozo Arts and Entertainment Law Journal, Cardozo Journal of International and Comparative Law*, and the *Cardozo Women's Law Journal*. The Moot Court Honor

Society is structured like a publication. Students also participate in three faculty-edited publications: *Cardozo Studies in Law and Literature, The Post-Soviet Media Law and Policy Newsletter*, and the *New York Real Estate Reporter*.

Student organizations include the Student Bar Association; the Unemployment Action Center; Cardozo Advocates for Battered Women; the *Forum* (student newspaper); Black, Asian, and Latino Law Student Associations; Cardozo Law Women; the Gay and Lesbian Alliance, and almost two dozen organizations devoted to particular areas of law.

■ Expenses and Financial Aid

➡ *tuition & fees—$21,780*
➡ *merit- & need-based scholarships available*
➡ *FAFSA and Need Access diskette required*

■ Placement

Ninety-six percent of the 1997 graduates who reported were employed within several months of graduation. The average overall starting salary was $56,667. Students were employed in private practice (62 percent); business (10 percent); government and public interest (15 percent); judicial clerkships (7 percent); academic (3 percent); and other (3 percent).

■ Further Information

Office of Admissions, Cardozo School of Law, 55 Fifth Avenue, New York, NY 10003, telephone: 212.790.0274; e-mail: lawinfo@ymail.yu.edu.

Applicant Group for the 1998-1999 Academic Year

Benjamin N. Cardozo School of Law Yeshiva University
This grid includes only applicants who earned 120-180 LSAT scores under standard administrations.

LSAT Score	3.75 +		3.50 - 3.74		3.25 - 3.49		3.00 - 3.24		2.75 - 2.99		2.50 - 2.74		2.25 - 2.49		2.00 - 2.24		Below 2.00		No GPA		Total	
	Apps	Adm	Apps	Adm	Apps	Adm	Apps	Adm	Apps	Adm	Apps	Adm	Apps	Adm	Apps	Adm	Apps	Adm	Apps	Adm	Apps	Adm
175-180	0	0	0	0	0	0	0	0	0	0	0	0	0	0	0	0	0	0	0	0	0	0
170-174	2	2	2	2	5	5	2	2	3	3	5	4	2	2	0	0	0	0	0	0	21	20
165-169	13	13	22	21	24	24	10	7	9	8	4	4	0	0	3	2	2	2	1	1	88	82
160-164	28	27	50	48	79	77	62	60	32	31	19	18	5	3	4	3	0	0	2	1	281	268
155-159	38	38	94	90	123	115	125	102	87	61	35	20	18	11	3	1	3	1	3	2	529	441
150-154	36	21	100	54	124	36	95	28	89	17	48	8	20	1	7	1	2	0	13	4	534	170
145-149	18	3	45	8	69	16	87	16	96	8	40	2	26	1	8	0	3	0	9	0	401	54
140-144	4	0	23	1	41	0	44	1	44	1	50	0	19	0	10	0	2	0	14	0	251	3
135-139	3	0	6	0	17	0	13	0	29	0	21	0	21	0	9	0	3	0	8	0	130	0
130-134	0	0	1	0	4	0	6	0	9	0	10	0	8	0	6	0	1	0	4	0	49	0
125-129	0	0	0	0	0	0	1	0	2	0	3	0	1	0	4	0	1	0	1	0	13	0
120-124	0	0	0	0	0	0	0	0	0	0	0	0	0	0	1	0	0	0	0	0	1	0
Total	142	104	343	224	486	273	445	216	400	129	235	56	120	18	55	7	17	3	55	8	2298	1038

Apps = Number of Applicants
Adm = Number Admitted
Reflects 98% of the total applicant pool.

Boston College Law School

Office of Admissions
885 Centre Street
Newton, MA 02459-1163

E-Mail: bclawadm@bc.edu
URL: http://www.bc.edu/lawschool
Phone: 617.552.4350

■ Introduction

Since its founding in 1929, Boston College Law School has earned a national reputation for educational excellence and the highest standards of professionalism while fostering a unique spirit of community among its students, faculty, and staff. The diverse curriculum is designed to help students develop the skills and knowledge needed to adapt successfully to changes in society and the legal profession. Boston College Law School is located on an attractive 40-acre campus in Newton, Massachusetts, just minutes from downtown Boston. It is fully accredited by both the American Bar Association and the Association of American Law Schools, and has a chapter of Order of the Coif, the prestigious national law school honorary society.

■ Enrollment/Student Body

➡ *4,480 applicants*   ➡ *1,275 admitted first-year class 1998*
➡ *260 enrolled first-year class 1998*   ➡ *full-time 25th/75th percentile GPA—3.21/3.64*   ➡ *full-time 25th/75th percentile LSAT—159/164*   ➡ *23% minority first-year class 1998*
➡ *47% women first-year class 1998*   ➡ *44 states & foreign countries represented*   ➡ *236 undergraduate schools represented*

■ Faculty

➡ *112 total*   ➡ *53 full-time*   ➡ *59 part-time or adjunct*
➡ *31 women*   ➡ *10 minority*

■ Library and Physical Facilities

➡ *382,629 volumes & equivalents*   ➡ *library hours: Mon.-Thurs., 8:00 A.M.-MIDNIGHT; Fri., 8:00 A.M.-11:00 P.M.; Sat., 9:00 A.M.-10:00 P.M.; Sun., 10:00 A.M.-MIDNIGHT*
➡ *LEXIS*   ➡ *NEXIS*   ➡ *WESTLAW*   ➡ *DIALOG*
➡ *9 full-time librarians*   ➡ *library seats 617*
➡ *member, New England Law Library Consortium*

Boston College Law School has just completed the second phase of an exciting $55 million dollar building program. In 1996, the Law School opened a new, $16.4 million multimedia law library. In January 1999, the Law School finished construction of a new $12.5 million classroom and faculty office wing, which includes five state-of-the-art lecture halls with data connections to every seat for use of the computers in the classroom.

All academic, administrative, library, and service facilities are accessible to disabled persons.

■ Curriculum

➡ *Academic Support Program*   ➡ *85 credits required to graduate*
➡ *110 courses available*   ➡ *degrees available: J.D.; J.D./M.B.A.; J.D./M.S.W.; J.D./M.Ed.*   ➡ *semesters, start in the fall*
➡ *range of first-year class size—30-90*
➡ *semester abroad at the University of London*

The faculty of Boston College Law School strongly believes in the importance of a general legal education designed to enable graduates to adapt to the changing demands of law practice. Areas of particular focus include constitutional law, business law, dispute resolution, environmental law, family law, international law, sports and entertainment law, and clinical programs.

In the first year, all students take traditional courses including Civil Procedure, Constitutional Law, Contracts, Property and Torts, as well as Legal Research and Writing and an innovative skills course titled Introduction to Lawyering and Professional Responsibility. More than 100 courses offered in the second and third years are elective.

■ Clinical Courses

The Law School is committed to making clinical experiences available to all students who desire them. The **Urban Legal Laboratory** is an externship program of individually designed placements with judges, government agencies, public interest organizations, and law firms in the greater Boston area. At the **Boston College Legal Assistance Bureau** (LAB), students assume responsibility for representation of indigent clients in civil cases.

Criminal Process offers the opportunity to prosecute or defend criminal cases in state court. The **Attorney General Law Clinic** provides a placement in the Massachusetts Attorney General's office and the **Judicial Process** course includes clinical placement with a specific Superior Court justice.

In **Juvenile Rights Advocacy**, students advocate for troubled youth and work toward juvenile justice policy reform. The **Immigration and Asylum Project** provides opportunities to advise clients and to work on administrative and appellate litigation under the supervision of practicing attorneys.

■ Student Activities

Selected students may participate in the following writing programs: *Boston College Law Review; Boston College Environmental Affairs Law Review; Boston College International and Comparative Law Review; Boston College Third World Law Journal*; and the *Uniform Commercial Code Reporter-Digest*.

Boston College Law School supports several annual moot court competitions that help students develop writing, courtroom-advocacy, and client-counseling skills. Over the years, Boston College has performed extremely well in the regional and national competitions, which are judged by faculty, state, and federal judges, and practicing attorneys.

■ Admission

➡ *Bachelor's degree from accredited college or university required*
➡ *application deadline—March 1 on a rolling admission basis, decisions sent Jan. to May 1*   ➡ *early notification program— submit application by Nov. 2, complete application by Nov. 25, decision mailed by Dec. 16*   ➡ *LSAT, LSDAS required*
➡ *application fee—$65*

The Law School has no minimum cutoff either for GPA or LSAT. Academic achievement and LSAT scores are extremely significant, but work and professional experience, college extracurricular activities, the quality of recommendations, and the personal statement also play an important role in decision making.

In evaluating GPA, class rank as well as courses taken are considered. If the LSAT has been taken more than once, scores are averaged unless a compelling reason is presented for considering a particular score. Less weight is given to the LSAT if the applicant has a history of poor standardized testing.

Minorities and Affirmative Action

Boston College Law School strongly encourages applications from qualified minority, disabled, or other students who have been socially, economically, or culturally disadvantaged. Each applicant is evaluated in an effort to ensure that all relevant credentials are favorably considered. The Law School has been very successful both in admitting minority and special students, and in retaining them to graduation. Both academic support and minority student mentor programs are available.

Expenses and Financial Aid

➡ *full-time tuition & fees—$23,420*   ➡ *estimated additional expenses—$11,000 (room, board, books, health insurance)*
➡ *need-based financial aid available*
➡ *FAFSA and Need Access or Profile forms required*
➡ *Students receiving grant assistance—43%*

All financial aid is processed through the university's Office of Financial Aid and the Law School Admissions Office.

The Financial Aid Office administers federal and private loan programs, the College Work-Study program, and the major Presidential and Law School Scholarship programs. The Law School has also developed a Loan Repayment Assistance program providing financial assistance to graduates taking lower-paying positions in government, nonprofit corporations, and legal services programs.

All applicants for financial aid must file the FAFSA (Free Application for Federal Student Aid) and either the Need Access or Profile form. Processed forms should be received in the Office of Financial Aid by March 15.

Housing

Housing assistance is provided through the university's Office of Off-Campus Housing. Applicants seeking resident assistantships should write the University Housing Office, Boston College, Chestnut Hill, MA 02167.

Career Services

The Office of Career Services is dedicated to helping students make the transition from law student to employed professional. The range of opportunities for graduates spans virtually the entire spectrum of legal practice. Each year more than 1,000 prospective employers solicit applications from Boston College law students. In 1998-1999, approximately 420 law firms, government agencies, corporations, and public interest organizations from 28 states visited the campus. Last year, 95 percent of graduates were employed either prior to or within several months of graduation. The 8,600 alumni are presently practicing in 48 states and a number of foreign countries.

Applicant Group for the 1998-1999 Academic Year

Boston College Law School
This grid includes only applicants who earned 120-180 LSAT scores under standard administrations.

LSAT Score	3.75 +		3.50 - 3.74		3.25 - 3.49		3.00 - 3.24		2.75 - 2.99		Below 2.75		No GPA		Total	
	Apps	Adm	Apps	Adm	Apps	Adm	Apps	Adm	Apps	Adm	Apps	Adm	Apps	Adm	Apps	Adm
175-180	4	4	6	6	5	5	2	0	1	0	0	0	0	0	18	15
170-174	18	18	28	28	34	29	22	16	12	6	6	0	2	2	122	99
165-169	89	81	165	149	161	114	87	46	48	16	20	4	4	3	574	413
160-164	169	132	350	216	360	135	192	54	86	14	37	4	13	5	1207	560
150-159	196	49	463	57	472	28	370	16	197	6	114	3	33	0	1845	159
140-149	31	3	73	6	138	5	115	5	107	3	104	1	18	2	586	25
Below 140	2	0	7	0	14	0	14	0	19	0	35	0	3	0	94	0
Total	509	287	1092	462	1184	316	802	137	470	45	316	12	73	12	4446	1271

Apps = Number of Applicants
Adm = Number Admitted
Reflects 99% of the total applicant pool.

Boston University School of Law

765 Commonwealth Avenue
Boston, MA 02215

E-Mail: bulawadm@bu.edu
URL: http://www.bu.edu/LAW
Phone: 617.353.3100

■ Introduction

Located in Boston, Massachusetts, overlooking a beautiful stretch of the Charles River, Boston University School of Law boasts a 126-year history of outstanding legal education. The school is committed to giving its students the broadest possible exposure to the practice and theory of law. Students graduate with a deep understanding of legal rules and principles, enriched by insights from related disciplines such as economics, philosophy, and history, and with strong analytical and practical skills that lay the foundation for a challenging and satisfying legal career. Boston University School of Law is located in one of the country's most vital intellectual and cultural centers. As a result, the school offers students a wide range of opportunities both inside and out-side of class that make for a memorable law school experience.

■ Enrollment/Student Body

➻ *4,233 applicants* ➻ *1,602 admitted first-year class 1998*
➻ *314 enrolled first-year class 1998* ➻ *full-time 25th/75th percentile GPA—3.09/3.58* ➻ *full-time 25th/75th percentile LSAT—158/163* ➻ *947 total full-time* ➻ *21% minority*
➻ *49% women* ➻ *56 states & foreign countries represented*
➻ *270 undergraduate schools represented*

■ Faculty

➻ *129 total* ➻ *58 full-time* ➻ *71 part-time or adjunct*
➻ *38 women* ➻ *12 minority*

■ Library and Physical Facilities

➻ *550,000 volumes & equivalents* ➻ *library hours:*
Mon.-Thurs., 8:00 A.M.-11:30 P.M.; Fri., 8:00 A.M.-10:00 P.M.;
Sat., 9:00 A.M.-9:00 P.M.; Sun., 10:00 A.M.-11:30 P.M.
➻ *LEXIS* ➻ *NEXIS* ➻ *WESTLAW* ➻ *DIALOG*
➻ *Internet* ➻ *10 full-time librarians* ➻ *library seats 797*

■ Curriculum

➻ *Academic Support Program* ➻ *84 credits required to graduate* ➻ *162 courses available* ➻ *degrees available:*
J.D.; J.D./M.B.A.; J.D./M.P.H.; J.D./M.S. (Law & Mass Communications); J.D./M.A. (Law & Preservation Studies; Philosophy; International Relations); LL.M. (American Banking Law, International Banking Law, Taxation, American Law)
➻ *semesters, start in late Aug.*
➻ *range of first-year class size—78-81*

During the first week, minority and first-year orientations introduce law students to the study of law. Most of the first-year curriculum is required. In the second and third years, the school offers a wide variety of courses and seminars in advanced areas. Legal ethics is taught through-out the curriculum and in a special intensive program.

Concentrations are available in Business Organizations and Finance Law, Environmental Law, Health Care Law, Intellectual Property, International Law, and Litigation and Dispute Resolution.

■ Business Organizations and Finance Law

The school provides a rich selection of courses, from the basics of corporate law to specialties such as trademark and unfair competition, bankruptcy and creditor rights, and federal regulation of banks and other financial institutions. The school offers a concentration in this area and dual-degree options with the School of Management. A student may graduate with advanced credentials within the normal three-year course of study through coursework in business and corporate law and by completing a major research paper in the area.

■ Environmental Law

The school offers a concentration with a particularly rich array of courses and seminars in the area of environmental law, augmented by many offerings in the Schools of Engineering, Environmental Health, Management, and other parts of Boston University.

■ Health Law

Home of the Center for Law and Health Sciences and the American Society of Law and Medicine, the school is well-known for its strong health law curriculum, distin-guished health law faculty, a concentration in health care law and two health-related dual-degree programs. The school's extremely broad selection of courses together with health-related offerings in the School of Public Health comprise one of the most comprehensive health law curricula in the country.

■ Law, Technology, and Innovation

Situated in an important high-technology area, the school offers a rich array of courses in the rapidly growing area of law, technology, and innovation, including offerings in patent law, copyright, trademark, computer law, communication law, art law, entertainment law, and environmental regulation and toxic torts. In addition, the school offers concentration in intellectual property and a dual J.D./M.S. degree in Mass Communication.

■ International Law

The school offers a concentration with an impressive selection of courses, seminars, and programs in interna-tional law, including the opportunity to study in this area during your first year. The school offers the opportunity to obtain a dual degree (M.A. in International Relations) as well as Study Abroad Programs at Oxford University in England; Université Jean Moulin in Lyon, France; the University of Leiden in the Netherlands; or at the University of Tel Aviv in Israel.

■ Litigation and Dispute Resolution

At Boston University School of Law, students acquire the skills of the litigator and negotiator in many ways. The solid foundation in legal theory acquired in class is enhanced by programs that allow the student to learn by doing—either through mock court experiences, legal internships, or through the representation of real clients in court and through agencies. The school offers the opportunity to concentrate in litigation and dispute resolution.

■ Clinical Programs

The school is known for some of the finest clinical offerings in the country. With ties to Greater Boston Legal Services and other organizations, these programs offer actual practice experience under the close supervision of a dedicated and highly accomplished group of full-time clinical faculty.

■ Admission

➽ Bachelor's degree required for admission ➽ application deadline—March 1 ➽ LSAT, LSDAS required ➽ application fee—$50

The Admissions Committee places primary emphasis on an applicant's cumulative undergraduate grade-point average and score on the LSAT. The committee also takes into account other factors, such as marked and sustained improvement in undergraduate grades, outstanding leadership ability, significant postgraduate experience, and motivation for law study. Letters of recommendation also can be very important.

■ Student Activities

Approximately one-third of upper-division students have an opportunity for professional writing experience by participating in one of six law journals. These include: Boston University Law Review, Annual Review of Banking Law, the American Journal of Law and Medicine, Boston University International Law Journal, the Public Interest Law Journal, and the Journal of Science and Technology Law.

The School of Law also encourages students to become active in student organizations. Reflecting our students' diverse interests and backgrounds, there are a number of active student organizations.

Upper-class students may participate in a number of moot court competitions.

■ Expenses and Financial Aid

➽ tuition & fees—$23,138 ➽ estimated additional expenses—$12,822 ➽ tuition grants available, primarily need-based ➽ minority scholarships: Martin Luther King Fellowships include tuition, fees, living expenses ➽ financial aid available; Profile, FAFSA, & school of law financial aid application due April 1, parental data required on all forms

■ Career Services

The Office of Career Development actively assists students and alumni/ae in securing employment. Each year more than 500 law firms, government agencies, public interest organizations, and corporations from all regions of the United States recruit law students for summer and permanent positions. The office maintains a comprehensive career resource library, provides career counseling and job listings, and sponsors career panels and interview workshops.

Over the past three years, approximately 90 percent of graduates reporting employment have secured positions or enrolled in an advanced-degree program within six to nine months of graduation. First-year and second-year law students have been similarly successful in securing summer employment.

Applicant Group for the 1998-1999 Academic Year

Boston University School of Law
This grid includes only applicants who earned 120-180 LSAT scores under standard administrations.

LSAT Score	3.75 +		3.50 - 3.74		3.25 - 3.49		3.00 - 3.24		2.75 - 2.99		2.50 - 2.74		2.25 - 2.49		2.00 - 2.24		Below 2.00		No GPA		Total	
	Apps	Adm	Apps	Adm	Apps	Adm	Apps	Adm	Apps	Adm	Apps	Adm	Apps	Adm	Apps	Adm	Apps	Adm	Apps	Adm	Apps	Adm
175-180	2	2	2	2	0	0	2	1	2	0	0	0	0	0	0	0	0	0	0	0	8	5
170-174	7	7	14	13	18	18	15	15	13	10	3	2	1	1	0	0	0	0	3	3	74	69
165-169	52	50	84	80	98	94	82	74	44	38	13	7	2	2	1	0	0	0	3	2	379	347
160-164	111	107	259	241	277	228	216	157	102	57	24	14	6	2	1	0	0	0	13	8	1009	814
155-159	129	86	280	85	316	31	237	23	120	11	45	6	24	2	5	0	1	0	13	4	1170	248
150-154	69	10	152	10	217	19	184	9	98	8	45	1	18	0	6	0	0	0	14	3	803	60
145-149	18	1	53	2	106	6	96	4	69	0	41	1	11	0	10	0	1	0	10	1	415	15
140-144	5	1	27	1	35	1	49	1	48	1	24	0	18	0	4	0	2	0	9	0	221	5
135-139	4	0	10	0	13	0	17	0	13	0	12	0	10	0	5	0	1	0	5	0	90	0
130-134	0	0	1	0	3	0	3	0	7	0	4	0	5	0	3	0	2	0	2	0	30	0
125-129	0	0	0	0	2	0	0	0	0	0	0	0	1	0	1	0	1	0	1	0	6	0
120-124	0	0	0	0	0	0	0	0	0	0	0	0	0	0	0	0	0	0	0	0	0	0
Total	397	264	882	434	1085	397	901	284	516	125	211	31	96	7	36	0	8	0	73	21	4205	1563

Apps = Number of Applicants
Adm = Number Admitted
Reflects 95% of the total applicant pool.

Brigham Young University—J. Reuben Clark Law School

340 JRCB
Box 28000
Provo, UT 84602-8000

E-Mail: wilcockl@lawgate.byu.edu
URL: http://www.law.byu.edu
Phone: 801.378.4277

■ Introduction

Brigham Young University, J. Reuben Clark Law School, located in Provo, Utah (about 50 miles south of Salt Lake City), is an integral part of the largest private university in the United States on the basis of full-time student enrollment. Brigham Young University is sponsored by The Church of Jesus Christ of Latter-day Saints (Mormon Church) and has a present enrollment of 30,000 students from all 50 states and more than 100 foreign countries. The Law School is fully accredited by the American Bar Association and is a member of the Association of American Law Schools. The school has a chapter of the Order of the Coif.

■ Enrollment/Student Body

➼ *663 applicants* ➼ *221 admitted first-year class 1998*
➼ *145 enrolled first-year class 1998* ➼ *full-time 25th/75th percentile GPA—3.42/3.77* ➼ *full-time 25th/75th percentile LSAT—157/164* ➼ *456 total full-time* ➼ *15% minority*
➼ *34% women* ➼ *44 states & foreign countries represented*
➼ *72 undergraduate schools represented*

■ Faculty

➼ *65 total* ➼ *28 full-time* ➼ *37 part-time or adjunct*
➼ *16 women* ➼ *3 minority*

■ Library and Physical Facilities

➼ *421,912 volumes & equivalents* ➼ *library hours:*
Mon.-Fri., 6:00 A.M.-MIDNIGHT; Sat., 8:00 A.M.-10:00 P.M.
➼ *LEXIS* ➼ *NEXIS* ➼ *WESTLAW* ➼ *RLIN*
➼ *Notis* ➼ *9 full-time librarians* ➼ *library seats 600*

The law building is designed to accommodate 500 students. In 1996, 39,000-square feet were added to the library. In addition to the law library facilities, the law building contains nine classrooms, three seminar rooms, rooms for group study, a four-room interviewing complex, a television studio, a student commons area, and ample space for student organizations and activities.

The law library provides public access by computer terminal to over 200 card catalogs of other institutions. The law library has a carrel for almost every student. These specially wired carrels allow students to access a full range of computer applications from word processing to legal research and data management. In addition to the access at the carrels, these applications are accessible from a number of student computers placed strategically around the library. In addition, the library has 26 study rooms.

■ Curriculum

➼ *Academic Support Program* ➼ *tutorials; Legal Writing Class*
➼ *90 credits required to graduate* ➼ *101 courses available*
➼ *degrees available: J.D.; J.D./M.B.A.; J.D./M.P.A.;*
J.D./M.A.C.C.; J.D./ Ed.D.; J.D./M.O.B.; J.D./M.Ed.

The Law School is operated on a semester basis. The fall semester runs from approximately the third week in August until the third week of December. Winter semester begins the first week in January and runs until the fourth week in April. The first-year course of study is prescribed and consists of approximately 15 hours per semester. A broad selection of elective courses and seminars is available in the second and third years. The law school offers a tutorial program for all students at no cost.

■ Special Programs

The Law School, in combination with the graduate school of the university, offers joint J.D./M.B.A., Master of Public Administration, Master of Accountancy, and Master of Organizational Behavior degrees; as well as J.D./M.Ed. and J.D./E.J.D. degrees. The Law School provides clinical opportunities for students by means of well-developed simulated programs in both civil and criminal matters and by extensive pro bono and externship experience. A number of innovative curricular and cocurricular programs are being used by the faculty and students: Lawyering Skills, Family Law Society, Natural Resources Law Forum, Government and Politics Legal Society, the International and Comparative Law Society, Negotiations Forum, and American Trial Lawyers Association.

■ Admission

➼ *Bachelor's degree required* ➼ *application deadline—Feb. 1*
➼ *LSAT, LSDAS required* ➼ *application fee—$30*

Students are admitted only in the fall semester and only for full-time study. Applications, which are processed on the basis of college work completed to date, may be made at any time after the beginning of the fall semester of the year preceding admission. College grades and the LSAT score are significant but not exclusive determinants of admissibility. The required written recommendations and personal statement are of significant influence.

■ Student Activities

Law schools have traditionally offered important additional training to a limited number of students through participation on a law review. The objective of the cocurricular programs offered at the J. Reuben Clark Law School is to make law review-quality experience available to a much larger number of students by extending its principles to more categories of activity. Comparable standards of excellence in research, writing, and editing are presently offered in four activities: *Journal of Public Law*, Board of Advocates, *Brigham Young University Education and Law Journal*, and the *Brigham Young University Law Review*.

■ Expenses and Financial Aid

➡ *full-time tuition & fees—in-state, $5,120; out-of-state, $7,680*
➡ *part-time tuition—$285 per sem. hr.* ➡ *estimated additional expenses—$11,720 (room & board, textbooks & supplies, personal expenses, transportation)* ➡ *scholarships available*
➡ *merit- & need-based minority scholarships available*
➡ *financial aid available: Federal Student Financial Aid, within 30 days of acceptance to the BYU Law School*

■ Career Services

Placement is regarded by the faculty as a matter of highest priority. A full-time law career services director, a full-time assistant director, a full-time recruiting coordinator, and one part-time student employee work with students and alumni in finding permanent and part-time employment in the legal profession. Over 143 law firms, government offices, and businesses recruit regularly at the Law School while over 200 other employers work closely with the Career Services Office in arranging off-campus interviews. Types of employment by the 1997 graduating class include private practice (53 percent), business (17 percent), government including judicial clerkships (26 percent), and other areas (4 percent). Job locations include Inter-mountain West (63 percent); East, South, and Midwest (17 percent); Pacific Coast, Hawaii (16 percent) and others (4 percent).

Applicant Profile for the 1998-1999 Academic Year

Brigham Young University—J. Reuben Clark Law School

LSAT Score	GPA								
	3.75 +	3.50 - 3.74	3.25 - 3.49	3.00 - 3.24	2.75 - 2.99	2.50 - 2.74	2.25 - 2.49	2.00 - 2.24	Below 2.00
175-180									
170-174									
165-169									
160-164									
155-159									
150-154									
145-149									
140-144									
135-139									
130-134									
125-129									
120-124									

Good Possibility   Possible   Unlikely

Brooklyn Law School

250 Joralemon Street
Brooklyn, NY 11201

E-Mail: admitq@brooklaw.edu
URL: http://www.brooklaw.edu
Phone: 718.780.7906

■ An Environment for Learning

Brooklyn Law School, a private, independent institution established in 1901, is flanked by the Brooklyn Heights Historic District and the Brooklyn Civic Center. Built up with grand mansions, stately rowhouses, diminutive carriage houses, and handsome educational and religious institutions, the Heights reflects what our city was like at the turn of the century. Lush gardens and almost-secret mews and tree-lined back streets make the Heights one of the most tranquil and beautiful neighborhoods of New York City. The school itself looks out over the U.S. District Court, the New York State Appellate Division Court, the State Supreme and Family Courts, and the City Civil and Criminal Courts. Within easy walking distance are the U.S. Attorney's Office, Kings County District Attorney's Office, Legal Aid Society, and numerous city, state, and federal governmental agencies. Just a few minutes away are Wall Street and its array of financial, legal, and corporate institutions.

■ Enrollment/Student Body

➡ *946 total full-time*   ➡ *484 total part-time*
➡ *448 enrolled first-year class 1998 (291 full-time, 157 part-time)*
➡ *full-time 25th/75th percentile GPA—2.95/3.49*
➡ *full-time 25th/75th percentile LSAT—152/158*
➡ *21.4% minority first-year class*
➡ *50.2% women first-year class*   ➡ *27 states, the District of Columbia, & 17 foreign countries represented*
➡ *153 colleges & universities represented*   ➡ *63 majors*

■ Faculty

➡ *62 full-time, almost 38% female*   ➡ *94 part-time*
➡ *20/1 student/faculty ratio*

A recent survey of law school faculty scholarship ranked Brooklyn Law School among the top 50 U.S. law schools for scholarly productivity.

Recently, two of our professors were appointed by the American Law Institute, one to serve as Reporter for the Restatement of the Law of Suretyship, the other as Co-Reporter for the Restatement of the Law of Torts (Third): Products Liability; they are among the very few faculty members from outside the ranks of the most highly rated national law schools to be so honored. Yet another professor has been named Reporter to the Advisory Committee on Federal Rules of Evidence.

■ Library and Physical Facilities

➡ *over 475,000 volumes & equivalents, over 1,000 periodicals*
➡ *LEXIS* ➡ *NEXIS* ➡ *WESTLAW* ➡ *DIALOG*
➡ *Internet* ➡ *21 full-time staff*
➡ *library seats 650 (approximately)*

Fall 1993 saw the opening of an 85,000-square-foot addition to our main building, including 3 reading rooms, 25 study rooms, 6 conference rooms, 2 computer research centers, a computer training/word processing center, wired carrels and tables to accommodate laptop computers, and multi-use classrooms wired at every seat for computer-assisted instruction.

■ Curriculum

➡ *Over 150 electives in 13 clusters, including criminal law, litigation, economic regulation, intellectual property, international law, & public interest law* ➡ *6 joint-degree programs* ➡ *2 study abroad options* ➡ *6 range of first-year class—15-125*

The core of the first-year curriculum is a Seminar Section Program that provides groups of 35-38 day students with a small-class experience in a substantive, required course during the first semester. This allows professors to depart from the standard lecture/Socratic dialogue format and to build a substantial skills training component into the course. This program is augmented by our first-year Legal Writing Program.

Our Professional Skills Program consists of an extensive array of in-house clinics, externships, Law in Practice internships, and simulation courses; so much so that in a recent article we were hailed as "a leader in the field."

In-house clinics include: **Consumer Counseling and Bankruptcy** (students interview and counsel clients contemplating bankruptcy and, where necessary, represent the debtor in Bankruptcy Court through final discharge); **Corporate/Real Estate** (students represent community groups or low income homesteaders in connection with the purchase of real estate from private owners or New York City); **Elderlaw Clinic** (students represent aged clients in connection with a variety of legal problems including benefits, health, and consumer matters); **Federal Litigation** (students represent clients in federal court); **Prosecutor's** (students prosecute misdemeanor cases in Brooklyn Criminal Court); **Safe Harbor** (students represent clients in a range of cases involving immigration status, deportation, naturalization and asylum, and international human rights); and **Securities Arbitration Clinic** (students represent clients with potential claims against broker-dealers before the NYSE or NASD).

Externships include: **Capital Defender** (students research challenges to various provisions of the New York Death Penalty statute); **Children's Law Center** (students represent children in custody/visitation and guardianship cases in Brooklyn Family Court); **Criminal Appeals** (two options: students represent clients of the Legal Aid Society's Criminal Appeals Bureau *or* handle respondent's appeals for the Manhattan District Attorney, arguing before the Appellate Division, First Department or the Appellate Terms); and **Mediation** (students train as mediators, learning the conceptual framework, range of application and normative constraints on nonjudicial processes—negotiation, mediation, and arbitration. Upon certification, they are placed in Civil, Family, or Small Claims court, as needed). *Law in Practice/Summer in Practice* internships include: **Civil Practice** (students assigned to assist attorneys in a variety of settings in federal, state, and city agencies—past placements include the S.E.C., U.S. Attorneys Office for both the Southern and Eastern District, and the New York State Attorney General's Office, as well as Legal Aid Society and Legal Services offices); **Criminal Practice** (students work in the office of either of the U.S. Attorneys, one of the District Attorneys, Victim Services Agency, or the Legal Aid Society); and **Judicial Clerkship** which, in the past three years, has averaged 143 placements annually, including (again an average) 65 at the federal level. Eleven **simulation courses** focus on discrete skills or on the application of certain skills to a particular area of practice, all in the context of prepared problems and case files.

■ Admission

➡ *average applicant volume 1995-1998—3,041*   ➡ *Bachelor's degree required*   ➡ *fall semester admission for entering class* ➡ *no application deadline; rolling admission favors early filing* ➡ *LSAT, LSDAS required*   ➡ *application fee—$60*

■ Housing

Brooklyn Law School has seven residence halls in historic Brooklyn Heights, offering affordable housing just a few blocks from the Law School for a limited number of students.

■ Career Center

With six attorney-counselors comprising one of the largest placement offices in the New York metropolitan area, the Career Center is able to offer unusually comprehensive services to students and alumni. The center emphasizes individualized counseling, including assistance with résumé/cover letter writing, interviewing skills, networking techniques, and strategic career planning. The professional

staff believes that maximizing the marketability of the school's students/graduates through an emphasis on job search skills and realistic career strategies is the linchpin of a successful placement program. Individual counseling is supplemented with skills workshops and panel discussions. The center has its own public service program, led by one of its counselors. The program encompasses both traditional public interest as well as government service. Of equal priority is an aggressive job development program supplementing a substantial on-campus interviewing program and computerized job listings. Employment rates have been very high. The employment rate (nine months after graduation) for the class of 1997 was 94 percent.

■ Special Programs

The school's **Center for the Study of International Business Law** trains lawyers to function globally, shaping international law and business policy. Our curriculum offers over 30 courses in the business law field, several of which focus on international and comparative law. The center sponsors a Fellowship Program and, with the cosponsorship of the University of London, biennially hosts a symposium in London and New York on international business issues; it also cosponsors summer programs in Italy and China.

Since 1985, the **Edward V. Sparer Public Interest Fellowship Program** has provided substantial stipends to students serving as legal interns in more than 70 public interest law offices nationwide. It also sponsors forums bringing prominent scholars, lawyers, and public policy advocates to the school to discuss current issues in public interest law.

An effective approach to maximizing our students' learning potential is a comprehensive **Academic Success Program** offered during the first year.

Applicant Group for the 1998-1999 Academic Year

Brooklyn Law School
This grid includes only applicants who earned 120-180 LSAT scores under standard administrations.

LSAT Score	3.75 +		3.50 - 3.74		3.25 - 3.49		3.00 - 3.24		2.75 - 2.99		2.50 - 2.74		2.25 - 2.49		2.00 - 2.24		Below 2.00		No GPA		Total	
	Apps	Adm	Apps	Adm	Apps	Adm	Apps	Adm	Apps	Adm	Apps	Adm	Apps	Adm	Apps	Adm	Apps	Adm	Apps	Adm	Apps	Adm
175-180	0	0	0	0	0	0	0	0	0	0	0	0	0	0	0	0	0	0	0	0	0	0
170-174	1	1	1	1	5	5	1	1	0	0	4	4	2	2	0	0	0	0	0	0	14	14
165-169	2	2	11	11	12	12	8	8	10	10	6	6	1	1	1	1	2	0	2	1	55	52
160-164	19	19	37	37	65	63	54	53	37	36	25	23	5	4	5	3	1	1	2	2	250	241
155-159	37	36	86	84	109	107	118	109	104	85	53	44	27	21	7	3	4	1	8	7	553	497
150-154	43	42	99	89	149	118	139	80	114	42	81	39	29	13	11	3	2	0	14	7	681	433
145-149	25	8	48	16	91	26	121	34	111	10	69	7	42	4	13	0	4	0	11	2	535	107
140-144	10	0	34	4	58	3	65	1	80	1	73	2	40	0	18	0	1	0	12	0	391	11
135-139	5	0	11	0	28	0	36	0	48	0	37	0	29	0	14	0	2	0	9	0	219	0
130-134	0	0	3	0	4	0	11	0	15	0	5	0	16	0	11	0	5	0	2	0	72	0
125-129	0	0	0	0	0	0	1	0	5	0	2	0	5	0	1	0	0	0	1	0	15	0
120-124	0	0	0	0	0	0	0	0	0	0	0	0	0	0	1	0	0	0	1	0	2	0
Total	142	108	330	242	521	334	554	286	524	184	355	125	196	45	82	10	21	2	62	19	2787	1355

Apps = Number of Applicants   Adm = Number Admitted   Reflects 99% of the total applicant pool.

University at Buffalo, State University of New York School of Law

Admissions Office
O'Brian Hall, Amherst Campus
Buffalo, NY 14260

E-Mail: mdmcleod@msmail.buffalo.edu
URL: http://www.buffalo.edu/law
Phone: 716.645.2907

■ Introduction

The University at Buffalo School of Law is the only law school in the SUNY system. The school provides a comprehensive curriculum similar to that of other major law schools, while at the same time affording students a broad range of curricular options and special programs. The Buffalo curriculum emphasizes the study of law in its social context, and a large number of interdisciplinary courses and programs support this emphasis. A strong clinical education program is closely tied to the core curriculum. The law school maintains close connections with other departments in the university and offers a wide array of dual-degree programs.

■ Enrollment/Student Body

➡ *full-time 25th/75th percentile GPA—2.90/3.47*
➡ *full-time 25th/75th percentile LSAT—149/156*

■ Library and Physical Facilities

➡ *517,226 volumes & equivalents*   ➡ *LEXIS*   ➡ *NEXIS*
➡ *WESTLAW*   ➡ *DIALOG*   ➡ *LRS*   ➡ *QL*

The school is housed in John Lord O'Brian Hall, a seven-story building completed in 1973. O'Brian Hall is located on the Amherst Campus of the University at Buffalo, which is one of the four university centers of the SUNY system. The classrooms, library, offices, and study space for the law school are in carpeted rooms which provide bright and comfortable work places and which provide access to computer technology for research and learning. The library contains a major collection of books, periodicals, and public documents; has an extensive collection of microforms, audiovisual equipment, and materials; and is a depository for U.S. government publications.

The Amherst Campus provides recreational and cultural space including two theaters, chamber music and concert halls, a ceramics and art center, and athletic facilities in a 10,000-seat field house.

■ Curriculum

➡ *Academic Support Program*   ➡ *87 credits required to graduate*   ➡ *two semesters and summer session*

Instruction is offered in two semesters from early September to May, including a January "bridge" term, and in a summer session from mid-May to mid-July. Six full-time semesters, or five full-time semesters plus two summer sessions, are required for graduation. A special program allows students to spread their work over eight semesters.

The first-year program includes instruction in civil procedure, contracts, constitutional law, criminal law, legal research and writing, property, and torts. These are the standard subjects in the first year at most ABA-accredited law schools. In addition, the first year affords an introduction to aspects of the social and economic context of the legal system and to legal institutions and processes, in a "perspectives" course and in an intensive, four-week bridge course.

Beyond the first year, students are required to complete 55 semester credit hours of work. Much of the upper-division program is elective, and students may choose from a full spectrum of survey and advanced courses covering the main fields of public and private law, from a very rich selection of seminars and small group courses in special or emerging areas of law study and research, and from clinics and simulations devoted to professional skills training. Upper-division students have the opportunity to select a curricular "concentration" for in-depth study that links theory with practice. Concentration subjects include Family Law, Finance Transactions, Community Development, Environmental Law, Civil Litigation, Criminal Law, Health Law, Regulatory Law and Policy, Law and Social Justice, and International Law.

■ Special Programs

The school offers special programs emphasizing interdisciplinary study and applications of law. The clinical program is distinguished in that the skills training is coordinated with substantive law courses to give students theoretical understanding of practical issues. The program allows students to serve clients and conduct research and field-work in such areas as economic development, housing, family law, criminal law, school and education law, and international protection of human rights.

The school also has an extensive dual-degree program, which permits students to earn credit toward a master's or Ph.D. degree and the J.D. In recent years, the most active dual-degree programs have been with political science, management, philosophy, social work, sociology, and economics. Special programs can be arranged with other departments. Interdisciplinary programs of the school are administered by the Baldy Center for Law and Social Policy. The center provides fellowship awards for outstanding J.D./Ph.D. students, offers advice and assistance to all dual-degree candidates, and supports interdisciplinary research and curriculum development.

The Legal Methods Program is a first-year program for students who are educationally disadvantaged. Based on the recognition that quantitative measurements of success in law school are not infallibly reliable predictors, the Admissions Committee reviews these applications for other signs of achievement that should lead to success in law school. Tutorial assistance in substantive courses is provided. Correspondence regarding the program should be directed to the Admissions Office.

■ Admission

➡ *application deadline—Feb. 15*   ➡ *LSAT, LSDAS required*

The school has no specific undergraduate course prerequisites. The school admits first-year students only in the fall semester; application materials are available the preceding September.

Transfer with advanced standing is open to students who have successfully completed one year of work in an ABA-accredited law school.

■ Student Activities

Law student extracurricular activities are managed by law students through an elected representative body, the Student Bar Association. SBA-sponsored activities include lectures and special education programs, coordination of student participation in law school governance, and social events for students and faculty. Other student organizations include the Moot Court Board, which sponsors mock appellate practice competitions; *The Opinion*, the student newspaper; the *Buffalo Law Review*, a professional journal edited by students; specialty journals in environmental law, affordable housing and community development, law and social policy concerning women, criminal law, and human rights; and special interest groups such as the Asian Law Students Association (ALSA), the Latin American Law Students Association (LALSA), the Black Law Students Association (BLSA), the Native American Law Students Association (NALSA), the Association of Women Law Students, and the National Lawyers Guild.

■ Expenses and Financial Aid

➨ *tuition & fees—resident, $7,850; nonresident, $12,500*
➨ *estimated additional expenses—$4,000-$5,000*

New York state residents are eligible for the Tuition Assistance Program (TAP) and State University Supplemental Tuition Awards (SUSTA). Students are eligible for Perkins (formerly NDSL) and federally insured loans offered through the New York State Higher Education Assistance Corporation (NYSHEAC). TAP and SUSTA are based on need.

For more information, write to the Financial Aid Office, 232 Capen Hall, North Campus, Buffalo, NY 14260.

■ Housing

Limited housing for students is available in the dormitory complex and in the townhouse apartments. A wide range of private apartments is available. Write to the University Housing Office, Richmond Quadrangle, University at Buffalo, Amherst Campus, Buffalo, NY 14261.

■ Career Services

The school's Career Services Office (CSO) guides students in career selection and serves as a liaison between students and prospective employers. In addition to providing services for third-year students, the CSO also aids first- and second-year law students in conducting their summer job search.

In recent years, over 90 percent of the eligible graduates in a class have been employed in legal work within nine months of graduation. New York and the northeastern states, as well as Washington, DC, are the most common locations for SUNY at Buffalo graduates. The southeastern, midwestern, and western states have also attracted graduates including Florida, Illinois, California, Arizona, and Georgia.

To obtain additional information, please contact the Assistant Dean of CSO, School of Law, O'Brian Hall, North Campus, Buffalo, NY 14260.

Applicant Group for the 1998-1999 Academic Year

University at Buffalo, State University of New York School of Law
This grid includes only applicants who earned 120-180 LSAT scores under standard administrations.

LSAT Score	GPA																				
	3.75 +		3.50 - 3.74		3.25 - 3.49		3.00 - 3.24		2.75 - 2.99		2.50 - 2.74		2.25 - 2.49		2.00 - 2.24		Below 2.00		No GPA		Total	
	Apps	Adm	Apps	Adm	Apps	Adm	Apps	Adm	Apps	Adm	Apps	Adm	Apps	Adm	Apps	Adm	Apps	Adm	Apps	Adm	Apps	Adm
175-180	0	0	0	0	0	0	0	0	0	0	0	0	0	0	0	0	0	0	0	0	0	0
170-174	1	1	1	1	0	0	0	0	1	1	0	0	2	2	0	0	0	0	0	0	5	5
165-169	5	5	6	6	7	7	2	2	1	1	1	1	0	0	0	0	0	0	1	0	23	22
160-164	13	13	10	10	11	11	16	16	10	10	4	4	3	2	2	1	0	0	2	2	71	69
155-159	8	8	22	22	32	30	28	25	18	15	17	15	12	10	3	2	1	1	6	3	147	131
150-154	14	14	28	23	56	49	56	44	37	27	19	6	13	4	2	1	2	1	5	3	232	172
145-149	6	5	17	11	32	15	40	20	44	11	27	3	15	3	6	0	2	0	1	0	190	68
140-144	4	3	14	7	15	1	14	3	19	3	18	1	9	0	11	0	2	0	5	2	111	20
135-139	0	0	4	0	3	0	18	2	12	0	9	0	8	0	2	0	1	0	0	0	57	2
130-134	0	0	2	0	0	0	3	0	5	0	1	0	5	0	3	0	1	0	0	0	20	0
125-129	2	0	0	0	0	0	0	0	2	0	1	0	0	0	1	0	0	0	0	0	6	0
120-124	0	0	0	0	0	0	0	0	0	0	0	0	0	0	0	0	0	0	0	0	0	0
No Score	1	1	0	0	0	0	1	0	1	1	0	0	0	0	0	0	0	0	20	1	23	3
Total	54	50	104	80	156	113	178	112	150	69	97	30	67	21	30	4	9	2	40	11	885	492

Apps = Number of Applicants
Adm = Number Admitted

University of California at Berkeley School of Law (Boalt Hall)

5 Boalt Hall
U.C., Berkeley, CA 94720-7200

E-Mail: admissions@mail.law.berkeley.edu
URL: http://www.law.berkeley.edu
Phone: 510.642.2274

■ Introduction

Boalt Hall is located on the campus of the University of
California at Berkeley. The campus is surrounded by
wooded, rolling hills and the city of Berkeley, which has
a long history as one of America's most lively, culturally
diverse, and politically adventurous cities. The surrounding
San Francisco Bay Area offers culture, entertainment, and
natural beauty without rival, much of which is accessible
by BART (the Bay Area Rapid Transit system). All of
Northern California, with its great variety of cultural and
recreational opportunities, is within easy reach. Boalt Hall
is one of the world's leading institutions of legal education
and research. The school is a member of AALS and is
approved by the ABA.

■ Enrollment/Student Body

➡ 4,587 applicants ➡ 857 admitted first-year class 1998
➡ 269 enrolled first-year class 1998 ➡ full-time 25th/75th
percentile GPA—3.66/3.87 ➡ full-time 25th/75th percentile
LSAT—161/169 ➡ 846 total full-time (no part-time)
➡ 33% minority ➡ 52% women ➡ 50 states & foreign
countries represented ➡ 106 undergraduate schools represented

The academic backgrounds and nonacademic experiences
of Boalt Hall students are varied, and there is a substantial
representation of various graduate and professional
degrees. An advanced graduate (LL.M.) program admits
20-25 students annually from foreign countries.

■ Faculty

➡ 65 full-time ➡ 87 part-time or adjunct ➡ 18 women
➡ 8 minority

■ Library and Physical Facilities

➡ 760,000 volumes & equivalents ➡ 14 full-time librarians
➡ LEXIS ➡ NEXIS ➡ WESTLAW ➡ INNOPAC
➡ MELVYL

The law library's collection includes the Robbins Collection
of Ancient, Canon, and Ecclesiastical Law, and extensive
special collections on comparative and international law,
natural resources, and the environment. The law library is
linked by computer to the collections at other national law
schools and to the combined university library holdings that
number more than seven million volumes. The late Chief
Justice Earl Warren, an alumnus of the school, designated
the law library as a depository for U.S. Supreme Court
records and briefs, and it is also a selective official depository
of U.S. government documents. The library maintains a
photocopying service and IBM and Macintosh PCs for
student word processing.
A studio apartment complex is reserved for law students.
The university also maintains limited housing for students
who are married or who have children. Most law students
live in rented apartments or houses in the area.

■ Admission

➡ Bachelor's degree required ➡ application deadline—Feb. 1,
early application strongly preferred ➡ LSAT, LSDAS required
➡ application fee—$40, fall admission only

Applications are evaluated primarily in terms of undergraduate academic work and LSAT score. Applicants
are encouraged to include in their personal statement a
discussion of their exceptional accomplishments, prior
employment, graduate study, or any other special characteristics, including nonacademic experiences, talents, and
ambitions. Two letters of recommendation submitted with
the application are advised. December is the last acceptable
test date to meet the February application deadline, and
repeated LSAT scores are averaged. Admission is highly
selective; approximately 20 applications are received
annually for each place in the first-year class. Some decisions
are made as early as January, and the bulk of decision
letters are mailed by May. Early application is advised.

■ Student Activities

Students edit and publish nine legal periodicals—the African-
American Law and Policy Report, the Asian Law Journal, the
Berkeley Journal of Employment and Labor Law, the California
Law Review, Ecology Law Quarterly, Berkeley Technology Law
Journal, Berkeley Journal of International Law, Berkeley Women's
Law Journal, and La Raza Law Journal.
Participation in moot court is compulsory for first-year
students; advanced students may participate in voluntary
moot court and in honors competitions. Other activities
include the Boalt Hall Student Association, the Boalt Hall
Women's Association, the Berkeley Law Foundation,
International Law Society, National Lawyers' Guild, and
many student cultural and affinity groups.
Student activities and educational programs are enriched
by the activities of the Earl Warren Legal Institute, an
interdisciplinary law-related research and public service
unit of the university.

■ Curriculum

➡ Academic Support Program ➡ 85 credits required
to graduate ➡ more than 150 courses available
➡ semesters, start in Aug.
➡ range of first-year class size—30-100

An orientation program introduces new law students to
the school and to legal learning at the beginning of the
fall term. The first-year curriculum is prescribed. Upon
completion of the first year, simulation-based courses
are available in legal interviewing, legal counseling, legal
accounting, and legal document drafting and are taught
by teams of lawyers from Bay Area law firms. Boalt Hall
also offers the following clinical programs that are integrated
with substantive courses—Disability Rights, Immigration
and Asylum, Environmental Law, Domestic Violence,
and The Berkeley Community Law Center. An inhouse

clinic offers hands-on work in International Human Rights or federal practice. Interested students may be placed for a full semester as law clerks to federal and state judges or with public interest, government, and private lawyers.

Special Programs

Concurrent-degree programs that allow students to earn the J.D. and a master's degree in another field in four years have been established with the following departments of the university—Asian studies, business administration, city planning, economics, information management and systems, international and area studies, journalism, public policy, and social welfare, as well as doctoral programs in economics and legal history. In addition, students may arrange concurrent programs with other campus departments.

Combined-degree programs are available with the Fletcher School of Law and Diplomacy at Tufts University or with the John F. Kennedy School of Government at Harvard University. Unique among American law schools is the graduate program in Jurisprudence and Social Policy, an interdisciplinary legal studies program leading to the Ph.D. that requires no prior legal training, and which also may be earned concurrently with a J.D.

Boalt Hall's concentration programs include Environmental Law, International and Comparative Legal Studies, and Law and Technology/Intellectual Property.

Expenses and Financial Aid

➡ *tuition & fees—full-time resident, $10,800; nonresident, $20,198* ➡ *estimated additional expenses—$12,958*
➡ *need-based financial aid available*
➡ *FAFSA form for need analysis due*
➡ *deadline for priority consideration—March 2*

All financial aid is need based and each package may consist of grants-in-aid, Perkins and Stafford loans, and work-study funds for continuing students. Nonresidents may become residents after one year if appropriate steps are taken and if certain eligibility requirements are met. All fees are subject to change without notice.

Career Services

The Boalt Hall Career Services Office serves as a resource for Boalt Hall students, alumni, and prospective employers. It operates one of the largest on-campus recruitment programs in the country; provides opportunities for part-time, summer, and full-time legal positions; and maintains extensive files on a wide variety of positions available throughout the nation. The career services staff announces career counseling, résumé workshops, and programs on opportunities for traditional and nontraditional law careers.

Applicant Group for the 1998-1999 Academic Year

University of California at Berkeley School of Law (Boalt Hall)
This grid includes only applicants who earned 120-180 LSAT scores under standard administrations.

LSAT Score	3.75 +		3.50 - 3.74		3.25 - 3.49		3.00 - 3.24		2.75 - 2.99		2.50 - 2.74		2.25 - 2.49		2.00 - 2.24		Below 2.00		No GPA		Total	
	Apps	Adm	Apps	Adm	Apps	Adm	Apps	Adm	Apps	Adm	Apps	Adm	Apps	Adm	Apps	Adm	Apps	Adm	Apps	Adm	Apps	Adm
175-180	50	50	39	33	18	8	12	1	6	0	0	0	0	0	0	0	0	0	4	2	129	94
170-174	150	140	172	80	105	13	42	2	14	0	9	0	2	0	0	0	0	0	7	3	501	238
165-169	288	178	354	77	215	17	89	3	40	1	12	0	9	0	1	0	1	0	22	8	1031	284
160-164	279	80	373	52	254	13	120	4	42	0	20	0	5	0	2	0	1	0	31	4	1127	153
155-159	166	28	228	21	174	2	118	1	65	1	26	0	9	0	1	0	2	0	30	0	819	53
150-154	71	12	103	9	110	0	85	0	57	0	22	0	17	0	3	0	0	0	26	0	494	21
145-149	21	4	44	2	46	0	42	0	33	0	17	0	14	0	2	0	0	0	21	0	240	6
140-144	9	0	11	0	11	0	25	0	20	0	13	0	5	0	4	0	1	0	7	0	106	0
135-139	2	0	3	0	9	0	13	0	12	0	8	0	6	0	3	0	1	0	3	0	60	0
130-134	0	0	0	0	3	0	2	0	5	0	3	0	4	0	1	0	0	0	1	0	19	0
125-129	0	0	0	0	0	0	0	0	1	0	2	0	0	0	1	0	1	0	1	0	6	0
120-124	0	0	0	0	0	0	0	0	0	0	0	0	0	0	0	0	0	0	0	0	0	0
Total	1036	492	1327	274	945	53	548	11	295	2	132	0	71	0	18	0	7	0	153	17	4532	849

Apps = Number of Applicants
Adm = Number Admitted
Reflects 99% of the total applicant pool.

School of Law, University of California—Davis

Admissions Office
Davis, CA 95616-5201

E-Mail: lawadmissions@ucdavis.edu
URL: http://kinghall.ucdavis.edu
Phone: 530.752.6477

■ Introduction

The School of Law at the University of California, Davis, was founded in 1965. It is accredited by the American Bar Association and is a member of the Association of American Law Schools. The school has a chapter of the Order of the Coif, the national honor society. The law building, King Hall, was named for Dr. Martin Luther King, Jr., in recognition of his efforts to bring social and political justice to disadvantaged peoples.

The Davis campus is 20 minutes from Sacramento and an hour-and-a-half from San Francisco, within easy reach of the major recreational areas of the Sierra Nevadas, Lake Tahoe, and the Mother Lode. The campus occupies 3,600 acres within the college town of Davis, where the small-town, friendly atmosphere is a welcome change from the distractions and stress usually associated with more urban environments.

The close proximity to the state capitol and the Bay Area provide both social and political stimulus necessary for a well-rounded educational experience. The campus also offers a full range of graduate and professional programs.

■ Enrollment/Student Body

➡ 2,288 applicants   ➡ 813 admitted first-year class 1998
➡ 183 enrolled first-year class 1998   ➡ full-time 25th/75th percentile GPA—3.24/3.62   ➡ full-time 25th/75th percentile LSAT—158/164   ➡ 505 total full-time   ➡ 23% minority
➡ 51% women   ➡ 142 undergraduate schools represented

■ Faculty

➡ 49 total   ➡ 29 full-time   ➡ 20 part-time
➡ 10 women   ➡ 6 minority   ➡ 1:17 faculty/student ratio (full-time faculty only)

■ Library and Physical Facilities

➡ 401,343 volumes & equivalents   ➡ Hours:
Mon.-Thurs., 8:00 A.M.-10:00 P.M.; Fri., 8:00 A.M.-5:00 P.M.;
Sat., NOON-5:00 P.M.; Sun., NOON-8:00 P.M.
➡ LEXIS/NEXIS   ➡ WESTLAW   ➡ MELVYL
➡ 5 full-time librarians   ➡ library seats 376

All faculty offices, classrooms, and the law library are housed in a single easily accessible building on the Davis campus. It has moot courtrooms, a pretrial-skills laboratory, an instructional computer and word-processing lab, study carrels, student journal offices, lounges, an infant care co-op, offices for student organizations, and is comfortably accessible to disabled students. Every law student has a key to the building and may use the facilities around the clock.

The law library has an open-stack system. All students are assigned to carrels, and books can be charged to carrels. The library is a federal and California documents depository and has an extensive collection of California and federal government documents.

■ Curriculum

➡ Academic Support Program   ➡ 88 credits required to graduate   ➡ 122 courses available   ➡ degrees available: J.D.; J.D./M.B.A.; J.D./M.A.; LL.M.   ➡ semesters, start in Aug.
➡ range of first-year class size—29-89 students

During the first year at King Hall, students study six basic areas of the law—civil procedure, constitutional law, contracts, crimes, property, and torts. In a major commitment to close student-faculty relation, one of these courses is taught in small sections of 30-31 students. The first year also includes a week-long introductory course and a course in legal research and writing. Second- and third-year programs are elective, except for a course on professional responsibility and a legal writing requirement. Courses may be selected within broad areas of concentration such as administration of criminal justice, business and taxation, civil litigation, estate planning and taxation, labor and employment law, environmental law, public interest law, and international law.

■ Special Programs

Second- and third-year students have the opportunity to work under the supervision of practicing lawyers in clinicals in civil rights, immigration law, environmental law, tax law, employment relations, public interest law, legislative, judicial, prison law, and criminal justice administration. Several also participate in judicial externships in trial and appellate courts.

King Hall has an integrated civil rights curriculum including a substantive course in civil rights law, a civil rights litigation skills seminar, and a clinic representing indigent persons in civil rights cases. Students participating in the King Hall Civil Rights Clinic are certified to appear in federal court, where they provide representation to people who would otherwise have no counsel and gain first-hand experience in constitutional litigation.

First-year students engage in oral argument as a part of the required legal research and writing course. This provides basic preparation for participation in the formal Moot Court Program, which emphasizes appellate advocacy skills. The program includes an honors competition and a series of regional, national, and international competitions.

Our moot court and trial competition teams have each advanced to the final rounds of the National Moot Court Competition and the National Mock Trial Competition in the last five years. We have also won other state, regional, and national competitions.

Skills courses cover the major elements of both litigation and nonlitigation practice. These include pretrial skills (interviewing, counseling, document drafting), negotiation and alternative dispute resolution, as well as introductory and advanced trial practice courses.

Students in the Public Interest Law Program receive a special certificate based on a combination of required coursework, practical experience, and community service. The program offers academic and career counseling.

■ Admission

➡ Bachelor's degree or equivalent from college or university of approved standing required ➡ application deadline—Feb. 1 ➡ rolling admission, early application encouraged ➡ LSAT, LSDAS required ➡ application fee—$40 (waivers available)

Undergraduate grades and LSAT score form the foundation of the admission evaluation. The Admission Committee seeks students of diverse backgrounds. Consideration is given to economic factors, advanced studies, significant work experience, and extracurricular and community activities. An applicant's maturity, capacity to grow, and commitment to law study are also major considerations. Multiple LSAT scores will be averaged. Admission Information Sessions are held at King Hall in October, November, December, and January. Law student guided tours can be arranged by contacting the Admission Office.

■ Cocurricular Activities

There are four student-run journals: the *UC Davis Law Review* and specialized journals in International Law, Environmental Law, and Juvenile Law. Membership is open to all students.

The Law Student Association coordinates law student activities. Students sit on the student-faculty Educational Policy, Faculty Appointments, and Admission Committees. Other active organizations include the International Law Society; Environmental Law Society; Entertainment and Sports Law; Women's Caucus; and Asian, Black, Christian, Jewish, La Raza, Native American, and Filipino Law Student Associations.

■ Expenses and Financial Aid

➡ tuition & fees—residents, $10,859; nonresidents, $20,243 ➡ additional expenses—$9,838 (room, board, books) ➡ some need-based scholarships available

Although grant monies are limited, the School of Law Financial Aid Office administers all nationally recognized aid programs, such as Perkins Loans and Work Study, and participates in the Federal Direct Student Loan Program. University student loans and grants are also available for child care. Financial aid applications must be submitted by March 1 of the year in which admission is sought. Applications are accepted after that date, but are not considered for grant or Perkins loan funding.

■ Housing

A wide variety of housing is available, but it is advisable to begin seeking preferred accommodations early. The university maintains on-campus apartments for all students and Leach Hall for single graduate students. Students desiring on-campus housing should apply well in advance of the April deadline.

■ Career Services

The law school maintains an active Career Services Office to help students secure permanent positions and summer work, as well as part-time or temporary employment during the academic year. Career counseling and strategy consultation are available to all students. Approximately 120 employers use the facilities of the office to interview Davis law students on campus. Special career workshops are scheduled throughout the year to provide students with employment information and to help them develop techniques useful in their job search.

Applicant Group for the 1998-1999 Academic Year

School of Law, University of California—Davis
This grid includes only applicants who earned 120-180 LSAT scores under standard administrations (98% of the total applicant pool).

LSAT Score	GPA																				
	3.75 +		3.50 - 3.74		3.25 - 3.49		3.00 - 3.24		2.75 - 2.99		2.50 - 2.74		2.25 - 2.49		2.00 - 2.24		Below 2.00		No GPA		Total	
	Apps	Adm	Apps	Adm	Apps	Adm	Apps	Adm	Apps	Adm	Apps	Adm	Apps	Adm	Apps	Adm	Apps	Adm	Apps	Adm	Apps	Adm
175-180	1	1	2	2	1	1	1	1	1	1	0	0	0	0	0	0	0	0	1	1	7	7
170-174	6	6	6	6	16	16	18	17	4	3	3	3	0	0	0	0	0	0	1	1	54	52
165-169	28	27	60	58	55	53	39	37	21	11	6	1	5	0	0	0	0	0	5	5	219	192
160-164	67	67	121	109	138	109	95	54	43	14	17	1	7	1	2	0	1	1	7	4	498	360
155-159	86	55	138	56	176	32	117	16	68	3	31	1	9	0	2	0	1	0	8	1	636	164
150-154	38	6	102	4	127	5	108	2	64	1	16	0	20	0	1	0	0	0	14	1	490	19
145-149	13	3	33	2	57	0	46	0	42	0	26	0	8	0	0	0	1	0	14	0	240	5
140-144	6	0	9	0	10	0	25	1	20	0	12	0	4	0	6	0	2	0	7	0	101	1
135-139	2	0	2	0	3	0	10	0	11	0	2	0	2	0	2	0	0	0	1	0	35	0
130-134	0	0	0	0	0	0	1	0	5	0	0	0	2	0	3	0	0	0	0	0	11	0
125-129	0	0	0	0	0	0	0	0	3	0	0	0	0	0	0	0	0	0	0	0	3	0
120-124	0	0	0	0	0	0	0	0	0	0	0	0	0	0	0	0	0	0	0	0	0	0
Total	247	165	473	237	583	216	460	128	282	33	113	6	57	1	16	0	5	1	58	13	2294	800

Apps = Number of Applicants
Adm = Number Admitted

University of California—Hastings College of the Law

200 McAllister Street
San Francisco, CA 94102

E-Mail: admiss@uchastings.edu
URL: http://www.uchastings.edu
Phone: 415.565.4623

■ Introduction

Since its founding in 1878 as the University of California's first school of law, Hastings College of the Law has been at the center of the legal community in the West. In addition to pursuing legal practice that covers the entire spectrum of law, Hastings graduates sit as judges on the California bench by a 3-to-1 margin over any other law school.

Located in San Francisco's Civic Center, Hastings provides students unparalleled access to legal institutions. The California Supreme Court, California Court of Appeals, and the U.S. Court of Appeals for the Ninth Circuit are nearby. Two blocks away is City Hall, as well as superior and municipal courts. With its central location and strong community links to many of the Bay Area's multicultural neighborhoods, Hastings offers students an educational experience that is virtually unlimited in its breadth and diversity.

■ Enrollment/Student Body

➡ *4,121 applicants*   ➡ *1,255 admitted first-year class 1998*
➡ *354 enrolled first-year class 1998*   ➡ *full-time 25th/75th percentile GPA—3.05/3.59*   ➡ *full-time 25th/75th percentile LSAT—159/164*   ➡ *1,130 total full-time*   ➡ *33% minority*
➡ *48% women*   ➡ *47 states & foreign countries represented*
➡ *over 200 undergraduate schools represented*

Many students come to Hastings from other career experiences. Though student ages range from 21-74, there are a significant number of students over 30; the average age of Hastings students is 27.

■ Faculty

➡ *90 total*   ➡ *46 full-time*   ➡ *44 part-time or adjunct*
➡ *24 women*   ➡ *18 minority*

■ Library and Physical Facilities

➡ *612,117 volumes & equivalents*   ➡ *library hours: Mon.-Fri., 8:00 A.M.-11:00 P.M.; Sat., 9:00 A.M.-10:00 P.M.; Sun., 9:00 A.M.-11:00 P.M.*   ➡ *LEXIS*   ➡ *NEXIS*
➡ *WESTLAW*   ➡ *DIALOG*   ➡ *INFOTRAC*
➡ *FIRST SEARCH*   ➡ *11 full-time librarians*
➡ *library seats 1,295*   ➡ *computer lab*

The law library houses an extensive collection of federal and California documents for which Hastings is an official depository. The breadth and depth of the library's collection, and its state-of-the-art computer-assisted research capabilities, draw local attorneys, court personnel, and government agency employees to use the library's resources.

■ Curriculum

➡ *Academic Support Program*   ➡ *Clinical Instruction Program*
➡ *6 scholarly publications*   ➡ *86 units/credits required to graduate*   ➡ *303 courses available; concentrations in civil*
litigation, international law, public interest law, & taxation
➡ *selected concurrent master's degree programs with U.C. Berkeley*   ➡ *full-time semesters, begin in Aug.*
➡ *range of first-year class size—9-100*

The Hastings curriculum offers a broad spectrum of courses, from those that are fundamental to all forms of practice to those that reflect increased specialization. After three years of successful study, the student will receive a Juris Doctor degree, conferred by the Regents of the University of California.

Students must complete six semesters in residence, earn 86 semester units, pass all required courses, and earn a cumulative G.P.A. of at least C (2.00). The program is designed for full-time students; new students are admitted only at the beginning of the fall semester.

■ Special Programs

Legal Education Opportunity Program—Initiated in 1969, the Legal Education Opportunity Program (LEOP) was designed to assist students in excelling academically at Hastings. Students admitted through LEOP are offered a number of academic support services throughout their three years of study, beginning with orientation for incoming students and ending with a supplemental bar review course.

To be eligible for LEOP, applicants must complete the LEOP application which includes questions regarding cultural, economic, educational, familial, geographic, linguistic, physical, or social issues/circumstances affecting preparation for law school.

Institutes and Exchanges Program—As part of the second- and third-year course of study, students at Hastings have the opportunity to participate in student-exchange programs with Leiden University, The Netherlands; the University of British Columbia; and Vermont Law School, as well as in the Land Conservation Institute, the Public Law Research Institute, and the Public Interest Clearinghouse.

■ Admission

➡ *B.A. or equivalent required*   ➡ *application deadline— Feb. 16*   ➡ *admission decisions made early Dec. to mid-April*   ➡ *LSAT, LSDAS required*
➡ *application fee—$40*

Although the selection process is highly competitive, each application is read with care and deliberation. Therefore, candidates are encouraged to provide a complete and candid picture of themselves.

The admission committee assesses the relative strength of each applicant's academic achievements; LSAT score; professional experience; community, volunteer, and extra-curricular activities; letters of recommendation; and writing ability. Residence is not a factor.

■ Cocurricular and Student Activities

Hastings publishes more journals that offer credit than most other U.S. law schools. Second- and third-year students may earn academic credit by working on one of six law journals: *Hastings Communications and Entertainment Law Journal*, *Hastings Constitutional Law Quarterly*, *Hastings International and Comparative Law Review*, *Hastings Law Journal*, *Hastings Women's Law Journal*, and *West-Northwest*.

Beyond the first-year moot court requirement, Hastings offers Appellate Advocacy as a second-year elective. Students write a brief and present oral arguments based on the record of an actual case pending in the California or the United States Supreme Court. Second- and third-year students represent Hastings in a number of state, national, and international advocacy competitions.

The Civil Justice Clinic, Criminal Practice Clinic, Worker's Rights Clinic, and Environmental Law Clinic offer students valuable experience in criminal and civil practice under the supervision of practicing attorneys and faculty.

The governing organization of the student body is the Associated Students of the University of California, Hastings. Additionally, students participate in approximately 40 different student groups.

■ Expenses and Financial Aid

➡ *full-time tuition & fees—residents, $11,167; nonresidents, $19,937* ➡ *limited number of scholarships available* ➡ *FAFSA and Entering Student Financial Aid Supplement required for financial aid; due by Feb. 16*

Typically, more than 80 percent of Hastings students receive financial assistance from college-administered sources. Scholarship awards are made to recognize and encourage the achievement, service, and professional promise of students.

In addition, students who pursue qualifying public interest and government sector employment may receive loan repayment assistance through the Public Interest Career Assistance Program (PICAP).

■ Housing

On-campus housing is available at McAllister Tower, a 24-story building. The 250 apartments include efficiencies, studios, one-bedroom, and a few two-bedroom apartments. Students with families are clustered together to provide mutual support and companionship. The Off-Campus Housing Office provides current listings in San Francisco and the Bay Area, as well as sample leases and other helpful publications.

■ Career Services

As part of its commitment to students and alumni, Hastings offers one of the most comprehensive law career services offices in the West. Students are assisted in clarifying their legal focus, acquiring job search skills, and developing law-related résumés, job-search strategies, and interviewing techniques.

Hastings annually lists 1,400-1,500 part-time and summer jobs for current students and alumni.

Through the fall and spring, more than 300 employers visit the campus to interview students for both summer associate positions and permanent postgraduation employment. An additional 200-300 employers from throughout the nation participate in the recruit-by-mail program.

Applicant Group for the 1998-1999 Academic Year

University of California—Hastings College of the Law
This grid includes only applicants who earned 120-180 LSAT scores under standard administrations.

LSAT Score	3.75 +		3.50 - 3.74		3.25 - 3.49		3.00 - 3.24		2.75 - 2.99		2.50 - 2.74		2.25 - 2.49		2.00 - 2.24		Below 2.00		No GPA		Total	
	Apps	Adm	Apps	Adm	Apps	Adm	Apps	Adm	Apps	Adm	Apps	Adm	Apps	Adm	Apps	Adm	Apps	Adm	Apps	Adm	Apps	Adm
175-180	3	3	5	5	4	4	2	2	1	1	0	0	0	0	0	0	0	0	1	1	16	16
170-174	15	15	22	21	26	24	19	18	15	13	9	5	0	0	1	1	0	0	3	3	110	100
165-169	47	47	79	77	90	87	76	69	51	36	18	9	11	4	2	0	2	1	10	7	386	337
160-164	96	90	219	211	216	137	184	59	69	17	44	9	11	2	6	0	1	0	12	6	858	531
155-159	107	66	211	56	284	23	198	8	133	7	56	0	25	1	7	0	1	0	23	1	1045	162
150-154	53	10	138	9	179	4	190	13	116	4	56	1	39	0	9	0	2	0	16	0	798	41
145-149	17	2	44	2	112	9	99	9	95	2	62	0	34	0	8	0	1	0	26	0	498	24
140-144	12	1	19	3	29	0	39	0	57	0	35	0	19	0	8	0	1	0	12	0	231	4
135-139	3	0	3	0	8	0	20	0	17	0	17	0	9	0	5	0	0	0	6	0	88	0
130-134	0	0	0	0	1	0	4	0	11	0	9	0	6	0	2	0	1	0	1	0	35	0
125-129	0	0	0	0	0	0	1	0	2	0	2	0	3	0	2	0	1	0	0	0	11	0
120-124	0	0	0	0	0	0	0	0	1	0	0	0	0	0	0	0	0	0	0	0	1	0
Total	353	234	740	384	949	288	832	178	568	80	308	24	157	7	50	1	10	1	110	18	4077	1215

Apps = Number of Applicants
Adm = Number Admitted
Reflects 99% of the total applicant pool.

University of California at Los Angeles School of Law

Law Admissions Office, 71 Dodd Hall
Box 951445
Los Angeles, CA 90095-1445

E-Mail: admissions@mail.law.ucla.edu
URL: http://www.law.ucla.edu
Phone: 310.825.4041

■ Introduction

The School of Law at the University of California, Los Angeles, is set on the beautiful UCLA campus, which is located in the foothills of the Santa Monica Mountains in the village of Westwood. Our location provides ready access to the exciting city of Los Angeles, while at the same time offering students an architecturally appointed and richly landscaped refuge from urban life.

■ Enrollment/Student Body

➥ 4,282 applicants ➥ 841 admitted first-year class 1998 ➥ 275 enrolled first-year class 1998 ➥ full-time 25th/75th percentile GPA—3.45/3.78 ➥ full-time 25th/75th percentile LSAT—161/166 ➥ 976 total full-time (no part-time) ➥ 34% minority (total student body) ➥ 49% women (total student body) ➥ 92 undergraduate schools represented in 1998 first-year class ➥ approximately 27% of the first-year class are non-California residents

■ Faculty

➥ 104 total ➥ 80 full-time ➥ 24 part-time or adjunct ➥ 30 women ➥ 11 minority

■ Library and Physical Facilities

➥ 554,000 volumes & equivalents ➥ library hours: Mon.-Thurs., 8:00 A.M.-11:30 P.M.; Fri., 8:00 A.M.-8:30 P.M.; Sat., 9:00 A.M.-5:30 P.M.; Sun., 1:00 P.M.-11:30 P.M. ➥ LEXIS ➥ NEXIS ➥ WESTLAW ➥ DIALOG ➥ CIS ➥ Internet ➥ 11 full-time librarians

The newly renovated and expanded law library, which opened in 1998, gives UCLA law students a spacious, electronically equipped and well-lighted facility for quiet study and reflection. The library's print collection of over a half a million volumes is complemented by the "virtual" library, which is accessible to the law school community in their offices, computer labs, and at home through the school's computer network.

■ Curriculum

➥ Academic Support Program ➥ 87 credits required to graduate ➥ degrees available: J.D.; J.D./M.B.A.; J.D./M.A. (Urban Planning); J.D./M.A. (American Indian Studies); J.D./M.S.W. (Social Welfare); J.D./M.A. (Public Policy—program approval pending); LL.M. (for foreign students planning to return to their native countries)

The law school offers a three-year, full-time course of study leading to a J.D. degree. Evening, summer, or part-time programs are not offered. The first-year curriculum corresponds to that in most leading U.S. law schools—the major common law subjects and constitutional law. However, UCLA differs from many other institutions in that it invests major resources in its first-year Lawyering Skills Program, which combines the beginning of skills

training, such as client interviewing and counseling, with traditional legal research and writing.

The school's distinguished and widely published faculty make it possible to offer outstanding classes in both traditional fields of study and in clinical education. Advanced students choose from a broad variety of courses, seminars, clinical programs, and independent studies.

The Clinical Education Program, housed in the law school's state-of-the-art clinical wing, provides extensive and rigorous practical training through simulated and actual client contact. Examples of clinical courses regularly offered are the Frank G. Wells Environmental Law Clinic, Street Law, Civil and Criminal Trial Advocacy and Interviewing, Counseling, and Negotiation.

■ Special Programs

Students and faculty often pioneer new programs together. Recent examples are the Public Interest Law and Policy Program and the program in Business Law. The Public Interest Law and Policy Program marks a distinct break with the way schools have traditionally trained lawyers for public interest careers. This program, which has a limited enrollment of 25 students, builds on the array of public interest oriented courses, programs, and activities open to all students while recognizing the need for coordinated and sequenced training. Participants take a special section of Lawyering Skills, participate in a first-year workshop, advanced seminars, and extracurricular programs.

Students may undertake a concentration in Business Law at the beginning of their second year of law school. Students must take three foundational courses in the first semester of their second year and then select one of four cores, or areas of specialization: corporate and securities, commercial and financing, taxation, and a general business field.

The law school also has an extensive full-time, semester-long Externship Program with placements in Los Angeles, San Francisco, and Washington, DC. Students are regularly placed in judges' chambers, governmental agencies, and nonprofit organizations where they experience lawyering firsthand.

■ Admission

➥ Bachelor's degree required ➥ application deadline—Feb. 1 ➥ LSAT, LSDAS required ➥ application fee—$40

All applicants must have a baccalaureate degree from an accredited university or college of approved standing. There are no specific undergraduate course or major requirements. Students are admitted for the fall semester only; applicants must take the LSAT no later than the December administration.

Admission is based primarily on proven outstanding academic and intellectual ability measured largely by the LSAT and the quality of undergraduate education as determined by not only the GPA, but also by such factors as the breadth, depth, and rigor of the undergraduate educational program. The admission committee may also consider additional factors such as whether economic, physical, or other hardships and challenges have been overcome, community or public service, letters of recommendation, work experience and career achievement, language ability, and career goals (with particular attention paid to the likelihood of the applicant representing underrepresented communities). UCLA invites transfer applications into the second-year class from students with excellent first-year credentials from an ABA-accredited law school. Transfer applications are available May 1 and due July 15.

■ Student Activities

Students edit and publish the *UCLA Law Review*, *Chicano/Latino Law Review*, *UCLA Pacific Basin Law Journal*, *Entertainment Law Review*, *Asian Pacific American Law Journal*, *UCLA Journal of Environmental Law and Policy*, *UCLA Women's Law Journal*, and the *UCLA Journal of International and Foreign Affairs*. Diverse student interests are represented in over 25 student organizations. The Moot Court Honors Program is open to all second-year students and offers a large and effective program of mock appellate advocacy. There is a very active Student Bar Association. Students also publish a law school newspaper, *The Docket*, and participate in an annual student/faculty musical.

■ Expenses and Financial Aid

➡ *tuition & fees—resident, $10,972; nonresident, $20,356*
➡ *scholarships available*   ➡ *need-based financial aid*

grants available   ➡ *FAFSA form & need analysis diskette must be filed by March 1*   ➡ *Supplemental Financial Aid Application due Feb. 1 with the law school application*

■ Residency

Applicants admitted to the law school as nonresident students for tuition purposes are eligible to be considered for resident classification if certain eligibility requirements are met. Most nonresident law students achieve residency status during the second year of law school.

■ Career Services

The Office of Career Services coordinates on-campus interviews during both the fall and spring semesters with nearly 400 interviewers from law firms, corporations, government agencies, and public interest organizations who visit the campus annually. In addition, the office maintains an internet site and extensive files containing job openings for permanent, part-time, and summer positions nationwide. Private counseling sessions are frequently utilized to discuss career choices, job-search strategies, and résumé and cover-letter preparation. The office also sponsors educational programs and receptions throughout the year, including a practice specialty series with practitioners, a mock-interview program, a government reception and information fair, and a small/mid-size law firm reception. UCLA School of Law had more than a 96 percent employment rate nine months after graduation (based on the Class of 1997 Employment Survey).

Applicant Group for the 1998-1999 Academic Year

University of California at Los Angeles School of Law
This grid includes only applicants who earned 120-180 LSAT scores under standard administrations.

LSAT Score	3.75 +		3.50 - 3.74		3.25 - 3.49		3.00 - 3.24		2.75 - 2.99		2.50 - 2.74		2.25 - 2.49		2.00 - 2.24		Below 2.00		No GPA		Total	
	Apps	Adm	Apps	Adm	Apps	Adm	Apps	Adm	Apps	Adm	Apps	Adm	Apps	Adm	Apps	Adm	Apps	Adm	Apps	Adm	Apps	Adm
175-180	14	14	12	12	7	6	7	5	4	0	0	0	0	0	0	0	0	0	0	0	44	37
170-174	49	49	57	56	48	30	22	7	8	0	3	0	0	0	0	0	0	0	4	1	191	143
165-169	133	131	200	151	154	45	81	7	41	3	17	1	4	0	0	0	2	0	13	2	645	340
160-164	202	134	336	87	312	26	145	10	60	1	22	0	6	0	3	0	0	0	18	1	1104	259
155-159	144	14	240	15	249	12	163	9	81	1	41	0	11	0	1	0	1	0	16	0	947	51
150-154	68	1	148	2	161	4	125	2	79	1	33	0	19	0	1	0	2	0	21	0	657	10
145-149	23	0	49	0	78	0	75	0	60	0	32	0	18	0	4	0	0	0	17	0	356	0
140-144	7	0	18	0	27	0	39	0	37	0	17	0	14	0	7	0	0	0	7	0	173	0
135-139	2	0	6	0	5	0	15	0	17	0	16	0	9	0	2	0	1	0	6	0	79	0
130-134	0	0	1	0	2	0	1	0	5	0	5	0	6	0	1	0	0	0	0	0	21	0
125-129	0	0	0	0	0	0	0	0	2	0	0	0	0	0	2	0	1	0	0	0	5	0
120-124	0	0	0	0	0	0	0	0	0	0	0	0	0	0	0	0	0	0	0	0	0	0
Total	642	343	1067	323	1043	123	673	40	394	6	186	1	87	0	21	0	7	0	102	4	4222	840

Apps = Number of Applicants
Adm = Number Admitted
Reflects 98% of the total applicant pool.

California Western School of Law

225 Cedar Street
San Diego, CA 92101

E-Mail: admissions@cwsl.edu; URL: http://www.cwsl.edu
Phone: 619.239.0391, 800.255.4252 ext. 1401 (admissions);
or 619.525.7083 (bulletin requests); Fax: 619.685.2916

■ Introduction

Located in downtown San Diego, one of the most beautiful cities in the world, the law school has a history of providing contemporary legal education. The law school's mission is to train creative, problem-solving lawyers who can devise innovative and responsible solutions to legal problems. The law school is constructing a new law library which will open in January 2000—the first new law library of the 21st century. The school is approved by the ABA and is a member of AALS.

■ Enrollment/Student Body

➤ 1,758 applicants   ➤ 1,224 admitted first-year class 1998
➤ 317 enrolled first-year class 1998   ➤ full-time 25th/75th percentile GPA—2.81/3.42   ➤ part-time 25th/75th percentile GPA—2.65/3.31   ➤ full-time 25th/75th percentile LSAT—146/153   ➤ part-time 25th/75th percentile LSAT—147/151
➤ 667 total full-time   ➤ 32 total part-time
➤ 27.5% minority   ➤ 53.5% women
➤ 42 states & 3 foreign countries represented
➤ 221 undergraduate schools represented

■ Faculty

➤ 89 total   ➤ 43 full-time   ➤ 33 full-/part-time women
➤ 6 minority

A young vibrant faculty, devoted to high quality teaching, are leading contributors to innovative research and practical legal education.

"We teach people how to be lawyers as well as how to think like them," says Professor Bill Lynch. "Students learn the practical side of becoming an attorney so that when they graduate they can practice the profession immediately and competently."

■ Library and Physical Facilities

➤ 265,077 volumes & equivalents   ➤ library hours:
7:00 A.M.-MIDNIGHT   ➤ LEXIS   ➤ NEXIS
➤ WESTLAW   ➤ DIALOG   ➤ 7 full-time librarians
➤ library seats 457   ➤ student computer center
➤ laptop computer room

Modern computer technology is strongly supported, with a sophisticated student LAN. Every student has Internet access.

■ Curriculum

➤ Academic Support Program   ➤ 89 credits required to graduate   ➤ 120 courses available   ➤ degrees available: J.D. & J.D./M.S.W.   ➤ starts in Aug. or Jan.   ➤ first-year class size—fall, 275; spring, 50   ➤ fall class divided into three sections   ➤ mid-year class starts spring trimester (Jan.)

Students have many options with the part-time division or the flexible trimester system, whereby students can graduate in two, two-and-one-half, or three years.

■ International Legal Studies Program

Publishing the third oldest *International Law Journal* in the United States, California Western also has one of the best collections of international, comparative, and foreign law resource materials in the Southwest.

■ Clinical Internship Program

Our nationally recognized program trains students in lawyering skills and provides the opportunity to put their academic skills into practice immediately. There are many opportunities locally and out of town. Jon Yonemitsu '97, who interned for the U.S. District Court, comments: "One of my best experiences in law school...gives you the opportunity to apply what you learn in the classroom and it is a good stepping stone to a permanent job."

■ Graduate Program

A dual-degree program with San Diego State University allows students to earn both the J.D. and M.S.W. with an emphasis on child welfare. Students can also take courses in other areas to enhance their legal education.

■ Specialty Courses and Programs

Strong programs in: international law, family law, advocacy, employment law, business law, telecommunications. Institutes include: Telecommunications Law Institute, the Interdisciplinary Training Program in Child Welfare, the Institute for Criminal Defense Advocacy, and the McGill Center for Creative Problem Solving. Specialty law courses include biotechnology, environmental, sports, entertainment, and health.

■ Summer Enrichment Program

A six-week law school class introducing you to the tasks of a law student and a better understanding of law school. Students admitted to California Western will receive three units of credit upon successful completion of the course. Students admitted to other law schools and college juniors and seniors may also enroll.

■ Admission Standards

➤ Bachelor's degree required   ➤ application deadline—fall class, April 1; spring class, Nov. 1
➤ LSAT, LSDAS required   ➤ application fee—$45

"Admission is competitive," according to Assistant Dean for Admissions Nancy Ramsayer, "but applicants receive full consideration by reviewing each file carefully." Performance on the LSAT and the academic record are the most important factors. However, substantial consideration is given to other factors such as work experience, personal achievements, and volunteer service.

■ Commitment to Ethnic and Cultural Diversity

California Western actively recruits students from current underrepresented groups in the legal profession. According to Director of Diversity Services, Carol Rogers, "Our institutional commitment to diversity resulted in 36 percent minority representation in the fall '98 class."

The academic support program includes (1) a two-week, skills-oriented class; (2) tutorials offered throughout the first year via small group and individual sessions; and (3) academic counseling.

■ Housing

The Housing Office works closely with students to locate attractive, convenient housing, assist with roommates, and offer information on services associated with relocation.

■ Student Activities

➡ *Publications include: Law Review (top 10%), International Law Journal, and Telecommunications Law Journal.*

Students share a spirit of cooperation. Study groups, the center of academic and emotional support, are common.

Students who relish the challenge of competition will find ample opportunity through appellate advocacy or trial competitions. Our teams consistently place in regional and national competitions.

■ Expenses and Financial Aid

➡ *tuition & fees—full-time, $20,500 + $70 (fees)*
➡ *estimated additional expenses—books, $650; rent, utilities, food, $6,850; transportation, $1,880; personal/misc., $3,740*

➡ *scholarships available: Academic Scholars Program, Scholarships for Ethnic & Cultural Diversity, Career Transition Scholarship, J.D. Scholarship for Librarians*
➡ *financial aid available*   ➡ *FAFSA need form required*

"Being a free-standing law school is a real advantage for us," says Financial Aid Executive Director Kyle Poston. "Law students are our only priority."

■ Career Services

Maximizing technological resources to facilitate career development and job searching, the Office of Career Services offers individual professional advice to each student about their own personal career interests and tailors strategies to meet those particular interests. "With on-campus recruiting programs, a vibrant practice area panel discussion series, extensive workshop offerings, a national alumni mentor program, a well-recognized Pro Bono Honors Program, and a wide range of valuable career resources, the Career Services Office received an "A" from our student newspaper, and does all within its power to help you achieve your professional goals," states Director Lou Helmuth.

■ Alumni

California Western has over 5,000 alumni located throughout the world. The Alumni Admissions Recruiter Program links alumni with prospective students in the area where they reside.

Applicant Group for the 1998-1999 Academic Year

California Western School of Law

LSAT Score	3.75 +		3.50 - 3.74		3.25 - 3.49		3.00 - 3.24		2.75 - 2.99		2.50 - 2.74		2.25 - 2.49		2.00 - 2.24		Below 2.00		No GPA		Totals	
	Apps	Adm	Apps	Adm	Apps	Adm	Apps	Adm	Apps	Adm	Apps	Adm	Apps	Adm	Apps	Adm	Apps	Adm	Apps	Adm	Apps	Adm
170-180	0	0	0	0	0	0	1	1	1	1	1	1	0	0	0	0	0	0	0	0	3	3
165-169	1	1	3	2	1	1	0	0	0	0	2	2	1	1	1	1	0	0	0	0	9	8
160-164	6	5	6	6	17	16	8	8	11	11	8	7	3	3	7	7	1	1	0	0	67	64
155-159	10	10	16	16	42	42	42	41	51	47	40	38	15	14	7	6	1	1	3	1	227	216
150-154	14	14	46	46	83	82	105	105	107	106	73	68	39	28	12	4	1	0	6	6	486	459
145-149	11	11	24	23	74	69	100	90	93	70	81	43	42	9	11	0	5	0	8	2	449	317
140-144	3	3	14	13	33	24	50	21	66	19	59	2	30	2	19	1	0	0	5	2	279	87
Below 140	1	0	4	0	8	2	16	2	18	0	22	0	23	0	9	0	6	0	1	0	108	4
Total	46	44	113	106	258	236	322	268	342	254	286	181	153	57	66	19	14	2	23	11	1628	1158

Apps = Number of Applicants
Adm = Number Admitted
Applicants with 120-180 LSAT scores earned under standard administrations   1,628
Miscellaneous applicants with no LSAT, nonstandard administration   6   (not in grid)
TOTAL   1,634

Campbell University—Norman Adrian Wiggins School of Law

P.O. Box 158
Buies Creek, NC 27506

Phone: 910.893.1754 or 1.800.334.4111

■ Introduction

Campbell University, Norman Adrian Wiggins School of Law admitted its charter class in August 1976. The School of Law was accredited by the North Carolina State Bar in 1978 and the American Bar Association in 1979.

Campbell University is located in the rural village of Buies Creek, 30 miles south of Raleigh, the state capital, and 30 miles north of Fayetteville—two of the most rapidly growing urban areas in the nation. Founded in 1887, the university's 1,450-acre campus offers programs for approximately 1,800 undergraduate and 800 graduate students.

While Campbell is a Southern Baptist university and establishment of the School of Law was conceived as a Christian mission, neither the School of Law nor the university, which also maintains a campus in Kuala Lumpur, Malaysia, is sectarian in the narrow sense of the word.

■ Enrollment/Student Body

➥ *655 applicants* ➥ *204 admitted first-year class 1998*
➥ *111 enrolled first-year class 1998* ➥ *full-time 25th/75th percentile GPA—2.96/3.49* ➥ *full-time 25th/75th percentile LSAT—152/156* ➥ *323 total full-time* ➥ *8% minority*
➥ *45% women*

■ Faculty

➥ *35 total* ➥ *20 full-time* ➥ *15 part-time or adjunct*
➥ *5 women*

■ Library and Physical Facilities

➥ *156,342 volumes & equivalents* ➥ *library hours:*
Mon.-Thurs., 7:00 A.M.-MIDNIGHT; Fri., 7:00 A.M.-11:00 P.M.;
Sat., 8:00 A.M.-6:00 P.M.; Sun., NOON-MIDNIGHT
➥ *LEXIS* ➥ *NEXIS* ➥ *WESTLAW*
➥ *1 full-time librarian* ➥ *library seats 414*

The School of Law is located in historic Kivett Hall in the center of the Campbell campus.

■ Curriculum

➥ *90 credits required to graduate*
➥ *degrees available: J.D./M.B.A.* ➥ *semesters, start in Aug.*

The law school conducts a seven-week summer session and does not operate a part-time program. A majority of the total hours of study consists of required courses. A broad range of electives, usually including several seminars of 10 or fewer students, is available. The curriculum has been carefully planned to coalesce the practical and theoretical. Jurisprudence is a required subject, and one-third of the third-year curriculum is devoted to an innovative advocacy and practice course designed to bridge the gap between law school and law practice. Fulfillment of an advanced writing requirement and completion of one of several planning courses are also prerequisites for graduation.

■ Special Programs

Campbell's first-year program is designed to maximize the opportunity for success in law school and law practice. Over one-half of the first-year classes are sectioned, ensuring an average size of 45 to 50 students in most classes, with each student participating in one section of only 25 students. Legal research and writing clinics of nine or ten students each are directed by teaching assistants under the supervision of faculty members.

The North Carolina State Bar's rule allows Campbell's second-year students to prosecute misdemeanors in state courts in conjunction with required criminal procedure and introductory trial advocacy courses.

Students also have the option of pursuing a J.D. and M.B.A. degree concurrently through a special arrangement with the Lundy-Fetterman School of Business at Campbell University.

In 1986, Campbell won the American College of Trial Lawyer's Emil Gumpert Award for the most outstanding trial advocacy program in the nation.

■ Admission

➥ *B.A./B.S. required* ➥ *rolling admission*
➥ *LSAT, LSDAS required* ➥ *application fee—$40*

Admission to the School of Law is granted on the basis of the faculty Admission Committee's evaluation of the probable contributions of the applicant to society and the legal profession. In an attempt to select objectively those who most possess traits essential for success in the practice of law, Campbell utilizes a comprehensive application questionnaire, including the LSAT/LSDAS reports and writing sample, and requires a personal interview as a prerequisite to admission.

Although a baccalaureate degree is generally required, students who have completed three-fourths of the work acceptable for the baccalaureate are also eligible to apply.

Each year, approximately 300 of those in the pool of qualified applicants are granted personal interviews. About 80 percent of those invited for interviews are selected on the basis of grade-point averages and LSAT scores, the balance primarily because of nonquantifiable factors. In past years, from 40 to 54 percent of those interviewed have been extended invitations for admission. Factors considered by the Admission Committee include the applicant's GPA, LSAT score, work experience, maturity, intellectual honesty, innovativeness, leadership, self-reliance, ability to overcome obstacles, pleasantness of personality, demonstrated moral and physical courage, sophistication in the sense of being able to function in varied contexts, and potential for unusual contributions to society.

■ Performance-based Admission Program

Since 1977, the School of Law has conducted a performance-based admission program during its summer session. Approximately 70 applicants take two regular law school courses for a total of six credit hours in the seven-week session. Students making a superior grade in each of the two courses are guaranteed positions in the first-year class in the fall. Students not making superior grades, but achieving a satisfactory average, are placed on a waiting list with qualified applicants not participating in the program. Performance in the program is a factor considered by the Admission Committee in filling vacancies from the waiting list.

■ Minority Admissions

The School of Law actively recruits minority students. Campbell's personalized admission and educational programs, equally available to minority and nonminority applicants and students, have resulted in the admission of minority students whose academic achievements have far surpassed projected class standing based solely on the LSAT/GPA statistics.

■ Student Activities

A chief goal in structuring a small law school was to afford every student an opportunity for meaningful participation in cocurricular activities. The student-edited *Campbell Law Review* was established in 1978. Students also publish the *Campbell Law Observer*, the nation's only student-edited newspaper for the legal profession, the circulation of which includes 10,000 North Carolina lawyers. The school has a full program of moot court activities, and students participate in regional and national moot court and trial court competitions. Delta Theta Phi and Phi Alpha Delta legal fraternities have established chapters at

Campbell, as have Women in Law, the Law Students Civil Rights Research Council, and the Christian Legal Society. The Student Bar Association maintains an extensive speakers program and coordinates student participation in law school activities. Law Partners is an organization composed of spouses of law students. The law school maintains an active intramural program, running its own basketball league and participating in university leagues in other sports. Golf tournaments are held on the campus at Keith Hills Golf Club, one of North Carolina's outstanding golf courses.

■ Expenses and Financial Aid

➡ *full-time tuition & fees—$16,500*   ➡ *10 full-tuition scholarships, partial scholarships, research & teaching assistantships available*   ➡ *minority scholarships available*
➡ *extensive financial aid program, including work-study, Law Student Assured Access, and National Director Student Loans*

The cost of living in Buies Creek and the surrounding communities is low by national and urban standards.

■ Career Services

The placement office corresponds with over 1,800 employers. About 98 percent of all Campbell law school alumni have passed at least one state bar examination. Approximately 10 to 20 alumni are admitted to the U.S. Supreme Court Bar yearly.

Applicant Profile Not Available

Capital University Law School

303 E. Broad St.
Columbus, OH 43215-3200

E-Mail: admissions@law.capital.edu
URL: http://www.law.capital.edu
Phone: 614.236.6310, Fax: 614.236.6972

■ Introduction

Capital University Law School, located in downtown Columbus, is in the heart of Ohio's legal community. Columbus is home to the Ohio Supreme Court, the state legislature, and numerous state agencies including the Ohio Attorney General's Office. In addition, a Federal District Court, the Ohio Court of Appeals, and various trial courts are within a short walk of the Law School. Our location provides a wealth of learning opportunities, through clinical and externship programs, and our new facility affords Capital University law students a state-of-the-art law school that is second to none.

As Capital University Law School prepares to celebrate its 100th year of excellence in educating lawyers, we invite you to take a closer look at the factors that distinguish this law school: an excellent teaching faculty, an ideal location, high placement rates, innovative institutes and programs, distinguished alumni, and reasonable tuition. As a result of its excellence, Capital enjoys full accreditation with the American Bar Association and membership in the Association of American Law Schools.

■ Enrollment/Student Body

➠ *836 applicants*   ➠ *420 admitted first-year day class 1999*
➠ *252 enrolled first-year class 1999*   ➠ *full-time 25th/75th percentile GPA—2.80/3.33*   ➠ *part-time 25th/75th percentile GPA—2.82/3.33*   ➠ *full-time 25th/75th percentile LSAT—146/154*   ➠ *part-time 25th/75th percentile LSAT—145/154*
➠ *430 total full-time*   ➠ *335 total part-time*
➠ *11% minority*   ➠ *45% women*   ➠ *40 states & foreign countries represented*   ➠ *150 undergraduate schools represented*

The Law School actively encourages applications from minority students, women, and students with disabilities, and admits without regard to race, creed, national origin, or gender.

■ Faculty

➠ *31 total full-time*   ➠ *53 part-time or adjunct*
➠ *9 women*   ➠ *4 minority*

■ Library and Physical Facilities

➠ *237,500 volumes & equivalents*   ➠ *24-hour access to law library*   ➠ *LEXIS*   ➠ *NEXIS*   ➠ *WESTLAW*
➠ *INFOTRAC*   ➠ *5 full-time librarians*

■ Curriculum

➠ *Academic Success Program*   ➠ *86 credits required to graduate*   ➠ *approx. 150 courses available*
➠ *degrees available: J.D.; J.D./M.B.A.; J.D./M.S. in Nursing; J.D./Masters of Sports Administration; J.D./LL.M. in Taxation; LL.M. in Business & Taxation; M.T. in Taxation*
➠ *semesters, start in Aug.*   ➠ *class sizes: 75-85 students per class in day program; 90-100 students per class in evening program; 25-30 students in legal writing sections*

The school's primary mission is to provide both day and evening division students with an excellent educational experience that combines competency-based legal education with a commitment to service and leadership in the profession and broader community. Capital is a forward-looking school. It combines a theoretical education with a program that emphasizes the skills and values necessary to practice in the 21st century, and combines the best of a traditional legal education with innovative programs. Our professors are accomplished scholars whose first and foremost duty is teaching.

For further details and specific course offerings, please consult the Law School viewbook available upon request.

■ Multicultural Affairs

Capital University Law School opened the doors to diversity nearly a century ago, and we continue to make gender, racial, ethnic, religious, and political diversity a priority in our faculty and administration as well as in our student body. Capital has many programs to aid in the retention of minority students; these include the presence of minority faculty, a director of multicultural affairs, availability of financial resources, and academic and nonacademic support as well as placement opportunities through the minority clerkship program.

■ Special Programs

Diversity of opportunity is a trademark of Capital University Law. Indicative of that trait are the certificate programs Capital offers in Governmental Affairs; Labor & Employment; Small Business Entities; Publicly-Held Companies; Dispute Resolution; and Environmental Law.

By devoting a portion of their studies to one of these areas, students may concentrate on developing their skills and knowledge in an area of particular interest to them. Further, students can take advantage of Capital's nationally known faculty and their experience in these areas to target career preparations.

Innovative programs give students an opportunity to explore various specialties within the legal profession, to improve their skills, and to provide a valuable service to the community. **The Institute for Citizen Education**'s Street Law Program uses Capital law students as instructors and role models in elementary and secondary school classrooms. As a result, thousands of Columbus area youngsters, including disadvantaged and minority youth, have a better understanding of the law and how it operates in their lives.

The Institute for International Education has made Capital the scene of a variety of projects, conferences, and ongoing activities related to international comparative law through its sister-school relationships with law schools in Scotland, Canada, and Germany; its Greek Summer Program; and the Study Abroad at Home Program.

The Center for Dispute Resolution is a multifaceted resource for the teaching, development, and implementation of various dispute resolution methods.

The Dave Thomas Center for Adoption Law at Capital, the first resource of its kind in the nation, creates programs and promotes activities focusing on all aspects of family law dealing with adoption.

Capital University offers the four following joint-degree programs:

In order to offer a joint **J.D./Master of Sports Admini-stration/Facility Management Degree**, Capital University has entered into agreement with Ohio University, one of the pioneers in the field of sports administration. This program allows a student to participate in one of the nation's most reputable sports administration programs while earning a law degree.

The Law School and the Graduate School of Administration cooperatively offer a joint **J.D./Master of Business Administration**. The curriculum allows simultaneous enrollment in both schools, and reduces by 18 hours the credits required for separate J.D. and M.B.A. degrees.

Capital's School of Nursing, in conjunction with the Law School, offers a joint **J.D./Masters of Science in Nursing Degree**. A graduate with a M.N.S./J.D. is exceptionally well prepared to address the needs of a health care system that require technical competence, compassionate care, and public accountability.

Under the combined **J.D./LL.M. in Taxation**, a student who has had Federal Personal Income Tax (FPIT) may take 12 hours in advanced tax courses while pursuing a J.D. degree. Upon graduation the student could matriculate and complete the LL.M. degree in one semester of full-time study (12 credit hours).

■ Admission

➡ *Bachelor's degree required for admission*
➡ *application deadline—May 1*   ➡ *LSAT, LSDAS required*
➡ *application fee—$35*

The Law School seeks applicants who ranked in the upper half of their undergraduate class and achieved an LSAT score above the 50th percentile. Other factors used in evaluation include the competitiveness and difficulty of the candidate's undergraduate school and course of study, any graduate coursework, employment history, writing ability, and general background.

■ Expenses and Financial Aid

➡ *tuition & fees—first-year full-time, $15,370; first-year part-time, $10,070*   ➡ *estimated additional expenses— $10,898 (includes books & living expenses)*   ➡ *merit-based scholarships; need- & merit-based grants available*
➡ *minority scholarships available (see viewbook)*
➡ *financial aid available; work-study, student loans, research assistants, & teaching assistants*
➡ *FAFSA required; forms are available after Jan. 1*

■ Student Activities

There are associations for African American, Hispanic, Asian, and Jewish students. The school has a Fellowship of Christian Law Students, a Women's Law Society, an International Law Society, three legal fraternities, as well as organizations for those interested in specific areas of the law.

■ Career Services

The Career Services Office provides counseling and information so individuals can explore the myriad of legal career options and make informed decisions about their future. It also serves as a resource to help students assess their skills and plan a productive job search strategy. The office also is responsible for developing an on-campus interview program and helping students "network" with employers.

Applicant Group for the 1998-1999 Academic Year

Capital University Law School

LSAT Score	GPA								
	3.75 +	3.50 - 3.74	3.25 - 3.49	3.00 - 3.24	2.75 - 2.99	2.50 - 2.74	2.25 - 2.49	2.00 - 2.24	Below 2.00
175-180									
170-174									
165-169									
160-164									
155-159									
150-154									
145-149									
140-144									
135-139									
130-134									
125-129									
120-124									

	Very Likely		Possible		Unlikely

Case Western Reserve University School of Law

11075 East Boulevard
Cleveland, OH 44106

E-Mail: lawadmissions@po.cwru.edu
URL: http://lawwww.cwru.edu/
Phone: 216.368.3600, 800.756.0036

■ Introduction

For more than 100 years, the law school has prepared men and women for leadership in the practice of law, public service, and commerce. Today our alumni are serving society in prominent positions throughout the nation and the world; their continuing interest in this school is embodied in generous scholarships and employment opportunities that benefit current students. Founded in 1892, the school is a charter member of the AALS and was among the first schools accredited by the ABA.

■ 1998 Entering Class

➡ 1,277 applicants   ➡ 201 enrolled
➡ full-time 25th/75th percentile GPA—2.99/3.50
➡ full-time 25th/75th percentile LSAT—153/161
➡ 10% students of color   ➡ 49% women   ➡ 33 states & foreign countries represented   ➡ 121 undergraduate schools represented   ➡ 46% outside Ohio

■ Curriculum and Faculty

➡ 105 courses available   ➡ degrees available: J.D./M.B.A. (Management); J.D./M.S.S.A. (Social Work); J.D./M.N.O. (Nonprofit Management); J.D./M.A. (Legal History); J.D./M.A. (Bioethics); J.D./M.D. (Medicine)   ➡ range of first-year class size—26-75   ➡ student-to-faculty ratio—14 to 1

The size and breadth of our curriculum offer students great flexibility, whether they choose to concentrate in an area or pursue a broader course of study. Students benefit from a powerful combination of theoretical learning and practical skills training that will provide a foundation for their careers. Our primary emphasis throughout the curriculum is on development of analytical, problem solving, and written and oral communication skills. Our faculty take their responsibility of educating tomorrow's leaders very seriously. Graduates often cite our faculty's commitment to excellent teaching and accessibility to our students—long a tradition at our school—as one of the most enriching and valuable aspects of their legal education.

■ Career Services

Our students' exposure to our Career Services Office begins during their very first semester, when they will meet one-on-one with one of our career counselors (all experienced attorneys) to begin to develop a plan for attaining their goals. Our extensive programs are designed to assist students in obtaining both summer employment and their first post-law school job, as well as helping them to develop skills to achieve long-term goals. Services provided include a comprehensive Career Services Guide, career options and résumé, cover letter and interview counseling, workshops on topics ranging from interviewing skills to obtaining a judicial clerkship to pursuing nontraditional careers, alumni mentor and mock interview

programs, an extensive on-campus interview program, participation in many off-campus job fairs, and computer access to state-of-the-art job search tools. The outstanding reputation of our school is reflected in the placement of our graduates throughout the country, in private practice, public service, and business.

■ Library and Physical Facilities

➡ 358,621 volumes & equivalents   ➡ LEXIS/NEXIS
➡ WESTLAW   ➡ CD-ROMS available on campus network: over 100 titles, most full-text   ➡ access to over 700 electronic services and library catalogs

Our award-winning law school building is handsome, contemporary, and comfortable. The law school is located in the heart of University Circle, one of the largest and richest cultural and educational centers in the nation, just 20 minutes away from downtown. The library's collection includes an extensive British collection and special collections in taxation, labor law, foreign investments, law-medicine, and international law. The library's professional and support staff places a heavy emphasis on assisting those who use the facilities. If we don't have what students need, we will get it. We have focused on the integration of modern technology with traditional research methods.

■ Professional Skills Program

Our skills training program is second to none. From the first-year Research, Analysis, and Writing ("RAW") program, which is uniquely designed to give them the communications tools that they need to distinguish themselves when they begin work, through upper-level courses such as The Lawyering Process, Appellate Advocacy, and Trial Tactics, culminating in our law clinic, students benefit from a cohesive, unified theory of how law ought to be practiced. The law clinic, with its student-faculty ratio of 9 to 1, operates as a modern law office right within the law school. Third-year students represent real clients in real cases, handling all aspects of the cases from intake to adjudication.

■ The Law-Medicine Center

Our long-established Law-Medicine Center focuses on the whole range of legal, social, economic, scientific, and ethical issues in which law and medicine are interrelated. The center also sponsors lectures, major conferences, and small forums, and is involved in the journal *Health Matrix* (see below).

■ International Law Program

We are preparing our students for a global practice in the 21st century. Our International Law Center has enabled us to strengthen even further our international law curriculum, sponsor visiting scholars from around the world, and provide study and work abroad opportunities for our students. The *Journal of International Law* is student-edited (see below). In addition, the Canada-U.S. Law Institute and the North American Legal Studies Program provide law students with the opportunity for work and study abroad.

■ Student Activities and Leadership

The school sponsors three student-edited scholarly journals—the *Case Western Reserve Law Review*; the *Journal of International Law*; and *Health Matrix: The Journal of Law-Medicine*. Our student Moot Court Board sponsors an intramural competition and three interscholastic competitions. A fourth moot court competition, the Jessup Competition, is administered by the Society of International Law Students. Finally, we have an intramural/extramural mock trial program. Our students bring intellectual talent, energy, and life experience to our law school community and are the driving force behind the many curricular and cocurricular activities that we support. There are over 40 professional, social, and academic student organizations supported by the Student Bar Association, reflecting the wide range of interest of our students. A partial listing includes: the Black Law Students Association; Women's Law Association; Student International Law Society; National Lawyers Guild; Student Public Interest Law Fellowship; LAMBDA; Second Career Students; Environmental Law Society; Jewish Law Students Association; and several legal fraternities.

■ Graduate Law Study

Our **LL.M. in United States Legal Studies** provides graduates from foreign law schools the opportunity to study the U.S. legal system and institutions. Students have weekly seminars on international business transactions with area practitioners and are paired with a student mentor and a practitioner mentor from a Cleveland firm or corporation.

The **LL.M. in Taxation** is designed as a part- or full-time program for practicing professionals who wish to gain a thorough understanding of the nation's increasingly complex tax laws and be better able to advise clients, particularly those involved in complicated transactions.

■ Admission

➡ *Bachelor's degree required* ➡ *application deadline—April 1*
➡ *LSAT, LSDAS required* ➡ *application fee—$40*

Our admission process is selective (and, as a result, the attrition rate is negligible). We weigh not only grade-point averages and LSAT scores, but also nonquantitative factors. Our standards are rigorous, but not rigid. We accept applications as early as October for admission in the following fall; our deadline is April 1, although early applicants have the best chance for admission and scholarships. As decisions are made, candidates are notified; most decisions are made between January 1 and May 15.

■ Expenses and Financial Aid

➡ *tuition & fees—full-time, $20,540; part-time/credit unit, $854* ➡ *estimated additional expenses—$5,365/semester (books, room & board, living expenses)* ➡ *scholarships available: merit-based scholarships & diversity grants* ➡ *financial aid loan programs available*

Thanks to the enthusiastic support of our alumni, we benefit from one of the largest endowments of any law school, enabling us to provide significant scholarship support to around one-quarter of each entering class. Our merit-based scholarships and diversity grants range in value. Each year, 10 exceptional entering students receive a full-tuition scholarship. In addition, we participate in government financial aid programs.

Applicant Group for the 1998-1999 Academic Year

Case Western Reserve University School of Law
This grid includes only applicants who earned 120-180 LSAT scores.

LSAT Score	GPA							
	3.75 +	3.50 - 3.74	3.25 - 3.49	3.00 - 3.24	2.75 - 2.99	2.50 - 2.74	Below 2.50	No GPA
164-180								
161-163								
158-159								
156-157								
154-155								
152-153								
150-151								
120-149								

■ Good Possibility   ■ Possibility   □ Slight Possibility

The Catholic University of America—Columbus School of Law

Office of Admissions
Washington, DC 20064

E-Mail: sokatch@law.edu
URL: http://www.law.edu
Phone: 202.319.5151

■ Introduction

Founded in 1897, the Columbus School of Law is located on the 154-acre campus of the university. Students and faculty have access to unique legal resources: the Supreme Court, the Congress, the United States and District of Columbia courts, and federal, executive, and administrative departments. Yet, while offering the advantages of the nation's capital, the campus is located in a pleasant, non-commercial area, and offers the scenic atmosphere of a suburban school. Classes are small and personal.

Although Catholic has religious affiliation, the school welcomes students of all religious, racial, and ethnic backgrounds to a program that emphasizes a commitment to community service and the ethical practice of law. The school has been a member of the AALS since 1921, and approved by the ABA since 1925.

■ Enrollment/Student Body

➡ 2,116 applicants   ➡ 1,062 admitted first-year class 1998
➡ 292 enrolled first-year class 1998   ➡ full-time 25th/75th percentile GPA—2.80/3.40   ➡ part-time 25th/75th percentile GPA—2.50/3.10   ➡ full-time 25th/75th percentile LSAT—151/157   ➡ part-time 25th/75th percentile LSAT—151/156
➡ 643 total full-time   ➡ 259 total part-time
➡ 19.6% minority   ➡ 49% women
➡ 50 states & foreign countries represented
➡ 276 undergraduate schools represented
➡ fewer than 50 percent of students enter directly from college

The first-year day and evening classes are sectioned in such a way that individual courses have 32 to 70 students. Upper-class courses range from 10 to 70 students. Individual faculty members are available for informal sessions, thus providing a personalized education.

■ Faculty

➡ 135 total   ➡ 47 full-time   ➡ 88 part-time or adjunct
➡ 15 women (full-time)   ➡ 7 minority (full-time)

The faculty brings a broad range of interests and experience to the academic setting. The adjunct faculty and professorial lecturers are selected from among local judges and practitioners for their expertise in given areas of law.

■ Library and Physical Facilities

➡ 300,000 volumes & equivalents   ➡ library hours: Mon.-Fri., 7:00 A.M.-11:45 P.M.; Sat. & Sun., 9:00 A.M.-11:45 P.M.
➡ LEXIS   ➡ NEXIS   ➡ WESTLAW   ➡ DIALOG
➡ computer lab, computer-equipped carrels
➡ 3 VCR playback rooms   ➡ 9 full-time librarians
➡ library seats 502

The Library of Congress and specialized law collections throughout the city complement the law school's legal collections. A new law school facility, completed in 1994, houses all components of the law school. It combines contemporary style with the rich architectural history of the campus. Law students have full access to other campus facilities, including a 40-acre athletic complex with pool, Nautilus equipment, sauna, tennis courts, and track.

■ Curriculum

➡ Academic Support Program   ➡ Law and Public Policy Program   ➡ 84 credits required to graduate
➡ 153 courses available   ➡ degrees available: J.D.; J.D./M.L.S.; J.D./M.S.W.; J.D./M.A.   ➡ semesters, start in Aug.
➡ range of first-year class size—32-70
➡ Comparative and International Law Institute
➡ Institute for Communications Law Studies
➡ Corporate and Securities Law Concentration

The prescribed first-year curriculum and method of teaching are designed to develop the analytical skills that characterize the able lawyer and to give the student familiarity with the major substantive areas of law. While lawyers traditionally have been heavily involved with the commercial interests of private or corporate clients, law is becoming increasingly responsive to problems that affect the public interest. The law school curriculum is designed to provide students with the basic knowledge to become effective lawyers in a changing legal environment.

■ Special Programs

The Institute for Communications Law Studies offers unique specialized training in communications law. The Institute currently offers nine courses and related externships to students who will receive the J.D. degree and a certificate from the Institute.

The Comparative and International Law Institute offers a concentration of courses in the public and private areas of international law. Externships and paid employment are also available in these areas. The institute also offers a six-week Summer Abroad Program at the Jagiellonian University in Cracow, Poland.

The Law and Public Policy Program uniquely combines classroom studies in legislative and administrative processes with externships in government agencies and advocacy organizations that affect national public policy.

■ Clinical Programs

The law school offers seven clinical programs, including five that emphasize client representation, case planning, and trial and administrative advocacy. The other two clinical offerings are: the Securities and Exchange Commission Training Program and the Legal Externship Program.

■ Admission

➡ Bachelor's degree from an accredited college or university required   ➡ application deadline—March 1
➡ LSAT, LSDAS required   ➡ application fee—$55
➡ admission decisions are made beginning in Dec. & continue until the class is filled

While heavy consideration is given to the applicant's grade-point average and LSAT scores, decisions are influenced by such other factors as leadership qualities, rank in class, improving performance, academic standards of the undergraduate school, the curriculum, potential for contributing to diversity, relevant work experience, and evidence of factors that adversely affected the student's grades. Special consideration is given to applicants from disadvantaged groups.

The Preface Program, a three-week summer program, is offered to entering students whose credentials indicate that an intensive introduction to law school would be especially beneficial.

Student Activities

The *Catholic University Law Review*, the *Journal of Contemporary Health Law*, and *COMMLAW CONSPECTUS: Journal of Communications Law and Policy* are scholarly law journals staffed by outstanding students. The Moot Court Board conducts five major competitions and a number of intraschool competitions each academic year. The Honor Board administers the student-created honor code of ethical standards of personal and professional conduct. The Student Bar Association provides a channel for student opinion and selects representatives to participate as voting members of faculty committees. Other activities include the Thurgood Marshall American Inn of Court, Black Law Students Association, Women's Organization, Latin American Law Students Association, Jewish Law Students Association, Asian-Pacific American Law Students Association, and many other student-interest groups.

Expenses and Financial Aid

➡ *tuition & fees—full-time, $23,014; part-time, $17,556*
➡ *estimated additional expenses—(room, board, books, transportation)—$14,274* ➡ *performance- & need-based scholarships are available* ➡ *performance- & need-based minority scholarships are available* ➡ *financial aid available*
➡ *registration with Need Access and FAFSA is required*

Financial aid decisions are made beginning in March.

Career Services

The Office of Legal Career Services actively supports students and graduates in their search for employment by providing counseling as well as activities that facilitate direct placement. On-campus interviews are provided. The school's small size permits individual counseling for each student desiring assistance. Our admission brochure lists employment statistics, including distribution by type of practice and by geographic location.

Housing

Graduate housing is available on campus. A variety of apartments and private rooms are within easy traveling distance. The Admissions Office assists students in locating apartments and roommates. Our location is convenient to public transportation, including the metrorail system.

Applicant Group for the 1998-1999 Academic Year

The Catholic University of America—Columbus School of Law
This grid includes only applicants who earned 120-180 LSAT scores under standard administrations.

LSAT Score	3.75 +		3.50 - 3.74		3.25 - 3.49		3.00 - 3.24		2.75 - 2.99		2.50 - 2.74		2.25 - 2.49		2.00 - 2.24		Below 2.00		No GPA		Total	
	Apps	Adm	Apps	Adm	Apps	Adm	Apps	Adm	Apps	Adm	Apps	Adm	Apps	Adm	Apps	Adm	Apps	Adm	Apps	Adm	Apps	Adm
175-180	0	0	0	0	1	1	0	0	0	0	1	1	0	0	0	0	0	0	0	0	2	2
170-174	1	1	1	1	2	2	0	0	1	1	2	2	0	0	0	0	0	0	0	0	7	7
165-169	1	1	4	4	7	7	7	6	6	6	4	4	2	2	1	1	1	0	1	1	34	32
160-164	9	8	15	14	27	27	27	27	25	23	10	8	4	4	8	5	0	0	0	0	125	116
155-159	35	34	52	47	80	80	115	103	93	84	47	42	28	23	10	6	2	1	4	3	466	423
150-154	30	27	63	50	129	87	147	77	121	49	61	17	20	4	16	8	3	1	11	1	601	321
145-149	13	8	42	10	54	17	97	20	100	16	74	10	40	2	18	4	3	0	5	0	446	87
140-144	6	2	14	4	34	9	54	6	47	4	54	3	30	0	11	0	5	0	11	0	266	28
135-139	2	0	8	0	9	0	11	0	20	0	20	0	17	0	10	0	4	0	2	0	103	0
130-134	0	0	1	0	0	0	2	0	5	0	7	0	13	0	6	0	0	0	1	0	35	0
125-129	0	0	0	0	0	0	0	0	1	0	2	0	1	0	3	0	1	0	2	0	10	0
120-124	0	0	0	0	0	0	0	0	0	0	0	0	0	0	0	0	0	0	1	0	1	0
Total	97	81	200	130	343	230	460	239	419	183	282	87	155	35	83	24	19	2	38	5	2096	1016

Apps = Number of Applicants
Adm = Number Admitted
Reflects 99% of the total applicant pool.
This grid should be used only as a general guide, as many nonnumerical factors are considered in admission decisions.

Chapman University School of Law

1240 South State College Boulevard
Anaheim, CA 92806

E-Mail: lawadm@chapman.edu
URL: http://www.chapman.edu/law/
Phone: 888.242.1913

■ Introduction

Chapman University is located in the Historic Old Towne District of Orange, California. Established in 1861, the university offers highly respected undergraduate and graduate programs. Chapman's new law school, inaugurated in 1995, received provisional approval by the American Bar Association in only its third year of operation. This approval entitles Chapman students to the same recognition accorded students at fully approved ABA law schools, including the right to take the bar examination in all 50 states.

Located in dynamic Orange County, the nation's fifth most populous county with nearly 3 million people, the law school affords its students the opportunity to perform externships in appellate and trial courts, and to develop advocacy skills in practice courses taught by outstanding judges and trial lawyers. The new $30 million law school building, to be completed in spring 1999, provides state-of-the-art learning facilities in its classrooms, law library, and courtrooms.

Chapman University School of Law enjoys the advantages of being the only law school in Orange County located on a university campus, with full recreational, cultural, and dining privileges.

■ Enrollment/Student Body

➡ 385 applicants ➡ 131 admitted first-year class 1998
➡ 59 enrolled first-year class 1998 ➡ full-time 25th/75th percentile GPA—2.70/3.36 ➡ part-time 25th/75th percentile GPA—2.61/3.42 ➡ full-time 25th/75th percentile LSAT—146/153 ➡ part-time 25th/75th percentile LSAT—147/157 ➡ 74 total full-time ➡ 113 total part-time
➡ 26% minority ➡ 48% women
➡ 18 states & foreign countries represented
➡ 52 undergraduate schools represented

■ Faculty

➡ 32 total ➡ 17 full-time ➡ 15 part-time or adjunct
➡ 6 women ➡ 4 minority

■ Library and Physical Facilities

➡ 219,386 volumes & equivalents ➡ library hours:
Mon.-Thur., 8:00 A.M.-11:00 P.M.; Fri., 8:00 A.M.-8:00 P.M.;
Sat., 9:00 A.M.-9:00 P.M.; Sun., 10:00 A.M.-9:00 P.M.
➡ LEXIS ➡ NEXIS ➡ WESTLAW ➡ OCLC
➡ 6 full-time librarians ➡ library seats 162

Law library holdings exceed 219,000 volumes and volume equivalents, all purchased within the last four years. The collection is fully accessible to students both in hard copy and through the law school's computer network. Terminals for access to LEXIS and WESTLAW as well as CD-ROM stations are located conveniently in the library. In addition, students utilize a well-equipped computer laboratory featuring both PCs and MacIntosh computers. Brightly lighted and efficiently arranged, the library has ample

seating for law students as well as private study areas for extended research. The university continues to emphasize funding for law library acquisitions, ensuring steady growth of the collection and enhanced diversity of its holdings.

In the late spring of 1999, the law school will move into the new $30 million law school complex under construction on Chapman University's main campus in Orange. The principal building, rising four stories and providing 130,000-square feet of floor space, offers an efficient and pleasant learning environment for students. Classrooms and seminar rooms are equipped with state-of-the-art technology for enhanced teaching and learning. The law library occupies one wing of the building and individualizes the research process by offering students carrels equipped with outlets for laptop computers and related electronic devices. Two courtrooms, one designed for trials and the other for appellate hearings, provide fully equipped facilities for trial advocacy exercises, mock trial and moot court competitions, and formal hearings by visiting courts. Computer laboratories on the second and third floors of the library offer each student convenient access to research and word processing programs. In addition, a new 720-car parking structure at the rear of the law building provides ample parking for students, faculty, and visitors.

■ Curriculum

➡ Academic Support Program ➡ curricular emphasis available in Taxation & in Environmental, Land Use, and Real Estate Law ➡ Externship Program; U.S. Tax Court Clinic
➡ 88 credits required to graduate ➡ 51 courses available
➡ J.D. ➡ semesters ➡ range of first-year class size—20-40

■ Special Programs

The School of Law offers invaluable practical training through several curriculum-related programs that complement the theoretical classroom experience. These include:

The Externship Program—Students enrolled in this program are placed in the offices of appellate justices, trial judges, district attorneys, and public defenders where they gain practical experience in the legal profession. Supervised by a full-time, tenure-track professor, the students also complete a classroom component and prepare written assignments.

The United States Tax Court Clinic—An exciting clinical experience awaits students enrolled in this course. Under the guidance of an attorney, the students perform all tasks involved in the representation of claimants against the Internal Revenue Service.

Trial Advocacy—Chapman offers a range of advocacy experiences to its students, including participation in mock trial, moot court, client counseling, international law, and negotiation competitions. Law school teams have won regional competitions and have performed competitively in national tournaments.

In addition, Chapman is quickly developing distinctive competencies in the areas of environmental, land use, real estate law, and taxation law.

Admission

➼ *Bachelor's or equivalent*   ➼ *rolling admission*
➼ *LSAT, LSDAS required*   ➼ *application fee—$40*
➼ *first year students admitted for fall only*   ➼ *transfer & visiting students admitted both fall & spring semesters*

For 1999, Chapman law seeks to enroll about 110 well-qualified and highly talented students for its full- and part-time programs. There are no numerical cut-off points and every file is reviewed in its entirety by at least one member of the Admission Committee. The committee considers—in addition to LSAT and academic record—the applicant's work history, community service, personal background, including a history of overcoming difficulties and unusual contributions or experiences. Applicants must submit letters of recommendation (two are required) through the LSDAS service. Early application is encouraged as the class is filled on a rolling basis and scholarship funds may be exhausted late in the admission cycle.

Student Activities

The law school offers many student-administered, cocurricular activities that enrich the academic program and provide important training in leadership. Two journals, *Nexus* and the *Chapman Law Review*, offer valuable experience in research, writing, and editing. The Student Bar Association is the general organization for all students and administers a full range of programs. Other organizations include the Public Interest Law Foundation and the student-run Honor Council. The Moot Court Board and the Mock Trial Board administer their respective programs and provide excellent practical training to a large number of students each semester.

Expenses and Financial Aid

➼ *$625/credit hr. in 1998-99 for all students*
➼ *$11,900 (room, board, transportation, books, & personal)*
➼ *merit scholarships available based on entering academic profile & class rank*   ➼ *financial aid available, FAFSA required*

Career Services

The Career Services Office aids students in making career decisions and assists them in reaching their career goals. The office provides assistance to students in résumé preparation, interviewing skills, networking, and job-search strategies. Workshops are held throughout the academic year to educate students in these areas.

The Career Services Office works with faculty and student organizations to develop programs and workshops. A student/attorney mentor program in conjunction with the Orange County Bar Association and the graduates of Chapman University matches students with local practitioners.

The office is open two evenings per week to accommodate evening students.

Applicant Group for the 1998-1999 Academic Year

Chapman University School of Law

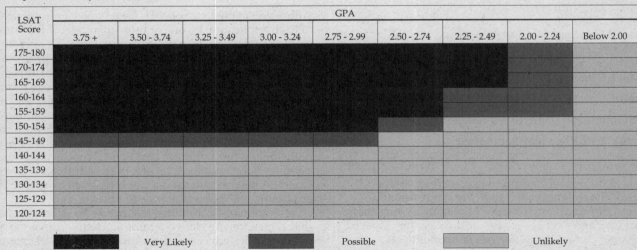

LSAT Score	GPA								
	3.75 +	3.50 - 3.74	3.25 - 3.49	3.00 - 3.24	2.75 - 2.99	2.50 - 2.74	2.25 - 2.49	2.00 - 2.24	Below 2.00
175-180									
170-174									
165-169									
160-164									
155-159									
150-154									
145-149									
140-144									
135-139									
130-134									
125-129									
120-124									

■ Very Likely   ■ Possible   ■ Unlikely

University of Chicago Law School

1111 E. 60th Street
Chicago, IL 60637

E-Mail: admissions@law.uchicago.edu
URL: http://www.law.uchicago.edu
Phone: 773.702.9484

■ Introduction

Legal education at the University of Chicago has long stressed the interdependence of legal and social studies in the training of lawyers. The school's program combines an emphasis on technical legal knowledge and professional skills with a concern for illuminating the connections between law and the social forces with which it interacts. Contributing to the first objective are opportunities for the application of formal knowledge to specific professional tasks. The school's model court facility provides students the opportunity to take part in moot trials and appellate arguments and to observe actual court sessions. A significant fraction of the faculty represents disciplines other than law, including economics, history, sociology, philosophy, and political science. The curriculum also devotes sub-stantial attention to relevant aspects of political theory, economics, legal history, comparative law, psychiatry, statistics, and other social science methodology. In addition to the student-edited University of Chicago *Law Review*, the University of Chicago *Legal Forum*, and the University of Chicago *Roundtable* the school is the home of four scholarly journals—*Supreme Court Review*; *Journal of Law and Economics*; *Journal of Legal Studies*; and *Crime and Justice: An Annual Review of Research*. It is also the home of the Center for Studies in Criminal Justice, the Legal History Program, the Law and Government Program, and the Law-Economics Program. The school is a charter member of the AALS and is on the approved list of the ABA.

■ Enrollment/Student Body

➡ *2,210 applicants*   ➡ *182 enrolled first-year class 1998*
➡ *full-time 25th/75th percentile GPA—3.55/3.81*
➡ *full-time 25th/75th percentile LSAT—167/171*
➡ *560 total full-time J.D.*   ➡ *40 graduate students*
➡ *19.5% minority*   ➡ *42% women*
➡ *46 states & 25 foreign countries represented*
➡ *182 undergraduate schools represented*

■ Faculty

➡ *49 full-time*   ➡ *39 part-time or adjunct*   ➡ *5 minority*

■ Library and Physical Facilities

➡ *628,000 volumes & equivalents*   ➡ *20 full-time library staff*

The Law School is located on the 203-acre, tree-lined campus of the university in Hyde Park, a residential community on the shore of Lake Michigan 15 minutes south of Chicago's business and cultural center. Most of the university's faculty, as well as its student body of 11,000, live in this community. The law quadrangle, designed by Eero Saarinen, consists of five connecting buildings surrounding an open court and reflecting pool. The library's collections are outstanding.

■ Curriculum

➡ *105 credits required to graduate*   ➡ *joint degrees offered*
➡ *quarters, begin in Sept.*   ➡ *typical upper-class curriculum: 70 courses (average size of 50 students) & 60 seminars (average size of 15 students)*

The basic program of study involves three years (nine quarters) of full-time study leading to the J.D. degree. Recesses between quarters occur in mid-December and mid-March. In addition to coursework, first-year students perform individual assignments under the direction of a tutor. The tutorial work emphasizes training in research, preparation of legal documents, and oral argument. Second- and third-year students are encouraged to substitute seminar work and individual research under faculty supervision for courses. Students may take a limited number of relevant courses in other departments of the university for credit toward the J.D. degree.

■ Special Programs

In cooperation with the Graduate School of Business, the Law School offers a joint program leading to the J.D. and M.B.A. degrees in four years. Joint programs in history, international relations, and economics are also available. The university's School of Public Policy Studies, which includes several Law School faculty members, offers a one-year program leading to the Master of Arts degree in public policy.

■ Admission

➡ *LSAT, LSDAS required*   ➡ *application fee—$60*
➡ *use evaluative interviews*

Admission to the Law School is based upon a careful review of each application by one or more members of the admis-sions committee. The committee considers all evidence that may indicate academic and professional promise. No automatic quantitative criteria are applied, although academic achievement as reflected in the college record and the evidence of intellectual ability provided by the LSAT are necessarily major determinants. The committee generally considers only a candidate's first LSAT score when multiple scores are presented unless a later score is substan-tially higher. Each year the Law School conducts evaluative interviews, by invitation, as part of the admissions process. One-year deferred admission will be granted to all admitted applicants who request it prior to June 15.

The admissions committee makes special efforts to ensure that each entering class contains students from a variety of geographic, educational, racial, and ethnic backgrounds, and is particularly interested in receiving applications from women and minority candidates, two groups that have traditionally been underrepresented in the profession.

■ Clinical Opportunities

A new clinical building, The Arthur Kane Center for Clinical Legal Education, was added to the Law School in 1998 and is the home for three clinical programs. The Mandel Legal Aid Clinic provides opportunities to learn litigation, lawyering, and other advocacy skills in five practice areas: criminal justice, employment discrimination, homeless assistance, mental health, and welfare work. The MacArthur Justice Center focuses on constitutional impact litigation in such areas as the death penalty, parole board discretion, and state public defender resources. The Clinic on Entrepreneurship provides a range of legal services, especially those for start-up businesses, to clients in economically disadvantaged communities. Every aspect of the clinical programs is the responsibility of students under the supervision of the nine clinical faculty members.

■ Student Activities

About 40 percent of the members of the second- and third-year classes in the Law School serve on one of the three student journals. They are selected on the basis of either academic achievement in the first year or performance in a writing competition open to all students and conducted each year. The Hinton Moot Court Committee conducts a two-year program in appellate advocacy open to all second- and third-year students. There are over 40 student organizations including a local chapter of the Black Law Students Association, Environmental Law Society, the Law Women's Caucus, the Federalist Society, International Comparative Law Society, the Law School Show, the Gay/Lesbian Law Students Association, Latino/a Law Students Association, and the Asian American Law Students Association.

■ Expenses and Financial Aid

➡ *tuition & fees—$25,149*
➡ *estimated additional expenses—$14,505 (living expenses)*

Through scholarship and loan funds, the Law School provides assistance to students who demonstrate financial need. Applicants for need-based scholarships must register with Need Access. The Law School also offers a number of merit scholarships that provide up to full tuition to a limited number of exceptional students.

■ Housing

A graduate residence hall, located two blocks from the Law School, is available for 140 graduate students from all areas of the university. Every first-year law student who wishes to do so, usually between 80 to 100 students, will live in this facility, which has mostly single rooms with private baths. The university has sufficient single and married student housing in Hyde Park to meet the needs of all students who request it. Campus buses run frequently during the day and evening between these buildings and the Law School.

■ Career Services

A full-time career services office assists students in obtaining permanent, summer, and part-time employment. During the 1998-1999 academic year, 350 employers scheduled interviews at the Law School. At the time of graduation, 97 percent of the class of 1998 was employed; 69 percent joined law firms, 26 percent obtained judicial clerkships, and the remainder were with government or legal services employers. Five graduates of the Law School clerked for justices on the United States Supreme Court during the 1998-1999 term. Ninety-nine percent of the class of 1999 and 89 percent of the class of 2000 had law-related positions during the summer of 1998.

Applicant Profile Not Available

Chicago-Kent College of Law—Illinois Institute of Technology

Office of Admissions and Financial Aid
565 West Adams Street
Chicago, IL 60661-3691

E-Mail: admitq@kentlaw.edu
URL: http://www.kentlaw.edu
Phone: 312.906.5020

■ Introduction

Chicago-Kent College of Law, Illinois Institute of Technology is nationally acclaimed for its innovative approaches to traditional legal education and its specialized programs within the law school curriculum.

The law school's unique affiliation with the Illinois Institute of Technology, one of the nation's largest scientific research centers, provides support for interdisciplinary programs including the Institute for Science, Law, and Technology; the Center for Law and Computers; and the certificate programs in Environmental and Energy Law and Intellectual Property Law.

Chicago-Kent is located in downtown Chicago, the heart of the city's commercial and legal communities. The new law school building, completed in 1992, is equipped with the latest technology and includes a four-story library and a complete courtroom. The college is fully accredited by the ABA and the AALS and is a member of the Order of the Coif.

■ Enrollment and Student Body

➼ *2,005 applicants* ➼ *832 total full-time* ➼ *344 total part-time* ➼ *17.3% minority* ➼ *49% women* ➼ *49 states & foreign countries represented* ➼ *294 enrolled first-year class 1998, day division* ➼ *108 enrolled first-year class 1998, evening division* ➼ *full-time 25th/75th percentile GPA—2.89/3.34* ➼ *part-time 25th/75th percentile GPA—2.64/3.32* ➼ *full-time 25th/75th percentile LSAT—150/157* ➼ *part-time 25th/75th percentile LSAT—148/156* ➼ *37% out-of-state in most recent entering class*

■ Faculty

➼ *178 total* ➼ *69 full-time* ➼ *109 part-time or adjunct* ➼ *52 women* ➼ *8 minority*

■ Library and Physical Facilities

➼ *530,000 volumes & equivalents* ➼ *library hours: Mon.-Thurs., 7:45 A.M.-11:00 P.M.; Fri., 7:45 A.M.-8:00 P.M.; Sat., 9:00 A.M.-8:00 P.M.; Sun., 10:00 A.M.-11:00 P.M.* ➼ *LEXIS* ➼ *NEXIS* ➼ *WESTLAW* ➼ *DIALOG* ➼ *EPIC* ➼ *ProQuest* ➼ *8 full-time librarians* ➼ *library seats 686*

The law library is among the largest national libraries. The collection includes the Library of International Relations and a wealth of material in environmental and energy law, intellectual property, international trade, and labor law.

An essential educational feature of the library and the classrooms is the extensive computer network in the building. Seats in the majority of classrooms, many library carrels, and numerous locations throughout the building are tied to the computer network, enabling students with their own laptop computers to connect into the network and the many legal databases. There are four computer laboratories with more than 100 personal computers reserved for student use.

Students have 24-hour access to the network and to LEXIS/NEXIS and WESTLAW through their home computers.

The new Marovitz Courtroom integrates design features from the best courtroom and trial advocacy training facilities in the nation.

■ Curriculum

➼ *Academic Support Program* ➼ *87 units/credits required to graduate* ➼ *over 100 courses offered each academic year* ➼ *degrees available: J.D.; J.D./M.B.A.; J.D./M.P.A.; J.D./LL.M. in Taxation; J.D./LL.M. in Financial Services Law; J.D./M.S. in Financial Markets & Trading; J.D./M.S. in Environmental Management; LL.M. in Taxation; LL.M. in Financial Services Law; LL.M. in International and Comparative Law* ➼ *range of first-year class size—30-100*

Day students usually complete the J.D. degree in three years. Evening students usually finish in four years. Students can transfer between divisions after completing their required courses in the division in which they originally enrolled.

■ Special Programs

Electronic Learning Project (E-Learn)—One-third of the students in the first-year class have color notebook computers with the electronic course materials for most of their classes. They can type notes directly into the materials, highlight crucial text in different colors, and create course outlines that contain their notes along with the highlighted materials.

Legal Research and Writing—Chicago-Kent has the most comprehensive legal research and writing program in the country. The three-year, five-course curriculum teaches students to analyze a wide range of legal problems and to write about them persuasively.

Environmental and Energy Law—The certificate program's interdisciplinary approach to the problems of environmental regulation and natural resources allocation prepares students for practice through a series of courses in law, economic and public policy analysis, and in the scientific aspects of environmental problems.

Clinical Education—The Law Offices of Chicago-Kent, one of the largest in-house clinical education programs in the country, offers eight clinical education programs that include civil, criminal, health, mediation, and tax law, and externships with government agencies and federal judges.

Trial Skills/Litigation and Alternative Dispute Resolution—The law school offers a two-semester sequence in trial advocacy and an intensive course. The courses are taught by skilled judges and experienced practitioners. There is a certificate program in Litigation and Alternative Dispute Resolution Studies.

International and Comparative Law—The certificate program encompasses study in international business and trade, international and comparative law, and international human rights. The Library of International Relations is one of few official depositories for United Nations and

European Community documents and the largest such public research collection in the Midwest.

Intellectual Property Law—The certificate program focuses on issues relating to patent, trademark, copyright, trade secrets, and unfair competition.

Labor and Employment Law—The certificate program provides students with theoretical and practical training in the law governing the work place.

■ Admission

➥ *B.A. or B.S. required for admission*   ➥ *suggested application deadline—April 1*   ➥ *LSAT, LSDAS required*   ➥ *application fee—$45*   ➥ *rolling admission, early application preferred*

Admission is highly selective. Decisions are based on a range of factors including quantitative and qualitative criteria. Each application is individually reviewed; there is no cut-off. Although the GPA and LSAT are important criteria, consideration also is given to nonnumerical factors such as the nature and rigor of the undergraduate curriculum, writing ability, graduate work and professional experience, extracurricular activities, diversity, and the personal statement. The admission requirements for the full- and part-time divisions are the same. Entering classes begin only in the fall. The law school is committed to attracting and retaining students from a variety of racial, ethnic, economic, geographic, and educational backgrounds.

■ Student Activities

The *Chicago-Kent Law Review* is published in symposium format by student editors and staff, in association with a faculty editor. Moot Court and Trial Advocacy teams successfully compete in local, regional, and national competitions every year, providing numerous opportunities to develop litigation expertise. Diverse student interests are represented in a wide variety of social, political, and professional student groups.

■ Expenses and Financial Aid

➥ *tuition & fees—full-time, $20,680; part-time, $14,915* ➥ *estimated additional expenses —$12,000*   ➥ *scholarships available*   ➥ *FAFSA, Chicago-Kent Institutional Application required for financial aid; priority deadline—April 15*

The Honors Scholars Program provides renewable scholarships of full-tuition and living expenses, research assistantships, and special seminars to a select group of students who demonstrate exceptional academic and leadership ability. Substantial scholarship assistance is offered to entering and continuing students based on need and merit. Federal and other loans are available.

■ Career Services

More than 92 percent of recent graduates found professional employment within six months of being licensed to practice.

The Office of Career Services, with seven full-time staff members and two part-time career strategists, sponsors fall and spring on-campus interview programs and offers individual counseling on résumé-writing, interview techniques, and job-search strategies.

■ Housing

Affordable housing is available in nearby urban and suburban neighborhoods. The law school is close to all public transportation.

Applicant Group for the 1998-1999 Academic Year

Chicago-Kent College of Law—Illinois Institute of Technology

LSAT Score	3.75 +		3.50 - 3.74		3.25 - 3.49		3.00 - 3.24		2.75 - 2.99		2.50 - 2.74		2.25 - 2.49		2.00 - 2.24		Below 2.00		No GPA		Total	
	Apps	Adm	Apps	Adm	Apps	Adm	Apps	Adm	Apps	Adm	Apps	Adm	Apps	Adm	Apps	Adm	Apps	Adm	Apps	Adm	Apps	Adm
170-180	3	3	3	3	3	3	2	2	1	1	0	0	0	0	0	0	0	0	0	0	12	12
165-169	3	3	6	6	14	10	11	11	11	10	4	4	2	2	0	0	0	0	1	1	52	47
160-164	17	16	26	25	27	25	37	36	40	36	15	12	6	6	4	4	1	0	5	3	178	163
155-159	18	17	45	45	73	71	89	83	79	75	35	30	23	21	10	5	3	0	5	4	380	351
150-154	27	27	56	51	81	79	118	114	103	92	69	53	41	18	16	7	4	1	10	5	525	447
145-149	8	8	42	41	53	45	91	72	90	56	57	17	43	9	14	1	5	0	10	2	413	251
140-144	9	3	8	0	27	3	56	10	37	1	46	1	35	0	14	0	2	0	10	0	244	18
Below 140	4	0	6	0	8	0	20	0	35	0	33	0	33	0	18	0	5	0	16	0	178	0
Total	89	77	192	171	286	236	424	328	396	271	259	117	183	56	76	17	20	1	57	15	1982	1289

Apps= Number of Applicants
Adm= Number Admitted
Reflects 99% of the total applicant pool.
This grid represents admission data for applicants to both the day and evening divisions.
The information in this grid is to be used only as an approximate gauge of the likelihood of admission and not as a guarantee.
Individual accomplishments and other nonnumerical factors are of significant importance to the Admissions Committee.

University of Cincinnati College of Law

P.O. Box 210040
Office of Admissions and Financial Aid
Cincinnati, OH 45221-0040

E-Mail: admissions@law.uc.edu
URL: http://www.law.uc.edu
Phone: 513.556.6805

■ Introduction

The College of Law at the University of Cincinnati was established in 1833. America's fourth-oldest law school, the college today is a national public law school serving an enrollment of 358 students—approximately 125 per class. The College of Law is a cornerstone on the University of Cincinnati campus in historic Clifton. This central location, approximately 10 minutes north of the city's downtown area, provides easy access to state, county, and federal courts, including the U.S. Court of Appeals for the Sixth Circuit. A charter member of the AALS, the University of Cincinnati was one of the first law schools to have a chapter of the Order of the Coif and to be approved by the ABA.

■ Enrollment/Student Body

Report on first-year class 1998   ➧ *917 applicants*
➧ *381 admitted*   ➧ *121 enrolled*
➧ *full-time 25th/75th percentile GPA—3.01/3.66*
➧ *full-time 25th/75th percentile LSAT—154/162*
➧ *21.4% minority*   ➧ *14% African American*
➧ *50% women*   ➧ *16 states & foreign countries represented*
➧ *70 undergraduate schools represented*
➧ *40 majors represented*   ➧ *average age—25*
➧ *11% of class age 30+ upon entrance*   ➧ *73% state residents*

The median LSAT is 159 and the median UGPA is 3.40.

■ Faculty

➧ *26 full-time*   ➧ *9 women*   ➧ *68 adjunct*
➧ *4 minority*

The law school has doubled the size of the faculty and constructed a new law building and library in the last 15 years. The resulting student-to-faculty ratio of 16:1 is one of the best nationally.

■ Library and Physical Facilities

➧ *379,242 volumes & equivalents*   ➧ *library hours:*
Mon.-Fri., 7:45 A.M.-11:00 P.M.; Sat.-Sun., 10:00 A.M.-11:00 P.M.
➧ *LEXIS*   ➧ *NEXIS*   ➧ *WESTLAW*   ➧ *UCLIO*
➧ *OHIOLINK*   ➧ *OCLC*   ➧ *DIALOG*   ➧ *EPIC*
➧ *DATATIMES*   ➧ *7 full-time librarians*
➧ *library seats 385*

The College of Law is one of the few law libraries large enough to seat its entire student body, if necessary. Two new student computer labs offer an excellent array of computer-assisted research aids and laser printers.

The library has built two databases already via the Internet: DIANA, a database of human rights materials, supports the work of the Urban Morgan Institute for Human Rights; and the Securities Lawyer's Deskbook supports the work of the newly established Center for Corporate Law.

■ Curriculum

➧ *90 credits required to graduate*   ➧ *60-80 courses available*
➧ *degrees available: J.D./M.B.A.; J.D./M.C.P.; J.D./M.A. in Women's Studies*   ➧ *semesters, Aug.-Dec., Jan.-May*
➧ *range of first-year class size—20-85*

The College of Law has well developed academic traditions in all major areas of the law. Especially strong programs exist in the areas of corporate, environmental, intellectual property law, human rights, and, in 1999-2000, Law and Psychiatry.

■ Special Programs

The College of Law recognizes that a lawyer needs both a firm grasp of subject matter and expertise in professional skills. The college has developed an extensive legal research and writing program that not only encompasses the first year, but upper-level courses as well. To involve students directly in the legal system, the Judge in Residence Program brings actual trials to the law school courtroom so that students can observe a visiting judge. The Public Service and Professional Development Program provides students with extern experience and the opportunity to work with practicing attorneys in public agencies. Additionally, the College of Law has centers in the international human rights and corporate law areas. Each center offers a fellowship program, research opportunities, and in-depth study in their respective areas. Additional information on the Urban Morgan Institute for Human Rights and the Center for Corporate Law can be received by contacting the Admissions Office.

■ Admission Standards

➧ *Bachelor's degree required*   ➧ *application deadline—April 1*
➧ *LSAT, LSDAS required*   ➧ *application fee—$35*

Applicants must have a baccalaureate degree from an accredited institution prior to enrollment. A valid LSAT score and the LSDAS subscription are required. Applications should be submitted before April 1. Admission to the college is based upon a selective review of each candidate's file. Although the admissions committee relies on the grade-point average and LSAT score to determine the applicant's academic potential, other non-quantitative factors believed to be relevant to success in law school are considered; i.e., the quality of the applicant's education, participation in community service, employment experience, graduate work, and letters of recommendation. The educational philosophy of the college reflects a belief that a quality legal education is enhanced by having a heterogeneous student body. The committee, therefore, also considers race, cultural background, unusual personal circumstances, and age. Admission decisions are made on a rolling basis.

Special consideration is given to competitive applications from members of minority groups who have been economically and culturally disadvantaged. Particular effort is made to provide adequate financial assistance for all students admitted.

Student Activities

The University of Cincinnati Law Review was founded in 1927 and was the first law review published by an Ohio law school. Edited quarterly by student editors, *Law Review* members are selected on the basis of both scholastic achievement and writing ability. The College's Moot Court Program participates in all national intercollegiate competitions and annually hosts the National Product Liabilities Competition. The Student Bar Association and Student Legal Education Committee participate in governance of the college, providing student members for law school committees. Additionally, the Volunteer Lawyers for the Poor (VLP) organization was founded in 1991.

Expenses and Financial Aid

➥ *tuition & fees—resident, $7,704; nonresident, $14,808*
➥ *scholarships available*
➥ *FAFSA required, March 1 priority deadline*

Living expenses are estimated at $10,454 for independent students. Scholarships are awarded to approximately 50-60 percent of the entering class on the basis of academic merit, merit/need and need. Priority deadline for receipt of the Scholarship Information forms is March 1. The FAFSA should also be filed by March 1 as a priority deadline.

Placement

The college maintains an active Career Planning and Placement Center with a professional staff available to counsel students seeking permanent, summer, and part-time employment. The Career Planning and Placement Office provides an on-campus recruiting program with over 60 law firms and agencies, businesses, corporations, and financial institutions participating. In recent years, over 90 percent of each graduating class has accepted employment within six months of graduation. Typically, one half of a graduating class will enter private practice; 10-15 percent, judicial clerkships; 10-20 percent, business/corporations; 2-10 percent, government; and 2-4 percent, public interest. While 60-65 percent of graduates accept employment in Cincinnati and 80 percent in the Midwest, an increasing number have accepted positions nationally. Graduates are employed in 48 states, the District of Columbia, and numerous foreign countries. The average salary for the class of 1997 was $42,265.

Applicant Group for the 1998-1999 Academic Year

University of Cincinnati College of Law
This grid includes only applicants who earned 120-180 LSAT scores under standard administrations.

LSAT Score	3.75 +		3.50 - 3.74		3.25 - 3.49		3.00 - 3.24		2.75 - 2.99		2.50 - 2.74		2.25 - 2.49		2.00 - 2.24		Below 2.00		No GPA		Total	
	Apps	Adm	Apps	Adm	Apps	Adm	Apps	Adm	Apps	Adm	Apps	Adm	Apps	Adm	Apps	Adm	Apps	Adm	Apps	Adm	Apps	Adm
175-180	0	0	1	1	1	1	1	1	0	0	0	0	0	0	0	0	0	0	0	0	3	3
170-174	1	1	2	2	0	0	1	1	0	0	0	0	0	0	0	0	0	0	0	0	4	4
165-169	5	5	7	7	10	10	4	4	11	11	4	4	0	0	1	1	0	0	0	0	42	42
160-164	14	14	27	27	24	24	26	26	15	14	3	3	5	4	1	1	0	0	1	1	116	114
155-159	27	27	48	45	49	30	44	17	22	4	8	1	7	0	7	1	1	0	2	1	215	126
150-154	28	23	44	18	51	7	47	4	32	4	23	8	14	1	2	0	0	0	2	0	243	65
145-149	6	3	15	2	29	3	23	3	30	5	20	4	9	0	1	0	0	0	3	0	136	20
140-144	6	2	6	1	16	2	14	0	13	0	15	1	10	0	3	0	0	0	0	0	83	6
135-139	1	0	4	0	2	0	9	0	6	0	5	0	8	0	2	0	1	0	4	0	42	0
130-134	0	0	0	0	0	0	2	0	3	0	2	0	1	0	1	0	0	0	0	0	9	0
125-129	0	0	0	0	0	0	0	0	0	0	0	0	1	0	1	0	0	0	0	0	2	0
120-124	0	0	0	0	0	0	0	0	0	0	0	0	0	0	0	0	0	0	0	0	0	0
Total	88	75	154	103	182	77	171	56	132	38	80	21	55	5	19	3	2	0	12	2	895	380

Apps = Number of Applicants
Adm = Number Admitted
Reflects 98% of the total applicant pool.

City University of New York School of Law at Queens College

65-21 Main Street
Flushing, NY 11367-1300

E-Mail: admissions@maclaw.law.cuny.edu
URL: http://web.law.cuny.edu
Phone: 718.340.4210; Fax: 718.340.4372

■ Introduction

CUNY School of Law at Queens College specializes in public service and public interest law. Fully accredited by the American Bar Association, it is the only publicly funded law school in New York City.

Founded in 1983, it is a unit of the City University of New York, one of the largest and most distinguished university systems in the nation. Queens College, on whose campus the law school is situated, is one of nine four-year colleges in the CUNY system.

■ Enrollment/Student Body

➥ 1,378 applicants ➥ 497 admitted first-year class 1998 ➥ 103 enrolled first-year class fall 1998 ➥ full-time 25th/75th percentile GPA—2.76/3.40 ➥ full-time 25th/75th percentile LSAT—143/153 ➥ 372 total full-time ➥ 44% minority ➥ 62% women ➥ 30 states & 12 foreign countries represented ➥ 219 undergraduate schools represented

The law school has been remarkably successful in recruiting the diverse, committed, and richly experienced student body that it has sought. The median age of matriculated students is 30. Approximately 65 percent of enrolled students are residents of New York State, and approximately one-third have attended one or more of the City University schools for undergraduate or graduate work. The academic credentials of our students run the full range of possible grades and scores. Where traditional indicators are low, applicants demonstrate academic potential through nonstandard indicia and very strong work or life experiences that are relevant to the school's mission.

■ Faculty

➥ 48 total ➥ 36 full-time ➥ 12 part-time or adjunct ➥ 30 women ➥ 17 minority

■ Library and Physical Facilities

➥ 242,632 volumes & equivalents ➥ library hours: open to public: Mon.-Thurs., 8:00 A.M.-8:00 P.M.; Fri., 8:00 A.M.-5:00 P.M. ➥ library hours open to students: 7:00 A.M.-MIDNIGHT, 7 days per week ➥ LEXIS ➥ NEXIS ➥ WESTLAW ➥ DIALOG ➥ 7 full-time librarians ➥ library seats 397

The law school's permanent facility is unique in that it allocates office space for student use. Each pair of offices, called a Section, comprises a suite of rooms. Two of these rooms are student work areas, with desks, bookshelves, and locking file drawers for each student. In addition, there are three faculty offices, a Section Library (with access to computer-assisted legal research databases), a secretarial/reception area, and photocopy and word processing equipment.

The main library combines a substantial print collection with extensive microform holdings and widely accessible computer databases.

■ Curriculum

➥ Academic Support Program ➥ 91 credits required to graduate ➥ J.D. degrees available ➥ semesters, start in Aug. & Jan. ➥ range of first-year class size—20-80

Our purpose is to create an educational program that honors students' aspirations toward a legal career built on a commitment to justice, fairness, and equality.

The overall theme of our integrated curriculum is especially reflected in our treatment of three areas that are given much heavier emphasis than has been traditional. These areas are legal theory, clinical education, and professional responsibility. The first three semesters consist almost entirely of required courses. The final three semesters allow the student to select from a number of elective courses, in a variety of doctrinal areas. In addition, in the final two semesters, the student is enrolled either in a concentration area (with classroom work and practice placement combined) or in a clinic (with virtually full-time live-client practice) with courtroom experience.

The school offers only a full-time day program.

■ Lawyering Seminars

Clinical work is comprehensively integrated into the course of study. Throughout the program students are organized into work units called Lawyering Seminars. These offices of 20 students provide a context for a series of simulated practice situations related to the substantive courses. Each Lawyering Seminar is affiliated with a faculty member. Through the simulations, the students engage in a wide range of lawyering tasks; they draft documents, interview and counsel clients, engage in negotiations, and make arguments before trial and appellate courts, often reviewing their work with the Lawyering Seminar teachers and other faculty.

We believe that grappling with issues of professional responsibility is at the heart of public interest practice, and that an awareness of personal and professional responsibility therefore should be integral to students' lawyering work.

■ Admission

➥ Bachelor's degree from accredited college or university required ➥ application deadline—March 15 for fall; Dec. 1 for spring ➥ LSAT, LSDAS required ➥ application fee—$40 ➥ early application preferred

We actively seek to recruit, retain, promote, and train students of all races, national origins, classes, and belief systems, without regard to gender or sexual preference.

We admit people based on several criteria. We look at academic performance and scores on the LSAT, and beyond these to other demonstrations of academic promise.

Assessment of academic ability alone does not dominate the admission process. We also assess some of the less tangible qualities that make an outstanding lawyer, including judgment, energy, initiative, and the ability to work both collaboratively and independently. We look for indications that the candidate has a special affinity for our particular program; people with a demonstrated commitment to the principles of justice, fairness, and equality in the legal process; people with a sensitivity to the diversity of society and the equal worth of each of its members; and people who manifest a regard for providing all groups the broadest participation in our public life. Finally, we select diverse groups of students, genuinely representative of the remarkable diversity of the city the school serves.

The school's admission process is described in detail in its application materials. In brief, all applications are read closely. The detailed personal statement that we require forms the core of most applications. Two recommendations are required and are also often a decisive part of the applicant's file. Tours, information sessions, and classroom visitations are encouraged for interested individuals who wish to learn more about the law school and its programs. They may be scheduled by contacting the Office of Admissions.

■ Expenses and Financial Aid

➥ *full-time tuition & fees—resident, $3,225.85/sem.; nonresident, $4,840.85/sem.* ➥ *estimated additional expenses—$9,000 (room & board, transportation, personal expenses, insurance)* ➥ *need- & merit-based grants available* ➥ *FAFSA plus special CUNY form (no cost to process) required for financial aid*

■ Career Services

The law school views the placement function as part of its academic program. Our placement program begins in the first year. We encourage students to reflect on the choices they make as they seek work and decide among employment opportunities. We also work actively to develop job opportunities during the year, during the summer, and after graduation.

Applicant Group for the 1998-1999 Academic Year

City University of New York School of Law at Queens College
This grid includes only applicants who earned 120-180 LSAT scores under standard administrations.

LSAT Score	3.75 +		3.50 - 3.74		3.25 - 3.49		3.00 - 3.24		2.75 - 2.99		2.50 - 2.74		2.25 - 2.49		2.00 - 2.24		Below 2.00		No GPA		Total	
	Apps	Adm	Apps	Adm	Apps	Adm	Apps	Adm	Apps	Adm	Apps	Adm	Apps	Adm	Apps	Adm	Apps	Adm	Apps	Adm	Apps	Adm
175-180	0	0	1	1	0	0	0	0	0	0	0	0	0	0	0	0	0	0	0	0	1	1
170-174	0	0	1	1	0	0	0	0	0	0	0	0	1	1	1	1	0	0	0	0	3	3
165-169	0	0	2	2	2	1	1	1	2	2	2	2	0	0	1	0	0	0	0	0	10	8
160-164	4	4	9	9	4	4	6	6	3	2	4	2	3	2	1	0	0	0	1	1	35	30
155-159	11	10	12	10	19	15	17	15	14	12	11	6	4	3	5	3	1	0	0	0	94	74
150-154	10	10	17	13	36	27	31	22	42	29	30	15	9	2	7	4	1	1	4	1	187	124
145-149	13	11	20	10	38	21	60	36	70	33	51	18	30	4	18	3	4	0	10	4	314	140
140-144	2	0	17	11	31	9	57	15	74	17	75	14	47	2	22	0	6	0	23	1	354	69
135-139	3	0	7	1	21	1	32	1	45	2	46	1	35	0	20	0	3	0	21	1	233	7
130-134	2	0	2	0	10	0	9	0	22	0	11	0	18	0	6	0	6	0	10	0	96	0
125-129	0	0	0	0	1	0	2	0	5	0	3	0	5	0	6	0	1	0	3	0	26	0
120-124	0	0	0	0	0	0	0	0	0	0	0	0	0	0	1	0	0	0	2	0	3	0
Total	45	35	88	58	162	78	215	96	277	97	233	58	152	14	88	11	22	1	74	8	1356	456

Apps = Number of Applicants
Adm = Number Admitted
Reflects 99% of the total applicant pool.

Cleveland State University—Cleveland-Marshall College of Law

E-Mail: mmcnally@sunshine.law.csuohio.edu
1801 Euclid Ave.
URL: http://www.csuohio.edu/law/
Cleveland, OH 44115-9984
Phone: 216.687.2304

■ Introduction

The Cleveland State University College of Law, located on the university's new urban campus in downtown Cleveland, is the largest law school in Ohio. It has been training lawyers since its forerunners, the Cleveland Law School and John Marshall Law School, were established in 1887 and 1916, respectively. Since becoming part of the state university system in 1969, the Cleveland-Marshall College of Law has maintained and enhanced its long-standing reputation for training attorneys dedicated to the service of their communities. The college operates a full-time day and part-time evening program, preparing students for practice in any jurisdiction. It is a member of AALS and the League of Ohio Law Schools and is approved by the ABA. Located on Lake Erie, Cleveland is an active cultural center, nationally renowned for its parks, libraries, and museums. The Cleveland Symphony Orchestra is one of the finest in the world. Cleveland is also a major industrial center and headquarters for many large corporations. An excellent rapid transportation system links downtown Cleveland and Cleveland State University to the eastern and western suburbs of the city.

■ Enrollment/Student Body

➡ *623 admitted first-year class 1998* ➡ *276 enrolled first-year class 1998* ➡ *full-time 25th/75th percentile GPA—2.83/3.44* ➡ *part-time 25th/75th percentile GPA—2.74/3.32* ➡ *full-time 25th/75th percentile LSAT—145/153*
➡ *part-time 25th/75th percentile LSAT—146/154*
➡ *555 total full-time* ➡ *311 total part-time*
➡ *15% minority* ➡ *47.6% women*
➡ *15-20 states & foreign countries represented*
➡ *110 undergraduate schools represented*

From 15 to 20 percent of each entering class is likely to be over 30 years old, with as many as 15 percent earning advanced degrees before beginning the study of law. From 15 to 20 percent of each class comes to Cleveland State from outside Ohio. Students of color and women are actively recruited and are encouraged to apply.

■ Faculty

➡ *75 total* ➡ *45 full-time* ➡ *30 part-time or adjunct*

■ Library and Physical Facilities

➡ *400,000 volumes & equivalents* ➡ *LEXIS*
➡ *NEXIS* ➡ *WESTLAW*

The Cleveland-Marshall College of Law library, with over 400,000 volumes, is a new facility readily accessible to law students. Other university facilities, including a bookstore, cafeterias, and modern gymnasium, are also available to law students and are within walking distance.

■ Curriculum

➡ *87 credits required to graduate* ➡ *degrees available: J.D.; J.D./M.B.A.; J.D./M.P.A.; J.D./M.U.P.D.D.*

In both day and evening programs, the core curriculum and most elective courses are taught by full-time faculty. The adjunct faculty, consisting of prominent judges and lawyers, teach in highly specialized areas. Typically, the J.D. program is completed by full-time day students in three academic years and by part-time evening students in four academic years and two summers. Full-time students may also attend summer sessions to accelerate their study.

Three Joint Degree programs are offered: the J.D./M.B.A. (Master of Business Administration); the J.D./M.P.A. (Master of Public Administration); and the J.D./M.U.P.D.D. (Master of Urban Planning, Design, and Development).

■ Special Programs

The urban setting of the college offers unusual opportunities to bring challenging legal experiences to students. Externship programs take the student out of the classroom and into the courtroom. A more specialized clinical opportunity is afforded the students who participate in these programs. The Fair Employment Practices Clinic provides credit for participation in litigation dealing with employment discrimination. The Judicial Externship Program offers upper-level students opportunities to work with state appellate and federal court judges. Each year lawyers, judges, and legal scholars of national renown are invited to the College of Law as Cleveland-Marshall Fund lecturers. Each of these distinguished visitors delivers a major address and spends two days at the College of Law meeting informally with students and faculty and conducting class sessions.

■ Admission

➡ *fall admission only* ➡ *LSAT, LSDAS required*

Applicants are admitted by the Dean upon the recommendation of an Admissions Committee composed of faculty members and students. Criteria for admission are identical for the full-time and part-time programs. Each applicant must have received a bachelor's level degree from a college or university accredited at the time of the applicant's graduation. Experience has shown that undergraduate grade-point averages and LSAT scores are generally the most reliable measures available for predicting success in law school. For this reason, most students are admitted primarily upon an index combining grades and test scores. However, under the Legal Careers Opportunity Program (LCOP), instituted by the law faculty in 1970, the admissions committee may consider many other factors in an effort to identify students who have faced adversity in the pursuit of their educational opportunities or who have accomplishments and experiences suggesting that they do have the ability to succeed in law school if given the opportunity. These factors include length of time since graduation from college, achievement after college, economic disadvantage, and extracurricular activity. LCOP applicants are required to submit a writing sample, three letters of recommendation, and a personal statement in addition to an LSDAS report. LCOP students are required to attend a summer program prior to fall admission. The application deadline is March 1.

Student Activities

The *Cleveland State Law Review* is edited and published by an editorial board consisting entirely of students of high academic standing and superior writing ability. The law review publishes articles by students and legal scholars for the practicing bar and for use in scholarly research. The *Journal of Law and Health* is an interdisciplinary publication that explores ideas in health law and policy. A Moot Court Program is offered to give students an understanding of the appellate process and of the work performed by lawyers at the appellate level. An extensive intramural competition is conducted each year, and outstanding students represent the college in nationwide competitions. All students are members of the Student Bar Association, an affiliate of the Law Student Division of the ABA. Phi Alpha Delta, Delta Theta Phi, and Tau Epsilon Rho, national legal fraternities, have active chapters on campus. Other student organizations include the Black Law Students Association, the National Lawyers Guild, and the Women's Caucus. In

addition, students of the College of Law publish a student newspaper, *The Gavel*.

Expenses and Financial Aid

➡ *tuition & fees—Ohio resident, $3,696/sem. ($285/credit hr.); nonresident, $7,391/sem. ($569/credit hr.)*
➡ *part-time students take 10 credits/sem.*
➡ *financial aid available; GAPSFAS due March 1*

The financial aid program at the college utilizes combinations of tuition grants, work-study employment awards, scholarships, and loans. Awards are made on the basis of merit or need. Forty-three percent of first-year students received scholarship awards. The college is able to meet a high proportion of the need of all students applying for aid.

Career Services

A full-time placement director provides placement services for students and alumni. Each year employers from law firms, corporations, business, government, legal services, and public interest groups interview students at the Cleveland-Marshall College of Law for part-time, summer, and full-time employment. It is estimated that approximately 50 percent of the attorneys practicing in greater Cleveland are graduates of Cleveland State and its predecessors. Our graduates continue to be highly visible on the northern Ohio bench, in business and industry, public service, government, and private practice.

Applicant Group for the 1998-1999 Academic Year

Cleveland State University—Cleveland-Marshall College of Law
This grid includes only applicants who earned 120-180 LSAT scores under standard administrations.

LSAT Score	3.75 +		3.50 - 3.74		3.25 - 3.49		3.00 - 3.24		2.75 - 2.99		2.50 - 2.74		2.25 - 2.49		2.00 - 2.24		Total	
	Apps	Adm	Apps	Adm	Apps	Adm	Apps	Adm	Apps	Adm	Apps	Adm	Apps	Adm	Apps	Adm	Apps	Adm
175-180	0	0	0	0	0	0	0	0	0	0	0	0	0	0	0	0	0	0
170-174	0	0	0	0	0	0	0	0	0	0	0	0	0	0	0	0	0	0
165-169	3	3	4	4	5	5	0	0	2	2	1	1	0	0	0	0	15	15
160-164	4	4	4	4	8	8	13	13	6	5	6	5	1	1	0	0	42	40
155-159	10	10	15	15	17	15	19	19	18	17	9	9	5	5	4	3	97	93
150-154	15	14	24	24	45	45	51	45	42	37	38	34	17	12	10	6	242	217
145-149	11	11	21	20	46	43	50	41	54	31	56	17	25	5	7	0	270	168
140-144	5	5	20	14	36	18	41	14	52	11	49	5	26	4	20	2	249	73
135-139	5	4	5	2	13	5	21	2	31	2	20	1	21	1	10	0	126	17
130-134	0	0	0	0	3	0	4	0	6	0	7	0	6	0	7	0	33	0
125-129	0	0	0	0	0	0	0	0	3	0	1	0	2	0	3	0	9	0
120-124	0	0	0	0	0	0	0	0	0	0	2	0	0	0	0	0	2	0
Total	53	51	93	83	173	139	199	134	214	105	189	72	103	28	61	11	1085	623

Apps = Number of Applicants
Adm = Number Admitted

University of Colorado School of Law

Fleming Law Building
Campus Box 403
Boulder, CO 80309-0403

URL: http://www.colorado.edu/law/
Phone: 303.492.7203; Catalog Request: press 5

■ Introduction

The School of Law is located on the Boulder campus of the University of Colorado and lies at the foot of the Rocky Mountains. High admission standards, combined with a relatively small student body and a favorable faculty-to-student ratio, assure a stimulating and challenging academic environment that encourages in-class participation and informal consultations with faculty. The school is a charter member of the AALS and is ABA approved.

■ Enrollment/Student Body

Report on first-year class 1998: ➡ *1,731 applicants* ➡ *592 admitted* ➡ *167 enrolled* ➡ *full-time 25th/75th percentile GPA—3.28/3.68* ➡ *full-time 25th/75th percentile LSAT—158/164* ➡ *95 undergraduate schools* ➡ *37 states Report on total enrollment:* ➡ *487 total full-time* ➡ *16% minority* ➡ *47% women*

■ Faculty

➡ *77 total* ➡ *35 full-time* ➡ *42 part-time or adjunct* ➡ *19 women* ➡ *11 minority*

■ Library and Physical Facilities

➡ *370,000 volumes & equivalents* ➡ *LEXIS* ➡ *NEXIS* ➡ *WESTLAW* ➡ *LEGISLATE* ➡ *DIALOG* ➡ *First Search* ➡ *CALI* ➡ *Internet* ➡ *7.5 full-time librarians* ➡ *library seats 360 (plus lounge seating)* ➡ *http://www.colorado.edu/Law/lawlib*

Professional librarians are available to assist students between 9:00 A.M. and 7:00 P.M. The university maintains a computer lab in the library providing word processing applications, Internet access, and CALR services. Students may elect to access computer services from their homes via modem. All computer resources are offered to law students at no charge.

■ Curriculum

➡ *Academic Support Program* ➡ *89 credits required to graduate* ➡ *100 courses available* ➡ *degrees available: J.D.; J.D./M.B.A.; J.D./M.P.A. (plus other joint degrees)* ➡ *semesters, start in Aug.* ➡ *range of first-year class size—28-80*

First semester runs from late August to mid-December, and second semester from mid-January to mid-May. An eight-week summer session is offered in June and July for students with advanced standing at any accredited law school. With a limited number of additional hours, a certificate in tax or environmental policy is attainable. The first-year curriculum is required of all students. During the second and third years, students may emphasize such areas as natural resources, environmental law, criminal law, business law, constitutional law, taxation, public law, American Indian law, litigation, intellectual property law, and jurisprudence.

■ Special Programs

The Natural Resources Law Center has three major areas of activity: research and publication, legal education, and the distinguished visitors and fellows program.

The National Wildlife Federation's Natural Resources Litigation Clinic involves students in complex environmental litigation, most of which reaches the state supreme court or federal appellate court level. A number of student-assisted clinic cases have set precedents and have been published in environmental law texts.

The Legal Aid and Defender Program allows students to represent low-income clients in actual civil and criminal cases in Colorado courts under the supervision of full-time faculty who are experienced trial attorneys.

The Indian Law Clinic provides students the opportunity to work with Native Americans on their unique legal problems.

The Appellate Advocacy Clinic is taught at the law school by a member of the Appellate Division of the Colorado State Public Defender's Office. Each student, under direct supervision of the instructor, is responsible for completing an appellate brief and attending the oral argument in the Colorado Supreme Court or the Colorado Court of Appeals. In addition, students meet in formal classes to discuss appellate procedure.

The Byron R. White Center for American Constitutional Study was established to further the study, teaching, and publication of Constitutional law. The White Center hosts the Ira C. Rothgerber Constitutional Law Conference annually, which exposes students to analysis and debate of contemporary constitutional issues.

■ Admission

➡ *Bachelor's degree from an accredited school required* ➡ *application deadline—Feb. 15 (earlier is recommended)* ➡ *rolling admission (first letters go out about Feb. 1; class is usually full about May/June; admission thereafter from the waiting list is limited)* ➡ *LSAT, LSDAS required* ➡ *application fee—$45*

Offers of admission are heavily based on GPA and LSAT, but these scores are considered in the context of the entire application. We give substantial weight to special qualities such as motivation; undergraduate program; diversity in economic, social, or cultural background; unusual employment or other experience; leadership; and perseverance in overcoming personal handicaps or disadvantages. The School of Law takes affirmative action to increase ethnic, cultural, and other diversity of its student body.

Several positions are offered each year to transfer and visiting students, based on space available in the second- and third-year classes. Criteria for these students are the same as for first-year students and include law school performance.

■ Housing

The university has dormitories for single students and apartments for married students. Inquiries should be sent to University Residence Halls, Room 80 Hallett, Boulder, CO 80310. Off-campus housing requests should be sent to University Memorial Center Room 336, CB 206, University of Colorado at Boulder, Boulder, CO 80309, or to Family Housing, 1350 20th Street, Boulder, CO 80302. Most law students live in private housing; students are advised to seek housing early.

■ Student Activities

Under the guidance of the faculty, students participate in The Rothgerber Moot Court Competition, The Jessup International Law Moot Court Competition, The Saul Lefkowitz Trademark Moot Court Competition, and other national moot court competitions. During the past several years CU teams have won regional, national, and international recognition in these events.

The *University of Colorado Law Review* is a professional journal edited entirely by students. The *Colorado Journal of International Environmental Law and Policy* is one of only two such journals in the nation.

Over 20 student organizations invite participation in projects, programs, and social activities.

■ Expenses and Financial Aid

➡ *tuition & fees—full-time resident, $5,411; full-time nonresident, $17,086* ➡ *estimated additional expenses— $12,556 (all living costs)* ➡ *scholarships available (limited state & private funds)* ➡ *merit, merit & financial need, and diversity scholarships available*

Colorado state grants are available on a limited basis to eligible resident students and are awarded on the basis of need. Nonresident students may establish Colorado residency by maintaining their legal residence in Colorado for 12 consecutive months. Once they have established Colorado residency, they qualify for the lower resident tuition rates. Students may not be employed during their first year, but limited outside employment may be compatible with second- and third-year schedules. Students applying for financial aid, including grants, must file the Free Application for Federal Student Aid. This form is available from all local high schools, colleges, and universities, and will be processed at no charge. The application must be properly completed and submitted to the processor as soon as possible after January 1.

■ Career Services

Career Services provides personal/group counseling to students/alumni regarding career direction, legal employers and alternatives to traditional legal careers. Workshops, symposia and table talk fora are held annually on résumé/interviewing skills, judicial clerkship applications and self-directed job search strategies. The office hosts on-campus interviews biannually and solicits legal employers nation-wide to recruit students through off-campus programs as well. Career Services has developed an aggressive marketing/recruiting strategy to entice legal employers in the Denver Metroplex area, the state of Colorado and the nation to hire our students/graduates. Almost 90 percent of our graduates were employed within six months of graduation over the past three years. The Bar Passage rate for first-time takers of the July 1997 Colorado Bar Examination was 97 percent.

Applicant Group for the 1998-1999 Academic Year

University of Colorado School of Law
This grid includes only applicants who earned 120-180 LSAT scores under standard administrations.

LSAT Score	3.75 +		3.50 - 3.74		3.25 - 3.49		3.00 - 3.24		2.75 - 2.99		2.50 - 2.74		2.25 - 2.49		2.00 - 2.24		Below 2.00		No GPA		Total	
	Apps	Adm	Apps	Adm	Apps	Adm	Apps	Adm	Apps	Adm	Apps	Adm	Apps	Adm	Apps	Adm	Apps	Adm	Apps	Adm	Apps	Adm
175-180	0	0	1	1	2	2	0	0	1	0	0	0	0	0	0	0	0	0	0	0	4	3
170-174	11	11	10	9	9	9	6	5	4	2	2	1	0	0	0	0	0	0	0	0	42	37
165-169	18	18	32	32	56	48	27	22	18	7	4	0	7	2	0	0	1	0	1	1	164	130
160-164	63	62	94	89	114	89	81	30	38	9	14	1	7	1	7	0	0	0	4	1	422	282
155-159	53	30	119	37	127	21	83	8	43	9	20	1	4	0	1	0	0	0	6	1	456	107
150-154	32	3	77	4	81	8	79	5	30	0	17	0	10	1	4	0	0	0	3	0	333	21
145-149	5	0	25	1	38	1	45	1	31	2	20	0	9	0	2	0	1	0	3	0	179	5
140-144	6	1	9	0	11	0	15	0	8	0	13	1	4	0	3	0	1	0	1	0	71	2
135-139	1	0	2	1	5	0	0	0	5	0	6	0	6	0	1	0	2	0	2	0	30	1
130-134	0	0	0	0	1	0	2	0	1	0	0	0	1	0	2	0	0	0	1	0	8	0
125-129	0	0	0	0	0	0	0	0	1	0	0	0	1	0	2	0	0	0	2	0	6	0
120-124	0	0	0	0	0	0	0	0	0	0	0	0	0	0	0	0	0	0	0	0	0	0
Total	189	125	369	174	444	178	338	71	180	29	96	4	49	4	22	0	5	0	23	3	1715	588

Apps = Number of Applicants
Adm = Number Admitted
Reflects 99% of the total applicant pool.

Columbia University School of Law

435 West 116th Street
New York, NY 10027

URL: http://www.law.columbia.edu
Phone: 212.854.2670

■ Introduction

Columbia School of Law, in the City of New York, is
distinguished, perhaps uniquely among leading American
law schools, as an international center of legal education
that stimulates its students to consider the full dimensions
of the possibility of the law—as an intellectual pursuit,
as a career, and as an instrument of human progress. The
character of academic and social life at Columbia, like that
of New York City, is fiercely democratic, dynamic, creative,
and innovative. The law school is especially committed
to educating students of differing perspectives, from
diverse backgrounds, and with varied life experiences.
Men and women choosing to study law at Columbia hail
from the small towns, farms, and suburbs of the West,
Midwest, and South; the industrial corridors and Ivy halls
of the Northeast; the inner cities of every major American
metropolis; and the international centers of Europe, Asia,
Africa, and Latin America.

Through our admission program, we seek to enroll an
entering class that reflects the broad range of economic,
ethnic, and cultural strains found in America. From around
the world, we welcome students who will enrich learning
at Columbia and thereafter advance the developing legal
cultures of their homelands.

Professional prospects for Columbia law graduates are
quite extraordinary. Not surprisingly, many of our graduates proceed to productive careers in every conceivable
arena of private practice. But, it should be emphasized
that while Columbia-trained attorneys are especially
well-regarded for their work in corporate law and finance,
an unusually high number also serve as state and federal
judges, prosecutors, civil and human rights advocates,
legal scholars, public defenders, business executives,
elected government officials, and national and international
leaders. Noteworthy also is the fact that many Columbia
law alumnae/i contribute significantly to the shaping of
American culture at large. Currently, our graduates serve
in leadership roles across the fields of art, music, film,
publishing, science, professional athletics, philanthropy, and
higher education. With an exceptionally talented student
body and faculty, and a strong tradition of encouraging
students with specialized interests to develop those interests
in depth, Columbia School of Law provides a legal
education that gives our students a singular capacity for
imagination, originality, and high responsibility in their
professional lives.

■ J.D. Enrollment/Student Body

➡ *5,719 applicants 1998*   ➡ *345 enrolled first-year class 1998*
➡ *full-time 25th/75th percentile GPA—3.38/3.74*
➡ *full-time 25th/75th percentile LSAT—164/171*
➡ *1,132 total full-time students*   ➡ *34% minority*
➡ *45% women*   ➡ *6% International*   ➡ *49 states, 22
foreign countries, & 206 undergraduate schools represented in*
J.D. student body   ➡ *13% earned at least one other graduate
or professional degree*   ➡ *40 foreign countries represented in
LL.M. program*

The median GPA is 3.60 and the median LSAT is 169.

■ Faculty

➡ *150 total*   ➡ *75 full-time (21 women, 11 minority)*
➡ *75 part-time or adjunct*

■ Library Resources and Research Facilities

➡ *980,461 volumes & equivalents*   ➡ *LEXIS*
➡ *NEXIS*   ➡ *WESTLAW*   ➡ *DIALOG*

The third largest law collection in this country, Columbia's
library is especially rich in American law and legal history,
international law, comparative law, Roman law, and the
legal literature of the major European countries, China,
and Japan. Connections through the Internet and CD-ROMs
provide additional resources with materials from Germany,
South Africa, and a wide range of international organizations. In addition, the many libraries of the university,
containing more than five million volumes, are available
to law students.

The law library's online catalog provides complete access
to the collection and acts as an index to the major legal
serials, as well as providing access to the online catalogs
of other major law school libraries. Columbia provides its
law students with some of the most sophisticated technologies of any law school in the nation. Facilities include
two major labs, one equipped for technical instruction,
and several other smaller labs. Many student services are
available via our Web site. The network and e-mail are
accessible through hundreds of jacks located throughout
the law school and remotely. The law library provides
facilities for visually impaired students.

■ Curriculum

➡ *Academic Support Program*   ➡ *83 total units required to
graduate*   ➡ *206 courses available*   ➡ *joint programs with
Columbia University's Arts and Sciences (M.A., M.Phil., Ph.D.);
Business (M.B.A.); International and Public Affairs (M.I.A.);
Journalism (M.S.); Theatre Arts (M.F.A.); Social Work
(M.S.W.); Architecture Planning and Preservation (M.S.);
and with Princeton University's Woodrow Wilson School of
Public and International Affairs (M.I.A.)*

The foundation of the Juris Doctor (J.D.) program consists
of legal methods, contracts, torts, constitutional law, civil
procedure, property, criminal law, foundations of the
regulatory state, and perspectives on legal thought. The
upper-class program is entirely elective, except for three
research and writing requirements, a course in professional
responsibility, and a pro bono service requirement. There
are approximately 100 seminars (normally limited to 18
students). In these small classes, students engage in
intensive study and individualized instruction.

Columbia has a special commitment to clinical education, which places the student in the role of a lawyer doing a lawyer's actual work under intensive faculty supervision. Some examples of clinical opportunities are Fair Housing, Law and the Arts, Non-Profit Organizations, Prisoners and Families, Child Advocacy, Mediation, and Human Rights. Unique to Columbia is a summer program which places 60-70 students in Civil Rights and Human Rights Internships in law firms and organizations throughout this country and around the world.

Especially distinguished are Columbia's offerings in international, foreign, and comparative law; constitutional law and theory; corporate and securities law; intellectual property; critical race theory; and human rights.

■ Special Programs

The school is well situated for developing a broad urban affairs program, since New York City is the home of an extraordinary variety of private and government agencies concerned with urban problems, ranging from legal service agencies to community development projects. In all, some 30 courses and seminars are offered in urban law, civil rights and liberties, and criminal law. A variety of legal training opportunities include federal and criminal court clerkships, and placement with such urban agencies as the Legal Aid Society, Neighborhood Defender Service, and the ACLU Immigrant Rights Project.

In the fields of international, comparative, and foreign law, Columbia offers approximately 40 courses and specialized seminars. In addition, Columbia is the home of the Parker School of Foreign and Comparative Law, a center for scholarly activity in foreign and comparative law that sponsors courses, publications, conferences, and scholarships.

Columbia's longstanding leadership in international law has been strengthened greatly in the last decade by the establishment of its Center for Chinese Legal Studies, its Center for Japanese Legal Studies, its Center for Korean Legal Studies, and a joint-degree program with the University of Paris I-Panthéon-Sorbonne.

Columbia is especially strong in the areas of constitutional law. Over 20 different members of the faculty teach at least one course or seminar in constitutional law or constitutional theory.

Other special Columbia programs, serving as catalysts for scholarly work, curricular development, and student enrichment include: the Kernochan Center for Law and the Arts; the Center for Law and Economic Studies; the Human Rights Internship Program; the Jaffin Program in Law and Social Responsibility; the Legislative Drafting Research Fund; the Samuel Rubin Program, advancing civic rights and civil liberties; the Julius Silver program in Law, Science, and Technology; the Feminism and Legal Theory Project; the Center for Law and Philosophy; and the Center for Public Interest Law.

■ Admission

➡ *LSAT, LSDAS required*   ➡ *application fee—$65*

All first-year students enter in late August. Candidates applying for regular admission should apply after September 1 of the year preceding their desired matriculation, but before February 15, the application deadline. Early Decision candidates must complete their applications by December 1 and are notified in late December.

■ Expenses and Financial Aid

➡ *tuition—$26,570/1998-99*   ➡ *estimated room, board, & personal expenses—$14,225*   ➡ *1998-99 average grant value—$12,378*   ➡ *financial aid application deadline— March 1*   ➡ *Public Interest Loan Forgiveness Program (LRAP) available*

Applicant Group for the 1998-1999 Academic Year

Columbia has chosen not to provide prospective students with an admission selectivity profile, based on LSAT scores and undergraduate GPA, because we believe it does not accurately portray our selection process. Ours is a comprehensive, multivariate evaluation of academic performance and professional promise. Unlike some law school admission programs which depend on LSAT/UGPA based formulas to select their entering class, Columbia evaluates every application individually—while carefully considering the candidate's background, interests, accomplishments, and goals. We are proud that Columbia is among the handful of the most highly selective law schools in the country, as measured by LSAT and UGPA statistics and other selectivity measures. But we wish to emphasize, by not reducing our selection process to a two-dimensional grid, that the recognized excellence of our student body and distinction of our alumnae/i are rooted not only in their intellectual power and outstanding academic records, but also in their personal strengths, professional skills, and diverse backgrounds.

University of Connecticut School of Law

55 Elizabeth Street
Hartford, CT 06105-2296

E-Mail: admit@law.uconn.edu
URL: http://www.law.uconn.edu
Phone: 860.570.5100

■ Introduction

Through several decades of sustained intellectual growth, the University of Connecticut School of Law has emerged as one of the leading public law schools in the United States. Because of Connecticut's extraordinary ratio of 11:1 full-time students to full-time faculty, 40 percent of the first-year curriculum is offered in seminar format and 70 percent of the advanced courses have 20 or fewer students. An intensive first-year skills program, a rich and varied curriculum, three student-edited journals, student organizations active across the spectrum of legal and social concerns, a regular flow of visiting lecturers, and a committed body of graduates all combine to make Connecticut a school of exceptional strength.

■ Enrollment/Student Body

➡ *936 day applicants*   ➡ *429 evening applicants*
➡ *367 admitted first-year day class 1998*   ➡ *189 admitted first-year evening class 1998*   ➡ *129 enrolled first-year day class 1998*   ➡ *full-time 25th/75th percentile GPA—3.08/3.54*
➡ *part-time 25th/75th percentile GPA—2.85/3.40*
➡ *full-time 25th/75th percentile LSAT—157/161*
➡ *part-time 25th/75th percentile LSAT—154/157*
➡ *61 enrolled first-year evening class 1998*   ➡ *420 total full-time*   ➡ *161 total part-time*   ➡ *16% minority*
➡ *46% women*   ➡ *20 states & foreign countries represented*
➡ *190 undergraduate schools represented*
➡ *37 undergraduate majors represented in first-year class*
➡ *7 foreign colleges & universities represented*

Our students constitute a culturally and intellectually diverse community. Their undergraduate majors include linguistics, math, and physics, in addition to the more usual fields such as history, economics, and philosophy.

■ Faculty

➡ *95 total*   ➡ *43 full-time*   ➡ *52 part-time or adjunct*
➡ *10 full-time women; 6 part-time women*
➡ *4 full-time minority; 2 part-time minority*

■ Library and Physical Facilities

➡ *461,903 volumes & equivalents*   ➡ *library hours: standard academic year hours excluding holiday weeks, break weeks, intersession, & exam periods: Mon.-Thurs., 8:30 A.M.-11:00 P.M.; Fri., 8:30 A.M.-9:00 P.M.; Sat., 9:00 A.M.-5:00 P.M.; Sun., 10:00 A.M.-11:00 P.M.*   ➡ *LEXIS*   ➡ *NEXIS*
➡ *WESTLAW*   ➡ *DIALOG*   ➡ *18 full-time library staff*
➡ *94,724 sq. ft., 797-seat library, including computer labs*
➡ *online catalog of all library holdings*
➡ *member of New England Law Libraries Consortium, RLG*

The campus, listed on the National Register of Historic Sites, is probably the most beautiful in the United States. The new library, completed in 1996 at a cost of over $23 million, is the finest—and, at 90,000-net-square feet, one of the largest in the country.

With its immediate neighbors—the Hartford Seminary, the Hartford College for Women, and the Connecticut Historical Society—the school is part of an academic enclave in a turn-of-the-century residential neighborhood.

Although the school has no dormitories, most students live within walking distance of the campus. Housing is plentiful and varied. The School maintains a comprehensive housing list, with information about accessibility for students with special physical requirements.

■ Curriculum

➡ *Academic Support Program*   ➡ *86 credits required to graduate*   ➡ *150 courses available*   ➡ *degrees available: J.D.; J.D./M.P.H.; J.D./M.S.W.; J.D./M.B.A.; J.D./M.P.A.; J.D./M.A. in Public Policy with Trinity College; J.D./M.L.S. with Southern Connecticut State University*

■ Special Programs

Connecticut was a pioneer in clinical legal education, and our clinics continue to be a distinguishing strength of the school. Students interested in fields as diverse as law and economics, feminist legal thought, and legal philosophy will find courses and specialists to meet their needs. Extensive offerings in environmental law are supplemented by a semester exchange program with the University of London and another with the Environmental Law Center at Vermont. International law occupies an increasingly prominent place in the curriculum, reinforced by the student-edited *Connecticut Journal of International Law*. Student-faculty exchange programs with Leiden (Netherlands), Exeter (U.K.), the University of Puerto Rico, Trinity College, Dublin (Ireland), Aix-en-Provence (France), and the Master's Program leading to the LL.M. for foreign lawyers all provide opportunities for our students to learn from and study with peers trained in different legal systems.

A new Insurance Law Center offers the nation's most extensive curriculum in this fast-changing field.

■ Services for Students With Disabilities

The Disabled Student Services Liaison (DSSL) at the School of Law works with students with disabilities in the development and implementation of reasonable accommodations to allow access to both its physical facilities and its educational and extracurricular programs. Associate Dean Laurie Werling serves as liaison. Her office hours are Monday-Friday, 8:30 A.M.-4:30 P.M.

Students with mobility impairments considering applying or admitted to the School of Law are invited to tour the campus. If assistance is required, please contact the DSSL. Students with other disabilities may contact the DSSL for discussion of accommodations.

■ Academic Support Program

Each year, the School of Law offers an Academic Support Program to entering first-year students who requested special admissions consideration, or whose admission files suggest that they would benefit from individual attention. The program is designed to promote the academic success of those who participate, as well as to demonstrate the School of Law's commitment to ensuring that all admitted students have a full opportunity to maximize their academic potential.

The program consists of a summer session and an academic-year tutorial program. The summer session is conducted during the week immediately prior to the beginning of classes.

■ Admission

➼ *Bachelor's degree required (or foreign equivalent)*
➼ *application deadline—April 1* ➼ *LSAT, LSDAS required*
➼ *application fee (day or evening) –$30*
➼ *application fee (day and evening)–$45*

■ Student Activities

The *Connecticut Law Review*, publishes approximately 1,000 pages of critical legal discussion each year. Managed entirely by a student Board of Editors, the *Law Review* sponsors a scholarly conference each year on a topic of national importance.

The *Connecticut Journal of International Law*, publishes up to three issues per year on topics concerning both public and private international law. Circulated internationally, the *Journal* is wholly student-managed and edited. The *Journal* also sponsors an international legal conference each year, and a number of campus lectures, panel discussions, and social events open to the entire law school community each semester.

The *Connecticut Insurance Law Journal*, published in conjunction with the Insurance Law Center, is the only academic law review in this field.

The **Connecticut Moot Court Board** provides students with the opportunity to practice oral advocacy in the challenging setting of intramural and interscholastic competitions.

The **Student Bar Association** is the representative student government of the school. It manages an annual budget consisting of funds derived from the Student Activities Fee and the university tuition to support the various student organizations, and to enhance generally the quality of student life.

In addition, a large number of organizations have active chapters on campus.

■ Expenses and Financial Aid

➼ *full-time tuition & fees—resident, $10,630; RI, MA, NH, or VT resident, $15,946; resident of any other state, $22,420*
➼ *part-time tuition & fees—resident, $371/credit hr.; RI, MA, NH, or VT resident, $556/credit hr.; resident of any other state, $782/credit hr.* ➼ *financial aid available; Tuition Remission Grant, opportunity scholarship, Stafford Loan*
➼ *law school financial aid application required by April 1*

■ Career Services

Connecticut operates a comprehensive career services office for the benefit of students and alumni/ae. The school offers a large and geographically diverse on-campus interviewing program, extensive individual and group counseling, a resource library, job listings, mentor programs, employment information sessions, newsletters, and job bulletins. Also, the School participates in several off-site public interest, minority, and patent intellectual property job fairs.

Applicant Group for the 1998-1999 Academic Year

University of Connecticut School of Law
This grid includes only applicants with a 3-digit LSAT score and a GPA (approximately 99% of all full-time applicants).

LSAT Score	GPA															
	3.75 - 4.00		3.50 - 3.74		3.25 - 3.49		3.00 - 3.24		2.75 - 2.99		2.50 - 2.74		Below 2.50		Total	
	Apps	Adm	Apps	Adm	Apps	Adm	Apps	Adm	Apps	Adm	Apps	Adm	Apps	Adm	Apps	Adm
175-180	0	0	1	1	0	0	0	0	0	0	0	0	0	0	1	1
170-174	0	0	1	0	1	1	1	1	1	1	2	2	1	0	7	5
165-169	5	5	4	3	16	15	6	6	3	3	1	1	0	0	35	33
160-164	6	5	26	25	47	47	41	40	19	15	9	8	5	3	153	143
155-159	20	15	60	45	80	45	72	36	38	13	12	2	8	2	290	158
150-154	9	2	26	1	58	6	57	3	36	2	18	0	10	0	214	14
145-149	4	2	16	3	25	2	28	2	22	0	14	0	12	0	121	9
140-144	2	0	9	0	14	1	11	0	27	0	11	0	12	0	86	1
Below 140	0	0	6	0	4	0	12	0	21	0	7	0	19	0	69	0
Total	46	29	149	78	245	117	228	88	167	34	74	13	67	5	976	364

Apps = Number of Applicants
Adm = Number Admitted
This is to be used as a general guide only. Nonnumerical factors are strongly considered for all applicants.

Cornell University Law School

Ithaca, NY 14853

E-Mail: lawadmit@law.mail.cornell.edu
URL: http://www.lawschool.cornell.edu

■ Introduction

Cornell is a national center of learning located in Ithaca, New York, the heart of the Finger Lakes region of New York State. The Law School's small classes, broad curriculum and distinguished faculty, combined with the advantages of being part of one of the world's leading research universities, make it ideal for those who value both depth and breadth in their legal studies. Students find Ithaca to be a safe and non-stressful, yet culturally rich, environment in which to pursue legal studies.

■ Enrollment/Student Body

➻ *3,000 applicants*　➻ *189 enrolled first-year class 1998*
➻ *full-time 25th/75th percentile GPA—3.30/3.70*
➻ *full-time 25th/75th percentile LSAT—163/166*
➻ *543 total full-time*　➻ *27.6% minority*
➻ *44% women*　➻ *58 states & foreign countries represented*
➻ *250 undergraduate schools represented*

Sixty percent of Cornell's entering students have taken one or more years between completion of their under-graduate degree and enrollment in law school. Selective admissions standards, combined with an emphasis on applicants' unique records and achievements, ensure that the student body is made up of people with wide-ranging interests, skills, concerns, and backgrounds.

■ Faculty

➻ *54 total*　➻ *39 full-time*　➻ *15 part-time or adjunct*
➻ *12 women*　➻ *4 minority*

Cornell's faculty are known not only as prolific scholars but also as great teachers. Tenured and tenure-track faculty teach and produce scholarship in their area of law; clinical faculty run client-focused and simulation courses centered around legal aid and several specialty clinics; and a large number of visitors, associated faculty from other university divisions, and adjunct faculty teach at the school each year. Many of the latter group are legal scholars and professors from other countries who teach in the law school's significant international program.

■ Library, Physical Facilities, and Computing

➻ *600,442 volumes & microform equivalents*
➻ *library hours: Mon.-Thurs., 8:00 A.M.-11:00 P.M.;*
Fri., 8:00 A.M.-5:00 P.M.; Sat., NOON-5:00 P.M.;
Sun., NOON-11:00 P.M.　➻ *LEXIS*　➻ *NEXIS*
➻ *WESTLAW*　➻ *7 full-time librarians*　➻ *library seats 407*

The Law School is located in the renovated and expanded Myron Taylor Hall, at the heart of the scenic 740-acre Cornell University campus. Hughes Hall, the Law School dormitory, is adjacent to the main Law School building and contains single rooms for about 80 students and a dining facility for breakfast and lunch.

Cornell is one of the nation's leaders in the development and support of electronic legal research. Students have access to the full array of Internet services, including sophisticated electronic mail. The Law School's multiple-node network and computer terminals are available to students for word processing, legal research, statistical analysis, and database management. Students also have access to the many satellite computer clusters and mainframe facilities located on the university campus.

■ Curriculum

➻ *Academic Support Program*　➻ *84 semester credit hours required to graduate*　➻ *degrees & joint/combined programs:*
J.D.; J.D. with specialization in international legal studies;
J.D./LL.M. in International Law and Comparative Law;
J.D./Maitrise en Droit; LL.M.; J.S.D.; J.D./M.B.A.;
J.D./M.P.A.; J.D./M.I.L.R.; J.D./M.R.P.; J.D./M.A.; J.D./Ph.D.
➻ *semesters, start in late Aug.*　➻ *first-year section size—32; other class ranges—70-100; first-year intensive writing classes average—32*

Cornell offers a national law curriculum leading to the J.D. degree. First-year students take a group of required courses and an intensive Practice Training course stressing a variety of legal research, writing, and advocacy techniques. After the first year, students may choose from a wide range of elective courses, including many seminars and problem courses. Optional concentrations are offered in four areas—advocacy, public law, business law and regulation, and general practice.

■ International Legal Studies

The Berger International Legal Studies Program is one of the country's oldest and most distinguished programs in international legal education. Cornell's comprehensive program features a unique J.D. specialization opportunity, a three-year J.D./LL.M. degree in International and Comparative Law, a four-year J.D./Maîtrise en Droit (French law degree) program, a four-year J.D./M.L.P. (German law degree) program, a Paris summer institute with the University of Paris I (Panthéon-Sorbonne), a comprehensive speaker series, a large number of visiting foreign professors and scholars, a weekly luncheon discussion series, and a leading journal of international and comparative law edited by students.

■ Clinical Studies

The Cornell Legal Aid Clinic, offering legal services to individuals financially unable to employ an attorney, provides students with the chance to engage in the super-vised practice of law under the direction of experienced attorneys. Clinical faculty also conduct a variety of other specialized clinics and skills courses within the regular curriculum. Over 50 percent of the Law School's graduates participate in a clinical program.

■ Admission

➡ *Bachelor's degree from accredited college or university required*
➡ *application deadline—Feb. 1*   ➡ *LSAT, LSDAS required*
➡ *application fee—$65*

Admission is highly competitive. The admissions committee bases its decisions on such nonquantifiable factors as extra-curricular and community activities, life experience, and work background. They also consider factors such as the LSAT score, undergraduate grades, graduate work, and recommendations. Diversity is considered a positive factor in an applicant's file, and applicants are encouraged to submit a separate statement describing their ethnic, cultural, social, and linguistic backgrounds.

■ Student Activities

Student-edited law journals include the *Cornell Law Review* (published continuously since 1916), the *Cornell International Law Journal* (established in 1967), and the newly established *Cornell Journal of Law and Public Policy*. Student organizations and activities include: American Indian Law Students Association; Asian American Law Students Association; Black Law Students Association; Herbert W. Briggs Society of International Law; Cornell Christian Legal Society; Cornell Criminal Justice Society; Cornell Law Student Association; Cornell Law Scales of Justice; Corporate Law Society; *The Tower*; Cornell Law School Peer Advising Center; Environmental Law Society; Federalist Society; James R. Withrow, Jr., Program on Legal Ethics; Jewish Law Student Association; Lambda Law Students; Latino American Law Students Association; Latter-Day Saint Law Student Association; Law Partners' Association;

Moot Court Program; National Lawyer's Guild; Phi Delta Phi; Public Interest Law Union; Science and Law Student Association; Women's Law Coalition.

■ Expenses and Financial Aid

➡ *tuition & fees—$24,100*   ➡ *estimated additional expenses—$7,400, room & meals; $760, books & supplies; $3,940, personal expenses*   ➡ *need-based scholarships offered*
➡ *Need Access Diskette required no later than March 15*

Cornell offers a need-based financial aid program. About 40 percent of students receive scholarship aid, with a higher percentage receiving government-backed loans. Minority and/or economically disadvantaged students are eligible for enhanced scholarship awards.
  A generous Public Interest Low Income Protection Plan assists those choosing qualifying public interest law jobs through the use of a moderated loan repayment plan and loan forgiveness.

■ Career Services

Cornell's students continue to be among the most recruited in the country. Every fall, hundreds of employers from across the country visit the law school and conduct employment interviews. Employers also participate in law school-sponsored job fairs in cities such as Boston, Los Angeles, New York, San Francisco, and Washington, DC. A professionally-staffed Career Office provides employment counseling to students and serves as a liaison with legal employers, both public and private.

Admission Profile Not Available

Creighton University School of Law

2500 California Plaza
Omaha, NE 68178

E-Mail: admit@culaw.creighton.edu
URL: http://www.creighton.edu/CULAW
Phone: 402.280.2872

■ Introduction

Creighton University, a privately endowed and supported Jesuit university, was founded in 1878. Creighton is the most diverse educational institution of its size in the nation. In addition to the School of Law, Creighton has a Medical School, Dental School, School of Pharmacy and Allied Health, School of Nursing, School of Business Administration, College of Arts and Sciences, and a Graduate School, making it the center of professional education in the Midwest. The university is located just blocks from downtown Omaha, a metropolitan area with a population of more than 600,000. Known as the River City, Omaha is the heart of the Midlands and the largest metroplex between Chicago and Denver.

■ The School of Law

The School of Law, established in 1904, has been a member of the AALS since 1907 and approved by the ABA for more than 60 years. Alumni from the law school are practicing in all 50 states and in more than 5 foreign countries. The law school's current enrollment is 424. Students come from over 35 states and more than 166 undergraduate institutions. Twenty-four full-time professors and a group of part-time specialists chosen from the bench and bar comprise the faculty.

■ Enrollment/Student Body

➡ *742 applicants*   ➡ *485 admitted first-year class 1998*
➡ *137 enrolled first-year class 1998*
➡ *full-time 25th/75th percentile GPA—2.74/3.42*
➡ *part-time 25th/75th percentile GPA—3.01/3.92*
➡ *full-time 25th/75th percentile LSAT—148/153*
➡ *part-time 25th/75th percentile LSAT—153/158*
➡ *409 total full-time*   ➡ *15 total part-time*
➡ *9.2% minority*   ➡ *42% women*   ➡ *36 states & foreign countries represented*   ➡ *166 undergraduate schools represented*

■ Faculty

➡ *60 total*   ➡ *24 full-time*   ➡ *36 part-time or adjunct*
➡ *16 women*   ➡ *2 minority*

■ Library and Physical Facilities

➡ *240,000 volumes & equivalents*   ➡ *library hours: Mon.-Thurs., 7:00 A.M.-MIDNIGHT; Fri., 7:00 A.M.-8:00 P.M.; Sat., 9:00 A.M.-8:00 P.M.; Sun., NOON-MIDNIGHT*   ➡ *LEXIS*
➡ *NEXIS*   ➡ *WESTLAW*   ➡ *6 full-time librarians*
➡ *library seats 386*

■ Curriculum

➡ *Academic Support Program*   ➡ *94 credits required to graduate*   ➡ *111 courses available*   ➡ *degrees available: J.D.; J.D./M.B.A.*   ➡ *semesters, start in Aug.*
➡ *range of first-year class size—10-75*

The first-year curriculum, required of all students, consists of Civil Procedure, Constitutional Law, Contracts, Legal Research, Legal Writing, Property, and Torts. Other than Professional Responsibility and advanced legal writing, required of all second-year students, second- and third-year students design their own program of studies from the numerous electives and seminars offered. The curriculum prepares students for the practice of law in any state.

■ Clinic and Internships

Third-year students selected to work in the Legal Clinic provide pro bono legal assistance to indigent citizens of Omaha. The School of Law also offers judicial and clinical internships in a number of city, county, federal, and Legal Aid offices.

■ Student Activities

The Student Bar Association is the student government of the law school. The purposes of the organization are to make law students aware of the obligations and opportunities existing for lawyers through Bar Association activities, promote a consciousness of professional responsibility, and provide a forum for student activities.

The school has chapters of the American Trial Lawyers Association and Phi Alpha Delta and Phi Delta Phi legal fraternities. Other student groups include the Black Law Students Association, the Latino Law Students Association, the Society of International Law, the Environmental Law Society, the Law Partners Association, Federalist Society, ACLU Chapter, Public Interest Law Forum, the Rutherford Institute, and the Women Law Students Association.

The *Creighton Law Review*, edited and managed by students, is a scholarly legal journal that is circulated nationally and internationally. The Review publishes articles contributed by prominent legal scholars, in addition to notes and comments written by students. Appellate brief writing and oral argument begin in the first-year Legal Writing program. During the second year, intraschool tournaments culminate in the selection of students for the domestic and international Moot Court Boards and the selection of teams to compete in regional and national moot court tournaments and the Philip C. Jessup International Law Moot Court program. The Client Counseling program promotes student knowledge and interest in the counseling and interviewing functions of law practice. An intraschool competition is held annually and culminates in students being selected for the Client Counseling Board and to represent Creighton in the national competition sponsored by the ABA's Law Student Division.

■ Admission

➡ *Bachelor's degree from accredited college or university required*
➡ *application deadline—May 1, rolling admission, early application preferred*   ➡ *LSAT, LSDAS required*
➡ *application fee—$40*

The applicant's LSAT score and undergraduate GPA are the primary factors in determining acceptance. Applicants with an LSAT percentile of 82-99 and a GPA range of 2.8 or higher have a very good chance of being admitted. Applicants with an LSAT percentile of 56-81 and a GPA of 3.1 or higher have a good chance of being admitted. Applicants with an LSAT percentile of 45 to 55 and a GPA of 3.25 or higher are also considered. Other factors that are considered by the Admission Committee include the personal statement, demonstrated leadership ability, employment and other experience, and graduate degrees. Two letters of recommendation are required.

■ Expenses and Financial Aid

➡ *tuition & fees—full-time, $15,684; part-time (per credit hour) $525* ➡ *estimated additional expenses—$10,870* ➡ *merit & merit-/need-based scholarships available* ➡ *minority scholarships available* ➡ *financial aid available* ➡ *FAFSA form for need analysis*

Most scholarships are awarded on the basis of superior academic achievement and LSAT scores. Continuation of scholarship aid after the first year is normally contingent upon academic achievement and participation in cocurricular activities of high academic worth. Once an applicant has been accepted, scholarship applications will be mailed to those applicants who meet merit guidelines. Long-term, low-interest loans under federal programs, as well as The Access Group and LAWLOANS are available. Those seeking loans and scholarship aid must use the FAFSA form. Additional information about scholarships and financial aid is available through the law school's Admission Office.

■ Minority Scholarship Program

The School of Law actively recruits minority students and has a substantial minority scholarship program. For the 1998-1999 school year 23 students have minority scholarships ranging from one-quarter to full tuition.

■ Career Services

The law school's Office of Career Service is committed to providing professional placement services for students and alumni. In addition to seminars and personal counseling, the office maintains a dynamic Web site that allows students to explore thousands of career opportunities throughout the world (www.creighton.edu/culaw/cso/).

Applicant Group for the 1998-1999 Academic Year

Creighton University School of Law
This grid includes only applicants who earned 120-180 LSAT scores under standard administrations in the 1996-1997 testing year.

LSAT Score	3.75 +		3.50 - 3.74		3.25 - 3.49		3.00 - 3.24		2.75 - 2.99		2.50 - 2.74		2.25 - 2.49		2.00 - 2.24		Below 2.00		No GPA		Total	
	Apps	Adm	Apps	Adm	Apps	Adm	Apps	Adm	Apps	Adm	Apps	Adm	Apps	Adm	Apps	Adm	Apps	Adm	Apps	Adm	Apps	Adm
175-180	0	0	0	0	0	0	0	0	0	0	0	0	0	0	0	0	0	0	0	0	0	0
170-174	1	1	0	0	0	0	0	0	0	0	0	0	0	0	0	0	0	0	0	0	1	1
165-169	2	2	0	0	0	0	1	1	2	2	0	0	0	0	0	0	0	0	1	0	6	5
160-164	5	5	6	5	6	5	3	3	3	3	1	1	1	1	0	0	0	0	0	0	25	23
155-159	11	11	5	5	19	18	13	13	16	14	7	6	7	5	4	3	0	0	1	0	83	75
150-154	13	12	21	21	35	32	51	47	30	27	24	22	6	5	3	1	1	1	3	2	187	170
145-149	11	10	27	25	45	32	53	38	50	27	27	17	10	8	3	1	2	0	0	0	228	158
140-144	8	1	18	7	17	3	25	4	28	5	17	1	12	0	3	0	0	0	6	3	134	24
135-139	2	0	3	0	4	0	9	1	6	0	11	0	4	0	5	0	2	0	5	0	51	1
130-134	0	0	1	0	0	0	1	0	1	0	0	0	4	0	2	0	0	0	1	0	10	0
125-129	0	0	0	0	0	0	2	0	1	0	0	0	2	0	1	0	0	0	1	0	7	0
120-124	0	0	0	0	0	0	0	0	0	0	0	0	0	0	0	0	0	0	0	0	0	0
Total	53	42	81	63	126	90	158	107	137	78	87	47	46	19	21	5	5	1	18	5	732	457

Apps = Number of Applicants
Adm = Number Admitted
Reflects 99% of the total applicant pool.

University of Dayton School of Law

300 College Park
Dayton, OH 45469-2760

E-Mail: lawinfo@udayton.edu
URL: http://www.udayton.edu/~law
Phone: 937.229.3555

■ Overview

The University of Dayton School of Law offers a single-division, full-time program of studies in a supportive and value-centered environment. The curriculum combines both traditional and innovative teaching methods, and it is designed to prepare graduates for the practice of law or for law-related careers nationwide. A private law school of 495 students, the University of Dayton School of Law continues to build a national reputation as alumni of the law school find employment in a variety of settings throughout the country. The School of Law is approved by the ABA and is a member of the AALS.

■ Mission

The mission of the University of Dayton School of Law is to enroll a diverse group of men and women who are intellectually curious, who possess self-discipline, and who are well motivated, and to rigorously train them in the substantive and procedural principles of public and private law. Faculty expect that graduates will become highly qualified and competent practicing attorneys who will uphold the highest professional standards.

■ Enrollment/Student Body

➥ 187 enrolled first-year class 1998   ➥ full-time 25th/75th percentile GPA—1.86/3.95   ➥ full-time 25th/75th percentile LSAT—133/169   ➥ 22% minority enrolled first-year class 1998   ➥ 112 undergraduate colleges represented in first-year class 1998   ➥ 54% of first-year class from 27 states other than Ohio   ➥ 16% of the first-year class had undergraduate majors in engineering & the sciences

■ Environment for Studying Law

Keller Hall—Joseph E. Keller Hall was dedicated in the fall of 1997 as the new center for legal education at the University of Dayton. With technology integrated through-out the building, this 122,500-square-foot complex features a dramatic atrium, state-of-the-art classrooms, and spacious law library. Keller Hall provides an outstanding environ-ment for studying law and enhances the school's tradition of preparing highly qualified legal professionals. Ready access is provided by 1,400 data and power outlets to the law school network from virtually any location in the law building.

The University—Founded in 1850, the University of Dayton today is the largest private university in Ohio and the eighth-largest Catholic university in the nation. More than 6,500 undergraduate students and 3,500 graduate students are enrolled at the university. The 110-acre campus is located in a residential neighborhood minutes from the city's center and includes a variety of student services, such as health care, on-campus housing, child care, meal plans, and banking.

The City—Law students have special opportunities available because the metropolitan area (population of

942,000) is home to a sizable judicial and legal community. Municipal courts, the Montgomery County Court of Common Pleas, the Second Ohio District Court of Appeals, and the U.S. District Court for the Southern District of Ohio are all located nearby. In addition, law students may find part-time employment with a number of the area's several Fortune 500 companies and their divisions (NCR, Standard Register, Mead, and LEXIS/NEXIS).

■ Law Library

➥ 262,739 volumes & equivalents   ➥ more than 5,500 legal serials   ➥ LEXIS   ➥ WESTLAW   ➥ computer center for word processing & database management   ➥ every seat in the law library has data & power, allowing access to the Internet and online research services   ➥ 11 full-time staff

■ Faculty

➥ 27 full-time   ➥ 30 part-time or adjunct

Student and alumni evaluations consistently give high marks to faculty of the law school. Faculty members are noted for being accessible to students, and it is this commitment that creates an environment which fosters faculty-student interaction. Faculty members at the School of Law bring a breadth of experience and research interests to the classroom.

■ Special Programs

Program in Law and Technology—The Program in Law and Technology allows upper-level students the opportunity to enroll in a number of specialized courses covering computer law, patent law, copyright law, trademark law, trade secrets, and transfers of technology and licensing. Additionally, qualified students may be placed as interns with area legal departments and law firms.

Joint-Degree Programs—The School of Law offers a joint J.D./Master of Business Administration degree. The degree is an integrated program of study that results in the conferral of both degrees at the time of graduation.

Law Clinic—The School of Law operates a law clinic which functions as a "typical" small, general-practice law office. Located within the law building, the clinic provides third-year students with the opportunity to represent actual clients in both civil and criminal matters.

Judicial Externships—Second- and third-year law students may participate in the law school's externship program offering the opportunity to clerk with area municipal, county, and federal judges. Externs undertake research for case decisions, thereby further developing research and writing skills, as well as gaining more direct knowledge of the judicial system.

Professional Skills Courses—Development of professional skills is offered through a variety of courses at the University of Dayton. These courses emphasize roles, situations, and problems that are commonly encountered by practicing attorneys. Professional skills courses include the three-semester Legal Profession course series, Negotiation and Mediation, Civil Trial Practice and Criminal Trial Practice, Mock Trial, Complex Litigation, and Land Use Planning.

Academic Excellence Program—The Academic Excellence Program includes a five-day orientation program prior to the start of the academic year, and a weekly tutorial session during both the first and second semesters. Entering students who are from economically or educationally disadvantaged backgrounds are especially encouraged to take part in the Academic Excellence Program.

■ Alumni and Placement Information

Graduates of the School of Law find success in a variety of career endeavors across the United States. A full-time placement director assists students in career planning and employment search activities. Counseling, career reference materials, position postings for direct contacts, and coordination of on- and off-campus interviews are provided as appropriate for those seeking clerkships, part-time and summer employment, further legal education, or permanent positions. Alumni of the School of Law include 2,950 men and women who are using their legal training in a variety of settings throughout the United States.

■ Activities

Student activities include the *University of Dayton Law Review*, Moot Court Board, Volunteer Income Tax Assistance, Asian Law Society, Student Bar Association, Women's Caucus, Black Law Students Association, Delta Theta

Phi, Phi Alpha Delta, Phi Delta Phi, Society of International Law, Hispanic Law Society, Association of Trial Lawyers of America, *Equitable Relief* newspaper, *Fiat Justia* yearbook, Law and Medicine Society, the Law and Technology Society, Christian Legal Society, the Jewish Student Union, St. Thomas More Society, the Federalist Society, and the Rutherford Institute.

■ Admission

➡ *candidates wishing to be considered for full or partial scholarships should submit admission materials by March 1*
➡ *Priority deadline for applications—May 1*

■ Expenses and Financial Aid

➡ *full-time tuition—$18,750*   ➡ *35 scholarship awards per year available (based on past academic performance & performance on the LSAT—ranging from full tuition to $2,500)*
➡ *loan programs available*
➡ *part-time employment available for upper-level students*

■ Questions Regarding the School of Law

Prospective students are invited to contact the School of Law Office of Admission with questions and concerns. The Office of Admission hours are Monday through Friday, 8:30 A.M. to 4:30 P.M. (Phone requests for admission materials may be made anytime throughout the week.)

Requests for materials also may be made via the Internet: lawinfo@udayton.edu or via the World Wide Web at http://www.udayton.edu/~law.

Applicant Group for the 1998-1999 Academic Year

University of Dayton School of Law
This grid provides a general sense of the admission decisions rendered by the Admission Committee. Candidates who have specific questions regarding admission criteria are welcome to phone the School of Law Admission Office.

LSAT Score	GPA									
	120-140		141-149		150-159		160-180		Total	
	Adm	Apps	Adm	Apps	Adm	Apps	Adm	Apps	Adm	Apps
3.50-4.00	4	15	68	78	100	104	26	26	198	226
3.00-3.49	7	47	103	165	191	198	18	18	319	428
2.50-2.99	3	79	55	183	83	87	8	10	149	359
2.49 & Below	1	47	4	54	34	44	5	6	44	151
Total	15	188	230	480	408	433	57	60	710	1164

University of Denver College of Law

7039 East 18th Avenue
Denver, CO 80220

E-Mail: admissions@adm.law.du.edu
URL: http://www.law.du.edu
Phone: 303.871.6135

■ Introduction

The University of Denver College of Law, a private institution, is located on a 33-acre site which is 15 minutes from downtown Denver. The Law Center, built in 1984, provides more than "state-of-the-art" library, classroom, and student facilities; it also reflects the tradition of the Inns of Court, where students learn the law in the company of members of the bench and bar. The campus is home to the National Center for Preventive Law, the Rocky Mountain Mineral Law Foundation, and other organizations which enhance the academic atmosphere.

■ Enrollment/Student Body

➼ *1,683 applicants*   ➼ *1,099 admitted first-year class 1998*
➼ *333 enrolled first-year class 1998*   ➼ *full-time 25th/75th percentile GPA—2.85/3.42*   ➼ *part-time 25th/75th percentile GPA—2.77/3.50*   ➼ *full-time 25th/75th percentile LSAT—151/157*   ➼ *part-time 25th/75th percentile LSAT—149/154*
➼ *751 total full-time*   ➼ *290 total part-time*
➼ *9% minority*   ➼ *52% women*   ➼ *54 states & foreign countries represented*   ➼ *170 undergraduate schools represented*

■ Faculty

➼ *91 total*   ➼ *42 full-time*   ➼ *49 part-time or adjunct*
   ➼ *16 women*   ➼ *5 minority*

■ Library and Physical Facilities

➼ *321,596 volumes & equivalents*   ➼ *library hours:*
Mon.- Thurs., 7:30 A.M.-MIDNIGHT; Fri., 7:30 A.M.-10:00 P.M.;
Sat., 8:00 A.M.-10:00 P.M.; Sun., 9:00 A.M.-MIDNIGHT
➼ *LEXIS*   ➼ *NEXIS*   ➼ *WESTLAW*   ➼ *DIALOG*
➼ *INFOTRAC*   ➼ *12 full-time librarians*
➼ *library seats 642*

■ Curriculum

➼ *Academic Support Program*   ➼ *90 credits required to graduate*   ➼ *117 courses available*   ➼ *degrees available: J.D.; J.D./M.B.A.; J.D. dual degree in International Studies, International Management, Psychology, History, Social Work, Sociology, and Mineral Economics*   ➼ *semesters, start in Aug.*
➼ *range of first-year class—20-87*

Lawyering Process Course—The first-year curriculum includes an innovative Lawyering Process Course which offers students, in small group law firm settings, experience with the standard operations and skills of the lawyer's craft in interviewing, counseling, negotiation, decision making, and litigation. The small groups replicate law firms and reinforce cooperative work. Coursework in legal research and writing is taught in the context of simulated client problems.

■ Special Programs

Drawing upon its location in one of the nation's natural resources and energy capitals, the University of Denver College of Law offers a rich program in natural resources and environmental law. Students can choose from a variety of courses. There are also abundant opportunities for independent research and internships in the local energy, environment, and natural resource community.

The International Legal Studies program is designed for students interested in international comparative law, international organization, or transnational business. Students in the program may work on the *Denver Journal of International Law and Policy* as staff members and editors. The International Law Society sponsors a rich schedule of outside speakers and an annual conference with invited guests from many organizations.

University of Denver has the only comprehensive program in transportation law in the United States. The program offers a unique opportunity to study the legal, regulatory, economic, and political developments in transportation. The basic course in Transportational Law offers an overview of all aspects of economic regulation of each of the domestic transport modes and also provides a survey of liability issues of the government's role in providing transport services. Students concentrating in Transportation Law are eligible for special scholarships that are awarded separately from other law scholarships.

The Business and Commercial Law program not only trains students to work with business entities but also prepares them for the specific needs of the corporate attorney. The program culminates in specialized seminars in business and commercial law. Corporate internships, highly prized one-semester assignments with large local corporations, are a valuable supplement to the coursework.

The Lawyering Skills program focuses on "what lawyers do." Courses in the regular curriculum are supplemented by the practical experience gained through public service legal work in the Student Law Office or through several internships or externships. The capstone of the program is the Student Law Office (Basic Civil Representation, Basic Criminal Representation, Advanced Public Interest Clinic) where students represent needy clients at all levels of the dispute resolution process. If the case reaches the litigation phase, the student handles all aspects of pretrial, trial preparation, and the trial itself—under faculty supervision. Focusing on one-to-one teaching and student responsibility, the program offers a rare opportunity to acquire lawyering skills.

■ Admission

➼ *Bachelor's degree required for admission*
➼ *application deadline—May 1*
➼ *rolling admission, application preferred Nov.-Jan.*
➼ *LSAT, LSDAS required*   ➼ *application fee—$45*

Applications should reach the College of Law between November and February to receive maximum consideration for admission the following August. Students may begin law study only in August. Applicants must take the

LSAT and subscribe to LSDAS. A baccalaureate degree from an approved college or university is required prior to registration. LSAT scores and records of academic performances are individually evaluated in the admission process. Of equal importance, however, are the applicant's work experience, significant personal accomplishments, interests, goals, and reasons for seeking admission to law school.

■ Student Activities

Student activities are sponsored by the Student Bar Association to which most students belong. The University of Denver's Moot Court program is designed to promote the necessary development of students' oral and written skills. D.U.'s law students have the opportunity to participate in six different Moot Court competitions. The Moot Court Board is comprised of students who have demonstrated merit in D.U.'s Moot Court program and have displayed a commitment to improving the oral and written skills of the student body. With faculty integrated support, the Moot Court Board organizes and runs D.U.'s Moot Court program.

Three scholarly journals are edited at the College of Law allowing students to participate in scholarly research in varied fields. Academic credit is awarded for work in the *Law Review, Journal of International Law and Policy*, and *Transportation Law Journal*. Many special interest organizations on campus are officially recognized by the Student Bar Association. Among those groups are the Asian American Law Students Association, the Black Law Students Association, the Entertainment Law Society, the Hispanic Law Students Association, the Native American Law

Students Association, the Public Interest Law Group, the Student Trial Lawyers Association, and the Women's Law Caucus/Children's Legal Issues in Perspective.

■ Expenses and Financial Aid

➨ *tuition & fees—full-time, $19,282; part-time, $12,440*
➨ *estimated additional expenses—$11,000 (health insurance, books, room & board, transportation)* ➨ *merit- & need-based scholarships available* ➨ *minority scholarships available*
➨ *FAFSA form due Feb. 1*

The Chancellor's Scholarship Program provides a unique educational experience to a limited number of motivated and qualified students committed to public service through law. These scholarships are awarded through open competition to entering first-year students. The annual scholarships are renewed for successive years based on satisfactory academic performance and full participation in all the activities of the program.

■ Career Services

The law school maintains a placement office staffed by a full-time director and two full-time assistants who aid both students and alumni in securing employment. The Career Services Office offers direct referral to part-time, full-time, summer, and career positions; arrangement of on-campus interviews each fall for second- and third-year students with law firms, governmental agencies, and corporations; and career counseling. The Career Services Office emphasizes its policy against discriminatory practices in the interviewing and hiring of its students and graduates.

Applicant Group for the 1998-1999 Academic Year

University of Denver College of Law
This grid includes only applicants who earned 120-180 LSAT scores under standard administrations.

LSAT Score	3.75 +		3.50 - 3.74		3.25 - 3.49		3.00 - 3.24		2.75 - 2.99		2.50 - 2.74		2.25 - 2.49		2.00 - 2.24		Below 2.00		No GPA		Total	
	Apps	Adm	Apps	Adm	Apps	Adm	Apps	Adm	Apps	Adm	Apps	Adm	Apps	Adm	Apps	Adm	Apps	Adm	Apps	Adm	Apps	Adm
175-180	0	0	0	0	0	0	0	0	0	0	0	0	0	0	0	0	0	0	0	0	0	0
170-174	1	1	2	2	2	2	1	1	1	1	0	0	0	0	0	0	0	0	0	0	7	7
165-169	5	4	9	8	8	7	3	3	3	3	4	4	1	1	0	0	1	1	1	1	35	32
160-164	11	11	16	13	23	18	30	29	23	20	15	14	4	3	8	8	1	1	2	0	133	117
155-159	20	17	50	49	92	87	84	81	66	64	41	39	18	17	5	5	0	0	2	0	378	359
150-154	18	18	75	71	98	92	104	96	97	87	43	38	25	19	9	0	2	2	6	2	477	425
145-149	6	4	33	24	45	26	106	38	73	16	52	3	19	2	12	0	3	0	9	2	358	115
140-144	3	1	12	1	15	1	35	1	33	0	22	0	20	0	13	0	1	0	8	0	162	4
135-139	1	0	5	0	9	0	10	0	6	0	16	0	12	0	4	0	2	0	2	0	67	0
130-134	0	0	0	0	2	0	3	0	3	0	2	0	7	0	3	1	1	1	3	0	24	2
125-129	0	0	0	0	0	0	0	0	0	0	0	0	1	0	1	0	0	0	3	0	5	0
120-124	0	0	0	0	0	0	0	0	0	0	0	0	0	0	0	0	0	0	0	0	0	0
Total	65	56	202	168	294	233	376	249	305	191	195	98	107	42	55	14	11	5	36	5	1646	1061

Apps = Number of Applicants
Adm = Number Admitted
Reflects 98% of the total applicant pool.

DePaul University College of Law

25 East Jackson Boulevard
Chicago, IL 60604

E-Mail: lawinfo@wppost.depaul.edu
URL: http://www.law.depaul.edu
Phone: 312.362.6831, toll-free: 800.428.7453

■ Introduction

DePaul University is the second largest private university in Illinois and enjoys the advantages of education conducted in a vibrant urban setting. Located in the heart of Chicago's business and legal communities, the College of Law is just a short walk from the Harold Washington Library, the largest municipal library in the world. Proximity to courts, government offices, and many law firms affords extensive contact with Chicago's legal community. Alumni include the Mayor of Chicago, state and federal judges, and managing partners of several Chicago law firms. The college offers full-time, part-time, and summer programs. DePaul is fully accredited by the ABA, is a member of AALS, and has an Order of the Coif chapter. The College of Law has completed its final phase of an ambitious $14 million fund-raising campaign to enhance its endowment and programs, including $6 million which was used for a complete renovation and expansion of its physical plant.

■ Enrollment/Student Body

➡ *1,939 applicants*　➡ *392 enrolled first-year class 1998 (293 full-time, 99 part-time)*　➡ *full-time 25th/75th percentile GPA—2.87/3.37*　➡ *part-time 25th/75th percentile GPA—2.69/3.13*　➡ *full-time 25th/75th percentile LSAT—149/155*
➡ *part-time 25th/75th percentile LSAT—146/153*
➡ *766 total full-time*　➡ *327 total part-time*
➡ *16% minority*　➡ *51% women*
➡ *31 states & foreign countries represented*
➡ *120 undergraduate schools represented in 1998 class*

The college has an increasingly national enrollment—48 percent of 1998 entering full-time students are from out-of-state. Each entering class brings a rich diversity in age, ethnicity, education, and career experience. For example, 35 students in the 1998 entering class had earned graduate and professional degrees. The average age of full-time day students and part-time evening students is 24 and 28, respectively. DePaul's bar passage rate has consistently exceeded the state average.

■ Faculty

➡ *134 total*　➡ *48 full-time*　➡ *86 part-time or adjunct*
➡ *54 women*　➡ *11 minority*

DePaul faculty are recognized scholars who represent a variety of professional backgrounds and interests as diverse as the curriculum. Many have advanced degrees in fields such as biology, political science, business, psychology, archaeology, theatre, public health, and philosophy.

■ Expenses and Financial Aid

➡ *tuition & fees—full-time, $19,800; part-time, $13,400*
➡ *additional expenses—approximately $10,000*
➡ *performance- & need-based scholarships available*
➡ *Free Application for Federal Student Aid due March 1*

■ Curriculum

➡ *Academic Support Program*　➡ *86 units required to graduate*　➡ *144 courses available*　➡ *degrees available: J.D. & J.D./M.B.A.*　➡ *semesters, start in early Aug.*
➡ *range of first-year class size—18-75 students*

■ Library and Physical Facilities

➡ *343,000 volumes & equivalents*　➡ *library hours: Mon.-Fri., 8:00 A.M.-11:00 P.M.; Sat., 8:00 A.M.-6:00 P.M.; Sun., NOON-10:00 P.M.*　➡ *LEXIS*　➡ *NEXIS*
➡ *WESTLAW*　➡ *DIALOG*　➡ *ILLINET On-line*
➡ *9 full-time librarians*

Holding extensive tax, health, and human rights law collections, the library is designated as an official government depository. Fully networked word processing and data management facilities include 95 personal computers. The college occupies six and one-half floors in both the 17-story Lewis Center and adjoining 15-story O'Malley Place in Chicago's Loop.

■ Special Specific Programs

Legal Clinic—An in-house component of the college, the legal clinic has a full-time staff of eight, including three clinical professors. Students serve clients from the initial interview through trial and acquire extensive experience.

Externships—Providing students with academic credit through supervised field work, externships are offered by federal and state judges, various municipal agencies, and a number of not-for-profit organizations.

International Human Rights Law Institute—This research institute sponsors conferences, engages in scholarly work, and cooperates with other human rights organizations and international bodies. This institute also houses the International Criminal Justice and Weapons Control Center, which is the only such center among U.S. law schools.

Center for Church/State Studies—An academic, nondenominational research institute, the center directs studies of the legal structures of American religious organizations.

Health Law Institute—This research institute sponsors national conferences on health law issues and works with community organizations on health policy and legislation. The centerpiece of the institute is the *Journal of Health and Hospital Law*.

Center for Law and Science—Established in 1997, this legal center is devoted to identifying, collecting and analyzing important scientific literature, trials and on-going appellate reviews of criminal and tort cases that address the intersection of the fields of law and science.

Study Abroad—DePaul and the University College Dublin have a student-exchange program whereby a small number of second-year students from both law schools undertake legal studies abroad for a semester.

J.D./M.B.A.—DePaul grants the combined Juris Doctor and Master of Business Administration degree.

Graduate Studies—DePaul was the first United States law school to offer courses toward the LL.M. in Health Law. The college also offers the LL.M. in Taxation program, featuring leading tax practitioners from Chicago law firms. DePaul educates about 100 graduate students in Health Law and Tax Law each year.

Professional Skills—DePaul is committed to education in professional skills. Among courses offered in dispute resolution are Arbitration, Dispute Resolution, Mediation, Mediation Clinic, Advanced Mediation, Interviewing, Counseling, and Negotiation. Courses in litigation skills include Product Liability, Juvenile Law, Pretrial Civil and Criminal Strategies, Trial Advocacy, Advanced Trial Advocacy, Complex Litigation, Law Clinic, Extern and Appellate Technique.

■ Admission

➡ *Bachelor's degree from an accredited college or university required* ➡ *application deadline—April 1*
➡ *rolling admission (first letters sent about March 1)*
➡ *LSAT, LSDAS required* ➡ *application fee—$40*

DePaul adheres to a policy of nondiscrimination and encourages applications from traditionally underrepresented minority groups. A faculty committee reviews applications. Undergraduate GPA and LSAT scores are highly significant admission criteria. When the LSAT is repeated, the average score is used. For the 1998-1999 academic year, 1,589 candidates applied for admission to the full-time (day) division; 350 candidates applied to the part-time (evening) division.

■ Student Activities

In addition to legal writing and research and senior research seminar courses, four student-edited law journals provide students with intensive legal research and writing training. The journals are *The DePaul Law Review*, the *Journal of Health and Hospital Law*, the *DePaul Business Law Journal*, and the *Journal of Art and Entertainment Law*. The Student Bar Association sponsors lectures and social functions. Through the Student Bar Association and student-faculty committees, students participate in the decision process of the college. Among the many student organizations are Moot Court Society; Women's Law Caucus; the Black, Latino, and Asian Law Student Associations; Public Interest Law Association; DePaul chapter of the ACLU; International Law Society; Decalogue Society; National Lawyers Guild; Computer Law Society; Federalist Society; and Environmental Law Society.

■ Career Services

Alumni, faculty, and students contribute to an active and aggressive career services network. The College of Law sponsors an extensive on-campus interviewing program and a series of career seminars for students. The teaching and publishing reputations of the faculty and the largest alumni/ae bench and bar network in the Chicago area complement three full-time DePaul career services officers.

Applicant Group for the 1998-1999 Academic Year

DePaul University College of Law
This grid includes all full-time applicants who earned LSAT scores on the 120-180 scale under standard test administrations and whose submission files were complete and reviewed by the faculty admission committee.

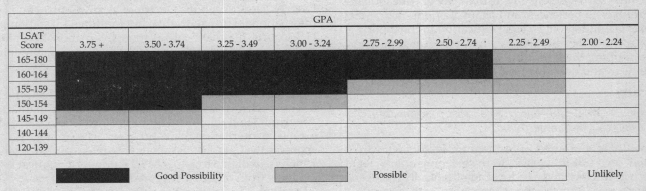

LSAT Score	GPA 3.75 +	3.50 - 3.74	3.25 - 3.49	3.00 - 3.24	2.75 - 2.99	2.50 - 2.74	2.25 - 2.49	2.00 - 2.24
165-180								
160-164								
155-159								
150-154								
145-149								
140-144								
120-139								

■ Good Possibility   ▨ Possible   ▢ Unlikely

This chart is to be used as a general guide only. Nonnumerical factors are also considered.

Detroit College of Law at Michigan State University

316 Law College Building
East Lansing, MI 48824

E-Mail: law@pilot.msu.edu
URL: http://www.dcl.edu
Phone: 517.432.0222

■ Introduction

Founded in 1891, Detroit College of Law at Michigan State University was the first law school established in Detroit. The college is a privately controlled and endowed coeducational institution devoted exclusively to professional education in law. For over 100 years it has continued to provide superior educational opportunities to qualified and ambitious men and women. Many of the most eminent lawyers, judges, public officials, and business executives in Michigan are graduates of this famous law school; four of the last six federal judges appointed to the bench of the United States District Court for the Eastern District of Michigan are alumni of the college. One of these four federal judges was elevated to the bench of the United States Court of Appeals for the Eastern District of Michigan.

Detroit College of Law at Michigan State University offers students the best of both worlds: the quality of exceptional legal tradition; the strength of a great international university.

Detroit College of Law at Michigan State University is fully accredited and approved by the American Bar Association (ABA) and is a member of the Association of American Law Schools (AALS).

■ Enrollment/Student Body

➦ 944 applicants   ➦ 206 enrolled first-year class 1998
➦ full-time 25th/75th percentile GPA—2.85/3.40
➦ part-time 25th/75th percentile GPA—2.80/3.42
➦ full-time 25th/75th percentile LSAT—147/154
➦ part-time 25th/75th percentile LSAT—145/154
➦ 555 total full-time   ➦ 186 total part-time
➦ 12% minority   ➦ 39% women
➦ 150 undergraduate schools represented

The students of the Detroit College of Law at Michigan State University represent a wide diversity of educational backgrounds, experiences, and national origin. DCL/MSU students are undergoing a legal education in the theory and purpose of the law, along with its practical application, thus equipping them to fulfill unique and complicated demands in and outside of the legal profession.

■ Faculty

➦ 62 total   ➦ 29 full-time   ➦ 33 part-time or adjunct
➦ 10 women   ➦ 3 minority

The faculty is composed of resident professors who are devoted, on a full-time basis, to the teaching of law; legal research instructors; and a cadre of adjunct faculty members and practicing attorneys who are specialists with extensive experience in the field of law they teach. By utilizing the talents of both the professional teacher and the practicing attorney, the academic viewpoint of the former is blended with the practical approach of the latter into a sound, well-balanced education in both theory and practice of the legal system.

■ Library and Physical Facilities

➦ over 200,000 volumes & equivalents   ➦ LEXIS
➦ NEXIS   ➦ WESTLAW   ➦ OCLC   ➦ Internet
➦ INFOTRAC   ➦ 11 full-time librarians

The library collection is designed to meet the educational needs of law students. This major research collection includes the statutes of the 50 states, the United States, and Canada, as well as collections of numerous decisions, legal periodicals, and treatises. The recently opened computer lab is equipped with 24 new computers—18 Value Point IBM PCs and six Macintosh Quadra 610 computers—linked to a Novell Local Area Network. The network supports a variety of programs, including word processing, Computer Assisted Legal Instruction (CALI), and Microsoft Mail, and e-mail system. The college has recently become an Internet affiliate through MERIT.

■ Curriculum

➦ 85 units/credits required to graduate
➦ over 125 courses available   ➦ J.D. degree, J.D./M.B.A., J.D./M.P.A.   ➦ first-year entry in Aug.   ➦ 3-year day, 4-year evening, & 5-year evening   ➦ 8-week summer session for both day & evening divisions   ➦ laptop classroom division optional   ➦ curriculum-related programs offered: Law Review, Moot Court, Externships, International and Comparative Law, Taxation, Lawyering Skills, Dean King Honors Program

■ Special Programs

International and Comparative Law—DCL/MSU students who wish to develop expertise in this field have the opportunity to study a wide variety of international legal issues. Some of the extensive course offerings include Admiralty, Chinese Law, Comparative Law, Immigration Law, International Business Transactions, International Criminal Law, Nuclear Weapons Doctrine: Arms Control and International Human Rights, International Litigation in U.S. Courts, International Taxation, International Wildlife and Environmental Law, Law of the European Community, Socialist Legal Systems, Transnational Legal Research, and U.S.-Canadian Taxation.

Center for Canadian-United States Law—The Center offers specific courses on Canadian law and Canadian-American legal relations within the law school's already extensive international law program. The Center also sponsors the Canadian Summer Law Internship Program which is available to DCL/MSU students and guest students from other ABA-accredited law schools.

Taxation—The college has extensive offerings in taxation designed to provide interested students with the opportunity to develop an expertise in taxation. Some of the courses include Basic Income Taxation, Estate and Gift Taxation, Partnership Taxation, Business Income Taxation, U.S.-Canadian Taxation, and International Taxation.

Lawyering Skills—Every substantive course develops legal analysis and reasoning; most of them develop other skills as well. DCL/MSU offers the following courses that focus directly on the development of lawyering skills beyond legal analysis and reasoning: Advanced Problems in Environmental Law, Advocacy I & II, Arbitration, Business Securities and Tax Planning, Contract Drafting, Counseling, Discovery and Trial Preparation, Transnational Legal Research, and Trial Advocacy and Litigation Seminar.

■ Admission

➡ *Bachelor's degree from an accredited college or university required*   ➡ *application deadline—Aug. entry, April 15*   ➡ *rolling admission*   ➡ *LSAT, LSDAS required*   ➡ *application fee—$50*

An admission decision is more complex than a mere ranking of applicants on the basis of a numerical formula. Detroit College of Law at Michigan State University is committed to a broad inquiry into the role and function of law in society and seeks a diverse student body as an integral part of its educational program. Accordingly, for purposes of discretionary admission, DCL/MSU will consider other subjective criteria in addition to an applicant's undergraduate grade-point average and LSAT score.

■ Curricular Activities

The *Detroit College of Law at Michigan State University Review* is a legal periodical, published by law students, in which recognized legal scholars contribute book reviews and articles of keen interest to the legal community. The college also publishes the *Journal of Medicine and Law, Journal of International Law and Practice*, and *Entertainment and Sports Law Forum*.

Moot Court at DCL/MSU is an extensive program of advocacy training in a competitive framework, permitting students to develop skills beyond those acquired in the first-year Research, Writing, and Advocacy course. The Moot Court Program participates in several national competitions, with teams researching a complex legal problem, writing and submitting a brief and then orally arguing before benches selected from judges and practitioners expert in the field.

Externship Programs are available in the Federal Defender's Office, County Circuit Courts, U.S. Attorney's Office, U.S. Department of Justice, U.S. District Court, U.S. Magistrate's Office, and County Prosecutor's Offices.

■ Student Activities

➡ *Student Senate*   ➡ *Wolverine Student Bar Association*
➡ *Federalist Society*   ➡ *Detroit Bar Association*
➡ *Women's Law Caucus*   ➡ *International Law Society*
➡ *Environmental Law Society*   ➡ *Phi Alpha Delta*
➡ *ABA Student Division*   ➡ *Delta Theta Phi*
➡ *Hands on Detroit*   ➡ *Entertainment & Sports Law Society*
➡ *National Lawyers Guild*   ➡ *Christian Law Society*
➡ *DCL Tax & Estate Planning Society*   ➡ *Triangle Bar*
➡ *Public Interest Law Society*   ➡ *Medical Legal Society*
➡ *Jewish Law Society*   ➡ *Asian Law Society*

Applicant Group for the 1998-1999 Academic Year

Detroit College of Law at Michigan State University
This grid includes only applicants who earned 120-180 LSAT scores under standard administrations.

LSAT Score	GPA																					
	3.75 +		3.50 - 3.74		3.25 - 3.49		3.00 - 3.24		2.75 - 2.99		2.50 - 2.74		2.25 - 2.49		2.00 - 2.24		Below 2.00		No GPA		Total	
	Apps	Adm	Apps	Adm	Apps	Adm	Apps	Adm	Apps	Adm	Apps	Adm	Apps	Adm	Apps	Adm	Apps	Adm	Apps	Adm	Apps	Adm
175-180	0	0	0	0	0	0	0	0	0	0	0	0	0	0	0	0	0	0	0	0	0	0
170-174	0	0	0	0	0	0	0	0	1	1	0	0	0	0	0	0	0	0	0	0	1	1
165-169	1	1	1	1	1	0	3	2	2	2	0	0	0	0	1	0	0	0	1	1	10	7
160-164	3	3	1	1	3	3	5	5	7	7	3	3	3	3	1	0	1	1	0	0	27	26
155-159	4	4	10	10	23	23	22	21	20	19	15	13	10	10	4	3	0	0	0	0	108	103
150-154	3	3	19	19	29	27	34	30	37	32	34	28	12	8	7	2	1	0	6	6	182	155
145-149	6	6	14	14	30	26	52	47	53	43	43	21	30	12	9	3	3	1	7	4	247	177
140-144	3	1	7	4	24	5	33	3	33	8	34	1	27	4	10	0	2	0	6	1	179	27
135-139	2	0	2	0	7	1	10	1	14	1	14	0	15	0	9	0	4	0	3	1	80	4
130-134	0	0	0	0	2	0	1	0	6	0	5	0	6	0	1	0	1	0	2	0	24	0
125-129	1	0	0	0	0	0	0	0	1	0	0	0	2	0	0	0	1	0	0	0	5	0
120-124	0	0	0	0	0	0	0	0	0	0	0	0	0	0	1	0	0	0	0	0	1	0
Total	23	18	54	49	119	85	160	109	174	113	148	66	105	37	43	8	13	2	25	13	864	500

Apps = Number of Applicants
Adm = Number Admitted
Reflects 97% of the total applicant pool.

University of Detroit Mercy School of Law

Office of Admissions
651 E. Jefferson Avenue
Detroit, MI 48226

E-Mail: udmlawao@udmercy.edu
URL: http://www.law.udmercy.edu/
Phone: 313.596.0264

■ Introduction

Founded in 1912, the University of Detroit Mercy School of Law is a well-established private school located opposite the Renaissance Center in a downtown Detroit riverfront complex of cultural, sports, convention, and residential facilities. The school is within walking distance of federal and state courts and downtown law firms. Windsor, Canada, is a five-minute drive across the river. A traditionally rich cultural center, with such renowned institutions as the Detroit Symphony and the Detroit Institute of Arts, the Detroit metropolitan area also provides a unique laboratory for the study of contemporary legal problems associated with urban and industrial redevelopment.

As a regional law school, with a faculty drawn from throughout the country and abroad, the school offers a broad curriculum and seeks to attract a geographically diverse student body. The school is a member of the AALS and is accredited by the ABA.

■ Student Body

➡ *full-time 25th/75th percentile GPA—2.77/3.42*
➡ *part-time 25th/75th percentile GPA—2.59/3.17*
➡ *full-time 25th/75th percentile LSAT—144/152*
➡ *part-time 25th/75th percentile LSAT—145/152*
➡ *over 400 total students*   ➡ *19% minority first-year class 1998*
➡ *48% women first-year class 1998*

The student body is drawn from diverse geographical, ethnic, and religious backgrounds. Two-thirds of the students in the entering class are in the full-time day program. Academic attrition among first-year students is traditionally about 11 percent.

■ Faculty

➡ *20 full-time*   ➡ *24 part-time or adjunct*

■ Library and Physical Facilities

➡ *298,557 volumes & equivalents*   ➡ *NEXIS*
➡ *WESTLAW*

The law school campus includes an architectural-prize-winning library building and a striking three-story interior atrium that serves as an unusually spacious student lounge.

The library is air-conditioned, and contains comfortable reading areas, typing and audiovisual rooms, and group study rooms, as well as individual study carrels.

Dowling Hall, a Detroit landmark, contains attractive classrooms, offices, and a bookstore; the atrium and adjoining cafeteria provide a congenial setting for informal student-faculty discussions.

■ Curriculum

➡ *Academic Support Program*   ➡ *90 credits required to graduate*   ➡ *degrees available: J.D.; J.D./M.B.A.*
➡ *semester system*

The school offers a three-year, full-time day program and a four-year, part-time evening program, both leading to the J.D. degree; academic standards in the two programs are identical. Basic courses in civil procedure, contracts, property, criminal law, torts, constitutional law, taxation, evidence, legal research and writing, and professional responsibility are required, and students must take at least one seminar in their final year. The remainder of the curriculum is elective. The academic year is divided into two semesters and a summer session. Students may accelerate by enrolling in the summer session.

■ Special Programs

The school's commitment to the concept of quality legal education as an approach to urban problems is reflected in opportunities to represent indigent clients under close faculty guidance and a variety of externship placements available through the Urban Law Clinic.

Our innovative Applied Legal Theory and Analysis Course (Applied Theory), sets us apart from other law schools. Applied Theory is a rigorous five-credit, two-semester course required of all first-year law students and is taught by full-time Applied Theory faculty. This ground-breaking program bridges the gap between the study of law and the practice of law by providing practical applications of theoretical concepts from first-year subject courses, especially Contracts.

The school provides an opportunity for qualified students to pursue a four-year joint J.D./M.B.A. degree. Additionally, the law school has a professorial exchange program with a French university (the University of Clermot—Ferrand), continuing legal education programs for lawyers and other professionals as well as a consortium of courses with other local law schools titled the Intellectual Property Law Institute.

The school also offers a special summer program for disadvantaged applicants who do not meet minimum standards for the entering class but nevertheless show potential for the study of law. Successful completion of the summer program permits admission as a regular student in the fall semester.

■ London Law Programme

The program offers second- and third-year law students an exceptional opportunity to study abroad for an academic semester. An integral part of the law school, the program provides for the study of international and comparative law at one of the world's leading centers of these disciplines and enables students to better understand our Anglo-American common law system and its origins.

University of Detroit Mercy is the only American law school to operate a foreign-based academic-year program organized on a semester basis. Although the program is primarily for University of Detroit Mercy law students, a limited number of spaces are available for students from other American and Canadian schools. Occasionally, qualified students from other countries like France and Mexico participate.

The program has been approved by the Council of the Section of Legal Education and Admissions to the Bar of the American Bar Association.

Admission

➡ *undergraduate degree from accredited institution required*
➡ *application deadline—April 15*   ➡ *fall admission only*
➡ *LSAT, LSDAS required*   ➡ *application fee—$50*

The school does not require a specific prelaw curriculum and agrees with the recommendations set forth in the introduction to this guide.

While the admissions committee considers the LSAT and undergraduate grades as the most important determinants of admission, it also considers factors such as letters of recommendation, evidence of maturity and leadership, graduate work, and work experience. Two letters of recommendation are required.

Applications are reviewed on a continuous basis and decisions are communicated as early as possible. Interviews, though not required, may be granted upon request. A $150 nonrefundable deposit is required of all admitted applicants and credited toward the first semester's tuition. A second deposit may be required. In general, transfer students must have a 3.0 GPA or be in the upper quarter of their law class.

The law school has nondiscrimination and affirmative action policies.

Activities

The *Law Review* is edited entirely by a student editorial board. Students edit and publish the *Michigan Business Law Journal*, which is the quarterly newsletter of the Business Law Section of the Michigan State Bar. A student moot court board helps to supervise the required appellate advocacy program and administers the school's Gallagher and Professional Responsibility competitions, as well as participation by students in regional and national competitions.

The Student Bar Association, affiliated with the Law Student Division of the ABA, plays a significant role in student affairs and program development. A student newspaper, *In Brief*, is published for the law school community. Some of the other approximately 25 student organizations include the Black Law Students Alliance; the Latin American Students Organization; the Women's Law Caucus; the Justice Frank Murphy Honor Society; the International Law Society; and chapters of two coeducational legal fraternities.

Expenses and Financial Aid

➡ *tuition—$600/credit hr.*   ➡ *estimated additional expenses—$9,790 (room, board, personal expenses)*
➡ *academic scholarships available*

Loans are available through the Federal Perkins Loan (formerly NDSL) and Michigan Guaranteed Loan Programs. Work-study positions are also available.

Placement

A Director of Career Services actively encourages law firms and other prospective employers to interview at the school and counsels and assists students in acquiring both temporary and full-time employment.

Applicant Group for the 1998-1999 Academic Year

University of Detroit Mercy School of Law
This grid includes only applicants who earned 120-180 LSAT scores under standard administrations.

LSAT Score	3.75 +		3.50 - 3.74		3.25 - 3.49		3.00 - 3.24		2.75 - 2.99		2.50 - 2.74		2.25 - 2.49		2.00 - 2.24		Below 2.00		No GPA		Total	
	Apps	Adm	Apps	Adm	Apps	Adm	Apps	Adm	Apps	Adm	Apps	Adm	Apps	Adm	Apps	Adm	Apps	Adm	Apps	Adm	Apps	Adm
175-180	0	0	0	0	0	0	0	0	0	0	0	0	0	0	0	0	0	0	0	0	0	0
170-174	1	1	0	0	0	0	0	0	1	1	0	0	0	0	0	0	0	0	0	0	2	2
165-169	1	1	1	1	0	0	2	1	0	0	0	0	0	0	0	0	0	0	0	0	4	3
160-164	4	4	2	2	2	2	4	4	2	2	2	2	0	0	0	0	1	1	0	0	17	17
155-159	5	5	11	11	19	18	14	12	12	11	11	11	2	2	3	2	1	0	0	0	78	72
150-154	2	2	15	15	22	21	28	27	15	15	20	18	6	4	6	4	0	0	5	4	119	110
145-149	5	5	10	10	31	29	44	42	36	32	36	25	16	9	5	2	1	0	3	2	187	156
140-144	2	2	5	4	30	22	21	11	20	12	21	2	28	3	6	1	4	1	7	1	144	59
135-139	1	0	4	0	8	0	9	0	15	1	15	1	9	1	9	0	2	0	3	0	75	3
130-134	0	0	0	0	1	0	3	0	5	0	6	0	5	0	5	0	2	0	2	0	29	0
125-129	1	0	0	0	0	0	1	0	2	0	1	0	1	0	1	0	0	0	0	0	7	0
120-124	0	0	0	0	0	0	0	0	0	0	0	0	0	0	0	0	0	0	1	0	1	0
Total	22	20	48	43	113	92	126	97	108	74	112	59	67	19	35	9	11	2	21	7	663	422

Apps = Number of Applicants
Adm = Number Admitted
Reflects 98% of the total applicant pool.

University of The District of Columbia—The David A. Clarke School of Law

4200 Connecticut Avenue, N.W.
Washington, DC 20008

URL: http://www.udc.edu/
Phone: 202.274.7341

■ Introduction

In 1986, the City Council of the District of Columbia authorized the establishment of the District of Columbia School of Law. The founding class was admitted in 1988. The Council created a dual mission for the School of Law and charged its Board of Governors with a special mandate to recruit and enroll, to the degree feasible, students from ethnic, racial, or other population groups that in the past have been underrepresented among persons admitted to the bar. It also charged the Board with representing the legal needs of low-income persons, particularly those who reside in the District of Columbia.

The DC School of Law, the only publicly funded law school in Washington, DC, formally merged with the University of the District of Columbia (UDC) in 1996, and became the University of the District of Columbia School of Law. Pursuant to legislation approved by the U.S. Congress in April 1998, the UDC School of Law is now the UDC David A. Clarke School of Law. The law school has a full-time program.

■ Enrollment/Student Body

➡ *61 full-time enrolled first-year class 1998*
➡ *full-time 25th/75th percentile GPA—2.30/2.75*
➡ *full-time 25th/75th percentile LSAT—141/147*
➡ *74% minority*   ➡ *53% full-time women*
➡ *60% full-time DC residents*   ➡ *full-time average age—30*
➡ *25 states represented*
➡ *100 undergraduate schools represented*

The School of Law prides itself in attracting a small, but extraordinary student body now totaling about 172. Our student body is a culturally and ethnically diverse group.

■ Faculty

➡ *30 total*   ➡ *21 full-time*   ➡ *9 part-time or adjunct*
➡ *10 women*   ➡ *9 minority*

■ Library and Physical Facilities

➡ *180,000 volumes & equivalents*   ➡ *LEXIS*
➡ *WESTLAW*   ➡ *CALI*   ➡ *DIALOG*
➡ *4 full-time librarians*   ➡ *library seats 142*

The School of Law occupies existing buildings at the University of the District of Columbia's Van Ness campus. The law school is located in a section of northwest Washington, DC known for its harmonious blend of residential and business communities.

In addition to the regular law volumes and volume equivalents, the library supports the Clinical Program by maintaining a small collection of clinical practice material and other materials pertinent to each of the clinics.

The Computer Center features terminals for student research, word processing, and computer-assisted tutorials in core subjects.

The campus is conveniently located on the Metro's Red Line at the UDC/Van Ness subway stop.

■ Curriculum

➡ *Academic Support Program*   ➡ *90 credits required to graduate*   ➡ *18 required courses*   ➡ *2 semesters of clinical work required for full time*   ➡ *6 clinics available*
➡ *49 total courses available*   ➡ *J.D. degree*
➡ *semesters, start in mid-Aug.*

Consistent with UDC law school's mission, the basic program is designed to equip students with the professional skills of practicing lawyers as well as the traditional substantive knowledge of law.

Orientation is a one-week program introducing first-year students to the study of law and the School of Law community. During orientation, students take the course Law and Justice, which addresses issues of justice; poverty law; the meaning, distinction between, and limitations on natural and positive law; identity; and diversity. They also meet administration, faculty, and continuing students. There is a dean's reception for first-year students in the fall semester. There are also other events planned by student organizations.

In the first year, students take a prescribed program consisting of required courses and one elective course. After the first year, students must also take courses in Evidence, Constitutional Law I and II, Professional Responsibility, and Moot Court.

In the second year, students begin their clinical experience by taking Clinic One. In the third year, they take Clinic Two. The clinics offered in the 1998-1999 academic year are Housing/Consumer, Public Entitlements/HIV, Juvenile, Legislation, and Government Accountability Project (GAP).

The School of Law offers a limited number of summer courses; it does not allow early graduation. Students normally complete the program in three calendar years.

UDC/DCSL considers academic support to be an integral part of its course of study. Students in academic difficulty at the end of their first semester may apply to be in the enhanced program, which may involve adjusting course-loads, counseling, and group and individual tutoring. In addition, faculty members hold extra review sessions during the semester in required courses and provide sample examination questions with model answers. During the first two weeks at the law school, students are given two diagnostic tests, one in reading and one in writing. Test results may be used to help students improve their skills.

The emphasis of the school is on public interest law; the overall curriculum—clinic and classroom—is designed to support that orientation. In addition, UDC/DCSL's goals are consistent with the objectives of legal education proposed by the Long-Range Planning Committee of the American Bar Association. These objectives include "training for [lawyering] competence...[and]... training in professional responsibility."

■ Internship Program

➤ *one semester internship, 8 credits*
➤ *internship seminar, 2 credits*

In addition to the clinic program, students in the second semester, second year, or third year may elect to do an internship in which they work 30 hours a week outside the law school in judicial, legislative, or Congressional offices, or in public interest legal organizations. Faculty members monitor each placement and students must attend a weekly Internship Seminar at the school. The School of Law emphasizes the importance of supervision, educational merit, and public service in each internship.

■ The Writing Program

Each UDC/DCSL student is required to produce significant pieces of writing each of the three years of study. In the first year students satisfy the writing requirement in the Lawyering Process course. In the second and third years, students may satisfy the legal writing requirement as part of a seminar, elective course, clinical practice, or independent study.

■ Admission

➤ *Bachelor's degree from accredited college or university required*
➤ *application deadline—April 1*
➤ *rolling admission, early application preferred*
➤ *LSAT, LSDAS required*   ➤ *application fee—$35*
➤ *fall admission, full-time, day*

Admission is based upon academic and nonacademic achievements and professional promise. Because the LSAT does not measure the skills, determination, and personal commitment that are vital to competence and success as a legal practitioner, UDC/DCSL looks at an applicant's LSAT scores and grades in tandem with other criteria that we believe may provide a more accurate measure of a candidate's potential for success in the study of law. This approach means that our Admissions Committee considers all submitted application material. It reviews closely the application essays and other information supplied with the application, including support documents and recommendations.

■ Student Activities

The first issue of the biannual *The District of Columbia Law Review* was published in 1992. *The Side-Bar* is the student newspaper which is published quarterly. Students participate in many of the decision processes of the law school. Numerous student organizations are active at the law school.

■ Expenses and Financial Aid

➤ *tuition & fees—DC residents, $7,000; nonresidents, $14,000*
➤ *additional expenses—$17,900 (room, board, books)*
➤ *need- & merit-based scholarships available*
➤ *FAFSA for need analysis due April 30*

■ Career Services

The Career Services Office provides employment information and career services to the School of Law's student body and graduates. The office maintains listings of permanent job openings, fellowships, summer clerkships, and part-time opportunities. The office also coordinates potential internship sites and invites employers to conduct on-campus interviews. The office provides resources for career planning, counseling sessions to assist students in developing their career goals, résumé workshops, and other relevant seminars.

Applicant Profile Not Available

Drake University Law School

2507 University Avenue
Des Moines, IA 50311-9979

E-Mail: lawadmit@drake.edu
URL: http://www.drake.edu/public/lawlib/top.html
Phone: 800.44.DRAKE, ext. 2782 or 515.271.2782

■ Introduction

Drake University Law School, a charter member of the AALS, is one of the 25 oldest law schools in the nation, tracing its history to 1865. Accredited by the ABA, the Law School became affiliated with Drake University, a private, independent institution of higher learning, at its founding in 1881.

Drake Law School is located in Iowa's capital, Des Moines, providing law students the opportunity to get hands-on experience with the executive, judicial, and legislative branches of government; the federal courts; administrative agencies; and a wide array of law firms and businesses.

■ Enrollment/Student Body

➡ 681 applicants   ➡ 410 admitted first-year class 1998
➡ full-time 25th/75th percentile GPA—2.86/3.50
➡ part-time 25th/75th percentile GPA—3.19/3.54
➡ full-time 25th/75th percentile LSAT—150/155
➡ part-time 25th/75th percentile LSAT—153/156
➡ 384 total full-time   ➡ 13 total part-time
➡ 12% minority   ➡ 44% women   ➡ 35 states & 4 foreign countries represented   ➡ 147 undergraduate schools represented

■ Faculty

➡ 63 total   ➡ 27 full-time   ➡ 36 part-time or adjunct
➡ 20 women   ➡ 3 minority

■ Library and Physical Facilities

➡ 275,000 volumes & equivalents   ➡ library hours:
Mon.-Thurs., 7:00 A.M.-MIDNIGHT; Fri., 7:00 A.M.-10:30 P.M.;
Sat., 9:00 A.M.-10:30 P.M.; Sun., NOON-MIDNIGHT
➡ LEXIS   ➡ NEXIS   ➡ WESTLAW
➡ 5 full-time librarians   ➡ library seats 700

The Dwight D. Opperman Hall and Law Library, built in 1993, has approximately 70,000-square feet and provides Drake law students with a state-of-the-art facility for legal research, class seminars, and studying. Opperman Hall is wired for computers and is equipped with online legal research training centers.

■ Legal Clinic

The Neal and Bea Smith Law Center, built in 1987, houses the Drake Law School Legal Clinic. The center is a state-of-the-art law office, with each student having access to the latest in computer technology. The center was selected as the national training and resource institute for public service attorneys. The $1.75 million addition, built in 1994, includes a fully computerized courtroom and training facilities for Drake law students.

■ Curriculum

➡ Academic Success Program   ➡ Tutorial Supplement
Program of Instruction   ➡ 90 credits required to graduate
➡ 121 courses available   ➡ additional summer agricultural

law and constitutional law program courses, which vary annually, are also offered   ➡ degrees available: J.D.; J.D./Pharmacy D.; J.D./M.B.A.; J.D./M.P.A.; J.D./M.A. (Mass Comm.); J.D./M.S. (Economics/Iowa State); J.D./M.A. (Pol. Sci./Iowa State); J.D./M.S.W. (Social Work/Iowa)   ➡ semesters, start in Aug. —first-year students may begin during summer session
➡ range of first-year class size—15-65

Educational excellence has long been achieved at Drake Law School through a balance of theory and practice that recognizes the need for both in a quality legal education. The J.D. curriculum at Drake is national in scope and emphasis.

Summer school is available for both incoming and continuing students, and may accelerate graduation.

■ Special Programs

Litigation Skills and Clinical Programs—Drake had one of the first clinics in the country and has built on that tradition. Drake students represent real clients out of their own fully computerized offices in the beautiful Smith Law Center, built especially for that purpose. In the first-year trial practicum, students view an actual trial and discuss it with professors and participants in break-out sessions.

The vast majority of Drake students do an internship, for academic credit, with a state or federal judge, administrative agency, legislature, or prosecutor. The quality of Drake's advocacy instruction is evident in the outstanding performance of the school's numerous trial and appellate advocacy teams.

Constitutional Law Programs—Drake is one of only four schools selected to receive a Congressional endowment for the establishment of a Constitutional Law Resource Center. The center sponsors a lecture series and symposia featuring nationally recognized constitutional scholars. In addition, the Opperman Lecture in Constitutional Law has brought seven U.S. Supreme Court justices to Drake in the past 10 years. The justices have taught classes, met with students, and participated in the intellectual life of the law school. A summer institute in Constitutional Law is offered annually for entering first-year students.

Agricultural Law—Drake has one of the few programs in the nation addressing the timely and important issues in American and international agricultural law and policy. The Agricultural Law Center hosts an annual Summer Agricultural Law Institute and conference, and students edit and write for the *Drake Journal of Agricultural Law.*

Legislative Practice Center—Drake is one of the few schools in the country to offer a special program geared toward students thinking of entering politics, working for the legislature, or becoming a lobbyist. Students earn a certificate in Legislative Practice by taking classes specially developed to teach legislative policy and practice and by completing two internships with legislators and legislative groups.

Admission

➡ Bachelor's degree required   ➡ priority application deadline—March 1   ➡ rolling admission
➡ LSAT, LSDAS required   ➡ application fee—$35

The Law School is committed to attracting, enrolling, retaining, and graduating an academically strong and diverse student body. All applications are reviewed by a faculty admission committee. Admission to Drake Law School is based upon an evaluation of an applicant's LSAT scores, undergraduate GPA, undergraduate institution, coursework, grade trend, writing skills as demonstrated in the LSAT writing sample and personal statement, community and extracurricular involvement, graduate school record, relevant work experience, and letters of recommendation.

Student Activities

Law students participate in many student organizations and cocurricular activities. The *Drake Law Review*, a student edited journal, is published quarterly. Drake moot court teams consistently win regional competitions and finish strong in national competitions. The Student Bar Association, Legal Research Service, and honorary societies provide students with leadership, public service, and learning opportunities. Drake students have also formed a variety of organizations around their special interests, including the Drake Law Women, Black Law Students Association, Latino Law Society, Asian-Pacific Islander Association, International Law Society, Christian Legal Society, Environmental Law Society, Federalist Society, National Lawyers Guild, and the Nontraditional Students Society.

Expenses and Financial Aid

➡ tuition & fees—full-time, $16,950; part-time, $565/credit
➡ estimated additional expenses—$10,125 (room & board, $5,900; personal expenses, $3,000; books, $900; transportation, $325)
➡ scholarships available: Law General (need & merit); Law Opportunity (disadvantaged); Opperman (merit awards); Public Interest Fellowships   ➡ minority scholarships available: Law Opportunity   ➡ financial aid available; FAFSA, all other forms are accepted   ➡ priority deadline for scholarships & financial aid—March 1

Career Services

The Law School Career Services Office offers career-planning and counseling services, assistance in résumé preparation, salary and geographical employment statistics, on-campus interviews, nationwide job postings, and state bar examination information. More than 90 percent of 1997 Drake Law School graduates were employed within six months of graduation. Law School alumni practice in all 50 states and several foreign countries.

Applicant Group for the 1998-1999 Academic Year

Drake University Law School
This grid includes only applicants who earned 120-180 LSAT scores under standard administrations.

LSAT Score	GPA 3.75 +		3.50 - 3.74		3.25 - 3.49		3.00 - 3.24		2.75 - 2.99		2.50 - 2.74		2.25 - 2.49		2.00 - 2.24		Below 2.00		No GPA		Total	
	Apps	Adm	Apps	Adm	Apps	Adm	Apps	Adm	Apps	Adm	Apps	Adm	Apps	Adm	Apps	Adm	Apps	Adm	Apps	Adm	Apps	Adm
175-180	0	0	0	0	0	0	0	0	0	0	0	0	0	0	0	0	0	0	0	0	0	0
170-174	0	0	2	2	0	0	0	0	0	0	0	0	0	0	0	0	0	0	0	0	2	2
165-169	2	2	1	1	1	1	0	0	0	0	0	0	0	0	0	0	0	0	1	0	5	4
160-164	9	9	6	6	7	7	2	2	7	7	2	2	1	1	0	0	1	1	0	0	35	35
155-159	8	8	18	18	24	23	20	20	14	14	11	11	8	7	3	3	0	0	4	2	110	106
150-154	18	17	19	18	38	36	42	40	28	26	21	19	7	5	6	5	0	0	5	1	184	167
145-149	9	8	25	20	34	23	40	21	29	11	20	5	13	1	5	0	5	0	1	0	181	89
140-144	5	0	12	1	12	1	23	0	10	0	19	4	10	0	3	0	0	0	2	1	96	7
135-139	0	0	2	1	5	0	6	0	6	0	7	0	3	0	3	0	0	0	3	0	35	1
130-134	0	0	1	0	0	0	1	0	1	0	3	0	2	0	0	0	1	0	1	0	10	0
125-129	0	0	0	0	0	0	0	0	0	0	1	0	0	0	1	0	1	0	0	0	3	0
120-124	0	0	0	0	0	0	0	0	0	0	0	0	0	0	0	0	0	0	0	0	0	0
Total	51	44	86	67	121	91	134	83	95	58	84	41	44	14	21	8	8	1	17	4	661	411

Apps = Number of Applicants
Adm = Number Admitted
Reflects 98% of the total applicant pool.

Duke University School of Law

Science Drive & Towerview Road
Box 90393
Durham, NC 27708-0393

E-Mail: admissions@law.duke.edu
URL: http://www.law.duke.edu
Phone: 919.613.7020

■ Introduction

Duke law school is distinguished by a learning environment that is similar to the professional environment in which students will work as lawyers. The school has a high level of intellectual engagement and interaction between students and faculty, a small student body, and a first-year small section program. The learning environment is characterized by an emphasis on professional values such as integrity, teamwork, and intellectual risk taking. The law school has been a pioneer in forging interdisciplinary relationships with other departments of the university. Through course-work and joint-degree programs in wide-ranging fields, students are able to broaden and specialize their legal education by utilizing the full intellectual resources of the university.

■ Enrollment/Student Body

- 3,443 applicants   - 212 enrolled first-year class 1998
- full-time 25th/75th percentile GPA—3.33/3.72
- full-time 25th/75th percentile LSAT—161/170
- 608 total full-time   - 21% minority   - 44% women
- 47 states & 21 foreign countries represented
- 196 undergraduate schools represented
- 61 foreign LL.M. students

The characteristic that most distinguishes the student body at Duke from that at other top law schools is the collegiality and collaborative spirit that consistently develops among its members.

■ Faculty

- 64 total faculty members   - 33 full-time
- 31 part-time or adjunct   - 27 women   - 5 minority

Faculty members' backgrounds and interests are as varied as they are distinguished. They bring to the classroom not only a love of teaching, but significant practical experience in both the public and private sectors. On the faculty are former Fulbright Scholars, Rhodes Scholars, and Marshall Scholars. A number of faculty members have served as Supreme Court clerks and one was the chief judge for the U.S. Court of Military Appeals. An exceptionally high number of our faculty members hold joint appointments with other departments within the university and have Ph.D.'s in a wide variety of subjects. The faculty also embodies a high degree of internationalization. A large number of visiting professors from abroad teach at Duke each year, and many faculty members have extensive international ties and connections.

■ Library and Physical Facilities

- 510,000 volumes & equivalents   - library open 24 hours/day
- LEXIS   - NEXIS   - WESTLAW   - First Search
- Uncover   - DIALOG   - 9 full-time librarians
- library seats 451   - Student Research Network

Duke Law Library's outstanding collection of materials is accessible to students through the law school's state-of-the-art computer network. Students have the use of over 100 student terminals in the library, 130 carrels which are wired to the network for students to plug in their own notebook computer, and network access from home.

Law students are encouraged to take advantage of the extensive resources of Duke University, equally renowned for its excellence in undergraduate, professional, and graduate schools, and research endeavors. With impressive Gothic architecture, 20 acres of formal and informal gardens, and 7,700 acres of undeveloped forest, the beauty of the Duke campus is unsurpassed.

■ Curriculum

- 84 credits required to graduate   - 96 courses available
- degrees available: J.D.; J.D./LL.M.; J.D./M.B.A.; J.D./M.E.M.; J.D./M.P.P.; J.D./Ph.D. (Pol. Sci.); J.D./M.A. or M.S. (in 11 departments); J.D./M.D.; J.D./M.T.S.   - semesters, start in Aug. with exception of selected joint-degree programs
- range of first-year class size—25-120

During the first year, students are divided into small sections of 25-35 students. Students have one substantive course in the small section and are in a small class for legal writing. All first-year classes are required.

Classes in the second and third years are entirely elective.

■ Special Programs

J.D./LL.M. in International and Comparative Legal Studies. Duke law school offers students enrolled in the J.D. program a unique opportunity to study concurrently for the Master of Laws (LL.M.) in Comparative and International Legal Studies. Students may earn these two degrees through extending legal study by only two summers. J.D./LL.M. students enroll at Duke in June and spend four weeks during the following summer at one of Duke's Institutes of Transnational Law in Geneva or in Hong Kong.

J.D./M.A. or M.S. Programs. Based on the idea that society will be best served by lawyers with diverse education, training, and background, Duke offers accelerated joint-degree programs through which students may obtain a J.D. and a master's degree in any of the following disciplines—Public Policy, Environmental Studies, Political Science, Economics, History, English, Philosophy, Psychology, Humanities, Cultural Anthropology, Romance Studies, or Mechanical Engineering. The only additional time necessary to obtain both degrees is the summer that precedes the first year of school. In addition to the accelerated programs, Duke offers four-year joint-degree programs combining law and Public Policy, Environmental Management, Business Administration, or Theological Studies.

■ Admission

➡ *early application deadline—Nov. 1*
➡ *suggested application deadline—Feb. 1*
➡ *LSAT, LSDAS required*   ➡ *application fee—$65*
➡ *encourage students to the LSAT no later than Dec.*

Admission to the law school is determined after careful consideration of all information presented in the application. Undergraduate grades, undergraduate institution, and LSAT scores are among the most important criteria in admission decisions. The committee also heavily weighs demonstrated leadership, community service, graduate study in another discipline, work experience, and other information indicating academic or professional potential. Students are encouraged to visit the school to see the campus, sit in on a class, and meet with students.

Students who want to take advantage of Duke's early action admission option must have taken the LSAT in June or earlier, and their applications must be complete by November 1. Early-action applications are judged by a higher than normal standard. Applicants who are admitted will be notified by December 31. All others will be considered with the rest of the pool. Admitted students are encouraged but not obligated to inform Duke as early as possible of their decision to attend.

■ Cocurricular Activities

The law school publishes four scholarly journals—*Duke Law Journal, Law and Contemporary Problems, Alaska Law Review,* and the *Duke Journal of Comparative and International Law,* and two annuals, *Duke Journal of Gender Law and Policy* and the *Duke Environmental Law and Policy Forum.* Particularly popular with students is the Pro Bono Project, an organization through which over 200 students provide volunteer legal service in the public, private, and nonprofit sectors.

■ Expenses and Financial Aid

➡ *full-time tuition & fees—$24,400*   ➡ *average additional expenses—$13,000*   ➡ *merit- & need-based scholarships available*   ➡ *financial aid available; FAFSA need analysis form should be filed in Feb.*

A generous loan forgiveness program assists students choosing to work in public interest or government jobs after graduation.

■ Career Services

The full-time staff of the Office of Career Services works actively to assist students in obtaining summer and permanent employment. In the fall of 1998, almost 450 employers came to Duke from 40 states to interview second- and third-year students. Another 800 employers requested résumés of students. Six months after graduation, 99 percent of the Class of 1997 was employed; 73 percent in private practice, 18 percent in judicial clerkships, and the remainder in public service, government, business, or academic study. Graduates found employment in 32 states; 47 percent of employed graduates went to the Northeast, 32 percent to the South, 7 percent to the Midwest, and 13 percent to the West.

Applicant Group for the 1998-1999 Academic Year

Duke University School of Law
This grid includes only applicants who earned 120-180 LSAT scores under standard administrations.

LSAT Score	GPA 3.75 +		3.50 - 3.74		3.25 - 3.49		3.00 - 3.24	
	Apps	Adm	Apps	Adm	Apps	Adm	Apps	Adm
175-180	22	20	21	19	16	14	11	4
170-174	121	109	112	95	76	56	39	19
165-169	266	156	330	141	187	61	76	14
160-164	243	52	285	32	188	16	93	7
155-159	106	13	131	13	138	8	74	7
150-154	58	10	96	14	75	5	62	4

Apps = Number of Applicants
Adm = Number Admitted
Reflects 99% of the total applicant pool.

Duquesne University School of Law

217 Hanley Hall
900 Locust Street
Pittsburgh, PA 15282

E-Mail: campion@duq.edu
URL: http://www.duq.edu/law
Phone: 412.396.6296

■ Introduction

The Duquesne University School of Law has been in existence since 1911 and is the only multiple-division law school in Western Pennsylvania. Admission requirements, instruction, and the nature and scope of the work required of students are identical for both the full-time day division and the part-time evening and part-time day divisions. The School of Law is approved by the ABA and is a member of the AALS.

Duquesne's 43-acre campus is uniquely situated, affording access, within walking distance, to the downtown legal, business, and government communities, and state and federal courts.

■ Enrollment/Student Body

➡ *first-year class enrollment–day, 125; evening, 87*
➡ *full-time 25th/75th percentile GPA—2.88/3.50*
➡ *part-time 25th/75th percentile GPA—2.74/3.39*
➡ *full-time 25th/75th percentile LSAT—147/154*
➡ *part-time 25th/75th percentile LSAT—144/154*
➡ *359 total full-time*   ➡ *332 total part-time*
➡ *4.7% minority*   ➡ *45% women*   ➡ *28 states & foreign countries represented*   ➡ *181 undergraduate schools represented*

The Duquesne University School of Law does not discriminate on the basis of race, creed, color, sex, national or ethnic origin, handicap, or age, nor in the administration of its admission and educational policies. The law school seeks diversity in the student body and encourages members of minority groups and others who have been underrepresented in the legal profession to apply. Out-of-state students typically comprise 30 percent of the full-time entering class.

■ Faculty

➡ *73 total*   ➡ *23 full-time plus 5 research and writing professors*   ➡ *44 part-time or adjunct*
➡ *8 women*   ➡ *5 minority*

■ Library and Physical Facilities

➡ *215,000 volumes & equivalents*   ➡ *library hours: Mon.-Thurs., 8:00 A.M.-MIDNIGHT; Fri., 8:00 A.M.-10:00 P.M.; Sat., 9:00 A.M.-9:00 P.M.; Sun., 1:00 P.M.-MIDNIGHT*
➡ *LEXIS*   ➡ *WESTLAW*   ➡ *5 full-time librarians*
➡ *library seats 325*

In 1982, the law school moved into the newly completed Edward J. Hanley Hall. This modern facility houses all classrooms, faculty offices, and study rooms for the law school, including the James P. McArdle Moot Court Room and the John E. Laughlin Memorial Library. The library contains group-study rooms, individual study carrels, and the law school's computer lab. All first-year students are trained on computer-assisted legal research.

■ Curriculum

➡ *Law Review (student-run tutoring program) offered*
➡ *86 credits required to graduate*   ➡ *123 courses available*
➡ *degrees available: J.D.; J.D./M.B.A.; J.D./M.Div.; J.D./M.S. Env. Sc. and Mgt.*   ➡ *semesters, start in Aug.*
➡ *range of first-year class size—20-100*

The course of study offered at the School of Law is sufficiently broad to prepare students for practice in all states. Three years are required for completion of the course of study in the day division, four years in the evening division.

Electives are offered after the first year of study in such developing areas as products and the consumer, environmental law, law and psychiatry, controlling medical therapy and experimentation, sex discrimination and the law, and legal medicine. An endowed chair in Law and Economics provides students with the opportunity to develop a knowledge of the application of economic principles to the study of law. These elective courses allow students to explore the more contemporary problems of law and society.

■ Special Programs

Students are afforded an opportunity to participate in numerous educational and professional activities, including moot court competitions and a wide variety of clinical programs. Part-time day division is offered.

■ Admission

➡ *Bachelor's degree required*   ➡ *application deadlines—day, April 1; evening, May 1; part-time day, June 1*
➡ *rolling admission*   ➡ *LSAT, LSDAS required*
➡ *application fee—$50*

All candidates for admission must take the LSAT, subscribe to LSDAS, and be graduates of an accredited college or university before enrolling in the law school. Personal interviews by members of the Admissions Committee are not granted, but applicants are encouraged to schedule an appointment to visit the school for an information session and/or a tour of the facilities.

The large number of applications received makes the admission process very selective. Most applicants apply well in advance of the deadlines. Students are admitted only for the fall semester.

In evaluating applications, the complete academic record is reviewed with consideration given to the competitiveness of the undergraduate institution, the college major, rank in class, and the overall academic performance. The LSAT is considered to be an important factor in assessing an applicant's ability to succeed in legal study. Graduate study, extracurricular activities, and recommendations also contribute to the committee's assessment. Work experience is considered when an applicant has been employed full-time for a significant length of time.

Student Activities

The Student Bar Association maintains a liaison between students and faculty and sponsors social and professional activities for the student body.

Membership in the *Duquesne Law Review* is based on the demonstrated academic ability of the student as well as his or her interest in becoming active in this publication.

Juris, the law school news magazine, is an ABA-award-winning publication containing articles of current interest to the entire legal community. Students also publish the *Duquesne Business Law Journal*.

There are also active chapters of the following organizations available to law students: Phi Alpha Delta legal fraternity, the Women Law Association (WLA), Black Law Students Association (BLSA), ABA/LSD American Bar Association/Law Student Division, International Law Society, Sports and Entertainment Law, Association of Trial Lawyers of America, Environmental Law Association, Health Care Law Society, Association for Public Interest Law, Corporate Law Society, and the Intellectual Property and Technological Law Society.

Expenses and Financial Aid

➡ *tuition & fees—full-time, $14,942; part-time, $11,378; fee, $660/yr.* ➡ *estimated additional expenses—$6,000 (books, room, & board)* ➡ *need- & merit-based scholarships available* ➡ *minority scholarships available (need- & merit-based)* ➡ *financial aid available* ➡ *Duquesne Financial Aid application due May 31* ➡ *PHEAA, FAFSA, and GAPSFAS accepted*

By maintaining a very competitive tuition rate, Duquesne consistently strives to ensure that the outstanding private legal education provided by the law school is within the reach of all qualified students. A number of merit scholarships are awarded to the most outstanding day-division applicants each year. Law school grants-in-aid are awarded primarily on the basis of need. A number of loans sponsored by the state and federal government are available to law students. For further information please write to the Financial Aid Office, Duquesne University, Pittsburgh, PA 15282.

Housing

Accommodations are available for single law students in the university dormitories. For off-campus residence information write to the Office of Commuter Affairs, Duquesne University, Pittsburgh, PA 15282. Off-campus accommodations are available nearby.

Career Services

The law school's Career Services Office staff offers assistance to students and alumni who are interested in obtaining full-time, part-time, and summer employment. The Career Services Office offers a fall and spring on-campus interview program in which law firms, government agencies, corporations, and accounting firms conduct individual interviews.

Duquesne University School of Law is a member of the National Association for Law Placement, the National Association for Public Interest Law Publication Network, and the Allegheny County Bar Association Minority Job Fair.

Graduates of the law school have consistently passed the Pennsylvania bar examination at a rate that well exceeds the statewide average. The law school has nearly 5,000 alumni throughout the United States and in several foreign countries, with the majority practicing in Pennsylvania and the northeastern United States.

Applicant Group for the 1998-1999 Academic Year

The law school recognizes the different strengths presented by our day division, evening division, and part-time day students and acknowledges that the diversity in the groups cannot be accurately or completely represented in a single grid of average and undergraduate GPA and LSAT scores. Graduate degrees, personal and professional accomplishments, and extensive employment experience predominate in the evening division, part-time, and day divisions.

These factors are considered crucial to an individual assessment of admissibility. Day-division applications are also reviewed individually, and factors such as leadership experience, community service, and other nonacademic experiences are considered. Applicants should contact the Admission Office for specific information on the current year's class—Phone: 214.396.6296. Applicants are encouraged to visit the law school.

Emory University School of Law

Gambrell Hall
1301 Clifton Road
Atlanta, GA 30322-2770

E-Mail: lawinfo@law.emory.edu
URL: http://www.law.emory.edu
Phone: 404.727.6801

■ Introduction

Emory's location in Atlanta, a national business and legal center, gives Emory law students the opportunity to take advanced classes from, and work with, some of the leading judges and lawyers in the United States. Atlanta is one of America's most beautiful and most livable cities.

The law school also benefits from the strength of Emory University, which was founded in 1836. Emory University School of Law is accredited by the American Bar Association, is a member of the Association of American Law Schools, and has a chapter of Order of the Coif.

■ Enrollment/Student Body

➡ *2,664 applicants* ➡ *1,077 admitted first-year class 1998*
➡ *233 enrolled first-year class 1998* ➡ *full-time 25th/75th percentile GPA—3.20/3.59* ➡ *full-time 25th/75th percentile LSAT—159/163* ➡ *635 total full-time* ➡ *21.3% minority*
➡ *50% women* ➡ *38 states & foreign countries represented*
➡ *over 100 undergraduate schools represented*

■ Faculty

➡ *86 total* ➡ *38 full-time* ➡ *48 part-time or adjunct*
➡ *5 women* ➡ *2 minority*

■ Library and Physical Facilities

➡ *300,000 volumes & equivalents* ➡ *library hours: Mon.-Fri., 8:00 A.M.-MIDNIGHT; Sat., 9:00 A.M.-MIDNIGHT; Sun., 10:00 A.M.-MIDNIGHT* ➡ *LEXIS* ➡ *WESTLAW*
➡ *6 full-time librarians* ➡ *library seats 400*

Our modern, air-conditioned building, Gambrell Hall, is a part of Emory's 630-acre campus in Druid Hills, six miles northeast of downtown Atlanta.

Gambrell Hall, constructed in 1972, contains the classrooms, faculty offices, administrative offices, student-organization offices, and a 450-seat auditorium. Gambrell Hall also houses a state-of-the-art courtroom television studio equipped for four-camera operation.

The Hugh F. McMillan Law Library sits adjacent to Gambrell Hall and is designed for easy student access. Students are trained on LEXIS and WESTLAW terminals and learn both the techniques of computer-assisted legal research and traditional research methods. Students may also use the library's computer labs—which offer MacIntosh and DOS-compatible computers.

■ Curriculum

➡ *88 credits required to graduate* ➡ *180 courses available*
➡ *degrees available: J.D.; J.D./M.B.A.; J.D./M.Div.; J.D./M.T.S.; J.D./M.P.H.; J.D./Ph.D. Religion; J.D./M.J.S.* ➡ *semesters, start in Aug.* ➡ *range of first-year class size—25-50*

The basic program of study involves three years of full-time study leading to the J.D. degree. The fall semester runs from late August to mid-December; the spring semester begins in early January and ends in mid-May.

The program of courses for the first year is prescribed. The program of courses for the second and third years is primarily elective. Students can sample a broad spectrum of courses and/or concentrate on a particular area of law.

All first-year courses and the basic second- and third-year courses are taught by full-time faculty members. A distinguished group of judges and practicing attorneys offer specialized courses.

■ Special Programs

The law school believes that its program of trial training is special. Emory's program uses as instructors many lawyers and judges from around the United States. For a two-week period, each second-year student works full-time with these lawyers and judges on each stage of the litigation of a simulated case.

Emory's affiliation with the Carter Center for Public Policy and its location in a city that is fast becoming an international legal center provide some unique opportunities in international law. Visiting international law professors from the former Soviet Union, Yugoslavia, and South Africa greatly enrich course offerings in that area.

The law school offers joint-degree programs with Emory's School of Business Administration, School of Theology, School of Public Health, and with the Graduate School of Arts and Sciences.

■ Admission

➡ *Bachelor's degree from an accredited college or university required* ➡ *application deadline—March 1*
➡ *LSAT, LSDAS required* ➡ *application fee—$50*
➡ *modified rolling admission, early application preferred*

The law school accepts beginning students for the fall term only. Prior to enrollment, a student must have earned a bachelor's degree from an approved institution.

Applications for admission must be received by Emory no later than March 1. Early applications are both encouraged and appreciated.

Many factors are considered in making admission decisions. Of particular importance are academic accomplishments and LSAT scores. Extracurricular activities, work experience, level of quality and difficulty of undergraduate courses, performance in graduate school, and letters of recommendation are also considered. Special consideration is given to members of minority groups, and members of such groups are encouraged to apply and to provide the Dean of Admission with any specific information about their background or accomplishments that would be of particular interest.

Applicants are encouraged to visit the law school. Upon acceptance, applicants are required to submit a nonrefundable $750 tuition deposit to reserve a space in the entering class.

■ Student Activities

A wide variety of organizations and activities are available to students. As there are three law reviews at Emory—*Emory Law Journal*, *Bankruptcy Developments Journal*, and *Emory International Law Review*—more than 30 percent of the second- and third-year students are involved in law review research, writing, and editing. Candidates for the reviews are selected from second- and third-year classes by the student editorial boards on the basis of scholarship and writing ability.

Students also participate in moot court. Each first-year student prepares a brief and presents an oral argument. In addition, many second- and third-year students compete in intramural and national moot court competitions.

There are numerous special interest and social groups and a very active Student Bar Association.

■ Expenses and Financial Aid

➡ *full-time tuition & fees—$23,375*
➡ *estimated additional expenses—$10,000 (room, board, & books)*
➡ *scholarships available: Robert W. Woodruff Fellowships (merit-based) & other merit/need*   ➡ *FAFSA form & profile due to the College Scholarship Service in early Feb. for financial aid*

■ Career Services

The law school regards career services as a matter of highest priority. A full-time career services office assists students in obtaining permanent, summer, and part-time employment. It arranges interviews with employers from many parts of the country and maintains extensive files on a wide variety of professional opportunities all over the United States. The great majority of Emory graduates join private law firms after graduation. Others work as judicial clerks, enter government service, or work for banks, corporations, or legal aid agencies. The career services office provides extensive training on résumés, interview skills, and job search techniques, as well as numerous opportunities to network with attorneys in a variety of practice areas and settings.

Emory School of Law provides a full range of career planning and placement services. The class of 1997 reported approximately 91.6 percent full- and part-time employment within nine months after graduation in the following fields: 59 percent in private practice; 11.8 percent in government; 9.2 percent in judicial clerkships; and 20.1 percent in business and industry, legal services, public interest, academic, and other fields. The geographic distribution reflected by these figures was as follows: Georgia, 48 percent; Southeast (excluding Atlanta), 18 percent; Northeast, 16 percent; Midwest, 3.4 percent; West, 4.8 percent; Southwest, 5.2 percent; and 3 percent outside the U.S.

Applicant Group for the 1998-1999 Academic Year

Emory University School of Law

LSAT Score	GPA								
	3.75 +	3.50 - 3.74	3.25 - 3.49	3.00 - 3.24	2.75 - 2.99	2.50 - 2.74	2.25 - 2.49	2.00 - 2.24	Below 2.00
175-180	■	■	■	■					
170-174	■	■	■	■					
165-169	■	■	■	■					
160-164	■	■	■	■					
155-159									
150-154									
145-149									
140-144									
135-139									
130-134									
125-129									
120-124									

■ Good Possibility   ☐ Possible   ▨ Unlikely

Note: This chart is to be used as a general guide in determining the chances for admittance.

University of Florida College of Law

Assistant Dean for Admissions
P.O. Box 117622, 325 Holland Hall
Gainesville, FL 32611-7622

E-Mail: willshan@law.ufl.edu; patrick@law.ufl.edu
URL: http://www.law.ufl.edu
Phone: 352.392.2087, Fax: 352.392.8727

■ Introduction

The University of Florida College of Law offers a three-year post-baccalaureate curriculum leading to the degree of Juris Doctor (J.D.), a number of joint-degree programs, and a post-J.D. program leading to the degree of Master of Laws in Taxation (LL.M.), and a Master of Laws in Comparative Law (LL.M.) for foreign lawyers. The study of law at the University of Florida prepares students for creative problem solving, dispute resolution, planning and counseling, and policy-making roles in contemporary society. With a student body consistently ranked among the nation's finest, the college is known for graduating leaders for Florida's legal, political, business, and educational sectors, and its faculty and alumni are recognized at the national and international level.

The University of Florida, occupying 2,000 acres mostly within Gainesville's 90,000-population urban area, is a member of the prestigious Association of American Universities and is recognized as one of the nation's leading research universities by the Carnegie Commission on Higher Education. Gainesville, with extensive educational, cultural, and recreational offerings, is consistently ranked among the best places to live in America.

■ History of the College of Law

➡ *founded in 1909* ➡ *Association of American Law Schools membership since 1920* ➡ *New York State Regents accreditation since 1917* ➡ *ABA approval since 1925*

■ Enrollment/Student Body

➡ *2,352 applicants* ➡ *475 admitted first-year class 1998*
➡ *203 enrolled first-year class 1998*
➡ *fall full-time 25th/75th percentile GPA—3.34/3.78*
➡ *spring full-time 25th/75th percentile GPA—3.23/3.58*
➡ *fall full-time 25th/75th percentile LSAT—153/162*
➡ *spring full-time 25th/75th percentile LSAT—152/159*
➡ *1,191 total full-time* ➡ *23% minority*
➡ *42.9% women* ➡ *99 undergraduate schools represented*
➡ *271 admitted spring 1999* ➡ *200 enrolled spring 1999*

■ Faculty

➡ *74 full-time* ➡ *12 part-time or adjunct* ➡ *26 women*
➡ *7 minority*

■ Library and Physical Facilities

➡ *591,800 volumes & equivalents* ➡ *library hours: Mon.-Fri., 7:30 A.M.-MIDNIGHT; Sat., 9:00 A.M.-5:00 P.M.; Sun., 11:00 A.M.-MIDNIGHT* ➡ *LEXIS* ➡ *WESTLAW*
➡ *Internet* ➡ *25 full-time librarians/staff* ➡ *library seats 800*

The College of Law is housed in two adjacent buildings on the University of Florida campus in North Central Florida. The Legal Information Center's extensive holdings rank it among the three largest law libraries in the Southeastern United States. The library long has been a national leader in audiovisual and microform services and computerized legal research. The library also offers PCs for student use, network access, and electronic mail accounts.

■ Curriculum

➡ *88 credits required to graduate* ➡ *over 100 courses & seminars available* ➡ *degrees available: J.D.; J.D./M.B.A.; J.D./M.A.; J.D./M.D.; & J.D./Ph.D.* ➡ *semesters, start in Aug., Jan., & May (8-week term)*

The College of Law curriculum includes traditional courses on law and legal analysis, skills training courses, international law offerings, and seminars on contemporary legal issues. Students generally are required to complete the first-year curriculum in sequence, and spring entrants are required to attend the first summer term. All students must complete a major research and writing project in the senior year.

Seventeen different joint-degree programs are currently being offered at the masters and doctoral levels. See our Web site under curriculum for a complete list. Newest additions to the joint-degree list are Doctorate of Medicine (MD), Environmental Engineering, and Latin American Studies. These new degrees and those listed on the Web site are available to students who meet the requirements of both the College of Law and the Graduate School.

■ Special Programs

The college is home to a nationally acclaimed Graduate Tax Program, leading to the degree LL.M. in Taxation. The program publishes the *Florida Tax Review*, which utilizes LL.M. student assistants. The college also offers a Master of Laws degree in Comparative Law (LL.M.) for foreign lawyers seeking to improve their understanding of American law.

Clinical programs provide J.D. students with the opportunity to represent actual clients in civil, criminal, and juvenile court cases, plus negotiation, mediation and other dispute resolution processes.

A number of "Centers & Institutes" have been established at the College of Law. They are the Institute for Dispute Resolution, Legal Technology, International Center for Automated Information Research (ICAIR), Legal Information Center, Holland & Knight Institute, Center for the Study of Race and Race Relations, Intellectual Property Institute, Environmental Land Use Law Program, Center for Governmental Responsibility, and the UF Centre for International Financial Crimes Studies. For details, please see Curriculum section on our Web site.

■ Admission

➡ *Bachelor's degree from accredited college or university required*
➡ *application deadline—fall, Feb. 1; spring, May 15*
➡ *rolling admissions, early application preferred*
➡ *LSAT, LSDAS required*

The College of Law enrolls only full-time students in the fall and spring. Approximately 95 percent of those entering successfully complete the first two semesters. The college subscribes to the suggestions on prelaw study included in this guide. In addition to the bulleted requirements above, the College of Law requests that each applicant provide a personal statement and three letters of evaluation. Admission standards are higher for non-Florida residents.

Approximately 50 percent of admission decisions are based primarily on the undergraduate grade-point average and LSAT score; however, multiple LSAT scores are considered by the Admissions Committee. The remainder of each class is selected on the basis of both quantitative and nonquantitative criteria. Applications cannot be processed more than one year in advance of the intended month of entry. However, early completion of applications is strongly recommended. Applicants must take the LSAT prior to application deadlines (December for fall; February for spring).

Students may transfer in August, January, or May from ABA law schools, but the Admissions Committee accepts only those transfer applicants who will have completed their first year of law school before enrolling at the University of Florida. Candidates must be in the upper one-third of their class to be considered. A letter of good standing from the dean is required. No more than 29 semester hours will be transferred.

The University of Florida and the College of Law actively recruit minority students. Scholarships and grants are available for qualified minority students. Inquiries should be addressed to the Assistant Director of Admissions, University of Florida College of Law, Gainesville, FL 32611-7622.

■ Student/Extracurricular Activities

Student activities include the *Florida Law Review*, *Florida Journal of International Law*, *Florida Journal of Law and Public Policy*, *Florida Tax Review*, Moot Court and Trial Team. More than 20 extracurricular organizations provide additional opportunities for student involvement.

■ Expenses and Financial Aid

➡ *tuition & fees—Florida residents, $154/sem. hr.; nonresidents, $518/sem. hr.*
➡ *estimated additional expenses—$10,650 room, board, books*
➡ *performance & need-based scholarships available*
➡ *deadlines—April 1 for fall applicants; July 1 for spring applicants (FAFSA required—see Prospectus)*

In addition to scholarships and awards, the College of Law provides short- and long-term loans to qualified students. Students applying for College of Law financial aid must have an undergraduate GPA of at least 3.2 and a single or average LSAT score of 158 or higher, and must submit the FAFSA. GPA and LSAT figures used are those reported by LSDAS. For information concerning federal, state, and Law Access loans, write to: Director of Financial Aid, College of Law, 164 Holland Hall, Gainesville, FL 32611-2038.

■ Housing

Housing is available for single students in university dormitories and for families in university apartments adjacent to the law school. Off-campus housing is also available. For more information, write to the Director of Housing, University of Florida, Gainesville, FL 32611.

■ Career Services

The Career Planning and Placement Office assists students in finding employment or clerkships. Approximately 150 employers recruit on campus each year. Approximately 85 percent of recent College of Law graduates seeking employment have jobs after taking the bar.

Applicant Group for the 1998-1999 Academic Year

University of Florida College of Law
This grid includes only applicants who earned 120-180 LSAT scores under standard administrations.

LSAT Score	3.75 +		3.50 - 3.74		3.25 - 3.49		3.00 - 3.24		2.75 - 2.99		2.50 - 2.74		2.25 - 2.49		2.00 - 2.24		Below 2.00		No GPA		Total	
	Apps	Adm	Apps	Adm	Apps	Adm	Apps	Adm	Apps	Adm	Apps	Adm	Apps	Adm	Apps	Adm	Apps	Adm	Apps	Adm	Apps	Adm
175-180	0	0	0	0	0	0	3	3	0	0	0	0	0	0	0	0	0	0	0	0	3	3
170-174	10	10	2	2	4	4	7	7	2	2	2	1	0	0	0	0	0	0	0	0	27	26
165-169	27	27	31	30	17	17	16	15	7	3	4	0	3	0	0	0	0	0	2	2	107	94
160-164	43	42	50	48	62	58	49	31	22	8	10	1	4	0	3	0	1	1	0	0	244	189
155-159	51	48	95	71	144	83	95	32	45	14	21	1	14	0	7	0	1	0	5	4	478	253
150-154	54	40	89	45	103	31	97	17	57	3	29	1	10	0	4	0	0	0	3	0	446	137
145-149	22	15	47	13	61	12	68	11	54	3	26	3	24	0	8	0	3	0	12	3	325	60
140-144	7	2	18	3	31	4	38	6	46	2	39	3	16	0	8	0	1	0	4	1	208	21
135-139	3	0	6	0	14	1	12	0	16	0	17	0	9	0	6	0	2	0	13	0	98	1
130-134	0	0	0	0	5	1	2	1	4	0	7	0	3	0	2	0	0	0	1	0	24	2
125-129	0	0	0	0	0	0	0	0	0	0	1	0	0	0	3	0	1	0	0	0	5	0
120-124	0	0	0	0	0	0	0	0	0	0	0	0	0	0	1	0	0	0	0	0	1	0
Total	217	184	338	212	441	211	387	123	253	35	156	10	83	0	42	0	9	1	40	10	1966	786

Apps = Number of Applicants   Adm = Number Admitted   Reflects 99% of the total applicant pool.

The Florida State University College of Law

College of Law
Tallahassee, FL 32306-1601

E-Mail: admissions@law.fsu.edu
URL: http://www.law.fsu.edu
Phone: 850.644.3787

■ Introduction

The Florida State University College of Law is widely recognized for both its commitment to teaching and its cutting-edge scholarship. The college subscribes to the idea that the best legal education is the result of a lively dialogue in an intimate learning environment. Our low student-to-faculty ratio allows for a diversity of class offerings while emphasizing a personalized legal education. The college is situated blocks from the Florida Capitol, the First District Court of Appeal, the Florida Supreme Court, the United States District Court, and other centers of judicial and administrative activity. Proximity to these institutions offers students a unique opportunity to observe firsthand the workings of the state government and courts. The curriculum is continually evolving to reflect changes in the practice of law. Three current areas of emphasis are environmental law, international law, and alternative dispute resolution. The college is a member of the Association of American Law Schools (AALS) and is ABA approved.

■ Enrollment

➧ 1,879 applicants   ➧ 625 admitted first-year class 1998
➧ 225 enrolled first-year class 1998   ➧ full-time 25th/75th percentile GPA—3.07/3.57   ➧ full-time 25th/75th percentile LSAT—153/159   ➧ 654 total full-time   ➧ 24.6% minority
➧ 45% women   ➧ 85 undergraduate schools represented

■ Faculty

➧ 58 total   ➧ 43 full-time   ➧ 15 adjunct
➧ 12 women   ➧ 6 minority

■ Library and Physical Facilities

➧ 401,020 volumes & equivalents   ➧ library hours: Mon.-Thurs., 7:30 A.M.-11:00 P.M.; Fri., 7:30 A.M.-8:00 P.M.; Sat., 10:00 A.M.-6:00 P.M.; Sun., 1:00 P.M.-11:00 P.M.
➧ LEXIS   ➧ NEXIS   ➧ WESTLAW
➧ 9 full-time librarians   ➧ library seats 429
➧ 5,441 serial subscriptions

The physical facilities of the College of Law consist of B.K. Roberts Hall opened in 1971; a separate, connected law library building opened in 1983; and the Village Green, completed in 1988.

Roberts Hall houses faculty, staff and student offices, lounges, classrooms, seminar rooms, and a practice courtroom making extensive use of video technology. Both Roberts Hall and the law library comply with all architectural regulations facilitating use for disabled students.

The law library's volumes and microform volume equivalents are all cataloged in the Florida State University libraries' online database, accessible through computer terminals located throughout the library and also available for remote access using computers with modems. Serial subscriptions exceed 5,400; holdings include a wide range of audiovisual materials. Individual and group study, video viewing, microform reading, and computer use and instruction are accommodated within the law library.

■ Curriculum

➧ Academic Support Program   ➧ 20-hour pro bono requirement   ➧ 88 credits required to graduate
➧ 124 courses available plus clinics and internships
➧ degrees available: J.D.; J.D./M.B.A.; J.D./M.P.A.; J.D./International Affairs; J.D./Urban & Regional Planning; J.D./Economics; J.D./M.S.W.
➧ range of first-year class size—30-70

The school operates on the semester basis. The first-year curriculum is mandatory. Current catalogs indicate the range of electives available. While the general curriculum is national in focus, some courses especially relevant to the Florida bar and Florida practice are offered.

■ Special Programs

The college's location in the state capital provides students with a variety of externship opportunities. Judicial externships are available with state trial and appellate courts, including the Florida Supreme Court and the federal courts. Externship opportunities with government agencies and commissions, the state attorney, the public defender, and legal services offices are also provided. The college's Children's Advocacy Center offers law students an opportunity to represent children in a variety of legal areas under the supervision of clinical faculty. The Florida Dispute Resolution Center, a joint project of the college and the Florida Supreme Court, encourages the use of alternate dispute resolution methods, and provides law students opportunities to gain hands-on knowledge of a rapidly growing area of the law. The college sponsors three summer law programs abroad, Oxford University in England, the University of the West Indies in Barbados, and Charles University in Prague. Faculty from Florida State and the host institutions participate in the programs, which are open to students who have completed the first year of law school. The college also coordinates a public service fellowship program that provides fellowships to students in return for a commitment to public service activities.

■ Admission Standards

➧ Bachelor's degree from accredited college or university required
➧ application deadline—Feb. 15   ➧ early application preferred
➧ LSAT, LSDAS required   ➧ application fee—$20

More than 1,800 applications are expected this year for the 200 places in the entering class.

Files are reviewed by a faculty committee. The committee considers the LSAT, UGPA, and the pattern of undergraduate performance from year to year as well as the school and coursework pursued by the applicant. Also, it weighs a number of other factors, including institutional interest in maintaining a student body as diverse as possible in the categories of ethnicity, gender, and educational background.

Transfer applicants may be admitted to any term after completion of the first year. Transcripts showing a full year's work and a dean's letter indicating the student's class rank and stating that the student is in good academic standing and eligible to return must be provided. Applicants must be enrolled in an ABA-approved law school. Applicants must be in the top 25 percent of their first-year class to be eligible for transfer.

■ Student Activities

One of the most attractive aspects of Florida State University's academic climate is the wide variety of educational and professional opportunities available outside the traditional classroom. The College of Law sponsors *Law Review*, the *Journal of Land Use and Environmental Law*, the *Journal of Transnational Law*, a nationally recognized moot court and trial advocacy program, and a variety of social and professional organizations. The college boasts active ACLU, NLG, PILSA, and STLA chapters; a Women's Law Society; a Black Law Students Association chapter; a Christian Legal Society; an Entertainment, Arts, and Sports Law Society; a Federalist Society; an International Law Society; Business Interest Society; Dispute Resolution Society; an Environmental Law Society; a Spanish-American Law Students Association chapter; and Law Partners, a law students' spouse and significant others support group. Both Phi Delta Phi and Phi Alpha Delta legal honoraries maintain a chapter on campus. F.S.U. was granted a chapter of

Order of the Coif in 1979. The Student Bar Association serves an active student government role and coordinates such services as the roommate referral program, a co-op bookstore, and coordination of many law school-sponsored social activities.

■ Expenses and Financial Aid

➡ *tuition & fees—full-time, in-state, $4,495; full-time, out-of-state, $14,874* ➡ *scholarships available (academic & need-based)* ➡ *minority scholarships available* ➡ *financial aid available; Federal Free Form (FAFSA) analysis preferred by March 1*

■ Housing

Housing is available for single and married students in university dormitories. Three private apartment complexes are located across the street from the College of Law building. Information may be obtained from the Director of Housing, 106 Cawthon Hall, Florida State University, Tallahassee, FL 32306.

■ Career Services

The College of Law is staffed with a full-time director of Career Planning and Placement, who assists both students and alumni in obtaining positions and also helps students find part-time and summer jobs. Students have many opportunities to make their talents known before graduation in both clinical programs and part-time work for law offices, state agencies, and legislators.

Applicant Group for the 1998-1999 Academic Year

The Florida State University College of Law
This grid includes only applicants who earned 120-180 LSAT scores under standard administrations.

LSAT Score	3.75 +		3.50 - 3.74		3.25 - 3.49		3.00 - 3.24		2.75 - 2.99		2.50 - 2.74		2.25 - 2.49		2.00 - 2.24		Below 2.00		No GPA		Total	
	Apps	Adm	Apps	Adm	Apps	Adm	Apps	Adm	Apps	Adm	Apps	Adm	Apps	Adm	Apps	Adm	Apps	Adm	Apps	Adm	Apps	Adm
175-180	0	0	0	0	0	0	1	1	0	0	0	0	0	0	0	0	0	0	0	0	1	1
170-174	0	0	1	1	1	1	3	3	2	2	1	1	1	1	0	0	0	0	0	0	9	9
165-169	10	10	4	4	4	4	5	5	3	1	4	2	2	2	0	0	0	0	0	0	32	28
160-164	21	20	21	21	33	30	39	33	23	17	11	4	4	1	2	0	1	0	0	0	155	126
155-159	37	36	64	56	101	78	84	54	48	19	22	6	17	0	7	1	2	0	4	0	386	250
150-154	40	27	87	43	115	40	109	23	71	8	28	0	16	1	6	0	1	1	3	1	476	144
145-149	23	5	53	7	79	8	99	7	68	5	44	3	23	0	11	0	0	0	12	3	412	38
140-144	8	0	18	1	31	0	54	2	51	0	46	0	12	0	9	0	4	0	3	0	236	3
135-139	1	0	9	0	12	0	18	0	25	0	21	0	11	0	7	0	3	0	3	0	110	0
130-134	0	0	2	0	4	0	2	0	7	0	6	0	4	0	4	0	1	0	4	0	34	0
125-129	0	0	0	0	0	0	0	0	3	0	0	0	1	0	1	0	2	0	2	0	9	0
120-124	0	0	0	0	0	0	0	0	1	0	0	0	0	0	0	0	0	0	0	0	1	0
Total	140	98	259	133	380	161	414	128	302	52	183	16	91	5	47	1	14	1	31	4	1861	599

Apps = Number of Applicants
Adm = Number Admitted
Reflects 99% of the total applicant pool.

Fordham University School of Law

140 West 62nd Street
New York, NY 10023

E-Mail: lawadmissions@mail.lawnet.fordham.edu
URL: http://www.fordham.edu
Phone: 212.636.6810

■ Introduction

Founded in 1841, Fordham University is a private institution, located in New York City, with an enrollment of some 13,000 students. The law school campus is immediately adjacent to Lincoln Center for the Performing Arts, in the heart of Manhattan. Fordham School of Law, founded in 1905, has been a member of the AALS since 1936 and is fully approved by the ABA.

■ Enrollment/Student Body

➡ *4,456 applicants*   ➡ *1,389 admitted first-year class 1998*
➡ *485 enrolled first-year class 1998 (351 full-time, 134 part-time)*
➡ *full-time 25th/75th percentile GPA—3.09/3.63*
➡ *full-time 25th/75th percentile LSAT—160/165*
➡ *1,108 total full-time*   ➡ *368 total part-time*
➡ *25% minority first-year class*   ➡ *45% women*
➡ *41 states, the District of Columbia, & 4 foreign countries represented*   ➡ *275 colleges and universities represented*

■ Faculty

➡ *214 total*   ➡ *62 full-time*   ➡ *152 part-time or adjunct*
➡ *17 women full-time, 42 women part-time or adjunct*
➡ *5 minority full-time, 13 minority part-time or adjunct*

■ Library and Physical Facilities

➡ *450,000 volumes & equivalents*   ➡ *library hours:*
Mon.-Fri., 7:00 A.M.-1:00 A.M.; Sat., 8:00 A.M.-1:00 A.M.;
Sun., 8:00 A.M.-1:00 A.M.   ➡ *LEXIS*   ➡ *NEXIS*
➡ *WESTLAW*   ➡ *DIALOG*   ➡ *11 full-time librarians*
➡ *library seats 560*

In addition to classroom, faculty, and administrative office space, the law school contains a large amphitheater, an atrium for special events and gatherings, a formal moot courtroom, a student lounge, a spacious cafeteria, and a library. The computer center contains Windows-based Pentium PCs emulated to both LEXIS and WESTLAW, and supported by laser printers and various word processing packages. These PCs run on the law school's LAN and will eventually allow access, through the Internet, to global information resources, in addition to the law libraries of several New York area law schools. Law students also have access to the University Computing Center, located within steps of the law school building, which contains nearly 100 DOS-based and Apple PCs, in addition to VAX mainframe terminals which run SPSS statistical and other sophisticated mainframe software packages.

■ Curriculum

➡ *Academic Support Program*   ➡ *83 credits required to graduate, of which 45 credits are required courses*
➡ *190 courses available*   ➡ *degrees available: J.D.; J.D./M.B.A.; J.D./M.S.W.; LL.M.*   ➡ *semesters, start in Aug.*   ➡ *range of first-year class size—18-122*

■ Special Programs

An extensive and growing clinical component is offered which includes a Trial Advocacy Program and clinics in Criminal Defense; Prosecution; Battered Women's Rights; Community Lawyering; Civil, Employment, and Disability Rights; Mediation; and Disability Law. Externships in federal, state, and city judges' offices, prosecutors' offices, the Legal Aid Society, the ACLU, the Children's Defense Fund, and many other public service settings throughout the city are also offered. A pilot program on lawyering skills introduces first-year students to a broad range of law practice skills, including negotiating, dispute resolution, client counseling, and witness interviewing. The Moot Court Program, considered by faculty to be one of the more important aspects of the student's law training, provides students with opportunities to participate in several intramural competitions as well as a variety of interschool competitions throughout the country.

   Fordham Public Service Programs—Fordham's commitment to producing graduates who will devote themselves to the public interest has resulted in the establishment of the Public Interest Resource Center, an administrative support base for the three public interest organizations in operation: The Fordham Law Community Service Project, The Fordham Student Sponsored Fellowship, and Fordham Pro Bono Students. The Stein Institute on Law and Ethics sponsors lectures and seminars throughout the year. The Stein Center for Ethics and Public Interest Law sponsors an annual symposium on current ethical issues; roundtable discussions among practitioners, scholars, and students engaged in public interest law; and the Stein Scholars Program, a three-year program for specially selected law students who will work in public interest law settings and undertake specialized academic work in legal ethics.

   The Fordham Center on European Community Law and International Antitrust provides a teaching and resource facility devoted to two overlapping areas of international law: European Community and international antitrust.

■ Admission

➡ *Bachelor's degree from accredited college or university required*   ➡ *application deadline—March 1*
➡ *LSAT, LSDAS required*

The selection of students is handled primarily by seven full-time faculty members, the Dean of Admissions, the Assistant Dean/Director of Admissions, and the Assistant Dean for Student Affairs, who together constitute the Admissions Committee. The Admissions Committee determines admissions criteria based on an evaluation of the applicant pool, comparison to the qualifications of recently admitted classes, and the first-year law school performance of the three most recently admitted classes as revealed in first-year performance validity/correlation studies. For the majority of applicants numeric indicators

(LSAT score and UGPA) are the principal criteria relied upon, and the majority of admitted students present an LSAT score above the 91 percentile and a UGPA above a 3.40. Qualitative factors including prior employment, student activities, service to the community, leadership ability, propensity for public service, and communication skills are also considered in selecting the incoming class. The law school makes an aggressive effort to identify and enroll applicants from the African American, Asian American, Latino, and Native American communities, in addition to applicants who are culturally, socially, or economically disadvantaged. Over the past five years the law school has received an average of 4,500 applications annually for approximately 470 seats, and its acceptance rate has varied from 13.9 percent to 31 percent.

■ Student Activities

Students publish five scholarly journals: the *Fordham Law Review*; the *Fordham Urban Law Journal*; the *Fordham International Law Journal*; the *Fordham Environmental Law Journal*; and the *Fordham Intellectual Property, Media, and Entertainment Law Journal*. Each contains lead articles by distinguished members of the profession as well as student notes and comments. These journals are cited in appellate court opinions throughout the country. Fordham is a member of the Order of the Coif, the national honor society for law students. Students who are in the top 10 percent of their graduating class are eligible for membership. Other activities and organizations include the American Bar Association, Law Student Division; Amnesty International; Asian American Law Students Association; Black Law Students Association; Christian Law Students; the Crowley Labor Guild; Fordham Democratic Law Students Association; Sports Law Society; Fordham Federalist Society; Fordham Follies; Gay and Lesbian Law Association; Jewish Law Students; Fordham Law Women; Older Law Students Association; Fordham Republican Law Students Association; Latin American Law Students Association; National Lawyers Guild; Phi Alpha Delta Law Fraternity; the *Advocate*; and the yearbook.

■ Expenses and Financial Aid

➧ *tuition & fees—full-time, $23,600; part-time, $17,700*
➧ *almost all aid is need-based, though a small number of donor scholarships are awarded on the basis of qualitative merit*
➧ *Profile and FAFSA required; due in early Feb.*

A 20-story dormitory, with 250 beds (in two- and three-bedroom apartments, some of which are double occupancy bedrooms) set aside for law students, and located on the Lincoln Center campus, opened in the summer of 1993. Rates for 1997-98 ranged from $6,400 to $7,500 per person, per academic year (single vs. double occupancy bedroom).

■ Career Services

The School of Law maintains a professionally staffed Career Planning Center which assists all students and alumni/ae in determining their career directions and opportunities and in developing effective employment search skills and strategies. Hundreds of law firms, governmental and public service agencies, and corporations interview at the law school each year. Applications are solicited by employers from almost every state. Employment trends for recent graduates have been about as follows: private practice, 68 percent; government and public interest, 11 percent; corporations, 11 percent; judicial clerkships, 9 percent; and academic, 1 percent.

Applicant Group for the 1998-1999 Academic Year

Fordham University School of Law
This data reflects the applicant pool for the fall 1998 entering class.

LSAT Score	No GPA		1.40 - 2.49		2.50 - 2.99		3.00 - 3.49		3.50 - 4.33		Totals	
	Adm	Apps	Adm	Apps	Adm	Apps	Adm	Apps	Adm	Apps	Adm	Apps
176-180	0	0	0	0	2	2	0	0	3	3	5	5
172-175	0	0	1	1	6	8	18	20	12	12	37	41
168-171	2	2	1	4	12	17	69	71	55	56	139	150
164-167	5	5	7	11	64	80	226	229	184	186	486	511
160-163	1	4	8	19	33	110	181	356	227	267	450	756
156-159	3	8	3	26	15	147	54	369	69	274	144	824
152-155	1	11	1	32	15	133	31	357	28	205	76	738
148-151	1	18	0	28	8	108	24	239	11	112	44	505
120-147	0	35	2	130	2	251	3	268	1	137	8	821
Applications That Never Became Complete											0	105
Total	14	73	23	251	157	856	606	1909	590	1252	1389	4456

Apps = Applications Received
Adm = Applications Accepted

Franklin Pierce Law Center

Admissions Office
2 White Street
Concord, NH 03301

E-Mail: admissions@fplc.edu
URL: http://www.fplc.edu
Phone: 603.228.9217

■ Introduction

Franklin Pierce Law Center is a private, ABA-approved national law school. Established in 1973 to encourage innovation in legal education, it remains the only law school in New Hampshire.

The Law Center's commitment to innovation in legal education is reflected in its emphasis on individually tailored legal education; a broad range of learning settings including lectures and seminars, real-client clinics, independent study, and externships with lawyers and judges; a community spirit of caring and compassion; and a close working relationship between students and faculty. Self-reliant students who know their own strengths and objectives thrive at Franklin Pierce and find the focus on personal pride and responsibility more motivating than fear, competition, or class rank.

The Law Center is one of the smallest private law schools in the United States. Each entering class numbers approximately 140 students. Classes tend to be small, especially after the first year. Thirty-five of the 50 elective courses enroll 35 or fewer students.

Located in New Hampshire's capital city of Concord (40,000 population), the Law Center is 25 minutes from Manchester, New Hampshire's largest city, and approximately one hour from Boston, the Atlantic seacoast, the state's lake region, and the White Mountains.

■ Enrollment/Student Body

➡ *759 applicants* ➡ *511 admitted first-year class 1998* ➡ *116 enrolled first-year class 1998* ➡ *full-time 25th/75th percentile GPA—2.60/3.31* ➡ *full-time 25th/75th percentile LSAT—146/155* ➡ *373 total full-time* ➡ *11 total part-time* ➡ *15% total minority first-year class 1998* ➡ *45% total women first-year class 1998* ➡ *45 states & 6 foreign countries represented* ➡ *237 undergraduate schools represented*

■ Faculty

➡ *75 total* ➡ *20 full-time* ➡ *55 part-time or adjunct* ➡ *25 women*

■ Library and Physical Facilities

➡ *213,019 volumes & equivalents* ➡ *library hours: Mon.-Thurs., 8:00 A.M.-MIDNIGHT; Fri., 8:00 A.M.-10:00 P.M.; Sat., 10:00 A.M.-10:00 P.M.; Sun., 10:00 A.M.-MIDNIGHT* ➡ *LEXIS* ➡ *NEXIS* ➡ *WESTLAW* ➡ *DIALOG* ➡ *6 full-time librarians* ➡ *library seats 247*

It is the largest law library in the state with special strength in intellectual property.

■ Curriculum

➡ *84 credits required to graduate* ➡ *82 courses available* ➡ *degrees available: J.D.; J.D./Master of Intellectual Property; J.D./Master of Education Law; LL.M.* ➡ *semesters, start in Aug.* ➡ *range of first-year class size—27-140*

■ Special Programs

Education Law—This unique program recognizes the large role law plays in education institutions from K–12 to universities. Courses and externship opportunities with government agencies, university counsel, school attorneys, and child advocates prepare students for this growing area of legal practice. The program offers a joint J.D./Master of Education Law and J.D./Certificate of Advanced Graduate Study.

Intellectual Property—The internationally recognized intellectual and industrial property specialization (patents, licensing, technology transfer, trade secrets, trademarks, cyberlaw, and copyrights) is supported by five full-time faculty members, all intellectual property lawyers. Training includes learning to advise clients regarding intellectual property protection, infringement, and technology transfer. Students with technical backgrounds may focus on patent law, many passing the patent bar exam prior to graduation. Other IP areas do not require a technical background.

Community Lawyering Program—This hands-on professional training program prepares students for public interest law in private practice, governmental service, social policy advocacy, and criminal practice.

Clinical opportunities include providing legal assistance in cases of divorce, neglect and abuse of children, through the Civil Practice Clinic; working with at-risk youth, small claims matters, and civil mediation in Dispute Resolution Clinics, and assisting with projects with the Health Policy and Non-profit Organizations Clinics.

Criminal Law—Courses, individual mentoring, clinics, and externships prepares students for careers in prosecution or defense. Criminal Practice Clinic students represent clients charged with misdemeanor and juvenile offenses at the district court level. In the Appellate Defender Program, students prepare briefs for the New Hampshire Supreme Court in criminal cases. Externship opportunities exist in prosecutorial positions at the local, state, and federal level and in defense positions with law firms and governmental agencies.

Health Law and Policy—Students are trained to represent clients seeking a more sensible, cost effective, and humane system for delivering health care. A professional collaboration with Law Center faculty members, Dartmouth Medical School, and the University of New Hampshire provide ongoing programs to encourage understanding and cooperation among the separate disciplines. In addition, students may participate in institute projects such as developing a plan for quality, cost effective elder care.

■ Admission

➡ *B.A. or B.S. degree required* ➡ *application deadline—May 1* ➡ *rolling admission* ➡ *LSAT, LSDAS required* ➡ *application fee—$45*

While LSAT scores and grade-point average are, of course, factors that must be considered in the decision-making process, neither alone is determinative.

Our Admissions Committee is composed of members of the faculty, student body, and admission staff. Every application receives a thorough and thoughtful review. The candidate's personal statement, letters of recommendation, and résumé are evaluated along with the "numbers." Community service, employment during college, and other nonacademic accomplishments are given weight to the extent that they reflect initiative, social responsibility, maturity, and other qualities. Franklin Pierce does not discriminate on the basis of age, sex, race, color, religion, national origin, marital status, sexual orientation, or disability, and encourages members of groups under-represented in the legal profession to seek admission.

■ Student Activities

Students prepare notes and comments for *IDEA: The Journal of Law and Technology*, published by the Center's Patent, Trademark and Copyright Research Foundation; *Risk Issues in Health & Safety*; and *Annual Survey of New Hampshire Law*, an annual publication consisting of six articles focusing principally on recent NH Supreme Court opinions. Articles are written by second-year and edited by third-year students. Student organizations include the Multicultural Law Student Association, the Law Students Cooperative, Public Interest Coalition, Women's Law Caucus, the Environmental Law Society, the International

Law Society, In-house Lawyering, BiGALLA (Bisexual, Gay, and Lesbian Alliance), and SIPLA (Student Intellectual Property Law Association), as well as chapters of the American Trial Lawyers Association, National Lawyers Guild, Phi Alpha Delta Fraternity, and the American Bar Association/Law Students Division.

■ Expenses and Financial Aid

➡ *tuition & fees—$16,475* ➡ *estimated additional expenses—books $600, living expenses $11,940* ➡ *scholarships available: Franklin Pierce Law Center Scholarships based on need* ➡ *merit scholarships available—award based upon academic & professional record* ➡ *diversity scholarships available—scholarships are awarded to members of underrepresented groups* ➡ *FPLC Financial Aid Application & FAFSA required* ➡ *application deadline—May 1* ➡ *decisions made on a rolling basis*

■ Career Services

The Career Services Center works with students and alumni to find the best match between their skills and interests and changing legal markets. The center provides extensive individual counseling and guidance; brings attorneys to campus to provide first-hand information about the practice of law; advises students of all resources through weekly publications and job boards; coordinates the efforts of faculty, staff, and student groups to provide information about opportunities to gain experience; and conducts outreach to employers.

Applicant Group for the 1998-1999 Academic Year

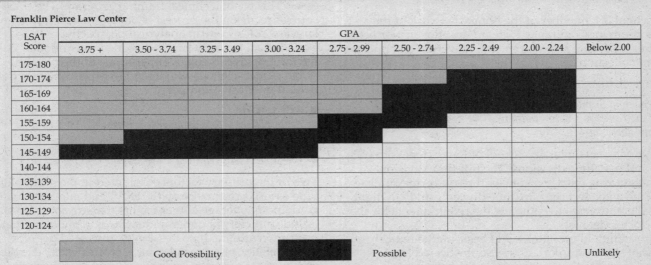

Franklin Pierce Law Center

LSAT Score	GPA								
	3.75 +	3.50 - 3.74	3.25 - 3.49	3.00 - 3.24	2.75 - 2.99	2.50 - 2.74	2.25 - 2.49	2.00 - 2.24	Below 2.00
175-180									
170-174									
165-169									
160-164									
155-159									
150-154									
145-149									
140-144									
135-139									
130-134									
125-129									
120-124									

Good Possibility   Possible   Unlikely

Note: This chart is to be used as a general guide in determining the chances for admittance. Nonnumerical factors are strongly considered for applicants

George Mason University School of Law

3401 North Fairfax Drive
Arlington, VA 22201-4498

E-Mail: lawadmis@gmu.edu
URL: http://www.gmu.edu/departments/law
Phone: 703.993.8010

■ Introduction

Located in Arlington, Virginia, George Mason University School of Law sits on the doorstep of the nation's capital. One of three public law schools in Virginia, it was established by authority of the Virginia General Assembly in 1979. George Mason is fully accredited by the ABA and is a member of the AALS.

■ Enrollment/Student Body

➡ *1,938 applicants* ➡ *665 admitted first-year class 1998*
➡ *209 enrolled first-year class 1998* ➡ *full-time 25th/75th percentile GPA—2.83/3.40* ➡ *part-time 25th/75th percentile GPA—2.74/3.38* ➡ *full-time 25th/75th percentile LSAT—156/161* ➡ *part-time 25th/75th percentile LSAT—153/160*
➡ *379 total full-time* ➡ *362 total part-time*
➡ *11.3% minority* ➡ *39% women* ➡ *35 states & foreign countries represented* ➡ *224 undergraduate schools represented*

George Mason University is an equal opportunity/ affirmative action institution.

■ Faculty

➡ *123 total* ➡ *33 full-time* ➡ *90 part-time or adjunct*
➡ *6 women* ➡ *2 minority*

■ Library and Physical Facilities

➡ *374,000 volumes & equivalents* ➡ *library hours: Mon.-Thurs., 8:00 A.M.-10:45 P.M.; Fri., 8:00 A.M.-9:45 P.M.; Sat., 10:00 A.M.-5:45 P.M.; Sun., NOON-10:45 P.M.*
➡ *LEXIS* ➡ *NEXIS* ➡ *WESTLAW*
➡ *7 full-time librarians* ➡ *library seats 342*

The school is a member of the library network of the Consortium for Continuing Higher Education in Northern Virginia, affording access to general university and public library collections.

■ Curriculum

➡ *Academic Support Program*
➡ *84 credits required to graduate* ➡ *degrees available: J.D.*
➡ *semesters, start in Aug.*

George Mason University School of Law offers both full-time and part-time divisions. The full-time division operates during the day and takes three years to complete. Students who elect the part-time division study at night and take four years to complete the requirements for the juris doctor degree.

A grounding in economics and basic mathematical and financial skills is important to a sophisticated legal education and to the development of a competent attorney. To ensure that George Mason graduates have this grounding, all students take a first-year course in Legal and Economic Methods.

George Mason law students complete a three-year legal writing program, which emphasizes the use of technology and continual practice of skills in the development of actual transactions and cases. A separate writing grade-point average further underscores the importance of good writing at George Mason.

The curriculum begins with exposure to the courses fundamental to a well-rounded legal education. Students at George Mason can also elect one of our specialty programs, thus demonstrating depth as well as breadth in their training. All specialties are offered in both the full-time and part-time divisions.

■ Special Programs

Corporate and Securities Law prepares students to work in a variety of fields related to corporate law and financial markets. By developing a thorough understanding of both law and underlying theory, students are prepared to deal with rapidly changing business and legal environments.

Regulatory Law prepares students for practice in and before the numerous agencies that regulate business and other activities. Students are taught economics, the economic analysis of law, administrative law, legislation, lobbying, and negotiation, as well as several substantive areas of regulatory law.

International Business prepares students for practice in the rapidly changing global business community, and provides them with a well-rounded legal education emphasizing analytical and writing skills.

Litigation Law provides an academic program for students interested in litigation and other dispute-resolution processes. This is not a clinical training program. The track courses focus on the processes of dispute resolution and lawyers' roles from an analytical perspective.

Intellectual Property Law is designed for students having a degree in engineering or one of the physical or biological sciences who intend to practice within the field of intellectual property.

■ Admission

➡ *Bachelor's degree required*
➡ *application deadline—March 1*
➡ *LSAT, LSDAS required* ➡ *application fee—$35*

Two of the primary factors considered in the admission process are performance on the LSAT and undergraduate grade-point average. Other factors that are considered include difficulty of undergraduate major, undergraduate institution attended, possession of advanced degrees, writing ability, recommendations, extracurricular activities, employment experience, demonstrated commitment to public and community service, leadership skills and experience, history of overcoming personal or professional challenges, and other academic, personal, and professional achievements.

■ Student Activities

George Mason University provides many services to enhance the law school experience and enable students to take full advantage of the university's educational and personal enrichment opportunities.

Student activities include the *George Mason University Law Review*, *Civil Rights Law Journal*, *Journal of International Legal Studies*, a newspaper, a yearbook, and numerous law-related organizations.

Because of the location of the School of Law, students have an unparalleled opportunity to gain experience in such varied settings as the Office of the U.S. Attorney for both the District of Columbia and the Eastern District of Virginia, as well as federal courts and agencies, local governments, and private firms. GMU's Work-Study Program provides eligible students with on-campus jobs. Eligibility is based partly on need.

Minority Student Services, Disability Support Services, and the Office of Veterans Services provide specialized assistance, as does the Counseling Center, where a staff of professionals helps students to reach personal, social, and academic goals.

The Patriot Center, a 10,000-seat arena, is home to GMU sports events and community programs. The Harris Theater and Center for Performing Arts provide world-class dance, music, and theater performances. The Sports and Recreation Complex offers indoor and outdoor tracks and playing fields, weight room, sauna, and other facilities.

■ Expenses and Financial Aid

➡ *tuition & fees—full-time resident, $7,644; full-time nonresident, $18,214; part-time resident, $273/sem. hr.; part-time nonresident, $650.50/sem. hr.; resident total annual average part-time tuition & fees, $5,733; nonresident total annual average part-time tuition & fees $13,660.50*
➡ *estimated additional expenses—$15,567*
➡ *merit-based scholarships available up to full-tuition*
➡ *financial aid available; FAFSA & institutional forms required*
➡ *need analysis done on a one-to-one basis*

George Mason University participates in the Direct Lending Program. There is no deadline for applying for financial aid, but applicants should complete the FAFSA as soon as possible in order to assure the timely award of aid.

In addition to loans available through the Direct Lending Program, George Mason students are eligible for a number of merit-based fellowships. These awards are available to both first-year and returning students.

■ Career Services

The Office of Career Services aids students and alumni in finding permanent, part-time, and summer jobs by serving as a clearinghouse for information on available positions. It also advises on résumé and interview preparation, and coordinates on-campus interviews. The office focuses on providing resources for career planning and development. As many as 150 firms, businesses, and government agencies recruit on campus each year. Graduates find employment in the legal profession throughout the country.

Applicant Profile Not Available

George Washington University Law School

2003 G Street, N.W.
Washington, DC 20052

E-Mail: jd@admit.nlc.gwu.edu
URL: http://www.law.gwu.edu
Phone: 202.994.7230

■ Introduction

Established in 1865, The George Washington University Law School is the oldest law school in the District of Columbia. Just four blocks from the White House and minutes away from Congress, the U.S. Supreme Court, and various federal departments and agencies, GW offers its students a special opportunity to study and observe lawmaking at the source.

The Law School is located on the main campus of The George Washington University, a private, nonsectarian institution established in 1821.

■ Enrollment/Student Body

➡ *6,271 applicants* ➡ *2,006 admitted first-year class 1998* ➡ *472 enrolled first-year class 1998* ➡ *full-time 25th/75th percentile GPA—3.21/3.57* ➡ *part-time 25th/75th percentile GPA—2.82/3.43* ➡ *full-time 25th/75th percentile LSAT—160/164* ➡ *part-time 25th/75th percentile LSAT—153/161* ➡ *1,165 total full-time J.D.* ➡ *238 total part-time J.D.* ➡ *30% minority* ➡ *43% women* ➡ *41 states, 15 foreign countries, and 215 undergraduate schools represented in entering class*

The student body of over 1,600 is a varied and interesting group representing nearly every state in the union and a number of foreign countries. Many enrollees come straight from their undergraduate universities, but the availability of a part-time evening program also attracts a number of students starting second careers.

■ Faculty

➡ *242 total* ➡ *65 full-time faculty* ➡ *177 part-time faculty* ➡ *65 women* ➡ *26 minority*

The full-time faculty teach all required and core courses. For some of its more specialized courses, the Law School calls upon leading experts from the large Washington, DC legal community to teach on an adjunct basis. These include many eminent government officials, judges, and highly regarded private practitioners.

■ Library and Physical Facilities

➡ *509,753 volumes & equivalents* ➡ *library hours: Mon.-Fri., 8:00 A.M.-11:45 P.M.; Sat.-Sun., 9:00 A.M.-11:45 P.M.* ➡ *LEXIS* ➡ *NEXIS* ➡ *WESTLAW* ➡ *DIALOG* ➡ *ALADIN* ➡ *16 full-time librarians* ➡ *library seats 703*

The Law School is housed in seven buildings, three of which adjoin to form the main complex of classrooms, the law library, faculty and administrative offices, and student lounges. Four town houses within one block of the main complex house the legal clinics, student publication offices, and additional administrative offices. The Jacob Burns Law Library provides a wide variety of traditional and automated research tools. The facility features three computer rooms providing students with access to LEXIS, WESTLAW, wordprocessing, e-mail, and Internet access, as well as an electronic reference room equipped with a CD-ROM network and automated catalogs.

■ Curriculum

➡ *Academic Support Program* ➡ *84 credits required to graduate* ➡ *250 courses available* ➡ *degrees available: J.D.; J.D./M.A.; J.D./M.B.A.; J.D./M.P.H.; J.D./M.H.S.A.; J.D./M.P.A.; LL.M.; LL.M./M.P.H.; S.J.D.* ➡ *semesters, start in Aug. & Jan.* ➡ *range of first-year class size—85-110*

One of GW's great strengths is the richness of its curriculum. With almost 200 electives offered each year, students have an opportunity to sample a broad array of legal subjects and to design a program of study that fits their individual interests and career plans. In addition to introductory and more advanced courses in a variety of fields, there are many highly specialized courses that allow students to develop expertise in a field, including international law, environmental law, intellectual property law, government regulation, and constitutional law. The school also offers 11 separate clinics and many skills-training courses.

The 84 credit hours required for the J.D. degree are usually completed in three years of full-time study. Part-time students usually attend for four academic years and one summer session. In some cases, summer school offerings permit a student to accelerate the program.

■ Clinical Programs

The Law School's extensive clinical programs include the Administrative Advocacy Clinic/Advocates for Older People; Civil Litigation Clinic; Consumer Mediation Clinic; Domestic Violence Clinic; Federal, Criminal, and Appellate Clinic; Immigration Clinic; Small Business Clinic; Vaccine Injury Clinic; Health Law Rights Clinic; Environmental Law Clinic; and Project for Older Prisoners. In addition, a wide variety of outside placement opportunities are available with more than 200 Washington, DC employers.

■ Special Programs

For J.D. students, joint-degree programs are offered with the university's schools of business and public management, international affairs, and medicine and health sciences.

The Master of Laws (LL.M.) degree is offered in the areas of environmental law, government procurement law, international and comparative law, litigation and dispute resolution, and intellectual property law, and the law school is regularly rated as one of the best—or the best—schools in these fields. Virtually all program courses are open to qualified J.D. candidates.

The Law School's summer Program in International Human Rights Law is offered jointly with the University of Oxford, and is held in Oxford in July. J.D. and LL.M. students may participate for credit.

■ Admission

➡ *Bachelor's degree required for admission*
➡ *application deadline—March 1*   ➡ *rolling admission*
➡ *LSAT, LSDAS required*   ➡ *application fee—$55*

The Law School receives about 6,300 applications per year for the entering class. The majority of those applicants are undoubtedly qualified for law study, but space limitations compel the Admission Committee to be highly selective. No inflexible standards are set; rather, the committee seeks to choose those whose undergraduate records and LSAT scores indicate probable success in law study. Other factors considered include the undergraduate school and major, the applicant's personal statement, and letters of recommendation, if submitted. In addition, the Admission Committee makes a positive effort to choose those applicants who will bring as broad a diversity of background as possible to the entering class. The committee begins to review completed applications in mid-January and makes decisions on a rolling basis. Decisions are reported to the applicants immediately, whether it is to admit, deny, or hold an applicant's file for later review.

■ Student Activities

Over 20 student groups are active at the Law School each year, sponsoring social, educational, career,

and public interest-related programs and events. The Student Bar Association, the Law School's elected student government, is active in school governance, and members serve on committees overseeing the curriculum, faculty appointments, computing, and other areas.

Membership is available on five publications: The *Law Review*, the *Journal of International Law and Economics*, the *Public Contract Law Journal* and the *Environmental Lawyer* (both cosponsored by ABA sections), and the *American Intellectual Property Association Quarterly Journal*, which is published by the AIPLA and housed at the Law School. In addition, the school newspaper, *Nota Bene*, is written and published biweekly by law students.

Three student skills boards, the Moot Court Board, the Alternative Dispute Resolution Board, and the Trial Court Board provide opportunities for students to participate in a number of competitions and to further develop their skills in client counseling, negotiation, trial advocacy, and appellate advocacy.

Each year the Law School's Enrichment Program brings a number of distinguished speakers to address the student body in an informal setting. Recent speakers have included Supreme Court justices, members of Congress, legal scholars, and leaders from public interest organizations.

Applicant Group for the 1998-1999 Academic Year

George Washington University Law School
This grid includes only applicants who earned 120-180 LSAT scores under standard administrations.

LSAT Score	3.75 +		3.50 - 3.74		3.25 - 3.49		3.00 - 3.24		2.75 - 2.99		2.50 - 2.74		2.25 - 2.49		2.00 - 2.24		Below 2.00		No GPA		Total	
	Apps	Adm	Apps	Adm	Apps	Adm	Apps	Adm	Apps	Adm	Apps	Adm	Apps	Adm	Apps	Adm	Apps	Adm	Apps	Adm	Apps	Adm
175-180	1	1	4	3	2	2	7	7	3	2	0	0	1	0	0	0	0	0	0	0	18	15
170-174	18	18	30	30	39	35	28	24	14	6	7	2	1	0	1	0	0	0	3	3	137	114
165-169	85	84	152	149	164	160	113	76	52	15	21	3	4	0	4	0	1	0	4	3	590	476
160-164	202	197	392	371	436	312	257	98	113	15	49	4	14	2	5	0	1	0	12	7	1479	989
155-159	157	41	349	64	432	48	317	34	166	17	67	9	28	3	9	0	1	0	11	0	1563	234
150-154	77	12	190	24	271	30	259	28	165	22	83	6	38	1	5	0	0	0	23	1	1118	123
145-149	28	3	67	12	116	11	113	4	102	4	75	2	36	1	9	0	2	0	14	0	579	42
140-144	8	0	28	0	44	0	51	0	52	0	50	0	22	0	10	0	2	0	16	0	290	0
135-139	3	0	6	0	6	0	18	0	17	0	20	0	12	0	5	0	1	0	9	0	102	0
130-134	0	0	0	0	4	0	4	0	7	0	5	0	10	0	3	0	0	0	0	0	33	0
125-129	0	0	0	0	0	0	0	0	1	0	4	0	0	0	2	0	2	0	3	0	12	0
120-124	0	0	0	0	0	0	1	0	0	0	0	0	0	0	0	0	0	0	2	0	3	0
Total	578	352	1215	641	1522	591	1167	271	698	80	389	26	165	7	55	0	12	0	123	25	5924	1993

Apps = Number of Applicants
Adm = Number Admitted
Reflects 99% of the total applicant pool.

Georgetown University Law Center

600 New Jersey Avenue, N.W.
Washington, DC 20001

E-Mail: admis@law.georgetown.edu
URL: http://www.law.georgetown.edu
Phone: 202.662.9010

■ Introduction

The Law Center is ideally situated to take advantage of the extensive legal resources of Washington. Its proximity to the courts, Congress, government departments, and administrative agencies provides the Georgetown student with an atmosphere for creative thought and learning. The Supreme Court, the District of Columbia's Judiciary Square, the U.S. Capitol, and the House and Senate Office buildings are a short walk from the Law Center. The excellent research facilities of the Library of Congress are easily accessible. One of the nation's largest law schools, Georgetown has been a member of the AALS since 1902 and was approved by the ABA in 1924.

■ Enrollment/Student Body

➡ *7,072 applicants*　➡ *1,964 admitted first-year class 1998*
➡ *579 enrolled first-year class 1998*　➡ *full-time 25th/75th percentile GPA—3.27/3.76*　➡ *part-time 25th/75th percentile GPA—3.20/3.71*　➡ *full-time 25th/75th percentile LSAT—163/168*　➡ *part-time 25th/75th percentile LSAT—159/166*
➡ *1,553 total full-time*　➡ *477 total part-time*
➡ *25.6% minority first-year class 1998*　➡ *50% women first-year class 1998*　➡ *48 states & 18 foreign countries represented*　➡ *204 undergraduate schools represented*

Georgetown is proud of the diversity of its student body and maintains that diversity by actively recruiting women and those from diverse ethnic, racial, economic, and educational backgrounds.

■ Faculty

➡ *276 total*　➡ *99 full-time*　➡ *177 part-time or adjunct*
➡ *61 women*　➡ *23% minority*

■ Library and Physical Facilities

➡ *933,290 volumes & equivalents*　➡ *library hours: Mon.-Fri., 8:00 A.M.-MIDNIGHT; Sat., 9:00 A.M.-10:00 P.M.; Sun., 10:00 A.M.-MIDNIGHT; extended hours during exams; Reading Room open until 2:00 A.M.; 24-hours during exams*
➡ *LEXIS*　➡ *NEXIS*　➡ *WESTLAW*　➡ *DIALOG*
➡ *21 full-time librarians*　➡ *library seats 1,260*

The library combines modern information delivery systems with the book collection of a major research library. Among its volumes are the reported decisions of all federal and state courts as well as federal administrative tribunals, all federal and state statutes, subscriptions to over 8,000 serial titles, and a growing collection of treatises. Also, there are special collections of microforms with all available Congressional publications, records and briefs of the U.S. Supreme Court and several other courts, and United Nations documents.

McDonough Hall, with its lecture halls, seminar rooms, faculty offices, bookstore, and student dining area and lounges is the academic center of the campus. The Law Center is accessible to students with disabilities.

■ Curriculum

➡ *Academic Support Program*　➡ *83 credits required to graduate*　➡ *221 courses available*　➡ *degrees available: J.D.; J.D./M.B.A.; J.D./M.S.F.S.; J.D./M.P.H.; J.D./Phil.; J.D./Gov't.*　➡ *range of first-year class size—20-130*
➡ *100+ graduate courses available to J.D. students*

Day and evening programs are offered leading to the J.D. degree. Entry to both programs is in the fall. During the first year, students are enrolled in either the "A" or "B" curriculum. Students in the "A" curriculum begin their studies with eight courses, including one elective course in the spring semester. The "B" curriculum, available to one section of full-time students, requires eight different courses, which emphasize the sources of law in history, philosophy, political theory, and economics. It also seeks to reflect the increasingly public nature of contemporary law. Electives satisfy the remaining degree requirements. A residency of six semesters is required for full-time students, eight semesters for part-time.

■ Tutorial Program

The tutorial program is structured to assist first-year students in analyzing fact patterns, identifying relevant legal issues, briefing cases, and taking class notes. First-year students who fall within guidelines for participation set by the faculty are invited to participate in the program. Other students may be admitted to the program for special reasons upon permission of the Dean. Tutorial groups are established for each of the five first-year sections. Each group is coordinated by an upper-class tutor who meets with participants at least once a week for two hours. Any unusual learning problem revealed by this process is then given individual attention.

■ The Writing Center

The Writing Center provides J.D. and graduate students with assistance on their written work. Senior Writing Fellows at the center provide feedback on making the transition from another field of expertise, approaching scholarly writing, using computer technology and word processing to improve legal research and writing, paying proper attention to legal citation form and footnotes, and mastering English grammar.

■ Special Programs

Georgetown Law Center, a pioneer in clinical legal education, offers an unmatched clinical program. Clinical programs are divided into two categories: (1) actual client representation programs that permit students to represent people in court or in administrative hearings and (2) other programs that allow students to participate in a nontrial context in federal and local agencies, schools, and other institutions. The Law Center also offers a Public Interest Law Scholars Program that gives special encouragement, in the form of enriched educational opportunities, career counseling, and a limited number of summer employment stipends to students who are committed to practice law in the public interest.

■ Admissions

➡ *B.A. or B.S. degree required*   ➡ *application deadline—day, Feb. 1; eve., March 1*   ➡ *rolling admission, early application encouraged*   ➡ *LSAT, LSDAS required*   ➡ *early action program—Nov. 1*   ➡ *application fee—$65*

Graduation from an accredited college is generally a prerequisite to admission, but mature students with compelling personal circumstances may be admitted after three years of college. Candidates are evaluated on two scales, academic or objective criteria and personal or subjective criteria. Academic information includes undergraduate records and LSAT scores. Personal factors include extracurricular activities, recommendations, work experience, and diversity of background. Other information giving insight into a candidate's potential for successful performance is also considered. Georgetown does not use numerical cutoffs. Upon acceptance, a prospective student must submit a nonrefundable deposit of $100 by May 1.

■ Student Housing

The Gewirz Student Center, opened in the fall of 1993, houses approximately 300 students. Priority for this housing is given to first-year students. The Gewirz Student Center offers a variety of apartment styles with one, two, and three private bedrooms. The apartments are air-conditioned and contain a kitchen and bathroom (the three-bedroom apartments have two bathrooms). Some apartments include a separate living room. Also available are apartments designed for students with disabilities.

For those who will not reside on campus, the Office of Student Affairs maintains a listing of available apartments, houses, and rooms to rent. During the summer, the office also offers an off-campus housing program.

■ Student Activities

The Law Center publishes eight student-edited scholarly journals. The *Law Weekly*, the school newspaper, is also printed under student direction. The Barristers' Council is responsible for the many appellate advocacy and trial practice programs, including intraschool and interschool competitions. Through the Student Bar Association and student/faculty committees, students participate in the decision processes of the Law Center. Over 58 student organizations and legal fraternities support personal and professional interests.

■ Financial Aid

➡ *tuition & fees—full-time, $24,530; part-time, $855/credit hr.*   ➡ *estimated additional expenses—$14,720 (room & board, books, transportation, & personal expenses)*   ➡ *financial aid available; FAFSA and/or Need Access Diskette/Aid Profile & institutional application due March 1*   ➡ *all GULC aid is need-based, awards combine federal & school loans & grant funds*

■ Career Services

Services include on-going consultation on job-search strategies, career decision-making and résumé writing assistance; interview skills training sessions; programs on law practice, opportunities in the legal profession, and trends in the legal job market; one of the largest on-campus interview programs in the country and off-campus interview opportunities; an extensive print and data resource center; and active current job listing resources. Intensive one-on-one counseling provided by professionals assigned as career advisors to entering class sections.

Applicant Profile Not Available

University of Georgia School of Law

Harold Hirsch Hall
225 Herty Drive
Athens, GA 30602-6012

E-Mail: ugajd@jd.lawsch.uga.edu
URL: http://www.lawsch.uga.edu
Phone: 706.542.7060

■ Introduction

The University of Georgia School of Law, established in 1859, is on the campus of the nation's first state-chartered university (1785). It is an excellent setting for the study of law with outstanding libraries and academic, cultural, social, and recreational opportunities. Located in Athens, the commercial and legal center for northeast Georgia, the campus is less than an hour from Atlanta. This location enables students to live and study in a university setting yet be in close proximity to one of the nation's outstanding metropolitan areas.

The School of Law is approved by the American Bar Association, is a member of the Association of American Law Schools, and has a chapter of the Order of the Coif.

■ Enrollment/Student Body

➡ *1,840 applicants* ➡ *577 admitted first-year class 1998*
➡ *190 enrolled first-year class 1998* ➡ *full-time 25th/75th percentile GPA—3.20/3.76* ➡ *full-time 25th/75th percentile LSAT—155/163* ➡ *633 total full-time* ➡ *12% minority*
➡ *46% women*

■ Faculty

➡ *73 total* ➡ *44 full-time* ➡ *29 part-time or adjunct*
➡ *12 women* ➡ *3 minority* ➡ *13 endowed chairs*

■ Library and Physical Facilities

➡ *462,731 volumes & equivalents* ➡ *library hours: Mon.-Fri., 7:30 A.M.-MIDNIGHT; Sat. & Sun., 8:00 A.M.-MIDNIGHT*
➡ *LEXIS* ➡ *NEXIS* ➡ *WESTLAW* ➡ *INFOTRAC*
➡ *INNOPAC* ➡ *9 full-time librarians* ➡ *library seats 456*

The Law Library is the only library in the Southeast designated as a Specialized European Documentation Center by the European Union.

The university's main library with over 3 million volumes is adjacent. The Institute of Continuing Judicial Education is located in the school; the Institute of Continuing Legal Education is located nearby. The shops, restaurants, and businesses of downtown Athens are about two blocks away.

■ Curriculum

➡ *Academic Support Program* ➡ *Legal Aid and Defender Clinic, Prosecutorial Clinic, Civil Clinic, Public Interest Practicum*
➡ *88 credits required to graduate* ➡ *degrees available: J.D.; LL.M.; J.D./M.B.A.; J.D./Masters of Historic Preservation; numerous concurrent degrees* ➡ *semesters, start in Aug.*
➡ *range of first-year class size—38-63*

The required first-year courses provide a basic foundation and are followed by a diverse offering of elective courses during the second and third years of full-time, day study.

Students are offered an outstanding clinical education in criminal and civil procedure. Certified third-year students are permitted to try cases in the civil and criminal courts and to appear before governmental administrative authorities.

International and Comparative Law—While the overall curriculum of the University of Georgia School of Law has gained a national reputation for high quality, the school's reputation as a center for international law goes beyond national boundaries. The Dean Rusk Center for International and Comparative Law conducts research and policy analyses relating to laws that affect international trade and development. Georgia law students edit and publish the *Georgia Journal of International and Comparative Law*. Summer clerkships with British law firms provide unique educational opportunities as does the annual Brussels Seminar at the University of Brussels.

The School of Law has formal exchange agreements with the University of Regensberg (Germany), Southampton University (Great Britain), the University of Brussels (Belgium), and the Universidad del Salvador (Argentina).

Scholarly Publications and Moot Court Activities—Georgia law students edit and publish three internationally circulated scholarly journals: The *Georgia Law Review*, the *Georgia Journal of International and Comparative Law*, and the *Journal of Intellectual Property Law*.

Moot court and mock trial teams successfully participate in numerous state, regional, and national events. In the 1990s, University of Georgia moot court teams have won six national championships and one world championship.

■ Admission

➡ *Bachelor's degree required*
➡ *application deadline—March 1*
➡ *LSAT, LSDAS required* ➡ *application fee—$30*

The School of Law seeks to enroll a talented, diverse student body. The Admissions Committee considers admission test scores and grade-point averages significant measures upon which to base admission decisions, but it also recognizes the importance of other components of the applicant's record. In reviewing an applicant's file, the committee members may take into consideration whether the applicant might contribute to the academic, cultural, ethnic, geographic, racial, or socioeconomic diversity of the law school.

■ Expenses and Student Financial Aid

➡ *tuition & fees—full-time resident, $4,200; nonresident, $14,940*
➡ *estimated additional expenses—$7,000 min. (room, board, books, supplies, etc.)* ➡ *scholarships and loans available*
➡ *FAFSA required for need-based financial aid*

Fees include charges for health services, transportation services, and most campus athletic and cultural activities.

School of Law scholarships include academic scholarships and need-based scholarships. Also available are tuition equalization scholarships which enable nonresidents to pay tuition at the resident tuition rate.

Candidates are encouraged to complete admission application files by January 31 to ensure full consideration for School of Law scholarships.

Candidates who may demonstrate financial need are encouraged to contact the university Office of Student Financial Aid regarding student loans and other student financial aid programs. Applications for Regents Opportunity Scholarships for economically disadvantaged applicants are available in late spring.

The University of Georgia participates in the Federal Direct Student Lending Program.

Limited part-time employment may be available on- or off-campus; however, first-year law students are not encouraged to work.

■ Housing

Law students may reside in university residence halls and family housing units. Students desiring university housing are encouraged to make early application.

Most law students choose to live in nearby off-campus rental units. Ample housing opportunities are available in Athens at rates below those in typical metropolitan areas.

■ Student Activities

Students participate in School of Law governance through the Student Bar Association and by way of representation on faculty and administrative committees. Intramural sports are available through law school leagues.

Student organizations are active on campus. The Equal Justice Foundation provides financial assistance to University of Georgia law clerks serving the public interest.

■ Legal Career Services

The School of Law maintains a Legal Career Services Office to assist students and alumni with employment matters. Alumni and faculty members actively support the employment efforts of the students.

Services of the Legal Career Services Office range from coordinating on-campus interviews and career seminars to an outreach program including participation in one of the most successful off-campus interview consortium programs in the United States.

In the past five years, an average of greater than 97 percent of the graduates have reported successful placement within six months of graduation.

The average first-time bar passage rate for Georgia graduates exceeds 94 percent over the last several years.

Applicant Group for the 1998-1999 Academic Year

University of Georgia School of Law
This grid includes only applicants who earned 120-180 LSAT scores under standard administrations.

LSAT Score	3.75 +		3.50 - 3.74		3.25 - 3.49		3.00 - 3.24		2.75 - 2.99		2.50 - 2.74		2.25 - 2.49		2.00 - 2.24		Below 2.00		No GPA		Total	
	Apps	Adm	Apps	Adm	Apps	Adm	Apps	Adm	Apps	Adm	Apps	Adm	Apps	Adm	Apps	Adm	Apps	Adm	Apps	Adm	Apps	Adm
175-180	1	1	2	2	1	1	2	2	1	1	0	0	0	0	0	0	0	0	0	0	7	7
170-174	5	5	5	5	5	5	5	5	2	1	2	1	2	0	0	0	0	0	0	0	26	22
165-169	19	18	28	27	35	33	27	26	13	6	10	5	3	1	0	0	0	0	0	0	135	116
160-164	66	61	63	56	65	49	78	54	38	8	19	0	7	2	5	0	1	0	4	4	346	234
155-159	49	34	88	34	120	16	77	5	48	3	27	0	13	1	6	0	2	0	3	0	433	93
150-154	46	16	72	13	91	10	85	6	51	2	19	3	15	1	3	0	1	0	6	1	389	52
145-149	13	2	34	2	45	8	42	5	37	3	23	0	15	0	6	0	1	0	10	0	226	20
140-144	11	1	17	2	16	3	29	3	31	0	17	0	19	0	8	0	1	0	8	1	157	10
135-139	1	0	2	1	10	0	9	0	18	0	9	0	5	0	3	0	0	0	3	0	60	1
130-134	0	0	1	0	2	0	2	0	3	0	7	0	4	0	2	0	0	0	3	0	24	0
125-129	0	0	0	0	0	0	0	0	0	0	2	0	2	0	1	0	0	0	0	0	5	0
120-124	0	0	0	0	0	0	0	0	0	0	0	0	0	0	0	0	0	0	0	0	0	0
Total	211	138	312	142	390	125	356	106	242	24	135	9	85	5	34	0	6	0	37	6	1808	555

Apps = Number of Applicants
Adm = Number Admitted
Reflects 99% of the total applicant pool.

Georgia State University College of Law

P.O. Box 4049
Atlanta, GA 30302-4049

E-Mail: admissions@gsulaw.gsu.edu
URL: http://law.gsu.edu
Phone: 404.651.2048

■ Introduction

Georgia State University College of Law is located in downtown Atlanta, the center of legal, financial, and governmental activities in the Southeast. This location provides easy access to federal, state, and local courts and agencies, the State Capitol, legislature, corporations, major law firms in the metropolitan area, and the library and other facilities of Georgia State University.

The College of Law began operation in 1982. The College of Law is accredited by the American Bar Association and is a member of the Association of American Law Schools.

■ Enrollment/Student Body

➡ *1,655 applicants* ➡ *497 admitted first-year class 1998*
➡ *198 enrolled first-year class 1998* ➡ *full-time 25th/75th percentile GPA—2.88/3.49* ➡ *part-time 25th/75th percentile GPA—2.85/3.49* ➡ *full-time 25th/75th percentile LSAT—153/160* ➡ *part-time 25th/75th percentile LSAT—153/160*
➡ *414 total full-time* ➡ *248 total part-time*
➡ *24.8% minority* ➡ *50.5% women*

■ Faculty

➡ *67 total* ➡ *40 full-time* ➡ *27 part-time or adjunct*
➡ *27 women* ➡ *14 minority*

■ Library and Physical Facilities

➡ *262,000 volumes & equivalents* ➡ *library hours: Mon.-Fri., 7:00 A.M.-11:00 P.M.; Sat., 9:00 A.M.-9:00 P.M.; Sun., 10:00 A.M.-11:00 P.M.* ➡ *LEXIS* ➡ *NEXIS*
➡ *WESTLAW* ➡ *DIALOG* ➡ *OLLI*
➡ *6 full-time librarians* ➡ *library seats 335*

Georgia State University College of Law is one of the leading law schools in the Southeast. Located on a 25-acre campus in the heart of downtown Atlanta, the College of Law building houses a moot courtroom equipped with state-of-the-art video technology and provides activities directed toward trial and appellate advocacy. Students have access to many other campus facilities including the athletic complex, which offers a variety of individual fitness opportunities and team sports.

■ Curriculum

➡ *Academic Support Program* ➡ *Summer Skills Program*
➡ *90 credits required to graduate* ➡ *202 courses available*
➡ *degrees & combined-degrees available: J.D.; J.D./M.B.A.; J.D./M.P.A.* ➡ *semesters, start in Aug.*
➡ *range of first-year class size—16-133*

The College of Law offers both a full-time, six-semester program and a part-time, nine-semester program leading to the degree of Juris Doctor. In addition, speakers such as Supreme Court Justices Sandra Day O'Connor and Antonin Scalia, International Court Judge Stephen Schwebel, U.S. Court of Appeals Judge Leon Higgenbotham, Derrick Bell, and others enrich our program. A four-day orientation program introduces first-year students to the study of law.

■ Special Programs

Tax Law Clinic—The Tax Law Clinic permits students to assist individual clients to prepare their cases for presentation before the Small Claims Division of U.S. tax Court and before the Appeals Office of the Internal Revenue Service. Under appropriate supervision, students will provide advice in a wide range of matters arising in regard to the Internal Revenue Code. Students will interview clients, research legal issues, analyze facts, and prepare protests and petitions.

Externships—Externships are designed to tie theoretical knowledge to a practical base of experience in the profession. Externships involve actual participation in rendering legal services. Enrollment may be limited and may involve a selection process. Students interested in the externship program should contact the Lawyer Skills Development Office.

Trial Advocacy—Trial advocacy has several components. Our litigation program, offered each spring, teaches students the basic skills of trial work in small seminar groups, where they receive intensive writing and simulation exercises.

The impressive performance of our trial teams has repeatedly placed Georgia State University among the nations top 16 trial advocacy programs. Georgia State teams have advanced to the national ABA and Atlanta Trial Lawyers Association (ATLA) Trial Competitions and have garnered invitations to the NACDL Trial Competition, the John Marshall National Tournament, and the Tournament of Champions. In 1989 and 1993, Georgia State students were selected Best Advocate at the Tournament of Champions. In 1994, a Georgia State team won the National NACDL Trial Competition, and a Georgia State student was selected Best Advocate. In 1997, the STLA teams won the intrastate and the southeastern invitational competitions. In 1998, Georgia State students were semi-finalists in the Criminal Justice Trial Advocacy Competition, and teams won awards at the Criminal Justice Trial Competition, the ABA Southeastern Regional Competition, and ATLA Regional Competition.

Moot Court—Each year, College of Law students compete in several of the most challenging and prestigious moot court competitions throughout the country to hone their appellate advocacy skills. The Moot Court Program at the College of Law has achieved substantial renown and success in its 16-year history.

The National Moot Court Competition, sponsored by the Association of the Bar of the City of New York, is the oldest and most recognized national competition, and in 1988 the College of Law became the first law school in Georgia to place first in that competition. Teams from the College of Law have since won numerous other competitions including the Regional National Appellate Advocacy Competition, the Georgia Intrastate Competition, the regional Thomas Tang

Competition, the Southeast Regional National Trademark Competition and the National Wagner Labor Law Competition. Georgia State teams also have garnered numerous second and third place finishes and have earned several awards for Best Brief and Best Oralist.

■ Admission

➤ *Bachelor's degree from accredited college or university required*
➤ *application deadline—March 15, rolling admission policy beginning in Jan., early application is encouraged*
➤ *LSAT, LSDAS required*　　➤ *application fee—$30*

The College of Law of Georgia State University actively seeks to enroll a student body with diversity in educational, cultural, and racial backgrounds that will enrich the educational experience of the entire group.

Applicants are encouraged to visit the College of Law. Please make arrangements through the Admissions Office to tour the campus; talk with students, faculty, and admissions staff; or attend a class.

■ Student Activities

The *Georgia State University Law Review* is published four times a year by students who have demonstrated outstanding writing and academic skills.

Student organizations include Asian-American Law Students Association, Association of Women Law Students, Black Law Students Association, Business Law Society, Christian Legal Society, Computer and Law Society, Delta Theta Phi Law Fraternity, Environmental Law Society,

Federalist Society, International and Comparative Law Society, Jewish Law Students Association, *Law Review*, National Association of Criminal Defense Lawyers, GSU Public Interest Law, Lesbian and Gay Law Students Association, Phi Delta Phi Law Fraternity, Phi Alpha Delta Law Fraternity, Sports and Entertainment Law Association, Student Health Lawyers Association, Student Trial Lawyers' Association, Student Bar Association, and Student Division of Federal Bar Association.

■ Expenses and Financial Aid

➤ *tuition & fees—full-time resident, $3,132/yr.; full-time nonresident, $12,528; part-time resident, $2,552; part-time nonresident, $10,208*　　➤ *estimated additional expenses— $9,514 (room, board, books)*　　➤ *performance- & need-based scholarships available*　　➤ *financial aid available; Free Application for Federal Student Aid form preferred*

■ Career Services

The Career Planning Office offers a broad range of services including individual career counseling, educational programs about career options, workshops to assist in the development of job-search skills, networking programs, current job listing services, on-campus interviews, and job fairs. Students may begin using the Career Planning Office in November of the first year of law school, and may continue utilizing career planning services throughout their careers. Specific programs geared toward minority students are the Atlanta Bar Association Minority Clerkship Program and the Southeastern Minority Job Fair.

Applicant Group for the 1998-1999 Academic Year

Georgia State University College of Law
This grid includes only applicants who earned 120-180 LSAT scores under standard administrations.

LSAT Score	GPA																					
	3.75 +		3.50 - 3.74		3.25 - 3.49		3.00 - 3.24		2.75 - 2.99		2.50 - 2.74		2.25 - 2.49		2.00 - 2.24		Below 2.00		No GPA		Total	
	Apps	Adm	Apps	Adm	Apps	Adm	Apps	Adm	Apps	Adm	Apps	Adm	Apps	Adm	Apps	Adm	Apps	Adm	Apps	Adm	Apps	Adm
175-180	0	0	0	0	0	0	1	1	0	0	0	0	0	0	0	0	0	0	0	0	1	1
170-174	0	0	2	2	2	2	1	1	1	1	0	0	0	0	0	0	0	0	0	0	6	6
165-169	6	5	8	7	1	0	6	6	2	2	5	5	1	1	2	1	0	0	2	2	33	29
160-164	8	8	7	7	14	11	18	17	21	19	14	12	5	3	1	1	1	1	1	1	90	80
155-159	13	12	40	38	51	45	62	50	40	26	28	13	20	9	6	1	2	0	2	0	264	194
150-154	27	20	69	35	90	36	90	22	74	15	45	4	21	5	12	5	5	0	7	2	440	144
145-149	9	1	33	7	56	6	67	7	70	4	64	5	42	1	16	1	4	0	16	0	377	32
140-144	7	1	14	0	32	1	54	2	49	1	57	1	47	0	14	0	2	0	15	2	291	8
135-139	2	0	8	0	18	0	15	0	21	0	19	1	25	0	7	0	3	0	7	0	125	1
130-134	0	0	1	0	1	0	6	0	14	0	15	0	12	1	3	0	1	1	6	0	59	2
125-129	0	0	0	0	0	0	3	0	0	0	3	0	0	0	2	0	2	0	1	0	11	0
120-124	0	0	0	0	0	0	0	0	0	0	0	0	0	0	0	0	0	0	0	0	0	0
Total	72	47	182	96	265	101	323	106	292	68	250	41	173	20	63	9	20	2	57	7	1697	497

Apps = Number of Applicants
Adm = Number Admitted
Reflects 98% of the total applicant pool.

Golden Gate University School of Law

536 Mission Street
San Francisco, CA 94105

E-Mail: lawadmit@ggu.edu
URL: http://www.ggu.edu/law/
Phone: 415.442.6630

■ Introduction

Founded in 1901, Golden Gate University School of Law is located in the heart of San Francisco's legal and financial district. The law school is noted for integrating practical skills training with legal theory. Golden Gate has a distinguished faculty who share a strong commitment to both excellence in teaching and accessibility to students.

The school is accredited by the ABA and is a member of the AALS.

■ Enrollment/Student Body

➡ *1,519 applicants*   ➡ *813 admitted first-year class 1998*
➡ *184 enrolled first-year class 1998*   ➡ *full-time 25th/75th percentile GPA—2.78/3.35*   ➡ *part-time 25th/75th percentile GPA—2.66/3.29*   ➡ *full-time 25th/75th percentile LSAT— 146/154*   ➡ *part-time 25th/75th percentile LSAT—147/155*
➡ *415 total full-time*   ➡ *170 total part-time*
➡ *26.2% minority*   ➡ *57.6% women*   ➡ *39 states & foreign countries represented*   ➡ *221 undergraduate schools represented*

■ Faculty

➡ *131 total*   ➡ *37 full-time*   ➡ *94 part-time or adjunct*
➡ *50 women*   ➡ *17 minority*

■ Library Facilities

➡ *226,140 volumes & equivalents*   ➡ *LEXIS*
➡ *WESTLAW*   ➡ *CALI*   ➡ *6 full-time librarians*
➡ *library seats 322*

■ Curriculum

➡ *Academic Assistance Program*   ➡ *88 credits required to graduate*   ➡ *133 courses available*

Golden Gate University School of Law affords students a practical legal education. The curriculum is designed to lay the foundations of modern legal theory, but also foster those lawyering skills necessary for a successful practice. Because writing is the lawyer's basic tool, the law school trains students to master the skills needed to draft a wide array of legal documents. Through its Academic Assistance Program, the law school provides all students with additional instruction in legal analysis and exam-writing skills.

■ Special Programs

Program Options—The law school offers both full-time and part-time programs. The full-time program normally involves three years of study; the part-time evening program takes four years. Golden Gate also offers mid-year admission, allowing full-time students to begin law school in January.

Integrated Professional Apprenticeship Curriculum (IPAC)—The program integrates classroom theory, skills, values, and practice. Two full-time, semester-long Professional Apprenticeships anchor the curriculum, which also utilizes traditional coursework and two intensive skill-based summer programs. IPAC students still complete law school in three years, pay the same tuition, and take the same number of units as students in the standard curriculum.

Specialty Areas—The law school's curriculum offers students the opportunity to concentrate in one of many specialty areas, including corporate and commercial law, criminal law, entertainment law, environmental law, intellectual property law, labor and employment law, real estate development, or public interest law. Students may also earn Certificates of Specialization in Business Law, Criminal Law, Labor and Employment Law, Real Estate Law, Environmental Law, International Legal Studies, and Public Interest Law.

Golden Gate offers study abroad programs in International Legal Studies in Istanbul, Turkey and in Bangkok, Thailand, where students study Pacific Rim issues at Chulalongkorn University. Golden Gate sponsors a student exchange program with the University of Paris at Nanterre.

Students who enroll in the Public Interest Law program work with the Public Interest Clearinghouse, which places students with the interest groups and agencies throughout the San Francisco Bay Area. The law school also offers the Public Interest Law Scholars Program, which provides scholarships, a summer employment stipend, and mentors to students planning a career in public interest law. A public interest loan forgiveness program for graduates who obtain employment in public interest law is also available.

The Environmental Law program includes basic courses in Environmental Law, but also offers clinical opportunities and advanced seminars. The law school sponsors an intensive summer program in Environmental Law.

The law school offers four graduate LL.M. programs: in Taxation, International Legal Studies, Environmental Law, and U.S. Legal Studies. Students may also earn an S.J.D. in International Legal Studies.

Advocacy Training—The law school offers an advocacy and dispute resolution curriculum that is one of the most comprehensive in the country. Its nationally recognized litigation program trains students in every aspect of litigation. Students with a serious interest in litigation may participate in trial advocacy and appellate advocacy competitions. In recent years, the law school's teams have won regional championships in trial competitions and eight were semifinalists in six others.

Besides learning courtroom tactics, students at Golden Gate may learn techniques of mediation and arbitration in Alternative Dispute Resolution. Students also receive training in the skills of client counseling and negotiating.

Clinics and Externships—Clinical programs, both on-site and field placement, are an integral part of the curriculum at Golden Gate. Through these programs, students may earn academic credit while working closely with practicing attorneys.

The law school houses three legal clinics. In the Women's Employment Rights Clinic, students represent low-income women with employment-related problems. Through the Environmental law and Justice Clinic, students assist Northern California communities in protecting their environmental interests. The Constitutional Law Clinic enables students to work on civil rights cases focusing on health care issues of institutionalized persons.

Students may also receive credit for participating in the Judicial Externship Program, which places students with the judges on the California Supreme Court, federal district courts, and the California state appellate and superior courts.

Combined Degrees—The law school offers the following combined-degree programs: J.D./M.B.A.; J.D./M.A. International Relations; and J.D./Ph.D. Clinical Psychology with the Pacific Graduate School of Psychology.

■ Admission

➤ *Bachelor's degree required* ➤ *April 15 deadline for fall; Nov. 14 for midyear* ➤ *application fee—$40*

Admission is competitive. The Admission Committee considers applicants' undergraduate GPA, LSAT score, and information contained in their personal statement. The committee also weighs such factors as graduate work, social and economic background, and personal and employment accomplishments.

■ Minority Students

Applications from minority students and other under-represented groups are encouraged and given special attention. Golden Gate participates in the CLEO Program. The law school works closely with minority student groups regarding issues such as admissions, academic assistance, and placement. In October 1993, the law school received the California Minority Counsel Program's

Second Annual Law School Racial and Ethnic Diversity Commitment Award.

■ Student Activities and Scholarship

The law school has over 15 student organizations, which range from groups representing minority students to groups focusing on specific areas of the law. In addition, a student editorial board publishes three issues of the *Golden Gate University Law Review* annually. In 1994, the law school began publishing the *Annual Survey of International and Comparative Law.*

■ Expenses and Financial Aid

➤ *tuition & fees—full-time, $19,981; part-time, $13,091* ➤ *estimated additional expenses—$11,190 (housing, transportation, insurance, books, food)* ➤ *financial aid available* ➤ *FAFSA, FAAP, Financial Aid Transcripts, & SAR due March 1 for priority*

Approximately 85 percent of the student body receives some form of financial aid. Golden Gate awards merit scholarships to many qualified entering students. Last year, Merit Scholarships ranged in amount from $6,000 to full tuition. The law school also has scholarships available to minority students in keeping with the law school's ongoing commitment to a diverse student body. In addition, the law school participates in federally subsidized and private loan programs.

■ Placement

The Career Services Office maintains listings of summer, part-time, and permanent positions and organizes on- and off-campus recruiting programs.

Applicant Group for the 1998-1999 Academic Year

Golden Gate University School of Law
This grid includes only applicants who earned 120-180 LSAT scores under standard administrations.

LSAT Score	GPA 3.75 +		3.50 - 3.74		3.25 - 3.49		3.00 - 3.24		2.75 - 2.99		2.50 - 2.74		2.25 - 2.49		2.00 - 2.24		Below 2.00		No GPA		Total	
	Apps	Adm	Apps	Adm	Apps	Adm	Apps	Adm	Apps	Adm	Apps	Adm	Apps	Adm	Apps	Adm	Apps	Adm	Apps	Adm	Apps	Adm
175-180	1	1	0	0	1	1	0	0	0	0	0	0	0	0	0	0	0	0	0	0	2	2
170-174	0	0	1	1	0	0	1	1	1	1	0	0	0	0	0	0	0	0	1	1	4	4
165-169	1	1	3	3	4	4	1	1	1	1	2	2	4	4	1	1	0	0	2	1	19	18
160-164	3	2	10	10	10	9	21	21	8	7	6	5	7	5	2	2	1	0	1	1	69	62
155-159	9	8	20	19	36	33	51	45	50	45	35	29	13	10	9	6	2	1	2	2	227	198
150-154	10	9	38	33	64	55	70	62	72	54	43	24	45	13	9	0	2	0	5	3	358	253
145-149	8	8	19	19	52	44	72	47	86	41	66	15	35	3	16	1	6	1	17	9	377	188
140-144	6	6	17	12	23	16	49	14	74	9	57	0	34	1	10	0	1	0	11	3	282	61
135-139	1	0	1	1	9	3	16	0	20	0	21	0	14	0	13	1	3	0	5	0	103	5
130-134	0	0	0	0	2	0	3	0	7	0	9	0	13	0	0	0	1	0	1	0	36	0
125-129	0	0	0	0	0	0	2	0	1	0	2	0	2	0	1	0	2	0	0	0	10	0
120-124	0	0	0	0	0	0	0	0	0	0	0	0	1	0	0	0	0	0	0	0	1	0
Total	39	35	109	98	201	165	286	191	320	158	241	75	168	36	61	11	18	2	45	20	1488	791

Apps = Number of Applicants
Adm = Number Admitted
Reflects 98% of the total applicant pool.

Gonzaga University School of Law

Box 3528
Spokane, WA 99220

E-Mail: admissions@lawschool.gonzaga.edu
URL: http://www.law.gonzaga.edu
Phone: 509.323.5532; Toll-free: 800.793.1710

■ Introduction

Gonzaga University School of Law belongs to a long and distinguished tradition of humanistic, Catholic, and Jesuit education. It is an integral part of Gonzaga University, which was founded in 1887 and continues to maintain the tradition of academic excellence in education that is at the heart of the mission of the 450-year-old Jesuit order. The School of Law was established in 1912. The campus is located in Spokane, a four-season city with the Spokane River flowing through its center. The metropolitan area of approximately 400,000 serves as the regional hub of the Inland Northwest, a large area running from the Cascade Mountains in the west to the Rockies in the east. Canada is a mere 100 miles to the north.

Spokane is not only an economic hub for manufacturing, agriculture, and light industry, but it is also a recreational sports area abundant with lakes, mountains, and forests. In minutes you can get away from the city's robust, rapidly growing business community to the surrounding pine covered hills, where there is an evergreen splendor unlike any place in America.

■ Enrollment/Student Body

➡ *875 applicants* ➡ *720 admitted first-year class 1998*
➡ *188 enrolled first-year class 1998* ➡ *full-time 25th/75th percentile GPA—2.74/3.30* ➡ *full-time 25th/75th percentile LSAT—145/154* ➡ *469 total full-time*
➡ *18 total part-time* ➡ *15% minority* ➡ *43% women*
➡ *40 states & foreign countries represented*
➡ *174 undergraduate schools represented* ➡ *average age—27*

■ Faculty

➡ *61 total* ➡ *34 full-time* ➡ *27 part-time or adjunct*
➡ *15 women*

The faculty are committed to teaching excellence and are accessible and approachable.

■ Library and Physical Facilities

➡ *225,400 volumes & equivalents* ➡ *library hours: Mon.-Thurs., 7:00 A.M.-MIDNIGHT; Fri., 7:00 A.M.-9:00 P.M.; Sat., 9:00 A.M.-9:00 P.M.; Sun., 10:00 A.M.-MIDNIGHT*
➡ *LEXIS* ➡ *NEXIS* ➡ *WESTLAW* ➡ *DIALOG, CARL* ➡ *5 full-time librarians* ➡ *library seats 468*

Students also have access to campus facilities such as the Foley Center, a new technology library; the University Health and Counseling Centers; the Student Union; and the Martin Athletic Center, complete with indoor running track, full-sized pool, state-of-the-art weight room, dance studio, basketball/volleyball courts, and racquetball courts.

■ Curriculum

➡ *Academic Support Program*
➡ *90 credits required to graduate* ➡ *75 courses available*

➡ *degrees available: J.D.; J.D./M.B.A. & J.D./M.Acc.*
➡ *semesters, start in Aug.*
➡ *range of Legal Writing sections—15-20*

There is a deliberate and delicate balance to legal education at Gonzaga. The rigorous, full, and rounded curriculum focuses on legal analysis, problem solving, values, and ethics. Equally as important is the emphasis on practical experience to develop real-world lawyering skills. As a capstone to its innovative approach to legal education, the School of Law offers Juris Doctor degrees with special concentrations in public interest law, environment/natural resource law, and business law (including tax law).

Gonzaga offers a favorable student-to-faculty ratio and an emphasis on positive rather than negative competition.

■ Special Programs

The first year of coursework is devoted to building a strong legal foundation for upper-division study. In order to ease the transition to the rigorous demands of law school, entering students may take advantage of the support offered through the student and attorney mentor programs, academic advisors, and special tutorials.

Joint programs leading to the J.D./M.B.A. and the J.D./M.Acc. degree are offered to prepare students who anticipate careers in other fields that require thorough knowledge of business, accountancy, and the law. Application must be made to the School of Business as well as to the School of Law.

An added dimension to the legal education for many Gonzaga law students is the opportunity to practice law while in school through the award-winning clinical law program.

■ Admission

➡ *Bachelor's degree required for admission*
➡ *application deadline—March 15*
➡ *LSAT, LSDAS required* ➡ *application fee—$40*

The School of Law endeavors to attract students with ambitious minds, professional motivation, and commitment to the highest ethics and values of the legal profession and to public service. A faculty committee reviews all applications. The consideration of applicants is not restricted to impersonal statistics. The enriching qualities of applicants such as work and life experiences, personal accomplishment, and opinions of others reflected in letters of recommendation will be considered.

The School of Law seeks to enroll a diverse student body to assure that the school and the legal profession are enriched through the participation of people from different cultural and ethnic backgrounds. Those individuals who desire diversity factors to be considered in their admission decision should include it in their application.

Students who have completed 45 semester credits or their equivalent or less and who are in good standing at another ABA law school may apply for admission to the School of Law with advanced standing.

Special Admission Program—The School of Law offers special acceptance to a limited number of applicants who do not meet regular admission requirements, but whose application file suggests there may be potential for success beyond what the statistics would normally predict. There is no special application procedure for this program, and applicants will be considered automatically. Those accepted will be admitted to a special summer program, which will consist of 10 weeks commencing the summer before entrance into the first year. Students who are successful in the summer program will continue with their studies in the fall semester.

■ Student Activities

Students find it easy to become involved in a broad range of activities at the School of Law. Gonzaga is a major player in moot court competition through five moot court teams. The student-run *Gonzaga Law Review*, more than 30 years in existence, is circulated throughout the country. The award-winning Student Bar Association is a strong, active organization which encourages student involvement. There is also an opportunity to participate in intraschool moot court competition, two legal fraternities, and other numerous organizations and activities.

Law students, representing many cultural heritages, join together in the Multi-Cultural Law Caucus and BALSA to provide a support network on campus and in the Spokane community for those students of diverse backgrounds.

■ Housing

The Gonzaga campus is in a residential area with housing within walking distance to the School of Law. Rental housing rates are reasonably priced compared to larger population centers. The University also provides two graduate/law housing complexes.

■ Expenses and Financial Aid

➼ *tuition & fees—full-time, $18,300 (30 credits/yr.); part-time, $12,200 (20 credits/yr.)* ➼ *estimated additional expenses—$11,100 (books, $900; room & board, $6,800; personal, $2,000; transportation, $1,400)* ➼ *academic & need-based scholarships available* ➼ *minority scholarships available: full tuition minority waivers, $2,000-$8,500 renewable scholarships, Thomas More public interest scholarships* ➼ *financial aid available; FAFSA (needed for all types) due May 1* ➼ *loans available—Stafford, SLS, LAL*

Law school is a career investment. For the tuition, fees, and other costs incurred to attend Gonzaga University, each student is offered an opportunity for a quality legal education and a rewarding legal career. For those who need financial assistance to help fund this investment, Gonzaga University will assist in identifying and obtaining financial aid packages.

■ Career Services

The active Career Services Office is dedicated to assisting law students and alumni in planning careers and seeking employment throughout law school and in the course of their professional career. The size of the school allows the Career Services director the opportunity to work individually with students and alumni in their job searches. Entering students are pleased to learn Gonzaga participates in federal and state work-study programs and provides interns to more than 200 Spokane law firms and numerous government agencies.

Applicant Group for the 1998-1999 Academic Year

Gonzaga University School of Law
This grid includes only applicants who earned 120-180 LSAT scores under standard administrations.

LSAT Score	3.75 +		3.50 - 3.74		3.25 - 3.49		3.00 - 3.24		2.75 - 2.99		2.50 - 2.74		Below 2.50		No GPA		Total	
	Apps	Adm	Apps	Adm	Apps	Adm	Apps	Adm	Apps	Adm	Apps	Adm	Apps	Adm	Apps	Adm	Apps	Adm
175-180	1	1	0	0	0	0	0	0	0	0	0	0	0	0	0	0	1	1
170-174	0	0	0	0	0	0	0	0	2	2	0	0	0	0	0	0	2	2
165-169	0	0	0	0	1	1	3	3	0	0	3	3	2	2	1	1	10	10
160-164	3	3	1	1	4	4	7	7	3	3	5	5	3	2	0	0	26	25
155-159	4	4	12	12	25	25	19	19	19	19	19	19	11	9	0	0	109	107
150-154	8	8	22	22	32	32	55	55	38	37	33	33	27	20	5	3	220	210
145-149	7	7	19	18	43	41	63	62	42	38	50	44	30	21	3	1	257	232
140-144	2	2	9	9	18	16	30	25	31	21	32	18	18	7	3	1	143	99
Below 140	1	1	3	3	4	1	18	7	8	2	22	4	20	0	3	0	79	18
Total	26	26	66	65	127	120	195	178	143	122	164	126	111	61	15	6	847	704

Apps = Number of Applicants
Adm = Number Admitted
Reflects 98% of the total applicant pool.

Hamline University School of Law

1536 Hewitt Avenue
St. Paul, MN 55104

E-Mail: lawadm@gw.hamline.edu
URL: http://web.hamline.edu/law/
Phone: 651.523.2461 or 800.388.3688

■ Introduction

Hamline University School of Law is responsive to the needs of the legal profession and the community, in both the public and private sectors. We have achieved national visibility for our expertise in Alternative Dispute Resolution; Law and Religion; Legal Research and Writing; and Trial and Advocacy skills. The school has also developed significant offerings in Business Law, Public Law, Government, and Ethics, and Child Advocacy and Family Law. The beautiful Hamline campus is located in a residential neighborhood midway between the downtowns of St. Paul and Minneapolis. The Twin Cities are frequently cited as two of the nation's "most livable" cities which claim to be home to several large corporate headquarters, complimented by a stimulating legal network and the state capital only minutes away.

■ Enrollment/Student Body

➡ *851 applicants* ➡ *199 enrolled first-year class 1998*
➡ *full-time 25th/75th percentile GPA—2.81/3.41*
➡ *part-time 25th/75th percentile GPA—2.64/3.55*
➡ *full-time 25th/75th percentile LSAT—146/156*
➡ *part-time 25th/75th percentile LSAT—145/154*
➡ *463 total full-time* ➡ *25 total part-time*
➡ *12.3% minority* ➡ *50% women* ➡ *49 states & foreign countries represented* ➡ *188 undergraduate schools represented*
➡ *average age first-year class 1998—26*

■ Faculty

➡ *28 full-time* ➡ *45 part-time or adjunct*
➡ *10 full-time women* ➡ *2 full-time minority*
➡ *6 legal writing instructors*

One hundred fifty practicum mentor-attorneys bring the experience of their day-to-day practice into the educational program.

■ Library and Physical Facilities

➡ *220,000 volumes & equivalents* ➡ *cooperative borrowing between local law libraries and local college libraries*
➡ *LEXIS* ➡ *NEXIS* ➡ *WESTLAW* ➡ *DIALOG*
➡ *6 full-time librarians, 4 with J.D./M.L.S.*
➡ *library seats 360* ➡ *computerized catalog system which also searches the holdings of local university and reference libraries*

The School of Law is accessible to persons with disabilities and housed in a modern, award-winning law center.

■ Curriculum

➡ *Academic Support Program* ➡ *120 courses available*
➡ *combined degrees available: J.D./M.A.P.A.; J.D./M.A.M.; J.D./M.A.N.M.; J.D./M.B.A. & J.D./A.M.B.A. with the University of St. Thomas* ➡ *full-time & part-time day programs* ➡ *semesters start in Aug.* ➡ *range of first-year class size—41-73* ➡ *3 daytime scheduling options first-year, 3-year program, 2-1/2 with summer school*

First-year students may select a traditional all-day schedule or may elect to block their classes in either the morning or the afternoon. First-year students may also choose to reduce their courseload by enrolling in our part-time day program.

Students with a clearly defined area of interest have the opportunity to declare a concentration at the beginning of their second year. Concentration areas are in Child Advocacy, Civil Dispute Resolution, Commercial Law, Corporate Law, Criminal Law, Government and Regulatory Affairs, International Law, and Labor and Employment Law.

■ General Practice Clinic

The School of Law operates a law clinic that functions as a typical small, general practice law office. Supervised by clinical instructors, students handle their own case load, from client counseling through the litigation, settlement, or mediation. Students represent clients in immigration, public interest, criminal defense, child advocacy, and family law mediation, and in the Small Business Planning Clinic.

■ Practicum Program

Guided by a seasoned judge or attorney, students serve as interns in law offices, public agencies, and courtrooms in specialized areas such as child advocacy, criminal work, corporate practice, administrative law, and public interest practice.

■ Public Law, Government, and Ethics

Extensive offerings in public law are available for those considering legislative, administrative, or public interest careers.

■ Business Law

Students considering a career in business and business law can attain special expertise in commercial law and corporate law through curriculum offerings in this field. The broad-based business environment of the Twin Cities provides practical experience opportunities in the specialty area.

■ Alternative Dispute Resolution (ADR)

In addition to course offerings, Hamline sponsors a summer Dispute Resolution Institute, taught by nationally recognized scholars and practitioners in the ADR field.

■ Student Activities

The *Hamline Law Review* publishes articles by students, leading members of the academic community, and practicing attorneys.

The *Hamline Journal of Public Law and Policy* is a forum for public policy articles on state and federal legislative, executive, and administrative functions.

The faculty-edited, *Journal of Law and Religion* has an international reputation and publishes articles, colloquia, and essays of interest to the legal, ethical, and religious communities.

Participation in the award-winning **moot court** teams offer students the opportunity to develop and refine writing and speaking skills for academic credit.

Student organizations are numerous and include organizations representing specialized areas of law.

■ Admission

➤ *Bachelor's degree required* ➤ *application deadline— May 15* ➤ *rolling admission, early application preferred* ➤ *LSAT, LSDAS required* ➤ *application fee—$40* ➤ *summer conditional program, acceptance by performance*

All applications are reviewed by an admission committee composed of faculty members, administrators, and students. Hamline's admission policy is designed to encourage and enhance the academic rigor, professional dedication, social concern, and diversity of the student body, including cultural, economic, racial, and ethnic composition.

The School of Law strives to maintain a selection process that emphasizes a fair examination of each person as an individual, not merely as a set of credentials. In addition to the LSAT and undergraduate GPA, the committee gives significant weight to motivation, personal experiences, employment history, graduate education, maturity, letters of recommendation, and the ability to articulate one's interest in and suitability for the study of law.

At the discretion of the Admission Committee, a limited number of students whose objective factors qualify them for entrance directly into the fall program are given the opportunity to demonstrate their ability and earn a position in the fall entering class by successfully completing summer coursework. This Acceptance by Performance program serves as part of the admission process, and participation in this program does not guarantee admission to Hamline as a degree candidate.

■ Expenses and Financial Aid

➤ *tuition & fees—$16,460* ➤ *estimated additional expenses— $3,322-$4,791 (on-campus housing & meal plan)* ➤ *a variety of scholarships are available*

■ Career Services

A wide variety of career-information programs and skills workshops are offered by our Career Services Office. Individualized counseling is also provided in areas such as interviewing, résumé writing, career assessment, and the development of job-search strategies. The office maintains extensive job listings for part-time, summer, and full-time employment. The 1997 Employment Survey showed 96 percent of those seeking employment employed in legally related positions six months after graduation.

Applicant Profile Not Available

Harvard University Law School

1563 Massachusetts Avenue
Cambridge, MA 02138

URL: http://www.law.harvard.edu
Phone: 617.495.3109

■ Introduction

Harvard Law School, established in 1817, is the oldest existing law school in the United States. It is located, along with most other parts of Harvard University, in Cambridge, Massachusetts. The school offers a diverse curriculum intended to provide comprehensive training for those who wish to become legal practitioners, as well as those interested in public service, law teaching, and legal scholarship. Through its faculty, students, and graduates, Harvard seeks to make substantial contributions toward solving the complex legal problems confronting our society.

■ Enrollment/Student Body

➠ *5,813 applicants*   ➠ *847 admitted first-year class 1998*
➠ *551 enrolled first-year class 1998*   ➠ *full-time 25th/75th percentile GPA—3.73/3.92*   ➠ *full-time 25th/75th percentile LSAT—166/173*   ➠ *1,656 total full-time J.D., 163 total LL.M.*
➠ *28% minority*   ➠ *42% women*   ➠ *50 states & 20 foreign countries represented (J.D.)*   ➠ *50 foreign countries (LL.M.)*
➠ *275 undergraduate schools represented*

■ Faculty

➠ *176 total*   ➠ *112 full-time*   ➠ *64 part-time or adjunct*
➠ *47 women*   ➠ *34 minority*

■ Library & Physical Facilities

➠ *1,962,871 volumes & equivalents*   ➠ *library hours: Mon.-Thurs., 8:30 A.M.-MIDNIGHT; Fri.-Sat., 8:30 A.M.-9:00 P.M.; Sun., NOON-MIDNIGHT*   ➠ *LEXIS (home access avail.)*
➠ *NEXIS (home access avail.)*   ➠ *WESTLAW (home access avail.)*   ➠ *34 full-time librarians*   ➠ *library seats 800*

The school occupies 21 buildings that include dormitories, dining facilities, classrooms, and offices. Through the public access catalog, many online research systems are available. Included are DIALOG, RLIN, Vu/Text, Dow-Jones News/Retrieval, Legi-Slate, and Legal Resources Index, among others.

■ Curriculum

➠ *Academic Support Program*   ➠ *82 credits required to graduate*   ➠ *250 courses available*   ➠ *degree available: J.D.; LL.M.; S.J.D.; J.D./M.B.A.; J.D./M.A.L.D.; J.D./ M.P.P.; J.D./Ph.D. & numerous other concurrent degrees*
➠ *cross-registration possibilities with other Harvard graduate schools*   ➠ *range of first-year class size—45-138*

Our basic aim is to train students to be lawyers. The emphasis is not on any particular type of law; the curriculum includes courses in civil liberties as well as corporate finance, international trade as well as criminal law, and taxation as well as legal services for the poor. Nor is the curriculum oriented toward mastering detail or teaching the law "as it is." Law reform, legal philosophy, the historical development of legal institutions—all of these subjects and many more are important fields of study for an educated

member of the profession. Because the law changes often and the problems lawyers face vary endlessly, our curriculum emphasizes mastery of the enduring principles of law, its methods of reasoning, and its process of development and change rather than the law as it is currently written.

The first-year curriculum is designed to give each student a thorough grounding in the basic intellectual processes of legal reasoning and analysis. It consists of criminal law, contracts, civil procedure, torts, property, a legal methods course including Ames moot court work, and an elective course during the second semester. Except for a required paper and a course in professional responsibility, the second and third years of the J.D. degree program are entirely elective.

■ Special Programs

Special research and study programs of particular interest to students in the J.D. program include the Clinical Legal Education Program; the East Asian Legal Studies Program; the Islamic Legal Studies Program, the Human Rights Program; the Program on International Financial Systems; the European Law Research Center; the International and Comparative Legal Studies Program; the Center for Law, Economics, and Business; the Program on the Legal Profession; and the Program on Negotiation.

■ Admission

➠ *Bachelor's degree from accredited college or university required*
➠ *rolling admission, early application encouraged*
➠ *LSAT, LSDAS required*
➠ *application fees—$60/$70/$80*

We consider each completed application in its entirety, including transcripts, extracurricular and community activities, work experience, personal background, letters of recommendation, personal statements, LSAT score(s), and LSAT writing sample. We seek to identify qualities in candidates that would contribute to the vitality, diversity, and intellectual excellence of our student body and to the educational experience at Harvard for all students.

Decisions are based on the Admission Committee's experienced judgment applied to individual cases. We use no computational methods for making admission decisions, and have no numerical "cut-offs" below which a candidate will not be considered. Our view is that individuals' academic, personal and professional achievements, and potential cannot be adequately summarized by undergraduate GPAs and LSATs alone. Grade-point averages do not account for difficulty of coursework, letters of recommendation from teachers, out-of-class commitments, differences in grading patterns among colleges, or other pertinent information. LSAT scores are evaluated in the context of other information about an individual, and are used as approximate indicators rather than precise measures of ability and promise for the study of law. Background factors such as demonstrated societal, financial, educational or personal disadvantage the candidate has overcome often help the committee to understand individual achievement.

Although we anticipate that the number of applicants for whom we would predict academic and professional success will greatly exceed the number of offers of admission available to us, we encourage all who would like to study law at Harvard to apply for admission.

■ Student Activities

Law-related activities at Harvard Law School are diverse and numerous. They include 12 law student publications —*Harvard Law Review, Harvard Journal on Legislation, Negotiation Journal, Harvard International Law Journal, Harvard Civil Rights-Civil Liberties Law Review, Harvard Environmental Law Review, Harvard Women's Law Journal, Harvard Journal of Law and Public Policy, Harvard Human Rights Journal, Harvard Latino Law Review, Harvard Blackletter Law Journal*, and *Harvard Journal of Law and Technology*— as well as the Board of Student Advisers (which administers the Ames moot court and alternative programs), the Legislative Research Bureau, International Law Society, Civil Liberties Union, and Law School Council. Massachusetts allows law students to represent the indigent of the Commonwealth in the district courts. There are three curricular-based organizations that represent indigent clients under this provision. They include the Criminal Justice Institute, the Legal Services Clinic, and the Immigration and Refugee Clinic. In addition, there are five extracurricular student-practice organizations which allow students similar opportunities—the Harvard Legal Aid Bureau, Harvard Defenders, Prison Legal Assistance Project, Tenant Advocacy Project, and the Harvard Mediation Program. Other activities are the *Law School Record* (America's oldest law school newspaper); Law School Forum;

Yearbook; Drama Society; Harvard Black Law Students Association; Harvard Environmental Law Society; Lambda; La Alianza; South Asian Association; Native American Law Students Association; Asian Pacific American Law Students Association; Women's Law Association, and more than 35 other student organizations not mentioned above.

■ Expenses and Financial Aid

➡ *tuition—full-time, $23,900*   ➡ *estimated additional expenses—$16,020 (room, board, living expenses, books & supplies)* ➡ *scholarships & financial aid available*

All students who demonstrate financial need according to a combination of federal and institutional guidelines receive assistance. Our program includes the Low Income Protection Plan, which provides partial forgiveness of loans to graduates who pursue public interest and other low-paid law-related careers.

■ Career Services

Our placement office assists students in obtaining permanent, part-time, and summer positions. Recently the employment pattern at graduation has been—law firms, 61 percent; judicial clerkships, 26 percent; federal, state, and local government, 2 percent; legal services, 2 percent; and teaching, further education, corporations, and other positions, 9 percent. Approximately 60 percent of each year's class locates in New York; Washington, DC; Massachusetts; or California; the remainder locates in about 38 other states and several foreign countries. In the past few years, 97 percent of the graduates have accepted offers for employment or further education by the time of graduation.

Applicant Group for the 1998-1999 Academic Year

We do not provide a profile chart of applicants considered and admitted because it would be based solely upon undergraduate GPA and LSAT scores. Decisions are based on the Admission Committee's experienced judgment applied to individual cases, and the committee takes account of many factors that are not represented by a two-factor profile. Because GPA and LSAT alone do not adequately summarize information about individuals that is important to admission decisions, GPA and LSAT alone often prove to be poor predictors of decisions on individual applications.

For example, although most admitted candidates graduated in the top 10 percent of their college classes and presented LSAT scores in the top five percentiles, a significant proportion of candidates who meet these characterizations are not offered admission. We admit some candidates who do not present as high college or LSAT standings but whose combined academic and other achievements are comparable nonetheless. While candidates with higher grades and scores tend to be admitted at higher rates than candidates with lower grades and scores, at no point on the GPA or LSAT scales are the chances for admission to Harvard Law School 0 or 100 percent.

University of Hawai'i at Mānoa—William S. Richardson School of Law

2515 Dole Street
Honolulu, HI 96822

E-Mail: lawadm@hawaii.edu
URL: http://www.hawaii.edu/law
Phone: 808.956.3000

■ Introduction

Established in 1973, the University of Hawai'i School of Law is located in Honolulu on the main campus of Hawai'i's nine-campus system. As the only law school in the state, its primary purpose is to equip degree candidates for active, effective, and creative participation as lawyers in both the private and public sectors. The school has ABA accreditation and membership in AALS.

Some unique and differentiating features of this law school are: its small size and close interaction among faculty, students, and the Hawai'i legal community; its emphasis on and resources for environmental/ocean law, Pacific-Asian legal systems, and elder law; its standing as perhaps the most racially and ethnically diverse law school in the country; and its graduation requirement of 60 hours of law-related community service.

■ Enrollment/Student Body

➤ 468 applicants   ➤ 168 admitted first-year class 1998
➤ 80 enrolled first-year class 1998   ➤ full-time 25th/75th percentile GPA—2.91/3.40   ➤ full-time 25th/75th percentile LSAT—154/162   ➤ 240 total full-time   ➤ 65% minority
➤ 53% women   ➤ 23 states & foreign countries represented
➤ 98 undergraduate schools represented

The student body reflects Hawai'i's diversity. Students represent the following racial/ethnic groups: Chinese, Filipino, Hispanic, Japanese, Korean, Native American, native Hawaiian, African-American, Caucasian, Chamorro, Micronesian, and Vietnamese. A number of students come from Japan, China, Guam, Commonwealth of the Northern Mariana Islands, and Micronesia.

■ Curriculum

➤ 89 credits required to graduate, 42 of which are nonelective
➤ approximately 80 courses available   ➤ degrees available: J.D.; J.D./M.B.A.; J.D./M.A. Asian Studies; J.D./Masters in Urban & Regional Planning   ➤ semesters, start in Aug. (new students) & Jan. (transfers & visiting students)
➤ range of first-year class size—12-75
➤ six semesters of full-time residency
➤ other dual degree programs can be arranged

The J.D. program is a three-year program of full-time day study. Full-time registration is defined as enrollment for a minimum of 12 credits each semester. First-year students begin with a one-week orientation; the first-year curriculum is entirely prescribed. All students must fulfill 60 hours of pro bono law-related community service in order to graduate.

■ Faculty

➤ 50 total   ➤ 17 full-time   ➤ 33 part-time or adjunct
➤ 16 women   ➤ 20 minority

■ Library and Physical Facilities

➤ 257,679 volumes & equivalents   ➤ library hours: Mon.-Thurs., 8:00 A.M.-11:00 P.M.; Fri., 8:00 A.M.-5:00 P.M.; Sat., 9:00 A.M.-5:00 P.M.; Sun., NOON-9:00 P.M.   ➤ LEXIS
➤ NEXIS   ➤ WESTLAW   ➤ 5 full-time librarians
➤ library seats 392

The library contains a study carrel for each student and seminar/discussion rooms for study groups. The classroom building houses a moot courtroom with video technology for support of clinical education programs. Law students have full access to all facilities of the university, including the health, counseling and computing centers, and athletic facilities.

■ Pacific-Asian Legal Studies

Because of Hawai'i's location, population, culture, and economic relationships, the law school offers a program in Pacific-Asian Legal Studies (PALS). The program has the two-fold purpose of conducting new research and enriching the J.D. curriculum. A number of faculty have expertise in Pacific/Asian research, teaching, and consultation. Recent and occasional course offerings in PALS have included Chinese Business Law, Chinese Law and Society, Pacific Island Legal Systems, Korean Law, Japanese Law and Society, and U.S.-Japan Business Transactions. The Certificate in Pacific-Asian Legal Studies allows students to focus elective coursework and earn the certificate in addition to the J.D.

A unique offering is the opportunity for selected students to do a full semester externship for academic credit with the court systems in certain Pacific Island nations or, with approval, in certain agencies or entities in Asia. Students may also arrange a semester of study with certain law faculties in Asia with prior approval.

■ Environmental/Ocean Law Programs

Students may focus their elective courses in the area of environmental law and earn the Certificate in Environmental Law along with the J.D. degree. Emphasis is on fresh water resources, oceans, coastal waters, and land use—all areas of special interest to Hawai'i and the Pacific.

The University of Hawai'i has unusually extensive programs in different types of marine research, and the law faculty is equally interested in ocean law and policy. Law students may elect to combine their J.D. studies with a university certificate program in Ocean Policy. The university also offers a certificate in Resource Management.

■ Admission

➤ Bachelor's degree from an accredited college or university required   ➤ application deadline—March 1 (firm)
➤ LSAT, LSDAS required   ➤ application fee—$30

Admission is determined by an applicant's academic achievement, aptitude for the study of law, and professional promise. Preference is given to residents of Hawai'i and to those nonresidents with strong ties to or special interest in Hawai'i, the Asia-Pacific region, or other programs in the law school. Up to 30 percent of the student body may be nonresidents.

Besides LSAT and undergraduate GPA and major, other factors considered are: academic work beyond the bachelor's degree, work experience, writing ability, community service, class diversity, hardship, and unusual accomplishments.

Applications from students wishing to transfer, or from those wishing to visit for a semester or two, are considered for both August and January admission.

■ Expenses and Financial Aid

➽ *1999-2000 tuition & fees—resident, $8,520; nonresident, $14,832* ➽ *estimated 9-month budget for off-campus living expenses—$9,800* ➽ *financial aid administered by Central University of Hawai'i Financial Aid Office, deadline—March 1* ➽ *FAFSA required for financial aid*

■ Student Activities

A student editorial board publishes the *University of Hawai'i Law Review* while other students participate in the moot court program, including national moot court competitions in international and environmental law. The 1993 Jessup International Moot Court Team placed first in the nation and second in the international competition. The 1994 and 1996 Jessup Teams won the Northwest Regional title, while the 1995 Jessup team captured the Pacific Regional championship and won first place for *Best Memorial* in the international competition. In 1998, the Jessup Team captured the *Richard R. Baxter Award* for best overall memorials in both the *Best Memorial—Applicant* and *Best Memorial—Respondent* categories surpassing 100 American teams and 70 international teams. The 1995 Environmental Team placed among the top ten (of 80) in the nation, while the 1996 Client Counseling Team placed second in the national competition.

Other students are active in a variety of organizations within the school and the Honolulu community including: Advocates for Public Interest Law (APIL), student divisions of the American Bar Association, National Lawyers Guild and American Trial Lawyers Association, American Inns of Court, Student Bar Association, Phi Delta Phi and Delta Theta Phi International Legal Fraternities, the Pacific Islands and Pacific-Asian Legal Studies Organizations, Association of Women Law Students, and Environmental Law Society. Student affinity groups include the Filipino Law Students Association and the *'Ahahui 'O Hawai'i*, an organization of native Hawaiian law students.

■ Career Services

Career counseling and services are provided to students and alumni for part-time, summer clerk, or associate positions in both the public and private sectors. On-campus facilities are available for interviews. Most large firms in Honolulu and many medium and small firms participate in the fall on-campus interview season for second- and third-year students. Recent graduating classes have had a 90 percent employment rate six months after graduation.

Applicant Group for the 1998-1999 Academic Year

University of Hawai'i at Mānoa—William S. Richardson School of Law
This grid includes only applicants who earned 120-180 LSAT scores under standard administrations in the 1994-1997 testing period.

LSAT Score	GPA 3.75 +		3.50 - 3.74		3.25 - 3.49		3.00 - 3.24		2.75 - 2.99		2.50 - 2.74		2.25 - 2.49		2.00 - 2.24		Below 2.00		No GPA		Totals	
	Apps	Adm	Apps	Adm	Apps	Adm	Apps	Adm	Apps	Adm	Apps	Adm	Apps	Adm	Apps	Adm	Apps	Adm	Apps	Adm	Apps	Adm
175-180	1	1	0	0	0	0	0	0	0	0	0	0	0	0	0	0	0	0	0	0	1	1
170-174	1	1	0	0	2	2	0	0	0	0	0	0	0	0	0	0	0	0	0	0	3	3
165-169	2	1	2	2	4	4	5	5	6	5	1	1	0	0	1	0	0	0	2	1	23	19
160-164	6	6	16	15	11	10	20	18	6	5	4	4	3	2	1	1	0	0	0	0	67	61
155-159	7	6	16	15	18	17	20	14	17	8	7	5	3	3	1	0	0	0	0	0	89	68
150-154	5	2	17	5	24	8	24	4	21	4	13	2	7	1	2	0	0	0	5	3	118	29
145-149	4	0	7	0	11	3	20	0	12	1	16	0	5	0	3	0	0	0	3	1	81	5
140-144	2	0	3	0	12	1	12	1	9	0	3	0	5	0	2	0	0	0	2	0	50	2
135-139	1	0	3	0	4	0	1	0	10	0	7	0	2	0	1	0	0	0	0	0	29	0
130-134	0	0	0	0	0	0	0	0	0	0	1	0	1	0	3	0	0	0	0	0	5	0
125-129	0	0	0	0	0	0	0	0	1	0	0	0	1	0	1	0	0	0	1	0	4	0
120-124	0	0	0	0	0	0	0	0	0	0	0	0	0	0	0	0	0	0	1	0	1	0
Total	29	17	64	37	86	45	102	42	82	23	52	12	27	6	15	1	0	0	14	5	471	188

Apps = Number of Applicants
Adm = Number Admitted
Reflects 98% of the total applicant pool.

Hofstra University School of Law

Hempstead, NY 11549

URL: http://www.hofstra.edu/law
Phone: 516.463.5916

■ Introduction

The Hofstra University School of Law is accredited by the ABA and is a member of the AALS. As a national law school, Hofstra provides a legal education designed to give students fundamental professional training and to prepare them for practice in any jurisdiction. Hofstra promotes considerable faculty/student contact and a strong sense of community.

■ Enrollment/Student Body

➡ *1,807 applicants*   ➡ *867 admitted first-year class 1998*
➡ *290 enrolled first-year class 1998*   ➡ *full-time 25th/75th percentile GPA—2.95/3.50*   ➡ *full-time 25th/75th percentile LSAT—150/158*   ➡ *799 total full-time*   ➡ *18% minority*
➡ *45% women*   ➡ *17 states & foreign countries represented*
➡ *110 undergraduate schools represented*

■ Faculty

➡ *75 total*   ➡ *40 full-time*   ➡ *35 part-time or adjunct*
➡ *14 women*   ➡ *4 minority*

One of Hofstra's greatest strengths is its faculty. The faculty are persons of academic distinction, and many of them are recognized as national authorities in their fields. They make it a point to be accessible to students outside of the traditional classroom setting. There are frequent lectures and scholarly activities emanating from the 17 endowed chairs and distinguished professorships.

■ Library and Physical Facilities

➡ *488,617 volumes & equivalents*   ➡ *library hours: Mon.-Thurs., 8:00 A.M.-MIDNIGHT; Fri., 8:00 A.M.-9:00 P.M.; Sat., 9:00 A.M.-6:00 P.M.; Sun., NOON-MIDNIGHT*
➡ *LEXIS*   ➡ *NEXIS*   ➡ *WESTLAW*   ➡ *DIALOG*
➡ *8 full-time librarians*   ➡ *library seats 595*

■ Curriculum

➡ *Academic Support Program*   ➡ *87 credits required to graduate*   ➡ *degrees and combined degrees available: J.D.; J.D./M.B.A.; LL.M.*   ➡ *semesters, start in late Aug.*
➡ *range of first-year class size—28-30 (small section); 117-120 (large section)*

■ Special Programs

Each entering student at Hofstra is placed in one small section of fewer than 30 students in a substantive course during the first semester of their first year. This small section experience enables a closer relationship between students and faculty in a seminar-like environment.

During the spring semester of their first year, students receive intensive instruction in legal research and writing. During the fall semester of their second year, students participate in the Appellate Advocacy Program, in which they receive instruction in persuasive writing and oral advocacy.

Each January, Hofstra students are able to select a three-credit course on trial techniques that is patterned on the program of the National Institute for Trial Advocacy. A carefully orchestrated sequence of exercises, covering every aspect of a trial from jury selection to closing arguments, builds the students' abilities so that they are able to conduct a full jury trial at the end of the course.

A courthouse of the United States District Court for the Eastern District of New York is located on the Hofstra campus. The court cooperates with the law school in various academic programs and offers the students additional educational and practical experiences.

Civil Externship Program—The Civil Externship Program provides students with opportunities to learn lawyering skills through placements in a variety of nonprofit organizations or government agencies.

Criminal Externship Program—The Criminal Externship Program provides an opportunity for students to learn about all phases of criminal law practice through placements in such agencies as Nassau, Queens, and Kings County District Attorneys' offices and New York City, Nassau County, and Suffolk Legal Aid offices. Students work approximately 15 hours per week.

Alternative Dispute Resolution Clinic—The goals of the Alternative Dispute Resolution Clinic are to teach mediation skills, provide clinically supervised mediation experience, and provide direction in the advanced study of theoretical, legal, ethical, and practical issues posed by the use of mediation as an alternative to litigation.

Criminal Justice Clinic—This program is a one-semester clinic in which students represent defendants in criminal cases in Nassau County District Court and in Hempstead and Mineola Village courts. Students represent clients in pretrial conferences, witness interviewing, motion and brief writing, case investigations, and trials—from jury selection through verdict.

Judicial Externship Program—The Judicial Externship Program provides an opportunity for students to serve as apprentices to state and federal judges for a semester. As judicial externs, for approximately 15 hours per week, students do research, write memoranda, observe court proceedings, and discuss cases with their judge.

Environmental Law Clinic—This program provides an opportunity to work on current environmental issues with public interest law firms, state or local environmental agencies, and private practitioners engaged in pro bono work in the field.

Housing Rights Clinic—Students handle a wide variety of housing cases for low-income clients, including defenses of eviction cases; actions by tenants against landlords challenging substandard conditions in their apartments; fair housing and exclusionary zoning cases; public utility shut-off cases; and work on behalf of community groups for housing rehabilitation. The course develops lawyering skills with special emphasis on litigation strategy, pretrial and trial preparation, and trial advocacy.

Pro Bono Student Lawyers Project—The Pro Bono Student Lawyers Project places students with a variety of existing agencies, service organizations, law firms, and private practitioners. Students in the program volunteer their time without compensation or credit to work on pro bono cases.

Unemployment Action Center—The Unemployment Action Center(UAC) is a nonprofit, student-run corporation that offers free advice and representation to persons denied unemployment benefits. The Unemployment Action Center received the New York State Bar Association Law Student Pro Bono Award for 1992.

■ Admission

➥ *Bachelor's degree required for admission*
➥ *application deadline—April 15*   ➥ *modified rolling admission*
➥ *LSAT, LSDAS required*   ➥ *application fee—$60*

■ Student Activities

Hofstra students publish four journals. The *Hofstra Law Review* enjoys national renown and an international circulation. The *Labor Law Journal* publishes scholarly articles on various aspects of labor and employment law. The *Law and Policy Symposium* focuses on an analysis of a single issue from various perspectives. The *Family and Conciliation Courts Review* is an international, interdisciplinary family law journal. Other student organizations include Asian Pacific American Law Students Association (APALSA); Black Law Students Association (BLSA); Coming Out

For Civil Rights; *Conscience* (the law school's student newspaper); Corporate Law Society; Democratic Law Students Association; *Environmental Law Digest*; Environmental Law Society; Federalist Society; Gaelic Law Students Society; Hofstra Law Women; Intellectual Property Association; Italian Law Students Association (ILSA); International Law Society; Jewish Law Students Association (JLSA); Lambda Alpha International; Latino-Latina American Law Students Association (LALSA); Phi Alpha Delta (PAD); *Pocket Part* (the law school yearbook); Public Justice Foundation; R.E.A.C.H. (Research, Education, and Advocacy to Combat Homelessness); Republican Law Students Association; Sports and Entertainment Law Group; Student Bar Association; Trial Advocacy Club; and Unemployment Action Center.

■ Expenses and Financial Aid

➥ *tuition & fees—$22,210*
➥ *financial aid and scholarships available*

■ Career Services

The Office of Career Services provides a wide range of services to facilitate job placement. The senior assistant dean for career services and the director organize recruitment programs, conduct job development campaigns, teach résumé writing and interviewing techniques, provide career counseling to students and alumni, and maintain employment statistics.

Admission Profile Not Available

University of Houston Law Center

Houston, TX 77204-6391

E-Mail: admissions@www.law.uh.edu
URL: http://www.law.uh.edu/
Phone: 713.743.1070

■ Introduction

The University of Houston Law Center is located at the University of Houston. Located three miles south of downtown, the campus extends over 550 acres of wooded terrain. The state-assisted Law Center, located in the nation's sixth largest legal market, is noted throughout the South and Southwest not only for its excellence, but for its progressive and innovative approach to the teaching of law. The College of Law, the academic branch of the Law Center, is fully accredited by the American Bar Association and the American Association of Law Schools and has a chapter of the Order of the Coif, the national legal honorary scholastic society. The Law Center confers a J.D. degree as a first degree in law and a Masters of Law (LL.M.) degree to students pursuing work beyond the J.D. degree.

■ Enrollment/Student Body

➠ 2,174 applicants ➠ 920 admitted first-year class 1997 ➠ 342 enrolled first-year class 1997 ➠ full-time 25th/75th percentile GPA—3.06/3.50 ➠ part-time 25th/75th percentile GPA—3.00/3.53 ➠ full-time 25th/75th percentile LSAT—155/160 ➠ part-time 25th/75th percentile LSAT—154/161 ➠ 773 total full-time ➠ 286 total first-year full-time ➠ 229 total part-time ➠ 56 total first-year full-time ➠ 22% minority ➠ 45% women ➠ 131 undergraduate schools represented ➠ 120 students enrolled in LL.M program

■ Faculty

➠ 123 total ➠ 46 full-time ➠ 77 part-time or adjunct ➠ 22 women ➠ 12 minority

■ Library and Physical Facilities

➠ 480,000 volumes & equivalents ➠ 11 full-time librarians ➠ LEXIS ➠ WESTLAW ➠ full access to Internet & World Wide Web ➠ large NT student network with 450 wired carrels, a CD-ROM network & a substantial World Wide Web presence ➠ special collections in International Law with emphasis on Latin America, Admiralty, Tax, Oil & Gas, and Mexican Law

■ Curriculum/Basic Program of Study

➠ 90 credits required to graduate ➠ Academic Enrichment Program ➠ 215 courses available ➠ full-time class starts early fall ➠ part-time (evening) class starts early summer

The first-year curriculum at the Law Center is prescribed. Students are also required to complete a course in professional responsibility and one major piece of legal research and writing before graduation. Emphasis is placed on legal theory and the varying approaches to the law.

■ Special Programs

➠ concurrent degree programs: J.D./M.B.A.; J.D./M.A. in History; J.D./M.P.H.; J.D./Ph.D. in Medical Humanities

➠ LL.M. degrees offered in Health Law, International Law, Intellectual Property Law; Energy, Environmental, and Natural Resources Law; & Tax Law

The University of Houston Law Center emphasizes current legal and administrative problems confronting the region and nation, including intellectual property law, environmental law, energy law, tax law, health law, and international law, with an emphasis on Latin America. The Law Center is home to the Health Law and Policy Institute, a research and instruction center on interdisciplinary issues. The Law Center is also host to the Intellectual Property Program, the Trial Advocacy Institute, the Environmental Liability Law Curriculum, the Institute for Higher Education Law and Governance, and the International Law Institute. The Law Center operates the Mexican Legal Studies Program, an annual summer school in Mexico for students interested in the Mexican legal system, particularly as it applies to foreign investors seeking to do business in Mexico. The Law Center also offers the broadest law curriculum of any law school in Texas.

■ Clinical Programs and Trial Advocacy

The Law Center offers a wide variety of clinical courses. Students can choose among different areas of concentration, such as agency or judicial internships; health or environmental law; and criminal prosecution or defense. The Law Center houses the Legal Aid Clinic, which gives students clinic opportunities in providing legal services to the indigent. The Law Center also offers skills training in both civil and criminal trial and appellate advocacy. The Trial Advocacy Institute oversees the design and implementation of trial advocacy courses at the Law Center.

■ Activities

The Student Bar Association has input into every facet of student life at the Law Center. The SBA participates in the first-year orientation, organizes the annual charity Fun-Run, aids in the selection of student representatives to sit on various faculty committees, and presents student attitudes and views both within and outside the Law Center.

The Law Center features an extensive moot court program, as well as the *Law Review* and the *Houston Journal of International Law*, two student-run scholarly publications.

Other student organizations include the Association of Women in Law, Black Law Students Association, Hispanic Law Students Association, Asian Law Students Association, Mandamus (Gay and Lesbian Student Organization), Lex Judaica (Jewish students), Public Interest Law Organization, Health Law Organization, Intellectual Property Student Organization, Environmental Law Society, Phi Delta Phi, Phi Alpha Delta, and Computer Law Society.

■ Student Body

The student body consists of approximately 1,000 persons from across the United States, although most students come from Texas and the Southwest. There is no provisional acceptance.

■ Admission

➼ *Bachelor's degree from an accredited university*
➼ *application deadline—Feb. 15*   ➼ *early decision—Nov. 1*
➼ *LSAT, LSDAS required*   ➼ *application fee—$50*

A completed application and LSDAS report must be furnished to the Law Center by February 1 to guarantee consideration for the following fall or summer semesters. Only LSAT scores graded on the 120-180 scale will be accepted for consideration.

The Law Center seeks candidates with demonstrated academic ability as evidenced by academic records and LSAT scores. In determining academic performance the committee may consider the following: the quality of the prior educational institutions attended; the rigor of the coursework and major; trends in improvement; whether academic achievement was made in spite of other commitments such as employment, family obligations, and service activities; graduate level academic performance; and academic performance in spite of weakness in prior preparation.

Other criteria are also considered in selecting students for admission. These criteria include: community or other service or volunteer work; overcoming hardships or other obstacles (such as family responsibilities, health problems, socioeconomic disadvantage, or disabilities); maturity; reliability; communication skills; responsibility; leadership; judgment; honesty; being ethical; work performance; military, peacekeeping, or law enforcement experience;

other personal talents relevant to the student or practice of law; accomplishments; and other factors in unusual cases.

It is important that you bring to our attention any information that you wish the Law Center to consider in evaluating your application through your personal statement, résumé, and letters of recommendation.

■ Expenses and Financial Aid

➼ *tuition & fees—full-time resident, $6,169; nonresident, $10,969*
➼ *estimated additional expenses (room, board, & books)—$9,970*
➼ *scholarships available*   ➼ *FAFSA for need analysis*

The Law Center forwards financial aid materials to applicants once they are accepted. The Financial Aid Advisor will assist accepted applicants with their questions. Once accepted, all applicants are automatically considered for merit scholarships.

■ Career Services

The Law Center's Career Services Office actively assists students and graduates in legal career planning. The office annually hosts prospective employers in on-campus interview and recruiting programs for second- and third-year students seeking summer clerkships and permanent positions. The Career Services Office receives notices of part-time and full-time positions available within the legal community, which are maintained for student review. The office also maintains a wide variety of resources such as legal directories, employers' résumés, and legal career planning publications.

Applicant Group for the 1998-1999 Academic Year

University of Houston Law Center
This grid includes only applicants who earned 120-180 LSAT scores under standard administrations.

LSAT Score	3.75 +		3.50 - 3.74		3.25 - 3.49		3.00 - 3.24		2.75 - 2.99		2.50 - 2.74		2.25 - 2.49		2.00 - 2.24		Below 2.00		No GPA		Totals	
	Apps	Adm	Apps	Adm	Apps	Adm	Apps	Adm	Apps	Adm	Apps	Adm	Apps	Adm	Apps	Adm	Apps	Adm	Apps	Adm	Apps	Adm
175-180	1	1	0	0	0	0	0	0	0	0	1	1	1	1	0	0	0	0	0	0	3	3
170-174	4	4	2	2	5	5	1	1	1	1	2	2	1	1	1	1	0	0	0	0	17	17
165-169	6	6	14	14	15	15	13	13	10	10	10	10	2	2	1	1	0	0	1	0	72	71
160-164	25	25	50	50	57	57	59	55	41	36	18	10	4	1	3	1	1	0	3	3	261	238
155-159	35	34	95	93	113	102	109	84	82	35	43	10	17	2	6	1	1	0	6	2	507	363
150-154	41	39	77	57	103	52	115	30	87	9	52	2	24	0	12	0	1	0	5	1	517	190
145-149	18	6	36	5	62	8	78	3	65	2	48	1	24	1	16	0	2	0	10	2	359	28
140-144	5	0	22	0	44	0	56	1	52	0	39	0	25	1	15	0	1	0	4	0	263	2
135-139	2	0	4	0	8	0	18	0	23	0	22	0	14	0	10	0	3	0	7	0	111	0
130-134	0	0	1	0	1	0	5	0	3	0	9	0	5	0	3	0	4	0	1	0	32	0
125-129	0	0	0	0	0	0	1	0	1	0	1	0	2	0	3	0	0	0	2	0	10	0
120-124	0	0	0	0	0	0	0	0	0	0	1	0	0	0	0	0	0	0	1	0	2	0
Total	137	115	301	221	408	239	455	187	365	93	246	36	119	9	70	4	13	0	40	8	2154	912

Apps = Number of Applicants
Adm = Number Admitted
Reflects 99% of the total applicant pool.

Howard University School of Law

Office of Admissions
2900 Van Ness Street, NW
Washington, DC 20008

E-Mail: kgray@law.howard.edu
URL: http://www.law.howard.edu
Phone: 202.806.8009

■ Introduction

Howard University, a coeducational, private institution in Washington, DC, was chartered by the U.S. Congress in 1867. Howard is a historically black institution that offers an educational experience of exceptional quality and value to students with high academic potential. Particular emphasis is placed on providing educational opportunities for promising African Americans and other persons of color who have been underrepresented in the legal profession, and nonminority persons with a strong interest in civil and human rights, as well as public service. The law school has a diverse student body and faculty. The main campus of Howard is located in northwest Washington. The law school is located on a separate 22-acre campus, also in northwest Washington, approximately three miles from the main campus. Howard University School of Law is fully approved by the American Bar Association and the Association of American Law Schools, and certifies its graduates for bar examination in all jurisdictions of the United States.

■ Enrollment (First-Year Class)

➡ *1,078 applicants*   ➡ *391 admitted*   ➡ *140 enrolled*
➡ *full-time 25th/75th percentile GPA—2.67/3.23*
➡ *full-time 25th/75th percentile LSAT—148/155*
➡ *405 total full-time*   ➡ *99.5% minority*   ➡ *57% women*
➡ *30 states & 4 foreign countries represented*
➡ *101 undergraduate schools represented*
➡ *28 different undergraduate majors represented*

■ Student Body

There are 392 full-time students in the J.D. Program. Another 13 students participate full-time in the LL.M. program. They come from all parts of the United States, as well as Asia, Africa, Canada, and the Caribbean. The academic attrition rate is 6 percent. Attrition for other reasons is approximately another 4 percent.

■ Faculty

➡ *56 total*   ➡ *31 full-time*   ➡ *25 part-time or adjunct*
➡ *20 women*

■ Library & Physical Facilities

➡ *250,000 volumes & equivalents*   ➡ *library hours: Mon.-Thurs., 8:00 A.M.-MIDNIGHT; Fri., 8:00 A.M.-9:00 P.M.; Sat., 9:00 A.M.-9:00 P.M.; Sun., NOON-MIDNIGHT; extended hours during reading & exam periods*   ➡ *LEXIS*   ➡ *NEXIS*
➡ *WESTLAW*   ➡ *CALI*   ➡ *DIALOG*   ➡ *OCLC*
➡ *LegalTrac*   ➡ *9 full-time librarians*   ➡ *17 total staff*

The Allen Mercer Daniel Law Library is both a working collection for law students and lawyers and a research institution for legal scholars. The civil rights archive contains briefs, working papers, and materials of the NAACP and other civil rights organizations. The library has a collection that emphasizes civil and political rights and literature to support study of the legal problems of the poor. Its collection has recently been expanded to also include considerable CD-ROM resources. The law library has been updated with an online catalogue system, e-mail capabilities, and Internet and CD-ROM access. The law library offers three computer labs containing both IBM and Macintosh personal computers with a 1:10 computer/student ratio. Howard University is a member of the Consortium of Universities of the Washington Metropolitan Area.

■ Curriculum

➡ *Academic Support Program*   ➡ *Elder Law Clinic*
➡ *Public Service Program*   ➡ *Criminal Justice Clinic*
➡ *internship*   ➡ *88 credits required to graduate, with a cumulative weighted average of not less than 70*
➡ *residence in the last full year is also a requirement for graduation*   ➡ *degrees available: J.D.; J.D./M.B.A.; LL.M.*
➡ *range of first year class size—30-50*

The curriculum leading to the first degree in law covers three academic years of two semesters each. Howard has no summer or evening program; it is a full-time day program. Experience has shown that beginning students must devote their entire time to their studies. During the first two years, emphasis is on the fundamental analytical concepts and skills of the law and the system by which it is administered; the functions required of a lawyer within a legal system based upon the common law. These courses afford rigorous training in the recognition of essential facts, in analysis and synthesis, and in the presentation of legal materials. The curriculum in the third year provides diversified experience and a solid foundation for whatever specialization is desired. There is an emphasis on effective legal writing throughout the law school curriculum. Howard is firmly committed to producing lawyers who have mastered the art of effective written communication. Students wishing to participate in the Joint J.D./M.B.A. program must be admitted both to the School of Law and the School of Business; one may use the law school application only to apply for the J.D./M.B.A. degree. Students interested in the LL.M. program should make inquiry to the School of Law.

■ Special Programs

The School of Law has a strong commitment to public service and to human and civil rights. Many programs and activities in the school reflect that fact. The school also provides an opportunity for clinical experience in civil and criminal litigation and employment law. Howard Law also offers a summer study abroad program in comparative and international law at the University of Western Cape in South Africa. The six-week program is approved by the ABA and offers constitutional, business, and trade law courses for credit.

Minority Programs

Howard University is a historically black institution, and has always had a strong, anti-discrimination policy. The School of Law, consistent with the mission and tradition of the university, believes in affirmative action both with regard to admissions and financial aid in order to ensure that all members of underrepresented groups may have access to the legal profession.

Admission

➤ Bachelor's degree from a college or university acceptable to the School of Law is required ➤ application deadline— April 30, rolling admission used; early application preferred (Oct. 30) ➤ LSAT, LSDAS required ➤ application fee—$60 ➤ letters of recommendation, undergraduate dean's survey, & personal statement should accompany application

The large number of applications received for the available spaces in the first-year class has made the admissions process highly selective. The School of Law admits only full-time students for entrance in the fall. Applicants must take the LSAT (and GMAT for the J.D./M.B.A.) and should arrange to take the LSAT no later than February of the year admission is sought to allow adequate processing time. Applicants must register with the LSDAS and must have obtained their college degrees before enrolling.

Student Activities

The *Howard Law Journal*, scheduled for publication three times a year, publishes legal materials of scholarly and professional interest. The national and international moot court teams, which sponsor intramural competitions and participate in competitions nationwide, have won numerous honors. The Student Bar Association (SBA) is the general student government organization. The *Barrister*, the student newspaper, publishes several issues a year. Other organizations represent students from diverse ethnic backgrounds, including, African Americans, Latinos, Africans, Caribbean Islanders, and Asian Pacific Islanders. Other activities include three legal fraternities and a legal sorority, as well as organizations that address a range of student needs and interests.

Expenses and Financial Aid

➤ tuition & fees—full-time, $12,425 ➤ additional expenses—$11,000 (room, board, & miscellaneous living expenses) ➤ merit scholarships are available ➤ financial aid available; financial aid forms due April 1 ➤ extensive list of loans available

Career Services

The Career Services Office is an integral part of the law school. To assist students, the office offers workshops on job search techniques and résumé writing, and seminars on career development and practice specialties. The office also maintains an extensive resource library with online employer research systems, newsletters, and updated listings of career opportunities. Howard affords its students varied career opportunities. Each year, the Career Services Office sponsors two on-campus interview programs and more than 250 recruiters from law firms, government agencies, and corporations visit the law school with offers of employment for promising students and graduates. Graduates work for courts; large and small private firms; federal, state, and local government agencies; public interest organizations; and public and private corporations throughout the United States.

Applicant Group for the 1998-1999 Academic Year

Howard University School of Law
This grid includes only applicants who earned 120-180 LSAT scores under standard administrations (reflects 99% of the total applicant pool).

LSAT Score	GPA																					
	3.75 +		3.50 - 3.74		3.25 - 3.49		3.00 - 3.24		2.75 - 2.99		2.50 - 2.74		2.25 - 2.49		2.00 - 2.24		Below 2.00		No GPA		Totals	
	Apps	Adm	Apps	Adm	Apps	Adm	Apps	Adm	Apps	Adm	Apps	Adm	Apps	Adm	Apps	Adm	Apps	Adm	Apps	Adm	Apps	Adm
175-180	0	0	0	0	0	0	0	0	0	0	0	0	0	0	0	0	0	0	0	0	0	0
170-174	0	0	0	0	0	0	0	0	1	1	0	0	0	0	0	0	0	0	0	0	1	1
165-169	0	0	1	1	1	1	2	2	0	0	0	0	1	1	2	1	0	0	2	2	9	8
160-164	0	0	4	4	1	1	1	1	4	3	3	3	3	2	0	0	0	0	0	0	16	14
155-159	2	2	7	7	7	6	12	10	12	12	7	6	5	4	2	1	0	0	3	2	58	51
150-154	4	3	14	10	20	15	31	26	26	21	22	17	16	10	7	2	1	0	4	1	145	105
145-149	5	3	14	6	29	15	45	23	54	25	45	11	25	5	21	6	5	0	7	1	250	95
140-144	4	1	19	0	27	2	67	7	57	4	71	4	41	3	21	1	1	0	4	0	312	22
135-139	2	0	9	0	13	0	28	1	33	0	33	2	35	0	19	0	5	0	5	0	182	3
130-134	1	0	4	0	2	0	11	0	20	0	8	0	10	0	5	0	1	0	4	0	66	0
125-129	0	0	0	0	0	0	1	0	5	0	5	0	3	0	7	0	3	0	2	0	26	0
120-124	0	0	0	0	0	0	0	0	1	0	0	0	0	0	1	0	0	0	0	0	2	0
Total	18	9	72	28	100	40	198	70	213	66	194	43	139	25	85	12	17	0	31	6	1067	299

Apps = Number of Applicants
Adm = Number Admitted

University of Idaho College of Law

Moscow, ID 83844-2321

E-Mail: tamaram@uidaho.edu
URL: http://www.uidaho.edu/law
Phone: 208.885.6423

■ Introduction

The College of Law is located on the main campus of the University of Idaho in the city of Moscow, about 90 miles southeast of Spokane, Washington, and about 8 miles east of Pullman, Washington. The Moscow-Pullman community is the cultural center of a vast inland area of the Northwest covering parts of Idaho, Washington, and Oregon. This area is renowned for outstanding opportunities for outdoor sports and activities. Washington State University and the University of Idaho are only 8 miles apart, and the two universities make their resources jointly available in many fields. The College of Law was established in 1909. It has been a member of the AALS since 1915 and has been on the approved list of the ABA since 1925.

■ Enrollment/Student Body

➡ *459 applicants*   ➡ *284 admitted first-year class 1998*
➡ *104 enrolled first-year class 1998*   ➡ *full-time 25th/75th percentile GPA—2.91/3.57*   ➡ *full-time 25th/75th percentile LSAT—149/156*   ➡ *300 total full-time*   ➡ *6% minority*
➡ *30% women*   ➡ *25 states & foreign countries represented*
➡ *85 undergraduate schools represented*

Students from Idaho constitute approximately 70 percent of the student body; the other 30 percent come from all regions of the United States. Although the total enrollment of the College of Law is relatively small (approximately 300), students typically represent over 70 different colleges and universities. Academic attrition is about 7 percent.

■ Faculty

➡ *27 total*   ➡ *21 full-time*   ➡ *6 part-time or adjunct*
➡ *8 women*

■ Library and Physical Facilities

➡ *174,395 volumes & equivalents*   ➡ *library hours: Mon.-Thurs., 7:30 A.M.-11:00 P.M.; Fri., 7:30 A.M.-8:30 P.M.; Sat., 9:30 A.M.-6:30 P.M.; Sun., 10:30 A.M.-11:00 P.M.*
➡ *LEXIS*   ➡ *NEXIS*   ➡ *WESTLAW*   ➡ *DIALOG*
➡ *Online Legal Periodical Indices*   ➡ *4 full-time librarians*
➡ *library seats 369*

The College of Law occupies an air-conditioned building designed for its use and completed in 1973. It contains a courtroom, classrooms, offices for the clinical training program, and the law library which houses two computer labs with access to the Internet, LEXIS/NEXIS, and WESTLAW/DIALOG. It is located across the street from the general library of the university.

The law library subscribes to CD-ROM libraries. Membership in the Western Library Network and the Inland Northwest Library Automation Network allows users to ascertain holdings of hundreds of libraries across the nation.

Law students have access to the other libraries of the University of Idaho, as well as to those of Washington State University.

■ Curriculum

➡ *In-house Clinical Program*   ➡ *88 credits required to graduate*
➡ *61 courses available*   ➡ *degree available: J.D.*
➡ *semesters, start in Aug., Jan., & May (summer)*
➡ *externships*

The school operates on a semester basis with six semesters and 88 semester credit hours required for the J.D. degree. A summer session is held for advanced students only, and the J.D. degree can be secured in five semesters and two summer sessions. The first-year curriculum is required and includes the traditional subjects of contracts, torts, procedure, property, and criminal law.

The focus is upon basic general principles widely applicable throughout the United States. Standard casebooks and other teaching materials are used, occasionally supplemented by references to the more localized problems of Idaho or the Northwest. No work is offered toward any degree other than the J.D.

■ Special Programs

The law school operates a variety of clinical programs. Law students in their third year may qualify as interns under the laws of Idaho and work in the in-house clinic. Interns are eligible to present cases in court under appropriate supervision. The in-house clinic includes a general practice unit, an appellate unit in which students practice in federal and state appellate courts, and a tribal court unit in which students serve as public defenders in the NezPerce Tribal Court.

Externships are available, for limited credit, with the Supreme Court and Court of Appeals of Idaho, the United States Court of Appeals for the Ninth Circuit, the United States District Court for the District of Idaho, the Attorney General of Idaho, the United States Attorney for the District of Idaho, and various county prosecutors and public defenders offices. Interns may also receive limited credit for work performed in law offices and selected public agencies.

A concurrent J.D./M.S. (Environmental Science) degree in cooperation with the University of Idaho College of Graduate Studies Environmental Science Program is available. The program allows students to obtain both degrees in four years rather than the five years it would take to earn them separately.

■ Admission

➡ *three years of undergraduate work or a Bachelor's degree required for admission*   ➡ *application deadline—Feb. 1, but all applications considered*   ➡ *LSAT, LSDAS required*
➡ *application fee—$40*

Applications are accepted beginning in September preceding the year in which enrollment is desired. Entering students are admitted only at the beginning of the fall semester. Applicants must submit LSAT scores and college transcripts for evaluation through LSDAS. Late fall application is recommended, and the deadline for being considered in the first wave of acceptances is February 1. In making decisions, the Admission Committee relies on the LSAT, the college record, references, and personal statement.

■ Student Activities

Students publish the *Idaho Law Review*, which is devoted particularly to state and regional problems, although articles of general national interest do appear. An intramural moot court competition is held on a voluntary basis and students are selected from the winning teams to participate in the National, International, and ABA Moot Court Teams. The Student Bar Association represents student interests, both educational and social. From its ranks come elected student members who sit on various faculty/student committees. There are chapters of the Phi Alpha Delta, Delta Theta Phi, and Phi Delta Phi legal fraternities at the College of Law, as well as the American Bar Association Law Student Division, the Board of Student Advocates, the Christian Legal Society, the Environmental Law Society, the Federalist Society, the *Idaho Law Review*, the Idaho Women's Law Caucus, the Idaho Trial Lawyers Association, the International Law Society, Law Students for Alternative Dispute Resolution, the Minority Law Student Association,

the Student Division of the Idaho State Bar's Corporate and Securities Section, the Public International Law Group, and the Law Student Spouse/Partner Association.

■ Expenses and Financial Aid

➡ *tuition & fees—resident, $4,076; nonresident, $10,076*
➡ *need- & achievement-based scholarships available*
➡ *minority scholarships available* ➡ *financial aid available; Financial Aid Application required* ➡ *FAF due Feb. 15*

■ Career Services

The law school sponsors a variety of activities designed to facilitate students' career planning and assist in their employment search as summer clerks or for permanent positions. Facilities are available for on-campus interviews and the school is able to work with employers who cannot visit the school but have indicated a desire to recruit by mail. More than 95 percent of graduates find employment within six months of graduation, with the majority finding employment in Idaho, although Washington and Oregon continue to be popular locations. Graduates are also employed throughout the United States and several foreign countries. In recent years students have followed the national averages in finding employment in positions requiring bar membership or extensive legal training.

Applicant Group for the 1998-1999 Academic Year

University of Idaho College of Law
This grid includes only applicants who earned 120-180 LSAT scores under standard administrations.

LSAT Score	3.75 +		3.50 - 3.74		3.25 - 3.49		3.00 - 3.24		2.75 - 2.99		2.50 - 2.74		2.25 - 2.49		2.00 - 2.24		Below 2.00		No GPA		Total	
	Apps	Adm	Apps	Adm	Apps	Adm	Apps	Adm	Apps	Adm	Apps	Adm	Apps	Adm	Apps	Adm	Apps	Adm	Apps	Adm	Apps	Adm
175-180	0	0	0	0	0	0	0	0	0	0	0	0	0	0	0	0	0	0	0	0	0	0
170-174	0	0	0	0	0	0	0	0	1	1	0	0	0	0	0	0	0	0	0	0	1	1
165-169	2	2	0	0	2	2	2	2	0	0	2	2	0	0	0	0	0	0	0	0	8	8
160-164	7	7	10	10	7	7	9	9	2	2	1	1	5	4	0	0	0	0	0	0	41	40
155-159	9	9	16	16	18	17	12	12	9	6	8	5	3	2	1	0	1	1	2	1	79	69
150-154	9	9	21	19	19	14	24	19	24	16	13	8	11	6	2	0	0	0	0	0	123	91
145-149	6	4	17	13	21	14	28	13	23	4	13	6	2	1	3	1	0	0	2	1	115	57
140-144	2	1	2	0	15	4	11	0	12	0	10	0	3	0	3	0	0	0	1	0	59	5
135-139	0	0	0	0	1	0	4	1	6	0	5	0	0	0	0	0	0	0	2	0	18	1
130-134	0	0	1	0	0	0	0	0	1	0	0	0	2	0	0	0	0	0	0	0	4	0
125-129	0	0	0	0	0	0	0	0	0	0	1	1	0	0	1	0	0	0	0	0	2	1
120-124	0	0	0	0	0	0	0	0	0	0	0	0	0	0	0	0	0	0	0	0	0	0
Total	35	32	67	58	83	58	90	56	78	29	53	23	26	13	10	1	1	1	7	2	450	273

Apps = Number of Applicants
Adm = Number Admitted
Reflects 98% of the total applicant pool.

University of Illinois College of Law

504 East Pennsylvania Avenue
Champaign, IL 61820

E-Mail: admissions@law.uiuc.edu
URL: http://www.law.uiuc.edu
Phone: 217.244.6415

■ Introduction

Established nearly a century ago, the University of Illinois College of Law fosters excellence in legal education through a close community of faculty members and students, where teaching goes hand in hand with scholarship. The resources —intellectual, cultural, and recreational—of one of the world's largest and best universities are readily available to our law students, as is the appealing ambience of a university community. The college's comparatively low tuition costs, as well as the area's moderate living costs, make our program an outstanding value.

■ Enrollment/Student Body

➡ *1,540 applicants* ➡ *194 enrolled first-year class 1998*
➡ *full-time 25th/75th percentile GPA—3.19/3.64*
➡ *full-time 25th/75th percentile LSAT—156/163*
➡ *592 total full-time* ➡ *30% minority* ➡ *40% women*
➡ *30 states & foreign countries represented*
➡ *160 undergraduate schools represented*

■ Faculty

➡ *78 total* ➡ *44 full-time* ➡ *34 part-time or adjunct*
➡ *22 women* ➡ *8 minority*

■ Library and Physical Facilities

➡ *687,963 volumes & equivalents* ➡ *LEXIS*
➡ *NEXIS* ➡ *WESTLAW* ➡ *3.5 full-time librarians*

In August 1993, the college completed a major addition and renovation that greatly increased the amount of space available for students.

The law library ranks sixth nationally in the number of titles held. The library has a substantial international collection and is one of the few American law libraries designated as a depository by the European Economic Community.

Directly across the street from the law school is one of the country's largest physical education buildings, with indoor and outdoor swimming pools, tennis courts, four gyms, weight and exercise equipment, archery, and ball courts of all kinds. The facility is free for students.

■ Curriculum

➡ *Academic Support Program*
➡ *90 credits required to graduate* ➡ *116 courses available*
➡ *degrees and combined degrees available: J.D.; LL.M.; J.D./M.B.A.; J.D./M.D.; J.D./D.V.M.; J.D./M.A. in Labor & Industrial Relations; J.D./M.A. in Urban Planning; J.D./Master of Education; Doctor of Education; J.D./M.S. in Journalism; J.D./M.S. in Chemistry; J.D./M.S. in Natural Resources & Environmental Sciences* ➡ *semesters, start in Aug.*
➡ *range of first-year class size—62-66*

In the second and third years, courses vary in size. Seminar enrollment is limited to 12 students, and trial advocacy sections are limited to 20 students each. Independent studies—in which students work individually with faculty on research topics of special interest—are also offered.

■ Special Programs

International Legal Studies—Students pursuing international legal studies can choose from 13 international and comparative law courses, ranging from European Community law to international human rights law. Faculty members have long-standing international connections, and some collaborate with international scholars and legal experts to teach these courses.

Trial Advocacy Program—The college's trial advocacy program is especially popular, enrolling about three-quarters of the third-year class. The year-long program teaches the art of courtroom litigation and concludes with students conducting a day-long mock trial.

Environmental Law—The college has an active program of environmental and planning studies. Beyond the first-year course in property, the college offers courses in environmental law, natural resources, and land-use planning.

An innovative computer-based course called Metro-Apex offers a semester-long simulation of environmental controversies and legal disputes. Students adopt and enforce regulations and conduct full-scale administrative and judicial proceedings.

Taxation—Illinois offers one of the strongest tax curricula in the country, with core courses that address all aspects of tax practice and advanced offerings that integrate tax problems with other fields of law.

Skills Training—The College offers a live-client Civil Clinic, as well as classes in legal drafting, business planning, advanced bankruptcy, environmental management, estate planning, and tax practice; all challenge students to solve concrete problems and draft legal documents in a variety of fields. Courses on computer applications in the law and quantitative methods in legal decision making familiarize students with sophisticated techniques necessary in today's law practice; these include computerized methods of document preparation and information retrieval, statistical analysis, the use of computer simulations in litigation, and the calculation of damage awards.

Offerings on alternative dispute resolution, the lawyer as negotiator, and collective bargaining and labor arbitration engage students in mock negotiations, arbitrations, and alternatives to traditional trials.

■ Admission

➡ *Bachelor's degree required* ➡ *application deadline—March 15* ➡ *rolling admission* ➡ *LSAT, LSDAS required*
➡ *application fee—$40*

In evaluating applications, the Admissions Committee places great weight on the undergraduate grade-point average and the Law School Admission Test score. Nevertheless, a thorough admission process, including individual review of all files by a committee, attempts to identify students whose grades or scores appear to under-predict their performance in law school, as well as students whose admission would contribute to diversity at the College of Law. The committee also considers graduate work in other fields, employment experience, and demonstrated leadership ability. Applicants are not judged on the basis of in-state residency.

■ Student Activities

Students can write for the *University of Illinois Law Review* or for the *Elder Law Journal*, the only law journal in the country to concentrate on the legal problems of the elderly. Illinois students also write analyses of recent court decisions for the monthly *Illinois Bar Journal*.

Students interested in appellate advocacy can compete in any of a number of moot court competitions and can gain practical experience through the client counseling and negotiation competitions, and the live-client clinic.

The small size of the college allows students to become actively involved in the college's more than 30 student organizations.

■ Expenses and Financial Aid

➤ *tuition & fees—full-time resident, $8,412; full-time non-resident, $18,786* ➤ *estimated additional expenses—$9,874 average (room, board, books, transportation, personal)* ➤ *merit-based scholarships available* ➤ *FAFSA due by March 15*

The College of Law offers a number of scholarships ranging from $900 to full tuition, and they are awarded to students who show the greatest promise in the study of law. Previous academic success is a primary consideration; the committee also considers other relevant factors. Complete Scholarship Application Form found in Application Booklet.

■ Career Services

The Office of Career Services works individually with students to help them decide which career choices are most attractive. Staff members arrange mock interviews with attorneys, assist with writing résumés and cover letters, and offer dozens of programs throughout the year. Faculty members counsel students on career goals, and attorneys regularly visit the college to discuss such topics as how to prepare for an interview or succeed as a summer associate.

Students participate in an active on-campus interviewing program and respond to requests for résumés from hundreds of employers nationwide. On average over the last five years, approximately 94.44 percent of our graduates known to be seeking employment accepted positions within six months of completing the J.D.

Applicant Group for the 1998-1999 Academic Year

University of Illinois College of Law
This grid includes only applicants who earned 120-180 LSAT scores under standard administrations.

LSAT Score	GPA																		
	3.75 +		3.50 - 3.74		3.25 - 3.49		3.00 - 3.24		2.75 - 2.99		2.50 - 2.74		2.25 - 2.49		2.00 - 2.24		Below 2.00		No GPA		Total	
	Apps	Adm	Apps	Adm	Apps	Adm	Apps	Adm	Apps	Adm	Apps	Adm	Apps	Adm	Apps	Adm	Apps	Adm	Apps	Adm	Apps	Adm
175-180	0	0	0	0	3	3	0	0	0	0	0	0	1	0	0	0	0	0	0	0	4	3
170-174	12	12	5	5	8	8	6	6	2	1	2	1	0	0	0	0	0	0	1	1	36	34
165-169	23	22	38	38	32	30	16	16	15	13	10	7	2	0	0	0	0	0	1	1	137	127
160-164	69	67	89	87	80	60	57	31	29	7	9	2	4	3	3	0	0	0	5	2	345	259
155-159	61	34	107	29	98	21	76	16	31	5	22	2	7	0	2	1	1	0	7	1	412	109
150-154	38	4	46	5	67	6	64	8	28	4	22	2	13	1	2	0	0	0	7	0	287	30
145-149	8	0	21	5	31	3	37	6	28	4	19	1	10	0	3	0	0	0	7	0	164	19
140-144	6	2	5	1	8	1	15	2	11	1	16	0	10	0	5	0	2	0	5	0	83	7
135-139	1	0	2	0	3	0	5	0	9	0	9	0	9	0	2	0	1	0	4	0	45	0
130-134	0	0	0	0	0	0	1	0	3	0	3	0	1	0	2	0	0	0	1	0	11	0
125-129	0	0	1	0	0	0	1	0	2	0	0	0	2	0	0	0	0	0	0	0	6	0
120-124	0	0	0	0	0	0	0	0	0	0	0	0	0	0	0	0	0	0	0	0	0	0
Total	218	141	314	170	330	132	278	85	158	35	112	15	59	4	19	1	4	0	38	5	1530	588

Apps = Number of Applicants
Adm = Number Admitted
Reflects 99% of the total applicant pool.
Note: This chart is to be used as a general guide only. Nonnumerical factors are strongly considered for all applicants.

Indiana University School of Law—Bloomington

211 S. Indiana Avenue
Admissions Office, Law Building, Room 230
Bloomington, IN 47405-1001

E-Mail: lawadmis@indiana.edu
URL: http://www.law.indiana.edu
Phone: 812.855.4765

■ Introduction

Founded in 1842, Indiana University School of Law—
Bloomington, is located on the beautifully wooded campus
of one of the nation's largest teaching and research universities. The presence of the university, including its world
famous School of Music, offers students cultural opportunities available in few urban areas, while retaining the
advantages of a small university town. The school is a
charter member of the AALS and is approved by the ABA.

■ Enrollment/Student Body

➡ *1,394 applicants*   ➡ *212 enrolled first-year class 1998*
➡ *594 admitted first-year class 1998*
➡ *full-time 25th/75th percentile GPA—3.00/3.60*
➡ *full-time 25th/75th percentile LSAT—155/163*
➡ *614 total full-time*   ➡ *8 total part-time*
➡ *16.2% minority*   ➡ *41% women*
➡ *43 states & foreign countries represented*
➡ *188 undergraduate schools represented*

■ Faculty

➡ *53 total*   ➡ *43 full-time*   ➡ *10 part-time or adjunct*
➡ *16 women*   ➡ *3 minority*

■ Library and Physical Facilities

➡ *610,000 volumes & equivalents*   ➡ *library hours: Mon.-
Wed., 7:30 A.M.-1:00 A.M.; Thurs.-Fri., 7:30 A.M.-MIDNIGHT;
Sat., 8:00 A.M.-10:00 P.M.; Sun., 9:00 A.M.-MIDNIGHT;
extended hours during exams*   ➡ *LEXIS*
➡ *WESTLAW*   ➡ *Internet*   ➡ *10 full-time librarians*
➡ *library seats 659*

With over 600,000 volumes, the Law Library is one of the 20
largest law libraries in the United States, and the largest in
the state of Indiana. The Law Library includes a first-rate
research collection in Anglo-American law as well as
outstanding holdings in international and foreign law. Law-
trained librarians give instruction in research techniques
and provide reference assistance. While continuing its
commitment to a high quality print collection, the Law
Library is a national leader in computer applications in legal
education. The records of the complete holdings of the Law
Library are accessible through its online catalog. A cluster
of three computer rooms provides the latest in computer
equipment, including a computer classroom. Additionally,
students can bring their own laptop computers and connect
to the university's network in all the conference rooms and
at many carrels. The school's award-winning Web site
provides both information about the law school and links
to legal information around the world.

■ Curriculum

➡ *86 credits required to graduate*   ➡ *136 courses available*
➡ *degrees and combined degrees available: J.D.; J.D./M.B.A.;
J.D./M.S.E.S.; J.D./M.L.S.; J.D./M.A. in Telecom.; J.D./M.P.A.-*
Pub. Aff.; J.D./M.P.A.-Pub. Acctg.; LL.M.; M.C.L.; S.J.D.
➡ *fall semesters start in Aug.*
➡ *range of first-year class size—26-100*

The curriculum does not emphasize the law of any state
and its many offerings include traditional courses as well
as specialized courses such as communications law, law
and biomedical advance, immigration law, international
business transactions, and environmental litigation. The
school also offers intensive training in litigation. Students
may also participate in clinics which enable them to deal
with client problems under close faculty supervision.

The Legal Education Opportunity Program (LEOP) is a
voluntary program designed to provide academic and
peer support to selected law students through a series of
voluntary workshops and classes. In addition, the School
offers a Peer Advisor Program which pairs upper-class
students with first-year students.

■ Joint-Degree Programs

Six formal joint J.D. and master's or doctoral degree programs are available with the School of Business, the
School of Public and Environmental Affairs, Department
of Telecommunications, and the School of Library and Information Science. Joint-degree programs in other
disciplines may be individually designed.

■ London Law Consortium

The School of Law participates in a consortium with seven
other law schools to offer a semester of study in London
during the spring. Classes are held at the Florida State
University London Study Center. Students are eligible to
participate during their second or third year in law school.

■ Accelerated/Summer Program

By starting law school in the summer session and attending
full summer sessions in the following two years, students
may complete degree requirements in 27 months. Students
who begin in the accelerated program are not required
to continue with the program. Students who do not
choose to begin their legal education in the accelerated
program may enroll in summer-session courses following
their first year.

■ Special Programs

The Center for the Study of Law and Society provides a
forum for those students and faculty across the Bloomington
campus interested in law-related research. Some of its
research projects include transnational disputing, the
role of courts, alternative dispute resolution, and the
regulation of markets.

■ Admission

➡ *Bachelor's degree required for admission*
➡ *application deadline—March 1 priority, rolling admission*
➡ *LSAT, LSDAS required*   ➡ *application fee—$35*

Generally, the quality and size of the applicant pool forces the Admissions Committee to rely heavily on the undergraduate grade-point average and the LSAT score. However, numerical indicators are not the only considerations used in evaluating applications. The committee considers the quality of the applicant's undergraduate institution, level and rigor of coursework, letters of recommendation (particularly from undergraduate or graduate faculty members), graduate work, employment during and after college, extracurricular activities, potential for service to the profession, educational diversity, and state of residence. Increasing the diversity of the student body, particularly with respect to minorities, is also important to the school.

■ Housing

Law students live both off campus and in graduate- or married-student campus housing. For information concerning campus housing contact Halls of Residence, 801 N. Jordan Ave., Bloomington, IN 47405-2107.

■ Student Activities

The *Indiana Law Journal* publishes articles by legal scholars, practitioners, jurists, and IU law students. Students edit the journal and publish it four times a year. Members are selected on the basis of academic achievement or through a writing competition. The *Federal Communications Law Journal* is the nation's oldest and largest communications law journal. A student-managed journal that publishes three times a year, the journal features articles of interest to those involved in federal communications law, telecommunications, intellectual property, and information policy. The *Indiana Journal of Global Legal Studies* is a multidisciplinary journal that specializes in international and comparative law articles. The editorial board consists of practitioners and faculty from the law, business, and public policy schools.

■ Expenses and Financial Aid

➡ *tuition & fees—resident, $6,717; nonresident, $17,229*
➡ *estimated additional expenses—$11,268 includes room & board, books, supplies, & personal expenses*
➡ *fellowships available: scholastic & need-based*
➡ *minority fellowship available* ➡ *financial aid available; separate application for fellowship; FAFSA for loan consideration*

■ Career Services

The Career Services Office actively assists with career planning and locating summer and permanent jobs. Typically, over 90 percent of each graduating class accepts employment within six months of graduation. Approximately one-half locate outside Indiana. Graduates are found in all 50 states.

Applicant Group for the 1998-1999 Academic Year

Indiana University School of Law—Bloomington
This grid includes only applicants who earned 120-180 LSAT scores under standard administrations.

LSAT Score	GPA																					
	3.75 +		3.50 - 3.74		3.25 - 3.49		3.00 - 3.24		2.75 - 2.99		2.50 - 2.74		2.25 - 2.49		2.00 - 2.24		Below 2.00		No GPA		Total	
	Apps	Adm	Apps	Adm	Apps	Adm	Apps	Adm	Apps	Adm	Apps	Adm	Apps	Adm	Apps	Adm	Apps	Adm	Apps	Adm	Apps	Adm
175-180	1	1	1	1	2	2	0	0	0	0	0	0	0	0	0	0	0	0	0	0	4	4
170-174	6	6	4	4	1	1	4	4	2	2	2	2	0	0	0	0	0	0	1	0	20	19
165-169	12	12	15	15	15	15	14	14	6	6	8	8	2	2	0	0	0	0	0	0	72	72
160-164	32	32	39	39	49	49	52	52	33	33	17	17	12	12	3	3	0	0	3	3	240	240
155-159	43	35	60	37	104	42	72	13	32	8	20	3	11	3	5	0	0	0	5	2	352	143
150-154	32	13	57	20	94	17	74	5	32	4	19	2	6	0	6	1	1	0	5	0	326	62
145-149	12	7	27	9	40	5	39	5	28	4	14	1	10	0	4	0	2	0	10	2	186	33
140-144	6	4	12	0	15	5	21	1	12	0	24	5	12	1	1	0	2	0	4	0	109	16
135-139	3	2	5	2	5	0	6	0	11	1	7	0	4	0	5	0	1	0	3	0	50	5
130-134	0	0	1	0	0	0	1	0	0	0	0	0	4	0	2	0	0	0	0	0	8	0
125-129	0	0	0	0	0	0	1	0	1	0	0	0	1	0	0	0	0	0	0	0	3	0
120-124	0	0	0	0	0	0	0	0	0	0	0	0	2	0	0	0	0	0	0	0	2	0
Total	147	112	221	127	325	136	284	94	157	58	111	38	64	18	26	4	6	0	31	7	1372	594

Apps = Number of Applicants
Adm = Number Admitted
Reflects 98% of the total applicant pool.

Indiana University School of Law—Indianapolis

735 W. New York Street
Indianapolis, IN 46202

E-Mail: khmiller@iupui.edu
URL: http://www.iulaw.indy.indiana.edu
Phone: 317.274.2459

■ Introduction

The law school is located on the Indianapolis campus of Indiana University and Purdue University. This location is also home to most of the professional schools of Indiana University including the Schools of Medicine, Dentistry, Nursing, and Social Work. The law school is just minutes away from the state's courts, legislature, and major law firms, giving students opportunities not only to observe the legal process in action, but also to participate in that process as law clerks, judicial interns, and legislative staff assistants. With approximately 800 students, the school is the largest in the state of Indiana and one of the few Big Ten law schools to offer the cultural, recreational, and professional advantages of an urban educational environment.

■ Enrollment/Student Body

➡ *1,009 applicants* ➡ *559 admitted* ➡ *288 enrolled first-year class 1998* ➡ *full-time 25th/75th percentile GPA—2.99/3.51* ➡ *part-time 25th/75th percentile GPA—2.85/3.49* ➡ *full-time 25th/75th percentile LSAT—150/156* ➡ *part-time 25th/75th percentile LSAT—149/157* ➡ *563 total full-time* ➡ *320 total part-time* ➡ *45% women* ➡ *35 states & 6 foreign countries represented* ➡ *178 undergraduate schools represented*

■ Faculty

➡ *67 total* ➡ *33 full-time* ➡ *34 part-time or adjunct* ➡ *13 women* ➡ *2 minority*

■ Library and Physical Facilities

➡ *492,000 volumes & equivalents* ➡ *library hours: Mon.-Thurs., 8:00 A.M.-MIDNIGHT; Fri., 8:00 A.M.-11:00 P.M.; Sat., 9:00 A.M.-7:00 P.M.* ➡ *LEXIS* ➡ *NEXIS* ➡ *WESTLAW* ➡ *8 full-time librarians* ➡ *library seats 412*

One of the largest in the nation, the library is a depository for the United States government and the United Nations publications. The library computer center features terminals from which students can conduct legal research.

■ Curriculum

➡ *Academic Support Program* ➡ *90 credits required to graduate, of the 90 hours, 37 are in prescribed courses* ➡ *112 courses available plus internships* ➡ *degrees available: J.D./M.B.A.; J.D./M.P.A.; J.D./M.H.A.* ➡ *semester, start in Aug.* ➡ *range of first-year class size varies with the class, some as few as 30, others 70-90*

■ Academic Support Programs

Students are offered assistance through the Dean's Tutorial Society and the Tutorial Study Group. Supervised by a tenured faculty member, the tutorial society is staffed by academically distinguished students who offer assistance in case briefing, exam preparation, and through individual tutoring. The Tutorial Study Group meets for two hours each week under the direction of a faculty member and assists students with their legal writing and analytical skills.

■ Special Summer Program

Summer admission is offered to a select group of applicants who can benefit from a class emphasizing writing and analytical skills. Applicants who have either an LSAT score or GPA that is outside of the median range of accepted students, persons who are returning to school after several years outside of the classroom, and students for whom English is a second language may be considered for the summer program. Summer admittees earn two credits toward their J.D. degree, and continuation in the fall is not contingent upon performance in the summer program. There is no special application form for summer admission. All applicants who are not presumptively admitted and whose file is completed by February 1 are considered for the summer program.

■ Clinical Experiences and Special Programs

The law school offers several clinical programs: The Civil Practice Clinic allows students the opportunity to represent clients in a variety of cases, including housing, dissolution of marriage, support, consumer, and administrative matters. In the Civil Practice Disability Clinic, students represent school-age children with special needs, as well as persons who are afflicted with the HIV virus, Alzheimer's disease, and AIDS. In the Criminal Defense Clinic, students represent clients in criminal cases involving a variety of misdemeanors or class D felony charges in the state of Indiana. Internships enable students to work with personnel in state agencies and state and federal judges.

The law school has a Center for Law and Health. The center provides an environment for the study of the critical issues relating to health care. The center interprets health care regulations and conducts research on law reform issues both nationally and locally. In addition, the law school has a center for State and Local Government and a program in Law and Education.

■ International Law

The law school offers several courses and seminars in the area of international law. Students can further cultivate their interest through participation in the professional journal, the *Indiana International and Comparative Law Review* and the International Law Society. Practical experience also can be gained through involvement in an internship in international law. The school also sponsors a month-long China Summer Program, which includes daily lectures in all major areas of Chinese law, and visits to local courts and institutions.

The law school also offers an opportunity for a month-long summer program in Lille, France in cooperation with the University of Lille II, which emphasizes legal study of the European Union.

The Program in International Human Rights Law has summer internships available in South Africa, Malaysia, India, Australia, Hong Kong, Switzerland, and Cambodia.

■ Admission

➡ *LSAT, LSDAS required*

The School of Law seeks to attain a culturally rich and diverse student body. To this end, admission decisions are based on a variety of factors. In addition to the LSAT and undergraduate GPA, the admissions committee considers the undergraduate institution attended and its distribution of grades, the undergraduate major and grade performance from year to year, extracurricular activities and work responsibilities while in school, postgraduate experience, and proven ability to overcome adversity. Letters of recommendation and a personal statement are also encouraged.

■ Student Activities

Students at the School of Law may participate in various activities, including the Student Bar Association, the Black Law Student Association, intramural and regional moot court, client counseling competitions, the student newspaper, legal fraternities, Women's Caucus, the *Indiana Law Review*, the *Indiana International and Comparative Law Review*, and the Dean's Tutorial Society. Students also serve as voting members on several faculty committees.

■ Expenses and Financial Aid

➡ *resident tuition & fees—full-time, $6,499.15; part-time, $4,193*
➡ *nonresident tuition & fees—full-time, $15,786.75; part-time, $10,185*

Financial aid is available. Scholarships are awarded on the basis of need and merit. Awards range from $1,000 to full tuition, regardless of residency status. While the law school does not grant fee waivers for applications, it will consider fee waivers for the LSAT.

■ Career Services and Bar Passage

The Career Services Office serves students interested in part-time, summer, and permanent employment. Services include, but are not limited to, inviting prospective employers to campus, staging mock interviews, a résumé review service, workshops, brown bag lunches with attorneys, judges and persons in alternative careers, and individual counseling sessions. The law school's graduates have an excellent record of achievement on the Indiana Bar Examination—better than a 91 percent passage rate since the early 1970s.

Applicant Group for the 1998-1999 Academic Year

Indiana University School of Law—Indianapolis
This grid includes only applicants who earned 120-180 LSAT scores under standard administrations.

LSAT Score	3.75 +		3.50 - 3.74		3.25 - 3.49		3.00 - 3.24		2.75 - 2.99		2.50 - 2.74		2.25 - 2.49		2.00 - 2.24		Below 2.00		No GPA		Total	
	Apps	Adm	Apps	Adm	Apps	Adm	Apps	Adm	Apps	Adm	Apps	Adm	Apps	Adm	Apps	Adm	Apps	Adm	Apps	Adm	Apps	Adm
175-180	0	0	0	0	0	0	0	0	0	0	0	0	0	0	0	0	0	0	0	0	0	0
170-174	0	0	0	0	0	0	2	2	0	0	1	1	0	0	0	0	0	0	0	0	3	3
165-169	3	3	2	2	7	7	3	3	2	2	1	1	0	0	0	0	0	0	1	1	19	19
160-164	5	5	9	8	9	9	11	11	9	9	5	5	8	7	4	1	0	0	2	2	62	57
155-159	17	17	25	24	49	48	40	40	33	28	17	12	8	2	2	0	1	0	6	4	198	175
150-154	23	22	37	33	74	66	53	42	40	20	33	6	16	3	12	4	0	0	3	0	291	196
145-149	10	8	26	17	32	15	29	9	41	10	30	5	10	0	8	1	3	0	8	1	197	66
140-144	5	3	12	5	18	3	31	6	20	4	29	4	19	1	13	1	2	0	8	4	157	31
135-139	2	1	7	3	7	1	8	1	7	1	3	1	7	0	7	0	1	0	2	0	51	8
130-134	0	0	0	0	0	0	2	0	3	0	2	0	4	2	1	0	1	0	0	0	13	2
125-129	0	0	0	0	0	0	1	0	0	0	1	0	0	0	1	0	0	0	0	0	3	0
120-124	0	0	0	0	0	0	0	0	0	0	0	0	0	0	0	0	0	0	0	0	0	0
Total	65	59	118	92	196	149	180	114	155	74	122	35	72	15	48	7	8	0	30	12	994	557

Apps = Number of Applicants
Adm = Number Admitted
Reflects 98% of the total applicant pool.

Inter American University School of Law

P.O. Box 70351
San Juan, PR 00936-8351

URL: http://www.inter.edu/derecho.html
Phone: 787.751.1912, exts. 2013, 2012

■ Introduction

The Inter American University School of Law is one of the
11 units of the Inter American University of Puerto Rico, a
private nonprofit educational corporation accredited by
the Middle States Association of Colleges and Secondary
Schools, the Puerto Rico Council of Higher Education,
and the Commonwealth of Puerto Rico Department of
Education. The School of Law is approved by the ABA
and is located in San Juan, the capital city of Puerto Rico.
Since its founding, the School of Law has successfully
strived to meet the needs of the legal profession in
particular, and Puerto Rico's society in general.

■ Enrollment/Student Body

➡ *1,058 applicants*   ➡ *331 admitted first-year class 1998*
➡ *full-time 25th/75th percentile GPA—2.82/3.25*
➡ *part-time 25th/75th percentile GPA—2.82/3.40*
➡ *full-time 25th/75th percentile LSAT—135/140*
➡ *part-time 25th/75th percentile LSAT—137/144*
➡ *226 enrolled first-year class 1998*   ➡ *376 total full-time*
➡ *352 total part-time*   ➡ *388 women*

The student body comes mainly from Puerto Rico,
although applicants from the mainland are encouraged
to apply.

■ Faculty

➡ *57 total*   ➡ *30 full-time*   ➡ *27 part-time or adjunct*
➡ *18 women*

■ Library and Physical Facilities

➡ *174,934 volumes & equivalents*   ➡ *100 library hours per
week: Mon.-Fri., 7:30 A.M.-11:00 P.M.; Sat.-Sun. & holidays,
9:00 A.M.-10:00 P.M.*   ➡ *LEXIS*   ➡ *NEXIS*
➡ *DIALOG*   ➡ *DOBIS/LUVEN*   ➡ *MICRO JURIS*
➡ *9 full-time librarians*   ➡ *library seats 329*

The Domingo Toledo Alamo Law School Library is a
fully developed learning resources and audiovisual center,
and contains two laboratories for computer-assisted legal
research and learning.
  Acquisitions, circulation, and cataloging functions are
fully automated, and an online union catalog contains the
resources of all the libraries of the university system.
  In January 1990, the library signed a collaboration
agreement to establish a consortium with the law school
library of the Catholic University of Puerto Rico and the
library of the Supreme Court of Puerto Rico, with the purpose of coordinating collection development and sharing
its resources through an automated bibliographic network,
interlibrary loans, and telecommunication services.

■ Curriculum

➡ *92 credits required to graduate*   ➡ *158 courses available
for J.D.*   ➡ *semesters, start in Aug. & Jan.*

The J.D. program covers three years in the day division
and four years in the evening division. Candidates must
complete a minimum of 92 credit hours with a GPA of not
less than 2.5 to qualify for graduation.
  Inter American University School of Law offers a three-
week preparation course to be taken during the summer
on a compulsory basis by students admitted to the school.
  Students who enter law school must be willing to make
a heavy commitment of time and energy. For its part, Inter
American University is willing to provide the best possible
professional educational experience through the careful
recruitment of a first-rate faculty, the development of a
progressive curriculum, and a willingness to create new
and exciting programs of clinical studies and research.

■ Admission

➡ *Bachelor's degree required*   ➡ *application deadline—
March 31*   ➡ *LSAT required*   ➡ *application fee—$63*

Proficiency in Spanish is essential in the program. Applicants must have a minimum grade index of 2.5, a medical
certificate for students 21 years or younger, a police department certificate of good conduct, and appear for a personal
interview, if required.
  Candidates are required to take the Prueba de Admision
para Estudios Graduados (PAEG), The Aptitude Test for
Graduate Education. Students should attain a 575 minimum
score on this test. Application forms and other relevant
information concerning the PAEG may be obtained from—
Educational Testing Service, G.P.O. Box 1271, San Juan,
PR 00936.

■ Housing

The university does not provide housing for law students.
However, the areas surrounding the School of Law contain
many private houses, apartments, and condominiums
for rent.

■ Student Activities

The Inter American School of Law Review is the official
publication of the School of Law. Leading articles are
prepared by academicians, student members of *Law Review*,
and practicing members of the profession. Its members
work under the supervision of an editorial board of four
students chosen on the basis of merit and dedication to
the *Review*, and an academic advisor who is a faculty
member appointed by the Dean.
  Student organizations include the Student Council, an
organization that represents the student body and participates in matters of administrative policy related to students'
interests. Council representatives serve on various faculty
committees, as well as the University Senate and the Board
of Trustees; the Law Student Division of the American Bar
Association; Phi Alpha Delta legal fraternity (composed
not only of law students of the school, but also of distinguished, honorary members who are Supreme Court

Justices, Federal District Court Judges, and other prominent attorneys); and the National Association of Law Students (which represents the three law schools of Puerto Rico and provides needed services to students, the legal profession, and the general community).

Guest speakers are invited to speak on topics of current concern in law and the social and behavioral sciences. The law review, *Revista Juridica de la Universidad Interamericana*, is written principally in Spanish by students, professors, and legal scholars on areas of current importance in the development of the law.

The Legal Aid Clinic Program of the Faculty is integrated with the Community Law Office through a combined effort of the U.S. Legal Service Corporation and Inter American University. Law students are provided with the opportunity to learn skills such as interviewing, negotiation and counseling, fact gathering and analysis, legal research and drafting, decision-making about alternative strategies, and preparation for trial and field practice. They also represent clients before administrative agencies and courts with the close supervision of the program's staff attorneys-professors, pursuant to rules of the Supreme Court of Puerto Rico. Students also gain practical experience by serving with Puerto Rico Legal Services, Inc.; San Juan Community Law Office, Inc.; Legal Aid Society of Puerto Rico; the district attorney's offices; and the Environmental Quality Board.

■ Expenses and Financial Aid

➡ *tuition & fees—full-time, $8,480; part-time, $6,360*
➡ *additional expenses (room & board, personal, books & supplies, transportation, & loan fees) full-time and part-time, $7,403*

➡ *scholarships available: State Student Incentive Grant Program, Legislature Educational Fund & merit (merit application due Aug. & Jan.)*
➡ *financial aid available; applications due—March 31*

The general university fee is $20 per semester. Students pay $125 to reserve a place in the class (after admission approval), $5 for the Law Review, and $10 per semester for student activities. There is a deferred-payment plan, and financial aid options include Federal Guaranteed Loan Program; Perkins Loan; Stafford; LAL; the Commonwealth Education Fund; the Students Incentive Grant program, and the College Work-Study Program. The university also has an Honor Scholarship program for law students based on academic accomplishment and financial need.

■ Career Services

The placement program's main purpose is to locate job opportunities for students and alumni, to orient students and alumni with regard to those job opportunities, and to advise prospective employees of placement services offered by the school.

The Dean of Students Office gives orientation and provides information concerning available graduate programs in Puerto Rico, the United States, and foreign countries. A collection of catalogues of law school graduate programs in the United States, Europe, and Canada is kept.

The Continuing Legal Education Program offers advanced courses and seminars concerning different fields of the law of interest to practicing lawyers as well as to the community in general.

Applicant Profile Not Available

University of Iowa College of Law

276 Boyd Law Building
Melrose at Byington Streets
Iowa City, IA 52242

E-Mail: law-admissions@uiowa.edu
URL: http://www.uiowa.edu/~lawcoll/
Phone: 319.335.9071

■ Introduction

The College of Law was founded in 1865 and is the oldest law school west of the Mississippi River. It has been continuously approved by the ABA and is a charter member of the AALS. Iowa's greatest strengths lie in its college-wide emphasis on writing skills, its international and comparative orientation, and its longstanding commitment to diversity. Located in Iowa City, a casual cosmopolitan community, which is home to 60,000 people from throughout the U.S. and some 90 foreign countries, Iowa City offers a rich cultural life, Big Ten athletic events, and is the home of the acclaimed Iowa Writer's Workshop.

■ Student Body

➥ *1,110 applicants* ➥ *522 admitted first-year class 1998*
➥ *229 enrolled first-year class 1998* ➥ *full-time 25th/75th percentile GPA—3.12/3.71* ➥ *full-time 25th/75th percentile LSAT—155/162* ➥ *654 total full-time* ➥ *18% minority*
➥ *39% women* ➥ *46 states & foreign countries represented*
➥ *193 undergraduate schools represented*

■ Faculty

➥ *56 total* ➥ *47 full-time* ➥ *9 part-time or adjunct*
➥ *12 women* ➥ *6 minority*

■ Library and Physical Facilities

➥ *909,842 volumes & equivalents* ➥ *library open 104 hours per week* ➥ *LEXIS* ➥ *NEXIS* ➥ *WESTLAW*
➥ *ILP* ➥ *12 full-time librarians* ➥ *library seats 672*
➥ *12 carrels for audio/video playback & microfilm reading/printing*
➥ *6 CD-ROM workstations with numerous databases*
➥ *41-station LAN* ➥ *381 individual study carrels*

The law building's central location on a bluff overlooking the Iowa River provides a professional enclave well suited to the college's intensive style of education, but with easy access to the academic, cultural, social, and recreational resources of the university.

■ Curriculum

➥ *Academic Support Program* ➥ *90 semester hours required to graduate* ➥ *190 courses available* ➥ *degrees available: J.D.; J.D./M.B.A.; J.D./M.A.; J.D./Ph.D., (joint-program students enrolled in law and 15 other departments)*
➥ *semesters, start in Aug.* ➥ *range of first-year class size—28-105* ➥ *accelerated program begins in mid-May*
➥ *graduate (LL.M.) program in International and Comparative Law*

■ Special Programs

Iowa is a leader among the nation's law schools in the development of a modern curriculum in which individual instruction in basic lawyer skills is integrated with the exploration of conceptual and institutional issues central to the legal process. The mainspring of this progressive curriculum is an ambitious writing program in which faculty-supervised writing exercises are provided in small classes each semester of a student's training. The lawyer-skills emphasis shifts from first-year concern with close analysis, research, precise expression, and advocacy to upper-class work on drafting, interviewing, counseling, negotiation, and litigation skills. The College of Law features a small-section program in the first year under which each student takes two courses in small sections of 30 or fewer. The first-year curriculum is required; thereafter, almost all courses are electives. The College of Law has a strong research orientation and students are encouraged to propose special projects in which they are interested.

■ Legal Clinic

Students who have completed the equivalent of three semesters (which may include a full summer session) toward their J.D. degrees (usually in excess of 37 credits) are eligible to participate in the College of Law's Legal Clinic Program. Students in the law school's in-house program work directly with faculty members on cases involving civil rights and liberties, statutory entitlements, criminal defense, immigration law, international human rights, consumer law, disability law, and general civil matters. Clinic interns participate fully in interviewing, fact investigation, negotiation, trials, and appellate proceedings.

■ International Law

The College of Law offers a strong program of study in international law. Over 50 percent of the faculty regularly teach or conduct research on international and comparative law subjects. In this era of accelerating global interdependence, virtually any lawyer may find herself or himself confronted by problems that require knowledge and understanding of international law and foreign legal systems. The study of international and comparative law provides unique insight into the nature of law and legal process and helps to establish the necessary theoretical foundations upon which superior lawyering skills depend.

■ Admission

➥ *Bachelor's degree from approved college or university required*
➥ *application deadline—March 1* ➥ *LSAT, LSDAS required*
➥ *application fee—$30* ➥ *foreign application fee—$50*

A faculty rule limits the college to no more than 30 percent nonresidents in the freshman class, so the resulting criteria for nonresidents are somewhat higher. Criteria other than the LSAT will be taken into account for applicants who demonstrate the inapplicability of the LSAT as a predictor of success for them. Included in this group are applicants from disadvantaged backgrounds as well as others. The College of Law strives to enroll a student body that reflects the diversity of a leading national law school.

The College's numbers plus policy, which looks beyond numerical indicators, utilizes a full file review to evaluate an applicant's potential contribution to classroom diversity through consideration of such factors as maturity, ability to overcome adversity, and family background.

This encompasses criteria such as growing up in a single parent household, coming from a family in which the parents did not attend college, and other life experiences that "promote beneficial educational pluralism."

■ Student Activities

Student-run cocurricular programs include the *Iowa Law Review*, the *Journal of Corporation Law*, the *Journal of Transnational Law and Contemporary Problems*, the *Iowa Journal of Gender, Race and Justice*, the Moot Court Board, Trial Advocacy, and Client Counseling. Other law student organizations are the Equal Justice Foundation, National Lawyers Guild, Iowa Student Bar Association, Iowa Society of International Law and Affairs, Environmental Law Society, Phi Delta Phi and Phi Alpha Delta (national law fraternities open to both men and women), the Black Law Students Association, the Chicano Hispanic Association for Legal Education, Asian American Law Student Association, Native American Law Student Association, The Outlaws (formerly known as the National Lesbian and Gay Law Association), Christian Law Students, Jewish Law Student Association, The Federalist Society, 21st Century Forum, and the Organization of Women Law Students and Staff.

■ Expenses and Financial Aid

➤ *tuition & fees—full-time resident, $6,510; nonresident, $16,426* ➤ *estimated additional expenses—$9,430 (books & supplies, room & board, personal, transportation)* ➤ *merit- & need-based scholarships available* ➤ *scholarships available for members of underrepresented groups* ➤ *financial aid available*

The Law Opportunity Fellowship program funds a limited number of three-year tuition and research assistant positions for members of traditionally underrepresented groups. Eligibility for financial aid is based on need established by completion of the Free Application for Federal Student Aid (FAFSA). FAFSA forms are available after January 1 and should be completed as soon as possible.

■ Career Services

Each year the Placement Office brings a variety of employers to campus from across the United States to conduct job interviews. During the 1996-1997 academic year (the most recent year for which we have complete statistics) just under 200 employers visited the campus. Of those graduates reporting, 96 percent were placed within six months of graduation. Nearly all of our second-year students (and a good number of our first-year students) seek and find law-related employment for the summer. While most work as clerks in law firms throughout the country, some work as prosecuting interns for county attorney's offices across the state and others serve as research assistants to faculty members here at the law school. The Placement Office actively encourages students' career growth by sponsoring weekly programs that explore the various employment options available, from small- and large-firm practice, judicial clerkships, and prosecution careers to the areas of public interest, government, and corporate legal counsel. The placement staff meets individually with all first-year students to make sure they get off to a good start.

Applicant Profile Not Available

The John Marshall Law School

315 South Plymouth Court
Chicago, IL 60604

E-Mail: admission@jmls.edu
URL: http://www.jmls.edu
Phone: 800.537.4280; 312.987.1406

■ Introduction

The John Marshall Law School is nationally respected for its intellectual property program, legal writing, and trial advocacy programs. Additionally, we offer a unique international program based on relationships with schools in Ireland, the Czech Republic, Lithuania, and China. Our long involvement in privacy issues means exciting courses in informatic law, and our fair housing and patent clinics provide unusual opportunities for students to put their learning to practice.

Located in the heart of Chicago's legal and financial district, The John Marshall Law School since 1899 has offered opportunities via a dynamic setting, stimulating classes, and an interactive faculty and staff to give our students a strong background in the law. JMLS is a member of AALS and is accredited by the ABA.

■ Enrollment/Student Body

➡ 1,659 applicants ➡ 246 admitted first-year class 1998
➡ full-time 25th/75th percentile GPA—2.64/3.20
➡ part-time 25th/75th percentile GPA—2.55/3.27
➡ full-time 25th/75th percentile LSAT—145/154
➡ part-time 25th/75th percentile LSAT—144/153
➡ 739 total full-time ➡ 428 total part-time
➡ 20% minority ➡ 44% women ➡ 35 states & foreign countries represented by first-year class ➡ 121 undergraduate schools represented by first-year class ➡ 38% out of state

■ Faculty

➡ 181 total ➡ 56 full-time ➡ 125 part-time or adjunct
➡ 46 women ➡ 17 minority

■ Library and Physical Facilities

➡ 362,000 volumes & equivalents ➡ 1,352 audiovisual tapes
➡ library hours: Mon.-Fri., 8:00 A.M.-11:00 P.M.; Sat.-Sun., 9:00 A.M.-9:00 P.M. ➡ LEXIS ➡ NEXIS ➡ WESTLAW
➡ CALI ➡ DIALOG ➡ 22.5 full-time staff
➡ library seats 624

The library's Center for Computerized Legal Instruction includes eight LEXIS terminals, eight WESTLAW terminals, and 17 PCs with CALI (Computer Assisted Legal Instruction) software. Seventeen PCs with WordPerfect software are available in two word processing centers. Special arrangements with LEXIS and WESTLAW permit students to access these services from their home computers.

■ Curriculum

➡ 90 semester hours required to graduate ➡ degrees available: J.D.; J.D./M.B.A.; LL.M.; J.D./M.P.A.; J.D./M.A.; J.D./LL.M. ➡ semesters, start in Aug. & Jan.
➡ range of first-year class size—10-60

The school has day and evening divisions, both requiring 90 semester hours to earn the J.D. degree. The instruction, course content, and scholastic requirements are identical in each division. Summer-term courses are also offered. A joint J.D./M.B.A. degree program in cooperation with Dominican University is also offered.

■ Special Programs

The Law School offers comprehensive professional skills training. Three interrelated programs comprise this training —the Legal Writing Program, the Center for Advocacy, and the Clinical Law Externship Program. The Legal Writing Program, formally known as Lawyering Skills, consists of a four-semester required sequence of courses taught in small sections, enabling faculty to work with students individually. The Center for Advocacy serves John Marshall students by providing a comprehensive and focused approach to attaining advocacy skills. The Clinical Law Externship Program places students with approved federal, state, and local agencies, law firms, the judiciary, and other legal organizations to gain practical experience outside the classroom.

The Center for Information Technology and Privacy Law was established in 1983 to carry on legal research and policy analysis regarding newly developing information and communications technology. Courses offered include Information Law and Policy, Computers and the Law, and Media Law and the Right of Privacy. Qualified students may apply after their first year of academic study to work for the center as research assistants. The Center for Intellectual Property Law offers extensive programs in this rapidly growing area of law. Courses in the J.D. program focus on patent and trade secrets; trademark, unfair competition, and copyright law; computer and franchising law; and entertainment law.

■ Admission

➡ B.A./B.S. required ➡ application deadline—March 1/Oct. 1, rolling admission ➡ LSAT, LSDAS required
➡ application fee—$50

Students are admitted in August and January. Applications for August entrance may be filed between October 1 and March 1; for January entrance, between May 1 and October 1. The LSAT score is evaluated together with the cumulative grade-point average and other relevant factors including difficulty of undergraduate program, postgraduate experience, leadership potential, business and professional background, and letters of recommendation. Applicants from minority and disadvantaged groups will be given special consideration in cases where their overall records are competitive with other applicants. Applicants with a B average overall and an LSAT score in the 60th percentile may be presumed to be within the range for favorable consideration. A Summer Conditional Program is offered to a limited number of candidates whose qualifications do not meet the usual standards, but whose discrepant predictors may be persuasive of probable success in law school. A special minority program, the Legal Education Access Program, is also offered during the fall semester. No separate application form is used for either of these programs.

■ Student Activities

The *John Marshall Law Review*, edited exclusively by students, publishes works on a broad range of current legal topics written by legal scholars, practitioners, and John Marshall law students. The *Journal of Computer and Information Law* is an international law review focusing on law and policy with regard to software, databases, and information networks. It is managed by a student editorial board. The John Marshall Moot Court Council and Executive Board are the student organizations that coordinate the various moot court activities, including participation in over 20 national and international competitions. The Law School sponsors a nationally respected moot court competition, the John Marshall National Moot Court Competition in Information Technology and Privacy. A new, national trial advocacy competition, cosponsored with the American Bar Association and focusing on criminal justice problems, is also held each spring at the Law School. Many fraternal, ethnic, and legal-interest organizations reflect the broad variety of interests among John Marshall students.

■ Expenses and Financial Aid

➡ *tuition & fees (1998-1999)—full-time, $19,500/yr.; part-time, $11,780*   ➡ *estimated additional expenses (1998-1999)—$13,778/yr. (books, $722; living expenses, $13,068)*

➡ *academic scholarships available*   ➡ *academic minority scholarships available*   ➡ *need-based financial aid available; JMLS financial aid form due on a rolling basis* ➡ *participates in federal Stafford and Access Group loan programs*

Tuition for the 1998-1999 academic year is $650 per semester hour. The regular day-division courseload is 15 hours and the regular evening-division courseload is 9-11 hours. Dean's scholarships and grants are awarded to entering students based upon academic achievement. Renewal of these awards is based on academic performance. All applicants for financial aid must file the Graduate and Professional School Financial Aid Service Free Application for Federal Student Aid (FAFSA) form.

■ Career Services

The Career Services Office assists students and graduates in obtaining permanent employment and helps students find summer and part-time positions. The office also offers a two-semester program in professional/personal development. There is an active on-campus interviewing program throughout the year and many employers who do not interview on campus do interview John Marshall students in their offices. Virtually all of the major Chicago law firms include John Marshall graduates among their associates and partners. In addition to private practice, John Marshall graduates can be found in government, corporate, and public interest sectors. Some of our most recent graduates have taken positions with the U.S. Department of Justice and other agencies of the federal government, in accounting firms, and as judicial clerks in federal courts of appeal, U.S. district courts, and state supreme and appellate courts.

Applicant Group for the 1998-1999 Academic Year

The John Marshall Law School
This grid includes only applicants who earned 120-180 LSAT scores under standard administrations.

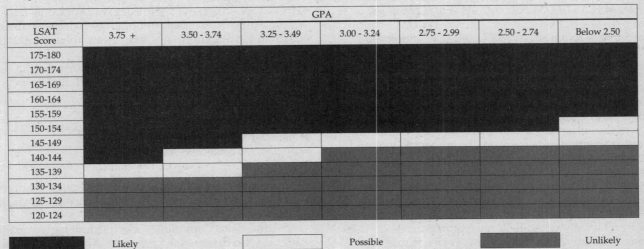

University of Kansas School of Law

205 Green Hall
Lawrence, KS 66045

E-Mail: admit@law.ukans.edu
URL: http://www.law.ukans.edu
Phone: 785.864.4378

■ Introduction

The University of Kansas School of Law was founded in 1891, replacing a Department of Law that had existed since 1878. The School of Law is located in Lawrence, Kansas, 40 miles west of Kansas City and 25 miles east of Topeka, the state capital. The school is a charter member of the AALS and is fully accredited by the ABA.

■ Enrollment/Student Body

➡ *758 applicants*   ➡ *417 admitted first-year class 1998*
➡ *171 enrolled first-year class 1998*   ➡ *full-time 25th/75th percentile GPA—3.16/3.68*   ➡ *full-time 25th/75th percentile LSAT—152/159*   ➡ *536 total full-time*   ➡ *10.8% minority*
➡ *41% women*   ➡ *40 states & foreign countries represented*
➡ *157 undergraduate schools represented*

The student body consists of 81 percent Kansas residents. The nonresidents come from all parts of the country.

■ Faculty

➡ *38 total*   ➡ *29 full-time*   ➡ *9 part-time or adjunct*
➡ *10 women*   ➡ *4 minority*

■ Library and Physical Facilities

➡ *325,000 volumes & equivalents*   ➡ *library hours: Mon.-Thurs., 7:30 A.M.-11:00 P.M.; Fri., 7:30 A.M.-10:00 P.M.; Sat., 9:00 A.M.-10:00 P.M.; Sun., 10:00 A.M.-11:00 P.M.*
➡ *LEXIS*   ➡ *NEXIS*   ➡ *WESTLAW*   ➡ *DIALOG*
➡ *3 full-time librarians*   ➡ *library seats 353*

The law library has ample reading areas and individual study carrels and maintains a microcomputer laboratory for student use.

■ Curriculum

➡ *Academic Support Program*   ➡ *90 credits required to graduate*   ➡ *131 courses available*   ➡ *degrees available: J.D.; J.D./M.B.A.; J.D./M.P.A.; J.D./M.A. in Economics; J.D./M.S. in Urban Planning; J.D./M.S.W.; J.D./M.S. in Health Services Administration; J.D./M.A. in Philosophy*
➡ *fall semester starts in Aug. & summer semester starts in May*   ➡ *range of first-year class size—20-100*

Six semesters of full-time study are required for graduation. Two summer sessions of five weeks each are available. Students may begin their law studies in either the summer session or the fall semester. Students who begin in the summer and are continuously enrolled in summer sessions and regular semesters can graduate in 26 months. The summer program is also open to students with advanced standing at an accredited law school other than the University of Kansas.

The first-year curriculum is prescribed. All first-year students take one course in a small section of about 20 students. Second- and third-year students are required to take courses in commercial law, constitutional law, evidence, and legal profession. Each student must also complete a faculty-supervised writing project in the second or third year. Upper-class students can choose from a wide variety of elective courses, workshops, and clinical programs. Many third-year courses offer intensive training in planning and supervising legal transactions and drafting legal documents.

■ Special Programs

The Legal Aid Clinic is operated for the benefit of the Douglas County Legal Aid Society. Third-year law students represent low-income clients in actual civil cases under the supervision of clinical faculty and practicing attorneys in Lawrence. Students in the Criminal Justice Clinic assist prosecutors in virtually all phases of the criminal process, including criminal trials. Participants in the Defender Project counsel and perform legal services for indigent inmates of the U.S. Penitentiary at Leavenworth, the Kansas State Penitentiary, and Kansas Correctional Institution at Lansing.

The Judicial Clerkship Clinic provides an opportunity for students to serve as part-time law clerks for judges in a district court, the Kansas Court of Appeals, or a federal court. The Legislative Clinic sends a number of students to work as legislative interns to Kansas state legislators.

The Elderlaw Clinic enables students to represent elderly individuals primarily in consumer, housing, and public benefit matters.

The Public Policy Clinic gives students practical experience in applying analytical policy methods to public policy issues.

The Media Law Clinic allows students the opportunity to prepare research reports on law, policy, regulation, and ethical issues relating to the rights and responsibilities of the communications media.

The Tribal Law and Government Center prepares a new generation of advocates for careers representing the legal interests of Indian nations and tribes. It provides a forum for research and scholarship on tribal legal and governance issues.

The school offers seven joint-degree programs. Each program allows a student to obtain two degrees in less time than it would normally take to earn them separately, generally four years.

The school offers two certificate programs: Media, Law, and Policy Certificate Program and the Tribal Lawyer Certificate Program.

■ Admission

➡ *Bachelor's degree required for admission*
➡ *application deadline—March 15*
➡ *LSAT, LSDAS required*   ➡ *application fee—$40*

The application deadline is March 15 for both the summer session and the fall semester. The school encourages students to apply by February 1.

The Admissions Committee seeks to admit highly qualified students with diverse backgrounds. Admission decisions are based on a variety of criteria. The committee considers and compares applicants' undergraduate coursework and grades, and LSAT scores as well as other factors, including race, ethnic background, employment or professional experience, undergraduate and graduate program of study, leadership in university and civic activities, unique individual qualities and achievements, and demonstrated ability to overcome cultural, financial, or other disadvantages. The committee also considers the applicant's state of residence; preference is given to Kansas residents. One letter of recommendation is required, two or three letters are encouraged. If possible, one letter should be from an academic reference. A personal statement is also required.

The School of Law is committed to the principle of providing access to the legal profession to men and women of all races, religions, ethnic backgrounds, and physical abilities. To that end, the School of Law engages in active recruitment of potential applicants with diverse backgrounds and characteristics, including those of minority race and ethnic background.

Admission decisions are made from January through April. After the class is filled, a waiting list is established. Each applicant offered admission pays a $100 deposit which is refunded to the student at enrollment.

■ Student Activities

The *Kansas Law Review*, published four times annually, is edited by third-year students. The *Kansas Journal of Law and Public Policy* is edited by third-year students and is published twice annually. The Moot Court Council operates all phases of the Appellate Advocacy program and also has responsibility for the Moot Court competition. The Student Bar Association is responsible for most student activities. There is an active chapter of Phi Alpha Delta legal fraternity, Black American Law Students Association, Hispanic American Law Students Association, Native American Law Student Association, Women-in-Law, Christian Legal Society, Jewish Law Students Association, Catholic Law Students, International Law Society, American Trial Lawyers Association, Federalist Society, National Lawyer's Guild, Sports and Entertainment Law Society, Environmental Law Society, J. Reuben Clark Law Society, and Order of the Coif.

■ Expenses and Financial Aid

➺ *tuition & fees—full-time resident, $5,729; nonresident, $12,820*
➺ *estimated additional expenses—$12,000 (books, room & board, transportation, & misc. expenses)* ➺ *merit-based scholarships available (generally first year only)*
➺ *minority scholarships available* ➺ *financial aid available: FAFSA Form—priority deadline March 1*

For more information: Office of Student Financial Aid, University of Kansas, 50 Strong Hall, Lawrence, KS 66045.

■ Career Services

The school has a full-time career services director and an aggressive placement program involving career counseling, a wide variety of workshops, and resource facilities for extensive legal and nontraditional job hunting research. Of the numerous placement opportunities available to law school graduates, law firms of all sizes attracted the highest percentage (42 percent) of those placed. By February 1, 1998, 94 percent of the 1997 class was employed. Students were placed in 15 states across the nation. The greatest percentage (75 percent) of those placed chose to remain in Kansas and the Kansas City metropolitan area.

Applicant Group for the 1998-1999 Academic Year

University of Kansas School of Law
This grid includes only applicants who earned 120-180 LSAT scores under standard administrations.

LSAT Score	3.75 +		3.50 - 3.74		3.25 - 3.49		3.00 - 3.24		2.75 - 2.99		2.50 - 2.74		2.25 - 2.49		2.00 - 2.24		Below 2.00		No GPA		Total	
	Apps	Adm	Apps	Adm	Apps	Adm	Apps	Adm	Apps	Adm	Apps	Adm	Apps	Adm	Apps	Adm	Apps	Adm	Apps	Adm	Apps	Adm
175-180	0	0	0	0	1	1	0	0	0	0	0	0	0	0	0	0	0	0	0	0	1	1
170-174	1	1	0	0	0	0	1	1	2	2	0	0	0	0	0	0	0	0	0	0	4	4
165-169	5	5	4	4	7	7	4	4	0	0	1	0	0	0	0	0	0	0	1	1	22	21
160-164	17	17	12	12	13	13	18	17	12	10	3	2	2	1	0	0	0	0	0	0	77	72
155-159	31	31	38	37	37	35	41	39	14	9	10	3	4	1	1	0	0	0	2	1	178	156
150-154	24	21	36	31	48	35	33	17	27	10	10	2	7	1	1	0	1	0	3	3	190	120
145-149	7	6	19	9	29	4	31	6	16	2	13	0	9	0	3	0	1	1	4	1	132	29
140-144	3	1	7	0	11	4	26	4	12	3	14	0	6	0	2	0	1	0	0	0	82	12
135-139	0	0	5	0	7	1	4	0	6	0	6	0	6	0	1	0	2	0	3	0	40	1
130-134	0	0	0	0	0	0	2	0	0	0	1	0	2	0	1	0	0	0	0	0	6	0
125-129	0	0	0	0	0	0	0	0	0	0	0	0	1	0	1	0	0	0	0	0	2	0
120-124	0	0	0	0	0	0	0	0	0	0	0	0	0	0	0	0	0	0	0	0	0	0
Total	88	82	121	93	153	100	160	88	89	36	58	7	37	3	10	0	5	1	13	6	734	416

Apps = Number of Applicants
Adm = Number Admitted
Reflects 99% of the total applicant pool.

University of Kentucky College of Law

Dean's Office, 209 Law Building
Lexington, KY 40506-0048

E-Mail: dbakert@pop.uky.edu
URL: http://www.uky.edu/Law
Phone: 606.257.7938 for catalogs; 606.257.1678 for other inquiries

■ Introduction

The University of Kentucky College of Law is a medium-sized, moderately priced, state-supported law school located on the main campus of the university in scenic Lexington, Kentucky, a city of approximately 250,000 in the center of the Bluegrass horse farm region. Founded in 1908, the college has been a member of the AALS since 1912 and has been approved by the ABA since 1925. The faculty has wide experience in law practice, research, teaching, and government service and provides a student-faculty ratio of 19 to 1. UK Law has a strong tradition of faculty knowing their students and of faculty concern about their students' progress and success. The curriculum offers broad training in the law and legal methods, drawing upon sources from all jurisdictions. Accordingly, UK Law graduates are prepared to practice in any of the 50 states.

■ Enrollment/Student Body

- ➼ *755 applicants*　➼ *145 enrolled first-year class 1998*
- ➼ *full-time 25th/75th percentile GPA—3.16/3.66*
- ➼ *full-time 25th/75th percentile LSAT—155/160*
- ➼ *418 total full-time (351 residents, 67 nonresidents)*
- ➼ *6% minority*　➼ *43% women*　➼ *25 states represented*
- ➼ *100 undergraduate schools represented*

■ Faculty

- ➼ *57 total*　➼ *27 full-time*　➼ *30 part-time or adjunct*
- ➼ *14 women*　➼ *3 minority*

■ Library and Physical Facilities

- ➼ *350,000 volumes & equivalents*　➼ *LEXIS*　➼ *NEXIS*
- ➼ *WESTLAW*　➼ *DIALOG*　➼ *library seats 392*

The college is self-contained in a contemporary brick and marble building that provides all facilities for a complete program of legal education, including a large courtroom. The law library is one of the largest in the southeast. Its newest additions are a 50-station computer laboratory for students and a study room with 42 carrels that are wired for laptop access to the Internet and all other law library computer research facilities.

■ Curriculum

- ➼ *Academic Support Program*　➼ *90 credits required to graduate*　➼ *98 courses available*　➼ *degrees available: J.D.; J.D./M.B.A.; J.D./M.P.A.*　➼ *range of first-year class size—10-70*

UK Law offers a full-time program only, designed to be completed over three academic years (six semesters). The first-year program is prescribed. In the second and third years, a full range of elective courses is offered in both traditional and newly developing legal fields. After the first year, the only specific requirements are that each student take a course in professional ethics and complete a seminar that involves substantial writing.

■ Special Programs

UK Law's Elder Law Clinic, located right across the street from the college, opened in 1997. Students are representing their clients in matters ranging from wills and trusts to guardianship hearings and bankruptcy petitions. The college's Mineral Law Center is now home to the Eastern Mineral Law Foundation, a center for research on environmental and natural resource issues. Second- and third-year students have the opportunity, in externships for credit, to serve as environmental mediators, clerks for state and federal judges, assistants to local prosecutors, and to represent federal prisoners. The college includes an Office of Continuing Legal Education that holds seminars for the bench and bar in which students can participate, including a national Equine Law seminar held the week of the Kentucky Derby. The college also hosts two lectureship series, bringing national figures to speak to its students and the community.

■ Student Activities

There are a variety of cocurricular activities at UK Law in which students may earn course credit. The *Kentucky Law Journal* is the 10th oldest American law review and is edited entirely by students, as is the *Journal of Natural Resources and Environmental Law*, which focuses on articles in the natural resources, mineral law, and environmental law areas. In 1997-98 the college fielded several moot court teams, which participated in both national and international competitions. The college's Trial Advocacy program teaches effective trial-level advocacy through student competition, and is coached by a faculty member with 10 years of trial experience. The UK trial advocacy team won the Sixth Circuit competition in 1998.

Chief among the college's 23 student groups is the Student Bar Association, which serves as the law student governing body and activities board. The SBA publishes a weekly student newspaper and sponsors regular student social events. UK's SBA was recognized by the ABA as one of the nation's best in 1992, 1994, 1995, and 1996.

The Student Public Interest Law Foundation, through grants and fundraising, sponsors 15-20 summer internships with public interest and public service organizations selected by the students who apply for SPILF grants. Other active student groups include the Women's Law Caucus, the Black Law Students Association, the International Law Society, the Environmental Law Society, the Equine Law Society, the Federalist Society, the American Civil Liberties Union, the Christian Legal Society, and three legal fraternities.

■ Admission

- ➼ *Bachelor's degree from accredited college or university required*
- ➼ *application deadline—March 1*　➼ *admission decisions begin in Nov. & continue weekly in the spring semester through April*　➼ *LSAT, LSDAS required*
- ➼ *application fee—$25*

Admission is considered and granted by the faculty admission committee, chaired by the Associate Dean for admission. Each file is reviewed completely before any action is taken and voted on by the full committee. While the candidate's undergraduate record and LSAT score are the primary indicators of potential for success in law school, all other factors presented are considered. The committee examines with particular care the candidate's grade-point average for the most recent semesters of undergraduate study, the nature and difficulty of coursework attempted, recommendations of faculty, the quality of the personal statement, work experience, community involvement, extracurricular activities, and postbaccalaureate experiences. Applicants are urged to read the full description of the admission process contained in the law school bulletin and to provide full information about their intellectual and nonacademic achievements. The February LSAT is the last examination accepted by the Admissions Committee for that year. Applicants are admitted for the fall term only.

■ Expenses and Financial Aid

➡ *1998-99 annual full-time tuition & fees—resident, $5,426; nonresident, $14,036* ➡ *estimated additional expenses—$9,800 annually* ➡ *merit scholarships available* ➡ *financial aid awards available* ➡ *FAFSA form due April 1 for Perkins loans & work-study; April 1 is priority deadline for other federal loans*

Scholarships for the first year of study are merit based and usually awarded to students whose credentials are exceptional. The largest and most prestigious are the Bert Combs Scholars, two of whom are chosen each year by an application and interview process, and the Ashland Inc. Legal Scholars, one of whom is chosen each year from among Kentucky residents by an application and interview process.

For all other first-year student scholarship awards, including the nonresident three-year tuition reduction

scholarships, no additional application is necessary. All students admitted to the college are considered automatically based upon their admission files. Just over one-third of the 1998 entering class received some form of scholarship award.

UK Law students are eligible for loan assistance through the Federal Direct Student Loan Program, as well as two national private loan programs specifically for law students. For more information, contact the UK's Student Financial Aid Office, 128 Funkhouser Building, University of Kentucky, Lexington, KY 40506-0054.

■ Career Services

UK Law students have the benefit of a large regional on-campus program and national placement through the college's participation in five off-campus interviewing conferences. UK is one of 12 member law schools, and the only Kentucky member, of the Southeastern Law Placement Consortium, the nation's oldest legal job fair, which attracts law firm, corporate, and government employers from across the country. UK also participates in the Southeastern Law Schools Minority Job Fair, the Mid-South Law Placement Consortium, the NAPIL Public Interest Job Fair, and the Patent Law Job Fair. Many local legal employers hire second- and third-year students to work part time during the school year and in the summers. The college's Career Planning Office, headed by a UK Law graduate who formerly practiced law, also uses alumni contacts and a unique computerized service to connect students with employment opportunities.

For the 1997 graduating class, the most recent for which full information is available at this writing, 97 percent were employed or in advanced-degree programs within nine months after graduation. A majority of UK Law graduates choose private practice, with 15-20 percent of each graduating class selected for state and federal judicial clerkships.

Applicant Group for the 1998-1999 Academic Year

University of Kentucky College of Law
Probability of admission to the University of Kentucky College of Law, based on admission decisions for the 1998 entering class.

LSAT Score	3.75 +	3.50 - 3.74	3.25 - 3.49	3.00 - 3.24	2.75 - 2.99	2.50 - 2.74	2.25 - 2.49	Below 2.25	GPA not scaled
165 +									
160-164									
155-159									
150-154									
145-149									
140-144									
Below 140									

Probable   Competitive   Possible   Unlikely

Lewis and Clark, Northwestern School of Law

10015 S.W. Terwilliger Blvd.
Portland, OR 97219

E-Mail: lawadmss@lclark.edu
URL: http://www.lclark.edu/LAW/
Phone: 503.768.6613

■ Introduction

Northwestern School of Law of Lewis and Clark College believes in a balanced approach to legal education that assures a solid theoretical foundation along with hands-on experience in practice. The campus is one of the most beautiful in the nation. Situated next to a state park, students are only a moment away from an extensive trail system used by joggers, walkers, and bicyclists.

■ Enrollment/Student Body

➡ *1,489 applicants* ➡ *956 admitted first-year class 1998*
➡ *237 enrolled first-year class 1998* ➡ *full-time 25th/75th percentile GPA—3.04/3.53* ➡ *part-time 25th/75th percentile GPA—2.94/3.59* ➡ *full-time 25th/75th percentile LSAT—155/162* ➡ *part-time 25th/75th percentile LSAT—153/161*
➡ *491 total full-time* ➡ *156 total part-time*
➡ *14% minority* ➡ *47% women*
➡ *approximately 43 states & foreign countries represented*
➡ *231 undergraduate schools represented*

The 630-680 students attending the law school represent a spectrum of ages, experiences, and priorities. Business executives, biologists interested in resources and environmental law, students of politics, musicians, school teachers—people from almost all of the analytical disciplines meet at the law school in a common pursuit. The atmosphere is one of mutual support during a time of academic challenge. Students and faculty can often be found discussing questions long after class has ended.

■ Faculty

➡ *98 total* ➡ *37 full-time* ➡ *61 part-time or adjunct*
➡ *29 women* ➡ *4 minority*

The full-time faculty were educated at the nation's most distinguished law schools. The faculty reflects a breadth of experience and interests that give depth and creative energy to their teaching. A number of faculty members have spent sabbaticals in recent years teaching in other countries; several have been Fulbright professors in such places as China, Greece, and Venezuela.

■ Library and Physical Facilities

➡ *443,000 volumes & equivalents* ➡ *library hours: Mon.-Thurs., 7:00 A.M.-MIDNIGHT; Fri., 7:00 A.M.-10:00 P.M.; Sat.-Sun., 9:00 A.M.-MIDNIGHT* ➡ *LEXIS* ➡ *NEXIS* ➡ *WESTLAW* ➡ *INFOTRAC, Internet access, PORTALS, CALI, OCLC, WLN, INNOVATIVE, ORBIS, FIRSTSEARCH, QL SYSTEM* ➡ *8 full-time librarians* ➡ *library seats 194*

The materials and staff of the Paul Boley Law Library, the largest law library in the state, the second largest in the northwest, well exceed the standards set by the Association of American Law Schools.

Our collection includes extensive materials in Environmental Law, Federal Legislative History, Tax, Commercial, Intellectual Property, and Legal History. It is also the only academic law library in the country to be a Patent and Trademark Depository Library. Supporting our collection is a sophisticated computer infrastructure of instruction labs and local area networks.

Framed by majestic fir trees, the campus is composed of contemporary buildings with both classrooms and a large state park within a moment's walk from the library. Traditional student needs and those of individuals with disabilities are met through a variety of facilities.

■ Curriculum

➡ *86 units/credits required to graduate*
➡ *142 courses available* ➡ *degrees available: J.D., LL.M. in Environmental & Natural Resources Law*
➡ *semester, start in Aug.* ➡ *range of first-year class size—27-78* ➡ *Academic Enhancement Program*

The law school confers both the J.D. degree and a specialized LL.M. in Environmental and Natural Resources Law. To earn a J.D., a student must take a prescribed first-year set of courses. In the upper division, students must take a seminar, constitutional law, and professionalism and fulfill two writing requirements. Students choose between a three-year day program and a four-year evening program. Admission criteria, faculty, academic opportunities, and graduation requirements are the same for each. After the first year, students may select courses in either division as their scheduling requirements suggest.

■ Specific Special Programs

Certificates: By taking a group of upper-division courses approved by the faculty, and by maintaining a superior grade-point average in those courses, a student may earn a certificate showing a concentration in environmental and natural resources law, in business law, or in tax law.

Clinical Opportunities, Externships, and Simulations: A student may create a schedule with precisely the mix of practical skills courses that fit that student's interests and needs. Students may choose among "live client" clinical experience, externships and internships, or simulation courses. The *legal clinic* located in downtown Portland offers students the opportunity to interview and counsel real clients, prepare documents, conduct trials, negotiate settlements, and prepare appeals. *Externships* place a student in full-time work for a semester or for a summer and require a substantial research paper and attendance at a special seminar. Externs are placed throughout the United States and in foreign countries. *Clinical internship seminars* and *environmental practicum* are similar to externships but the student works only part-time, attending other classes during the semester. Clinical internship seminars include placements with in-house counsel, government agencies, law firms, and public interest, nonprofit organizations. Other courses such as *moot courts, advanced advocacy, trial advocacy, criminal law seminar, estate planning seminar, corporate transactions seminar*, and *family mediation seminar* involve extensive simulations.

Admission

➡ *Bachelor's degree required*   ➡ *application deadline—*
March 15, rolling admission   ➡ *LSAT, LSDAS required*
➡ *application fee—$50*

Lewis and Clark affirmatively seeks a diverse student body. The Admission Committee makes a serious effort to consider each applicant as an individual. Factors such as college, program, length of time since the degree was obtained, experience, writing ability, and community activities are taken into consideration. Only those candidates with excellent professional promise are admitted. Academic attrition is low, averaging 2 to 4 percent.

Student Activities

These include two law reviews, *Environmental Law*, and *Journal of Small and Emerging Business Law*; numerous speakers on campus; an endowed program that brings an outstanding legal scholar to campus for lectures and seminars; and many student organizations reflecting the diverse make-up of the student body.

Expenses and Financial Aid

➡ *tuition & fees—full-time, $18,265; part-time, $13,697*
➡ *estimated additional expenses—$10,500 (books, rent, transportation, living expenses)*   ➡ *scholarships available*
➡ *financial aid available; FAFSA application due Feb. 1*

Approximately 40 percent of the students at Lewis and Clark receive some scholarship support during their law school career. The school annually awards Dean's Fellowships, Natural Resources Scholarships, and Public Interest Fellowships for up to $10,000 apiece. In addition, loan money and work-study funds are available. There is no separate application procedure for scholarship funds. Scholarship consideration is part of the admission process. Students are considered on the basis of undergraduate record, LSAT score, activities, and writing ability.

Students interested in loans need to apply for financial aid as early as possible and should not wait for an admission decision to begin the financial aid application.

Career Services

The Career Services Office maintains and runs an extraordinary number and variety of programs. In addition to posting clerk positions for law students and running the on-campus interviews, the office maintains an extensive mentoring program, runs dozens of panels each year on various areas of practice, and counsels individual students from the first year onward.

Applicant Group for the 1998-1999 Academic Year

Lewis and Clark, Northwestern School of Law
This grid includes only applicants who earned 120-180 LSAT scores under standard administrations.

LSAT Score	GPA																		
	3.75 +		3.50 - 3.74		3.25 - 3.49		3.00 - 3.24		2.75 - 2.99		2.50 - 2.74		2.25 - 2.49		Below 2.25		No GPA		Total
	Apps	Adm	Apps	Adm	Apps	Adm	Apps	Adm	Apps	Adm	Apps	Adm	Apps	Adm	Apps	Adm	Apps	Adm	Apps Adm
170-180	1	1	7	7	10	10	4	4	3	3	5	3	0	0	0	0	1	1	31 29
160-169	47	46	69	68	78	76	80	79	43	43	26	25	9	9	7	6	7	7	366 359
150-159	38	38	143	135	175	143	183	115	112	54	73	24	22	3	14	1	19	13	779 526
140-149	14	4	26	4	49	5	54	5	56	8	36	2	13	0	4	0	6	2	258 30
120-139	0	0	3	0	1	0	7	0	9	0	10	0	4	0	3	0	1	0	38 0
Total	100	89	248	214	313	234	328	203	223	108	150	54	48	12	28	7	34	23	1472 944

Apps = Number of Applicants
Adm = Number Admitted
Reflects 98% of the total applicant pool.

Louis D. Brandeis School of Law at the University of Louisville

E-Mail: glendajoyce@louisville.edu
URL: http://www.louisville.edu/brandeislaw/
Louisville, KY 40292
Phone: 502.852.6364

■ Introduction

Founded in 1846, the Louis D. Brandeis School of Law at the University of Louisville is Kentucky's oldest law school and America's fifth oldest in continuous operation. Heir to the legacy of Justice Louis D. Brandeis, the school is distinguished by a rich history, national outreach, and profound dedication to public service. It is an integral part of the University of Louisville, a public institution and major research center founded in 1798. The metropolitan area, with a population of approximately one million, combines a gracious ambience of southern hospitality with cultural, aesthetic, and recreational attractions that have put Louisville on the "Places Rated Almanac" top ten list of most livable American cities. Historic Churchill Downs, the acclaimed Kentucky Center for the Arts, the J.B. Speed Art Museum, and the university's outstanding sports facilities are near the law school or within a few minutes drive.

■ Enrollment/Student Body

➡ *839 completed applications* ➡ *294 admitted first-year class 1998* ➡ *121 enrolled first-year class 1998 (86 day division/35 evening division)* ➡ *full-time 25th/75th percentile GPA—2.85/3.57* ➡ *part-time 25th/75th percentile GPA—2.74/3.53* ➡ *full-time 25th/75th percentile LSAT—154/159* ➡ *part-time 25th/75th percentile LSAT—149/157* ➡ *313 total full-time* ➡ *105 total part-time* ➡ *10% minority* ➡ *40% women* ➡ *25 states & foreign countries represented* ➡ *over 100 undergraduate schools represented*

The Brandeis School of Law promotes equal opportunity, geographical and cultural diversity, and a positive learning environment for all students.

■ Faculty

➡ *40 total* ➡ *30 full-time* ➡ *10 part-time or adjunct* ➡ *11 women (including 4 adjunct faculty)* ➡ *4 professors of color*

Based on full-time equivalency standards, the law school has the extremely attractive faculty-student ratio of 1 to 13.9. Law faculty recently have acted as consultants to the Kentucky General Assembly, the U.S. Securities and Exchange Commission, the State Justice Institute, the U.S. Administrative Office of the Courts, and the constitutional drafting commissions of the former Soviet republics of Belarus and Kyrghystan.

■ Library and Physical Facilities

➡ *over 300,000 volumes & equivalents (over 5,000 serials)* ➡ *library hours: Mon.-Thurs., 8:00 A.M.-11:00 P.M.; Fri., 8:00 A.M.-6:00 P.M.; Sat., 9:00 A.M.-6:00 P.M.; Sun., 1:00 P.M.-11:00 P.M.* ➡ *LEXIS* ➡ *WESTLAW* ➡ *OCLC* ➡ *4 full-time librarians* ➡ *library seats 391*

The modern law library contains two computer rooms; OCLC, LEXIS, and WESTLAW services; CD-ROM; and interactive instructional workstations. The library also houses the Brandeis Rare Book Room and, by direction of Justice Brandeis, a collection of original Supreme Court briefs.

■ Curriculum

➡ *90 units/credits & public service component required for J.D. degree (3 years full-time, 4 years part-time)* ➡ *over 100 courses available; 6 externship programs; 13 moot court, mock trial, & other professional skill competitions; 2 law reviews; & independent studies* ➡ *degrees available: J.D. & two combined degrees (M.B.A./J.D. and J.D./M.Div.)* ➡ *semesters start in Aug. & Jan.; summer term in May* ➡ *range of first-year class size—35 to 45 (in three sections)*

The law school full-time day division and part-time evening division share the same curriculum, faculty, and academic standards. After basic courses in the first year, students take "core" courses in doctrinal subjects, advanced research and writing, and professional responsibility. Students also may choose among a rich variety of specialized and interdisciplinary electives. The Brandeis School of Law conducts an innovative summer enrichment program for selected, newly admitted students. A highly successful academic support office serves students throughout the year.

■ Special Programs

The Brandeis School of Law contains a Center for Environmental Policy, which promotes interdisciplinary studies. National speakers present the annual Brandeis Lecture, Harlan Lecture, Petrilli Family Law Seminar, and the Carl A. Warns Labor/Employment Law Institute. The school operates clinical internship programs in which upper-class students, with supervision, represent clients and appear in court. The school has active faculty and/or student international exchanges with law schools in England, France, Germany, Japan, Australia, Finland, Peoples Republic of China, and South Africa.

The M.B.A/J.D. program is offered jointly by the School of Law and the School of Business. The law school, in concert with the Louisville Presbyterian Theological Seminary, also offers a M. Div./J.D. dual degree.

■ Samuel L. Greenebaum Public Service Program

Reflecting the spirit of Justice Louis D. Brandeis, the School of Law was one of America's first five law schools to adopt public service as part of the prescribed course of study. Through this public service work, students develop lawyering skills, serve their communities, and establish professional values.

■ Admission

➡ *Baccalaureate degree (candidacy) required* ➡ *priority deadline—March 1* ➡ *application fee—$30*

➧ *LSAT, LSDAS required (letter of recommendation service preferred)*

Applicants are encouraged to submit their files no later than March 1. Later applications ordinarily will be considered only if space becomes available. In truly exceptional circumstances, the law school may consider applicants who have taken the LSAT in June immediately preceding the fall semester of expected enrollment. Admitted applicants with nontraditional credentials may be required to attend a four-week enrichment program prior to matriculation.

■ Expenses and Financial Aid

➧ *annual tuition & fees—full-time resident, $5,330; full-time nonresident, $13,940; part-time resident, $4,789; part-time nonresident, $12,559* ➧ *estimated additional expenses— $9,886 (includes full housing, board, books & supplies, transportation, & personal expenses)* ➧ *moderate cost housing available near university* ➧ *merit & need scholarships available* ➧ *financial aid over $500,000 in 1998-1999* ➧ *FAFSA required*

■ Publications and Professional Skills

The Brandeis School of Law publishes three student-edited periodicals with national or international circulation: the *Brandeis Law Journal* (the school's law review, published quarterly, including an international edition), the *Journal of Law and Education*, published jointly by the law schools of the University of Louisville and the University of South Carolina, and *The Brandeis Brief*, a magazine-style publication containing interdisciplinary articles in the Brandeis tradition and news of the law school.

The Brandeis School of Law emphasizes professional skill programs. It participates in 13 different national moot court competitions including an international moot court program, a negotiations competition sponsored by the ABA, a mock trial program sponsored by the ABA, and a mock trial program sponsored by the Association of Trial Lawyers of America. All students are thoroughly trained in legal writing and oral argument in their first year, and they may participate in the intraschool Pirtle-Washer Competition.

Honor students are recognized by membership in the law school's Brandeis Society. The Society awards the prestigious Brandeis Medal to America's outstanding lawyers and jurists. Recipients have included Supreme Court Justices Sandra Day O'Connor and Harry Blackman, Judge Leon Higginbotham, Senator Christopher Dodd, civil rights attorney Morris Dees, and Professor Charles Ogletree.

■ Career Opportunities

Graduates have enjoyed a higher Kentucky bar passage rate than the overall average, and they have been successful in other states as well. The most recent (1997) national survey of law graduates showed over 98 percent of the Brandeis law graduates had obtained law (or alternative use) employment within six months of graduation. Practical experience, through law clerking opportunities in the greater Louisville area, is abundant. Job listings, various databases, informational sessions, hard copy resources, job fairs, and individual counseling are available to assist students and alumni throughout the development of their professional careers.

Applicant Group for the 1998-1999 Academic Year

Louis D. Brandeis School of Law at the University of Louisville
Our faculty admission committee reads all files very carefully. Beyond numerical indicators (LSAT scores and grade-point averages), the committee looks for individuals with unique attributes who will bring diversity to the entering class and good character to the legal profession. No numerical quantifiers are automatic grounds for admission or denial.

LSAT Score	GPA								
	3.75 +	3.50 - 3.74	3.25 - 3.49	3.00 - 3.24	2.75 - 2.99	2.50 - 2.74	2.25 - 2.49	2.00 - 2.24	Below 2.00
175-180									
170-174									
165-169									
160-164									
155-159									
150-154									
145-149									
140-144									
135-139									
130-134									
125-129									
120-124									

■ Probable   ■ Competitive   □ Possible with special attributes

Louisiana State University, Paul M. Hebert Law Center

E-Mail: lwregs@unix1.sncc.lsu.edu
URL: http://www.lsu.edu/guests/lsulaw/
Baton Rouge, LA 70803
Phone: 225.388.8646

■ Introduction

The Louisiana State University Law Center was originally established as the Louisiana State University Law School in 1907, pursuant to an authorization contained in the university charter. In 1979, the Law Center was renamed the Paul M. Hebert Law Center of Louisiana State University. The Law Center holds membership in the AALS and is on the approved list of the ABA.

■ Enrollment/Student Body

➡ *965 applicants* ➡ *630 admitted first-year class 1998*
➡ *310 enrolled first-year class 1998* ➡ *full-time 25th/75th percentile GPA—3.10/3.53* ➡ *full-time 25th/75th percentile LSAT—147/156* ➡ *658 total full-time*
➡ *9% minority* ➡ *46% women*

■ Faculty

➡ *47 total* ➡ *33 full-time* ➡ *14 part-time or adjunct*
➡ *5 women* ➡ *2 minority*

■ Library and Physical Facilities

➡ *578,034 volumes & equivalents* ➡ *library hours: Mon.-Fri., 7:00 A.M.-11:00 P.M.; Sat., 9:00 A.M.-5:00 P.M.; Sun., NOON-11:00 P.M.* ➡ *LEXIS* ➡ *NEXIS*
➡ *WESTLAW* ➡ *Internet* ➡ *9 full-time librarians*
➡ *library seats 464*

The Law Center Building, completed in October 1969, adds extensive facilities to the original Law Center Building dedicated in 1938. This complex provides classroom areas, seminar rooms, discussion rooms, and meeting areas as well as a practice courtroom. Special offices for student research and student activities such as the *Louisiana Law Review*, Moot Court Board, and Student Bar Association are included in the facility. The law library, housed in the complex, provides one of the most complete collections of Roman and modern civil law reports and materials in the country. Library resources include reading rooms, discussion rooms, study carrels, personal computers, and audiovisual facilities. Students also have access to other campus facilities including the Student Health Center, residential housing, and the Sports Recreational Complex.

■ Curriculum

➡ *97 units required to graduate* ➡ *87 courses available*
➡ *degrees available: J.D.; J.D./M.P.A.; LL.M.; & M.C.L.*
➡ *semesters start in Aug.*
➡ *range of first-year class size—75-80*

First-year students have a prescribed curriculum and thereafter students may choose a wide variety of electives in addition to the core of civil law courses. An orientation program and library tour introduces the first-year class to the study of law. The Law Center's dedication to the study of both the civil and the common law prepares its graduates to practice in any state and in some foreign

countries. Students receive a unique insight with the comparison of the two legal systems. Seven semesters of resident study are required for the degree. In addition to its full-time law faculty, the LSU Law Center each semester invites a number of special lecturers, including practicing attorneys and legal scholars, to teach courses in which they are particularly distinguished. A number of faculty have law degrees from foreign countries. This serves to promote the study of international law and an understanding of the policies of foreign law.

■ Summer Session Abroad

The Law Center conducts a summer program in France at the University of Aix-Marseille III Law School, Aix-en-Provence, France. All classes of the six-week summer program are conducted in English and are designed to meet the requirements of the ABA and AALS.

■ Special Programs

A wide variety of courses affords each student the opportunity to participate in the preparation and trial of mock cases, both civil and criminal, and also to develop skill in legal negotiations and counseling. LSU sponsors and encourages student participation in national trial and appellate competitions throughout the school year.

In cooperation with the Center of Continuing Professional Development, the Law Center presents several seminars, institutes, and conferences for practicing lawyers.

The LSU Law Center admits candidates for the degrees of Master of Laws (LL.M.) and Master of Civil Law (M.C.L.). The program is highly selective and admits students with exceptional ability.

■ Admission

➡ *Bachelor's degree from accredited college or university required*
➡ *application deadline—Feb. 1, rolling admission, early applications preferred* ➡ *LSAT, LSDAS required*
➡ *application fee—$25*

No specific prelaw curriculum is required for admission. Applicants are chosen mainly on the basis of the combination of their GPA and LSAT score. Applicants are advised to take the LSAT in October or no later than December prior to the year in which they seek admission to the Law Center. When the LSAT is repeated, the highest score received is used. The Law Center admits students only in the fall and only for full-time study. There are no night courses offered. Written recommendations are not required, and personal interviews are not encouraged. Because of the great number of applicants, only a few nonresidents are accepted. Transfer applications may be made, but only students who originally would be admissible to the Law Center and have excellent law school records are accepted.

Louisiana State University assures equal opportunity for all qualified persons without regard to race, color, religion, sex, national origin, age, disability, marital status, or veteran's status in the admission to, participation in, or employment in the programs and activities that the university operates.

■ Student Activities

The *Louisiana Law Review* was established to encourage high-quality legal scholarship in the student body, to contribute to the development of the law by scholarly criticism and analysis, and to serve the bar of Louisiana by comments and discussion of current cases and legal problems. It is edited by a board of student editors with faculty cooperation.

The Louisiana Chapter of the Order of the Coif, a national honorary law fraternity, was established in the Law Center in 1942. Election to the Order of the Coif is recognized as the highest honor a law student may receive.

Since a large number of graduates of the Law Center go directly into practice, the LSU Law Center has an extensive Trial Advocacy Program in which moot court training is offered both for trial work and in appellate argument.

All students in the Law Center are eligible to join the Student Bar Association. This association promotes and coordinates student activities within the Law Center and serves as an instructional medium for postgraduate bar association activities.

■ Expenses and Financial Aid

➡ *tuition & fees—full-time/semester resident students, $1,976; full-time/semester nonresident students, $4,654*
➡ *estimated additional expenses—$350/semester books*
➡ *performance- & need-based scholarships available*
➡ *ACT form for need analysis due to financial aid office in March*

A number of loan funds are available to help deserving students who need financial assistance to continue their education. All such funds are subject to the policies and regulations authorized by the LSU Student Loan Fund Committee. Detailed information on all loan funds may be secured by contacting the Student Loan Section, LSU Office of Financial Aid and Scholarships, 202 Himes Hall, Baton Rouge, LA 70803.

■ Career Services

The Career Services Office of the Law Center provides job opportunities for students and graduates. It serves as a liaison between the numerous firms, businesses, and governmental agencies in providing on-campus interviews each year. This office offers a series of workshops and individual counseling to help meet the career needs of all students.

Applicant Group for the 1998-1999 Academic Year

Louisiana State University, Paul M. Hebert Law Center
This grid includes only applicants who earned 120-180 LSAT scores under standard administrations.

LSAT Score	GPA																					
	3.75 +		3.50 - 3.74		3.25 - 3.49		3.00 - 3.24		2.75 - 2.99		2.50 - 2.74		2.25 - 2.49		2.00 - 2.24		Below 2.00		No GPA		Total	
	Apps	Adm	Apps	Adm	Apps	Adm	Apps	Adm	Apps	Adm	Apps	Adm	Apps	Adm	Apps	Adm	Apps	Adm	Apps	Adm	Apps	Adm
175-180	0	0	0	0	1	1	0	0	0	0	0	0	1	1	0	0	0	0	0	0	2	2
170-174	1	1	0	0	1	1	0	0	0	0	0	0	0	0	0	0	0	0	0	0	2	2
165-169	7	7	3	3	1	1	3	3	0	0	1	1	1	1	0	0	0	0	0	0	16	16
160-164	15	15	15	15	13	13	7	7	10	9	6	5	2	1	0	0	0	0	0	0	68	65
155-159	20	19	16	15	41	38	48	47	30	28	15	10	8	4	1	0	1	0	0	0	180	161
150-154	21	21	36	35	63	61	56	50	44	24	24	5	10	1	4	0	0	0	4	0	262	197
145-149	9	9	26	26	63	61	47	32	42	4	20	2	12	1	8	0	1	0	3	0	231	135
140-144	2	1	17	13	29	15	30	10	28	2	17	0	11	0	2	0	0	0	4	1	140	42
135-139	3	2	6	5	3	1	10	3	7	1	9	0	8	1	2	0	0	0	2	0	50	13
130-134	1	1	0	0	1	0	2	0	1	0	3	0	2	0	2	0	0	0	3	0	15	1
125-129	0	0	0	0	0	0	0	0	1	0	0	0	0	0	0	0	0	0	0	0	1	0
120-124	0	0	0	0	0	0	0	0	0	0	0	0	0	0	0	0	0	0	0	0	0	0
Total	79	76	119	112	216	192	203	152	163	68	95	23	55	10	19	0	2	0	16	1	967	634

Apps = Number of Applicants
Adm = Number Admitted
Reflects 98% of the total applicant pool.

Loyola University Chicago School of Law

One East Pearson Street
Chicago, IL 60611

E-Mail: law-admissions@luc.edu
URL: http://www.luc.edu/schools/law/
Phone: 312.915.7170, 1.800.545.5744

■ Introduction

Loyola University Chicago is the second largest private institution of higher learning in Illinois. The School of Law is located on the Water Tower campus of the university, a few blocks north of the Chicago Loop. This campus adjoins Michigan Avenue at the historical Water Tower, a Chicago landmark, in approximately the center of the renowned "Magnificent Mile," a commercial center over which the John Hancock Center towers. This location provides ready access to the state and federal courts and to the offices of most other institutions of federal, state, and local government as well as the cultural centers of Chicago. The school is a member of the AALS and is approved by the ABA.

■ Enrollment/Student Body

➡ *2,231 applicants* ➡ *861 admitted first-year class 1998*
➡ *241 enrolled first-year class 1998* ➡ *full-time 25th/75th percentile GPA—3.06/3.56* ➡ *part-time 25th/75th percentile GPA—2.78/3.34* ➡ *full-time 25th/75th percentile LSAT— 155/160* ➡ *part-time 25th/75th percentile LSAT—150/156*
➡ *725 total J.D. students* ➡ *518 total full-time J.D. students*
➡ *207 total part-time J.D. students*
➡ *21.2% minority J.D. students* ➡ *53% women J.D. students*
➡ *40 states & 23 foreign countries represented in the student body*
➡ *119 undergraduate schools represented in the student body*

■ Faculty

➡ *139 total faculty members* ➡ *36 full-time*
➡ *103 part-time or adjunct* ➡ *57 women* ➡ *6 minority*

■ Library and Physical Facilities

➡ *over 346,663 volumes & equivalents* ➡ *library hours (including weekends & evenings): 99 hours/week*
➡ *LEXIS* ➡ *NEXIS* ➡ *WESTLAW*
➡ *7 full-time librarians* ➡ *library seats 370*

■ Curriculum

➡ *Academic Support Program* ➡ *86 units/credits required to graduate* ➡ *101 courses available* ➡ *degrees available: J.D.; LL.M.; M.J.; S.J.D.; D.Law; J.D./M.B.A.; J.D./M.S.W.; J.D./M.A.; J.D./H.R.I.R.* ➡ *semesters, start in Aug.*
➡ *range of first-year class size—60-75*
➡ *first-year legal writing sections of 15 maximum*

■ Foreign Study Programs

Since 1983 the School of Law has offered a program of international and comparative law courses at the Rome Center for Liberal Arts, the university's campus in Rome, Italy. Each summer, for approximately five weeks, law students from the United States and elsewhere can take one or more of the courses offered in Rome by members of the full-time Loyola law faculty.

In 1997, the law school added a program in Strasbourg at the Internation Human Rights in the Council of Europe and at NATO and the European Union in Brussels, Belgium. Coursework is completed through Loyola's summer program in Nottingham, England.

In January 1989, Loyola inaugurated its London Advocacy Program in which students travel to London for approximately 15 days to become immersed in the world of the British barrister.

■ Dual-Degree Programs

The School of Law has multi-degree programs with Loyola's School of Social Work, the Graduate Program of the Department of Political Science, the Graduate School of Business, and the Institute of Human Resources and Industrial Relations. The multi-degree programs are structured to allow completion after four years.

■ ChildLaw Center

The Loyola ChildLaw Center was created in 1993 to prepare law students to represent abused and neglected children. The center is the first of its kind at any American law school; was the recipient of the National Association of Counsel for Children 1996 Outstanding Legal Advocacy Award; and draws on the full resources of Loyola University, including the schools of medicine, social work, and education. The scope of the program has grown to include an LL.M. degree and a master's degree program for nonlawyers.

Annually eight fellows are selected from the entering law class. Each fellow receives financial support. At the conclusion of the three-year J.D. program, students are trained thoroughly to serve as skilled litigators and advocates for children.

■ Institute for Health Law

The Institute for Health Law was created in 1984, in recognition of the need for an academic forum to study the field of health law and to act as a vehicle to foster dialogue between the law and the health sciences. Through the Institute, the law school offers an S.J.D. in Health Law and Policy, and an LL.M. in health law. In addition, it offers the first Master of Jurisprudence (M.J.) in health law and Doctor of Law (D.Law) in Health Law and Policy, providing health care professionals with an intensive overview in health law. More than two dozen health law classes are offered in the law school.

■ Corporate Law Center

The Corporate Law Center was created in 1996 to further enhance Loyola's corporate law curriculum by offering more specialized and practical skills classes to its students. The center offers corporate externships for law students; an international corporate law program for foreign lawyers; and sponsors continuing education programs for both corporate attorneys and employees.

■ Institute for Consumer Antitrust Studies

The Institute for Consumer Antitrust Studies is an independent, academically based institute designed to explore the impact of antitrust and consumer law enforcement on the individual consumer and the general public. The institute was founded by a grant from the United States District Court for the Northern District of Illinois, and is supported by Loyola University and private donors.

▪ Admission

➤ B.A. degree required   ➤ application deadline—April 1
➤ rolling admission, early application preferred
➤ early decision deadline—Jan. 15
➤ LSAT, LSDAS required   ➤ application fee—$45

Factors other than LSAT scores and college grades are considered. Such factors include work experience, personal goals, specialized education, and other evidence of ability to contribute invaluable insight to law classes.

▪ Cocurricular Activities

Students are encouraged to participate in cocurricular activities, especially after completion of the first year. There are nine student and faculty edited publications at Loyola. The *Loyola Law Journal* is a quarterly professional journal edited by students who are selected on a competitive basis. Articles, comments, and notes on both state and federal developments in law are published. *The Loyola Consumer Law Review* is devoted to legal analyses of current issues affecting consumers. Students compete in approximately 18 interschool and intraschool moot court and mock trial competitions. All students are members of the Loyola Student Bar Association, the principal instrument of student government. There are over 25

student organizations, including a law fraternity (Phi Alpha Delta), groups devoted to particular areas of legal practice, and ethnic groups.

▪ Expenses and Financial Aid

➤ full-time tuition & fees—$22,000   ➤ part-time tuition & fees—$16,500   ➤ estimated additional expenses— $12,500 (books, rent, food, clothing, & transportation)
➤ scholarships available: average $4,000, academic, public interest, ethnic, Law Journal, & Consumer Law Review
➤ minority scholarships available: black & Hispanic
➤ financial aid available   ➤ FAFSA required, priority deadline March 1

▪ Career Services

The Career Services Office assists students and alumni with career planning and employment selection.

A year-round on-campus employer interview and recruitment program provides employment opportunities for students. In addition, there is daily posting of employment opportunities for legal and nonlegal positions.

Seminars by practicing attorneys and alumni; résumé preparation, review, and critique; interviewing techniques and strategies; individual counseling sessions; and job-search strategies are just some of the many programs for students and alumni administered by the Career Services Office.

The School of Law is a member of the National Association for Law Placement (NALP) and participates in research projects applicable to law students and graduates such as the annual survey of graduates concerning their employment choices and salaries.

Applicant Group for the 1998-1999 Academic Year

Loyola University Chicago School of Law
This grid includes only applicants who earned 120-180 LSAT scores under standard administrations.

LSAT Score	GPA																						
	3.75 +		3.50 - 3.74		3.25 - 3.49		3.00 - 3.24		2.75 - 2.99		2.50 - 2.74		2.25 - 2.49		2.00 - 2.24		Below 2.00		No GPA		Total	
	Apps	Adm	Apps	Adm	Apps	Adm	Apps	Adm	Apps	Adm	Apps	Adm	Apps	Adm	Apps	Adm	Apps	Adm	Apps	Adm	Apps	Adm
175-180	0	0	0	0	0	0	0	0	0	0	0	0	0	0	0	0	0	0	0	0	0	0
170-174	3	3	5	5	1	1	2	2	3	3	1	1	0	0	0	0	0	0	1	1	16	16
165-169	8	7	10	10	21	21	12	12	16	15	9	9	2	2	0	0	0	0	1	0	79	76
160-164	36	36	47	47	67	66	52	51	43	40	16	12	3	3	6	4	1	0	2	2	273	261
155-159	50	42	107	93	146	120	120	78	88	49	29	12	21	7	10	1	2	0	4	4	577	406
150-154	40	25	88	30	117	39	140	37	98	17	60	15	23	2	8	1	3	0	5	2	582	168
145-149	7	3	43	9	68	12	95	13	82	5	47	1	29	0	5	1	6	0	5	1	387	45
140-144	11	2	13	2	27	0	47	1	37	4	34	1	24	1	8	0	2	0	5	1	208	12
135-139	2	0	7	0	9	0	15	0	15	0	12	0	18	0	7	0	3	0	7	1	95	1
130-134	0	0	1	0	1	0	4	0	6	0	5	0	5	0	1	0	0	0	0	0	23	0
125-129	0	0	0	0	1	0	1	0	0	0	1	0	1	0	2	0	1	0	0	0	7	0
120-124	0	0	0	0	0	0	0	0	0	0	0	0	1	0	0	0	0	0	0	0	1	0
Total	157	118	321	196	458	259	488	194	388	133	214	51	127	15	47	7	18	0	30	12	2248	985

Apps = Number of Applicants
Adm = Number Admitted
Reflects 99% of the total applicant pool.

Loyola Law School, Los Angeles, Loyola Marymount University

919 S. Albany Street
Los Angeles, CA 90015

E-Mail: admissions@lls.edu
URL: http://www.lls.edu
Phone: 213.736.1180

■ Introduction

Loyola Law School, established in 1920, is one of the oldest law schools in Southern California. The Law School has strong ties with the city of Los Angeles, one of the world's most important legal, political, and financial centers. Loyola is a member of the Order of the Coif and provides the highest standards of education and professional development in the context of the university's deeply held ethical and moral values. Recognized for the teaching excellence of its faculty, Loyola offers a comprehensive academic program with the opportunity for both in-depth scholarly development and intensive preparation for the practice of law.

■ Enrollment/Student Body

➥ *3,105 applicants* ➥ *1,201 admitted first-year class 1998*
➥ *453 enrolled first-year class 1998* ➥ *full-time 25th/75th percentile GPA—3.03/3.48* ➥ *part-time 25th/75th percentile GPA—3.00/3.46* ➥ *full-time 25th/75th percentile LSAT—154/160* ➥ *part-time 25th/75th percentile LSAT—151/158*
➥ *968 total full-time* ➥ *375 total part-time*
➥ *41.7% minority* ➥ *47% women*
➥ *approximately 40 states & foreign countries represented*
➥ *over 100 undergraduate schools represented*

■ Library and Physical Facilities

➥ *475,000 volumes & equivalents* ➥ *library hours: Mon.-Thurs., 7:00 A.M.-MIDNIGHT; Fri., 7:00 A.M.-8:30 P.M.; Sat., 9:00 A.M.-8:30 P.M.; Sun., 9:00 A.M.-MIDNIGHT; Extended hours during reading & exam periods*
➥ *WESTLAW* ➥ *LEXIS-NEXIS* ➥ *DIALOG*
➥ *C.CALI* ➥ *13 full-time librarians* ➥ *library seats 683*

Loyola's modern and dynamic campus was designed by the internationally renowned architect Frank Gehry. Encompassing an entire city block, the Law School occupies eight buildings, including a new parking structure, classrooms, courtrooms, advanced audiovisual and computer centers, dining facilities, and offices. The "academical village" design with its many courtyards, plazas, rooftop terraces, and grassy knolls, has become the focal point for outdoor group study, social activities, and various participation sports. The William M. Rains Law Library features large reading areas, open stacks, individual study carrels, group-study areas, and extensive online and database resources. Large computer research and word processing centers equipped with personal computers and laser printers are designated solely for student use. With one of the largest budgets in the nation and an aggressive schedule for expansion, Loyola is committed to maintaining one of the country's finest law libraries. Major renovation and expansion of the William M. Rains Law Library is planned.

■ Faculty

➥ *148 total* ➥ *64 full-time* ➥ *84 part-time or adjunct*
➥ *63 women* ➥ *21 minority*

■ Curriculum

Loyola's curriculum is designed to provide the knowledge and skills that will enable students to become excellent practicing lawyers. The curriculum integrates traditional instruction in legal doctrine and theory with a special commitment to innovative skills education. The first-year curriculum includes a rigorous grounding in basic subjects and includes an intensive course in legal writing, taught by the full-time faculty. The required upper-division curriculum includes Ethics, Counseling, and Negotiation, in which simulated negotiation and counseling exercises provide students with an opportunity to apply the principles of legal ethics in a practical context.

Because of its large faculty, the Law School has a wide variety of course offerings, ranging from comprehensive offerings in the traditional subjects to a wide variety of advanced courses in many areas, including environmental law, entertainment law, international law, and the protection of civil and constitutional rights.

The 87-unit course of study for the J.D. can be completed in three years by full-time day students, and in four years by part-time evening students. The day and evening programs have identical admission standards and academic requirements.

■ Special Programs

Loyola's extensive externship program offers students an opportunity to explore the nature of the attorney-client relationship, experience the operation of legal institutions, and, particularly, to refine and enhance lawyering skills. In addition to an extensive program of externship placements in courts, government, and legal service agencies throughout the region, the Law School supports an on-campus clinic, the Western Center for Disability Rights, which is nationally recognized for excellence in the representation of disabled persons.

The Law School offers a summer program in Central America that enables students to take courses in Costa Rica on international environmental law and the protection of human rights. The Central American program includes a variety of study trips to neighboring countries.

■ Admission

➥ *Baccalaureate degree required* ➥ *application deadline—day, Feb. 1; evening, April 15* ➥ *LSAT, LSDAS required*
➥ *application fee—$50*

The Law School is nonsectarian and is committed to maintaining the diversity of its student population. Members of all religious, ethnic, and cultural groups are actively recruited and encouraged to apply. All applications are reviewed in their entirety and many factors, both academic and nonacademic, are considered. Applicants are encouraged to provide information about extracurricular activities and awards, educational history, cultural background, and other life experiences. Applicants are strongly urged to take the LSAT no later than the December administration. At least one academic letter of evaluation is recommended. Decisions are made on a rolling basis.

■ Student Activities

Three journals are published by Loyola students: the *Loyola of Los Angeles Law Review*; the *International and Comparative Law Journal*; and the *Entertainment Law Journal*. Membership on intramural and intermural moot court and trial advocacy teams is highly sought. Students can participate in student bar associations and the monthly newspaper, as well as in a number of student organizations including the Black Law Students Association, Asian-Pacific American Law Students Association, La Raza de Loyola, Christian Legal Society, Jewish Law Students Association, Lesbian and Gay Law Union, St. Thomas More Legal Honor Society, Phi Alpha Delta Professional Legal Fraternity, Phi Delta Phi Honor Fraternity, the Women's Law Association, Native American Law Student Association, and the Middle Eastern Law Student Association.

■ Expenses and Financial Aid

➡ *tuition & fees—full-time, $21,674; part-time, $14,526*
➡ *scholarships available*
➡ *financial aid available; FAFSA forms due March 2*

Loyola offers a number of full- and partial-tuition scholarships to entering students based on academic achievement.

Additional scholarship funds are set aside for continuing students who are in approximately the top 10 percent of their class at the end of the first year. Applicants should complete the FAFSA by March 2.

■ Career Services

The Office of Career Services provides a professional staff to counsel students and graduates and to assist them in job searches in a variety of ways. Many major national and regional firms recruited in the On-Campus Interviewing Program in 1998, and students and graduates are employed by the nation's most prestigious private and public legal institutions.

■ Alumni

Loyola Law School has graduated more than 10,000 alumni since its founding. Many of these graduates play significant roles in major national and international law firms, government offices, public interest agencies, the entertainment industry, and the judiciary both in California and throughout the United States.

Some of Loyola's prominent alumni include Bob Miller '71, Governor of Nevada; Mary Orozco '61, first Latina member of the California Bar; Johnnie Cochran '62, criminal defense attorney; Deidre Hill '85, first female African American president of the Los Angeles Police Commission; Robert Shapiro '68, defense attorney.

Applicant Group for the 1998-1999 Academic Year

Loyola Law School, Los Angeles, Loyola Marymount University
This grid includes only applicants who earned 120-180 LSAT scores under standard administrations.

GPA	120-142		143-148		149-153		154-157		158-162		163-169		170-180		Total	
	Apps	Adm	Apps	Adm	Apps	Adm	Apps	Adm	Apps	Adm	Apps	Adm	Apps	Adm	Apps	Adm
3.75 & above	3	0	16	2	38	11	43	37	51	49	18	17	3	3	172	119
3.74-3.50	17	0	52	6	95	29	73	55	102	99	42	40	5	5	386	234
3.49-3.25	40	0	94	8	138	49	115	69	133	127	65	64	5	4	590	321
3.24-3.00	59	0	148	8	159	36	144	60	115	109	55	55	6	6	686	274
2.99-2.75	73	0	116	1	106	16	82	29	84	73	33	30	3	3	497	152
2.74-2.50	54	0	71	0	67	3	47	11	36	30	19	16	2	2	296	62
2.49-2.25	51	0	37	0	33	2	24	5	16	9	9	7	0	0	170	23
2.24-2.00	23	0	17	0	8	0	6	0	11	3	2	0	0	0	67	3
1.99-1.00	5	0	2	0	1	0	1	0	0	0	0	0	0	0	9	0
CES-P/F	12	0	17	3	12	3	7	2	2	1	6	4	0	0	56	13
Total	337	0	570	28	657	149	542	268	550	500	249	233	24	23	2929	1201

Apps = Number of Applicants (Grid represents 95% of applicant pool)
Adm = Number Admitted (Grid represents 100% of admit pool)

Loyola University—New Orleans, School of Law

7214 St. Charles Avenue
New Orleans, LA 70118

E-Mail: ladmit@nadal.loyno.edu
URL: http://www.loyno.edu/law.admissions/index.html
Phone: 504.861.5575

■ Introduction

The School of Law was established at Loyola University in 1914. It has been approved by the ABA since 1931 and has been a member of the AALS since 1934. The university is a member of the Southern Association of Colleges and Schools and is operated by the Jesuits of the Southern Province. The campus is located in uptown New Orleans approximately five miles from the historic French Quarter and the Central Business District.

■ Enrollment/Student Body

➤ 1,341 applicants ➤ 702 admitted first-year class 1998
➤ 239 enrolled first-year class 1998 ➤ full-time 25th/75th percentile GPA—2.67/3.25 ➤ part-time 25th/75th percentile GPA—2.62/3.28 ➤ full-time 25th/75th percentile LSAT—148/153 ➤ part-time 25th/75th percentile LSAT—148/157
➤ 493 total full-time ➤ 167 total part-time
➤ 24% minority ➤ 46% women
➤ 26 states & 7 foreign countries represented in first-year class
➤ 103 undergraduate schools represented in first-year class

■ Faculty

➤ 77 total ➤ 36 full-time ➤ 41 part-time or adjunct
➤ 12 women ➤ 6 minority

■ Library and Physical Facilities

➤ 265,089 volumes & equivalents ➤ library hours: Mon.-Thurs., 7:30 A.M.-MIDNIGHT; Fri., 7:30 A.M.-9:00 P.M.; Sat., 10:00 A.M.-10:00 P.M.; Sun., 11:00 A.M.-11:00 P.M.
➤ LEXIS ➤ NEXIS ➤ WESTLAW ➤ DIALOG
➤ 7 full-time librarians ➤ library seats 529

In 1986, the School of Law moved to a new and larger facility on the Broadway Campus of Loyola University. Located approximately six blocks from the main campus, the facility houses all academic and research components of the School of Law, including the Gillis W. Long Law Poverty Center. The law school is designed to accommodate the needs of people with disabilities. Law students also have complete access to the facilities located on the main campus.

The library's collection of over 265,089 volumes supports the curriculum and research needs of the law school faculty and students. Its working collection contains legal authorities of international law, comparative law, and laws of individual foreign countries, as well as materials dealing with law-related subjects. In addition to conventional resources, the library has extensive computer facilities for students' use.

■ Curriculum

➤ Academic Support Program ➤ 90 credits required to graduate ➤ 126 courses available ➤ degrees available: J.D./M.B.A.; J.D./M.A.—Religious Studies; J.D./Master of Urban and Regional Planning; J.D./M.A.—Communications; J.D./Master of Public Administration ➤ semesters, start in Aug. ➤ range of first-year class size—12-100

■ Special Programs

The State of Louisiana is governed in the area of private (property) law by the civil law tradition as found in the provisions of the Louisiana Civil Code. The common law tradition, however, is predominant throughout most of the United States. The School of Law offers both traditions. The full-time student may select from two separate and distinct curricula while still maintaining sufficient flexibility to elect courses in the other. Such a system allows the student to study the private law by the comparative method. The part-time (evening) program offers the civil law tradition as found in the State of Louisiana.

In addition to the regular curriculum, each student entering the School of Law must accumulate a number of lawyering-skills points in order to graduate. Lawyering-skills points, including trial practice, client counseling, and negotiation and document drafting, may be earned by taking certain skills courses for which normal academic credit is given; by participating in other skills-related activities such as moot court and trial competitions; and by participating in short extracurricular courses that will be offered by the School of Law from time to time.

Full-time students are required to be in residence for a minimum of six full semesters. The normal time frame for part-time students is eight semesters and two summer sessions.

Loyola offers four 5-week summer-abroad programs. Courses are taught in Cuernavaca, Mexico; Kyoto, Japan; Capetown, South Africa; and Eastern Europe. In addition, Loyola offers three 2-week programs in Vienna, Austria; Costa Rica; and Brazil. All students, after completion of their freshman year, are permitted to enroll in summer school classes.

The Law Clinic, celebrating over 25 years of service to the community, is a vital component to the law school. Students chosen to participate in the senior-year program will be assigned cases, civil and criminal, and will be expected to prepare them for trial. Thereafter, they will actually participate in the trial process. Upper-division students also have an opportunity to serve as judicial clerks in the federal extern program sponsored in conjunction with the U. S. District Court for the Eastern District of Louisiana.

The Public Law Center represents a new departure in American legal education. The center takes legislative initiatives from the conceptual stage through research and drafting into the actual legislative process, then beyond into administrative rulemaking following the enactment of new statutes. In addition, the center offers a vital program of legislative and administrative assistance to community and public interest groups, thereby providing access to two nonlitigation advocacy methodologies traditionally underutilized by the poor and disadvantaged interests of society.

■ Admission

➡ *Bachelor's degree generally required*   ➡ *rolling admission, priority given to applications completed by May 1*
➡ *LSAT, LSDAS required*   ➡ *application fee—$20*

■ Student Activities

The *Loyola Law Review* is published by a student editorial board and includes student work and articles written by specialists from the practicing bar, as well as from the academic community. Staff membership is based on scholarship and interest in legal writing.

The *Poverty Law Journal* is open to qualified students and is devoted to issues faced by the poor, children, the elderly, and all others who are unable to afford legal representation. The Moot Court Board, selected from prior years' competitions, is responsible for the Moot Court Program. Teams are entered each year in competitions.

The Student Bar Association is comprised of all students enrolled in the day and evening divisions of the law school. It provides a professional program for students and appoints members to attend faculty meetings and to sit on the student-faculty relations committee. The law school newspaper, *The Code*, is published by a student editorial board. Three legal fraternities, Delta Theta Phi, Phi Alpha Delta, and Phi Delta Phi have active chapters within the school. Other organizations include BLSA, SALSA, Association of Women Law Students, Native American Law Society, Asian Pacific American Law Students Association, Maritime Law Association, St. Thomas More Law Club, Environmental Law Society, Association of Trial Lawyers of America (ATLA), and the Sports and Entertainment Law Society.

■ Expenses and Financial Aid

➡ *first-year tuition & fees—full-time, $19,391; part-time, $13,281*
➡ *estimated additional expenses—$11,000 (books, room & board, transportation, misc.)*   ➡ *scholarships available; based on academic merit only*   ➡ *minority scholarships available; based on academic merit only*   ➡ *financial aid available; FAFSA analysis, no deadline, priority given to those applications completed by May 1*

■ Career Services

The School of Law Career Services Office offers a variety of services to both students and alumni. Staffed by the director and an assistant, the office maintains and operates a career-planning center, assists students in preparing résumés, videotapes mock interviews, and conducts seminars on career planning, employment opportunities, and interviewing techniques. The office actively solicits job opportunities for summer and school-term clerkships, as well as employment options for each year's graduating class.

Applicant Group for the 1998-1999 Academic Year

Loyola University—New Orleans, School of Law
This grid includes only applicants who earned 120-180 LSAT scores under standard administrations.

LSAT Score	3.75 +		3.50 - 3.74		3.25 - 3.49		3.00 - 3.24		2.75 - 2.99		2.50 - 2.74		2.25 - 2.49		2.00 - 2.24		Below 2.00		No GPA		Total	
	Apps	Adm	Apps	Adm	Apps	Adm	Apps	Adm	Apps	Adm	Apps	Adm	Apps	Adm	Apps	Adm	Apps	Adm	Apps	Adm	Apps	Adm
175-180	0	0	0	0	0	0	0	0	0	0	0	0	0	0	0	0	0	0	0	0	0	0
170-174	0	0	0	0	1	1	0	0	0	0	0	0	0	0	1	0	0	0	0	0	2	1
165-169	2	2	2	2	2	2	3	3	2	2	1	1	1	1	0	0	0	0	1	1	14	14
160-164	6	6	3	3	4	4	4	3	6	6	4	4	3	3	0	0	0	0	1	1	31	30
155-159	9	9	11	10	21	20	25	25	34	34	24	23	17	15	6	6	1	1	1	1	149	144
150-154	15	15	28	28	46	44	51	48	71	70	52	45	32	19	10	5	1	0	7	4	313	278
145-149	7	6	33	27	58	37	70	43	83	42	61	29	34	10	19	1	4	0	6	3	375	198
140-144	5	3	7	1	26	3	39	4	74	11	43	7	36	1	15	0	2	0	11	2	258	32
135-139	2	0	7	0	3	0	22	1	23	0	21	1	19	0	8	0	3	0	11	0	119	2
130-134	1	0	1	0	1	0	2	0	5	0	8	0	2	0	4	0	3	0	5	0	32	0
125-129	0	0	0	0	0	0	0	0	1	0	0	0	0	0	0	0	1	0	1	0	3	0
120-124	0	0	0	0	0	0	0	0	0	0	0	0	0	0	1	0	0	0	0	0	1	0
Total	47	41	92	71	162	111	216	127	299	165	214	110	144	49	64	12	15	1	44	12	1297	699

Apps = Number of Applicants
Adm = Number Admitted
Reflects 97% of the total applicant pool.

University of Maine School of Law

246 Deering Ave.
Portland, ME 04102

URL: http://www.law.usm.maine.edu
Phone: 207.780.4341

■ Introduction

The University of Maine School of Law is an administrative unit of the University of Southern Maine, a part of the University of Maine System. The law school is located in Portland, which, though the largest metropolitan area in northern New England, is a "livable" city that retains many elements of an attractive seacoast community. A distinctive feature of the school is its small size, which engenders close working relationships between students and faculty and a strong sense of community among students. The school is a charter member of the AALS and is fully approved by the ABA.

■ Enrollment/Student Body

➼ *506 applicants*   ➼ *282 admitted first-year class 1998*
➼ *104 enrolled first-year class 1998*   ➼ *full-time 25th/75th percentile GPA—2.98/3.51*   ➼ *full-time 25th/75th percentile LSAT—150/158*   ➼ *289 total full-time*   ➼ *5% minority*
➼ *42% women*   ➼ *30 states & foreign countries represented*
➼ *111 undergraduate schools represented*

■ Faculty

➼ *26 total*   ➼ *18 full-time*   ➼ *8 part-time or adjunct*
➼ *9 women*

■ Library and Physical Facilities

➼ *300,000 volumes & equivalents*   ➼ *library hours: Sun.-Thurs., 8:00 A.M.-11:00 P.M.; Fri., 8:00 A.M.-9:00 P.M.; Sat., 9:00 A.M.-8:00 P.M.*   ➼ *LEXIS*   ➼ *NEXIS*
➼ *WESTLAW*   ➼ *6 full-time librarians*

■ Curriculum

➼ *89 credits required to graduate*   ➼ *98 courses available*
➼ *degrees available: J.D.; joint-degrees program with USM in Public Policy and Management, Community Planning and Development*   ➼ *semesters, start in late Aug.*

The first-year curriculum is a structured program of courses prescribed for all first-year students. A primary objective of the first-year curriculum is the development of students' legal analytical skills and their ability to read and understand cases and statutory material. The program also provides an introduction to legal research and writing. Most courses after the first year are elective. However, all students are required successfully to complete Professional Responsibility, Constitutional Law II, and one of the upper-level courses designated by the faculty as a "perspective" course—one which places the law in a broader philosophical, historical, or comparative context. In addition, each student must fulfill the Independent Writing Requirement, which may be done in several ways: through an Independent Writing Project (a substantial research project under the direction of a faculty member), or through membership on the *Maine Law Review, Ocean and Coastal Law Journal*, or the Moot Court Board. The school does

not purport to offer specialization in any one area of the law; rather the faculty believes that the most effective legal education is broad and general. Maine does, however, possess unique curricular strength in its clinical programs in environmental/marine, business, and international law.

■ Special Programs

The University of Maine School of Law has initiated an Integrated Clinical Education Program through the Cumberland Legal Aid Clinic. Third-year law students represent clients under faculty supervision in this approved legal assistance office. A number of clinical courses are offered, including the General Practice Clinic, Criminal Law Practicum, and the Family Law Clinic. The practicum courses include, in addition to client representation, a classroom component emphasizing direct application of substantive and procedural law to a specific area of practice.

The school's Marine Law Institute conducts research on laws and policies affecting ocean and coastal resources. Law students have an opportunity to participate as research assistants in this work.

The law school sponsors a statewide law-related education program which provides resources for teachers who use the law in their classroom teaching. The Teachers/Law Students Project trains up to 20 law students and pairs them with middle and high school teachers.

The school coordinates *pro bono* opportunities for law students in various public interest endeavors, such as CASA (Court Appointed Special Advocates), Volunteer Lawyers Project, Maine Pre-Trial Services, and the Family Law Project of Pine Tree Legal Assistance.

■ Admission

➼ *Bachelor's degree from an accredited college or university required*   ➼ *application deadline—Feb. 15*
➼ *LSAT, LSDAS required*   ➼ *application fee—$25*

■ Student Activities

The *Maine Law Review*, published twice a year, concerns itself with national, regional, and state legal problems, with emphasis on matters of current interest. The *Ocean and Coastal Law Journal*, published by the law school's Marine Law Institute, includes student articles on marine resource, environmental, and ocean legal issues. The moot court board represents the school at regional and national competitions with other law schools.

Law students participate as voting members on many law school and university committees. The Student Bar Association performs the varied functions of student government, and acts as an umbrella organization, coordinating the activities of a number of student organizations: the Black Law Students Association, Business Law Association, La Cofradía, Environmental Law Society, Federalist Society, Health Law Association, International Law Society, Lesbian/Gay/Bisexual Law Caucus, Maine Association for Public Interest Law, Maine Law and

Technology Association, National Lawyers Guild, Native American Law Students Association, Phi Alpha Delta, Second Amendment Association, Sports and Entertainment Law Society, and Women's Law Association.

■ Expenses and Financial Aid

➡ *tuition—residents, $9,360; nonresident, $17,012*
➡ *annual fees—$300*   ➡ *estimated additional expenses (room, board, books)—$7,930*   ➡ *need-based scholarships available*
➡ *minority scholarships available*   ➡ *financial aid available*
➡ *FAFSA due at processing center by Feb. 1*

■ Career Services

➡ *1997 placement rate (6 months after graduation)—88%*
➡ *1997 first-time bar passage rate—70%*

The Career Services Office provides a full range of services including counseling; career resource materials; specific summer, full-time, part-time, and work/study job listings; and extensive on-campus recruiting. The small enrollment of the law school ensures services tailored to meet the specific needs of students. In addition to individual counseling, a series of workshops and panel discussions with practitioners is held each year. The full-time Career Services Director is happy to provide further information to interested applicants.

Applicant Group for the 1998-1999 Academic Year

University of Maine School of Law
This grid includes only applicants who earned 120-180 LSAT scores under standard administrations.

LSAT Score	3.75 +		3.50 - 3.74		3.25 - 3.49		3.00 - 3.24		2.75 - 2.99		2.50 - 2.74		2.25 - 2.49		2.00 - 2.24		Below 2.00		No GPA		Total	
	Apps	Adm	Apps	Adm	Apps	Adm	Apps	Adm	Apps	Adm	Apps	Adm	Apps	Adm	Apps	Adm	Apps	Adm	Apps	Adm	Apps	Adm
175-180	0	0	1	1	0	0	1	1	0	0	0	0	0	0	0	0	0	0	0	0	2	2
170-174	0	0	1	1	3	3	1	1	0	0	0	0	1	1	0	0	0	0	0	0	6	6
165-169	4	3	3	3	2	2	1	1	3	3	0	0	2	2	1	0	0	0	1	0	17	14
160-164	4	4	10	9	5	5	15	15	7	7	4	2	1	1	0	0	0	0	0	0	46	43
155-159	5	5	21	20	17	15	20	17	19	15	10	5	1	1	1	0	2	1	5	2	101	81
150-154	4	4	15	13	29	20	28	21	28	13	9	3	5	1	1	0	0	0	3	1	122	76
145-149	4	3	10	6	20	9	29	11	16	6	9	0	11	1	2	0	1	0	2	1	104	37
140-144	2	0	7	0	8	2	13	0	15	1	9	1	5	0	1	0	1	0	1	0	62	4
135-139	1	1	2	0	2	1	2	0	7	1	5	1	3	0	0	0	1	0	1	0	24	4
130-134	0	0	0	0	0	0	1	0	0	0	1	0	1	0	1	0	0	0	0	0	4	0
125-129	0	0	0	0	0	0	0	0	1	0	0	0	0	0	1	0	0	0	0	0	2	0
120-124	0	0	0	0	0	0	0	0	0	0	0	0	1	0	1	0	0	0	0	0	2	0
Total	24	20	70	53	86	57	111	67	96	46	47	12	31	7	9	0	5	1	13	4	492	267

Apps = Number of Applicants
Adm = Number Admitted

Marquette University Law School

Office of Admissions, Sensenbrenner Hall
1103 W. Wisconsin Ave, P.O. Box 1881
Milwaukee, WI 53201-1881

E-Mail: law.admission@marquette.edu
URL: http://www.marquette.edu/law/
Phone: 414.288.6767

■ Introduction

For more than a century, Marquette University Law School has been committed to training men and women to serve the public interest by becoming highly skilled, ethical, and moral attorneys. Traditionally, the Law School's curriculum has emphasized the practical aspects of legal practice. In recent years that emphasis has expanded to include particular excellence in the areas of intellectual property, international law, business law, criminal law and procedure, children and the law, and litigation-related courses. The National Sports Law Institute, the premiere sports law program in the U.S., is part of the Law School. Our 5,500 alumni and alumnae serve in a broad range of legal, public, and corporate positions throughout the United States.

The Law School is located on the university's campus—two blocks from the state courthouse and a short walk to the federal courthouse and downtown Milwaukee. Marquette is the only Law School in Milwaukee and in southeast Wisconsin. Marquette University—a Catholic, Jesuit, urban, and national university—is the largest private university in Wisconsin. The Catholic and Jesuit nature of the institution translates into a specific concern for the well-being of each individual, whether he or she is a law student, a legal client, or the victim of a crime. Persons of all religious backgrounds attend Marquette, serve on our faculty, and are valued in our Law School community. The Law School is committed to academic freedom, the broadest possible scope of inquiry, and the examination of any subject.

Milwaukee is a lively city on Lake Michigan, 90 miles north of Chicago. It is Wisconsin's largest city, with a population of 630,000, but it retains the appeal of a small town. Remarkably clean and well-run, it's known for its many ethnic festivals and the variety and quality of its cuisine.

■ Enrollment/Student Body

➡ *855 applicants*   ➡ *548 admitted first-year class 1998*
➡ *207 enrolled first-year class 1998 (150 full time, 57 part time)*   ➡ *full-time 25th/75th percentile GPA—2.82/3.35*   ➡ *part-time 25th/75th percentile GPA—2.79/3.47*
➡ *full-time 25th/75th percentile LSAT—152/157*
➡ *part-time 25th/75th percentile LSAT—151/159*
➡ *449 total full-time*   ➡ *93 total part-time*
➡ *7.4% minority*   ➡ *44% women*   ➡ *30 states & one foreign country represented*   ➡ *147 U.S. & foreign undergraduate schools represented in student body*

The Law School is actively committed to increasing diversity and encourages applications from members of groups historically disadvantaged in the U.S. and underrepresented in the legal profession.

■ Faculty

➡ *72 total*   ➡ *31 full-time*   ➡ *41 part-time or adjunct*
➡ *16 women faculty*   ➡ *7 minority faculty*

■ Library and Physical Facility

➡ *262,540 volumes & equivalents*   ➡ *library hours: Mon.-Thurs., 7:00 A.M.-MIDNIGHT; Fri., 7:00 A.M.-8:00 P.M.; Sat., 9:00 A.M.-8:00 P.M.; Sun., 10:00 A.M.-MIDNIGHT*
➡ *LEXIS*   ➡ *NEXIS*   ➡ *WESTLAW*   ➡ *DIALOG*
➡ *MARQCAT*   ➡ *LegalTrac*   ➡ *CALI*
➡ *WISCAT*   ➡ *OCLC*   ➡ *9 full-time librarians*
➡ *library seats 315*

The Law School is located in Sensenbrenner Hall, an attractive, comfortable, four-story, air-conditioned building that houses faculty offices, classrooms, two courtrooms, and administrative offices. The law library, a modern, four-level facility, is connected to the Law School. The law library has two computer labs and provides students access to computer-assisted legal research systems and computer-assisted legal instruction exercises. The law library is a federal document depository and is the largest legal research facility in southeastern Wisconsin. Law students have access to all Marquette University campus facilities, including the university computer center.

■ Curriculum

➡ *Academic Support Program*   ➡ *90 credits required to graduate*   ➡ *102 courses available*   ➡ *degrees available: J.D.; J.D./M.B.A.; J.D./M.A. Pol. Sci.; J.D./M.A. International Affairs*   ➡ *semesters, start in Aug.*   ➡ *range of first-year class size—15-80*

The Law School curriculum is designed to prepare students to practice law in the twenty-first century. This means an explicit emphasis on a strong core curriculum that includes consideration of the theoretical underpinnings of the law, as well as the practical application of substantive legal concepts. The Law School's curriculum is national in focus and scope, and emphasizes the skills and values necessary to be a competent and ethical lawyer, as well as a contributing citizen and community leader. The Law School takes advantage of its location to include on its adjunct faculty many of the state's outstanding practitioners who supplement required and core courses with a broad range of elective and specialty courses.

■ Special Programs

Our comprehensive trial-practice courses are an excellent complement to the curriculum and provide an exceptional opportunity for students to develop trial skills. Distinctive clinics include the Prosecutor and Defender Clinics, Judicial Internships (Appellate and Trial), Municipal Ordinance Defense Clinic, Children with Special Health Needs Project, and supervised fieldwork opportunities in specialized areas.

The Law School and the University of Queenland, Australia, jointly sponsor a program in international, foreign, and comparative law.

■ Admission

➠ *Bachelor's degree from an accredited college or university required* ➠ *application deadline—April 1 (full time); May 1 (part time); rolling notification, early application preferred* ➠ *LSAT, LSDAS required* ➠ *application fee—$40*

Review of completed applications begins after October 1 and continues through the spring. Although the applicant's LSAT score and academic record are the principal considerations in the selection process, the Admission Committee also considers other factors, such as personal accomplishments and characteristics that contribute to the diversity of the school, the legal community, and the profession. Accepted applicants are required to submit nonrefundable tuition deposits in April and June. These are applied to the student's fall semester tuition. Applicants are welcome to visit the Law School (arranging for tours in advance) or contact the Admissions Office with any questions. Interviews are not part of the application process.

■ Diploma Privilege

Since 1933, graduates of the Law School who qualify have been admitted to the practice of law in Wisconsin without having to take the Wisconsin Bar Examination. Marquette graduates are entitled to sit for bar examinations in any American jurisdiction.

■ Student Privilege

The Law School publishes the *Marquette Law Review*, the *Marquette Sports Law Journal*, and the *Marquette Intellectual Property Law Review*. All students may develop advocacy skills in moot court competitions. Marquette moot court teams have won regional titles and championships in National Moot Court and National Labor Law competitions. A wide variety of student organizations are active at the Law School.

■ Expenses and Financial Aid

➠ *tuition & fees—full-time, $18,370; part-time, $760/credit hr.* ➠ *estimated additional expenses—$10,000 (room & board, personal, medical)* ➠ *renewable scholarships available (performance & diversity tuition-based awards)* ➠ *financial aid available; FAFSA required—Federal Stafford Loan, Federal Unsubsidized Stafford Loan, Federal Perkins*

■ Career Services

The Office of Career Planning processes hundreds of listings of employment opportunities, coordinates campus interviews, and provides counseling assistance to students. Marquette law alumni practice law in virtually every state of the Union. In recent years over 90 percent of our graduates had secured employment within seven months of graduation.

■ Housing

There are many university and campus area apartments within six blocks of the Law School. Ample, affordable housing is also available throughout Milwaukee and its suburbs. Applications for university housing may be obtained from the Office of Residence Life, Tower Hall, Marquette University, Milwaukee, WI 53201-1881 (phone: 414.288.7208).

Applicant Group for the 1998-1999 Academic Year

Marquette University Law School
This grid includes only applicants who earned 120-180 LSAT scores under standard administrations.

LSAT Score	3.75 +		3.50 - 3.74		3.25 - 3.49		3.00 - 3.24		2.75 - 2.99		2.50 - 2.74		2.25 - 2.49		2.00 - 2.24		Below 2.00		No GPA		Total	
	Apps	Adm	Apps	Adm	Apps	Adm	Apps	Adm	Apps	Adm	Apps	Adm	Apps	Adm	Apps	Adm	Apps	Adm	Apps	Adm	Apps	Adm
160-180	10	10	10	10	15	14	11	11	13	13	10	10	4	4	3	2	0	0	1	0	77	74
155-159	18	18	16	16	49	48	42	37	45	45	15	14	10	7	5	5	1	1	1	1	202	192
150-154	13	11	24	23	55	55	59	59	45	42	20	20	13	13	3	2	2	1	2	2	236	228
145-149	5	3	11	2	23	9	35	14	44	15	26	8	18	3	1	0	1	0	1	0	165	54
Below 145	2	0	8	0	13	0	36	0	28	0	30	0	22	0	10	0	7	0	1	0	157	0
Total	48	42	69	51	155	126	183	121	175	115	101	52	67	27	22	9	11	2	6	3	837	548

Apps = Number of Applicants
Adm = Number Admitted
Reflects 99% of the total applicant pool.

University of Maryland School of Law

500 West Baltimore Street
Baltimore, MD 21201

E-Mail: admissions@law.umaryland.edu
URL: http://www.law.umaryland.edu
Phone: 410.706.3492

■ Introduction

The University of Maryland School of Law is distinguished as a powerful source of the knowledge, experience, and expertise that prepares students for professional leadership as lawyers, business executives, legislators and public policy makers, community advocates, and agents of social, political, and economic progress.

The law school is an integral part of the Baltimore/Washington/Annapolis legal-business community. Located in downtown Baltimore, just a few blocks from the Inner Harbor's tourist attractions, Oriole Park at Camden Yards, and the Baltimore Ravens football stadium, the school's proximity to the nation's capitol affords opportunities for extensive interaction with local, state, and national governments, as well as many law firms, agencies, and organizations of prominence.

Students entering Maryland law school join an especially collegial and supportive community and a network of dedicated graduates who occupy positions of professional leadership throughout the state, region, and nation.

■ Enrollment/Student Body

➡ 2,439 applicants   ➡ 993 admitted first-year class 1998
➡ 257 enrolled first-year class 1998   ➡ 847 total enrollment—581 day, 266 evening   ➡ full-time 25th/75th percentile GPA—3.06/3.51   ➡ part-time 25th/75th percentile GPA—2.89/3.39
➡ full-time 25th/75th percentile LSAT—152/158
➡ part-time 25th/75th percentile LSAT—152/159
➡ 28.7% minority   ➡ 53% women
➡ 37 states; Washington, DC; Puerto Rico; & several foreign countries represented   ➡ 257 undergraduate schools represented

■ Faculty

➡ 113 total   ➡ 53 full-time (20 women, 9 minority)
➡ 60 adjunct   ➡ faculty/student ratio—1:14

■ Library and Physical Facilities

➡ 375,304 volumes & equivalents   ➡ 4,086 serials
➡ LEXIS   ➡ WESTLAW   ➡ CARL   ➡ UNCOVER
➡ Legal Resource Index   ➡ OCLC First Search
➡ access to any other databases through online catalog & the Internet   ➡ 9 full-time librarians

In the summer of 1999, construction will begin on the new University of Maryland School of Law building. During the construction period, the law school and law library will be housed in quarters specifically renovated to accommodate their needs. The renovated facility is at the heart of the campus, adjacent to the new campus library and the Student Union. The new building will provide state-of-the-art accommodations for faculty and students engaged in one of the nation's leading programs integrating theory and practice, classroom and experiential learning.

■ Curriculum

➡ Juris Doctor (J.D.) program   ➡ 3-year day, 4-year part-time day & evening programs   ➡ 85 credits required to graduate   ➡ fall & spring semesters, summer session (evening classes only) open to students in good standing at any ABA-approved law school   ➡ 160 elective courses
➡ Academic Support Program   ➡ range of first-year class size—24-100

Each first-semester student is assigned to a fall-semester course with enrollment averaging 25, combining an introduction to legal institutions and processes, an understanding of the skills necessary in the professional use of case law and legislation, and one of the traditional substantive courses. Elective courses include a wide range of courses, seminars, independent studies, simulations, clinics, and externships. Specialization in a number of subject areas is available but not required. Each student must produce at least one substantial paper based on extensive research.

Maryland integrates traditional classroom study of legal theory with clinical practice "live client" representation. Students meet regularly with their instructors to review the substantive, professional, ethical, and craft issues raised by their work and to explore the connections between what is taught in the classroom and the practice of law as they are experiencing it.

Maryland's strong academic programs in business, environment, health, international, public interest and public policy, and a developing specialty in intellectual property and technology, enable students to develop expertise and experience in fields of critical importance to the future. By having among the most extensive clinical law and externship programs in the nation, Maryland provides real-world lawyering experiences to students in a wide variety of settings ranging from start-up companies and community services organizations to major corporations and law firms.

■ Dual Degrees and Interdisciplinary Study

➡ dual degrees with Applied and Professional Ethics, Business Administration, Community Planning, Criminal Justice, Liberal Education, Policy Sciences, Public Management, Social Work

Maryland's interdisciplinary programs, including environment, health care, technology transfer, and entrepreneurship, offer students the opportunity to work with lawyers and professionals in related disciplines toward the resolution of problems that transcend traditional disciplinary boundaries. Supplementing the dual-degree programs, students are encouraged to explore the connection between law and other disciplines by enrolling in as many as nine credits in related graduate level programs.

■ Admission

➡ *application deadline—March 1, rolling admission*
➡ *application fee—$50*

First-year students are admitted only for the fall. Applicants should file applications as early as possible after September 1 of the year preceding enrollment and prior to March 1. Later receipt of the application, the LSAT score, or LSDAS report may seriously prejudice the applicant's chances of acceptance. February 2000 LSAT scores will be considered on time for August 2000 admission. Admission decisions are made by a faculty committee. Multiple test scores normally are averaged. Residency may be a factor in close cases. Applicants are welcome to visit the school, but interviews are not part of the admission process.

We expect applicants to come from different backgrounds, have different experiences, and have many reasons for wanting to study law. We do not seek to cast students into any particular acceptable mold. In addition to academic ability, the qualities of the students we seek may be reflected in their personal background as demonstrated through such characteristics as national and geographic origin; cultural and language background; racial, disability, social, and economic barriers overcome; interpersonal skills, as demonstrated by extracurricular pursuits, work or service experience, and leadership activities; potential for intellectual and social growth, as demonstrated by personal talents and skills, maturity, and compassion; and other special circumstances and characteristics which, when combined with academic skills necessary for sound legal education, promise to make a special contribution to the community. The personal statement and letters of recommendation are the primary means for candidates to convey this information and these characteristics to the admissions committee.

■ Student Activities

Maryland law students participate in a variety of activities, including four journals (*Business Lawyer, Journal of Health Care Law and Policy, Journal of International Law and Trade, Maryland Law Review*) and dozens of social, political, and professional student groups.

■ Expenses and Financial Aid

➡ *full-time tuition & fees 1998-99—resident, $9,842; nonresident, $17,735* ➡ *evening tuition & fees— resident, $7,393; nonresident, $13,311* ➡ *FAFSA* ➡ *State of Maryland Loan Repayment Assistance for some public interest employment*

■ Career Development

Maryland law students benefit from an extensive set of connections to the bar, judiciary, business and industry, government, and community organizations in the state of Maryland; Washington, DC; and beyond, which provide practice oriented learning experiences and access to a large and well-placed network of contacts for career placement and advancement.

The Career Development Office assists law students and graduates in developing successful job search strategies. Career Development markets the University of Maryland School of Law and its graduates to a diverse group of employers and facilitates interviewing opportunities through its on-campus interview program, job-posting system, and other venues. Career Development staff presents workshops and seminars which address issues related to students' professional development. Ninety-nine percent of the 239 graduates in the Class of 1997 reported employment in the following categories: 38 percent private practice; 17 percent judicial clerkship; 19 percent business and industry; 20 percent government and public interest; 1 percent academia; and 5 percent other.

Applicant Group for the 1998-1999 Academic Year

University of Maryland School of Law
Approximately 2,400 candidates applied for admission to Maryland's 1998 entering class. Figures in the chart below reflect 1998 admission decisions as of June 1, 1998 for all applicants with LSAT score on the 120-180 score scale (approximately 99% of all applicants).

	LSAT Score											
	151 & Below		152-154		155-157		158-160		161-163		164 & Above	
GPA	Apps	Adm	Apps	Adm	Apps	Adm	Apps	Adm	Apps	Adm	Apps	Adm
3.75-4.00	32	9	23	21	39	39	25	25	16	15	19	18
3.50-3.74	88	21	49	33	60	57	39	38	16	15	14	14
3.25-3.49	176	35	93	33	94	56	61	59	35	35	23	23
3.00-3.24	215	29	96	27	88	32	52	34	38	38	33	32
2.75-2.99	202	16	68	14	59	19	38	17	25	19	21	21
2.74 & Below	335	10	52	3	52	8	32	8	30	14	19	12
Total	1048	120	381	131	392	211	247	181	160	136	129	120

Apps = Number of Applicants
Adm = Number Admitted

McGeorge School of Law, University of the Pacific

3200 Fifth Avenue
Sacramento, CA 95817

E-Mail: admissionsmcgeorge@uop.edu
URL: http://www.mcgeorge.edu
Phone: 916.739.7105

■ Introduction

McGeorge School of Law of the University of the
Pacific is located in Sacramento, California, the capital
of the nation's most populous state. Established in 1924,
the school offers both full-time day and part-time
evening programs as well as graduate law programs.
McGeorge is a member of the AALS, is accredited by
the ABA and the State Bar of California, and has a
chapter of the Order of the Coif.

■ Enrollment/Student Body

➺ *1,756 applicants*   ➺ *1,204 admitted first-year class 1998*
➺ *25th/75th percentile GPA—2.70/3.34*
➺ *25th/75th percentile LSAT—148/155*
➺ *370 enrolled first-year class 1998 (270 day, 100 evening)*
➺ *745 total full-time*   ➺ *350 total part-time*
➺ *30% minority first-year class 1998*   ➺ *48% women*
➺ *215 U.S. and 7 foreign undergraduate schools represented*

■ Faculty

➺ *111 total*   ➺ *49 full-time*   ➺ *62 visiting or adjunct*
➺ *15 women*   ➺ *4 minority*

■ Library and Physical Facilities

➺ *436,384 volumes & equivalents*   ➺ *library hours: Sun.-
Thurs., 8:00 A.M.-MIDNIGHT; Fri. & Sat., 8:00 A.M.-11:00 P.M.*
➺ *LEXIS*   ➺ *NEXIS*   ➺ *WESTLAW*   ➺ *DIALOG*
➺ *7.5 full-time librarians*   ➺ *library seats 615*

McGeorge's unique 22-acre law school campus in
Sacramento is separate from the university's main
campus in Stockton. The McGeorge campus includes
a variety of classroom settings, the law library,
the Courtroom of the Future, the Institutes for
Administrative Justice and for Legislative Practice,
clinical facilities, the Student Center, student
apartments, and recreational facilities.

  McGeorge's law library provides spacious and
well-lighted reading rooms with a variety of study
carrels, tables, and group-study rooms. Terminals
for access to LEXIS and WESTLAW as well as
CD-ROM stations are located throughout the library.
A well-equipped and staffed Law Lab provides
terminals for access to Internet and intracampus
communications, computer-assisted legal instruction,
and word processing.

■ Curriculum

➺ *Minority Student Program; Student Bar Association
Tutorial Program*   ➺ *88 credits required to graduate*
➺ *138 courses available*   ➺ *45 clinical offerings*
➺ *degrees available: J.D.; J.D./M.B.A.; J.D./M.P.P.A.; LL.M.—
Transnational Business Practice*   ➺ *semesters, start in Aug.*
➺ *range of first-year class size—32-102*

Completion of the J.D. program requires six semesters
for day division students. Evening division students
normally require eight semesters although an accelerated
program is available through attendance at summer
sessions. Special areas of curricular strength, in addition
to those listed below, are business; criminal justice;
family, juvenile justice, and child protection law;
practice and litigation skills; and alternative dispute
resolution mechanisms.

■ Special Programs

Governmental Affairs—A specialized curriculum leads
to a J.D. degree with a separate certificate in Governmental
Affairs. Legislation and administrative rule making at
the federal, state, and local levels affect issues ranging
from the environment and land use to education, civil
rights, and business structuring. Sacramento is home for
the California legislature, the governor's office, and many
state and federal administrative agencies. A broad range
of student externships complement foundational and
advanced elective courses in the areas of legislative
policy making and governmental affairs.

  Clinical and Internship Opportunities—The importance
McGeorge places on clinical experiences is evidenced by
the number and breadth of on- and off-campus clinics and
externships. Legal employers value realistic practice
experience that enables a recent graduate to begin work
with a firm or agency as an effective participant. The
McGeorge Admissions Bulletin provides an overview of the
school's extensive clinical offerings in civil and criminal
practice settings.

  Tax Concentration—Tax considerations are important
and often controlling factors in many business
transactions and personal decisions. McGeorge's Tax
Concentration provides students with the needed
foundation to enter business or estate planning
practice upon earning the J.D. degree. Those who
wish to go on, either immediately upon graduation or
after several years of practice, to acquire an LL.M. for a
more specialized tax practice will be well-prepared for
graduate study.

  **Environmental, Natural Resources, and Land Use
Planning**—California's environmental statutes have
served as models for other states and, in some respects,
for the federal government as well. More than any
other state, California is the forum in which the major
environmental policy disputes of the era are being heard.
McGeorge offers an integrated classroom and externship
curriculum which takes advantage of the school's location
in the state's capital.

  International Business Transactions—For over 20 years,
McGeorge has been training lawyers capable of practicing
in the international sphere. In addition to offering a solid
core of business law courses, there is an extensive array
of international courses. The unique LL.M. program in

Transnational Business Practice combines advanced international business coursework with an internship period in a foreign law firm or agency.

■ Admission

➤ *Bachelor's degree or senior standing from accredited college or university required* ➤ *application deadline—day division, May 15* ➤ *LSAT, LSDAS required* ➤ *application fee—$40*

An applicant's undergraduate record and LSAT results are important factors in the decision process. When there are multiple LSAT scores, the highest is accorded significant weight. Other factors considered are grade patterns or trends, employment and career accomplishments, graduate work, and extracurricular or community activities. Ethnic, cultural, and experiential backgrounds that contribute to student body diversity are valued.

■ Student Activities

➤ *McGeorge Law Review* ➤ *The Transnational Lawyer Journal* ➤ *student moot court, international moot court, & community legal services boards* ➤ *over 30 professional, social, & academic student organizations*

■ Expenses and Financial Aid

➤ *first-year tuition & fees—full-time, $20,724; part-time, $13,286*
➤ *estimated additional expenses—$13,910 (housing, food, books, utilities, transportation, medical insurance, personal expenses)*
➤ *academic merit scholarships & grants available for first-year entering students & advanced students*
➤ *financial aid office provides individual counseling*

■ Housing

McGeorge has 158 on-campus apartments, including efficiencies and one- or two-bedroom units. Early application is advised. The Housing Office assists in locating off-campus accommodations which are readily available in Sacramento.

■ Career Services

The well-staffed Career Development Office offers a full range of counseling and resource services for students and alumni. Fall and spring interview seasons bring employers to campus, and other employers from throughout the country use the CDO facilities to solicit applications from McGeorge students. Among the services provided by CDO are résumé, job search, and interview workshops, a program of speakers with firsthand information about traditional and nontraditional law careers, and individual counseling about career paths.

Applicant Group for the 1998-1999 Academic Year

McGeorge School of Law, University of the Pacific
This grid includes only applicants who earned 120-180 LSAT scores under standard administrations.

LSAT Score	GPA																					
	3.75 +		3.50 - 3.74		3.25 - 3.49		3.00 - 3.24		2.75 - 2.99		2.50 - 2.74		2.25 - 2.49		2.00 - 2.24		Below 2.00		No GPA		Total	
	Apps	Adm	Apps	Adm	Apps	Adm	Apps	Adm	Apps	Adm	Apps	Adm	Apps	Adm	Apps	Adm	Apps	Adm	Apps	Adm	Apps	Adm
165-180	3	3	4	4	6	6	10	10	9	9	7	6	4	4	3	3	1	0	0	0	47	45
160-164	9	9	19	19	20	19	29	28	16	15	14	13	9	8	8	7	0	0	2	2	126	120
155-159	24	23	26	24	66	66	80	78	74	71	39	33	18	15	10	8	0	0	3	3	340	321
150-154	15	15	52	47	99	93	97	90	100	96	45	37	52	43	10	6	1	1	7	6	478	434
145-149	14	11	32	24	60	46	69	41	81	47	59	29	32	17	9	2	1	1	9	3	366	221
120-144	8	6	21	7	38	11	71	10	63	2	66	4	45	6	24	0	5	0	20	4	361	50
Total	73	67	154	125	289	241	356	257	343	240	230	122	160	93	64	26	8	2	41	18	1718	1191

Apps = Number of Applicants
Adm = Number Admitted
Reflects 98% of the total applicant pool.

The University of Memphis—Cecil C. Humphreys School of Law

Campus Box 526513
Memphis, TN 38152-6513

E-Mail: uofmlaw@profnet.law.memphis.edu
URL: http://www.people.memphis.edu/~law/
Phone: 901.678.2073

■ Introduction

The School of Law, located on The University of Memphis campus, was established in 1962 and was accredited by the ABA in 1965. The school is located in the pleasant surroundings of residential neighborhoods away from the hustle of the city. With a population of over 1,000,000, Memphis provides an excellent location for local, state, and federal courts, and the various judicial administrative offices associated with them.

■ Enrollment/Student Body: 1998-99

➡ *803 applicants*   ➡ *318 admitted first-year class 1998*
➡ *165 enrolled first-year class 1998*   ➡ *full-time 25th/75th percentile GPA—2.84/3.63*   ➡ *part-time 25th/75th percentile GPA—2.81/3.46*   ➡ *full-time 25th/75th percentile LSAT—150/157*   ➡ *part-time 25th/75th percentile LSAT—141/151*   ➡ *153 first-year, full-time*   ➡ *12 first-year, part-time*   ➡ *16% minority, first-year class*   ➡ *43% women, first-year class*   ➡ *65 undergraduate schools represented, first-year class*   ➡ *11% nonresidents, first-year class*   ➡ *average age, first-year class—26*

■ Faculty

➡ *64 total*   ➡ *26 full-time*   ➡ *38 part-time or adjunct*
➡ *21 women*   ➡ *4 minority*

■ Library and Physical Facilities

➡ *272,454 volumes & equivalents*   ➡ *library hours: Mon.-Thurs., 7:30 A.M.-MIDNIGHT; Fri., 7:30 A.M.-10:30 P.M.; Sat., 9:00 A.M.-10:00 P.M.; Sun., 11:00 A.M.-MIDNIGHT*
➡ *LEXIS*   ➡ *NEXIS*   ➡ *WESTLAW*   ➡ *DIALOG*
➡ *6 full-time librarians*   ➡ *library seats 275*
➡ *library designated as a federal depository—2,295 active serial subscriptions*

■ Curriculum

➡ *Academic Support Program*   ➡ *90 credits required to graduate*   ➡ *78 courses available*   ➡ *degrees available: J.D.; J.D./M.B.A.*   ➡ *range of first-year class size—80-85*

The school offers a full-time day program on the semester system. Students normally graduate in three years, although summer classes are available and some students graduate after five semesters plus two summers. A total of 90 semester hours are required for graduation; 56 are required, and 34 are electives that may be chosen from a wide selection of elective courses, seminars, externships, law review or moot court participation, and independent research.

A part-time day program is available for up to 10 percent of the entering class. This program, unlike the full-time program, permits students to be employed more than 20 hours per week while attending law school.

The faculty-to-student ratio of 1:20 enables the faculty to take a personal interest in the welfare and education of our students. In addition, approximately 33 distinguished practicing attorneys offer upper-level elective courses and participate in the first-year legal research and writing program.

■ Special Programs

In cooperation with the College of Business and Economics, a joint J.D./M.B.A. program is available.

Upper-class law students are eligible to enroll in practice skills courses which are under the supervision of the full-time faculty. Several clinics provide students with the opportunity to represent clients under the supervision of an attorney.

The school has externship programs in conjunction with several federal agencies such as the United States Attorney's Office for the Western District of Tennessee, the National Labor Relations Board, and the U.S. Bankruptcy Court. These programs allow a limited number of students to earn two credit-hours by working in one of these agencies 10 hours a week for one semester.

■ Admission

➡ *Bachelor's degree required for admission*
➡ *application deadline—Feb. 15*   ➡ *LSAT, LSDAS required*
➡ *application fee—$15*   ➡ *fall entrance only for first-year class*

A completed file includes application form, domicile certificate, LSDAS report, dean's certification form, recommendation with waiver form, and personal statement. An applicant must have taken the LSAT within three years prior to enrollment, and must have utilized LSDAS. Students are admitted only in the fall semester.

Approximately 85 percent of admissions are based on a weighted combination of the LSAT score and the cumulative undergraduate GPA. Approximately 15 percent of the entering class will be selected by the Faculty Admission Committee through the subjective admission process. In this process, the committee takes into consideration nonquantifiable subjective factors, such as undergraduate institution, performance in "core" and "major" curriculum, public or community service, personal background, employment history, and performance in graduate school. Offers of acceptance are then extended to those applicants in the subjective pool whom the committee feels have the best chance of successfully competing in law school.

In an effort to increase the number of African Americans admitted to law school in Tennessee, the Tennessee PreLaw Fellowship Program (TPLF) is offered. TPLF is a preparatory and developmental effort available to African American Tennessee residents only. Students participate in an eight-week intensive summer program. Students who successfully complete the summer program, and who meet minimum requirements for admission, will be offered admission to the law school. Aside from TPLF, the law school encourages applications from members of racial and ethnic groups who have been underrepresented in the legal profession. A student who has done acceptable work at a law school on the approved list of the ABA may be admitted to advanced standing under a transfer student program.

■ Student Activities

The University of Memphis Law Review is written, edited, and published quarterly by a student staff with contributions made by legal specialists in various fields. Students also participate in national, regional, and intraschool moot court and mock trial activities. All students are members of the Student Bar Association, which organizes many social and law-related activities. There are also active chapters of the Black Law Students Association, legal fraternities, and other special-interest organizations.

■ Expenses and Financial Aid

➡ *full-time tuition & fees—resident, $4,580; nonresident, $11,376*
➡ *part-time tuition & fees—resident, $206/credit hr.; nonresident, $501/credit hr.* ➡ *estimated additional expenses—$6,570, room & board; $1,300, books & supplies*
➡ *scholarships available* ➡ *minority scholarships available: African American Law Student Stipends available to enrolled African American students who are Tennessee residents*
➡ *financial aid available; Free Application for Federal Student Aid (FAFSA) required, priority deadline—April 1*

Financial aid is available in the form of scholarships, loans, and on-campus jobs. During 1998-1999, 100 students received approximately $400,000 in scholarship awards. Scholarships may range from $1,000 to $8,000 for the academic year.

■ Career Services

The School of Law's Career Services Office assists students and alumni by developing their interest in specific areas of the law, by enhancing their professional skills, and by providing information about opportunities for part-time and full-time employment in their law careers. The office receives a high volume of job listings each month for clerk and associate positions, and it keeps an extensive number of publications available to assist students and alumni with career and professional development. A comprehensive network of alumni mentors is available to help students who are interested in law careers outside the Memphis area. The office also conducts monthly seminars on job searching skills, résumé writing, and interviewing techniques as well as seminars bringing in outside private, corporate, and government attorneys to discuss how a student or alumni can make a successful career in their particular field of law.

In addition to hosting a large number of firms, corporations, and public interest/governmental employers for fall and spring on-campus interviewing, the School of Law is a member of several organizations that conduct annual recruiting conferences that provide second- and third-year law students and judicial law clerks with the opportunity to interview with law firms, government agencies, and corporations throughout the nation.

According to NALP statistics for the 1997 graduating class employment survey, more than 98 percent of those graduates responding reported employment within nine months of graduation.

Applicant Group for the 1998-1999 Academic Year

The University of Memphis—Cecil C. Humphreys School of Law
This grid includes only applicants who earned 120-180 LSAT scores under standard administrations.

LSAT Score	GPA																					
	3.75 +		3.50 - 3.74		3.25 - 3.49		3.00 - 3.24		2.75 - 2.99		2.50 - 2.74		2.25 - 2.49		2.00 - 2.24		Below 2.00		No GPA		Total	
	Apps	Adm	Apps	Adm	Apps	Adm	Apps	Adm	Apps	Adm	Apps	Adm	Apps	Adm	Apps	Adm	Apps	Adm	Apps	Adm	Apps	Adm
175-180	0	0	0	0	0	0	0	0	0	0	0	0	0	0	0	0	0	0	0	0	0	0
170-174	0	0	0	0	0	0	0	0	0	0	0	0	0	0	0	0	0	0	0	0	0	0
165-169	1	1	1	1	1	1	2	1	1	1	2	2	2	2	1	1	0	0	2	0	13	10
160-164	3	3	5	4	6	3	7	6	7	6	6	6	1	1	1	1	2	0	0	0	38	30
155-159	8	6	12	12	19	18	28	24	18	18	17	15	11	7	2	0	1	0	1	0	117	100
150-154	7	7	25	25	29	26	39	29	36	19	23	9	11	1	8	0	1	0	1	0	180	116
145-149	13	10	20	12	34	9	37	4	34	3	32	3	10	2	7	0	2	0	1	0	190	43
140-144	3	1	12	2	23	2	27	3	29	3	22	1	11	1	7	0	1	0	1	0	136	13
135-139	2	0	2	0	7	0	4	0	13	1	9	0	7	0	3	0	2	0	0	0	49	1
130-134	2	0	1	0	2	0	1	0	6	0	3	0	4	0	1	0	1	0	0	0	21	0
125-129	0	0	0	0	0	0	1	0	1	0	1	0	0	0	0	0	2	0	0	0	5	0
120-124	0	0	0	0	0	0	0	0	0	0	0	0	0	0	1	0	0	0	0	0	1	0
Total	39	28	78	56	121	59	146	67	145	51	115	36	57	14	31	2	12	0	6	0	750	313

Apps = Number of Applicants
Adm = Number Admitted
Reflects 99% of the total applicant pool.

Mercer University—Walter F. George School of Law

Office of Admissions
Macon, GA 31207

E-Mail: rollis_sd@mercer.edu
URL: http://www.law.mercer.edu
Phone: (toll-free) out-of-state, 800.MERCER-U, ext. 2605; in-state 800.342.0841, ext. 2605

■ Introduction

The Walter F. George School of Law of Mercer University is located in Macon, about 80 miles south of Atlanta. Founded in 1873, it is one of the oldest private law schools in the South. Named for a distinguished alumnus who served as a United States Senator for 36 years, the school became a member of AALS in 1923 and has been ABA-approved since 1925. In 1987, George Woodruff bequeathed the school $15 million, making possible the curricular and programmatic renaissance now enjoyed by Mercer law students. Two major initiatives were pursued as a result of Mr. Woodruff's beneficence: enrollment was reduced to approximately 400 students, and a new curriculum was put in place. The new curriculum emphasizes small classes, a progression in the course of study, and a unique sixth semester designed to facilitate the transition from student to lawyer.

■ Enrollment/Student Body

➡ *935 applicants* ➡ *133 admitted first-year class 1998*
➡ *full-time 25th/75th percentile GPA—2.87/3.48*
➡ *full-time 25th/75th percentile LSAT—150/156*
➡ *407 total full-time* ➡ *12.5% minority*
➡ *49% women* ➡ *21 states & foreign countries represented*
➡ *142 undergraduate schools represented*

■ Faculty

➡ *45 total* ➡ *27 full-time* ➡ *18 part-time or adjunct*
➡ *7 women* ➡ *4 minority*

■ Library and Physical Facilities

➡ *273,000 volumes & equivalents* ➡ *library hours: Mon.-Thurs. 8:30 A.M.-9:00 P.M.; Fri., 8:30 A.M.-5:00 P.M.; Sat., 11:00 A.M.-5:00 P.M.* ➡ *LEXIS* ➡ *NEXIS*
➡ *WESTLAW* ➡ *DIALOG* ➡ *6 full-time librarians*
➡ *library seats 326* ➡ *library keys provide 24-hour access*

Mercer School of Law enjoys the use of one of the finest law buildings in the country. The library contains a computer learning center. The computer learning center offers 24-hour access to all legal research databases, and the new computer lab offers Internet access along with CALI, word processing, LEXIS/NEXIS, and WESTLAW/DIALOG.

■ Admission

➡ *Bachelor's degree required for admission* ➡ *application deadline—March 15* ➡ *rolling admission, early application preferred* ➡ *LSAT, LSDAS required* ➡ *application fee—$45*

The Admissions Committee weighs a wide range of factors, including LSAT score and undergraduate GPA. Letters of recommendation are required and are considered along with other evidence of nonacademic experiences. Other factors that influence the admission decision include (1) undergraduate activities and honors; (2) work/military experience; (3) quality of the applicant's undergraduate institution; (4) postgraduate work; (5) factors that indicate an unusual degree of motivation or maturity; and, (6) factors that would contribute to the overall diversity of the entering class.

■ Student Activities

The *Mercer Law Review* is the oldest and most widely circulated student-staffed legal journal in the state of Georgia.

In addition to the Student Bar Association, the law school has chapters of Phi Alpha Delta and Phi Delta Phi legal fraternities, Black Law Students Association, Hispanic Bar Association, Environmental Law Society, International Law Society, Christian Legal Society, Jewish Legal Society, Asian-American Law Student Association, Association of Women Law Students, Federalist Society, Honor Council, Law School PC User's Group, Law Spouses, The Janus Chronicle, and the Public Interest Society, as well as student chapters of the American Trial Lawyers Association and National Association of Criminal Defense Lawyers.

■ Curriculum

➡ *Academic Support Program*
➡ *90 credits required to graduate* ➡ *over 100 courses available*
➡ *degrees & combined degrees available: J.D.; J.D./M.B.A.*
➡ *range of first-year class size—25-75*

Mercer School of Law offers an innovative curriculum, known as the Woodruff Program, leading in an orderly fashion toward the practice of law. Each year begins with an introductory week-long course exploring one role of the practicing lawyer. The first-year course, Introduction to Law Study, focuses on the lawyer as legal analyst and initiates the student into the law school routine of briefing and analyzing appellate case options. Introduction to Counseling, featuring the lawyer as problem-solver for the client, kicks off the second year. Introduction to Dispute Resolution launches the final year by teaching the lawyering skills of negotiation and mediation in the lawyer's roles as an advocate representing the client.

First-semester courses immerse the student in case-method study of the classic subjects of the common law. The focus broadens from case analysis to include constitutional and statutory analysis in the second semester. The middle semesters of legal study offer a wide array of electives along with required courses that ensure a thorough grounding in the core elements of the general practice of law. Students are required to select electives from three blocks of courses so that every Mercer graduate has the breadth of legal background to adapt to the changing demands of modern practice. Mercer offers enough small sections of a very popular Trial Practice Course, which enables each student to learn trial techniques through individual videotaped performances and one-on-one tape reviews with the professor.

One pervasive skill needed for law practice is the ability to write clearly and convincingly. In each year of law study, students sharpen their powers of written persuasion. In the spring semester of the first year, students take the basic course in Legal Writing, followed by a Legal Writing II in the second year, and a writing seminar on a topic of current interest in the final year.

The last semester of study offers students a unique opportunity to make the transition from law school to law practice. An intensive session features advanced courses in a variety of practical lawyering skills such as negotiation, business planning, and advanced criminal trial techniques. Also during this session, a number of outstanding judges and lawyers offer Mercer students a variety of "Practice Electives," courses exploring particular areas of specialized practice. Noted lawyers are called upon to provide the benefit of their experience and perspective in a special pre-practice course titled Perspectives on Lawyering. The course of study at Mercer is a logical progression of preparation for the practice of law.

■ Special Programs

The Woodruff Program is one of the most innovative and exciting education programs available, and unlike special programs at other schools, it is offered to every Mercer student. A more complete description of the program is available from the Office of Admissions. The National Criminal Defense College sponsors summer practice institutes that bring several hundred criminal defense attorneys to Mercer from across the United States. Selected students are given the opportunity to meet, observe, and work with some of the most prominent criminal defense attorneys in the nation.

■ Expenses and Financial Aid

➠ *full-time tuition & fees—$18,590*   ➠ *merit scholarships available*   ➠ *financial aid available; FAFSA due April 1*

The tuition rate is guaranteed to remain the same for students in good standing for three consecutive years. Tuition for the 1998 entering class will be set in May. For entering students, scholarships and loans are available to applicants with strong admissions credentials and demonstrated need. The school has its own scholarships and loan funds, including the Woodruff Scholarship, which covers full tuition and has an annual stipend of $5,000. Three of these are awarded annually.

■ Career Services

Mercer Law School has an active placement office headed by the Assistant Dean for Career Services. Alumni and faculty members support students in their efforts to find satisfying employment. The office assists students in obtaining permanent, summer, and part-time employment.

Services of the office include arranging on-campus interviews with employers, career planning seminars, and off-campus interviewing consortia. Individual career counseling and résumé and cover letter writing workshops also comprise much of the work of the office. There is an extensive library of career resources available for student use.

The class of 1997 reported 91.5 percent employed within six months of graduation. Members of the class of 1998 who took the Georgia Bar Examination passed the exam at a rate of over 92.5 percent.

Applicant Group for the 1998-1999 Academic Year

Mercer University—Walter F. George School of Law
This grid includes only applicants who earned 120-180 LSAT scores under standard administrations.

LSAT Score	GPA 3.75 +		3.50 - 3.74		3.25 - 3.49		3.00 - 3.24		2.75 - 2.99		2.50 - 2.74		2.25 - 2.49		2.00 - 2.24		Below 2.00		No GPA		Total	
	Apps	Adm	Apps	Adm	Apps	Adm	Apps	Adm	Apps	Adm	Apps	Adm	Apps	Adm	Apps	Adm	Apps	Adm	Apps	Adm	Apps	Adm
175-180	0	0	0	0	0	0	0	0	0	0	0	0	0	0	0	0	0	0	0	0	0	0
170-174	0	0	0	0	0	0	0	0	0	0	0	0	0	0	1	1	0	0	0	0	1	1
165-169	3	3	2	2	2	2	3	3	2	2	1	1	2	1	1	1	0	0	1	1	17	16
160-164	15	15	4	4	11	11	12	12	10	10	7	7	2	2	0	0	0	0	0	0	61	61
155-159	17	17	23	23	20	19	28	28	15	15	20	20	14	14	5	3	1	0	2	1	145	140
150-154	11	11	27	27	42	39	53	38	61	39	22	9	13	4	6	2	2	0	2	1	239	170
145-149	6	4	25	16	36	13	36	8	33	7	29	2	20	0	6	0	3	0	5	2	199	52
140-144	5	0	7	0	10	1	29	0	27	1	30	0	21	0	7	0	1	0	3	0	140	2
135-139	1	0	4	0	5	0	9	0	15	0	10	1	9	0	2	0	1	0	2	0	58	1
130-134	0	0	0	0	0	0	3	0	3	0	5	0	3	0	3	0	0	0	2	0	19	0
125-129	0	0	0	0	0	0	1	0	0	0	1	0	0	0	1	0	0	0	0	0	3	0
120-124	0	0	0	0	0	0	0	0	0	0	0	0	0	0	1	0	0	0	0	0	1	0
Total	58	50	92	72	126	85	174	89	166	74	125	40	84	21	33	7	8	0	17	5	883	443

Apps = Number of Applicants
Adm = Number Admitted
Reflects 99% of the total applicant pool.

University of Miami School of Law

P.O. Box 248087
Coral Gables, FL 33124-8087

E-Mail: admissions@law.miami.edu
URL: http://www.law.miami.edu
Phone: 305.284.2523

■ Introduction

Established in 1926 in Coral Gables, Florida, the University of Miami School of Law is part of one of the largest private research universities in the United States. The school's location, in a city of 40,000 south of Miami, allows students to attend the law school in a tranquil subtropical setting while gaining legal experience in the nearby international business center of Miami. The school is accredited by the ABA and is a member of the Association of American Law Schools. The school has a chapter of the Order of the Coif, the legal profession's most prestigious scholastic honor society.

■ Enrollment/Student Body

➡ *2,294 applicants*   ➡ *1,191 admitted first-year class 1998*
➡ *326 enrolled first-year class 1998*   ➡ *full-time 25th/75th percentile GPA—2.92/3.41*   ➡ *part-time 25th/75th percentile GPA—2.77/3.51*   ➡ *full-time 25th/75th percentile LSAT—151/157*   ➡ *part-time 25th/75th percentile LSAT—148/155*
➡ *1,043 total full-time*   ➡ *211 total part-time*
➡ *34.2% minority*   ➡ *43% women*
➡ *67 states & foreign countries represented*   ➡ *380 undergraduate schools represented*   ➡ *45% out-of-state residents*

■ Faculty

➡ *151 total .*   ➡ *52 full-time*   ➡ *99 part-time or adjunct*
➡ *14 full-time women*   ➡ *7 full-time minority*

The quality of a University of Miami legal education is directly attributable to the faculty, whose expertise covers the wide spectrum of the law, from jurisprudence to the law of the sea, from labor law to land use, from legal ethics to the law of international sales, and from Latin American legal systems to British legal history.

■ Library and Physical Facilities

➡ *over 490,000 volumes & equivalents*   ➡ *library hours: Mon.-Thurs., 7:00 A.M.-12:30 A.M.; Fri., 7:00 A.M.-MIDNIGHT; Sat., 8:30 A.M.-MIDNIGHT; Sun., 8:30 A.M.-12:30 A.M.*
➡ *LEXIS*   ➡ *NEXIS*   ➡ *WESTLAW*   ➡ *CIS Universe*
➡ *10 full-time librarians; 26 full-time staff*   ➡ *library seats 663*

Comfortable, spacious, and technologically advanced, the library is the largest legal research facility in the Southeast.

■ Curriculum

➡ *88 units required to graduate*   ➡ *170+ courses, workshops, & seminars*   ➡ *degrees available: J.D.; J.D./M.B.A.; J.D./M.P.H.; J.D./M.S.; LL.M.*   ➡ *semesters, start in Aug.*
➡ *range of first-year class size—90 day/50 evening divisions; one first-year class will be approximately 45 students; legal writing and research will be approximately 23 students*

Students ordinarily satisfy the requirements for the J.D. degree in three academic years of full-time study. An evening program and summer sessions are available. Joint J.D./Masters in Business Administration, J.D./Masters in Public Health, and J.D./Masters in Marine Affairs programs are also available.

The school also offers Master of Laws (LL.M.) degree programs for students specializing in inter-American law, international law, ocean and coastal law, taxation, estate planning, real property development, and comparative law.

Applicants to the LL.M. program must have earned a J.D. degree or its equivalent from an accredited law school and demonstrated the capacity for graduate law work. The school also offers an LL.M. for foreign students.

■ Special Programs

The law school offers one of the most comprehensive and sophisticated skills-training programs in the nation, integrating trial, pretrial, and clinical experiences into one program. Directed by a full-time faculty member, more than 50 distinguished trial attorneys and judges, from both state and federal courts, assist with the trial and pretrial courses and help to supervise the clinical placements. Additional skills training is available in Alternative Dispute Resolution, Mediation, and Domestic and International Legal Research.

Two seven-week summer study abroad programs are offered: the London Summer Program, held at the University College London; and the Tour de Espana, held in Barcelona (10 nights), Fuengirola (26 nights), and Madrid (10 nights).

The Children and Youth Law Clinic provides representation primarily to abused and neglected children and youth in the foster care system.

The James Weldon Johnson Summer Institute, held for five weeks before the fall semester, acquaints selected students with the discipline necessary to succeed in law school.

The law school makes a major contribution toward increasing the representation of minorities in the legal profession, with one of the largest minority enrollments in the nation. To that end, the Professional Opportunities Program for Black Law Students, a coalition of local bar organizations, established attorneys, law firms, and the school, assists students in securing federal or judicial clerkships, summer associate positions, and internships, and provides a mentor program with attorneys.

■ Admission

➡ *Bachelor's degree from a regionally accredited college or university required*   ➡ *application deadline—March 8 (priority)*
➡ *rolling admissions, early application preferred*
➡ *LSAT, LSDAS required*
➡ *nonrefundable application fee—$50*

Admission is competitive and will be more selective as enrollment goals decrease. LSAT scores and undergraduate averages are used in the selection process. Letters of recommendation are required. Also considered are the applicant's work and extracurricular history, special skills, and background. The school encourages members of minority groups to apply. Entering students are admitted only in the fall semester. Applicants are urged to apply for admission as early as possible after September 1. Applications received after March 8 will be considered on a space-available basis. Applications will be accepted until July 31. Transfer applications are welcomed from students with competitive records who have completed at least, but no more than, one full year of work at an ABA-accredited law school.

■ Student Activities

The school's many student activities include a Student Bar Association; an Honor Council; publications such as the *University of Miami Law Review*; *Inter-American Law Review*; *Yearbook of International Law*; *Entertainment and Sports Law Review*; *Psychology, Public Policy, and Law Review*; and *Business Law Journal*; and about 40 diverse student organizations.

The school runs one of the nation's largest mock trial competitions, involving over 200 experienced lawyers who coach some 100 students. The school is distinguished by winning state, regional, and national competitions in moot court, mock trial, negotiation, and client counseling.

■ Expenses and Financial Aid

➡ *yearly tuition & fees—full-time, $21,956; part-time, $16,168* ➡ *estimated additional expenses—$9,025 min. (room, board, books) plus $4,722 (personal & transportation)* ➡ *merit- & need-based scholarships available* ➡ *financial aid available; FAFSA form for need analysis due in Jan. or early Feb.*

Scholarship aid available through the law school normally does not exceed the cost of tuition. Most scholarships are awarded on the basis of merit, although need is sometimes considered. Admitted applicants are automatically considered for scholarship awards. Those admitted by February 1 are considered for the Harvey T. Reid and Soia Mentschikoff and Miami Scholars scholarships. Loan funds are available through the Financial Aid Office. The priority deadline for all financial assistance is March 1.

Scholarships are also available through the Florida Minority Participation in Legal Education Program. Eligible applicants are Florida resident U.S. citizens, members of a historically disadvantaged minority group, and who have been accepted for full-time admission to a participating Florida law school. Recipients agree to apply for the Florida Bar and practice a minimum of three years in Florida. For further information contact: The Florida Education Fund, MPLE Offices, 15485 Eagle Nest Lane, Suite 200, Miami Lakes, FL 33014.

On-campus, furnished three-bedroom apartments are available for law students. The approximate annual cost of $5,424 includes utilities, local phone service, and television cable. Off-campus housing information is available from the Office of Student Recruiting.

■ Career Services

The Career Planning Center provides career counseling and career resources to law students and alumni. The Career Planning Center's fall On-Campus Interviewing Program attracts local and national employers, providing opportunities to interview with firms, corporations, government, the courts, public interest employers, and public service organizations. The Center offers access to a resource library, research terminals, and job postings on our Web site.

Applicant Group for the 1998-1999 Academic Year

University of Miami School of Law
This grid includes only applicants who earned 120-180 LSAT scores under standard administrations

LSAT Score	GPA								
	3.75 +	3.50 - 3.74	3.25 - 3.49	3.00 - 3.24	2.75 - 2.99	2.50 - 2.74	2.25 - 2.49	2.00 - 2.24	Below 2.00
175-180									
170-174									
165-169									
160-164									
155-159									
150-154									
145-149									
140-144									
135-139									
130-134									
125-129									
120-124									

■ Good Possibility   □ Possible   ▨ Unlikely

Reflects 98% of the total applicant pool.
When reviewing the grid, it is important to note that admission to the school is based upon all aspects of an applicant's background, and not limited to the LSAT and undergraduate grade-point average.

University of Michigan Law School

Hutchins Hall
Ann Arbor, MI 48109-1215

URL: http://www.law.umich.edu
Phone: 734.764.0537

■ Introduction

The University of Michigan Law School, founded in 1859, has long been one of the nation's finest institutions of legal education. The school is home to a distinguished and diverse faculty, many of its scholars preeminent in their fields. It is recognized as a leader in interdisciplinary legal studies; the insights and methods of other fields of study are apparent throughout the broad curriculum offerings.

Graduates' careers also speak eloquently for the value of the education offered. Michigan law graduates are found serving with distinction in all sectors of law, business, and government around the world.

Above all, the Law School takes special pride in its student body. Students from across the nation and around the globe contribute their remarkable talents and accomplishments to make the Law School a community that exudes a sense of serious purpose, high academic achievement, and social commitment.

■ Enrollment/Student Body

➼ 3,476 applicants ➼ 341 enrolled first-year class 1998
➼ full-time 25th/75th percentile GPA—3.36/3.73
➼ full-time 25th/75th percentile LSAT—163/168
➼ 1,030 total full-time ➼ 37 full-time graduate students
➼ 22.5% students of color ➼ 39% women
➼ 41 states & foreign countries represented J.D.;
27 foreign countries graduate students
➼ 129 undergraduate schools represented

The first-year class includes approximately 340 J.D. candidates who are joined each year by about 35 new graduate students, most of them young law faculty from a score of foreign countries. Students routinely come from all 50 states. In 1998, 29 percent of the first-year students were classified as Michigan residents.

■ Faculty

➼ 120 total ➼ 68 full-time ➼ 52 part-time or adjunct
➼ 37 women ➼ 10 minority

There are 68 full-time faculty members; many distinguished visiting scholars and practitioners further enhance course offerings. While maintaining a long tradition of eminence in constitutional, criminal, international, and comparative law, as well as the law of international trade, the faculty have expanded legal scholarship with the insights of such fields as economics, history, philosophy, psychiatry, psychology, and sociology.

■ Library and Physical Facilities

➼ 826,766 volumes & equivalents ➼ library hours:
8:00 A.M.-MIDNIGHT daily ➼ LEXIS ➼ NEXIS
➼ WESTLAW ➼ LEXCALIBUR
➼ 12 full-time librarians ➼ library seats 843

■ Curriculum

➼ Academic Support Program ➼ Minority Affairs Program
➼ 83 credits minimum required to graduate ➼ 103 courses available ➼ 71 seminars ➼ 5 clinical offerings
➼ degrees available: J.D.; LL.M.; M.C.L.; S.J.D.; J.D./Ph.D. in Economics; J.D./M.B.A.; J.D./M.H.S.A.; J.D./M.P.P.; J.D./M.S.W.; J.D./M.S. Natural Resources; J.D./A.M. World Politics; J.D./M.A. Russian & East European Studies; J.D./A.M. Modern Middle Eastern & North African Studies; J.D./M.S.I. in Information

The first-year program is designed to give all students mastery of the basic methods of legal analysis, and of the processes of reasoning used by lawyers, while introducing major areas of legal specialization. A small-section program emphasizes the importance of collegiality between faculty and students, as does the unusually large number of students hired as research assistants with the help of the William Cook endowment. The first-year curriculum is presented to four sections of first-year students. One section begins work in late May, and three start in the fall. The Legal Practice Program affords another opportunity for small-group work and for unique learning in the art of persuasive legal writing. Every student has the option of taking at least one elective course during the first year. The second and third years are entirely elective, the only requirements being that each student elect before graduation one seminar and a course meeting the professional responsibility requirement.

In addition to the joint J.D. programs with other disciplines, other concurrent programs may be arranged. The Belfield-Bates Overseas Travel Fellowships provide funds for legal studies abroad or professional internships with international or governmental agencies or law firms. Externships provide individual students with advanced training in their areas of interest.

■ Clinical Opportunities

The Law School offers a variety of clinical courses including: a large General Clinic in which students may elect a civil, criminal, poverty, or neighborhood-based concentration; the Child Advocacy Law Clinic; the Legal Assistance for Urban Communities Program; the Environmental Law Clinic; and the Criminal Appellate Seminar.

The Family Law Project, Asylum and Refugee Project, and Project for Older Prisoners are student-run advocacy programs in which students volunteer to represent clients.

■ Admission

➼ Bachelor's degree required ➼ application deadline—
Feb. 15, modified rolling (strongest applications evaluated earliest)
➼ LSAT, LSDAS required ➼ application fee—$70

Michigan seeks to form a class which comprises an exciting and productive mix of students who will enhance the educational experience for each other. Law School Admission Test scores and the quality of the applicant's educational experience (particularly the nature of and performance in coursework) are relied on heavily. Serious regard also is given to one's promise of making a notable contribution to the class by way of a particular strength in one or more of the many attainments and characteristics examined in the application process. Selections among applicants are guided by the purpose of making the school a better and livelier place in which to learn, and improving its service to the profession and the public.

■ Student Activities

The *Michigan Law Review* covers significant research in all areas of law. The *Journal of Law Reform* focuses on the law as it has changed and as it ought to be, while the *Michigan Journal of International Law* concentrates on international and comparative law. The *Michigan Journal of Gender and Law* publishes feminist perspectives on gender issues in the law. The *Michigan Telecommunication and Technology Law Review* is among the first solely electronic, online legal journals, dedicated to exploring complex issues surrounding regulation of communication technology. The *Michigan Journal of Race and Law* focuses on critical race theory and related scholarly study. Students interested in combining oral argument with experience as writers of briefs may choose to enter the Campbell Moot Court Competition or the Philip C. Jessup International Moot Court Competition. The Law School Student Senate funds over 50 student organizations. Students enjoy speakers and social support through groups defined by religion, ethnicity, sexual orientation, age, gender, or personal interests.

■ Expenses and Financial Aid

➡ *tuition & fees—resident, $17,910; nonresident, $23,880*
➡ *estimated additional expenses—$13,165*
➡ *financial aid available; Need Access & FAFSA forms required*

Nearly all financial aid is need-based and consists of a combination of loans and grants. The school's Financial Aid Program is very substantial, drawing on a variety of Law School Scholarship and Loan Funds, as well as funds from the federal government and other external sources. Parental information is necessary in order to be considered for grant aid. We endeavor to provide financial assistance to all full-time students seeking the J.D. degree who would be unable to meet the costs of their law school education if drawing only on their own and family resources.

Merit scholarships are also available each year. They are awarded to outstanding candidates remarkable for their anticipated contribution to the Law School and the legal profession. They vary in amount from several thousand dollars per year to full tuition plus a stipend for three years.

A post-graduate Debt Management Program enhances law graduates' freedom to pursue public interest or other positions in which salaries are lower than many alternatives.

■ Career Services/Public Service

The Office of Career Services schedules nearly 8,000 interviews each year with over 650 employers from all over the country. It also informs students of announcements of some 2,000 other employment opportunities with employers who do not visit the school. This year employers from 49 states, the District of Columbia, and 20 foreign countries notified the Office of Career Services of available positions. The Office of Public Service works with students interested in employment in public interest organizations and government. The majority of Michigan graduates accept positions with private law firms, and a substantial proportion accept judicial clerkships for their initial professional position.

Admission Profile Not Available

University of Minnesota Law School

229 19th Avenue South
Minneapolis, MN 55455

E-Mail: umnlsadm@tc.umn.edu
URL: http://www.law.umn.edu/
Phone: 612.625.5005

■ Introduction

The University of Minnesota Law School has entered its 110th year in vigorous health. The quality of Minnesota's faculty, the academic credentials of its students, and the caliber of its library collection and physical facilities are the strongest in the history of the school. This vitality is a result of thoughtful and forward-looking development of the school's century-old tradition of excellence in legal education. The law school provides a personal, collegial environment for the study of law; at the same time, students have access to the academic, professional, and cultural resources of the larger university, and the Twin Cities of St. Paul and Minneapolis, one of the most progressive and livable metropolitan communities in the country.

■ Enrollment/Student Body

➡ *1,467 applicants* ➡ *240 enrolled first-year class 1998*
➡ *full-time 25th/75th percentile GPA—3.34/3.80*
➡ *full-time 25th/75th percentile LSAT—159/164*
➡ *789 total full-time* ➡ *19% minority* ➡ *50% women*
➡ *35 states & foreign countries represented*
➡ *219 undergraduate schools represented*

■ Faculty

➡ *144 total* ➡ *44 full-time* ➡ *100 part-time or adjunct*
➡ *15 women* ➡ *5 minority*

The faculty's wide-ranging expertise allows students to choose from a curriculum that offers traditional legal training as well as innovative clinical and computer-assisted programs.

■ Library and Physical Facilities

➡ *850,000 volumes & equivalents* ➡ *library hours:
open 365 day/year, 24 hours/day; staffed, Mon.-Fri., 8:00 A.M.-10:00 P.M.; Sat., 9:00 A.M.-6:00 P.M.; Sun., NOON-6:00 P.M.*
➡ *LEXIS* ➡ *NEXIS* ➡ *WESTLAW* ➡ *LUMINA*
➡ *29 full-time librarians* ➡ *library seats 934*

The award-winning Law Center on the west bank of the university's Minneapolis Campus, dedicated in 1978, remains a model for new law school complexes. The Law Library is the sixth largest academic law library in the United States and offers an exceptional international collection, comprehensive primary and secondary legal materials, and computerized connections to WESTLAW, LEXIS, and the entire University of Minnesota library system.

■ Curriculum

➡ *Academic Support Program*
➡ *88 credits required to graduate* ➡ *130 courses available*
➡ *degrees available: J.D.; J.D./M.B.A.; J.D./M.P.A. (Public Affairs); joint degrees are available with most graduate programs*
➡ *semesters, start in late Aug.*
➡ *range of first-year class size—14-108*

The traditional Socratic teaching method appears in all three years of the J.D. curriculum. Tutorial seminars, computer-assisted instruction, and clinical and simulated skills training are offered in various forms throughout a student's law school career. Students must fulfill a legal writing requirement in each of their three years and take one class in professional responsibility, but otherwise their second and third years are entirely elective. The first-year writing class and the various moot courts, journals, and writing seminars all provide students with small-group instruction, editing, and supervision.

■ Clinical Legal Education

The Law School has developed one of the country's largest and most active clinical programs. Each year, over 160 students receive academic credit for participating in negotiations, client interviews, court appearances, and other casework supervised by clinic faculty. Clinic course offerings include domestic abuse, bankruptcy, appellate practice, civil litigation, federal taxation, criminal prosecution and defense, asylum law, public interest law, worker's compensation, child advocacy, social security disability, gender and the law, family law, and prisoner assistance in civil matters.

■ International Law

International programs are supported by a broad comparative and international law curriculum taught by Minnesota's own faculty experts on GATT, Public and Private International Law, and International Human Rights, and by visiting international scholars. This year, law professors and students from the People's Republic of China, Mexico, Poland, France, Germany, and Sweden are engaged in research, J.D., and graduate studies, and scholars from many other countries will visit for special programs. Summer sessions abroad in alternate years offer the study of comparative law at Lyon, France or Uppsala, Sweden. School-year study is possible in several countries for students possessing fluency in the language of the host institution.

■ Computer-Assisted Study and Research

The Law School is a home to and founding member of CCALI, the Center for Computer-Assisted Legal Instruction, a consortium of more than 116 law schools, which develops computer-assisted exercises for legal education. Students complete these tutorials, drills, and simulation exercises as assignments or supplements for classroom instruction. The Law School computer lab provides student access to personal computers for CCALI exercises, computer-based legal research, and word processing.

■ Admission

➡ *Bachelor's degree required* ➡ *application deadline—March 1; rolling admissions, early application preferred starting Nov. 1* ➡ *LSAT, LSDAS required*
➡ *application fee—$40*

The Admissions Committee seeks to enroll 250 highly qualified, widely talented full-time students each fall. The class is selected on the basis of numerical indicators of potential success in law school. The committee also considers individual scholastic honors, extracurricular activities, personal statements, recommendations, work experience, unusual life experiences, and other factors that indicate a potential for success as a law student and lawyer. Minnesota is committed to equal educational opportunities for women and minorities and strongly encourages their applications. Applicants are encouraged to visit the Law School. Arrangements can be made through the Office of Admissions to sit in on a class, tour the Law Center, and meet with an admissions representative.

■ Student Activities

Members of the *Minnesota Law Review*, founded in 1917; *The Journal of Law and Inequality*, established in 1982; *The Minnesota Journal of Global Trade*, established in 1991; *Constitutional Commentary*; and *Crime and Justice*; publish scholarly legal articles, refining their writing skills under close editorial supervision. Minnesota's eight moot court teams have built a strong record of success in regional and national competition. Extracurricular organizations focus on international human rights, minority concerns, public interest law internships, environmental law, law and religion, and other areas.

■ Expenses and Financial Aid

➡ *tuition & fees—full-time resident, $9,630; nonresident, $15,930*
➡ *estimated additional expenses—$9,400*
➡ *scholarships available (performance & need-based)*
➡ *minority scholarships available (performance & need-based)*
➡ *financial aid available*   ➡ *FAFSA form for need analysis should be filed before March 1*

In recent years more than 85 percent of the student body has received financial aid, primarily in loans, but including scholarships, grants, and work-study programs. Forms are available from the Office of Student Financial Aid, 210 Fraser Hall, 106 Pleasant Street, S.E., University of Minnesota, Minneapolis, MN 55455.

■ Career Services

Our graduates are leaders in federal and state judiciary and government, academics, law practice, legal services, and business. In 1997-1998, approximately 100 law firms, corporations, and governmental agencies from around the United States will interview on campus. In addition, more than 900 employers send notices for posting in the Career Services Office. While a majority of graduates accept positions in the Midwest, the national composition of our student body is attractive to employees across the country. The Career Services Office provides numerous career-planning seminars and services, and maintains a resource library.

Applicant Group for the 1998-1999 Academic Year

University of Minnesota Law School

LSAT Score	3.75 +		3.50 - 3.74		3.25 - 3.49		3.00 - 3.24		2.75 - 2.99		2.50 - 2.74		2.25 - 2.49		2.00 - 2.24		Below 2.00		No GPA		Total	
	Apps	Adm	Apps	Adm	Apps	Adm	Apps	Adm	Apps	Adm	Apps	Adm	Apps	Adm	Apps	Adm	Apps	Adm	Apps	Adm	Apps	Adm
175-180	2	2	6	6	2	2	1	1	2	2	0	0	1	0	0	0	0	0	0	0	14	13
170-174	9	8	10	10	8	8	4	3	4	4	0	0	2	1	0	0	0	0	1	1	38	35
165-169	47	45	41	39	46	45	18	18	13	9	6	4	2	0	0	0	0	0	1	1	174	161
160-164	79	76	97	81	86	53	42	22	28	10	7	1	5	2	0	0	0	0	13	7	357	252
155-159	78	53	98	30	96	18	62	11	26	0	8	2	9	0	3	0	0	0	12	3	392	117
150-154	39	7	54	11	74	14	45	3	30	1	12	1	5	0	2	0	0	0	10	2	271	39
145-149	12	0	30	3	29	2	21	0	13	0	12	0	4	0	1	0	0	0	7	1	129	6
140-144	2	0	6	0	11	1	15	0	8	0	10	0	2	0	2	0	1	0	3	1	60	2
135-139	0	0	6	0	0	0	3	0	3	0	10	0	2	0	2	0	3	0	1	0	30	0
130-134	0	0	0	0	0	0	1	0	3	0	1	0	0	0	1	0	0	0	0	0	6	0
125-129	0	0	0	0	1	0	1	0	0	0	1	0	0	0	1	0	1	0	0	0	5	0
120-124	0	0	0	0	0	0	0	0	0	0	0	0	1	0	0	0	0	0	0	0	1	0
Total	268	191	348	180	353	143	213	58	130	26	67	8	33	3	12	0	5	0	48	16	1477	625

Apps = Number of Applicants
Adm = Number Admitted
This grid includes all applicants who earned 120-180 LSAT scores.
This chart is to be used as a general guide only. Nonnumerical factors are strongly considered for all applicants.

The University of Mississippi School of Law

E-Mail: lawmiss@olemiss.edu
URL: http://www.olemiss.edu/depts/law_school/law-hom.html
University, MS 38677
Phone: Admission: 601.232.6910, Main: 601.232.7361

■ Introduction

Recognizing the need for formal law instruction in the state of Mississippi, the legislature in 1854 established the Department of Law at The University of Mississippi. Over the years, the law department has evolved into today's modern Law Center. Located in Oxford, Mississippi, on the main campus of the University of Mississippi, the Law Center is housed in Lamar Hall, named in honor of the late Mississippian, L.Q.C. Lamar, former Associate Justice of the United States Supreme Court and first law professor at the university. Oxford, a small town of approximately 10,000 people, lies nestled in the quiet hills of North Mississippi, just 75 miles southeast of bustling Memphis, Tennessee, and 180 miles north of the state capital of Jackson.

The University of Mississippi is the fourth oldest state-supported law school in the nation. The School of Law is fully approved by the American Bar Association and is a long-standing member of the Association of American Law Schools.

■ Enrollment/Student Body

➡ *1,203 applicants* ➡ *446 admitted first-year class 1998*
➡ *158 enrolled first-year class 1998*
➡ *full-time 25th/75th percentile GPA—3.01/3.63*
➡ *full-time 25th/75th percentile LSAT—150/157*
➡ *481 total full-time* ➡ *4 total part-time*
➡ *13% minority* ➡ *37% women* ➡ *21 states represented*
➡ *107 undergraduate schools represented*

■ Faculty

➡ *37 total* ➡ *27 full-time* ➡ *10 part-time or adjunct*
➡ *7 women* ➡ *5 minority*

■ Library and Physical Facilities

➡ *287,000 volumes & equivalents* ➡ *library hours: 115*
➡ *LEXIS* ➡ *NEXIS* ➡ *WESTLAW* ➡ *DIALOG*
➡ *6 full-time librarians* ➡ *library seats 395*

In August 1978, the law school moved into a new and modern five-story structure which contains, among many other features, five large classrooms with tiered seating and video capabilities, two fully equipped moot courtrooms, office space for several auxiliary law programs and their staff, and individual faculty offices.

The law library collection consists of over 287,000 volumes, 138,500 of which are in microform equivalents. During the 1995-1996 academic year, the law library installed a major upgrade of its online catalog, making it available to Internet users. The law library also added the first federal district court opinions to the Web when it became the host site for the Northern District of Mississippi court opinions. During the '96/'97 academic year, the computer lab was upgraded to include 14 multimedia pentium computers.

■ Special Programs

The law school actively recruits minority students and provides counseling and support programs for minority students both before and after enrollment. At present, 63 minority students are pursuing a law degree.

■ Curriculum

➡ *Academic Support Program* ➡ *90 credits required to graduate* ➡ *123 courses available* ➡ *degrees available: J.D.; J.D./M.B.A.* ➡ *semesters, start in June and Aug.*

■ Admission

➡ *Bachelor's degree required for admission*
➡ *application deadline—March 1*
➡ *LSAT, LSDAS required* ➡ *application fee—$25*

Admission to law school is gained by committee approval based upon an applicant's credentials. These credentials include a satisfactory Law School Admission Test (LSAT) score and an acceptable academic record at the undergraduate level. A bachelor's degree from an accredited school is required before an applicant can register for law school.

There are no prelaw requisites. Every applicant must take the LSAT and subscribe to the LSDAS. An LSAT score obtained more than three years before application is not valid, and the applicant will be required to retake the test. Applications are available the September preceding admission, with the application deadline for both summer and fall enrollment being March 1. However, early application is encouraged. Applicants who file late risk being placed on a waiting list.

Although the LSAT and GPA are obviously the most important factors in the admission process, other considerations are: (1) grade patterns and progression; (2) quality of undergraduate institution; (3) difficulty of major field of study; (4) number of years since bachelor's degree was earned; (5) job experience; (6) social, personal, or economic circumstances that may have affected college grades or performance on the LSAT or academic record; (7) nonacademic achievements; (8) letters of recommendation; and (9) residency.

■ Student Activities

The *Mississippi Law Journal* is edited and published by law students. Students also administer the Moot Court program. Membership in each is competitive with grade and writing requirements.

■ Expenses and Financial Aid

➡ *tuition & fees—full-time resident, $3,581/yr.; full-time nonresident, $7,503/yr.* ➡ *estimated additional expenses— $7,000 (books & living expenses)* ➡ *scholarships available*
➡ *minority scholarships available*
➡ *financial aid available; FAF due March 1*

■ Career Services

A full-time Director of Career Services assists students in finding permanent, summer, or part-time employment. Seventy-five to 100 law firms and other prospective employers interview at the law school each year. Approximately 60 percent of graduating seniors are employed prior to graduation, with the remaining num-ber being placed within six months of graduation. The law school is an active member of the National Association of Law Placement (NALP) and annually participates in the Mid-South Placement Consortium (Nashville), the National Public Interest Law Career Fair (Washington, DC), and the Minority Job Fair (Atlanta).

Applicant Group for the 1998-1999 Academic Year

The University of Mississippi School of Law
This grid includes only applicants who earned 120-180 LSAT scores under standard administrations.

LSAT Score	GPA 3.75 +		3.50 - 3.74		3.25 - 3.49		3.00 - 3.24		2.75 - 2.99		2.50 - 2.74		2.25 - 2.49		2.00 - 2.24		Below 2.00		No GPA		Total	
	Apps	Adm	Apps	Adm	Apps	Adm	Apps	Adm	Apps	Adm	Apps	Adm	Apps	Adm	Apps	Adm	Apps	Adm	Apps	Adm	Apps	Adm
175-180	0	0	0	0	0	0	0	0	0	0	0	0	0	0	0	0	0	0	0	0	0	0
170-174	2	2	1	1	0	0	1	1	1	1	2	2	1	1	0	0	0	0	0	0	8	8
165-169	3	3	1	1	2	2	2	2	4	4	2	2	2	2	0	0	0	0	1	0	17	16
160-164	10	10	8	8	12	12	8	7	11	11	8	7	6	4	0	0	0	0	0	0	63	59
155-159	25	25	23	23	36	36	39	37	33	28	18	12	13	5	6	0	1	0	1	1	195	167
150-154	18	16	55	40	70	34	61	27	60	12	36	5	20	2	6	0	0	0	3	2	329	138
145-149	16	9	35	9	56	10	64	10	51	2	42	2	26	2	5	0	3	0	5	1	303	45
140-144	8	2	9	0	24	1	33	1	37	1	26	0	11	0	9	0	2	0	3	0	162	5
135-139	2	0	6	1	10	1	11	2	19	0	13	0	7	0	0	0	1	0	1	0	70	4
130-134	1	0	1	0	2	1	4	0	5	0	4	0	5	0	2	0	2	0	3	0	29	1
125-129	0	0	0	0	0	0	1	0	1	0	0	0	3	0	1	0	1	0	1	0	8	0
120-124	0	0	0	0	0	0	0	0	0	0	0	0	0	0	0	0	0	0	1	0	1	0
Total	85	67	139	83	212	97	224	87	222	59	151	30	94	16	29	0	10	0	19	4	1185	443

Apps = Number of Applicants
Adm = Number Admitted
Reflects 99% of the total applicant pool.

Mississippi College School of Law

151 E. Griffith St.
Jackson, MS 39201

E-Mail: law-admissions@mc.edu
URL: http://www.mc.edu/organizations/acad/LAW/
Phone: 800.738.1236 or 601.925.7150

■ Introduction

Mississippi College School of Law is conveniently located in downtown Jackson, the state capital, and is within walking distance of the legislature, as well as all federal and state administrative agencies and courts. Jackson is the legal and commercial center of the state and has a metropolitan population of approximately 400,000. The main campus of Mississippi College, with an enroll-ment of more than 3,000 students, is located in Clinton, a suburb 12 miles west of Jackson. Mississippi College School of Law is fully accredited by the American Bar Association and is a member of the Association of American Law Schools.

■ Enrollment/Student Body

➸ *693 applicants*   ➸ *414 admitted first-year class 1998*
➸ *141 enrolled first-year class 1998*   ➸ *full-time 25th/75th percentile GPA—2.81/3.39*   ➸ *full-time 25th/75th percentile LSAT—145/152*   ➸ *401 total full-time*   ➸ *10% minority*
➸ *38% women*   ➸ *30 states & foreign countries represented*
➸ *115 undergraduate schools represented*

■ Faculty

➸ *38 total*   ➸ *20 full-time*   ➸ *18 part-time or adjunct*
➸ *7 women*   ➸ *2 minority*

■ Library and Physical Facilities

➸ *293,000 volumes & equivalents*   ➸ *library hours: Mon.-Thurs., 7:30 A.M.-MIDNIGHT; Fri., 7:30 A.M.-9:00 P.M.; Sat., 9:00 A.M.-9:00 P.M.; Sun., NOON-MIDNIGHT*
➸ *LEXIS/NEXIS*   ➸ *WESTLAW*
➸ *6 full-time librarians*   ➸ *library seats 207*

The Law Library is housed on the second and third floors of the facility in attractive space that makes generous use of natural light and affords pleasing views of the park-like law school grounds. Carpeted throughout, the library has separate rooms for individual and group study, audiovisual equipment, and photocopying. A chief feature is the modern computer lab that provides computer-assisted legal instruc-tion and word processing using WordPerfect software. The library is a government depository and serves bench and bar, along with its students, by providing access to primary and secondary authority for legal research in federal and state law, in addition to selective foreign and international materials.

■ Curriculum

➸ *Academic Support Program*   ➸ *88 credits required to graduate*   ➸ *81 courses available*   ➸ *degrees available: J.D.; J.D./M.B.A.*   ➸ *semesters, start in Aug.*
➸ *range of first-year class size—12-75*

Mississippi College School of Law is an institution that provides superior academic instruction with a curriculum

that is national in focus. The school is operated on a semester basis. A beginning student must enter in the fall semester. A summer term is available to second- and third-year students who wish to accelerate and/or enrich their studies.

■ Special Programs

In order to assist students in choosing elective courses, four areas of concentration have been developed. These areas consist of general practice, commercial and corporate practice, government-related practice, and litigation practice. These groupings, however, are not intended to provide specialization during a student's first degree in law. Recognizing the importance of developing lawyering skills, Mississippi College School of Law has a curriculum that includes instruction in both theoretical and practical skills. Students have an opportunity to put into practice what they have learned in courses such as Pretrial Practice, Trial Practice, Counseling and Negotiation, Appellate Advocacy I and II, Legal Drafting, and Real Estate Transactions.

■ Minority Program

The law school offers a variety of programs to assist minority students: dedicated scholarships/stipends; Academic Support Program; Minority Interaction Placement in conjunction with the state bar; and CLEO participation. Minority students are strongly encouraged to apply and each applicant's entire record will be care-fully considered.

■ Admission

➸ *Bachelor's degree required*   ➸ *application deadline—May 1*
➸ *LSAT, LSDAS required*   ➸ *application fee—$25*
➸ *rolling admission*

The admissions standards are set annually by the faculty. They are based on the college undergraduate grade-point average, the LSAT score, and personal and/or academic achievements or honors. A degree from an accredited four-year college or university is a prerequisite to admission. Every applicant must take the LSAT and subscribe to the LSDAS prior to being considered for admission. The school makes admissions decisions without discrimina-tion against any person on the basis of race, religion, sex, or national origin. A $25 application fee must accompany the application. The LSAT scores should reach the Admissions Office by May 1 for fall admission. When an applicant is accepted, a deposit of $100 is required to reserve a seat in the entering class. A second deposit of $200 must be received by July 1. Upon enroll-ment, these nonrefundable payments are credited to the applicant's tuition.

■ Student Activities

The *Mississippi College Law Review* is a legal journal edited and published by law students selected on the basis of scholarship and the ability to do creative, scholarly research and writing. The students write comments and notes on legal developments and significant cases and edit lead articles and book reviews written by professors, lawyers, judges, legislators, and other scholars. Membership on the *Law Review* staff is recognized as both an honor and a unique educational experience. Mississippi College School of Law also provides an appellate advocacy program administered by the Moot Court Board, composed of second- and third-year students. This required program provides students with instruction and practice in both brief writing and oral argument. The Law Student Bar Association (LSBA) is the organized student government of the law school. All students are members and are eligible to hold office in the association. Other student activities include: three national legal fraternity chapters, Phi Alpha Delta, Delta Theta Phi, and Phi Delta Phi; a student chapter of the Mississippi Trial Lawyers Association; the Women's Student Bar; Christian Legal Society; Black Law Students Association; the Law School Speakers Program; and Environmental Law Club.

■ Expenses and Financial Aid

➡ *tuition & fees—full-time, $14,615*
➡ *estimated additional expenses—$13,990 (room & board, $7,400; books, $850; travel, $2,500; personal, $3,240)*
➡ *performance-based scholarships available*
➡ *performance-based minority scholarships available*
➡ *financial aid available*   ➡ *FAFSA financial aid form due May 1*   ➡ *MS College financial aid application*

■ Career Services

The Dean for Student Services and the Coordinator of Career Services work together to assist in placement activities. In addition to the traditional on-campus interviews, the law school participates in regional interviews and a clerkship interaction program to help students find employment prior to graduation. Graduates are locating employment with major law firms, corporations, and government agencies throughout the United States, with a primary focus in the Southeast. Students have received clerkships with the United States Circuit Court of Appeals, United States District Courts, and the Supreme Courts of various states.

Applicant Group for the 1998-1999 Academic Year

Mississippi College School of Law

LSAT Score	GPA																					
	3.75 +		3.50 - 3.74		3.25 - 3.49		3.00 - 3.24		2.75 - 2.99		2.50 - 2.74		2.25 - 2.49		2.00 - 2.24		Below 2.00		No GPA		Total	
	Apps	Adm	Apps	Adm	Apps	Adm	Apps	Adm	Apps	Adm	Apps	Adm	Apps	Adm	Apps	Adm	Apps	Adm	Apps	Adm	Apps	Adm
175-180	0	0	0	0	0	0	0	0	0	0	0	0	0	0	0	0	0	0	0	0	0	0
170-174	0	0	0	0	0	0	0	0	0	0	0	0	1	1	0	0	0	0	0	0	1	1
165-169	1	1	1	1	1	1	1	1	0	0	0	0	0	0	0	0	0	0	1	1	5	5
160-164	0	0	3	3	1	1	0	0	1	1	0	0	0	0	0	0	0	0	0	0	5	5
155-159	9	9	3	3	5	5	7	7	5	5	9	9	3	3	4	4	1	1	1	1	47	47
150-154	7	7	15	15	16	15	17	17	27	25	20	19	18	17	8	5	0	0	5	2	133	122
145-149	5	5	19	19	36	31	38	37	41	36	40	31	20	8	8	0	5	0	5	2	217	169
140-144	3	3	16	10	19	12	34	13	34	9	34	1	16	2	8	0	3	0	2	0	169	50
135-139	0	0	8	5	11	3	15	3	14	1	12	0	12	1	2	0	1	0	2	0	77	13
130-134	1	0	3	0	2	0	0	0	3	0	0	0	6	0	3	0	0	0	0	0	18	0
125-129	0	0	0	0	0	0	0	0	1	0	0	0	2	0	2	0	2	0	0	0	7	0
120-124	0	0	0	0	0	0	0	0	0	0	0	0	0	0	0	0	0	0	0	0	0	0
Total	26	25	68	56	91	68	112	78	126	77	115	60	77	31	36	10	12	1	16	6	679	412

Apps = Number of Applicants
Adm = Number Admitted
Reflects 98% of the total applicant pool.

University of Missouri—Columbia School of Law

103 Hulston Hall
Columbia, MO 65211

E-Mail: gregorys/@missouri.edu
URL: http://www.law.missouri.edu
Phone: 573.882.6042, 888.MULAW4U; Fax: 573.882.9625

■ Introduction

The University of Missouri (now called the University of Missouri—Columbia or Mizzou) was founded in 1839 and was the first state university established west of the Mississippi. The School of Law in Columbia was established in 1872. The faculty consists almost entirely of full-time teachers with prior experience in the practice of law. The school has an enviable history of service to the state and the nation. It is a charter member of the AALS and is fully accredited.

The new law building, completed in the fall of 1988, has tripled the space available to the law school and serves as a focal point of the Mizzou campus.

■ Enrollment/Student Body

➡ *798 applicants*   ➡ *410 admitted first-year class 1998*
➡ *169 enrolled first-year class 1998*   ➡ *full-time 25th/75th percentile GPA—3.07/3.67*   ➡ *full-time 25th/75th percentile LSAT—153/159*   ➡ *550 total full-time*   ➡ *12% minority first-year class 1998*   ➡ *47% women first-year class 1998*
➡ *27 states & foreign countries represented*
➡ *75 undergraduate schools represented*

■ Faculty

➡ *47 total*   ➡ *35 full-time*   ➡ *12 part-time or adjunct*
➡ *11 women*   ➡ *3 minority*

■ Library and Physical Facilities

➡ *315,000 volumes & equivalents*   ➡ *library hours: Mon.-Thurs., 8:00 A.M.-10:00 P.M.; (building hours 7:30 A.M.-MIDNIGHT); Fri., 8:00 A.M.-6:00 P.M.; Sat., 9:00 A.M.-8:00 P.M.; Sun., 10:00 A.M.-10:00 P.M.*   ➡ *LEXIS*   ➡ *NEXIS*
➡ *WESTLAW*   ➡ *INFOTRAC*   ➡ *MERLIN/OCLC*
➡ *6 full-time librarians*   ➡ *library seats 475*
➡ *22 private 3L study rooms*

The law library is a focal point to the new law building, with windows overlooking most of the campus. The library also includes a state-of-the-art computer lab with 23 individual and 6 laptop work stations for word processing, database searching, and other uses.

■ Curriculum

➡ *89 credits required to graduate*   ➡ *90 courses available*
➡ *degrees available: J.D.; J.D./M.B.A.; J.D./M.P.A.; J.D./M.A. in Economics; and J.D./M.A. in Human Dev. & Family Studies*   ➡ *semesters, start in Aug.*
➡ *usually admit 5-10 second-year transfer students*

The program of study leading to the J.D. degree consists of six semesters of study. There is one seven-week semester each summer.

The first-year curriculum is prescribed. A substantial portion of the second-year curriculum is also prescribed. There is writing instruction in each year of study. A student must complete the 89 semester hours with a minimum average of 70 on a 55 to 100 scale for graduation.

■ Special Programs

The Center for the Study of Dispute Resolution is a unique feature of the law school, and provides national leadership in this rapidly developing area of law. The school's dispute resolution program is unique and highly ranked. Beginning in the 1999 fall semester, the law school will offer a Master of Law (LL.M.) Degree in Dispute Resolution.

The School of Law has established joint-degree programs with the graduate programs in Business Administration (J.D./M.B.A.), Public Administration (J.D./M.P.A), Human Development and Family Studies (J.D./M.A. Human Development & Family Studies), and Economics (J.D./M.A. in Economics). In addition, the school will consider fashioning a joint-degree program to meet individual student interests. The joint-degree programs enable students to earn two degrees concurrently, the Juris Doctor and the Master's. Traditionally, joint-degree students spend their first year in the School of Law. The joint-degree student must fulfill all entrance requirements of both schools, including the graduate school's entrance exam as well as the LSAT.

The School of Law recognizes the importance of providing students with experience to enhance lawyering skills and promote awareness of ethical issues. Two clinical programs and an externship program have been developed to meet this need. The Family Violence Clinic allows students to represent indigent victims of domestic abuse. The Criminal Prosecution Clinic allows students to represent the state at felony preliminary hearings and misdemeanor trials. Both clinics provide intensive faculty supervision and emphasize client contact and courtroom experience. Additionally, the School of Law offers student internships that place students with public and not-for-profit agencies, as well as with judges.

The School of Law participates in the London Law Consortium. A semester in London, each January through May, is available to second- and third-year law students in good standing. The courses are taught by regular faculty from the participating American universities. Students also may enroll in classes taught by British professors.

■ Admission

➡ *Bachelor's degree required for admission*
➡ *rolling admission*   ➡ *preference given to applications before March 1*   ➡ *LSAT, LSDAS required*
➡ *application fee—$40*
➡ *nonrefundable deposit to hold seat—$200*

A faculty committee reviews all applications. No one is automatically accepted or rejected. In many cases, factors other than GPA or LSAT score prove to be determinative. When the LSAT is repeated, the school will use an average of those scores for its evaluation.

Qualifications of applicants with a disadvantaged background (cultural or economic) are specially evaluated.

Students should apply very early in the year. Applicants are encouraged to visit the School of Law. Arrangements can be made through the Admissions Office to attend a law class, meet with an admissions counselor, or tour the facilities.

■ Student Activities

The School of Law publishes the *Missouri Law Review*, a respected periodical, four times each year. The review contains articles written by legal specialists and by students. It is edited by a student editorial board. Law students become eligible to participate in the review after their first year in law school.

The School of Law also maintains a very active appellate advocacy program under the supervision of a specially selected student Board of Advocates. These programs are open to all law students. Students are involved in a wide variety of advocacy competitions.

The school has chapters of the Order of the Coif; the Order of Barristers; Student Bar Association; BLSA; Women's Law Association; and Phi Delta Phi, Phi Alpha Delta, and Delta Theta Phi legal fraternities. There are numerous other student organizations that encompass almost every aspect of social and academic life at the law school.

■ Expenses and Financial Aid

➡ *tuition & fees—residents, $8,842; nonresidents, $17,116*
➡ *estimated additional expenses—$12,158 (books/supplies, room & board, personal expenses, & transportation)*
➡ *scholarships available: mostly academic, some need-based—usually range from $500/yr. to full tuition*
➡ *minority scholarships available: academic & need-based—usually range from $500/yr. to full tuition*
➡ *financial aid available: Stafford, Supplemental, Law Access, & university loan programs* ➡ *highly recommended that Free Application Form for Student Aid (FAFSA) be submitted by March 1*

Although it is necessary to apply for scholarships on an annual basis, scholarships are normally renewed each year for those students who have need and maintain academic achievement.

■ Career Services

The Career Services Office serves as a liaison between students and prospective employers. As many as 85 firms, businesses, government agencies, and judges interview on campus each year. Graduates find employment in the legal profession in Missouri and throughout the country, and the world.

The office focuses on providing resources for career planning and development. A series of workshops, seminars, and individual counseling sessions help students develop their career goals and locate employment.

Applicant Group for the 1998-1999 Academic Year

University of Missouri—Columbia School of Law
This grid includes only applicants who earned 120-180 LSAT scores under standard administrations.

LSAT Score	3.75 +		3.50 - 3.74		3.25 - 3.49		3.00 - 3.24		2.75 - 2.99		2.50 - 2.74		2.25 - 2.49		2.00 - 2.24		Below 2.00		No GPA		Total	
	Apps	Adm	Apps	Adm	Apps	Adm	Apps	Adm	Apps	Adm	Apps	Adm	Apps	Adm	Apps	Adm	Apps	Adm	Apps	Adm	Apps	Adm
175-180	0	0	0	0	0	0	0	0	0	0	0	0	0	0	0	0	0	0	0	0	0	0
170-174	1	1	0	0	0	0	0	0	1	1	0	0	1	1	0	0	0	0	1	1	4	4
165-169	4	4	7	7	4	4	4	4	1	1	3	3	2	2	0	0	0	0	0	0	25	25
160-164	12	11	16	16	18	17	10	9	14	14	5	4	0	0	4	1	0	0	6	5	85	77
155-159	24	24	23	22	22	21	48	43	13	10	10	6	14	9	1	0	0	0	9	9	164	144
150-154	18	17	26	25	43	39	34	23	38	10	15	4	12	3	5	2	1	1	7	3	199	127
145-149	7	7	19	10	27	5	26	5	15	3	16	3	6	0	9	0	1	0	11	2	137	35
140-144	1	0	6	0	5	0	10	0	18	0	9	1	9	0	2	0	0	0	4	0	64	1
135-139	1	0	1	0	6	0	3	0	4	0	5	0	2	0	3	0	1	0	2	0	28	0
130-134	0	0	0	0	1	0	0	0	2	0	3	0	2	0	1	0	1	0	0	0	10	0
125-129	0	0	1	0	0	0	0	0	2	0	0	0	0	0	0	0	0	0	0	0	3	0
120-124	0	0	0	0	0	0	0	0	0	0	0	0	0	0	0	0	0	0	0	0	0	0
Total	68	64	99	80	126	86	135	84	108	39	66	21	48	15	25	3	4	1	40	20	719	413

Apps = Number of Applicants
Adm = Number Admitted
Reflects 99% of the total applicant pool.
This chart is to be used as a general guide only. Nonnumerical factors are strongly considered for all applicants.

University of Missouri—Kansas City School of Law

5100 Rockhill Road
Kansas City, MO 64110

E-Mail: klostermanm@umkc.edu
URL: http://www.law.umkc.edu
Phone: 816.235.1644

■ Introduction

The University of Missouri—Kansas City (UMKC) School of Law was founded in 1895 as the Kansas City School of Law. It merged with the University of Kansas City in 1938 and affiliated with the University of Missouri in 1963. It is fully accredited by the ABA and the AALS.

■ Enrollment/Student Body

- 712 applicants
- 173 enrolled first-year class 1998
- full-time 25th/75th percentile GPA—2.91/3.46
- part-time 25th/75th percentile GPA—2.65/3.48
- full-time 25th/75th percentile LSAT—148/157
- part-time 25th/75th percentile LSAT—151/155
- 454 total full-time
- 31 total part-time
- 11.5% minority
- 53% women
- 25 states & foreign countries represented
- 59 undergraduate schools represented

■ Faculty

- 31 full-time
- 47 part-time or adjunct
- 15 women
- 2 minority

■ Library and Physical Facilities

- 277,843 volumes & equivalents
- LEXIS/NEXIS
- WESTLAW/DIALOG
- Internet
- Virtual Classroom
- extensive CD-ROM and electronic database collection
- 8 full-time librarians/tech support
- library seats 521

The School of Law is housed on the UMKC campus, in the center of a metroplex that is, itself, in the center of the nation. Its location offers convenient access to downtown law offices, courts, and government agencies. The law building contains modern classrooms equipped with audiovisual aids, a large student lounge, and offices for student organizations. A fully equipped Electronic Resource Center houses a student computer lab and a virtual classroom for use in training students in the use of the Internet, LEXIS/NEXIS, and WESTLAW.

A unique feature of the building is the placement of student study stations in office suites shared by faculty. These student stations include study carrels and private or double-occupancy student offices available to all second- and third-year students. This suite arrangement provides considerable study space and facilitates student-student and student-faculty interaction.

■ Curriculum

- Academic Support Program
- full-time & flex (part-time day) programs
- 91 credits required to graduate
- large selection of courses available
- degrees available: J.D.; J.D./M.B.A.; LL.M. (Tax and General); and J.D./LL.M. (Tax)
- semesters, start in Aug.
- range of first-year class size—15-60

The first-year J.D. program is prescribed. First-year courses are taught in classes of fewer than 60 students each. Students take a year-long intensive course in Introduction to Law

and Lawyering Processes that includes instruction in legal analysis, research, writing, and advocacy. Classes in this course are taught in groups of fewer than 30, with workshops of 15. The upper-level program includes seven required courses, as well as familiarity requirements in federal agency law and jurisprudence. Students must also complete an intensive research and writing project. Students may elect from a broad selection of elective courses, including approved nonlaw courses in other UMKC divisions. No class offered is larger than 80 students, and most are significantly smaller.

Courses at UMKC are taught in a variety of formats, but all have in common high-quality teaching and student-faculty interaction. Many of the substantive required and elective courses include problem-solving and skills components, and there are many smaller skills courses offered as well.

The school is committed to the success of its students. An academic enrichment program in the form of supervised, structured study groups and periodic lectures is offered to all first-year students. Additional opportunities include a week-long summer program and weekly enrichment sessions made available on a more limited basis.

Students may graduate in two-and-one-half years by attending two summer sessions. An LL.M. degree is available, including concentrations in taxation and health law. Courses in the LL.M. program are available to J.D. candidates as electives.

■ J.D./M.B.A. Dual-Degree Program

The School of Law has a dual-degree program with the School of Business and Public Administration. The program allows students to earn a J.D. degree and a Master of Business Administration degree on an accelerated basis through cross-acceptance of credit hours. Applicants must satisfy the admission requirements of each school and, if admitted, may enroll in the first year of law school either before or after beginning M.B.A. courses.

■ J.D./LL.M. (Tax) Combined-Degree Program

The School of Law has a combined-degree program that allows qualified J.D. students to apply up to 12 hours of approved J.D. tax courses toward an LL.M. degree. This will allow the student to earn the LL.M. on an accelerated basis, generally requiring only one additional semester (or two summers) beyond that required for the J.D.

■ Student Activities

UMKC's location in a metropolitan area provides many opportunities for student participation in clinical programs, including judicial clerkships, Legal Aid, Public Defender, and death penalty clinics. Missouri and Kansas Supreme Court rules permit senior law students to appear in court on behalf of indigent persons. Students write and edit a substantial portion of the UMKC *Law Review*, a scholarly legal journal, and also serve as assistant editors of the

Urban Lawyer, published by the ABA Section of Local Government Law, and of the *Journal of the American Academy of Matrimonial Lawyers*.

All students develop skills in appellate advocacy through Introduction to Law, with further opportunity to participate in a sequenced upper-level program. UMKC also has an extensive trial advocacy program. Both offer opportunities for participation in national competition. UMKC also participates in the ABA Negotiation and Client Counseling competitions, as well as several specialized moot court competitions. UMKC competition teams have won regional or national honors in the past several years.

The law school has an active Student Bar Association affiliated with the Law Student Division of the ABA. Students are represented at faculty and committee meetings and play an important role in establishing school policy. Three national fraternities, Delta Theta Phi, Phi Alpha Delta, and Phi Delta Phi, have chapters at the school, as do BLSA, HLSA, Association of Women Law Students, and other organizations that specialize in particular areas of interest.

■ Admission

➡ *Bachelor's degree from accredited school required; combined degree admission without undergrad degree possible*
➡ *rolling admission, early application preferred*
➡ *LSAT, LSDAS required*   ➡ *application fee—$25*

Some students are chosen based primarily on an index formula determined by combining an applicant's cumulative undergraduate grade-point average with the LSAT score. Other candidates are admitted based on a combination of factors designed to ensure that the entering class contains persons of diverse background whose index scores and other achievements qualify them for law study.

Students may be admitted with a bachelor's degree from an approved institution or, in appropriate cases, with 90 hours of acceptable academic work. A $100 seat deposit is payable by April 1, or within 20 days of admission, whichever comes later. Applicants are encouraged to visit the school. Arrangements can be made through the Admissions Office to meet with students and faculty, visit a class, or tour the law school.

■ Expenses and Financial Aid

➡ *full-time tuition & fees—resident, $8,824; nonresident, $17,098*   ➡ *estimated additional expenses—$10,200 (room & board, transportation, medical, & personal expenses)*
➡ *merit- & need-based scholarships available*
➡ *merit- & need-based diversity scholarships available*
➡ *government loan program available through UMKC Financial Aid Office*   ➡ *FFS, UMKC financial aid form & financial aid transcripts required*

■ Career Services

The Career Services Office assists law students and graduates in exploring and defining career options through individual counseling, workshops, and seminars. Law firms, businesses, and government agencies interview students on campus for summer clerkships and post-graduate employment. Additionally, area law firms list available clerk and attorney positions with the office. In cooperation with area bar associations, a mentor program pairs first-year students with practicing attorneys. The Career Services Office also provides resources for career planning and development.

Applicant Group for the 1998-1999 Academic Year

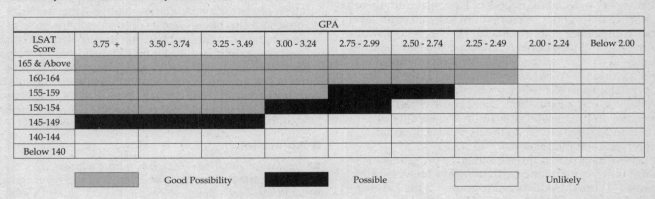

University of Missouri—Kansas City School of Law

LSAT Score	GPA								
	3.75 +	3.50 - 3.74	3.25 - 3.49	3.00 - 3.24	2.75 - 2.99	2.50 - 2.74	2.25 - 2.49	2.00 - 2.24	Below 2.00
165 & Above									
160-164									
155-159									
150-154									
145-149									
140-144									
Below 140									

Good Possibility   Possible   Unlikely

The School of Law considers many factors beyond LSAT score and GPA. This chart should be used only as a general guide.

University of Montana School of Law

Missoula, MT 59812

E-Mail: lawadmis@selway.umt.edu
URL: http://www.umt.edu/law/homepage.htm
Phone: 406.243.4311

■ Introduction

The University of Montana is located in Missoula, on the west slopes of the Rocky Mountains. Missoula is situated halfway between Yellowstone and Glacier National Parks and is surrounded by several of the largest designated wilderness areas in the continental United States. The city is known for its outdoor opportunities and quality of life.

The University of Montana School of Law was established in 1911. It has been accredited by the AALS since 1914 and by the ABA since 1923. As one of the smallest law schools in the nation, students enjoy a congenial academic, intellectual, and social environment. The law school serves as a legal center for the state.

■ Enrollment: First-Year Class

➡ *408 applicants*   ➡ *226 admitted*   ➡ *92 enrolled*
➡ *full-time 25th/75th percentile GPA—2.93/3.50*
➡ *full-time 25th/75th percentile LSAT—152/159*
➡ *10% minority*   ➡ *35% women*
➡ *37 states, countries, and Indian tribes represented*
➡ *55 undergraduate schools represented*

■ Faculty

➡ *39 total*   ➡ *16 full-time*   ➡ *23 part-time*
➡ *8 women*

■ Library and Physical Facilities

➡ *101,990 volumes & equivalents*   ➡ *LEXIS*
➡ *WESTLAW*   ➡ *two computer labs*
➡ *computer research integrated with class assignments*

■ Curriculum

➡ *90 semester hours required to graduate*
➡ *73 courses available*   ➡ *degrees available: J.D.;*
J.D./M.P.A.; J.D./M.S.   ➡ *semesters, start in late Aug.*

The University of Montana School of Law integrates theory and practice throughout its curriculum to instill entry level practice competence in its graduates. The law school's curriculum, teaching methodology, and assessment techniques are designed to address the following components of a lawyer's work: (1) knowledge of the law; (2) the ability to apply legal rules to resolve problems; 3) ability to use lawyer skills (e.g., negotiation, client counseling); (4) perspective on the societal role and responsibility of lawyers; and (5) sensitivity to the dynamics of social and interpersonal interaction.

The school has created three distinctive programs to acquaint first-year students with the ways lawyers think and work: (1) the Introductory Program, (2) the Lawyer Skills Program, and (3) the Law Firm Program. In the introductory program, students are initiated into the legal culture by surveying legal history, the American legal system, the litigation process, legal writing, and legal analysis and jurisprudence. The law school is one of the few to introduce first-year students to the skills involved in dispute resolution, including client counseling, legal drafting, and oral argument. The innovative "law firm" program encourages students to cooperate and collaborate rather than compete as they begin to think and work as lawyers. From the beginning of law school, entering students belong to "law firms," groups of six students, called associates, directed by specially trained upper-class students.

The school has long emphasized performance in its curriculum. The school's legal writing and dispute resolution programs represent a coherent and comprehensive approach to lawyer skills. Students master specific transactional skills such as planning an estate, drafting a contract, and creating a small business.

The upper-division clinical training program provides students with a wide range of opportunities to earn required academic credit by working on actual cases under the supervision of faculty and practicing attorneys in Missoula. The clinical offerings include the Natural Resource Clinic, Indian Law Clinic, Montana Legal Services Association, ASUM Legal Services, Missoula County Attorney's Office, Forest Service Clinic, University of Montana Legal Counsel's Office, Missoula City Attorney's Office, and Disability Law Clinic.

■ Special Programs

The law school also offers students wishing to specialize several clusters of courses. Because of Montana's natural setting, many students enroll in the natural resource and environmental law courses. The school offers basic and advanced courses in resource and environmental law, as well as natural resource clinics and the opportunity to participate on the *Public Land and Resources Law Review*.

Montana is home to seven Indian reservations. The law school's Indian Law courses, Indian Law Clinic, and Native American Law Student Association provide opportunities for students to learn about and participate in the administration of justice for Montana's Native Americans.

The school also offers clusters of courses in the areas of business and tax (with emphasis on the problems of small businesses), public law, and individual and property rights.

The school offers two joint-degree programs. A joint program in law and environmental studies allows students to earn both their J.D. and an M.S. in as little as four years. A joint program in law and public administration leads to both the J.D. and M.P.A. degrees in four years.

■ Admission

➡ *application deadline—March 1, rolling admission,*
early application preferred   ➡ *LSAT, LSDAS required*
➡ *application fee—$60*

A committee of the law faculty passes on all applications. Candidates must be of good moral character, have intellectual promise, and have a baccalaureate degree from an approved college or university prior to matriculation.

As a state-assisted institution, the School of Law gives some preference in admissions to residents. The school seeks a diverse student body and welcomes applications from members of groups historically underrepresented in the legal profession.

The most important admissions criteria are the cumulative undergraduate GPA and the LSAT score. The admissions committee weighs such factors as writing ability, experience prior to application to law school including graduate study, college attended, trend in grades, quality of work in difficult courses, ability to overcome economic or other disadvantage, and change in performance after an absence from college.

The school recognizes a commitment to providing full opportunities for the study of law and entry into the legal profession of qualified members of groups (notably racial and ethnic minorities) which have been victims of discrimination in various forms. This commitment is implemented by special recruitment and retention efforts.

If the LSAT is repeated, the average of the scores will be used in computing the applicant's prediction index. No test score achieved later than the February administration of the LSAT can be considered in decisions for the subsequent September.

■ Student Activities

All students are members of the Student Bar Association. Its programs contribute to the professional development and the social life of the student body. Clayberg Inn of Phi Delta Phi national law fraternity encourages scholarship, promotes fellowship, and fosters the ideals of the profession. The Women's Law Caucus is part of the SBA,

and other organizations include a Christian Legal Society, a student chapter of the American Trial Lawyers— Montana Trial Lawyers Association, the Environmental Law Group, the Native American Law Student Association, the Federalist Society, the University of Montana Public Interest Law Coalition, Edna Rankin Law Society, and Montana Defense Trial Lawyers Association. The *Montana Law Review* and the *Public Land and Resources Law Review* afford supplementary training in analyzing legal problems precisely and presenting legal issues cogently. The UMLS team placed first and third in the nation in the 1991-92 and 1995-96, respectively, American Trial Lawyers Association trial competition and first in the 1990-91 American Bar Association Client Counseling Competition. The UMLS National Moot Court Competition teams have advanced from regional to the national finals ten times in the last 14 years.

■ Expenses and Financial Aid

➡ *tuition & fees—residents, $6,742; nonresidents, $12,113*
➡ *estimated additional expenses—$8,500 (room, board, books)* ➡ *performance- & need-based scholarships available (primarily to second- & third-year students)*
➡ *file FAFSA financial aid applications by March 1*

■ Career Services

The School of Law maintains a career service to assist students in finding part-time and summer employment, and attorney positions upon graduation. The job placement rate for the 1996 class for the period not less than 18 months after graduation was 94 percent.

Applicant Group for the 1998-1999 Academic Year

University of Montana School of Law
This grid includes only applicants who earned 120-180 LSAT scores under standard administrations.

LSAT Score	3.75 +		3.50 - 3.74		3.25 - 3.49		3.00 - 3.24		2.75 - 2.99		2.50 - 2.74		2.25 - 2.49		2.00 - 2.24		Below 2.00		No GPA		Total	
	Apps	Adm	Apps	Adm	Apps	Adm	Apps	Adm	Apps	Adm	Apps	Adm	Apps	Adm	Apps	Adm	Apps	Adm	Apps	Adm	Apps	Adm
175-180	0	0	0	0	0	0	0	0	0	0	0	0	0	0	0	0	0	0	0	0	0	0
170-174	0	0	0	0	0	0	1	1	1	1	0	0	0	0	0	0	0	0	0	0	2	2
165-169	0	0	2	2	3	3	3	3	1	1	0	0	0	0	0	0	0	0	0	0	9	9
160-164	9	8	8	8	8	8	6	6	6	5	3	3	2	2	0	0	0	0	0	0	42	40
155-159	6	6	17	17	24	22	19	17	14	14	7	6	4	4	1	0	2	0	0	0	94	86
150-154	7	7	19	17	27	20	23	14	17	7	12	6	6	1	4	0	0	0	1	0	116	72
145-149	2	0	13	3	16	3	21	2	14	3	9	0	6	0	0	0	0	0	2	0	83	11
140-144	1	1	1	0	7	1	6	1	7	0	5	0	7	1	4	0	0	0	1	0	39	4
135-139	0	0	2	0	3	0	3	0	1	0	3	0	1	0	1	0	1	0	0	0	15	0
130-134	0	0	0	0	0	0	0	0	0	0	0	0	1	0	0	0	0	0	0	0	1	0
125-129	0	0	0	0	1	0	0	0	0	0	0	0	0	0	0	0	0	0	1	0	2	0
120-124	0	0	0	0	0	0	0	0	0	0	0	0	0	0	0	0	0	0	0	0	0	0
Total	25	22	62	47	89	57	82	44	61	31	39	15	27	8	10	0	3	0	5	0	403	224

Apps = Number of Applicants
Adm = Number Admitted
Reflects 99% of the total applicant pool.

University of Nebraska College of Law

P.O. Box 830902
Lincoln, NE 68583-0902

E-Mail: lawadm@unl.edu
URL: http://www.unl.edu/lawcoll/
Phone: 402.472.2161

■ Introduction

The University of Nebraska College of Law offers an excellent legal education at a reasonable cost. It is large enough to provide students with a diverse curriculum, yet small enough to ensure that students are not lost in a faceless crowd. The college was founded in 1888 and is accredited by both the AALS and the ABA. It is located on the East Campus of the University of Nebraska in Lincoln, a city of approximately 208,000, and the state capital.

■ Enrollment/Student Body

➡ *568 applicants*   ➡ *373 admitted first-year class 1998*
➡ *150 enrolled first-year class 1998*   ➡ *full-time 25th/75th percentile GPA—3.18/3.73*   ➡ *full-time 25th/75th percentile LSAT—149/157*   ➡ *392 total full-time*   ➡ *8% minority*
➡ *41% women*   ➡ *38 states & foreign countries represented*
➡ *118 undergraduate schools represented*

■ Faculty

➡ *59 total*   ➡ *28 full-time*   ➡ *31 part-time or adjunct*
➡ *6 women*   ➡ *2 minority*

■ Library and Physical Facilities

➡ *349,419 volumes & equivalents*   ➡ *library hours: Mon.-Fri., 7:30 A.M.-12:30 A.M.; Sat., 9:00 A.M.-10:00 P.M.; Sun., 11:00 A.M.-12:30 A.M.*   ➡ *LEXIS*   ➡ *NEXIS*
➡ *WESTLAW*   ➡ *DIALOG*   ➡ *6 full-time librarians*
➡ *library seats 339*

The law college building offers the best in modern facilities, including two multimedia classrooms. The college's courtroom addition features a fully equipped teaching courtroom and facilities for the civil clinical program.

In the law library, students have access to a student computer laboratory as well as e-mail, audio and video materials, CD-ROM network, the Internet, and the LEXIS and WESTLAW computerized research systems.

■ Curriculum

➡ *Academic Resource Program*   ➡ *96 credits required to graduate*   ➡ *90 courses available*   ➡ *degrees available: J.D.; M.L.S.; J.D./M.B.A.; J.D./M.P.A. (Accounting); J.D./Ph.D. (Psychology); J.D./Econ.; J.D./ Poli.Sci.; J.D./M.C.R.P. (Community and Regional Planning); J.D./Ph.D. (Ed. Admin); J.D./M.A. (International Affairs, with the University of Denver); J.D./individually designed programs*   ➡ *semesters, start in Aug.*
➡ *range of first-year class size—22-70*

The academic year runs from late August to early May. A two-day orientation before the beginning of the fall semester introduces first-year students to the law school and the study of law. Although completing the requirements for a J.D. degree normally takes three years, it is possible to graduate in two and one-half years by attending summer school during two summers. The college offers

no night classes and only rarely accepts part-time students. Students receiving the J.D. degree are qualified to practice law in any state upon passage of that state's bar examination.

The first-year curriculum is 18 hours per semester and includes civil procedure, contracts, criminal law, legal process, legal writing, property, and torts. Courses in the second and third years are elective, with the exception of required courses in constitutional law, professional responsibility, and a research seminar. The curriculum encompasses a broad range of areas, from taxation and securities to Native American law, legal control of discrimination, and international transactions. The curriculum offers particular depth in the areas of litigation, taxation, and environmental law. The average upper-class student takes 15 hours per semester.

■ Special Programs

Skills and Clinical Education. The college offers professional skills courses in pretrial litigation, trial advocacy, advanced trial advocacy, appellate advocacy, mediation, negotiations, alternative dispute resolution, client interviewing and counseling, business planning, and civil and criminal clinic. These classes allow second- and third-year students to develop lawyering skills and to learn strategic and practical skills in simulated settings or in the handling of real cases for actual clients. In civil clinic, third-year students represent clients in and out of court in a wide range of matters including bankruptcy, tax audits, domestic relations, immigration, adoption, and landlord-tenant disputes. Students in criminal clinic prosecute misdemeanor cases in Lancaster County, including drug possession, assault, trespass, forgery, escape, arson, and extortion.

Joint-degree Programs. The college's interdisciplinary program in Law and Psychology is recognized as one of the finest in the nation. The college also participates in seven other joint-degree programs and will work with students to individually design programs in disciplines not covered by a formal program. In each program, students will earn two degrees with fewer credit hours and in less time than if the degrees were pursued separately.

■ Admission

➡ *Bachelor's degree from accredited institution required*
➡ *application deadline—March 1*   ➡ *rolling admission, early application preferred*   ➡ *LSAT, LSDAS required*
➡ *application fee—$25*

The college starts reviewing applications in early January. Although an applicant's undergraduate GPA and LSAT score weigh heavily in the admission decision, the college also takes into account the applicant's personal statement, the quality of the applicant's undergraduate institution, course of study, work experience, graduate study, extracurricular activities, recommendations, and other information supplied by the applicant. The college will waive the application fee upon demonstration of financial need. To visit a law class, meet with admission personnel, or tour the law college, contact the Admissions Office.

The college takes special care in evaluating applications from members of minority groups that have been under-represented in the legal profession. The college participates in the CLEO program and looks favorably upon candidates for admission who have successfully completed the program.

The college provides an Academic Resource Program to assist first-year students in developing and improving fundamental skills such as note taking, case briefing, outlining, analyzing, and exam taking. The college also offers a skills class to focus on these skills. Participation in the class is by invitation or on a space-available basis.

■ Student Activities

The *Nebraska Law Review*, published by a student editorial board, publishes leading articles from well-known authorities in their fields, as well as student notes and comments. The *Nebraska Transcript*, includes articles by students about the college and is published three times a year for students, faculty, and alumni. Other student activities and organizations include the National Moot Court Competition, Client Counseling Competition, National Trial Competition, Student Bar Association, Women's Law Caucus, Community Legal Education Project, Black Law Students Association, Civil Liberties

Group, Equal Justice Foundation, Nebraska Fund for Clerkships in the Public Interest, Multi-Cultural Legal Society, Natural Resources Law Society, Nontraditional Law Students Group, Christian Legal Society, Federalist Society, The Rutherford Institute, Association of Trial Lawyers of America, International Law Society, Volunteer Income Tax Assistance Program, and two national legal fraternities.

■ Expenses and Financial Aid

➡ *tuition & fees—resident, $5,050; nonresident, $11,116*
➡ *estimated additional expenses—$9,851 (books, living expenses, transportation, personal)* ➡ *academic scholarships, need-based grants, nonresident scholarships, & opportunity grants available*
➡ *FAFSA forms and College of Law need-based grant application forms for need-based aid required, preferably by March 1*

For the 1998-1999 academic year, resident tuition is $107.50 per hour, and nonresident tuition is $276 per hour. Fees total $590 per semester.

■ Career Services

The college operates its own career services office for students seeking full-time employment or summer clerkships. The office provides students with a variety of placement-related services and also organizes on-campus interviews by private law firms, governmental agencies, corporations, and other potential employers. As of December 1997, approximately 95 percent of the members of the class of 1997 were employed or were enrolled in advanced degree programs.

Applicant Group for the 1998-1999 Academic Year

University of Nebraska College of Law
This grid includes only applicants who earned 120-180 LSAT scores under standard administrations.

LSAT Score	GPA 3.75+		3.50-3.74		3.25-3.49		3.00-3.24		2.75-2.99		2.50-2.74		2.25-2.49		2.00-2.24		Below 2.00		No GPA		Total	
	Apps	Adm	Apps	Adm	Apps	Adm	Apps	Adm	Apps	Adm	Apps	Adm	Apps	Adm	Apps	Adm	Apps	Adm	Apps	Adm	Apps	Adm
175-180	0	0	0	0	0	0	1	1	0	0	0	0	0	0	0	0	0	0	0	0	1	1
170-174	1	1	2	2	2	2	0	0	0	0	0	0	0	0	0	0	0	0	0	0	5	5
165-169	5	5	0	0	1	1	2	2	2	2	2	2	0	0	0	0	0	0	1	1	13	13
160-164	14	14	10	10	7	7	7	7	8	8	4	3	1	0	0	0	0	0	2	2	53	51
155-159	20	20	19	19	25	24	35	33	10	9	6	6	2	1	2	1	0	0	1	1	120	114
150-154	23	23	27	27	39	36	31	22	14	6	13	6	4	1	1	0	0	0	0	0	152	121
145-149	8	6	25	21	22	11	21	6	16	6	15	3	12	0	0	0	2	1	2	0	123	54
140-144	3	1	9	4	9	3	12	4	10	0	5	1	7	0	3	1	0	0	3	1	61	15
135-139	0	0	2	0	2	0	4	1	2	0	7	0	1	0	1	0	1	0	2	0	22	1
130-134	0	0	0	0	1	0	2	0	1	0	3	0	0	0	0	0	1	0	1	0	9	0
125-129	0	0	0	0	0	0	1	0	0	0	2	0	0	0	2	0	1	0	0	0	6	0
120-124	0	0	0	0	0	0	0	0	0	0	0	0	0	0	0	0	0	0	0	0	0	0
Total	74	70	94	83	108	84	116	76	63	31	57	21	27	2	9	2	5	1	12	5	565	375

Apps = Number of Applicants
Adm = Number Admitted
Reflects 99% of the total applicant pool.

New England School of Law

154 Stuart Street
Boston, MA 02116

E-Mail: admit@admin.nesl.edu
URL: http://www.nesl.edu
Phone: 617.422.7210

■ Introduction

New England School of Law was founded in 1908 as Portia Law School, the first school in the nation dedicated exclusively to the legal education of women. The institution became coeducational in 1938, but it has remained sensitive to the needs of those underrepresented in the legal profession. New England is fully accredited by the American Bar Association, and is a member of the Association of American Law Schools.

Boston is an ideal city in which to study law. Our school occupies two completely modern, downtown facilities near Boston's government, business, and theater districts.

New England capitalizes on its advantageous location by providing an extensive clinical program and by utilizing members of the city's legal community as adjunct faculty and lecturers. The school has attracted a number of distinguished speakers through its lecture series and other events. Most notably, we have welcomed in recent years United States Supreme Court Justices Sandra Day O'Connor, Harry A. Blackmun, Clarence Thomas, and Attorney General Janet Reno.

■ Enrollment/Student Body

➡ *1,901 applicants* ➡ *1,457 admitted first-year class 1998*
➡ *350 enrolled first-year class 1998* ➡ *full-time 25th/75th percentile GPA—2.69/3.25* ➡ *part-time 25th/75th percentile GPA—2.66/3.26* ➡ *full-time 25th/75th percentile LSAT—142/151* ➡ *part-time 25th/75th percentile LSAT—143/153*
➡ *573 total full-time* ➡ *364 total part-time*
➡ *19.6% minority* ➡ *50% women* ➡ *48 states & foreign countries represented* ➡ *342 undergraduate schools represented*

■ Faculty

➡ *112 total* ➡ *36 full-time* ➡ *76 part-time or adjunct*
➡ *9 full-time women* ➡ *3 minority*

■ Library and Physical Facilities

➡ *290,000 volumes & equivalents* ➡ *library hours: Mon.-Fri., 8:00 A.M.-11:00 P.M.; Sat., 9:00 A.M.-10:00 P.M.; Sun., 10:00 A.M.-11:00 P.M.* ➡ *LEXIS* ➡ *NEXIS*
➡ *WESTLAW* ➡ *DIALOG* ➡ *OCLC* ➡ *CALI*
➡ *9 full-time librarians* ➡ *library seats 398*

The tri-level law library incorporates computerized legal research equipment, study carrels, typing space, and consultation and lounge areas. Offering access to Internet, e-mail, and Web searches, the library also has audio and video collections, several trials on Interactive Videodisc, and numerous CD-ROM indexes.

■ Curriculum

➡ *Academic Support Program* ➡ *84 units/credits required to graduate* ➡ *154 courses available*
➡ *J.D. degree offered* ➡ *semesters, start in Aug.*
➡ *range of first-year class size—15-120*

As a national law school, New England's curriculum is designed to prepare graduates to practice in any jurisdiction in the United States. The school has both a day and evening division, each offering the J.D. degree. The day program requires 84 credit hours over three academic years. The work of the first year is prescribed. Second-year students are required to take criminal law and procedure, evidence, and law and ethics of lawyering. Remaining courses are elective.

The evening program requires 84 credit hours over four academic years. The evening program curriculum is prescribed for the first and second years; the third and fourth years are elective.

In addition to its day and evening programs, New England offers a third program of study for persons whose child-care responsibilities permit only part-time study with more flexibility.

■ Special Programs

New England prides itself on the great variety of high quality clinical programs available to its students. The school offers 18 clinics and maintains its own fully equipped Clinical Law Office, in which supervised students handle actual cases. Besides its civil and criminal practice clinics, the school offers clinical programs in such diverse areas of law, as health, mental health, immigration, tax, employment, land use, environmental, administrative, prisoners' rights, government, and domestic violence.

■ Admission

➡ *Bachelor's degree required for admission*
➡ *application deadline: March 15—priority deadline; June 1—extended deadline* ➡ *LSAT, LSDAS required*
➡ *application fee—$50*

New England requires the LSAT, use of the LSDAS, and two letters of recommendation. Applications received by March 15 are generally given priority consideration. If received between March 16 and June 1 they will be completely reviewed, but are subject to space availability.

Like most law schools in desirable urban locations, New England receives applications from many more qualified individuals than it can accommodate. The Admission Committee makes decisions to provide stability and diversity in the entering class. Factors that reflect stability are the GPA and the LSAT score. Factors weighted heavily for diversity include, but are not limited to, undergraduate major and institution, extracurricular activities and/or work experience, geographic distribution, minority status, gender, and exceptional characteristics.

■ Student Activities

Upper-class students are selected for membership on the *New England Law Review* on the basis of academic achievement or success in a writing competition. Our other scholarly journal, *The New England Journal of Criminal and Civil*

Confinement, is the only student publication in the country devoted solely to this field. Another student publication is the *International and Comparative Law Annual*. Our school participates in several moot court programs, including the National Moot Court, the Jessup (international law), the National Environmental Law, and National Tax Moot Court competitions. The 1997 Jessup team advanced to the regional finals and won the Best Oralist Award. The Environmental Moot Court Team advanced to the national semi-finals in 1997. The school's team in the National Tax Moot Court competition won Best Appellate Brief in 1997.

The Student Bar Association (SBA) is the school's student government, with members serving as student representatives on faculty and law school committees. The SBA also sponsors social events, community participation including a partnership with Boston High School, and a lecture series. Other student organizations include the Lesbian, Bisexual, Gay, Transexual Caucus; Minority Students' Association; Public Interest Law Association; Women's Law Caucus; and others.

■ Minority Programs

As part of fulfilling its continued pledge to those under-represented in the legal profession, New England has developed a recruitment program, funded additional allocations of financial aid, and established the Charles Hamilton Houston Enrichment Program (CHHEP). The CHHEP has three components that involve first-year students: the speaker series, the first-year discussion groups, and the academic support program.

■ Expenses and Financial Aid

➦ *tuition & fees—full-time, $15,100 part-time, $11,360*
➦ *estimated additional expenses—books, $850; health insurance, $690; living expenses, $12,600*   ➦ *scholarships available: NESL grant, MacLean grant, Arthur Getchell grants, Trustee Scholars, NESL Merit Scholarships*   ➦ *minority scholarships available: Jacqueline Lloyd grant*   ➦ *financial aid available*
➦ *Free Application for Federal Student Aid (FAFSA) and New England School of Law Financial Aid Application required, due April 15*

The school participates in the Federal Perkins Loan and Federal Work-Study programs. Limited institutional employment, grants, and scholarships are also available to needy applicants, including the MacLean Grant for students from extremely disadvantaged backgrounds and the Jacqueline Lloyd grant for students from minority backgrounds.

■ Placement

The law school maintains a Career Services Office to assist students and alumni in securing law-related employment both prior to and after graduation. The services provided by the office include individual and group career counseling, résumé preparation, maintenance of a career-resource library, and specific job listings for students and graduates. In addition, information is disseminated concerning summer internships, part-time and full-time employment, judicial clerkships, and graduate programs.

Respondents to the employment survey of the class of 1997 indicated an overall employment rate of 89.2 percent. Of the employed graduates, 40.8 percent were working in private law practice.

Applicant Group for the 1998-1999 Academic Year

New England School of Law
This grid includes only applicants who earned 120-180 LSAT scores under standard administrations.

LSAT Score	3.75 +		3.50 - 3.74		3.25 - 3.49		3.00 - 3.24		2.75 - 2.99		2.50 - 2.74		2.25 - 2.49		2.00 - 2.24		Below 2.00		No GPA		Total	
	Apps	Adm	Apps	Adm	Apps	Adm	Apps	Adm	Apps	Adm	Apps	Adm	Apps	Adm	Apps	Adm	Apps	Adm	Apps	Adm	Apps	Adm
175-180	0	0	0	0	0	0	0	0	0	0	0	0	0	0	0	0	0	0	0	0	0	0
170-174	0	0	0	0	0	0	0	0	1	1	0	0	0	0	0	0	0	0	0	0	1	1
165-169	1	1	1	1	2	2	3	2	6	4	0	0	1	1	1	0	1	1	1	0	17	12
160-164	2	2	3	3	9	8	8	7	12	12	2	2	4	3	5	3	0	0	1	1	46	41
155-159	9	9	20	20	27	26	41	35	44	37	37	31	19	19	10	7	3	0	0	0	210	184
150-154	8	8	29	27	64	57	80	74	96	87	80	71	36	32	14	11	2	0	1	0	410	367
145-149	10	9	48	46	83	77	124	109	143	120	112	83	64	44	36	20	5	0	10	6	635	514
140-144	6	6	23	19	50	42	87	63	97	55	93	48	64	24	25	2	3	0	15	8	463	267
135-139	3	2	9	2	18	6	19	3	49	7	46	1	32	1	19	1	5	0	7	3	207	26
130-134	0	0	1	0	4	0	9	0	20	0	10	0	10	1	6	0	3	0	2	0	65	1
125-129	1	0	0	0	2	0	0	0	3	0	5	0	0	0	4	0	1	0	2	0	18	0
120-124	0	0	0	0	0	0	0	0	0	0	0	0	2	0	1	0	0	0	1	0	4	0
Total	40	37	134	118	259	218	371	293	471	323	385	236	232	125	121	44	23	1	40	18	2076	1413

Apps = Number of Applicants
Adm = Number Admitted
Reflects 98% of the total applicant pool.

University of New Mexico School of Law

1117 Stanford Drive, N.E.
Albuquerque, NM 87131-1431

E-Mail: CARTER@law.unm.edu
URL: http://lawschool.unm.edu
Phone: 505.277.0572

■ Introduction

The University of New Mexico is the state's major university with over 24,000 students. The law school, located on the north campus of the university in Albuquerque, is just minutes from the downtown area and 60 miles from Santa Fe, the state's capital. This proximity to local, state, and federal courts, key government offices, and law firms allows students opportunities to observe and participate in the practice of law. In their leisure, students have access to symphony, theater, the Santa Fe Opera, galleries, museums, and the beauty of outdoor New Mexico. The combination of Indian, Spanish, and Anglo cultures reflected in food, music, art, architecture, and local customs heightens Albuquerque's appeal.

The University of New Mexico School of Law is known for its small classes, easy student-faculty interaction, and innovative education and research. The School of Law has an 11:1 student-faculty ratio, one of the best in the country. This ratio allows the school to offer more courses with smaller enrollments.

The school offers a comprehensive curriculum and has special programs in clinical law, natural resources law, and American Indian law. It also has a summer legal education equal opportunity program. It is a member of the AALS and is fully approved by the ABA.

■ Enrollment/Student Body

➡ *791 applicants* ➡ *267 admitted first-year class 1998*
➡ *114 enrolled first-year class 1998* ➡ *full-time 25th/75th percentile GPA—2.86/3.44* ➡ *full-time 25th/75th percentile LSAT—150/158* ➡ *335 total full-time*
➡ *38% minority* ➡ *53% women*
➡ *52 undergraduate schools represented in first-year class*

■ Faculty

➡ *67 total* ➡ *32 full-time* ➡ *35 part-time or adjunct*
➡ *15 women* ➡ *9 minority*

■ Library and Physical Facilities

➡ *346,000 volumes & equivalents* ➡ *library hours: Mon.-Thurs., 7:30 A.M.-MIDNIGHT; Fri., 7:30 A.M.-10:00 P.M.; Sat., 9:00 A.M.-10:00 P.M.; Sun., NOON-MIDNIGHT*
➡ *LEXIS* ➡ *NEXIS* ➡ *WESTLAW* ➡ *Q/L*
➡ *DIALOG* ➡ *Michie Law on Disk*
➡ *4 full-time librarians* ➡ *library seats 380*

The law school is housed in Bratton Hall. In addition to classrooms, seminar rooms, the moot courtroom, the library, and faculty and student organization offices,Bratton Hall also houses the American Indian Law Center and the Law Practice Clinic.

The UNM Law Library is the primary New Mexico legal research center. The library includes comprehensive collections of British, federal, and state court reports, and annotations, session laws, current state and federal statutes, legal treatises, periodicals, encyclopedias, digests, administrative reports, and other classes of legal materials. Special collections are being developed in American Indian law, Mexican and Latin American law, community land grant law, and natural resources law.

Over 100 carrels are available to students and faculty engaged in ongoing research. Pocket lounges and browsing areas, audiovisual carrels, group study rooms, a photocopy facility, and a computer lab are available for students' use.

■ Curriculum

➡ *Academic Support Program* ➡ *programs offered: Orientation, Mentor, Summer Academic Support/Academic Year Tutorials* ➡ *86 credits required to graduate*
➡ *over 120 courses available* ➡ *degrees available: J.D.; J.D./M.B.A.; J.D./M.P.A.; J.D./M.A. (Latin American Studies)*
➡ *semesters, start in Aug. & Jan. (15 weeks), May (clinic)*
➡ *range of first-year class size—18-59*

First-year students must take a full first-year curriculum, including basic courses in torts, contracts, civil procedure, property, and criminal law. Emphasis is also placed on the skills of advocacy; legal writing, oral argument, litigation, counseling, and negotiation. Second- and third-year courses are elective except for Ethics, Introduction to Constitutional Law, and a clinical program. Students normally complete the requirements for the J.D. degree in three academic years (six semesters).

Unlike most other law schools, UNM requires six credit hours of clinical work for graduation. In 1970, the New Mexico Supreme Court adopted a rule permitting students to practice before state courts. Today, the UNM Program in Clinical Law is regarded as one of the finest practical-lawyering programs in the country. The program is based at the school, and includes the Law Practice Clinic, Community Lawyering clinics, the District Attorney Clinic, and the Southwest Indian Law Clinic. The clinical program also operates an extern placement program. Students may elect assignment to a judge's office, the Public Defender's Office, federal and state administrative offices, and private practitioners.

■ Special Programs

Four research and training institutes are a part of the law school—the American Indian Law Center; the Institute of Public Law; the International Transboundary Center, and the U.S. Mexico Law Institute. The American Indian Law Center is an independent institute devoted to strengthening Indian tribal government. It has worked closely with the tribes and pueblos to assist them in improving their judicial systems. The Institute of Public Law serves New Mexico and the Southwest in an advisory capacity and provides training programs and research for state and local governments. Recent activities by its centers include projects in bioethics, environmental clean-up, and wildlife law.

The U.S. Mexico Law Institute promotes research on legal problems common to the U.S. and Mexico. It is particularly interested in the study of the administration of justice, the modernization of commercial laws, and immigration law and regulations. The International Transboundary Center is research oriented and concerns itself with the management of natural resources complicated by political divisions.

UNM law students may earn an Indian Law Certificate. Students must complete 21 hours of coursework in Indian law and fulfill the J.D. writing requirement in a study focused on an Indian law subject. Students may also earn a Natural Resources Certificate. The School of Law is a member of a consortium which offers six weeks of summer law study in Guanajuato.

■ Admission

➡ *Bachelor's degree from an accredited college or university required* ➡ *application deadline—Feb. 16*
➡ *LSAT, LSDAS required* ➡ *application fee—$40*
➡ *admittance fall semester only*
➡ *no deposit required of accepted applicants*

Applicants should take the LSAT no later than December before the year in which they wish to enroll.

A five-member committee reviews all applications from residents and all competitive applications from nonresidents. Substantial weight is given to the applicant's personal statement, prior work experience, extracurricular activities, recommendations, and other background information supplied by the applicant.

The profile printed below does not make any distinction between residents and nonresidents, but applications from New Mexico residents are given very decided preference.

■ Student Activities

Extracurricular activities include the *Natural Resources Journal*, the *New Mexico Law Review*, the *U.S.-Mexico Law Journal*, and several moot court and mock trial competitions. All law students are members of the university's Graduate/Professional Student Association and the Student Bar Association. Students may participate in more than 20 law-student organizations.

■ Expenses and Financial Aid

➡ *full-time tuition & fees—resident, $3,984/yr.; nonresident, $13,338/yr.* ➡ *estimated additional expenses—room & board, $6,328; books & supplies, $810; transportation, $1,252; personal expenses, $2,292* ➡ *grants available*
➡ *Native American grants available* ➡ *financial aid available*
➡ *FAFSA due March 1*

The law school awards a significant number of need-based grants to full-time students each year.

Applicant Group for the 1998-1999 Academic Year

University of New Mexico School of Law
This grid includes only applicants who earned 120-180 LSAT scores under standard administrations.

LSAT Score	3.75 +		3.50 - 3.74		3.25 - 3.49		3.00 - 3.24		2.75 - 2.99		2.50 - 2.74		2.25 - 2.49		2.00 - 2.24		Below 2.00		No GPA		Total	
	Apps	Adm	Apps	Adm	Apps	Adm	Apps	Adm	Apps	Adm	Apps	Adm	Apps	Adm	Apps	Adm	Apps	Adm	Apps	Adm	Apps	Adm
175-180	0	0	0	0	0	0	0	0	0	0	0	0	0	0	0	0	0	0	0	0	0	0
170-174	2	2	2	2	0	0	2	2	1	1	1	0	0	0	0	0	0	0	1	1	9	8
165-169	4	4	4	4	7	7	3	1	1	1	2	1	0	0	0	0	0	0	0	0	21	18
160-164	9	9	13	12	11	10	13	10	14	10	4	4	3	2	1	0	0	0	1	0	69	57
155-159	10	7	31	20	35	19	28	15	26	7	16	6	7	1	5	1	0	0	3	1	161	77
150-154	10	5	21	8	41	15	32	12	35	6	22	4	9	3	4	0	1	0	4	3	179	56
145-149	9	2	14	5	27	8	33	11	41	7	22	4	9	0	4	0	0	0	2	0	161	37
140-144	6	2	10	0	12	4	20	2	24	1	23	1	7	0	6	0	0	0	1	0	109	10
135-139	0	0	2	0	4	0	3	0	4	0	11	0	5	0	5	0	1	0	5	0	40	0
130-134	0	0	1	0	0	0	3	0	2	0	2	0	3	0	0	0	0	0	1	0	12	0
125-129	0	0	0	0	0	0	0	0	1	0	2	0	2	0	3	0	1	0	1	0	10	0
120-124	0	0	0	0	0	0	0	0	0	0	0	0	0	0	0	0	0	0	0	0	0	0
Total	50	31	98	51	137	63	137	53	149	33	105	20	45	6	28	1	3	0	19	5	771	263

Apps = Number of Applicants
Adm = Number Admitted
Reflects 97% of the total applicant pool.

New York Law School

57 Worth Street
New York, NY 10013-2960

E-Mail: admissions@nyls.edu
URL: http://www.nyls.edu
Phone: 212.431.2888

■ Introduction

New York Law School has been an integral part of New York's legal community for over 100 years. Founded in 1891, the school's approach to law study combines practical perspectives with theoretical analysis to produce a "lawyer-centered" legal education. The school's central location and proximity to courts, government agencies, major law firms, corporations, and financial institutions provides invaluable educational and practical experiences for students. The Law School offers clerkship and externship opportunities in numerous courts, law offices, and government agencies within walking distance of the Law School. The Law School is located in TriBeCa, one of the city's most colorful and dynamic communities and the home of film studios, art galleries, fine restaurants, and numerous other cultural and entertainment resources.

The school's success is reflected in the many leaders of the legal and business community who are New York Law School graduates. It offers a full-time day program, a part-time day program, and a part-time evening program. New York Law School is a member of the Association of American Law Schools, is fully approved by the ABA, and is chartered by the New York State Board of Regents.

■ Enrollment/Student Body

➡ 4,240 applicants ➡ 1,989 admitted first-year class 1998 ➡ 503 enrolled first-year class 1998 ➡ full-time 25th/75th percentile GPA—2.77/3.27 ➡ part-time 25th/75th percentile GPA—2.78/3.24 ➡ full-time 25th/75th percentile LSAT—148/154 ➡ part-time 25th/75th percentile LSAT—147/154 ➡ 921 total full-time ➡ 484 total part-time ➡ 24% minority ➡ 47% women ➡ 42 states & foreign countries represented ➡ 194 undergraduate schools represented ➡ 32 first-year students hold advanced degrees

New York Law School has a long-standing and continuing interest in enrolling students from varied backgrounds, including older students, minority students, women, career changers, and public servants. Students range in age from 21 to 65, with the average age of 26.

■ Faculty

➡ 121 total ➡ 51 full-time ➡ 70 part-time or adjunct ➡ 42 women ➡ 12 minority

The school's broad curriculum of more than 200 elective courses and seminars is taught by a distinguished faculty. Leading jurists and attorneys who work in nearby offices are members of the adjunct faculty and teach courses in their areas of practice and expertise. Collectively, the faculty offers exceptional breadth and depth in their backgrounds and professional interests.

■ Library and Physical Facilities

➡ 451,199 volumes & equivalents ➡ library hours: Mon.-Thurs., 8:00 A.M.-11:00 P.M.; Fri., 8:00 A.M.-10:00 P.M.; Sat. and Sun., 10:00 A.M.-10:00 P.M.; expanded hours during exams ➡ LEXIS/NEXIS ➡ Law Schools Online ➡ WESTLAW/DIALOG/Dow Jones News Retrieval ➡ OCLC ➡ RLIN ➡ CD-ROM Tower ➡ 23 staff members, including 13 full-time librarians ➡ library seats 616

The Mendik Library reflects the latest developments in information technology. Designed to be a functional, comfortable environment in which to study, it features separate rooms for computer terminals, spacious study areas, and informal lounges. Of particular interest is the Communications Library, devoted to material related to the school's Media Law Program. The Law School's facilities occupy a group of four connected buildings in Lower Manhattan near the courts, city, state, and federal offices, and the financial district.

■ Curriculum and Special Programs

➡ Academic Support Program ➡ 86 units/credits required to graduate ➡ 225 courses available ➡ degrees available: J.D.; J.D./M.B.A. with Baruch College (City University of New York); & Bachelor's/J.D. with Stevens Institute of Technology ➡ range of first-year class size—15-120

The curriculum is designed to prepare students to be effective, productive, and responsible members of the legal profession. The required curriculum, comprising the entire first year and part of the second year, provides a foundation in legal reasoning and in areas of law that are considered indispensable building blocks of a legal education. In the second year and thereafter, students may design their programs with elective courses chosen from an extraordinarily rich array.

The Lawyering Skills Program—Elements such as legal analysis and legal writing, counseling, interviewing, negotiating, advocacy, planning, and strategizing form the core subject areas of the school's Lawyering Skills Program. Among the key elements of the Lawyering Skills Program are the following:

The New York Law School Civil and Human Rights Clinic—The Civil and Human Rights Clinic offers students the opportunity to represent real clients who are suffering real or threatened deprivations of a right or who are seeking political asylum.

Workshops—The Law School offers a number of workshop courses, which link a seminar in a specialized body of law to field placements for seminar participants in offices and agencies practicing in that area of law.

The Externship and Judicial Internship Programs—These programs permit students to do actual lawyering work at placements in law offices.

■ Centers for Specialized Study

Communications Media Center—Established in 1977, the center promotes education, discussion, research, and writing about mass communications law. It is headed by

Professor Michael Botein, whose background includes extensive experience in the telecommunications industry.

Center for New York City Law—In 1993, New York Law School established the Center for New York City Law to focus on governmental and legal processes in the urban setting. Professor Ross Sandler, a former New York City Commissioner and Special Advisor to the Mayor, directs the center.

Center for International Law—Established in 1996, this center focuses on legal issues relating to international trade and finance. Sydney M. Cone, III, professor and director of the Center, was, until joining the Law School this year, a partner of a major New York City law firm specializing in international law.

■ Admission

➡ *Bachelor's degree from accredited college or university required for admission* ➡ *application deadline—April 1*
➡ *rolling admission, early application preferred*
➡ *LSAT, LSDAS required* ➡ *application fee—$50*

In the admission process a range of factors is taken into account, including the applicant's academic record and Law School Admission Test scores. The school seeks to admit students who, in addition to possessing strong academic credentials, also have demonstrated leadership ability, motivation, and a sense of service and responsibility to society. In evaluating applicants, excellence in a particular field of study, motivation, progression of grades, strength of undergraduate curriculum, work and community-service experience, graduate study in other disciplines, and extracurricular activities all are considered. Writing ability receives particular attention.

The school seeks to enroll a diverse student body made up of individuals who, through their backgrounds, experiences, perspectives, and ambitions, promise to enrich the law school community and, ultimately, the larger society.

■ Student Activities

There is a Moot Court Board with active and successful participation in intermural competitions, as well as three scholarly publications, edited and staffed by students, that are integral parts of the Law School's program— *New York Law School Law Review*, *New York Law School Journal of International and Comparative Law*, and *New York Law School Journal of Human Rights*. Students have established some 32 interest organizations as well.

■ Expenses and Financial Aid

➡ *tuition & fees—full-time, $22,114; part-time, $16,588*
➡ *average additional expenses—$10,745 (room, board, books)*
➡ *merit- & need-based scholarships available*
➡ *minority scholarships available* ➡ *financial aid available*

New York Law School has established a program of financial aid to assist students in meeting the costs of a legal education. Financial assistance is available in the form of grants, scholarships, work-study awards, and loans. New York Law School awards scholarships on the basis of academic merit and financial need. Complete information may be obtained from the Office of Financial Aid.

■ Career Services

The Career Services Office provides an array of services, including individual career counseling; on-campus interview programs; numerous career panels and workshops; alumni services and network/mentoring programs; law firm lists categorized by specialty areas and size; computerized legal employer databases; and information on summer, full-time, and part-time positions and alternative career opportunities.

Applicant Group for the 1998-1999 Academic Year

New York Law School
This grid includes only applicants who earned 120-180 LSAT scores under standard administrations.

LSAT Score	GPA 3.75 +		3.50 - 3.74		3.25 - 3.49		3.00 - 3.24		2.75 - 2.99		2.50 - 2.74		2.25 - 2.49		2.00 - 2.24		Below 2.00		No GPA		Total	
	Apps	Adm	Apps	Adm	Apps	Adm	Apps	Adm	Apps	Adm	Apps	Adm	Apps	Adm	Apps	Adm	Apps	Adm	Apps	Adm	Apps	Adm
165-180	3	3	8	8	13	13	8	6	8	8	4	4	3	3	2	2	1	0	0	0	50	47
155-164	37	35	90	89	133	132	185	176	142	136	94	89	42	34	18	15	5	0	8	0	754	706
145-154	64	56	175	151	304	253	406	329	417	317	300	201	142	66	38	10	12	0	9	0	1867	1383
Below 145	23	2	54	2	115	2	179	2	225	2	204	1	146	0	74	0	17	0	15	0	1052	11
Total	127	96	327	250	565	400	778	513	792	463	602	295	333	103	132	27	35	0	32	0	3723	2147

Apps = Number of Applicants
Adm = Number Admitted
Reflects 88% of the total applicant pool.

New York University School of Law

110 West Third Street
New York, NY 10012

URL: http://www.law.nyu.edu/index.html
Phone: 212.998.6060; Fax: 212.995.4527

■ Introduction

Founded in 1835, New York University School of Law has a record of academic excellence and national scholarly influence extending back into the nineteenth century. More than 100 years ago it became one of the first law schools routinely to admit women and those from groups discriminated against by many other institutions.

NYU has been a pioneer in such widely diverse areas as the clinical education programs for all interested students, programs to train lawyers for public service, and interdisciplinary colloquia in fields including jurisprudence, criminal law and criminology, legal history, and international legal studies.

These traditions remain vibrant today as the School of Law, located on the university's campus in Greenwich Village—a residential neighborhood with its own rich history—continues to use its position in New York City to create a twenty-first century legal education in global justice, grounded in solid sociological and jurisprudential training and reflected in sensitive professional service to the world's peoples.

■ Enrollment/Student Body

➡ 6,479 applicants   ➡ 448 enrolled first-year class 1998
➡ full-time 25th/75th percentile GPA—3.56/3.81
➡ full-time 25th/75th percentile LSAT—166/171
➡ 1,368 total full-time   ➡ 23% minority
➡ 50% women   ➡ 69 states & foreign countries represented
➡ 226 undergraduate schools represented
➡ 15% hold advanced or professional degrees

■ Faculty

➡ 95 full-time faculty and instructors (36 women, 10 minority & foreign)   ➡ 97 part-time or adjunct faculty (20 women, 38 minority & foreign)

■ Library and Physical Facilities

➡ 944,969 volumes & equivalents   ➡ 100 library hours per week   ➡ LEXIS   ➡ NEXIS   ➡ WESTLAW
➡ DIALOG   ➡ 17 full-time librarians

In addition to its classroom and clinical buildings, the School of Law owns two modern apartment buildings which provide housing for more than 900 people, including law students, their spouses, their partners, and their children.

■ Curriculum

➡ 82 credits required to graduate   ➡ 187 courses available beyond first year   ➡ degrees available: J.D./LL.M. in Taxation; J.D./M.A. (sociology, politics, history, philosophy, economics, French, Latin/Caribbean studies, Law & Society); J.D./M.B.A.; J.D./M.P.A. with Princeton or NYU; J.D./M.S.W.; J.D./M.U.P.; LL.M.; M.C.J.; J.S.D.   ➡ semesters, start in Aug.
➡ range of first-year class size—18-100

NYU School of Law's Law Center includes the J.D. and graduate divisions, the Global Law Program, the Center for International Studies, the Center for Research in Crime and Justice, the Arthur Garfield Hays Civil Liberties Program, the Program for the Study of Law, Philosophy and Social Theory, the Program on Philanthropy and the Law, the Public Interest Center, and the Institute for Judicial Administration.

NYU's curriculum is distinguished by its strength in traditional areas of legal study, interdisciplinary study, and clinical education, and has long been committed to educating lawyers who will use their degrees to serve the public. The **Root-Tilden-Snow Program** and the **Public Interest Center**, with seven full-time staff members, sponsor speakers, offer academic and career counseling, and administer summer internship, volunteer, and mentoring programs.

The interdisciplinary programs combine a resident faculty, distinguished visitors, and courses at entry through advanced levels.

The J.D. Program is enriched by the graduate program, which offers advanced degrees. Attorneys, law teachers, and judges from over 30 countries enroll each year in degree programs in corporations, international, tax, trade regulation, and individual specialties.

■ Admission

➡ baccalaureate degree or its foreign equivalent required
➡ application deadline—early action, Oct. 15; regular, Feb. 1
➡ LSAT, LSDAS required   ➡ application fee—$65

The admissions process is highly selective. The Committee on Admissions selects candidates with the strongest combination of qualifications and the greatest potential to contribute to NYU and to the legal profession. The committee bases its decisions on intellectual potential, academic achievement, character, community involvement, and work experience.

New York University has one of the largest and most competitive applicant pools in the country; only about one in six of those who apply is admitted. An applicant's undergraduate record and LSAT, while important, are not the sole determinants for admission. No index or cut-off is used in reviewing applications. An applicant's transcripts are analyzed for breadth and depth of coursework, trend in grades, and rank; the competitiveness of the school and major are taken into account, as are special honors and awards.

A strong undergraduate record and LSAT are most important for those applying to law school directly after graduating from college. In all cases, however, other aspects of the application significantly influence the decision. Letters of recommendation, activities, and work experience are reviewed for evidence of significant non-academic or professional achievement, and for qualities including rigor of thought, maturity, judgment, motivation, leadership, imagination, and social commitment. Factors beyond the undergraduate record are particularly important for older applicants, for international students, for those who have experienced educational or socioeconomic disadvantage, and for those who have racial or ethnic identities that are underrepresented in the student body and the legal profession.

In making its decisions the committee aims to enroll an entering class of students with diverse experience, backgrounds, and points of view. Applicants are encouraged to provide information to help the committee reach thoughtful, informed decisions on their applications.

▣ Student Activities

Student-edited publications are *New York University Law Review, Annual Survey of American Law, Environmental Law Journal, Journal of International Law and Politics,* and *New York University Review of Law and Social Change. The Commentator* is the law school newspaper. There are more than 50 active student organizations in 1998-1999, and in most years.

▣ Expenses and Financial Aid

➡ *full-time tuition—$26,100* ➡ *an average amount of additional expenses—$17,995 (rent, food, utilities, personal expenses, books, & course expenses)* ➡ *scholarships available* ➡ *FAFSA form required for federal aid*

NYU will award a number of Root-Tilden-Snow Scholarships to entering students who will spend their careers in low-paying public service jobs. Other financial aid is provided on the basis of need. Aid awarded to first-year students is automatically renewable depending on student's summer earnings. Federal and private loans provide the majority of funding. Seventy-eight percent of the class entering in 1996 received NYU or federal aid.

Loan Forgiveness Program—Graduates who pursue careers in public service or other low-paying sectors of the legal profession will receive post-graduation benefits through NYU's Loan Repayment Assistance Program. The program will pay benefits based on salary to assist our graduates in the repayment of Law School educational debt. Low income is currently defined as $52,020 in determining LRAP eligibility.

▣ Career Services

NYU has an extensive placement program. Career planning for first-year students includes personal career counseling, workshops on all aspects of the search, specialty panels featuring speakers from all areas of practice, and a videotape mock interview program. In 1997-1998, almost 600 private law firms, public interest organizations, government agencies, corporations, and public accounting firms came to NYU to interview students. Two-thirds of these employers were from outside New York.

In summer 1997, 96 percent of first-year students and almost 100 percent of second-year students reported law-related employment. Each summer more than 100 first- and second-year students receive grants from the School of Law to work in public interest positions.

Ninety percent of the 1998 graduating class reporting indicated that they secured their first choice of employment. An additional eight percent reported securing their second choice.

The Career Services Office sponsors recruitment programs in several cities, and, with area law schools, a public service symposium, and a recruiting conference for students of color.

Admission Profile Not Available

University of North Carolina School of Law

Campus Box 3380, 101 Van Hecke-Wettach Hall
Chapel Hill, NC 27599-3380

E-Mail: law_admission@unc.edu
URL: http://www.law.unc.edu
Phone: 919.962.5109

■ Introduction

The University of North Carolina, the first state university chartered in the United States, has offered degrees in law since 1845. The School of Law has been a member of the AALS since 1920 and has been an approved school since the ABA began its accreditation activities in 1923. The School of Law is one of the outstanding institutions in the United States, and the University of North Carolina is recognized as being among the nation's leaders in graduate and professional education. The school aims to provide quality legal education that will prepare students to practice successfully in any jurisdiction. Chapel Hill is a university community close to the metropolitan and industrial centers of Greensboro and Durham, the Research Triangle Park, and the state capital, Raleigh. The immediate area offers an attractive blend of an academic atmosphere in a cosmopolitan setting.

■ Enrollment/Student Body

➡ *2,192 applicants*   ➡ *603 admitted first-year class 1998*
➡ *231 enrolled first-year class 1998*   ➡ *full-time 25th/75th percentile GPA—3.32/3.81*   ➡ *full-time 25th/75th percentile LSAT—153/164*   ➡ *690 total full-time*   ➡ *19.7% minority*
➡ *50.5% women*   ➡ *30 states plus 1 foreign country represented in entering class of 1998*
➡ *104 undergraduate schools represented in entering class*
➡ *12.6% 30 years or older in first-year class of 1998*

■ Faculty

➡ *84 total*   ➡ *44 full-time*   ➡ *40 part-time*
➡ *32 women*   ➡ *5 minority*

■ Library and Physical Facilities

➡ *456,558 volumes & equivalents*   ➡ *library hours: Mon.-Fri., 7:30 A.M.-MIDNIGHT; Sat., 9:00 A.M.-9:00 P.M.; Sun., 10:00 A.M.-MIDNIGHT*   ➡ *LEXIS*   ➡ *NEXIS*
➡ *WESTLAW*   ➡ *19 full-time library staff*
➡ *library seats 407*

The school occupies a contemporary complex within walking distance of residence halls, dining halls, athletic facilities, student union, and the main libraries. The law library, wholly contained within the complex, includes microforms, CD-ROM, interactive video, and other specialized items. Also included within the library wing is a microcomputer laboratory with 20 workstations and electronic resources learning centers with 28 workstations to access computer-assisted legal research systems and CD-ROM libraries.

■ Admission

➡ *Bachelor's degree from accredited college or university required*   ➡ *application deadline—Feb. 1*
➡ *early decision deadline—Oct. 15*
➡ *LSAT, LSDAS required*   ➡ *application fee—$60*

Admission is a competitive process, and applicants with the strongest records are given priority. Admission decisions are based on all the information revealed during a careful and thorough consideration of an applicant's entire admission file. Every file is carefully evaluated. No applicant is granted or denied admission exclusively on the basis of an LSAT score or grade-point average. Every applicant's file is individually assessed on the basis of both quantifiable and qualitative criteria. Applications are examined with the goals of (a) assessing the overall competitive strength of the applicant's record as compared with all other applicants within that applicant's pool and (b) achieving a class that as a whole will have depth in quality, richness of background, wide variety of experience, breadth of perspective, and substantial diversity of viewpoint.

Each year 70 to 75 percent of entering students are legal residents of the state of North Carolina. Admission decisions are made progressively on a rolling basis from November into late spring and are controlled to ensure that all applications submitted by February 1 are given equal consideration.

Applicants are encouraged to visit the law school to attend a class and then tour the campus. Guided tours and self-guided tours are both available. Regular group sessions are conducted throughout the year. Personal meetings are also available with the admissions dean.

■ Student Activities

Students can write for three prominent student legal publications—*The North Carolina Law Review, The North Carolina Journal of International Law and Commercial Regulation,* and *The North Carolina Banking Journal.* The Student Bar Association sponsors a full range of professional, athletic, and social events; a speakers program; minority recruitment events; a legal research service for practicing lawyers; and participation in school governance. The Moot Court Program is student operated and fields a number of successful teams in regional, national, and international competitions; moot court teams compete in client counseling, negotiation, trial practice, appellate advocacy, constitutional law, international law, and environmental negotiation. Students serve on most faculty committees. The extensive array of student organizations include many devoted to public service and social justice issues such as domestic violence, child advocacy, homelessness, AIDS, workers rights, and race relations. Over 40 student organizations are active in the law school, including the American Indian Law Students Association, Asian Pacific American Law Students Association, Black Law Students Association, Christian Legal Society, Jewish Law Student Association, Women in Law, Second Careers in Law, and Parents Active in Law School.

■ Expenses and Financial Aid

➡ *full-time tuition & fees—resident, $3,169; nonresident, $15,269*
➡ *estimated additional expenses—$10,584*

➥ *Chancellors Scholars Program scholarship available*
➥ *need-based scholarships available (FAFSA due March 1)*

Most scholarships are awarded based on a combination of need and merit. Admitted applicants are automatically considered for merit-based scholarships.

Recipients of the Chancellors Scholars awards benefit from substantial financial support which generally includes full tuition and fees, a stipend toward living expenses, and special research and mentoring opportunities with law faculty. Awards are made only on a merit basis.

Financial aid sources available to law students include need-based sources. Some research assistance grants are available for second- and third-year students. Applications for scholarships and loans must be completed by March 1.

■ Housing

There are graduate dormitories near the law school for single students. University student family housing and private apartments are available. Information may be obtained from the University Housing Office, Carr Building CB 5500, Chapel Hill, NC 27599-5580, 919.962.5401.

■ Placement

The Career Development and Services Office, with a full-time director, assistant director, and staff, assists students and alumni with summer and permanent positions. Interviews are held in the law school, and contact is maintained with law offices and agencies throughout the country.

In 1997-98, over 220 employers from throughout the United States and the District of Columbia interviewed on campus; 1997 graduates are employed in 23 states plus the District of Columbia and one foreign country. Of those 1997 graduates reporting to the Placement Office, 98 percent had accepted employment within nine months; 36 percent accepted employment outside of North Carolina. Fifty-five percent of 1997 graduates entered private practice, 13.5 percent accepted judicial clerkships, 9 percent entered business-related fields, 3 percent entered government practice, and 10 percent entered public interest work.

■ Correspondence

Admissions Office, University of North Carolina, School of Law, Van Hecke-Wettach Hall CB 3380, Chapel Hill, NC 27599-3380. Phone: 919.962.5109.

Applicant Group for the 1998-1999 Academic Year

University of North Carolina School of Law
This grid includes only applicants who earned 120-180 LSAT scores under standard administrations.

LSAT Score	3.75 +		3.50 - 3.74		3.25 - 3.49		3.00 - 3.24		2.75 - 2.99		2.50 - 2.74		2.25 - 2.49		2.00 - 2.24		Below 2.00		No GPA		Total	
	Apps	Adm	Apps	Adm	Apps	Adm	Apps	Adm	Apps	Adm	Apps	Adm	Apps	Adm	Apps	Adm	Apps	Adm	Apps	Adm	Apps	Adm
175-180	0	0	1	1	2	2	2	2	2	2	0	0	0	0	0	0	0	0	0	0	7	7
170-174	9	8	11	11	11	9	8	7	5	1	0	0	1	1	0	0	0	0	1	1	46	38
165-169	42	42	46	44	50	34	41	10	24	4	5	0	3	0	0	0	1	0	2	1	214	135
160-164	87	86	113	82	119	36	78	7	43	2	13	1	3	0	5	0	0	0	7	3	468	217
155-159	101	86	146	41	148	15	108	10	63	3	43	1	9	1	4	0	1	0	4	3	627	160
150-154	54	16	83	18	117	17	99	6	60	2	32	1	13	1	4	0	0	0	5	0	467	61
145-149	13	4	38	4	48	6	50	7	41	2	28	0	17	0	7	0	0	0	7	0	249	23
140-144	6	1	14	2	26	2	32	1	28	0	24	0	14	1	8	0	1	0	4	0	157	7
135-139	1	0	2	0	3	0	17	0	13	0	11	0	5	0	0	0	1	0	0	0	53	0
130-134	0	0	1	0	1	0	5	0	6	0	3	0	4	0	2	0	1	0	1	0	24	0
125-129	0	0	0	0	0	0	0	0	1	0	4	0	0	0	2	0	0	0	0	0	7	0
120-124	0	0	0	0	0	0	0	0	0	0	0	0	0	0	0	0	0	0	0	0	0	0
Total	313	243	455	203	525	121	440	50	286	16	163	3	69	4	32	0	5	0	31	8	2319	648

Apps = Number of Applicants
Adm = Number Admitted
Reflects 99% of the total applicant pool.

North Carolina Central University School of Law

1512 South Alston Avenue
Durham, NC 27707

Phone: 919.560.6333

◼ Introduction

The North Carolina Central University School of Law was established in 1939. The School of Law is located in Durham, which, along with Raleigh and Chapel Hill, forms North Carolina's thriving "Research Triangle." The school has been accredited by the American Bar Association since 1950.

North Carolina Central University (NCCU) was chartered in 1909 as a private institution and opened to students in July of 1910. In 1923, when the General Assembly of North Carolina appropriated funds for the purchase and maintenance of the school, the institution became the first state-supported liberal arts college for African Americans in the United States. In July 1972, NCCU became one of the constituent institutions of the University of North Carolina system. Today, the School of Law is one of the most diverse in the country.

◼ Enrollment/Student Body

➡ *838 applicants* ➡ *242 admitted first-year class 1998*
➡ *93 enrolled first-year class 1998 (day)* ➡*33 enrolled first-year class 1998 (evening)* ➡ *full-time 25th/75th percentile GPA—2.70/3.20* ➡ *part-time 25th/75th percentile GPA—2.90/3.30* ➡ *full-time 25th/75th percentile LSAT—143/152* ➡ *part-time 25th/75th percentile LSAT—152/161*
➡ *265 total full-time* ➡ *108 total part-time*
➡ *58.7% minority* ➡ *55.8% women*

◼ Faculty

➡ *39 total* ➡ *19 full-time* ➡ *20 part-time or adjunct*
➡ *20 women* ➡ *12 minority*

◼ Library and Physical Facilities

➡ *126,803 volumes & 888,687 pieces* ➡ *library hours: Mon.-Thurs., 8:00 A.M.-MIDNIGHT; Fri., 8:00 A.M.-9:00 P.M.; Sat., 10:00 A.M.-9:00 P.M.; Sun., 1:00 P.M.-10:00 P.M.*
➡ *LEXIS* ➡ *NEXIS* ➡ *WESTLAW* ➡ *DIALOG*
➡ *5 full-time librarians*

◼ Curriculum

➡ *Academic Support Program* ➡ *88 credits required to graduate* ➡ *degrees available: J.D.; J.D./M.B.A.; J.D./M.L.S.*
➡ *semesters, start in Aug.*
➡ *range of first-year class size—45-55 (day); 25-35 (evening)*

◼ Special Programs

The joint degree J.D./M.L.S. program allows students interested in a career in law librarianship to simultaneously pursue the J.D. degree and a masters degree in library and information sciences. Application to and acceptance by both the School of Law and the School of Library and Information Sciences are required.

The School of Law and the NCCU School of Business offer a J.D./M.B.A. program enabling a student to receive the J.D. and M.B.A. degrees in four years rather than the usual five. Students must be accepted into both programs.

The Clinical Legal Experience Program (the clinic) is comprised of a Criminal Litigation Clinic, a Civil Litigation Clinic, and a Family Law Clinic. The purpose of the clinic is to provide an opportunity for law students to learn practical lawyering skills under the supervision of clinical professors, all of whom are outstanding trial lawyers, appellate lawyers, and jurists. With the assistance of supervising attorneys, clinic students represent indigent clients in civil matters and misdemeanor criminal cases. The Clinical Legal Experience Program is housed in a state-of-the-art model law office facility located in the law school's basement.

The School of Law offers the only part-time evening law program in North Carolina. This four-year program offers a unique opportunity for motivated professionals to pursue a legal education while maintaining their current daytime commitments.

◼ Admission

➡ *Bachelor's degree required for admission*
➡ *application deadline—April 15* ➡ *rolling admission*
➡ *LSAT, LSDAS required* ➡ *application fee—$30*

North Carolina Central University School of Law welcomes students of all races to contribute to its diversity as it continues to pursue with vigor its historic mission of producing a substantial percentage of minority attorneys for the state and nation. The school gives considerable weight to the traditional criteria of the LSAT score and UGPA, but it also considers evidence that an applicant has demonstrated in other ways a likelihood of succeeding in the legal profession.

The School of Law seeks students who are more likely to contribute affirmatively to the learning of others by reason of their intellectual attainments, demonstrated emotional maturity and self-discipline, social background, or exceptional capacity to benefit from the school's educational program. For this reason, applicants are asked to provide full information about their intellectual attainments, their personal achievements, employment experience, and social background.

◼ Student Activities

The *North Carolina Central Law Journal*, published semi-annually, is devoted to articles by legal scholars and to case notes and comments by students. Invitations to join the *Law Journal* are extended to students on the basis of academic achievement and writing ability.

The School of Law has a complete moot court and trial advocacy program. Intra- and interscholastic competitions provide students with an opportunity to write appellate briefs and to participate in mock trials and appellate oral arguments.

Student organizations at the School of Law include the Student Bar Association, Moot Court Board, American Bar Association/Law Students Division, Black Law Students

Association, Entertainment and Sports Law Association, Intellectual Property Society, Women's Caucus, National Lawyers Guild, and F.A.C.E.S. (Future Attorneys Challenging Elementary Students). There are chapters of three legal fraternities—Delta Theta Phi; Phi Alpha Delta; and Phi Delta Phi.

■ Expenses and Financial Aid

➤ *tuition & fees—resident, $2,700.50; nonresident, $10,997.50; part-time tuition & fees—resident, $2,700.50; nonresident, $10,997.50* ➤ *estimated additional expenses—$13,438 (books, supplies, & living expenses)* ➤ *merit- & need-based scholarships available* ➤ *merit- & need-based minority scholarships available* ➤ *financial aid available* ➤ *application for Federal Student Aid (FAFSA) form for need analysis due by Feb. 1*

■ Housing

There is a graduate dormitory near the law school for single students. Information may be obtained by writing to the University Housing Director, North Carolina Central University, P.O. Box 19382, Durham, NC, 27707.

■ Career Services

The Placement Office offers a range of services to students and prospective employers. These services include career counseling, interview preparation and résumé writing workshops, firm and résumé referral banks, a placement information booklet and resource library, and an on-campus interview program. Graduates typically find employment in judicial clerkships, government agencies, law firms, legal service organizations, and the Judge Advocate General's Corps.

Admission Profile Not Available
Applicants should feel free to contact the Admission Office for additional information.

University of North Dakota School of Law

Office of the Dean
Grand Forks, ND 58202

E-Mail: mark.brickson@thor.law.und.nodak.edu
URL: http://www.law.und.nodak.edu
Phone: 701.777.2104

■ Introduction

The University of North Dakota School of Law was established in 1899, and has been a member of the AALS since 1910. In 1923, it was approved by the ABA; it is a fully accredited graduate professional school of the university awarding the J.D. degree. The School of Law is located on the main campus of the university in Grand Forks, a city of approximately 50,000, in the northeastern part of the state. The third largest city in the state, Grand Forks is a center of commerce for the Upper Great Plains, as well as a large legal community, including county, state, and federal trial courts.

■ Enrollment/Student Body

➠ *full-time 25th/75th percentile GPA—2.95/3.43*
➠ *full-time 25th/75th percentile LSAT—148/154*
➠ *204 total full-time*

While a large percentage of the entering students are North Dakota residents, the School of Law enrolls students from all parts of the country.

■ Library and Physical Facilities

➠ *255,991 volumes & equivalents*

The Thormodsgard Law Library, constructed in 1973 as an addition to the classroom and office building, offers generous seating and study space on its four levels. The Baker Moot Court Room, completed in 1973, provides facilities for trial and appellate arguments, and is occasionally used by the North Dakota Supreme Court, United States Court of Appeals for the Eighth Circuit, United States District Court for the District of North Dakota, and other state and federal courts.

■ Curriculum

➠ *90 credits required to graduate*

The curriculum of the School of Law covers a period of three full academic years. All the work of the first year is prescribed. Courses in the second and third years are elective, except for the course in Professional Responsibility.

■ Special Programs

The size of the student body is ideally suited for close professional contact with the faculty. Students are given ample opportunity to participate in the governance of the school. Elected members of the Student Bar Association attend regularly scheduled faculty meetings and are active voting participants in most law school committees. Participation by students in the State Bar Association of North Dakota is encouraged, and students are eligible to serve on selected state bar committees.

The School of Law is committed to the principle that all students should have an opportunity to elect, as a portion of their educational development, clinical legal education.

This is not intended to diminish the law school's responsibility for education in legal analysis and legal principles, but adds an additional responsibility, providing experience in the application of analysis and theory.

The clinical program provides training in practical skills through simulation training and client representation. Under supervision, law students work with clients in cases, as permitted under the rule of the North Dakota Supreme Court. Training is received in such skills as interviewing, counseling, negotiating, fact gathering, and advocacy.

The school has an extensive Trial Advocacy Program, in which students learn trial skills in a simulated advocacy setting under the close supervision of experienced trial lawyers. Each student in this course is responsible, with one student advocate cocounsel, for the trial of at least one full civil or criminal case during the semester. This program has received the Emil Gumpert Award of the American College of Trial Lawyers for excellence in the teaching of trial advocacy.

During sessions of the state legislature, selected students serve as legislative interns at the state capital in Bismarck.

Central Legal Research, directed by an attorney under the supervision of the Dean, is housed in the School of Law. This bureau is the research arm for the criminal justice system of the State of North Dakota. Competitively hired students perform original legal research upon request for judges, prosecutors, court-appointed defense counsel, police, and others.

In 1982 the law school initiated a new foreign exchange program, the UND-University of Oslo Program. The Norwegian program provides for exchange of students and faculty between these two fine law schools.

■ Admission

➠ *undergraduate degree from accredited college or university required* ➠ *application deadline—April 1*
➠ *LSAT, LSDAS required*

The School of Law has no specific undergraduate course prerequisites and agrees with the observations in the introduction to this guide. The school admits students only in August, and only for full-time study. Applications are available upon request. The policy of the faculty of the School of Law is to admit those applicants who, in the determination of the faculty, will be able to satisfactorily complete the law school program. The admissions committee utilizes the following criteria to achieve this goal: (1) LSAT score; (2) undergraduate GPA; (3) past performance in an academic environment; (4) past performance in activities that would tend to predict the applicant's ability to complete successfully the law school program; and, (5) other evidence relevant to predicted success and prospective professional responsibility. The total number of students admitted is, of course, limited by considerations involving space and faculty courseload.

The law school does not have a nonresident quota; however, preference is given to residents.

Students who have begun the study of law in other accredited law schools may be admitted in exceptional circumstances to advanced standing, provided they have fulfilled the requirements for admission to the University of North Dakota School of Law. Ordinarily, no transfer credit will be allowed for more than two semesters of work completed elsewhere, nor will transfer credit be given for any courses in which an unsatisfactory or failing grade has been received. Moreover, admission maybe conditioned upon meeting such additional requirements as the faculty may prescribe. No student will be admitted as a transfer student with advanced standing who is not eligible to continue as a student at his or her present law school.

■ Student Activities

The *North Dakota Law Review* and Agricultural Law Research program provide research and writing opportunities. Students also participate in various moot court activities, including regional and national competitions. Student organizations include the Christian Legal Society, Environmental Law Society, International Law Society, Law Women's Caucus, Native American Law Students Association, Student Trial Lawyers Association, *Rhadamanthus*

(newsletter) and an active Student Bar Association. The School of Law also has chapters of the Order of the Coif and Phi Alpha Delta and Delta Theta Phi legal fraternities.

■ Expenses and Financial Aid

➡ *full-time tuition & fees—resident, $2,125/semester; nonresident, $4,448/semester (1998-99)*
➡ *scholarships available*   ➡ *financial aid available*

The semester fees include student activity and university fees totaling $184 per semester, a $50 per semester technology fee, and a $500 per semester professional fee. The student activity and university fees cover payment for health services, the university center, campus publications, and drama and athletic events. The professional fee is a fee assessed by the School of Law and is used to support and improve the law school program. Fees are subject to change without notice. Loan funds for all qualified students are available through the university Student Financial Aids Office, Twamley Hall.

■ Housing

The university's family housing facilities are open to law students. University residence halls are open to single law students. Inquiries should be directed to the Housing Office, Post Office Box 9029, Grand Forks, ND 58202.

Applicant Group for the 1998-1999 Academic Year

University of North Dakota School of Law
This grid includes only applicants who earned 120-180 LSAT scores under standard administrations.

LSAT Score	GPA																					
	3.75 +		3.50 - 3.74		3.25 - 3.49		3.00 - 3.24		2.75 - 2.99		2.50 -2.74		2.25 - 2.49		2.00 - 2.24		Below 2.00		No GPA		Total	
	Apps	Adm	Apps	Adm	Apps	Adm	Apps	Adm	Apps	Adm	Apps	Adm	Apps	Adm	Apps	Adm	Apps	Adm	Apps	Adm	Apps	Adm
175-180	0	0	0	0	0	0	0	0	0	0	0	0	0	0	0	0	0	0	0	0	0	0
170-174	0	0	0	0	0	0	0	0	0	0	0	0	0	0	0	0	0	0	0	0	0	0
165-169	0	0	0	0	1	1	0	0	0	0	1	1	0	0	0	0	0	0	0	0	2	2
160-164	1	0	3	3	1	1	2	1	0	0	0	0	0	0	0	0	0	0	1	1	8	6
155-159	5	4	2	1	5	5	6	6	4	4	0	0	1	0	1	1	2	0	0	0	26	21
150-154	4	4	9	9	15	14	15	15	8	7	7	5	4	2	4	2	0	0	1	0	67	58
145-149	5	4	7	7	12	10	19	15	10	7	16	6	6	1	2	1	2	0	1	0	80	51
140-144	1	0	1	0	9	3	7	0	9	0	8	0	2	0	1	0	0	0	0	0	38	3
135-139	0	0	3	1	2	0	2	0	2	0	3	0	0	0	1	0	0	0	4	0	17	1
130-134	0	0	0	0	0	0	1	0	2	0	3	0	2	0	0	0	0	0	0	0	8	0
125-129	0	0	0	0	0	0	0	0	0	0	0	0	0	0	0	0	0	0	0	0	0	0
120-124	0	0	0	0	0	0	0	0	0	0	0	0	0	0	0	0	0	0	0	0	0	0
Total	16	12	25	21	45	34	52	37	35	18	38	12	15	3	9	4	4	0	7	1	246	142

Apps = Number of Applicants
Adm = Number Admitted
Reflects 98% of the total applicant pool.

Northeastern University School of Law

P.O. Box 728
Boston, MA 02117-0728

E-Mail: lawadmissions@nunet.neu.edu
URL: http://www.slaw.neu.edu/NUSL.htm
Phone: 617.373.2395

■ Introduction

Located in Boston, Massachusetts, Northeastern is a small law school with a unique program combining rigorous academic study with practical legal work experience and a strong tradition of public service. While maintaining the highest academic standards, it enables students to learn the skills of actual practice across a broad spectrum of the law. The cooperative legal education program ensures that no graduate will enter the practice of law without having first spent half of his or her second and third years as a full-time apprentice or legal assistant to cooperating employers, generally in several diverse areas of legal practice. Through this program, students have an unusual opportunity to learn an array of practical skills, to observe various approaches to the practice of law, and to determine which areas of the law interest them most. The law school is accredited by the ABA and is a member of the AALS.

■ Enrollment/Student Body

➡ *1,733 applicants*   ➡ *756 admitted first-year class 1998*
➡ *230 enrolled first-year class 1998*   ➡ *full-time 25th/75th percentile GPA—2.80/3.40*   ➡ *full-time 25th/75th percentile LSAT—151/158*   ➡ *614 total full-time*   ➡ *26% minority*
➡ *66% women*   ➡ *40 states & foreign countries represented*
➡ *229 undergraduate schools represented*

■ Faculty

➡ *67 total*   ➡ *29 full-time*   ➡ *38 part-time or adjunct*
➡ *28 women*

■ Library and Physical Facilities

➡ *285,000 volumes & equivalents*   ➡ *library hours: Mon.-Thurs., 8:00 A.M.-11:00 P.M.; Fri., 8:00 A.M.-9:00 P.M.; Sat., 9:00 A.M.-9:00 P.M.; Sun., NOON-10:00 P.M.*
➡ *LEXIS*   ➡ *NEXIS*   ➡ *WESTLAW*   ➡ *DIALOG*
➡ *7 full-time librarians and 2 paraprofessional staff*
➡ *library seats 371*

■ Curriculum

➡ *99 credits required to graduate*   ➡ *public interest graduation requirement*   ➡ *85-95 total courses available*
➡ *degrees available: J.D.; J.D./M.B.A.; J.D./M.S./M.B.A. in Accounting; J.D./Ph.D. in Law, Policy, & Society*
➡ *first-year class starts late Aug.*
➡ *range of first-year class size—8-200*

■ Special Programs

The **Cooperative Legal Education Program** is an integral part of each student's experience at Northeastern: academic credit is awarded for successful completion of four quarters of legal "co-op" work. Students earn their J.D. degree in the same time as their counterparts at other law schools.

First-year students begin in late August and follow a traditional full-time academic program for nine months until the end of May. The second year starts in June. Half the class undertakes work as full-time interns for the summer quarter; the other half undertakes the first academic period of the second year. At the end of the summer, the sections exchange places. They continue this process of alternating work and academic periods through the 24 months of the second and third years.

Students work for large and small firms, judges, government agencies, legal assistance and public defender organizations, corporate law departments, unions, and practically every type of legal practitioner. There are over 700 participating employers throughout the United States, including Alaska and Hawaii, and increasing numbers of students work in foreign nations. Currently, students have completed co-ops in over 30 different countries.

The cooperative program is not a way to "work your way through law school." However, earnings from cooperative employment may somewhat reduce the net cost of attending school during the second and third years. Salaries range from a nominal amount to $1,400 per week. Each year the school provides roughly $370,000 in funding to students engaged in public interest work and judicial internships.

The school offers clinical courses including the Certiorari/Criminal Appeals Clinic, the Domestic Violence Clinic, the Poverty Law and Practice Program, the Criminal Advocacy Program, the Prisoner's Rights Program, and the Tobacco Control Clinic.

The **Domestic Violence Clinic**, which combines classroom instruction with supervised clinical practice, is offered each quarter.

The course integrates theory, substantive law, and skills training. The substantive law focus is on the Massachusetts Abuse Prevention Act, related areas of family law, benefits, and the criminal process as it relates to domestic violence. Skills training focuses on interviewing, counseling, and preparation and presentation of cases.

The **Poverty Law and Practice Program** combines classroom instruction with clinical practice under the supervision of experienced clinical instructors. All course and clinical work takes place at the new clinical offices on campus.

The clinic supports community organizations struggling with issues of urban poverty. The focus of the clinic concentrates on the intersection of work and welfare and involves both individual and group representation.

■ Admission

➡ *Bachelor's degree required*   ➡ *application deadline— modified rolling (final deadline is March 1)*
➡ *LSAT, LSDAS required*   ➡ *application fee—$55*

Northeastern University operates a full-time day program only. Students are enrolled only in late August.

Admission decisions for each fall entering class are made in three rounds. Deadlines for three rounds are December 1, January 15, and March 1. Applicants in the first round may also apply for Early Decision.

An applicant should ordinarily have undergraduate grades and LSAT scores in the 80th percentile. In addition to attempting to assess a candidate's academic achievement to date, the Admissions Committee considers other factors that indicate his or her potential. These include professional work experience, involvement in extracurricular or community activities, and clear indications of unusual determination, motivation, and accomplishment. The School of Law recommends, but does not require, evaluative interviews for admission. Interviews are conducted on-campus from July 1 to February 15. No alumni/ae interviews are available.

■ Student Activities

Students are elected to serve as representatives on all standing committees within the school. Through the Black Law Students Association, Asian Pacific American Law Students Association, and the Latina/o American Law Students Association, students work closely with the school in an effort to recruit minority students. Other student groups include the Environmental Law Forum; Critical Legal Theory Study Group; Women's Caucus; Lesbian, Gay, and Bisexual Caucus; the National Lawyers Guild; the Business Law Forum; Entertainment, Arts, and Sports Law Society; Jewish Law Students Association; Older Wiser Law Students; the International Law Society;

the Cooperative Income Sharing Program; the Coalition for the Public Interest; Moot Court Society; the Student of Color Coalition; High Tech Law Society; Immigration Law Task Force; Intellectual Property Society; and the Student Bar Association.

■ Expenses and Financial Aid

➡ *full-time tuition & fees—$22,500 (1998-99)*
➡ *estimated additional expenses—$13,440 (living expenses & books)* ➡ *merit- & need-based scholarships available*
➡ *FAFSA & NUSL Financial Aid Form*

■ Career Services

The Office of Career Services assists students with all phases of the job-search process. Northeastern graduates are employed throughout the United States and abroad with private firms, government agencies, legal services and public defender organizations, the judiciary, labor unions, and corporate law departments. In 1997, 43 percent of NUSL graduates accepted post-graduate positions with their former co-op employers. In recent years, over 20 percent of NUSL graduates, almost twice the national average, began their legal careers as judicial clerks. Graduates of the School of Law have entered public interest work at a rate nearly five times the national average. In addition, for the last seven years, NUSL graduates have been among the 25 recipients nationwide to be awarded the prestigious Skadden Fellowship, enabling them to pursue careers in public interest law.

Applicant Group for the 1998-1999 Academic Year

Northeastern University School of Law
This grid includes only applicants who earned 120-180 LSAT scores under standard administrations.

LSAT Score	3.75 +		3.50 - 3.74		3.25 - 3.49		3.00 - 3.24		2.75 - 2.99		2.50 -2.74		2.25 - 2.49		2.00 - 2.24		Below 2.00		No GPA		Total	
	Apps	Adm	Apps	Adm	Apps	Adm	Apps	Adm	Apps	Adm	Apps	Adm	Apps	Adm	Apps	Adm	Apps	Adm	Apps	Adm	Apps	Adm
175-180	0	0	1	1	2	2	0	0	0	0	0	0	0	0	0	0	0	0	0	0	3	3
170-174	3	3	1	1	2	2	2	1	1	1	0	0	0	0	0	0	0	0	0	0	9	8
165-169	5	5	12	12	11	9	11	10	4	1	5	5	0	0	0	0	1	0	2	2	51	44
160-164	16	15	41	34	49	42	45	40	19	16	6	6	4	4	1	1	0	0	3	3	184	161
155-159	26	20	79	68	87	54	92	62	52	39	31	21	17	11	8	5	1	1	2	2	395	283
150-154	15	8	57	15	104	30	101	36	66	25	48	20	16	8	7	3	0	0	6	2	420	147
145-149	7	2	39	9	53	6	73	12	48	6	38	3	19	2	16	1	2	0	6	1	301	42
140-144	8	1	18	5	34	7	50	12	38	0	37	6	21	1	6	0	1	0	6	1	219	33
135-139	0	0	10	0	13	0	15	0	22	0	11	2	10	0	5	0	2	0	4	1	92	3
130-134	0	0	0	0	1	0	4	0	9	0	2	0	2	0	2	0	0	0	1	0	21	0
125-129	0	0	0	0	1	0	0	0	0	0	2	0	0	0	1	0	1	0	3	0	8	0
120-124	0	0	0	0	0	0	0	0	0	0	0	0	1	0	0	0	1	0	1	0	3	0
Total	80	54	258	145	357	152	393	173	259	88	180	63	90	26	47	10	8	1	34	12	1706	724

Apps = Number of Applicants
Adm = Number Admitted
Reflects 99% of the total applicant pool.

Northern Illinois University College of Law

DeKalb, IL 60115

E-Mail: lawadm@niu.edu
URL: http://www.niu.edu/claw/index.htm
Phone: 800.892.3050 or 815.753.8595

■ Introduction

The College of Law is located on the 546-acre main campus of NIU in DeKalb. The community of DeKalb, known as the "Barb City" is conveniently located approximately 60 miles west of Chicago and 25 miles outside of the suburban area on the Illinois Research and Development Corridor. It is close enough to the Chicago metropolitan area to draw on its resources, yet retain its own college-town flavor— a safe and low-cost environment with a high quality of life.

The College of Law seeks to prepare its graduates not only for the traditional role of lawyers, but for the tasks we can now only speculate will be assumed by the law-trained.

■ Enrollment/Student Body

➡ *814 applicants*   ➡ *full-time 25th/75th percentile GPA— 2.78/3.30*   ➡ *part-time 25th/75th percentile GPA—2.87/3.82*
➡ *full-time 25th/75th percentile LSAT—151/156*
➡ *part-time 25th/75th percentile LSAT—149/154*
➡ *107 enrolled first-year class 1998*   ➡ *290 total enrollment*
➡ *23 total part-time*   ➡ *22% total minority*
➡ *38% total women*   ➡ *22 states & foreign countries represented*   ➡ *11 undergraduate schools represented*
➡ *22,252 total university enrollment*

The current student body reflects broad geographic, cultural, and economic diversity.

■ Faculty

➡ *42 total*   ➡ *29 full-time*   ➡ *13 part-time or adjunct*
➡ *10 women*   ➡ *8 minority*

The school has a diverse and professionally distinguished faculty dedicated to teaching and scholarship.

■ Library and Physical Facilities

➡ *204,000 volumes & equivalents*
➡ *LEXIS*   ➡ *NEXIS*   ➡ *WESTLAW*
➡ *Illinois State Legislative Information System (LIS)*

The College of Law is located at the center of campus in Swen Parson Hall, an impressive gothic building that combines the distinction of the traditional with the sleek lines of the modern in its architectural design. The classrooms are designed to maximize interaction between students and their professors. The law school provides an atmosphere of shared goals and achievement and a genuine sense of community. The David C. Shapiro Memorial Law Library provides one of the best ratios of library resources to students. The Founders Memorial Library, adjacent to the College of Law, contains nearly 1.5 million volumes and an additional 1.2 million federal, state, and international governmental documents.

■ Curriculum

➡ *Academic Support Program*   ➡ *90 units/credits required to graduate*   ➡ *80 courses available*   ➡ *degrees available: J.D.; J.D./M.B.A.*   ➡ *semesters, start in Aug.*

The College of Law provides its students with the type of curriculum that will make them well-rounded legal professionals. The first year consists of the traditional ABA required courses. A second course in constitutional law in the second year and a course in legal ethics in the third year are required. Students select the remainder of the 85 hours required for graduation from a wide range of electives.

The law school recognizes that a rigorous analytical legal education taught from traditional materials can be enriched by a breadth of exposure, in all areas of the curriculum, to supervised training in the skills of law practice. Clinical lawyering skills programs offer students the opportunity to acquire essential techniques needed in pretrial and trial work through structured simulations in the classroom and professional experiences in a variety of legal settings. The Externship Program provides students with sound educational experience under the supervision of a practicing attorney, or as a law clerk for a judge.

The summer program in Agen, France offers valuable experience for those interested in international law.

■ Student Activities

The College of Law affords its students a wide variety of educationally and professionally oriented activities. Among these are the *Law Review*, a forum for the expression of serious legal scholarship, and *The Advocate* a newspaper published by law students. Students compete in an extensive selection of moot court and client counseling competitions at the national, regional, state, and local levels. Third-year students can participate in the American Inn of Court program. Due to the small size of the law school, students can become involved in a wide variety of student organizations, many of which provide peer-support/mentoring programs.

■ Admission

➡ *B.S./B.A. required for admission*   ➡ *suggested application deadline—May 15*   ➡ *rolling admission; early application recommended*   ➡ *LSAT, LSDAS required*
➡ *application fee—$40*   ➡ *separate part-time application*

The College of Law grants admission strictly on a competitive basis through an evaluation of an applicant's aptitude and professional promise. Prospective students are encouraged to visit. Such visits, however, will not play a role in the evaluation process.

An application, application fee, personal statement are required in addition to LSDAS. To be considered for the part-time option, an additional application—obtainable from the Admission Office—must be submitted. The applicant's undergraduate record and LSAT score are of principal importance to the Admission Committee, but the committee is also interested in other factors such as an applicant's reasons for seeking admission, the applicant's school or community activities and accomplishments, employment background, and the applicant's ability to add diversity to the law school community.

■ Expenses and Financial Aid

➡ *full-time tuition & fees—resident, $6,388; nonresident, $12,776* ➡ *merit-based scholarships & need-based grants available* ➡ *FAFSA priority deadline for loans March 1* ➡ *in-state residency qualification—6 months*

Many partial- and full-tuition waivers, scholarships, and grants are available, some with monthly stipends. Second- and third-year students qualify for research assistantships both in and outside of the law school.

■ Housing

Affordable housing is available both on campus and off campus. Neptune Hall, one block from the law school, designates its first floor just for law students. Married and handicapped housing is also available on campus. The law school floor is $4,354 per academic year depending on the meal plan chosen. Housing information is sent to admitted students.

■ Career Opportunities

The College of Law Career Opportunities Office provides a service for law students to improve awareness and provide assistance in the selection of suitable employment opportunities. The office refers qualified applicants to prospective employers and conducts on-campus interviews. The Office maintains listings of opportunities in the legal profession as well as information on judicial clerkships and fellowships.

The staff of career opportunities actively counsels and advises students on all phases of career and placement activity and provides assistance with résumé preparation, job-search strategy, and interviewing skills. A library of placement resources is maintained for both students and alumni.

■ Correspondence

Northern Illinois University, College of Law, DeKalb, IL 60115. Phone: toll free 800.892.3050 or 815.753.8595.

Applicant Group for the 1998-1999 Academic Year

Northern Illinois University College of Law
This grid includes only applicants who earned 120-180 LSAT scores under standard administrations.

LSAT Score	3.75 +		3.50 - 3.74		3.25 - 3.49		3.00 - 3.24		2.75 - 2.99		2.50 - 2.74		2.25 - 2.49		2.00 - 2.24		Below 2.00		Total	
	Apps	Adm	Apps	Adm	Apps	Adm	Apps	Adm	Apps	Adm	Apps	Adm	Apps	Adm	Apps	Adm	Apps	Adm	Apps	Adm
175-180	0	0	0	0	0	0	0	0	0	0	0	0	0	0	0	0	0	0	0	0
170-174	0	0	0	0	0	0	0	0	0	0	0	0	0	0	0	0	0	0	0	0
165-169	0	0	2	2	0	0	1	1	3	3	0	0	0	0	0	0	1	1	7	7
160-164	6	6	4	4	5	5	6	6	5	5	7	7	3	3	1	1	0	0	37	37
155-159	7	7	17	16	26	23	25	23	29	27	13	11	15	14	7	5	3	3	142	129
150-154	15	15	16	14	28	20	38	28	35	22	26	18	18	7	7	4	9	2	192	130
145-149	6	4	11	5	23	9	41	6	43	12	27	8	15	3	8	1	6	0	180	48
140-144	4	0	4	1	20	4	24	4	25	2	31	2	15	0	5	0	5	0	133	13
135-139	3	0	1	0	3	0	11	0	6	0	10	0	12	0	3	0	8	0	57	0
130-134	0	0	1	0	1	0	7	0	4	0	3	0	2	0	2	0	3	0	23	0
125-129	0	0	0	0	0	0	1	0	2	0	0	0	2	0	1	0	2	0	8	0
120-124	0	0	0	0	0	0	0	0	0	0	1	0	0	0	0	0	0	0	1	0
Total	41	32	56	42	106	61	154	68	152	71	118	46	82	27	34	11	37	6	780	364

Apps = Number of Applicants
Adm = Number Admitted

	App	Adm
Applicants with 120-180 LSAT scores earned under standard administrations	708	364
Applicants with no LSAT or Nonstandard Administration LSAT	34	1
Total	814	365

Northern Kentucky University—Salmon P. Chase College of Law

Office of Admissions
Nunn Dr.
Highland Heights, KY 41099

E-Mail: brayg@nku.edu
URL: http://www.nku.edu/~chase/
Phone: 606.572.6476

■ Introduction

The Salmon P. Chase College of Law of Northern Kentucky University, founded in 1893 in Cincinnati, Ohio, is located in Highland Heights, Kentucky, eight miles southeast of Cincinnati. The campus is situated on 300 acres of rolling countryside in the largest metropolitan area of any state university in Kentucky. The curriculum not only provides instruction aimed at developing competent legal practitioners, but also includes courses that will enable students to become especially proficient in certain areas of the law. Day and evening programs are offered. Apartment and traditional student housing is available on campus.

■ Enrollment/Student Body

➥ 648 applicants ➥ 119 enrolled first-year class 1998
➥ full-time 25th/75th percentile GPA—3.09/3.57
➥ part-time 25th/75th percentile GPA—2.79/3.63
➥ full-time 25th/75th percentile LSAT—150/154
➥ part-time 25th/75th percentile LSAT—151/156
➥ 67 full-time first-year class 1998 ➥ 52 part-time first-year class ➥ 4 minority students in first-year class
➥ 57 women enrolled in first-year class ➥ 77 residents
➥ 42 nonresidents ➥ average age of first-year student—28
➥ age range—21-47 ➥ 55 undergraduate institutions represented ➥ 14 students in first-year class hold advanced degrees ➥ total enrollment—392

The College of Law is operated under the auspices of the Commonwealth of Kentucky; thus, some preference is given to Kentucky residents.

■ Faculty

➥ 24 full-time ➥ 7 women ➥ 1 minority
➥ 3 emeriti faculty ➥ 105 adjunct faculty

The Chase College Foundation brings in outstanding legal scholars, judges, and practitioners to enrich the education of the student body.

■ Library and Physical Facilities

➥ 248,646 volumes & equivalents ➥ library hours: Mon.-Thurs., 8:00 A.M.-MIDNIGHT; Fri., 8:00 A.M.-10:00 P.M.; Sat., 9:00 A.M.-9:00 P.M.; Sun., NOON-10:00 P.M.
➥ extended hours during exams, shortened hours during academic breaks ➥ LEXIS ➥ NEXIS ➥ WESTLAW
➥ DIALOG ➥ 5 full-time librarians ➥ library seats 200

The extensive law library has a liberal borrowing policy and participates in interlibrary lending programs.

Students also have access to excellent recreational facilities at A.D. Albright Health Center on campus, including basketball and racquetball courts, Nautilus and other exercise equipment, indoor running track and pool, and sauna. University Center, including a cafeteria, snack bar, and bookstore, is near the College of Law.

■ Curriculum

➥ 90 credits required to graduate ➥ 85 courses available
➥ degrees available: J.D.; J.D./M.B.A. ➥ semesters, start in Aug. ➥ range of first-year class size—13-67

The program of study may be completed in three years for full-time students and four years for part-time students. A week-long course introduces first-year students to the study of law. Forty-one semester hours of coursework are prescribed. Students must also select 19 hours from a list of core courses. Two additional courses developing legal research and drafting skills are required. The remaining hours may be chosen from a broad offering of electives.

Informal academic support is available to all students. Students may earn credit for work as law clerks in federal courts.

■ Special Programs

The J.D./M.B.A. degree is designed for students who seek to expand their expertise in the increasingly dynamic and complex business area. Selected courses in the College of Law serve as electives for 9 of the 36 hours required for the M.B.A. degree while M.B.A. courses count for 14 of the 90 hours required in the J.D. program. Thus, the number of hours required to obtain the joint degree is less than the number required if each degree were pursued independently.

The College of Law operates a prestigious Moot Court Program, entering teams in the National Moot Court, Tri-School Moot Court, and other competitions. Degree credit may be earned for participation in this program.

The College of Law has established the Ohio Valley Environmental and Natural Resources Law Institute which will sponsor annually both a national environmental law moot court competition and an environmental law symposium.

A course in Trial Advocacy based upon a national model allows students to practice and participate in every part of a trial. The course ends with its students conducting an entire civil and criminal trial including jury selection and jury deliberation.

Students may participate in the Children's Law Clinic representing clients under attorney supervision.

A local government law clinic has recently been established.

■ Admission

➥ Bachelor's degree from accredited college or university required ➥ application deadline March 1
➥ LSAT, LSDAS required ➥ application fee—$30
➥ rolling admission, early application preferred

First-year students are admitted for the fall semester only. In measuring academic potential for admission, the Admissions Committee relies primarily on the applicant's undergraduate GPA and the applicant's performance on the LSAT. Each file is reviewed for motivational factors, which include rising trend in academic performance, college and/or course selection, graduate study, employment pressures, competence in another profession or vocation, significant changes in the LSAT, leadership ability, cultural or educational deprivation, and evidence of oral or written linguistic ability. The committee seeks diversity in the student body by considering, in no particular order, sex, age, minority status, and cultural or geographic background.

Persons in good academic standing at another ABA-accredited school may apply for admission as transfer students. Transfer determinations are based upon the quality of the applicant's performance at the other law school and the reason for the applicant's desire to transfer.

■ Student Activities

The *Northern Kentucky Law Review*, published by the students of the College of Law, devotes space to national and regional law problems. The Student Bar Association (SBA) sponsors many activities, including a student mentor program, as well as student-faculty mixers and other social events. The SBA also selects students to participate on several faculty committees. There are chapters of the Black American Law Students Association, Delta Theta Phi Law Fraternity, Phi Alpha Delta Law Fraternity, and the Law Student Division of the American Bar Association. Other groups at the College of Law include the Chase Trial Lawyers Association, Christian Legal Society, Environmental Law Society, International Law Society, and Women's Law Caucus. Additionally, the Kentucky Municipal Law Center, the Academy of Criminal Justice Sciences, and the Ohio Valley Environmental and Natural Resources Law Institute are housed in Nunn Hall.

■ Expenses and Financial Aid

➡ *tuition & fees—resident, $227/sem. hr. (not to exceed $2,695/sem.; nonresident, $584/sem. hr. (not to exceed $7,000/sem.)*

➡ *estimated additional expenses—$1,800-$5,396/sem. (books & supplies, room & board, transportation, personal)*
➡ *one-year and multiyear performance & need-based scholarships available*   ➡ *one-year and multiyear performance & need-based minority scholarships available*
➡ *appropriate form for need analysis due to national processing organization in Jan.; form required may vary from year to year*

Northern Kentucky University financial aid application forms are due February 1. The latter forms are available from the Financial Aid Office, Northern Kentucky University at 606.572.5144. Certain scholarships and stipends have been established specifically to aid students from Kentucky or designated counties in Ohio.

All tuition and fees are due and payable prior to the first day of classes.

■ Career Services

With the support of a Placement Advisory Board, made up of practitioners in Ohio and Kentucky, and a Student Placement Board, Chase has a strong program to assist students in planning their legal careers. This includes scheduling on-campus interviews, posting job notices from law firms throughout Kentucky and greater Cincinnati, holding career seminars, and publishing a placement newsletter. Students participate in the All-Kentucky Legal Job Fair, a public interest job fair, a federal job options program, and the Minority Access Program. Reciprocal agreements with career services offices at other law schools assist those students who are looking for opportunities in different parts of the country. Chase alumni are employed in 45 states and throughout the world. Further, the Career Development Office houses a career opportunity library and provides access to several employment databases.

Applicant Group for the 1998-1999 Academic Year

Northern Kentucky University—Salmon P. Chase College of Law
This grid includes only applicants who earned 120-180 LSAT scores under standard administrations.

LSAT Score	3.75 +		3.50 - 3.74		3.25 - 3.49		3.00 - 3.24		2.75 - 2.99		2.50 - 2.74		2.25 - 2.49		2.00 - 2.24		Below 2.00		No GPA		Total	
	Apps	Adm	Apps	Adm	Apps	Adm	Apps	Adm	Apps	Adm	Apps	Adm	Apps	Adm	Apps	Adm	Apps	Adm	Apps	Adm	Apps	Adm
175-180	0	0	0	0	0	0	0	0	0	0	0	0	0	0	0	0	0	0	0	0	0	0
170-174	0	0	0	0	0	0	0	0	0	0	0	0	0	0	0	0	0	0	0	0	0	0
165-169	0	0	1	0	2	1	1	1	2	0	0	0	0	0	0	0	0	0	1	0	7	2
160-164	2	2	6	2	5	2	6	5	7	2	1	1	4	3	0	0	0	0	0	0	31	17
155-159	9	5	12	4	20	7	18	8	14	6	7	2	4	1	1	1	2	1	1	1	88	36
150-154	12	4	29	21	43	24	31	18	23	15	21	10	12	3	4	0	3	0	1	0	179	95
145-149	7	2	19	6	23	6	31	5	30	1	20	0	12	1	6	1	0	0	4	1	152	23
140-144	3	1	6	1	16	1	19	0	27	0	13	0	11	0	7	0	1	0	1	0	104	3
135-139	0	0	2	1	2	0	10	1	9	0	6	0	4	0	5	0	1	0	4	0	43	2
130-134	0	0	0	0	1	0	1	0	3	0	2	0	0	0	0	0	0	0	1	0	8	0
125-129	0	0	0	0	0	0	0	0	0	0	0	0	2	0	0	0	0	0	0	0	2	0
120-124	0	0	0	0	0	0	0	0	0	0	0	0	0	0	0	0	0	0	0	0	0	0
Total	33	14	75	35	112	41	117	38	115	24	70	13	49	8	23	2	7	1	13	2	614	178

Apps = Number of Applicants   Adm = Number Admitted   Reflects 99% of the total applicant pool.

Northwestern University School of Law

357 East Chicago Avenue
Chicago, IL 60611

E-Mail: nulawadm@nwu.edu
URL: http://www.law1.nwu.edu/
Phone: 312.503.8465

■ Introduction

Northwestern University School of Law, founded in 1859, is a nationally-oriented private institution dedicated to advancing the understanding of law and to producing graduates prepared to excel in a rapidly changing world. Legal education at Northwestern uniquely blends a rigorous intellectual environment within a collegial and supportive community. With one of the lowest student-faculty ratios in the country, Northwestern provides students with unusually close contact with full-time professors who are noted scholars.

Northwestern's lakefront location in the heart of downtown Chicago provides a truly spectacular setting in which to study law. The law school's proximity to courts, commerce, and public interest activities enables students to experience the practice of law as well as its theory.

■ Enrollment/Student Body

➡ *3,557 applicants*   ➡ *755 admitted first-year class 1998*
➡ *204 enrolled first-year class 1998*   ➡ *full-time 25th/75th percentile GPA—3.28/3.67*   ➡ *full-time 25th/75th percentile LSAT—162/167*   ➡ *642 total full-time*
➡ *no part-time program*   ➡ *25% minority*
➡ *51% women*   ➡ *40 states & 10 foreign countries represented*
➡ *178 undergraduate schools represented*

The law school is characterized by an energetic and diverse student body, where each entering class enriches and revitalizes the community. A significant number of J.D. candidates enter with full-time work experience and many possess other graduate or professional degrees. Most of the international students are enrolled in the LL.M. program, where J.D. candidates have the advantage of interacting with them in combined classes.

■ Faculty

➡ *216 total*   ➡ *54 full-time*   ➡ *162 part-time or adjunct*
➡ *43 women (16 full-time, 27 part-time/adjunct)*
➡ *14 minority (5 full-time, 9 part-time/adjunct)*

The Northwestern faculty is composed of a group of the finest scholars, diverse in background and perspective, whose research and writing make major contributions to important academic and public policy debates. Northwestern professors have a passion for teaching and for engaging students in both theoretical and practical legal applications.

The faculty includes scholars with advanced degrees in economics, history, philosophy, and political science as well as law; it includes a former chairman of the Securities and Exchange Commission, a former deputy solicitor general of the United States, the first American attorney to argue before the European Court of Human Rights and the senior author of the most widely used casebook on American legal history. The full-time faculty is supplemented by a distinguished group of adjunct professors who teach a wide variety of specialized courses.

■ Library and Physical Facilities

➡ *634,272 volumes & equivalents*   ➡ *library hours: Mon.-Thurs., 7:30 A.M.-MIDNIGHT; Fri., 7:30 A.M.-8:00 P.M.; Sat., 9:00 A.M.-8:00 P.M.; Sun., 9:00 A.M.-MIDNIGHT*
➡ *LEXIS*   ➡ *NEXIS*   ➡ *WESTLAW*   ➡ *CCH Access*
➡ *DIALOG*   ➡ *12 full-time librarians*   ➡ *library seats 750*

Northwestern's law library collection is known as one of the finest in the nation. The library has an excellent, service-oriented staff and study carrels and tables wired so that students can take advantage of a network that includes Internet access, word processing software, and legal research databases. The law school's three interconnected buildings along Chicago's lakefront also house the national headquarters of the American Bar Association and the American Bar Foundation.

■ Curriculum

➡ *86 credits required to graduate*   ➡ *more than 130 courses available*   ➡ *degrees available: J.D.; J.D./M.M.; J.D./Ph.D.; LL.M.; S.J.D.*   ➡ *semesters, start in Aug.*
➡ *range of first-year class size—25-100*
➡ *senior writing requirements for graduation*
➡ *clinical program available*
➡ *senior research program available*

Northwestern offers a curriculum designed to develop fundamental legal skills and an understanding of the contexts in which the law operates. Northwestern's broad and flexible curriculum gives students the opportunity to take a wide variety of courses and also allows them to specialize in particular areas of legal interest.

The law school's size enables students to have one-on-one relationships with professors. Over half of the required first-year courses are taught in sections of 50 or fewer students. The Senior Research Program enables third-year students to do individual research under the supervision of a professor, using library, field, and interdisciplinary research methods.

Northwestern's nationally recognized clinical program includes six full-time professors and six staff attorneys, and enables students not only to obtain experience representing clients, but also allows them to learn legal practice skills in highly regarded simulation courses or in externships. Clinic attorneys and students handle both civil and criminal cases representing indigents and prisoners on death row and are intensively involved in a major reform of the juvenile justice system.

■ Special Programs

A combined program in law and management is offered with Northwestern's J. L. Kellogg Graduate School of Management in which students earn both a J.D. from the law school and a master of management (M.M.) degree from Kellogg. Students may also enroll in a joint J.D./Ph.D. program with the law school and one of Northwestern's social sciences departments.

The Graduate and International Program awards a masters of law (LL.M.) degree to outstanding graduates of foreign law schools who pursue a one-year program of advanced study to expand their knowledge of American law and legal processes as well as international law. The Graduate Program in Law and Business, a joint program of the law school and the J. L. Kellogg Graduate School of Management, offers students educated outside the United States an opportunity to study both business law and management techniques. Graduates of this 12-month program are awarded an LL.M. degree from the law school and a certificate in management from Kellogg.

■ **Student Activities**

Northwestern law students take an intense and energetic interest in their community and their education. Several scholarly journals are available for research, writing, and editing, including the *Northwestern University Law Review*, *Journal of Criminal Law and Criminology*, and *Northwestern Journal of International Law and Business*.

■ **Admission**

➼ *Bachelor's degree or its equivalent from accredited college or university required* ➼ *application deadline—Feb. 15*
➼ *rolling admission; early completion of application encouraged*
➼ *LSAT, LSDAS required* ➼ *application fee—$70 ($80 after Jan. 1)* ➼ *two letters of recommendation required*
➼ *personal statement required* ➼ *interviews encouraged*

The admission process at Northwestern is highly selective. Northwestern seeks a student body diverse in experience, background, and perspective. Northwestern looks at the total applicant—no one element is determinative. Each application is reviewed regardless of the LSAT score or the GPA.

In addition to academic prowess and achievement, Northwestern seeks students with strong interpersonal skills, ambition, life experience, and substantial maturity. Northwestern maintains an active interviewing program, both on campus and through its alumni network throughout the nation and world. Applicants are encouraged to provide information about their personal background and special characteristics.

■ **Expenses and Financial Aid**

➼ *tuition & fees—$23,974* ➼ *estimated additional expenses—$16,024 (room, board, books, transportation, personal)*
➼ *merit- & need-based scholarships available*
➼ *FAFSA required* ➼ *University Application required*
➼ *Loan Repayment Assistance Program available*
➼ *deadline for financial aid application—March 15*

Northwestern is committed to enrolling students, regardless of ability to pay. The law school annually awards $2.5 million in grants and scholarships in addition to long-term, low-interest institutional loans. These resources enable the law school to cover 100 percent of a student's calculated financial need. Approximately 70 percent of the students currently enrolled are receiving financial aid.

■ **Career Services**

The full-time staff of the Office of Career Services works actively to assist students in obtaining summer and permanent employment. The office schedules student interviews with employers and offers training workshops, individual counseling, and other services to help students pursue their professional goals. In the fall of 1998, over 250 employers came to Northwestern from all parts of the country—40 percent Midwest, 28 percent Northeast, 24 percent West, and 8 percent South. Seventy-two percent of the graduates accepted positions in private practice, 10 percent in judicial clerkships, and the remainder in public service, government, business, or academic study.

Applicant Group for the 1998-1999 Academic Year

Our Admission Committee considers many factors beyond test scores and GPAs when evaluating applicants and, although they are not required, interviews are encouraged for all applicants. Interviews can take place on campus with a member of our Admission Committee or off campus with an alumnus. To request an interview, please contact our admission office.

Notre Dame Law School

P.O. Box 959
Notre Dame, IN 46556-0959

E-Mail: law.bulletin.1@nd.edu
URL: http://www.nd.edu/~ndlaw/
Phone: 219.631.6626, Fax: 219.631.3980

■ Introduction

Notre Dame Law School is one of the oldest law schools in the country, and the nation's oldest Catholic law school. Since 1869, students have come from every state and several foreign nations to participate in the rich heritage and ancient traditions that form the core of legal education at Notre Dame. The Law School occupies a handsome Gothic Tudor-style structure near the center of the university campus near South Bend, Indiana.

The Notre Dame Law School educational experience focuses on professional competence inspired by enduring values. With one of the highest bar-passage rates in the nation, the academic programs equip students to practice law competently in any jurisdiction in the United States. A Notre Dame Law School education transcends mere professional competence. With its focus on heritage and tradition, faith and values, and community spirit, the Notre Dame experience inspires students to examine their practice of law within the context of their responsibilities as members of the bar, as participants in an active faith community, and as citizens of a global community.

Critical to this process is the close interaction of students and faculty—both in and outside the classroom. Students enjoy a variety of opportunities for learning from renowned legal authorities through research assistanceships, individualized directed readings, and extracurricular or cocurricular activities.

Approximately three-quarters of the student body who identify a religious affiliation are Roman Catholics, but members of all faiths find a welcoming community open to inquiry and exploration of other faith traditions.

The Notre Dame Law School is accredited by the American Bar Association and is a member of the Association of American Law Schools.

■ Enrollment/Student Body

➡ *185 enrolled first-year class 1998*   ➡ *full-time 25th/75th percentile GPA—3.20/3.67*   ➡ *full-time 25th/75th percentile LSAT—160/165*   ➡ *550 total full-time, including LL.M. & J.S.D. candidates*   ➡ *20% minority*   ➡ *40% women*   ➡ *200 undergraduate schools represented*

■ Faculty

➡ *35 full-time teaching and research faculty*   ➡ *5 full-time clinical faculty*   ➡ *26 part-time or adjunct faculty*

Faculty members come to the Notre Dame Law School with extensive experience in private practice and government service, and represent a wide range of undergraduate institutions, law schools, and state bars.

■ Library and Physical Facilities

➡ *485,000 volumes & microform equivalents*
➡ *library hours: 24 hours/day, 7 days/week*   ➡ *LEXIS/NEXIS*
➡ *WESTLAW*   ➡ *9 full-time librarians*

Long considered a good working library, the Kresge Law Library sits among the top-tier of American law-school research libraries. The library is considered a national leader in legal-research techniques using automated technology.

The Law School maintains computer facilities in the Kresge Law Library, including a 20-workstation wordprocessing facility and a 10-workstation instructional facility, which may be used for word-processing or other computer functions when not scheduled for instructional use. The computers are connected to the university's sophisticated NT@ND local-area network, which allows access to e-mail, the World Wide Web, WESTLAW and LEXIS/NEXIS, dozens of application programs, and individual automatically backed-up electronic storage space for every student. In addition, the library has 48 computer drops for use with a student's own laptop.

Classrooms continue to be converted to include multimedia capabilities such as computer-assisted learning.

■ Curriculum

➡ *90 credits required to graduate*   ➡ *degrees available: J.D.; J.D./M.B.A.; J.D./M.E.; J.D./M.A. (in Peace Studies or English); LL.M. & J.S.D. in international human-rights law; LL.M. in international & comparative law (London campus only); other joint-degree programs to suit individual needs*   ➡ *semesters, start in Aug.; London campus—trimesters, start in Sept.*

The Law School awards the J.D. degree after three years (six semesters) of full-time residential day study. The rigorous curriculum includes 52 hours of required courses designed to expose students to the important legal issues they will encounter in whatever type of law they choose to practice.

■ London Programs

Notre Dame Law School recognizes that today's legal practice increasingly involves matters of international significance, and thus, matters of international law.

J.D. candidates may augment their legal education by participating in one of two programs offered by the Law School through its London Law Centre. Second-year students who wish to immerse themselves in comparative and international law, as well as in the traditions of the American and British common-law systems, can study in the only ABA-approved year-long overseas program offered by an American law school. Students who desire a shorter international-study experience and who have completed their first year of law school can spend six weeks in London during the summer studying with students from many different American law schools in Notre Dame's summer program.

The Law School also offers a year-long LL.M. program in international and comparative law—the only LL.M. offered overseas by an American law school.

■ Admission

➡ *Bachelor's degree required for admission*   ➡ *application deadline—March 1 for regular admission; Nov. 15 for early*

admission ➡️ *LSAT, LSDAS required*
➡️ *application fee—$50 prior to Feb. 1; $65 after Feb. 1*

Admission results from recommendations by a faculty committee that considers each application individually. The faculty and the Dean make their decisions based on the whole-person concept, including academic performance, work experience, recommendations, extracurricular activities, commitment to service, and leadership, as well as GPA, academic program, and LSAT scores.

■ Student Activities

Student-run academic publications include *Notre Dame Law Review, Notre Dame Journal of Law, Ethics and Public Policy; Journal of College and University Law*, and *Journal of Legislation*. Students who write for and edit these journals benefit from significant opportunities for in-depth research and writing on topics of special interest, as well as from meaningful interaction with specialists in various legal disciplines.

Clinical programs offered include Legal Aid Clinic, Immigration Clinic, and Mediation Clinic. Students, who work as attorneys under the supervision of five clinical faculty and local volunteer attorneys, gain valuable experience in direct representation of low-income clients before local courts, the United States Immigration and Naturalization Service, and other judicial and administrative bodies. Significant related coursework strengthens the academic value of these service-oriented programs.

Other opportunities to turn scholarship into service include: an externship program with the local public defender's office; an appellate advocacy program through which students, under the direct supervision of faculty members, brief and argue before the U.S. Court of Appeals for the Seventh Circuit; and Street Law, through which students teach law-related courses at local high schools.

Students also benefit from the Law School's involvement with three research and study institutes and centers. The Center for Civil and Human Rights brings together lawyers from all around the world to study for LL.M. and J.S.D.

degrees in international human rights. J.D. candidates can take courses through the center, and learn from those who practice human-rights law around the world. The Natural Law Institute explores the fundamental notions of natural law in determining or assessing the validity of all positive law. J.D. candidates benefit from the National Institute for Trial Advocacy faculty who teach in Notre Dame's renowned trial-advocacy program, honored in 1995 by the American College of Trial Lawyers with its Emil T. Gumpert Award for the nation's most outstanding trial-advocacy program.

■ Expenses and Financial Aid

➡️ *tuition & fees—$21,500*   ➡️ *fellowships available (need- & merit-based)*   ➡️ *financial aid available; FAFSA required*   ➡️ *work-study available*

The Law School awards fellowships to students on the basis of need as well as on a demonstrated ability to achieve in law school. The Law School reserves its Dean's Fellowships and several other prestigious fellowships for exceptional academic performers and community leaders.

■ Housing

Many single law students choose to live on campus in graduate-student housing. Married students with children can live in the unfurnished University Village apartments. Students who wish to live off campus can find reasonably priced accommodations near the campus, and can secure on-campus parking for a nominal additional charge.

■ Career Services

The Career Services Office offers students the opportunity to interview on campus with more than 150 law firms annually. A national network of over 7,000 law school alumni and friends assist students and graduates in finding employment opportunities across the country.

Applicant Profile Not Available

Nova Southeastern University—Shepard Broad Law Center

3305 College Avenue
Fort Lauderdale, FL 33314-7721

E-Mail: admission@nsu.law.nova.edu
URL: http://www.nsulaw.nova.edu
Phone: 954.262.6117; Fax: 954.262.3844

■ Introduction

Nova Southeastern Law Center opened in 1974 as part of Nova Southeastern University, a private, nonsectarian institution. We are accredited by the American Bar Association and belong to the AALS. We are located in the western suburbs of Fort Lauderdale, just a short drive from the airport and from all parts of Dade, Broward, and Palm Beach counties.

■ Enrollment/Student Body

➥ *full-time 25th/75th percentile GPA—2.59/3.19*
➥ *part-time 25th/75th percentile GPA—2.54/3.12*
➥ *full-time 25th/75th percentile LSAT—144/151*
➥ *part-time 25th/75th percentile LSAT—144/150*

■ Faculty

➥ *113 total*   ➥ *48 full-time*   ➥ *65 part-time or adjunct*
➥ *19 women full-time*   ➥ *9 minority full-time*

Faculty members are committed to teaching excellence and maintain an open-door policy for students. By limiting first-year section size, we can offer each student individualized attention. Our faculty is relatively young and represents numerous practice fields. Their expertise is reflected in scholarly articles and texts and in their public service activities. Distinguished practicing attorneys join our full-time faculty, particularly for courses in our lawyering skills curriculum.

■ Library and Physical Facilities

➥ *300,689 volumes & equivalents*   ➥ *library hours:*
Mon.-Thurs., 7:45 A.M.-MIDNIGHT; Fri., 7:45 A.M.-10:00 P.M.;
Sat., 8:30 A.M.-9:00 P.M.; Sun., 10:00 A.M.-MIDNIGHT
➥ *LEXIS*   ➥ *NEXIS*   ➥ *WESTLAW*   ➥ *DIALOG*
➥ *Lois Law*   ➥ *12 full-time librarians*   ➥ *library seats 565*

Our classroom/student activities area includes the Clinic, Disability Law Institute, and Mediation Program. Our courtrooms are used by students in our trial advocacy and moot court program, by National Institute for Trial Advocacy programs, and by state appellate court judges.

The library's extensive holdings include special collections in tax, criminal law, law and popular culture, admiralty, and international law. The library has over 200 computer ports and provides wired and wireless networked access to word processing and computerized legal research programs. Computer-assisted instruction is available, and numerous publications are available on CD-ROM. The library is a depository for state, federal, and United Nations documents.

■ Curriculum

➥ *Academic Support Program*   ➥ *90 units/credits required to graduate*   ➥ *120 courses available*   ➥ *degrees available: J.D.; J.D./M.B.A.; J.D./M.S. (Psych.); J.D./M.S. (Dispute Resolution); J.D./M.U.R.P (Urban Regional Planning)*
➥ *range of first-year class size—30-60*

Day division students can earn the J.D. degree after three years of study; evening division students can complete their requirements in four years. After completing their first year of law studies, joint-degree students take classes in both programs. All students are guaranteed a full-semester clinic in their final year of study. All students have laptop computers, which can be used throughout the building.

■ Special Programs

Lawyering Skills and Values—Every student completes a four-semester lawyering skills and values sequence that introduces interviewing, counseling, negotiating, research, drafting, and other critical skills in the context of a simulated law firm experience. In the second LSV year, students select between a litigation track and a business/transactional track.

Clinics—We guarantee all students the opportunity to enroll in a full-semester clinic during their final year. Clinical opportunities, located throughout the United States and in foreign countries, include Business Practice, Children and Families, Criminal Justice, Environmental, International, and Personal Injury and Alternative Dispute Resolution. The clinical semester includes advanced skills training, interdisciplinary coursework, and an advanced substantive course. Students work for 12 weeks at their clinical placements and meet weekly—in person or by compressed video—to learn from each other's experiences.

Internships—Our Judicial Internship Program, Mediation Program, Guardian Ad Litem Program, and Individuals with Disabilities Project provide valuable academic experiences, and students in our Street Law Program introduce middle and high school students to the legal system.

Summer Study—Students who attend two eight-week summer sessions can accelerate their graduation by one semester. The typical summer term includes as many as 20 courses. Students may also attend our summer programs in Caracas, Venezuela, and Cambridge, England.

■ Admission

➥ *Bachelor's degree from accredited college or university required for admission*   ➥ *priority application deadline—March 1*
➥ *applications completed after May 31 are at a disadvantage*
➥ *LSAT, LSDAS required*   ➥ *application fee—$50*

In passing upon applications, the admissions committee reviews undergraduate grades, the LSAT score, and the writing sample. Committee members also consider the applicant's personal statement, work experience, and letters of recommendation. While no single factor is determinative, applicants who fail to demonstrate academic promise on both the LSAT score and the GPA are unlikely to be offered regular admission.

Selected applicants who otherwise would be rejected may receive an opportunity to compete for admission by taking two three-credit courses during May through July. Summer Conditional Acceptance Program courses are taught by experienced full-time faculty members. Applicants earning at least a 2.5 average for the summer are admitted to the entering class.

We are committed to diversity in our student body. Approximately 46.1 percent of the 1998 entering class is female; over 28 percent are members of minority groups. The average age of first-year day students is 27; of evening students, 32.

We encourage applicants to visit the campus, either for an Admissions Open House or for a classroom visit. Alumni in many regions are available to answer applicant questions about the Nova Southeastern experience.

■ Student Activities

Students can join either the *Nova Law Review* or the *Journal of International and Comparative Law*. Both publications accept students based on grades as well as through a write-on competition.

In addition to sponsoring two intramural competitions and a national competition, Moot Court Society members participate in a variety of national competitions. Our ATLA and American Bar Association/LSD chapters compete in several trial, client counseling, and negotiations competitions.

Students participate on faculty committees and with organizations such as BLSA, JLSA, HLSA, Lambda, Florida Association for Women Lawyers, and International Law Society. The Student Bar Association and the National Association for Public Interest Law chapters are quite active,

and we have several legal fraternities and Inns of Court chapters. Ad hoc groups form for various sports activities.

■ Expenses and Financial Aid

➡ *tuition & fees—full-time, $19,770; part-time, $14,832*
➡ *estimated additional expenses—$8,500-$13,500 (room, board, books, transportation)* ➡ *scholarships available*
➡ *financial aid available (FAFSA & Nova Southeastern forms required)*

The admissions committee awards a number of three-year tuition waivers. These waivers are available to accepted applicants on the basis of academic merit. In addition to work-study opportunities, upper-class students can serve as faculty research assistants, receiving salaries that approximate those for law clerks.

■ Career Services

Our Career Development Office assists students and alumni with career counseling and the employment process. In addition to facilitating on-campus interviews and résumé distributions, the director coordinates career-option seminars and interviewing workshops. The Career Development Office sponsors a number of law office management and other skills courses through its Career Development Academy. In addition, the office assists students interested in pro bono placements with firms and agencies throughout the country.

Applicant Group for the 1998-1999 Academic Year

Nova Southeastern University—Shepard Broad Law Center
This grid includes only applicants who earned 120-180 LSAT scores under standard administrations.

LSAT Score	3.75 +		3.50 - 3.74		3.25 - 3.49		3.00 - 3.24		2.75 - 2.99		2.50 - 2.74		2.25 - 2.49		2.00 - 2.24		Below 2.00		No GPA		Total	
	Apps	Adm	Apps	Adm	Apps	Adm	Apps	Adm	Apps	Adm	Apps	Adm	Apps	Adm	Apps	Adm	Apps	Adm	Apps	Adm	Apps	Adm
175-180	0	0	0	0	0	0	0	0	0	0	0	0	0	0	0	0	0	0	0	0	0	0
170-174	0	0	0	0	0	0	0	0	0	0	0	0	0	0	0	0	0	0	0	0	0	0
165-169	0	0	2	1	1	1	0	0	1	1	0	0	2	2	0	0	1	0	0	0	7	5
160-164	1	1	3	3	9	9	1	1	5	5	1	1	4	2	0	0	1	1	0	0	25	23
155-159	4	4	7	6	17	17	21	19	20	18	13	11	15	13	6	5	1	1	1	0	105	94
150-154	6	6	19	17	35	29	63	59	52	47	39	35	28	22	15	14	5	1	5	3	267	233
145-149	16	16	22	21	39	35	86	72	73	61	82	56	52	26	28	15	8	3	9	6	415	311
140-144	4	2	16	7	30	8	63	16	95	25	91	27	53	11	38	5	9	1	9	3	408	105
135-139	5	1	5	0	17	2	36	4	45	0	43	3	49	0	16	1	7	0	14	6	237	17
130-134	0	0	3	0	7	0	7	0	13	0	14	0	11	0	10	0	3	0	10	1	78	1
125-129	0	0	0	0	2	0	1	0	5	0	3	0	4	0	3	0	3	0	2	0	23	0
120-124	0	0	0	0	0	0	0	0	0	0	0	0	0	0	0	0	1	0	1	0	2	0
Total	36	30	77	55	157	101	278	171	309	157	286	133	218	76	116	40	39	7	51	19	1567	789

Apps = Number of Applicants
Adm = Number Admitted
Reflects 98% of the total applicant pool.

Ohio Northern University—Claude W. Pettit College of Law

525 South Main Street
Ada, OH 45810

E-Mail: n-wright@onu.edu
URL: http://www.law.onu.edu
Phone: 419.772.2211

■ Introduction

Founded in 1885, the Claude W. Pettit College of Law of Ohio Northern University is fully accredited by the American Bar Association and is a member of both the Association of American Law Schools and the League of Ohio Law Schools.

The university of 3,000 students is small enough to provide individual attention to student needs, yet large enough to provide the amenities of a major research institution. The 280-acre campus is located in Ada, a small and picturesque college town in the midwest. Ada is approximately 70 to 90 miles from the Ohio cities of Dayton, Toledo, and Columbus, as well as Fort Wayne, Indiana.

■ Enrollment/Student Body

➤ *818 applicants* ➤ *557 admitted first-year class 1998*
➤ *131 enrolled first-year class 1998* ➤ *full-time 25th/75th percentile GPA—2.59/3.12* ➤ *full-time 25th/75th percentile LSAT—143/150* ➤ *305 total full-time* ➤ *18.7% minority*
➤ *36% women* ➤ *30 states & foreign countries represented*
➤ *203 undergraduate schools represented*

■ Faculty

➤ *43 total* ➤ *20 full-time* ➤ *23 part-time or adjunct*
➤ *10 women*

The faculty strives for excellence in both teaching and scholarship. All faculty members have practiced law, bringing a wealth of practical experience gained from law firms, corporate law departments, and government to the classroom. The faculty also maintains a high level of scholarly productivity and professional service.

Small classes and individual attention are the hallmarks of the college. First-year classes are generally limited to 45 or fewer students. Faculty maintain open-door policies to foster good communication with students.

■ Library and Physical Facilities

➤ *265,000 volumes & equivalents* ➤ *library hours: Mon.-Fri., 8:00 A.M.-MIDNIGHT; Sat., 9:00 A.M.-MIDNIGHT; Sun., 11:00 A.M.-MIDNIGHT* ➤ *LEXIS* ➤ *NEXIS*
➤ *WESTLAW* ➤ *4 full-time librarians*
➤ *library seats 325*

The College of Law is housed in Tilton Hall, a modern state-of-the-art building containing classrooms, faculty and administrative offices, student organization offices, moot courtrooms, a student lounge, and the law library. The Taggart Law Library, a federal government depository, houses online card cataloguing and an excellent computer lab.

Law students also have access to the other campus facilities, including a wide variety of entertainment programs at the Freed Center for the Performing Arts and the athletic facilities in the recently expanded Sports Center.

■ Curriculum

➤ *Academic Support Program* ➤ *full-time program*
➤ *87 credits required to graduate* ➤ *80 courses available*
➤ *degrees available: J.D.* ➤ *semesters, start in Aug.*
➤ *range of first-year class size—21-52*

Students may choose from over 67 elective courses, including advanced courses and seminars. Each student must complete a research paper in the second or third year under the supervision of a faculty member.

■ Special Programs

Clinical Education—The College of Law offers many opportunities for experiential learning through its clinical education program. The variety of clinical experiences available to Ohio Northern students include the Enterprise Development Clinic, Legislative Clinic, Bankruptcy Clinic, Environmental Clinic, and Governmental Clinic. Legal Aid Clinics which focus on the concerns of the economically disadvantaged and elderly are offered at offices in Ada and nearby Lima. Students also participate in Criminal and Judicial Externships with judges, legal aid societies, public defender offices, and prosecutors' offices.

Icelandic Exchange Program—The college shares a study exchange program with the law school at the University of Iceland. Participating students travel to Iceland to experience its culture and legal system. ONU students can spend a semester studying at the university in Reykjavik.

■ Admission

➤ *Bachelor's degree from accredited college or university required*
➤ *no application deadline* ➤ *rolling admission, early application preferred* ➤ *LSAT, LSDAS required*
➤ *application fee—$40*

While Ohio Northern gives significant weight to the LSAT and undergraduate GPA, the Admissions Committee may consider other nonquantifiable factors such as candidates' undergraduate program and grade trends, completion of other graduate degrees, professional accomplishments, and socioeconomic or cultural barriers faced by the applicant. Letters of recommendation are not required, but letters from persons who have a basis to assess the candidate's intellectual ability and potential for success in law school, such as former professors or employers, are encouraged.

Ohio Northern University is committed to a culturally and socially diverse student body. Applications from women, minority group members, and persons with disabilities are strongly encouraged. The College of Law is a contributing supporter of the Council on Legal Education Opportunity (CLEO) Program. The facilities of the College of Law are accessible to physically disabled students.

■ Student Activities

Students can choose from a variety of extracurricular activities. The College of Law publishes the *Ohio Northern University Law Review*, a student-edited commentary on legal issues. Students also serve on the staffs of *The Environmental Law Journal* and *The Women's Law Journal*.

Intraschool, regional, and national moot court competitions are open to all students. Ohio Northern University students participate in at least 10 national and regional moot court competitions each year. Ohio Northern hosts the National Administrative Law Moot Court Competition.

Through the Student Bar Association, students participate in a variety of extracurricular activities such as the Environmental Law and International Law societies. Students volunteer their services through the Volunteer Income Tax Assistance program. Ohio Northern has active chapters of BLSA (Black Law Students Association), LAW (Legal Association of Women), Christian Legal Society, and the Cardozo Law Student Association. Ohio Northern also offers membership in Phi Kappa Phi (national honorary society), the Willis Society (honorary society), Phi Alpha Delta, Delta Theta Phi, and Phi Delta Phi.

■ Expenses and Financial Aid

➦ *full-time tuition & fees—$18,980* ➦ *average additional expenses—$5,000 (books, living expenses, transportation)* ➦ *merit-based scholarships & need-based grants are available, renewable for second & third years* ➦ *financial aid available* ➦ *FAFSA required, FAF accepted for financial aid* ➦ *students who apply after March 15 may be disadvantaged in consideration for scholarship or grant aid*

Our Legal Scholar Program provides scholarship awards for students whose undergraduate records demonstrate academic excellence. The scholarship amounts range from $3,000 to $18,000 and are renewable provided the student remains in good scholarship academic standing. Additionally, substantial scholarships are awarded to students who excel in their first year of law school. Diversity awards, subject to the availability of funds, are also made available to selected students.

■ Career Services

Through individualized counseling, students and graduates obtain valuable guidance in obtaining summer jobs and permanent positions. The Office of Career Services assists in the application and interviewing processes; provides current listings of positions in law firms, governmental agencies, and corporations; and hosts on-campus interviews.

Applicant Group for the 1998-1999 Academic Year

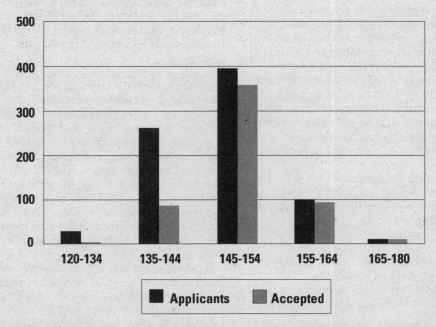

Ohio Northern University—Claude W. Pettit College of Law

This chart is to be used as a general guide only. Nonnumerical factors are strongly considered for all applicants.

The Ohio State University College of Law

John Deaver Drinko Hall
55 West 12th Avenue
Columbus, OH 43210

URL: http://www.acs.ohio-state.edu/units/law/index.htm
Phone: 614.292.8810

■ Introduction

Founded in 1891, the College of Law is located on the main campus of The Ohio State University, one of the largest comprehensive institutions of higher education in the world. In addition to being the state capital, Columbus is a commercial and cultural center that has expanded dramatically in the past decade. The curriculum and experiences of law students are enriched by the opportunities presented by interaction with the university, state government, the bar, the bench, and community organizations.

■ Enrollment/Student Body

➡ *enrollment: first-year class, 214; total, 639*
➡ *full-time 25th/75th percentile GPA—3.29/3.75*
➡ *full-time 25th/75th percentile LSAT—152/160*
➡ *21.9% minority first-year class* ➡ *52.33% women*
➡ *33 states, 3 countries, & over 108 colleges and universities represented*

■ Faculty

➡ *40 full-time faculty* ➡ *36 adjuncts*
➡ *11 women full-time faculty* ➡ *6 minority full-time faculty*
➡ *student/full-time faculty ratio: 17.6 to 1*

■ Library and Physical Facilities

➡ *665,317 volumes & equivalents* ➡ *LEXIS*
➡ *WESTLAW* ➡ *12 other databases including 232 CD-ROM and equivalent titles* ➡ *8.75 full-time librarians*
➡ *10 support staff* ➡ *carrels for 350*
➡ *computer lab for student use*

Renovation of the existing building was completed in 1993. The result is a state-of-the-art teaching and research facility that includes three comfortably furnished lounges for students. The building has an abundance of natural light, which creates a bright and cheerful environment. Attractive landscaping and a covered colonnade invite students to spend time studying and just relaxing outdoors in good weather. The law library, the largest in the state and the 13th largest in the nation, has an extensive research collection. The collection of foreign law materials is very strong. The library is a selective government depository for federal documents.

The new library has a computer laboratory for students and comfortable study and seating space for all students. Students also have immediate access to the vast collections housed in the university libraries.

■ Curriculum

➡ *summer program at Oxford University* ➡ *joint degrees: J.D./M.B.A.; J.D./M.P.A.; J.D./M.H.A., and others*
➡ *88 semester hours required* ➡ *clinical programs*
➡ *legal writing* ➡ *dispute resolution courses & journal*

After the first-year, the curriculum is largely elective. Class size in most first-year courses is between 50 and 70 students;

first-year students also take two courses in which there are only 30-35 students. The curriculum offers great depth in specialized areas such as commercial, constitutional, dispute resolution, labor and employment, international, and criminal law. In addition, offerings extend beyond the traditional curriculum into areas such as legislation, legal history, natural resources, law and social sciences, children's rights, and international trade.

■ Special Programs

The College offers a summer program at the Oxford University for upper-level students. In addition, the College has been designated a Comprehensive National Resources Center by the U.S. Department of Education. This designation provides funding for fellowships for law students to study foreign languages, study-abroad opportunities, and electronic linkages with foreign universities. The College also offers a certificate program in International Business Transactions and a Public Service Fellows program.

Ohio State has one of the oldest clinical programs in the country. Second-year students can enroll in courses that simulate litigation practice and procedure. Third-year students can enroll in civil, criminal, or dispute resolution clinics to represent clients under the close supervision of an attorney and a faculty member. The newest clinic, children's rights, started in January 1998.

The College offers joint-degree programs in business administration, public administration, and health administration. In addition, students may earn joint degrees in individually designed programs.

During their second year, all students participate in the moot court program. Following that course, students may compete for positions on teams the College places in national interschool competitions.

■ Activities

Students have played a major role in shaping the law school. The College of Law was established in 1891 in response to requests from Columbus law clerks for formal legal training. Students organized the *Ohio State Law Journal* and were instrumental in establishing the Legal Clinic, the *Ohio State Journal on Dispute Resolution*, and the Public Interest Law Foundation. In 1997, students formed the Pro Bono Research Group to offer legal research and writing assistance to Ohio lawyers representing lower-income clients. Students serve on all standing faculty committees. The Student Bar Association serves as the students' governing body, hosts social events and speakers, and runs the bookstore.

There are many student organizations, including two legal fraternities; associations of Asian American Law Students, Black Law Students, Hispanic Law Students, and Jewish Law Students; Christian Legal Society; Environmental, Law and Technology, and Sports and Entertainment Law associations; International Law Society; Federalist

Society; Women's Law Caucus; Gay, Lesbian, and Bisexual Law Caucus; Health Care Organization; Public Interest Law Foundation; a student newspaper; a Street Law Program; and a Volunteer Income Tax Assistance Program.

■ Admission

➡ *Bachelor's degree required* ➡ *application deadline—March 15* ➡ *LSAT, LSDAS required*
➡ *application fee—$30* ➡ *rolling admission*

Each candidate's file is carefully reviewed. The most important factor is the candidate's academic potential, which is usually best evidenced by the LSAT score and undergraduate transcript. Some factors believed relevant to success in law school may also be considered, such as trend in academic performance; letters of recommendation that address the candidate's intellectual potential; achievement in graduate school; caliber of the under-graduate college or university; unusually time-consuming extracurricular activities or work experience; and rigor of coursework selected. The College desires to enroll a diverse student body and, consistent with that objective, those from disadvantaged backgrounds, who have unusual or extensive work experience, or who have over-come severe or unusual obstacles to obtain an education are thought by the Admissions Committee to add diversity. For the same reason, the College has an affirmative action program. Applicants are encouraged to visit the College.

■ Expenses and Financial Aid

➡ *1998-99 tuition & fees—residents, $7,692; nonresidents, $17,086* ➡ *estimated additional expenses—$10,180*
➡ *financial aid—mostly need-based; competition for merit-based awards is strong* ➡ *Free Application for Federal Student Aid (FAFSA) required; March 1 deadline*
➡ *64 percent of the entering class to receive grants*

■ Housing

The university has dormitories for single graduate and professional students as well as married students. The College provides assistance in locating off-campus housing. Columbus, a major metropolitan area, offers a wide variety of housing.

■ Placement

The placement office helps all students secure summer and permanent positions, and also helps second- and third-year students find part-time employment during the academic year. Under the supervision of a full-time director, the program provides a wide range of services including individual counseling in career selection, resume preparation, and interviewing techniques. The office runs the largest on-campus interview program in the state and posts hundreds of openings from employers who cannot visit the campus. Although national law firms constitute the largest category of employers in the on-campus interviewing program, opportunities to interview with employers from all levels of government and corporate legal departments are also available. Typically, more than 90 percent of each graduating class accept law-related employment within six months of graduation. Generally, 55 percent go into private practice and 15 percent into government work, 10-15 percent into judicial clerkships, with the remainder divided among corporate law positions, and public interest organizations. Graduates are currently practicing in all 50 states, the District of Columbia, and more than a dozen foreign countries.

Applicant Group for the 1998-1999 Academic Year

The Ohio State University College of Law
This grid includes only applicants who earned 120-180 LSAT scores under standard administrations.

LSAT Score	3.75 +		3.50 - 3.74		3.25 - 3.49		3.00 - 3.24		2.75 - 2.99		2.50 - 2.74		2.25 - 2.49		2.00 - 2.24		Below 2.00		No GPA		Total	
	Apps	Adm	Apps	Adm	Apps	Adm	Apps	Adm	Apps	Adm	Apps	Adm	Apps	Adm	Apps	Adm	Apps	Adm	Apps	Adm	Apps	Adm
175-180	1	1	0	0	1	1	1	0	0	0	0	0	0	0	0	0	0	0	0	0	3	2
170-174	5	5	5	5	3	3	2	2	2	2	2	2	0	0	0	0	0	0	1	0	20	19
165-169	17	16	13	13	21	21	7	6	10	8	3	1	0	0	0	0	0	0	0	0	71	65
160-164	34	32	37	33	41	35	35	20	20	12	8	3	2	0	0	0	0	0	2	2	179	137
155-159	57	54	86	64	89	46	73	16	35	6	11	2	9	0	2	0	0	0	9	4	371	192
150-154	39	26	76	28	90	19	80	9	53	5	29	4	16	1	7	0	0	0	9	3	399	95
145-149	17	10	31	10	50	7	56	4	50	8	20	1	20	1	5	0	1	0	6	2	256	43
140-144	10	3	15	5	25	4	24	2	21	0	19	0	15	0	8	1	0	0	8	3	145	18
135-139	6	2	5	1	5	0	9	0	8	0	9	0	4	0	3	0	0	0	3	0	52	3
130-134	0	0	0	0	0	0	3	0	2	0	3	0	4	0	1	0	0	0	2	0	15	0
125-129	0	0	0	0	0	0	1	0	0	0	1	0	0	0	0	0	0	0	0	0	2	0
120-124	0	0	0	0	0	0	0	0	0	0	0	0	0	0	0	0	0	0	0	0	0	0
Total	186	149	268	159	325	136	291	59	201	41	105	13	70	2	26	1	1	0	40	14	1513	574

Apps = Number of Applicants
Adm = Number Admitted

University of Oklahoma College of Law

300 Timberdell Road
Norman, OK 73019

E-Mail: law@hamilton.ou.edu
URL: http://www.law.ou.edu
Phone: 405.325.4726

■ Introduction

The University of Oklahoma College of Law is located on the main campus of the university in Norman, a city of 89,000 in the Oklahoma City metropolitan area. The college was founded in 1909. The only state-supported law school in Oklahoma, it has been a member of the AALS since 1911 and ABA-approved since that list was first published in 1923. The Law Center, on the south campus of the University of Oklahoma, is within walking distance of dormitories, apartments, book exchange, and recreational facilities.

■ Enrollment/Student Body

➡ 526 applicants ➡ 311 admitted first-year class 1998
➡ 204 enrolled first-year class 1998 ➡ full-time 25th/75th percentile GPA—2.74/3.42 ➡ full-time 25th/75th percentile LSAT—146/154 ➡ 575 total full-time ➡ 17% minority
➡ 41% women ➡ 27 states & foreign countries represented
➡ 52 undergraduate schools represented

■ Faculty

➡ 50 total ➡ 34 full-time ➡ 16 part-time or adjunct
➡ 6 women ➡ 3 minority

■ Library and Physical Facilities

➡ 300,896 volumes & equivalents ➡ library hours:
Mon.-Thurs., 7:30 A.M.-11:00 P.M.; Fri., 7:30 A.M.-8:00 P.M.;
Sat., 8:00 A.M.-8:00 P.M.; Sun., 1:00 P.M.-11:00 P.M.
➡ LEXIS ➡ WESTLAW ➡ 7 full-time librarians
➡ Native Peoples Collection

The law library features three computer labs (one for LEXIS and WESTLAW, and two for word processing and other computer activities), as well as a variety of automated indexes and CD-ROMs. Records for all materials in the law library are contained in OLIN (Oklahoma Library Information Network) which serves as the online catalog for the entire University of Oklahoma campus.

■ Curriculum

➡ Academic Support Program ➡ Summer Abroad Program, Oxford, England ➡ 90 credits required to graduate
➡ 144 courses available ➡ degrees available: J.D.;
J.D./M.B.A.; J.D./Master of Public Health; J.D./M.S. in Environmental Mgmt., J.D./M.S. in Occupational Health
➡ semesters, start in Aug. & Jan.
➡ summer session, starts mid-May

Each fall, first-year students attend a two-day required orientation conducted on the Thursday and Friday before classes begin on Monday. The first-year curriculum is prescribed. Students are assigned all of their first-year classes in one of four sections. Students are assigned a faculty advisor for their first year of law study.

■ Special Programs

The American Indian Law and Policy Center of the College of Law provides a resource on historic and contemporary matters relating to Native Americans. The center supports the work of the *American Indian Law Review* and the Native American Law Students Association.

The Oxford Summer Program in Law is cosponsored by the College of Law and the Department for Continuing Education of Oxford University. The program affords students an opportunity to live and study in stimulating and beautiful surroundings under the guidance of American and English legal educators.

The Enrichment Program brings outstanding individuals in law and public service to the school to speak on a variety of subjects.

The Jurist-in-Residence Program brings distinguished justices and judges to the College of Law as resident scholars providing instruction in the areas of criminal law, constitutional law, and trial techniques.

The International Law Professor-in-Residence appoints distinguished international visiting scholars.

The Clinical Legal Education Program is designed to provide law students an opportunity to prepare for the practice of law by working with actual clients with real legal problems. Clinical opportunities include the Cleveland County Legal Aid Office, the Criminal Defense Clinic, the Externship Clinic, and the Judicial Clinic.

Students may receive course credit for participation in all clinical programs. Supervision of students is provided by the director and assistant director of the clinical legal education program.

■ Admission

➡ Bachelor's degree required ➡ application deadline—
April 15 ➡ rolling admission, fall semester only
➡ LSAT, LSDAS required ➡ application fee—$50

A faculty committee reviews all applications. In evaluating an applicant, undergraduate grade-point average and the LSAT score are each given great weight. Consideration is also given to employment experience, achievements in graduate study, extracurricular activities, and other relevant factors. In evaluating grade-point averages, consideration is given to distinct trends or discrepancies among the applicant's grades, time commitments while attending, and other relevant factors.

The College of Law conducts a special admission program each summer. Admission to this program is offered to a select group of about 20 students whose grade-point averages and LSAT scores do not meet the current standards for regular admission, but whose records reveal past performance affected by adverse circumstances or disadvantage and other factors, and whose records indicate possible future success. Factors considered by the Admissions Committee include, but are not limited to, social, cultural, or physical handicaps. Students in the program are required to complete six hours of summer coursework beginning in mid-May.

■ Student Activities

The *Oklahoma Law Review*, a quarterly publication, is a student publication that is scholarly in tone and gives expression to legal scholarship. Each issue has major articles by authorities in the field and sections written by the student members of the *Review* on significant topics and recent developments in the law.

The *American Indian Law Review*, published biannually, includes articles by authorities in the field; student-written sections; and addresses by noted speakers on Indian law, special recent developments in the area of Indian law, and recent federal developments of interest to tribal attorneys.

The Student Bar Association, affiliated with the Law Student Division of the American Bar Association, elects the Board of Governors to supervise activities and to present the students' viewpoints to the faculty and administration. Students sit as voting members on most of the College of Law faculty-administration committees. There are two legal fraternities and numerous student organizations.

The College of Law participates in several competitions including the National Moot Court, National Appellate Advocacy, National Trial Advocacy, American Client

Counseling, Jessup International Law, and Thomas Tang. Course credit may be earned for participation in these teams.

■ Expenses and Financial Aid

➡ *full-time tuition—resident, $4,140; nonresident, $12,924*
➡ *estimated additional expenses—$8,000 (room & board, books)*
➡ *performance- & need-based scholarships available*
➡ *Oklahoma State Regents Professional Study Grants*
➡ *financial aid available; FAFSA requested by March 1*

■ Career Services

The Office of Legal Career Services is involved in a variety of activities designed to assist students seeking employment as summer clerks and attorneys. While the most visible activity sponsored by the college is its fall on-campus interview program, many students benefit from the office's collection of materials about legal employers and legal careers, available positions, and bar membership requirements.

Typically 93 percent of our graduating students accept positions within twelve months of graduation.

The College of Law participates in two Minority Job Fairs each year. They are held in Dallas and Atlanta. We also participate in the National Association of Public Interest Law job fair held annually in Washington, DC.

Applicant Group for the 1998-1999 Academic Year

University of Oklahoma College of Law
This grid includes only applicants who earned 120-180 LSAT scores under standard administrations.

LSAT Score	3.75 +		3.50 - 3.74		3.25 - 3.49		3.00 - 3.24		2.75 - 2.99		2.50 - 2.74		2.25 - 2.49		2.00 - 2.24		Below 2.00		No GPA		Total	
	Apps	Adm	Apps	Adm	Apps	Adm	Apps	Adm	Apps	Adm	Apps	Adm	Apps	Adm	Apps	Adm	Apps	Adm	Apps	Adm	Apps	Adm
175-180	0	0	0	0	0	0	0	0	0	0	0	0	0	0	0	0	0	0	0	0	0	0
170-174	1	1	0	0	1	0	0	0	1	1	0	0	0	0	0	0	0	0	0	0	3	2
165-169	2	1	2	2	0	0	1	1	3	3	1	1	0	0	0	0	0	0	1	1	10	9
160-164	10	10	5	5	8	6	4	4	2	2	1	1	1	1	1	0	0	0	1	1	33	30
155-159	10	10	16	16	14	13	12	10	12	12	9	7	3	2	1	1	0	0	1	0	78	71
150-154	14	14	17	14	22	22	29	28	23	20	12	6	13	2	2	0	0	0	0	0	132	106
145-149	6	6	12	11	23	21	28	24	21	13	12	4	13	4	4	0	0	0	4	1	123	84
140-144	2	2	15	10	15	8	18	8	15	7	13	1	3	0	0	0	2	0	5	2	88	38
135-139	2	0	1	1	5	0	4	1	4	1	5	0	1	0	2	0	2	0	5	1	31	4
130-134	0	0	0	0	0	0	2	0	2	0	4	0	2	0	1	0	1	0	2	0	14	0
125-129	0	0	0	0	0	0	0	0	2	0	0	0	2	0	2	0	1	0	0	0	7	0
120-124	0	0	0	0	0	0	0	0	1	0	0	0	1	0	0	0	0	0	0	0	2	0
Total	47	44	68	59	88	70	98	76	86	59	57	20	39	9	13	1	6	0	19	6	521	344

Apps = Number of Applicants
Adm = Number Admitted
Reflects 99% of the total applicant pool.

Oklahoma City University School of Law

P.O. Box 61310
Oklahoma City, OK 73146-1310

E-Mail: lawadmit@lec.okcu.edu
URL: http://www.okcu.edu/law/admi.htm
Phone: 1.800.633.7242 or 405.521.5354

■ Introduction

Oklahoma City University School of Law is located within a metropolitan area of over 950,000, only minutes from several of Oklahoma's largest law firms, corporations, banks, city and state government agencies, and the federal courts.

The School of Law is fully accredited by the American Bar Association, the Supreme Court of Oklahoma, and the Oklahoma Board of Bar Examiners.

■ Enrollment/Student Body

➡ *754 applicants*   ➡ *565 admitted first-year class 1998*
➡ *187 enrolled first-year class 1998*   ➡ *full-time 25th/75th percentile GPA—2.58/3.18*   ➡ *part-time 25th/75th percentile GPA—2.57/3.36*   ➡ *full-time 25th/75th percentile LSAT—142/148*   ➡ *part-time 25th/75th percentile LSAT—144/152*
➡ *364 total full-time*   ➡ *145 total part-time*
➡ *19% minority*   ➡ *41% women*   ➡ *41 states & foreign countries represented*   ➡ *191 undergraduate schools represented*

■ Faculty

➡ *30 full-time*   ➡ *33 part-time or adjunct*
➡ *9 women*   ➡ *2 minority*

■ Library and Physical Facilities

➡ *262,000 volumes & equivalents*   ➡ *LEXIS*   ➡ *NEXIS*
➡ *WESTLAW*   ➡ *DIALOG*   ➡ *CONGRESSIONAL UNIVERSE*   ➡ *INFOTRAC*   ➡ *LEGAL TRAC*
➡ *FIRST SEARCH*   ➡ *Internet*   ➡ *CALI (Computer Assisted Instruction)*   ➡ *INDEX MASTER*
➡ *7 full-time librarians*   ➡ *library seats 365*

The library has primary and secondary federal and state resources and special collections in health law, dispute resolution, mediation, Native American, and foreign and international law. The state-of-the-art main computer lab has 25 workstations—some are multimedia—laser printers and scanners. Each student has a personal e-mail account. Other computer resources besides LEXIS and WESTLAW are CALI, word processing applications, and CD-ROM libraries including tax, patent health, and immigration law. The Harvard Interactive lessons help students learn trial skills. Carrels on the lower level are wired enabling students to use their own laptops to connect to the law library network. The online catalog, OLIB, gives access to the holdings of the law library and the university library.

■ Curriculum

➡ *90 credits required to graduate*   ➡ *99 courses available*
➡ *degrees available: J.D.; J.D./M.B.A.*   ➡ *semesters, start in Aug.*   ➡ *range of first-year class size—20-83*

The School of Law offers J.D. programs during both the day and evening hours, requiring the completion of 90 semester hours. The school operates two 16-week semesters and one eight-week summer term. Day students may complete their degree requirements in two-and-a-half years, and evening students in four years, by attending summer sessions.

All students take Civil Procedure, Constitutional Law, Contracts, Criminal Law, Criminal Procedure, Legal Research and Writing, Legal Analysis, Legal Profession, Property, Torts, and Evidence. The remaining 44 hours of work may be selected from electives and seminars. Many upper-level courses are designed to blend substance and practice. Externships and clinical opportunities are available. All upper-class students are required to complete a substantial written project.

The law school faculty consists of full-time and adjunct professors and five full-time writing instructors. Full-time faculty members hail from many states and hold degrees from 27 different graduate or professional schools. Law degrees among faculty members represent a diversity of law schools, including the nation's most prestigious.

■ Special Programs

Three times each year, the student-edited *Law Review* is published. The School of Law also enters student teams in such interscholastic competitions as the ABA Moot Court Competition, the Philip C. Jessup International Moot Court Competition, the Benton Moot Court Competition, and the American Trial Lawyers Association Student Trial Advocacy Competition. OCU students have placed high in regional, national, and international competitions.

Oklahoma has one of the most liberal policies toward limited licenses for legal interns. Students who have completed at least 50 hours are eligible, and those who qualify may appear in court under certain circumstances.

The School of Law operates the Native American Legal Resource Center, an institution which seeks to improve the quality of legal representation for individuals with problems in the field of Native American law. The center is designed to provide high quality basic and advanced training and resource support in varied areas of Native American law. It is also active in providing direct services to tribal court personnel and practitioners.

The School of Law also operates the Native American Legal Assistance Externship, a for-credit clinical program currently operated in conjunction with Legal Aid of Western Oklahoma and Oklahoma Indian Legal Services. This externship provides students with the opportunity for supervised, hands-on experience in dealing with real-life problems in the field while receiving training for which academic credit is awarded.

The School of Law is also home to the Center on Alternative Dispute Resolution. The center provides mediation services to courts, tribes, and government entities, and provides training so that students can become certified mediators. The range of mediation services provided by the center continues to grow. The Mediation Clinic provides for-credit mediation experience.

In the summer, the school offers, as part of its curriculum, intensive tracks of for-credit programs in such areas as civil litigation, criminal practice, and alternative dispute resolution. The school is also home to the week-long Oklahoma Trial Lawyers Academy; students may assist and participate.

■ Admission

➡ *Bachelor's degree required*   ➡ *application deadline—July 15*
➡ *LSAT, LSDAS required*   ➡ *application fee—$40*

Admission decisions are determined by a faculty committee that considers each application separately. Many factors are considered, including academic performance, undergraduate institution and curriculum, advanced degrees, work experiences, background, activities, recommendations, and LSAT scores.

Regular students are admitted only in the fall term. Transcript evaluation by LSDAS is required, as are recommendations.

The Summer Alternate Admissions Program offers approximately 45 students who cannot meet ordinary admission requirements for law school an opportunity to earn their way academically into regular fall admission.

■ Student Activities

Active student organizations include the *Law Review*, Moot Court Board, Federalist Society, Black American Law Students Association, Hispanic American Law Student Association, Intellectual Property Student Association, National Women's Law Student Association, Phi Alpha Delta, Phi Delta Phi, an award-winning ABA-LSD chapter, Iota Tau Tau, Native American Law Students Association, American Inns of Court, Merit Scholars, and the Trial Lawyers Association. The social year culminates in the annual spring dance and Gridiron (the Gridiron is a student roast of faculty and administrators).

■ Expenses and Financial Aid

➡ *tuition & fees—full-time, $15,624; part-time, $10,080*
➡ *estimated additional expenses—$4,180 (on-campus housing, $950/semester; meal plan, $1,140*   ➡ *scholarships available: Hatton Sumners & University Merit*   ➡ *minority scholarships available*   ➡ *financial aid available; FAFSA forms*

In addition to the nonrefundable $40 application fee, when accepted a student is required to pay a $250 nonrefundable tuition deposit, credited toward the first semester's tuition.

Scholarships for first-year and upper-class students are available. Financial need and academic promise/performance are considered in awards. The Hatton W. Sumners Foundation offers up to five full scholarships each year to outstanding beginning students. The scholarships cover full tuition, books, fees, and a stipend for room/board. Minority applications are encouraged. The Kerr Foundation provides scholarship assistance to upper-class students on the basis of academic performance, participation in school activities, exemplary character, and need. Other scholarships and loan funds are also available. Students with need who are seeking financial aid should contact the Office of Financial Aid.

■ Career Services

The Office of Career Services assists students, beginning in their first year, seeking employment or legal internship positions and graduates seeking positions.

All students have access to notices of job opportunities, campus interviews, and general placement information issued by Career Services. Registration with the office affords them individual attention and access to opportunities available in their fields of interest. More details are provided on the career services portion of the law school's Web site.

Applicant Group for the 1998-1999 Academic Year

Oklahoma City University School of Law

LSAT Score	3.75 +		3.50 - 3.74		3.25 - 3.49		3.00 - 3.24		2.75 - 2.99		2.50 - 2.74		2.25 - 2.49		2.00 - 2.24		Below 2.00		No GPA		Total	
	Apps	Adm	Apps	Adm	Apps	Adm	Apps	Adm	Apps	Adm	Apps	Adm	Apps	Adm	Apps	Adm	Apps	Adm	Apps	Adm	Apps	Adm
175-180	0	0	0	0	0	0	0	0	0	0	0	0	0	0	0	0	0	0	0	0	0	0
170-174	0	0	0	0	0	0	0	0	0	0	0	0	0	0	0	0	0	0	0	0	0	0
165-169	3	3	0	0	1	1	0	0	0	0	0	0	0	0	0	0	0	0	0	0	4	4
160-164	4	4	2	2	2	2	4	4	0	0	0	0	0	0	1	0	0	0	0	0	13	12
155-159	6	6	7	7	5	4	6	6	4	4	6	6	4	4	3	3	0	0	1	1	42	41
150-154	3	3	6	6	9	7	17	17	21	21	26	21	22	20	3	3	0	0	4	1	111	99
145-149	8	8	20	19	30	28	35	31	45	38	33	30	33	29	9	9	2	0	7	4	222	196
140-144	2	2	16	14	24	21	34	30	47	44	30	20	11	6	13	3	6	1	9	4	192	145
135-139	5	4	4	3	5	4	15	7	19	8	21	6	11	1	14	0	3	0	6	0	103	33
130-134	0	0	2	1	2	1	8	3	3	0	12	0	4	0	5	0	2	0	6	0	44	5
125-129	0	0	1	0	0	0	1	0	2	0	1	0	2	0	2	0	0	0	2	0	11	0
120-124	0	0	0	0	0	0	0	0	0	0	0	0	0	0	0	0	0	0	0	0	0	0
Total	31	30	58	52	78	68	120	98	141	115	129	83	87	60	50	18	13	1	35	10	742	535

University of Oregon School of Law

Office of Admissions, Room 201
1221 University of Oregon
Eugene, OR 97403-1221

E-Mail: admissions@law.uoregon.edu
URL: http://www.law.uoregon.edu
Phone: 541.346.3846

■ Introduction

Eugene, Oregon is nestled in the southern Willamette Valley, which is outlined by the Coast Range and the Pacific Ocean to the west and the Cascade mountain range to the east. Eugene is the home of an internationally ranked research institution—the University of Oregon. The School of Law was founded in 1884 and continues to promote the joy of learning, creative scholarship, public service, ethics, and commitment to human diversity as well as providing a broad level of legal training for a wide variety of professional interests. The University of Oregon School of Law recently broke ground for the new William W. Knight Law Center which will be completed in 1999. The building will support our commitment to ensuring students a technical education as well as a legal education. We will continue our laptop computer requirement, and the new building will be extensively wired to promote electronic research as well as the sharing of knowledge among teachers and students. Easy-to-reach faculty offices will ensure that the relatively informal relationships between students and their professors at Oregon will remain intact.

■ Enrollment/Student Body

➡ 1,050 applicants   ➡ 548 admitted first-year class 1998
➡ 170 enrolled first-year class 1998   ➡ full-time 25th/75th percentile GPA—3.13/3.60   ➡ full-time 25th/75th percentile LSAT—152/159   ➡ 499 total full-time
➡ 12% minority   ➡ 51% women
➡ 95 undergraduate schools represented in first year class 1998

■ Faculty

➡ 54 total   ➡ 43 teaching   ➡ 38 full-time
➡ 16 part-time or adjunct   ➡ 26 women
➡ 6 minority   ➡ 7 endowed professorships

■ Library and Physical Facilities

➡ 360,000 volumes & equivalents   ➡ LEXIS   ➡ NEXIS
➡ WESTLAW   ➡ Janus   ➡ 6 full-time librarians
➡ library seats 297

The library's collection is accessed through Janus, an online catalog that is an important tool for researchers. The online Legal Resource Room in the law library contains 21 computer workstations which can be used to access information, information management, electronic communication, and word processing.

The Law Center's facilities include spacious classrooms, seminar rooms, a courtroom with videotape facilities, Student Bar Association office, student organization offices, *Oregon Law Review* and *Journal of Environmental Law and Litigation* (JELL) offices, offices for clinical programs, and a student lounge and courtyard.

■ Curriculum

➡ Academic Support Program   ➡ 85 credits required to graduate   ➡ degrees available: J.D.; J.D./M.B.A.
➡ semesters, start in Aug.

The School of Law core curriculum emphasizes rigorous courses in all traditional legal subjects: civil procedure, contracts, criminal law, legal research and writing, legislative and administrative processes, property, and torts. The elective curriculum allows students to concentrate their studies in particular areas such as business and corporate law, international law, estate planning, taxation, litigation, constitutional law, intellectual property law, environmental law, and administrative law.

■ Academic Programs

The Business Law Program offers second- and third-year students an opportunity to receive a Business Law Statement of Completion or an Estate Planning Statement of Completion upon successfully completing a number of specific courses. Statements of completion are also available in Ocean and Coastal Law and Environmental Law.

The School of Law and the Graduate School of Management offer a concurrent J.D./M.B.A. degree program. The Law and Entrepreneurship Center provides an innovative forum to advance understanding of how lawyers create value for entrepreneurial clients.

An intensive year-long research and writing program is required of all first-year students. Students present final oral arguments at the end of the second semester in a courtroom setting.

The location of the school in the Pacific Northwest has led to a strong program in environmental law and ocean and coastal law offerings. Courses in water resources law, land use law, environment and pollution, ocean and coastal law, law of the sea, public land law, Indian law, and wildlife law give students insight into legal problems involved in these specific areas. Statements of Completion offered in Environmental and Natural Resources and Ocean and Coastal Law give the school the distinction of being one of only a few schools in the nation to offer such programs.

The School of Law offers five clinical programs: Civil Practice, Criminal Defense, Prosecution, Environmental Law, and Mediation and Appropriate Dispute Resolution.

In addition to the broad range of courses, externships, and clinics, the University of Oregon School of Law is committed to providing students with a working knowledge of computer technology. Laptop computers are required and considered as essential as "books and supplies." Seminars and training classes are provided for students throughout the year to help students learn how to use their laptops for research, Internet, and network use. The services, support, and training provided by the Computer Department are an integral part of the academic environment at the University of Oregon School of Law. The law school also provides students the opportunity to study in Australia at the University of Adelaide School of Law.

■ Admission

➡ *Bachelor's degree required* ➡ *application deadline—March 1*
➡ *LSAT, LSDAS required* ➡ *application fee—$50*

Over 1,000 applications were received for the 170 openings in the fall 1998 entering class. While the applicant's entire background is considered, quantitative indicators are given considerable weight. Entering students are accepted for admission in the fall only. The University of Oregon is an equal opportunity employer, affirmative action institution committed to cultural diversity and compliance with the Americans with Disabilities Act.

■ Student Activities

The *Oregon Law Review* is published by a student editorial board and has been in continuous publication since 1921. The *Journal of Environmental Law and Litigation* (JELL) is published by students and focuses on current issues in environmental law. The Moot Court Board sponsors five in-house school competitions each year from which teams are selected to represent the school in regional and national competitions. The Student Bar Association represents the student body by serving on faculty committees and sponsoring numerous activities. Other organizations include Asian-Pacific Americans Law Student Association; Black Law Students Association; Christian Legal Society; FACT; Federalist Society; International Law Society; Jewish Law Students Association; Journal of Environmental Law and Litigation; Land Air Water; Lesbian and Gay Law Student Association; Minority Law Students Association; *Monitor*; National Lawyers Guild; Oregon Law Students' Public Interest Fund; Oregon Women Lawyers; Parents at Law School, Partners in Law, Lovers and Relatives Support; Peer Advising Board; People's Law School; Phi Alpha Delta; Phi Delta Phi; Sports Club; *The Weekly Dissent*; Entertainment Law Club; and the Women's Law Forum.

■ Expenses and Financial Aid

➡ *full-time tuition & fees—resident, $10,238/yr.; nonresident, $13,986/yr.* ➡ *estimated additional expenses—$7,000 (books, room & board, personal)* ➡ *academic & need-based scholarships available* ➡ *academic & need-based minority scholarships available*
➡ *financial aid available; FAFSA due Feb. 1*

■ Career Services

The Career Services Office provides counseling, assistance with résumé preparation, job-search strategy, and interviewing skills. It offers a library of career planning resources for use by students and alumni. Law firms, corporations, government organizations, and public interest agencies visit the campus for on-site interviews each year. Graduates have risen to prominent positions in the state and federal court systems, have served with distinction in state and national legislative and executive offices, and have distinguished themselves in private practice and in business.

Applicant Group for the 1998-1999 Academic Year

University of Oregon School of Law

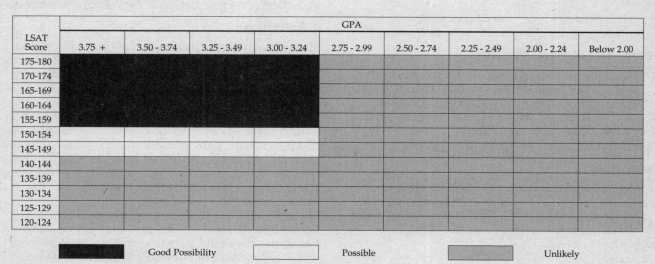

LSAT Score	GPA								
	3.75 +	3.50 - 3.74	3.25 - 3.49	3.00 - 3.24	2.75 - 2.99	2.50 - 2.74	2.25 - 2.49	2.00 - 2.24	Below 2.00
175-180									
170-174									
165-169									
160-164									
155-159									
150-154									
145-149									
140-144									
135-139									
130-134									
125-129									
120-124									

■ Good Possibility □ Possible ▨ Unlikely

Pace University School of Law

78 North Broadway
White Plains, NY 10603

E-Mail: admissions@genesis.law.pace.edu
URL: http://www.law.pace.edu/
Phone: 914.422.4210

■ Introduction

The Pace University School of Law, a division of a multi-campus university, is fully accredited by the American Bar Association and is a member of the Association of American Law Schools. Located in White Plains, NY, the law school provides convenient access to metropolitan New York, Connecticut, and New Jersey. In the area are the headquarters of some of the nation's largest corporations, as well as a large legal community and county, state, and federal courts. This concentration of resources and the law school's proximity to New York City have enabled Pace to attract highly qualified professors, speakers, and advisors.

The programs of the law school, including the J.D., LL.M., and S.J.D. in Environmental Law, are national in perspective and are based on the concept that rigorous standards and high quality teaching can coexist with an atmosphere congenial to learning and enjoyment. The aspirations of the students and faculty are high: to achieve national recognition and to reflect the range and level of the varied resources of the metropolitan New York City area.

The law school has just expanded into new buildings on its verdant campus setting. The school is noted for its community atmosphere and the closeness of students, faculty, and alumni.

■ Enrollment/Student Body

➡ 1,903 applicants ➡ 778 admitted first-year class 1998 ➡ 258 enrolled first-year class 1998 ➡ full-time 25th/75th percentile GPA—2.84/3.41 ➡ part-time 25th/75th percentile GPA—2.72/3.60 ➡ full-time 25th/75th percentile LSAT—147/154 ➡ part-time 25th/75th percentile LSAT—146/154 ➡ 449 total full-time ➡ 308 total part-time ➡ 51% women

■ Faculty

➡ 98 total ➡ 34 full-time ➡ 64 part-time or adjunct ➡ 2 emeriti in residence ➡ 15 women ➡ 3 minority

■ Library and Physical Facilities

➡ 318,430 volumes & equivalents ➡ library hours: Mon.-Thurs., 8:00 A.M.-MIDNIGHT; Fri., 8:00 A.M.-10:00 P.M.; Sat., 9:00 A.M.-9:00 P.M.; Sun., 11:00 A.M.-11:00 P.M. ➡ LEXIS ➡ NEXIS ➡ WESTLAW ➡ DIALOG ➡ RLIN ➡ OCLC ➡ WebPALS ➡ 8 full-time librarians ➡ library seats 358

■ Curriculum

➡ Academic Support Program ➡ 90 credits required to graduate ➡ 134 courses available ➡ degrees available: J.D.; J.D./M.B.A.; J.D./M.P.A.; LL.M.; S.J.D. in Environmental Law ➡ semesters, first-year begin in mid-Aug. ➡ range of first-year class size—25-80

■ Special Programs

Certificates in Environmental Law, Health Law, and International Law are awarded when students complete a sequence of courses with specified GPAs in the applicable area. Clinics are available in appellate and civil (health) litigation, criminal prosecution (domestic violence) and criminal defense, a Securities Arbitration Clinic, as well as trial courses and externships. The environmental litigation clinic run by Robert F. Kennedy, Jr., has achieved national recognition. Pace has the unique London Program largely taught by the Faculty of Law, University College, London. The program includes the opportunity for clinical internships with members of Parliament, law firms, and corporations.

Pace offers the opportunity to pursue the joint J.D./M.B.A. or joint J.D./M.P.A. degree programs. The programs are typically completed in four years of full-time study; evening study is also possible.

■ Admission

➡ Bachelor's degree required ➡ application deadline—Feb. 15 ➡ rolling admission ➡ application fee—$55 ➡ 2 letters of recommendation & a personal statement ➡ LSAT, LSDAS required

The law school received over 1,903 applications for 1998 admission. It enrolls approximately 170 day and 90 part-time students annually. Admission is very competitive. The GPAs of the admitted classes average 3.20, and the mean LSAT score is around the 67th percentile. The GPA and LSAT are the most important criteria for admission. However, many additional factors (e.g., schools attended, grade progression, courses, experiences) are also considered.

Minority students are encouraged to apply. Pace encourages diverse representation in the school and profession.

■ Activities

Students may participate in the writing, editing, and production of three law journals: the *Pace Law Review*; the *Pace Environmental Law Review*; and the *Pace Journal of International Law*. Other law student organizations at Pace include *Hearsay*, the student newspaper, Moot Court Board, Student Bar Association, Women's Association of Law Students, Minority Student Association, Entertainment and Sports Law, Labor and Employment Law, Environmental Law, and International Law Clubs, and other special-interest groups. Special activities such as workshops and speakers sponsored by these groups, as well as social events, enrich Pace's offerings.

In addition, Pace students compete in the Philip C. Jessup International Moot Court, the National Moot Court, the National Client Counseling Competition, and the National Trial Competition. Pace hosts the annual National Environmental Law Moot Court Competition and an international commercial law arbitration moot in Vienna. Students may also attend our Continuing Legal Education (CLE) programs.

■ Expenses and Financial Aid

➡ *tuition & fees—full-time, $21,600; part-time, $16,300*
➡ *estimated additional expenses—$9,395 (off-campus living allowance)* ➡ *merit- & need-based scholarships available*
➡ *financial aid available* ➡ *FAFSA required completed by March 15, Profile Form or the Need Access Application*

■ Career Services

The school's reputation continues to grow and, over the course of the past 20 years, Pace has succeeded in firmly establishing itself in the legal marketplace. That success is due largely to the achievements of our graduates and continued employer satisfaction. Pace graduates typically go on to careers with national, regional, and local law firms; government agencies; county prosecutors; and public interest organizations. Pace students are awarded federal and state judicial clerkships each year.

The Office of Career Development provides guidance and assistance to students as they engage in the search for legal employment. The office serves as a liaison between law students and legal employers. It solicits and identifies employment opportunities; develops and maintains resources for student use in their job search; and encourages employers to accept student résumés and to interview on campus. The office provides counseling on résumé and cover letter preparation, interviewing techniques, and career options as well as advice on how best to conduct a job search.

Applicant Group for the 1998-1999 Academic Year

Pace University School of Law
This grid includes only applicants who earned 120-180 LSAT scores under standard administrations.

LSAT Score	3.75 +		3.50 - 3.74		3.25 - 3.49		3.00 - 3.24		2.75 - 2.99		2.50 -2.74		2.25 - 2.49		2.00 - 2.24		Below 2.00		No GPA		Total	
	Apps	Adm	Apps	Adm	Apps	Adm	Apps	Adm	Apps	Adm	Apps	Adm	Apps	Adm	Apps	Adm	Apps	Adm	Apps	Adm	Apps	Adm
175-180	0	0	0	0	0	0	0	0	0	0	0	0	0	0	0	0	0	0	0	0	0	0
170-174	0	0	0	0	1	1	0	0	0	0	1	1	0	0	0	0	0	0	0	0	2	2
165-169	2	2	4	4	2	2	1	1	0	0	3	3	1	1	2	2	2	0	1	1	18	16
160-164	7	7	4	4	5	5	15	14	11	11	5	5	1	1	0	0	1	0	1	1	50	48
155-159	11	11	20	19	25	25	43	41	29	28	28	28	10	9	6	6	2	0	4	4	178	171
150-154	21	21	32	32	68	68	68	68	74	71	61	58	22	19	8	4	1	0	4	3	359	344
145-149	11	10	34	34	76	73	99	90	92	69	68	42	39	16	18	7	4	1	5	3	446	345
140-144	10	7	23	8	52	24	80	17	84	5	85	3	40	0	14	0	12	0	6	0	406	64
135-139	3	0	13	0	9	0	30	0	41	0	42	0	41	0	18	0	5	0	7	0	209	0
130-134	0	0	3	0	2	0	8	0	23	0	8	0	14	0	8	0	3	0	3	0	72	0
125-129	0	0	3	0	0	0	3	0	2	0	1	0	1	0	2	0	2	0	0	0	14	0
120-124	0	0	0	0	0	0	0	0	0	0	1	0	0	0	1	0	0	0	0	0	2	0
Total	65	58	136	101	240	198	347	231	356	184	303	140	169	46	77	19	32	1	31	12	1756	990

Apps = Number of Applicants
Adm = Number Admitted

University of Pennsylvania Law School

3400 Chestnut Street
Philadelphia, PA 19104-6204

E-Mail: admissions@oyez.law.upenn.edu
URL: http://www.law.upenn.edu
Phone: 215.898.7400

■ Introduction

The study of law at the University of Pennsylvania began in 1790 and the Law School was formally organized in 1852. The Law School is a charter member of the AALS and is on the approved list of the ABA. The university is a private institution. The Law School, located on the university campus, is convenient to the many places of cultural and historical interest in Philadelphia.

■ Enrollment/Student Body

➡ 3,771 applicants   ➡ 1,178 admitted first-year class 1998
➡ 271 enrolled first-year class 1998   ➡ full-time 25th/75th percentile GPA—3.41/3.73   ➡ full-time 25th/75th percentile LSAT—163/167   ➡ 767 total full-time   ➡ 25% minority
➡ 43% women   ➡ 58 states & foreign countries represented
➡ 181 undergraduate schools represented

The student body is a diverse group of J.D. candidates plus a number of full-time graduate students from the United States and abroad. In recent years, 55 percent of the J.D. candidates did not matriculate directly from undergraduate study; 14 percent possess other graduate or professional degrees.

■ Faculty

➡ 110 total   ➡ 51 full-time   ➡ 59 part-time or adjunct
➡ 9 women   ➡ 3 minority

■ Libraries and Physical Facilities

➡ 672,000 volumes & equivalents   ➡ library hours:
Mon.-Thurs., 7:30 A.M.-MIDNIGHT; Fri., 7:30 A.M.-11:00 P.M.;
Sat., 9:00 A.M.-11:00 P.M.; Sun., 9:00 A.M.-MIDNIGHT
➡ LEXIS   ➡ NEXIS   ➡ WESTLAW   ➡ DIALOG
➡ BRS   ➡ VUTEXT   ➡ Dow Jones
➡ 14 full-time librarians   ➡ library seats 525
➡ 657 computer ports

The Law School is a modern, self-contained complex of buildings. A new library adjacent to the Law School was completed in 1993. Law students also have ready access to the university's other libraries, which contain an additional three million books.

■ Curriculum

➡ Degrees available: J.D.; J.D./M.B.A.; J.D./M.S.W.;
J.D./M.C.P.; J.D./M.A. Economics; J.D./M.A. Middle Eastern Studies; J.D./M.D.; J.D./M.A. Public Policy; J.D./Ph.D. Philosophy; LL.M.; S.J.D.; J.D./M.Ed.; J.D./M.G.A.

The Law School awards the J.D. degree upon the successful completion of three academic years. There are no summer or night classes. The school operates on the semester basis.
    The prescribed program of the first year includes courses based on statutory and administrative law, as well as the traditional common law courses. In a small group, each student receives individualized instruction in legal research and writing. In the second and third years the work is elective, with opportunity for in-depth work in particular areas, including nonclassroom study. Additionally, second- and third-year students are required to perform 35 hours of unpaid professional service each year. This public service is a graduation requirement. Under rules on the practice of law in the Commonwealth, students in the Law School's clinical programs are permitted to represent clients in a variety of judicial and administrative tribunals. All third-year students write a major senior research paper. The programs of graduate study lead to the degree of Master of Laws (LL.M.), Master of Comparative Law (LL.C.M.), and Doctor of Juridical Science of Law (S.J.D.).

■ Special Programs

The Law School's sensitivity to the problems confronting contemporary society is reflected in its programs. Among these are four-year programs with the Department of City Planning, leading to the J.D. and Master of City Planning degrees; the Wharton School of Business Administration, leading to the J.D. and M.B.A. or J.D. and M.A./Ph.D. in Public Policy and Management; the Department of Economics leading to the J.D. and M.A. or, through a very rigorous program, a combined J.D./Ph.D.; the School of Social Work leading to the J.D. and Master of Social Work; and the Department of Philosophy leading to a J.D./Ph.D. in Philosophy. In conjunction with the university's Middle East Center, the Law School offers a program designed for law students who wish to focus their attention on legal issues arising in the Islamic Middle East. Through arrangements with the graduate faculty, well-qualified J.D. candidates may pursue a joint program in other law-related graduate disciplines. Selected students may spend one semester working and studying in externship programs away from the Law School. The Law School maintains a Legal Assistance Office where students represent clients under the supervision of experienced attorneys. A small-business clinic has been established in conjunction with the Wharton School.

■ Admission

➡ Bachelor's degree from accredited institution required
➡ application deadline—March 1   ➡ LSAT, LSDAS required
➡ application fee—$65

Admission is highly selective. The school lays prime emphasis upon overall undergraduate performance and LSAT score. It may also take into account maturity, extracurricular records, and other personal qualifications. Recommendations, preferably from former instructors, are required. Personal interviews are not required, but students contemplating law study are encouraged to visit the school. For the class that entered in August 1997, the median LSAT score was in the 95th percentile. The Law School strongly encourages applications from members of minority groups. The deadline for admission and financial aid applications is March 1. The school admits students only in the fall and only for full-time study. The school accepts a number of transfer students each year from applicants with superior undergraduate and law school records.

■ Housing

Facilities for single and married students are available in the Graduate Towers and International House, which are adjacent to the Law School. A wide range of off-campus facilities is also available. For information students may write to the Office of Graduate Housing, 3901 Locust Walk, Philadelphia, PA 19104.

■ Student Activities

The *University of Pennsylvania Law Review* is edited by a board of student editors. It dates from 1896 and is a lineal successor to the *American Law Register*, which originated in 1852. The Law School also publishes a *Journal of International Business Law* and the *Comparative Labor Law Journal*. There is a chapter of the Order of the Coif. Student representatives participate in the governance of the Law School by participating in committee and faculty meetings. There is a full program of moot court activities. Other activities include the National Lawyer's Guild, the Federalist Society, and the Environmental Law Group. There are organizations for women, black, Asian-American, Latino, and gay and lesbian students, and various professional interests.

■ Expenses and Financial Aid

➡ *tuition & fees—full-time, $25,780*   ➡ *estimated additional expenses—$12,320*   ➡ *scholarships available (Public Interest Scholarships)*   ➡ *need-based grants available*   ➡ *financial aid available*   ➡ *FAFSA required for need-based scholarships, as well as institutional application*

The school maintains a substantial program of both scholarship and loan aid based entirely on need. Over 75 percent of the student body receives some type of financial aid.

Entering students may apply for several Public Interest Scholarships. These cover two-thirds of tuition and fees for three years. Applicants are selected on the basis of previous work experience in the public sector and commitment to employment in the public sector after graduation. Applications for the scholarships are contained in our admission material.

The Law School has a loan forgiveness program to assist graduates in repaying law school debts if they choose to work in the public sector.

■ Career Services

The Career Planning and Placement Office is staffed by four professionals who assist law students in finding employment and counsel students and alumni on employment opportunities. We offer specialized counseling for public interest work, first-year job searches, minority students' concerns, and judicial clerkships. Of the recent classes, about 67 percent entered private practice; 19 percent held judicial clerkships; and 7 percent were in government and public interest positions.

Applicant Group for the 1998-1999 Academic Year

University of Pennsylvania Law School
This grid includes only applicants who earned 120-180 LSAT scores under standard administrations.

LSAT Score	3.75 +		3.50 - 3.74		3.25 - 3.49		3.00 - 3.24		2.75 - 2.99		2.50 -2.74		2.25 - 2.49		2.00 - 2.24		Below 2.00		No GPA		Total	
	Apps	Adm	Apps	Adm	Apps	Adm	Apps	Adm	Apps	Adm	Apps	Adm	Apps	Adm	Apps	Adm	Apps	Adm	Apps	Adm	Apps	Adm
175-180	17	15	22	21	13	10	7	1	3	0	1	0	0	0	0	0	0	0	2	2	65	49
170-174	68	62	96	87	78	60	34	16	11	1	7	1	2	0	0	0	0	0	3	2	299	229
165-169	219	198	296	252	224	126	74	10	27	2	9	0	3	0	0	0	1	1	16	8	869	597
160-164	221	68	378	57	259	17	119	7	44	5	13	0	7	1	1	0	0	0	18	3	1060	158
155-159	106	11	165	14	179	19	118	14	63	4	15	1	7	0	5	0	0	0	18	0	676	63
150-154	58	5	86	6	98	6	71	7	36	0	20	1	8	0	0	0	1	0	20	1	398	26
145-149	17	1	36	2	44	0	33	1	35	0	16	0	8	0	4	0	0	0	10	0	203	4
140-144	9	0	14	0	17	0	16	0	20	0	15	0	6	0	4	0	1	0	10	0	112	0
135-139	2	0	3	0	2	0	6	0	7	0	6	0	6	0	3	0	1	0	4	0	40	0
130-134	0	0	1	0	0	0	0	0	1	0	2	0	2	0	1	0	0	0	0	0	7	0
125-129	0	0	0	0	0	0	1	0	0	0	0	0	0	0	1	0	1	0	0	0	3	0
120-124	0	0	0	0	0	0	0	0	0	0	0	0	0	0	0	0	0	0	0	0	0	0
Total	717	360	1097	439	914	238	479	56	247	12	104	3	49	1	19	0	5	1	101	16	3732	1126

Apps = Number of Applicants
Adm = Number Admitted
Reflects 99% of the total applicant pool.

The Pennsylvania State University, The Dickinson School of Law

150 South College Street
Carlisle, PA 17013

E-Mail: dsladmit@psu.edu
URL: http://www.dsl.edu
Phone: 800.840.1122; 717.240.5000

■ Introduction

In 1997 The Dickinson School of Law, affiliated with Penn State, became The Dickinson School of Law of The Pennsylvania State University. As part of Penn State, the law school acquired enhanced technological capabilities and now offers its students opportunities for combined-degree programs in a number of fields. The law school recently acquired an 11-acre tract of land, three miles from our main building. This new property will provide expansion space for library materials storage, additional offices, and space that can be devoted to skills education and to continuing education programs.

Founded in 1834, Dickinson has been a pioneer in providing skills training and comparative law curricula and has been recognized nationally for the excellence of its advocacy program. Small class sizes and easy accessibility to faculty help to foster an academic atmosphere that, while competitive, is friendly and cooperative. Our rigorous academic program includes opportunities for real-life, hands-on experience in clinical settings and moot court competitions. Students may compete to work on three scholarly journals and may participate in a wide array of extra- and cocurricular activities which enhance the law school experience. Our location provides easy access to Pittsburgh, Philadelphia, New York, Washington, DC, and Baltimore. Located less than 20 miles from the state capital of Harrisburg, the school affords opportunities for part-time work in state government agencies and private law firms during the school year and in the summer.

■ Enrollment/Student Body

➡ *1,150 applicants*   ➡ *full-time 25th/75th percentile GPA—2.90/3.50*   ➡ *full-time 25th/75th percentile LSAT—150/155*   ➡ *185 enrolled first-year class 1998*   ➡ *508 total full-time*   ➡ *7% minority*   ➡ *43% women*   ➡ *26 states & foreign countries represented*   ➡ *190 undergraduate schools represented*

■ Faculty

➡ *91 total*   ➡ *31 full-time*   ➡ *60 part-time or adjunct*   ➡ *10 full-time women*   ➡ *2 full-time minority*

■ Library and Physical Facilities

➡ *393,000 volumes & equivalents*   ➡ *library hours (public use): Mon.-Thurs., 8:00 A.M.-9:00 P.M.; Fri., 8:00 A.M.-5:00 P.M.; students have 24-hour access*   ➡ *LEXIS*   ➡ *NEXIS*   ➡ *WESTLAW*   ➡ *OCLC*   ➡ *LIAS*   ➡ *7 full-time librarians*   ➡ *library seats 444*

The computer lab offers access to LEXIS and WESTLAW computerized legal research systems, as well as word processing capabilities. A local area network links students' personal computers to the library catalog and other research resources, including yearlong access to the Internet through Penn State's university-wide computer system. The addition of two new classroom/computer laboratories and a computer training area more than doubles the number of computer terminals available. As a result of our affiliation with Penn State, we have acquired a satellite dish, which will enable us to pipe transmissions into our classrooms; we will have an interactive video/audio system for small classes and meetings; and our students have access to Penn State's four-million-volume library as well as access to other research databases.

Some accommodations for single students are available in the Levinson Curtilage, a dormitory quadrangle located next to the Trickett Hall complex. Reasonably priced off-campus housing is readily available.

The law school's Community Law Center in downtown Carlisle houses state-of-the-art clinic facilities similar to real law offices. It includes an 1,800-square-foot law library for use by students in the Disability and Family Law clinics.

■ Programs of Study/Degree Requirements

Dickinson School of Law graduates receive a broad-based theoretical and practical legal education that prepares them to practice law anywhere in the United States. Skills preparation in trial and appellate advocacy, client counseling, and legal writing complement the standard coursework. With a distinguished record in interscholastic moot court competitions, Dickinson's advocacy program has been recognized for excellence by the American College of Trial Lawyers.

Cooperative programs with Penn State's Smeal College of Business Administration and Penn State Harrisburg allow students to earn both a J.D. degree and a master's degree in either the business administration, public administration, or environmental pollution control programs. Our newly-developed Agricultural Law Research and Education Center, a joint enterprise with the Pennsylvania Department of Agriculture and Penn State's College of Agricultural Sciences, provides service to the public, as well as special learning opportunities for our students.

Foreign lawyers with law degrees not founded substantially on the English Common Law system may apply for admission to the Master of Laws in Comparative Law degree program, which requires successful completion of an academic year in residence.

■ Summer Sessions Abroad

In the early 1980s, Dickinson became one of the first law schools to establish an overseas comparative law program for American students. Dickinson offers two, four-week summer credit programs: one in Florence, Italy; the other in Vienna, Austria; Brussels, Belgium; and Strasbourg, France. Distinguished guest lecturers in recent years have included U.S. Supreme Court Justices Ruth Bader Ginsburg, Antonin Scalia, and Sandra Day O'Connor, and Judge Anthony J. Scirica of the Third Circuit Court of Appeals.

■ Special Programs and Activities

Dickinson was a pioneer in providing hands-on, clinical experiences to assist students in developing the skills necessary to counsel clients effectively. The school's in-house clinics include the Family Law Clinic, which handles matters involving divorce, child custody, visitation, protection from abuse, and other family-related matters; and the Disability Law Clinic. The Art, Sports, and Entertainment Law Clinic provides free services to individuals in art, sports, and entertainment fields. Services include educational information and, when appropriate, legal representation. There are also many field placement opportunities in Legal Services, public defenders' and district attorneys' offices, judges' chambers, and legal departments of state agencies.

■ Admission

➡ *Bachelor's degree required*   ➡ *application deadline—March 1*
➡ *LSAT, LSDAS required*   ➡ *application fee—$50*

Prior to enrollment, applicants must complete work for an undergraduate degree from an accredited college or university and must submit all college transcripts and LSAT scores. All relevant factors will be considered by the Admissions Committee to identify those applicants who are most likely to make a substantial and constructive contribution to the law school and the legal profession. There are no automatic admissions or denials based on numbers.

Through participation in CLEO, implementation of a minority visitation weekend, and recruiting efforts, Dickinson is working to broaden the diversity of its student body.

Personal interviews are not a part of the admissions process, but applicants are invited to visit campus and attend a class, preferably in the fall.

Students with an outstanding first-year performance at another AALS school may be considered for admission as

second-year students. Transfer applications must be received on or before June 15. No action will be taken on these applications until first-year grades and class standing are received.

The Pennsylvania State University is committed to the policy that all persons shall have equal access to programs, facilities, admission, and employment without regard to personal characteristics not related to ability, performance, or qualifications as determined by University policy or by state or federal authorities. The Pennsylvania State University does not discriminate against any person because of age, ancestry, color, disability or handicap, national origin, race, religious creed, sex, sexual orientation, or veteran status.

■ Cocurricular Activities

Founded in 1897, the quarterly *Dickinson Law Review* ranks as one of the oldest law school publications in the country. The *Dickinson Journal of International Law* publishes articles on private and public international law. The *Dickinson Journal of Environmental Law & Policy* is a forum for articles that treat aspects of environmental law. The Student Bar Association promotes the interests of the many student organizations both within the law school and in the community.

■ Expenses and Financial Aid

Dickinson is one of the best buys in legal education. The current annual tuition is $15,040. The estimated annual cost for an unmarried student living in school housing, excluding personal expenses, is $25,965. Tuition and fees are subject to change. FAFSA is required of all applicants for federal loans. FAFSA and Need Access are required of applicants for need-based grants.

Applicant Group for the 1998-1999 Academic Year

The Pennsylvania State University, The Dickinson School of Law
This grid includes only applicants who earned 120-180 LSAT scores under standard administrations.

LSAT Score	3.75 +		3.50 - 3.74		3.25 - 3.49		3.00 - 3.24		2.75 - 2.99		2.50 -2.74		2.25 - 2.49		2.00 - 2.24		Below 2.00		No GPA		Total	
	Apps	Adm	Apps	Adm	Apps	Adm	Apps	Adm	Apps	Adm	Apps	Adm	Apps	Adm	Apps	Adm	Apps	Adm	Apps	Adm	Apps	Adm
175-180	0	0	0	0	0	0	0	0	0	0	0	0	0	0	0	0	0	0	0	0	0	0
170-174	3	3	0	0	0	0	1	1	1	1	1	1	0	0	0	0	0	0	0	0	6	6
165-169	5	4	2	2	4	2	2	1	3	3	2	1	0	0	0	0	0	0	1	1	19	14
160-164	14	14	16	15	10	10	15	13	9	7	5	5	2	2	2	2	0	0	1	1	74	69
155-159	19	18	29	27	32	30	39	38	38	37	18	15	9	8	0	0	1	1	0	0	185	174
150-154	21	20	64	62	88	78	79	70	61	43	32	21	12	6	10	5	1	1	4	1	372	307
145-149	13	5	25	8	52	14	51	3	43	7	35	4	17	2	5	1	1	0	1	0	243	44
140-144	2	0	14	4	28	5	37	0	29	1	23	1	10	0	4	0	1	0	2	0	150	11
135-139	4	0	8	0	7	0	11	0	12	0	8	0	11	0	2	0	2	0	6	0	71	0
130-134	0	0	1	0	1	0	3	0	1	0	3	0	1	0	2	0	0	0	0	0	12	0
125-129	0	0	0	0	1	0	0	0	1	0	0	0	0	0	0	0	2	0	0	0	4	0
120-124	0	0	0	0	0	0	0	0	0	0	0	0	0	0	0	0	0	0	0	0	0	0
Total	81	64	159	118	223	139	238	126	198	99	127	48	62	18	25	8	8	2	15	3	1136	625

Apps = Number of Applicants
Adm = Number Admitted
Reflects 99% of the total applicant pool.

Pepperdine University School of Law

24255 Pacific Coast Highway
Malibu, CA 90263

E-Mail: soladmis@pepperdine.edu
URL: http://law-www.pepperdine.edu
Phone: 310.456.4631

■ Introduction

Pepperdine University School of Law is located in the Odell McConnell Law Center on the university's 830-acre Malibu campus in Los Angeles County. This campus is the site of Seaver College, the university's undergraduate school, the School of Business and Management's Residential M.B.A. program, and the School of Public Policy. The natural beauty of the Malibu campus combines the majesty of the rugged Santa Monica Mountains with a breathtaking view of the Pacific Ocean. Known for its clean air and almost rural setting, Malibu is less than a half hour's drive from the heavily populated San Fernando Valley; the business and legal communities of Santa Monica, Westwood, and Century City; and the fast-growing Thousand Oaks/Conejo Valley areas in nearby Ventura County. It is less than a 45-minute drive from downtown Los Angeles.

The School of Law is approved by the ABA and is a member of the AALS. With 45 percent of its students coming from states other than California, the school has a national reputation for excellence. Pepperdine offers a unique opportunity for the student who wishes to pursue a legal education in an institution that stresses academic excellence while supporting Christian values. Pepperdine is an independent, private university with a long-standing relationship with churches of Christ.

■ Enrollment/Student Body

➡ *2,514 applicants* ➡ *1,071 admitted first-year class 1998*
➡ *233 enrolled first-year class 1998* ➡ *full-time 25th/75th percentile GPA—3.02/3.51* ➡ *full-time 25th/75th percentile LSAT—153/160* ➡ *652 total full-time* ➡ *16% minority*
➡ *45% women* ➡ *42 states & foreign countries represented*
➡ *255 undergraduate schools represented*

The school actively recruits minority students.

■ Faculty

➡ *81 total* ➡ *39 full-time* ➡ *42 part-time or adjunct*
➡ *9 women* ➡ *4 minority* ➡ *12 women part-time*

The full-time opportunity for a personal relationship between faculty and students increases the effectiveness of the entire educational experience.

■ Library and Physical Facilities

➡ *265,000 volumes & equivalents* ➡ *library hours: Mon.-Fri., 7:00 A.M.-10:00 P.M.; Sat., 10:00 A.M.-10:00 P.M.; Sun., NOON-MIDNIGHT* ➡ *LEXIS* ➡ *NEXIS*
➡ *WESTLAW* ➡ *5 full-time librarians* ➡ *library seats 500*

The Jerene Appleby Harnish Law Library maintains an online public catalog as well as online, CD-ROM, and book indexes to provide access to the monograph and serials collections. All first-year students receive extensive training in both the LEXIS/NEXIS and the WESTLAW/DIALOG computer-assisted legal research systems, administered through the library.

■ Curriculum

➡ *Academic Support Program* ➡ *88 credits required to graduate* ➡ *149 courses available* ➡ *degrees available: J.D.; J.D./M.B.A.; J.D./M.D.R., J.D./M.P.P.*
➡ *semesters, start in Aug., Jan., May*

The School offers a three-year, full-time Juris Doctor program, a four-year, full-time JD/MBA and JD/MPP joint degrees program, and a concurrent JD/MDR degrees program.

An eight-week summer session is available for interested continuing students. It is possible to accelerate graduation one semester by taking appropriate courseloads for two summer sessions. During the summer session, classes are offered in the evenings to allow students employment opportunities during the day.

■ Special Programs

Through extensive clinical programs and the California State Bar Legal Intern Program, students engage in a wide variety of practical legal activities under the supervision of experienced attorneys.

■ Institute for Dispute Resolution

In 1986, the School of Law established the Institute for Dispute Resolution, recognizing the needs for effective, timely, and affordable justice. The most comprehensive dispute resolution program in the country, the institute's activities include academic programs, research, publications, national training, and actual dispute resolution activities. In 1988, the institute began its unique certificate program, which recognizes students who complete special coursework in the dispute-resolution field. In 1995, the institute expanded its program to offer a Masters in Dispute Resolution. Through the institute, the School of Law has received national recognition as a leader in the field of dispute resolution.

■ London Program

The School of Law offers a limited selection of courses in London, England, with an emphasis on international law in the fall and summer semesters. Second- and third-year students are given the opportunity to take courses in London under the direction of Pepperdine faculty and London adjunct professors. Several students from other law schools also participate.

■ Student Activities

Students are involved in a number of challenging activities, such as publication of the *Pepperdine Law Review*. The school operates one of the finest moot court programs in the country, with Pepperdine students excelling in statewide and national competitions. There are also successful trial advocacy and client-counseling competitions. Student organizations and legal fraternities offer additional opportunities for activities centered around the profession of law.

■ Admission

➡ *four-year undergraduate degree required*
➡ *application deadline—March 1*   ➡ *rolling admission*
➡ *LSAT, LSDAS required*   ➡ *application fee—$50*

No specific prelaw curriculum is required. First-year students are admitted only in the fall. Applications should be received by March 1.

Pepperdine University does not discriminate on the basis of race, color, national or ethnic origin, religion, age, sex, disability, or prior military service. Evaluation is based on GPA, LSAT score, personal references, and extracurricular activities. The GPA and LSAT scores provide the objective factors in the selection process. In addition, intangible and personal factors are weighed to ensure diversity among the student body and to meet institutional objectives. Admission is limited to those who show substantial promise of successfully completing the study of law.

A limited number of transfer students may be accepted each year. Transfer applicants must be in good academic standing (top 15 percent of class) at a law school approved by the ABA and holding membership in the AALS, and must complete their last 58 units in residence at Pepperdine.

■ Housing

A limited number of law students can be housed in the on-campus School of Law apartment complex, which is located directly across the street from the Law Center.

■ Expenses and Financial Aid

➡ *tuition & fees—$22,830 full-time; $845/unit part-time*
➡ *estimated additional expenses—$15,234 (room & board, $9,200; books, $700; travel, $1,800; personal, $3,534)*
➡ *merit- & need-based scholarships available*
➡ *diversity scholarships available*
➡ *financial aid available; FAFSA*

An active financial aid program provides over 85 percent of the student body with some type of financial assistance. Scholarship grants are available to students with outstanding academic credentials and to those with demonstrated financial need. The school's catalog contains loan and scholarship information. The deadline for students to complete applications for financial aid is May 1 of the entering year. The financial aid application is included in the application for admission.

■ Career Services

The Career Services Center offers individual counseling to develop personalized career strategies as well as coordinate on-campus interview programs, workshops, guest speakers, and a spring job fair. A successful alumni mentor program allows students to gain valuable insight into the legal profession. A staff with both legal and business contacts throughout the country gives students maximum career opportunities.

Applicant Group for the 1998-1999 Academic Year

Pepperdine University School of Law
This grid includes only applicants who earned 120-180 LSAT scores under standard administrations.

LSAT Score	3.75 +		3.50 - 3.74		3.25 - 3.49		3.00 - 3.24		2.75 - 2.99		2.50 -2.74		2.25 - 2.49		2.00 - 2.24		Below 2.00		No GPA		Total	
	Apps	Adm	Apps	Adm	Apps	Adm	Apps	Adm	Apps	Adm	Apps	Adm	Apps	Adm	Apps	Adm	Apps	Adm	Apps	Adm	Apps	Adm
175-180	1	1	2	2	1	1	0	0	1	1	0	0	0	0	0	0	0	0	0	0	5	5
170-174	4	4	8	8	5	4	9	9	2	2	2	1	1	1	0	0	0	0	1	1	32	30
165-169	19	19	15	14	23	23	16	16	20	20	6	5	2	2	1	1	0	0	3	3	105	103
160-164	42	39	48	48	60	55	68	65	33	29	21	19	6	3	5	1	0	0	0	0	283	259
155-159	42	39	86	82	127	124	125	111	90	61	66	25	18	2	11	0	0	0	7	5	572	449
150-154	29	16	92	53	146	69	183	36	120	14	65	3	27	0	10	1	2	0	1	0	675	192
145-149	15	1	37	3	96	9	108	5	95	6	68	2	36	2	7	0	2	0	6	0	470	28
140-144	4	0	14	0	36	1	62	4	57	4	45	3	37	0	19	0	1	0	7	0	282	12
135-139	1	0	5	0	10	0	18	0	19	0	22	0	11	0	9	0	2	0	5	0	102	0
130-134	0	0	1	0	0	0	2	0	7	0	6	0	13	0	3	0	0	0	2	0	34	0
125-129	0	0	0	0	0	0	0	0	2	0	0	0	0	0	1	0	1	0	1	0	5	0
120-124	0	0	0	0	0	0	0	0	0	0	0	0	0	0	1	0	0	0	0	0	1	0
Total	157	119	308	210	504	286	591	246	446	137	301	58	151	10	67	3	8	0	33	9	2566	1078

Apps = Number of Applicants
Adm = Number Admitted
Reflects 99% of the total applicant pool.

University of Pittsburgh School of Law

3900 Forbes Avenue
Pittsburgh, PA 15260

E-Mail: miller@law.pitt.edu
URL: http://www.law.pitt.edu
Phone: 412.648.1415

■ Introduction

Tradition: Law teaching at the University of Pittsburgh began in 1843, making Pittsburgh one of the first universities in the United States to offer a legal education. **Reputation:** The University of Pittsburgh remains one of the finest law schools in the country, featuring a broad and varied curriculum, an internationally renowned, enthusiastic faculty, first-rate physical facilities, and a talented, diverse student body. **Venue:** The School of Law is located in its own modern building on the university campus in Oakland, the cultural and educational center of the city of Pittsburgh. State and federal courts, major corporate headquarters, and hundreds of large and small law firms are located nearby in downtown Pittsburgh, minutes from the campus. The Oakland area is home to four colleges and universities, the seven-hospital University Health Center, scientific and high-tech research centers, museums, art galleries, and libraries. The university campus abuts a safe and attractive city park, and desirable and affordable residential areas are less than a mile away.

■ Enrollment/Student Body

➼ *1,228 applicants*   ➼ *826 admitted first-year class 1998*
➼ *250 enrolled first-year class 1998*   ➼ *full-time 25th/75th percentile GPA—2.80/3.50*   ➼ *full-time 25th/75th percentile LSAT—150/156*   ➼ *717 total full-time*   ➼ *10 total flex-time*
➼ *11.4% minority*   ➼ *42% women*   ➼ *23 states & foreign countries represented*   ➼ *114 undergraduate schools represented*

■ Faculty

➼ *80 total*   ➼ *42 full-time*   ➼ *38 part-time or adjunct*
➼ *16 women*   ➼ *4 minority*

■ Library and Physical Facilities

➼ *375,000 volumes & equivalents*   ➼ *library hours: Mon.-Thurs., 8:00 A.M.-MIDNIGHT; Fri., 8:00 A.M.- 11:00 P.M.; Sat., 9:00 A.M.-8:00 P.M.; Sun., NOON-MIDNIGHT*
➼ *LEXIS*   ➼ *NEXIS*   ➼ *WESTLAW*
➼ *7 full-time librarians*   ➼ *library seats 442*

Faculty offices ring the perimeter of the library. This encourages ease of interaction between students and faculty.

■ Curriculum

➼ *Academic Support Program*   ➼ *88 credits required to graduate*   ➼ *108 courses available*   ➼ *20 are seminars with limited enrollment (12 students)*   ➼ *5 clinics*
➼ *degrees available: J.D./M.P.A., Law and Urban and Public Administration; J.D./M.P.I.A., Law and International Affairs; J.D./M.U.R.P., Law and Urban and Regional Planning; J.D./M.B.A., Law and Business Administration; J.D./M.P.H., Law and Public Health; J.D./M.A., Law and Medical Ethics; J.D./M.S.I.A., Law and Industrial Management; J.D./M.S., Law and Public Management, Law and Arts Management*
➼ *range of first-year class size—10-75*

The first-year class is divided into three sections. For each section, one course is taught in a small class of fewer than 30 students. Upper-level students may enroll in seminars, limited to 12 students, where they complete a faculty-supervised writing project. The upper-level curriculum is extremely varied, and the courses have been grouped into 19 practice areas, permitting students to develop a specialization, if they choose.

■ Special Programs

Clinical Programs—Law school is much more than analyzing cases. It is also working with people and applying what you have learned from your legal studies and from other disciplines. Pitt Law students have the opportunity for "hands on" experience in several different clinical programs.

   The Family Support Clinic is a trial practice clinic designed to enhance students' client counseling, pretrial preparation, negotiation, and litigation skills. Students analyze and strategize on how best to handle the legal concerns for their real-life clients under the supervision of their faculty/supervising attorney. Upon enrolling in the clinic, students concentrate and represent live clients in one of three substantive areas of law.

   1. Health Law and Related Matters—Students represent clients in a variety of health areas, physical or mental, such as mental retardation, AIDS, depression, prenatal care, and senior citizen health issues.

   2. Elder Law and Related Matters—Students participate in a geriatric practicum and are part of the assessment process for determining capacity of their elderly clients. Ethical issues are analyzed in the context of dealing with elderly clients who are incapacitated.

   3. Disability Law and Related Matters—Students work on cases involving persons infected with and affected by HIV/AIDS. The legal, ethical, and medical issues explored will range from insurance coverage to future care and custody planning, and from job discrimination to child custody disputes.

   The Child Welfare Clinic—Students prepare and conduct in court all opening statements, direct examination questions, cross examination questions, and closing arguments.

   The Corporate Counsel Clinic—Students serve as legal counsel to MBA students at Carnegie Mellon University.

   Health Law Certificate (HLC)—A student who elects to participate in the HLC program takes a minimum of 18 credits in required and elective health law courses. To fulfill the requirements, students must take the basic course in health law, one health law clinical experience, at least three health law electives, and a health law seminar. Certain graduate courses outside of the School of Law may fulfill one of the electives.

   Academic Support (The Mellon Legal Writing Program)—The Mellon Legal Writing Program provides academic support to minority students through intensive training in legal analysis and writing. The program has been so successful in enhancing the performance of minority students that it was expanded to include other under-represented groups, including older students and students with disabilities.

Students in the Mellon program participate in a week-long orientation prior to the start of classes. Throughout the academic year, students receive close, individual attention in class meetings of only 10-12 people.

International Law—Pitt's Center for International Legal Education allows students to learn from some of the brightest legal minds in the world by attracting visiting scholars and lecturers from the U.S. and abroad, and convening a first-rate faculty to teach more than 15 comparative law courses and unique classes in French, Chinese, German, and Spanish for lawyers. The Center also provides opportunities for students to study and work abroad during the summer and/or school year. Two annual international moot court competitions and an international arbitration competition give students first-hand experience with the law as it applies in other countries. The Center also benefits from a close relationship with other highly respected international programs at the University of Pittsburgh.

■ Admission

➡ *Bachelor's degree from accredited college or university required*
➡ *application deadline—March 1* ➡ *LSAT, LSDAS required*
➡ *application fee—$50*

This School of Law is committed to providing opportunities for individuals in all segments of society: minorities, women, older students, and students with disabilities.

Since some individuals do not score well on standardized tests, in accepting students we look at all factors and all information submitted to see if an individual has the potential and capacity to study law.

■ Student Activities

The *Law Review* is a quarterly legal periodical published by second- and third-year law students. Each issue contains articles by law faculty, lawyers, and public officials throughout the country. The *Journal of Law and Commerce* reflects the law school's strength in the commercial, business, tax, and corporate law areas.

There are more than 25 organizations under the Student Bar Association representing the many social and intellectual experiences of our students. Among them is The Environmental Law Council, Feminist Law Forum, the Christian Legal Society, Black Law Students Association, Lesbian-Gay Rights Organization, and the Sports and Entertainment Law Society.

■ Expenses and Financial Aid

➡ *full-time tuition & fees—resident, $12,354; nonresident, $19,060* ➡ *additional expenses (room, board, other living expenses)—$9,970* ➡ *scholarships available: need-based & academic* ➡ *minority scholarships available*
➡ *financial aid available; FAFSA required for loans, law school financial aid form required for scholarship*

■ Career Services

The Placement Office provides year-round assistance to the school's students and graduates. The office serves as a clearinghouse for information on summer, part-time, and permanent work with law firms, corporations, accounting firms, government agencies, judges, and other legal employers. Placement rate for the class of 1996 was 81.5 percent.

Applicant Group for the 1998-1999 Academic Year

University of Pittsburgh School of Law
This grid includes only applicants who earned 120-180 LSAT scores under standard administrations.

LSAT Score	3.75 +		3.50 - 3.74		3.25 - 3.49		3.00 - 3.24		2.75 - 2.99		2.50 - 2.74		Below 2.50		No GPA		Total	
	Apps	Adm	Apps	Adm	Apps	Adm	Apps	Adm	Apps	Adm	Apps	Adm	Apps	Adm	Apps	Adm	Apps	Adm
165+	2	2	6	6	1	1	4	4	7	7	3	3	1	1	0	0	24	24
160-164	10	10	19	19	26	25	13	13	16	15	11	11	10	9	1	0	106	102
155-159	24	24	29	29	45	45	63	62	37	36	35	35	18	18	4	1	255	250
150-154	20	20	52	51	85	84	88	84	53	50	46	40	21	14	5	1	370	344
145-149	15	10	20	14	59	27	48	17	41	11	35	8	24	2	7	1	249	90
Below 145	5	2	17	0	21	1	44	3	41	4	33	0	53	1	11	0	225	11
Total	76	68	143	119	237	183	260	183	195	123	163	97	127	45	28	3	1229	821

Apps = Number of Applicants
Adm = Number Admitted
Reflects 99% of the total applicant pool.

Pontifical Catholic University of Puerto Rico, Faculty of Law (1997/1998 information)

Ponce, PR 00732   Phone: 787.841.2000 ext. 339 or 340

■ Introduction

The School of Law of the Pontifical Catholic University of Puerto Rico was founded in 1961. It is located within the main campus of the Pontifical Catholic University of Puerto Rico, on the southern part of the island in the historical city of Ponce, one of the most beautiful places in Puerto Rico.

The primary objective of the Pontifical Catholic University of Puerto Rico School of Law is the formation of lawyers imbued with a deep love and concern for their Catholic faith and steeped in the redeeming truths of Christian philosophy and ethics. The law school of the Pontifical Catholic University of Puerto Rico hopes to contribute to upholding the high ethical, cultural, and literary accomplishments of the Puerto Rican bar, which historically represents a tradition of moral austerity, intellectual achievement, and professional competence.

■ Enrollment/Student Body

➡ *518 total part-time & full-time students*
➡ *most students are from Puerto Rico*
➡ *25th/75th percentile GPA—2.83/3.33*
➡ *25th/75th percentile LSAT—133/141*

■ Library and Physical Facilities

➡ *176,914 volumes of Puerto Rican, Hispanic, Anglo-American, and foreign legal publications* ➡ *LEXIS* ➡ *NEXIS* ➡ *WESTLAW* ➡ *DIALOG* ➡ *MICROJURIS*

The School of Law occupies the Spellman Building. Its location on the campus of Pontifical Catholic University of Puerto Rico enables the students to study related academic disciplines, to participate in the intellectual life, and to enjoy many other facilities of the university.

Among the materials in the library is a comprehensive and growing collection of legal treatises, tests, monographs, and periodicals, including the most important and recent publications in civil, common, and comparative law. Modern audiovisual equipment and computerized services are also available. The library is an authorized depository for United Nations documents as well as for United States documents. In addition, it offers the services of the computerized WESTLAW and LEXIS/NEXIS systems, which permit computer-assisted legal research.

■ Curriculum

➡ *94 credits required to graduate* ➡ *degrees available: J.D.; J.D./M.B.A.* ➡ *semesters system*

The required subjects are Introduction to Law, Constitutional Law, Torts, Property Law, Legal Ethics and Professional Responsibility, Theology, Family Law, Successions and Donations, Penal Law, Criminal Procedure, Administrative Law, Obligations, Contracts, Notary Law, Civil Procedure, Evidence, Mortgages, Trial Practice, Legal Aid Clinic, Corporations, Mercantile Law,

Negotiable Instruments, Federal Jurisdiction, Special Legal Proceedings, Computers and the Legal Profession, Analysis of Jurisprudence, Legal Document Workshop, and Legal Bibliography. The basic program covers three years in the day division or four years in the evening division.

The school curriculum includes a clinical program for third-year students. Pursuant to a rule approved by the Supreme Court of the Commonwealth of Puerto Rico in 1974, students practice trial advocacy under the supervision of law school professors in the superior and district courts and in administrative agencies.

The required credits for the joint degree are as follows: J.D. degree, 88 credits (82 required credits and 6 elective credits) and an additional 6 approved elective credits in the Graduate Program of the School of Business Administration, for a total of 94 credits; M.B.A. degree, 37 credits (31 required credits and 6 elective credits) and an additional 6 approved elective credits in J.D., for a total of 43 credits, plus four hours of Theology.

■ Admission

➡ *Bachelor's degree required for admission*
➡ *application deadline—April 15* ➡ *LSAT and PAEG required* ➡ *beginning students admitted in Aug.*

Application for admission is open to men and women of good character who have received a bachelor's degree from a qualified institution with substantive content or training and a 2.5 grade-point average. Students without a bachelor's degree are not admitted.

The required forms of application and all other information may be obtained upon request from the registrar of the law school and should be filed with all supporting documents before May 15 in order to ensure consideration. The School of Law admits beginning students in August for both the full-time and part-time programs.

Applicants are required to take both the LSAT and the Prueba de Admision para Estudios Graduados (PAEG).

Test scores are not the only factor considered. Besides the objective factors, there are many intangible and personal considerations, such as strong motivation, disadvantaged circumstances, evidence of improving performance, and relevant work experience. A personal interview of the applicant by a committee is essential before a decision is made. Applicants of both sexes and from all religious, racial, social, and ethnic backgrounds are encouraged to apply.

All courses are offered only in Spanish. Consequently, students are required to be proficient in Spanish.

■ Student Activities

The law review, *Revista de Derecho Puertorriqueño*, is devoted to scholarly analysis and discussion of development of the law. It publishes student notes, comments, and surveys, as well as articles of outstanding quality submitted by attorneys, judges, and other members of the legal profession. We have a student council, a chapter of the National Association of Law Students of Puerto Rico, and an Association Pro Women's Rights. Local chapters of Phi Alpha Delta international law fraternity, the Delta Theta Phi law fraternity, and the Law Student Division of the ABA are also active and well organized in the law school.

■ Housing

Students live either in the university residences or in private housing. Inquiries concerning housing facilities should be addressed to the Housing Office, Pontifical Catholic University of Puerto Rico, Ponce, Puerto Rico 00732.

■ Expenses and Financial Aid

➡ *tuition—$250/credit hour, $266.50 fees*
➡ *estimated additional expenses—$3,570/sem.*
➡ *scholarships available* ➡ *financial aid available*

There is a deferred plan for students who have financial difficulties at the time of registration. The university has made available for law students several full-tuition scholarships to be awarded on the basis of scholastic excellence and financial need. The university also has an office for loans and other types of financial aid for students.

Admission Profile Not Available

University of Puerto Rico School of Law

P.O. Box 23349, UPR Station
Rio Piedras, PR 00931-3349

Phone: 787.764.1655

■ Introduction

The University of Puerto Rico School of Law was founded in 1913 at its present site on the University Campus at Rio Piedras, within the metropolitan area of San Juan. The School of Law has been accredited by the American Bar Association since 1945 and the University of Puerto Rico is accredited by the Middle States Colleges Association. In 1948, the school was approved by the Association of American Law Schools. It is also accredited by the Council on Higher Education and the Puerto Rico Supreme Court.

■ Enrollment/Student Body

➡ *720 applicants*   ➡ *179 admitted first-year class 1998*
➡ *153 enrolled first-year class 1998*   ➡ *full-time 25th/75th percentile GPA—3.26/3.79*   ➡ *part-time 25th/75th percentile GPA—3.14/3.79*   ➡ *full-time 25th/75th percentile LSAT—143/151*   ➡ *part-time 25th/75th percentile LSAT—142/149*
➡ *352 total full-time*   ➡ *221 total part-time*
➡ *55% women*   ➡ *3 states & foreign countries represented*
➡ *more than 20 undergraduate schools represented*

■ Faculty

➡ *66 total*   ➡ *33 full-time*   ➡ *33 part-time or adjunct*
➡ *20 women*

■ Library and Physical Facilities

➡ *328,113 volumes & equivalents*   ➡ *library hours: Mon.-Fri., 7:30 A.M.-11:45 P.M.; Sat. & Sun., 8:00 A.M.-10:15 P.M.*
➡ *LEXIS*   ➡ *NEXIS*   ➡ *WESTLAW*   ➡ *DIALOG*
➡ *COMPUCLERK*   ➡ *CUMPULEY*   ➡ *LEGALTRAC*
➡ *INFOTRAC*   ➡ *MICROJURIS*   ➡ *PRONLINX*
➡ *10 full-time librarians*   ➡ *library seats 407*

The law library is the largest law library in the Caribbean. Its collection reflects both the Romano-Germanic civil law and Anglo-American common law traditions. The law library is in the process of developing a comprehensive collection of legal materials from the Caribbean Basin including resources from Mexico, Central America, Venezuela, and Colombia, as well as the island jurisdictions. In addition to hard-copy and microform materials, the law library subscribes to a variety of computerized legal research services. The law library has been designated as a European Documentation Centre by the European Communities and is also a selective depository for U.S. government documents.

■ Curriculum

➡ *92 credits required to graduate*   ➡ *124 courses available*
➡ *J.D. degree available*   ➡ *semesters, start in Aug.*
➡ *range of first-year class size—10-50*

The basic program covers three years in the day division and four years in the evening division. Seventy credits consist of required courses and 22 are elective. Students are required to take two seminars (two credit-hours each).

■ Special Programs

The curriculum includes a clinical program for third-year students. The Legal Aid Clinic handles upwards of 1,300 cases per year. Rules for the participation of students before the local courts were approved by the Puerto Rico Supreme Court in March 1974 and by the U.S. District Court in 1991.

■ Student Exchange Programs

The law school has Student Exchange Programs with the University of Arizona College of Law and the University of Connecticut School of Law. Under these programs, the students will register at their home institution but will take a full courseload at the host institution. The credits and grades earned during a single semester will be awarded by the home institution according to the standard procedure of the home law school.

The law school also sponsors the UPR Summer Law Program at the University of Barcelona, Spain (June 28 to August 2, 1998).

There is a second program with the University of Barcelona. It is a four year program. Three years will be studied at the University of Puerto Rico, School of Law and one year will be abroad at the University of Barcelona. At the end of the four years, the students will receive the Juris Doctor and a degree of law from Barcelona.

■ Admission

➡ *Bachelor's degree from accredited college or university required*
➡ *application deadline—Feb. 16*   ➡ *LSAT, LSDAS required*
➡ *median PAEG—659*

The admissions procedure is absolutely nondiscriminating. There is no preference toward undergraduates from the University of Puerto Rico, nor toward men or women.

The University of Puerto Rico School of Law does not have a minority group breakdown since approximately 98 percent of our students are Puerto Rican, which would be considered a minority in stateside institutions, but certainly not in Puerto Rico. Racial composition is highly mixed due to the historical circumstances of the island.

Applicants must take the LSAT and the Prueba de Admision para Estudios Graduados (PAEG) no later than the year of application, and must complete their undergraduate degree before enrolling in the law school. The LSAT, the PAEG, and the graduating index are given the same weight.

The cases of applicants with disabilities, who, by reason of their disability cannot take the required aptitude tests, are considered individually by the Admissions Committee.

■ Expenses and Financial Aid

➡ *tuition & fees—full-time, $2,320; part-time, $1,570*
➡ *estimated additional expenses—$4,700 (books, room & board, & transportation)*   ➡ *performance- & need-based scholarships available*   ➡ *financial aid available*
➡ *FAF due April 15*

Resident law students pay tuition and fees amounting to $75 per credit each semester. Nonresident students who are American citizens pay the same amount that would be required from Puerto Rican students if they were to study in the state from which the nonresidents come, thus establishing a reciprocity principle.

Regular fees for medical services amount to $130 for the first semester and $165 for the second semester, which includes summer. The medical fee for the summer session only is $46.

Nonresident students—Nonresident students who are not American citizens pay tuition and fees amounting to $1,750 for eight or more credits for each semester. Regular fees for basic medical services amount to $115 for the first semester and $161 for the second semester, which includes summer.

All financial aid for the University of Puerto Rico is administered by the Office of Financial Aid, Dean of Students,

Rio Piedras Campus, University of Puerto Rico, San Juan, PR 00931. Each student is considered on his or her own merit and need. Awards are made only after an applicant has been admitted.

■ **Career Services**

Since 1981, the school has had an Office of Student Affairs under an assistant dean that offers a variety of services, including placement. The Placement Officer, with the aid of the Puerto Rico Bar Association, the Department of Justice, and other government agencies, helps students obtain part-time jobs, regular jobs, or scholarships.

The Office of Student Affairs has initiated a series of statistical studies on the school's graduates and will continue to do so. Among the school's alumni are a former Governor of Puerto Rico, the Secretary of Justice, Puerto Rico Supreme Court justices, and many cabinet members, judges, and legislators.

Applicant Group for the 1998-1999 Academic Year

University of Puerto Rico School of Law
This grid includes only applicants who earned 120-180 LSAT scores under standard administrations.

LSAT Score	3.75 +		3.50 - 3.74		3.25 - 3.49		3.00 - 3.24		2.75 - 2.99		2.50 -2.74		2.25 - 2.49		2.00 - 2.24		Below 2.00		No GPA		Total	
	Apps	Adm	Apps	Adm	Apps	Adm	Apps	Adm	Apps	Adm	Apps	Adm	Apps	Adm	Apps	Adm	Apps	Adm	Apps	Adm	Apps	Adm
175-180	0	0	0	0	0	0	0	0	0	0	0	0	0	0	0	0	0	0	0	0	0	0
170-174	0	0	1	1	1	1	0	0	0	0	0	0	0	0	0	0	0	0	0	0	2	2
165-169	0	0	0	0	1	1	0	0	0	0	0	0	0	0	0	0	0	0	0	0	1	1
160-164	1	1	0	0	1	1	0	0	1	1	1	1	1	1	0	0	0	0	0	0	5	5
155-159	4	4	1	1	2	1	1	1	1	1	1	1	0	0	2	0	0	0	0	0	12	9
150-154	9	9	10	10	9	8	6	4	3	3	1	1	4	1	1	0	0	0	1	0	44	36
145-149	12	12	11	8	17	11	23	15	11	5	13	1	6	0	1	0	3	0	4	0	101	52
140-144	11	11	16	12	31	19	41	4	18	0	23	1	9	0	3	0	5	0	2	0	159	47
135-139	12	8	22	5	34	1	31	0	26	0	24	0	11	0	7	0	3	0	9	0	179	14
130-134	17	1	20	0	31	0	37	0	35	0	25	0	12	0	7	0	3	0	3	0	190	1
125-129	2	0	10	0	12	0	17	0	22	0	17	0	9	0	3	0	0	0	11	0	103	0
120-124	0	0	1	0	5	0	4	0	8	0	3	0	3	0	1	0	0	0	5	0	30	0
Total	68	46	92	37	144	43	160	24	125	10	108	5	55	2	25	0	14	0	35	0	826	167

Apps = Number of Applicants
Adm = Number Admitted

Quinnipiac College School of Law

275 Mt. Carmel Avenue
Hamden, CT 06518-1948

E-Mail: ladm@quinnipiac.edu
URL: http://law.quinnipiac.edu/law.htm
Phone: 203.287.3400

■ Introduction

Dedicated in the fall of 1995, the new, award winning Quinnipiac College School of Law Center is located on the idyllic Hamden Campus of Quinnipiac College. Adjacent to a beautiful pond and across the road from Sleeping Giant State Park, the Law Center complex provides a modern, relaxed, and secure environment in which to study. The new Law Center is designed to provide a 21st-century facility for students and faculty. The center completes a Quinnipiac College quadrangle, which includes all of the major academic buildings on campus.

Quinnipiac is considered one of the most beautiful college campuses in New England. It offers a spacious 180-acre campus, yet it is only 90 minutes from New York and two-and-one-half-hours from Boston. Eight miles from metropolitan New Haven, students have easy access to the area's diverse resources. The area offers many excellent employment and residential opportunities as well as extensive cultural and recreational facilities.

■ Enrollment/Student Body

➡ 1,795 applicants   ➡ 937 admitted first-year class 1998   ➡ 261 enrolled first-year class 1998   ➡ full-time 25th/75th percentile GPA—2.52/3.19   ➡ part-time 25th/75th percentile GPA—2.49/3.08   ➡ full-time 25th/75th percentile LSAT—145/152   ➡ part-time 25th/75th percentile LSAT—144/150   ➡ 491 total full-time   ➡ 267 total part-time   ➡ 14% minority   ➡ 43% women   ➡ 22 states & foreign countries represented   ➡ 155 undergraduate schools represented

Traditionally, the fall class is taught in three sections, two day and one evening. The law school seeks to enroll 225 students in the fall and 25 students in January.

■ Faculty

➡ 82 total   ➡ 42 full-time   ➡ 40 part-time or adjunct   ➡ 30 women   ➡ 4 minority

Although the fundamental strength of the law school lies in the faculty's dedication to academic excellence, the rigors of its programs are tempered by the personal attention and individual regard that students receive. Indeed, the care with which members of the faculty demonstrate their interest in each student's progress and success is a distinguishing characteristic of Quinnipiac College School of Law.

In addition to teaching, members of the faculty devote considerable attention to scholarly research. Before joining the faculty, many enjoyed successful legal careers in a variety of areas including corporate, governmental, tax, and general practice.

■ Library and Physical Facilities

➡ 339,979 volumes & equivalents   ➡ library hours: Mon.-Thurs., 8:30 A.M.-11:00 P.M.; Fri.-Sat., 8:30 A.M.-9:00 P.M.; Sun., 10:00 A.M.-11:00 P.M.   ➡ LEXIS   ➡ NEXIS   ➡ WESTLAW   ➡ DIALOG   ➡ 6 full-time librarians   ➡ library seats 400

■ Curriculum

➡ 86 total units/credits required to graduate   ➡ 185 courses available   ➡ J.D. degree available (upon completion of 6 full-time or 8 part-time semesters)   ➡ semesters, start in Aug. & Jan.   ➡ range of first-year class size—15-65

The law school is fully accredited by the ABA, and is a member of AALS. Full-time students are admitted in the fall (day only), while part-time students are admitted in the fall and in the spring.

The first- and second-year curriculum is traditional and prescribed. There is flexibility within the electives scheme to allow students to fashion their own programs of concentration. A flex-time program is also possible. Concentrations include business and tax law, health care law, public interest law, and litigation. The J.D./M.B.A. and J.D./M.H.A. (Master in Health Care Administration) degree programs are also available. The law school sponsors a summer abroad program with Trinity College in Dublin, Ireland. It provides a comparative study of selected subjects in Irish and American law.

■ Special Programs

A total of nine clinical and externship programs are available to students after completion of their second semester. These programs represent tangible work experience to employers and often provide an important service to the community.

The four clinical programs are appellate, health care, civil, and tax. The five externship programs are Corporate Counsel, Public Interest, Legislative, Judicial, and Criminal Justice.

An Academic Support Program and a writing program are made available to students of the law school.

■ Admission

➡ Bachelor's degree required   ➡ LSAT, LSDAS required   ➡ application fee—$40   ➡ rolling admission, early application preferred   ➡ Pre-Admission Summer Program

Admission is based on a variety of factors—undergraduate scholastic record, scores on the Law School Admission Test, and other evidence such as advanced degrees, employment, experience, and extracurricular activities. Although the best indicator for performance in law school is past performance, this may be rebutted in certain cases when factors in the background of an individual, such as economic, cultural, and physical considerations, indicate that past performance may not be a reliable guide.

In the Pre-Admission Summer Program, students not admitted through the regular admissions process attend a small seven-week session taught by a full-time faculty member, applying normal standards to assess students' performance. Students who attain the acceptable grade are admitted to the regular part-time program. The offering of the Pre-Admission Summer Program is determined on a year-to-year basis.

Admission decisions are made by a faculty admissions committee which reviews every application. The law school places special emphasis on minority recruitment. Application fee waivers are available.

■ Student Activities

The Law School publishes *QLR (the Law Review)* two to four times a year. The journal is organized and edited by a board of student editors under the guidance of faculty advisors. The *Quinnipiac Health Law Journal* is also published at the school.

The *Quinnipiac Probate Law Journal* is the result of a cooperative effort with the Connecticut Probate Assembly that chose Quinnipiac, from the three law schools in the state, to produce it.

The Moot Court Board organizes an annual intramural moot court competition for entry onto the Board. The Moot Court Board edits briefs and supervises its own members as they participate in regional and national competitions. In the past, the Mock Trial Society competed in the National Association of Criminal Defense Lawyers Cathy G. Bennett Criminal Trial Competition, and won two of three Best Advocate awards.

Quinnipiac has a very active Student Bar Association, and students publish their own newspaper titled the *Quinnipiac Legal Times.* The law school has local chapters of three international professional law fraternities—Delta Theta Phi, Phi Delta Phi, and Phi Alpha Delta. In addition, it has chapters of BLSA, LALSA, Jewish Law Students' Association, and Law Women's Association.

■ Expenses and Financial Aid

➤ *tuition & fees—full-time, $19,992; part-time, $833/credit* ➤ *estimated additional expenses—Student Bar Association fee, $75; student fee, $370* ➤ *academic need-based scholarships available* ➤ *diversity scholarships available* ➤ *FAFSA & Quinnipiac Financial Aid application required* ➤ *work/study program*

In 1998-1999, approximately 85 percent of the student body receives some form of financial aid. Total scholarship funding exceeded $1 million.

■ Housing

There is ample, affordable housing available throughout Fairfield and New Haven counties. The School of Law Admissions Office and the Quinnipiac College Office of Residential Life assist in securing off-campus accommodations.

■ Career Services

The office assists students on an individual basis, as well as in workshops on topics such as writing résumés and cover letters, interviewing techniques, and other employment-related topics. It sponsors extensive on- and off-campus recruitment programs for summer internships as well as for permanent jobs. In addition, it holds career symposia to expose students to more diverse areas of work and to apprise them of employment trends.

Placement statistics attest to the success of the law school's students in the contemporary job market. A number of the law school's alumni/ae are judicial clerks, Justice Department attorneys, and associates in prestigious metropolitan firms.

Applicant Group for the 1998-1999 Academic Year

Quinnipiac College School of Law
This grid includes only applicants who earned 120-180 LSAT scores under standard administrations.

LSAT Score	3.75 +		3.50 - 3.74		3.25 - 3.49		3.00 - 3.24		2.75 - 2.99		2.50 - 2.74		2.25 - 2.49		2.00 - 2.24		Below 2.00		No GPA		Total	
	Apps	Adm	Apps	Adm	Apps	Adm	Apps	Adm	Apps	Adm	Apps	Adm	Apps	Adm	Apps	Adm	Apps	Adm	Apps	Adm	Apps	Adm
175-180	0	0	0	0	0	0	0	0	0	0	0	0	0	0	0	0	0	0	0	0	0	0
170-174	0	0	0	0	0	0	0	0	0	0	0	0	0	0	0	0	0	0	0	0	0	0
165-169	2	2	0	0	0	0	1	1	1	1	0	0	0	0	1	1	0	0	2	2	7	7
160-164	3	3	7	7	5	5	8	8	4	4	6	6	3	2	1	1	0	0	0	0	37	36
155-159	2	1	10	10	16	16	22	20	17	17	15	14	7	7	3	3	6	5	2	2	100	95
150-154	10	10	17	17	43	41	35	31	51	50	52	46	28	27	17	14	6	2	5	4	264	242
145-149	7	6	24	22	46	41	73	70	110	94	100	86	56	46	30	24	7	0	11	3	464	392
140-144	7	4	11	3	40	16	62	16	114	38	115	31	72	12	45	5	8	0	19	0	493	125
135-139	4	0	16	2	21	1	39	2	54	3	62	2	69	1	25	0	10	1	14	0	314	12
130-134	0	0	2	0	3	0	11	0	20	0	17	0	14	0	13	0	6	0	6	0	92	0
125-129	0	0	0	0	0	0	5	0	3	0	4	0	4	0	6	0	0	0	4	0	26	0
120-124	0	0	0	0	0	0	0	0	0	0	1	0	1	0	2	0	0	0	3	0	7	0
Total	35	26	87	61	174	120	256	148	374	207	372	185	254	95	143	48	43	8	66	11	1804	909

Apps = Number of Applicants
Adm = Number Admitted
This total number reflects dual applicants/accepts for the spring/fall terms (97% of the total applicant pool).

Regent University School of Law

1000 Regent University Drive
Virginia Beach, VA 23464-9880

E-Mail: lawschool@regent.edu
URL: http://www.regent.edu/acad/schlaw
Phone: 757.226.4584; Fax: 757.226.4139

■ Introduction

The School of Law is one of seven academic programs at Regent University, America's premier Christian graduate institution. The foremost objective of the School of Law is to train lawyers to participate effectively in a variety of legal careers in the private and public sectors. The School of Law, as well as other graduate programs at the university, is unique in that its mission includes the nurturing of students' Christian faith. In addition to the traditional legal education found at other ABA-approved schools, Regent provides students with the historical and biblical foundation and framework for our Anglo-American legal system.

Regent law students come from across the United States and bring to their legal studies a variety of personal, professional, and educational backgrounds. Law students develop strong and collegial relationships with one another as a result of their Christian commitment and concern for one another. Regent students have earned top honors in recent national negotiations competitions and for the quality of the school's *Law Review*.

The School of Law enjoys a special relationship with the American Center for Law and Justice, the nation's foremost religious-liberty, public interest organization. Typically, 10-12 Regent law students serve as externs with ACLJ each year. Located in the same facility as the law school, the ACLJ helps to develop legal strategies to defend life, liberty, and the family.

In addition to the J.D., the School of Law offers the nation's only ABA-approved online, graduate-level law degree. Focusing on international tax law, this LL.M. allows students the ability to load weekly online lectures and utilizes electronic chat rooms to communicate with faculty and fellow students.

Regent University is located on a beautiful campus in Virginia Beach, which is famed for its 28 miles of ocean and bay beaches. It is within an hour's drive from historic Yorktown, Jamestown, and Colonial Williamsburg and within four hours of Washington, DC, the Blue Ridge Mountains, and North Carolina's Outer Banks.

■ Enrollment/Student Body

➡ *406 applicants* ➡ *248 admitted first-year class 1998* ➡ *143 enrolled first-year class 1998* ➡ *full-time 25th/75th percentile GPA—2.64/3.50* ➡ *part-time 25th/75th percentile GPA—2.33/3.05* ➡ *full-time 25th/75th percentile LSAT—145/153* ➡ *part-time 25th/75th percentile LSAT—145/152* ➡ *14% minority* ➡ *50% women* ➡ *35 states & foreign countries represented* ➡ *105 undergraduate schools represented*

■ Faculty

➡ *58 total* ➡ *28 full-time* ➡ *30 part-time or adjunct* ➡ *25% of full-time faculty are of a minority background*

Adjunct faculty includes judges, private practitioners, and public prosecutors.

■ Library and Physical Facilities

➡ *300,000 volumes & equivalents* ➡ *library hours: Mon.-Fri., 7:30 A.M.-MIDNIGHT; Sat., 8:00 A.M.-MIDNIGHT* ➡ *LEXIS* ➡ *NEXIS* ➡ *WESTLAW* ➡ *DIALOG* ➡ *INFOTRAC* ➡ *FIRSTSEARCH* ➡ *Internet access* ➡ *LegalTrac* ➡ *CALI* ➡ *5 full-time librarians* ➡ *library seats 280*

The law school is located in Robertson Hall. Completed in 1993, this four-story, 143,000-square-foot building includes the latest technological equipment.

Robertson Hall is adjacent to the 150,000-square-foot university library which houses the law library on the third floor. The law library contains all the materials necessary for training students for the practice of law plus significant materials for advanced research in public policy and law.

■ Curriculum

➡ *90 units/credits required to graduate* ➡ *76 courses available* ➡ *International Human Rights Summer Program in Strasbourg, France* ➡ *degrees available: J.D.; J.D./M.B.A.; J.D./M.A. in Public Policy; J.D./M.A. in Management; J.D./M.A. in Communications; J.D./M.P.A.* ➡ *semesters, start in Aug.* ➡ *part-time program available* ➡ *range of first-year class size—50-75*

■ Externship Opportunities

In addition to the regular course offerings, students have the opportunity to receive academic credit through legal externships. A standing extern program has been established with the local U.S. Attorney's Office, Tidewater Legal Aid. Students may also seek approval for externships with judges, prosecutors, and public defenders.

■ Admission

➡ *Bachelor's degree required for admission* ➡ *priority application deadline—March 1; regular deadline—June 1* ➡ *LSAT, LSDAS required* ➡ *application fee—$40*

The law school admission committee assesses the qualifications of each applicant by examining his or her undergraduate record, LSAT score, any graduate study or work experience, the applicant's statement of goals, three recommendations and, in many cases, an interview. The committee further determines if the educational experience at Regent University will meet a mutually shared goal discerned by the committee and the student. A student must be willing to receive a legal education in accordance with the university's Community Life Form.

■ Student Activities

The *Regent University Law Review* provides a forum for a Christian perspective on law in a traditional legal periodical. Student editors and staff members, chosen on the basis of academic achievement and writing ability, gain valuable experience by writing and editing the *Law Review* under the guidance of the law faculty. Both the Moot Court Board and the Dispute Resolution and Client Counseling Board involve students in the professional skills program. These student-managed boards plan and prepare for intramural and national competitions.

In addition to an active student bar association, law students are involved in the American Inns of Court, the Grotius International Law Society, the Christian Legal Society, the Federalist Society, the American Center for Law and Justice, the Black Law Students Association (BLSA), the Rutherford Institute, the American Trial Lawyers Association (ATLA), and the American Bar Association. Other student-initiated groups include the Women's Legal Society and Law Wives. Law students also are involved in the university-wide Council of Graduate Students.

■ Expenses and Financial Aid

➡ *full-time tuition & fees—$15,840* ➡ *part-time tuition & fees—$12,870* ➡ *estimated additional expenses—$550 (books & supplies)* ➡ *scholarships available: performance- & need-based, as well as several institutionally funded scholarships and grants, & several named and endowed scholarships* ➡ *minority scholarships available* ➡ *financial aid application due March 1*

Regent University has one of the largest endowments for an institution of its size. Law students who have a demonstrated record of academic achievement, financial need, and/or who plan a career as a public interest attorney may qualify for financial assistance covering up to 100 percent of tuition. This past year, more than three-fourths of the first-year class received some form of financial aid from the School of Law and/or the university.

■ Career Services

The law school at Regent University has developed a three-year placement strategy including self-assessment, an investigation of career opportunities, and a specific career search. Workshops are conducted to assist students with résumé writing, interviews, and career selection. The Law Career Services Department offers both on-campus interviewing and a Non-Visiting Employers Program. Regent law students also participate in Virginia law school job fairs. The career services program has a national focus, with graduates employed in a variety of capacities including judicial clerks, criminal prosecutors, public interest attorneys, corporate counsel, and as partners and associates in firms across the nation.

Applicant Group for the 1998-1999 Academic Year

Regent University School of Law
This grid includes only applicants who earned 120-180 LSAT scores under standard administrations

LSAT Score	GPA								
	3.75 +	3.50 - 3.74	3.25 - 3.49	3.00 - 3.24	2.75 - 2.99	2.50 - 2.74	2.25 - 2.49	2.00 - 2.24	Below 2.50
175-180									
170-174									
165-169									
160-164									
155-159									
150-154									
145-149									
140-144									
135-139									
130-134									
125-129									
120-124									

■ Strong Possibility   □ Possible   ▨ Unlikely

This grid is intended to provide prospective applicants a general sense of our admission standards, as based upon competition for entry into the class entering in 1998. This grid does not adequately describe the numerous nonquantifiable factors that are considered by our Admission Committee. Prospective applicants are encouraged to review our admission materials for a fuller understanding of the admission-review standards used by Regent University School of Law.

University of Richmond School of Law

University of Richmond, VA 23173

E-Mail: admissions@uofrlaw.richmond.edu
URL: http://law.richmond.edu
Phone: 804.289.8189

■ Introduction

The University of Richmond School of Law, founded in 1870, enjoys an established reputation for preparing its graduates for legal careers throughout the U.S. Accredited by the ABA and a member of the AALS, its J.D. qualifies graduates to seek admission to the bar of all 50 states and the District of Columbia.

Situated on the university's beautiful suburban campus, the law school community thrives on the stimulation found only in such an academic setting. Yet, the campus is within a 20-minute drive of Richmond's pulsating legal community.

■ Enrollment/Student Body

➡ *1,305 applicants* ➡ *564 admitted first-year class 1998*
➡ *168 enrolled first-year class 1998* ➡ *full-time 25th/75th percentile GPA—2.73/3.41* ➡ *full-time 25th/75th percentile LSAT—153/158* ➡ *475 total full-time* ➡ *1 total part-time*
➡ *21% minority* ➡ *54% women* ➡ *44 states & foreign countries represented* ➡ *175 undergraduate schools represented*

■ Faculty

➡ *95 total* ➡ *27 full-time* ➡ *68 part-time or adjunct*
➡ *32 women* ➡ *5 minority*

■ Library and Physical Facilities

➡ *267,224 volumes & equivalents* ➡ *library hours: 105.5 per week—Mon.-Thurs., 7:30 A.M.-MIDNIGHT; Fri., 7:30 A.M.-9:00 P.M.; Sat., 9:00 A.M.-9:00 P.M.; Sun., 10:00 A.M.-MIDNIGHT* ➡ *LEXIS* ➡ *NEXIS*
➡ *WESTLAW* ➡ *VA Legislative Bill Service*
➡ *6 full-time librarians* ➡ *library seats 602*

The law school building provides technically-equipped classrooms, seminar rooms, a state-of-the-art law library, a magnificent courtroom, faculty offices, administrative offices, lounges, and offices for student organizations.

University of Richmond was the first law school in the country, in 1995, to require that entering first-year students own a laptop computer. Every student is assigned their own study carrel in our expansive law library. Each carrel consists of a desk with a sliding tray for a laptop computer and a secure storage area allowing students ready access to books and notes. These carrels are linked via students' personal computers to a school-wide computer system giving instant access to the electronic age in law.

■ Curriculum

➡ *clinical programs offered* ➡ *86 units/credits required to graduate* ➡ *111 courses available* ➡ *degrees available: J.D.; J.D./M.B.A.; J.D./M.U.R.P.; J.D./M.H.A.; J.D./M.S.W.*
➡ *range of first-year class size—80-84*

Courses in environmental law, contracts, torts, criminal law, procedure, property, and constitutional law comprise the first-year curriculum. Required upper-level courses include professional responsibility and a third-year writing seminar.

Elective courses in a variety of areas are available to satisfy each student's interests.

In addition, all students complete a program in legal reasoning, writing, research, and fundamental lawyering skills and values. In mock law offices, students interview and counsel clients, negotiate simulated transactions, and resolve legal disputes through trial and appeal.

■ International Program

You may choose to further your international studies through one of Richmond Law's study-abroad programs. The university has exchange relationships with more than 20 universities worldwide, nine of which have acclaimed law programs. Additionally, Richmond Law offers a summer program at Emmanuel College in Cambridge, England, and an exchange program with the University of Paris.

■ Special Programs

Several dual-degree programs are offered that allow students to earn the J.D. degree as well as a master's degree in a related discipline. Students can reduce the time and cost associated with obtaining two degrees while enjoying the study of two fields of interest. Dual-degree programs are available in Business Administration, Health Administration, Social Work, and Urban Studies and Planning.

The law school operates the Youth Advocacy, Mental Disabilities Clinics, and DC Summer Environmental Internship Program in which qualified third-year law students represent clients. These clinics are staffed by teaching, practicing attorneys who work together with students to represent clients in civil, criminal, and administrative proceedings. Students receive assistance in developing trial strategies and guidance in courtroom procedure while handling several court cases each semester.

The law school also arranges exciting clinical placements for academic credit in the nearby courts and law offices. Among the opportunities available are positions in various Commonwealth, city, and county attorneys' offices; the Virginia Attorney General's Office; the U.S. Attorney's Office; the ACLU; environmental organizations; and the Alternative Dispute Resolution Center.

■ Student Activities

A student board publishes *The University of Richmond Law Review* on a quarterly basis. The *Law Review* presents scholarly articles by professors, judges, attorneys, and students on matters of current interest in the law.

The *Richmond Journal of Law and Technology*, the first student edited scholarly journal to be published exclusively in electronic form, went online April 10, 1995.

Perspectives on Law and the Public Interest is a second online journal published by our students. This journal provides a forum for all who contemplate the issues that face the human community as it approaches the 21st century.

Richmond's moot court activities allow students to test their research, brief-writing, trial, and appellate advocacy skills. Students participate in intraschool tournaments that lead to membership on the Moot Court Board and on teams that represent the law school in regional and national competitions.

The Client Counseling and Negotiation Board organizes intra- and interschool competitions. It most recently hosted the National Environmental Negotiation Competition.

Other student organizations play a vital role in the law school community.

■ Admission

➡ *B.S./B.A. degree required for admission*
➡ *application deadline—Jan. 15*
➡ *LSAT, LSDAS required*   ➡ *application fee—$35*

Applications are reviewed as they become complete. All decisions are released by May 15. The undergraduate GPA and LSAT are two important items considered by the admissions committee, although the committee is also interested in extracurricular and community-service activities and employment experience. The law school provides an equal educational opportunity without regard to race, color, national origin, age, sex, handicap, or religion. The university practices reflect the belief that sexual orientation is a private matter, and, as such, it is not a relevant characteristic to consider in determining an individual's participation in the life of the university. The university has developed policies to protect all persons from various forms of harassment.

Admission conferences are available in November, December, and January. Although these conferences do not impact on the committee's decision, they are invaluable in providing information and answering questions. Class visits are encouraged. Law students are available to give tours and to speak with. Student representatives may be reached at LSAR@richmond.edu.

■ Expenses and Financial Aid

➡ *tuition & fees—full-time, $19,195; part-time, $960/credit hour*
➡ *estimated additional expenses—books, $900; room & board, $6,660; personal expenses, $1,665*   ➡ *merit- & need-based scholarships available*   ➡ *minority scholarships available*
➡ *financial aid available; FAFSA form & **university supplemental forms** are due to be **received** by Feb. 25*

John Marshall Scholars Program—The law school's most prestigious awards offer $10,000 annual stipends, as well as other honors, and are renewable annually if criteria is met. The general application must be **completed** by February 1. If invited to compete for these awards, a separate application must be submitted by March 10. Committee consideration for these scholarships is based solely on merit and personal attributes. Some applicants may be able to demonstrate the required attributes by having successfully overcome serious disadvantages or obstacles.

■ Career Services

The role of the Career Services Office is to serve law students and alumni in obtaining employment by helping develop the skills and the knowledge necessary to conduct successful job searches. In addition, the office provides opportunities for students to identify and explore career options. Employment opportunities for students and alumni are obtained and posted. The office organizes a comprehensive, on-campus interview program which includes law firms, government agencies, corporations and public-interest organizations. For the last several years, our graduates have reported an average of 95 percent employment within nine months of graduation. Of those seeking employment in the 1997 graduating class, 100 percent were employed within six months of graduation.

Applicant Group for the 1998-1999 Academic Year

University of Richmond School of Law
This grid includes only applicants who earned 120-180 LSAT scores under standard administrations.

LSAT Score	3.75 +		3.50 - 3.74		3.25 - 3.49		3.00 - 3.24		2.75 - 2.99		2.50 - 2.74		2.25 - 2.49		2.00 - 2.24		Below 2.00		No GPA		Total	
	Apps	Adm	Apps	Adm	Apps	Adm	Apps	Adm	Apps	Adm	Apps	Adm	Apps	Adm	Apps	Adm	Apps	Adm	Apps	Adm	Apps	Adm
175-180	0	0	0	0	0	0	0	0	0	0	0	0	0	0	0	0	0	0	0	0	0	0
170-174	0	0	1	1	2	2	2	2	1	1	0	0	1	1	1	0	0	0	0	0	8	7
165-169	0	0	4	4	4	4	11	11	7	7	6	6	3	3	1	0	0	0	1	1	37	36
160-164	10	10	25	25	34	32	28	27	25	24	19	18	7	6	9	9	0	0	1	1	158	152
155-159	21	21	24	24	67	57	65	53	56	42	37	25	16	13	5	2	4	0	1	1	296	238
150-154	17	14	31	20	67	16	78	18	72	10	32	10	20	5	7	0	3	0	6	1	333	94
145-149	2	0	20	4	39	5	40	5	49	5	36	5	17	3	9	0	5	0	2	2	219	29
140-144	3	0	11	0	12	0	26	0	37	1	26	0	20	0	7	0	1	0	3	0	146	1
135-139	1	0	3	1	3	0	6	0	6	0	12	0	6	0	8	0	1	0	5	0	51	1
130-134	0	0	1	0	3	0	3	0	7	0	4	0	2	0	2	0	1	0	2	0	25	0
125-129	0	0	0	0	1	0	1	0	3	0	0	0	1	0	1	0	0	0	1	0	8	0
120-124	0	0	0	0	0	0	0	0	1	0	0	0	0	0	0	0	0	0	0	0	1	0
Total	54	45	120	79	232	116	260	116	264	90	172	64	93	31	50	11	15	0	22	6	1282	558

Apps = Number of Applicants   Adm = Number Admitted   Reflects 98% of the total applicant pool.

Roger Williams University School of Law

Ten Metacom Avenue
Bristol, RI 02809

E-Mail: admissions@rwulaw.rwu.edu
URL: http://www.rwu.edu/law
Phone: 800.633.2727 or 401.254.4555

■ Introduction

Roger Williams University Ralph R. Papitto School of Law is located on a peninsula in the historic seacoast community of Bristol, Rhode Island, a small New England town providing an ideal place to study law. The School of Law is a private entity and the only law school in the state of Rhode Island. While the academic environment is challenging, a collegial atmosphere exists. As a small school, there is a strong sense of camaraderie among the students, and the faculty is both accessible and approachable.

■ Enrollment/Student Body

➡ *700 applicants*   ➡*114 matriculated first-year class 1998*
➡ *75 enrolled first-year full-time 1998*   ➡*39 enrolled first-year part-time 1998*   ➡ *full-time 25th/75th percentile GPA—2.64/3.42*   ➡ *part-time 25th/75th percentile GPA—2.83/3.43+*
➡ *full-time 25th/75th percentile LSAT—142/151*
➡ *part-time 25th/75th percentile LSAT—141/155*
➡ *10% minority first-year class 1998*   ➡ *44% women*
➡ *17 states represented*
➡ *134 undergraduate schools represented*

The LSAT median is 150 and the GPA median is 3.0.

■ Faculty

➡ *26 total full-time*   ➡ *28 adjunct*   ➡ *10 women*
➡*16 men*   ➡ *3 minority*

■ Library

➡ *220,000 volumes & equivalents*   ➡ *library hours:*
Mon.-Thur., 7:30 A.M.-MIDNIGHT; Fri., 7:30 A.M.-10:00 P.M.;
Sat., 9:00 A.M.-10:00 P.M.; Sun., 9:00 A.M.-MIDNIGHT
➡ *LEXIS*   ➡ *NEXIS*   ➡ *WESTLAW*   ➡ *DIALOG*
➡ *6 full-time librarians*   ➡ *library seats 380*
➡ *member, CRIARL (Consortium of RI Academic and Research Libraries)*

■ Physical Facilities

A new School of Law building, at a cost of $12 million, was opened in 1993. The state-of-the-art law school building features both an appellate and trial moot courtroom, law practice center including a mock law firm, class and seminar rooms, faculty offices, administrative suites, student services offices, café, post office, bookstore, copy center, and student organization offices. The school is conveniently located in the center of Rhode Island. Providence, the state's capital and legal center, is only 20 minutes away and offers employment and externship opportunities. The resort town of Newport is located close by and is the hub of significant cultural, sporting, and recreational events. Boston, Cape Cod, and the seasonal activities of New England are all in close proximity to Bristol.

■ Curriculum

➡ *90 credits required to graduate*   ➡ *degrees available:*
J.D.; J.D./M.C.P.; J.D./M.M.A.   ➡ *range of first-year class size—15-60*   ➡ *evening program available*
➡ *summer session available*   ➡ *Academic Advising Program*

The study of law at Roger Williams University School of Law features a combination of a rigorous core curriculum designed to instill in students fundamental lawyering knowledge and a comprehensive practical-skills training program.

Skills Training Curriculum—A significant aspect of Roger Williams University School of Law's curriculum is its comprehensive skills training program. To satisfy a complex society and ever-changing legal profession, practitioners must master not only traditional legal analysis, but also the ability to elicit and convey information. The School of Law has carefully planned a legal skills program which is designed to give the student, in a small-group setting, intensive training in the practical skills critical to lawyering. The four-semester Legal Methods program enables all students to develop the lawyering skills necessary to solve problems and communicate both orally and in writing. The program provides practical training in legal research and writing, appellate advocacy, interviewing and client counseling, and trial advocacy.

■ Special Programs

Established by a generous contribution, the Feinstein Institute for Legal Service has been designed to produce an enduring culture of public service whereby each entering student must complete 20 hours of volunteer community service prior to graduation.

The Louis Feinstein Legal Clinic in downtown Providence houses the School of Law's Family Law and Criminal Defense Clinics. Under the supervision of full-time faculty members, students represent low-income clients before various agencies and courts in a range of matters.

The Marine Affairs Institute, established in 1996, has a three-fold emphasis—traditional admiralty law and practice, environmental regulation, and the international law of the sea. The Institute also provides a forum for discussion through lectures, faculty exchanges, scholarly publications, and an annual symposium.

The law school operates two foreign summer-study programs, one in London in conjunction with the Inns of Court School of Law and the other in Lisbon in conjunction with the Catholic University of Portugal.

The Honors Program is an educational enrichment program featuring special seminars and classes as well as opportunities for faculty research assistantships and mentoring from members of the Rhode Island legal community. Participation is by invitation only, during the admission process, and strictly merit-based. A stipend is included.

■ Admission

→ *Bachelor's degree or equivalent required for admission*
→ *application deadline—May 15* → *LSAT, LSDAS required*
→ *application fee—$60* → *admission to fall term only*

Admission is competitive at Roger Williams University School of Law and is based on the undergraduate grade-point average and the Law School Admission Test (LSAT) score, as well as other indicators of probable success in the study of law such as: graduate degree, work experience, undergraduate extracurricular activities, and community services. All applicants must register with the Law School Data Assembly Service (LSDAS). Code: #3081.

Students are admitted only in the fall. Admission is offered on a rolling basis. Applicants improve their opportunity for favorable decisions by applying early. The deadline for admission is May 15. A personal statement and the $60 fee must accompany all applications. Letters of recommendation are not required, but will certainly be considered by the admission committee if submitted. Personal interviews are not part of the regular admission process. Multiple LSAT scores are averaged. Admission criteria are identical for both the regular and extended divisions.

■ Student Activities

Cocurricular Activities—*Law Review*—Membership on *Law Review* is considered one of the most valuable and prestigious of the student activities. *Roger Williams University Law Review* is staffed and primarily administered by students who are selected by their academic achievement and superior writing ability. This group publishes annual editions which consist of scholarly papers written by both students and members of the legal academic community.

Moot Court Honor Society—Moot Court Honor Society is comprised of students possessing superior appellate advocacy and writing ability. This prestigious organization sponsors speakers and programs on appellate advocacy, organizes an intraschool competition, and sends moot court teams to interschool competitions.

Extracurricular Activities—The School of Law recognizes the importance of extracurricular activities in law school life. Participation in such organizations enhances the curriculum and affords students valuable opportunities to refine skills and access information.

Although participation in extracurricular activities is voluntary, Roger Williams University School of Law students have chosen to become very involved. The students have formed many organizations, concentrating on both social and academic activities. The student governing body is the Student Bar Association (SBA), which is run by an executive board selected through schoolwide elections. The SBA has instituted several events including: Mentor/ Mentee program (between upper-class students and incoming first-year students); annual golf tournament and Barrister's Ball; Volunteer Income Tax Assistance Program; awards banquet; and an annual Spring Fling. Additionally, the SBA supports *The Docket*, which is the student newspaper. Students are eligible to become a student member of the American Bar Association—Law Schools Division.

■ Expenses and Financial Aid

→ *full-time tuition—$19,100* → *part-time tuition—$14,655*
→ *$635 per credit* → *Roger Williams University Law School Financial Aid Form and FAFSA required by April 30 for full consideration*

■ Career Services

Roger Williams University School of Law provides students with the most comprehensive career services available. The objective of the Career Services Office is to aid students in making career decisions and assist them in reaching their goals. Knowledgeable professionals help match the students' educational and experiential skills with employment opportunities on a national level.

Admission Profile Not Available

Rutgers—The State University—School of Law—Camden

406 Penn Street
Camden, NJ 08102

E-Mail: admissions@camlaw.rutgers.edu
URL: http://www-camlaw.rutgers.edu
Phone: 609.225.6102 or 800.466.7561; Fax: 609.225.6537

■ Introduction

Set against a center-city Philadelphia backdrop, Rutgers University's thriving 25 tree-lined acre urban campus in Camden, NJ is a handsome blend of converted Victorian buildings and newly constructed facilities. The School of Law shares the spacious campus mall with two undergraduate colleges, the Graduate School, and the School of Business. A member of the Association of American Law Schools, the school is included on the list of approved schools of the American Bar Association.

■ Enrollment/Student Body

➡ *1,444 applicants*   ➡ *716 admitted first-year class 1998*
➡ *267 enrolled first-year class 1998*   ➡ *full-time 25th/75th percentile GPA—2.87/3.39*   ➡ *part-time 25th/75th percentile GPA—2.70/3.27*   ➡ *full-time 25th/75th percentile LSAT—151/155*   ➡ *part-time 25th/75th percentile LSAT—150/157*
➡ *592 total full-time*   ➡ *159 total part-time*
➡ *18% minority*   ➡ *46% women*
➡ *31 states & 10 foreign countries represented*
➡ *230 undergraduate schools represented*

■ Faculty

➡ *41 full-time*   ➡ *57 part-time or adjunct*
➡ *11 full-time women*   ➡ *2 full-time minority*

The law school faculty is engaged in a dynamic program of scholarship, teaching, and service to the bar and community. Faculty scholarship has been cited by numerous courts, including the New Jersey and United States Supreme Courts. Faculty members also serve as consultants and reporters for the American Bar Association, the American Law Institute, and several federal and state commissions, and are counsel in important public interest litigation. Faculty members are engaged in innovative teaching enterprises to enhance the students' educational experiences.

■ Library and Physical Facilities

➡ *404,075 volumes & equivalents*   ➡ *library hours: Mon.-Thurs., 8:00 A.M.-MIDNIGHT; Fri., 8:00 A.M.-10:00 P.M.; Sat., 9:00 A.M.-5:00 P.M.; Sun., 10:00 A.M.-MIDNIGHT*
➡ *LEXIS*   ➡ *NEXIS*   ➡ *WESTLAW*
➡ *7 full-time librarians*   ➡ *library seats over 400*

Noted for its extensive collection of East European legal materials, the law library, with its especially broad holdings in government documents and legal periodicals, provides comprehensive research support for students and faculty. Students receive extensive training in the use of computers in legal research. A major renovation to the building for additional library space has been completed.

■ Curriculum

➡ *Academic Support Program*   ➡ *84 credits required to graduate*   ➡ *160 courses available; 87 upper-level courses available for 1998 academic year*   ➡ *degrees available:*
J.D./M.B.A.; J.D./M.A. (Pol. Sci.); J.D./M.C.R.P. (Urban Planning); J.D./M.P.A.; J.D./M.S.W.; J.D./M.D.; J.D./M.P.A. (Health Care Mgmt.)   ➡ *semesters, start in Aug. & Jan.*

The full-time program requires six semesters; the part-time day or evening program is completed in eight semesters, plus one summer session. Both programs are subject to the same admission and academic standards, and are taught by the same faculty. After the core curriculum is completed, students select their own courses. Courses in both Professional Responsibility and Introduction to Federal Income Taxation and the completion of three courses with significant writing components are required for graduation. The general curriculum prepares students for work in any jurisdiction of the United States.

■ Special Programs

The law school offers an unusually comprehensive range of courses including innovative courses in business, commercial, public interest, criminal, and family law. Central to the curriculum is the lawyering program that engages students in various issues that arise in the practice of law. Simulated lawyering activities are incorporated throughout the curriculum.

The Externship Program offers third-year students an opportunity to work in various federal and state judicial chambers, public agencies, or public interest organizations. Students in the in-house Civil Practice Clinic represent low income elderly and disabled clients and counsel small businesses.

The active pro bono program provides opportunities for students to represent clients in many areas including domestic violence and bankruptcy cases. Students may also serve as mediators in the alternative dispute resolution program of Camden Municipal Court.

The student-directed *Rutgers Law Journal* offers in-depth training in independent research and analysis of current legal problems. One issue of the journal each year is devoted to a symposium on state constitutional law.

The extensive moot court programs provide trial experience before panels of judges and practicing attorneys.

The law school, in conjunction with the Society for the Reform of Criminal Law, also publishes a refereed scholarly journal devoted to international and comparative criminal law, *The Criminal Law Forum*. The law school also offers a faculty and student exchange program with the University of Graz, Austria.

■ Admission

➡ *Baccalaureate degree required for admission*
➡ *application deadline—March 1*
➡ *LSAT, LSDAS required*   ➡ *application fee—$50*

Entering class size is approximately 230. A few places are available for applicants with advanced standing; transfer students may be admitted at the beginning of either semester only upon completion of one full year of law study. Occasionally, special qualities may overcome an applicant's lower numbers.

■ Student Activities

Among the numerous student organizations are the Hispanic Students Association, Asian/Pacific American Law Students Association, Association for Public Interest Law, Black Law Students Association, Christian Legal Society, Community Outreach Group, Environmental Law Students Association, Francis Deak International Law Society, Gay and Lesbian Students Association, Human Rights Group, Italian-American Law Students Organization, Jewish Law Students Association, Law Journal (publishes the *Rutgers Law Journal*), Phi Alpha Delta law fraternity, Pro Bono/Public Interest Steering Committee, and the Women's Law Caucus.

In addition, there are active intramural programs in various sports for men and women. The gymnasium offers recreational swimming, tennis, racquetball, squash, and basketball.

■ Expenses and Financial Aid

➡ *full-time tuition & fees—resident, $10,780; nonresident, $15,304*   ➡ *part-time tuition—resident, $401 per credit; nonresident, $591 per credit*
➡ *student fee—$236 per semester*   ➡ *scholarships available*
➡ *minority scholarships available*   ➡ *financial aid available; FAFSA form due March 1 for full consideration*

In the 1997-98 academic year, the Federal Direct Loan Program provided almost $9 million in financial aid to Rutgers law students. Additional money was distributed to students in the law school through grants, scholarships, and work study. The average financial aid package was $16,800, with 80 percent of the student body receiving some form of assistance.

■ Housing

The air-conditioned and carpeted residence hall has 62 apartments: 12 two-bedroom and 50 four-bedroom. There also are abundant housing opportunities in the nearby suburbs or in Philadelphia, made more convenient by an excellent transportation system. First-year admitted students are invited to utilize the law school's housing Web page and to attend Housing Day in the spring of each year.

■ Career Services

As a direct result of the quality of legal education at Rutgers, typically more than 95 percent of each year's class obtains employment in the legal profession within nine months of graduation. All major Philadelphia, New Jersey, and Delaware firms recruit from Rutgers, as do prestigious firms from New York City, California, and Washington, DC. In 1998, Rutgers ranked third in the nation in placing its law graduates in highly desirable state and federal judicial clerkships. The school's more than 6,000 alumni are leading members of the judiciary, government, and bar throughout this nation.

Applicant Group for the 1998-1999 Academic Year

Rutgers—The State University—School of Law—Camden
This grid includes only applicants who earned 120-180 LSAT scores under standard administrations.

LSAT Score	GPA																				
	3.75 +		3.50 - 3.74		3.25 - 3.49		3.00 - 3.24		2.75 - 2.99		2.50 - 2.74		2.25 - 2.49		2.00 - 2.24		Below 2.00		No GPA		Total	
	Apps	Adm	Apps	Adm	Apps	Adm	Apps	Adm	Apps	Adm	Apps	Adm	Apps	Adm	Apps	Adm	Apps	Adm	Apps	Adm	Apps	Adm
175-180	0	0	0	0	0	0	0	0	0	0	0	0	0	0	0	0	0	0	0	0	0	0
170-174	1	1	0	0	0	0	0	0	0	0	0	0	0	0	0	0	0	0	0	0	1	1
165-169	4	4	0	0	1	1	3	3	3	3	2	2	1	1	2	2	0	0	0	0	16	16
160-164	3	3	9	9	8	8	16	16	14	14	7	6	5	5	1	0	0	0	0	0	63	61
155-159	10	10	29	29	49	49	58	58	41	40	22	22	6	4	10	7	1	0	5	3	231	222
150-154	15	15	35	33	78	77	80	76	60	57	41	33	22	14	9	3	2	1	8	7	350	316
145-149	7	4	32	18	44	25	77	22	58	8	42	3	28	0	9	0	4	0	9	1	310	81
140-144	5	2	25	6	42	1	45	1	48	1	49	0	18	0	12	0	4	0	17	0	265	11
135-139	2	0	5	1	14	1	16	0	24	0	11	0	27	0	10	0	3	0	12	0	124	2
130-134	0	0	1	0	1	0	4	0	10	0	12	0	7	0	3	0	3	0	2	0	43	0
125-129	0	0	1	0	1	0	2	0	5	0	3	0	2	0	3	0	1	0	3	0	21	0
120-124	0	0	0	0	0	0	0	0	0	0	0	0	0	0	0	0	0	0	0	0	0	0
Total	47	39	137	96	238	162	301	176	263	123	189	66	116	24	59	12	18	1	56	11	1424	710

Apps = Number of Applicants
Adm = Number Admitted
Reflects 99% of the total applicant pool.

Rutgers University School of Law—Newark

S.I. Newhouse Center for Law & Justice
15 Washington Street
Newark, NJ 07102

E-Mail: geddis@andromeda.rutgers.edu
URL: http://info.rutgers.edu/RUSLN/rulnindx.html
Phone: 973.353.5557/4

■ Introduction

The Rutgers School of Law—Newark is the oldest law school in New Jersey. The School of Law is accredited by the American Bar Association and registered by the Board of Regents of New York. It has a chapter of the Order of the Coif.

The School of Law is located on the urban campus of Rutgers University in Newark. The social, cultural, vocational, and educational opportunities of the New York-Newark area combine to provide a fitting location for the study of law.

Qualities that typify the Rutgers School of Law—Newark include its informal atmosphere, its nationally recognized faculty, a comparatively favorable tuition, a public interest focus, and a very diverse student body. Almost 80 percent of the students are New Jersey residents, but all parts of the country are represented.

■ Enrollment/Student Body

➡ *2,059 applicants*   ➡ *686 admitted first-year class 1998*
➡ *213 enrolled first-year class 1998*   ➡ *full-time 25th/75th percentile GPA—2.88/3.42*   ➡ *part-time 25th/75th percentile GPA—2.93/3.32*   ➡ *full-time 25th/75th percentile LSAT—151/159*   ➡ *part-time 25th/75th percentile LSAT—152/159*
➡ *493 total full-time*   ➡ *195 total part-time*
➡ *31.9% minority*   ➡ *45.2% women*
➡ *16 states & 4 foreign countries represented*
➡ *120 undergraduate schools represented*

■ Faculty

➡ *46 full-time*   ➡ *27 part-time or adjunct*
➡ *12 women*   ➡ *10 minority*

■ Library and Physical Facilities

➡ *419,259 volumes (including 147,607 microform equivalents)*
➡ *library hours: Mon.-Fri., 8:00 A.M.-MIDNIGHT; Sat., 9:00 A.M.-MIDNIGHT; Sun., NOON-MIDNIGHT*   ➡ *LEXIS*
➡ *NEXIS*   ➡ *WESTLAW*   ➡ *CALI*
➡ *10 full-time librarians*   ➡ *12 support staff*
➡ *library seats 397*

The Justice Henry Ackerson Library has an extensive collection of primary and secondary legal materials and associated finding tools for the federal law of the United States and the law of all fifty states, international law, and the law of England. The library is a depository for federal and New Jersey government publications. A training program in WESTLAW and LEXIS automated legal research programs is offered to each student as part of the course in Legal Research and Writing I & II. Library includes student computer lab with 22 workstations.

■ Curriculum

➡ *Academic Support Program*   ➡ *84 credits required to graduate*   ➡ *research and teaching assistantships*

➡ *152 courses available*   ➡ *degrees available: J.D./M.A., Criminal Justice; J.D./M.C.R.P.; J.D./M.A. Pol. Sci.*
➡ *semester available in U. of Leiden, Holland*
➡ *semesters, start in Aug.*

Following the required courses, the law school allows the student substantial freedom in the selection of courses and seminars. During the four upper-class terms, approximately 200 class and seminar hours are available to satisfy the 53 credit-hours required.

Second- and third-year clinics include the Urban Legal Clinic, Constitutional Litigation Clinic, Women's Rights Clinic, Environmental Law Clinic, Animal Rights Clinic, Federal Tax Law Clinic, Special Ed Clinic, and Community Law Program.

Only limited summer courses are available. The first-year curriculum is prescribed except for one enrichment elective; the second and third years are fully elective.

A part-time program permits students to earn a J.D. degree in the evening over a four or four-and-one-half year period. Evening summer classes are available and are necessary for those students who wish to complete their program in four years. The summer after the first year is required.

The law school permits limited cross-registration with other Rutgers graduate programs, such as business, social work, sociology, economics, and political science. Law students may enroll in certain courses in these graduate schools and receive up to six credits toward the law degree.

With permission, upper-class students may engage in independent research projects under the supervision of a member of the faculty and may earn credit for work in the chambers of federal and state judges.

■ Admission

➡ *B.A. required for admission—in exceptional cases, 3/4 of B.A. acceptable*   ➡ *application deadline—March 15*
➡ *LSAT, LSDAS required*   ➡ *application fee—$50*

While factors other than undergraduate GPAs and LSAT scores are given significant weight in admissions decisions, applicants should be aware that approximately 10 applications are received for each seat. The mean scores of the classes entering in the last five years under the regular admissions program have been around a 3.3 GPA and the 80th percentile LSAT ranges.

There is a Minority Student Admission Program for minority and disadvantaged applicants. Minorities include Black/African, Asian, Hispanic, and Native Americans. Disadvantaged applicants include non-minorities who grew up as members of low-income families with a history of poverty or who can demonstrate that for other reasons they are educationally disadvantaged. The mean scores of persons entering under the Minority Student Program were around the 48th percentile range (LSAT), and 3.0 (GPA). Inquiries concerning this program should be directed to the Dean of the Minority Student Program.

LSAT scores older than three years from date of application to law school are not accepted. Applications received after March 15 have little prospect of favorable action. Applicants whose files do not contain all required documentation by June 1 will be denied admission. First-year students are accepted for classes commencing in the fall only. Transfer and visiting student applications are also accepted for the spring term, but only students with excellent law school records are accepted at any time.

Personal interviews are not a part of the admissions process, and applicants are requested not to seek them. Periodically during the academic year, the Director of Admissions conducts group meetings to answer questions of general interest and to explain admissions procedures. Any interested person should call the Office of Admissions to make an appointment for one of these meetings.

■ Student Activities

Publications—Students contribute to the *Rutgers Law Review*, the *Rutgers Journal of Computers, Technology and the Law*, the *Rutgers Race and the Law Review*, the *Rutgers Law Record*, and the *Women's Rights Law Reporter*.

Organizations—The variety of student-run organizations reflects the varied professional, political, social, and community interests of the student body. There are approximately 24 such organizations.

■ Expenses and Financial Aid

➧ *full-time tuition & fees—resident, $10,740; nonresident, $15,264* ➧ *part-time tuition & fees—resident, $401/credit hr., plus student fee of $452/year; nonresident, $592/credit hr., plus student fee of $452/year* ➧ *estimated additional expenses—$5,500-$12,000* (living expenses, books, travel, miscellaneous)
➧ *need-based & merit scholarships available*
➧ *Graduate Law Fellowships (1-year tuition)*
➧ *minority scholarships & Dean's scholarships*
➧ *Clyde Ferguson Scholarships* ➧ *Ralph Bunche Fellowships (full tuition and stipend)* ➧ *financial aid available; FAFSA and Rutgers Institutional Form (FA005) due March 1*

The school participates in the Direct Lending Program and administers an aid program for full-time and part-time students that integrates scholarships, loans, and college work-study based on the student's financial needs and the funds available. In most cases, students are expected to provide for most of their personal living expenses.

■ Housing

An eight-story university apartment complex offers 22 two-bedroom units and 66 four-bedroom units, as well as 10 apartments for married students of the graduate schools of Rutgers University in Newark. Other accommodations are available in the vicinity of the school, as well as in nearby suburban areas and New York City. Public transportation is readily available.

■ Career Services

The Office of Career Services provides information, job-hunting strategy training (including interview workshops and résumé review), and contacts, both direct (through on-campus interviews, résumé collection and job postings), and indirect (through lists, directories and alumnae/i records).

For the class of 1997, 97 percent of the graduates seeking employment obtained jobs within eight months of graduation.

Applicant Group for the 1998-1999 Academic Year

Rutgers University School of Law—Newark
This grid includes only applicants who earned 120-180 LSAT scores under standard administrations.

LSAT Score	3.75 +		3.50 - 3.74		3.25 - 3.49		3.00 - 3.24		2.75 - 2.99		2.50 - 2.74		2.25 - 2.49		2.00 - 2.24		Below 2.00		No GPA		Total	
	Apps	Adm	Apps	Adm	Apps	Adm	Apps	Adm	Apps	Adm	Apps	Adm	Apps	Adm	Apps	Adm	Apps	Adm	Apps	Adm	Apps	Adm
175-180	0	0	0	0	0	0	0	0	0	0	0	0	0	0	0	0	0	0	0	0	0	0
170-174	3	3	2	2	5	5	3	3	2	2	1	1	0	0	0	0	0	0	0	0	16	16
165-169	14	14	10	9	17	16	15	13	9	8	5	5	1	1	2	2	3	1	2	2	78	71
160-164	26	26	40	40	40	38	38	36	30	27	11	10	5	5	3	2	0	0	4	4	197	188
155-159	23	17	71	56	86	62	87	58	51	33	23	13	10	5	9	1	2	0	9	4	371	249
150-154	24	6	48	9	89	18	90	17	62	15	44	8	19	3	9	3	1	0	12	3	398	82
145-149	11	1	31	3	60	7	78	8	73	10	51	7	31	2	8	1	6	0	16	2	365	41
140-144	8	1	17	0	47	1	52	2	55	1	50	1	26	0	14	0	2	0	7	0	278	6
135-139	3	0	12	1	16	0	27	0	30	0	22	0	25	0	12	0	1	0	13	0	161	1
130-134	0	0	0	0	5	0	5	0	14	0	9	0	11	0	4	0	5	0	6	0	59	0
125-129	0	0	0	0	1	0	1	0	3	0	1	0	1	0	4	0	1	0	4	0	16	0
120-124	0	0	0	0	0	0	1	0	0	0	0	0	0	0	1	0	0	0	0	0	2	0
Total	112	68	231	120	366	147	397	137	329	96	217	45	129	16	66	9	21	1	73	15	1941	654

Apps = Number of Applicants
Adm = Number Admitted
Reflects 99% of the total applicant pool.

St. John's University School of Law

8000 Utopia Parkway
Jamaica, NY 11439

E-Mail: RSVP@SJUlaw.stjohns.edu
URL: http://www.stjohns.edu/law
Phone: 718.990.6611

■ Introduction

St. John's University School of Law is a forceful presence and an integral part of the New York metropolitan area. It imparts to its students training and competency in the basic skills and techniques of the legal profession, a grasp of the history and the system of common law, and a familiarity with important statutes and decisions in federal and state jurisdictions, including the state of New York.

The recently completed expansion of the law school produced a state-of-the-art facility with a gross total square footage of 179,400, one of the highest space per student ratios in the country. Some highlights of the new addition include expanded facilities for student activities, new alumni function areas, a student lounge, faculty offices, and classrooms for teaching clinical and lawyering skills.

The School of Law is located on the Queens Campus of St. John's University. Situated on almost 100 rolling acres in a residential area, the campus boasts a spectacular view of the Manhattan skyline. St. John's School of Law is approved by the ABA and is a member of the AALS.

■ Enrollment/Student Body

➥ 2,388 applicants   ➥ 1,173 admitted first-year class 1998
➥ 268 enrolled first-year class 1998   ➥ full-time 25th/75th percentile GPA—2.87/3.50   ➥ part-time 25th/ 75th percentile GPA—2.85/3.36   ➥ full-time 25th/75th percentile LSAT—151/158   ➥ part-time 25th/75th percentile LSAT—149/156
➥ 752 total full-time   ➥ 282 total part-time
➥ 23% minority   ➥ 39% women
➥ 110 undergraduate schools represented in 1998 entering class

■ Faculty

➥ 80 total   ➥ 53 full-time   ➥ 27 part-time or adjunct
➥ 11 full-time women   ➥ 5 full-time minority

■ Library and Physical Facilities

➥ 440,000 volumes & equivalents   ➥ library hours: Mon.-Fri., 7:30 A.M.-MIDNIGHT; Sat., 10:00 A.M.-8:00 P.M.; Sun., 12:00 NOON-11:00 P.M.   ➥ LEXIS   ➥ NEXIS
➥ WESTLAW   ➥ DIALOG   ➥ 7 full-time librarians
➥ library seats 607

The showpiece of the law school building is its beautiful new library which incorporates the most recent advances in law library science and technology. It contains a 22-terminal computer classroom, a 30-terminal computer laboratory, and eight study rooms for student conferences. The library occupies approximately 60,000 square feet on five of the seven building levels. It has been designated a depository library for U.S. government documents.

■ Curriculum

➥ Academic Support Program   ➥ 85 credits required for J.D. degree; 30 credits for LL.M. degree   ➥ over 150 courses available
➥ degrees available: J.D.; B.A./B.S. & J.D.; J.D./M.A.

Gov't. & Politics; M.B.A./J.D.; LL.M. in Bankruptcy
➥ semesters, start in Aug. & Jan.

■ Special Programs and LL.M. in Bankruptcy

An elective clinical program is available to second- and third-year full-time students.

In the Civil Clinical Seminar, students work 12 hours per week in (1) a legal services office assisting lawyers who provide legal representation to the poor; or (2) a public service or governmental agency such as the United States Attorney's Office, the Securities and Exchange Commission, and the New York Legal Aid Society.

In the Criminal Clinical Seminar, students work 12 hours per week in a District Attorney's office, a Legal Aid office, or in the law department of the Supreme Court or Criminal Court.

In the Judicial Clinical Seminar, students work 12 hours per week in the federal, state, or city court system.

The Estate Administration Clinical Component is offered in conjunction with the elective Estate Administration. Participants assist the Surrogate in nearby counties and receive practical insight into the functioning of the Surrogate's Court, which is responsible for the judicial administering of decedent's estates.

St. John's has started the nation's first master's program in bankruptcy. It is designed to meet an important and special educational need in the field of bankruptcy law. Matriculating students will be required to complete 30 credits, including the preparation and defense of a major thesis on a current significant bankruptcy topic. Students may matriculate on a full- or part-time basis. An Advisory Board, consisting of leading bankruptcy judges, practitioners, and insolvency professionals, will advise on the scope of the program and the course offerings.

■ Elder Law Clinic

This in-school, live client clinic allows students to represent actual clients in real cases under the close supervision of a faculty member. Students interview clients, draft pleadings and litigation papers, perform legal research, participate in discovery proceedings, prepare for trial, engage in settlement negotiations, and try cases, while honing skills such as decision making and office management. The three-credit per semester clinic is open to second- and third-year students who must enroll for a full academic year and devote a minimum of 15 hours per week.

■ Special Diversity Admissions Program

The law school sponsors a program for individuals who have suffered the effects of discrimination, chronic financial hardship, and/or other social, educational, or physical disadvantages to such an extent that their undergraduate performance or LSAT score would not otherwise warrant unconditional acceptance into the entering class. This program, which is available at no additional charge to the participants, consists of a substantive course taught and graded according to the same qualitative standard applied to all first-year courses, as well as a legal writing course. The program enables individuals whose LSAT score and/or GPA are not reliable predictors of their success to demonstrate that they have the ability to succeed in the study of law.

■ Admission Standards

➡ *Bachelor's degree required for J.D. program; J.D. degree required for LL.M. program*   ➡ *application deadlines— J.D.: March 1 & Nov. 1; LL.M.: June 1*
➡ *LSAT, LSDAS required*   ➡ *application fee—$50*

■ Student Activities

Publications—*St. John's Law Review, The Catholic Lawyer, Journal of Legal Commentary, International Law Review of the New York State Bar Association, American Bankruptcy Institute Law Review.*

Mock Trial and Appellate Activities—Moot Court, Criminal Law Institute, Civil Trial Institute.

Specialized Legal Activities—The Student Bar Association, Admiralty Law Society, Women's Law Association, Bankruptcy Law Society, Environmental Law Club, Entertainment and Sports Club, International Law Society, Intellectual Property, Labor and Employment Club, Real Property Club, the Black Law Students Association, the Asian American Law Students Association, the Latino American Law Students Association, and Client Counseling Competition. The school also maintains chapters in two legal societies, Phi Delta Phi and Phi Alpha Delta and the Black, Asian, and Latino Law Students Association.

■ Expenses and Financial Aid

➡ *tuition & fees—full-time, $22,000; part-time, $16,500*
➡ *scholarships available: St. Thomas More, University Scholarships, & Law School Scholarships*
➡ *diversity minority scholarships available*
➡ *financial aid available; FAFSA by April 1*

There are brand new dormitory facilities on campus and many students find other suitable living accommodations in the vicinity of the university. (A housing service, for all St. John's students is provided by the university's Office of Student Life.) In addition, the Admission Office coordinates a housing network for students. Students with housing needs are invited to contact the Admission Office for assistance and information. Average housing costs run approximately $600 per month.

■ Career Services

Career Services provides an array of services including résumé and cover letter critiquing, mock interview coaching, career job openings and judicial clerkships, newsletters, lists of prospective employers, interview programs, and career education panels. Recent graduates have obtained employment in many areas of the legal profession. Annually, 5 to 8 percent accept federal and state judicial clerkships.

Alumni of the School of Law are currently practicing throughout the United States and its territories. Many have achieved positions of prominence in executive and legislative branches of the government, as members of the judiciary, and in both private and corporate practice. The governor of the U.S. Virgin Islands, two recent governors of New York, and a former governor of California, and three of the seven judges on the NYS Court of Appeals are graduates of St. John's.

Applicant Group for the 1998-1999 Academic Year

St. John's University School of Law

LSAT Score	GPA								
	3.75 +	3.50 - 3.74	3.25 - 3.49	3.00 - 3.24	2.75 - 2.99	2.50 - 2.74	2.25 - 2.49	2.00 - 2.24	Below 2.00
175-180									
170-174									
165-169									
160-164									
155-159									
150-154									
145-149									
140-144									
135-139									
130-134									
125-129									
120-124									

Good Possibility   Possible   Unlikely

Saint Louis University School of Law

3700 Lindell Blvd.
St. Louis, MO 63108

E-Mail: admissions@lawlib.slu.edu
URL: http://lawlib.slu.edu/
Phone: 314.977.2800

■ Introduction

At Saint Louis University School of Law, you will find a unique character and atmosphere that are the result of a number of factors, including Jesuit institutional traditions and goals, the law faculty and students, and the quality of life in a thriving midwestern city. The School of Law is known for its open and friendly atmosphere, for the rapport among students and between students and faculty, and for its inviting physical plant. It is located on the main campus of Saint Louis University in midtown. The campus is just a block from the Fox Theatre and Powell Symphony Hall, just minutes from St. Louis Union Station, the Arch, the riverfront, and downtown. There is a wide choice of affordable rental housing for students in the neighborhoods around the university. St. Louis offers the amenities of urban living without the inconveniences and high costs normally associated with living in a major metropolitan area.

■ Enrollment/Student Body

➥ *995 applicants*   ➥ *613 admitted first-year class 1998*
➥ *248 enrolled first-year class 1998*   ➥ *full-time 25th/75th percentile GPA—3.00/3.60*   ➥ *part-time 25th/75th percentile GPA—2.77/3.41*   ➥ *full-time 25th/75th percentile LSAT—150/157*   ➥ *part-time 25th/75th percentile LSAT—148/156*
➥ *563 total full-time*   ➥ *261 total part-time*
➥ *15% minority*   ➥ *46% women*
➥ *43 states & foreign countries represented*
➥ *125 undergraduate schools represented*

■ Faculty

➥ *54 total*   ➥ *39 full-time*   ➥ *15 part-time or adjunct*
➥ *10 women*   ➥ *4 minority*

The offices of individual faculty members are located in the law library, and all classrooms, administrative offices, and clinical facilities are housed within this same building complex for convenience and collegiality.

■ Library and Physical Facilities

➥ *530,000 volumes & equivalents*   ➥ *library hours: Mon.-Thurs., 9:00 A.M.-MIDNIGHT; Fri., 8:00 A.M.-11:00 P.M.; Sat., 9:00 A.M.-8:00 P.M.; Sun., 10:00 A.M.-MIDNIGHT*
➥ *LEXIS*   ➥ *NEXIS*   ➥ *WESTLAW*   ➥ *DIALOG*
➥ *9 full-time librarians*   ➥ *library seats 437*

■ Curriculum

➥ *Academic Support Program*   ➥ *88 credits required to graduate*   ➥ *100+ courses available*   ➥ *degrees available: J.D.; J.D./M.B.A.; J.D./M.H.A.; J.D./M.U.A.; J.D./M.S.W.; J.D./M.P.H.; others as requested*   ➥ *semesters, start in Aug.*
➥ *range of first-year class size—30-90*

A cumulative grade-point average (GPA) of 2.0 is required to earn the J.D. degree. The part-time program of legal education involves the same degree of academic quality and rigor, and the same admissions standards in evaluating applicants, as the full-time program. The same faculty members are involved in teaching both the full- and part-time programs.

The school has gained national recognition in the areas of health law, lawyering skills, employment law, and international law.

■ Special Programs

The Center for Health Law Studies—The Center's faculty work closely with Saint Louis University's School of Medicine, School of Nursing, School of Allied Health Professions, Graduate Department of Hospital and Health Care Administration, and the Medical Center.

The school's health law program is unique in that there are seven full-time faculty members teaching in the health law area. Its endowed library collection in health law provides an outstanding research facility. Many special programs are offered throughout the year to bring students information about the many opportunities in health law. Saint Louis University health law alumni are particularly helpful in this area.

The Center for International and Comparative Law—The strength of the international law program at Saint Louis University School of Law is a result of the combination of curricular and extracurricular offerings, permanent and visiting faculty, and a strong library collection.

The school also has developed cooperative agreements with Sichuan University in Chengdu, People's Republic of China, and the University of Warsaw.

To complement the course offerings in international law, the school has a number of special study opportunities in European countries. Through the Brussels Seminar and the Ruhr University Exchange Program, the school offers its qualified students four to five weeks of high quality instruction in Europe, at no charge for tuition and accommodations.

The Center for Employment Law—The center offers interested students an opportunity to specialize in the subject of the employment relationship as a unifying thread for their study of law.

■ Admission

➥ *Bachelor's degree required*   ➥ *preferential application deadline—March 1*   ➥ *LSAT, LSDAS required*
➥ *application fee—$40*

Factors considered by the committee in addition to the GPA and LSAT score are strength of the undergraduate program, work experience, any extraordinary circumstances that may have affected a student's performance in college, and motivation.

There are 175 spaces available for full-time students and 65 spaces available for part-time students in the fall entering class.

The admissions committee is composed of the Assistant Dean for Admissions, three faculty members, and three law students. The committee uses an admission index in preliminary evaluations of applicants. With the exception of those applications whose index falls in a clearly defined upper or lower percentile and whose application is reviewed by the assistant dean and the faculty committee chair, the committee reviews the entire application of each applicant. No action is taken without the consensus of the committee.

The School of Law is committed to increasing the number of minorities in the legal profession. Accordingly, the School of Law actively seeks applications from qualified minorities.

A special admissions program is conducted each summer at the School of Law. The Summer Institute is designed to identify students who have suffered the effects of cultural or racial discrimination, cultural deprivation, or economic or other disadvantages to such an extent that their undergraduate work or performance on standardized tests is affected.

■ Student Activities

Student organizations play a vital role in meeting the many special interests of the student body. Programs and publications sponsored by these organizations add considerable depth to the overall program.

■ Expenses and Financial Aid

➤ *tuition & fees—full-time, $19,170; part-time, $14,360/$872*
➤ *estimated additional expenses—$8,000 (includes room & board)*
➤ *academic merit scholarships to 50% of class*
➤ *financial aid available; FAFSA required*

The majority of law students receive some form of financial assistance. Most awards are need-based, with the exception of the academic scholarships and grants administered directly by the School of Law.

■ Career Services

The Career Planning and Placement Office is designed to assist students, alumni, and employers. Students and alumni are welcome to utilize the services of the office throughout their academic and legal careers. These services include career counseling, assistance in developing résumés and letters, access to job postings, an alumni job bulletin, assistance in the job search in other geographic areas, and on-campus interviews for current students. The office houses a career library which has information on a wide range of employers and career choices, including government job bulletins, books, and brochures on a variety of practice areas and placement bulletins from law schools throughout the United States. The office lists positions for student clerks, summer positions, full-time positions for recent graduates, and positions for attorneys with experience. In order to assist students in finding additional information about employers, the LEXIS, NEXIS, and WESTLAW computer research services are also available in the Career Library.

The distribution of graduates by types of employment is comparable to that of many law schools. Approximately 70 percent of the graduates enter private practice. Within six months of graduation, 92.3 percent of the class is employed, with salaries ranging from $24,000 to $80,000. Although there are alumni practicing in all 50 states and several foreign countries, the majority are practicing in the midwest region, especially in the states of Illinois and Missouri.

Applicant Group for the 1998-1999 Academic Year

Saint Louis University School of Law

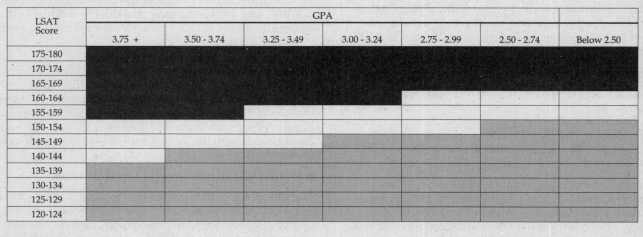

LSAT Score	GPA						
	3.75 +	3.50 - 3.74	3.25 - 3.49	3.00 - 3.24	2.75 - 2.99	2.50 - 2.74	Below 2.50
175-180							
170-174							
165-169							
160-164							
155-159							
150-154							
145-149							
140-144							
135-139							
130-134							
125-129							
120-124							

Likely   Possible   Unlikely

St. Mary's University School of Law

One Camino Santa Maria
San Antonio, TX 78228-8601

Phone: 210.436.3523

■ Introduction

St. Mary's University School of Law, founded in San Antonio, Texas in 1927, is maintaining its strength as an institution that offers a solid curriculum of traditional legal studies and teaches its students the practical skills and habits of mind that enable them to become effective advocates. As part of a Catholic institution founded by the Society of Mary (Marianists), the mission of the law school is to give its students the knowledge and attributes of mind and character essential to the effective rendition of public service, while developing new methodologies to prepare students for the practice of law in a changing world. St. Mary's University School of Law was the recipient of the 1996-97 ABA Public Interest Award.

■ Enrollment/Student Body

➤ 1,094 applicants ➤ 665 admitted first-year class 1998 ➤ 269 enrolled first-year class 1998 ➤ full-time 25th/75th percentile GPA—2.61/3.12 ➤ full-time 25th/75th percentile LSAT—146/152 ➤ 733 total full-time ➤ 45% minority ➤ 50% women ➤ 22 states & foreign countries represented ➤ 61 undergraduate schools represented

■ Faculty

➤ 79 total ➤ 36 full-time ➤ 43 part-time or adjunct ➤ 10 women ➤ 11 minority

■ Library and Physical Facilities

➤ 320,000 volumes & equivalents ➤ library hours: Mon.-Thurs., 7:00 A.M.-MIDNIGHT; Fri., 7:00 A.M.-10:00 P.M.; Sat., 9:00 A.M.-10:00 P.M.; Sun., 10:00 A.M.-MIDNIGHT ➤ LEXIS ➤ NEXIS ➤ WESTLAW ➤ DIALOG ➤ 8 full-time librarians ➤ library seats 446

The Sarita Kennedy East Law Library is a modern, recently constructed, award-winning building. The collection includes legal documents from the United Nations that provide access to American, British, Canadian, and International law.

■ Curriculum

➤ Academic Support Program ➤ 90 credits required to graduate ➤ 145 courses available ➤ degrees available: J.D.; J.D./M.B.A.; J.D./M.P.A.; J.D./EC.; J.D./IR.; J.D./TH.; J.D./ Engineering; J.D./Justice Administration; J.D./Computer Science ➤ semesters, start in Aug. ➤ range of first-year class size—90 students in each of 3 sections

Required first-year courses are Constitutional Law, Contracts, Criminal Law, Legal Research and Writing, Procedure I, Property, and Torts. In addition to other electives, all students must take the following required courses: Professional Responsibility; Evidence; Texas Civil Procedure; and one course chosen from Jurisprudence, American Legal History, Legal Philosophy, or Law and Economics, and complete one research paper. Texas Civil Procedure is only required of those planning to take the Texas bar examination.

■ Clinical Legal Education

The Civil Justice Clinic introduces students to the skills and responsibilities of lawyering through supervised representation of low-income, including homeless, clients in four areas of civil law cases: family law, public benefits, landlord-tenant disputes, and wills and probate.

The Criminal Justice Clinic provides legal services to indigents of all ages who are charged with crimes ranging from misdemeanors to capital offenses.

The Immigration Rights Clinic engages students in the representation of indigent foreign nationals in a variety of immigration cases. The Human Rights Clinic works on cases and projects involving violations of internationally protected human rights.

The Community Development Clinic involves students in capacity-building economic development activities in San Antonio and the colonias of South Texas.

■ International Law

The St. Mary's Institute on World Legal Problems is conducted at the University of Innsbruck in Austria during July and August. The program is designed to provide law students with a broader understanding of global issues and the role that law can play in their peaceful resolution.

Other international programs include: Centre for Conciliation and Arbitration; Institute on International Human Rights; Abogados de las Americas; Center for International Legal Studies; Inter-American Legal Studies Program; and two LL.M. programs: international and comparative law and American legal studies for foreign students.

Visiting lecturers have included the Honorable William H. Rehnquist, Chief Justice of the United States, during the 1991 and 1994 Institutes, and the Honorable Ruth Bader Ginsburg, Distinguished Visiting Lecturer, (1995).

■ Judicial Internships

St. Mary's students are eligible to apply for an internship with the Supreme Court of Texas, where they work under the supervision of a justice, preparing memoranda and making oral presentations in conferences with the Court. Similar programs exist with the Texas Court of Criminal Appeals and with the Texas Court of Appeals, both located in Austin, Texas.

■ Center for International Legal Studies

The Center for International Legal Studies was established as part of the law school's strategic plan for the development of a strong concentration in international and comparative law, particularly the law of the Americas. The center's Foreign Visiting Scholars program has attracted legal scholars from several other nations, including Nigeria, Russia, and Mexico.

■ Admission Standards

➡ *Bachelor's degree required* ➡ *application deadline—March 1* ➡ *LSAT, LSDAS required*
➡ *application fee—$45*

St. Mary's goal is to create an intellectually stimulating student body comprised of persons with diverse backgrounds who share a desire for academic excellence and accomplishment in the practice of law. In addition to academic ability, we seek evidence of qualities such as leadership ability, maturity, community organization skills, knowledge of other languages and cultures, a history of overcoming disadvantage, public interest accomplishments, or success in a previous career. Participants in the CLEO program are especially encouraged to apply. A faculty committee reviews all applications. No one is automatically rejected. All files are read.

■ Student Activities

Student organizations include the American Civil Liberties Union; Asian-Pacific American Law Student Association; Black Allied Law Students Association; Board of Advocates; Christian Legal Society; Criminal Law Association; Delta Alpha Delta; Delta Theta Phi; Environmental Law Society; Family Law Association; Federalist Society; Harlan Society; Hispanic Law Students Association; International Law Association; Jewish Law Students Association; Legal Education Association for Gay and Lesbian Issues; Native American Law Students Association; Law Student Division, San Antonio Bar Association; Phi Alpha Delta; Phi Delta Phi; Public Interest Law Association; Republican Law Students Association; Society of Legal Entrepreneurs; Sports and Entertainment and Arts Law; *St. Mary's Law Journal*; St. Thomas More Society; Student Aggie Bar Association; Student Bar Association; William Sessions American Inn of Court; and Women's Law Association.

■ Expenses and Financial Aid

➡ *tuition & fees—$545/credit hr.* ➡ *student service fee—$86*
➡ *University Center fee—$20* ➡ *parking fee—$30*
➡ *performance- & need-based scholarships available*
➡ *donated funds may be earmarked for minority scholarships*
➡ *financial aid available; financial aid forms must be filed with the University Office of Financial Assistance between Jan. 1 and April 1 of the year for which student is enrolling*

■ Career Services

The Office of Career Services is under the direction of an associate dean with 10 years of recruiting experience on a hiring committee in a major law firm. The mission of the office is to provide personal, individualized assistance to all students as they seek employment during and after law school. Confidential strategy sessions provide a unique opportunity for students to develop a personal plan to assess and meet their career goals. The office publishes a weekly job newsletter for students, and a monthly job newsletter for graduates. The office's Student Résumé Center offers an extensive and up-to-date library of career resources and directories of attorneys, as well as computer terminals with employer databases to help students direct and begin their careers in legal and nontraditional positions. A diverse and active alumni association offers mentors and career programs throughout the year.

For the class of 1997, who reported employment status, over 77 percent were employed in a legal job.

Applicant Group for the 1998-1999 Academic Year

St. Mary's University School of Law
This grid includes only applicants who earned 120-180 LSAT scores under standard administrations.

LSAT Score	GPA																							
	3.75 +		3.50 - 3.74		3.25 - 3.49		3.00 - 3.24		2.75 - 2.99		2.50 - 2.74		2.25 - 2.49		2.00 - 2.24		Below 2.00		No GPA		Total	
	Apps	Adm	Apps	Adm	Apps	Adm	Apps	Adm	Apps	Adm	Apps	Adm	Apps	Adm	Apps	Adm	Apps	Adm	Apps	Adm	Apps	Adm
175-180	0	0	0	0	0	0	0	0	0	0	0	0	0	0	0	0	0	0	0	0	0	0
170-174	0	0	0	0	1	1	0	0	0	0	0	0	0	0	0	0	0	0	0	0	1	1
165-169	0	0	0	0	0	0	1	1	0	0	2	2	0	0	0	0	0	0	0	0	3	3
160-164	2	2	2	2	4	4	12	12	2	2	3	3	2	2	1	1	0	0	1	0	29	28
155-159	3	3	13	13	12	12	30	30	26	26	13	13	8	8	4	3	1	0	1	0	111	108
150-154	6	6	21	21	29	29	53	53	52	49	41	40	26	24	14	12	1	1	1	1	244	236
145-149	7	7	21	20	40	34	58	49	63	49	54	44	30	17	14	7	3	1	3	0	293	228
140-144	2	0	12	4	25	4	43	9	51	13	55	11	28	5	16	1	2	0	4	0	238	47
135-139	0	0	3	0	10	1	27	2	17	3	24	2	14	1	12	0	3	0	5	0	115	9
130-134	1	0	0	0	1	0	5	0	4	0	10	0	6	0	6	0	2	0	1	0	36	0
125-129	0	0	0	0	0	0	0	0	1	0	1	0	4	0	3	0	1	0	0	0	10	0
120-124	0	0	0	0	0	0	0	0	0	0	0	0	0	0	0	0	0	0	0	0	0	0
Total	21	18	72	60	122	85	229	156	216	142	203	115	118	57	70	24	13	2	16	1	1080	660

Apps = Number of Applicants (Reflects 99% of the total applicant pool.)
Adm = Number Admitted

St. Thomas University School of Law

16400 NW 32nd Avenue
Miami, FL 33054

E-Mail: admitme@stu.edu
URL: http://www.stu.edu/lawschool/lawmain.htm
Phone: 305.623.2310

■ Introduction

St. Thomas University School of Law, founded in 1984, is one of the newest and most technologically-oriented law schools in the country. The only Catholic law school in the Southeastern United States, St. Thomas emphasizes professional ethics throughout its programs, provides intensive academic support on an individual and small-group basis, and offers a broad curriculum, including an array of clinical experiences.

St. Thomas University is located on a 140-acre campus in northwest suburban Miami. Fifteen miles southeast in downtown Miami stands the new federal courthouse, the location of the United States District Court for the Southern District of Florida. State trial and appellate courts are several blocks away. Approximately 20 miles to the north of the law school is the city of Ft. Lauderdale, another venue for state trial and appellate courts.

■ Enrollment/Student Body

➼ *1,835 applicants* ➼ *1,308 admitted first-year class 1998*
➼ *170 enrolled first-year class 1998* ➼ *full-time 25th/75th percentile GPA—2.36/3.03* ➼ *full-time 25th/75th percentile LSAT—145/151* ➼ *487 total full-time* ➼ *41.8% minority*
➼ *39.6% women* ➼ *15 states & foreign countries represented*
➼ *107 undergraduate schools represented*

■ Faculty

➼ *59 total* ➼ *22 full-time* ➼ *37 part-time or adjunct*
➼ *8 women* ➼ *7 minority*

■ Library and Physical Facilities

➼ *287,385 volumes & equivalents* ➼ *library hours: Mon.-Thurs., 8:00 A.M.-MIDNIGHT; Fri., 8:00 A.M.-10:00 P.M.; Sat., 9:00 A.M.-9:00 P.M.; Sun., 9:00 A.M.-MIDNIGHT*
➼ *LEXIS* ➼ *NEXIS* ➼ *WESTLAW*
➼ *6 full-time librarians, 9 full-time support staff*
➼ *library seats 313, study rooms available*
➼ *computer lab and other locations with 65+ PCs & printers*

■ Curriculum

➼ *Academic Support Program* ➼ *90 credits required to graduate* ➼ *over 100 courses available*
➼ *J.D. degree available* ➼ *semesters, start in Aug.*

The curriculum of the School of Law covers a period of three academic years. The first-year curriculum is fully prescribed, while the second-year curriculum is partially prescribed, with third-year courses being electives.

■ Clinical Legal Education Programs

St. Thomas University School of Law has four clinical programs. Three—the Field Placement Clinic, the Immigration Clinic, and the Appellate Litigation Clinic—are year-long programs for which third-year students receive eight hours of credit. The Family Court Clinic is offered for one semester with three hours of credit. Each clinic also has a weekly classroom component. In the **Family Court Clinic**, students learn the inner workings and explore the basis for family court matters in Florida. Students will work in the Family Court Self-Help Unit interviewing *pro se* litigants and *pro se* documents filed with the court.

The Field Placement Clinic involves 20 students working as interns in public defender, states attorneys, city and county attorneys, and Legal Services offices. Supervising attorneys are assigned by the offices involved and general supervision, including a classroom component, is provided by a full-time, tenure-track professor. Many students in this clinic try cases or participate in trials conducted by the supervising attorneys.

In the **Immigration Clinic**, students, under the supervision of an experienced faculty member, represent indigent immigrants detained at a federal facility in deportation and exclusion hearings and other immigration matters before immigration judges.

In the **Appellate Litigation Clinic**, which also has offices at the law school, students represent indigents in appellate cases before courts of appeals under the supervision of a tenure-track faculty member. The students brief and argue the cases on appeal.

In the **Peter T. Fay American Inn of Court at St. Thomas**, the first of its kind in South Florida, students are able to interact professionally with distinguished members of the local bench and bar.

Street Law is a two-hour-per-week course in which law students teach local high school students in areas of the law of practical importance in the daily lives of community members. Selected topics include consumer, housing, and constitutional law, as well as criminal law and procedure.

The **St. Thomas Public Service Fellowship Program**, sponsored by the Florida Bar Foundation Interest on Trust Accounts program, places selected law students in various public service agencies where they provide legal assistance to indigents under the supervision and direction of attorneys working in the agencies involved. The fellows are paid for their work and receive no course credit.

Legal Assistance Wednesday, L.A.W., is a pro bono program sponsored by St. Thomas University School of Law and Greater Bethel A.M.E. Church, with additional support from the Florida Bar Foundation. Every Wednesday, students and attorneys volunteer their time to provide legal assistance and representation to members of the community who cannot afford legal counsel.

■ Admission

➼ *Bachelor's degree required*
➼ *application deadline—April 30, early application preferred*
➼ *LSAT, LSDAS required* ➼ *application fee—$40*

Applicants must possess a bachelor's degree from a regionally accredited college or university. While no particular program of prelaw study is required, the undergraduate transcript should reflect a strong aptitude for study in a challenging academic field. The School of Law does not discriminate on the basis of sex, age, race, color, disability, religion, sexual orientation, or national origin in its educational programs, admission policies, employment policies, financial aid, or other school-administered programs. The School of Law is committed to a policy of enhancing the diversity of its student body and encouraging applications for admission from members of all minority groups.

In determining which applicants will be accepted for admission, the Admissions Committee will look for both demonstrated academic ability and diversity of background. Consideration will be given to a variety of factors beyond the Law School Admission Test score and the undergraduate grade-point average. Those factors include work experience, honors or awards, extracurricular activities, a strong letter of recommendation from an instructor or someone familiar with the applicant's academic abilities, and ethnic diversity.

■ Student Activities

The *St. Thomas Law Review* is a student-operated scholarly journal publishing articles submitted by law faculty and members of the bench and bar nationwide. Membership is determined on the basis of academic excellence and/or demonstrated writing ability.

The student-operated Student Bar Association is active in matters concerning law students and in selecting representative student members to serve on faculty committees. Numerous student organizations are active on campus, and students publish the newspaper, *Opinio Juris*.

■ Expenses and Financial Aid

➡ *full-time tuition & fees—$19,975*
➡ *estimated additional expenses—$11,325 (books & supplies, $800; room & board, $7,300; transportation, $1,425; personal expenses, $1,800)*   ➡ *scholarships available*
➡ *financial aid available; FAFSA due April 15 (priority)*

The awarding of financial aid is administered by the University Financial Aid Office. Inquiries regarding financial aid programs should be directed to the University Financial Aid Office, St. Thomas University, 16400 NW 32nd Avenue, Miami, FL 33054, or call 305.628.6547.

■ Career Services

The Career Services Office is dedicated to assisting law students in articulating, developing, and eventually attaining their professional goals. It offers a range of traditional and innovative services and programs to facilitate the career planning efforts of our students and to maximize their potential for employment.

Career and personal development workshops are scheduled regularly and the office maintains a Career Services Library for students' use. Employers from the legal, government, and corporate sectors are invited on campus during the fall semester to conduct a recruitment interview with students. Contact the Assistant Dean for Career Services for more information, 305.623.2351.

Applicant Group for the 1998-1999 Academic Year

St. Thomas University School of Law
This grid includes only applicants who earned 120-180 LSAT scores under standard administrations.

LSAT Score	GPA																				
	3.75 +		3.50 - 3.74		3.25 - 3.49		3.00 - 3.24		2.75 - 2.99		2.50 - 2.74		2.25 - 2.49		2.00 - 2.24		Below 2.00		No GPA		Total	
	Apps	Adm	Apps	Adm	Apps	Adm	Apps	Adm	Apps	Adm	Apps	Adm	Apps	Adm	Apps	Adm	Apps	Adm	Apps	Adm	Apps	Adm
175-180	0	0	0	0	0	0	0	0	0	0	0	0	0	0	0	0	0	0	0	0	0	0
170-174	0	0	0	0	0	0	0	0	0	0	0	0	0	0	0	0	0	0	0	0	0	0
165-169	0	0	1	1	1	1	2	2	2	2	0	0	1	1	0	0	0	0	0	0	7	7
160-164	6	5	17	15	18	16	15	14	5	5	6	6	5	4	0	0	2	2	1	1	75	68
155-159	17	17	30	26	35	33	48	44	54	52	32	28	12	12	19	17	2	2	2	1	251	232
150-154	14	13	54	46	71	64	95	87	96	92	79	69	60	52	30	28	8	8	8	2	515	461
145-149	13	11	28	26	41	38	80	74	78	66	75	65	64	55	36	29	7	6	11	3	433	373
140-144	1	0	14	4	18	8	38	18	66	33	72	34	44	24	24	11	6	1	7	1	290	134
135-139	2	0	5	0	13	0	25	1	30	1	38	1	33	1	10	0	2	0	5	0	163	4
130-134	0	0	1	0	2	0	4	0	6	0	16	0	16	0	5	0	4	0	10	1	64	1
125-129	0	0	0	0	3	0	1	0	4	0	2	0	2	0	3	0	2	0	4	0	21	0
120-124	0	0	0	0	0	0	0	0	0	0	0	0	1	0	1	0	1	0	0	0	3	0
Total	53	46	150	118	202	160	308	240	341	251	320	203	238	149	128	85	34	19	48	9	1822	1280

Apps = Number of Applicants
Adm = Number Admitted
Reflects 99% of the total applicant pool.

Samford University, Cumberland School of Law

800 Lakeshore Drive
Birmingham, AL 35229

E-Mail: law.admissions@samford.edu
URL: http://cumberland.samford.edu
Phone: 205.870.2702, 800.888.7213

■ Introduction

The Cumberland School of Law, established in 1847 as a part of Cumberland University in Lebanon, Tennessee, is one of the oldest law schools in the country. The school was acquired by Samford University in 1961 and is now known as the Cumberland School of Law at Samford University. Today, Samford University is the largest privately supported and fully accredited institution of higher learning in Alabama. The beautiful campus is located in a suburban area of Birmingham, Alabama's largest city. Birmingham is the state's industrial, business, and cultural center. The Cumberland School of Law has been a member of the Association of American Law Schools (AALS) since 1952, and has been accredited by the American Bar Association (ABA) since 1949.

■ Enrollment/Student Body

➡ 843 applicants ➡ 217 enrolled first-year class 1998
➡ full-time 25th/75th percentile GPA—2.72/3.31
➡ full-time 25th/75th percentile LSAT—148/153
➡ full-time only ➡ 7.9% minority
➡ 36.9% women ➡ 26 states represented
➡ 186 undergraduate schools represented
➡ 59.18% of 1998 first-year class from outside Alabama
➡ fall semester enrollment only

Since more than half of the entering class come from other states, the Student Bar Association (SBA) actively assists each student who desires help in relocating to Birmingham by providing a number of services. For example, students may join the Phoenix Organization for a one-time fee of $30, thereby relieving them of the need to pay deposits to local utility companies.

■ Faculty

➡ 64 total ➡ 32 full-time ➡ 32 part-time
➡ 7 women (full-time) ➡ 4 minority (full-time)

A strength of the law school, the 32 full-time faculty members hail from 21 law schools. The academic credentials, scholarly achievements, and publications of each faculty member are highlighted in the Admissions Prospectus.

■ Library and Physical Facilities

➡ 247,324 volumes & equivalents ➡ library hours: Mon.-Fri., 7:30 A.M.-MIDNIGHT; Sat., 9:00 A.M.-10:00 P.M.; Sun., 1:00 P.M.-MIDNIGHT ➡ 3 computer labs providing 30 work stations, includes LEXIS, WESTLAW, Internet, and WordPerfect
➡ LegalTrac CD-ROM ➡ 7 full-time librarians
➡ library seats 474 ➡ 12 conference rooms
➡ laptop computers available for checkout

The Lucille Stewart Beeson Law Library, an $8.4 million, free-standing, Georgian structure, opened in March of 1995. The library is visually stunning as well as superbly functional. This 61,000-square-foot, three-and-one-half story

building is connected to the law school by a second-story breezeway. The building's design is intended to make all facilities easily accessible to students with disabilities.

Complete training on WESTLAW, LEXIS, and Legal-Trac is a part of the first-year curriculum through the Legal Research and Writing Program. All study carrels and conference rooms are wired for data transmission. In addition, law students have full access to the university's four campus libraries as well as six computer labs.

■ Curriculum

➡ 90 credits required for J.D. ➡ 147 courses offered (courses are 2-,3-, or 4-hour courses) ➡ 53 credit hours in prescribed courses required ➡ supervised analytical writing required ➡ 6 joint degrees available: J.D./M.Acc.; J.D./M.B.A.; J.D./M.P.A.; J.D./M.P.H.; J.D./M.Div.; J.D./M.S. (Environmental Management) ➡ semesters, start in Aug. ➡ range of first-year class size—5-70

■ International Law

Cumberland conducts two ABA-approved international summer programs that are offered at the University of Durham, Durham, England and the University of Victoria, Victoria, British Columbia. The graduate degree of M.C.L., Master of Comparative Law, is offered to international law school graduates. New for summer, Cumberland's first study-abroad program in the Southern Hemisphere is expected to take place at Faculdade de Direito de Universidade de São Paulo in Brazil.

■ Special Programs

Cumberland has an exceptional record of recent trial-advocacy competition victories, winning both the ABA and ATLA national championships (including several national second- and third-place awards); winning 24 regional championships; and winning the coveted American College of Trial Lawyers' Emil Gumpert Award for Excellence in the Teaching of Trial Advocacy.

Cumberland students have the chance to get class credit, and a professional leg-up, working for Birmingham's major law firms, judges' offices, and corporate legal departments. The clinical curriculum offers second- and third-year students judicial and corporate externships, as well as externships in the offices of the I.R.S. and the U.S. Attorney. In addition, the Alabama Third-Year Practice Rule gives third-year students a chance to practice law under the supervision of a licensed attorney.

The law school also has an active intellectual life. Students may participate in faculty-run colloquia and the student-run Cordell Hull Speakers Series as well as many other student organizations.

■ Admission

➡ Bachelor's degree from accredited college or university required
➡ LSAT, LSDAS required ➡ application fee—$40

➼ *reactivation fee—$40* ➼ *applications accepted between Oct. 1 & May 1* ➼ *applicants admitted on a rolling admission basis* ➼ *priority application deadline—Feb. 28; final—May 1*

Cumberland School of Law of Samford University does not use a number index system or formula when choosing who will be admitted. Every applicant's file is thoroughly reviewed by the Faculty Admissions Committee. In addition to the LSAT score and undergraduate GPA, other important factors considered are: undergraduate school grade trend and difficulty of major; extracurricular activities and/or employment while in undergraduate school; graduate work; employment experience; personal statement; and letters of recommendation.

Admitted applicants are required to pay a nonrefundable $400 seat deposit that is credited toward tuition. The first installment of $150 is due April 1; the second installment of $250 is due June 15.

■ Student Activities

The Student Bar Association (SBA) is the foundation of student organization at the law school and functions as the first professional organization of a law student's career. Student Bar chapters keep students in touch with job opportunities and bar requirements. In addition to many outstanding organizations, students may also be invited to join one of three national legal fraternities and be inducted into two honorary societies, Order of the Barrister, and Curia Honoris. Student-run publications include *Cumberland Law Review*, *American Journal of Trial Advocacy*, and *Pro Confesso*.

■ Expenses and Financial Aid

➼ *1998-1999 tuition—$18,350 (flat rate)*
➼ *additional expenses—locker rental, $10; parking decal, $20; graduation fee, $37* ➼ *Guaranteed Student Loan Program available through the Financial Aid Office*
➼ *financial aid filing deadline—March 1*
➼ *26.2% of enrolled students awarded scholarships*

All admitted applicants are automatically considered for merit- and recruiting-scholarship awards. Various other scholarships are available to outstanding students who distinguish themselves academically, or who make outstanding contributions through leadership in the law school's programs.

■ Career Services

Through the Career Services Office (a member of the National Association for Law Placement), the law school assists all law students in locating summer clerkships and part-time and permanent employment upon graduation. Students also receive individual counseling and take part in workshops on everything from career choices to interviewing techniques and networking. The office schedules on-campus interview programs during the fall and spring semesters. Off-campus recruiting programs also are available. Cumberland students and graduates are encouraged to attend well-known recruiting conferences in Chicago, Atlanta, Nashville, and Washington, DC. The Career Services Office also surveys each graduating class nine months after graduation, and based on data collected from the most recent graduates (Class of '97), 91 percent had successfully obtained employment.

Applicant Group for the 1998-1999 Academic Year

Samford University, Cumberland School of Law

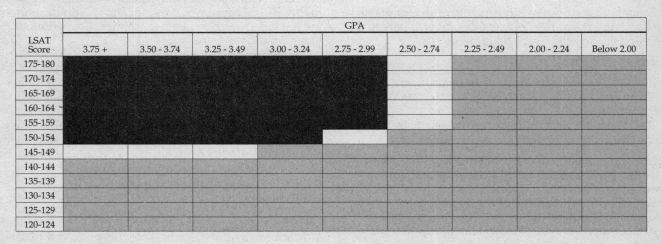

LSAT Score	GPA								
	3.75 +	3.50 - 3.74	3.25 - 3.49	3.00 - 3.24	2.75 - 2.99	2.50 - 2.74	2.25 - 2.49	2.00 - 2.24	Below 2.00
175-180									
170-174									
165-169									
160-164									
155-159									
150-154									
145-149									
140-144									
135-139									
130-134									
125-129									
120-124									

■ Good Possibility   □ Possible   ▦ Unlikely

University of San Diego School of Law

5998 Alcalá Park
San Diego, CA 92110-2492

E-Mail: jdinfo@acusd.edu
URL: http://www.acusd.edu/~usdlaw/
Phone: 619.260.4528

■ Introduction

Only 49 years old, USD School of Law is already recognized as a leading center of legal education. Set in a landmark location overlooking San Diego's spectacular shoreline, the School of Law fosters a climate of stimulating and rigorous intellectual exchange between professors and students. The university and the San Diego community offer a wealth of cultural, social, and athletic activities. The graceful Spanish Renaissance architecture and year-round ideal climate make this an attractive place to live and study. The School of Law has strong ties in the Southern California legal community— one in four lawyers practicing in the San Diego area is a USD graduate. The curriculum and student experience is enhanced by eminent visitors, specialized clinical programs, and research institutes. The law school is part of a private, values-based university and the educational environment supports the broader personal and ethical development of students. USD School of Law is accredited by the ABA and is a member of the AALS and the Order of the Coif.

■ Enrollment/Student Body

➡ 2,742 applicants   ➡ 341 enrolled first-year class 1998
➡ full-time 25th/75th percentile GPA—2.86/3.35
➡ part-time 25th/75th percentile GPA—2.86/3.45
➡ full-time 25th/75th percentile LSAT—157/161
➡ part-time 25th/75th percentile LSAT—153/156
➡ 788 total full-time   ➡ 345 total part-time
➡ 26% minority first-year; 23% minority all years
➡ 43% women   ➡ 32 states & 4 foreign countries represented first-year class 1998   ➡ 129 undergraduate schools represented first-year class 1998   ➡ age range first-year class 1998—20-46

■ Faculty

➡ 60 full-time   ➡ 56 part-time or adjunct
➡ 36 women   ➡ 11 minority

The School of Law offers a large faculty with experts in virtually every major field of law from diverse personal, professional, and academic backgrounds.

■ Library and Physical Facilities

➡ 445,000 volumes & equivalents   ➡ library hours: Sun.-Thurs., 8:00 A.M.-MIDNIGHT; Fri.-Sat., 8:00 A.M.-10:00 P.M.
➡ LEXIS   ➡ NEXIS   ➡ WESTLAW
➡ CALI (Computer Assisted Legal Instruction)   ➡ Dialog
➡ LegalTrac   ➡ 10 librarians   ➡ library seats 600

Regarded as one of the finest academic law libraries in the nation, USD's Pardee Legal Research Center offers state-of-the-art services and facilities to law students. The School of Law holds one of the major legal research collections in Southern California. The Pardee Legal Research Center features an instructional computer lab with networked computers replicating lawyers' workstations. Standard computer applications are enhanced by access to the Internet, interactive video instruction, computer-assisted legal instruction, and an online library automation system.

■ Curriculum

➡ Academic Support Program   ➡ 85 credits required to graduate   ➡ more than 150 total courses available
➡ degrees available: J.D.; J.D./M.B.A.; J.D./M.I.B.; J.D./M.A.; LL.M. in Comparative Law for Foreign Lawyers; LL.M. General, Tax, & International Law   ➡ semesters, start in Aug.
➡ range of first-year class size—20-85

Students in the day division normally require six semesters to complete the J.D., while evening-division students normally complete it in eight semesters plus one summer session. Attendance at two summer sessions may accelerate graduation by one semester. The first-year curriculum is prescribed. There are many small classes, including a legal research and writing program with a student faculty ratio of 20:1. Legal writing instructors work with students to develop research and writing, computer, and oral advocacy skills.

■ Special Programs

Institute on International and Comparative Law—The School of Law, in cooperation with foreign universities, sponsors the Institute on International and Comparative Law. The Institute has conducted summer law programs in England, France, Ireland, Italy, Russia, and Spain. The programs introduce American law students to foreign law and legal institutions and provides intensive study during four- to six-week sessions.

Clinical Education Program—The Clinical Education Program is recognized as one of the most extensive and successful in the nation. The law school received the Emil Gumpert Award from the American College of Trial Lawyers for excellence in trial advocacy training. Students represent clients in actual cases including work in the areas of consumer, housing, family, administrative, mental health, environmental, immigration, criminal, juvenile, and land use law.

Research and Advocacy Institutes—The Center for Public Interest Law (CPIL) and Children's Advocacy Institute (CAI) offer unique research and clinical opportunities. Other programs that offer practical experience include judicial internships and the Pro Bono Legal Advocates organization.

Joint Degrees—The School of Law offers joint-degree programs whereby students earn a J.D. degree along with a Master of Business Administration (M.B.A.), a Master of International Business (M.I.B.), or a Master of Arts in International Relations (M.A.). Separate admission is required, and the GMAT or GRE must be taken for acceptance into the appropriate joint-degree program.

Distinguished Visitors and Speakers—The School of Law attracts an outstanding array of speakers and senior Distinguished Professors, who are drawn from the nation's elite law schools; Practitioners-in-Residence, from the nation's outstanding law firms; and internationally renowned visiting scholars.

■ Admission

➡ *Bachelor's degree from an approved college or university required for admission* ➡ *application priority deadline—Feb. 1* ➡ *rolling admission, early application preferred* ➡ *LSAT, LSDAS required* ➡ *application fee—$40*

The educational mission of the University of San Diego embraces a commitment to academic excellence, individual dignity, and the need to develop the knowledge, values, and skills of its students to prepare them for service to their professional, global, civic, and faith communities. As a Roman Catholic institution, USD has a moral and theological commitment to educating a diverse student body. Accordingly, USD welcomes and respects those whose lives are formed by different traditions, recognizing that diversity of viewpoint, background, and experience (including race, ethnicity, cultural diversity, gender, religion, age, socioeconomic status, and disability) among its student body is essential to the full and informed exchange of ideas and to the quality of legal education it seeks to provide.

■ Student Activities

Student activities range from writing for a legal publication and doing scholarly research to participating in the law school student/faculty intramural sports activities. The *San Diego Law Review* is a student-run legal periodical of articles and comments addressing major issues and topics in law. The USD Moot Court team is considered one of the best in the nation. The USD team was best in the nation in the 1995 Jessup International Law Competition. The 1994 Jessup International law team came home with best brief and best oralist in the world. The USD Mock Trial team

competes in the ABA's National Trial competitions and has placed first in the Western Regionals for the past six years.

■ Housing

USD offers limited on-campus graduate housing. Early application is advised. The Housing Office and the Admissions Office assist in providing information and resources in locating off-campus accommodations.

■ Expenses and Financial Aid

➡ *tuition & fees—full-time, $20,980; part-time, $14,890* ➡ *financial aid available* ➡ *over 300 scholarships available— Dean's Outstanding Scholar Awards, entering merit awards, academic achievement scholarships, diversity scholarships, & activity grants* ➡ *Institutional financial aid application required* ➡ *Loan Repayment Assistance Program available* ➡ *FAFSA form for need analysis required; priority date March 2*

■ Career Services

The University of San Diego School of Law Career Services Office offers to all our law students, through its services, programs, and resources, the opportunity to learn about law careers, define personal career objectives, consider and apply for a broad range of legal employment opportunities, and plan for a successful transition into the legal profession. Each year Career Services lists hundreds of law clerking, intern, and attorney positions with law firms, public interest, government, corporate, and academic employers. Additionally, legal job bulletins and online resources provide students with listings and information on a broad range of career opportunities. Annually, 250 affiliated and on-campus interviewers from 27 states participate in the fall and spring recruiting process. USD's students and graduates work throughout the nation and internationally with prestigious law firms and with government, public interest, corporate, and academic employers.

Applicant Group for the 1998-1999 Academic Year

University of San Diego School of Law

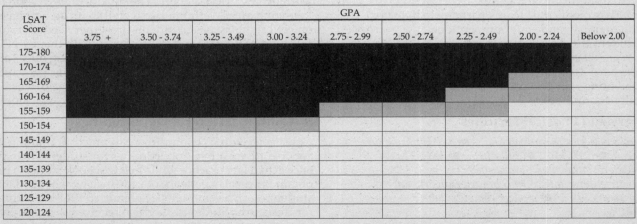

LSAT Score	GPA								
	3.75 +	3.50 - 3.74	3.25 - 3.49	3.00 - 3.24	2.75 - 2.99	2.50 - 2.74	2.25 - 2.49	2.00 - 2.24	Below 2.00
175-180									
170-174									
165-169									
160-164									
155-159									
150-154									
145-149									
140-144									
135-139									
130-134									
125-129									
120-124									

■ Very Likely   ▨ Possible   ☐ Unlikely

University of San Francisco School of Law

2130 Fulton Street
San Francisco, CA 94117-1080

URL: http://www.usfca.edu/law
Phone: 415.422.6586

■ Introduction

The University of San Francisco School of Law is situated on a 51-acre residential campus adjacent to Golden Gate Park and a short distance from downtown San Francisco. Its graduates play leading roles on the bench and in the bar of the San Francisco Bay Area and in over 40 states and 20 foreign countries. The university was founded by the Jesuit fathers in 1855. The law school dates from 1912 and is located in its own modern building, which was constructed in 1962.

The school's close proximity to the San Francisco Civic Center makes it convenient for students to engage in clerkships with the federal and state courts. San Francisco, the concentrated center for legal activity in the western United States, includes numerous administrative clerking opportunities. The school is fully accredited by the ABA and is a member of the AALS.

■ Enrollment/Student Body

➡ 2,242 applicants ➡ 997 admitted first-year class 1998
➡ 248 enrolled first-year class 1998 ➡ full-time 25th/75th percentile GPA—3.03/3.45 ➡ part-time 25th/75th percentile GPA—2.76/3.39 ➡ full-time 25th/75th percentile LSAT—154/159 ➡ part-time 25th/75th percentile LSAT—151/159
➡ 518 total full-time ➡ 127 total part-time
➡ 24% minority ➡ 56% women ➡ 31 states & foreign countries represented ➡ 95 undergraduate schools represented

At the time of admission the median age of the day and evening students is 26. Students in the two divisions merge into an integral unit of organizations for mutual activities.

■ Faculty

➡ 92 total ➡ 24 full-time ➡ 68 part-time or adjunct
➡ 20 women ➡ 12 minority

The school also draws from the finest Bay Area lawyers to teach in their area of expertise. The faculty is further supplemented by visiting faculty from throughout the United States, Europe, and China.

Upper-class moot court teams participate in major national, regional, and state competitions.

The Student Bar Association is responsible for student activities and liaison with the faculty and administration. Students participate directly in the school's governance through voting representation at faculty meetings and on faculty committees.

■ Library and Physical Facilities

➡ 288,678 volumes & equivalents ➡ 100 library hours per week ➡ LEXIS ➡ NEXIS ➡ WESTLAW
➡ INNOPAC automated library system
➡ 6 full-time librarians ➡ 6 library support staff
➡ library seats 293 ➡ student computer lab
➡ CD-ROM

The law school and law library are self-contained in a modern three-story structure. The library's collection includes approximately 288,678 volumes of Anglo American legal materials in print and microformat. A student computer center, group-study conference rooms, and copier facilities are also located in the law library. CD-ROM titles and workstations are available to students.

■ Admission

➡ B.A./B.S. required for admission ➡ application deadline—Feb. 15 (priority) ➡ LSAT, LSDAS required
➡ application fee—$40

The School of Law does not discriminate on the basis of sex, race, color, creed, age, handicap, or national origin. Beginning students are admitted only in the fall semester, and applicants must present a baccalaureate degree prior to registration. No application is considered until all supporting documents have been received. The admission committee employs a rolling admissions procedure. The committee strives to bring together an entering class that represents a variety of social, educational, geographical, and cultural backgrounds. Students from economically disadvantaged backgrounds are encouraged to apply through the Special Admission Program.

■ Curriculum

➡ 86 units/credits required to graduate ➡ degrees available: J.D.; J.D./M.B.A. ➡ semesters, start in Aug. & Jan.
➡ summer session starts in June ➡ range of first-year class size—day, 85; evening, 60

The first-year program begins with a four-day orientation program featuring a "minicourse," seminars, and a practice exam. The first-year curriculum includes the traditional curriculum plus Moot Court. The upper-class curriculum permits students to pursue their particular areas of interest.

■ Clinical Education—Law Clinic

The in-house Law Clinic gives students an alternative to learning law in a classroom. The clinic accepts cases in the following areas—criminal, and civil (with an emphasis on civil rights issues). Students are supervised by four full-time professors and work closely with them while meeting with clients, taking depositions, writing briefs, and making court appearances. In addition, all clinic participants meet in a weekly briefing session where they discuss current cases and share ideas, strategies, and "war stories."

■ Additional Clinical Opportunities

Consistent with its commitment to practical training, the School of Law offers opportunities for students to experience actual law practice while in law school. Students may obtain practical experience outside the law school. Many students earn a semester's academic credit by clerking for the courts. Students may also receive academic credit by clerking for governmental agencies, state and federal courts, public interest law firms, corporate legal departments, and private firms.

The School of Law pioneered and now directs a program in "Street Law." Under the program, students from five Bay Area law schools receive academic credit for teaching a course on the basics of our legal system to pupils in local high schools.

■ Student Activities

➡ *University of San Francisco Law Review*
➡ *University of San Francisco Maritime Law Journal*
➡ *The FORUM, student newspaper*
➡ *over 20 professional, social, and academic student organizations under the auspices of the Student Bar Association*

■ Intensive Advocacy Program

A two-week Intensive Advocacy Program is offered each summer. This unique program provides outstanding training in both pretrial and trial skills. The program features over 80 hours of lecture, demonstration, and practice workshops. At the conclusion of the program each student will conduct a jury trial. The faculty for the program will be made up of over 100 distinguished judges, practitioners, and professors from around the United States.

■ International Law and Study Abroad

The school offers an extensive list of courses in International Law. The faculty exchange program offers students the opportunity to study with faculty visiting USF from Irish, Czech, and Chinese universities. Summer study abroad programs are available in Ireland, the Czech Republic, and Indonesia.

The Asian Pacific Legal Studies program at the University of San Francisco School of Law is unique among Bay Area Law Schools and is one of only a few Asian law programs currently offered in the United States. The program has four components—curriculum, research and publication, academic exchange, and community outreach.

■ Expenses and Financial Aid

➡ *tuition & fees—full-time, $21,018; part-time, $748 per unit*
➡ *$12,769 average additional expenses (housing, board, books, misc. for 9 months)* ➡ *scholarships available* ➡ *financial aid available (grants and low-interest subsidized loans)*

■ Career Services

The Career Services Office facilitates the job search process for law school students and alumni. The office features a complete resource library, including in-depth dossiers on legal employers, and an aggressive placement program. Workshops, individual counseling, and panel presentations enable students to discern which areas of practice and types of employers best suit their individual career goals. In addition to listings for externships; part-time, permanent, and summer employment with law firms, corporations, accounting firms, governmental agencies, the judiciary, and other legal employers; USF also features fall and spring on-campus interview programs. Students are encouraged to consider employment in public interest law and may join the Public Interest Law Program sponsored by the Public Interest Clearinghouse. The law school is a member of the National Association for Law Placement.

Applicant Group for the 1998-1999 Academic Year

University of San Francisco School of Law
This grid includes only applicants who earned 120-180 LSAT scores under standard administrations.

LSAT Score	3.75 +		3.50 - 3.74		3.25 - 3.49		3.00 - 3.24		2.75 - 2.99		2.50 - 2.74		2.25 - 2.49		2.00 - 2.24		Below 2.00		No GPA		Total	
	Apps	Adm	Apps	Adm	Apps	Adm	Apps	Adm	Apps	Adm	Apps	Adm	Apps	Adm	Apps	Adm	Apps	Adm	Apps	Adm	Apps	Adm
175-180	1	1	0	0	0	0	0	0	0	0	0	0	0	0	0	0	0	0	1	1	2	2
170-174	0	0	1	1	2	2	3	2	1	1	3	2	0	0	0	0	0	0	2	2	12	10
165-169	6	6	10	9	6	4	7	7	5	5	2	2	4	2	3	2	0	0	4	3	47	40
160-164	8	7	31	30	50	48	62	56	27	23	18	15	6	5	8	3	1	0	1	1	212	188
155-159	23	21	59	56	101	96	130	118	102	70	57	23	22	9	11	2	1	0	6	4	512	399
150-154	21	16	81	57	117	71	170	73	119	29	52	7	38	6	5	0	2	0	6	2	611	261
145-149	11	3	41	14	70	8	93	12	109	9	66	5	31	0	11	0	1	0	9	0	442	51
140-144	8	1	12	0	28	3	41	3	67	1	47	1	28	0	7	1	0	0	17	0	255	10
135-139	1	0	3	1	8	1	17	0	20	1	19	0	11	0	9	0	3	0	6	0	97	3
130-134	0	0	0	0	0	0	1	0	9	0	2	0	6	0	2	0	2	0	0	0	22	0
125-129	0	0	0	0	0	0	2	0	3	0	3	0	3	0	0	0	1	0	0	0	12	0
120-124	0	0	0	0	0	0	0	0	0	0	0	0	0	0	0	0	0	0	0	0	0	0
Total	79	55	238	168	382	233	526	271	462	139	269	55	149	22	56	8	11	0	52	13	2224	964

Apps = Number of Applicants
Adm = Number Admitted
Reflects 99% of the total applicant pool.

Santa Clara University School of Law

500 El Camino Real
Santa Clara, CA 95053

E-Mail: lawadmission@scu.edu
URL: http://www.scu.edu/law
Phone: 408.554.4800

■ Introduction

Santa Clara University School of Law is located 46 miles from San Francisco, near the southern tip of San Francisco Bay. It is situated on the university campus, which was founded by the Jesuit fathers in 1851 and which surrounds the Mission of Santa Clara de Asis, the eighth of California's original 21 missions. The School of Law was added to the Santa Clara College in 1912 when the college became a university. The school is approved by the ABA and is a member of the AALS.

For more than 145 years, Santa Clara has fostered an exceptional academic program based on the Jesuit tradition. Located adjacent to San Jose and situated in the midst of one of the nation's greatest concentrations of high technology industry, internationally known as Silicon Valley, the law school has established a curriculum that addresses the fundamental demands of law practice and the evolving needs of society.

■ Enrollment/Student Body

➡ *2,530 applicants first-year class 1998*   ➡ *1,281 admitted first-year class 1998*   ➡ *293 enrolled first-year class 1998*
➡ *full-time 25th/75th percentile GPA—2.96/3.49*
➡ *part-time 25th/75th percentile GPA—2.85/3.32*
➡ *full-time 25th/75th percentile LSAT—153/158*
➡ *part-time 25th/75th percentile LSAT—153/160*
➡ *629 total full-time*   ➡ *288 total part-time*
➡ *34.2% minority*   ➡ *49% women*
➡ *105 undergraduate schools represented in entering class*

Santa Clara is consistently among the top 20 law schools nationwide in terms of ethnic diversity.

■ Faculty

➡ *76 total*   ➡ *32 full-time*   ➡ *44 part-time*
➡ *25 women*   ➡ *7 minority*

■ Library and Physical Facilities

➡ *275,160 volumes & equivalents*   ➡ *library hours: Mon.-Fri., 8:00 A.M.-MIDNIGHT; Sat., 9:00 A.M.-8:00 P.M.; Sun., 10:00 A.M.-MIDNIGHT*   ➡ *hours extended during exam periods*   ➡ *LEXIS*   ➡ *NEXIS*   ➡ *WESTLAW*
➡ *OSCAR*   ➡ *online catalog*
➡ *18 full-time librarians and staff*   ➡ *library seats 448*

The School of Law is on the 105-acre university campus. Towering palm trees, spacious lawns, and extensive flower gardens surround the Heafey Law Library. A traditional moot courtroom provides the setting for advocacy training and activities of the Edwin A. Heafey, Jr. Center for Trial and Appellate Advocacy. Other facilities include Bergin Hall faculty office building, Bannan Hall with its technology-equipped classrooms, and Law House where law career services is located. Students also have access to other campus facilities including computer laboratories, Cowell Student Health Center, Benson Memorial Center, and Leavey Activities Center with its pool; basketball; volleyball and racquetball courts; and steamroom and sauna.

■ Curriculum

➡ *full-time and part-time programs*   ➡ *Academic Success Program*   ➡ *86 semester units required to graduate*
➡ *138 courses available*   ➡ *degrees available: J.D. & J.D./M.B.A.*   ➡ *semesters, start in Aug.*

An academic orientation introduces first-year students to the study of law. The first-year curriculum is prescribed. The Academic Success Program has been used as a model academic assistance program by Law School Admission Council. All students of color are encouraged to participate in a special Pre-Law Orientation, a First-Year Program, an Upper-Division Program, and an Introduction to the Bar Program.

The J.D./M.B.A. Combined Degree Program offers students the opportunity to earn both degrees in three-and-one-half to four years. This means a savings in both time and tuition fees.

■ International Law Certificate

A specialized curriculum allows students to earn a Certificate in International Law. The Institute of International and Comparative Law sponsors summer law study programs in Munich, Germany; Budapest, Hungary; Strasbourg, France; Geneva, Switzerland; Oxford, England; Hong Kong; Singapore; Seoul, Korea; Bangkok, Thailand; Ho Chi Minh City, People's Republic of Vietnam; Beijing, People's Republic of China; Kuala Lumpur, Malaysia; and Tokyo, Japan. All of the programs, with the exception of Oxford, offer internships with law offices, corporations, or groups particularly suited to give students on-site observation and participation in areas of international law.

■ Computer and High-Technology Law Certificate

Santa Clara has capitalized on its Silicon Valley location by establishing a specialized curriculum that emphasizes computer and high-technology law. Students seeking an emphasis on high technology issues can enroll in courses such as patent law, copyright, biotechnology law, and technology licensing. They may also intern with a leading high tech firm and may earn a certificate in High Technology law.

■ Public Interest Law Certificate

Students concerned with social issues and public service can receive a Certificate in Public Interest Law through the Public Interest Law Program. The Public Interest Endowment funds a limited number of scholarships, summer work fellowships, and income supplement grants for graduates. Students may also enroll in selected graduate counseling courses for credit.

554-
5040

■ Clinical Programs

The Santa Clara University Law Clinic allows students to practice law under the supervision of an experienced attorney. Students participate in all phases of a case from the initial client interview through the trial.

Students have the opportunity to earn credit for work as law clerks with public agencies such as the district attorney or public defender, with legal aid offices, or with private law offices. Students may also work as judges' clerks in appellate courts including the California Supreme Court, or trial courts including the United States District Court and local superior and municipal courts.

■ Student Activities

The school's quarterly, *Santa Clara Law Review*, is published by a student editorial board. The *Computer and High Technology Law Journal* provides a practical resource for high technology industry and the corresponding legal community.

Through the Student Bar Association and student-faculty committees, students participate in the decision processes of the law school.

■ Admissions

➡ *Baccalaureate degree from accredited college or university required* ➡ *application deadline—March 1*
➡ *rolling admission, early application preferred*
➡ *early action deadline—Nov. 1* ➡ *LSAT, LSDAS required*
➡ *application fee—$40 ($60 international)*

A faculty committee reviews all applications. No one is automatically accepted or rejected. When the LSAT is repeated, the highest score received is used.

Recognizing the critical need for persons from underrepresented groups to gain access to the legal profession, the School of Law has adopted a policy for special admission. Applicants may request a special consideration because of race, disadvantaged background, or other factors. Over 32 percent of the entering class is composed of students of color and 53 percent are women.

Applicants are encouraged to visit the School of Law. Arrangements can be made through the Admissions Office to attend a law class, meet with an admission counselor, or tour the campus.

■ Expenses and Financial Aid

➡ *tuition & fees—$20,782, full-time; $15,078, part-time*
➡ *additional expenses—$8,000 min. (room, board, books)*
➡ *academic & need-based scholarships available*
➡ *public interest scholarships, summer fellowships,*
& income supplement grants ➡ *FAFSA form for needs analysis should be completed in Jan. or early Feb.*
➡ *financial aid counselor available for individual counseling*

■ Career Services

The Career Services Office serves as a liaison between students and prospective employers. Firms, businesses, and government agencies interview on campus each year. Graduates find employment in the legal profession throughout the 50 states. Office services include individual career counseling and a series of workshops in job-search strategies. Strong alumni support assists students in all stages of their career exploration and development.

Applicant Group for the 1998-1999 Academic Year

Santa Clara University School of Law
This grid includes only applicants who earned 120-180 LSAT scores under standard administrations.

LSAT Score	3.75 +		3.50 - 3.74		3.25 - 3.49		3.00 - 3.24		2.75 - 2.99		2.50 - 2.74		2.25 - 2.49		2.00 - 2.24		Below 2.00		No GPA		Total	
	Apps	Adm	Apps	Adm	Apps	Adm	Apps	Adm	Apps	Adm	Apps	Adm	Apps	Adm	Apps	Adm	Apps	Adm	Apps	Adm	Apps	Adm
170-180	4	4	6	6	7	7	10	10	0	0	4	4	1	1	0	0	0	0	0	0	32	32
165-169	7	7	8	8	16	16	23	23	11	11	7	7	5	3	2	1	0	0	1	1	80	77
160-164	22	22	49	48	65	65	56	56	32	30	16	12	4	3	6	4	0	0	8	7	258	247
155-159	50	47	94	93	148	145	138	133	91	72	48	28	19	9	8	1	1	1	8	6	605	535
150-154	32	29	108	75	170	104	154	67	115	32	54	10	35	5	7	0	1	0	15	7	691	329
145-149	16	9	41	11	78	8	101	9	98	6	58	2	20	0	10	0	2	0	12	2	436	47
140-144	6	0	14	0	31	0	47	0	71	0	50	0	26	0	11	0	2	0	9	0	267	0
Below 140	1	0	5	0	11	0	23	0	21	0	20	0	17	0	7	0	3	0	10	0	118	0
Total	138	118	325	241	526	345	552	298	439	151	257	63	127	21	51	6	9	1	63	23	2487	1267

Apps = Number of Applicants
Adm = Number Admitted

Seattle University School of Law

900 Broadway **after July 1, 1999
Seattle, WA 98122-4340

E-Mail: lawadmis@seattleu.edu
URL: http://www.law.seattleu.edu
Phone: 253.591.2252

■ Introduction

When the founders of our School of Law set its direction more than two decades ago, they envisioned a school with rigorous academic standards and impeccable ethics, a solid commitment to public service, and a firm resolve to serve as a school of opportunity for persons from diverse backgrounds and socioeconomic circumstances. The law school, informed by Jesuit values and traditions, is a superb center for teaching and learning, an ethical training ground, and a place to prepare for a lifetime of service.

After 25 years in Tacoma, the School of Law will be moving to new, state-of-the-art facilities on the Seattle University campus in fall 1999. The campus, a state-designated backyard wildlife sanctuary, is located on historic First Hill, overlooking downtown Seattle and the Pacific Northwest's largest legal community. Seattle, a major port city and part of the "gateway to Asia," offers students a lively urban environment that represents an ideal setting for our brand of legal education—a student body from throughout the nation and a blend of traditional textbook and innovative hands-on legal education.

■ Enrollment/Student Body

➡ *1,125 applicants*   ➡ *708 admitted first-year class 1998*
➡ *242 enrolled first-year class 1998*   ➡ *full-time 25th/75th percentile GPA—3.04/3.50*   ➡ *part-time 25th/75th percentile GPA—2.68/3.37*   ➡ *full-time 25th/75th percentile LSAT—151/157*   ➡ *part-time 25th/75th percentile LSAT—147/156*
➡ *652 total full-time*   ➡ *189 total part-time*
➡ *22% minority*   ➡ *60% women*   ➡ *45 states & foreign countries represented*   ➡ *245 undergraduate schools represented*

Seattle University law students range in age from 19 to 71. While their average age at entry is 30, about 30 percent choose to pursue legal studies directly after undergraduate school. The remainder come to us from an impressive array of professional careers. On average, they rank in the top quarter of their graduating class and their performance on the LSAT is solidly in the 70th percentile.

■ Faculty

➡ *87 total*   ➡ *36 full-time*   ➡ *51 adjunct*
➡ *29 women*   ➡ *9 minority*

When the law faculty meet to decide on faculty selection, promotion, and tenure, they first consider teaching aptitude and performance. Against this backdrop, the professors' production of significant scholarship is impressive, earning them a place among the "top 50" law faculties in the nation (1st/1989 and 2nd/1992 Editions, *Faculty Scholarship Survey*).

■ Library

➡ *322,520 volumes & equivalents*   ➡ *library hours: 7:00 A.M.-MIDNIGHT, daily*   ➡ *LEXIS*   ➡ *NEXIS*
➡ *WESTLAW*   ➡ *DIALOG*   ➡ *BRS*   ➡ *VUTEXT*
➡ *WILSONLINE*   ➡ *36 other CD-ROM databases*

➡ *DATATIMES*   ➡ *8 full-time librarians*
➡ *library seats 600*

The Law Library houses one of the largest law collections in the Northwest. Ranked among the top law libraries in the West, the SU Law Library offers students superb resources for legal research.

■ Curriculum

➡ *90 credits required to graduate*   ➡ *143 courses available*
➡ *J.D. degree*   ➡ *semesters, start in late Aug.*   ➡ *optional early start in June*   ➡ *range of first-year class size—15-100*

In the first intensive year, the curriculum concentrates on the highly traditional and prescribed basic courses, and on an intensive, year-long course refining legal analysis and writing skills which the ABA has called "among the finest legal writing programs in the nation." The upper-level courses allow for choice, innovation, and diversity. Students may choose either a broad, balanced program of study, or focus on a particular area such as Business, Corporate, and Tax Law (35 related courses plus clerkship opportunities with over 100 law firms, government agencies, and corporations in Western Washington); Law in the Public Sector (40 course offerings); or Environmental Law (10 courses plus internships with the Port of Seattle, Sierra Club Legal Defense Fund, U.S. Environmental Protection Agency, and Washington Environmental Council, among others). An innovative clinic program allows students to integrate a live client component with a substantive course.

■ Academic Resource Center

The law school's Academic Resource Center offers a range of academic support services designed to maximize every student's success. Workshops and seminars for new students emphasize self-evaluation techniques and support-group strategies. Representative programs include the following workshops—Effective Study Techniques; How to Outline; Preparing for Exams; and Organizing Your Time. The center is staffed by a full-time director (a J.D. graduate) and second- and third-year law students who serve as advisors and teaching assistants.

■ Expanded Scheduling

One of the most distinctive and popular features of the academic program is what we term "expanded scheduling." Seattle University, unlike any other school in the region, offers courses from 8:00 A.M. to 10:00 P.M., all year, for all students. At entry, students have the option of completing first-year studies over nine, twelve, or fifteen months. They may commence their studies in the summer or in the fall.

■ Admission

➡ *Bachelor's degree from an accredited college or university*
➡ *application deadline—April 1*   ➡ *rolling admission, early application preferred*   ➡ *LSAT, LSDAS required*

➡ *application fee—$50*   ➡ *typed personal statement and two letters of recommendation required*

The Faculty Admission Committee places primary emphasis on three factors: (1) LSAT scores; (2) undergraduate academic performance; and (3) personal accomplishments.

Each applicant file is reviewed individually by a minimum of two evaluators. Personal achievements weigh heavily in each admission decision.

Candidates for admission are advised to apply as early as possible and complete their files no later than April 1. A very few spaces in the class are held for persons taking the June LSAT.

The law school is committed to a wholly nondiscriminatory admission policy and philosophy.

■ Alternative Admission

A select group of applicants is admitted each year through an alternative-admission program established by the law school based on recognition that traditional admission criteria are, in some cases, inadequate predictors of success in law school and the legal profession. The majority of individuals considered for this program are members of historically disadvantaged groups. Enrollment is strictly limited to 10 percent of the entering class.

■ Student Activities

A partial listing of student organizations illustrates the scope of interests held by law students—Alaska Student Bar Association; Asian/Pacific Islander Law Student Association; Black Law Student Association; Christian Legal Fellowship; Entertainment/Sports Law Association; Environmental Law Society; Hispanic Organization for Legal Advancement; Inn of Court; International Law Society; Jewish Law Society; Law Review; Lesbian and Gay Legal Society; Moot Court; Native American Student Bar Association; Public Interest Law Foundation; Student Bar Association; and Women's Law Caucus.

■ Expenses and Financial Aid

➡ *tuition & fees—$17,880 1998-99/yr.*   ➡ *estimated additional expenses—$11,008 (books, room, board, & living expenses)*
➡ *performance and/or need-based scholarships available*
➡ *minority scholarships available*

Well over 80 percent of the student body receives some form of financial assistance. A full 35 percent of students receive law school-funded scholarships which total over $1 million per year. Information on scholarships, grants, loans, and employment opportunities is mailed to all applicants.

■ Career Services

More than 90 percent of law students have been employed in at least one law firm, legal agency, or other law-related position prior to graduation. Many have held two or three such jobs in order to strengthen and diversify their resumes. Our alumni/ae are employed throughout the U.S. and in 19 foreign countries. Seventy-nine percent of 1997 graduates passed the Washington bar exam on their first attempt (five points higher than the statewide average).

Applicant Group for the 1998-1999 Academic Year

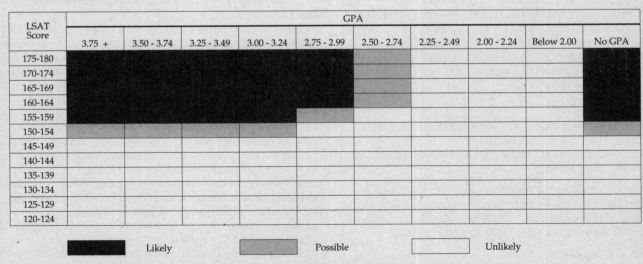

Seattle University School of Law

LSAT Score	GPA									
	3.75 +	3.50 - 3.74	3.25 - 3.49	3.00 - 3.24	2.75 - 2.99	2.50 - 2.74	2.25 - 2.49	2.00 - 2.24	Below 2.00	No GPA
175-180	■	■	■	■	■					■
170-174	■	■	■	■	■					■
165-169	■	■	■	■	■					■
160-164	■	■	■	■	■					■
155-159	■	■	■	■						■
150-154	▨									
145-149										
140-144										
135-139										
130-134										
125-129										
120-124										

■ Likely   ▨ Possible   ☐ Unlikely

Of applicants in the Unlikely category, about one in 20 candidates was admitted to the Alternative Admission Program.

Seton Hall University School of Law

Office of Admissions
One Newark Center
Newark, NJ 07102-5210

E-Mail: admitme@shu.edu
URL: http://www.shu.edu/law
Phone: 888.415.7271; 973.642.8747

■ Introduction

Founded in 1951, Seton Hall University School of Law is the only private law school in the state of New Jersey. While it values its Catholic identity as a division of the university, the law school is a pluralistic community representing a diversity of racial, cultural, religious, and socioeconomic backgrounds. The school was recently recognized for its high level of student satisfaction and its high rate of judicial clerkship placement. The law school building is architecturally dynamic fostering a congenial atmosphere and incorporating technological sophistication for the study of law. The school location puts our students in the midst of federal, appellate, state and county courts, the Legal Center, hundreds of law firms and legal agencies, and the New Jersey Performing Arts Center.

■ Enrollment/Student Body

➡ 2,116 applicants ➡ 970 admitted first-year class 1998
➡ 376 enrolled first-year class 1998 ➡ full-time 25th/75th percentile GPA—2.83/3.41 ➡ part-time 25th/75th percentile GPA—2.55/3.28 ➡ full-time 25th/75th percentile LSAT—151/157 ➡ part-time 25th/75th percentile LSAT—150/157
➡ 920 total full-time ➡ 335 total part-time
➡ 25% minority ➡ 44% women
➡ 24 states represented in first-year class
➡ 161 undergraduate schools represented in first-year class

■ Faculty

➡ 147 total ➡ 51 full-time ➡ 96 part-time or adjunct
➡ 19 women ➡ 7 minority

■ Library and Physical Facilities

➡ 386,000 volumes & equivalents ➡ library hours: Mon.-Thurs., 8:00 A.M.-11:00 P.M.; Fri., 8:00 A.M.-8:00 P.M.; Sat., 9:00 A.M.-6:00 P.M.; Sun., 10:00 A.M.-9:00 P.M.
➡ LEXIS/NEXIS ➡ WESTLAW ➡ LegalTrac
➡ GPO Access ➡ 9 professional librarians;
14 library assistants ➡ library seats 600
➡ computer lab for student use

■ Curriculum

➡ Academic Support Program ➡ 85 credits required to graduate ➡ 216 courses available
➡ degrees available: J.D.; J.D./M.B.A.; LL.M.-Health Law; M.S.J.
➡ semesters, start in Aug.

The program emphasizes humanistic principles and encourages their synthesis with knowledge of the law and professional responsibility. The law school is committed to in-depth training in legal writing and research.

■ Special Programs

Clinics—Seton Hall law school is committed to clinical education and is at its forefront. The 24 years of service performed by the law school's clinics was recognized by Congress and the President in the form of a $5.4 million grant. With this grant, the school has created the Center for Social Justice, a clinical legal education center that serves as a national model. The school's litigation clinics presently represent more than 3,000 disadvantaged and underrepresented clients each year in a wide range of litigation such as housing and shelter, consumer protection, family law, public entitlement, juvenile justice, disability law, immigration, and inmate advocacy.

Judicial Internships—The law school also offers judicial internships with justices of the New Jersey Supreme Court; judges of the New Jersey Appellate Division, Chancery and Law Courts, the Third Circuit Court of Appeals, the U.S. District Courts, and the U.S. Bankruptcy Courts. There are internship programs with the Environmental Protection Agency, the Office of the U.S. Trustee for Bankruptcy, and the Internal Revenue Service.

Journals—The law school offers students an opportunity to advance legal scholarship through four student journals—The Seton Hall Law Review, Seton Hall Legislative Journal, Seton Hall Constitutional Law Journal, and the Seton Hall Sports Law Journal.

Concentrations—The law school offers concentrations with certificates in health, employment, environmental, criminal, and corporate law.

Foreign Study—Each summer the law school cosponsors, with the University of Parma, a course of international studies for American law students in Parma, Italy. The law school also sponsors studies in Cairo, Egypt.

M.B.A./J.D. Program—Students may be admitted to the joint M.B.A./J.D. program during the first year of their law school career. The M.B.A. degree consists of 60 credits, and a maximum of 12 credits may be applied to both degree requirements. The LSAT and GMAT examinations are both required.

Health Law—Seton Hall offers an LL.M. degree in Health Law, which provides attorneys the opportunity to broadly explore health law and policy or focus more narrowly on courses designed for the lawyer planning to represent the health provider, payer or regulator, the pharmaceutical company, or the biotechnology company.

Seton Hall also offers a Master of Science in Jurisprudence (M.S.J.) degree in Health Law, which provides health care professionals with a solid foundation in legal aspects of health care delivery and regulation. Such a concentrated exposure to health law issues can be vital to medical directors, regulatory and contract compliance officers, risk and case managers, employee benefits personnel, lobbyists, and pharmaceutical employees.

Full- and part-time programs are available for both the LL.M. and M.S.J. degrees.

LEO Institute—The Monsignor Thomas Fahy Legal Education Opportunities (LEO) Institute provides an intense, summer-long classroom experience for educationally or economically disadvantaged students. Applicants from disadvantaged groups, regardless of race, religion, age, sex, sexual orientation, or national origin, may wish to inquire into this program.

Moot Court Program—Students represent the law school in the National Moot Court Competition as well as in nine interschool competitions focusing on specific areas of law.

■ Admission

➤ *B.A./B.S. from accredited college or university required* ➤ *application deadline—April 1*
➤ *LSAT, LSDAS required* ➤ *application fee—$50*
➤ *rolling admission, early application preferred*

An early decision program is available with an application deadline of November 27 and notification in late December. TOEFL is required of applicants whose precollege education was not in English. A minimum score of 600 is recommended.

The law school recognizes the desirability of bringing together an entering class of diverse cultural, social, and educational backgrounds. Nonquantifiable indicators of success in law school may surface in one's demonstrated skills. These skills can be reflected in things such as the employment record, meaningful community endeavors, and unusual cocurricular service projects of a candidate.

General decision notification begins in January and continues through May. A $500 tuition deposit is required by April 1. A second tuition deposit of $1,000 is due in June.

■ Student Activities

Student organizations flourish at Seton Hall. Many are related to specific areas of practice; others related to student governance and student representation on faculty standing committees. International law fraternities have chapters here. Several organizations, including the St. Thomas More Society, are committed to community service. Many other groups represent a wide range of professional interests, religious commitments, and cultural identities found among an enormously diverse student population.

The law school is also very involved in encouraging the study of law and the pursuit of legal careers among college and high school students, through the Mentor and Pre-Legal programs.

■ Expenses and Financial Aid

➤ *tuition & fees—full-time, $21,980; part-time,$16,096 ($698/credit hour)* ➤ *recommended budget including tuition —full-time, $36,500; part-time, $30,461* ➤ *merit- & need-based scholarships available* ➤ *FAFSA due April 15th*

In 1998-99, an estimated $21 million was awarded to law students. The first-year class was awarded $1.7 million of merit money.

■ Career Services

Seton Hall School of Law maintains a Career Services Office staffed by two full-time counselors who assist students in defining their career objectives and goals and establishing contact with employers. Every fall, law firm, corporate, public interest, and government employers conduct interviews through the school's On-Campus Interview Program. The placement ratio for 1997 graduates was 94 percent. Alumni of the School of Law are practicing in many states.

Applicant Group for the 1998-1999 Academic Year

Seton Hall University School of Law
This grid includes only applicants who earned 120-180 LSAT scores under standard administrations.

LSAT Score	3.75 +		3.50 - 3.74		3.25 - 3.49		3.00 - 3.24		2.75 - 2.99		2.50 - 2.74		2.25 - 2.49		2.00 - 2.24		Below 2.00		No GPA		Total	
	Apps	Adm	Apps	Adm	Apps	Adm	Apps	Adm	Apps	Adm	Apps	Adm	Apps	Adm	Apps	Adm	Apps	Adm	Apps	Adm	Apps	Adm
175-180	0	0	0	0	0	0	0	0	0	0	0	0	0	0	0	0	0	0	0	0	0	0
170-174	0	0	0	0	3	3	1	1	0	0	1	1	0	0	0	0	0	0	0	0	5	5
165-169	3	3	5	5	5	5	5	5	4	4	5	5	2	0	1	1	2	2	1	1	33	31
160-164	6	6	13	13	26	26	25	25	21	20	11	11	3	3	4	4	0	0	1	1	110	109
155-159	18	18	51	51	56	56	77	77	60	60	37	37	13	12	7	7	3	1	4	3	326	322
150-154	23	22	48	47	100	95	133	119	104	74	79	41	20	10	11	6	1	0	5	0	524	414
145-149	12	6	37	12	70	15	100	14	97	6	68	9	39	4	7	0	4	0	4	0	438	66
140-144	5	1	22	1	44	2	66	2	56	3	63	3	29	1	18	0	3	0	4	0	310	13
135-139	2	0	11	0	13	2	25	2	40	4	25	1	36	0	15	1	3	0	5	0	175	10
130-134	0	0	3	0	4	0	6	0	16	0	8	0	11	0	5	0	3	0	3	0	59	0
125-129	0	0	0	0	1	0	0	0	5	0	3	0	2	0	4	0	0	0	2	0	17	0
120-124	0	0	0	0	0	0	0	0	0	0	0	0	0	0	0	0	0	0	0	0	0	0
Total	69	56	190	129	322	204	438	245	403	171	300	108	155	30	72	19	19	3	29	5	1997	970

Apps = Number of Applicants
Adm = Number Admitted
Reflects 94% of the total applicant pool.

University of South Carolina School of Law

Columbia, SC 29208

E-Mail: usclaw@law.law.sc.edu
URL: http://www.law.sc.edu/
Phone: 803.777.6605 or 6606

■ Introduction

The University of South Carolina School of Law, established in 1867, is located in Columbia, South Carolina. Situated in the state capital in the center of the state, there is easy access to the mountains and to the coast. The school is within close proximity of state and federal courts, government agencies, the State Capitol, and large law firms. The School of Law is fully accredited by the American Bar Association and has been a member of the Association of American Law Schools since 1924.

■ Enrollment/Student Body

→ *1,230 applicants*   → *415 admitted first-year class 1998*
→ *228 enrolled first-year class 1998*   → *full-time 25th/75th percentile GPA—2.85/3.53*   → *full-time 25th/75th percentile LSAT—152/159*   → *746 total full-time*   → *10% minority*
→ *43% women*   → *13 states & foreign countries represented*
→ *75 undergraduate schools represented*
→ *85% residents of South Carolina*

■ Faculty

→ *69 total*   → *44 full-time*   → *25 part-time or adjunct*
→ *4 women*   → *2 minority*

■ Library and Physical Facilities

→ *326,000 volumes & equivalents*   → *library hours: open 111 hours/week under regular schedule; Mon.-Thurs., 7:00 A.M.-MIDNIGHT; Fri., 7:00 A.M.-10:00 P.M.; Sat., 9:00 A.M.-10:00 P.M.; Sun., 9:00 A.M.-MIDNIGHT*
→ *LEXIS*   → *NEXIS*   → *WESTLAW*   → *DIALOG*
→ *RLIN*   → *OCLC*   → *USCAN (online card catalog)*
→ *5.5 full-time librarians*   → *library seats 645*
→ *South Carolina Legal History Collection is housed in the School of Law Library*

Closed carrels are available for assignment to students for year-long use.

■ Curriculum

→ *Academic Support Program*   → *90 total units/credits required to graduate*   → *121 courses available*
→ *joint-degree programs: J.D./Masters Business Administration; J.D./Masters Criminal Justice; J.D./Masters Public Administration; J.D./Masters International Business; J.D./Masters Employee Personnel Relations; J.D./Master of Accountancy; J.D./Master of Arts in Economics*
→ *two semesters, begin in Aug. and Jan.*
→ *one summer session*   → *beginning students admitted for fall semester only*   → *range of first-year class size—20-80*

Transfer students are accepted in limited numbers.

■ Special Programs

Clinical Legal Education Program. Under special court rule, third-year law students in South Carolina may represent clients and appear in court when enrolled in a clinical legal education course. The clinical education program offers courses designed to develop lawyering skills. The program, through the use of simulation techniques, offers training in trial advocacy, negotiation, settlement, interviewing, and counseling. Clinics include domestic practice, criminal practice, administrative litigation, and bankruptcy. Judicial internship clinics place students with trial and appellate court judges.

■ Admissions

→ *Bachelor's degree from an accredited college or university required for admission*   → *application deadline—Feb. 15*
→ *fall admission only*   → *transfer application deadline—May 15*   → *LSAT, LSDAS required*

The Faculty Committee on Admissions reviews applications to the School of Law. Factors considered include LSAT, GPA, degree-granting institution, major, work and/or military experience, extracurricular activities, letters of recommendation, and the personal statement. When multiple LSAT scores are presented, the average of the scores is used.

The fall 1997 entering class was 11 percent minority, 45 percent women, and 85 percent South Carolina residents.

Visits to the Office of Admissions and the School of Law to discuss specific questions and concerns are welcomed.

■ Student Activities

Order of the Coif—National legal honorary society which recognizes outstanding student academic achievement.

Order of Wig and Robe—Local legal scholastic organization organized in 1935.

South Carolina Law Review—Published quarterly and contains articles by distinguished scholars, members of the bar, and students.

South Carolina Environmental Law Journal—Published regularly by students of the School of Law. Each issue, containing articles written by attorneys, professors, and professionals in the field, provides updates on current developments in environmental law.

Real Property, Probate, and Trust Journal—The School of Law serves as the host affiliate for this ABA journal.

Pro Bono Program—Directed by a student board, the Pro Bono Program offers students an opportunity to be involved in activities such as income tax assistance, legal research, and teaching law-related courses to juveniles.

Moot Court—Teams are sponsored in the National, International, American Bar Association, and Labor Law Moot Court competitions and National Trial Competition.

Other student organizations include the Student Bar Association, which is the student government for the School of Law, the Black Law Student Association, the Association of Women Law Students, the Christian Legal Society, and the Environmental Law Society.

■ Expenses and Financial Aid

➡ *full-time tuition & fees—SC resident, $6,864/year; non-SC resident, $13,606* ➡ *average amount of additional expenses—$9,000 (rent, transportation, utilities, books, food, misc.)* ➡ *scholarships available (merit-based full- & half-tuition scholarships, need-based scholarships* ➡ *minority scholarships available (merit-based full- & half-tuition scholarships)* ➡ *financial aid available* ➡ *priority deadline for applications for federal student loan programs—April 15* ➡ *Free Application for Federal Student Aid (FAFSA) required*

Candidates who want to be considered for merit scholarships should complete their application to the School of Law by February 1.

■ Office of Career Services

The Office of Career Services serves as liaison between students and legal employers and offers services to equip students with the skills and information necessary for a successful employment search. Services available include individual counseling, résumé writing, and interviewing seminars, on-campus interviews, participation in job fairs including the Southeastern Law Placement Consortium in Atlanta, GA; the South Atlantic Recruiting Conference in Washington, DC; the Southeastern Minority Job Fair; and the Southeastern Public Interest Job Fair.

Applicant Group for the 1998-1999 Academic Year

University of South Carolina School of Law
This grid includes only applicants who earned 120-180 LSAT scores under standard administrations.

LSAT Score	3.75 +		3.50 - 3.74		3.25 - 3.49		3.00 - 3.24		2.75 - 2.99		2.50 - 2.74		2.25 - 2.49		2.00 - 2.24		Below 2.00		No GPA		Total	
	Apps	Adm	Apps	Adm	Apps	Adm	Apps	Adm	Apps	Adm	Apps	Adm	Apps	Adm	Apps	Adm	Apps	Adm	Apps	Adm	Apps	Adm
175-180	0	0	0	0	0	0	0	0	0	0	0	0	0	0	0	0	0	0	0	0	0	0
170-174	0	0	3	3	0	0	0	0	1	1	1	1	1	1	1	1	0	0	0	0	7	7
165-169	2	2	3	3	6	5	5	3	3	3	0	0	2	2	1	1	0	0	1	1	23	20
160-164	10	10	16	13	17	17	18	18	20	18	12	11	4	3	1	0	0	0	1	0	99	90
155-159	20	18	32	27	48	39	55	32	41	22	23	12	11	4	8	5	1	0	1	0	240	159
150-154	28	20	49	17	75	25	83	13	50	7	36	7	16	3	7	2	0	0	0	0	344	94
145-149	12	4	28	11	48	11	59	6	29	1	34	2	11	3	8	2	2	0	3	2	234	42
140-144	8	0	16	1	26	3	29	5	30	0	33	1	11	0	8	0	2	0	5	1	168	11
135-139	2	0	4	0	6	0	13	0	13	0	13	0	10	0	4	0	3	0	2	0	70	0
130-134	0	0	2	0	0	0	2	0	2	0	1	0	0	0	2	0	1	0	1	0	11	0
125-129	0	0	0	0	0	0	0	0	0	0	1	0	1	0	1	0	0	0	0	0	3	0
120-124	0	0	0	0	0	0	0	0	0	0	0	0	0	0	0	0	0	0	0	0	0	0
Total	82	54	153	75	226	100	264	77	189	52	154	34	67	16	41	11	9	0	14	4	1199	423

Apps = Number of Applicants
Adm = Number Admitted
Reflects 99% of the total applicant pool.

University of South Dakota School of Law

Admissions/Office of the Dean
414 E. Clark
Vermillion, SD 57069-2390

E-Mail: request@jurist.law.usd.edu
URL: http://www.usd.edu/law/legal.html
Phone: 605.677.5443

■ Introduction

The School of Law, located on the university campus in Vermillion, is noted for its contributions in training distinguished leaders for the bench, the bar, and the lawmaking bodies of the state and region. Founded in 1901, the school is accredited by both the ABA and the AALS.

Approximately 214 students are enrolled at USD School of Law, with a total university population of approximately 6,500. The city of Vermillion, with a population of approximately 10,000, provides a small-town atmosphere for students, faculty, and staff.

■ Enrollment/Student Body

➡ *251 applicants* ➡ *129 admitted first-year class 1998*
➡ *61 enrolled first-year class 1998* ➡ *full-time 25th/75th percentile GPA—3.01/3.54* ➡ *full-time 25th/75th percentile LSAT—146/156* ➡ *214 total full-time* ➡ *5.6% minority* ➡ *40.6% women* ➡ *21 states & foreign countries represented* ➡ *70 undergraduate schools represented*

■ Faculty

➡ *17 total* ➡ *15 full-time* ➡ *2 part-time or adjunct* ➡ *3 women*

Excellent student-faculty ratio fosters a close relationship between students and teaching faculty.

■ Library and Physical Facilities

➡ *182,522 volumes & equivalents* ➡ *library hours: Mon.-Thurs., 7:30 A.M.-MIDNIGHT; Fri., 7:30 A.M.-6:00 P.M.; Sat., 10:00 A.M.-5:00 P.M.; Sun., NOON-MIDNIGHT* ➡ *LEXIS* ➡ *NEXIS* ➡ *WESTLAW* ➡ *DIALOG* ➡ *SDLN* ➡ *CALI* ➡ *Internet* ➡ *CD-ROM network* ➡ *5 full-time librarians* ➡ *library seats 227*

The law school has been housed in its present facility since 1981. It contains three classrooms, each containing a data drop; three seminar rooms; a student computer room; a spacious student lounge; offices for faculty, administration, and student organizations; and a teaching courtroom with judges' chambers and an audiovisual control room. The courtroom doubles as an assembly hall.

The library occupies a substantial portion of all three floors of the facility, and provides study carrels for students and group study space. Many library functions are automated providing easy access to the library's own collection and to the collection of more than 30 other libraries in South Dakota and 18 other law libraries in the region.

■ Curriculum

➡ *90 credits required to graduate* ➡ *62 courses available* ➡ *degrees available: J.D.; J.D./Masters offered in 9 areas including Bus., Educ., Arts & Science* ➡ *semesters, start in Aug.* ➡ *range of first-year class size—61*

There is a three-semester core curriculum and three semesters of advanced studies. Ninety semester credits are required for the J.D. degree. The first-year curriculum is required of all students. In the second and third years, electives are available in addition to required courses. An optional clinical externship/academic course semesters available for 15 credit hours during the spring semester. Also, during the summer a clinical externship program is offered for 6 credit hours. Clinical interns learn by doing under the close supervision of an attorney and the clinical law director. Skills training is also available to second- and third-year students in the trial techniques course, negotiations, and other courses, each of which utilizes to the fullest extent the audiovisual capabilities of the law school.

■ Special Programs

The school has joint programs with other departments of the graduate school, with joint degrees available in professional accountancy, business administration, history, English, psychology, education, political science/public administration, and political science, public administration, and administrative studies. Students may transfer nine hours of approved interdisciplinary coursework for J.D. credit. For students not enrolled in a joint-degree program, up to six interdisciplinary credits may be applied toward the 90-credit J.D. requirement.

Various paid, summer legal internships both within and outside of South Dakota are available in both private firms and public agencies. The South Dakota Supreme Court has adopted a student-practice rule that allows students who have completed their second year to represent clients in court under the supervision of a member of the bar.

■ Admission Standards

➡ *Bachelor's degree required* ➡ *preferred application deadline —March 1* ➡ *rolling admission, early application preferred* ➡ *LSAT, LSDAS required* ➡ *application fee—(first time applications only)* ➡ *application form, 2 letters of recommendation, personal statement required*

Accepted students are required to pay a $50 nonrefundable deposit to reserve a position in the entering first-year class, and to submit two photographs and an official transcript reflecting their undergraduate degree.

Students who do not meet regular admission criteria may be invited to participate in the Summer Screening Program. Program participants are enrolled in two noncredit law school courses during a five-week summer session. Up to 10 students who receive the highest cumulative grade-point average while maintaining a grade of 70 or better in both courses are offered admission to the entering first-year class. The program provides a valuable proving ground for applicants whose abilities are not accurately reflected in past undergraduate or LSAT performance.

USD School of Law is committed to providing full opportunity for the study of law and entry into the profession by qualified members or groups (notably racial and ethnic minorities, including Native Americans) that have been victims of discrimination in various forms.

Transfer students may apply for admission with advanced standing only if they are in good standing and eligible to return to the transferor law school.

Foreign students who attended undergraduate programs in which English was not the dominant language must also submit a TOEFL score as part of their application package.

■ Student Activities

The *South Dakota Law Review* presents articles by second- and third-year students, lawyers, judges, and professors. The *Great Plains Natural Resources Journal* provides articles dealing with environmental law and natural resources law. Cocurricular activities include a Moot Court Board and Clinical Counseling and Negotiations Board. Competitions in all activities are held at the intramural, regional, and national levels.

The school is active in the Law Student Division of the ABA. Two legal fraternities—Delta Theta Phi and Phi Alpha Delta—are active at the school. Other organizations with chapters at the school include Women in Law, the Native American Law Students Association, the Christian Legal Society, the Environmental Law Society, the International Law Students Association, International Law Students Association, the Federalist Society, and the R.D. Hurd Pro Bono Society.

■ Expenses and Financial Aid

➡ *tuition & fees—full-time resident, $5,291*
➡ *estimated additional expenses—$3,500 (books, room & board)*
➡ *academic performance & need-based scholarships available*
➡ *financial aid available; FAFSA needs analysis must be submitted through central University Financial Aid Office*

Scholarships and grants were awarded to 39 percent of the student body for 1997-98.

A limited number of teaching and research assistantships are available for academically qualified second- and third-year students. A research service provided by the McKusick Law Library for practicing attorneys also provides employment opportunities for several law students during the academic year.

Student loans are available through the university's Office of Student Financial Aid (605.677.5446). For information about minority scholarship programs, applicants should contact Minority Student Financial Aid Coordinator, 14 Slagle Hall, USD, 414 E. Clark St., Vermillion, SD 57069-2390 (605.677.5446).

■ Career Services

The placement opportunities for third-year law students have been excellent both in South Dakota, the surrounding areas, and throughout the United States. Approximately one-third of the graduates of the school practice law outside of South Dakota. The law school also has an active program to place first- and second-year students in summer internship programs with law firms.

Applicant Group for the 1998-1999 Academic Year

University of South Dakota School of Law

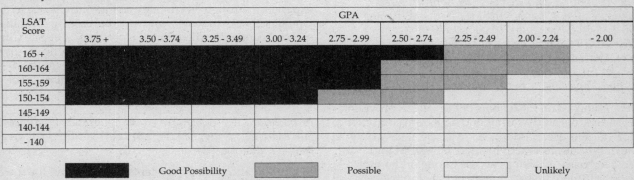

LSAT Score	GPA								
	3.75 +	3.50 - 3.74	3.25 - 3.49	3.00 - 3.24	2.75 - 2.99	2.50 - 2.74	2.25 - 2.49	2.00 - 2.24	- 2.00
165 +	■	■	■	■	■	■	▨	▨	
160-164	■	■	■	■	■	▨	▨	▨	
155-159	■	■	■	■	■	▨	▨		
150-154	■	■	■	■	▨	▨			
145-149									
140-144									
- 140									

■ Good Possibility   ▨ Possible   ☐ Unlikely

USD School of Law considers many factors beyond LSAT score and GPA. This chart should be used only as a general rule.

For Fall 1998:				
Applicants:	251	25th/75th percentile LSAT:	148/156
Accepted:	119	25th/75th percentile GPA:	3.06/3.54
Accepted from Summer Screening:	10		
Total accepted:	129		
Matriculated:	62		

South Texas College of Law affiliated with Texas A&M University

1303 San Jacinto Street
Houston, TX 77002-7000

E-Mail: acramer@stcl.edu
URL: http://www.stcl.edu
Phone: Main: 713.659.8040; Admission: 713.646.1810

■ Introduction

South Texas College of Law affiliated with Texas A&M University is a private, nonprofit, independent institution located in downtown Houston. Founded in 1923, is the oldest law school in the metropolitan area and one of the larger private law schools in the nation. The college offers both full-time and part-time study leading to the Doctor of Jurisprudence degree. South Texas' historic alliance with Texas A&M University paves the way for the development of joint programs and degrees while preserving the private, independent status of the law school. South Texas is accredited by the ABA and holds membership in the AALS.

■ Enrollment/Student Body

➡ *1,656 applicants* ➡ *1,025 admitted first-year class 1998* ➡ *465 enrolled first-year class 1998* ➡ *full-time 25th/75th percentile GPA—2.67/3.14* ➡ *part-time 25th/75th percentile GPA—2.67/3.29* ➡ *full-time 25th/75th percentile LSAT—146/153* ➡ *part-time 25th/75th percentile LSAT—146/152* ➡ *812 total full-time* ➡ *394 total part-time* ➡ *21% minority* ➡ *44% women* ➡ *33 states & foreign countries represented* ➡ *247 undergraduate schools represented*

The student-to-faculty ratio is approximately 21 to 1, with the median age of the student body at approximately 27 years. Many students are pursuing law as a second career or to complement their current employment.

■ Faculty

➡ *89 total* ➡ *57 full-time* ➡ *32 part-time or adjunct* ➡ *24 women* ➡ *7 minority*

■ Library and Physical Facilities

➡ *357,491 volumes & equivalents* ➡ *library hours: Mon.-Thurs., 7:30 A.M.-MIDNIGHT; Fri., 7:30 A.M.-10:00 P.M.; Sat., 8:30 A.M.-7:00 P.M.; Sun., 10:00 A.M.-10:00 P.M.* ➡ *LEXIS/NEXIS (home access available)* ➡ *WESTLAW (home access available)* ➡ *CALI* ➡ *Epic* ➡ *Internet (home access available)* ➡ *9 full-time librarians* ➡ *library seats 586*

The library is housed on three floors of the college, providing space for individual study carrels and a modern computer center for student use. Students have access to a variety of online databases; interactive video; CD-ROM and laserdisc databases; as well as access to one of the most advanced multimedia departments in the country.

Located in the law school complex are hearing rooms and chambers for the First and Fourteenth Texas Courts of Appeals (intermediate appellate tribunals with both civil and criminal jurisdiction), making the only American law school to house two appellate courts on a permanent basis.

■ Curriculum

➡ *Academic Support Program* ➡ *90 credits required to graduate* ➡ *166 courses available* ➡ *J.D. degree available* ➡ *semesters, start in Aug. and Jan.* ➡ *summer session available* ➡ *range of first-year class size—20-95*

The curriculum at South Texas combines traditional classroom instruction with innovative simulated and clinical courses. The full-time program requires a minimum of 90 weeks of study generally requiring three years, and the part-time program requires a minimum of 120 weeks of study generally requiring four years.

South Texas offers a class scheduling system whereby students may select convenient class times rather than having to choose between day and evening divisions. To accommodate part-time working students, a complete curriculum of classes is scheduled after 5:30 P.M. A few classes are also scheduled on Saturday.

■ Special Programs

South Texas administers an academic assistance program to eligible students in their first 30 hours of coursework. These individual and small-group sessions provide weekly reviews of study techniques, such as taking class notes, outlining, briefing cases, and reviewing for examinations. The program is augmented by periodic seminars covering similar topics, which are open to all interested students.

The Center for Legal Responsibility at South Texas College of Law promotes conflict resolution outside the traditional judicial system, fostering opportunities for students to develop skills in alternative dispute resolution procedures. The center seeks to prepare law students to follow *The Texas Lawyer's Creed—A Mandate for Professionalism.*

South Texas provides students with practical legal experience through its On-Site and Off-Site Clinics. In the On-Site Clinics, students work on actual cases and simulated exercises under the direction of a professor. Off-Site Clinics involve hands-on experience in prosecutors' offices, governmental agencies, and with members of the state and federal judiciary, both at the trial and appellate level.

■ Admission Standards

➡ *Bachelor's degree required* ➡ *application deadlines— fall, March 1; spring, Oct. 1* ➡ *LSAT, LSDAS required* ➡ *application fee—$40*

Beginning and transfer students are admitted for the fall and spring terms, and early application is encouraged. Students are admitted primarily on the basis of their LSAT score and undergraduate grade-point average. A significant percentage of each class, however, is selected on the basis of other additional factors, such as exceptional personal or academic achievement (not necessarily demonstrated in academic or testing assessments); letters of recommendation;

work, community service, or life experiences; leadership potential; a history of overcoming adversity and hardship; and a talent for communicating effectively. Every attempt is made to evaluate each applicant as an individual, a prospective student, and a future professional.

South Texas College of Law affiliated with Texas A&M University does not discriminate on the basis of race, color, religion, national or ethnic origin, sex, sexual orientation, age, or disability in the administration of its educational policies, admission policies, scholarship and loan programs, or other school-administered rights, privileges, programs, or activities generally accorded or made available to the students at the college.

■ Student Activities

The *South Texas Law Review* is a scholarly periodical published and edited by a staff of law school students selected for membership on the basis of outstanding scholarship or writing ability. In addition, South Texas law students edit and publish the *Corporate Counsel Review* on behalf of the Corporate Counsel Section of the State Bar of Texas, and *Currents*, a journal of international trade law, which focuses on the latest legislation, treaties, cases, and trends affecting international trade.

Each year, South Texas is represented by student teams at various state, national, and international moot court competitions, as well as mock trial, client counseling, and negotiation and settlement competitions. Since 1980, these teams have earned an unmatched record, leading the nation in victories with an array of state, regional, and national championships, as well as numerous individual honors.

The Student Bar Association is an active organization composed of the entire student body. South Texas has a local honor society, the Order of the Lytae; a chapter of the national Order of Barristers; three legal fraternities; and numerous special-interest student organizations.

■ Expenses and Financial Aid

➡ *tuition & fees—full-time, $15,450; part-time, $10,500* ➡ *estimated additional expenses—$12,372 (room & board, books, transportation, & other expenses)* ➡ *academic merit & financial need scholarships available* ➡ *FAFSA form for need analysis due to central processor in Feb. or early March for fall, and July or early Aug. for spring*

South Texas offers a deferred tuition payment program. In addition, various financial aid programs are available. Depending on the circumstances, students may be eligible for Tuition Equalization Grants and State Student Incentive Grants for Texas residents, Stafford Loans, the Law Access Loan, and Federal work-study. An expanding variety of merit- and need-based scholarships, tuition waivers, grants, and emergency loans are also offered. Deadlines for these assistance programs vary. Interested applicants may contact the Office of Scholarships and Financial Aid at 713.646.1820.

■ Career Services

The Career Services Office (CSO) offers a full range of services to meet the needs of students while remaining responsive to changes in hiring trends and patterns. The CSO is committed to providing personalized service by being available on a daily basis to assist students and alumni with career guidance and job search strategies. The CSO facilitates the job search process by offering skills seminars (résumé writing, interviewing skills, etc.), coordinating the fall recruiting program and job fairs, offering career counseling, and providing a variety of written and electronic resources to both students and alumni.

Applicant Group for the 1998-1999 Academic Year

South Texas College of Law affiliated with Texas A&M University

GPA	No LSAT		120 - 124		125 - 129		130 - 134		135 - 139		140 - 144		145 - 149		150 - 154		155 - 159		160 - 164		165 - 169		170 - 180		Total	
	Apps	Adm	Apps	Adm	Apps	Adm	Apps	Adm	Apps	Adm	Apps	Adm	Apps	Adm	Apps	Adm	Apps	Adm	Apps	Adm	Apps	Adm	Apps	Adm	Apps	Adm
3.75-4.00	0	0	0	0	0	0	0	0	1	0	2	2	9	9	7	7	5	4	4	4	0	0	0	0	28	26
3.50-3.74	1	0	0	0	0	0	3	0	4	1	12	9	28	26	35	33	22	20	5	5	1	1	0	0	114	95
3.25-3.49	1	1	0	0	1	0	0	0	15	1	46	25	52	48	62	58	30	29	11	10	2	1	0	0	220	173
3.00-3.24	1	1	0	0	0	0	9	0	28	2	69	32	81	72	74	68	31	30	9	9	3	1	0	0	314	215
2.75-2.99	1	0	0	0	3	0	10	0	34	0	70	22	86	74	79	75	46	45	16	14	2	2	0	0	357	232
2.50-2.74	0	0	0	0	0	0	10	0	31	0	65	8	72	57	65	55	37	33	9	8	2	2	0	0	301	163
2.25-2.49	2	0	0	0	0	0	6	0	28	0	43	0	50	23	44	36	28	22	7	6	0	0	0	0	214	87
2.00-2.24	0	0	0	0	2	0	3	0	15	0	25	1	17	3	18	6	11	4	2	0	2	2	1	1	99	17
No GPA	11	0	1	0	0	0	0	0	0	0	2	0	1	1	0	0	1	0	0	0	1	0	0	0	17	1
Total	17	2	1	0	6	0	41	0	156	4	334	99	396	313	384	338	211	187	63	56	13	9	1	1	1664	1009

Apps = Number of Applicants
Adm = Number Admitted
Note: This chart is to be used as a general guide only. Nonnumerical factors are considered for all applicants.

University of Southern California Law School

USC Law School
University of Southern California
Los Angeles, CA 90089-0071

E-Mail: admissions@law.usc.edu
URL: http://www.usc.edu/law
Phone: 213.740.7331

■ Introduction

The University of Southern California Law School is a nationally oriented, private institution offering an innovative program focusing on the law as an expression of social values and as an instrument for implementing social goals. The Law School is small and informal, boasting an unusually advantageous student/faculty ratio of better than 14:1. Instruction is both highly theoretical and highly practical, emphasizing in various courses both a critical understanding of how law functions in society and a practical knowledge of how lawyers function within the legal system. The school has achieved national recognition both for its innovative, interdisciplinary-oriented young faculty and for its leadership in clinical education.

The Law School's location on the main campus of the University of Southern California, University Park, facilitates access to instruction in law-related disciplines. University Park is located five miles from the center of Los Angeles, a dynamic city which itself is the core of an internationally important region.

Fully accredited nationwide, the USC Law School has been a member of the AALS since 1907, and was included in the first group of schools to be accredited by the ABA.

■ Enrollment/Student Body

- ➤ 3,500 applicants ➤ 205 enrolled first-year class 1998
- ➤ full-time 25th/75th percentile GPA—3.30/3.65
- ➤ full-time 25th/75th percentile LSAT—159/165
- ➤ 620 total full-time ➤ 40% minority
- ➤ 46% women ➤ 40 states represented
- ➤ 125 undergraduate schools represented

Typically, the size of the entering class is between 195 and 205 students, divided for first-year instructional purposes into two, three, or four sections.

■ Faculty

- ➤ 46 full-time ➤ 40 part-time or adjunct

■ Library and Physical Facilities

- ➤ 340,000 volumes & equivalents ➤ LEXIS
- ➤ WESTLAW ➤ 10 full-time librarians

The law library has an excellent, service-oriented professional staff. Law librarians teach special programs such as Accelerated Legal Research, an optional summer course for entering first-year students, and Summer Associates' Survival Skills, a spring-semester program that prepares students for summer employment. Study carrels and tables throughout the library are wired so that students can attach their own laptop computers to the network.

■ Curriculum

- ➤ Academic Support Program
- ➤ 88 credits required to graduate ➤ joint degrees offered

The USC Law School operates on a semester basis, and admits only full-time students. The first-year curriculum consists of required courses; the remaining two years are elective, enabling students to concentrate on subjects of special interest. Numerous courses are offered by faculty experts in international law, corporations and business-government relationships, bioethics, civil rights and liberties, and judicial administration. The curriculum draws upon several related disciplines such as philosophy, linguistics, economics, psychology, sociology, international relations, and urban planning to provide an integrated approach to legal study.

■ Special Programs

Dual Degrees—The Law School offers dual-degree programs that enable qualified students to earn a law degree and a Master's degree in the following fields: Business Administration, Business Taxation, Economics, Communications Management, Gerontology, International Relations, Philosophy, Political Science, Public Administration, Public Policy, Real Estate Development, Religion, and Social Work. The Law School also maintains a dual-degree program with the California Institute of Technology, enabling students to receive a J.D. from USC and a Ph.D. in Social Science from Cal Tech, or to complete the requirements for the Graduate Certificate in the USC Program in Gender Studies.

Legal Clinics—The Post-Conviction Justice Project, Children's Legal Issues, and the Business Legal Advice Clinic, taught by faculty members with substantial practical experience, enable students to gain valuable advocacy skills and learn first-hand about access to justice, children's rights, and business/employment law by representing real clients. In addition, the school arranges placements for academic credit with federal and state court judges, and numerous government and public interest law offices.

Research Centers—The Law School supports several research centers including the Center for Communications Law and Policy, the Pacific Center for Health Policy and Ethics, and the Olin Program in Law and Rational Choice.

■ Admission

- ➤ Bachelor's degree from an accredited college required
- ➤ application deadline—Feb. 1; early application encouraged
- ➤ application fee—$60

Students applying for admission should take the LSAT no later than the December administration. Admissions decisions are made on the basis of the student's academic record, LSAT score, personal statement, and letters of recommendation. The Admissions Committee gives primary consideration to outstanding academic and professional promise and to qualities which will enhance the diversity of the student body, or will enrich the Law School educational environment. Two letters of recommendation are required. Applicants are strongly urged to submit at least one academic recommendation letter.

The committee focuses on the student's college grades, academic major, selection of courses, and significant scholarly achievements. The Law School does not require applicants to take any specific college courses of study. Whatever the discipline, the student should concentrate on developing strong writing and analytic skills.

■ Student Activities

The school's *Law Review* has one of the largest circulations in the nation. Students also publish the *Southern California Interdisciplinary Law Journal*, and the *Review of Law and Women's Studies*. The Moot Court competition sends participants to national and state competitions; recently the final rounds at the Law School have been judged by justices of the U.S. Supreme Court. The Order of the Coif, the national legal scholastic honor society, has a local chapter at the school.

Public service activities abound. The Public Interest Law Foundation provides financial assistance for summer and postgraduate public-service employment and volunteer opportunities. The school provides annual awards to students who excel in public and community service, and who author the best essay on a social-justice topic.

Asian, African American, and Latino law students are represented by associations. Other student organizations include international and entertainment law societies, chapters of major legal fraternities, a Women's Law Association, Gay and Lesbian Law Union, Christian Legal Society, Jewish Law Students, and chapters of the ACLU and Federalist Society.

■ Expenses and Financial Aid

➡ *1998-99 tuition—$12,526/semester*

A significant financial commitment is made each year to assist worthy applicants so that they may attend. No student should refrain from applying because of financial need.

To assist in the partial payment of educational loans, the Law School offers funds to graduates who accept employment with low-paying public interest organizations.

For more information, please call Mary Bingham, Director of Financial Aid at 213.740.7331.

■ Housing

University housing is available for law students in various university dormitories and apartments.

■ Career Services

The Law School maintains a career services office to assist students and alumni in securing professional employment. The office provides a variety of services including arranging on-campus interviews by legal employers, assisting students in summer and part-time job searches, and maintaining a file and monthly newsletter for alumni seeking a change of employment. In addition, programs designed to provide guidance concerning career selection are offered during the year. The career services office maintains a public interest and government employment directory listing all available positions. Each year, several hundred private firms, government agencies, public interest agencies, and corporations from throughout the country come to USC Law School to interview students for summer and permanent employment. Historically, more than 95 percent of each graduating class has found employment.

Applicant Group for the 1998-1999 Academic Year

University of Southern California Law School
This grid includes only applicants who earned 120-180 LSAT scores under standard administrations.

LSAT Score	3.75 +		3.50 - 3.74		3.25 - 3.49		3.00 - 3.24		2.75 - 2.99		Below 2.75		No GPA		Total	
	Apps	Adm	Apps	Adm	Apps	Adm	Apps	Adm	Apps	Adm	Apps	Adm	Apps	Adm	Apps	Adm
175-180	6	6	4	4	1	1	3	2	3	0	0	0	0	0	17	13
170-174	26	25	25	24	31	25	22	6	12	4	5	0	1	0	122	84
165-169	65	65	134	127	122	92	84	13	40	2	27	2	13	5	485	306
160-164	110	80	221	122	237	68	129	20	52	2	27	0	15	3	791	295
155-159	94	25	172	23	201	21	155	20	75	4	51	4	17	0	765	97
150-154	60	6	122	11	130	9	154	10	73	0	55	0	19	0	613	36
Below 150	23	1	70	0	125	4	148	0	122	0	157	0	24	0	669	5
Total	384	208	748	311	847	220	695	71	377	12	322	6	89	8	3462	836

Apps = Number of Applicants
Adm = Number Admitted
Reflects 98% of the total applicant pool.

Southern Illinois University School of Law

Lesar Law Building
1150 Douglas Drive
Carbondale, IL 62901-6804

E-Mail: lawadmit@siu.edu
URL: http://www.siu.edu/~lawsch
Phone: 800.739.9187 or 618.453.8858 or 8767

■ Introduction

Southern Illinois University School of Law is located in Carbondale, a community of 27,000 people in the hilly, wooded Ozark area of Illinois. Carbondale's quality of life has recently been rated as number one among all small cities in Illinois. The School of Law is one of many colleges of Southern Illinois University-Carbondale, a comprehensive state university with a total student enrollment of over 20,000. The law school is fully accredited by the ABA and is a member of the Association of American Law Schools.

■ Enrollment/Student Body

➡ *737 applicants*   ➡ *425 admitted first-year class 1998*
➡ *full-time 25th/75th percentile GPA—2.67/3.38*
➡ *part-time 25th/75th percentile GPA—3.34/3.34*
➡ *full-time 25th/75th percentile LSAT—150/155*
➡ *part-time 25th/75th percentile LSAT—164/164*
➡ *145 enrolled first-year class 1998*   ➡ *376 total full-time*
➡ *5 total part-time*   ➡ *12% minority*   ➡ *36% women*
➡ *50+ states & foreign countries represented*
➡ *120+ undergraduate schools represented*

■ Faculty

➡ *33 total*   ➡ *23 full-time*   ➡ *10 part-time or adjunct*
➡ *7 women*   ➡ *1 minority*

■ Library and Physical Facilities

➡ *350,000 volumes & equivalents*   ➡ *library hours:*
Mon.-Fri., 8:00 A.M.-6:00 P.M.; Sat., 9:00 A.M.-5:00 P.M.;
Sun., 1:00 P.M.-9:00 P.M.   ➡ *LEXIS*   ➡ *NEXIS*
➡ *WESTLAW*   ➡ *LEGALTRAC*
➡ *7 full-time librarians*   ➡ *library seats 407*

The law library's professional staff provides a wide range of services to patrons. The online public catalog available via the Internet provides immediate and detailed information about the monographs and journals available in the library collection. A LAN-based computer lab provides access to computer-assisted research systems, both legal (e.g. WESTLAW, LEXIS) and nonlegal, as well as computer-aided instruction, word processing, and other application software. Ample seating in a variety of settings, including tables, unreserved carrels, and locked carrels for research assistants and seminar students, help make the library an activity center of the law school. All facilities are fully accessible to individuals with disabilities. Students have 24-hour keyed access to the library and other facilities.

■ Curriculum

➡ *Academic Support Program*   ➡ *90 credits required to graduate*   ➡ *79 courses available*   ➡ *degrees available: J.D.; J.D./M.D.; J.D./M.B.A.; J.D./M. Acc.; J.D./M.P.A.; J.D./M.S.W.; J.D./Ph.D. in Political Science*
➡ *semesters, start in Aug.*
➡ *range of first-year class size—20-65*

All students have a uniform first-year Lawyering Skills curriculum. A broad range of courses and seminars are offered in the second and third years. Throughout the curriculum the faculty emphasize the inculcation of professional skills such as writing, oral argumentation, drafting documents, interviewing, negotiating, and counseling.

■ Special Programs

The school's clinical programs enable senior law students to have various "real-life" experiences with clients and the legal system under the supervision of clinical faculty members, judges, and licensed attorneys. The Elderly Clinic provides direct legal assistance to persons over 60 years of age in the 13 southernmost counties of Illinois. Students may participate in an Externship Program in which they obtain academic credit while working in a publicly funded law office or agency. The ADR Clinic allows students to learn more about alternative dispute resolution techniques and mediate in court and community programs. A Domestic Violence Clinic allows students to assist victims in obtaining legal relief.

Concurrent J.D./Masters Degree programs (M.B.A., M.P.A., M. Acc., M.S.W., Ph.D. Political Science) are offered in conjunction with the Graduate School. An innovative six-year program offered in cooperation with the School of Medicine permits selected students to concurrently obtain J.D. and M.D. degrees.

The school has a very strong health law curriculum, featuring five courses in this specialty. Environmental law is a prominent subject in the law school's curriculum, with six elective courses as well as a National Environmental Law Moot Court team.

The school provides a comprehensive moot court program, sponsoring teams that compete in various national moot court as well as interviewing/counseling and negotiation competitions. SIU law students have enjoyed tremendous success in these competitions.

As part of its mission to emphasize leadership skills, the law school sponsors an active public speakers' program focusing on important national and regional issues. In addition, the school sponsors a major symposium each year bringing a large number of prominent legal educators to Carbondale. Recent symposia have addressed the legal ramifications of the rising prison population, Bill of Rights, Justice Oliver Wendell Holmes, Brown v. Board of Education, and Tobacco Litigation.

■ Admission

➡ *Bachelor's degree required*   ➡ *rolling admission, early application (before March 1) recommended*
➡ *LSAT, LSDAS required*   ➡ *application fee—$25*

Admission decisions are based on a number of factors, the LSAT score and undergraduate GPA being most prominent. The highest LSAT score is used. There is no formal cutoff for either the LSAT score or GPAs. Other factors considered by the admissions committee include trends in academic performance, writing ability, leadership and maturity, letters of recommendation, employment, or community service experience, and obstacles imposed by religious, ethnic, gender, or disability discrimination. The admissions committee actively recruits minority students.

■ Student Activities

The school publishes the *SIU Law Journal*, which provides editorial and writing experience for a number of upper-class students. Students with a particular interest in health law can also publish articles in *The Journal of Legal Medicine*.

All students automatically belong to the Student Bar Association. The SBA schedules lectures and social affairs, provides services to its members, and serves as a channel of communication between students and faculty. Students play an active role in law school governance, serving on most faculty committees. Other student organizations include Phi Alpha Delta, the International Law Society, the Women's Law Forum, the Environmental Law Society, the Black Law Student Association, Lesbian and Gay Law Students, Phi Delta Phi, the Law and Medicine Society, the Christian Legal Society, the Hispanic Law Student Association, the Asian Pacific Law Student Association, and law student divisions of the Illinois State Bar Association and the ABA.

■ Expenses and Financial Aid

➡ *full-time tuition & fees—resident, $5,654/yr.; nonresident, $14,894/yr.* ➡ *estimated additional expenses—$8,226 (books, supplies, room & board, transportation & misc.)* ➡ *scholarships available* ➡ *financial aid available; Free Application for Federal Student Aid (FAFSA) need form is required*

Currently, students can qualify for the in-state tuition rate after they have been a bona fide Illinois resident for at least three consecutive months. Student loans, work-study opportunities, and most other forms of financial aid are administered by the university's Financial Aid Office. Information concerning loans and financial aid procedures may be obtained for the Financial Aid Office, Woody Hall, Southern Illinois University-Carbondale.

■ Career Services

The Career Services Office provides services for both enrolled students and alumni. Students have the opportunity to participate in a variety of regional and national job fairs and career conferences throughout the year. Other programs and services provided include individual career counseling, an on-campus interview program, a research pool service, and career workshops.

The Career Services Office also provides a job-listing service, subscribes to a variety of job newsletters, publishes a biweekly job vacancy bulletin, and exchanges job bulletins with other law schools. The career library contains diverse career materials including firm résumés, corporate brochures, and directories.

Applicant Group for the 1998-1999 Academic Year

Southern Illinois University School of Law
This grid includes only applicants who earned 120-180 LSAT scores under standard administrations.

LSAT Score	GPA																				
	3.75 +		3.50 - 3.74		3.25 - 3.49		3.00 - 3.24		2.75 - 2.99		2.50 - 2.74		2.25 - 2.49		2.00 - 2.24		Below 2.00		No GPA		Total	
	Apps	Adm	Apps	Adm	Apps	Adm	Apps	Adm	Apps	Adm	Apps	Adm	Apps	Adm	Apps	Adm	Apps	Adm	Apps	Adm	Apps	Adm
175-180	0	0	0	0	0	0	0	0	0	0	0	0	0	0	0	0	0	0	0	0	0	0
170-174	0	0	0	0	0	0	0	0	0	0	1	1	0	0	0	0	0	0	0	0	1	1
165-169	2	2	5	5	1	1	1	1	1	1	0	0	1	1	0	0	0	0	1	1	12	12
160-164	4	4	5	5	10	10	6	6	5	5	2	2	2	2	0	0	0	0	0	0	34	34
155-159	11	10	10	10	25	24	24	23	8	8	21	20	8	8	2	2	1	1	3	2	113	108
150-154	16	15	21	20	34	33	40	40	26	25	21	21	11	9	6	5	1	0	1	1	177	169
145-149	4	3	20	17	29	17	37	19	23	12	26	9	12	4	4	1	0	0	4	2	159	84
140-144	9	5	12	4	13	3	23	1	21	0	26	0	14	0	12	0	2	0	8	2	140	15
135-139	3	1	4	0	8	0	12	0	9	0	12	0	10	0	4	0	1	0	7	0	70	1
130-134	1	0	0	0	0	0	5	0	2	0	3	0	2	0	1	0	2	0	2	0	18	0
125-129	0	0	1	0	0	0	0	0	2	0	0	0	1	0	1	0	0	0	0	0	5	0
120-124	0	0	0	0	0	0	0	0	0	0	0	0	0	0	0	0	1	0	0	0	1	0
Total	50	40	78	61	120	88	148	90	97	51	112	53	61	24	30	8	8	1	26	8	730	424

Apps = Number of Applicants
Adm = Number Admitted
Reflects 99% of the total applicant pool.

Southern Methodist University School of Law

Assistant Dean for Admissions
P.O. Box 750110
Dallas, TX 75275-0110

E-Mail: lawadmit@mail.smu.edu
URL: http://www.law.smu.edu
Phone: 214.768.2550

■ Introduction

SMU law school is located just five miles north of downtown Dallas, one of the 10 largest cities in the U.S.A. The campus is situated in a beautiful, residential neighborhood, an intimate learning community within a vibrant urban center.

Consistently recognized as one of the top 40 law schools in the country by the practicing bar, SMU law school provides its graduates the opportunity to become part of a professional community of over 9,000 graduates practicing in all 50 states and 65 foreign countries.

■ Enrollment/Student Body

➡ *1,640 applicants* ➡ *230 enrolled first-year class 1998*
➡ *full-time 25th/75th percentile GPA—2.94/3.49* ➡ *full-time 25th/75th percentile LSAT—154/160* ➡ *16% minority*
➡ *49.5% women* ➡ *30 states and the District of Columbia represented* ➡ *103 undergraduate schools represented*
➡ *total enrollment—751* ➡ *total minority—15%*

Each year, SMU attracts students from the top 25 percent of the national applicant pool. This small and selective student body is the core of our close-knit learning community.

■ Faculty

➡ *96 total* ➡ *36 full-time* ➡ *58 part-time or adjunct*
➡ *10 women (full-time)* ➡ *7 minority (full-time)*

At SMU, students receive individual attention from nationally- recognized faculty who have practical experience as attorneys in addition to experience in the classroom.

■ Library and Physical Facilities

➡ *500,000 volumes & equivalents* ➡ *computer center with WESTLAW and LEXIS* ➡ *11 full-time librarians*
➡ *library seats 700*

The Law School Quadrangle, a six-acre self-contained corner of a beautiful, tree-lined campus, offers students easy and convenient access to all law school facilities. The four buildings in the quad house state-of-the-art classrooms, student lounges, faculty offices, expansive student affairs and career services offices, and a library where students have open-stack access to holdings ranked in the top 25 in the nation. The larger SMU campus offers law students a variety of housing options, a child-care facility, a health center, and a fitness/wellness center.

■ Curriculum

➡ *Tutorial Services & Academic Support Program*
➡ *90 credits required to graduate* ➡ *over 170 courses available* ➡ *degrees available: J.D.; J.D./M.B.A.; J.D./M.A. in Economics; LL.M.; LL.M. (Taxation); LL.M. (International and Comparative Law—for foreign attorneys only)*

Students find a sophisticated curriculum at the SMU School of Law that complements its wide breadth of offerings with extensive depth of focus.

The classroom requirements consist of 90 hours of course study completed over three years. In the first year students study a prescribed set of courses that lay a solid foundation for advanced study and for development of essential lawyering skills, including an innovative, hands-on course designed to develop students' interviewing and negotiating skills. In the second and third years, students have limited requirements.

The classroom requirements are complemented by the public service requirement. Following completion of the first year, students are required to complete 30 hours of law-related public service prior to graduation. Students may choose from a wide variety of pre-approved public service placements or design one of their own.

During the three years, students have a mix of lecture and seminar courses. In the first year, the entering class is divided into sections of 75-80 students. All of the substantive law courses are taken with the section. In the second and third years, the lecture courses have an average of 40 students and the seminar courses have an average of 15 students.

Externships and Clinics—Externships offer students opportunity to work at a government agency for up to two hours of course credit. Popular externships include those with the U.S. Attorney, the SEC, and the EPA.

Clinics offer students an opportunity to engage in the practice of law for up to five hours of course credit. Currently SMU has three clinical programs: civil, criminal, and tax.

Overseas Study—SMU offers students an opportunity to study law for six weeks at University College at Oxford University in England.

■ Admission Standards

➡ *Bachelor's degree required* ➡ *application deadline: Dec. 1 —early decision; Feb. 1—regular decision; April 1—late decision*
➡ *LSAT, LSDAS required* ➡ *application fee—$50*

The goal of the admissions process is to identify applicants who have the ability to handle a rigorous intellectual challenge, a capacity to acquire lawyering skills, and the potential for success as a law student and a lawyer. In the admission process, the Admission Committee wants to know about each applicant's unique abilities, accomplishments, and personality. To that end, each application is considered in its entirety: LSAT scores, undergraduate performance, graduate studies, work experience, activities, a personal statement, and letters of recommendation are all read and evaluated.

■ Student Activities

SMU offers selected students opportunities to write and research for five legal publications: *SMU Law Review*, *Journal of Air Law and Commerce, International Lawyer*, *Computer Section Reporter*, and *NAFTA: Law and Business Review of the Americas*.

SMU students who are aspiring advocates develop and showcase their lawyering skills in over 20 regional, national, and international competitions annually, including mock trial, client counseling, negotiation, and moot court competitions. As team members, students are coached by faculty members and local lawyers.

Student organizations offer students opportunities to develop friendships, to find support and advice, and to learn about legal topics. The following student organizations are active at SMU: Student Bar Association; Asian Law Students Association; Black Law Students Association; Hispanic Law Students Association; Women in Law; Law Students with Families; Jewish Law Students Association; Christian Legal Society; Environmental Law Society; International Law Society; Intellectual Property Society; and three legal fraternities.

■ Expenses and Financial Aid

➡ *full-time tuition & fees—$21,908*
➡ *estimated additional expenses—$7,372 (room & board, $4,508; books, $930; misc., $1,942)*

A legal education at SMU is an investment in the future. Recognizing that most students do not have sufficient personal resources to pay for this investment, SMU provides more than $2 million in scholarships annually and access to both federal and private loan programs.

The scholarships are awarded on the basis of merit and need.

■ Career Services

SMU provides students with job placement assistance throughout their legal careers. The Career Services Office helps students develop their job search and career development skills and partner with students in locating summer and permanent job opportunities.

SMU graduates fare well in the legal job market. Within nine months of graduation the class of 1997 had a placement rate of 98 percent and a median starting salary of $55,000. Graduates who accept jobs in the public sector may be eligible to receive assistance repaying their law school debts.

Applicant Group for the 1998-1999 Academic Year

Southern Methodist University School of Law
This grid includes only applicants who earned 120-180 LSAT scores under standard administrations.

LSAT Score	GPA																					
	3.75 +		3.50 - 3.74		3.25 - 3.49		3.00 - 3.24		2.75 - 2.99		2.50 - 2.74		2.25 - 2.49		2.00 - 2.24		Below 2.00		No GPA		Total	
	Apps	Adm	Apps	Adm	Apps	Adm	Apps	Adm	Apps	Adm	Apps	Adm	Apps	Adm	Apps	Adm	Apps	Adm	Apps	Adm	Apps	Adm
175-180	0	0	0	0	1	1	0	0	1	1	0	0	1	1	0	0	0	0	0	0	3	3
170-174	2	2	3	3	4	4	1	1	0	0	3	3	0	0	0	0	0	0	1	0	14	13
165-169	14	13	9	9	8	8	7	7	11	11	5	5	1	1	1	1	0	0	2	2	58	57
160-164	22	22	35	34	45	45	31	31	28	27	16	16	8	6	6	6	0	0	2	2	193	189
155-159	30	30	62	60	83	79	97	74	67	34	27	13	20	12	9	4	1	0	4	1	400	307
150-154	22	16	61	36	77	35	97	9	62	2	39	2	16	1	8	0	1	0	6	1	389	102
145-149	13	4	27	5	52	10	59	7	54	3	29	1	25	0	9	0	1	0	11	1	280	31
140-144	6	1	14	0	21	1	31	0	42	0	28	0	17	0	6	0	1	0	5	0	171	2
135-139	4	0	4	0	5	0	13	0	10	0	11	0	8	0	4	0	4	0	3	0	66	0
130-134	0	0	1	0	0	0	0	0	5	0	6	0	3	0	4	0	1	0	1	0	21	0
125-129	0	0	0	0	0	0	1	0	2	0	1	0	2	0	4	0	1	0	2	0	13	0
120-124	0	0	0	0	1	0	1	0	0	0	1	0	0	0	0	0	0	0	0	0	3	0
Total	113	88	216	147	297	183	338	129	282	78	166	40	101	21	51	11	10	0	37	7	1611	704

Apps = Number of Applicants
Adm = Number Admitted
Reflects 98% of the total applicant pool.

Southern University Law Center

Admissions Office
P.O. Box 9294, Southern Branch Post Office
Baton Rouge, LA 70813

E-Mail: simmons@sus.edu
Phone: 504.771.5340 or 800.537.1135

■ Introduction

In September 1947, the Southern University School of Law was officially opened. Accredited by the American Bar Association, the Supreme Court of Louisiana, and the Southern Association of Colleges and Secondary Schools, the Law Center maintains a high standard of professional education. It is fully approved by the Veterans Administration for the training of eligible veterans. The Southern University Law Center adheres to the principle of equal opportunity without regard to race, sex, color, creed, national origin, age, handicap, or marital status.

■ Enrollment/Student Body

➡ *762 applicants*   ➡ *207 admitted first-year class 1998*
➡ *118 enrolled first-year class 1998*   ➡ *full-time 25th/75th percentile GPA—2.40/3.11*   ➡ *full-time 25th/75th percentile LSAT—141/146*   ➡ *311 total full-time*   ➡ *66% minority*
➡ *50% women*   ➡ *22 states & foreign countries represented*
➡ *50 undergraduate schools represented*

■ Faculty

➡ *41 total*   ➡ *30 full-time*   ➡ *11 part-time or adjunct*
➡ *10 women*   ➡ *25 minority*

■ Library and Physical Facilities

➡ *400,270 volumes & equivalents*   ➡ *library hours: Mon.-Thurs., 7:30 A.M.-MIDNIGHT; Fri., 7:30 A.M.-5:00 P.M.; Sat., 9:00 A.M.-5:00 P.M.; Sun., 2:00 P.M.-10:00 P.M.*
➡ *LEXIS*   ➡ *NEXIS*   ➡ *WESTLAW*   ➡ *DIALOG*
➡ *Legal Trac*   ➡ *6 full-time librarians*   ➡ *library seats 284*

The Law Center building is located on the parent campus of the Southern University system. A $4 million expansion and improvement program has been completed. The new facility gives the Law Center a total area of approximately 80,000-square feet.

Special arrangements have been made with the Louisiana State University Library, which has one of the largest collections of Anglo-American and civil law materials in the South, to make its resources available for research purposes through the Southern University Law Library.

Training sessions are conducted each semester by library staff to assist students in the proper utilization of the WESTLAW system.

■ Curriculum

➡ *Academic Support Program*   ➡ *Pre-Law Success offered*
➡ *96 credits required to graduate*   ➡ *81 courses available*
➡ *fall semester—Aug.-Dec.*   ➡ *spring semester—Jan.-May*
➡ *summer session—June-July*

The program of study is designed to give students a comprehensive knowledge of both the civil law and common law. While emphasis is given to the substantive and procedural law of Louisiana with its French and Spanish origins, Anglo-American law is strongly integrated into the curriculum. Fundamental differences in method and approach and the results reached in the two systems are analyzed.

The civil law system of Louisiana offers the law student a unique educational opportunity. The program of instruction examines the historical background of the civil law system and its development in the Anglo-American setting.

Students are trained in the art of advocacy, legal research, and the sources and social purposes of legal principles. Techniques to discipline the students' minds in legal reasoning are an integral part of the educational objectives of the Law Center. Students are instructed in the ethics of the legal profession and the professional responsibility of the lawyer to society.

The three-year curriculum is based upon the standard professional courses usually given in ABA-approved member schools. The curriculum requires a full six semesters of residence. Any study undertaken in a summer session shall not count toward residence requirements. Electives have been integrated as part of the curriculum, and students are required to take courses specified for the respective years.

■ Admission

➡ *Bachelor's degree required*
➡ *application deadline—March 31*   ➡ *LSAT, LSDAS required*
➡ *application fee—$25*

The Law Center does not prescribe any prelegal courses but strongly recommends a foundation in such courses as English, speech, political science, history, economics, psychology, logic, mathematics and analytical courses, and science.

Students beginning the study of law are admitted only in the fall semester. The Law Center operates a full-time day program. Applicants are advised to take the LSAT prior to the February test date of the expected year of enrollment. Under no circumstances will a score received on the test administered more than three years prior to the anticipated date of acceptance be considered. All applications for admission are reviewed by a special committee. Though many variables are taken into consideration for admission, primary emphasis is given to the undergraduate grade-point average and scores from the LSAT. Work experience and past pursuits are also reviewed.

Completed application forms, in addition to two letters of recommendation and one copy of official transcript, should be filed with the Admissions Office during the fall semester prior to the year in which admission is sought.

■ Housing

Limited dormitory accommodations are available for law students. All students desiring to live in campus housing are required to submit an application to the Housing Office, in addition to a security deposit of $50. Applications should be made to the Director of Housing, Southern University, as early as possible.

■ Student Activities

Students with advanced standing are eligible to enroll in the Clinical Education Program, which allows students to handle cases under the direct supervision of a full-time faculty member of the Law Center.

The *Southern University Law Review* is a scholarly periodical published under the auspices of the Southern University Law Center. Editorial administration and managerial responsibilities are handled by the student members of the *Law Review* staff with guidance from a faculty advisor. Membership is conditional on the submissions by each candidate, or other interested students, of a manuscript deemed by the editorial board to be publishable. *Law Review* membership provides eligible students with a wealth of experience in legal research and writing.

The purpose of the Student Bar Association is to promote the general welfare of the Law Center, encourage among its members high scholarship, and cultivate rapport and cooperation among the students, faculty, and members of the legal profession.

■ Other Student Organizations

➡ *Moot Court board*   ➡ *Law Student Division, ABA*
➡ *Black Law Students Association*   ➡ *Delta Theta Phi Law Fraternity*   ➡ *Phi Alpha Delta Law Fraternity, International*

➡ *Women in Law*   ➡ *Environmental Law Society*
➡ *Sports & Entertainment Legal Association*
➡ *Student Trial Lawyers Association*

■ Expenses and Financial Aid

➡ *full-time tuition & fees—resident, $3,128/yr.; nonresident, $3,128 + $4,600*   ➡ *estimated additional expenses—$6,900 (books, lodging, food, transportation, misc.)*   ➡ *limited merit- & need-based scholarships available*   ➡ *financial aid available; Student Aid Report (SAR) required*   ➡ *deadline April 15*

A limited number of direct stipends and jobs are available. Direct stipends are awarded on the basis of the applicant's academic standing and demonstrated financial need. Applications for stipends should be directed to the Scholarship Committee, Southern University Law Center. Short-term loans to meet emergency needs are available from the Law Center loan fund. All students are expected to pay the required fees on the day of registration.

■ Career Services

The placement office assists students and alumni in obtaining meaningful employment opportunities. Information on part-time employment before graduation is available through this office. Assistance is also given in job-seeking skills and interviewing techniques.

Admission Profile Not Available

Southwestern University School of Law

675 South Westmoreland Avenue
Los Angeles, CA 90005-3992

E-Mail: admissions@swlaw.edu
URL: http://www.swlaw.edu
Phone: 213.738.6717

■ Introduction

The only law school with four courses of study leading
to the J.D. degree, Southwestern University School of Law
offers traditional full-time and part-time programs as well
as a unique two-year alternative curriculum. The campus,
which includes a new 83,000-square-foot law library, is
located among Los Angeles' major law firms and corporate
headquarters, and is just a short distance from the courts
and government offices in the downtown district. Many
public officials and members of the California judiciary
are among the outstanding Southwestern graduates who
practice law throughout the U.S. and abroad. Southwestern
was founded in 1911 as an independent, nonprofit, nonsectarian institution, is approved by the ABA, and holds
membership in the AALS.

■ Enrollment/Student Body

➤ *2,140 applicants* ➤ *334 enrolled first-year class 1998*
➤ *full-time 25th/75th percentile GPA—2.69/3.20*
➤ *part-time 25th/75th percentile GPA—2.61/3.22*
➤ *full-time 25th/75th percentile LSAT—149/153*
➤ *part-time 25th/75th percentile LSAT—148/153*
➤ *616 total full-time* ➤ *286 total part-time*
➤ *37.1% minority* ➤ *51.3% women*
➤ *over 240 undergraduate schools represented*

Southwestern students come from virtually every state
as well as from a dozen foreign countries. More than
two-thirds have prior work experience or have already
completed advanced degrees in such diverse disciplines
as accounting, business, chemistry, engineering, international relations, medicine, and urban planning.

■ Faculty

➤ *84 total* ➤ *47 full-time* ➤ *37 part-time or adjunct*
➤ *25 women* ➤ *14 minority*

The full-time faculty brings to the classroom an average of
seven years of law practice and well over a dozen years of
law teaching experience, and includes several nationally
recognized experts on the law. Distinguished judicial officers
and practicing attorneys on the adjunct faculty offer courses
in a number of legal specialties.

■ Library and Physical Facilities

➤ *394,090 volumes & equivalents* ➤ *over 100 weekly
library hours* ➤ *LEXIS* ➤ *NEXIS* ➤ *WESTLAW*
➤ *RLIN* ➤ *WILSONLINE* ➤ *LegalTrac*
➤ *8 full-time librarians* ➤ *library seats 610*
➤ *state and federal government depository*

Encompassing nearly two city blocks, the campus features
modern classrooms and moot court facilities, and a beautifully landscaped student commons, as well as the second
largest law library facility of all the ABA-approved law
schools in California. The library is located on four levels

of Southwestern's newly restored and adapted former
Bullocks Wilshire building, a nationally recognized historic
Art Deco landmark. The new facilities feature state-of-the-art
technology, including a 50-station computer lab and two
15-station computer learning centers, as well as custom-
designed carrels and study tables cabled for access to online
database services and the Internet.

■ Curriculum

➤ *Academic Support Program* ➤ *87 units/credits required
to graduate* ➤ *more than 140 courses available*
➤ *J.D. degree* ➤ *semesters, begin mid-Aug. (July for
SCALE program)* ➤ *range of first-year class size—27-117*
➤ *8-week on-campus summer session including Entertainment
Law Summer Program* ➤ *Foreign Summer Law Programs
in Argentina, Canada, & Mexico* ➤ *Extensive courses &
related programs in international and entertainment/sports law*

Southwestern's four courses of study include a three-year,
full-time day division; a four-year, part-time evening
division; a four-year, part-time day division known as
PLEAS (Part-time Legal Education Alternative at Southwestern), designed to accommodate students with child-care
responsibilities; and an intensive, two-calendar-year alternative program known as SCALE (Southwestern's
Conceptual Approach to Legal Education; see below).

The required curriculum for students in the day, evening,
and PLEAS divisions includes 19 courses ranging from
Business Associations to Torts. Over 120 elective courses on
a wide range of topics and more than 100 externship settings
allow students to design a broad-based legal education or
emphasize an area of law in which they plan to practice.

Legal Research and Writing is required of all first-year
students. Students must also fulfill an advanced writing
requirement later in their course of studies.

■ SCALE Program

SCALE, introduced in 1974, is an alternative, innovative J.D.
course of study offered exclusively at Southwestern. Its two
calendar years of instruction are equivalent to three full
academic years in the traditional curriculum. The program
design presents the law as an integrated whole rather than
as a series of discrete courses, incorporating instruction in
lawyering skills throughout. In the second year, the classroom functions as a "teaching law office" using simulated
client files as the primary instructional vehicle. SCALE
students also undertake off-campus externships to acquaint
them with the working life of the lawyer and judge.

■ Public Interest Involvement

A member school of the National Association for Public
Interest Law, Southwestern encourages students to pursue
public interest service through special scholarship funds, a
Loan Forgiveness Program for new graduates involved in
public interest careers, summer grants for students
working with public-service agencies, student volunteer

work with local schools and community organizations, and a variety of externships.

■ Expenses and Financial Aid

➡ *tuition & fees—$21,040 (SCALE program, $27,600; part-time, $13,362)* ➡ *estimated additional expenses— housing, food, transportation, $1,200/mo.; books & supplies, $430-650/yr.* ➡ *loans, scholarships, & work-study available* ➡ *financial aid application, FAFSA, Need Access form due June 1*

Among the more than 55 institutional scholarship funds are the Paul W. Wildman Scholarship Program and the John J. Schumacher Minority Leadership Scholarship Program, which have been established to provide up to full-tuition re-newable scholarships to members of the entering class who demonstrate exceptional academic and leadership potential.

■ Career Services

The career planning and placement program at South-western helps prepare students to succeed in a changing legal job market and assists them in obtaining permanent, part-time, and summer employment. Individual and small-group sessions on résumé writing, interview techniques, and job-search strategies are conducted. Special panel presenta-tions, seminars, and individual mock interview sessions featuring alumni and other attorneys representing a variety of law practice and legal specialization options are also offered. In addition, the Placement Office sponsors intensive on- and off-campus interview programs with prospective employers and maintains comprehensive job listings.

■ Admission

➡ *Bachelor's degree required for admission* ➡ *application deadline—June 30 (May 31 for SCALE)* ➡ *LSAT, LSDAS required* ➡ *rolling admission, early application advised*

Southwestern does not require a particular prelaw major or curriculum. Primary emphasis is placed upon GPA and LSAT scores earned within the past three-year period. Factors considered in the assessment of each applicant's file include nonacademic work, community involvement, motivation, recommendations, and diversity. Transfer applications are considered from students who have successfully completed at least one year at another ABA-approved law school.

■ Student Activities

Southwestern has one of the most active and successful interscholastic Moot Court Honors programs in the country, with teams participating in 15 competitions a year. Teams also compete through the Interscholastic Trial Advocacy Program. The *Southwestern University Law Review* and the *Southwestern Journal of Law and Trade in the Americas* feature scholarly articles and commentary on current legal issues contributed by noted jurists, attorneys, academicians, and students, and sponsor Distinguished Lecture Series and symposia on campus.

An ABA award winner and National Student Bar Associa-tion award winner, Southwestern's Student Bar Association sponsors student welfare programs and community out-reach projects. There are also over 35 on-campus student organizations including three legal fraternities; minority, cultural, and religious groups; and a variety of associations concerned with specific areas of law.

■ Alumni

Among Southwestern's 8,900 alumni are a U.S. Senator, two U.S. Congressmen, the California State Treasurer, the senior member of the California Supreme Court, the past three mayors of Los Angeles, and numerous other civic leaders.

Applicant Group for the 1998-1999 Academic Year

Southwestern University School of Law

GPA	LSAT Score										
	120-124	125-129	130-134	135-139	140-144	145-149	150-154	155-159	160-164	165-169	170 +
3.75 +											
3.50-3.74											
3.25-3.49											
3.00-3.24											
2.75-2.99											
2.50-2.74											
2.25-2.49											
2.00-2.24											
Below 2.00											
No GPA											

■ Likely   ▨ Possible   □ Unlikely

Note: This chart is to be used as a a general guide only in determining chances for admittance. Nonnumerical factors are strongly considered for all applicants.

Stanford University Law School

Office of Admissions
Stanford, CA 94305-8610

E-Mail: Law.Admissions@forsythe.stanford.edu
URL: http://www.stanford.edu/group/law/
Phone: 650.723.4985

■ Introduction

Stanford Law School is a privately funded institution dedicated to professional and graduate education and to the advancement of legal knowledge. Part of world-renowned Stanford University, it is located on Stanford's 8,180-acre campus, 35 miles south of San Francisco, California. The Law School admitted its first students in 1893 and granted its first LL.B. degree in 1901.

The school is small and intimate, enabling students to pursue personalized courses of study. In addition to providing a top-flight education, Stanford strives to maintain an environment in which diverse students feel welcome and respect one another's backgrounds and views.

■ Enrollment/Student Body

➡ *4,022 applicants* ➡ *426 admitted first-year class 1998*
➡ *180 enrolled first-year class 1998* ➡ *full-time 25th/75th percentile GPA—3.55/3.91* ➡ *full-time 25th/75th percentile LSAT—164/170* ➡ *541 total full-time* ➡ *31% minority*
➡ *43% women* ➡ *45 states & 11 foreign countries represented*
➡ *133 undergraduate schools represented*

■ Faculty

➡ *51 total* ➡ *42 full-time faculty; includes 9 emeriti*
➡ *76 visiting and lecturers* ➡ *10 women* ➡ *6 minority*

■ Library and Physical Facilities

➡ *470,000 volumes & equivalents* ➡ *library hours: Mon.-Thurs., 8:00 A.M.-MIDNIGHT; Fri., 8:00 A.M.-6:00 P.M.; Sat., 9:00 A.M.-5:00 P.M.; Sun., 10:00 A.M.-MIDNIGHT*
➡ *LEXIS* ➡ *NEXIS* ➡ *WESTLAW*
➡ *numerous other online research systems available*
➡ *8 full-time librarians* ➡ *assignable library carrels*

Robert Crown Law Library is one of this nation's most efficient and comfortable legal-research facilities. Features include a computer-assisted research center, online catalogs, open stacks, and rooms for conferences and joint work. The law library resources are augmented by the interdisciplinary 6.9-million volume Stanford University collections.

■ Curriculum

➡ *86 units/credits required to graduate* ➡ *semesters, start in Sept.* ➡ *range of first-year class size—10-60*

Stanford Law School offers a day curriculum leading to the Doctor of Jurisprudence (J.D.), or one of three other degrees. The J.D., the basic professional degree, normally requires three years of full-time study. The first-year curriculum allows two to four elective courses. Each first-year student also participates in a small-section class in research and legal writing. The second and third years are fully elective.

The Law School has special strengths in business law, high technology law, intellectual property, environmental and natural resources law, constitutional law, public policy, law and economics, problem solving, dispute resolution, legal history and theory, international law, and certain areas of public interest practice. Law students may also take relevant courses in other university departments.

■ Special Programs

Stanford Law School is a participant in a number of interdisciplinary programs, including joint-degree programs with Stanford's Graduate School of Business and other departments including economics, history, and political science, and a program leading to a J.D. and masters degree in International Policy Studies (J.D./I.P.S.); joint-degree programs with the Woodrow Wilson School of Public and International Affairs at Princeton University (J.D./M.P.A.) and with the Johns Hopkins School of Advanced Studies (J.D./M.A.); graduate level research and policy-oriented work at the Stanford Center on Conflict and Negotiation, John M. Olin Program in Law and Economics Law & Technology Policy Center, and Cyberspace Law Institute (a joint venture with Georgetown University Law Center); and supervised practice with clients at the East Palo Alto Community Law Project and other legal service entities in the Bay Area.

■ Admission

➡ *B.A. required for admission* ➡ *application deadline—Feb. 1* ➡ *rolling admission* ➡ *LSAT, LSDAS required*
➡ *application fee—$65*

Admission to Stanford Law School is based primarily upon superior academic achievement and potential to contribute to the development of the law. Competition is severe: the 180 members of the Class of 2001 were selected from among 4,022 applicants. The largest part of each class is drawn from the upper 4 percent of their undergraduate colleges and the upper 4 percent of the LSAT pool.

In evaluating individual files, the faculty considers both the record of undergraduate and graduate education and the applicant's nonacademic experience, talents, and aspirations.

Recent classes included many persons who have chosen to study law in order to enhance their contribution to fields like finance, academics, computer and natural sciences, medicine, the arts, and government. Because of its strong belief in the value of diversity, the school especially encourages applications from African Americans, Mexican Americans, American Indians, and Puerto Ricans, as well as others whose ethnic and social background provide additional dimensions that will enhance the school's program.

Applications must be postmarked after September 15 and before February 1 to meet the application deadline.

■ Student Activities

Thirty student organizations enrich the law school experience. Opportunities for scholarly work are provided through *Stanford Law Review; Stanford Journal of Interna-*

tional Law; *Stanford Journal of Law, Business and Finance*; *Stanford Law and Policy Review*; and *Stanford Environmental Law Journal*. Courtroom skills are developed in moot court. Other student-run activities include the newspaper (*Stanford Law Journal*), conferences, and Stanford Law Students Association.

Students who are female, Asian, African American, Latino, Native American, Christian, Jewish, older, bisexual, gay, or lesbian will all find groups with their particular concerns. Other organizations focus on environmental law, international law, the J.D./M.B.A. program, law and technology, and public interest law. Local affiliates of the Federalist Society and National Lawyers Guild are also present.

■ Expenses and Financial Aid

➡ *1998-99 full-time tuition, $25,080*   ➡ *estimated additional expenses (housing & misc.)—single students, $11,472; married students, $21,069*   ➡ *scholarships awarded on the basis of financial need*   ➡ *financial aid available; Need Access diskette and FAFSA forms required*

The purpose of student financial aid is to assist students who would otherwise be unable to pursue a legal education at Stanford. Approximately 80 percent of the student body receives tuition fellowship or loan assistance.

Stanford law students planning public service careers may obtain Public Service Fellowships for their second and third years of school. The school also offers grants to students who dedicate a law school summer to qualified public-service work. And for graduates who take low-paying public interest jobs and have substantial educational debt, the school has a loan relief program—Public Interest Loan Repayment Assistance Program (LRAP).

■ Career Services

The Office of Career Services helps students find both permanent employment following graduation and part-time and summer employment during law school. Over 300 employers representing over 500 offices from throughout the country participate in the spring and fall on-campus interview programs. The office also offers counseling and information on traditional and nontraditional careers and employers. The school encourages students to consider public interest and public-sector employment, and assists students to secure such positions.

A survey of students graduating in the Class of 1998 showed the following employment patterns: law firm associates, 59 percent; judicial clerks, 25 percent; business/nonlegal, public interest, government, or law teaching, 16 percent.

Applicant Group for the 1998-1999 Academic Year

Our admission process takes into consideration many factors besides the undergraduate GPA and the LSAT score. A statistical grid, as is typically provided here, only takes into consideration these two factors. We have chosen not to provide applicants with such a grid because our admission process would not be accurately portrayed.

Stetson University College of Law

1401 61st Street South
St. Petersburg, FL 33707

E-Mail: lawadmit@law.stetson.edu
URL: http://www.law.stetson.edu
Phone: 727.562.7802

■ Introduction

Stetson University College of Law, founded in 1900 in DeLand, is Florida's first law school. The College of Law was relocated in 1954 to St. Petersburg, Florida, a metropolitan area that includes Tampa and Clearwater. The Tampa Bay community is a growing commercial area that includes many law firms and courts which provide College of Law students additional educational opportunities. The College of Law is approved by the ABA and became a member of the AALS in 1931.

Stetson University College of Law is an equal opportunity educational institution.

■ Enrollment/Student Body

→ *1,716 applicants* → *802 admitted first-year*
→ *291 enrolled first-year* → *full-time 25th/75th percentile GPA—2.91/3.40* → *full-time 25th/75th percentile LSAT—146/154* → *644 total full-time* → *21% minority*
→ *57% women*

The number of applicants, admitted and enrolled, represents the spring, summer, and fall 1998 entering classes.

■ Faculty

→ *78 total* → *44 full-time* → *34 adjunct*
→ *10 women* → *4 minority*

■ Library and Physical Facilities

→ *350,000 volumes & equivalents* → *library hours: Mon.-Thurs., 7:00 A.M.-MIDNIGHT; Fri., 7:00 A.M.-7:00 P.M.; Sat., 10:00 A.M.-7:00 P.M..; Sun., 10:00 A.M.-MIDNIGHT*
→ *LEXIS* → *NEXIS* → *WESTLAW*
→ *8 full-time librarians* → *library seats 487*

The College of Law buildings reflect an early type of Spanish architecture featuring plazas, palm trees, fountains, and massive arcades after the plan of ancient monasteries. Modern in every educational aspect, the facilities include four model courtroom/classrooms, two of which are used by state courts and administrative boards for periodic sessions. The new Law Library, constructed in the same architectural style, opened with the Fall 1998 class. The library provides students with access to the world through the latest in technology. New students are required to have a laptop computer.

■ Curriculum

→ *Academic Support Program*
→ *88 credits required to graduate* → *over 100 courses available*
→ *joint J.D./M.B.A., LL.M. in International Law and Business*
→ *Scandinavian-Baltic Summer Institute in Tallinn, Estonia*
→ *semester system, new classes enroll in Jan., May, & Aug.; curriculum for first 3 semesters is prescribed*
→ *range of first-year class size—30-70*

The academic program at Stetson devotes significant attention to the lawyering process. The Stetson faculty believes that the teaching of substantive law is enhanced by extensive training in criminal and civil procedure, and by coursework or related experiences in client counseling, drafting legal papers, trial practice, and actual representation of clients—all under close faculty supervision. Stetson is a pioneer and a national leader in the development of trial practice, in which students perform the functions of a lawyer in close collaboration with a faculty member. The College of Law's courtrooms, equipped with closed-circuit video systems, allow students to observe and evaluate their own performances.

This laboratory aspect of learning is complemented by the presentation of actual sessions of court in the college's courtrooms. The District Court of Appeals, Second District of Florida, periodically convenes in the college's courtrooms to hear oral arguments from actual cases on appeal from the area's trial courts.

■ Special Programs

Trial Advocacy: Stetson is recognized as one of the best law schools in the nation for the study of trial and appellate advocacy. Student teams from Stetson routinely win national, regional, and state mock trial competitions, and in 1994, Stetson became the first law school to win all five of the major national mock trial competitions in a single academic year.

Clinics, internships, and practicums at Stetson offer a wide range of legal venues where upper-level law students can work, including the State Attorney's Office, Office of the Public defender, office of the U.S. Equal Employment Opportunity Commission, the National Labor Relations Board, the Federal Bureau of Investigation, the Department of Veteran Affairs, and local legal service offices.

Civil Government Clinic: Students gain exposure to governmental law practice and work on a variety of issues, including municipal liability, zoning, and ordinances.

Civil Poverty Law Clinic: Students advise and represent low-income individuals on issues such as family law, domestic violence, landlord-tenant, and consumer and government benefits.

Elder Law Clinic: Students get hands-on experience in the representation of elderly clients and gain exposure to a variety of legal topics which impact and address the special needs of the elderly.

Labor Law Clinic: Students gain practical experience working in the regional offices of the National Labor Relations Board and the Florida Public Employee Relations Committee.

Prosecution Clinic: Students work in the State Attorney's Office in the preparation and trial of both felony and misdemeanor cases. Students are certified with the Florida Supreme Court and actively participate during the trials and hearings.

Public Defender Clinic: Students assist in the Office of the Public Defender to render legal aid to indigent defendants in criminal prosecutions. These students are also certified to appear before the court, often following a case from inception to conclusion.

Federal Litigation Practicum: Students work with federal agencies such as the Federal Bureau of Investigation and the Department of Veterans Affairs.

Federal and State Judicial Internships: Students gain valuable insight into the judicial process by working with federal, county, and circuit judges in various divisions.

Employment Discrimination Clinic: Students assist the office of the U.S. Equal Employment Opportunity Commission in investigating charges of employment discrimination.

Environmental Law Practicum: Students work on environmental issues under the supervision of government attorneys in both state and federal agencies.

Alternative Dispute Resolution Clinic: Students get practical experience in the mediation and arbitration of a wide variety of disputes.

■ Expenses and Financial Aid

➡ *full-time tuition & fees—$19,890*   ➡ *estimated additional expenses—$10,000 (room, board, and expenses of a single student living on campus)*   ➡ *all students screened for merit scholarships which are available for first-year entering students; no application form required*   ➡ *need-based grants available; supplemental application form required; deadlines are fall— Feb. 15; Spring—Aug. 15; Summer—Feb. 15*

■ Career Services

The College of Law's firm commitment to helping students achieve their ultimate goals, either as practicing attorneys or in other lifetime positions, is reflected in its strong career services and placement programs. The Office of Career Services assists students and graduates in securing all types of legal employment and provides group seminars and individual counseling on subjects ranging from interviewing techniques and placement strategies to letter and résumé writing. The Office of Career Services, a liaison between students and legal employers, brings many legal organizations to the campus each year to interview second- and third-year students. This office posts many other legal employment opportunities for legal associates, part-time and summer positions throughout the year. The office maintains an up-to-date reference library including materials and information on law firms, graduate programs, government agencies, judicial clerkships, alternative careers, and teaching opportunities. Stetson also participates in regional job fairs, where a diverse pool of legal employers grant on-the-spot interviews.

■ Florida Bar Exam

Students who successfully complete the College of Law's course of study are eligible to sit for the bar examination in the state of Florida and all other states. Stetson ranks consistently high in passage rates and maintains the highest cumulative passing rate of all Florida law schools over the past 10 years.

Applicant Group for the 1998-1999 Academic Year

Stetson University College of Law
This grid includes only applicants who earned 120-180 LSAT scores under standard administrations.

LSAT Score	3.75 +		3.50 - 3.74		3.25 - 3.49		3.00 - 3.24		2.75 - 2.99		2.50 - 2.74		2.25 - 2.49		2.00 - 2.24		Below 2.00		No GPA		Total	
	Apps	Adm	Apps	Adm	Apps	Adm	Apps	Adm	Apps	Adm	Apps	Adm	Apps	Adm	Apps	Adm	Apps	Adm	Apps	Adm	Apps	Adm
175-180	0	0	0	0	0	0	1	1	0	0	0	0	0	0	0	0	0	0	0	0	1	1
170-174	0	0	0	0	0	0	1	1	0	0	1	0	0	0	1	0	0	0	0	0	3	1
165-169	5	5	5	5	5	5	3	3	1	0	2	1	1	0	0	0	0	0	1	0	23	19
160-164	9	9	9	7	17	15	19	18	14	9	5	3	0	0	0	0	0	0	0	0	73	61
155-159	16	14	22	19	51	42	44	34	53	33	28	11	15	3	9	1	2	0	4	1	244	158
150-154	29	25	50	44	92	75	98	70	91	40	46	14	30	6	14	2	5	1	6	4	461	281
145-149	14	12	48	32	72	44	92	38	85	15	69	9	41	3	13	1	3	0	7	4	444	158
140-144	7	5	20	4	37	13	60	9	67	8	51	2	23	0	12	0	1	0	6	0	284	41
135-139	1	0	8	1	11	3	31	5	29	2	25	1	30	1	12	0	4	0	7	2	158	15
130-134	1	0	1	0	3	0	5	1	8	1	5	1	4	0	3	0	1	0	4	1	35	4
125-129	0	0	0	0	0	0	0	0	2	0	2	0	1	0	2	0	0	0	0	0	7	0
120-124	0	0	0	0	0	0	1	0	1	0	1	0	0	0	0	0	0	0	0	0	3	0
Total	82	70	163	112	288	197	355	180	351	108	235	42	145	13	66	4	16	1	35	12	1736	739

Apps = Number of Applicants
Adm = Number Admitted
Reflects 98% of the total applicant pool.

Suffolk University Law School

David J. Sargent Hall
120 Tremont St.
Boston, MA 02108

E-Mail: lawadm@admin.suffolk.edu
URL: http://www.suffolk.edu/law
Phone: 617.573.8144

■ Introduction

June 1999 will mark the opening of Suffolk University Law School's new, technologically state-of-the-art facility. This 300,000-square-foot cutting-edge law school will be America's most advanced legal education facility and will be a milestone in the school's 92-year history. Founded in 1906, Suffolk, long a major school in the Northeast, is reaching into the new millennium through its new facility, technology, and faculty.

The school is accredited by the ABA and is a member of the Association of American Law Schools. Emphasis on academic excellence, ethics, and advancing the legal profession have always been at the forefront of a Suffolk University Law School education.

Located in the heart of historic Boston, Suffolk University Law School offers its students a unique opportunity to participate in many facets of the law as part of a legal education. Boston is a major center for political, financial, technological, and medical advances which students may use to their advantage by choosing one of Suffolk Law's five concentrations.

■ Enrollment/Student Body

➡ 2,000 applicants ➡ 375 enrolled first-year class 1998, day division ➡ 200 enrolled first-year class 1998, evening division ➡ full-time 25th/75th percentile GPA—2.81/3.40 ➡ part-time 25th/75th percentile GPA—2.65/3.35 ➡ full-time 25th/75th percentile LSAT—146/154 ➡ part-time 25th/75th percentile LSAT—146/156 ➡ 1,050 total full-time ➡ 650 total part-time ➡ 12% minority ➡ 50% women ➡ 50 states & foreign countries represented ➡ 322 undergraduate schools represented

■ Faculty

➡ 155 total ➡ 60 full-time ➡ 95 part-time or adjunct ➡ 33 women ➡ 11 minority ➡ 14 full-time writing instructors

■ Library and Physical Facilities

➡ 300,080 volumes & equivalents ➡ library hours: Mon.-Fri., 8:00 A.M.-11:00 P.M.; Sat. & Sun., 9:00 A.M.-11:00 P.M. ➡ LEXIS ➡ NEXIS ➡ WESTLAW ➡ DIALOG ➡ 8 full-time librarians ➡ library seats 743

■ Curriculum

➡ Academic Support Program ➡ 84 credits required to graduate ➡ 200 courses available ➡ 4 joint degrees available: J.D.; J.D./M.B.A.; J.D./M.P.A., Public Administration; J.D./M.S.F., Finance; J.D./M.S.I.E., International Economics

■ Special Programs

The High Technology Intellectual Property Law Concentration—Students in this concentration have the opportunity to design a program of study to follow their interest in high technology and to gain recognition upon graduation as a distinguished student in this high-demand field of law.

The Tax Law Concentration allows students to distinguish themselves in a very competitive area of legal practice. The Tax Law Concentration enriches the student's law school experience and gives the student a competitive edge in the fields of tax and business law.

The Civil Litigation Concentration—Litigation is a traditional area of practice for Suffolk University Law School graduates. SULS is one of the premier training grounds for civil litigators in the country, and among its alumni are many prominent judges, outstanding litigators, and trial lawyers. Curricular offerings in the civil litigation field are among the most extensive in the nation.

The Financial Services Concentration capitalizes on the Law School's location in Boston, the national leader in the financial services industry. Courses are taught by both resident and adjunct faculty with extensive financial service expertise. Students have a diverse and growing number of advanced financial service courses from which to select to prepare themselves for a career in this rapidly growing field of legal practice.

The Health and Biomedical Law Concentration—Because a large number of the nation's most prominent teaching hospitals, health maintenance organizations, and research facilities are headquartered in the area, Boston is a focal point for advances in health care and biomedicine. This program encompasses a wide variety of topics and allows each student to design a course of study that meets his or her specific goals for a future in health and biomedical law.

The key component of Suffolk's first-year curriculum is the Legal Practice Skills Program (LPS). Each year, 10 full-time, highly qualified instructors teach small (18-20) groups of first-year students the basics of legal research and writing.

Clinical legal education is an area of primary interest at Suffolk University Law School.

Suffolk Voluntary Defenders—This program consists of a field and classroom component. Students receive thorough training in trial practice skills in their second year, and represent indigent adult and juvenile criminal defendants in the Massachusetts District Courts in their third year.

The Prosecutor Program—Students in their final year are assigned to a court where they work under the supervision of an assistant district attorney. They appear weekly, are assigned cases, and handle all aspects of prosecution.

Suffolk University Legal Assistance Bureau (SULAB)—This civil clinical program is designed for students in their final year. It has two components, the Family Unit and the Housing Unit, both located in a law office setting.

S.U. Clinica Legal—This program provides legal assistance in housing cases to indigent tenants. The program is staffed by second- and third-year students fluent in either Spanish or an Asian language, who can provide legal representation to the growing Latino and Asian populations. The students assume full responsibility for their cases.

Battered Women's Advocacy Program (BWAP)—BWAP combines classroom lectures/discussions with actual client representation under the supervision of an attorney. Students staff a "crisis line" at the Law School, giving legal advice to domestic violence victims.

Legal Internship Program—The following internships are available: Administrative Law Internship, AIDS and the Law Internship, Children's Law Internship, Employment Law Internship, Government Litigation Internship, Immigration Law Internship, Judicial Research and Writing Internship, Legal Profession Internship, Mediation Internship, and On "Being" A Lawyer Internship.

Simulation and Trial Advocacy Programs—SULS has long been known for graduating outstanding trial lawyers.

■ Admission

➥ *B.A./B.S. required for admission* ➥ *modified rolling admission, early application encouraged; application deadline—March 1* ➥ *LSAT, LSDAS required* ➥ *application fee—$50*

Admission to the Law School is highly competitive. Applicants must submit both a dean's certification of good standing and a letter of recommendation.

Candidates applying for admission must take the LSAT no later than February. The admission committee does not use a minimum cut-off system in its evaluation of an applicant's LSAT score or GPA. The subjective review includes analysis of class rank, grade trends, year of graduation, range as well as depth of courses, and extracurricular activities. Work experience since graduation is evaluated on the basis of achievement since college, maturity, and responsibility. Applicants are required to submit a personal statement discussing any subjective factors they feel are particularly important to a review of their application.

The review of completed files begins in early November. While the application deadline is March 1, it is clearly to the applicant's advantage to complete his or her file early.

A student who has maintained a satisfactory academic record at another accredited law school and who meets the admission requirements of Suffolk University Law School may apply for admission as a transfer student. Students applying for transfer must do so by June 2.

Admitted applicants reserve a place by paying a two-part deposit totaling $500. No payment is required before April 15.

■ Student Activities

Law students edit and publish the *Suffolk University Law Review, Transnational Law Journal*, and the *Trial Law Journal*. Other publications include *The Advocate* and *Dicta*, the Law School newspaper.

Participation in the Moot Court Program is compulsory for first-year students; upper-class students may participate in a voluntary Moot Court Program or on the school's national or international moot court teams.

Over 30 student organizations are active on campus.

■ Expenses and Financial Aid

➥ *1998-99 tuition & fees—full-time, $20,250; part-time, $15,188* ➥ *estimated additional expenses—books & supplies, $976; health insurance, $520* ➥ *scholarships available* ➥ *David J. Sargent Fellowship available (full-time)* ➥ *need- & merit-based financial aid available* ➥ *FAFSA, Profile, Suffolk Financial Aid Application, financial aid transcripts, tax returns, & W2 forms (students and parents, if applicable) required by March 1*

■ Career Services

A professional staff of eight assists students and alumni/ae in securing part-time, summer, and permanent employment. Assistance is also provided for students seeking volunteer and work-study positions. A special feature of the service is an alumni network of over 14,000 Suffolk University Law School graduates.

Applicant Group for the 1998-1999 Academic Year

Suffolk University Law School

LSAT Score	GPA								
	3.75 +	3.50 - 3.74	3.25 - 3.49	3.00 - 3.24	2.75 - 2.99	2.50 - 2.74	2.25 - 2.49	2.00 - 2.24	Below 2.00
175-180	■	■	■	■	■		▨	▨	▨
170-174	■	■	■	■	■		▨	▨	▨
165-169	■	■	■	■	■		▨	▨	▨
160-164	■	■	■	■	■		▨	▨	▨
155-159	■	■	■				▨	▨	▨
150-154						▨	▨	▨	▨
145-149				▨	▨	▨	▨	▨	▨
140-144	▨	▨	▨	▨	▨	▨	▨	▨	▨
135-139	▨	▨	▨	▨	▨	▨	▨	▨	▨
130-134	▨	▨	▨	▨	▨	▨	▨	▨	▨
125-129	▨	▨	▨	▨	▨	▨	▨	▨	▨
120-124	▨	▨	▨	▨	▨	▨	▨	▨	▨

■ Very Likely   ☐ Possible   ▨ Unlikely

Syracuse University College of Law

Office of Admissions and Financial Aid, Suite 340
Syracuse, NY 13244-1030

E-Mail: admissions@law.syr.edu
URL: http://www.law.syr.edu
Phone: 315.443.1962

■ Introduction

Syracuse University College of Law was established in 1895. The college is a charter member of the AALS and is fully approved by the ABA. It is one of the oldest of the 15 academic units comprising Syracuse University, a major teaching and research institution. The College of Law is located on the 200-acre Syracuse University campus, which overlooks the scenic upstate city of Syracuse, New York.

■ Enrollment/Student Body

➡ *1,714 applicants first-year class 1998*   ➡ *1,022 admitted*
➡ *288 enrolled*   ➡ *full-time 25th/75th percentile GPA—*
2.95/3.40   ➡ *part-time 25th/75th percentile GPA—3.23/3.38*
➡ *full-time 25th/75th percentile LSAT—147/154*
➡ *part-time 25th/75th percentile LSAT—152/155*
➡ *736 total full-time*   ➡ *15 total part-time*
➡ *24% minority*   ➡ *46% women*   ➡ *46 states & 6 foreign*
countries represented   ➡ *300 undergraduate schools represented*
➡ *25—average age*   ➡ *8% possess advanced degrees*

■ Faculty

➡ *82 total*   ➡ *38 full-time*   ➡ *44 part-time or adjunct*
➡ *23 women*   ➡ *6 minority*

■ Library and Physical Facilities

➡ *368,407 volumes & equivalents*   ➡ *LEXIS*   ➡ *NEXIS*
➡ *WESTLAW*   ➡ *DIALOG*   ➡ *16 full-time librarians*
& staff   ➡ *library seats 531*   ➡ *computer clusters with a*
total of 68 IBM PCs   ➡ *42-title CD-ROM network*
➡ *69 additional workstations throughout library*

■ Curriculum

➡ *Academic Support Program*   ➡ *Legal Education*
Opportunity Program   ➡ *87 credits required for J.D. degree*
➡ *degrees available: J.D.; J.D./M.B.A.; J.D./M.P.A.;*
J.D./M.S.; J.D./M.A.; J.D./Ph.D.

Syracuse University College of Law's mission is guided by the philosophy that the best way to train lawyers to practice in today's world is to teach them to apply what they learn in the classroom to real legal issues, problems, and clients. Beginning in the first year and continuing throughout the curriculum, the Syracuse Applied Learning Program creates educational settings that integrate opportunities for students to acquire a better understanding of legal theory and doctrine, develop professional skills, and get exposure to the values and ethics of the legal profession. The Applied Learning Program does not replace the traditional educational program. Rather, it adds experiences that allow students to draw on all that they have studied. Upon graduation, Syracuse students are better prepared for the practice of law.

■ Applied Learning Centers

Center for Law and Business Enterprise—Students take foundation courses in business associations, commercial transactions, and federal income taxation, followed by advanced business law courses, and participate in a skills seminar or a clinic or externship related to business practice. Additional options include seminars such as Law and Economics or one of the year-long Applied Learning Seminars.

Family Law and Social Policy Center—the Center provides a dynamic way for students to combine in-depth classroom learning with actual problem solving. Through courses, programs, and research, the center involves an interdisciplinary group of students, faculty members, and practitioners interested in a range of issues from divorce, domestic violence, and special education to housing accessibility, public benefits, and AIDS.

Center for Global Law and Practice—the Center provides a broad variety of opportunities both in and out of the classroom for students interested in global law. A sampling of course offerings includes comparative law, immigration law, international human rights, and national security law. Cocurricular activities include moot court competitions, the International Law Society, and the *Syracuse Journal of International Law and Commerce*. Summer abroad programs are offered in Hong Kong, London, and Zimbabwe.

Center for Law, Technology, and Management —the Center emphasizes interdisciplinary and applied research approaches to the study of commercial development of new technologies. Coursework involves the study of intellectual property, licensing, patents and copyrights, tax consequences of technology, and business management. Law students work with management and engineering graduate students on projects that involve development and distribution of new technologies.

■ Other Opportunities for Specialization

Clinical Programs—Students enrolled in our clinical programs work on real cases under faculty supervision for course credit. Diverse clinical opportunities at the College of Law include: the Children's Rights and Family Law Clinic, the Criminal Law Clinic, the Housing and Finance Clinic, and the Public Interest Law Firm. The College of Law also offers four distinct externship courses in which students have the opportunity to work in judicial chambers, or in governmental or public interest law offices for course credit. The D.C. Externship places students in Congressional offices, federal agencies, and at national public interest organizations.

Joint-Degree Programs—Formal joint degree options are offered with many graduate programs of Syracuse University, including the Maxwell School of Citizenship and Public Affairs, the S.I. Newhouse School of Public Communications, and the School of Management, among many others. Joint degrees may also be designed to fit special career objectives.

Advocacy Skills Training—Syracuse Law is recognized for its exceptional advocacy programs. Students are actively involved, and have been highly successful in national moot court competitions. Syracuse students participate in intraschool programs throughout the year, in trial and appellate competitions covering a wide variety of areas, including criminal law, tax law, environmental law, intellectual property law, and international law. Trial practice courses, among the most popular elective offerings, concentrate on the elements of trial processes and techniques, jury selection, expert witness examination, direct and cross-examination, and summation.

■ Admission

➧ *Bachelor's degree required* ➧ *application deadline—April 1* ➧ *rolling admission, early application encouraged* ➧ *LSAT, LSDAS required* ➧ *application fee—$50*

The experience of Syracuse reveals that undergraduate grades and LSAT scores are reliable measures, in most cases, for predicting probable success in law study. Thus, an index combining grades and test scores becomes a factor in most admission decisions. However, recognizing that numerical indicators are not always the best predictors of success in law school—even when considered in combination with other factors—the college admits a limited number of students each year through its Legal Education Opportunity (LEO) Program. A goal of the LEO program is the admission of persons who may have been deprived of equal education opportunities for reasons of race, gender, poverty, or other factors beyond their control.

■ Expenses and Financial Aid

➧ *tuition & fees—$22,224* ➧ *estimated additional expenses—$11,820 (room, board, books & personal)* ➧ *merit scholarships & need-based grants available* ➧ *forms required: FAFSA; Syracuse internal application; applicant & parent federal tax returns; and W-2s* ➧ *FAFSA due to processor by Jan. 31; internal application, applicant & parent federal tax returns, and W-2s due by March 1*

The College of Law makes awards from a variety of sources, including tuition grants and scholarships; University fellowships; and federal sources such as the work-study program, and the Perkins and Stafford Loan programs. Private loan programs are available to assist law students with supplemental financing for legal education expenses. Approximately 85 percent of the student body receives some form of financial aid.

■ Career Services

Syracuse graduates are employed throughout the United States and overseas. The Office of Career Services administers a comprehensive program that utilizes the most current resources available to assist students in developing a career plan and employment search strategy. A broad mix of innovative and traditional support, provided by the professional Career Services staff, empowers students with the confidence and skills necessary to conduct an effective job search in a competitive marketplace.

The Grant Opportunity (GO) Program, administered through the Career Services Office, provides summer grants to a limited number of students to financially assist them while they work in public interest summer positions.

Applicant Group for the 1998-1999 Academic Year

Syracuse University College of Law
This grid includes only applicants who earned 120-180 LSAT scores under standard administrations.

LSAT Score	GPA 3.75 +		3.50 - 3.74		3.25 - 3.49		3.00 - 3.24		2.75 - 2.99		2.50 - 2.74		2.25 - 2.49		2.00 - 2.24		Below 2.00		No GPA		Total	
	Apps	Adm	Apps	Adm	Apps	Adm	Apps	Adm	Apps	Adm	Apps	Adm	Apps	Adm	Apps	Adm	Apps	Adm	Apps	Adm	Apps	Adm
170-180	2	2	0	0	0	0	0	0	3	3	0	0	0	0	0	0	0	0	0	0	5	5
165-169	5	5	4	4	6	6	2	2	2	2	1	1	0	0	0	0	0	0	2	2	22	22
160-164	8	8	10	9	14	14	12	12	11	11	5	5	2	2	4	0	1	0	4	2	71	63
155-159	18	17	22	22	47	47	53	51	42	39	19	17	17	12	8	4	1	0	4	3	231	212
150-154	18	17	50	47	105	100	118	113	78	59	48	28	19	4	7	1	3	0	8	4	454	373
145-149	7	7	52	42	100	80	100	52	85	31	60	18	29	3	13	0	2	0	11	4	459	237
Below 145	13	4	38	15	58	21	87	18	94	14	74	3	41	0	28	0	9	0	16	2	458	77
Total	71	60	176	139	330	268	372	248	315	159	207	72	108	21	60	5	16	0	45	17	1700	989

Apps = Number of Applicants
Adm = Number Admitted
Reflects 99% of the total applicant pool.
This chart is provided as a general guide in assessing an applicant's possibility of admission based solely on quantitative factors. It should be noted that nonquantitative factors are also considered in all admission decisions.

Temple University School of Law

1719 North Broad Street
Philadelphia, PA 19122

E-Mail: law@astro.ocis.temple.edu
URL: http://www.temple.edu/lawschool
Phone: 800.560.1428

■ Introduction

Temple law school stands apart from other law schools. We have a unique student-centered curriculum that integrates both critical thinking and practical legal skills. Rigorous study is complemented by actual practice experience. Students at Temple build lawyering skills both in the classroom and in the readily accessible law firms, courts, civic organizations, and financial institutions of center city Philadelphia and the surrounding region. As a result, our graduates have a head start. They graduate ready to perform skillfully in the legal marketplace.

■ Student Body

➡ *2,738 applicants*   ➡ *1,052 admitted first-year class 1998*
➡ *345 enrolled first-year class 1998*   ➡ *full-time 25th/75th percentile GPA—3.02/3.52*   ➡ *part-time 25th/75th percentile GPA—2.80/3.35*   ➡ *full-time 25th/75th percentile LSAT—150/157*   ➡ *part-time 25th/75th percentile LSAT—150/155*
➡ *758 total full-time*   ➡ *346 total part-time*
➡ *25% minority*   ➡ *49% women*   ➡ *61 states & foreign countries represented*   ➡ *309 undergraduate schools represented*
➡ *day & evening divisions, full- & part-time*

■ Faculty

➡ *220 total*   ➡ *55 full-time (17 women, 12 minority)*
➡ *165 part-time or adjunct*

The faculty is an outstanding group of teacher-scholars who embody the law school's philosophical diversity. Their experience brings a rich and varied quality to classroom discussion and they continually strive to develop new and creative methods of instruction.

■ Curriculum

➡ *86 credits required to graduate*   ➡ *200 courses available*
➡ *degrees available: J.D.; J.D./M.B.A.; J.D./LL.M. in Taxation; J.D./LL.M. in Transnational Law*   ➡ *semesters, start in Aug. only*   ➡ *range of first-year class size—10-91*

Temple's extensive clinical program and our innovative skills courses for both prospective trial lawyers and transactional lawyers are evidence of Temple's philosophy that a legal education must provide both practical and theoretical knowledge.

Temple law school has a national reputation for its prize-winning **trial advocacy** programs. In an overwhelming show of strength, Temple's National Trial Team swept all four major national trial competitions in 1997-98, including its third consecutive win in the National Invitational Tournament of Champions. Temple's successful trial advocacy curriculum is anchored by the innovative "Integrated Program," which combines the teaching of trial advocacy, evidence, and professional responsibility.

In the uncharted territory of cyberspace law, Temple is one of the mapmakers, preparing students to succeed in the virtual world. Through coursework in **technology** law and **intellectual property**, hands-on activities outside the classroom, and faculty members who are experts in the field, students learn how to meet the challenges of practicing law in a world without borders.

Temple offers superior training in **business and tax law**, including a creative program which combines the teaching of professional responsibility, substantive law courses, and business skills, such as interviewing, negotiating, and drafting. Students use these skills in several clinicals, including the Community Nonprofit Organizations Clinical, the Federal Estate and Gift Tax Clinical, and the Business Law Clinical. Prospective business lawyers can also pursue the J.D./M.B.A. dual-degree program, offered in conjunction with the School of Business and Management, or the J.D./LL.M. in Taxation.

For students interested in **international law**, Temple offers a unique semester abroad program in Tokyo, Japan (see below). The Japan program capitalizes on Temple's strengths in international law—a distinguished international law faculty; a diverse curriculum in international and comparative law; the opportunity for summer study in Rome, Athens, and Tel Aviv; a Master of Laws (LL.M.) program for international students holding foreign law degrees; and active student organizations, such as the International Law Journal and the International Law Society. Temple's strength in international law has been enhanced by the newly created J.D./LL.M. in Transnational Law.

Public service is a Temple tradition. Students provide much needed legal services in the Philadelphia area through the clinical program, the Temple Legal Aid Office, located in the law school building, and the Temple Law, Education and Participation Program (LEAP), which offers programs designed to teach children about the law. Public interest careers are supported by the Student Public Interest Network which provides grants for summer internships, and the Barrack Public Interest Fellowships, a loan repayment assistance program for Temple graduates in public interest jobs.

■ Semester Abroad Program—Japan

Recognizing that an international experience is best gained by actually living, learning, and working abroad, the law school has established a semester-abroad program in Tokyo, Japan. This is the first and only ABA-accredited semester abroad program offered by an American law school in Asia. The curriculum, taught by U.S. and Japanese law professors to U.S. and Japanese students, includes a mix of standard law courses and specialty courses focusing on comparative, Japanese, and Asian legal studies. Internships in Japanese law firms and corporations are also available.

■ Library and Physical Facilities

➡ *497,575 volumes & equivalents*   ➡ *library hours: Mon.-Thurs., 8:00 A.M.-11:00 P.M.; Fri., 8:00 A.M.-10:00 P.M.; Sat., 9:00 A.M.-5:00 P.M.; Sun., 1:00 P.M.-10:00 P.M.*
➡ *LEXIS*   ➡ *NEXIS*   ➡ *WESTLAW*   ➡ *RLN*

➡ *INNOVAC* ➡ *DIALOG* ➡ *CALI*
➡ *9 full-time librarians* ➡ *library seats 644*

Technology is an essential feature of the educational process at Temple. Computer labs and kiosks are located throughout the building and 170 library carrels are wired to the computer network, allowing students with their own computers, or those rented through the law school's affordable PC loaner program, access to legal research databases, the library card catalog, word processing, and other software. Students make use of their free e-mail accounts to communicate with faculty and students and, via the Web, students can check their grades, registration, financial aid, and billing information. A "smart classroom" is equipped with a powerful arsenal of cutting edge technology, including video, audio, and Internet access. In the near future, the law school will expand its facilities into Barrack Hall, creating a state-of-the-art educational environment in an architecturally historic building.

■ Student Activities

Students are an integral part of policy-making and governance at the law school. The Student Bar Association is the umbrella organization that oversees over 30 student groups. Student publications include the *Temple Law Review*, the *Temple Environmental Law and Technology Journal*, the *Temple International and Comparative Law Journal*, and the *Temple Political and Civil Rights Law Review*. Students who excel in trial advocacy may participate in the National Trial Team, the Moot Court Honor Society, and the Barrister's Society. Temple law students belong to a variety of student organizations, including the Women's Law Caucus; the Black Law Students Association; the Asian/Pacific Islander American Law Student Association; the Latino Law Students Association; Law Students for Lesbian, Gay, Bisexual, and Transgender Rights; the Student Public

Interest Network; the International Law Society; and the Technology Law Society.

■ Career Planning

The Career Planning Office provides one-on-one counseling, administers several on-campus and off-campus interview programs, publishes a weekly newsletter, sponsors workshops and programs on job search skills, and maintains the Career Planning Resources Center. According to the responses of 97 percent of its members, the 1997 graduating class had a placement rate of 91 percent.

■ Admission

➡ *Bachelor's degree from accredited college or university required*
➡ *application deadline—March 1* ➡ *LSAT, LSDAS required*
➡ *application fee—$50* ➡ *rolling admission, early application preferred*

At the discretion of the faculty Admissions Committee, applications may be considered under Temple's discretionary admissions process, called the Sp.A.C.E. Program. The Sp.A.C.E. Program was established by the faculty over 25 years ago in fulfillment of Temple's mission of offering opportunities to students who might otherwise be foreclosed from pursuing a high quality legal education. Under the Sp.A.C.E. Program, the faculty carefully and individually selects applicants who have outstanding performance records and exceptional aptitudes for the study and practice of law, not necessarily reflected by grades and LSAT scores.

■ Expenses and Financial Aid

➡ *tuition—$8,926 full-time, resident; $15,632 full-time, nonresident; $7,140 part-time, resident; $12,506 part-time, nonresident* ➡ *merit scholarships & need-based grants available* ➡ *loan repayment assistance program*
➡ *FAFSA need analysis form due March 1*

Applicant Group for the 1998-1999 Academic Year

Temple University School of Law
This grid includes only applicants who earned 120-180 LSAT scores under standard administrations.

LSAT Score	3.75 +		3.50 - 3.74		3.25 - 3.49		3.00 - 3.24		2.75 - 2.99		2.50 - 2.74		2.25 - 2.49		2.00 - 2.24		Below 2.00		No GPA		Total	
	Apps	Adm	Apps	Adm	Apps	Adm	Apps	Adm	Apps	Adm	Apps	Adm	Apps	Adm	Apps	Adm	Apps	Adm	Apps	Adm	Apps	Adm
170-180	1	1	3	3	3	3	2	1	3	3	1	1	0	0	0	0	0	0	1	1	14	13
165-169	8	8	9	9	10	10	4	4	6	5	5	5	0	0	2	1	0	0	1	1	45	43
160-164	14	14	34	34	29	28	38	38	28	27	11	9	6	5	2	2	0	0	0	0	162	157
155-159	23	23	51	51	91	85	118	107	73	48	52	35	17	9	6	2	1	0	3	2	435	362
150-154	29	26	73	59	139	73	165	79	112	44	80	24	26	6	9	3	1	0	7	3	641	317
145-149	21	15	56	22	104	29	131	25	135	21	93	7	40	1	14	1	1	0	13	4	608	125
140-144	6	0	15	0	30	1	53	0	61	0	55	0	50	0	27	0	11	0	21	0	329	1
Below 140	0	0	0	0	0	0	0	0	0	0	0	0	1	0	1	0	0	0	1	0	3	0
Total	114	93	275	185	466	239	599	258	502	150	386	81	174	21	79	9	21	0	64	13	2680	1049

Apps = Number of Applicants
Adm = Number Admitted
Reflects 99% of the total applicant pool.

University of Tennessee College of Law

Admissions Office
1505 W. Cumberland Avenue, Suite 161
Knoxville, TN 37996-1810

E-Mail: lawadmit@libra.law.utk.edu
URL: http://www.law.UTK.edu
Phone: 423.974.4131

■ Introduction

For more than a century, the University of Tennessee College of Law has offered a strong combination of practical and theoretical legal training. Established in 1890, the College of Law is a charter member of the AALS and is ABA approved.

■ Enrollment/Student Body

➡ *1,096 applicants*   ➡ *394 admitted first-year class 1998*
➡ *159 enrolled first-year class 1998*   ➡ *489 total enrollment*
➡ *full-time 25th/75th percentile GPA—3.20/3.69*
➡ *full-time 25th/75th percentile LSAT—153/160*
➡ *12.5% minority*   ➡ *45% women enrolled in 1998*
➡ *78 undergraduate schools represented*

Traditionally, Tennessee residents account for approximately 80 percent of the student body; however, our students are from every region of the United States.

■ Faculty

➡ *31 full-time*   ➡ *23 part-time or adjunct of prominent area attorneys*

The quality of our faculty is evidenced by their legal training at some of the finest law schools in the United States, the significance of their scholarly writings, their activity in professional associations, and their involvement in public service.

■ Library and Physical Facilities

➡ *452,892 volumes & equivalents*   ➡ *LEXIS*   ➡ *NEXIS*
➡ *WESTLAW*   ➡ *INFOTRAC legal data retrieval systems*
➡ *21 full-time library staff, 1 part-time*   ➡ *ready access to vast collection at the University of Tennessee main library system*

The new law center at The University of Tennessee—a melding of the old with the new—is an exceptional setting for legal education in the 21st century. The library increased to over 58,000-square feet in size. The Legal Clinic has both the space and the equipment to function technologically as a modern law firm, to compliment the instruction and supervision that has made the Legal Clinic one of the most highly regarded clinical programs in the nation.

■ Location

The University of Tennessee College of Law is located on the main campus of the University of Tennessee at Knoxville, the largest city in east Tennessee and the third largest in the state. More than 25,000 students attend UTK. Knoxville has the natural advantage of being located in the foothills of the Great Smokey Mountains, making hiking, biking, golf, and fishing popular and accessible activities. Members of the law school community enjoy access to campus facilities for sports and recreation, leisure, the performing arts, entertainment, and other activities and services.

■ Curriculum

➡ *Academic Support Program*   ➡ *89 credits required to graduate*   ➡ *degrees available: J.D.; J.D./M.B.A.; J.D./M.P.A.*   ➡ *semesters, start in Aug. only*

First-year students begin law school with a week-long Introductory Period, a series of minicourses to introduce students to the study of law. Second- and third-year students may choose from over 75 elective courses.

The College of Law offers two optional programs for students. The **Center for Entrepreneurial Law** allows second- and third-year students to focus on the legal aspects of the conduct of public and private enterprise, emphasizing the needs of small- and intermediate-sized business concerns.

The **Center for Advocacy and Dispute Resolution** allows interested students to focus their second- and third-year experience toward preparation for a career in advocacy, commonly thought of as litigation or trial practice.

UT was recognized by the American College of Trial Lawyers for the 1996 Emil Gumpert Award for Excellence in Teaching Trial Advocacy. The award is given annually to a law school deemed to have achieved a superior level of excellence in the teaching of trial advocacy as measured by the strength of the institution's clinical programs, teaching methods, mock trial competitions, student clerkships, and special instructional programs.

■ Special Programs

The Civil and Criminal Advocacy Clinic—Established in 1947, this is one of the oldest continually operating clinical programs in the United States. It provides an ideal opportunity for third-year students to examine the parameters and demands of law practice while working cooperatively with other students and teachers in a supportive environment.

Moot Court Program—University of Tennessee teams have distinguished themselves by winning the National Moot Court Competition. The Evidence Moot Court Team finished second in the nation and won the award for the best brief at the 1997 competition. The 1997 National Moot Court team advanced to the national competition as one of the top 16 teams out of 152 law schools that participated. The National Trial Team won the National Association of Criminal Defense Lawyers Trial Competition in 1993. The 1993 Jerome Prince Evidence team took first place in the national competition. The Environmental Law Moot Court team placed second in the U.S. in the National Environmental Competition in 1992 and 1993.

Mediation Clinic—Participants work in teams to mediate real civil and misdemeanor cases in the lower courts. Students gain valuable first-hand experience in this emerging form of conflict resolution.

Student Activities

The *Tennessee Law Review* offers participants an excellent opportunity to conduct legal research and writing of a scholarly and practical nature. The Student Bar Association and various other student organizations offer numerous programs, services, and special events. The national honor fraternity, Order of the Coif, and two leading professional fraternities, Phi Delta Phi and Phi Alpha Delta, have local chapters here.

Admission

➡ *Bachelor's degree from accredited 4-year institution required*
➡ *apply between Oct. 1 but before Feb. 1*
➡ *application fee—$15*

Admission to the College of Law is competitive. The Admissions Committee places substantial emphasis on traditional indicators of performance—the undergraduate GPA and the LSAT score. The committee also considers factors such as improvement in undergraduate grades and graduate school performance; strength of undergraduate institution and major course of study; extracurricular activities; community service; and employment and professional experience. Also considered are circumstances that may have affected an applicant's grades or LSAT score, and economic, social, or cultural background or success in overcoming social or economic disadvantages. Applicants are required to submit two letters of recommendation and write a personal statement and an essay.

The College of Law also recognizes its obligation to assure meaningful access to legal education to qualified applicants who are members of groups that have been historically underrepresented in the legal profession. Members of historically underrepresented minority groups are encouraged to apply. The College of Law encourages applications from such students. Successful completion of the Council on Legal Education Opportunity (CLEO) summer institute and the Tennessee Pre-Professional Program may also be considered by the Admissions Committee.

Expenses, Financial Aid, and Housing

➡ *annual full-time tuition & fees—residents, $4,502; nonresidents, $11,424* ➡ *scholarships available (merit- and/or need-based)* ➡ *minority scholarships available* ➡ *financial aid available: Perkins Loans, Stafford Loans, Law Access, Law Loans, work-study*

Students who wish to receive priority consideration for need-based scholarships must complete FAFSA by February 14. There is no application form to complete for most merit-based scholarships. Eligible students are automatically considered.

Campus apartment and residence hall housing is open to law students. Knoxville also has ample private apartment housing available.

Career Services

Through Career Services, our students and alumni can acquire the skills and knowledge necessary for their first job search and for long-term career planning, as well as useful information about the many professional arenas in which a law degree can be used. These efforts have contributed to the consistently high employment rate for graduates, above the national average in recent years. There are approximately 6,000 alumni in 49 states, the District of Columbia, and a dozen foreign countries.

Applicant Group for the 1998-1999 Academic Year

University of Tennessee College of Law
This grid includes only applicants who earned 120-180 LSAT scores under standard administrations.

LSAT Score	3.75 +		3.50 - 3.74		3.25 - 3.49		3.00 - 3.24		2.75 - 2.99		2.50 - 2.74		2.25 - 2.49		2.00 - 2.24		Below 2.00		No GPA		Total	
	Apps	Adm	Apps	Adm	Apps	Adm	Apps	Adm	Apps	Adm	Apps	Adm	Apps	Adm	Apps	Adm	Apps	Adm	Apps	Adm	Apps	Adm
175-180	0	0	0	0	0	0	0	0	0	0	0	0	0	0	0	0	0	0	0	0	0	0
170-174	3	3	0	0	1	1	1	1	0	0	0	0	0	0	0	0	0	0	0	0	5	5
165-169	7	7	6	6	8	8	11	10	4	4	1	1	1	0	1	0	0	0	1	0	40	36
160-164	25	25	20	19	22	20	25	20	20	9	9	3	3	2	2	0	0	0	2	0	128	98
155-159	34	32	50	40	51	37	50	18	31	5	23	1	5	1	0	0	0	0	2	1	246	135
150-154	30	29	59	31	72	20	72	10	44	2	27	2	9	1	3	0	1	0	4	3	321	98
145-149	8	1	23	3	43	5	29	4	36	1	26	2	15	0	4	0	0	0	1	0	185	16
140-144	5	1	9	0	13	1	27	2	25	1	17	0	10	0	3	0	0	0	3	0	112	5
135-139	3	1	3	0	3	0	3	0	7	0	7	0	4	0	0	0	5	0	2	0	37	1
130-134	1	0	0	0	1	0	1	0	4	0	1	0	2	0	1	0	2	0	1	0	14	0
125-129	0	0	0	0	0	0	1	0	1	0	0	0	1	0	0	0	0	0	0	0	3	0
120-124	0	0	0	0	0	0	0	0	0	0	0	0	0	0	0	0	1	0	0	0	1	0
Total	116	99	170	99	214	92	220	65	172	22	111	9	50	4	14	0	9	0	16	4	1092	394

Apps = Number of Applicants
Adm = Number Admitted
Reflects 99% of the total applicant pool.

The University of Texas School of Law

Post Office Box 149105
Austin, TX 78714-9105

E-Mail: admissions@mail.law.utexas.edu
URL: http://www.utexas.edu/law
Phone: 512.232.1200

■ Introduction

The School of Law is located on the University of Texas campus in Austin, the state capital. This location provides ready access to the state legislature, the Supreme Court of Texas, federal trial and appellate courts, offices of state and federal agencies, and the libraries and other facilities of the University of Texas campus. Long recognized as having a distinguished faculty and educational program, the law school has been a member of the AALS since 1907, and is fully accredited.

Austin is situated in the hill country of Texas, allowing for easy access to lakes and wilderness areas. The University of Texas plays an important role in this metropolitan area of over one million, and many of the entertainment and cultural activities cater to the student population.

■ Enrollment/Student Body

➼ *3,184 applicants*   ➼ *468 admitted first-year class 1998*
➼ *full-time 25th/75th percentile GPA—3.40/3.77*
➼ *full-time 25th/75th percentile LSAT—158/164*
➼ *1,394 total full-time*   ➼ *20.7% minority*
➼ *45% women*   ➼ *over 250 undergraduate schools represented*   ➼ *nonresident enrollment limited to 20%*

■ Library and Physical Facilities

➼ *927,000 volumes & equivalents*
➼ *19 full-time librarians*

Recent additions and alterations to the law school complex have made it one of the most attractive and spacious educational facilities of any law school in the nation. Eight large classrooms, numerous seminar rooms, and spacious student lounge areas provide an attractive setting for law study. Federal and state courts hold trial and appellate cases in the moot courtroom on a regular basis. The Tarlton Law Library is the fifth largest in the nation. Open stacks and the most modern computer and audiovisual equipment available make the library facilities accessible to students, scholars, and practicing lawyers.

■ Curriculum

➼ *86 credits required to graduate*
➼ *joint-degree programs offered*   ➼ *semesters*
➼ *Freshlaws start the last week of Aug.*

All first-year students (except those in the Extended First-Year Program for parents of young children and disabled students) are required to take a full courseload of 15 hours per week in contracts, property, torts, civil procedure, criminal law, constitutional law, brief writing and oral advocacy, and legal research and writing. After the first year, the only required courses are professional responsibility, advanced constitutional law, and a writing and research seminar. The student may design his or her course of study from an array of course offerings in many fields of law. These offerings include interdisciplinary and advanced public and private law courses. There is also a large summer program enabling the student to complete degree requirements in less than three years.

The school offers a Master of Laws (LL.M.) program for foreign law school graduates. There are several established joint-degree programs: J.D./Master of Public Administration with the LBJ School of Public Affairs; J.D./Master in Business Administration with the Graduate School of Business; J.D./Master of Arts in Latin American Studies; J.D./Master of Science in Community and Regional Planning; J.D./Master of Arts in Post-Soviet and East European Studies; and J.D./Master of Arts in Middle Eastern Studies.

■ Special Programs

The school offers clinical education courses for credit in such fields as capital punishment, children's rights, criminal defense, domestic violence, elder law, housing law, immigration law, juvenile justice, mediation, and mental health. Internships are available to qualified students with the Texas Supreme Court, the Texas Court of Criminal Appeals, and the Third Court of Appeals. The law school also has an extensive trial advocacy program.

■ Admission

➼ *early decision deadline—Nov. 1*
➼ *regular decision deadline—Feb. 1*   ➼ *application fee—$65*
➼ *in-state 25th/75th percentile GPA—3.39/3.74*
➼ *in-state 25th/75th percentile LSAT—158/165*
➼ *out-of-state 25th/75th percentile GPA—3.56/3.84*
➼ *out-of-state 25th/75th percentile LSAT—161/166*

To be eligible for admission, an applicant must hold a baccalaureate degree from an accredited college or university and must have a competitive grade-point average and LSAT score. In 1998, only one of every three resident applicants was offered admission, and one of four non-resident applicants was offered admission. A diverse student body is sought. Special facilities are available for students who have disabilities. A $250 seat deposit is required from an applicant who is offered admission. This fee is subject to change without notice.

The law school accepts a limited number of transfer students who have completed the first-year curriculum at an accredited law school and who have compiled a superior academic record at their original law school.

■ Student Activities

The School of Law offers many student-administered, cocurricular activities that enhance the law students' regular studies. Student-edited journals include *American Journal of Criminal Law; Hispanic Law Journal; Texas Environmental Law Journal; Texas Forum on Civil Liberties and Civil Rights; Texas Intellectual Property Law Journal; Texas*

International Law Journal; Texas Journal of Business Law; Texas Journal of Women and the Law; Texas Law Review; Texas Review of Law and Politics; and *The Review of Litigation.*

Other activities include the Legal Research Board, whose members research actual legal problems for practicing attorneys; the Student Bar Association, which includes the entire student body and promotes student social and professional activities; the Women's Law Caucus; the Chicano Law Students Association; the Thurgood Marshall Legal Society; the Teaching Quizmaster Program in which qualified second- and third-year students teach the first-year courses in legal research and writing; the Board of Advocates, which administers the mock trial and moot court programs; and chapters of legal fraternities. The Mock Trial and Moot Court Program consists of 11 voluntary intramural competitions involving both trial and appellate advocacy and 19 interscholastic competitions. The following competitions are also offered—Alternative Dispute Resolution, Client Counseling, Mediation, Negotiations, and Voir Dire. Interscholastic teams consistently achieve a high degree of success in competition and have won several national championships.

■ Expenses and Financial Aid

➡ *tuition & fees—resident, $7,234/yr.; nonresident, $15,034/yr. (subject to change without notice)*
➡ *scholarships available (up to 3 years)*

A limited number of scholarships are awarded to first-year students on the basis of performance in undergraduate studies, academic promise in the study of law, and financial need. The prestigious Rice Scholarship is designed to support eight outstanding law students with full tuition and fees for all three years of law school. Scholarships and research assistantships are available for second- and third-year students. The law school administers several short- and long-term loan funds for students with financial need, and the university offers substantial federally funded loan programs. Information on these programs is given in the Law School Application/Bulletin.

■ Housing

The large majority of our students select off-campus housing. The law school is within 25 minutes by car of almost any point in Austin, and good housing is available within walking distance. Arrangements must be made by the student. For information concerning university dormitories, write to: The University of Texas Housing Division, Kinsolving Dormitory, Austin, TX 78712, or call 512.471.3136.

■ Career Services

Each year, the law school's active placement service arranges interviews with over 500 employers from throughout the country, including law firms, judges, corporations, government agencies, and public interest organizations. The service is available to students and alumni seeking part-time jobs, summer clerkships, and full-time employment. Within six months after graduation, 96.5 percent of the 1997 graduates were employed.

Applicant Group for the 1998-1999 Academic Year

The University of Texas School of Law
This grid includes only applicants who earned 120-180 LSAT scores under standard administrations.

LSAT Score	3.75 +		3.50 - 3.74		3.25 - 3.49		3.00 - 3.24		2.75 - 2.99		2.50 - 2.74		2.25 - 2.49		2.00 - 2.24		Below 2.00		No GPA		Total	
	Apps	Adm	Apps	Adm	Apps	Adm	Apps	Adm	Apps	Adm	Apps	Adm	Apps	Adm	Apps	Adm	Apps	Adm	Apps	Adm	Apps	Adm
175-180	10	10	12	12	3	3	3	0	2	1	1	0	0	0	0	0	0	0	0	0	31	26
170-174	27	27	37	37	36	33	20	10	6	2	5	0	0	0	0	0	0	0	0	0	131	109
165-169	95	92	109	99	107	68	60	18	25	3	12	2	4	1	1	0	0	0	4	2	417	285
160-164	166	147	202	154	185	92	148	34	58	2	18	1	9	0	3	0	0	0	10	1	799	431
155-159	108	77	207	101	177	36	152	11	82	2	30	1	16	0	3	0	1	0	10	1	786	229
150-154	49	19	97	25	109	13	101	4	63	0	31	0	18	0	7	0	0	0	9	1	484	62
145-149	17	5	44	2	51	5	55	0	51	0	29	1	16	0	6	0	1	0	8	0	278	13
140-144	4	0	18	0	27	0	31	0	23	0	19	0	12	0	5	0	0	0	2	0	141	0
135-139	3	0	6	0	3	0	11	0	7	0	7	0	3	0	6	0	3	0	4	0	53	0
130-134	0	0	2	0	2	0	3	0	3	0	3	0	4	0	3	0	0	0	0	0	20	0
125-129	0	0	0	0	0	0	0	0	0	0	0	0	1	0	3	0	1	0	3	0	8	0
120-124	0	0	0	0	0	0	0	0	0	0	2	0	0	0	0	0	0	0	1	0	3	0
Total	479	377	734	430	700	250	584	77	320	10	157	5	83	1	37	0	6	0	51	5	3151	1155

Apps = Number of Applicants
Adm = Number Admitted
Reflects 99% of the total applicant pool.

Texas Southern University—Thurgood Marshall School of Law

Office of Admissions
3100 Cleburne Street
Houston, TX 77004

E-Mail: cgardner@tsulaw.edu
URL: http://www.tsulaw.edu
Phone: 713.313.7114

■ Introduction

The Thurgood Marshall School of Law, a state institution founded in 1947, seeks to provide a legal education and an opportunity to excel to students from a wide range of backgrounds, including those who otherwise would not have an opportunity for legal training. The law school is accredited by the ABA. The student body is truly multi-ethnic and multicultural. The law school is housed in a tri-level structure and is located just outside downtown Houston. Near campus housing is available in the form of modern apartments for single and married students. The school makes extensive use of legal facilities in Houston through its clinical programs.

■ Enrollment/Student Body

➡ *937 applicants*   ➡ *511 admitted first-year class 1998*
➡ *280 enrolled first-year class 1998*   ➡ *full-time 25th/75th percentile GPA—2.37/3.00*   ➡ *full-time 25th/75th percentile LSAT—139/144*   ➡ *600 total full-time*   ➡ *87% minority*
➡ *49% women*   ➡ *29 states & foreign countries represented*
➡ *123 undergraduate schools represented*

A majority of the students are from Texas, but all parts of the country are represented. Approximately 57 percent of the students are black, 23 percent Chicano, 13 percent Caucasian, and 3 percent Asian and Native American. The median age range is about 25 to 35 years.

■ Faculty

➡ *53 total*   ➡ *32 full-time*   ➡ *21 part-time or adjunct*
➡ *9 women*   ➡ *26 minority*

■ Library and Physical Facilities

➡ *300,000 volumes & equivalents*   ➡ *library hours: Mon.-Thurs., 7:00 A.M.-MIDNIGHT; Fri., 7:00 A.M.-10:00 P.M.; Sat., 9:00 A.M.-10:00 P.M.; Sun., NOON-MIDNIGHT*
➡ *LEXIS*   ➡ *NEXIS*   ➡ *WESTLAW*   ➡ *DIALOG*
➡ *CALI*   ➡ *LegalTrac*   ➡ *6 full-time librarians*
➡ *library seats 335*   ➡ *student computer labs and study rooms*
➡ *laptop computer connections*

Students receive individual and/or group orientation and intensive training in the use of the library. The law school has undergone approximately $3 million in renovations, expanding the available space from 16,000- to 32,000-square feet.

■ Curriculum

➡ *Academic Support Program*   ➡ *Moot Court, Law Review, & Legal Clinics offered*   ➡ *90 credits required to graduate*
➡ *74 courses available*   ➡ *J.D. degree available*
➡ *semesters, start in Aug.*
➡ *range of first-year class size—67-77*

Upon entry to the School of Law, all students in the first-year class are required to attend a week-long orientation program. Attention is given to examanship, briefing cases, outlining, and an overview of law school life and expectations.

The law school offers a three-year, full-time J.D. program. The minimum courseload is 12 hours. Required courses for the first year are Case Analysis and Legal Writing, Civil Procedure, Property, Contracts, Torts, Constitutional Law, and Criminal Law. Second-year students must take Evidence, Criminal Procedure, Trial Simulation, Appellate Litigation, Business Associations, Commercial Law, Professional Responsibility, and Wills and Trusts. Second- or third-year students are required to take Federal Jurisdiction and Procedure, a seminar/independent research project, Basic Federal Taxation, and Consumer Rights. Third-year students are required to take Texas Practice. The remaining hours required to complete the degree may be selected from a number of areas of interest.

The law school operates a full-time, in-house clinic in which students work under the supervision of faculty and adjunct faculty members. Internships are available with the Harris County District Attorney's Office, the Federal Magistrates, Gulf Coast Legal Foundation, the Federal Bankruptcy Court, the Harris County Attorney's Office, the Internal Revenue Service, and the U.S. District Court. The school operates a number of clinics, including advanced skills, basic skills, civil and criminal externships, environmental justice, family law, and housing law. A judicial externship with state and federal judges is available to academically outstanding third-year students. The summer session offers a different series of related courses each year. A six-week summer pre-enrollment (L.E.A.P.) program, by invitation, and a tutorial program for all first-year classes are provided.

■ Admission

➡ *Baccalaureate degree required*   ➡ *LSAT, LSDAS required*
➡ *application fee—$40*

The GPA and LSAT (or average LSAT if attempted more than once on same scale) are factored into a formula which places more weight on the LSAT. The number derived, the index, is used to determine an applicant's initial competitiveness.

No particular undergraduate major is preferred, but the school looks for applicants with broad backgrounds in the social sciences, natural sciences, humanities, and business sciences. Admission decisions are based primarily on the applicant's motivation and intellectual capacity, undergraduate GPA, and LSAT scores. Newly admitted students must send two seat deposits ($150 upon acceptance and $100 in June), which are refundable upon matriculation. The law school's student body represents one of the most culturally and ethnically diverse student bodies in the country. Transfer applications are accepted; students must submit a transcript and letter from the dean of their former law school stating that they are in good standing. All newly admitted students must submit an official transcript from the baccalaureate degree-granting institution as well as all law schools attended. No application will be evaluated by the Admissions Committee until the LSDAS report has been received. In order to ensure complete review, applications must be received by the Office of Admissions no later than April 1, although earlier submission is encouraged. Entering students are admitted only in August (fall semester). Students are notified of acceptance after the Admissions Committee has reviewed the complete file. Early completion of applications is especially important for the L.E.A.P. interview process. Admission decisions are made on a rolling basis.

■ Student Activities

Numerous law school organizations are active on campus. A student board edits the *Thurgood Marshall Law Review*. Moot court competitions are held in trial and appellate work, labor law, and client counseling.

■ Expenses and Financial Aid

➡ *full-time tuition—resident, $132/sem. hr.; nonresident, $262/sem. hr.* ➡ *estimated additional expenses per semester—fees, $700; room, board, books & supplies, $4,936* ➡ *law school & university scholarships available* ➡ *financial aid available; forms due May 1; FAFSA for need analysis*

About 90 percent of the students receive some form of aid. The law school administers its own scholarship program, which is competitive. Scholarships are awarded on the basis of both need and merit, and may range up to full tuition. The university also offers additional scholarship aid, and the law school and the university offer loan assistance. Ten to fifteen percent of the students hold assistantships. The aid application deadline is May 1.

The scholarship program makes several awards (approximately 60) each year. The awards have enabled out-of-state residents to qualify for resident-tuition rates. In addition, a number of law students each year qualify for the federal work study and loan programs. Additional limited scholarship aid is available to students after they have completed a year of law study. An applicant in need of other financial assistance should make arrangements for financial aid through the Director of Financial Aid, Thurgood Marshall School of Law, Texas Southern University, 3100 Cleburne St., Houston, TX 77004.

■ Career Development

The law school employs a full-time career development officer. Graduates are placed primarily with law firms, federal and state agencies, legal services, judges, and businesses. The Career Development Office also conducts a major national effort to encourage legal employers in every major city in the United States to recruit Texas Southern University Thurgood Marshall School of Law graduates.

Applicant Group for the 1998-1999 Academic Year

Texas Southern University—Thurgood Marshall School of Law
This grid includes only applicants who earned 120-180 LSAT scores under standard administrations.

LSAT Score	3.75 +		3.50 - 3.74		3.25 - 3.49		3.00 - 3.24		2.75 - 2.99		2.50 - 2.74		2.25 - 2.49		2.00 - 2.24		Below 2.00		No GPA		Total	
	Apps	Adm	Apps	Adm	Apps	Adm	Apps	Adm	Apps	Adm	Apps	Adm	Apps	Adm	Apps	Adm	Apps	Adm	Apps	Adm	Apps	Adm
175-180	0	0	0	0	0	0	0	0	0	0	0	0	0	0	0	0	0	0	0	0	0	0
170-174	0	0	0	0	0	0	0	0	0	0	0	0	0	0	0	0	0	0	0	0	0	0
165-169	0	0	0	0	0	0	0	0	0	0	0	0	0	0	1	0	0	0	0	0	1	0
160-164	0	0	0	0	0	0	1	1	1	0	0	0	0	0	0	0	0	0	0	0	2	1
155-159	0	0	0	0	1	0	1	1	4	3	4	4	4	3	1	1	1	1	0	0	16	13
150-154	0	0	1	1	5	5	2	2	8	8	11	9	9	7	10	10	1	1	1	1	48	44
145-149	3	3	8	8	11	11	17	15	28	25	30	27	23	18	17	13	4	2	3	2	144	124
140-144	3	2	8	5	28	23	37	34	53	46	68	59	54	43	39	25	4	3	6	0	300	240
135-139	2	1	8	2	17	5	38	15	41	11	43	19	48	17	25	4	13	1	16	6	251	81
130-134	0	0	5	3	5	1	15	2	23	4	27	2	20	2	11	0	6	0	2	0	114	14
125-129	0	0	0	0	0	0	2	0	7	0	3	0	2	0	8	0	5	0	7	0	34	0
120-124	0	0	0	0	0	0	0	0	0	0	0	0	1	0	2	0	0	0	0	0	3	0
Total	8	6	30	19	67	45	113	70	165	97	186	120	161	90	114	53	34	8	35	9	913	517

Apps = Number of Applicants
Adm = Number Admitted
Reflects 98% of the total applicant pool.

Texas Tech University School of Law

Box 40004
Lubbock, TX 79409

E-Mail: xydaw@ttacs.ttu.edu
URL: http://www.law.ttu.edu
Phone: 806.742.3791

■ Introduction

The School of Law, which accepted its first class in 1967, is located on the main campus of Texas Tech University in Lubbock. It is fully accredited, having received approval from the Supreme Court of Texas and the ABA and membership in the AALS at the earliest dates possible under the rules of those organizations. As a result, its graduates are eligible to take the bar examination in any state in the nation, and many are engaged in practice throughout the United States. In 1974, a chapter of the Order of the Coif, the national legal honorary society, was established at the School of Law.

■ Enrollment/Student Body

➡ *1,068 applicants* ➡ *510 accepted first-year class 1998*
➡ *217 enrolled first-year class 1998* ➡ *full-time 25th/75th percentile GPA—3.12/3.59* ➡ *full-time 25th/75th percentile LSAT—151/158* ➡ *619 total full-time* ➡ *16% minority*
➡ *43% women* ➡ *79 undergraduate schools represented*

■ Faculty

➡ *35 total* ➡ *22 full-time* ➡ *13 part-time or adjunct*
➡ *13 women* ➡ *3 minority*

■ Library and Physical Facilities

➡ *250,000 volumes & equivalents* ➡ *library hours:*
Mon.-Thurs., 7:30 A.M.-MIDNIGHT; Fri., 7:30 A.M.-6:00 P.M.;
Sat., NOON-6:00 P.M.; Sun., 2:00 P.M.-MIDNIGHT ➡ *LEXIS*
➡ *NEXIS* ➡ *WESTLAW* ➡ *5 full-time librarians*
➡ *library seats 475*

The law school is housed in a beautiful and functional building designed to comfortably accommodate a student body of about 600 and a full-time faculty of 22. A renovation of the law library, completed in 1994, added 12,000 square-feet of stack and study space. Two hundred fifty study carrels housing 500 students are equipped with 250 PCs offering access to WESTLAW and LEXIS, as well as to the library's online catalog. Word processing capabilities are also provided. Student organizations occupy spacious offices on the third floor. Two other notable features of the building are the beautiful and functional courtroom where the Texas Court of Appeals sits each year, and the Forum, which serves as a student lounge and the site of various law school social functions. As a result of the remodeling, the building now complies with ADA standards.

■ Curriculum

➡ *Academic Support Program* ➡ *90 semester hours required to graduate* ➡ *degrees available: J.D.; J.D./M.B.A.; J.D./M.P.A.; J.D./AG. ECON.; J.D. Master of Taxation; J.D./Master of Environmental Health (pending)*
➡ *semesters, start in Aug. & Jan.* ➡ *range of first-year class size—60-70* ➡ *summer sessions available*

The program of study is planned to equip the student to practice law as advocate, counselor, judge, or law teacher. At the same time, recognition is given to the use of law training as a stepping-stone to a career in government, politics, or business. All of the courses in the first year and some of the courses in the advanced years are required. The remainder of the courses are electives.

■ Special Programs

In addition to the basic program of study for the J.D. degree, qualified students may elect to pursue one of four joint-degree programs: the J.D./Master of Business Administration; the J.D./Master of Public Administration; the J.D./Master of Science in Agricultural Economics; and the J.D./Master of Taxation. The joint-degree programs allow a student to complete the requirements for both degrees in less than four academic years instead of the five required if both degrees were pursued separately.

The School of Law offers opportunities to practice various lawyering skills in courses such as trial advocacy, appellate advocacy, arbitration, skills development, and others.

In recognition of the lack of representation of minority groups in the legal profession, the School of Law participates actively in programs designed to increase the number of minority group lawyers.

■ Admission

➡ *Bachelor's degree from accredited college or university required*
➡ *application deadline—Feb. 1*
➡ *LSAT, LSDAS required* ➡ *application fee—$50*
➡ *rolling admission, early application preferred*

Written recommendations are not required, but in borderline cases may prove helpful. Anyone filing an application after February 1 will be at a disadvantage in competing for the limited number of places available. Accepted applicants must pay a $200 deposit to hold a place in the entering class. This acceptance deposit will be refunded to the applicants upon matriculation at the law school. One-half of the deposit is refundable upon timely written notice of a change in plans. Such notice is due May 1 for fall admission. In June, accepted applicants must pay one-half of their tuition and fees for the fall semester.

Admissions decisions are made by the Admissions Committee and are based on an evaluation of the LSAT score, the quality of the undergraduate coursework and performance, and other criteria including background and employment experience, graduate work, and evidence of leadership qualities in campus and community activities. The LSAT score and the undergraduate GPA are weighted about equally.

■ Student Activities

In addition to activities available to all students of the university, there are many extracurricular activities provided for the law student.

The *Texas Tech Law Review*, published four times a year, consists of articles written by students and leading jurists, practitioners, and faculty. Membership is based on academic qualification.

The Board of Barristers supervises and conducts an extensive moot court program, in which the student develops skills in brief writing and in the art of oral advocacy. The school enters teams in interschool competition in mock trial, moot court, client counseling, and negotiation.

The Legal Research Board is a student organization that offers attorneys a service similar to that of a briefing staff. The board methodically researches requested legal topics and then compiles the information in a memorandum of law.

The Student Bar Association is the focal point for many student activities, both professional and social. The SBA cooperates closely with the faculty in bringing speakers and programs to the law school. In addition, the SBA sponsors numerous student social events.

The legal fraternities at the school sponsor professional and social functions. They admit both men and women to membership.

■ Expenses and Financial Aid

➡ *tuition & fees—$6,520* ➡ *average additional expenses—$5,750 (room & board and books)* ➡ *merit- & need-based scholarships available* ➡ *FAFSA, financial aid transcripts, and loan applications required for financial aid*

More than 80 scholarships are available, ranging in value from $1,000 to a full scholarship. Long-term educational loan funds are available through the Office of the Director of Financial Aid, and short-term loans are available through the Law School Foundation.

■ Housing

A variety of housing convenient to the campus is available for single and married students. Information on campus housing may be obtained from the Housing Office, Texas Tech University.

■ Career Services

The Placement Office of the School of Law is under the direction of the assistant dean. Graduates of the law school find employment in every area of practice in the public and private sectors. Historically, a significant majority of graduates are employed within six months of graduation. The law school is a member of the National Association of Law Placement, which provides information on opportunities for placement nationally to students.

Academic Group for the 1998-1999 Academic Year

Texas Tech University School of Law
This grid includes only applicants who earned 120-180 LSAT scores under standard administrations.

LSAT Score	3.75 +		3.50 - 3.74		3.25 - 3.49		3.00 - 3.24		2.75 - 2.99		2.50 - 2.74		2.25 - 2.49		2.00 - 2.24		Below 2.00		No GPA		Total	
	Apps	Adm	Apps	Adm	Apps	Adm	Apps	Adm	Apps	Adm	Apps	Adm	Apps	Adm	Apps	Adm	Apps	Adm	Apps	Adm	Apps	Adm
175-180	0	0	0	0	0	0	0	0	1	1	0	0	0	0	0	0	0	0	0	0	1	1
170-174	2	2	2	2	0	0	1	1	0	0	0	0	0	0	0	0	0	0	0	0	5	5
165-169	2	2	2	2	3	3	3	2	4	4	2	2	0	0	0	0	0	0	1	1	17	16
160-164	15	15	9	9	15	15	18	18	11	11	9	8	2	2	1	0	0	0	0	0	80	78
155-159	23	23	38	37	39	38	64	57	32	23	17	4	10	2	5	0	2	0	3	2	233	186
150-154	26	26	44	41	64	56	71	33	42	9	33	2	17	0	8	0	0	0	2	0	307	167
145-149	14	14	23	10	42	15	47	5	39	1	24	0	15	0	5	0	1	1	10	0	220	46
140-144	2	2	10	1	18	5	31	2	27	0	22	0	4	0	6	0	1	0	3	0	124	10
135-139	1	0	2	1	5	0	5	0	10	0	12	0	6	0	6	0	0	0	6	0	53	1
130-134	0	0	0	0	1	0	1	0	1	0	2	0	2	0	1	0	0	0	0	0	8	0
125-129	0	0	0	0	1	0	0	0	3	0	0	0	0	0	4	0	0	0	1	0	9	0
120-124	0	0	0	0	0	0	0	0	0	0	0	0	0	0	0	0	0	0	0	0	0	0
Total	85	84	130	103	188	132	241	118	170	49	121	16	56	4	36	0	4	1	26	3	1057	510

Apps = Number of Applicants
Adm = Number Admitted
Reflects 99% of the total applicant pool.

Texas Wesleyan University School of Law

1515 Commerce Street
Fort Worth, TX 76102

URL: http://www.law.txwes.edu
Phone: 800.733.9529; 817.212.4000; Fax: 817.212.4002

■ Introduction

Established in 1989, the law school became part of Texas Wesleyan University in 1992. A comprehensive university, Texas Wesleyan was founded in 1890 and offers degrees in business, education, fine arts, humanities, sciences, and law. In August of 1994, the law school received provisional accreditation by the American Bar Association, which entitles students to the same recognition as students of fully-approved ABA law schools, including the right to sit for the bar exam in every state upon graduation. Texas Wesleyan offers both full-time and part-time study leading to the Juris Doctor degree.

Texas Wesleyan is committed to educating students of diverse backgrounds with varied life experiences and educational perspectives. Many Wesleyan students are nontraditional, seeking a legal education at a later stage in life. For the entering class of 1998, the median age was 29 with students ranging in age from 21 to 59. Many Wesleyan students have backgrounds in business, accounting, health sciences, education, and public service.

■ Enrollment/Student Body

➡ 843 applicants ➡ 438 admitted first-year class 1998
➡ 195 enrolled first-year class 1998 ➡ full-time 25th/75th percentile GPA—2.66/3.19 ➡ part-time 25th/75th percentile GPA—2.75/3.26 ➡ full-time 25th/75th percentile LSAT—145/153 ➡ part-time 25th/75th percentile LSAT—146/154 ➡ 303 total full-time ➡ 255 total part-time
➡ 15.4% minority (entering class) ➡ 40% women (225 women) ➡ 89 undergraduate schools represented

■ Faculty

➡ 57 total ➡ 26 full-time ➡ 31 part-time or adjunct
➡ 16 women ➡ 6 minority

The 26 members of the full-time faculty hold 72 degrees from 37 educational institutions. Law schools represented by the faculty's degrees include Columbia, Chicago, George Washington, Harvard, Texas, and Yale, with graduate law degrees from such schools as Columbia, Harvard, New York University, Virginia, and Yale. Nonlaw doctoral and master's degrees include Stanford, Michigan, Chicago, Harvard, and Wisconsin. Faculty members have contributed numerous articles, essays, and other material for legal publishers and law journals around the country. Adjunct professors provide a considerable range of academic and professional experience as well.

■ Library and Physical Facilities

➡ 147,750 volumes & equivalents ➡ library hours: Mon.-Fri., 7:30 A.M.-MIDNIGHT; Sat., 9:00 A.M.-MIDNIGHT; Sun., 10:00 A.M.-MIDNIGHT ➡ LEXIS ➡ NEXIS
➡ WESTLAW ➡ 7 full-time librarians
➡ library staff of 14 ➡ library seats 254

The law school boasts first-rate facilities including spacious classrooms, impressive courtrooms, an in-house law clinic, as well as a state-of-the-art library. The law library's mission is to provide student access to the legal information resources needed to practice law in the digital age. In addition to its law book collection, the law library subscribes to major online electronic legal information services and several CD-ROM research tools. Students are furnished software and passwords for use on home computers to provide them access to online legal information beyond the law library walls. Complementing book and electronic sources, an extensive collection of U.S. Congressional documents, including full transcripts of all Congressional hearings, is available on microfiche. The law library is open more than 100 hours a week, during 80 of which at least one professional reference librarian is on duty.

During the summer of 1997 the school moved to a new location in downtown Fort Worth, Texas, in close proximity to the Tarrant County legal and judicial community. The Dallas/Fort Worth Metroplex, with a population of 3.8 million, offers a relatively low cost of living and a growing economy and has rapidly grown to be one of the largest and most diversified metropolitan areas in the country.

Fort Worth's downtown is "urban complete" since a virtual renaissance began there in the 1980s, and the relocation of Texas Wesleyan's law school is a continuation of redevelopment efforts. The city is home to the world-renowned Kimbell and Amon Carter museums; Sundance Square; a downtown center for business, the arts and residential living; the historic Stockyards District; and a beautiful natural-environment zoo. Dallas offers diverse entertainment options such as a vibrant arts district, an arboretum/botanical gardens complex, and teams from all five major athletic leagues.

■ Curriculum

➡ Academic Support Program ➡ 88 credits required to graduate ➡ 98 courses available ➡ degree available: J.D.

Eighty-eight hours of academic instruction are required for completion of the three-year full-time, or four-year part-time program leading to the Juris Doctor degree. The part-time program is offered for students who wish to work full-time while pursuing their legal education.

■ Skills Training

Wesleyan considers skills training to be a significant component of legal education. By participation in such skills courses as trial advocacy, moot court, pretrial practice, appellate practice, dispute resolution, mediation, negotiations, commercial arbitration, family mediation and crisis management, and estate planning, students develop strengths in oral advocacy, writing, and drafting. Additionally, the Externship Program enables students to work with practicing attorneys for academic credit and provides a supervised context in which students will be exposed to front-line practice before the bar and governmental agencies.

Students also have the opportunity to gain hands-on professional experience representing clients through an in-house clinic.

■ Admission

➡ *Bachelor's degree from an accredited college or university required* ➡ *application date—preferably by Feb. 15, later applications may be considered* ➡ *LSAT, LSDAS required* ➡ *application fee—$50*

In addition to addressing academic achievements and aptitude, the Admissions Committee endeavors, on the basis of the applicant's education and other experiences, to determine the professional promise of the applicant. In this connection, the committee looks for evidence of high achievement in various endeavors, prior employment, military experience, graduate study, community service, and other factors. The diversity of the student body is also an important consideration with respect to the variety of undergraduate institutions and the cultural and geographic breadth represented in an entering class. Inquiries as to credentials and timing should be directed to the law school's Admission Office 817.212.4040. Wesleyan may admit students with advanced standing who are in good standing at a law school approved by the American Bar Association.

■ Activities

Student activities, complementing traditional academic programs, include the *Texas Wesleyan Law Review*, a scholarly periodical published by a staff of law students with membership based on outstanding grades and writing ability, Moot Court, Order of the Barristers, Mediation

Clinics, and the Pro Bono Board. Cocurricular activities such as the Student Bar Association, the Criminal Justice Society, International Law Society, Intellectual Property Society, the Christian Legal Society, Black Law Students Association, Hispanic Law Students Association, Asian and Pacific American Law Students Association, Organization of Women Law Students, Wesleyan Law Democrats, Wesleyan Law Republicans, ADR Bar, Texas Aggies Legal Society, Environmental Law Society, and ABA/Law Student Division. Two legal fraternities also serve to broaden the student experience.

■ Expenses and Financial Aid

➡ *1998-1999 tuition & fees—$450/credit hr., plus $87/fees per semester* ➡ *approximate additional expenses—$500/semester (books & study guides)* ➡ *scholarships available* ➡ *financial aid available*

FAFSA, financial aid transcripts, and loan applications required for financial aid. Loan information is available through the Office of Financial Aid, 817.212.4090.

■ Career Services

The Wesleyan Law School Career Services Office assists students, graduates, and employers in their mutual efforts to link those seeking legal positions with those providing employment opportunities. In addition to assisting with full-time employment opportunities, Career Services supports students securing part-time or temporary employment while attending law school. A range of services, such as career counseling, résumé writing, and on-campus interviewing are available. The law school also offers a career planning library. The school is a member of the National Association of Law Placement.

Applicant Group for the 1998-1999 Academic Year

In addition to addressing academic achievement and aptitude, the Admission Committee looks for evidence of substantial achievement in various endeavors, prior employment, graduate study, and community and public service. The diversity of the student body is an

important consideration with respect to age, culture, and geographic background. We do not provide a profile chart of applicants considered and admitted because it is based solely upon undergraduate GPA and LSAT scores.

Thomas M. Cooley Law School

217 S. Capital Avenue
Post Office Box 13038
Lansing, MI 48901

E-Mail: cooleyadm@aol.com
URL: http://www.cooley.edu
Phone: 517.371.5140

■ Introduction

Thomas M. Cooley Law School, one of the nation's largest law schools, was established in 1972 in Lansing, Michigan, by former Supreme Court Chief Justice Thomas E. Brennan and a group of dedicated lawyers and judges.

Named for Michigan's renowned Judge Cooley, the school is committed to liberal admissions, practical scholarship, and uncompromising professionalism. The American Bar Association approved Thomas Cooley Law School in 1975.

As an independent, graduate college, Thomas Cooley enjoys the reputation of a tough law school, run by experienced lawyers and judges. Its faculty, students, and alumni take pride in the school's close contacts with the bench and bar.

The *Thomas M. Cooley Law Review* has received national recognition for promoting the use of plain English lawsuit papers.

■ Enrollment/Student Body

➡ *2,901 applicants for all 1998 classes*   ➡ *2,413 accepted*
➡ *879 matriculated first-year class 1998*   ➡ *full-time 25th/75th percentile GPA—2.66/3.20*   ➡ *part-time 25th/75th percentile GPA—2.63/3.20*   ➡ *full-time 25th/75th percentile LSAT—139/145*   ➡ *part-time 25th/75th percentile LSAT—139/147*
➡ *406 total full-time*   ➡ *1,288 total part-time*
➡ *28% minority*   ➡ *44% women*

Of Thomas Cooley's diverse student body, 63 percent hail from out-of-state and 10 percent hold advanced degrees. The median age of entering students is 26.

■ Faculty

➡ *58 full-time*   ➡ *100 part-time or adjunct*
➡ *17 women*   ➡ *5 minority*

■ Library and Physical Facilities

➡ *395,151 volumes & equivalents*   ➡ *library is open 120 hours/wk. including weekends*   ➡ *LEXIS*
➡ *NEXIS*   ➡ *WESTLAW*   ➡ *10 full-time librarians*
➡ *library seats 530*

Cooley's research facility is designed to meet the research needs of today's law student. The library features a large computer lab, two electronic classrooms for computer-assisted legal instruction and Innopac, an integrated automated library system.

Occupying nearly 65,000-square feet and five levels, the library collection includes standard state and federal legal materials. Primary research materials from every state are maintained and updated. Nearby, the State Law Library and the general libraries of the city of Lansing, state of Michigan, Lansing Community College, and Michigan State University are available to Thomas Cooley students.

■ Curriculum

➡ *J.D. degree*   ➡ *3 semesters per year, beginning Jan., May, & Sept.*   ➡ *90 credits required to graduate*

Thomas Cooley Law School is organized on a 12-month academic year, consisting of three full 15-week terms of school. Each term meets the definition of a full semester. Like the terms of the English Courts of Common Law, Thomas Cooley's three academic terms are designated Hilary Term (January to April), Trinity Term (May to August), and Michaelmas Term (September to December).

Cooley Law School offers students more scheduling options than most other law schools. Students may choose from either full- or part-time programs, weekday or evening programs, and schedules spanning from two to four years. Classes are offered seven days a week. There is a scheduling option to fit most any individual's needs, and each of Cooley's programs offers a J.D. degree to its graduates. Final-year elective concentrations are available in several areas of the law.

■ Special Programs

The Sixty-Plus Law Center, Thomas Cooley's award-winning clinic for elderly citizens, permits students to earn academic credit while representing real clients.

Directed studies, trial workshops, law review, and moot court programs enrich the curriculum. Because Thomas Cooley has a national student body, civil and criminal practice courses for New York, New Jersey, Pennsylvania, Florida, Indiana, Arizona, Texas, Wisconsin, and Illinois are offered.

■ Admission

➡ *Bachelor's degree required in most cases*
➡ *rolling admission*   ➡ *LSAT, LSDAS required*
➡ *$25 non-refundable fee upon acceptance*

The admissions office uses a simple index (15 times undergraduate grade-point average [UGPA] + LSAT) to determine admissibility. All applicants with an index of 180 or more are virtually assured of acceptance.

Candidates otherwise qualified may be rejected for specific negative factors by the Faculty Admissions Committee. Morning, afternoon, and evening divisions are organized in September, January, and May, respectively. Students with index scores below 180 are usually urged to retake the LSAT.

■ Student Activities

All students are members of the Student Bar Association, and chapters of two national legal fraternities have been established. In addition, students publish a newspaper, supervise the Student Tutorial Service, edit and publish *The Thomas M. Cooley Law Review*, *The Thomas M. Cooley Journal of Practical and Clinical Law*, and conduct an active intramural sports program.

The Thomas M. Cooley Law Review focuses upon legal questions of significance to state governments, state court jurists, and state public policy matters. The *Review* prepares and publishes three issues per year. Each issue features articles written by practicing attorneys, judges, and professors; casenotes and comments written by Thomas Cooley students; and distinguished briefs argued before the Michigan Supreme Court.

The Thomas M. Cooley Journal of Practical and Clinical Law is a new publication at the Law School. It takes the practical view of legal issues and provides articles of interest and use to assist the practicing attorney.

Cooley Law School has an extensive externship program in which students are placed with various law offices and agencies to garner real-life experience. There are 32 clubs and organizations for students. They include the International Law Society, Women's Law Alliance, Black Law Students Association, Christian Legal Society, the Environmental Law Society, Jewish Law Caucus, Hispanic Law Society, and Asian Pacific American Law Students Association.

■ Expenses and Financial Aid

➡ *tuition & fees—full-time/part-time, $550/credit hr.*
➡ *estimated additional expenses—$11,103 (room & board, books, personal, transportation)* ➡ *honors, academic standing, & special-factor scholarships available* ➡ *financial aid available*

Honors Scholarships reward academic excellence, they are offered to qualified incoming students based on their admissions index and to qualified continuing students based on their academic performance at Cooley. Honors Scholarships are awarded based upon the following admissions index levels:

Index	Honors Scholarship
220+	100%
215-219	75%
210-214	50%
205-209	25%
195-204	10%

The initial Honors Scholarship is continued as a minimum award for the duration of the student's enrollment at the Law School, so long as the student remains in good standing academically and is not subject to sanction under the Honor Code or Disciplinary Procedures and so long as Cooley Law School continues the Honors Scholarship program.

It is possible that a student earning an Honors Scholarship of less than 50 percent may increase the scholarship amount up to 50 percent if his or her class rank improves. The new, higher scholarship award is continued as a minimum award for the duration of the student's enrollment in good standing at Cooley.

■ Housing

The Law School does not operate residence facilities. There is an ample supply of living accommodations available nearby in all price ranges.

■ Career Services

The Career and Student Services Office provides a wide variety of services to students and graduates of the Law School. Job postings (updated weekly) provide listings for full-time positions in both in- and out-of-state, as well as listings for legally related part-time work in the greater Lansing area. Reciprocal agreements with law school placement offices in other parts of the country are maintained for those students and graduates who wish to practice in other states. Workshops and seminars, focusing on topics ranging from interviewing skills to business etiquette, are open to all students. Services for students and alumni include the Thomas Cooley Placement Hotline, a 24-hour recording of the most recent week's listings. The office also maintains a credential file system for graduates, utilized by employers who wish the Career and Student Services Office to supply résumés of interested candidates.

Acceptance and Scholarship Range

Thomas M. Cooley School of Law

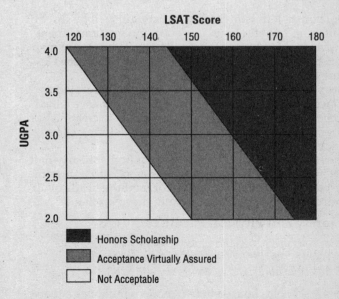

Thomas Jefferson School of Law

2121 San Diego Avenue
San Diego, CA 92110

E-Mail: adm@tjsl.edu
URL: http://www.tjsl.edu
Phone: 619.297.9700; 800.956.5070

■ Introduction

The Thomas Jefferson School of Law is a private, independent law school that emphasizes an individualized approach to legal education. This approach features small classes, and close student/faculty interaction in a supportive environment. It also features a flexible curriculum that allows students to start law school in January or August, attend full time or part time, and accelerate graduation by attending classes in the summer.

Thomas Jefferson is located in the spectacular city of San Diego, California, which boasts what many consider to be the finest climate in the continental United States. At the same time, as the sixth largest city in the nation, San Diego offers all of the professional, social, and cultural opportunities of a major metropolitan area.

The law school was provisionally approved by the ABA on August 6, 1996, which entitles its students to the same recognition that students at fully-approved law schools receive, including the right to sit for the bar exam in all 50 states upon graduation.

■ Enrollment/Student Body

➼ *563 enrolled*   ➼ *full-time 25th/75th percentile GPA—2.45/3.12*   ➼ *part-time 25th/75th percentile GPA—2.50/3.19*
➼ *full-time 25th/75th percentile LSAT—145/155*
➼ *part-time 25th/75th percentile LSAT—145/153*
➼ *1998 entering class is 22.1% minority*   ➼ *1998 entering class is 55.4% out-of-state*   ➼ *37 states & 14 foreign countries represented*   ➼ *115 undergraduate schools represented*

■ Faculty

➼ *52 total*   ➼ *26 full-time (12 women)*   ➼ *26 adjunct*
➼ *2 minority*

The Thomas Jefferson faculty is distinguished by three features: its qualifications, its youth, and its commitment to teaching. Members of the faculty were educated at many of the finest law schools in the nation and all practiced law before turning to academic careers.

The youth and vitality of the faculty are suggested by the fact that about three-fourths of the faculty have joined Thomas Jefferson since 1990. All contribute to creating the student-centered environment that is a defining characteristic of Thomas Jefferson.

The full-time faculty is very unusual in that nearly half of its members are women, as are the associate dean, both assistant deans, the library director, and the heads of all administrative departments within the law school.

■ Library and Physical Facilities

➼ *library is open 105 hours/wk.*   ➼ *LEXIS*
➼ *NEXIS*   ➼ *WESTLAW*   ➼ *Internet access*
➼ *6 full-time librarians*   ➼ *library seats 283*

The law school is housed in two modern buildings situated in the beautiful and historic Old Town section of San Diego.

The library includes the law school's five computer labs and numerous private study rooms that students may reserve for group or individual study.

■ Curriculum

➼ *Academic Support Program*   ➼ *88 units required to graduate*   ➼ *more than 90 courses available*   ➼ *J.D. degree available*   ➼ *entering classes begin in Jan. or Aug.*   ➼ *day & evening program*   ➼ *range of first-year class size—20-60*

Students may commence their studies at Thomas Jefferson in either August or January. The law school offers a three-year full-time program and a four-year part-time program. Full-time students generally take their courses during the day, while part-time students may attend either the day or the evening division. Students may accelerate graduation under either program by one semester by taking additional classes during the summer.

All programs have the same admission standards and graduation requirements. The full-time faculty teaches the same proportion of courses in both the day and evening divisions.

The first-year curriculum is prescribed. All first-year class sections are small by American law school standards, typically with 35-50 students in doctrinal courses and about 25 students in legal writing courses. All first-year students are invited to attend optional weekly survival skills workshops, which are small group study sessions led by successful upper-level students.

■ Special Programs

The law school offers, each year, a large number of courses that train students in professional skills, supplemented by a variety of field placement programs. The judicial internship program allows students to work for a semester with local federal and state judges, gaining experience in drafting opinions and observing courtroom proceedings. Students also may work for credit at a variety of public agencies. California law allows law students who have completed certain coursework to obtain certification to appear in court.

In addition to solid curricula in traditional areas such as business and criminal law, the law school has developed special concentrations in international law, intellectual property, and constitutional/civil rights law. Elective courses also are available in newer fields such as bioethics, entertainment law, health law, sports law, women and the law, and sexual orientation and the law.

■ Admission

➼ *LSAT, LSDAS required*   ➼ *application fee—$35*
➼ *fall & spring admission available*
➼ *personal interviews available*

Thomas Jefferson conducts a rolling admission process under which applicants are considered when their applications are complete. Because the law school admits two entering classes each year, the admission committee meets continuously throughout the year and there are no formal application deadlines. Early applications are encouraged, however, and those who apply early increase their chance of a favorable decision.

The admission committee gives each applicant careful, thorough, and personalized consideration. In addition to the LSAT score, the committee considers the applicant's undergraduate record, extracurricular activities, work experience, and history of overcoming adversity.

The law school accepts applications from transfer students in both the fall and spring semesters. Transfer students must be in good academic standing at their current law school.

■ Expenses and Financial Aid

➡ *tuition & fees—full-time, $18,780; part-time, $11,580*
➡ *estimated additional expenses—$14,000*
➡ *merit-based scholarships available*
➡ *need-based financial assistance available*

All entering students with an average LSAT score of 150 or higher automatically receive a partial or full scholarship for the first year. Partial and full tuition scholarships also are automatically awarded after the first year, but are based on academic performance at the end of the prior year rather than on LSAT scores. Generally, all students in the top 30 percent are on scholarship.

Student loans and work-study funds also are available. Students interested in these programs should apply as early as possible and should not wait for an admission decision before applying for financial assistance.

■ Student Activities

Student activities at Thomas Jefferson include both cocurricular and extracurricular activities. The most prestigious cocurricular activity is the *Thomas Jefferson Law Review*, a semiannual journal of legal scholarship edited and managed by students.

Cocurricular programs at Thomas Jefferson also include the moot court and mock trial competitions. Extracurricular activities serve a variety of student interests and needs. Some student organizations are organized around substantive areas of law practice such as the International Law Society, the Intellectual Property Law Society, and the Sports and Entertainment Law Society. Many student organizations provide a source of mutual support for various groups of students such as the Black Law Student Association, La Raza, and the Pan Asian Law Students Association. The law school also has campus chapters of two national fraternities, Delta Theta Phi and Phi Alpha Delta, and the National Lawyers Guild.

■ Career Services

The Thomas Jefferson Career Services Office assists students and alumni in finding temporary and permanent law related employment. The career services director counsels students individually on résumé preparation, interviewing skills, and job-search strategies. The office maintains listings of employment opportunities and schedules on-campus interviewing. It also assists students in obtaining placement with state and federal judges and with various public agencies, where they can work during the year for academic credit.

The Career Services Office has developed an alumni mentoring program, through which Thomas Jefferson students can obtain advice and assistance from some of the law school's more than 4,000 alumni.

Admission Profile Not Available

The University of Toledo College of Law

2801 West Bancroft Street
Toledo, OH 43606

E-Mail: law0046@uoft01.utoledo.edu
URL: http://www.utoledo.edu/law/
Phone: 419.530.4131

■ Introduction

The University of Toledo is a state university of more than 20,000 students, conveniently located on the western edge of Toledo, Ohio, in one of the city's nicest residential areas.

The College of Law, located on the main campus of the University of Toledo, is accredited by the ABA and is a member of the AALS and the League of Ohio Law Schools. It has been training lawyers since 1906 and in 1984 was awarded a chapter of the Order of the Coif. Toledo, at the western end of Lake Erie, is conveniently located to Ann Arbor, Detroit, Cincinnati, Cleveland, Columbus, and Chicago.

■ Enrollment/Student Body

➡ 595 applicants   ➡ 396 admitted first-year class 1998
➡ 166 enrolled first-year class 1998
➡ full-time 25th/75th percentile GPA—2.69/3.34
➡ part-time 25th/75th percentile GPA—2.81/3.36
➡ full-time 25th/75th percentile LSAT—146/156
➡ part-time 25th/75th percentile LSAT—146/154
➡ 387 total full-time   ➡ 163 total part-time   ➡ 8% minority
➡ 45% women   ➡ 31 states & foreign countries represented
➡ 200 undergraduate schools represented

The college seeks a diverse student body. Approximately 30 percent of the entering students come from outside Ohio. The day-division entering class ranges from 135 to 140; evening, from 35 to 40.

■ Faculty

➡ 56 total   ➡ 33 full-time   ➡ 23 part-time or adjunct
➡ 10 women   ➡ 3 minority

The full-time faculty hold law degrees from some of the most outstanding universities in the country. Many have advanced law degrees.

While legal scholarship is important and many faculty members have national reputations for scholarship, the College of Law places a high priority on effective teaching and accessibility to students.

■ Library and Physical Facilities

➡ 306,450 volumes & equivalents   ➡ library hours:
Mon.-Fri., 7:30 A.M.-MIDNIGHT; Sat.-Sun., 9:00 A.M.-MIDNIGHT
➡ LEXIS   ➡ NEXIS   ➡ WESTLAW
➡ 6.5 full-time librarians   ➡ library seats 430

The spacious, modern Law Center includes tiered classrooms, a striking student lounge, state-of-the-art moot courtroom, law office classroom, and amphitheater auditorium.

The law library contains six group-study rooms, video-taping facilities, and 53 computers and printers for use by law students.

■ Curriculum

➡ Academic Support Program   ➡ 89 credits required
to graduate   ➡ 150 courses available   ➡ degrees available:
J.D.; J.D./M.B.A.   ➡ semesters, start in Aug.
➡ range of first year class size—20-55

Both a full-time and a part-time program are available. The first-year curriculum is prescribed. Prior to graduation, all students are required to complete the course in Evidence and in Legal Ethics and Professional Responsibility, as well as a scholarly paper within the context of a seminar.

■ Special Programs

The college was a pioneer in clinical legal education. Under a rule of the Ohio Supreme Court, upper-class students appear in court under close faculty supervision in both civil and criminal cases. Through the Dispute Resolution Clinic, mediation experience also is available in a variety of matters, including unruly child complaints and custody and visitation issues in parentage cases in juvenile court.

The college has a long-standing interest in international legal studies.

■ The Legal Institute of the Great Lakes

The Institute supports research, special studies, and conferences on legal issues of greater than ordinary import to the Great Lakes Region of the United States and Canada. The Institute sponsors a course of study on Law and the Great Lakes which integrates major topical areas including environmental law, natural resources law, transportation law, agricultural law, commercial and corporate law, and international and comparative Canadian law. It publishes a newsletter and a multidisciplinary, peer-reviewed journal.

■ Admission

➡ Bachelor's degree from an accredited college or
university required   ➡ application deadline—full-time,
March 15; part-time, May 15   ➡ LSAT, LSDAS required
➡ application fee—$30

Grades and LSAT scores are the most important determinants of admission. Evidence showing that the GPA and LSAT score understate an applicant's ability is carefully considered. Letters of recommendation are important.

Prospective students are encouraged to visit the College of Law and sit in on classes. Appointments can be made through the Admission Office.

■ Student Activities

The *University of Toledo Law Review* is published four times a year by students selected on the basis of scholarship. Students may also qualify by submitting a publishable article. Training and practice in brief writing and oral argument beyond the required appellate advocacy course are obtained in the Charles Fornoff Intramural Moot Court Competition and in several national and regional competitions. Client counseling and trial practice programs are also stressed. All students are members of the Student Bar Association. The Black Law Students Association, Business Law Society, Environmental Law Society, Federalist Society, Health Care Law Association, Hispanic Law Student Association, International Law Society, Sports Law Association, and the Women Law Students Association are among several active student organizations.

■ Expenses and Financial Aid

➡ *full-time tuition & fees—$7,351, resident; $14,174, nonresident* ➡ *part-time tuition & fees— $5,207, resident; $10,040, nonresident*
➡ *per semester hr. tuition & fees—$306.27, resident; $590.57, nonresident* ➡ *estimated additional expenses— $10,250 (room, board, books, personal expenses, transportation)*
➡ *merit- & merit-/need-based scholarships available*
➡ *financial aid available; need analysis form due to Financial Aid Office by April 1*

Under the terms of an agreement entered into by the states of Ohio and Michigan, residents of Monroe County, Michigan, who are attending the University of Toledo are treated as in-state residents for tuition purposes. Although the university has no housing for law students, housing near the university is plentiful. Newly admitted students desiring assistance in obtaining housing receive help from the Student Bar Association and the university's Off-Campus Living Office.

■ Career Services

The College places top priority on providing comprehensive career planning and placement for its students and graduates. The office assists students through workshops, videotapes, and counseling, and provides guest speakers on legal career options.

As a result of both on- and off-campus interviews, second- and third-year students in 1997-1998 accepted summer or attorney positions in all major cities of Ohio and Michigan as well as other locations throughout the U.S.

The College's Judicial Clerkship Program places graduates as clerks with federal courts of appeals and district courts, and with state trial and appellate courts around the country. Second- and third-year students have the opportunity to participate in internships in federal and Ohio appellate courts.

College of Law graduates take the bar examination in many states. The college's first-time takers of the Ohio Bar Examination consistently pass the exam with scores above the state's average.

Applicant Group for the 1998-1999 Academic Year

The University of Toledo College of Law
Graph reflects admission decisions as of 9/1/98.

LSAT (10) Percentile Intervals									
GPA	0-20	21-30	31-40	41-50	51-60	61-70	71-80	81-90	91-99
3.75 Above									
3.74 3.50									
3.49 3.25									
3.24 3.00									
2.99 2.75									
2.74 2.50									
2.49 2.25									
2.24 2.00									
Below 2.00									

■ Highly Likely   ▪ Possible   □ Unlikely

Touro College—Jacob D. Fuchsberg Law Center

300 Nassau Road
Huntington, NY 11743

E-Mail: admissions@tourolaw.edu
URL: http://www.tourolaw.edu
Phone: 516.421.2244, ext. 312

■ Introduction

Touro Law Center is located in the vibrant suburban community of Huntington, Long Island, a short drive or convenient commuter train ride from New York City. Touro is best known for its accessible faculty, intensive practical training, and acclaimed international programs. The focus of the Law Center's practical training is its clinics, all of which give students the opportunity to work on real cases under the supervision of experienced attorneys. The centerpiece of Touro's international emphasis is its summer programs in India and Russia. A unique international summer internship program is also offered. The Law Center is fully accredited by the ABA and is a member of the AALS.

■ Enrollment/Student Body

➡ *1,616 applicants*   ➡ *799 admitted first-year class 1998*
➡ *243 enrolled first-year class 1998*   ➡ *full-time 25th/75th percentile GPA—2.73/3.20*   ➡ *part-time 25th/75th percentile GPA—2.69/3.31*   ➡ *full-time 25th/75th percentile LSAT—144/151*   ➡ *part-time 25th/75th percentile LSAT—144/153*
➡ *419 total full-time*   ➡ *285 total part-time*
➡ *24% minority*   ➡ *46.6% women*   ➡ *13 states & 2 foreign countries represented in first-year class 1998*
➡ *105 undergraduate schools represented in first-year class 1998*
➡ *average age in the full-time class is 27; part-time is 30*

■ Faculty

➡ *67 total*   ➡ *37 full-time*   ➡ *30 part-time or adjunct*
➡ *13 women*   ➡ *2 minority*

■ Library and Physical Facilities

➡ *380,000 volumes & equivalents*   ➡ *library hours: Mon.-Thurs., 8:00 A.M.-11:45 P.M.; Fri., 8:00 A.M.-2:45 P.M.; Sat., closed; Sun., 9:00 A.M.-11:45 P.M.*   ➡ *LEXIS*
➡ *NEXIS*   ➡ *WESTLAW*   ➡ *DIALOG*
➡ *DOWJONES*   ➡ *Internet*   ➡ *7 full-time librarians*
➡ *library seats 395*

■ Curriculum

➡ *87 credits required to graduate*   ➡ *120 courses available (not offered every semester)*   ➡ *J.D.; J.D./M.B.A.; J.D./M.S. (Taxation); J.D./M.P.A. (Health); LL.M. (for Foreign Law Graduates) degrees available*   ➡ *fall semester begins mid-Aug.; spring semester begins early Jan.*
➡ *range of first-year class size—16-60*

The full-time J.D. program takes three years (six semesters) and the part-time J.D. program—available day or evening—takes four years (eight semesters). In each case, the program can be shortened by one semester by attending two summer sessions. The entire first-year curriculum is required. Some required courses continue into the second year for full-time students and into the third year for part-time students. Over 100 elective courses allow students to specialize in such areas as business, criminal, elder, family, health, intellectual property, international, and public interest.

■ Special Programs

Clinics. Clinics include Criminal Law, Elder Law, Family Law, Civil Rights Litigation, International Human Rights Asylum (available to evening students), Judicial Clerkship, and Civil Practice. In the latter, students earn academic credit in for-profit settings, including private law firms and corporate law departments.

Dual Degree Programs. Students may combine the Juris Doctor degree with either a Master of Business Administration, a Master of Science (Taxation), or a Master of Public Administration (Health).

Part-time Day Program. Touro's part-time day program is designed to enable people with child-care and elder-care responsibilities to attend law school. Special schedules are arranged between 10 A.M. and 2 P.M., while students follow the required curriculum and may graduate in three and one-half or four years.

Academic Support Programs. The Law Center provides a unique program of outside-the-classroom assistance. Teaching Assistants (TAs), assigned to most required courses, present weekly review sessions on the material covered in class. TAs also offer sessions on basic study skills and strategies. For graduating students, there is a series of workshops to review the multi-state bar examination topics. In addition, the Legal Education Access Program (LEAP) is designed to offset barriers to success that are often experienced by students of color. LEAP includes a three-week summer program prior to the start of classes, TAs, a mentor program, and individualized assistance for all participants.

International Internships. Law firms, courts, and government law offices in London, Paris, Brussels, Lisbon, Tel Aviv, and Jerusalem make available summer positions exclusively for Law Center students.

Moscow and India Summer Programs. The former is based at, and offered in cooperation with, Moscow State University, the oldest, largest, and most prestigious university in the former Soviet Union. The "New India" program, the first of its kind to be conducted by an American law school on the Indian subcontinent, is based in Shimla, in the foothills of the Himalayas. Both programs include the option to work in local law offices at the end of the school session.

Specialized Institutes. The Law Center hosts the Institute of Local and Suburban Law and the Institute of Jewish Law. The former is dedicated to research and education in municipal, environmental, planning, and local government law. The latter, in keeping with Touro's establishment under Jewish auspices, is concerned with research, scholarship, and publications in Jewish law.

LL.M. for Foreign Law Graduates. This 27-credit program is available to graduates of non-U.S. law schools who seek familiarity with U.S. law and legal institutions. Recipients of the degree are generally eligible to sit for the New York Bar examination.

■ Student Activities

Students play an active role in governing the entire institution through the Student Bar Association and service on faculty committees. There are more than 30 professional and social organizations, most notably the *Touro Law Review* and the Moot Court Board. The Law Center also sponsors the Trial Advocacy Competition Board, as well as two other student-edited publications: the *Touro International Law Review* and the *Journal of the Suffolk Academy of Law*.

■ Admission

➡ *Bachelor's degree from accredited college/university required*
➡ *priority deadline—May 1* ➡ *early application preferred, rolling admission* ➡ *LSAT, LSDAS required*
➡ *application fee—$50* ➡ *personal statement required*

New students are admitted to the full-time day, part-time day, and part-time evening divisions for the fall semester each year. Transfer students are admitted to summer, fall, or spring semesters. The admission process seeks to identify those applicants who evidence an ability to pursue the study of law successfully and to make a significant contribution to the educational program of the law school.

Two important criteria used in the admission process are the cumulative undergraduate grade-point average and the LSAT score. The selection process, however, recognizes that other factors—course selection, graduate study, work experience, and character—may also be indicators of potential.

While they are not required, letters of recommendation from those with direct personal knowledge of an applicant can contribute to the admission decision.

The Law Center does not discriminate against any applicant for admission because of race, color, religion, gender, sexual orientation, national origin, age, marital status, financial status, or physical disability.

Applicants are encouraged to visit the campus, to sit in on classes, and to meet faculty and students. Advance arrangements should be made through the Admissions Office.

■ Housing

A 42-unit apartment building for Law Center students forms an integral part of the Touro campus. In addition, the Office of Admissions operates a Housing Information Network to help students locate suitable off-campus housing in the Huntington area.

■ Expenses and Financial Aid

➡ *tuition & fees—full-time, $20,370; part-time, $15,900*
➡ *estimated additional expenses—(approximate cost of books & supplies in the first year)—$500* ➡ *scholarships available*
➡ *financial aid available; FAFSA due May 1*

The Law Center provides access to federal and private loans, and to the New York Tuition Assistance Program. Ninety percent of all students receive financial aid and approximately 50 percent of entering students receive tuition scholarships. Institutional aid includes the College Work-Study Program, the Touro Grant Program, Dean's Fellowships (100 percent tuition), merit and achievement scholarships (5-80 percent tuition), Incentive Awards (5-50 percent tuition), and Administrative Grants (for books and materials). In addition, the Law Center offers Public Interest Law Fellowships for summer employment and a Public Interest Loan Forgiveness Program for graduates.

■ Career Services

The Office of Career Planning and Counseling functions as a career center, offering a variety of services to students and employers. The office assists students in their efforts to secure employment upon graduation, as well as part-time and full-time employment during the school year and summer.

Applicant Group for the 1998-1999 Academic Year

Touro Law Center does not provide an Admission Profile for its applicant group because at no point on a purely objective scale is an applicant assured of a particular disposition or result.

Tulane University Law School

John Giffen Weinmann Hall
6329 Freret Street
New Orleans, LA 70118

E-Mail: admissions@law.tulane.edu
URL: http://www.law.tulane.edu
Phone: 504.865.5930, Fax: 504.865.6710

■ Introduction

Located in one of the most interesting cities in the United States, Tulane Law School was established in 1847. By offering a comprehensive curriculum in the common law, in all federal subjects, and in the civil law, Tulane offers its students a unique opportunity, if they so choose, to pursue comparative education in the world's two major legal systems. Tulane's location in uptown New Orleans provides ready access to the downtown activities of the U.S. Court of Appeals for the Fifth Circuit, the Louisiana Supreme Court, and lower federal and state civil and criminal courts. In addition to cultural events at Tulane University, students enjoy the advantages of city life and many aspects of New Orleans.

■ Enrollment/Student Body

➡ *2,325 applicants*   ➡ *1,194 admitted first-year class 1998*
➡ *347 enrolled first-year class 1998*   ➡ *full-time 25th/75th percentile GPA—3.01/3.53*   ➡ *full-time 25th/75th percentile LSAT—155/161*   ➡ *942 total full-time*   ➡ *22.6% minority*
➡ *46.7% women*   ➡ *62 states & foreign countries represented*
➡ *333 undergraduate schools represented*

■ Faculty

➡ *106 total*   ➡ *58 full-time*   ➡ *48 part-time or adjunct*
➡ *17 women*   ➡ *6 minority*

Assistant or associate deans oversee admission and financial aid, student life, continuing legal education, community service, and the Office of Career Services.

■ Library and Physical Facilities

➡ *501,000 volumes & equivalents*   ➡ *library hours:*
Mon.-Fri., 7:30 A.M.-MIDNIGHT; Sat.-Sun., 9:00 A.M.-MIDNIGHT
➡ *LEXIS*   ➡ *NEXIS*   ➡ *WESTLAW*   ➡ *DIALOG*
➡ *EELS*   ➡ *ORBIT*   ➡ *QUICKLAW*   ➡ *VUTEXT*
➡ *DATATIMES*   ➡ *Internet*   ➡ *MARC*
➡ *WILSONDISC*   ➡ *INFOTRAC*   ➡ *CALI*
➡ *several cataloging systems*   ➡ *10 full-time librarians*
➡ *library seats 596*   ➡ *130 computers available for student use*

The law library has both national and international collections. The university's Howard-Tilton Library houses over one million volumes.

The Law School's 160,000-square-foot building, John Giffen Weinmann Hall, opened in the spring of 1995. Designed to integrate classrooms, other student spaces, and faculty offices with a state-of-the-art library and computer facilities, the building is centrally located on campus.

On-campus housing is available. Off-campus housing is also plentiful and nearby.

■ Curriculum

➡ *Academic Support Program*   ➡ *88 credits required to graduate*   ➡ *175 courses available*   ➡ *degrees available:*
J.D.; J.D./M.B.A.; J.D./M.H.A.; J.D./M.A.; J.D./M.P.H.; J.D./M.S.W.; LL.M.; S.J.D.   ➡ *semesters, start in Aug.*
➡ *range of first-year class size—80-90*

Six semesters in residence, at least a C average, and fulfillment of a 20-hour community service obligation are required for graduation from the J.D. program. The first-year curriculum comprises eight required courses and one elective. Thereafter, all courses are elective. All first-year and many upper-class courses are taught in multiple sections to allow for smaller classes, and faculty members teach advanced courses and seminars in their fields of specialty.

The first-year Legal Research and Writing program is taught by four instructors with significant experience as lawyers and writers, each assisted by four senior fellows. This arrangement results in more personalized attention for students.

■ Special Programs

Among the strengths for which the school is known are international and comparative law, admiralty and maritime law, and environmental law. The school offers four optional "concentration" programs which allow J.D. students to receive a certificate of studies in (a) European Legal Studies, (b) Environmental Law, (c) Maritime Law, or (d) Sports Law. Tulane's Eason-Weinmann Center for Comparative Law, its Maritime Law Center, and its Institute for Environmental Law and Policy add depth to the curriculum.

The annual Tulane Tax Institute and Corporate Law Institute, and the biennial Admiralty Law Institute, are recognized for their excellence. The school offers a strong intellectual property curriculum. Tulane conducts a summer school in New Orleans and offers summer-study programs abroad in Canada, England, Israel, The Netherlands, France, Italy, and Greece. All summer programs are open to law students enrolled at Tulane or other law schools.

■ Clinical Programs

The school offers eight different live clinical programs—civil, criminal, juvenile, immigration, environmental, appellate, legislative advocacy, and administrative advocacy. In addition, there is a Trial Advocacy program, and selected third-year students may do externships with federal and state judges. The school was the first to institute a mandatory pro bono program, requiring that each student complete at least 20 hours of community-service work prior to graduation.

■ Joint-Degree and Graduate Programs

Joint-degree programs are offered in conjunction with Tulane's Freeman School of Business, (J.D./M.B.A.), School of Public Health and Tropical Medicine, (J.D./M.H.A. or M.P.H.), and Graduate School (J.D./M.A.), in a variety of fields including Latin American Studies and International Affairs. At the graduate level, the Law School offers a general LL.M. program, LL.M. programs in Admiralty, in Energy and Environmental Law, and in International and Comparative Law, and the S.J.D.

■ Admission

➨ *Bachelor's degree from accredited university or college required; strong candidates who have completed 3/4 of work toward undergraduate degree are also considered* ➨ *application deadline—May 1; application by end of Feb. strongly recommended* ➨ *rolling admission, early application preferred* ➨ *LSAT, LSDAS required* ➨ *application fee—$50*

Competition is keen, and a combination of the average LSAT score and the UGPA is relied upon heavily. Tulane seeks to individualize the admissions process by also considering factors such as grade trends, courseload, undergraduate school, nonacademic activities, the student's background and experience, and the personal statement.

The Law School receives applications for admission starting October 1 and begins to announce decisions after December 1.

■ Student Activities

Credit may be earned for work on the student-edited *Tulane Law Review*, *Tulane Maritime Law Journal*, or for participation in the several moot court appellate and trial competitions. Other journals include the *Tulane Environmental Law Journal*, the *Journal of Law and Sexuality*, the *Tulane European and Civil Law Forum*, *Sports Lawyers'*

Journal, and the *Tulane Journal of International and Comparative Law*. An online journal of technology and intellectual property is scheduled to begin publication in 1998-99. The Law School has a chapter of the Order of the Coif. Over 20 student organizations are represented at Tulane including Tulane Law Women, Black Law Students Association, La Alianza del Derecho, Asian Pacific American Law Student Association, and the Environmental Law Society. The Tulane Public Interest Law Foundation raises funds, matched by the Law School, to support as many as 45 students each summer in public interest fellowships with a variety of organizations.

■ Expenses and Financial Aid

➨ *1998-99 full-time tuition & fees—$23,588* ➨ *estimated additional expenses—$11,540 (room, board, health, books, transportation, misc.)* ➨ *scholarships available: mainly merit-based* ➨ *financial aid available; FAFSA due Feb. 15; LRAP for eligible graduates in certain public interest employment*

■ Career Services

The Office of Career Services at the Law School assists both students and alumni in finding employment in the legal profession. A large career services library is available to students, as well as a full range of counseling services. Tulane offers both on- and off-campus interview programs.

The office has taken a proactive stance in assisting students with their job searches, with the result that Tulane graduates find law-related employment throughout the United States.

Applicant Group for the 1998-1999 Academic Year

Tulane University Law School

LSAT Score	3.75 +		3.50 - 3.74		3.25 - 3.49		3.00 - 3.24		2.75 - 2.99		2.50 - 2.74		2.25 - 2.49		2.00 - 2.24		Below 2.00		No GPA		Total	
	Apps	Adm	Apps	Adm	Apps	Adm	Apps	Adm	Apps	Adm	Apps	Adm	Apps	Adm	Apps	Adm	Apps	Adm	Apps	Adm	Apps	Adm
175-180	1	1	0	0	1	0	1	0	1	0	0	0	1	1	0	0	0	0	0	0	5	2
170-174	4	3	2	1	2	2	5	5	6	5	5	4	0	0	1	1	0	0	1	1	26	22
165-169	11	8	13	10	25	23	26	18	17	16	9	9	3	2	1	0	1	0	2	2	108	88
160-164	50	45	72	56	102	88	87	79	62	53	33	24	12	7	6	2	0	0	4	2	428	356
155-159	47	43	90	81	184	168	155	113	105	44	60	15	13	3	11	4	2	0	5	4	672	475
150-154	33	30	79	54	121	43	120	21	99	23	37	2	22	2	2	0	2	0	9	1	524	176
145-149	8	4	33	11	70	17	80	14	47	6	28	0	17	0	5	0	2	0	7	1	297	53
140-144	8	2	14	5	15	1	22	2	31	1	23	0	22	0	7	0	2	0	10	0	154	11
135-139	1	0	3	0	5	0	6	0	15	0	9	0	8	0	6	0	1	0	7	0	61	0
130-134	0	0	1	0	0	0	1	0	1	0	7	0	3	0	1	0	1	0	3	0	18	0
125-129	0	0	0	0	0	0	1	0	0	0	0	0	0	0	0	0	1	0	0	0	2	0
120-124	0	0	0	0	0	0	0	0	1	0	0	0	0	0	0	0	0	0	0	0	1	0
Total	163	136	307	218	525	342	504	252	385	148	211	54	101	15	40	7	12	0	48	11	2296	1183

Reflects 99% of the total applicant pool.

University of Tulsa College of Law

3120 East Fourth Place
Tulsa, OK 74104

E-Mail: law_vls@centum.utulsa.edu
URL: http://www.utulsa.edu/law
Phone: 918.631.2709

■ Introduction

The College of Law, a private, nonsectarian institution, with an enrollment of about 655 students, is located on the main campus of the University of Tulsa about two miles from downtown Tulsa, providing the benefits of a quiet, residential campus and an active urban center. Tulsa is a flourishing city of approximately 725,000 located in the northeast quarter in the green country of Oklahoma, with lakes and hills nearby. The college is accredited by the ABA and the AALS. The university is accredited through the doctoral level and consists of five colleges and a graduate school.

■ Enrollment/Student Body

➡ *792 applicants*   ➡ *524 admitted first-year class 1998*
➡ *201 enrolled first-year class 1998*   ➡ *full-time 25th/75th percentile GPA—2.64/3.20*   ➡ *part-time 25th/75th percentile GPA—2.62/3.33*   ➡ *full-time 25th/75th percentile LSAT—144/154*   ➡ *part-time 25th/75th percentile LSAT—145/154*
➡ *459 total full-time*   ➡ *124 total part-time*
➡ *19% minority*   ➡ *44% women*   ➡ *48 states & foreign countries represented*   ➡ *175 undergraduate schools represented*

Approximately 57 percent of the first-year class is from out-of-state. Typically, an entering class represents students from about 30 states and 120 colleges and universities.

■ Faculty

➡ *71 total*   ➡ *37 full-time (includes one full-time chair)*
➡ *34 part-time or adjunct*   ➡ *14 women*   ➡ *7 minority*

■ Library and Physical Facilities

➡ *270,325 volumes & equivalents*   ➡ *library hours: Mon.-Thurs., 7:30 A.M.-MIDNIGHT; Fri., 7:30 A.M.-9:00 P.M.; Sat., 9:00 A.M.-9:00 P.M.; Sun., 9:00 A.M.-MIDNIGHT*
➡ *LEXIS*   ➡ *WESTLAW*   ➡ *many CD-ROM databases*
➡ *77 computers for student use, 22 with web browsers*
➡ *Legal Track & Wilson Disk (legal periodical indexes on CD-ROM)*   ➡ *8 full-time librarians*
➡ *7 full-time support staff*   ➡ *library seats 485*

The College of Law occupies John Rogers Hall, which provides convenient facilities for the library, classes, seminars, model courtroom, faculty, admission, placement, and other support services.

The library has a strong basic legal collection, and specialized collections in energy and environmental law and policy and in Native American law. Computer labs for word processing, computer-assisted legal instruction, and other law-related database and World Wide Web searching are available.

Groundbreaking for a new Legal Information Center and renovated library facilities occurred September 21, 1998, with completion date scheduled for early-2000. The new Legal Information Center will enable the College of Law to better serve not only its students and faculty, but also Tulsa's professional community, which uses the library extensively. The addition will permit the College of Law to nearly double its collection, increase seating capacity, introduce expanded library technologies, and meet programmatic needs. In the interim, full library services will be provided in campus buildings close to the College of Law.

■ Curriculum and Special Programs

➡ *Academic Support Program*
➡ *88 credits required to graduate*   ➡ *95 courses available*
➡ *degrees available: J.D.; J.D./M.A. in History, Modern Letters, Industrial/Organizational Psychology; J.D./M.S. in Geosciences, Biological Sciences, Anthropology; J.D./M.B.A.; J.D./Master of Accountancy; J.D./Master of Taxation*

The College of Law offers opportunities for students to specialize or concentrate their studies after completing the first-year required curriculum. For these students and for those who wish to have a broad grounding in a wide range of coursework, the College of Law offers students an array of curriculum choices.

The college is on a semester system. Students may pursue their studies either in a full- or part-time program of study. Students, too, may choose to continue their studies through the summer months either at the College of Law during one of the 4-, 6- or 12-week sessions, or abroad participating in one of a series of study-abroad programs sponsored by the college.

The law school offers certificate programs in **Alternative Methods of Dispute Resolution**; **Comparative and International Law**; **Health Law**; **Native American Law**; **Public Policy and Regulation**; and **Resources, Energy, and Environmental Law**. Students, of course, are free to select individual courses within these programs without completing the requirements for a certificate.

In addition, the faculty has defined two other areas of concentration: General Practice and Corporate Practice. As with the certificate programs, students may freely select among the courses within these areas of concentration to construct a curriculum reflecting their needs and interests.

General Practice courses cover a wide range of subjects, and many advanced courses build on them. Because of the number of general practice courses, students pursuing a normal 88 semester-hour program of study will be unable to complete them all. Students should select courses from this area to meet their individual career interests.

Corporate Practice courses include those that are basic to a corporate or corporate-related practice. Basic corporate-practice courses include business structures, governmental control of business, taxes, financing, and planning.

■ Practical Experience

Legal and Judicial Internship programs are available and provide valuable "hands-on" experience.

Through the Oklahoma Bar Association, students who have completed 50 hours and certain prerequisites may be granted a limited license to practice law under the supervision of a practicing attorney.

The College of Law, in cooperation with both state and federal courts located in Tulsa, also offers a Judicial Internship Program wherein students work in the court system.

Our **Legal Clinic** gives students an opportunity to handle actual cases and develop professional skills under the close supervision of faculty supervisors.

■ Admission

➡ *B.A. or B.S. degree required*   ➡ *application deadline— Jan. 15 (for full consideration on scholarship awards)*
➡ *LSAT, LSDAS required*   ➡ *application fee—$30*

Application may be made by anyone who will be, by the time of enrollment, a graduate of a regionally accredited college. No applicant will be required to make a final decision on an offer prior to April 1. There is no firm application cutoff date; however, early applications are preferable. Tulsa is committed to an affirmative action program. Special care is taken in evaluating applications from members of minority groups traditionally not well represented in the profession.

■ Student Activities

The *Tulsa Law Journal*, edited by students, is published four times per year. The *Energy Law Journal*, the *Tulsa Journal of Comparative and International Law*, and the *Natural Resources Law Monograph Series* are also produced. Student competitions include national and international moot court, national trial advocacy, negotiations, and client counseling. The University of Tulsa's Student Bar Association has consistently been named an outstanding chapter by the American Bar Association. The student newspaper, *Baculus*, has achieved national recognition also for the efforts of its law school journalists. Student groups include American Bar Association/Law Student Division; Black Law Student Association; Board of Advocates; Christian Legal Society; Delta Theta Phi; *Energy Law Journal*; Entertainment and Sports Law Society; Environmental Law Society; Hispanic Law Society; International Law Society; Law and Medicine Society; Moot Court Board; Native American Law Student Association; Oklahoma Intercollegiate Legislature; Phi Alpha Delta; Phi Delta Phi; Public Interest Law Society; Rutherford Institute; Significant Others Society; Student Bar Association; Tulsa Law and Technology Association; Tulsa University Trial Lawyers Association; Volunteer Income Tax Assistance; and Women's Law Caucus.

■ Housing

Housing is available in both residence halls and university apartments. Accommodations are available in nonuniversity facilities at reasonable cost.

■ Expenses and Financial Aid

➡ *tuition & fees—31 credit hrs., $16,000; 21 credit hrs., $10,600*   ➡ *estimated additional expenses—on-campus, $8,400 off-campus, $9,710 (room & board, transportation, books & supplies)*   ➡ *merit scholarships available*
➡ *financial aid available*
➡ *FAF, FFS, GAPSFAS, or USAF accepted*

Tuition and fees are the same for resident and nonresident students.

■ Career Services

The University of Tulsa College of Law class of 1997 had an employment rate of approximately 83 percent six months after graduation. Approximately 3 percent of the class entered an advanced-degree program.

Of the approximately 83 percent employed, the types of employment were as follows: private practice, 60 percent; business & industry, 20 percent; government, 15 percent; judicial clerkships, 3 percent; public interest, 1 percent; and academia, 1 percent.

University of Tulsa College of Law

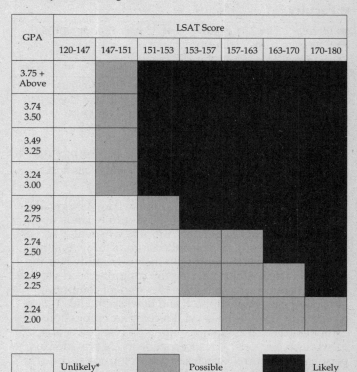

* Individual accomplishments crucial

This chart is to be used as a general guide in determining the chances for admittance.

University of Utah College of Law

Admissions Office
332 South 1400 East Front
Salt Lake City, UT 84112-0730

E-Mail: admissions@law.utah.edu
URL: http://www.law.utah.edu
Phone: 801.581.7479

■ Introduction

The University of Utah College of Law, approved by the ABA and a member of AALS, is situated in the foothills of the picturesque Wasatch Mountain Range of the Rocky Mountains, and is a five-minute drive from downtown Salt Lake City, the seat of federal, state, and local governmental bodies. The College of Law is nationally recognized for its academic reputation, innovative curriculum, and favorable faculty/student ratio. As indicated in a 1996 student survey, there is a prevailing sense of community among students fostered by a faculty and administration that is friendly, open, and service oriented. A 1997 university accreditation review confirmed our students have a high level of satisfaction with virtually every facet of their law school experience.

■ Enrollment/Student Body

➡ *302 admitted first-year class 1998* ➡ *123 enrolled first-year class 1998* ➡ *full-time 25th/75th percentile GPA—3.19/3.76* ➡ *full-time 25th/75th percentile LSAT—155/162* ➡ *360 total full-time* ➡ *13% minority* ➡ *38% women* ➡ *39 states & 11 foreign countries represented* ➡ *138 undergraduate schools represented*

■ Faculty

➡ *60 total* ➡ *27 full-time* ➡ *33 part-time or adjunct* ➡ *9 women* ➡ *5 minority*

■ Library and Physical Facilities

➡ *300,000 volumes & equivalents* ➡ *library hours: Mon.-Thurs., 7:00 A.M.-11:00 P.M.; Fri., 7:00 A.M.-8:00 P.M.; Sat., 9:00 A.M.-8:00 P.M.; Sun., 11:00 A.M.-11:00 P.M.* ➡ *LEXIS* ➡ *NEXIS* ➡ *WESTLAW* ➡ *VuText* ➡ *Internet* ➡ *World Wide Web Services* ➡ *Utah Courts Information* ➡ *Xchange* ➡ *PACER* ➡ *7 full-time librarians; 5 of the full-time librarians hold law degrees* ➡ *library seats 381*

The College of Law and the S.J. Quinney Law Library are located in the lower portion of the beautifully landscaped 1,500-acre University of Utah campus, which also serves as the site of the official state arboretum. The law building provides first-year students with their own study hall and personal carrels, which have laptop computer access to the campus network. It also houses two student computing labs, other computer support, and newly remodeled class rooms with state-of-the-art video-computer projection equipment as well as laptop computer access power and network access ports. Advanced students are provided a personal study carrel, which also has laptop access nodes in the adjacent S.J. Quinney Law Library—a modern, spacious facility with functional compact shelving to house its collection and the latest technological equipment and library research services.

■ Curriculum

➡ *Academic Support Program* ➡ *88 credits required to graduate* ➡ *111 courses available* ➡ *degrees available: J.D.; J.D./M.B.A.; J.D./M.P.A.; LL.M. (Environmental Law)* ➡ *semesters, start in Aug.* ➡ *full-time, day program; 10-week summer term* ➡ *range of first-year class size—10-62*

The innovative curriculum is designed to allow more efficient and rational sequencing of legal education that responds to the evolving legal, social, and ethical needs of our society. The entering students are first offered an intensive four-day Introduction to Law course before they begin the required first-year curriculum. Second-year students select from a variety of foundational Cornerstone courses. In the third year, students may take year-long intensive Capstone courses that provide the opportunity for in-depth study, research, and practicum in a focused area of law. In addition, students may select from more than 50 advanced courses and seminars, a variety of clinical and skills courses, and numerous cocurricular opportunities. The curriculum is geared to prepare students to practice in any state.

■ Special Programs

The Wallace Stegner Center for Land, Resources, and the Environment provides opportunities for J.D. candidates, while at Utah, to engage in academic courses and related law activities focusing on public lands, environment, natural resources, and energy. Regular courses offered include Natural Resource Law, Oil and Gas, Mining and Minerals, Water Law, Public Land Use, and Environmental Law. The law school offers a specialized LL.M. degree in natural resource and environmental law.

The clinical programs offer both live and simulated opportunities for students to assume the lawyering role. In the Civil Clinic and the Criminal Clinic, students directly represent clients, investigate cases, and appear in court. In the Judicial Clinic students act as clerks to judges, researching issues and drafting opinions in pending cases. The Judicial Extern Program allows students to spend a semester away from the school working as full-time clerks for certain courts.

■ Admission Standards

➡ *Bachelor's degree required* ➡ *application deadline—Feb. 1* ➡ *rolling admission* ➡ *LSAT, LSDAS required* ➡ *application fee—$40* ➡ *begin fall only*

No applicant is accepted or rejected without a member of the Admission Committee having first fully considered the entire application. The Personal Statement should expand on the applicant's biographic and academic background and motivations for seeking a legal education. The College of Law makes a special effort to attract nontraditional students from diverse cultural, educational, economic, and ethnic backgrounds. Each applicant is evaluated for the contribution that person can make to the student body or the legal profession, in addition to evidence of demonstrated high academic ability. Qualified candidates may be invited to participate in the Academic Support Program.

■ Student Activities

The *Utah Law Review*, the *Journal of Law and Family Studies*, and *Journal of Land, Resources, and Environmental Law* are professional journals edited and published by students.

Student organizations include the Student Bar Association, the Women's Law Caucus, Natural Resources Law Forum, the Moot Court Society, the Minority Law Caucus, the International Law Society, Health Law Coalition, Christian Legal Society, Intramural Sports, the Federalist Society, the Gay and Lesbian Law Student Alliance, Native American Law Student Association, and the Public Interest Law Organization.

■ Expenses and Financial Aid

➡ *1998-99 tuition & fees—$4,856/yr., resident; $10,822/yr., nonresident* ➡ *need-based & merit scholarships available* ➡ *minority scholarships available: Minority Law Caucus Scholarship, Immigration & Refugee Scholarship, need- &*

merit-based scholarships, diversity intern stipends
➡ *financial aid available; Free Application for Federal Student Aid (FAFSA) due Feb. 15, may submit after Jan. 1*

Students who wish to apply for need-based scholarships or long-term loans such as Perkins Loans (formerly NDSL), Stafford Loans (formerly GSL), or others, must submit a FAFSA and should contact the Financial Aid Office, 105 SSB, University of Utah, Salt Lake City, UT 84112, (801) 581-6211. The deadline for submitting a FAFSA to begin the application process for financial aid is February 15. The law school also has an endowed Loan Forgiveness Program for qualified graduates who practice in the public sector.

■ Career Services

The College of Law and its graduates have access to one of the most technologically advanced Legal Career Services programs in the country. The LCS office transmits information to prospective employers, both on and off campus. The LCS office also offers personal counseling, maintains a resource library, and sponsors numerous seminars throughout the year.

Applicant Group for the 1998-1999 Academic Year

University of Utah College of Law
This grid includes only applicants who earned 120-180 LSAT scores under standard administrations.

LSAT Score	3.75 +		3.50 - 3.74		3.25 - 3.49		3.00 - 3.24		2.75 - 2.99		2.50 - 2.74		2.25 - 2.49		2.00 - 2.24		Below 2.00		No GPA		Total	
	Apps	Adm	Apps	Adm	Apps	Adm	Apps	Adm	Apps	Adm	Apps	Adm	Apps	Adm	Apps	Adm	Apps	Adm	Apps	Adm	Apps	Adm
175-180	3	3	0	0	0	0	0	0	0	0	0	0	0	0	0	0	0	0	0	0	3	3
170-174	2	2	2	2	1	1	4	4	1	1	0	0	1	1	0	0	0	0	0	0	11	11
165-169	15	15	9	9	11	11	12	11	1	1	0	0	0	0	1	0	0	0	1	1	50	48
160-164	24	23	25	25	25	21	27	20	14	9	3	0	4	0	1	1	0	0	3	1	126	100
155-159	30	24	49	31	43	17	36	12	18	3	8	1	3	0	1	0	0	0	3	2	191	90
150-154	16	5	27	7	35	3	31	5	26	3	6	0	5	0	0	0	1	0	6	1	153	24
145-149	6	3	19	5	21	2	15	1	23	0	9	2	4	0	0	0	2	0	4	2	103	15
140-144	0	0	5	1	6	1	16	0	14	0	10	0	3	1	2	0	0	0	3	0	59	3
135-139	0	0	3	1	1	0	4	0	5	1	4	0	1	0	2	0	0	0	3	0	23	2
130-134	0	0	0	0	0	0	1	0	0	0	1	0	3	0	3	0	1	0	1	0	10	0
125-129	0	0	0	0	0	0	0	0	1	0	0	0	0	0	0	0	0	0	0	0	1	0
120-124	0	0	0	0	0	0	0	0	0	0	0	0	0	0	0	0	0	0	0	0	0	0
Total	96	75	139	81	143	56	146	53	103	18	41	3	24	2	10	1	4	0	24	7	730	296

Apps = Number of Applicants
Adm = Number Admitted
Reflects 98% of the total applicant pool.

Valparaiso University School of Law

Wesemann Hall
Valparaiso, IN 46383

E-Mail: valpolaw@valpo.edu
URL: http://www.valpo.edu/law
Phone: 888.825.7652 or 219.465.7829

■ Introduction

Valparaiso University School of Law was founded in 1879 and is accredited by the American Bar Association and the Association of American Law Schools. Valparaiso University is a private university located 55 miles southeast of Chicago in suburban northwest Indiana. The university is affiliated with the Lutheran church. Valparaiso is a small law school, with a total enrollment of approximately 425 students, which allows for a learning atmosphere in which the rigors of legal education are experienced in a supportive setting. Valparaiso offers a broad curriculum touching upon all the major areas of practice, balancing intellectual and analytical preparation with a strong, skills-oriented clinical program.

■ Enrollment/Student Body

➠ *726 applicants*   ➠ *494 admitted entering-class fall 1998*
➠ *143 full-time, 23 part-time, enrolled first-year class 1998*
➠ *full-time 25th/75th percentile GPA—2.92/3.55*
➠ *part-time 25th/75th percentile GPA—2.45/3.11*
➠ *full-time 25th/75th percentile LSAT—148/157*
➠ *part-time 25th/75th percentile LSAT—143/151*
➠ *367 total full-time enrollment*   ➠ *53 total part-time enrollment*   ➠ *15% minority*   ➠ *46% women*
➠ *29 states & 2 foreign countries represented*
➠ *149 undergraduate schools represented*

■ Faculty

Valparaiso law professors have been Fulbright scholars, clerks to federal appellate and state supreme court judges, and have served in federal, state, and local government. They bring to their teaching significant practical experience in both public and private sectors. Their scholarly interests span a broad range and include such areas as environmental law, intellectual property law, civil rights and constitutional law, health and elder law, securities regulation, tax, race relations, and feminist legal theory. Several faculty maintain active law practices and some involve students in current representation.

■ Library and Physical Facilities

➠ *262,000 volumes & equivalents*   ➠ *library hours: Mon.-Thurs., 7:30 A.M.-1:00 A.M.; Fri., 7:30 A.M.-10:00 P.M.; Sat., 9:00 A.M.-10:00 P.M.; Sun., 9:00 A.M.-MIDNIGHT*
➠ *LEXIS*   ➠ *NEXIS*   ➠ *WESTLAW*   ➠ *DIALOG*
➠ *6 full-time librarians*   ➠ *library seats 347*

The law library collection includes hard copy and micro-form formats. Individual and group study carrels are available for student use; a computer lab provides facilities for word processing, Internet, and World Wide Web access. All students receive e-mail accounts.

■ Curriculum

➠ *90 credit hours attempted, 85 earned to graduate, of which 46 are required courses*   ➠ *J.D. & LL.M. programs*

➠ *academic calendar is semesters, which begin in Aug.*
➠ *first-year class size ranges 45-65 students per class section*

Valparaiso provides a comprehensive and intensive study of the foundations of the law, an introduction to the many substantive areas of the law, and the opportunity for advanced study in areas of specific student interest. The curriculum provides a thorough grounding in legal analysis, legal writing and research, practical skills training, perspectives on the law, and professional ethics. The legal writing program extends across the full three years of law study. The first-year class is divided into small legal writing groups of 9-12 students enabling legal writing professors and members of the teaching assistant staff to work closely with each student. The School of Law is committed to the highest standards of professional ethics and to an inquiry into values, and is concerned that students not view the legal system as unchangeable and untouched by their own ethical and intellectual analyses.

A 20-hour commitment of pro bono legal service is required of all students for graduation. Through the pro bono requirement, students help to meet the need for legal service to the poor and gain valuable practical experience and contacts within the legal community.

■ Special Programs

Clinical Law Program—Students enrolled in the live client law clinic participate in all stages of representation from interview to trial/hearing; the law clinic represents indigent criminal defendants and clients in need of general civil representation in matters such as divorce, landlord/tenant disputes, and public entitlements.

There is also a mediation clinic, juvenile clinic, and environmental clinic.

Current Representation—Faculty members invite students to work in connection with legal representation provided by the faculty member.

Externships—Externship programs available to second- and third-year students include: Americans United for Life, Bankruptcy Externship, Business and Professional People for the Public Interest, County Attorney Externship, County Prosecutor's Externship, Equal Employment Opportunity Commission Externship, Environmental Insurance Externship, Environmental Protection Agency Externship, Federal Judicial Externship, Immigration and Naturalization Externship, Indiana Department of Environmental Management Externship, Indiana Human Rights Externship, Internal Revenue Service Externship, LaPorte County Prosecutors Externship, Oakland Raiders Externship, Public Guardian Externship, Public Welfare Externship, Special Education Externship, State Judicial Externship, and U.S. Attorney Externship.

Summer Study Abroad—Valparaiso's interest in international and comparative law are enhanced with its Summer Study Abroad Program in Cambridge, England.

385

Honors Program—The Honors Program is designed to offer a special academic challenge to highly talented students. Candidates are selected based on excellent academic credentials and demonstrated leadership skills. Personal interviews are required.

■ Admission Standards

➡ *Bachelor's degree from accredited college or university required*
➡ *application deadline—April 15*   ➡ *rolling admission*
➡ *LSAT, LSDAS required*   ➡ *application fee—$30*

The commitment to student-centered education is expressed in the admission policy. While the LSAT and GPA weigh heavily in determining the applicant's academic ability, the Admissions Committee also considers nonquantifiable factors. Work and life experience, evidence of perseverance, and records of outstanding community service and other subjective factors are considered. Two letters of recommendation, while not required, are strongly encouraged.

Valparaiso values diversity in its student body, and minorities, women, and nontraditional students are strongly encouraged to apply.

Valparaiso offers a voluntary Academic Support Program for select students identified by the Academic Support Program Committee; this includes a summer preparatory program and tutorial sessions during the semester.

■ Student Activities

The *Valparaiso University Law Review* is published four times per year by a student editorial board selected on the basis of academic achievement and quality of writing skills. Students interested in enhancing advocacy skills may try out to join the Moot Court Society, Client Counseling team, Mock Trial team, and Negotiation team.

The Student Bar Association conducts professional programs and social activities, and funds more than 20 student organizations. Students participate in academic, literary, musical, social, and athletic events including intramural sports.

■ Expenses and Financial Aid

➡ *tuition & fees—full-time, $17,580; part-time, $10,150/yr.*
➡ *estimated additional expenses—$10,390 (room, board, books, travel, & miscellaneous)*   ➡ *full- & partial-tuition merit scholarships available, including minority scholarships*
➡ *public-service grants, summer public-service grants available*

Approximately 40 percent of the entering class were awarded scholarships and about two-thirds received assistance through university law grants and loan programs. Valparaiso offers a Public Interest Loan Repayment Assistance program and a summer public interest scholarship program.

■ Career Services

Ninety-seven percent of the class of 1997 found law-related employment within six months of passing a bar—the majority in private practice in small to mid-sized law firms, or in government service, primarily as prosecutors. Valparaiso's Career Services Office offers career planning and counseling including résumé/cover letter preparation and state bar examination information as well as placement assistance; maintains an extensive resource library; coordinates an on-campus interview program; and participates in regional and national job fairs.

Applicant Group for the 1998-1999 Academic Year

Valparaiso University School of Law

LSAT Score	3.75 +	3.50 - 3.74	3.25 - 3.49	3.00 - 3.24	2.75 - 2.99	2.50 - 2.74	2.25 - 2.49	2.00 - 2.24	Below 2.00
175-180									
170-174									
165-169									
160-164									
155-159									
150-154									
145-149									
140-144									
135-139									
130-134									
125-129									
120-124									

■ Acceptance Likely   □ Acceptance Possible   ▨ Acceptance Unlikely

Vanderbilt University Law School

Admissions Office
131 21st Avenue, South
Nashville, TN 37203

E-Mail: admissions@law.vanderbilt.edu
URL: http://www.vanderbilt.edu/Law/
Phone: 615.322.6452

■ Introduction

Vanderbilt Law School offers the Juris Doctor degree to a small group of talented students who learn in an environment combining rigorous intellectual challenge with collegial relationships. The faculty is committed to excellence in both teaching and scholarship. Prolific writers who publish regularly in leading law reviews and journals, Vanderbilt professors bring a breadth of interdisciplinary training and research interests to their classrooms. The favorable student/faculty ratio and the faculty open-door policy encourage regular interaction between students and their professors.

More than 225 colleges and universities are represented in the 550-member student body. A typical class will have students from 40 states and several other countries.

Founded in 1874, the Law School is part of the beautiful university campus, designated a National Arboretum, and is two miles from Nashville's business center. Vanderbilt is a major research university with approximately 10,000 students in its undergraduate, graduate, and professional schools. A city of nearly a million, the state capitol is home to the executive and legislative branches of state government and many federal agencies. Trial and appellate courts at both the state and federal levels are accessible to students.

Nashville is listed regularly among the best cities in which to live and work and is growing rapidly. It has the vitality and attractions of a major city—professional sports, theater, ballet, symphony—and the grace of a smaller town with friendly and welcoming citizens.

■ Enrollment/Student Body

➡ 2,230 applicants ➡ 718 admitted first-year class 1998 ➡ 190 enrolled first-year class 1998 ➡ full-time 25th/75th percentile GPA—3.42/3.81 ➡ full-time 25th/75th percentile LSAT—157/164 ➡ 550 total full-time ➡ 27% minority first-year class 1998 ➡ 47% women first-year class 1998 ➡ 48 states & foreign countries represented

■ Faculty

➡ 64 total ➡ 34 full-time ➡ 30 part-time or adjunct ➡ 16 women ➡ 5 minority

■ Library and Physical Facilities

➡ 521,151 volumes & equivalents ➡ library hours: Mon.-Sun., 7:00 A.M.-MIDNIGHT ➡ LEXIS ➡ NEXIS ➡ WESTLAW ➡ INFOTRAC ➡ CD-based systems ➡ 10 full-time librarians ➡ library seats 431

A major expansion and renovation of the law building is scheduled to be completed by the fall of 2001. The Alyne Queener Massey law library is one of the primary research centers in the Southeast. The collection primarily supports the curriculum and research interests of the faculty, and its strengths include intellectual property law, bioethics, international trade, and general international and foreign

law. All other university libraries, containing more than 2.3 million volumes, are available to law students. Ten library professionals provide a full range of research and library services, and legal research training is incorporated into the first-year writing program.

■ Curriculum

➡ 88 credits required to graduate ➡ 125 courses available ➡ degrees available: J.D./M.Div.; J.D./M.B.A.; J.D./M.T.S.; J.D./M.A.; J.D./Ph.D. ➡ semesters, start in Aug. ➡ range of first-year class size—24-90

The first-year required courses are the foundation courses of legal study in addition to an innovative course on legal process and the institutions of lawmaking. The year-long legal writing course, teaching the fundamentals of writing, analysis, and research, is taught in small groups of 24 students. With the exception of Professional Responsibility, all upper-level courses are electives.

The curriculum is broad and deep, offering students the opportunity to gain exposure to the fundamental knowledge necessary to become a competent professional while focusing on areas of special interest.

■ Special Programs

Clinical programs offer students the chance to represent clients in civil, criminal, and juvenile cases while earning academic credit. Through cooperative arrangements with the Legal Aid Society of Middle Tennessee, the District Attorney's Office, the Public Defender, and juvenile court, students perform a number of legal services under the supervision of clinical professors.

The Joe C. Davis Foundation Program in Law and Economics features regular workshops involving leading scholars from around the nation.

Vanderbilt University is home to the First Amendment Center, a nationally recognized institute where journalists and legal scholars do research and write on issues involving freedoms granted in the first amendment to the Constitution. The Vanderbilt Institute for Public Policy Studies offers faculty and students from departments throughout the university a place to work cooperatively on issues ranging from health care policy to international trade.

The Hyatt Speakers Fund has been established to enhance the intellectual experience of students by supporting the educational programs of student organizations.

■ Admission

➡ Bachelor's degree from an accredited college or university required ➡ application deadline—March 1 ➡ LSAT, LSDAS required ➡ application fee—$50

The Admission Committee thoroughly evaluates each application, considering the academic record, LSAT score, letters of recommendation, personal statements, extracurricular/civic activities, and work experience. The committee takes into account any elements in the applicant's background that will add depth and diversity to the student body or which indicate promise of leadership in the legal profession.

The full-file review process yields a group of students which has developed the ability to read and comprehend accurately, thoroughly and rapidly; to speak and write clearly and correctly; to think precisely; and to analyze complex situations. A broad cultural background is also important since lawyers must serve a complex society. The entering class is limited to approximately 180 students. Because the students work in a cooperative and mutually respectful environment, Vanderbilt attracts students from many racial and ethnic groups.

■ Student Activities

Students continue their learning outside the classroom through opportunities to serve on the editorial boards of the *Vanderbilt Law Review* and *The Journal of Transnational Law*; participation on moot court teams and the Moot Court Board; and through the activities of more than 25 student groups. Educational programs enliven the intellectual life of the school and social events bring students together regularly.

The Moot Court Board administers a program of brief writing and oral advocacy to enhance students' courtroom lawyering skills. Four moot court teams compete in national tournaments each year and the board hosts the nationally acclaimed First Amendment Moot Court competition which draws teams from 32 other law schools each year. The student government body, the Vanderbilt Bar Association, publishes a newsletter and sponsors a variety of activities, both professional and social.

■ Expenses and Financial Aid

➡ *full-time tuition & fees—$22,780* ➡ *estimated additional expenses—$13,400 (housing, food, books, travel, etc.)*
➡ *need-based & merit-based scholarships available*
➡ *participation in several government & private loan programs; FAFSA CSS Profile & law school loan forms required by Feb. 28*

A substantial amount of scholarship aid is available for law students. Financial aid packages are awarded before admission response deadlines. Scholarship awards are made for the three law school years conditioned on good-standing status. Approximately 40 percent of entering students receive scholarship assistance. Vanderbilt participates in government, university, and private loan programs to assist students in funding their legal education. A good credit history is essential for borrowing from private loan programs.

Vanderbilt offers a loan forgiveness program to graduates who elect to practice in public interest.

■ Career Services

Vanderbilt graduates enjoy an outstanding reputation in the legal profession. In addition to the on-campus recruiting program, several hundred employers write annually to solicit résumés from Vanderbilt students.

In the fall of 1998 nearly 500 employers visited Vanderbilt to recruit the 220 students participating in the on-campus recruiting program. They came from more than 30 states, and Vanderbilt graduates accepted positions throughout the country. The Career Services Office maintains a staff of professional counselors to assist students individually with their career goals. The placement rate, six months following graduation, is 98 percent. The same percentage of second-year students worked in legal jobs during the summer. A limited on-campus interviewing program is held for first-year students in the spring and more than 92 percent had a legal job last summer, 60 percent of which were paid positions.

■ Housing

While the university offers limited on-campus housing, most law students elect to live in apartments and houses off campus. The Admission Office assists incoming students during the summer months with roommate lists and housing options.

Applicant Profile Not Available

Vermont Law School

Chelsea Street
South Royalton, VT 05068-0096

E-Mail: admiss@vermontlaw.edu
URL: http://www.vermontlaw.edu
Phone: toll free: 888.APPLY.VLS or 802.763.8303, ext. 2239

■ Introduction

Five features distinguish legal education at Vermont Law School—a core J.D. curriculum that emphasizes the broader social context of the law in addition to focusing on legal doctrine and analysis; clinical/experiential programs that complement traditional classroom instruction; the internationally recognized Master of Studies in Environmental Law program; the informal atmosphere of a beautiful rural setting; and a real sense of community and commitment to public service. The school is accredited by the American Bar Association, the Association of American Law Schools, and the New England Association of Schools and Colleges.

Situated in a National Register Historic District along Vermont's scenic White River, the school's 13-acre campus is an integrated complex of renovated turn-of-the-century buildings, a new computer center, and a modern library and community center. A new 25,000-square-foot classroom building was completed in summer 1998. Nearby Dartmouth College complements the law school's social and cultural offerings. Ample housing is available in the area and the law school maintains an extensive landlord list.

■ Enrollment/Student Body

➡ *894 applicants*   ➡ *194 enrolled first-year class 1998*
➡ *full-time 25th/75th percentile GPA—2.70/3.30*
➡ *full-time 25th/75th percentile LSAT—148/156*
➡ *500 total full-time students*   ➡ *8% students of color*
➡ *48% women*   ➡ *49 states, Puerto Rico, and DC represented*
➡ *over 300 undergraduate and graduate institutions represented*

Vermont Law School is one of the most geographically diverse law schools in the country. Students bring a remarkable range of experience and backgrounds. Their ages range from 20 to over 50 years, with the average being 27. Twenty-four percent are 30 years or older.

Diversity—Vermont Law School is committed to enrolling a diverse student body. Diversity organizations include the Lesbian, Gay, Bisexual, Transgender, and Straight Alliance; Asian Pacific American Law Students Association; Black Law Students Association; Jewish Students Group; National Latino Law Students Association; Native American Law Society; Women's Law Group.

■ Faculty

➡ *38 full-time*   ➡ *30 adjunct*   ➡ *30 summer*
➡ *5 visiting*   ➡ *40% female full-time*

Vermont Law School attracts faculty who are committed to teaching and scholarship. Recent faculty books have included the topics of capital punishment, national security and the environment, Oliver Wendell Holmes, publicity and privacy, environmental law, and federal taxation.

■ Library and Technology

➡ *library hours: Mon.-Fri., 8:00 A.M.-MIDNIGHT;*
Sat.-Sun., 9:00 A.M.-MIDNIGHT   ➡ *LEXIS*   ➡ *NEXIS*

➡ *WESTLAW*   ➡ *DIALOG*
➡ *member, New England Law Library Consortium*
➡ *access to Dartmouth College Library*

Opened in 1991, the 33,000-square-foot Cornell Library houses all primary sources needed for student research. The library subscribes to some 2,650 periodicals and serials, and features an exceptionally fine environmental law collection. It also serves as a selective depository for United States government documents. The library catalog is online and accessible from all computers on the network. Vermont Law School has a fully networked computer environment with remote e-mail access available and one classroom equipped with interactive TV facilities used for distance learning.

■ Curriculum

➡ *Academic Support Program*   ➡ *84 credits required to graduate*   ➡ *100 courses available*   ➡ *degrees available: J.D.; M.S.E.L.; J.D./M.S.E.L.*   ➡ *summer session available (36 courses)*   ➡ *range of first-year class sizes—18-70*

The curriculum prepares graduates to practice law in all 50 states. A wide variety of clinical programs, electives, seminars, and opportunities for supervised independent research are important adjuncts to a strong core curriculum.

Environmental Law Center—Vermont Law School's Environmental Law Center is recognized internationally as a preeminent center for the study of environmental law and policy. The Environmental Law Center offers a one-year program leading to a Master of Studies in Environmental Law (M.S.E.L.) degree based upon a multidisciplinary curriculum of law, science, policy, and economics, and a joint J.D./M.S.E.L. degree program that can be completed in three academic years and two summers. The center offers over 50 environmental courses and an Environmental Semester in Washington, DC, and sponsors conferences and research.

General Practice Program—The optional General Practice Program has classes structured to operate as a law firm, with professors in the role of senior partners. Because it teaches the range of skills generally required of new associates in most types of legal environments, the program is also valuable to students who ultimately plan to specialize.

Special Programs—The **Semester in Practice Program** allows students to participate in a full-credit, supervised clinical program in a legal environment outside the law school. Students currently work throughout the Northeast, including New York, Boston, and Washington, DC. In the **Legislation Clinic**, students work under the direction of a legislative committee chair on research and drafting projects directly related to legislation pending before the Vermont General Assembly. Students working with the **South Royalton Legal Clinic** develop legal skills while providing legal assistance to low-income clients. The **Dispute Resolution Project** introduces students to nonlitigious approaches to dispute resolution, such as arbitration, mediation, and negotiation. Through the **Law School Exchange Program** students may spend a semester at one of eight participating law schools across the U.S. and aboard.

■ Admission

➡ *Bachelor's degree or equivalent required for admission*
➡ *application deadline—Feb. 1* ➡ *LSAT, LSDAS required*
➡ *application fee—$50*
➡ *first-year admission to fall term only*

The school seeks candidates who will bring diverse perspectives and talents to the law school community and the community-at-large. Successful applicants demonstrate substantial ability, motivation, life experience, and unique personal attributes. Two of the more important admission criteria are the undergraduate record and application personal statements. Multiple LSAT scores are averaged. The school responds favorably to community and college involvement and work experience, and is committed to attracting people traditionally underrepresented in the legal profession.

■ Student Activities

A community-oriented and active student body supports more than 30 official organizations, including *Vermont Law Review*, Douglas M. Costle Environmental Moot Court Competition, *Guardians ad Litem*, Habitat for Humanity, International Law Society, National Lawyers Guild, Thomas M. Debevoise Moot Court Competition, and Volunteer Income Tax Assistance Program, among others. Student organizations and the law school sponsor a full

range of social, cultural, and academic events. Students also field several athletic teams.

■ Expenses and Financial Aid

➡ *full-time tuition & fees—$19,490* ➡ *$12,595 average additional expenses* ➡ *merit scholarships, grants,& fellowships (primarily need-based)* ➡ *need-based diversity scholarships* ➡ *private, government, & school-funded loans* ➡ *Vermont Law School Financial Aid Application & FAFSA required by Feb. 15 for full consideration*

Combinations of loans, tuition grants, and work-study employment are used to meet demonstrated financial need. About 90 percent of the student body receives some form of assistance and about 35 percent receive VLS grant aid. The Vermont Law School Loan Repayment Assistance Program aids graduates entering lower-paying public interest positions to repay educational debts.

■ Career Services

The Career Services office is directed by an attorney and provides a broad range of counseling and placement services. The school aggressively pursues employment opportunities nationwide and graduates work in the full range of legal and nonlegal positions throughout the U.S. A Cooperative Legal Education program facilitates the transition from academics to legal practice.

Our 1997 J.D. graduates have been very successful after graduation—83 percent passed a bar exam in 30 different states on the first attempt; 84 percent were employed or in a degree program within six months of graduation.

Applicant Group for the 1998-1999 Academic Year

Vermont Law School
This grid includes only applicants who earned 120-180 LSAT scores under standard administrations.

LSAT Score	GPA																					
	3.75 +		3.50 - 3.74		3.25 - 3.49		3.00 - 3.24		2.75 - 2.99		2.50 - 2.74		2.25 - 2.49		2.00 - 2.24		Below 2.00		No GPA		Total	
	Apps	Adm	Apps	Adm	Apps	Adm	Apps	Adm	Apps	Adm	Apps	Adm	Apps	Adm	Apps	Adm	Apps	Adm	Apps	Adm	Apps	Adm
175-180	0	0	0	0	0	0	0	0	0	0	0	0	0	0	0	0	0	0	0	0	0	0
170-174	0	0	0	0	0	0	0	0	2	1	2	2	1	1	0	0	0	0	0	0	5	4
165-169	3	3	2	2	5	4	6	6	8	5	5	5	1	1	1	0	1	1	0	0	32	27
160-164	7	7	12	8	19	17	15	15	17	14	9	8	3	2	2	1	0	0	1	1	85	73
155-159	16	13	28	27	38	33	46	43	40	34	28	21	11	9	6	4	2	1	1	0	216	185
150-154	10	9	30	28	49	44	65	49	51	35	41	29	16	11	7	3	2	0	1	1	272	209
145-149	0	0	10	8	20	15	42	31	25	13	22	12	14	7	4	0	2	2	9	1	148	89
140-144	3	0	4	3	10	8	21	7	17	6	17	3	10	0	8	2	1	0	4	1	95	30
135-139	0	0	1	1	0	0	6	1	3	1	3	1	5	2	1	0	0	0	1	0	20	6
130-134	0	0	1	0	1	0	1	0	4	0	3	0	1	0	1	0	0	0	0	0	12	0
125-129	0	0	1	0	0	0	0	0	0	0	1	0	0	0	1	0	1	0	1	0	6	0
120-124	0	0	0	0	0	0	0	0	0	0	0	0	0	0	0	0	0	0	0	0	1	0
Total	39	32	89	77	142	121	202	152	168	109	131	81	63	33	31	10	9	4	18	4	892	623

Apps = Number of Applicants
Adm = Number Admitted
Reflects 99% of the total applicant pool.
Vermont Law School does not use cutoff LSAT scores or GPAs.

Villanova University School of Law

299 North Spring Mill Road
Villanova, PA 19085

E-Mail: admit@law.vill.edu
URL: http://vls.law.vill.edu
Phone: 610.519.7010

■ Introduction

Today, as never before, there is a need for law schools to teach far more than the letter of the law. They must give future lawyers a sense of the importance of their role in the larger society, and they must prepare lawyers to work in an environment of burgeoning technology with issues of global importance.

With its Catholic roots, Villanova offers a legal education designed to teach the rules of law and their application; to demonstrate how lawyers analyze legal issues and express arguments and conclusions; to inculcate the skills of the counselor, advocate, and decision maker; and to explore the ethical and moral dimensions of law practice and professional conduct. The school is also providing leadership in information technology, law and psychology, taxation, and international law, among other fields.

Villanova's Center for Information Law and Policy is shaping the future of law and technology. Its Center for Information Law and Policy (www.cilp.org) is the most visited legal Web site on the Internet, giving lawyers everywhere access to information and discussion. Around the world, Villanova is improving lives and building legal systems through its Global Democracy Project in Bosnia, Costa Rica, Macedonia, Slovenia, and Rwanda.

Few law schools are located in a more beautiful and tranquil environment. Adjacent to the university campus on Philadelphia's Main Line, the school is at the approximate midpoint of East Coast legal centers in New York and Washington, and only 20 minutes by commuter rail from the center of Philadelphia.

Opened in 1953, the school is approved by the American Bar Association and is a member of the Association of American Law Schools. Students are graduates of more than 124 colleges and universities; many have significant work experience outside of law. The atmosphere of the school is noted for its collegiality.

■ Enrollment/Student Body for Incoming Class

➨ *1,245 applicants*   ➨ *780 admitted first-year class 1998*
➨ *238 enrolled first-year class 1998*   ➨ *full-time 25th/75th percentile GPA—3.09/3.50*   ➨ *full-time 25th/75th percentile LSAT—152/158*   ➨ *713 total full-time*   ➨ *11% minority*
➨ *43% women*   ➨ *26 states & foreign countries represented*
➨ *124 undergraduate schools represented*

■ Faculty

➨ *77 total*   ➨ *42 full-time*   ➨ *35 part-time or adjunct*
➨ *10 women*   ➨ *6 minority*

While Villanova faculty members are recognized nationally and internationally for their legal scholarship and for their contributions to the study and practice of law, they are also deeply committed to teaching. The student-faculty ratio is 15 to 1.

■ Library and Physical Facilities

➨ *430,000 volumes & equivalents*   ➨ *library hours: 100 hours/wk., including 24 hour access for law students*
➨ *LEXIS*   ➨ *NEXIS*   ➨ *WESTLAW*   ➨ *DIALOG*
➨ *10 full-time librarians*   ➨ *library seats 368*

In the newly renovated library, students have access to the 88 Pentium computers and may use any one of the 62 portals to link their laptop computers to the network or the Internet. More than 130 additional computers are located elsewhere in the library, in classrooms, and in student organization offices. The library's online catalog provides access to more than 30,000 records and is connected to a database of more than 20 million records from major American law library collections.

■ Curriculum

➨ *Academic Support Program*   ➨ *87 credits required to graduate*   ➨ *151 courses available*   ➨ *degrees available: J.D.; LL.M.; J.D./M.B.A.; J.D./Ph.D.*   ➨ *semesters, start in Aug.*

■ Joint J.D./M.B.A. Program

The Villanova University School of Law and College of Commerce and Finance offer a joint program permitting simultaneous study for the Juris Doctor and the Master of Business Administration degrees. The College of Commerce and Finance is one of the few colleges of business in the nation whose Master of Business Administration and Department of Accountancy program have been approved by the American Assembly of Collegiate Schools of Business.

Credit is given in the program for certain courses by both the School of Law and the College of Commerce and Finance. Degrees may be completed in less time than it would take to obtain them separately.

■ Joint J.D./Ph.D. Program in Law and Psychology

In cooperation with Allegheny University of the Health Sciences, Villanova Law School offers an integrated program in law and psychology leading to a Juris Doctor from Villanova and a Ph.D. in clinical psychology from Allegheny. Villanova offers the only program in the country with a Ph.D. component in clinical psychology, which is fully accredited by the American Psychological Association.

The program has three major purposes—(1) to produce lawyer-psychologists who can participate in the development of mental health policy in the legislature and the courts; (2) to develop scientist-practitioners who will produce legally sophisticated social science research to assist the legal system in making better, more empirically based decisions; and (3) to educate highly trained clinicians who can contribute to the advancement of forensic psychology in such areas as criminal law, domestic relations, and civil commitment.

■ LL.M. in Taxation

This interdisciplinary program is conducted under the auspices of the School of Law and Villanova's College of Commerce and Finance. The program enriches the tax curriculum available to J.D. candidates, who are able to enroll in LL.M. courses.

■ Special Programs

Beyond the skills of written and oral expression developed in the first-year writing program and the required upper-level moot court program, drafting, and seminar courses, Villanova students acquire the fundamental skills of the practicing lawyer—including counseling, negotiation, advocacy, mediation, dispute resolution, conciliation, and mature judgment. Hands-on clinical opportunities allow students to apply classroom experiences to real-world client representation, often while performing public service. Clinical programs include the Tax, Juvenile Justice, and Information Law Clinics. Villanova Community Legal Services, and the Law and Entrepreneurship Program offer unusual externship opportunities.

Students may also work with faculty on Villanova's Global Democracy Project, which aims to improve lives and legal systems in countries with tenuous democratic governments. In one year alone, students and faculty have made four trips to the former Soviet Union, and law students have participated in externships in the region.

■ Admission

➡ *Bachelor's degree required* ➡ *application deadline—March 1* ➡ *rolling admissions, most decisions made after application deadline* ➡ *LSAT, LSDAS required* ➡ *application fee—$75*

■ Student Activities

The *Villanova Law Review* is a scholarly journal prepared and edited by law students. Members are selected on the basis of academic rank or through an open writing competition. The *Villanova Environmental Law Journal* publishes both student and outside articles dealing with environmental issues. Students are selected for member-ship by an open writing competition.

The Villanova *Sports and Entertainment Law Journal* contains articles prepared by practitioners and professors in sports and entertainment law as well as by students. Membership is earned by selection through an open writing competition.

Each year, second- and third-year students have the opportunity to practice lawyering skills through the Client Interviewing and Counseling Competition, the Reimel Moot Court Competition, and several outside moot court competitions.

Student organizations include Asian-Pacific American Law Students, Black Law Students Association, Catholic Law Students, Christian Legal Society, Civil Rights Law Society, Corporate Law Society, Court Jesters, Criminal Law Society, *The Docket*, Environmental Law Society, Family Law Society, Health Law Society, Intellectual Property Protection Society, International Law Society, Jewish Law Students Association, Latin American Law Student Association, National Italian-American Bar Association, Justian Society, Phi Delta Phi, Public Interest Law Society, St. Thomas More Society, Sports and Entertainment Law Society, Tax Law Society, Women's Law Caucus.

■ Expenses and Financial Aid

➡ *full-time tuition & fees—$19,410* ➡ *estimated additional expenses—$13,440 (room, board, books, & living expenses for off-campus students)* ➡ *scholarships & fellowships available* ➡ *financial aid available; FAFSA priority deadline is March 1*

■ Career Services and Placement

Villanova graduates go on to become partners of major law firms, corporate lawyers, leaders in government, advocates for the underrepresented, judicial clerks, and more. Of the 220 J.D. graduates in a recent class, 58 percent were working in private practice, 24 percent in judicial clerkships, 4 percent in government, and 1 percent in public interest law. Villanova's Career Services Center helps students find full-time, part-time, clerkship, and graduate positions.

Admission Profile Not Available

University of Virginia School of Law

Admissions Office
Charlottesville, VA 22901

URL: http://www.law.virginia.edu
Phone: 804.924.7351

■ Introduction

The University of Virginia School of Law continues to uphold Thomas Jefferson's ideal of the lawyer as public citizen, advancing Jefferson's belief that lawyers should be educated to promote the ideals of leadership, integrity, and community service. Founded in 1826 as one of Jefferson's eight original faculties, the law school is a world-renowned training ground for distinguished lawyers and public servants, and an integral part of a great university.

Located in Charlottesville, Virginia, a picturesque and thriving metropolitan community about two hours southwest of Washington, DC, the law school draws its 1,105 J.D. students from across the nation and around the globe. Virginia is widely recognized for the collegial environment it affords both students and faculty, and student satisfaction is consistently cited as among the highest in American law schools. Students subscribe to the University of Virginia's student-run honor system, in place for more than 150 years, which enables law students to enjoy the kind of personal freedom that is possible only in an environment where mutual respect and trust exist.

■ Enrollment/Student Body

➡ 3,443 applicants   ➡ 957 admitted first-year class 1998
➡ 358 enrolled first-year class 1998   ➡ full-time 25th/75th percentile GPA—3.51/3.78   ➡ full-time 25th/75th percentile LSAT—163/168   ➡ 1,105 total full-time   ➡ 13% minority
➡ 37% women   ➡ 45 states, District of Columbia, and 2 foreign countries represented   ➡ 254 undergraduate schools represented   ➡ 52% residents   ➡ 48% nonresidents

■ Faculty

➡ 129 total   ➡ 64 full-time   ➡ 65 part-time or adjunct
➡ 27 women   ➡ 6 minority

■ Library and Physical Facilities

➡ 788,674 volumes & equivalents   ➡ library hours:
Mon.-Sat., 8:00 A.M.-MIDNIGHT; Sun., 10:00 A.M.-MIDNIGHT
➡ LEXIS   ➡ NEXIS   ➡ WESTLAW
➡ 12 full-time librarians   ➡ library seats 815

The David A. Harrison III Law Grounds, completed in 1997, is a $30 million expansion and renovation of the law school facilities funded entirely by alumni and friends. Expansion of the grounds has created three new moot courtrooms, seven seminar rooms, additional offices for student journals and organizations, a larger library, and an 86-seat computer lab.

■ Curriculum

➡ Academic Support Program   ➡ 86 credits required to graduate
➡ 160 course titles, of which 55 are seminars & 8 are clinical programs   ➡ degrees available: J.D.; LL.M.; J.D./M.B.A.;
J.D./M.A.; J.D./M.P.; J.D./M.S.; J.D./Ph.D.   ➡ semesters, start in Aug.   ➡ range of first-year class size—30-90

The first-year curriculum is arranged so that each entering student takes one of five courses in the first semester in a class of only 30 students. This "small section" concept, plus numerous second- and third-year electives, seminars, and individual research projects, assure every student a great deal of contact and interaction with the faculty.

The first-semester curriculum of torts, contracts, civil procedure, criminal law, and legal writing is required of all students. Property, constitutional law, and another section of legal writing are required in the spring semester of the first year. The only other required course is Professional Responsibility. More than 150 electives are offered each year; these are outlined in the law school catalog. The Principles and Practice Program offers a unique blend of substantive and practical learning by pairing full-time faculty with full-time practitioners in semester-long courses in a variety of topic areas.

■ Special Programs

The law school offers combined-degree programs with the Department of Economics, the Department of History, the Department of English, the Department of Sociology, the Darden Graduate School of Business Administration, the School of Medicine, the School of Architecture in Urban and Environmental Planning, the McIntire School of Commerce in Accounting, the Department of Philosophy, and the Department of Government and Foreign Affairs. A student not enrolled in one of these programs may take up to six credit hours of graduate courses in other schools and departments of the university.

In addition, the school offers opportunities for clinical experience under the direction of a clinical director and also offers interdisciplinary courses in law and medicine, law and economics, and law and social science.

■ Admission

➡ Bachelor's degree from accredited college or university required
➡ application deadline—Jan. 15   ➡ LSAT, LSDAS required
➡ application fee—$65

The Admissions Committee believes that absolute standards based on a combination of LSAT score and grade-point average (GPA) cannot be the only criteria for selection. Recognizing that the real meaning of GPA will vary with such factors as quality of the institution attended, rigor of courses selected, and degree of grade inflation, the committee considers an array of elements in addition to the essential LSAT and GPA, with a view toward assembling a diverse class while arriving at a fair appraisal of the individual applicant.

Although it is difficult to predict what action the committee will take on an individual application, the LSAT and GPA remain the primary determinants for admission. However, the committee takes other elements into account, including the maturing effect of some years away from formal education; trends in academic performance versus solid but unexceptional work; employment during the under-graduate years; significant personal achievement in extracurricular work at college or in a work or military situation; and/or unusual prior training, background, or ethnicity, which promises a contribution to the law school community. The applicant who has successfully overcome economic, social, or educational obstacles is more likely to receive favorable consideration.

It is clear, though, that unless an applicant has a high LSAT score and strong GPA, the chances of admission are severely reduced. Each year, the committee chooses a few applicants whose GPA and LSAT are lower than the prevailing averages, but who present other impressive credentials for admission, and rejects some whose performance on these two predictors is quite high.

The charts provided below track the selection process during the 1998 admissions year. To interpret the charts, one must understand the Admission Index. This number results from combining LSAT score(s) with the under-graduate GPA for each applicant, using weights for each chosen by this school. The formula used at Virginia for applicants with test scores on the 120-180 scale is $(4.1590 \times UGPA) + (.240 \times LSAT) + (2.0) = Index$. Thus, an applicant with a 3.62 UGPA and a 168 LSAT would receive a 57 Admissions Index, while a 3.17 UGPA and a 158 LSAT would produce a 53 Admissions Index. The index provides the law school with a convenient method for simultaneously reviewing LSAT score(s) and undergraduate GPAs.

The law school seeks to maintain a diverse student body in which the free exchange of ideas and viewpoints can flourish, creating a rich learning experience for all law school students. Therefore, the active recruitment of minority students is important to our admissions process.

■ Student Activities

Popular student activities include the Asian Law Student Association, Black Law Student Association, Environmental Law Forum, Federalist Society, First Year Council, Gay and Lesbian Law Students Association, *Journal of Law and Politics*, Legal Assistance Society, Libel Show, moot court competitions, Post-Conviction Assistance Project, Student Bar Association, Student Peer Advisors, Students United to Promote Racial Awareness, Virginia Health Law Forum, *Virginia Journal of International Law*, *Virginia Environmental Law Journal*, *Virginia Journal of Social Policy and the Law*, Virginia Law Women, *Virginia Law Review*, *Virginia Tax Review*, *Virginia Law and Technology Journal*, and *Voz Latina*.

■ Expenses and Financial Aid

➡ *full-time tuition & fees—residents, $14,533; nonresidents, $20,633* ➡ *estimated additional expenses—$11,800 (room, board, books)* ➡ *need-based scholarships available* ➡ *financial aid available* ➡ *FAFSA form for need analysis due to Federal Student Aid Center in Feb.*

■ Career Services

The School of Law actively assists students seeking employ-ment. More than 90 percent of the Class of 1998 reported to the Office of Career Services at graduation that they had obtained permanent employment, and over 96 percent of the class will be employed within six months of graduation. More than 95 percent of the second-year class obtained internships during the summer of 1997, primarily through the Career Services Office. Virginia students obtain a wide variety of positions that are located in many places. For example, 1998 graduates who reported by graduation that they had accepted jobs are employed in 33 states and the District of Columbia.

Profile of the Entering Class—Fall 1998

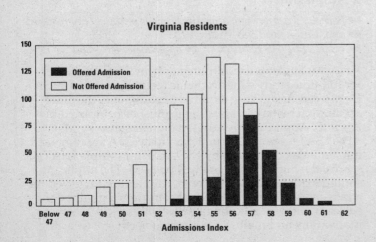

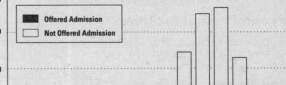
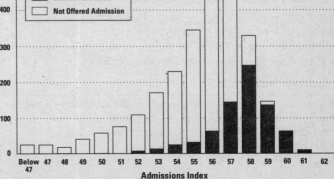

Wake Forest University School of Law

P.O. Box 7206
Reynolda Station
Winston-Salem, NC 27109

E-Mail: admissions@law.wfu.edu
URL: http://www.law.wfu.edu
Phone: 336.758.5437

■ Introduction

The Wake Forest University School of Law, established in 1894, is a member of AALS and is ABA-approved. In 1998 the law school was awarded a Chapter of the Order of the Coif, a national honorary society. Wake Forest is located in Winston-Salem, North Carolina, a city of 170,000 and a center for recreation, education, and the arts.

The philosophy at Wake Forest law school embodies meaningful promises for the future. The school's undertaking embraces seven principal commitments. They are—(1) To maintain a school of the right size that begins with a first-year class of 160 students comprised of four sections of 40 students each. (2) To develop and retain a faculty strong in teaching, strong in experience, and strong in current scholarly writing. (3) To assure that students are taught substantive law and to research through maximum use of leading-edge technology. (4) To continue the school's emphasis on dispute resolution and the development of litigation skills through instruction, competition, and comprehensive clinical practice. (5) To build a bridge between law and management communities by an enhanced curriculum, the sharing of resources, and collaborative instruction. (6) To seek to provide placement opportunities for our students and graduates that match their potential. (7) To teach the transcendence of ethics and to inculcate in graduates the importance of doing good while doing well throughout their professional lives.

Our goal is to graduate students who are not only eligible to practice law but qualified as well.

■ Enrollment/Student Body

➼ *1,219 applicants* ➼ *541 admitted first-year class 1998*
➼ *160 enrolled first-year class 1998* ➼ *full-time 25th/75th percentile GPA—3.04/3.57* ➼ *full-time 25th/75th percentile LSAT—156/162* ➼ *475 total full-time* ➼ *7.7% minority*
➼ *39% women* ➼ *40 states & foreign countries represented*
➼ *180 undergraduate schools represented*

■ Faculty

➼ *69 total* ➼ *34 full-time* ➼ *35 adjunct* ➼ *20 women*
➼ *6 minority* ➼ *30 supervising clinical attorneys*

■ Library and Physical Facilities

➼ *330,585 volumes & equivalents* ➼ *109 library hours/wk.*
➼ *LEXIS* ➼ *NEXIS* ➼ *WESTLAW*
➼ *DIALOG* ➼ *EPIC* ➼ *ACES* ➼ *Dow Jones*
➼ *6 full-time librarians* ➼ *library seats 568*

■ Curriculum

➼ *89 units/credits required to graduate* ➼ *100 courses available*
➼ *degrees available: J.D.; J.D./M.B.A.; and LL.M. in American Law* ➼ *semesters, start in Aug. & Jan.*
➼ *first-year class size—approx. 40*

Three academic years are divided into two semesters of 15 weeks each. A solid core of first-year courses is required, with strong emphasis on legal research and writing. Advanced elective courses are offered in specialty areas such as securities regulation, taxation, corporations, environmental law, clinic, and trial advocacy.

■ Special Programs

The law school offers two clinical programs. The first is a program of academic instruction, skills training, and live client representation, and is a cooperative venture of the bench, bar, and law school. Clinical students participate in an integrated program of both civil and criminal law practice. They are placed with supervising attorneys in the following areas—private practice, legal aid, the United States Attorney, district attorney, public defender, National Labor Relations Board, or corporate general counsel. The classroom component includes interviewing, counseling, negotiation, and discovery. The second clinical program is an in-house legal clinic for the elderly operating as an interdisciplinary element in the Sticht Center for the Aging.

The joint J.D./M.B.A. degree program permits the student to obtain both degrees in four years.

The School of Law offers an LL.M. Program in American Law for foreign law graduates. Students who have received their law degrees in countries other than the United States are eligible for admission. For more information write to the Director of Admissions.

■ Computer Instruction and Services

Wake Forest provides a wide range of computer services to students, faculty, and staff, and ranks among the top five law schools nationally for computers per student.

The Computerized Legal Research and Instruction Center contains 53 Pentium workstations, laser printers, and programs that allow students to access WESTLAW and LEXIS, use word processing and other legal software, and access computer-assisted legal research instruction programs.

■ Admission

➼ *Bachelor's degree from accredited college or university required*
➼ *application deadline—March 15*
➼ *LSAT, LSDAS required* ➼ *application fee—$60*

First-year students are admitted only in the fall semester for full-time study. One academic recommendation and a Dean's certification are required in addition to the other application materials, and the file must be completed by April 15. Applicants are advised of their status by May 15.

The LSAT score and the undergraduate GPA are combined into an index computed by LSDAS. For multiple LSAT scores, the higher test score will be used. The applicant should explain disparate scores. All files are reviewed on a case-by-case basis. The school considers a number of subjective factors indicating intellectual capacity, character, motivation, and maturity with the objective of selecting those most likely to succeed in law study and in the legal profession and also those who would contribute to the diversity essential to a rich educational experience.

The School of Law is committed to providing access to men and women of all races, religions, ethnic backgrounds, and physical abilities. Scholarships are available. One of the purposes of these scholarships is to enhance student body diversity and to encourage applicants, including those from minority or disadvantaged groups, who demonstrate substantial academic and professional promise. Inquiries should be addressed to the Director of Admissions and Financial Aid of the Law School.

Applicants admitted for the entering class in 1999 are required to pay a $300 nonrefundable deposit by April 15, and an interim tuition deposit on July 1 (both fees are applicable toward tuition and fee charges).

Personal interviews are not required, but may be arranged upon request. Individual applicants or groups are encouraged to visit the campus.

Transfer students who meet law school admission requirements are accepted on a space-available basis after the successful completion of one year at an AALS or ABA-approved law school.

■ Student Activities

All students are members of the Student Bar Association. A number of other organizations allow students to pursue a variety of interests.

The *Wake Forest Law Review* is a recognized scholastic journal. Selection to the *Law Review* is based on academic performance or demonstrated writing and academic ability.

The Moot Court Board and Student Trial Bar assist in the administration of the school's strong trial and appellate advocacy program through various intramural and inter-collegiate competitions.

■ Expenses and Financial Aid

➡ *tuition & fees—$20,450*   ➡ *estimated living expenses—$5,500-7,000*   ➡ *merit- & need-based scholarships available*   ➡ *diversity scholarships available*   ➡ *FAF, Federal Needs Analysis, due May 1*

Approximately 78 percent of the students receive financial assistance from scholarships, loans, work-study funds, and assistantships.

■ Placement Services

The Placement Program seeks to provide opportunities for our students and graduates that match their potential.

The Office of Placement Services conducts workshops in résumé preparation, interviewing techniques, and career planning to help prepare students to find employment.

Firms and corporations who cannot send a representative to the campus may request résumés and invite students to interview. These services are provided for those seeking permanent employment, and for summer work, clerkships, and part-time employment.

The Office of Placement Services encourages employers to notify the director of openings for experienced attorneys. Placement maintains a list of Law School graduates seeking a change in employment. A listing of opportunities is mailed to these graduates each month.

Applicant Group for the 1998-1999 Academic Year

Wake Forest University School of Law

LSAT Score	3.75 +		3.50 - 3.74		3.25 - 3.49		3.00 - 3.24		2.75 - 2.99		2.50 - 2.74		2.25 - 2.49		Below 2.25		Total	
	Apps	Adm	Apps	Adm	Apps	Adm	Apps	Adm	Apps	Adm	Apps	Adm	Apps	Adm	Apps	Adm	Apps	Adm
175-180	0	0	0	0	0	0	0	0	0	0	0	0	0	0	0	0	0	0
170-174	3	3	5	5	1	1	4	4	3	2	1	1	0	0	1	1	18	17
165-169	7	7	12	11	14	14	16	14	14	13	5	5	1	1	0	0	69	65
160-164	27	27	39	39	56	52	61	54	31	24	11	8	6	1	0	0	231	205
155-159	41	41	70	66	90	59	78	24	35	5	30	5	7	0	1	0	352	200
150-154	13	9	32	11	71	11	65	8	45	4	11	0	6	0	3	0	246	43
145-149	6	1	13	0	25	3	25	4	13	0	10	0	9	0	0	0	101	8
140-144	2	0	10	1	13	1	19	1	20	0	10	0	6	0	3	0	83	3
135-139	0	0	1	0	4	0	6	0	3	0	6	0	6	0	3	0	29	0
130-134	0	0	1	0	0	0	1	0	1	0	0	0	1	0	1	0	5	0
Below 130	0	0	0	0	0	0	0	0	0	0	2	0	0	0	0	0	2	0
Total	99	88	183	133	274	141	275	109	165	48	86	19	42	2	12	1	1136	541

Apps = Number of Applicants
Adm = Number Admitted
This grid includes only applicants with 120-180 LSAT scores earned under standard administrations.

Washburn University School of Law

1700 College
Topeka, KS 66621

E-Mail: admissions@washburnlaw.edu
URL: http://washburnlaw.edu
Phone: 888.WASHLAW or 888.927.4529

■ Introduction

Washburn University began as Lincoln College in 1865 and became Washburn College in 1868. The School of Law opened its doors in 1903, and in 1905 became one of the early members of the Association of American Law Schools. In 1923, Washburn was among the first law schools to be fully accredited by the American Bar Association. Washburn University today is an urban university serving 6,500 students. It is located in Topeka, the capital city of Kansas, about 60 miles west of Kansas City.

■ Enrollment/Student Body

▶ 500 applicants   ▶ 340 admitted first-year class 1998
▶ 158 enrolled first-year class 1998   ▶ full-time 25th/75th percentile GPA—2.85/3.49   ▶ full-time 25th/75th percentile LSAT—146/153   ▶ 435 total full-time   ▶ 12.6% minority
▶ 43.2% women   ▶ 45 states & foreign countries represented
▶ 180 undergraduate schools represented

■ Faculty

▶ 27 full-time   ▶ 9 women   ▶ 7 minority
▶ 35 part-time or adjunct

■ Library and Physical Facilities

▶ 311,932 volumes & equivalents   ▶ library hours:
Mon.-Thurs., 7:30 A.M.-11:00 P.M.; Fri., 7:30 A.M.-9:00 P.M.;
Sat., 8:00 A.M.-8:00 P.M.; Sun., NOON-11:00 P.M.
▶ LEXIS   ▶ WESTLAW   ▶ Internet (including e-mail)
▶ 7 full-time librarians   ▶ library seats 346
▶ 41-station computer lab

Library highlights include a 41-station microcomputer lab, individual study carrels, group study rooms, lounge seating areas, and a richly furbished special collections room. The law building has a barrier-free design. Washburn's clinical program, one of the first in the nation, is housed in an attached model law office. A beautiful moot courtroom is regularly used for administrative law hearings and occasional sittings by the Kansas Court of Appeals and the U.S. Tenth Circuit Court of Appeals.

The law library has a national reputation for leadership in the use of new information technologies. The 1997 edition of Don MacLeod's *The Internet Guide for the Legal Researcher* describes WashLaw, created by the Washburn law library staff, as "the best all-around law resource on the Internet, period." The author advises that if "only one law-related index page were allowed on the Internet, this one would be the one to choose." Washburn also hosts over 400 law-related listservs (online discussion groups), more than any other law school worldwide. Each law student receives a password for accessing LEXIS, WESTLAW, Internet, and e-mail from home or school. A local area network provides convenient access to one of the largest law-related networked CD-ROM collections in the nation, computer-assisted learning exercises, and computer software.

The library collection has had nearly two decades of vigorous growth, ranking in the top quarter of all law school libraries for new titles added since 1979. A strong law-related videotape collection is used to supplement classroom instruction. Specialized research facilities include U.S. and Kansas government document depositories, a local public document room for the U.S. Nuclear Regulatory Commission, and a satellite reference center for the Kansas Patent Depository Library. Law students have access to the 200,000-volume Kansas Supreme Court Law Library.

■ Curriculum

▶ Academic Support Program   ▶ 90 credits required to graduate   ▶ 122 courses available   ▶ semesters, start in Aug. & Jan.   ▶ range of first-year class size—25-75
▶ two six-week summer sessions

Students may begin their study in either the fall or spring semester. The first-year curriculum is prescribed. To complete the upper-level program, students must meet distributional requirements in six areas of study plus writing and oral presentational requirements.

■ Certificate Programs

A Certificate in Law and Mental Health is awarded jointly by Washburn and the world-renowned Menninger Foundation psychiatric center to students who graduate with 96 credit hours and receive a B average in at least 15 hours of credit in the Mental Health Law area. Students participate in a colloquium with psychiatric residents at Menninger and represent clients in mental disability cases in the Washburn Law Clinic.

Certificates in Tax Law, Family Law, Agricultural Law, and Environmental Law are awarded to students graduating with 96 credit hours who achieve a B average in at least 15 hours of credit in the Tax, Family, Agricultural, or Environmental Law area.

■ Special Programs

Washburn has gained national recognition through its Law Clinic, a general practice firm of senior law students representing indigent clients. The clinic experience includes direct client representation in a wide range of civil and criminal litigation and provision of mediation services.

Valuable academic and work opportunities are provided by the state legislature, state executive offices, state and federal district courts, state supreme court, court of appeals, bankruptcy court, and state and federal agencies.

Washburn sponsors a six-credit-hour, six-week program abroad each summer. Washburn faculty team teach classes with faculty members from the host school.

The Rural Law Center focuses teaching and research on aspects of the law affecting the rural environment.

■ Admission

➡ *Bachelor's degree from accredited college or university*
➡ *application deadline—fall, March 15; spring, Sept. 15*
➡ *LSAT, LSDAS required*   ➡ *application fee—$30*

Significant factors that the Admissions Committee considers are the LSAT score and grade-point average. There is no automatic cutoff for LSAT score or GPA. Other factors which are evaluated are work experience, graduate work, cultural background, extracurricular activities, and the need for diversity in the student body. Late applications are accepted but applicants may be at a disadvantage. Admitted applicants pay a $100 admission deposit which applies toward tuition when the student enrolls. Applicants are encouraged to visit the school and attend a law class.

■ Student Activities

Students are selected to membership on the Board of Editors of the *Washburn Law Journal* on the basis of academic standing and performance in a writing competition.

Washburn has assumed editorial responsibility for publication of the Family Law Quarterly of the American Bar Association's Family Law Section. The Quarterly provides a second editorial experience for Washburn students.

The Washburn Student Bar Association directs student affairs, sponsoring a wide variety of educational and social activities. Students participate in Moot Court, Client Counseling, Negotiations, and Trial Advocacy competitions. There are more than 25 active student organizations, including two law fraternities, Asian, Hispanic American, Native American, and Black Law Student Associations, Women's Legal Forum, and societies for students interested in Environmental, International, Public Interest, Tax, and Sports and Entertainment Law.

■ Expenses and Financial Aid

➡ *full-time tuition—residents, $7,170 ($239/credit hr.); nonresidents, $10,740 ($358/credit hr.)*   ➡ *fees—$40 per year* ➡ *books & supplies—$700*   ➡ *academic- & need-based scholarships available*   ➡ *College Scholarship Service PROFILE required for need-based scholarships, Free Application for Federal Student Aid (FAFSA) required for loans*   ➡ *financial aid forms due April 1 for fall & Sept. 15 for January admission*

Scholarships may be awarded on a combination of academic performance and need. Diversity is considered as a factor in making scholarship awards. Second- and third-year students appreciate the availability of research-assistant positions within the law school and the abundance of law-related jobs in Topeka.

Housing costs vary, but are quite reasonable: dormitory room and board from $3,110 per year; university apartments for families, 1 bedroom—$180. Most students live in apartments in the residential areas surrounding the campus.

■ Career Services

Washburn provides students and alumni with professional career-planning services. Programs emphasize assessment of career goals, exploration of varied applications of a legal education, and support for the transition into the professional marketplace. Extensive resources are available regarding local, regional, national, and international legal employment in the public and private sectors, graduate and foreign study, and judicial clerkships.

Washburn graduates' employment experiences are consistent with national law placement averages within one year of graduation. Alumni are located in every state in the nation and several foreign countries.

Applicant Group for the 1998-1999 Academic Year

Washburn University School of Law

LSAT Score	3.75 +		3.50 - 3.74		3.25 - 3.49		3.00 - 3.24		2.75 - 2.99		2.50 - 2.74		2.25 - 2.49		Below 2.25		Total	
	Apps	Adm	Apps	Adm	Apps	Adm	Apps	Adm	Apps	Adm	Apps	Adm	Apps	Adm	Apps	Adm	Apps	Adm
175-180	0	0	0	0	0	0	0	0	0	0	0	0	0	0	0	0	0	0
170-174	0	0	0	0	0	0	0	0	0	0	0	0	0	0	1	0	1	0
165-169	0	0	0	0	2	2	1	1	0	0	0	0	0	0	0	0	3	3
160-164	4	4	2	2	2	2	2	2	1	1	2	2	3	3	0	0	16	16
155-159	8	8	15	14	7	7	13	12	12	11	9	6	4	3	2	2	70	63
150-154	10	10	17	17	19	17	27	27	21	21	8	8	6	4	2	2	110	106
145-149	5	5	16	15	25	22	30	27	20	14	25	10	12	7	3	2	136	102
140-144	4	4	9	5	16	10	24	10	17	6	11	1	5	0	3	1	89	37
Below 140	1	1	2	1	3	1	7	1	10	1	10	0	9	0	5	0	47	5
Total	32	32	61	54	74	61	104	80	81	54	65	27	39	17	16	7	472	332

Apps = Number of Applicants
Adm = Number Admitted
This chart is to be used for general information only. Nonnumerical factors are weighed heavily in all admission decisions.
This chart represents only completed applications.

University of Washington School of Law

316 Condon Hall
1100 N.E. Campus Parkway
Seattle, WA 98105-6617

E-Mail: admissions@law.washington.edu
URL: http://www.law.washington.edu
Phone: 206.543.4078

■ Introduction

Established in 1899, the School of Law is part of the main campus of the University of Washington, approximately four miles from downtown Seattle. The university, the largest single campus institution in the western United States, with an enrollment of 33,500 students, offers nearly every discipline for study. The School of Law has 47 full-time faculty members and about 500 J.D. students. Because of the favorable student-to-faculty ratio, classes are generally small, with frequent opportunities for student-teacher contacts. Each first-year student is usually in at least one class of 30 or fewer students, in addition to the Basic Legal Skills course. The school is a member of the AALS, is approved by the ABA, and has a chapter of the Order of the Coif.

■ Enrollment/Student Body

➡ 1,717 applicants   ➡ 493 admitted first-year class 1998
➡ 173 enrolled first-year class 1998   ➡ full-time 25th/75th percentile GPA—3.38/3.72   ➡ full-time 25th/75th percentile LSAT—158/166   ➡ 500 total full-time J.D.
➡ 29% minority   ➡ 53% women
➡ 20 states and 3 foreign countries represented
➡ 85 undergraduate schools represented

■ Faculty

➡ 92 total   ➡ 47 full-time   ➡ 45 part-time or adjunct
➡ 18 women   ➡ 5 minority

■ Library and Physical Facilities

➡ 508,000 volumes & equivalents   ➡ library hours:
Mon.-Thurs., 8:00 A.M.-11:00 P.M.; Fri., 8:00 A.M.-6:00 P.M.;
Sat., 10:00 A.M.-6:00 P.M.; Sun., NOON-11:00 P.M.
➡ LEXIS   ➡ NEXIS   ➡ CD-ROM & full Internet accessibility   ➡ 11.5 full-time librarians   ➡ library seats 454

■ Curriculum

➡ 135 quarter credits required to graduate   ➡ 115 courses available; full-time day program only   ➡ degrees available: J.D./M.B. A.; J.D./International Studies; LL.M. in Asian Law, Law and Marine Affairs, International Environmental Law, Law of Sustainable International Development, and Taxation
➡ quarters, begin in Oct.
➡ range of first-year class size—30-120

The first-year curriculum is prescribed. After that, except for an analytical writing requirement and a class in professional responsibility, all courses in the second and third years are elective. In addition to traditional courses and seminars, advanced students may participate in a criminal, mediation, family and employment law, immigration, affordable housing or refugee advocacy clinic, or in courses in trial advocacy. Judicial, legislative, agency, and public interest externships are available. Students must also perform 60 hours of public service legal work.

Students are encouraged to rely on their initiative and to develop their own powers of perception. Classroom discussion in which students participate fully is one means used to assist this development. Independent research projects, either in the context of a seminar or through individualized study under faculty supervision, are also emphasized. Although it is a state law school, Washington state law is not emphasized unduly. Graduates of the school are prepared to practice law anywhere in the United States or in other common law countries.

■ Special Programs

Students studying for the J.D. program may take courses in any of the LL.M. programs during the second and third years. The UW also offers a master's degree in Law Librarianship.

■ Admission Standards

➡ Bachelor's degree required   ➡ application deadline—Jan. 15; applicants must take the LSAT no later than Dec.
➡ decisions made from Jan. 15 to April 1
➡ LSAT, LSDAS required   ➡ application fee—$50

In selecting the entering class, the law school does not make all of its admission decisions solely on the basis of predicted academic performance. Important academic objectives are furthered by classes comprised of students having talents and skills derived from diverse backgrounds believed to be relevant to a rich and effective study of law.

Nearly twenty-nine percent of the incoming class consists of students of color, for whom the school provides student, faculty, and professional mentoring programs.

■ Student Activities

The *Washington Law Review* and *Pacific Rim Law and Policy Journal* are edited and published by students. The University of Washington is consistently among the top scoring Moot Court teams in the nation.

Through the Student Bar Association and student/faculty committees, students participate in the decision processes of the law school. Student organizations include the Law Women's Caucus; Minority Law Students Association; Asian Pacific American Law Students; Coalition of Black Law Students; Filipino Law Students Association; Latino/Latina Law Students Association; Native American Law Students Association; Environmental Law Society; International Law Society; Christian Legal Society; National Lawyer's Guild; Law, Science, and Technology Group; Lesbian and Gay Legal Society; Phi Alpha Delta; ABA Student Division; Federalist Society; Public Interest Law Association; Phi Delta Phi; Law and Alternative Dispute Resolution; Law Kids; Center for Advanced Study and Research on Intellectual Property (CASRIP); Jewish Law Students Association; the UW Law Outreach; *Docket*; Immigrant Families Advocate Project; Labor Law Society;

Law and Economics Society; Law Poets; Sports and Entertainment Law Club; and Street Youth Legal Advocates of Washington.

■ Expenses and Financial Aid

➤ *full-time tuition & fees—resident, $5,800; nonresident, $14,200* ➤ *estimated additional expenses—$11,650 (books $900; room & board, $8,000; transportation/personal $2,700—includes $350 health insurance)* ➤ *need-based scholarships available* ➤ *financial aid available; FAFSA due Feb. 28*

■ Career Services

The Career Services Office serves as a liaison between students and prospective employers. Firms, agencies, and other potential employers are invited to interview at the school and to list job openings in the regularly published placement bulletin. About 90 percent of the graduates choose to remain in Washington state.

Applicant Group for the 1998-1999 Academic Year

University of Washington School of Law
This grid includes 100% of all applications reviewed with scores on the 120-180 score scale.

GPA Range	Average LSAT Score														
	120-153		154-156		157-159		160-162		163-165		166-168		169-180		Total	
	Adm	Apps	Adm	Apps	Adm	Apps	Adm	Apps	Adm	Apps	Adm	Apps	Adm	Apps	Adm	Apps
3.75 & Above	6	27	2	25	13	41	21	39	40	41	27	27	33	33	142	233
3.50-3.74	10	81	7	54	13	64	34	91	36	65	41	45	30	30	171	430
3.25-3.49	2	90	11	59	7	72	22	69	18	53	27	48	31	34	118	425
3.00-3.24	2	100	2	33	10	56	4	39	5	38	3	11	9	15	35	292
2.75-2.99	0	54	0	26	0	22	6	22	0	13	0	7	3	9	9	153
2.50-2.74	0	35	0	5	1	8	0	4	2	6	0	3	0	3	3	64
Below 2.50	0	25	0	2	0	5	0	3	0	1	0	4	0	1	0	41
LSAT only	2	30	0	8	1	7	2	7	4	8	3	6	3	3	15	69
Total	22	442	22	212	45	275	89	274	105	225	101	151	109	128	493	1707

Apps = Number of Applicants
Adm = Number Admitted
In cases where an applicant presented multiple LSAT scores, the average score was used.

This information is presented to give applicants some idea of the likelihood of admission. It should be noted, however, that these data can and do change from year to year. In addition, there is some latitude within each category, so that a person presenting credentials at the upper limits of one cell might have an excellent chance for admission, while another applicant at the lower limits might only have a marginal chance. For these reasons, this chart should be used as an approximate gauge of the likelihood of admission and **NOT** as a guarantee.

Washington and Lee University School of Law

Lewis Hall
Lexington, VA 24450

E-Mail: lawadm@wlu.edu
URL: http://www.wlu.edu/law/
Phone: 540.463.8504

■ Introduction

Washington and Lee University School of Law is a private institution located in Lexington, Virginia, approximately 175 miles southwest of Washington, DC, in the Blue Ridge Mountains. Founded in 1849, the school is a member of the AALS and is fully accredited by the ABA.

As a small, selective private law school, Washington and Lee takes pride in offering a nationally oriented legal education that is professionally rigorous and intellectually challenging. The size of the school is carefully controlled to achieve a generous faculty-to-student ratio and a closely knit community of students and faculty, in which the opportunity for informal contact and collaboration in ongoing research enhances the educational process. The school seeks to limit its total enrollment to 360 students; there are 33 regular faculty members and 12 adjunct members.

■ Enrollment/Student Body

➡ 1,267 applicants   ➡ 463 admitted first-year class 1998
➡ 122 enrolled first-year class 1998   ➡ full-time 25th/75th percentile GPA—3.05/3.75   ➡ full-time 25th/75th percentile LSAT—161/166   ➡ 367 total full-time   ➡ 9% minority
➡ 40% women   ➡ 46 states & foreign countries represented
➡ 193 undergraduate schools represented

■ Faculty

➡ 45 total   ➡ 33 full-time   ➡ 12 part-time or adjunct
➡ 8 women   ➡ 4 minority

■ Library and Physical Facilities

➡ 350,065 volumes & equivalents   ➡ library open 24 hours / day, 7 days/week, year-round   ➡ LEXIS   ➡ NEXIS
➡ WESTLAW   ➡ 7 full-time librarians   ➡ library seats 400

The School of Law is located on the campus of Washington and Lee University in Lewis Hall, originally built in 1976 and expanded in 1991 with the addition of the Lewis F. Powell, Jr. Archives, which house the Supreme Court and professional papers of retired Supreme Court Justice Powell, a graduate of the University's college and law school. Each student is provided his or her own study carrel or office space in Lewis Hall. Training in the use of all online research services is provided to all first-year students. Students have access to the library collection on an open-stack basis. The school makes extensive use of state-of-the-art video and computer technology in classroom settings and in trial advocacy training.

■ Curriculum

➡ Academic Support Program   ➡ 85 credits required to graduate   ➡ 120 courses available   ➡ J.D. degree available
➡ range of first-year class size—20-60
➡ average class size after first-year—23

■ Special Programs

Second- and third-year law students may elect to participate in a number of clinical or specialized practice programs offered by the School of Law, including the Legal Aid Society, providing legal services to indigent civil clients; the Legal Practice Clinic, an in-house clinic that represents the mentally ill and coal miners with federal black-lung claims; the Alderson Legal Assistance Program, providing legal services to inmates of a major federal institution for female offenders; and the Public Defender Program, providing legal services to indigent persons charged with crimes. In the U.S. Attorney's Program, students participate in prosecutorial trial work in the federal court system. The Judicial Clerkship Program provides opportunities to clerk for trial or appellate judges in the Virginia court system.

The International Environmental Law Program was founded with a grant from the Creswell Foundation, and provides students with an opportunity to participate in a program of seminars, directed research, and summer internships in the field of international environmental law. Governmental organizations, corporations, or public interest entities submit project proposals; program participants select the project and entity of their choice. In recent years, students have worked for the Natural Resources Defense Council, the government of Hungary, the Community Nutrition Institute, for public interest groups concerned with development in the Arctic, and in environmental issues dealing with human rights, among others.

The Virginia Capital Case Clearinghouse was established to provide research and litigation support to attorneys appointed to represent persons charged with capital crimes, or who are pursuing appeals of cases in which the death penalty has been imposed. Students pursue in-depth research into developments in current death-penalty law and assist with the preparation of pleadings, legal memoranda, and briefs in ongoing cases. Students write and edit the *Capital Case Digest*, a journal dealing with the complex and important area of capital sentencing.

■ Admission

➡ undergraduate degree required for admission
➡ application deadline—Feb. 1   ➡ applications received after Feb. 1 will be considered but cannot be guaranteed a response by April 1   ➡ LSAT, LSDAS required
➡ application fee—$40

Students enter the School of Law only in the fall semester, which begins in late August. There is no part-time program.

Although the LSAT score and undergraduate grade-point average are important factors considered by the Admissions Committee, other, more subjective factors, such as trends in grades, the rigor of an applicant's academic program, achievement in extracurricular or community service activities, work experience, and evaluations from professors are a significant part of an admissions decision. An applicant may request an interview with a member of the Admissions

Committee. Applicants are encouraged to visit the school to sit in on classes, tour the facility, and talk with students and faculty if it is convenient for them to do so.

The School of Law actively seeks a diversified student body whose members are of different religious, racial, ethnic, economic, and geographic backgrounds. Applications from persons considering a change in career are encouraged.

■ Student Activities

The *Washington and Lee Law Review*, managed and published by students, is a quarterly journal for scholarly discussion of important legal problems. A variety of moot court and advocacy competitions, both intra- and interschool, provide students with opportunities to hone advocacy, counseling, negotiation, and trial skills.

All students are members of the Student Bar Association, which represents students in the ongoing affairs of the school and sponsors professional programs and social activities. Law students also participate in university intramural sports, drama, music, and political programs. The Black Law Student Association, Women Law Student Association, the National Lawyers Guild, the Federalist Society, the Environmental Law Forum, the International Law Society, and three national professional fraternities all present programs addressing matters of special concern to their members.

■ Expenses and Financial Aid

➥ *tuition—$17,470*   ➥ *full-time fees—$241*
➥ *estimated additional expenses—$8,000 (room, board,*

books, misc. expenses)   ➥ *need- & merit-based*
scholarships available   ➥ *merit-based fellowships available*
➥ *FAFSA required for financial aid*

■ Housing Opportunities

On-campus housing is available in the Woods Creek Apartments, adjacent to the law school. The law school provides an off-campus housing referral service to interested students.

■ Career Services

The Placement Office acts as a liaison between law students and legal employers. Workshops, brown-bag lunches, and panel presentations focus on special topics or skills, but individual counseling with personal attention to each student is the hallmark of the placement effort. An active alumni network is in place to assist students. In 1997, 53 percent of graduates entered the private practice of law immediately following graduation. Twenty-six percent served a judicial clerkship. Other graduates go into business-related employment, including corporate law staffs, banks, and accounting firms; take positions in various federal, state, or local governmental agencies; serve in public interest law, or in the JAG Corps; and some pursue advanced law degrees. Graduates are employed throughout the country; in the last three years, students have accepted employment in 44 states and seven foreign countries. In the class of 1997, 95.6 percent reported employment within nine months of graduation.

Applicant Group for the 1998-1999 Academic Year

Washington and Lee University School of Law
This grid includes only applicants who earned 120-180 LSAT scores under standard administrations.

LSAT Score	3.75 +		3.50 - 3.74		3.25 - 3.49		3.00 - 3.24		2.75 - 2.99		2.50 - 2.74		2.25 - 2.49		2.00 - 2.24		Below 2.00		No GPA		Total	
	Apps	Adm	Apps	Adm	Apps	Adm	Apps	Adm	Apps	Adm	Apps	Adm	Apps	Adm	Apps	Adm	Apps	Adm	Apps	Adm	Apps	Adm
175-180	4	3	2	2	1	1	1	1	1	1	0	0	1	1	0	0	0	0	0	0	10	9
170-174	9	8	11	9	7	6	9	9	4	3	2	2	1	1	0	0	0	0	0	0	43	38
165-169	38	35	59	56	42	41	24	23	14	13	11	10	2	2	0	0	1	1	3	2	194	183
160-164	53	51	69	51	70	24	53	22	29	7	17	4	2	2	0	0	0	0	3	1	296	162
155-159	52	32	58	13	60	1	69	0	24	1	8	0	3	1	4	0	0	0	7	0	285	48
150-154	29	1	33	5	45	2	45	3	26	0	6	1	8	1	3	0	1	0	7	0	203	13
145-149	5	0	10	2	21	1	18	0	18	0	13	0	12	1	4	0	1	0	2	0	104	4
140-144	3	0	13	0	10	0	18	0	18	0	13	0	5	0	1	0	0	0	1	0	82	0
135-139	1	0	5	0	1	0	5	0	5	0	4	0	2	0	1	0	0	0	2	0	26	0
130-134	0	0	0	0	0	0	1	0	0	0	0	0	4	0	0	0	0	0	0	0	5	0
125-129	0	0	0	0	0	0	0	0	0	0	2	0	0	0	0	0	0	0	0	0	2	0
120-124	0	0	0	0	0	0	0	0	0	0	0	0	0	0	0	0	0	0	0	0	0	0
Total	194	130	260	138	257	76	243	58	139	25	76	17	40	9	13	0	3	1	25	3	1250	457

Apps = Number of Applicants
Adm = Number Admitted
Reflects 99% of the total applicant pool.

Washington University School of Law

Box 1120
One Brookings Drive
St. Louis, MO 63130

E-Mail: admiss@wulaw.wustl.edu
URL: http://ls.wustl.edu
Phone: 314.935.4525

■ Introduction

Founded in 1867, Washington University School of Law is the oldest private law school in continuous operation west of the Mississippi River. A charter member of the AALS and approved by the ABA, the school was one of the first accredited law schools to graduate women. The law school is located on the beautiful and serene 169-acre Hilltop Campus bordered by Forest Park, the site of the 1904 World's Fair, and the lovely suburban communities of Clayton and University City.

■ Enrollment/Student Body

➡ 1,640 applicants ➡ 885 admitted first-year class 1998 ➡ 213 enrolled first-year class 1998 ➡ full-time 25th/75th percentile GPA—3.12/3.58 ➡ full-time 25th/75th percentile LSAT—155/163 ➡ 627 total full-time ➡ 22% minority ➡ 47% women ➡ 42 states & 5 foreign countries represented ➡ 110 undergraduate schools represented

The law school has a national approach to legal education and attracts students from throughout the United States and several foreign countries. The wide variety of undergraduate academic disciplines enriches the Socratic method of teaching.

■ Faculty

➡ 125 total ➡ 48 full-time ➡ 77 part-time or adjunct ➡ 20 women ➡ 14 minority

Our student-to-faculty ratio (including only full-time faculty) is 14 to 1.

■ Library and Physical Facilities

➡ 563,292 volumes & equivalents ➡ library hours: Mon.-Thurs., 7:00 A.M.-1:00 A.M.; Fri., 7:00 A.M.-MIDNIGHT; Sat., 9:00 A.M.-MIDNIGHT; Sun., 9:00 A.M.-1:00 A.M. ➡ LEXIS ➡ NEXIS ➡ WESTLAW ➡ Congressional Information System ➡ LEGI-SLATE ➡ assorted CD-ROMs ➡ 8 full-time librarians ➡ library seats 519

The new law school facility, which opened in January 1997 is traditional in its architecture, but state-of-the-art in its facilities.

■ Curriculum

➡ 85 credits required to graduate ➡ 143 courses available ➡ degrees available: J.D./Asian studies; J.D./M.B.A.; J.D./M.A.-Econ.; J.D./M.A.-Pol. Sci.; J.D./M.H.A.; J.D./M.S.W.; J.D./M.A. or M.S.-Environmental Policy; J.D./M.A.-European studies

A three-year, full-time course of study leads to the J.D. degree. The prescribed first-year courses are sectioned to ensure individualized instruction. In addition, all first-year students participate in a year-long legal research and writing program. Coursework in the second and third years is chosen by the student. A Congressional Clinic and a Federal Administrative Agency Clinic offered in the spring semester of the third year allow a small group of students to work in Washington, DC, with individual members of Congress, congressional committees, and federal agencies. Other areas of strength include environmental, international, corporate, clinical education, constitutional, taxation, criminal, labor, and intellectual property.

■ Special Programs

➡ Congressional Clinic (Washington, DC)—spring sem., 3rd yr. ➡ 8 joint-degree programs available

The School of Law offers a Master's degree (LL.M.) in Taxation. Combined-study programs exist between the law school and School of Social Work (J.D./M.S.W.), the Health Administration Department of the School of Medicine (J.D./M.H.A.), the School of Business (J.D./M.B.A.), and the Department of Economics (J.D./M.S.Ec.), Political Science (J.D./M.A.), the Asian Studies department (J.D./M.A.), the European Studies department (J.D./M.A.), and the Department of Engineering and Policy of the School of Engineering and Applied Science. This degree (J.D./M.S. or M.A.) places an emphasis on environmental law and policy.

Additional combined-degree programs are available by arrangement with other departments.

■ Admission

➡ Bachelor's degree required ➡ application deadline—March 1 ➡ LSAT, LSDAS required ➡ application fee—$50

While there is no formal deadline for applying to the school of law, applications received after March 1 may not receive full consideration. The Admissions Committee informs applicants of their status by April 15. Decisions on transfer applications are made in midsummer and considered only if the student has an outstanding record at another AALS-ABA approved school.

Admission decisions are based on a wide range of factors, including undergraduate record, the Law School Admission Test score, and personal statement. Letters of recommendation are encouraged but not required, and should be limited to no more than three. Applicants are also advised to visit the law school; arrangements can be made by contacting the Admissions Office.

The committee makes a conscientious effort to examine the more personal variables that have a real impact on the quality of life and the quality of education in this institution, such as energy, motivation, self-discipline, and character. Insight into these variables is derived from careful examination of the undergraduate record, personal statement, résumé, and/or letters of recommendation, and other items in the applicant's file.

■ Housing

A wide range of affordable private housing is available near the School of Law. For housing information, students should contact the University Housing Office (314.935.5050).

■ Student Activities

The School of Law publishes two student-edited law review periodicals, the *Law Quarterly* and the *Journal of Urban and Contemporary Law*. A very active moot court program, mock trial competition, and competitions in negotiation and client counseling are available. Law students participate in a variety of other programs, including the Women's Law Caucus, the Pro Bono Law Association, the Black Law Students Association, the Asian American Law Student Association, and the Student Bar Association. The student body is self-regulated through the Law School Honor Council. Students are eligible for election to the Order of the Coif. Students also serve on many joint committees with faculty members.

■ Opportunities for Minority & Women Students

The environment for minority law students is excellent at Washington University. Minority students have been actively involved in law review publications, moot court, mock trial competitions, legal fraternities, student government, and other academic and extracurricular activities. Minorities with strong academic records will automatically be considered for the Minority Scholars in Law Program.

One of the first women to receive a degree from an American law school graduated from Washington University in 1871. The school successfully continues to recruit outstanding women, although admission decisions are made on a nondiscriminatory basis. Women with exceptional academic records are encouraged to apply for an Olin Fellowship, which provides full tuition and some stipends for eight women pursuing graduate degrees at Washington University. Application deadline for this award is February 1.

■ Expenses and Financial Aid

➡ *tuition & fees—$23,080 (1998-99)*
➡ *estimated additional expenses—$11,000 (housing, food, etc.)*
➡ *scholarships available: Scholars in Law, Minority Scholars in Law, Olin Fellowship (for women), Buder Scholarship (for Native Americans), Farmer Scholarship (for African Americans), Fisse Scholarship, Chancellor's Fellowship*
➡ *financial aid available; FAFSA due March 1*

The school offers merit scholarships that are awarded to entering students with exceptional credentials without regard to financial need.

Most student aid is in the form of government and privately sponsored loans. One-half of the students receive some scholarship assistance; two-thirds receive loans. (Virtually all those receiving scholarships also receive loans.)

■ Career Services

An aggressive and efficient Career Services Office serves both students and employers. For the class of 1997, 96 percent of the graduating class found employment within six months of graduation. Sixty percent accepted positions outside Missouri, 60 percent entered private practice, and 27 percent found positions in the public sector. Others are employed in corporate legal departments, accounting firms, banks, and commercial businesses.

Applicant Group for the 1998-1999 Academic Year

Washington University School of Law
This grid includes only applicants who earned 120-180 LSAT scores under standard administrations.

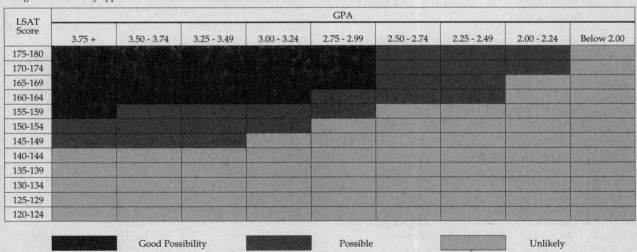

LSAT Score	GPA								
	3.75 +	3.50 - 3.74	3.25 - 3.49	3.00 - 3.24	2.75 - 2.99	2.50 - 2.74	2.25 - 2.49	2.00 - 2.24	Below 2.00
175-180									
170-174									
165-169									
160-164									
155-159									
150-154									
145-149									
140-144									
135-139									
130-134									
125-129									
120-124									

■ Good Possibility   ■ Possible   ■ Unlikely

Reflects 98% of the total applicant pool.

Wayne State University Law School

Admissions Office
468 W. Ferry Mall
Detroit, MI 48202

E-Mail: inquire@novell.law.wayne.edu
URL: http://www.law.wayne.edu
Phone: 313.577.3937

■ Introduction

Wayne State University Law School was established in 1927, is accredited by the ABA, is a member of the AALS, and has a chapter of the Order of the Coif, the national honor society of the legal profession.

The Law School is a flagship unit of Wayne State University, a major metropolitan research university, located in the Detroit Cultural Center. The Law School's three-building complex is situated at the north end of the university's campus, which covers 185 beautifully landscaped acres and is highlighted by famous Yamasaki-designed buildings.

■ Enrollment/Student Body

➡ 1,040 applicants   ➡ 509 admitted first-year class 1998
➡ 261 enrolled first-year class 1998   ➡ full-time 25th/75th percentile GPA—3.06/3.46   ➡ part-time 25th/75th percentile GPA—2.86/3.36   ➡ full-time 25th/75th percentile LSAT—151/157   ➡ part-time 25th/75th percentile LSAT—151/158   ➡ 516 total full-time   ➡ 220 total part-time
➡ 16% minority   ➡ 46% women   ➡ 13 states & foreign countries represented   ➡ 99 undergraduate schools represented
➡ age range—20-57

Approximately 750 students are enrolled in the J.D. program, including individuals from diverse racial, ethnic and socioeconomic backgrounds. Student life, both social and academic, is unusually friendly.

When compared with graduates of other law schools, Wayne State law graduates consistently have the highest or the second highest passing rate on the Michigan Bar Examination.

■ Faculty

➡ 83 total   ➡ 35 full-time   ➡ 48 part-time or adjunct
➡ 10 women   ➡ 4 minority

The members of the full-time faculty are committed to teaching, research, and publishing yet remain accessible to students. One-fourth of the faculty are elected members of the American Law Institute. Many are nationally or internationally recognized experts in their fields of specialization.

Judges and attorneys prominent in specific areas of law, and professors from the United States and other countries serve as adjunct faculty and visiting professors.

■ The Arthur Neef Law Library

➡ 500,000 volumes & equivalents   ➡ library hours: Mon.-Thurs., 8:00 A.M.-11:00 P.M.; Fri., 8:00 A.M.-9:00 P.M.; Sat., 9:00 A.M.-9:00 P.M.; Sun., 11:00 A.M.-11:00 P.M.; exam periods until MIDNIGHT   ➡ LEXIS   ➡ NEXIS
➡ WESTLAW   ➡ CALI   ➡ 6 full-time librarians
➡ library seats 456   ➡ 32-station computer lab
➡ interactive video   ➡ full Internet access
➡ Federal Depository Web-based online catalog with links to full-text electronic resources. Students have access to over

500,000 volumes in the libraries on campus and in the Detroit Public Library.

■ Curriculum

➡ Academic Support Program (Summer Institute)
➡ 86 credits required to graduate   ➡ 103 total courses available   ➡ degrees available: J.D.; J.D./M.A. History; J.D./M.A. Public Policy; J.D./M.B.A   ➡ semesters, start in Aug.   ➡ range of first-year class size—30-90

The first-year curriculum includes the required basic courses: civil procedure, contracts, criminal law, property, torts, and legal research and writing.

The legal research and writing course is one of the best in the nation. The research and writing proficiency of Wayne State law students is highly valued by law firms and other employers. The course is taught by full-time instructors, who are attorneys with experience in the courts, legal practice, and teaching.

Upper-class students are required to take a semester each of constitutional law and professional responsibility. Other courses may be chosen from a broad and diverse range of elective courses, seminars, and skills training classes.

The Law School offers LL.M. programs in the areas of taxation, labor law, and corporate planning.

■ Admission

➡ Bachelor's degree required   ➡ application priority filing date—March 15   ➡ rolling admission
➡ LSAT, LSDAS required   ➡ application fee—$20

Most of the class is admitted strictly on the basis of superior undergraduate GPA and LSAT scores. Others are admitted on the basis of academic credentials and other discretionary factors.

Transfer applications may be made, but only students from ABA-approved law schools with excellent academic credentials will be accepted.

■ Minority Students and Other Special Programs

Wayne State Law School has a commitment to enroll a diverse student body and maintains an affirmative action admissions policy for minority group members. Our goal is to assure that every individual we admit has the potential to be successful at our Law School.

Minority students admitted to Wayne State Law School have a high graduation and bar passage rate. Qualified minority students are considered for the Kenneth Cockrel, Wade McCree, and Law Alumni Scholarship.

The Supportive Services Program, under the full-time supervision of an Assistant Dean, offers academic and related support to all students. The Summer Institute Program allows entering students to complete a first-year required course prior to the beginning of the regular academic year.

Student Activities

The *Wayne Law Review*, a scholarly legal journal with nationwide circulation, is published by upper-class law students selected on the basis of their superior academic achievement and/or writing ability.

The Wayne Moot Court Program enjoys national recognition and is affiliated with the Order of the Barristers, a national honorary organization.

The Student Trial Advocacy Program (STAP) provides basic instruction in evidence and the techniques of trial advocacy.

Many students work in the Free Legal Aid Clinic representing indigent clients in court under attorney supervision. Students in the Criminal Appellate Practice Program, in cooperation with the Michigan State Appellate Defender Office, prepare briefs and other pleadings for indigent clients with pending felony appeals.

Second- and third-year students may intern on a part-time basis for distinguished judges and in a variety of governmental and nonprofit agencies.

The Student Board of Governors plays a significant role in the decision-making process of the school and also sponsors social activities for law students. Other student organizations include the Black Law Students Association, Hispanic Law Student Association, Jewish Law Students Association, Federalist Society, Women's Law Caucus, National Lawyers Guild, Environmental Law Society, International Law Society, Arab and Chaldean Law Student Association, Parents-In-Law, ABA Law Student Division, and legal fraternities.

Study Abroad

The Law School sponsors three study abroad programs: Wayne/Warwick, England Student Exchange Program; Utrecht University (The Netherlands) Student Exchange Program; and the Freeman Fellowship for Study at the Hague Academy of International Law, The Netherlands.

Intellectual Property Law Institute (I.P.L.I.)

The I.P.L.I. offers an exceptional and rich curriculum for law students and lawyers in such areas of intellectual property as patents, copyrights, trademarks, trade secrets, computers and related technology, communications and media, entertainment, technology transfer, trade regulation, and the arts.

Expenses and Financial Aid

➡ *full-time tuition & fees—resident, $7,698; nonresident, $15,828* ➡ *part-time tuition & fees—resident, $4,170; nonresident, $8,506* ➡ *estimated additional expenses—$15,020 (books, room & board, transportation, miscellaneous expenses)* ➡ *merit- & need-based scholarships available* ➡ *merit- & need-based minority scholarships available* ➡ *financial aid available* ➡ *FAFSA priority date—April 30*

Applicant Group for the 1998-1999 Academic Year

Wayne State University Law School
This grid includes only applicants who earned 120-180 LSAT scores under standard administrations.

LSAT Score	3.75 +		3.50 - 3.74		3.25 - 3.49		3.00 - 3.24		2.75 - 2.99		2.50 - 2.74		2.25 - 2.49		2.00 - 2.24		Below 2.00		No GPA		Total	
	Apps	Adm	Apps	Adm	Apps	Adm	Apps	Adm	Apps	Adm	Apps	Adm	Apps	Adm	Apps	Adm	Apps	Adm	Apps	Adm	Apps	Adm
175-180	0	0	0	0	0	0	0	0	0	0	0	0	0	0	0	0	0	0	0	0	0	0
170-174	3	3	1	1	1	1	1	1	1	1	0	0	1	1	0	0	0	0	2	1	10	9
165-169	3	3	2	2	4	4	8	8	5	5	0	0	0	0	0	0	0	0	1	0	23	22
160-164	15	15	17	17	19	19	16	15	11	10	6	6	4	1	1	0	1	0	0	0	90	83
155-159	5	5	35	34	54	54	39	36	22	16	18	7	5	0	1	0	1	0	2	2	182	154
150-154	8	8	41	41	50	45	58	53	36	21	25	4	2	0	4	0	1	0	6	5	231	177
145-149	9	8	22	11	39	12	58	18	42	6	34	3	16	1	4	0	3	0	3	0	230	59
140-144	2	0	11	0	23	1	28	1	20	1	20	0	20	0	3	0	6	0	5	0	138	3
135-139	0	0	6	0	10	0	11	0	15	0	19	0	9	0	10	0	2	0	1	0	83	0
130-134	0	0	0	0	2	0	2	0	3	0	5	0	4	0	2	0	0	0	5	0	23	0
125-129	1	0	0	0	0	0	0	0	1	0	2	0	4	0	1	0	1	0	1	0	11	0
120-124	0	0	0	0	0	0	0	0	0	0	0	0	0	0	1	0	0	0	0	0	1	0
Total	46	42	135	106	202	136	221	132	156	60	129	20	65	3	27	0	15	0	26	8	1022	507

Apps = Number of Applicants
Adm = Number Admitted
Reflects 98% of the total applicant pool.

West Virginia University College of Law

P.O. Box 6130
Morgantown, WV 26506-6130

E-Mail: lawaply@wvu.edu
URL: http://www.wvu.edu/~law
Phone: 304.293.5304

■ Introduction

The College of Law was established in 1878 and is the oldest professional school at West Virginia University. The university is located in Morgantown, West Virginia, a community of 50,000, and is easily accessible by interstate highways, commercial airlines, and bus services. The College of Law has been a member of the AALS since 1914 and was fully accredited by the ABA in 1923. The college has had a chapter of the Order of the Coif since 1925.

Since its founding in 1867, West Virginia University has become the center of graduate and professional education, research, and extension programs in West Virginia. The university's rural setting makes for an ideal learning environment for its 20,000 full-time students.

The College of Law has established itself as a national leader in legal issues relating to the development and production of energy resources, and annually publishes the *National Coal Issue* of the *West Virginia Law Review* and sponsors conferences and continuing legal education seminars on legal issues in mineral law.

West Virginia University provides a full range of both athletic and cultural facilities. The Personal Rapid Transit System (PRT) provides convenient, modern transportation among the university's three campuses.

■ Enrollment/Student Body

➡ *full-time 25th/75th percentile GPA—2.96/3.62*
➡ *full-time 25th/75th percentile LSAT—150/156*
➡ *423 total full-time*   ➡ *16 total part-time*
➡ *27 minority*   ➡ *207 women*

■ Faculty

➡ *25 full-time*   ➡ *25 part-time or adjunct*
➡ *16 women*   ➡ *2 African American*

■ Library and Physical Facilities

➡ *255,000 volumes & equivalents*   ➡ *LEXIS*
➡ *WESTLAW*   ➡ *CALI*   ➡ *4 full-time librarians*
➡ *library seats 296*

The three-floor library features open stacks, group study rooms, study carrels, a rare book room, labs for word processing and computer-assisted legal instruction, and terminals to access legal research databases and the campus-wide, online catalog. All students have access to e-mail and to the Internet, and student carrels and classrooms are wired for computer use. A Co-op Day Care Center is located at the Law Center.

■ Curriculum

➡ *93 credits required to graduate*
➡ *degrees available: J.D.; J.D./M.B.A.; J.D./M.P.A.*

The first-year curriculum is required. The second- and third-year programs offer a number of course options and possibilities for concentration. No summer programs are regularly scheduled. The college does accept a limited number of transfer students only after the first year. The college has long stressed advocacy and training in lawyerly skills. Each student is trained in counseling and interviewing, legal drafting, and negotiation, and completes the trial of a mock suit before a jury prior to graduation. The Appalachian Center for Law and Public Service and the Law Clinic offer opportunities to work for real clients under the supervision of professors and lawyers.

Students have the option of attending the College of Law on a part-time basis during the day, along with full-time students. There is not a separate nighttime track.

The academic assistance program offers students an opportunity to become paired with a member of our faculty during their entire law school experience.

■ Student Activities

Candidates for the *West Virginia Law Review* are selected on the basis of performance during their first year in law school and a writing competition.

An active Moot Court Program is conducted at the law school under the supervision of the Moot Court Board. Members competed in five interscholastic regional and national moot court competitions last year.

The Student Bar Association is the student government of the school.

The college hosts several other organizations representing the varied interests of students.

■ Opportunities for Minority Students

The opportunities available to minority students at the College of Law evolve from our institution's commitment to promote an academic environment comprised of student representation from all segments of society.

This commitment is furthered by the financial aid that is made available to our minority students. First of all, the Board of Trustees makes available full tuition and fees scholarships. Second, there is the W.E.B. Dubois Fellowship that provides full tuition, fees, and a yearly living stipend to qualified African American professional or graduate students. Third, the Mountain State Bar Association, an African American–founded professional association, provides available funds in the form of fellowships to African American students. Finally, the contributions from our alumni have contributed significantly to the total amount of money made available to minority students so they may finance their education.

Additional opportunities for minority students involve the academic support provided by our student-initiated Student/Faculty Academic Assistance Program and the social and professional support provided by our Black Law Students Association (BLSA).

Our Book Loan Program, which provides free textbooks and other materials, is a popular feature of BLSA's support to our students. It cuts down on expenditures that would ordinarily be between $200 and $300 a semester.

Our Bridging the Gap Program involves seminars on the LSAT; financial aid, career planning, and legal research and writing; mock law school classes, and opportunities to speak with minority students and faculty about issues and concerns.

■ Placement

The Meredith Career Services Center actively assists students and alumni in securing employment, including employment in nontraditional legal careers such as legal aid societies, business, insurance companies, and government agencies.

■ Admission

➽ *Baccalaureate degree from regionally accredited college or university required* ➽ *application deadline—March 1* ➽ *LSAT required* ➽ *application fee—$45*

No specific prelaw curriculum is required for admission. The college subscribes to the suggestions on prelaw study in this handbook, and stresses the value of college courses that require extensive analytic skills and writing assignments.

In addition, undergraduate grades and performance on the LSAT are carefully and objectively evaluated and compared against that of all other applicants. Applicants must arrange for the timely submission of at least three letters of recommendation from a college professor to the LSAC recommendation service. Preference is given to West Virginia residents. The College of Law receives many more applications for admission than it has been able to accommodate.

Applications are accepted beginning in September of each year for the class to be admitted in the following August. As soon as applicant files can be completed,

they will be notified of the final decision. Those accepted are required to make a deposit of $100 against tuition and fees within a designated period, but not before April 1.

■ Expenses and Financial Aid

➽ *full-time tuition & fees—residents, $5,296; nonresidents, $12,568* ➽ *estimated additional expenses for books & supplies—$800* ➽ *living allowance for 9 months—$9,130* ➽ *estimated budget: residents, $15,735; nonresidents, $23,007* ➽ *Free Application for Federal Student Aid (FAFSA) due by March 1* ➽ *scholarship application due by April 1*

Applicants for admission can seek financial assistance by contacting Joanna Hastings, Financial Aid Counselor, P.O. Box 6130, Morgantown, WV 26506-6130, phone: 304.293.5302, jhasting@wvu.edu.

Note: It is suggested that students apply for financial aid assistance before being accepted.

■ Housing

The University Housing Office (304.293.3621) provides information concerning university-owned housing, including dormitories and apartments. Off-campus privately owned housing information may be obtained by calling the main campus (304.293.5613). The university maintains 361 furnished and unfurnished apartments for graduate students, married students, faculty, and staff. There is usually a waiting list for apartments, so application should be made as early as possible. Listings for privately owned rentals change daily.

Admitted students are urged to visit Morgantown during the summer prior to registration to secure housing.

Applicant Group for the 1998-1999 Academic Year

West Virginia University College of Law
This grid includes only applicants who earned 120-180 LSAT scores under standard administrations.

LSAT Score	3.75 +		3.50 - 3.74		3.25 - 3.49		3.00 - 3.24		2.75 - 2.99		2.50 - 2.74		2.25 - 2.49		2.00 - 2.24		Below 2.00		No GPA		Total	
	Apps	Adm	Apps	Adm	Apps	Adm	Apps	Adm	Apps	Adm	Apps	Adm	Apps	Adm	Apps	Adm	Apps	Adm	Apps	Adm	Apps	Adm
175-180	0	0	0	0	0	0	0	0	0	0	0	0	0	0	0	0	0	0	0	0	0	0
170-174	0	0	0	0	0	0	0	0	0	0	0	0	0	0	0	0	0	0	0	0	0	0
165-169	1	1	1	1	4	4	1	1	1	1	0	0	0	0	0	0	0	0	1	0	9	8
160-164	7	6	4	4	6	6	5	4	3	3	0	0	1	0	0	0	0	0	1	1	27	24
155-159	11	9	10	9	8	7	16	14	14	12	9	7	4	3	2	0	0	0	0	0	74	61
150-154	20	19	17	13	21	17	34	23	25	15	13	3	3	2	2	1	1	0	2	1	138	94
145-149	10	9	14	6	23	10	22	6	26	5	19	1	7	0	2	0	3	0	4	1	130	38
140-144	5	2	4	1	7	0	21	2	20	2	7	0	9	0	7	0	0	0	5	2	85	9
135-139	2	0	1	0	1	0	3	1	9	1	6	0	4	0	1	0	0	0	3	1	30	3
130-134	0	0	1	0	1	0	1	0	2	0	3	0	0	0	0	0	0	0	3	1	11	1
125-129	0	0	0	0	0	0	0	0	0	0	0	0	0	0	0	0	1	0	0	0	1	0
120-124	0	0	0	0	0	0	0	0	0	0	0	0	0	0	0	0	0	0	1	0	1	0
Total	56	46	52	34	71	44	103	51	100	39	57	11	28	5	14	1	5	0	20	7	506	238

Apps = Number of Applicants
Adm = Number Admitted
Reflects 99% of the total applicant pool.

Western New England College School of Law

Office of Admissions
1215 Wilbraham Road
Springfield, MA 01119-2684

E-Mail: lawadmis@wnec.edu
URL: http://www.law.wnec.edu
Phone: 800.782.6665, 413.782.1406

■ Introduction

For more than three quarters of a century, Western New England College School of Law has been preparing men and women to enter the legal profession. We are fully accredited by the ABA and are a member of the AALS. Our 6,000 alumni live in almost all 50 states and several foreign countries and are judges, private practice attorneys, corporate lawyers, and armed services personnel. We offer both full- and part-time programs and are conveniently located 90 miles west of Boston and 150 miles north of New York City.

■ Enrollment/Student Body

➼ 1,017 applicants   ➼ 185 enrolled first-year class 1998
➼ full-time 25th/75th percentile GPA—2.78/3.36
➼ part-time 25th/75th percentile GPA—2.61/3.31
➼ full-time 25th/75th percentile LSAT—142/151
➼ part-time 25th/75th percentile LSAT—140/151
➼ 357 total full-time   ➼ 242 total part-time
➼ 19% students of color in first-year class
➼ 53% women in first-year class

Currently enrolled students come from 31 different states and Canada and from over 200 undergraduate institutions.

■ Faculty

➼ 60 total   ➼ 26 full-time (9 women)
➼ 34 adjunct (10 women, 1 minority)

Our faculty members all share a love of teaching and take pride in their ability to engage students in rigorous law study in a collaborative, not bitterly competitive, environment. They are productive scholars who are consistently praised by our students for their accessibility.

■ Library and Physical Facilities

➼ 351,000 volumes & equivalents   ➼ library normally open 103 hours/wk., extended hours during exams
➼ LEXIS   ➼ NEXIS   ➼ WESTLAW   ➼ MEDIS
➼ DIALOG   ➼ OCLC   ➼ 6 full-time library administrators
➼ library seats 400 patrons

We participate in the New England Law Library Consortium, so students have access to an additional 13 academic, one private, and three government law libraries.

The law school building is located on Western New England College's 185-acre campus in a residential section of Springfield. Ramps and elevators give students with disabilities access to all parts of the Law Center, and ample, on-campus, free parking is available to all students.

Springfield is a small city offering a wide array of recreational, social, and cultural attractions. The Pioneer Valley provides our students with a range of affordable housing options in a variety of settings. As the only law school in Western Massachusetts, Western New England College School of Law students receive accessibility to a host of internship and clinical opportunities throughout the region.

■ Curriculum

➼ Legal Education Assistance Program (LEAP) available for additional academic support   ➼ 88 units/credits required to graduate   ➼ 74 courses, including 5 clinics, available in 1998-99   ➼ J.D./M.R.P. (Master's in Regional Planning) combined-degree program with the University of Massachusetts at Amherst available; J.D./M.S.W. (Master's in Social Work) combined-degree program with Springfield College available   ➼ recent first-year class size approximately 65 students per section

All required courses, both day and evening, are taught by full-time, tenure-track faculty members. Some upper-level courses are taught through classroom discussions of judicial decisions and statutes. Others are taught through simulations in which students perform the roles of lawyers in life-like situations and through clinics where students represent actual clients.

Part-time day and part-time evening programs are also available. These programs take four years to complete, including summer sessions, or four and one-half years without summer study. Many evening students commute from Albany, Hartford, and other parts of Massachusetts.

While we do not offer specialization programs, faculty advisors assigned in the first year can assist in selecting elective courses that build upon your particular area of interest.

■ Clinical Programs

Criminal Law Clinic—Under direct faculty supervision, students are appointed as student assistant district attorneys in the Hampden County District Attorney's office. Students represent the Commonwealth in bail hearings, plea negotiations, pretrial motions, and trials.

Discrimination Law Clinic—Students represent complainants in cases brought before the Massachusetts Commission Against Discrimination. Students plan case strategy, conduct discovery, and where applicable, negotiate settlements and/or conduct trials before the Commission.

Legal Services Clinic—Through the office of Western Massachusetts Legal Services, Inc., which provides free civil legal services to low-income and elderly persons, students handle all phases of actual cases, including client interviews, legal research and factual development, and representation of clients in court and in administrative proceedings.

Consumer Protection Clinic—This clinical program provides an introduction to consumer complaint mediation procedures through fieldwork at the Consumer Action Center and weekly classroom meetings.

Disability Law Clinic—The Disability Law Clinic provides free legal representation to developmentally disabled clients who are residents of the Monson Developmental Center and Charles River Hospital/West. Students learn to deal with the legal issues, but also the practical and ethical issues, in the representation of handicapped persons.

Clinical Internship—To permit students to acquire substantive legal knowledge and skills in a practical situation, clinical internships allow students to work in the office of an attorney, judge, or magistrate.

■ Admission

➺ *B.A./B.S. required for admission*   ➺ *March 15 preferred deadline; rolling admission*   ➺ *LSAT, LSDAS required* ➺ *application fee—$45*

Every application is personally read by an admissions staff member or member of the Admissions Committee. Half-hour evaluative interviews are available to applicants. All facets of the application are carefully considered, including racial, gender, physical, language, educational, social, and economic obstacles overcome in the applicant's pursuit of higher education. We seek candidates with well-developed writing ability and analytical skills who will contribute to classroom discussions and the law school community.

■ Student Activities

The law school's *Law Review* is published by a student editorial board with faculty supervision. Students sit on faculty committees such as the Admissions Committee and the Academic Standards Committee, and two students attend regular faculty meetings. Student organizations include the Student Bar Association; the Multi-Cultural Law Students Association; the Women's Law Association; the Lesbian/Gay/Bisexual Alliance; the Christian Legal Society; and the Jewish Law Students Association. Other groups include the National Lawyer's Guild; the Environmental Law Coalition; the International Law Society; the Sports and Entertainment Law Society; the Criminal Law Society; the Federalist Society; Phi Alpha Delta; a chapter of the American Bar Association's Law Student Division; the newspaper *Lex Brevis*; and a yearbook.

Student teams also compete against other law schools in the National Moot Court, the ABA National Trial, the Jessup International Moot Court, the Vale Corporate Moot Court, and the Environmental Moot Court Competitions.

■ Expenses and Financial Aid

➺ *1998-99 tuition—full-time, $17,750; part-time, $13,312* ➺ *estimated additional first-year expenses—books, $585; fees, $644*   ➺ *In-house academic scholarships available, along with several endowed scholarships* ➺ *Free Application for Federal Student Aid (FAFSA) required*

Four to five full-tuition and many partial-tuition academic scholarships are granted by the Admissions Committee to applicants who demonstrate the most promise for a high level of achievement in their law studies.

■ Career Services

Individual attention to each student is of great importance at Western New England College School of Law, and counseling is an important function of the Office of Career Services. Students discuss potential career paths, employment application strategies, and review their résumés, cover letters, and other application materials with a professional counselor.

During the on-campus interview program, students interview with some of the most prestigious employers in Western Massachusetts and Connecticut. Students have additional opportunities throughout the academic year to interview with various employers.

Applicant Group for the 1998-1999 Academic Year

Western New England College School of Law
This grid includes only applicants who earned 120-180 LSAT scores under standard administrations.

LSAT Score	3.75 +		3.50 - 3.74		3.25 - 3.49		3.00 - 3.24		2.75 - 2.99		2.50 - 2.74		2.25 - 2.49		2.00 - 2.24		Below 2.00		No GPA		Total	
	Apps	Adm	Apps	Adm	Apps	Adm	Apps	Adm	Apps	Adm	Apps	Adm	Apps	Adm	Apps	Adm	Apps	Adm	Apps	Adm	Apps	Adm
175-180	0	0	0	0	0	0	0	0	0	0	0	0	0	0	0	0	0	0	0	0	0	0
170-174	0	0	0	0	0	0	0	0	0	0	0	0	0	0	1	1	0	0	0	0	1	1
165-169	0	0	0	0	0	0	0	0	1	1	1	1	1	1	0	0	0	0	1	1	4	4
160-164	2	2	2	1	2	1	5	5	6	6	0	0	1	1	0	0	0	0	0	0	18	16
155-159	5	4	12	12	13	12	16	15	18	17	14	14	6	5	4	2	1	1	3	3	92	85
150-154	3	3	8	8	30	30	23	23	42	40	28	20	19	17	13	7	4	1	7	3	177	152
145-149	2	2	22	22	39	35	49	45	48	41	58	46	29	17	18	5	5	0	6	5	276	218
140-144	7	5	13	11	30	26	47	33	55	34	50	23	29	9	16	0	1	0	8	2	256	143
135-139	1	1	11	7	6	3	17	6	33	5	22	3	22	1	12	0	1	0	5	2	130	28
130-134	0	0	1	0	0	0	6	1	11	0	10	0	7	0	4	0	4	0	3	0	46	1
125-129	1	0	1	0	2	0	1	1	1	0	1	0	0	0	2	0	0	0	0	0	9	1
120-124	0	0	0	0	0	0	0	0	0	0	0	0	3	0	0	0	0	0	1	0	4	0
Total	21	17	70	61	122	107	164	129	215	144	184	107	117	51	70	15	16	2	34	16	1013	649

Reflects 98% of the total applicant pool.

Western State University—College of Law

1111 North State College Boulevard
Fullerton, Orange County, CA 92831-3014

E-Mail: adm@wsulaw.edu
URL: http://www.wsulaw.edu
Phone: 714.738.1000 ext. 2600 or 800-WSU-4LAW

■ Introduction

Western State University College of Law, founded in 1966, is the oldest law school in Orange County, a southern California community known for its beautiful beaches, Mediterranean climate, and dynamic economy. The school's tradition of providing superior legal education spans four decades. Its alumni have distinguished themselves as jurists, lawmakers, district attorneys, public defenders, and civil practitioners.

Western State is a diverse community. The law school ranks second among California law schools in percentage of women faculty.

Western State's hands-on curriculum emphasizes the effective combination of legal theory and professional skills. The faculty tailors specific courses to assist students in bridging the gap between classroom learning and real-time practice. Students have the opportunity to apply their skills training in several externship programs. Externs spend 15-40 hours per week working directly with a supervising attorney or judge. These one-on-one apprenticeships give students a crucial insider's perspective into the law.

■ Enrollment/Student Body

➡ 590 applicants   ➡ 320 admitted first-year class 1998
➡ 173 enrolled first-year class 1998   ➡ full-time 25th/75th percentile GPA—2.45/3.17   ➡ part-time 25th/75th percentile GPA—2.49/3.13   ➡ full-time 25th/75th percentile LSAT—142/151   ➡ part-time 25th/75th percentile LSAT—142/151
➡ 231 total full-time   ➡ 501 total part-time
➡ 33% minority   ➡ 42% women
➡ 204 undergraduate schools represented

■ Faculty

➡ 64 total   ➡ 20 full-time   ➡ 44 part-time or adjunct
➡ 9 women   ➡ 6 minority

■ Library and Physical Facilities

➡ 149,000 volumes & equivalents   ➡ library hours: 7:00 A.M.-11:30 P.M. seven days a week   ➡ LEXIS
➡ NEXIS   ➡ WESTLAW   ➡ DIALOG   ➡ Internet
➡ 7 full-time librarians   ➡ library seats 340

Western State is situated in the heart of Fullerton's university district, giving students access to a wealth of research and recreational resources at four neighboring campuses. The main building houses classrooms, administrative offices, student study areas, the cafeteria, and a lounge. Across the library plaza stands the law library, a tri-level, state-of-the-art facility with a computer lab and network ports at virtually every seat. Nonglare lighting illuminates the entire building. The library collection boasts a solid and fast-growing collection covering all 50 states, with the full range of traditional printed, microform, CD-ROM, Internet, and online legal materials. In addition, the library supports the law school's commitment to skills training by supplying all legal interactive video programs from PLI and Harvard Interactive, and a strong skills collection of books and audiovisual materials. The electronic resources include legal software, hundreds of CD-ROM titles, CALI legal tutoring programs, Internet, and the online public access catalog—all instantly available on the campus network. Our librarians serve the research needs of the students by maintaining long hours and providing extensive reference services and training in legal bibliography, online research, software, and CD-ROM services.

■ Curriculum

➡ Academic Support Program   ➡ 88 units required to graduate
➡ 137 courses available   ➡ degree available: J.D.
➡ two 16-week semesters, an 8-week summer session
➡ full-time and part-time students admitted to start in fall and spring   ➡ range of first-year class size—16-65

Western State is committed to preparing graduates for rewarding careers as practicing attorneys. The successful practice of law requires a balance of three equally important elements: understanding the theories underlying the legal system, detailed knowledge of the rules of law, and proficiency in the fundamental professional skills necessary to help clients win cases. We teach all three. The curriculum is designed to help graduates make the transition from law student to lawyer swiftly and easily. By interweaving courtroom and law office scenarios into courses, we equip our graduates with the training necessary for a lifetime of legal practice in a constantly changing environment.

■ Special Programs

Professional Skills Curriculum—Skills training focuses on the techniques and strategies needed for client representation. Through our integrative curriculum, students acquire a solid grounding in analytical and theoretical knowledge as they master the techniques and acquire the insights essential to the successful practice of law. Western State's emphasis on professional skills creates an active, positive learning environment by making the study of law directly relevant to the student's life and personal experiences.

Judicial Trial/Judicial Appellate Externship—Students work closely with Superior and Municipal Court judges and with U.S. and California appellate judges. The externs research civil and criminal case laws and constitutional case law issues, write legal memoranda, and draft opinions. Students work closely with the judges and their staff attorneys. As externs they are privy to the judges' thinking and often are invited to offer their own perspectives.

Civil Practice Externship—Students work with public agencies, attorneys in general practice firms, and corporate law offices. Under the direct supervision of experienced attorneys, externs interview clients, research cases, and write briefs. By preparing for litigation that involves contracts, torts, property, constitutional law, and civil procedure, externs apply what they have learned in the classroom to the actual practice of civil law.

Public Defender/District Attorney Externship—Working with a deputy public defender or deputy district attorney, student externs write trial memoranda and trial motions and appear before judges in municipal and superior courts. Students also observe firsthand the workings of the crime lab and the coroner's office.

Journals—The *Western State University Law Review* offers students opportunities to showcase their abilities and to refine their research, writing, analytical, and editing skills.

Part-time Program—Both a part-time day and a part-time evening program and the option to apply for fall or spring admission are offered. Our full-time faculty teaches both day and evening courses, ensuring the same high quality of legal education for all students. Students normally complete the part-time program in four years. It is possible to complete the program in three and one-half years.

Public Service Program—Through Western State's voluntary public service program, many of our students choose to use their legal skills in service to underrepresented members of the community. They volunteer at government agencies, legal service organizations, charitable organizations, and private law firms that undertake *pro bono* cases. Each year the school honors students—and faculty members—who have provided outstanding public service.

■ Admission

➠ *Bachelor's degree required*   ➠ *application deadline—Aug. 1*
➠ *LSAT, LSDAS required*   ➠ *application fee—$50*

The Admission Committee bases its decisions on a variety of factors, including the student's LSAT scores, undergraduate GPA, and letters of recommendation. Because Western State strives for a diverse student body, the committee seeks to admit individuals who through their personal, intellectual, or professional background and experience will contribute to the diversity of the law school community, the legal profession, and society as a whole.

■ Student Activities

The Student Bar Association is the official law student organization. The SBA charters all student organizations, as well as arranging speakers' forums and social and community service activities. Students participate in a wide range of cocurricular activities and organizations through which they maintain a strong network of peer support.

■ Expenses and Financial Aid

➠ *full-time tuition & fees—$18,900*   ➠ *part-time—$12,600 for fall & spring semester; $625 per credit hr. for summer*
➠ *estimated additional expenses—$14,781 for books and supplies, room & board, transportation, & personal expenses*
➠ *scholarships available: merit & need-based*
➠ *minority scholarships available*   ➠ *financial aid available*

The Financial Assistance Office helps students obtain loans, grants, and scholarships from state, federal, institutional, and private funding services. Students receive scholarships for their first year of study based on their average LSAT score. The scholarships are renewable, provided the student maintains a cumulative GPA of 2.50. Limited need-based scholarships are also available.

■ Career Services

The Career Services Office provides assistance in obtaining law-related employment both during and after law school through law clerking and attorney listings, on-campus interviews, the Career Services Internet Web site, employment publications, and bar associations and consortium career fairs. Other resources available to students and graduates include an extensive career library, assistance in writing résumés, and computer terminals with Internet access.

Applicant Group for the 1998-1999 Academic Year

Western State University—College of Law
This grid includes only applicants who earned 120-180 LSAT scores under standard administrations.

LSAT Score	3.75 +		3.50 - 3.74		3.25 - 3.49		3.00 - 3.24		2.75 - 2.99		2.50 - 2.74		2.25 - 2.49		2.00 - 2.24		Below 2.00		No GPA		Total	
	Apps	Adm	Apps	Adm	Apps	Adm	Apps	Adm	Apps	Adm	Apps	Adm	Apps	Adm	Apps	Adm	Apps	Adm	Apps	Adm	Apps	Adm
170-180	0	0	0	0	0	0	0	0	0	0	0	0	0	0	0	0	0	0	0	0	0	0
165-169	0	0	0	0	0	0	3	2	1	1	0	0	0	0	0	0	0	0	0	0	4	3
160-164	2	2	0	0	5	5	2	2	1	1	0	0	2	2	0	0	0	0	0	0	12	12
155-159	2	2	2	2	7	7	6	6	9	9	7	7	3	3	0	0	0	0	0	0	36	36
150-154	3	2	6	6	6	6	14	13	12	12	14	13	11	11	6	5	1	1	0	0	73	69
145-149	2	2	1	1	11	11	18	16	17	15	20	15	20	19	13	10	1	0	1	1	104	90
140-144	2	2	6	4	16	13	22	14	22	11	35	24	18	14	16	5	1	0	1	0	139	87
Below 140	0	0	5	1	7	4	20	3	28	1	36	5	21	0	7	1	4	0	3	0	131	15
Total	11	10	20	14	52	46	85	56	90	50	112	64	75	49	42	21	7	1	5	1	499	312

Apps = Number of Applicants
Adm = Number Admitted

Whittier Law School

3333 Harbor Boulevard
Costa Mesa, CA 92626

E-Mail: info@law.whittier.edu
URL: http://www.law.whittier.edu
Phone: 714.444.4141 ext. 123

■ Introduction

Whittier College is a nationally recognized, independent college of arts and sciences founded in 1887 in Whittier, California. The Law School, now located in Orange County, was established in 1975.

The Whittier tradition of concern for students as individuals is reflected in admission practices, a close student-to-faculty ratio (approximately 20:1), small classes, and continuous student counseling and placement services. Affiliation with Whittier College ensures a continuing commitment to academic excellence and individual attention.

Now entering its third decade, Whittier Law School has established a permanent home in the city of Costa Mesa on a beautiful 15-acre campus with exceptional facilities, such as the largest academic law research library in the region. Nearly three times the size of the previous campus in Los Angeles, the Law School is comprised of four buildings totaling 130,000-square feet.

Whittier Law School is fully accredited by the ABA and is a member of the AALS.

■ Enrollment/Student Body

➡ *1,456 applicants*   ➡ *226 enrolled first-year class 1998*
➡ *full-time 25th/75th percentile GPA—2.68/3.24*
➡ *part-time 25th/75th percentile GPA—2.62/3.25*
➡ *full-time 25th/75th percentile LSAT—146/153*
➡ *part-time 25th/75th percentile LSAT—146/152*
➡ *392 total full-time*   ➡ *259 total part-time*
➡ *37% minority*   ➡ *48% women*
➡ *42 states & 2 foreign countries represented*
➡ *84 undergraduate schools represented*   ➡ *18% nonresident*

■ Faculty

➡ *62 total*   ➡ *27 full-time*   ➡ *35 part-time*
➡ *22 women*   ➡ *6 minority*

The full-time faculty is drawn from law schools throughout the country so that the school's perspective is a national one, preparing students to pursue legal careers anywhere in the United States.

Faculty members recognize that their teaching obligation includes considerable interaction with students. The new campus provides a noninstitutional atmosphere conducive to this interaction.

■ Library and Physical Facilities

➡ *310,000 volumes & equivalents*   ➡ *library hours:*
Mon.-Thurs., 8:00 A.M.-MIDNIGHT; Fri., 8:00 A.M.-10:00 P.M.;
Sat., 10:00 A.M.-8:00 P.M.; Sun., 10:00 A.M.-MIDNIGHT
➡ *LEXIS*   ➡ *NEXIS*   ➡ *WESTLAW*   ➡ *DIALOG*
➡ *8 professionals*   ➡ *library seats 386*

The library has a rapidly growing legal research collection and serves as a state and federal depository. The Student Computer Center, located in the Law School Library, is available to students free of charge. The center houses computer hardware and a variety of software to aid students with computer-assisted instruction and legal research.

The Law School also offers plentiful on-site parking.

■ Curriculum

➡ *J.D. degree available*   ➡ *semesters, start in Aug., Jan., & June*
➡ *range of first-year class size—70-90*

Typically, the J.D. is completed in three years of full-time study; for part-time (day and evening) students, four years, including two summer sessions, will be necessary.

First- and second-year part-time (day and evening) students generally attend classes three days a week. Standards for admission and retention are identical for all students, and the full-time faculty serve both the full-time and part-time programs.

Required courses total 40 of the 87 units needed to graduate. The remainder of the requirement is met from a wide variety of elective courses reflecting the diversity of careers and activities of modern lawyers.

■ Special Programs

Whittier Law School offers a variety of externships with trial and appellate judges and government agencies. Students perform lawyering tasks and apply their academic studies to real client cases, gaining valuable insights into the operation of legal institutions.

The externship program is coordinated by a full-time, tenured professor who assures that students receive significant legal experience in interviewing and counseling clients, negotiating, participating in alternative dispute resolutions, drafting documents, or litigating in administrative hearings and trials.

The Center for Children's Rights enrolls up to 25 students yearly who receive fellowships and summer stipends to prepare for careers in children's rights advocacy. In addition to the regular curriculum, special classes, symposia, and extern opportunities are offered.

■ Admission

➡ *Bachelor's degree required*   ➡ *application deadline—*
March 15 (fall admission), Nov. 1 (January admission)
➡ *rolling admission, early application preferred*
➡ *LSAT, LSDAS required*   ➡ *application fee—$50*
➡ *Summer Performance Program*

In rare instances, an applicant will be admitted as a special student without a baccalaureate degree upon showing an unusually high LSAT score, excellence in college work completed, a statement of personal factors indicating maturity, and capacity for legal studies and professional achievement.

Consistent with Whittier Law School's tradition of concern for students as individuals, no magic numbers are used to determine admission decisions. In addition to the objective criteria of the LSAT score and the undergraduate GPA, subjective factors such as undergraduate school, course of study, graduate work, social and economic background, and personal accomplishments are considered. Thus, objective criteria are balanced with subjective factors. Applicants are encouraged to discuss these factors in their written personal statements.

Summer Performance—Whittier permits a select group of applicants to be admitted based upon their performance during an eight-week, full-time Summer Performance Admission Program. Applicants are chosen from those individuals who have not demonstrated aptitude for the study of law according to the traditional criteria, but who the faculty believes should be given an opportunity to perform based on other factors. Successful completion of this summer work will result in regular admission for the fall semester.

■ Student Activities

The Law School's location in the center of one of America's busiest and most diverse legal communities affords many opportunities for law-related experiences as students pursue their legal education.

The *Whittier Law Review*, published by a board of student editors selected from among those with superior academic records in the Law School, is open to all students on the basis of a writing competition. The *Review* stresses the highest standards of legal scholarship.

Moot court competition develops skills in written and oral advocacy. Students who perform well are invited to the Moot Court Honors Board. Members compete in school, regional, state, and national competitions.

The Student Bar Association is an independent student organization with officers elected by fellow students. Its

activities include a speakers' program, publication of the student newspaper, various social functions, and participation in student-faculty committees for school governance.

Other student organizations represent the numerous and varied interests of Whittier law students.

■ Expenses and Financial Aid

➤ *tuition & fees—full-time, $21,030; part-time, $12,618*
➤ *estimated additional expenses—$14,698 (books & supplies, room & board, personal & transportation)*
➤ *scholarships available: need-based, merit-based, and diversity*
➤ *financial aid available; FAFSA required*

The Law School offers several alternatives for financial assistance, including loan programs, scholarships, and employment opportunities.

After notification of admission, applicants will receive detailed information and instructions on applying for financial aid.

■ Career Services

Whittier Law School provides assistance to students and alumni in obtaining law clerking, externship, and attorney positions. The Career Services Office offers its services and resources to students beginning their first year of study. In addition to individual assistance in résumé and cover letter preparation, career goal identification and career planning strategies, the office hosts on-campus interviews, matches students in an alumni mentor program, arranges panels and symposia on career-related topics, prepares a weekly student newsletter, maintains a comprehensive library of career resources and offers a mock interview program.

Applicant Group for the 1998-1999 Academic Year

Whittier Law School
This grid includes only applicants who earned 120-180 LSAT scores under standard administrations.

LSAT Score	GPA								
	3.75 +	3.50 - 3.74	3.25 - 3.49	3.00 - 3.24	2.75 - 2.99	2.50 - 2.74	2.25 - 2.49	2.00 - 2.24	Below 2.00
175-180									
170-174									
165-169									
160-164									
155-159									
150-154									
145-149									
140-144									
135-139									
130-134									
125-129									
120-124									

■ Very Likely   ▨ Possible   ☐ Unlikely

Widener University School of Law

P.O. Box 7474, Wilmington, DE 19803-0474
P.O. Box 69381, Harrisburg, PA 17106-9381

E-Mail: law.admissions@law.widener.edu
URL: http://www.widener.edu/law/law.html
Phone: 302.477.2162, 717.541.3903

■ Introduction

Widener University School of Law is unique among American law schools. Widener has two campuses—one in Wilmington, Delaware, the corporate and banking center of the United States, and the other in Harrisburg, Pennsylvania, the state capital and a major center of government and commerce. Each campus offers a comprehensive curriculum of basic and advanced courses complemented by one of the most extensive clinical and skills programs in the country. The Harrisburg campus features a unique admissions and academic cooperative program with the Pennsylvania State System of Higher Education.

Widener's first-year curriculum provides greater emphasis on individual work in legal writing and more concentrated study in courses essential to current developments in legal practice. The intensity of study throughout the curriculum is balanced by the strong commitment of faculty members to personal attention and individual counseling so that all students will be encouraged to fulfill their potential.

■ Enrollment/Student Body

➡ 1,926 applicants ➡ 1,253 admitted first-year class 1998 ➡ 478 enrolled first-year class 1998 ➡ full-time 25th/75th percentile GPA—2.65/3.26 ➡ part-time 25th/75th percentile GPA—2.53/3.24 ➡ full-time 25th/75th percentile LSAT—144/149 ➡ part-time 25th/75th percentile LSAT—145/153 ➡ 885 total full-time ➡ 625 total part-time ➡ 8% minority ➡ 45% women ➡ 37 states & foreign countries represented ➡ 306 undergraduate schools represented

■ Faculty

➡ 162 total ➡ 78 full-time ➡ 84 part-time or adjunct ➡ 59 women ➡ 6 minority

Our full-time faculty (59 percent male, 41 percent female) represents the broadest possible range of interests, expertise, and accomplishments.

■ Library and Physical Facilities

➡ 572,000 volumes & equivalents ➡ LEXIS ➡ NEXIS ➡ WESTLAW ➡ DIALOG ➡ LEGALTRAC ➡ INFOTRAC ➡ Internet ➡ PRO QUEST ➡ CIS CONGRESSIONAL COMPASS ➡ 15 full-time librarians

The attractive 40-acre Wilmington campus is located in the heart of the beautiful Brandywine River Valley. A major construction project is underway that will result in a state-of-the-art moot courtroom, new classrooms, attractive space for the legal clinics, and a completely renovated and modernized legal information center. A large number of supervised externships permit students to work as neophyte lawyers in nonprofit corporations and with state and county government agencies. Students wishing to pursue careers as prosecutors can enroll in the Prosecutors Extern Program. The scenic 21-acre Harrisburg campus is located

in four modern buildings along the foothills of the Blue Ridge Mountains.

The combined libraries house one of the most significant legal collections in the region and incorporate the latest in legal information technologies. More than 100 high-speed computers are available to students throughout the law school and represent our commitment to keep pace with advanced technologies to improve the quality of information access.

■ Curriculum

➡ Academic Support Program ➡ 87 credits required to graduate ➡ 229 courses available ➡ degrees available: J.D.; J.D./M.B.A.; J.D./Psy.D.; LL.M.; M.J.; D.L.; S.J.D. ➡ range of first-year class size—25-110 ➡ summer school ➡ day and evening programs

To meet the needs of today's law students, the law school will offer a limited number of seats in a part-time day program. Both campuses provide a full range of classes for day and evening students. The first-year core curriculum is the foundation for second- and third-year electives that meet students' personal needs.

■ Special Programs and Institutes

Widener is a leader in developing a coordinated lawyering skills program. The program includes clinical practice, externship placement, and comprehensive simulations.

Clinics are designed to permit students to actually represent clients under the supervision of the clinic director before courts, administrative boards, and the state legislature. Widener operates an Environmental Law Clinic and Criminal Defense and Juvenile Justice Clinics. Indigent persons with family law cases are also served by the PA and DE Civil and Domestic Violence Clinics.

An extensive judicial externship program, under the general supervision of former judges, places students with state and federal courts at both the trial and appellate levels in DC, DE, MD, NJ, PA, and VA.

The Trial Advocacy Institute conducts a seven-day Intensive Trial Advocacy Program (ITAP), supervised by outstanding local trial lawyers and judges. A semester-long course is also available. Appellate and pre-trial practice, advanced trial skills, and alternative dispute resolution simulations complement the basic level lawyering skills courses offered at Widener.

An extensive moot court program that prepares students to compete in regional and national interschool competitions exists on both campuses. Moot court teams from Widener reached the ABA National Appellate Advocacy final round in past academic years. In addition, Widener's Moot Court Team won the 22nd Annual Irving R. Kaufman Memorial Securities Law Moot Court Competition and also won Best Oralist Award at Fordham University.

The law school's Health Law Institute provides research, policy analysis, and specialty education.

The graduate programs at the law school grant LL.M. degrees in Corporate Law and Finance and in Health Law. A joint J.D./M.B.A. degree is offered in cooperation with the Widener School of Business Administration. The J.D./Psy.D. program is offered in cooperation with the Widener University Institute for Graduate Clinical Psychology and requires six years of study.

The M.J. (Master of Juriprudence) and the D.L. (Doctor of Laws) are designed for health care and other professionals who desire to broaden their understanding of the legal and policy health care environment. The S.J.D. (Doctor of Juridical Science) is designed for lawyers who hold the LL.M. and have a strong scholarly interest in health care law and policy.

■ International Law Programs

Widener students have the opportunity to study international and comparative law while living abroad. The Geneva International Law Institute, held at Webster University, provides a range of courses including International Trade Law. The Nairobi International Law Institute offers courses in International Environmental Law and other areas. The Sydney International Law Institute at Macquarie University offers courses in Comparative Constitutional Law, International Environmental Law, and other disciplines.

■ Student Activities

Selected Delaware students publish the *Delaware Journal of Corporate Law* and *The Widener Law Symposium Journal*. Selected Harrisburg students publish the *Widener Journal of Public Law*.

Student organizations provides opportunities for intra-scholastic and interscholastic competitions, public service, and association with others who share the same interests.

■ Admission

➡ *baccalaureate degree required* ➡ *application deadline—May 15* ➡ *rolling admission* ➡ *LSAT, LSDAS required* ➡ *application fee—$60*

While there are no fixed admission criteria, great weight is given to the applicant's LSAT score and undergraduate grade-point average. The Admissions Committee carefully considers an applicant's personal statement. Graduate

degrees, writing samples, extracurricular activities, and community and professional service may enhance the application. The law school encourages those with diverse backgrounds to apply.

Each summer, Widener conducts the Trial Admission Program for a small number of carefully selected applicants who show potential for success in law school despite a relatively low score on the LSAT or a lower undergraduate grade-point average. TAP is a conditional admittance program. TAP participation is not considered admission to the law school. Rather, participants are enrolled in a six-week summer program designed to assess their ability to succeed in law school. Participants who successfully complete the program are offered admission to the fall entering class.

Interested candidates are encouraged to visit either campus of the law school.

■ Expenses and Financial Aid

➡ *tuition & fees—full-time, $18,550; part-time, $13,930* ➡ *estimated additional expenses—$11,970 (living expenses & books)* ➡ *Widener Achievement Scholarships available for qualified majority and minority applicants* ➡ *Loan Repayment Assistance Program available to selected graduates pursuing a career in public service* ➡ *financial aid available; FAFSA required for need analysis* ➡ *need-based loans and grants available to students who demonstrate exceptional financial need* ➡ *on-campus housing available in Delaware* ➡ *safe and affordable housing available adjacent to campus in both locations*

■ Career Development

The Career Development Office is strongly committed to helping students obtain the positions that best suit their individual needs and ambitions.

Widener's placement statistics evidence its success in assisting graduates in finding a niche in the contemporary job market. Widener alumni have become judges in DE, NJ, and PA; members of the legislature; partners in major regional law firms; hospital administrators; legal educators; and broadcast journalists.

Admission Profile Not Available

Willamette University College of Law

Truman Wesley Collins Legal Center
900 State Street
Salem, OR 97301

E-Mail: law-admission@willamette.edu
URL: http://www.willamette.edu/wucl/
Phone: 503.370.6282

■ Introduction

In 1883, Willamette University established the first law school in the Pacific Northwest, Willamette University College of Law. Today, it remains one of the smallest and most intellectually intimate law schools in the West. In its 115-year history, more than 4,600 alumni have benefited from a program of legal education that is traditional in content and approach.

Willamette University is located in Salem, Oregon's capital city, 45 minutes from metropolitan Portland and four hours south of Seattle, Washington. The peaceful 61-acre campus is situated adjacent to the state capitol and courts. A city of 125,000, Salem is "small town" in feel. It is bordered by pastures, farmland, and vineyards. The Cascade Mountains and Pacific Ocean are about a one-hour drive.

The College of Law has long been accredited by the ABA and is a member of the Association of American Law Schools.

■ Enrollment/Student Body

➡ *full-time 25th/75th percentile GPA—2.78/3.33*
➡ *full-time 25th/75th percentile LSAT—150/157*

Students are drawn to Willamette principally from the West. Twenty-three states and 69 colleges were represented in the entering class. The average age of the entering class is 26. About 15 percent of the class is 30 years of age or older.

■ Faculty

Praised for their professional experience and commitment to teaching, Willamette's faculty includes four recent Fulbright Scholars whose research brought them to Australia, Bulgaria, India, and Namibia; the former vice president and general counsel for one of the nation's largest hi-tech companies; the "Thomas B. Stoel Professor of Law" endowed chair; and the former chief justice and a former associate justice of the Oregon State Supreme Court.

■ Library and Physical Facilities

➡ *280,076 volumes & equivalents* ➡ *library hours: 24-hour access to library* ➡ *LEXIS* ➡ *NEXIS* ➡ *WESTLAW* ➡ *DIALOG* ➡ *Internet* ➡ *CALI* ➡ *6 full-time librarians, 2 half-time* ➡ *library seats 500*

The 61-acre campus of Willamette University, noted for its wide lawns, meandering mill stream, and traditional brick architecture, is among the most beautiful in the Pacific Northwest. The award-winning Truman Wesley Collins Legal Center is a technologically advanced and student-oriented facility. It houses the courtroom, classrooms, offices, and the spacious J.W. Long Library, the only 24-hour law library in the Pacific Northwest. The Long Library offers special collections in public international law, tax law, and labor law. It is also a selective federal government document depository. Also available is the Willamette University

Mark O. Hatfield Library and within walking distance, the resources of Oregon's judicial, legislative, and executive offices.

■ Admission

➡ *B.A. required for admission* ➡ *application deadline— April 1 (preferred)* ➡ *LSAT, LSDAS required* ➡ *application fee—$50*

The Committee on Admission is particularly interested in applicants who seek a smaller, more intimate community for their legal education and who appreciate the importance of both competition and collaboration in the learning environment.

■ Curriculum

➡ *Academic Support Program* ➡ *88 units/credits required to graduate* ➡ *100 courses available* ➡ *degrees available: J.D.; J.D./M.M.* ➡ *semesters, start in Aug.* ➡ *range of first-year class size—30-120*

Though one of the smallest law schools in the West, Willamette's curriculum is unusually comprehensive. Sample practice interest areas include corporate and commercial law, criminal law, environmental/natural resources law, estate planning, individual rights (family law, immigration, civil rights, torts), international law, labor and employment law, litigation and dispute resolution, real estate development, tax law, government practice.

■ Law and Government

A number of opportunities at Willamette University College of Law reflect its unique location in Salem, the nerve center of state, county, and municipal government.

An extensive curriculum combining learning with practical experience in a variety of settings permits the study of the public sector from many perspectives, and to observe and act as advocate before the state legislature, the courts, and a wide range of government agencies.

■ Joint-Degree Program

The nation's only joint-degree program accredited for law, business, and government, this opportunity leads to the simultaneous awarding of the Doctor of Jurisprudence (J.D.) and Master of Management (M.M.) degrees in four years rather than the usual five. Admission to this program is selective and candidates must make separate applications to the Atkinson School and to the College of Law. The Atkinson School is accredited by the American Assembly of Collegiate Schools of Business (AACSB) and the National Association of Schools of Public Affairs and Administration (NASPAA).

■ Center for Dispute Resolution

The Center for Dispute Resolution embodies Willamette's long-standing recognition of the need for legal training in an array of dispute resolution methods, ranging from negotiation, mediation and arbitration, to traditional litigation. The

Center serves the legal community and the public through work with the Oregon Department of Justice, local school districts, the Marion County Family court, and other agencies. Law students may elect a certificate in dispute resolution as a part of the J.D. program.

■ International Programs

Since 1984, Willamette has lead the China Program, conducted at the East China Institute of Politics and Law in Shanghai. Willamette law students, with ABA approval and on an individual basis, may elect to spend a semester studying law in Quinto, Ecuador at the Pontifical Catholic University of Ecuador.

The College of Law, in addition to *Willamette Law Review*, also publishes the *Willamette Journal of International Law and Dispute Resolution*.

■ Ethnic Student Programs

Willamette encourages applications from students interested in building a diverse community of attorneys to help meet the future needs of our region. Trustee scholarships are available to those demonstrating academic success and leadership in their college or community.

The Oregon State Bar Affirmative Action Program provides ethnic law students with opportunities for support and professional development. For more information, contact the Office of Admission or the Oregon State Bar, 503.620.0222.

■ Expenses, Financial Aid, and Scholarships

Willamette's reputation as one of the best educational values in the West is well-deserved. Its facilities are among the finest and its tuition ranks among the lowest of any private law school on the West Coast. Trustee scholarships are awarded at admission to a wide-range of first-year students who demonstrate a combination of strong academic achievement, outstanding professional promise, and a potential to make a noteworthy contribution to the character of the Willamette community. No separate application for scholarship is required. Scholarships are renewed for the remaining two years so long as the student remains in good academic standing (2.00/4.00 scale).

In addition to scholarships, the first-year class also receives assistance in the form of student loans. Federal and private loans are administered through the Willamette University Office of Financial Aid. Students are eligible for work-study positions in the second and third year. To contact the Office of Financial Aid, call 503.370.6273.

■ Housing

Housing options in Salem and in the neighboring community of Keizer are many and range from older historic homes to modern apartment complexes.

University-owned apartments, one block from the College of Law, are also open to single law students. For more information, call the Office of Residential Life, 503.370.6212.

■ Career Services

Willamette graduates emerge in positions of influence, not only in private practice and in government, but throughout the professions. To meet the varied goals of our law students, the Office of Career Services oversees a busy on-campus interviewing program and provides a comprehensive program which trains and supports students through the clerkship and job-seeking process. To contact Career Services, call 503.370.6057.

Admission Profile Not Available

College of William and Mary School of Law

Law Admission
P.O. Box 8795
Williamsburg, VA 23187-8795

E-Mail: lawadm@facstaff.wm.edu
URL: http://www.wm.edu/law
Phone: 757.221.3785, Fax: 757.221.3261

■ Introduction

The College of William and Mary School of Law is located in historic Williamsburg in the tidewater area of Virginia, within easy reach of the metropolitan areas of Norfolk, Richmond, and Washington, DC. A small, selective public law school, William and Mary offers a nationally recognized legal education program. Its origin dates from 1779, when George Wythe was appointed professor of law, making the College of William and Mary America's first educational institution to offer instruction in law. It is accredited by the ABA, is a member of the AALS, is registered by the New York State Department of Education, and has a chapter of the Order of the Coif.

■ Enrollment/Student Body

➡ *2,176 applicants* ➡ *732 admitted first-year class 1998*
➡ *175 enrolled first-year class 1998* ➡ *full-time 25th/75th percentile GPA—3.03/3.53* ➡ *full-time 25th/75th percentile LSAT—159/164* ➡ *533 total full-time* ➡ *21% minority*
➡ *45% women* ➡ *40 states, DC, & foreign countries represented* ➡ *220 undergraduate schools represented*

■ Faculty

➡ *66 total* ➡ *27 full-time* ➡ *39 part-time or adjunct*
➡ *8 women* ➡ *3 minority*

■ Library and Physical Facilities

➡ *350,000 volumes & equivalents*
➡ *library hours: 6:00 A.M.-1:30 A.M. daily*
➡ *LEXIS* ➡ *NEXIS* ➡ *WESTLAW*
➡ *DIALOG* ➡ *Virginia Legislative Service*
➡ *7 full-time librarians* ➡ *library seats 446*
➡ *student ID cards provide access 19 hours/day*

The law school's modern facility is located adjacent to the National Center for State Courts. The law school houses Courtroom 21, the world's most technologically advanced courtroom. The university's new apartment complex for graduate students is located adjacent to the law school. The law library contains a comprehensive collection of over 350,000 volumes and several legal and nonlegal computer-generated databases, as well as other CD-ROM information sources. The library houses two computer labs with 32 personal computers. Additional PCs are available in small study rooms, and students may connect to the Internet with their own notebooks from other library locations. Law students also have access to the other university libraries.

■ Curriculum

➡ *Academic Support Program* ➡ *90 credits required to graduate* ➡ *127 courses available*
➡ *degrees available: J.D.; J.D./M.B.A.; J.D./M.P.P.; J.D./M.A. (American Studies); LL.M.*
➡ *semesters, start in Aug. & Jan.*

■ Special Programs

Successful completion of 90 semester credit hours of law studies and 90 weeks of residence is required. Required first-year courses include studies in constitutional law, contracts, torts, civil procedure, property, criminal law, legal skills, and statutory law. Prior to graduation, students must take a second year of legal skills, which includes professional ethics. Through simulated law firms, students in the Legal Skills Program experience and refine many lawyering skills such as interviewing, negotiation, legal briefing, and trial techniques. The school's Legal Skills Program was the first to be awarded the American Bar Association's Gambrell Award for excellence in professional training. A fully accredited summer session is offered at the University of Madrid in Spain. The law school also offers an LL.M. in the American Legal System for foreign attorneys. The law school provides a wide variety of externships, including the Legal Aid Clinic and the Environmental Practice, Employee Relations, Attorney General Practice, and the Virginia Court of Appeals Externships. In addition, second- and third-year students are encouraged to work in a variety of legal settings, such as private firms and public law offices and legal clinics. The curriculum is enriched by the Institute of Bill of Rights Law, a privately funded organization. The Institute's central focus is scholarship and education on freedom of speech and of the press, with interests also in legal history, legal writing, and professional responsibility.

■ Admission

➡ *Bachelor's degree from accredited college or university*
➡ *application deadline—March 1*
➡ *LSAT, LSDAS required* ➡ *application fee—$40*

The William and Mary School of Law is committed to providing opportunities for the study of law and entry into the legal profession to qualified students, and students who, because of socio or economic factors, may have been denied access to advantageous educational experiences. This commitment includes a special concern for determining the potential of these applicants through the admission process and special recruitment efforts. Applicants must take the LSAT and complete their college degree prior to enrolling in the law school. Transcript evaluation by LSDAS is required. Two written recommendations are required, one of which should be from a college professor or dean. Applications, which will be processed upon completion of three years of academic work, are available the September preceding admission. Personal interviews are not required; however, they are granted upon request. Group meetings to answer general questions, introduce the School of Law facilities and curriculum, and discuss admission procedures are offered several times during the winter months. Interested persons should contact the Office of Admission to reserve a seat. February 1 is the deadline for completing the registration process with LSDAS. Admission to the College of William and Mary School of Law is offered to those applicants who, in the opinion of the faculty admission committee, will make the most significant contribution to society as members of the legal profession. Factors such as general academic ability based on undergraduate work, capacity for the study of law based on the LSAT, work experience, and other personal qualities are considered.

■ Student Activities

William and Mary law students may participate in over 30 student organizations and writing experiences. Our student-managed law reviews and journals include: *William and Mary Bill of Rights Journal, William and Mary Environmental Law and Policy Review, William and Mary Journal of Women and the Law,* and the *William and Mary Law Review.* William and Mary students' diverse interests are illustrated by the following example list of student organizations: Law Students Involved in the Community, Public Service Fund, Student Legal Services, Asian Law Students Association, Black Law Students Association, Lesbian and Gay Law Association, Christian Law Fellowship, Jewish Law Students' Association, Federalist Society, Marshall-Wythe Democrats, Republican Graduate/Professional Students, the Phi Delta Phi and Phi Alpha Delta Legal Fraternities, and International Law Society. The law school curriculum is additionally enhanced by the extracurricular activities such as the National Trial Team and the Moot Court Program. Both programs involve students in intraschool, interschool, and national competitions. William and Mary moot court teams are extremely competitive on all levels. Our students have often placed and won

Best Brief and Best Oral Argument at the Annual National Moot Court Competition, sponsored by the Association of the Bar of the City of New York, the profession's oldest and most prestigious moot court competition.

■ Expenses and Financial Aid

➡ *full-time tuition & fees—resident, $8,494; nonresident, $17,940* ➡ *estimated additional expenses—living allowance, $11,830; books, $1,000* ➡ *merit- and need-based scholarships available* ➡ *financial aid available; FAFSA due Feb. 15*

■ Career Services

Employers from 26 states and the District of Columbia conducted on-campus interviews during 1997. The Career Services office posted job notices from over 1,600 additional nonvisiting employers from 48 states, the District of Columbia, and several foreign countries. William and Mary students have the opportunity to participate in 15 off-campus job fairs with a national employer base, including specialized programs for intellectual property law, public interest and government positions, and small regional firms. The law school offers a variety of funding programs to assist students working in low-paying or nonpaying public-service positions during the summer. The class of 1997 reported employment in virtually all areas of the country. Approximately 32 percent remained in Virginia, the other 68 percent accepted positions in 24 states, the District of Columbia, and three foreign countries.

Applicant Group for the 1998-1999 Academic Year

College of William and Mary School of Law
This grid includes only applicants who earned 120-180 LSAT scores under standard administrations.

LSAT Score	GPA																				
	3.75 +		3.50 - 3.74		3.25 - 3.49		3.00 - 3.24		2.75 - 2.99		2.50 - 2.74		2.25 - 2.49		2.00 - 2.24		Below 2.00		No GPA		Total	
	Apps	Adm	Apps	Adm	Apps	Adm	Apps	Adm	Apps	Adm	Apps	Adm	Apps	Adm	Apps	Adm	Apps	Adm	Apps	Adm	Apps	Adm
175-180	0	0	2	2	1	1	1	1	3	2	0	0	0	0	0	0	0	0	0	0	7	6
170-174	6	6	10	9	9	9	8	8	2	2	2	2	2	1	0	0	0	0	0	0	39	37
165-169	26	26	41	41	47	47	37	35	25	23	17	15	8	7	0	0	1	0	2	2	204	196
160-164	65	57	116	101	143	106	98	47	55	24	22	5	9	2	8	2	0	0	2	2	518	346
155-159	62	24	102	25	135	22	117	7	61	7	37	3	13	2	5	0	0	0	5	4	537	94
150-154	28	7	73	9	103	6	88	13	57	2	23	1	8	0	7	0	0	0	12	0	399	38
145-149	10	2	32	5	49	2	48	3	38	1	29	1	16	0	7	0	1	0	5	0	235	14
140-144	8	0	18	0	16	0	24	0	22	0	20	0	11	0	5	0	1	0	3	0	128	0
135-139	2	0	6	0	9	0	11	0	10	0	8	0	6	0	3	0	3	0	7	0	65	0
130-134	0	0	1	0	1	0	2	0	2	0	2	0	4	0	2	0	0	0	0	0	14	0
125-129	0	0	0	0	0	0	1	0	0	0	0	0	1	0	0	0	0	0	0	0	2	0
120-124	0	0	0	0	0	0	0	0	0	0	0	0	0	0	0	0	0	0	0	0	0	0
Total	207	122	401	192	513	193	435	114	275	61	160	27	78	12	37	2	6	0	36	8	2148	731

Apps = Number of Applicants
Adm = Number Admitted
Reflects 99% of the total applicant pool.

William Mitchell College of Law

Office of Admissions
875 Summit Avenue
St. Paul, MN 55105

E-Mail: admissions@wmitchell.edu
URL: http://www.wmitchell.edu
Phone: 651.290.6476; toll-free: 888.WMCL.LAW

■ Introduction

William Mitchell College of Law provides practical and theoretical legal skills training in addition to a strong traditional academic curriculum. It is the only program in the upper Midwest that offers students the flexibility to work full- or part-time while pursuing a law degree either in the day or evening. We also offer a full-time program. Among the college's 6,500 alumni/ae are these distinguished members of the judiciary: Warren E. Burger, '31, former Chief Justice of the United States; Douglas K. Amdahl, '51, retired Chief Justice of the Minnesota Supreme Court; Peter Popovich, '47, former Chief Justice of the Minnesota Supreme Court; Rosalie Wahl, '67, recently-retired justice on the Minnesota Supreme Court; and Esther Tomljanovich, '55, a justice on the Minnesota Supreme Court.

The college is accredited by the ABA, is a member of the Association of American Law Schools, and is approved by the U.S. Veterans Administration.

■ Enrollment/Student Body

➡ *290 enrolled first-year class 1998*   ➡ *full-time 25th/75th percentile GPA—2.90/3.44*   ➡ *part-time 25th/75th percentile GPA—2.71/3.45*   ➡ *full-time 25th/75th percentile LSAT—147/155*   ➡ *part-time 25th/75th percentile LSAT—148/156*   ➡ *471 total full-time*   ➡ *550 total part-time*   ➡ *10.8% minority*   ➡ *48% women*

William Mitchell is committed to correcting the historical problem of too few minority persons in the legal profession. We work to facilitate the admission of minority students and have minority-oriented organizations, curriculum, academic, and financial support.

■ Faculty

➡ *33 full-time faculty*   ➡ *100 part-time or adjunct*

The excellent full-time and part-time faculty bring extensive practice experience to the classroom. The faculty's expertise is particularly valuable in areas of instruction on the practical application of law through its legal writing and trial practice skills training.

■ Library and Physical Facilities

➡ *286,000 volumes & equivalents*   ➡ *LEXIS*   ➡ *WESTLAW*   ➡ *9 full-time librarians*

Our campus, located in St. Paul, Minnesota, provides space for high-tech classrooms, seminar rooms, moot courtrooms, the Law Clinic, library and study areas, a student lounge, and offices for student organizations. Students also have access to materials from other law libraries in the Twin Cities and, through the MINITEX interlibrary loan network, to libraries throughout the United States and Canada. Students are trained to use online computer terminals for legal research.

■ Curriculum

➡ *Academic Support Program*
➡ *86 credits required to graduate*

William Mitchell offers 3-, 3 1/2-, and 4-year programs of morning, afternoon, and evening classes leading to a J.D. degree.

Students in the full-time program take 12 to 15 hours of classroom instruction per week over a three-year period. Students in the four-year, part-time program take a maximum of 11 hours of classroom instruction per week over a period of four years, allowing them to work up to full time while attending school. Full-time faculty teach in both the day and evening. All students must complete their degree requirements within six academic years of their original matriculation.

The college is not committed to any single system or method of instruction. The case method involves the study and analysis of selected cases, as well as classroom discussion of the rules of law established or illustrated by the cases. The problem method, seminars, written assignments, and simulated exercises are employed in certain courses. The use of videotapes and computers adds another learning dimension.

The curriculum has a broad national focus, and numerous elective courses enable advanced students to specialize.

■ Special Programs

The William Mitchell Law Clinic produces graduates who are ready to immediately begin to practice law. Since its beginning in 1972, the Law Clinic has become a nationally recognized leader in trial advocacy teaching methods and clinical education. In 1981, the college received the prestigious Emil Gumpert Award for excellence in the teaching of trial advocacy. Students are eligible to participate in any of a broad range of clinical courses. The clinics are taught by full-time professors and supervisory attorneys. Students can also participate in Legal Practicum, a simulated law office experience where student "law firms" handle cases ranging from criminal to tort personal injury matters.

The Legal Writing Program has been singled out for praise by the American Bar Association and the Association of American Law Schools as an excellent legal writing program. The legal writing text written by William Mitchell faculty members has been adopted by many law schools throughout the country. One of the strengths of the program is the 13 to 1 student-faculty ratio.

The Child Care Center meets the needs of our students who must have child care available at more flexible times than traditional child care facilities. The center is on campus.

■ Admission

➥ *Bachelor's degree required for admission*
➥ *application deadline—July 1* ➥ *LSAT required*
➥ *application fee—$45*

Admission decisions are based upon academic factors such as the applicant's LSAT score and undergraduate GPA, as well as nonacademic factors such as work experience, interpersonal skills, motivation, extracurricular activities/community service, and overcoming disadvantage. The college does not require any particular area of undergraduate study, but does prefer applicants with strong written communication and analytical skills. William Mitchell College of Law admits students of either sex and of any race, color, religion, national or ethnic origin, and sexual orientation.

■ Expenses and Financial Aid

➥ *tuition & fees—four-year program, $12,510; three-year program, $17,230* ➥ *estimated additional expenses— books, $500 per year* ➥ *need-based scholarships available* ➥ *financial aid available—federal Stafford loans (subsidized and unsubsidized), federal Perkins loans, Law Access loans, SELF loans, and other alternative loans*

Over one-third of the entering class will receive significant renewable merit-based scholarship assistance. The scholarships are awarded at the time of acceptance.

■ Housing

The college maintains no dormitories or housing facilities, but the college's location in an urban residential area assures students of the availability of private apartment housing. A monthly *Housing Bulletin* is published by the Student Service Office.

■ Career Services

William Mitchell graduates are highly employable. The college attracts a special kind of student: motivated, industrious, mature, and serious about a legal education. Many William Mitchell students hold full- or part-time jobs while in school and have valuable work experience to offer the employer. Also, because the college combines practical skills with legal theory, students have much to offer the employer. William Mitchell provides a complete career services office with a full-time Assistant Dean and staff, on-campus interviews, a computerized résumé search service, career counseling, programs, publications, and job postings.

According to recent surveys of graduates, 93 percent of those responding were employed within one year after graduation; 40.2 percent of those were in private practice; 28.2 percent were in business and corporations; 28.2 percent were in government, including judicial clerkships; and the rest were in graduate school, teaching, or the military.

Applicant Group for the 1998-1999 Academic Year

William Mitchell College of Law
This grid includes only applicants who earned 120-180 LSAT scores under standard administrations.

LSAT Score	3.75 +		3.50 - 3.74		3.25 - 3.49		3.00 - 3.24		2.75 - 2.99		2.50 - 2.74		2.25 - 2.49		2.00 - 2.24		Below 2.00		No GPA		Total	
	Apps	Adm	Apps	Adm	Apps	Adm	Apps	Adm	Apps	Adm	Apps	Adm	Apps	Adm	Apps	Adm	Apps	Adm	Apps	Adm	Apps	Adm
175-180	0	0	0	0	0	0	0	0	0	0	0	0	0	0	0	0	0	0	0	0	0	0
170-174	0	0	1	1	0	0	0	0	1	1	0	0	0	0	0	0	0	0	0	0	2	2
165-169	2	2	3	3	4	4	3	3	0	0	0	0	0	0	0	0	0	0	1	1	13	13
160-164	7	7	10	10	12	12	13	13	11	10	7	6	1	1	1	1	0	0	2	2	64	62
155-159	11	11	31	31	31	31	37	37	24	24	15	15	9	9	1	1	2	2	4	4	165	165
150-154	14	14	31	31	41	41	45	44	37	35	29	29	10	10	10	4	1	1	2	2	220	211
145-149	11	11	16	15	43	35	47	32	46	27	37	18	19	9	6	2	2	0	4	4	231	153
140-144	3	2	10	7	16	11	29	12	27	11	25	7	20	4	13	3	0	0	10	8	153	65
135-139	0	0	0	0	3	1	10	1	7	1	11	2	7	0	3	0	3	0	0	0	44	5
130-134	0	0	1	0	0	0	3	0	4	0	3	0	3	0	2	0	1	0	1	0	18	0
125-129	0	0	0	0	1	0	0	0	1	0	2	0	1	0	2	0	1	0	0	0	8	0
120-124	0	0	0	0	0	0	0	0	0	0	0	0	0	0	0	0	0	0	0	0	0	0
Total	48	47	103	98	151	135	187	142	158	109	129	77	70	33	38	11	10	3	24	21	918	676

Apps = Number of Applicants
Adm = Number Admitted

University of Wisconsin Law School

975 Bascom Mall
Madison, WI 53706-1399

E-Mail: admissions@law.wisc.edu
URL: http://www.law.wisc.edu
Phone: 608.262.5914

■ Introduction

The University of Wisconsin Law School, with its new world class building addition, is a part of one of the world's largest, most honored, and most diversified universities. The central focus of the new building is a dramatic four-story atrium, giving the Law School an imposing new presence on Bascom Hill, the heart of the campus. In Madison, a particularly interesting and livable city of just under 200,000, the school is located in the center of the main campus, close to downtown and the state capital. The school pioneered the belief that the law must be studied in action, as it relates to society, not as a self-contained system. Close connections with other departments and facilities of the university and research and service projects with state and federal governments have given concrete meaning to this law-in-action emphasis and provide students a set of significant additional opportunities in the study and practice of law. The school has a national reputation, is a charter member of the AALS, and is ABA approved.

■ Enrollment/Student Body

➡ 1,544 applicants ➡ 725 admitted first-year class 1998 ➡ 281 enrolled first-year class 1998 ➡ full-time 25th/75th percentile GPA—3.25/3.66 ➡ part-time 25th/75th percentile GPA—2.64/3.56 ➡ full-time 25th/75th percentile LSAT—154/160 ➡ part-time 25th/75th percentile LSAT—154/162 ➡ 757 total full-time ➡ 48 total part-time ➡ 23% minority ➡ 47% women ➡ 33 states & foreign countries represented ➡ 124 undergraduate schools represented ➡ loss of first-year students due to academic failure runs less than 1%

■ Faculty

➡ 47 total, all full-time ➡ 11 women ➡ 6 minority

■ Library and Physical Facilities

➡ 400,000 volumes & equivalents ➡ library hours: Mon.-Thurs., 8:00 A.M.-MIDNIGHT; Fri., 8:00 A.M.-9:00 P.M.; Sat., 9:00 A.M.-9:00 P.M.; Sun., 9:00 A.M.-MIDNIGHT ➡ LEXIS ➡ NEXIS ➡ WESTLAW ➡ DIALOG ➡ 13+ full-time librarians ➡ library seats 600

With its reopening in September 1996, we believe the University of Wisconsin Law Library is one of the most technically advanced and architecturally beautiful in the country. With a two-story glass front facing Bascom Hill, the Main Reading Room is truly a site to behold.

The library's print collections are strong in all areas of U.S. state and federal law, international law, and the law of select foreign jurisdictions, and they support research and document requests from practitioners and legal scholars throughout the world. These print collections are complemented with distributed access to online legal information from virtually anywhere in the library. Additionally, the library's online catalog ties into a campus rich in library resources, including the 5 million volumes

located in the nearby main campus library and Historical Society Library.

■ Curriculum

➡ Academic Support Program ➡ 90 credits required to graduate ➡ semesters, start in Aug. ➡ range of first-year class size—20-89

The first semester runs from late August to shortly before Christmas; the second, from January to May. A total of 13 weeks of summer school are available each year, making it possible for a student to complete credit and residence requirements in five regular semesters and two summer semesters. Summer school is available for advanced students only, including students in good standing at other law schools. The first-year curriculum consists of required courses plus one elective choice. A broad selection of elective courses and seminars is available in the second and third years. Students who wish admission to the state bar of Wisconsin without bar examination must elect some advanced courses in traditional areas. In addition to the J.D., research-oriented LL.M. and S.J.D. programs are available on an individual basis. There are formalized dual-degree programs in Law and Public Administration, Law and Library Service, Law and Ibero-American Studies, Law and Environmental Studies, Law and Industrial Relations, Law and Business Master's Degree, Ph.D. in Philosophy, and Ph.D. in Sociology.

■ Special Programs

The Law School's clinical programs provide a variety of opportunities including public interest work, administrative and environmental law practices, judicial clerkships, legal services to institutionalized persons, representation of indigent defendants, and advocacy for disadvantaged persons.

Further, a number of exchange programs in South America, Asia, Europe, and Africa provide students additional opportunities to study the law in action in many transnational contexts.

■ Admission

➡ Bachelor's degree from accredited college or university required ➡ application deadline—Feb. 1 ➡ LSAT, LSDAS required ➡ application fee—$45

The Law School has no specific undergraduate course prerequisites and agrees with the suggestions in the introduction of this handbook. Although most students attend on a full-time basis, part-time attendance opportunities are available to those admitted students who cannot or do not wish to attend full time. It is faculty policy to encourage women and members of minority and disadvantaged groups to apply for admission. An active program for recruitment, admission, and financial aid for minority and disadvantaged students is important to the school. Applications are available the September preceding admission. Written recommendations are welcomed but not required; interviews are not part of the admissions process. A carefully prepared personal statement reflecting consideration of our admission criteria is often very helpful to the Admissions Committee. An application deadline of February 1 is enforced. No statement of intention to enroll is required until after April 1. College grades and LSAT score are significant, but many other factors are considered. Large numbers of applications from highly qualified Wisconsin residents have forced Wisconsin's only state-supported law school to reserve approximately 70 to 80 percent of the available places for Wisconsin residents, with the result that criteria are somewhat higher for nonresidents.

Transfer applications may be made, but only students with excellent law school records can be accepted. The deadline for transfer applicants for fall admission is June 1, but a decision cannot be expected until the full year's law school record is available.

■ Student Activities

In addition to the myriad of university activities, there are many activities especially for law students. The *Wisconsin Law Review*, edited by students, devotes substantial space to national and international problems and Wisconsin law. Written by both professionals in the field and law students, the student-edited *Wisconsin International Law Journal*, *Women's Law Journal*, and *Environmental Law Journal* offer articles of scholarly and practical interest in various areas of law. The Student Bar Association sponsors activities and nominates students for student/faculty committees such as curriculum,

tenure, and admissions. Further, the Law School has four constituent student associations for students of color.

■ Expenses and Financial Aid

➡ *full-time tuition & fees—residents, $6,206; nonresidents, $16,382*

Scholarship grants are awarded to students on the basis of need and merit. Need-based scholarships are determined through application to the Campus Office of Student Financial Services. Scholarship money is limited, and will not meet the student's total needs. Entering students must apply for financial aid as early as possible after January 1, and, therefore, should not wait until acceptance to apply. The Law School participates in Free Application for Federal Student Aid and will not accept GAPSFAS applications. Loan funds from government and private sources to law students in 1998-99 amounted to approximately $10,000,000. The Law School has an emergency short-term loan fund available for qualified students.

■ Career Services

The Office of Career Services operates full time to assist law students and alumni seeking summer, part-time or permanent employment. Each fall, O.C.S. conducts an on-campus interview program with about 100 employers. Numerous career-related workshops, speakers, and seminars are offered throughout the academic year.

Applicant Group for the 1998-1999 Academic Year

University of Wisconsin Law School
This grid includes only applicants who earned 120-180 LSAT scores under standard administrations.

LSAT Score	GPA 3.75 +		3.50 - 3.74		3.25 - 3.49		3.00 - 3.24		2.75 - 2.99		2.50 - 2.74		2.25 - 2.49		2.00 - 2.24		Below 2.00		No GPA		Total	
	Apps	Adm	Apps	Adm	Apps	Adm	Apps	Adm	Apps	Adm	Apps	Adm	Apps	Adm	Apps	Adm	Apps	Adm	Apps	Adm	Apps	Adm
175-180	0	0	1	0	0	0	1	1	1	1	0	0	1	0	0	0	0	0	0	0	4	2
170-174	6	6	2	2	6	6	3	3	6	6	1	1	2	2	0	0	0	0	0	0	26	26
165-169	19	19	20	19	26	26	13	12	8	6	6	5	0	0	1	0	0	0	1	1	94	88
160-164	54	54	63	63	66	66	58	39	28	8	12	1	4	1	1	0	0	0	4	2	290	234
155-159	51	48	107	99	131	76	74	15	38	3	18	3	6	1	2	0	0	0	7	2	434	247
150-154	25	20	61	25	92	14	67	6	38	5	19	3	8	1	2	1	0	0	12	3	324	78
145-149	15	5	26	4	35	10	49	6	36	5	22	1	10	2	2	0	1	0	5	0	201	33
140-144	2	0	9	1	15	2	17	6	14	0	15	1	8	2	6	1	0	0	7	0	93	13
135-139	3	1	1	0	5	0	3	0	11	0	10	0	10	0	3	0	1	0	6	1	53	2
130-134	1	0	0	0	1	0	0	0	3	0	2	0	0	0	1	0	0	0	2	0	10	0
125-129	0	0	0	0	0	0	0	0	0	0	0	0	1	0	0	0	0	0	1	0	2	0
120-124	0	0	0	0	0	0	0	0	0	0	0	0	0	0	1	0	0	0	0	0	1	0
Total	176	153	290	213	377	200	285	88	183	34	105	15	50	9	19	2	2	0	45	9	1532	723

Apps = Number of Applicants
Adm = Number Admitted
Reflects 99% of the total applicant pool.
This grid should be used only as a general guide since nonnumerical factors are also taken into account in admission decisions.

University of Wyoming College of Law

Post Office Box 3035
Laramie, WY 82071-3035

E-Mail: lawadmis@uwyo.edu
URL: http://www.uwyo.edu/law/law.htm
Phone: 307.766.6416

■ Introduction

The College of Law is located on the campus of the University of Wyoming in Laramie. The university, the only four-year institution of higher learning in Wyoming, comprises eight colleges, a graduate school, and several organized research units. The university has a student body of 11,000 in Laramie.

The College of Law, founded in 1920, is a member of the AALS and is accredited by the ABA. The college has approximately 230 students, a faculty of 14 full-time teachers, and several lecturers. The small student body and the excellent student-to-faculty ratio make possible a congenial atmosphere and a great amount of informal communication between students and faculty.

Laramie is a town of 30,000 located in the southeastern part of Wyoming at an altitude of 7,200 feet, on the high plains between two mountain ranges. Laramie's proximity to the mountains provides a variety of recreational activities including skiing, backpacking, rock climbing, hiking, camping, fishing, and hunting.

■ Enrollment/Student Body

➡ *376 applicants* ➡ *263 admitted first-year class 1998*
➡ *86 enrolled first-year class 1998* ➡ *full-time 25th/75th percentile GPA—3.01/3.56* ➡ *full-time 25th/75th percentile LSAT—148/157* ➡ *226 total full-time* ➡ *4% minority*
➡ *40% women* ➡ *29 states & foreign countries represented*
➡ *70 undergraduate schools represented*

■ Faculty

➡ *17 total* ➡ *14 full-time* ➡ *3 part-time or adjunct*
➡ *6 women*

■ Library and Physical Facilities

➡ *174,000 volumes & equivalents* ➡ *library hours: Mon.-Thurs., 7:30 A.M.-MIDNIGHT; Fri., 7:30 A.M.-9:00 P.M.; Sat., 9:00 A.M.-9:00 P.M.; Sun., 10:00 A.M.-MIDNIGHT*
➡ *LEXIS* ➡ *NEXIS* ➡ *WESTLAW* ➡ *INFOTRAC*
➡ *3 full-time librarians* ➡ *library seats 181*

The College of Law first occupied its new building in 1977. The facility provides ample classroom, library, and student study space, and furnishes a pleasant environment for study. A new three-story library addition was completed in the fall of 1993. This addition doubled the existing square footage of the law library. All law students are trained in computerized legal research, as well as in traditional research methods.

■ Curriculum

➡ *Academic Support Program* ➡ *88 credits required to graduate* ➡ *60 courses available* ➡ *degrees available: J.D.; J.D./M.B.A.; J.D./M.P.A.* ➡ *semesters, start in Aug.*
➡ *range of first-year class size—20-80*

The first year consists entirely of required courses. During the second year, students must take additional required courses including evidence, professional responsibility, and a second semester of constitutional law and civil procedure. Students must also complete an advanced writing requirement prior to graduation. As a condition of graduation from the College of Law, all students must successfully complete at least two of the following three courses—administrative law, business organizations, and trusts and estates. In addition, all students must successfully complete at least one of the following three courses—creditors' rights, income taxation, or secured transactions.

In both the second and third years, practical legal training is available through courses in legal research, legal skills and problems, trial practice, and clinical work. The college has no summer session; however, graduation may be accelerated one semester by summer work at other accredited law schools.

■ Special Programs

The College of Law has a strong program of elective courses in natural resources law. Courses are regularly offered in environmental law, hazardous waste and water pollution, oil and gas, mining law, public land resources, and water rights. Other electives include coverage of trial and appellate practice, business planning, estate planning, corporate and commercial law, administrative law, consumer law, and Indian law.

Students may obtain practical experience and receive academic credit for work in three clinical programs: (1) a defender aid program in which students brief and argue criminal appeals on behalf of indigent persons and assist penitentiary inmates in postconviction cases; (2) a prosecution assistance program in which students work directly with prosecuting attorneys and the United States Attorney in criminal cases; and, (3) a legal services program in which students provide legal assistance to economically disadvantaged persons. All clinical programs operate under faculty supervision.

■ Admission Standards

➡ *Bachelor's degree from accredited college or university required*
➡ *application deadline—March 15* ➡ *early application preferred* ➡ *early review of applications begins in mid-Feb.*
➡ *LSAT, LSDAS required* ➡ *application fee—$35*

The College of Law restricts the entering class to 80. Approximately 55 of these students are Wyoming residents, and 25 are nonresidents. In recent years, about 85 percent of the entering class have successfully completed law study and received the J.D. degree. The school does not discriminate on the basis of race, sex, or age in making admission decisions.

Students are admitted only for the fall semester. The college begins to accept applications in October for the class entering the following August. The entering class is selected from applications completed and on file by March 15. Applications are accepted after March 15, but only to fill vacancies that occur in the class initially selected. To meet the March 15 deadline, applicants should take the LSAT no later than February and should subscribe to LSDAS and arrange for forwarding of official transcripts no later than mid-January.

As a general rule, applicants must have received an undergraduate degree prior to registration. In very exceptional cases, a candidate without an undergraduate degree who possesses extraordinary experience and training may be admitted.

Written recommendations are not required. Selection of the entering class is based primarily on LSAT score and undergraduate grade-point average. As a limited number of places are assigned to nonresidents, out-of-state applicants who do not have a 3.00 grade average on a 4.0 scale and an LSAT score in the 50th percentile have little chance of serious consideration. However, a lower grade-point average or LSAT score may be offset by a higher LSAT score or grade average.

■ Student Activities

The College of Law publishes the *Land and Water Law Review*, a student-edited journal devoted to legal problems of natural resources, environmental issues, questions of Wyoming jurisprudence, and legal topics of general interest.

Student professional organizations include Potter Law Club, which provides student government and social activities and affiliation with the Law Student Division of the ABA, three legal fraternities, Christian Legal Society, Minority Law Student Association, Natural Resources Law Forum, Women's Law Forum, and the Wyoming Trial Lawyers Association. Students represent the college each year in the National Moot Court Competition, National Environmental Law Moot Court Competition, National Client Counseling Competition, ATLA National Student Trial Advocacy Competition, and the Natural Resources Law Moot Court Competition. Student organizations include two law school honoraries: the Order of the Coif, and the Order of the Barrister.

■ Expenses and Financial Aid

➡ *tuition & fees—resident, $4,234; nonresident, $9,322*
➡ *estimated additional expenses—$7,000 (room, board, books)*
➡ *academic and need-based scholarships available*
➡ *financial aid available; FAF for need analysis due to College Board in Jan. or early Feb.* ➡ *College of Law Scholarship Application due May 15*

■ Career Services

The placement service, under the direction of the Career Services Director, coordinates job placement for law students and recent graduates who seek permanent or summer employment; disseminates information to potential employers; collects résumés and employer information; and arranges interviews and conferences. Advice is given on the various opportunities for legal employment, résumé preparation, job interview dynamics, and techniques for obtaining employment.

Applicant Group for the 1998-1999 Academic Year

University of Wyoming College of Law
This grid includes only applicants who earned 120-180 LSAT scores under standard administrations.

LSAT Score	GPA 3.75 +		3.50 - 3.74		3.25 - 3.49		3.00 - 3.24		2.75 - 2.99		2.50 - 2.74		2.25 - 2.49		2.00 - 2.24		Below 2.00		No GPA		Total	
	Apps	Adm	Apps	Adm	Apps	Adm	Apps	Adm	Apps	Adm	Apps	Adm	Apps	Adm	Apps	Adm	Apps	Adm	Apps	Adm	Apps	Adm
175-180	0	0	0	0	0	0	0	0	0	0	0	0	0	0	0	0	0	0	0	0	0	0
170-174	0	0	0	0	2	2	0	0	0	0	0	0	0	0	0	0	0	0	0	0	2	2
165-169	1	1	0	0	6	6	1	1	1	1	3	3	0	0	0	0	0	0	0	0	12	12
160-164	4	4	3	3	6	6	8	7	4	4	2	2	0	0	0	0	0	0	0	0	27	26
155-159	8	8	12	11	19	17	9	9	11	11	6	6	0	0	1	1	1	0	0	0	67	63
150-154	13	13	21	18	23	21	20	20	14	13	7	3	4	3	3	3	3	0	0	0	105	94
145-149	4	4	16	15	17	15	21	13	12	3	8	3	6	0	3	0	0	0	2	1	89	54
140-144	2	1	2	0	7	3	16	2	9	1	6	1	4	1	4	0	0	0	1	0	51	9
135-139	0	0	3	0	1	0	5	0	3	0	1	0	2	0	0	0	0	0	0	0	15	0
130-134	0	0	0	0	0	0	1	0	0	0	2	0	2	0	0	0	1	0	0	0	6	0
125-129	1	1	0	0	0	0	0	0	1	0	0	0	1	0	0	0	0	0	0	0	3	1
120-124	0	0	0	0	0	0	0	0	0	0	0	0	0	0	0	0	0	0	0	0	0	0
Total	33	32	57	47	81	70	81	52	55	33	35	18	19	4	11	4	2	0	3	1	377	261

Apps = Number of Applicants
Adm = Number Admitted
Reflects 98% of the total applicant pool.

Yale Law School

P.O. Box 208329
New Haven, CT 06520-8329

E-Mail: admissions.law@yale.edu
URL: http://www.law.yale.edu
Phone: 203.432.4995

■ Introduction

Yale Law School is an extraordinary community in which to study law. Our unmatched faculty-to-student ratio allows us to offer a vast array of courses, an average class size of under 20 students, and countless opportunities for independent research, writing, and student-organized seminars. Easy student-faculty interaction and institutional flexibility are hallmarks of the school. Law students have access to scholars in all of Yale's departments, to the university's nine-million-volume library system, and to its cultural, social, intellectual, and athletic activities. At the same time, Yale Law School has ties to the city of New Haven, a small, lively urban center with the attractions and problems of an American city. New Haven has two of the finest repertory theaters in the country, commercial theaters that bring in touring shows and performers, several first-rate museums, and the best pizza in America. Students are involved with New Haven's less prosperous side through the legal services organization.

■ Enrollment/Student Body

➡ 3,269 applicants ➡ 309 admitted first-year class 1998 (including previously deferred) ➡ 185 enrolled first-year class 1998 ➡ full-time 25th/75th percentile GPA—3.75/3.97 ➡ full-time 25th/75th percentile LSAT—168/175 ➡ 594 total full-time J.D. ➡ 30.8% minority ➡ 43% women ➡ 76 states & foreign countries represented (1997-1998) ➡ 183 undergraduate schools represented (1997-1998)

The vitality of Yale Law School depends as much on the knowledge, experience, and expertise of the students as it does on the faculty, the library, the university, or the alumni. The school selects its students from applicants with the highest academic qualifications in the country; within this group, it seeks diversity of background and experience. Most of the international students in the school are enrolled in the LL.M. program. The Law School welcomes older students and students with disabilities.

■ Faculty

➡ 117+ total ➡ 53 full-time ➡ 64 part-time or adjunct ➡ 14 women full-time ➡ 7 minority full-time

The Law School faculty is as broad-ranging in its interests and expertise as it is distinguished. It includes prominent scholars of economics, philosophy, and psychoanalysis, as well as leading specialists in every area of law. Approximately 50 full-time professors are joined each year by visiting lecturers, adjunct professors from other parts of the university, and practicing lawyers who assist the full-time clinical faculty as tutors in the clinical program. In addition, dozens of guest lecturers from around the world help to make Yale Law School a vibrant intellectual community.

■ Library and Physical Facilities

➡ 800,000 volumes & equivalents ➡ library hours: 24 hours a day, 7 days a week during academic year ➡ LEXIS ➡ NEXIS ➡ WESTLAW ➡ DIALOG ➡ 17 full-time librarians ➡ library seats 380

The Sterling Law Buildings occupy one city block at the heart of Yale University and close to downtown New Haven. Constructed in 1929-1931, they were modeled on the idea of the English Inns of Court. Classrooms, offices, the law library and the international law library, two student computer labs, dormitory rooms for about 70 law students, and the dining hall surround a pleasant courtyard. A day-care center is located off-site.

■ Curriculum

➡ 82 credits required to graduate ➡ 140 courses available ➡ degrees available: J.D./M.P.A.; M.S.L.; LL.M.; J.S.D.; J.D.; J.D./M.P.P.M.; J.D./M.A.; J.D./Ph.D.; J.D./M.D.; J.D./M.E.S.; J.D./M.F.S.; J.D./M.DIV. ➡ semesters, start in Aug. ➡ range of first-year class size—15-90

In the fall semester, all first-year students take classes in constitutional law, contracts, procedure, and torts. After the first term, the only required course is criminal law. A supervised analytic paper, a substantial paper, and attendance at a series of lectures on professional responsibility are also required. For the first term, all grades are credit/fail. After that, grades are honors, pass, low pass, and fail, with credit/fail options.

■ Special Programs

Yale Law School sees the study of law as interrelated with other intellectual disciplines and with practical experience. The Law School encourages special programs, including joint-degree opportunities with many other departments at Yale and with some other universities, intensive semester experiences outside the Law School, work with state legislative committees drafting legislation and preparing reports, and work with local organizations such as schools, human rights, and civil rights agencies under the aegis of student-run programs.

■ Transfer Students and Advanced Degrees

Yale Law School welcomes applications for transfer. Students who wish to transfer may be granted residence and academic credit for up to two semesters of study. Transfer students must do at least two years of work at Yale Law School.

In addition to the J.D., Yale Law School offers an LL.M. degree, for those who are interested in teaching law. The Master of Studies in Law degree (M.S.L.) is a one-year program designed for professionals in other fields who desire an intensive introduction to the law.

■ Admission

➥ Bachelor's degree from accredited college or university required
➥ application deadline—Feb. 15   ➥ LSAT, LSDAS required
➥ application fee—$65

The admissions process at Yale Law School is an intensely competitive one in which the totality of available information about the applicant is taken into account. No one element is decisive. The competition is stiff; nevertheless, we encourage all those who desire to be a part of the Yale Law School community to submit applications. Each application file is first read by the Dean or Director of Admissions. A group of the most highly rated files is then considered by faculty file readers. On the basis of the faculty ratings we admit candidates and establish a waiting list. Use of the waiting list varies from year to year; the list is not ranked until offers are to be made from the list. A number of waiting-list candidates are held for consideration through registration day. Faculty file readers' ratings are based on their own criteria, and the relative weight to be given to experience versus academic achievement is within each file reader's discretion. A 250-word essay, on a subject of your choice, is required. Personal statements of any length are welcome. Two letters of recommendation are required; additional letters are welcome. The Law School begins to issue decisions in late February. Minority applicants are evaluated in the same fashion as and along with nonminority applicants. Applicants are encouraged to bring to our attention aspects of their personal background and other special characteristics that they believe to be pertinent.

■ Student Activities

Yale Law students are very active outside the classroom. In any given year, as many as 40-50 student organizations may be active. Included in that group are six student-run journals.

■ Expenses and Financial Aid

➥ $25,550 full-time tuition & fees   ➥ average amount additional expenses—$12,100 (room & board, books, and personal expenses)   ➥ need-based scholarships available for all eligible students   ➥ financial aid available ➥ Loan Forgiveness Program (COAP) ➥ Need Access required   ➥ FAFSA required

Financial aid is awarded solely on the basis of need. Admission decisions are made before and independently of financial aid decisions. Approximately 74 percent of the student body now receives some form of financial assistance; about 35 percent receive loans only. A financial aid award consists of a portion in gift and a portion in loan; typically the higher the total financial need, the higher the proportion of gift.

■ Career Services

Yale Law School graduates occupy positions of leadership in a tremendous range of endeavors. The Career Development Office, staffed by six full-time employees including three attorney counselors, helps students explore the unparalleled diversity of opportunities they face.

Applicant Group for the 1998-1999 Academic Year

Yale Law School

Average LSAT Score on the 120-180* Scale

Undergraduate GPA	Below 154		155-159		160-164		165-169		170-174		175-180		Total	
	Apps	Adm	Apps	Adm	Apps	Adm	Apps	Adm	Apps	Adm	Apps	Adm	Apps	Adm
3.75 +	71	1	127	5	227	22	357	33	292	95	127	76	1201	232
3.50-3.74	93	0	100	0	196	6	245	20	206	21	71	10	911	57
3.25-3.49	87	0	79	0	121	3	120	11	72	1	30	0	509	15
3.00-3.24	80	0	46	0	46	0	45	0	27	1	6	0	250	1
Below 3.00	120	0	45	0	29	0	25	0	17	0	4	0	240	0
No GPA	54	0	14	1	17	0	17	1	5	0	4	0	111	2
Total	505	1	411	6	636	31	809	65	619	118	242	86	3222	307*

Apps = Number of Applicants
Adm = Number Admitted
* Because only applicants with scores on the 120-180 scale are included above, the grid includes only 98% of applicants and 99.4% of admitted applicants. Total applicants for the fall of 1998 were 3269; total admitted applicants, 309.

Appendix A: Canadian LSAC-Member Law Schools

University of Alberta
Faculty of Law
Room 484B, Admissions Office
Edmonton, Alberta
CANADA T6G 2H5

University of British Columbia
Faculty of Law
1822 East Mall
Vancouver, British Columbia
CANADA V6T 1Z1

University of Calgary
Faculty of Law
Murray Fraser Hall
Calgary, Alberta
CANADA T2N 1N4

Dalhousie Law School
6061 University Avenue
Halifax, Nova Scotia
CANADA B3H 4H9

University of Manitoba
Faculty of Law
Robson Hall
Winnipeg, Manitoba
CANADA R3T 2N2

McGill University
Faculty of Law
3674 Peel
Montreal, Quebec
CANADA H3A 1W9

University of New Brunswick
Faculty of Law
P.O. Box 44271
Fredericton, New Brunswick
CANADA E3B 6C2

University of Ottawa
Faculty of Law
57 Louis Pasteur
P.O. Box 450
Station A
Ottawa, Ontario
CANADA K1N 6N5

Queen's University
Faculty of Law
Registrar of Law, Macdonald Hall
Kingston, Ontario
CANADA K7L 3N6

University of Saskatchewan
College of Law
Admissions Committee
15 Campus Drive
Saskatoon, Saskatchewan
CANADA S7N 5A6

University of Toronto
Faculty of Law
78 Queen's Park
Toronto, Ontario
CANADA M5S 2C5

University of Victoria
Faculty of Law
P.O. Box 2400
Victoria, British Columbia
CANADA V8W 3H7

University of Western Ontario
Faculty of Law
London, Ontario
CANADA N6A 3K7

University of Windsor
Faculty of Law
401 Sunset Ave.
Windsor, Ontario
CANADA N9B 3P4

York University
Osgoode Hall Law School
4700 Keele Street
North York, Ontario
CANADA M3J 1P3

Appendix B: U.S. Law Schools Not Approved by the ABA

Alabama

Birmingham School of Law
823 Frank Nelson Bldg.
205 North 20th Street
Birmingham, AL 35203

Jones School of Law
5345 Atlanta Highway
Montgomery, AL 36109

Miles Law School
P.O. Box 3800
Birmingham, AL 35208

California

American College of Law
1717 S. State College Blvd.
Suite 100
Anaheim, CA 92806

CAL Northern School of Law
1395 Ridgewood Drive
Suite 100
Chico, CA 95973

California Pacific School of Law
1600 Truxton Avenue
Bakersfield, CA 93301

California Southern Law School
3775 Elizabeth Street
Riverside, CA 92506

Empire College
3033 Cleveland Avenue
Suite 102
Santa Rosa, CA 95403

Glendale University
College of Law
220 North Glendale Avenue
Glendale, CA 91206

Humphreys College—School of Law
6650 Inglewood Avenue
Stockton, CA 95207

John F. Kennedy University School of Law
12 Altarinda Road
Orinda, CA 94563

University of LaVerne
College of Law at San Fernando Valley
21300 Oxnard Street
Woodland Hills, CA 91367

University of LaVerne
College of Law
1950 3rd Street
LaVerne, CA 91750

Lincoln Law School of Sacramento
3140 J Street
Sacramento, CA 95816

Lincoln Law School
of San Jose
2160 Lundy Avenue
San Jose, CA 95131

Monterey College of Law
404 West Franklin Street
Monterey, CA 93940

New College of California
School of Law
50 Fell Street
San Francisco, CA 94102

University of Northern California
Lorenzo Patino School of Law
1012 J Street
Sacramento, CA 95814

Oakland College of Law
120 11th Street
Suite 103
Oakland, CA 94607-4806

Pacific West College of Law
1380 Southern Sanderson Avenue
Anaheim, CA 92806

Peninsula University College of Law
436 Dell Avenue
Mountain View, CA 94043

San Francisco Law School
20 Haight Street
San Francisco, CA 94102

San Joaquin College of Law
901 Fifth Street
Clovis, CA 93612

Santa Barbara College of Law
20 E. Victoria Street
Santa Barbara, CA 93101

Trinity Law School
2200 North Grand Avenue
Santa Ana, CA 92705

Ventura College of Law
4475 Market Street
Ventura, CA 93003

University of West Los Angeles
School of Law
1155 W. Arbor Vitae Street
Inglewood, CA 90301-2902

Western Sierra Law School
8376 Hercules Street
La Mesa, CA 91942

William Howard Taft University
201 East Sandpoint Avenue
Santa Ana, CA 92707-5703

Florida

Florida Coastal School of Law
7555 Beach Boulevard
Jacksonville, FL 32216

University of Orlando School of Law
6441 E. Colonial Drive
Orlando, FL 32807

Georgia

John Marshall Law School, Atlanta
1422 W. Peachtree Street, N.E.
Suite 400
Atlanta, GA 30309

Massachusetts

Massachusetts School of Law
at Andover
500 Federal Street
Andover, MA 01810

Southern New England School of Law
333 Faunce Corner Road
North Dartmouth, MA 02747

Nevada

William S. Boyd School of Law
at the University of Nevada
4505 Maryland Parkway
Box 451003
Las Vegas, NV 89154-1003

Puerto Rico

Eugenio Maria de Hostos School of Law
P.O. Box 1900
Mayaguez, Puerto Rico 00681-1900

Tennessee

Nashville School of Law
2934 Sidco Drive
Nashville, TN 37204

Appendix C: LSAC Statement of Good Admission Practices

Introduction

This Statement of Good Admission Practices is designed to focus attention on principles that should guide law school admission programs. No attempt has been made to develop "legislative" guidelines, because no absolute rules apply to every situation. The statement is intended to improve the admission process in law schools and to promote fairness for all participants.

General Principles

1. The primary purpose of the law school admission process is to serve law school applicants, law schools, and the legal profession by making informed judgments about those who seek legal education. The responsibility that role carries with it demands the highest standards of professional conduct.

2. Law school admission professionals should avoid impropriety and the appearance of impropriety, as well as any conflict of interest or the appearance of conflict. They should not accept anything for themselves or the law school or pursue any activity that might compromise or seem to compromise their integrity or that of the admission process.

3. Law schools should strive to achieve and maintain the highest standards of accuracy and candor in the development and publication of print and other materials designed to inform or influence applicants. A law school should provide any applicant or potential applicant with information and data that will enable the applicant to assess his or her prospects for successfully (1) seeking admission to that school, (2) financing his or her education at that school, (3) completing the educational program at that school, and (4) seeking employment with degree from that school. If statistics are provided regarding admissions, financial aid, and placement, law schools should provide the most current information and should present it in an easily understood form. Sig-nificant errors of fact, as well as errors of omission, should be corrected promptly and prominently.

4. Law schools should establish application procedures that inform applicants of relevant criteria, processes, and deadlines, respect the confidentiality of student records and admission data, and provide for timely notification of admission decisions. Law schools should also ensure that all parties concerned with the admission process are familiar with and observe relevant laws, accreditation standards, and institutional guidelines, including the *Cautionary Policies Concerning LSAT Scores and Related Services* developed by Law School Admission Council (Law Services).

5. In making admission decisions, law schools should give special consideration to applicants who are members of cultural, ethnic, or racial groups that have not had adequate opportunities to develop and demonstrate potential for academic achievement and would not otherwise be meaningfully represented in the entering class. Schools should also make reasonable accommodations to the special needs of disabled applicants. Law schools should make a special effort to provide the information noted in Number 3 above to those applicants who are members of minority groups or who are disabled.

Admission Policy

1. Law schools should develop coherent and consistent admission policies. The admission policies should serve law school applicants by clearly setting forth the criteria on which admission decisions are made and the manner in which the criteria will be applied.

Law schools should develop and promulgate concise and coherent admission policies designed both to regularize the admission process and to inform fully prospective applicants and prelaw advisors of the means used to select new law students. The policies should include consideration of the various criteria and processes used to make admission decisions, such as the Law School Admission Test (LSAT), prior academic performance, professional and other work experiences, equal opportunity considerations, disabled status, geographical diversity, letters of recommendation, personal statements, and personal interviews, if required. These and other considerations related to a law school's institutional mission or objectives may result in a preference for certain applicants. Each law school's admission policies should be adequately disclosed to all prospective applicants at the outset of the admission process.

Scores obtained on the LSAT and undergraduate grade-point averages are factors by which applicants are judged by virtually all law schools. Law schools should ensure that all application materials accurately describe the manner in which LSAT scores, prior academic performance, and other factors are used in the admission process.

The LSAT is designed to measure some, but certainly not all, of the mental and academic abilities that are needed for successful law study. Within limits, it provides a reasonable assessment of these factors. LSAT scores provide at best a partial measure of an applicant's ability and should be considered in relation to the total range of information available about a prospective law student. Thus, the LSAT score should be used as only one of several criteria for evaluation and should not be given undue weight.

Use of cut-off LSAT scores below which no candidate will be considered is explicitly discouraged in the Law Services Cautionary Policies. However, a particular law school may discover evidence that applicants scoring below a certain point have substantial difficulty in performing satisfactorily in its program of studies. Based on that evidence, the law school may rationally choose to implement a policy of discouraging applications with LSAT scores below a certain point. Should a law school make that determination, applicants should be informed of that fact.

Similar considerations govern the evaluation of the applicant's prior academic record. Undergraduate grades are a significant indicator of potential success in law school. In addition to being one measure of academic ability, a strong scholastic record may indicate perseverance, organization, and motivation, all important factors which have few direct measures. There are, of course, measures of intellectual ability other than the cumulative grade-point average. Unusual creativity, exceptional research skills, analytical prowess, and other factors may not be reflected on a candidate's college transcript.

In evaluating the academic record, law schools may choose to consider factors such as grade inflation, the age of the grades, discrepancies among the applicant's grades, the quality of the college attended, difficulty of coursework, and time commitments while attending college.

Law schools may also take into consideration additional factors when choosing among various law school candidates. Letters of recommendation often have a significant impact on admission decisions. Some schools believe that letters of recommendation are usually more candid when the subject of the letter waives access to them and recommend that applicants limit their rights to inspect this portion of their admission files. However,

waiver of access to letters of recommendation or of any part of the student's record should not be made a mandatory prerequisite to admission. The Buckley Amendment specifically mandates that U.S. law schools must not require such a waiver.

As with members of cultural, ethnic, and racial groups, law schools should also recognize the importance of providing equal educational opportunity for disabled individuals. Sometimes the applicant's disability may prevent the assembly of a complete admission file. For example, some applicants can take the LSAT only under special conditions, making it difficult to interpret their test scores. Others may seek to have certain admission requirements waived entirely. In these circumstances, law schools can properly give weight to the disabled applicant's demonstrated ability to overcome obstacles in building a record of academic and professional performance.

Admission of applicants from a wide variety of academic, cultural, ethnic, and racial backgrounds, and the resulting diversity, enhances and enriches the educational experience of all students and faculty.

It is proper to prefer students who have taken courses such as those that develop skills in both written and oral communications, develop analytical and problem-solving skills, or promote familiarity with the humanities and social sciences to understand the human condition and the social context in which legal problems arise. The decision to prefer either a classical liberal arts education or a more narrowly focused one should rest within the sound discretion of the law school.

2. Law schools that accept transfer applications should state clearly the application procedures for transfer applicants and inform them of all relevant deadlines, necessary documents and records, courses accepted for credit, and, to the extent possible, course equivalency.

Recruitment and Promotion

1. Law schools are responsible for all people they involve in admission, promotional, and recruitment activities (including graduates, students, and faculty), and for educating them about the principles of good practice outlined in this Statement, as well as all relevant laws, accreditation standards, and institutional policies. Law schools that use admission management firms or consulting firms are responsible for assuring that these firms adhere to sound admission practices.

The oversight role entrusted to law schools includes supervision of all personnel involved in the admission process. Law school personnel, students, and graduates who represent the law school at recruitment and other promotional activities should be informed of current law school programs and activities. They should be knowledgeable about

the academic and financial requirements of attending the law school, and they should honestly and forthrightly respond to inquiries.

Professional recruiting organizations, though not formally affiliated with law schools, nonetheless are part of the admission process when they are engaged by law schools. Law schools engaging outside services are responsible for ensuring the integrity and the accuracy of the work performed for them. For example, errors or misleading statements appearing in recruitment brochures and law school catalogs may not be ascribed to the company performing the service. Law schools cannot abdicate the responsibility for accuracy by shifting blame to third parties.

2. Admissions publications should contain an accurate and current admission calendar and information about financial aid opportunities and requirements.

In addition to containing a complete listing of all relevant admission and financial aid deadlines, admission material should also convey accurate information about optimum dates, if any, for submitting admission materials. Among the items that might usefully be included are: dates for taking the Law School Admission Test; dates for submission of financial aid applications, including the best time for submission of materials to a financial aid need analysis service, if used; and the most useful date for submission of letters of recommendation. This information is particularly useful when law schools begin to make admission decisions prior to the deadline date for receipt of application materials under a "rolling" admission system.

Law schools should notify applicants about deadlines for financial aid applications and the criteria used in awarding aid. To the extent reasonably practicable, law schools should disclose how parental income will affect the financial aid determination. Similarly, the availability of need-based and of merit-based aid should be disclosed.

3. Law school admission professionals should be forthright and accurate in providing information about their institutions. Law school publications and any statements submitted for publication should contain current and accurate descriptions and representations of law school programs, campus life, and the surrounding community. Law schools should provide accurate, candid, and comprehensive information

with respect to the law school opportunities sought by students and available to them.

Law school recruitment activities, e.g., law school forums, prelaw days, caravans, and law school fairs, provide an opportunity for law school representatives to engage in personal contact with applicants. In many instances, these activities are not only the first, but often the only direct contact applicants have with law schools until registration. In all of these instances, law school representatives should conduct themselves in a professional manner. Representatives attending these activities have an obligation to familiarize themselves with all aspects of the admission process at their respective schools. Recruitment activities should not include unreasonable and unfounded comparisons with other law schools.

4. Law schools should provide prelaw advisors and other educational and career counselors with accurate and appropriate information to assist them in counseling applicants about law school opportunities.

Issues of law school recruitment and enrollment require the cooperative efforts of college and university personnel working with law school admission counselors. Prelaw colleagues and other college counselors daily encounter students who are or may be interested in pursuing legal education. To serve the undergraduate population effectively, law schools should keep interested prelaw advisors, minority and other counselors informed of their admission requirements and institutional programs.

Application Procedures

1. Law schools should promptly notify applicants of admission decisions.

2. Law schools should respect the confidential nature of information received about applicants.

While a policy of openness and accessibility should form the basis for all communications with law school applicants, law schools should be scrupulous in maintaining the privacy of applicants. Without the expressed consent of the applicant involved and the author of the material in question, admission information relating to an applicant, such as LSAT scores, prior academic record, letters of recommendation, and dean's reports, should not be released to persons other than admission decision makers, the candidate and others with a legitimate interest in the admission process. This restriction would not prevent schools from sharing information that is not in a personally identifiable form, but even in this case, law schools should take care that the information is released with appropriate discretion.

From time to time, information about law school applicants at a particular law school is provided by Law

Services. Information contained in many of these periodic reports is also confidential and should not be released to persons outside of the admission process, except as required by law.

3. A law school application should state clearly what information is being sought. The application should also state the applicant's obligation to provide accurate, current, and complete information. Further, the application should define the consequences of providing false, misleading, or incomplete information.

If the law school believes that false or misleading information has been provided by an applicant, that allegation should be submitted to the LSAC Misconduct and Irregularities in the Admission Process Subcommittee for investigation. Then, if misconduct is found, all law schools to which the applicant has applied, or may apply, will be notified.

4. Except under early decision plans, law schools should not require applicants or other persons to indicate the order of applicants' law school preferences.

Law schools should allow applicants the freedom to explore as many opportunities to pursue legal education as possible. To preserve applicant options, law schools should not base admission decisions on the order of applicants' law school preferences, unless the school has established an early decision plan. An early decision plan is one under which an applicant and a law school mutually agree at the point of application that the applicant will be given an admission decision at a date earlier than usual in return for the applicant's commitment, at that date, to attend the school and withdraw all applications pending at other law schools, and not initiate new applications.

5. Except under early decision plans, law schools should permit applicants to choose among offers of admission as well as offers of scholarships, grants, and loans without penalty until April 1. Admitted applicants who have submitted a timely financial aid application should not be required to commit to enroll until notified of financial aid awards that are within the control of the law school.

6. No law school has an obligation to maintain an offer of admission if it discovers that the applicant has accepted an offer at another institution. Except under early decision plans, law schools should not suggest that acceptance of their offer of admission creates a moral or legal obligation to register at that school. Every accepted applicant should be free to deal with all law schools and to accept an offer from one of them even though a deposit has been paid to another school. To provide applicants with an uncoerced choice among various law schools, no excessive fee should be required solely to maintain a place in the class. Law schools should give applicants sufficient warning and ample time before withdrawing offers.

7. Law schools should maintain a waiting list of reasonable length and only for a reasonable length of time.

Law schools using waiting lists should ensure that the lists are of reasonable length and that final decisions about applicants placed on the waiting lists are made and communicated to the applicant as soon as possible.

Appendix D: Preparation for Legal Education

Introduction

The following statement was prepared in 1996 by the members of the American Bar Association Prelaw Committee. It has been reviewed by many members of the legal education community and the legal profession.

It provides general advice from knowledgeable people about how to prepare for law school and the legal profession.

Preparation for Legal Education

Students who are successful in law school, and who become accomplished lawyers or use their legal education successfully in other areas of professional life, come to their legal education from widely differing educational and experiential backgrounds. As undergraduate students, some have majored in subjects that are traditionally considered paths to law school, such as history, English, philosophy, political science, economics or business. Other successful law students, however, have focused their undergraduate studies in areas as diverse as art, music theory, computer science, engineering, nursing or education. Many law students enter law school directly from their undergraduate studies and without having had any substantial work experience. Others begin their legal education significantly later in life, and they bring to their law school education the insights and perspectives gained from those life experiences.

Thus, the ABA does not recommend any particular group of undergraduate majors, or courses, that should be taken by those wishing to prepare for legal education; developing such a list is neither possible nor desirable. The law is too multifaceted, and the human mind too adaptable, to permit such a linear approach to preparing for law school or the practice of law. Nonetheless, there are important skills and values, and significant bodies of knowledge, that can be acquired prior to law school and that will provide a sound foundation for a sophisticated legal education. This Statement presents the recommendations of the American Bar Association Section of Legal Education and Admissions to the Bar concerning preparation for a good law school experience.

Prospective law students should also consult closely with the prelaw advisor at their undergraduate institution. That individual may be able to assist current students in selecting courses or professors that will particularly assist in developing the skills and knowledge foundation that is emphasized in this Statement. Taking difficult courses from demanding instructors is the best generic preparation for legal education. The prelaw advisor can also assist current and former students in choosing law schools to which to apply that are appropriate in light of a prospective student's interests and credentials. Finally, prospective law students should also consult the publications and admissions personnel of the schools to which they are considering applying for any specific recommendations that individual schools may have concerning preparation for law school.

There are numerous skills and values that are essential to success in law school and to competent lawyering.

There also is a large body of information that law students, and attorneys, should possess. The three or four years that a student spends in obtaining a quality legal education can and do provide much of the information that a lawyer needs. Good legal education also aids in developing the many skills and values essential to competent lawyering. Sound legal education, however, must build upon and further refine skills, values and knowledge that the student already possesses. Even though a student may well be able to acquire in law school some specific fundamental skills and knowledge that the student's prelaw school experience has not provided, the student who comes to law school lacking a broad range of basic skills and knowledge will face an extremely difficult task.

■ Skills and Values

The core skills and values that are essential for competent lawyering include analytic and problem solving skills, critical reading abilities, writing skills, oral communication and listening abilities, general research skills, task organization and management skills, and the values of serving faithfully the interests of others while also promoting justice.[1] Thus, individuals who wish to prepare adequately for legal education, and for a career in law or for other professional service that involves the use of lawyering skills, should seek educational, extracurricular and life experiences that will assist them in developing those attributes.[2] Some brief comments about each of the listed skills and values follow.

Analytic and Problem-Solving Skills

Students should seek courses and other experiences that will engage them in critical thinking about important issues, that will engender in them tolerance for uncertainty, and that will give them experience in structuring and evaluating arguments for and against propositions that are susceptible to reasoned debate. Students also should seek courses and other experiences that require them to apply previously developed principles or theories to new situations, and that demand that they develop solutions to new problems. Good legal education teaches students to "think like a lawyer," but the analytic and problem-solving skills required of lawyers are not fundamentally different from those employed by other professionals. The law school experience will develop and refine those crucial skills, but one must enter law school with a reasonably well developed set of analytic and problem-solving abilities.

Critical Reading Abilities

Preparation for legal education should include substantial experience at close reading and critical analysis of complex textual material, for much of what law students and lawyers do involves careful reading and sophisticated comprehension of judicial opinions, statutes, documents, and other written materials. As with the other skills discussed in this Statement, the requisite critical reading abilities may be acquired in a wide range of experiences, including the close reading of complex material in literature, political or economic theory, philosophy, or history. The particular nature of the materials examined is not crucial; what is important is that law school not be the first time that a student has been rigorously engaged in the enterprise of carefully reading and understanding, and critically analyzing, complex written material of substantial length. Potential law students should also be aware that the study and practice of law require the ability to read and assimilate large amounts of material, often in a short period of time.

Writing Skills

Those seeking to prepare for legal education should develop a high degree of skill at written communication. Language is the most important tool of a lawyer, and lawyers must learn to express themselves clearly and concisely. Legal education provides good training in writing, and particularly in the specific techniques and forms of written expression that are common in the law. Fundamental writing skills, however, should be acquired and refined before one enters law school. Those preparing for legal education should seek as many experiences as possible that will require rigorous and analytical writing, including preparing original pieces of substantial length and revising written work in response to constructive criticism.

Oral Communication and Listening Abilities

The ability to speak clearly and persuasively is another skill that is essential to success in law school and the practice of law. Lawyers also must have excellent listening skills if they are to understand their clients and others with whom they must interact daily. As with writing skills, legal education provides excellent opportunities for refining oral communication skills, and particularly for practicing the forms and techniques of oral expression that are most common in the practice of law. Before coming to law school, however, individuals should seek to develop their basic speaking and listening skills, such as by engaging in debate, making formal presentations in class, or speaking before groups in school, the community, or the workplace.

General Research Skills

Although there are many research sources and techniques that are specific to the law, an individual need not have developed any familiarity with these specific skills or materials before entering law school. However, the individual who comes to law school without ever having undertaken a project that requires significant library research and the analysis of large amounts of information obtained from that research will be at a severe disadvantage. Those wishing to prepare for legal education should select courses and seek experiences that will require them to plan a research strategy, to undertake substantial library research, and to analyze, organize and present a reasonably large amount of material. A basic ability to use a personal computer is also increasingly important for law students, both for word processing and for computerized legal research.

Task Organization and Management Skills

The study and practice of law require the ability to organize large amounts of information, to identify objectives, and to create a structure for applying that information in an efficient way in order to achieve desired results. Many law school courses, for example, are graded primarily on the basis of one examination at the end of the course, and many projects in the practice of law require the compilation of large amounts of information from a wide variety of sources, frequently over relatively brief periods of time. Thus, those entering law school must be prepared to organize and assimilate large amounts of information in a manner that facilitates the recall and application of that information in an effective and efficient manner. Some of the requisite experience can be obtained through undertaking school projects that require substantial research and writing, or through the preparation of major reports for an employer, a school, or a civic organization.

The Values of Serving Others and Promoting Justice

Each member of the legal profession should be dedicated both to the objectives of serving others honestly, competently, and responsibly, and to the goals of improving fairness and the quality of justice in the legal system. Those thinking of entering this profession would be well served by having some significant experience, before coming to law school, in which they devoted substantial effort toward assisting others. Participation in public service projects or similar efforts at achieving objectives established for common purposes can be particularly helpful.

■ Knowledge

In addition to these fundamental skills and values, there are some basic areas of knowledge that are important to a sophisticated legal education and to the development of a competent lawyer. As law becomes more pervasive in our society, an increasingly broad range of knowledge and information from other disciplines become relevant to lawyering and to any full understanding of the legal system. Some of that knowledge, particularly that most directly relevant to particular areas of the law, can be acquired in law school or when necessary for a particular project.

There are, however, generic types of knowledge that one should possess in order to have a full appreciation of the legal system in general, to understand how disputes might be resolved, to understand and apply various legal principles and standards, and to appreciate the context in which a legal problem or dispute arises. Some of the types of knowledge that are most useful, and that would most pervasively affect one's ability to derive the maximum benefit from legal education, include the following:

- A broad understanding of history, particularly American history, and the various factors (social, political, economic, and cultural) that have influenced the development of the pluralistic society that presently exists in the United States;

- A fundamental understanding of political thought and theory, and of the contemporary American political system;

- A basic understanding of ethical theory and theories of justice;

- A grounding in economics, particularly elementary micro-economic theory, and an understanding of the interaction between economic theory and public policy;

- Some basic mathematical and financial skills, such as an understanding of basic pre-calculus mathematics and an ability to analyze financial data;

- A basic understanding of human behavior and social interaction; and
- An understanding of diverse cultures within and beyond the United States, of international institutions and issues, and of the increasing interdependence of the nations and communities within our world.

As law has become more woven into the fabric of our society, and as that society is increasingly influenced by disparate national and global forces, a broad knowledge base is essential for success in law school and for competence in the legal profession. Knowledge of specific areas of law can and will be acquired during a good legal education, but students must come to law school with much fundamental knowledge upon which legal education can build. Thus, those considering law school should focus their substantive preparation on acquiring the broad knowledge and perspectives outlined above.

■ Conclusion

The skills, values and knowledge discussed in this Statement may be acquired in a wide variety of ways. One may take undergraduate, graduate, or even high school courses that can assist an individual in acquiring much of the requisite information, skills and perspectives. One may also gain much of this essential background through self-learning (another essential lawyering skill), by reading, in the workplace, or through various other life experiences. Moreover, it is not essential that everyone come to law school having fully developed all of the skills, values and knowledge suggested in this Statement. Some of that foundation can be acquired during the initial years of law school. However, one who begins law school having already acquired most of the skills, values and knowledge listed in this Statement will have a significant advantage and will be well prepared to benefit fully from a sophisticated and challenging legal education.

[1]These core skill and value areas are drawn, in substantial part, from the Statement of Skills and Values contained in the 1992 Report of the American Bar Association Task Force on Law Schools and the Profession, *Legal Education and Professional Development—An Educational Continuum.*

[2]People with various disabilities, such as visual or hearing limitations, have been successful in law school and in the practice of law. Persons with such disabilities, however, should be cognizant of the particular challenges that they may face in law school and in the profession.

Think About Law School

LAW SCHOOL
F O R U M S ℠

If you're considering law school, come to a Law School Forum. Free admission. No preregistration. In one place, you can

- talk with representatives of LSAC–member law schools from across the United States;

- obtain admission materials, catalogs, and financial aid information;

- view video programs about the law school admission process, legal education and careers, and minority perspectives on legal education;

- attend informational sessions on the law school admission process, financing a legal education, and issues of importance to minority applicants; and

- purchase Law Services publications and LSAT® preparation materials.

Atlanta, GA	Friday, September 24: NOON-6 P.M. Saturday, September 25: 10 A.M.-4 P.M. Grand Hyatt Atlanta 3300 Peachtree Road Atlanta, GA
Boston, MA	Friday, October 29: NOON-6 P.M. Saturday, October 30: 10 A.M.-4 P.M. Marriott Copley Place 110 Huntington Avenue Boston, MA
Chicago, IL	Friday, November 12: NOON-6 P.M. Saturday, November 13: 10 A.M.-4 P.M. Chicago Marriott Downtown 540 North Michigan Avenue Chicago, IL
Houston, TX	Saturday, October 23: 10 A.M.-4 P.M. JW Marriott 5150 Westheimer Road Houston, TX
Los Angeles, CA	Friday, November 5: NOON-6 P.M. Saturday, November 6: 10 A.M.-3 P.M. Los Angeles Airport Marriott 5855 West Century Boulevard Los Angeles, CA
New York, NY	Friday, September 17: NOON-7 P.M. Saturday, September 18: 10 A.M.-4 P.M. New York Marriott World Trade Center Three World Trade Center New York, NY
Oakland, CA (San Francisco Bay Area)	Monday, November 8: 1 P.M.-7 P.M. Oakland Marriott City Center 1001 Broadway Oakland, CA
Washington, DC	Saturday, July 17: 10 A.M.-5 P.M. Omni Shoreham Hotel 2500 Calvert Street, NW Washington, DC

For further information contact:
Law School Forums
Law Services
Box 40
Newtown, PA 18940-0040
215.968.1001
Internet: http://www.LSAC.org

Free Time

You'll have more of it if you use your computer to search for and apply to law schools using these great TOOLS.

LSACD 2000 — Available September 1999!

Computerized Law School Applications and Official Guide to U.S. Law Schools

CD-ROM for Windows

$59

Including the:

Official Guide to U.S. Law Schools

This is the searchable, electronic version of the nationally recognized *Official Guide to U.S. Law Schools*. Find the schools that are the best bet for you using the wealth of data, photographs, and descriptions for each of the 181 ABA-approved law schools. Search for law schools based on location, key words, LSAT/GPA credentials, or specific criteria such as size, cost, affiliation, and more. Customize your search to suit your interests.

Computerized Law School Applications

Our common information section and flow-as-you-go technology saves you time and trouble. You answer the common questions once, select the schools to which you want to apply, and let the program place the answers in the proper fields. The CD-ROM includes official applications for all 181 ABA-approved law schools, and all of the schools welcome applications generated by the *LSACD*. You print out your completed applications, enclose all required fees and materials, and mail your applications to the schools.

LSACD on the Web

$49

The *LSACD* on the Web is the Web-based version of the LSACD-ROM and includes the Computerized Law School Applications and the *Official Guide to U.S. Law Schools*, as well as the many other features included on the *LSACD*. It also allows you to save your applications on LSAC's secure central database instead of your computer's hard drive, so you can access it from anywhere. Subscribers get unlimited use for the entire year-2000 admission cycle.

Official Guide to U.S. Law Schools on the Web

$20

This is the Web-based version of the nationally recognized *Official Guide to U.S. Law Schools*. It is the same searchable guide that is found on the *LSACD* and *LSACD* on the Web, but without the Computerized Law School Applications. Subscribers get unlimited use of the latest version.

Computerized Law School Applications on the Web

$35

This is the Web-based version of the Computerized Law School Applications found on the *LSACD* and *LSACD* on the Web, but without the *Official Guide to U.S. Law Schools*. Subscribers get the convenience of the Common Information Form and flow-as-you-go technology for the entire year-2000 admission cycle. Application data is safely stored on LSAC's secure central database. You print out your completed applications to any of the 181 ABA-approved law schools, enclose all required fees and materials, and mail your applications to the schools.

Index

These cards are for your convenience in writing to law schools for information. They are not applications for admission. At the beginning of each institution's *Official Guide* description, you will find the name and address of the office to which the card should be addressed.

If you wish to request information or application materials from more than six law schools, please use the postcards found in the *LSAT/LSDAS Registration and Information Book,* or prepare your own postcards in a similar format. You may also copy these cards and mail them in envelopes if you wish to request information from additional schools.

Request for Information

Please Print Clearly

I am interested in information about your law school. I will be ready to enter law school in:

Month _____ Year _____

I am interested in a ☐ full-time and/or ☐ part-time program

Please send me:

☐ a catalog ☐ financial information

☐ admission material ☐ other _____
(please specify)

Name _____

Mailing Address _____

City   State/Province   Country   Zip/Postal Code

Undergraduate College _____

Year of Graduation _____

Request for Information

Please Print Clearly

I am interested in information about your law school. I will be ready to enter law school in:

Month _____ Year _____

I am interested in a ☐ full-time and/or ☐ part-time program

Please send me:

☐ a catalog ☐ financial information

☐ admission material ☐ other _____
(please specify)

Name _____

Mailing Address _____

City   State/Province   Country   Zip/Postal Code

Undergraduate College _____

Year of Graduation _____

Request for Information

Please Print Clearly

I am interested in information about your law school. I will be ready to enter law school in:

Month _____ Year _____

I am interested in a ☐ full-time and/or ☐ part-time program

Please send me:

☐ a catalog ☐ financial information

☐ admission material ☐ other _____
(please specify)

Name _____

Mailing Address _____

City   State/Province   Country   Zip/Postal Code

Undergraduate College _____

Year of Graduation _____